The Book History Reader

Since the invention of the printing press in the fifteenth century, books and print culture have been central to the shaping of culture and society. *The Book History Reader* was the first comprehensive volume to bring together a variety of work – much of which is now out of print or impossible to access – examining key aspects of book history. This second edition contains a larger number of extracts covering issues of gender, material culture and bibliographical matters and a completely new section on the future of the book in the electronic age.

The Book History Reader is an essential collection of writings examining different aspects of the history of books and print culture: the development of the book, the move from spoken word to written texts, the commodification of books and authors and the power and profile of readers. Arranged in thematic sections and featuring a general introduction to the *Reader* as well as an introduction to each section, the editors illustrate how book history studies have developed a broad approach which incorporates social and cultural considerations governing the production, dissemination and reception of print and texts.

International in scope and interdisciplinary in nature, book history studies is a rapidly growing subject which analyses books and print as cultural artefacts. This pioneering book will be a vital resource for all those involved in publishing studies, library studies and book history and also those studying English literature, cultural studies, sociology and history.

Featuring essays by: Thomas R. Adams and Nicolas Barker, Richard Altick, Roland Barthes, C. A. Bayly, Pierre Bourdieu, Fredson Bowers, John Brewer, Roger Chartier, Robert Darnton, Paul Duguid, Elizabeth Eisenstein, Stanley Fish, Kate Flint, Michel Foucault, Wolfgang Iser, Adrian Johns, Harold Love, Paula McDowell, Jerome McGann, Elizabeth McHenry, D. F. McKenzie, Jayne Marek, E. Jennifer Monaghan, Jan-Dirk Müller, Scott B. Noegel, Geoffrey Nunberg, Walter Ong, Robert L. Patten, Mark Poster, Leah Price, Janice Radway, Jonathan Rose, Mark Rose, John Sutherland, Marcel Thomas, Jane Tompkins, James L. W. West III.

David Finkelstein is Research Professor of Media and Print Culture at Queen Margaret University College, Edinburgh. He is author of *The House of Blackwood: Author–Publisher Relations in the Victorian Era* and co-author (with Alistair McCleery) of *An Introduction to Book History*.

Alistair McCleery is Professor of Literature and Culture at Napier University, Edinburgh, and Director of the Scottish Centre for the Book. He is co-editor of *The Bibliotheck*.

The Book History Reader

SECOND EDITION

Edited by David Finkelstein and
Alistair McCleery

Routledge
Taylor & Francis Group

LONDON AND NEW YORK

First published 2002
by Routledge

This edition published 2006
by Routledge
2 Park Square, Milton Park, Abingdon, Oxon OX14 4RN

Simultaneously published in the USA and Canada
by Routledge
270 Madison Ave, New York NY 10016

Reprinted 2008, 2009

Routledge is an imprint of the Taylor & Francis Group, an informa business

Editorial selection and material © 2006 David Finkelstein and Alistair McCleery
Chapters © 2006 Contributors

Typeset in Perpetua and Bell Gothic by Refine Catch Limited, Bungay, Suffolk
Printed and bound in Great Britain by TJ International Ltd, Padstow, Cornwall

British Library Cataloguing in Publication Data
A catalogue record for this book is available from the British Library

Library of Congress Cataloging in Publication Data
The book history reader / edited by David Finkelstein and Alistair McCleery.
   p. cm.
   Includes bibliographical references and index.
1. Book—Social aspects—History.   2. Books and reading—Social aspects—History.
3. Authorship—Social aspects—History.   I. Finkelstein, David, 1964– II. McCleery,
Alistair.
   Z4.B647 2006
   00—dc22   2006009669

ISBN10: 0–415–35947–3 (hbk)
ISBN10: 0–415–35948–1 (pbk)

ISBN13: 978–0–415–35947–4 (hbk)
ISBN13: 978–0–415–35948–1 (pbk)

CONTENTS

PART FIVE
The future of the book

ILLUSTRATIONS

PREFACE

In 2001 we published the first edition of the *Book History Reader*. The impetus for its development came from our experiences of teaching book history courses; preparing material for such courses often involved tedious and lengthy gathering together of out-of-print or inaccessible book extracts and articles. Given the interest in the area that was beginning to manifest itself in new and continuing university courses on the subject, we asked why it was not possible to publish a reader that made these texts more widely available. The goal was to help students, teachers and interested general readers gather a sense of what book history is, and of how it is being practised at the moment. We drew on the expertise of colleagues and members of such organisations as the Society for the History of Authorship, Reading and Publishing to come up with a master list of desired examples, which we duly presented to Routledge. Space limitations prevented us from publishing the full wish list at the time.

The popularity of the Reader over the intervening years, however, has given us the opportunity to produce an expanded second edition. We have revised the volume to include touchstone texts as well as cutting-edge new work, and to respond to the comments and constructive criticisms made about the original *Reader*. In particular, section headings have been changed to reflect more accurately the general themes covered in the extracts; a new, short section on 'The future of the book' has been included; thirteen new works have been added to the original list of twenty-seven extracts, increasing our coverage of topics such as analytical bibliography, manuscript and scribal culture, oral and textual interaction, religious and periodical publishing, and gender and ethnic interests. Some reviewers of the first edition called for more in-depth introductions to the extracts. We have written *An Introduction to Book History* (Routledge, 2005) in response. This can be used either in conjunction with the Reader or as a stand-alone text; it provides a comprehensive critical overview of the general theories and issues currently dominating the study of the history of the book and print culture studies.

That the *Reader* and *An Introduction to Book History* have been so well received attests to the growing strength and interest in the area of book history and print culture studies. The works featured in this edition of the Reader are just a small sample of the important work being published in the field. Book history is developing rapidly and this volume is developing with it.

We would like to express our gratitude to all the contributors to the Reader and their original publishers and, while it might seem inappropriate to single out any of them, we do need to thank Christine Ferdinand, Robert L. Patten and Jonathan Rose for their continued support. Benjamin Brabon was of great assistance in the final preparation of the volume for the press.

David Finkelstein
Alistair McCleery
March 2006

ACKNOWLEDGEMENTS

The editors and publisher gratefully acknowledge permission to reproduce copyright material from the following:

Nicolas Barker, and the British Library for permission to reprint Thomas Adams and Nicolas Barker, 'A New Model for the Study of the Book', from *A Potencie of Life: Books in Society*, London: British Library, 1993, pp. 1–15, 37–9.

Richard Altick, Chicago University Press, and Ohio State University Press for permission to reprint from Richard Altick, *The English Common Reader*, Chicago: Chicago University Press, 1957; revised edition, Ohio State University Press, 1998.

Éditions du Seuil for permission to reprint Roland Barthes, 'The death of the author', from *Oeuvres complètes*, Tome 2. 1966–1973, Éditions du Seuil, 1994.

Cambridge University Press for permission to reprint C. A. Bayly, 'The Indian ecumene: An indigenous public sphere', from *Empire and Information: Intelligence Gathering and Social Communication in India 1780–1870*, Cambridge University Press, 1996.

Blackwell/Polity Press for permission to reprint an extract from Pierre Bourdieu, *The Field of Cultural Production*, ed. Randal Johnson, Cambridge: Polity Press, 1993, pp. 27–73.

The Bibliographical Society of America for permission to reprint Fredson Bowers, 'Bibliography, Pure Bibliography, and Literary Studies', *Papers of the Bibliographical Society of America* 46 (1952): 186–208.

The author and his agent for permission to reprint John Brewer, 'Authors, publishers and the making of literary culture', from *The Pleasures of the Imagination: English Culture in the Eighteenth Century*, Glasgow: HarperCollins, 1997, pp. 125–66.

Roger Chartier and Johns Hopkins University Press for permission to reprint Roger Chartier, 'Labourers and voyagers: From the text to the reader', *Diacritics* 22.2 (1992): 49–61. © Johns Hopkins University Press. Reprinted with the permission of The Johns Hopkins University Press.

Roger Chartier and Harvard University Press for permission to reprint Roger Chartier, 'The practical impact of writing', from *A History of Private Life*, volume 3, Harvard University Press, 1989, pp. 111–59. Reprinted by permission of the publisher from *A History of Private Life, volume 3: Passions of the Renaissance*, Roger Chartier, vol. ed., translated by Arthur Goldhammer, Cambridge, Mass.: The Belknap Press of Harvard University Press. © 1989 by the President and Fellows of Harvard College.

The author for permission to reprint Robert Darnton, 'What is the history of books?', from *The Kiss of Lamourette: Reflections in Cultural History*, London: Faber and Faber, revised edition 1990, pp. 107–36.

xii ACKNOWLEDGEMENTS

Paul Duguid and University of California Press for permission to reprint Paul Duguid, 'Material Matters: the Past and Futurology of the Book' from G. Nunberg ed., *The Future of the Book*, Berkeley, Ca.: University of California Press, 1996, pp. 63–102.

Cambridge University Press for permission to reprint Elizabeth Eisenstein, 'Defining the initial shift: Some features of print culture', from *The Printing Press as an Agent of Change*, Cambridge University Press, 1979, pp. 43–71.

Stanley Fish and Chicago University Press for permission to reprint Stanley Fish, 'Interpreting the Variorum', from 'Is there a text in this class?', *Critical Enquiry*, 2.3 (Winter 1976): 465–86.

Oxford University Press for permission to reprint Kate Flint, 'Reading practices', from *The Woman Reader, 1837–1914*, Oxford University Press, 1993, pp. 187–249. © Kate Flint 1993.

Cornell University Press for permission to reprint Michel Foucault, 'What is an author?'.

Princeton University Press for permission to reprint Wolfgang Iser, 'Interaction between text and reader', from Susan K. Suleiman and Inge Crosman, eds, *The Reader in the Text: Essays on Audience and Interpretation*, New Jersey: Princeton University Press, 1980, pp. 106–19. © 1980 by Princeton University Press.

Adrian Johns and the University of Chicago Press for permission to reprint from Adrian Johns, *The Book of Nature and the Nature of the Book*, Chicago: The University of Chicago Press, 1998, pp. 1–36.

The author for permission to reprint Harold Love, 'Early Modern Print Culture: Assessing the Models', *Parergon*, 20,1 (2003): 45–64.

Oxford University Press for permission to reprint from Paula McDowell, *The Women of Grub Street: Press, Politics and Gender in the Literary Marketplace 1678–1730*, Oxford: Clarendon Press, 1998, pp. 128–179.

Princeton University Press for permission to reprint Jerome McGann, 'The Socialization of Texts', from *The Textual Condition*, Princeton University Press, 1991, pp. 69–83. © 1991 by Princeton University Press.

Duke University Press for permission to reprint from Elizabeth McHenry, *Forgotten Readers: Recovering the Lost History of African American Literary Societies*, Durham and London: Duke University Press, 2002.

The Estate of the late D. F. McKenzie for permission to reprint D. F. McKenzie, 'The book as an expressive form', from D. F. McKenzie, *The Panizzi Lectures, 1985: Bibliography and the Sociology of Texts*, London: British Library, 1986, pp. 1–20; and D. F. McKenzie, 'The sociology of a text: Orality, literacy and print in early New Zealand', *The Library*, Sixth Series, 6.4 (December 1984): 333–65.

The University Press of Kentucky for permission to reprint Jayne Marek, 'Toward International Cooperation: The Literary Editing of H. D. and Bryher', from *Women Editing Modernism*, Lexington: The University Press of Kentucky, 1995, pp. 101–137.

The Johns Hopkins University Press and E. Jennifer Monaghan for permission to reprint E. Jennifer Monaghan, 'Literacy instruction and gender in Colonial New England', from Cathy N. Davidson, ed., *Reading in America: Literature and Social History*, Johns Hopkins University Press, 1989, pp. 53–80. © 1989 Johns Hopkins University Press.

Stanford University Press for permission to reprint Jan-Dirk Müller, 'The body of the book: The media transition from manuscript to print', reprinted from *Materialities of Communication*, edited by Hans Ulrich Gumbrecht and K. Ludwig Pfeiffer, translated by William Whobrey, with the permission of the publisher, Stanford University Press. © 1994 by the Board of Trustees of the Leland Stanford Junior University.

University of Washington Press and the Simpson Center for the Humanities for permission to reprint Scott B. Noegel, 'Text, Script, and Media: New Observations on Scribal Activity in the

Ancient Near East', from Raimonda Modiano, Leroy F. Searle and Peter Shillingsburg, eds., *Voice, Text, Hypertext: Emerging Practices in Textual Studies*, Seattle: University of Washington Press, 2004, pp. 133–143.

University of California Press for permission to reprint Geoffrey Nunberg, 'Farewell to the Information Age' from G. Nunberg ed., *The Future of the Book*, Berkeley, Ca.: University of California Press, 1996, pp. 103–138.

Taylor and Francis Books Ltd for permission to reprint Walter Ong, 'Writing restructures consciousness', *Orality and Literacy: The Technologizing of the Word*, Routledge, rev. edn 1997, pp. 78–138.

The author for permission to reprint a revised version of Robert L. Patten, 'When is a book not a book?', *Biblion*, 4.2 (Spring 1996): 35–63.

University of Minnesota Press for permission to reprint Mark Poster, 'The Digital Subject and Cultural Theory', from *What's the Matter with the Internet?* Minneapolis, Mn.: University of Minnesota Press, 2001, pp. 60–77.

Cambridge University Press for permission to reprint Leah Price, 'Cultures of the Commonplace' from *The Anthology and the Rise of the Novel: From Richardson to George Eliot*, Cambridge: Cambridge University Press, 2000, pp. 67–77.

University of North Carolina Press for permission to reprint Janice Radway, 'A feeling for books: The Book-of-the-Month Club, literary taste and middle-class desire', from *A Feeling for Books: The Book of the Month Club, Literary Taste, and Middle Class Desire* by Janice A. Radway, Chapel Hill: University of North Carolina Press, 1997, pp. 263–79. © 1997 by the University of North Carolina Press.

Jonathan Rose and Johns Hopkins University Press for permission to reprint Jonathan Rose, 'Rereading the English common reader: A preface to a history of audiences', *Journal of the History of Ideas* 53 (1992): 47–70. © The Journal of the History of Ideas, Inc. Reprinted by permission of The Johns Hopkins University Press.

Mark Rose and Harvard University Press for permission to reprint Mark Rose, 'Literary property determined', from *Authors and Owners: the invention of copyright*, Cambridge, Mass.: Harvard University Press, 1993, pp. 92–112. © 1993 by the President and Fellows of Harvard College.

Macmillan Press Ltd for permission to reprint John Sutherland, 'The Victorian novelists: Who were they?', from *Victorian Fiction: Writers, Publishers, Readers*, Basingstoke: Macmillan Press, 1995, pp. 151–64. © Macmillan Press Ltd.

Editions Albin Michel for permission to reprint Marcel Thomas, 'Manuscripts' from Lucien LeFebvre and Henri-Jean Martin, *The Coming of the Book: The Impact of Printing, 1450–1800* tr. D. Gerard, London: Verso, 1976, pp. 15–29.

Oxford University Press, Inc. for permission to reprint Jane Tompkins, 'Masterpiece theater: The politics of Hawthorne's literary reputation', from *Sensational Designs: The Cultural Work of American Fiction 1790–1860*, New York: Oxford University Press, 1985, pp. 20–34. © 1985 by Oxford University Press, Inc.

James L. W. West III for permission to reprint 'The magazine market' from *American Authors and the Literary Marketplace since 1900*, Philadelphia, PA.: University of Pennsylvania Press, 1990, pp. 103–13.

Every attempt has been made to obtain permission to reproduce copyright material. If any proper acknowledgement has not been made, we would invite copyright holders to inform us of the oversight.

Chapter 1

David Finkelstein and Alistair McCleery

INTRODUCTION

Take two novels. In Ray Bradbury's *Fahrenheit 451* (1953) a society is described in which books are prohibited objects to be burnt when discovered (the title is the ignition point of paper). Books are regarded as carriers of social dissent; but the story ends on a generally comforting note with its description of living books, men and women who have committed classic texts to memory and preserve in themselves that cultural heritage. In pursuing his theme, Bradbury makes a common distinction between texts, composed of words, and books, composed of paper and ink, which act only as vehicles for texts. Books can be replaced by memory and oral recitation, or in contemporary terms by digitised and downloadable text. Printed books, from this latter viewpoint, are a passing phase, albeit one which has lasted over five hundred years. The setting of Umberto Eco's novel *The Name of the Rose* (1983), a monastery before the coming of print, provides a view of the reproduction and conservation of texts in manuscript in which the authority of the author is sacrosanct. Indeed, the murders in the monastery which the Sherlock Holmes-like Baskerville (itself an allusion to the eighteenth-century English typographer) investigates originate in a concern to preserve the reputation of Aristotle. The author's authority and the accuracy of his texts represent central tenets of the textual scholars. Both these novels address issues which form part of the substance of this Reader. These are issues, on the one hand, of the significance of the book as a physical object, and, on the other, of authorial status, which in their historical development fall within the field of Book History.

Book History has emerged as a field of study in relatively recent times. Although its ancestors can be traced through prior disciplines such as Bibliography and Social History, it achieves its relative distinctiveness from both through its emphasis upon print culture and the role of the book as material object within that culture. The use of the term 'culture' also underpins a recurrent emphasis within the field upon broad social movements drawing on detailed statistical evidence, a methodology heavily influenced by the French *annales* school of historians. This aspect of Book History stands in contrast to both the technical analysis of individual books or editions characteristic of Bibliography in the Anglo-American tradition and the narrow remit of most publishing 'house histories', themselves also typified by an often adulatory attitude towards their subjects.

Bibliography traditionally dealt with the recension of manuscripts in order to produce the most complete and least corrupted version of a text possible. The intervention of agents other than the author in the transmission of the text was seen as part of that corrupting process. This approach was applied by scholars such as McKerrow (1927), Greg (1966) and Bowers (1949) to the printed book. The operation of agents in the printing process, including editors and proof-readers, was painstakingly retraced in order to distinguish their interference and establish the text which most accurately reflected the author's final intention. How the author's final intention was itself to be deciphered was the subject at times of a much less rigorous analysis and doubt remains whether the author's intention existed only as an editorial concept disguising the editor's own predilections and decisions (see Tanselle, 1979). However, two key elements were inherited from Bibliography by book History: the very recognition that a book is a result of a collaborative, albeit for bibliographers an often corrupting, process; and a detailed system for describing books on the basis of their production attributes which provided a universal standard drawing attention to the material object rather than its contents.

The vogue for producing publishing 'house histories', on the other hand, characterised a self-satisfied industry desirous of ensuring its own immortality through promotion of its role in Literature. If there is anything of value to be salvaged from these self-congratulatory tomes, it is not so much the recognition of the publisher's role in the gestation of great works but the emphasis upon the entrepreneurial and dynamic individuals responsible for the establishment of our oldest publishing houses and the slow trajectory from family to corporate ownership through succeeding generations. If Book History were to be represented by these histories alone, then it would be fairly criticised as a field lacking in objectivity and rigour. That it cannot may be due to the purgative value of social history.

The application of *annales* methodology, of quantitative social history drawing on detail to produce the overall pattern, was found in Robert Escarpit's *Sociologie de la Littérature* (1958) and also in the same year in Febvre and Martin's *L'Apparition du Livre* (1958). Escarpit's work is notable for his attempt to isolate models of book production, dissemination and reception from the accumulation of data in a manner taken up by Darnton (Chapter 2 in this *Reader*) and Adams and Barker (Chapter 5 in this *Reader*). The *annales* approach differs, moreover, from attempts such as Elizabeth Eisenstein's to relate the development of the printed book to broader social and political movements in what has more recently been criticised as an over-determinist and simplistic approach, itself indicated in the title of her major work, *The Printing Press as an Agent of Change* (1979) (see Johns, Chapter 18 in this *Reader*). Febvre and Martin are perhaps more accurate in their chapter headed 'The Book as a Force for Change'. For them, the printing press is only one of a number of actors in a social and political drama; Lucien Febvre offers the alternative title for their study of 'The Book in the Service of History'. These various intellectual and scholarly strands from Bibliography, Business History and Social History began to blend in the 1980s to produce the current field of Book History.

That Book History as a field of study has come to prominence in the last few decades partly derives from both a recognition of the key role print has played in our culture for the past five hundred years and a realisation that the role has now been usurped by other media. The book will continue as a cultural component (it will not die), but its dominance has disappeared and this in some way has licensed the study of its past. Perhaps the very ubiquity of printed texts in our history prevented previous scholars from appreciating and evaluating the fuller complexities of textual functions, procedures and nature.

Since Darnton's formulation of the 'communication circuit' as a means of examining the role of texts in society, and the subsequent modifications suggested by critics such as Adams and Barker, Book History has begun increasingly to focus on what McGann has described as the 'socialization of texts', that is, the impact of books as artefacts travelling from private to public spaces (see Chapter 6 in this *Reader*). In this formulation, production becomes very much part of a process of, as Duguid notes, 'producing a public artifact and inserting it in a particular social circuit' (Chapter 39 in this *Reader*). But at the same time, the picture has become more complex and more interesting. Textual production is no longer to be viewed simply as a straightforward linear paradigm of production, progressing from composition to publication and reception. Rather, in the words of Jordan and Patten, what are now become increasingly important are conceptions of 'the activity of producing and consuming books that decenter the principal elements and make them interactive and inter-dependent: publishing history, in other words, as hypertext' (Jordan and Patten, 1995: 11).

While past traditions in bibliographic and textual studies have sought to establish stable texts and precise textual intentions, the field of Book History now operates within a context of unstable texts. With new media practices and the World Wide Web challenging the fixity of print and creating new links between visual, oral and textual communication forms, print culture studies is shifting to acknowledge the need to view texts, past and present, in wider contexts. In order to do this, Book History is drawing on and borrowing from a combination of analytical tools and insights derived from various disciplines, ranging from literary studies to history, media and communication studies. Book History is no longer simply the province of bibliographers or literary critics, but rather can be seen as an integral part of the history of human communication.

Even if the book in the future will no longer be the main form of human communication, this does not signify, as some critics would have us believe, the death of the book. Nor does it lessen the impact of print on social formations. Book History is important for what it says about human development. For well over five hundred years, print has been central to the shaping of Western society, and to the transmission of its values outwards (whether imposed or voluntarily) into colonised and connected societies and territories (as extracts in this *Reader* by Bayly and McKenzie suggest). Without the portability and reach of print and texts, social, cultural, legal, humanistic and religious formations would not have developed, been transmitted and shaped beliefs and systems around the world.

In 1984, Robert Darnton surveyed the field of Book History and declared that it was so scattered in approach it resembled 'interdisciplinarity run riot'. At the same time, he predicted it was an area that 'seems likely to win a place alongside fields like the history of science and the history of art in the canon of scholarly discipline' (Chapter 2 in this *Reader*). The explosion in studies in Book History since Darnton's pronouncement bears him out, as the selections in this *Reader* demonstrate. However, in order to restrain riotous diversity, this revised *Reader* is divided into five major sections covering definitions of book history, the impact of print, texts and authors, texts and their readers, and the future of the book. Each section has its own introduction drawing out specific themes and issues touched on briefly in this preliminary editorial introduction. There is also a concluding bibliography of further readings both general and section specific.

On reviewing the variety of texts represented in this *Reader*, we feel it is fair to conclude that this very interdisciplinarity is a key strength of Book History. This may well be one of its attractions for students, as the various undergraduate and graduate studies courses in Book History that are now developing provide witness. At the same time, Book History has emerged as a field in which common structures, methodologies and frameworks for investigating texts are now being embedded, offering a combination of empirically informed and theoretically grounded approaches to the subject. There is much here for future scholars to take advantage of.

PART ONE

What is book history?

EDITORS' INTRODUCTION

Throughout the first half of the twentieth century, the study of the nature of books in Anglo-American circles was dominated by a preoccupation with the physical materiality of books. The works of Ronald McKerrow (1927), W. W. Greg (1966) and Fredson Bowers (1949) are classic exemplars of this tradition of scholarly endeavour, still utilised today to a certain extent in courses on bibliographic methods. Bowers's later (1952) piece, reproduced here, establishes the parameters under which bibliography was defined in the first half of the twentieth century. It summarises and categorises the practices of bibliography as they were understood by scholars, librarians and antiquarian bookdealers of the time. Book history studies thereafter evolved over the last half of the twentieth century to incorporate work on the social and cultural conditions governing the production, dissemination and reception of print and texts. Much of this shift is a result of critical authorities represented in this part's extracts.

Crucial to any student's understanding of book history is Robert Darnton's piece which, borrowing from French sociological models, was one of the first to suggest a practical model of study for the 'newly' constituted book history field, one which emphasised locating cultural and social investigations of texts within an overarching cycle of print production, dissemination and reception. His 'communications circuit', a processive and circular model of the 'life cycle' of books, running between and returning to author, reader and publisher, has been a point of departure for much work undertaken on print culture history. Similarly, Don McKenzie's Panizzi Lectures of 1985, of which we have extracted the first section, offered the resonating clarion call to view book history in sociological contexts, to delve into 'the sociology of texts'. This too has become central to the formation of new directions in book history studies.

An influential reassessment and redevelopment of these models has since been provided by Adams and Barker (1993), who refer to McKenzie while at the same time expanding on Darnton's work to suggest stronger linkages of social investigations of print culture to textual conditions and bio-bibliographical evidence. Jerome McGann is among those whose fusion of literary history and bibliographical methods has also been influential in moving textual editing and bibliographic activity towards integrating social and cultural considerations in the shaping of the production of texts. McGann's 'socialization of the text' echoes Darnton's 'communications circuit' and Don McKenzie's 'sociology of the text' as memorable phrases used to encapsulate what book history is now about. These attempts to define the field are surveyed in Harold Love's assessment of the ways in which the terms 'print culture' and 'age of print' have been conceptualised since the 1970s. Love elaborates on Ong's concept of print culture as 'noetic' (see Part Two 'The Impact of Print' below): that is, having the ability to restructure the way in which we think and perceive; he examines the nature of social relationships within print culture production and consumption; and he places print culture within larger information economy frameworks (what C. A. Bayly terms the 'social ecumene' in his contribution to this Reader).

One of the most influential and prolific exponents of book history as a physical and social phenomenon over the past twenty years has been the French analyst Roger Chartier. Chartier's work on reading and the reception of texts in particular follows the traditions of the *annales* school of literary historiography, and has been tremendously influential in focusing attention on the importance of integrating readership studies into book history studies. The extract included here is one of his best-known pieces. Taking his inspiration from the historian and ethnologist Michel de Certeau, Chartier offers an examination of the possibilities for a history of reading. His proposal for a definition of print culture intertwined with studies of readership expresses and explores some of the tensions to be found between the material and cultural analyses of textual production which demarcate bibliographic and sociological views of book history.

Finally, an extract is included of Pierre Bourdieu's sociological theorisation of the 'literary field'. Bourdieu's theory of the field has gained much currency recently among book historians, stressing as it does the juncture between culture, society and material production. In this case, the literary field is seen as representing self-contained literary, artistic and social microcosms with their own structures and codes, operating within and affected indirectly by changing social, economic, political and technological conditions. Like Darnton, Bourdieu is interested in the material production and distribution of textual culture; unlike him, however, Bourdieu uses these as a starting point for investigating how 'cultural status' is acquired and retained for aesthetic products and by literary elites.

There is no doubt that current approaches to the study of book history will continue to evolve as further work is done in the areas demarcated in these extracts. What is also true is that book history studies no longer rely solely on the simple paradigm of linear production from author to publishers to reader. In an era dominated by new technology, the study of texts acquires new significance, as a past survey effectively suggests: book historians now have theoretical models to choose from that offer 'conceptions of the activity of producing and consuming books that decenter the principal elements and make them interactive and interdependent: publishing history, in other words, as hypertext' (Jordan and Patten, 1995: 11).

Chapter 2

Robert Darnton

WHAT IS THE HISTORY OF BOOKS?

'*Histoire du livre*' in France, '*Geschichte des Buchwesens*' in Germany, 'history of books' or 'of the book' in English-speaking countries – its name varies from place to place, but everywhere it is being recognized as an important new discipline. It might even be called the social and cultural history of communication by print, if that were not such a mouthful, because its purpose is to understand how ideas were transmitted through print and how exposure to the printed word affected the thought and behavior of mankind during the last five hundred years. Some book historians pursue their subject deep into the period before the invention of movable type. Some students of printing concentrate on newspapers, broadsides, and other forms besides the book. The field can be extended and expanded in many ways; but for the most part, it concerns books since the time of Gutenberg, an area of research that has developed so rapidly during the last few years that it seems likely to win a place alongside fields like the history of science and the history of art in the canon of scholarly disciplines.

Whatever the history of books may become in the future, its past shows how a field of knowledge can take on a distinct scholarly identity. It arose from the convergence of several disciplines on a common set of problems, all of them having to do with the process of communication. Initially, the problems took the form of concrete questions in unrelated branches of scholarship: What were Shakespeare's original texts? What caused the French Revolution? What is the connection between culture and social stratification? In pursuing those questions, scholars found themselves crossing paths in a no-man's land located at the intersection of a half-dozen fields of study. They decided to constitute a field of their own and to invite in historians, literary scholars, sociologists, librarians, and anyone else who wanted to understand the book as a force in history. The history of books began to acquire its own journals, research centers, conferences, and lecture circuits. It accumulated tribal elders as well as Young Turks. And although it has not yet developed passwords or secret handshakes or its own population of Ph.D.s, its adherents can recognize one another by the glint in their eyes. They belong to a common cause, one of the few sectors in the human sciences where there is a mood of expansion and a flurry of fresh ideas.

To be sure, the history of the history of books did not begin yesterday. It stretches back to the scholarship of the Renaissance, if not beyond; and it began in earnest during the nineteenth century when the study of books as material objects led to the rise of analytical bibliography in England. But the current work represents a departure from the established strains of scholarship, which may be traced to their nineteenth-century origins through back issues of *The Library* and *Börsenblatt für den Deutschen Buchhandel* or theses in the Ecole des Chartes. The new strain developed during the 1960s in France, where it took root in institutions like the Ecole Pratique des Hautes Etudes and spread through publications like *L'Apparition du livre* (1958), by Lucien Febvre and Henri-Jean Martin, and *Livre et société dans la France du XVIIIe siècle* (two volumes 1965 and 1970) by a group connected with the VIe section of the Ecole Pratique des Hautes Etudes.

The new book historians brought the subject within the range of themes studied by the 'Annales school' of socioeconomic history. Instead of dwelling on fine points of bibliography, they tried to uncover the general pattern of book production and consumption over long stretches of time. They compiled statistics from requests for *privilèges* (a kind of copyright), analyzed the contents of private libraries, and traced ideological currents through neglected genres like the *bibliothèque bleue* (primitive paperbacks). Rare books and fine editions had no interest for them; they concentrated instead on the most ordinary sort of books because they wanted to discover the literary experience of ordinary readers. They put familiar phenomena like the Counter-Reformation and the Enlightenment in an unfamiliar light by showing how much traditional culture outweighed the avant-garde in the literary fare of the entire society. Although they did not come up with a firm set of conclusions, they demonstrated the importance of asking new questions, using new methods, and tapping new sources.[1]

Their example spread throughout Europe and the United States, reinforcing indigenous traditions, such as reception studies in Germany and printing history in Britain. Drawn together by their commitment to a common enterprise, and animated by enthusiasm for new ideas, book historians began to meet, first in cafés, then in conferences. They created new journals – *Publishing History*, *Bibliography Newsletter*, *Nouvelles du livre ancien*, *Revue française d'histoire du livre* (new series), *Buchhandelsgeschichte*, and *Wolfenbütteler Notizen zur Buchgeschichte*. They founded new centers – the Institut d'Etude du Livre in Paris, the Arbeitskreis für Geschichte des Buchwesens in Wolfenbüttel, the Center for the Book in the Library of Congress. Special colloquia – in Geneva, Paris, Boston, Worcester, Wolfenbüttel, and Athens, to name only a few that took place in the late 1970s – disseminated their research on an international scale. In the brief span of two decades, the history of books had become a rich and varied field of study.

So rich did it prove, in fact, that it now looks less like a field than a tropical rain forest. The explorer can hardly make his way across it. At every step he becomes entangled in a luxuriant undergrowth of journal articles and disoriented by the crisscrossing of disciplines – analytical bibliography pointing in this direction, the sociology of knowledge in that, while history, English, and comparative literature stake out overlapping territories. He is beset by claims to newness – '*la nouvelle bibliographie matérielle*', 'the new literary history' – and bewildered by competing methodologies, which would have him collating editions, compiling statistics, decoding copyright law, wading through reams of manuscript, heaving at the bar of a reconstructed common press, and psychoanalyzing the mental processes of readers. The history of books has become so crowded with ancillary disciplines that one can no longer see its general contours. How can the book historian neglect the history of libraries, of publishing, of paper, type, and reading? But how can he master their technologies, especially when they appear in imposing foreign formulations, like *Geschichte der Appellstruktur* and *Bibliométrie bibliologique*? It is enough to make one want to retire to a rare book room and count watermarks.

To get some distance from interdisciplinarity run riot, and to see the subject as a whole, it might be useful to propose a general model for analyzing the way books come into being and spread through society. To be sure, conditions have varied so much from place to place and from time to time since the invention of movable type that it would be vain to expect the biography of every book to conform to the same pattern. But printed books generally pass through roughly the same life cycle. It could be described as a communications circuit that runs from the author to the publisher (if the bookseller does not assume that role), the printer, the shipper, the bookseller, and the reader. The reader completes the circuit because he influences the author both before and after the act of composition. Authors are readers themselves. By reading and associating with other readers and writers, they form notions of genre and style and a general sense of the literary enterprise which affects their texts, whether they are composing Shakespearean sonnets or directions for assembling radio kits. A writer may respond in his writing to criticisms of his previous work or anticipate reactions that his text will elicit. He addresses implicit readers and hears from explicit reviewers. So the circuit runs full cycle. It transmits messages, transforming them en route, as they pass from thought to writing to printed characters and back to thought again. Book history concerns each phase of this process and the process as a whole, in all its variations over space and time and in all its relations with other systems, economic, social, political, and cultural, in the surrounding environment.

That is a large undertaking. To keep their task within manageable proportions, book historians generally cut into one segment of the communications circuit and analyze it according to the procedures of a single discipline – printing, for example, which they study by means of analytical bibliography. But the parts do not take on their full significance unless they are related to the whole, and some holistic view of the book as a means of communication seems necessary if book history is to avoid being fragmented into esoteric specializations cut off from each other by arcane techniques and mutual misunderstanding. The model shown in Figure 2.1 provides a way of envisaging the entire communication process. With minor adjustments, it should apply to all periods in the history of the printed book (manuscript books and book illustrations will have to be considered elsewhere), but I would like to discuss it in connection with the period I know best, the eighteenth century, and to take it up phase by phase, showing how each phase is related to (1) other activities that a given person has underway at a given point in the circuit, (2) other persons at the same point in other circuits, (3) other persons at other points in the same circuit, and (4) other elements in society. The first three considerations bear directly on the transmission of a text, while the last concerns outside influences, which could vary endlessly. For the sake of simplicity, I have reduced the latter to the three general categories in the center of the diagram.

Models have a way of freezing human beings out of history. To put some flesh and blood on this one, and to show how it can make sense of an actual case, I will apply it to the publishing history of Voltaire's *Questions sur l'Encyclopédie*, an important work of the Enlightenment, and one that touched the lives of a great many eighteenth-century bookmen. One could study the circuit of its transmission at any point – at the stage of its composition, for example, when Voltaire shaped its text and orchestrated its diffusion in order to promote his campaign against religious intolerance, as his biographers have shown; or at its printing, a stage in which bibliographical analysis helps to establish the multiplication of editions; or at the point of its assimilation in libraries, where, according to statistical studies by literary historians, Voltaire's works occupied an impressive share of shelf space.[2] But I would like to consider the least familiar link in the diffusion process, the role of the bookseller, taking Isaac-Pierre Rigaud of Montpellier as an example, and working through the four considerations mentioned above.[3]

I

On August 16, 1770, Rigaud ordered thirty copies of the nine-volume octavo edition of the *Questions*, which the Société typographique de Neuchâtel (STN) had recently begun to print in the Prussian principality of Neuchâtel on the Swiss side of the French–Swiss border. Rigaud generally preferred to read at least a few pages of a new book before stocking it, but he considered the *Questions* such a good bet that he risked making a fairly large order for it, sight unseen. He did not

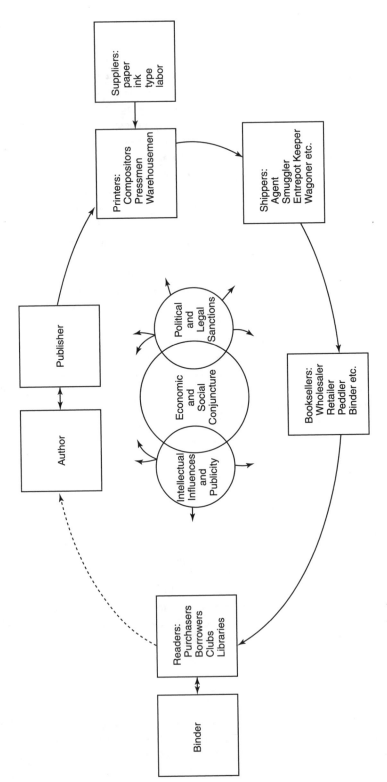

Figure 2.1 The communications circuit

have any personal sympathy for Voltaire. On the contrary, he deplored the philosophe's tendency to tinker with his books, adding and amending passages while cooperating with pirated editions behind the backs of the original publishers. Such practices produced complaints from customers, who objected to receiving inferior (or insufficiently audacious) texts. 'It is astonishing that at the end of his career M. de Voltaire cannot refrain from duping booksellers', Rigaud complained to the STN. 'It would not matter if all these little ruses, frauds, and deceits were blamed on the author. But unfortunately the printers and still more the retail booksellers are usually held responsible'.[4] Voltaire made life hard for booksellers, but he sold well.

There was nothing Voltairean about most of the other books in Rigaud's shop. His sales catalogues show that he specialized somewhat in medical books, which were always in demand in Montpellier, thanks to the university's famous faculty of medicine. Rigaud also kept a discreet line of Protestant works, because Montpellier lay in Huguenot territory. And when the authorities looked the other way, he brought in a few shipments of forbidden books.[5] But he generally supplied his customers with books of all kinds, which he drew from an inventory worth at least forty-five thousand livres, the largest in Montpellier and probably in all Languedoc, according to a report from the intendant's *subdélégué*.[6]

Rigaud's way of ordering from the STN illustrates the character of his business. Unlike other large provincial dealers, who speculated on a hundred or more copies of a book when they smelled a best seller, he rarely ordered more than a half dozen copies of a single work. He read widely, consulted his customers, took soundings by means of his commercial correspondence, and studied the catalogues that the STN and his other suppliers sent to him (by 1785 the STN's catalogue included seven hundred and fifty titles). Then he chose about ten titles and ordered just enough copies of them to make up a crate of fifty pounds, the minimum weight for shipment at the cheaper rate charged by the wagoners. If the books sold well, he reordered them; but he usually kept his orders rather small, and made four or five of them a year. In this way, he conserved capital, minimized risks, and built up such a large and varied stock that his shop became a clearinghouse for literary demand of every kind in the region.

The pattern of Rigaud's orders, which stands out clearly from the STN's account books, shows that he offered his customers a little of everything – travel books, histories, novels, religious works, and the occasional scientific or philosophical treatise. Instead of following his own preferences, he seemed to transmit demand fairly accurately and to live according to the accepted wisdom of the book trade, which one of the STN's other customers summarized as follows: 'The best book for a bookseller is a book that sells'.[7] Given his cautious style of business, Rigaud's decision to place an advance order for thirty-nine volume sets of the *Questions sur l'Encyclopédie* seems especially significant. He would not have put so much money on a single work if he had not felt certain of the demand – and his later orders show that he had calculated correctly. On June 19, 1772, soon after receiving the last shipment of the last volume, Rigaud ordered another dozen sets; and he ordered two more two years later, although by then the STN had exhausted its stock. It had printed a huge edition, twenty-five hundred copies, approximately twice its usual press run, and the booksellers had fallen all over themselves in the rush to purchase it. So Rigaud's purchase was no aberration. It expressed a current of Voltaireanism that had spread far and wide among the reading public of the Old Regime.

II

How does the purchase of the *Questions* look when examined from the perspective of Rigaud's relations with the other booksellers of Montpellier? A book-trade almanac listed nine of them in 1777:[8]

Printer-Booksellers:	Aug. Franç Rochard
	Jean Martel
Booksellers:	Isaac-Pierre Rigaud
	J. B. Faure
	Albert Pons
	Tournel
	Bascon
	Cézary
	Fontanel

But according to a report from a traveling salesman of the STN, there were only seven.[9] Rigaud and Pons had merged and completely dominated the local trade; Cézary and Faure scraped along in the middle ranks; and the rest teetered on the brink of bankruptcy in precarious boutiques. The occasional binder and under-the-cloak peddler also provided a few books, most of them illegal, to the more adventuresome readers of the city. For example, the demoiselle Bringand, known as 'the students' mother', stocked some forbidden fruit 'under the bed on the room to the right on the second floor', according to the report of a raid that was engineered by the established booksellers.[10] The trade in most provincial cities fell into the same pattern, which can be envisaged as a series of concentric circles: at the center, one or two firms tried to monopolize the market; around the margin, a few small dealers survived by specializing in chapbooks and old volumes, by setting up reading clubs (*cabinets littéraires*) and binderies, or by peddling their wares in the back country; and beyond the fringe of legality, adventurers moved in and out of the market, selling forbidden literature.

When he ordered his shipment of the *Questions*, Rigaud was consolidating his position at the center of the local trade. His merger with Pons in 1770 provided him with enough capital and assets to ride out the mishaps – delayed shipments, defaulting debtors, liquidity crises – that often upset smaller businesses. Also, he played rough. When Cézary, one of the middling dealers, failed to meet some of his payments in 1781, Rigaud drove him out of business by organizing a cabal of his creditors. They refused to let him reschedule the payments, had him thrown in prison for debt, and forced him to sell off his stock at an auction, where they kept down the prices and gobbled up the books. By dispensing patronage, Rigaud controlled most of Montpellier's binderies; and by exerting pressure on the binders, he produced delays and snags in the affairs of the other booksellers. In 1789 only one of them remained, Abraham Fontanel, and he stayed solvent only by maintaining a *cabinet littéraire*, 'which provokes terrible fits of jealousy by the sieur Rigaud, who wants to be the only one left and who shows his hatred of me every day',[11] as Fontanel confided to the STN.

Rigaud did not eliminate his competitors simply by outdoing them in the dog-eat-dog style of commercial capitalism of early modern France. His letters, theirs, and the correspondence of many other booksellers show that the book trade contracted during the late 1770s and 1780s. In hard times, the big booksellers squeezed out the small, and the tough outlasted the tender. Rigaud had been a tough customer from the very beginning of his relations with the STN. He had ordered his copies of the *Questions* from Neuchâtel, where the STN was printing a pirated edition, rather than from Geneva, where Voltaire's regular printer, Gabriel Cramer, was producing the original, because he had extracted better terms. He also demanded better service, especially when the other book-sellers in Montpellier, who had dealt with Cramer, received their copies first. The delay produced a volley of letters from Rigaud to the STN. Why couldn't the STN work faster? Didn't it know that it was making him lose customers to his competitors? He would have to order from Cramer in the future if it could not provide quicker shipments at a lower price. When volumes one through three finally arrived from Neuchâtel, volumes four through six from Geneva were already on sale in the other shops. Rigaud compared the texts, word for word, and found that the STN's edition contained none of the additional material that it had claimed to receive on the sly from Voltaire. So how could he push the theme of 'additions and corrections' in his sales talk? The recriminations flew thick and fast in the mail between Montpellier and Neuchâtel, and they showed that Rigaud meant to exploit every inch of every advantage that he could gain on his competitors. More important, they also revealed that the *Questions* were being sold all over Montpellier, even though in principle they could not circulate legally in France. Far from being confined to the under-the-cloak trade of marginal characters like 'the students' mother', Voltaire's work turned out to be a prize item in the scramble for profits at the very heart of the established book trade. When dealers like Rigaud scratched and clawed for their shipments of it, Voltaire could be sure that he was succeeding in his attempt to propel his ideas through the main lines of France's communications system.

III

The role of Voltaire and Cramer in the diffusion process raises the problem of how Rigaud's operation fits into the other stages in the life cycle of the *Questions*. Rigaud knew that he was not getting a first edition; the STN had sent a circular letter to him and its other main customers explaining that it would reproduce Cramer's text, but with corrections and additions provided by the author himself, so that its version would be superior to the original. One of the STN's directors had visited Voltaire at Ferney in April 1770 and had returned with a promise that Voltaire would touch up the printed sheets he was to receive from Cramer and then would forward them to Neuchâtel for a pirated edition.[12] Voltaire often played such tricks. They provided a way to improve the quality and increase the quantity of his books, and therefore served his main purpose – which was not to make money, for he did not sell his prose to the printers, but to spread Enlightenment. The profit motive kept the rest of the system going, however. So when Cramer got wind of the STN's attempt to raid his market, he protested to Voltaire, Voltaire retracted his promise to the STN, and the STN had to settle for a delayed version of the text, which it received from Ferney, but with only minimal additions and corrections.[13] In fact, this setback did not hurt its sales, because the market had plenty of room to absorb editions, not only the STN's but also one that Marc Michel Rey produced in Amsterdam, and probably others as well. The booksellers had their choice of suppliers, and they chose according to whatever marginal advantage they could obtain on matters of price, quality, speed, and reliability in delivery. Rigaud dealt regularly with publishers in Paris, Lyon, Rouen, Avignon, and Geneva. He played them off against each other and sometimes ordered the same book from two or three of them so as to be certain of getting it before his competitors did. By working several circuits at the same time, he increased his room for maneuver. But in the case of the *Questions*, he was outmaneuvered and had to receive his goods from the circuitous Voltaire–Cramer–Voltaire–STN route.

   That route merely took the copy from the author to the printer. For the printed sheets to reach Rigaud in Montpellier from the STN's shop in Neuchâtel, they had to wind their way through one of the most complex stages in the book's circuit. They could follow two main routes. One led from Neuchâtel to Geneva, Turin, Nice (which was not yet French), and Marseille. It had the advantage of skirting French territory – and therefore the danger of confiscation – but it involved huge detours and expenses. The books had to be lugged over the Alps and pass through a whole army of middlemen – shipping agents, bargemen, wagoners, entrepôt keepers, ship captains, and dockers – before they arrived in Rigaud's storeroom. The best Swiss shippers claimed they could get a crate to Nice in a month for thirteen livres, eight sous per hundredweight; but their estimates proved to be far too low. The direct route from Neuchâtel to Lyon and down the Rhône was fast, cheap, and easy – but dangerous. The crates had to be sealed at their point of entry into France and inspected by the booksellers' guild and the royal book inspector in Lyon, then reshipped and inspected once more in Montpellier.[14]

Always cautious, Rigaud asked the STN to ship the first volumes of the *Questions* by the roundabout route, because he knew he could rely on his agent in Marseille, Joseph Coulomb, to get the books into France without mishap. They left on December 9, 1771, but did not arrive until after March, when the first three volumes of Cramer's edition were already being sold by Rigaud's competitors. The second and third volumes arrived in July, but loaded down with shipping charges and damaged by rough handling. 'It seems that we are five or six thousand leagues apart', Rigaud complained, adding that he regretted he had not given his business to Cramer, whose shipments had already reached volume six.[15] By this time, the STN was worried enough about losing customers throughout southern France to set up a smuggling operation in Lyon. Their man, a marginal bookdealer named Joseph-Louis Berthoud, got volumes four and five past the guild inspectors, but then his business collapsed in bankruptcy; and to make matters worse, the French government imposed a tax of sixty livres per hundredweight on all book imports. The STN fell back on the Alpine route, offering to get its shipments as far as Nice for fifteen livres per hundredweight if Rigaud would pay the rest of the expenses, including the import duty. But Rigaud considered the duty such a heavy blow to the international trade that he suspended all his orders with foreign suppliers. The new tariff policy had made it prohibitively expensive to disguise illegal books as legal ones and to pass them through normal commercial channels.

In December, the STN's agent in Nice, Jacques Deandreis, somehow got a shipment of volume six of the *Questions* to Rigaud through the port of Sète, which was supposed to be closed to book imports. Then the French government, realizing that it had nearly destroyed the foreign book trade, lowered the tariff to twenty-six livres per hundredweight. Rigaud proposed sharing the cost with his suppliers: he would pay one third if they would pay two thirds. This proposal suited the STN, but in the spring of 1772 Rigaud decided that the Nice route was too expensive to be used under any conditions. Having heard enough complaints from its other customers to reach the same conclusion, the STN dispatched one of its directors to Lyon, and he persuaded a more dependable Lyonnais dealer, J.-M. Barret, to clear its shipments through the local guild and forward them to its provincial clients. Thanks to this arrangement, the last three volumes of Rigaud's *Questions* arrived safely in the summer.

It had required continuous effort and considerable expense to get the entire order to Montpellier, and Rigaud and the STN did not stop realigning their supply routes once they had completed this transaction. Because economic and political pressures kept shifting, they had constantly to readjust their arrangements within the complex world of middlemen, who linked printing houses with bookshops and often determined, in the last analysis, what literature reached French readers.

How the readers assimilated their books cannot be determined. Bibliographical analysis of all the copies that can be located would show what varieties of the text were available. A study of notarial archives in Montpellier might indicate how many copies turned up in inheritances, and statistics drawn from auction catalogues might make it possible to estimate the number in substantial private libraries. But given the present state of documentation, one cannot know who Voltaire's readers were or how they responded to his text. Reading remains the most difficult stage to study in the circuit that books follow.

IV

All stages were affected by the social, economic, political, and intellectual conditions of the time; but for Rigaud, these general influences made themselves felt within a local context. He sold books in a city of thirty-one thousand inhabitants. Despite an important textile industry, Montpellier was essentially an old-fashioned administrative and religious center, richly endowed with cultural institutions, including a university, an academy of sciences, twelve Masonic lodges, and sixteen monastic communities. And because it was a seat of the provincial estates of Languedoc and an intendancy, and had as well an array of courts, the city had a large population of lawyers and royal officials. If they resembled their counterparts in other provincial centers,[16] they probably provided Rigaud with a good many of his customers and probably had a taste for Enlightenment literature. He did not discuss their social background in his correspondence, but he noted that they clamored for the works of Voltaire, Rousseau, and Raynal. They subscribed heavily to the *Encyclopédie*, and even asked for atheistic treatises like *Système de la nature* and *Philosophie de la nature*. Montpellier was no intellectual backwater, and it was good book territory. 'The book trade is quite extensive in this town', an observer remarked in 1768. 'The booksellers have kept their shops well stocked ever since the inhabitants developed a taste for having libraries.'[17]

These favorable conditions prevailed when Rigaud ordered his *Questions*. But hard times set in during the early 1770s; and in the 1780s Rigaud, like most booksellers, complained of a severe decline in his trade. The whole French economy contracted during those years, according to the standard account of C. E. Labrousse.[18] Certainly, the state's finances went into a tailspin: hence the disastrous book tariff of 1771, which belonged to Terray's unsuccessful attempt to reduce the deficit accumulated during the Seven Years' War. The government also tried to stamp out pirated and forbidden books, first by more severe police work in 1771–74, then by a general reform of the book trade in 1777. These measures eventually ruined Rigaud's commerce with the STN and with the other publishing houses that had grown up around France's borders during the prosperous mid-century years. Foreign publishers produced both original editions of books that could not pass the censorship in Paris and pirated editions of books put out by the Parisian publishers. Because the Parisians had acquired a virtual monopoly over the legal publishing industry, their rivals in the provinces formed alliances with the foreign houses and looked the other way when shipments from abroad arrived for inspection in the provincial guild halls (*chambres syndicales*). Under Louis XIV the government had used the Parisian guild as an instrument to suppress the illegal trade: but under Louis XV it became increasingly lax, until a new era of severity began with the fall of Choiseul's ministry (December 1770). Thus Rigaud's relations with the STN fit perfectly into an economic and political pattern that had prevailed in the book trade since the early eighteenth century and that began to fall apart just as the first crates of the *Questions* were making their way between Neuchâtel and Montpellier.

Other patterns might show up in other research, for the model need not be applied in this manner, nor need it be applied at all. I am not arguing that book history should be written according to a standard formula but trying to show how its disparate segments can be brought together within a single conceptual scheme. Different book historians might prefer different schemata. They might concentrate on the book trade of all Languedoc, as Madeleine Ventre has done; or on the general bibliography of Voltaire, as Giles Barber, Jeroom Vercruysse, and others are doing; or on the overall pattern of book production in eighteenth-century France, in the manner of François Furet and Robert Estivals.[19] But however they define their subject, they will not draw out its full significance unless they relate it to all the elements that worked together as a circuit for transmitting texts. To make the point clearer, I will go over the model circuit once more, noting questions that have been investigated successfully or that seem ripe for further research.

I Authors

Despite the proliferation of biographies of great writers, the basic conditions of authorship remain obscure for most periods of history. At what point did writers free themselves from the patronage of wealthy noblemen and the state in order to live by their pens? What was the nature of a literary career, and how was it pursued? How did writers deal with publishers, printers, booksellers, reviewers, and one another? Until those questions are answered, we will not have a full understanding of the transmission of texts. Voltaire was able to manipulate secret alliances with pirate publishers because he did not depend on writing for a living. A century later, Zola proclaimed that a writer's independence came from selling his prose to the highest bidder.[20] How did this transformation take place? The work of John Lough begins to provide an answer, but more systematic research on the evolution of the republic of letters in France could be done from police records, literary almanacs, and bibliographies (*La France littéraire* gives the names and publications of 1,187 writers in 1757 and 3,089 in 1784). The situation in Germany is more obscure, owing to the fragmentation of the German states before 1871. But German scholars are beginning to tap sources like *Das gelehrte Teutschland*, which lists four thousand writers in 1779, and to trace the links between authors, publishers, and readers in regional and monographic studies.[21] Marino Berengo has shown how much can be discovered about author–publisher relations in Italy.[22] And the work of A. S. Collins still provides an excellent account of authorship in England, although it needs to be brought up to date and extended beyond the eighteenth century.[23]

II Publishers

The key role of publishers is now becoming clearer, thanks to articles appearing in the *Journal of Publishing History* and monographs like Martin Lowry's *The World of Aldus Manutius*, Robert Patten's *Charles Dickens and His Publishers*, and Gary Stark's *Entrepreneurs of Ideology: Neoconservative Publishers in Germany, 1890–1933*. But the evolution of the publisher as a distinct figure in contrast to the master bookseller and the printer still needs systematic study. Historians have barely begun to tap the papers of publishers, although they are the richest of all sources for the history of books. The archives of the Cotta Verlag in Marbach, for example, contain at least one hundred and fifty thousand documents, yet they have only been skimmed for references to Goethe, Schiller, and other famous writers. Further investigation almost certainly would turn up a great deal of information about the book as a force in nineteenth-century Germany. How did publishers draw up contracts with authors, build alliances with booksellers, negotiate with political authorities, and handle finances, supplies, shipments, and publicity? The answers to those questions would carry the history of books deep into the territory of social, economic, and political history, to their mutual benefit.

The Project for Historical Biobibliography at Newcastle upon Tyne and the Institut de Littérature et de Techniques Artistiques de Masse at Bordeaux illustrate the directions that such interdisciplinary work has already taken. The Bordeaux group has tried to trace books through different distribution systems in order to uncover the literary experience of different groups in contemporary France.[24] The researchers in Newcastle have studied the diffusion process through quantitative analysis of subscription lists, which were widely used in the sales campaigns of British publishers from the early seventeenth to the early nineteenth centuries.[25] Similar work could be done on publishers' catalogues and prospectuses, which have been collected in research centers like the Newberry Library. The whole subject of book advertising needs investigation. One could learn a great deal about attitudes toward books and the context of their use by studying the way they were presented – the strategy of the appeal, the values invoked by the phrasing – in all kinds of publicity, from journal notices to wall posters. American historians have used newspaper advertisements to map the spread of the printed word into the back reaches of colonial society.[26] By consulting the papers of publishers, they could make deeper inroads in the nineteenth and twentieth centuries.[27] Unfortunately, however, publishers usually treat their archives as garbage. Although they save the occasional letter from a famous author, they throw away account books and commercial correspondence, which usually are the most important sources of information for the book historian. The Center for the Book in the Library of Congress is now compiling a guide to publishers' archives. If they can be preserved and studied, they might provide a different perspective on the whole course of American history.

III Printers

The printing shop is far better known than the other stages in the production and diffusion of books because it has been a favorite subject of study in the field of analytical bibliography, whose purpose, as defined by R. B. McKerrow and Philip Gaskell, is 'to elucidate the transmission of texts by explaining the processes of book production'.[28] Bibliographers have made important contributions to textual criticism, especially in Shakespearean scholarship, by building inferences backward from the structure of a book to the process of its printing and hence to an original text, such as the missing Shakespeare manuscripts. That line of reasoning has been undercut recently by D. F. McKenzie.[29] But even if they can never reconstruct an Ur-Shakespeare, bibliographers can demonstrate the existence of different editions of a text and of different states of an edition, a necessary skill in diffusion studies. Their techniques also make it possible to decipher the records of printers and so have opened up a new, archival phase in the history of printing. Thanks to the work of McKenzie, Leon Voet, Raymond de Roover, and Jacques Rychner, we now have a clear picture of how printing shops operated throughout the handpress period (roughly 1500–1800).[30] More work needs to be done on later periods, and new questions could be asked: How did printers calculate costs and organize production, especially after the spread of job printing and journalism? How did book budgets change after the introduction of machine-made paper in the first decade of the nineteenth century and Linotype in the 1880s? How did the technological changes affect the management of labor? And what part did journeymen printers, an unusually articulate and militant sector of the working class, play in labor history? Analytical bibliography may seem arcane to the outsider, but it could make a great contribution to social as well as literary history, especially if it were seasoned with a reading of printers' manuals and autobiographies, beginning with those of Thomas Platter, Thomas Gent, N. F. Restif de la Bretonne, Benjamin Franklin, and Charles Manby Smith.

IV Shippers

Little is known about the way books reached bookstores from printing shops. The wagon, the canal barge, the merchant vessel, the post office, and the railroad may have influenced the history of literature more than one would suspect. Although transport facilities probably had little effect on the trade in great publishing centers like London and Paris, they sometimes determined the ebb and flow of business in remote areas. Before the nineteenth century, books were usually sent in sheets, so that the customer could have them bound according to his taste and his ability to pay. They traveled in large bales wrapped in heavy paper and were easily damaged by rain and the friction of ropes. Compared with commodities like textiles, their intrinsic value was slight, yet their shipping costs were high, owing to the size and weight of the sheets. So shipping often took up a large proportion of a book's total cost and a large place in the marketing strategy of publishers. In many parts of Europe, printers could not count on getting shipments to booksellers in August and September because wagoners abandoned their routes to work the harvest. The Baltic trade frequently ground to a halt after October, because ice closed the ports. Routes opened and shut everywhere in response to the pressures of war, politics, and even insurance rates. Unorthodox literature has traveled underground in huge quantities from the sixteenth century to the present, so its influence has varied according to the effectiveness of the smuggling industry. And other genres, like chapbooks and penny dreadfuls, circulated through special distribution systems, which need much more study, although book historians are now beginning to clear some of the ground.[31]

V Booksellers

Thanks to some classic studies – H. S. Bennett on early modern England, L. C. Wroth on colonial America, H.-J. Martin on seventeenth-century France, and Johann Goldfriedrich on Germany – it is possible to piece together a general picture of the evolution of the book trade.[32] But more work needs to be done on the bookseller as a cultural agent, the middleman who mediated between supply and demand at their key point of contact. We still do not know enough about the social and intellectual world of men like Rigaud, about their values and tastes and the way they fit into their communities. They also operated within commercial networks, which expanded and collapsed like alliances in the diplomatic world. What laws governed the rise and fall of trade empires in publishing? A comparison of national histories could reveal some general tendencies, such as the centripetal force of great centers like London, Paris, Frankfurt, and Leipzig, which drew provincial houses into their orbits, and the countervailing trend toward alignments between provincial dealers and suppliers in independent enclaves like Liège, Bouillon, Neuchâtel, Geneva, and Avignon. But comparisons are difficult because the trade operated through different institutions in different countries, which generated different kinds of archives. The records of the London Stationers' company, the Communauté des Libraires et Imprimeurs de Paris, and the Leipzig and Frankfurt book fairs have had a great deal to do with the different courses that book history has taken in England, France, and Germany.[33]

Nevertheless, books were sold as commodities everywhere. A more unabashedly economic study of them would provide a new perspective to the history of literature. James Barnes, John Tebbel, and Frédéric Barbier have demonstrated the importance of the economic element in the book trades of nineteenth-century England, America, and France.[34] But more work could be done – on credit mechanisms, for example, and the techniques of negotiating bills of exchange, of defense against suspensions of payment, and of exchanging printed sheets in lieu of payment in specie. The book trade, like other businesses during the Renaissance and early modern periods, was largely a confidence game, but we still do not know how it was played.

VI Readers

Despite a considerable literature on its psychology, phenomenology, textology, and sociology, reading remains mysterious. How do readers make sense of the signs on the printed page? What are the social effects of that experience? And how has it varied? Literary scholars like Wayne Booth, Stanley Fish, Wolfgang Iser, Walter Ong, and Jonathan Culler have made reading a central concern of textual criticism because they understand literature as an activity, the construal of meaning within a system of communication, rather than a canon of texts.[35] The book historian could make use of their notions of fictitious audiences, implicit readers, and interpretive communities. But he may find their observations somewhat time-bound. Although the critics know their way around literary history (they are especially strong on seventeenth-century England), they seem to assume that texts have always worked on the sensibilities of readers in the same way. But a seventeenth-century London burgher inhabited a different mental universe from that of a twentieth-century American professor. Reading itself has changed over time. It was often done aloud and in groups, or in secret and with an intensity we may not be able to imagine today. Carlo Ginzburg has shown how much meaning a sixteenth-century miller could infuse into a text, and Margaret Spufford has demonstrated that still humbler workmen fought their way to mastery over the printed word in the era of

Areopagitica.[36] Everywhere in early modern Europe, from the ranks of Montaigne to those of Menocchio, readers wrung significance from books; they did not merely decipher them. Reading was a passion long before the '*Lesewut*' and the '*Wertherfieber*' of the romantic era; and there is *Sturm und Drang* in it yet, despite the vogue for speed-reading and the mechanistic view of literature as the encoding and decoding of messages.

But texts shape the response of readers, however active they may be. As Walter Ong has observed, the opening pages of *The Canterbury Tales* and *A Farewell to Arms* create a frame and cast the reader in a role, which he cannot avoid no matter what he thinks of pilgrimages and civil wars.[37] In fact, typography as well as style and syntax determine the ways in which texts convey meanings. McKenzie has shown that the bawdy, unruly Congreve of the early quarto editions settled down into the decorous neoclassicist of the *Works* of 1709 as a consequence of book design rather than bowdlerization.[38] The history of reading will have to take account of the ways that texts constrain readers as well as the ways that readers take liberties with texts. The tension between those tendencies has existed wherever men confronted books, and it has produced some extraordinary results, as in Luther's reading of the Psalms, Rousseau's reading of *Le Misanthrope*, and Kierkegaard's reading of the sacrifice of Isaac.

If it is not possible to recapture the great rereadings of the past, the inner experience of ordinary readers may always elude us. But we should at least be able to reconstruct a good deal of the social context of reading. The debate about silent reading during the Middle Ages has produced some impressive evidence about reading habits,[39] and studies of reading societies in Germany, where they proliferated to an extraordinary degree in the eighteenth and nineteenth centuries, have shown the importance of reading in the development of a distinct bourgeois cultural style.[40] German scholars have also done a great deal in the history of libraries and in reception studies of all kinds.[41] Following a notion of Rolf Engelsing, they often maintain that reading habits became transformed at the end of the eighteenth century. Before this '*Leserevolution*', readers tended to work laboriously through a small number of texts, especially the Bible, over and over again. Afterwards, they raced through all kinds of material, seeking amusement rather than edification. The shift from intensive to extensive reading coincided with a desacralization of the printed word. The world began to be cluttered with reading matter, and texts began to be treated as commodities that could be discarded as casually as yesterday's newspaper. This interpretation has recently been disputed by Reinhart Siegert, Martin Welke, and other young scholars, who have discovered 'intensive' reading in the reception of fugitive works like almanacs and newspapers, notably the *Noth- und Hülfsbüchlein* of Rudolph Zacharias Becker, an extraordinary best seller of the *Goethezeit*.[42] But whether or not the concept of a reading revolution will hold up, it has helped to align research on reading with general questions of social and cultural history.[43] The same can be said of research on literacy,[44] which has made it possible for scholars to detect the vague outline of diverse reading publics two and three centuries ago and to trace books to readers at several levels of society. The lower the level, the more intense the study. Popular literature has been a favorite topic of research during the last decade,[45] despite a growing tendency to question the notion that cheap booklets like the *bibliothèque bleue* represented an autonomous culture of the common people or that one can distinguish clearly between strains of 'elite' and 'popular' culture. It now seems inadequate to view cultural change as a linear, or trickle-down, movement of influences. Currents flowed up as well as down, merging and blending as they went. Characters like Gargantua, Cinderella, and Buscon moved back and forth through oral traditions, chapbooks, and sophisticated literature, changing in nationality as well as genre.[46] One could even trace the metamorphoses of stock figures in almanacs. What does Poor Richard's reincarnation as *le Bonhomme Richard* reveal about literary culture in America and France? And what can be learned about German–French relations by following the Lame Messenger (*der hinkende Bote, le messager boiteux*) through the traffic of almanacs across the Rhine?

Questions about who reads what, in what conditions, at what time, and with what effect, link reading studies with sociology. The book historian could learn how to pursue such questions from the work of Douglas Waples, Bernard Berelson, Paul Lazarsfeld, and Pierre Bourdieu. He could draw on the reading research that flourished in the Graduate Library School of the University of Chicago from 1930 to 1950, and that still turns up in the occasional Gallup report.[47] And as an example of the sociological strain in historical writing, he could consult the studies of reading (and nonreading) in the English working class during the last two centuries by Richard Altick, Robert Webb, and Richard Hoggart.[48] All this work opens onto the larger problem of how exposure to the printed word affects the way men think. Did the invention of movable type transform man's mental universe? There may be no single satisfactory answer to that question because it bears on so many different aspects of life in early modern Europe, as Elizabeth Eisenstein has shown.[49] But it should be possible to arrive at a firmer understanding of what books meant to people. Their use in the taking of oaths, the exchanging of gifts, the awarding of prizes, and the bestowing of legacies would provide clues to their significance within different societies. The iconography of books could indicate the weight of their authority, even for illiterate laborers who sat in church before pictures of the tablets of Moses. The place of books in folklore, and of folk motifs in books, shows that influences ran both ways when oral traditions came into contact with printed texts, and that books need to be studied in relation to other media.[50] The lines of research could lead in many directions, but they all should issue ultimately in a larger understanding of how printing has shaped man's attempts to make sense of the human condition.

One can easily lose sight of the larger dimensions of the enterprise because book historians often stray into esoteric byways and unconnected specializations. Their work can be so fragmented, even within the limits of the literature on a single country, that it may seem hopeless to conceive of book history as a single subject, to be studied from a comparative perspective across the whole range of historical disciplines. But books themselves do not respect limits, either linguistic or national. They have often been written by authors who belonged to an international republic of letters, composed by printers who did not work in their native tongue, sold by booksellers who operated across national boundaries, and read in one language by readers who spoke another. Books also refuse to be contained within the confines of a single discipline when treated as objects of study. Neither history nor literature nor economics nor sociology nor bibliography can do justice to all the aspects of the life of a book. By its very nature, therefore, the history of books must be international in scale and interdisciplinary in method. But it need not lack conceptual coherence, because books belong to circuits of communication that operate in consistent patterns, however complex they may be. By unearthing those circuits, historians can show that books do not merely recount history; they make it.

Notes

This essay first appeared in *Daedalus* (Summer 1982): 65–83. Since then I have attempted to develop its themes further in an essay on the history of reading in 'Histoire du livre – Geschichte des Buchwesens: An Agenda for Comparative History', *Publishing History*, no. 22 (1987): 33–41.

1   For examples of this work, see, in addition to the books named in the essay, Henri-Jean Martin, *Livre, pouvoirs et société à Paris au XVII* siècle (1598–1701)* (Geneva, 1969), 2 volumes; Jean Quéniart, *L'Imprimerie et la librairie à Rouen au XVIII* siècle* (Paris, 1969); René Moulinas, *L'Imprimerie, la librairie et la presse à Avignon au XVIII* siècle* (Grenoble, 1974); and Frédéric Barbier, *Trois cents ans de librairie et d'imprimerie: Berger-Levrault, 1676–1830* (Geneva, 1979), in the series 'Histoire et civilisation du livre', which includes several monographs written along similar lines. Much of the French work has appeared as articles in the *Revue française d'histoire*

du livre. For a survey of the field by two of the most important contributors to it, see Roger Chartier and Daniel Roche, 'Le livre, un changement de perspective', *Faire de l'histoire* (Paris, 1974), III: 115–36, and Chartier and Roche, 'L'Histoire quantitative du livre', *Revue française d'histoire du livre* 16 (1977): 3–27. For sympathetic assessments by two American fellow travelers, see Robert Darnton, 'Reading, Writing, and Publishing in Eighteenth-Century France: A Case Study in the Sociology of Literature', *Daedalus* (Winter 1971): 214–56, and Raymond Birn, 'Livre et Société After Ten Years: Formation of a Discipline', *Studies on Voltaire and the Eighteenth Century* 151 (1976): 287–312.

2   As examples of these approaches, see Theodore Besterman, *Voltaire* (New York, 1969), pp. 433–34; Daniel Mornet, 'Les Enseignements des bibliothèques privées (1750–1780)', *Revue d'histoire littéraire de la France* 17 (1910): 449–92; and the bibliographical studies now being prepared under the direction of the Voltaire Foundation, which will replace the outdated bibliography by Georges Bengesco.

3   The following account is based on the ninety-nine letters in Rigaud's dossier in the papers of the Société typographique de Neuchâtel, Bibliothèque de la ville de Neuchâtel, Switzerland (henceforth referred to as STN), supplemented by other relevant material from the vast archives of the STN.

4   Rigaud to STN, July 27, 1771.

5   The pattern of Rigaud's orders is evident from his letters to the STN and STN's 'Livres de Commission', where it tabulated its orders. Rigaud included catalogues of his major holdings in his letters of June 29, 1774, and May 23, 1777.

6   Madeleine Ventre, *L'Imprimerie et la librairie en Languedoc au dernier siècle de l'Ancien Régime* (Paris and The Hague, 1958), p. 227.

7   B. André to STN, August 22, 1784.

8   *Manuel de l'auteur et du libraire* (Paris, 1777), p. 67.

9   Jean-François Favarger to STN, August 29, 1778.

10   The *procès-verbal* of the raids is in the Bibliothèque Nationale, Ms. français 22075, fo. 355.

11   Fontanel to STN, March 6, 1781.

12   STN to Gosse and Pinet, booksellers of The Hague, April 19, 1770.

13   STN to Voltaire, September 15, 1770.

14   This account is based on the STN's correspondence with intermediaries all along its routes, notably the shipping agents Nicole and Galliard of Nyon and Secrétan and De la Serve of Ouchy.

15   Rigaud to STN, August 28, 1771.

16   Robert Darnton, *The Business of Enlightenment: A Publishing History of the Encyclopédie 1775–1800* (Cambridge, Mass., 1979), pp. 273–99.

17   Anonymous, 'Etat et description de la ville de Montpellier, fait en 1768', in *Montpellier en 1768 et en 1836 d'après deux manuscrits inédits*, edited by J. Berthelé (Montpellier, 1909), p. 55. This rich contemporary description of Montpellier is the main source of the above account.

18   C. E. Labrousse, *La Crise de l'économie française à la fin de l'Ancien Régime et au début de la Révolution* (Paris, 1944).

19   Ventre, *L'Imprimerie et la librairie en Languedoc*; François Furet, 'La "librairie" du royaume de France au 18ᵉ siecle', *Livre et société*, 1, 3–32; and Robert Estivals, *La Statistique bibliographique de la France sous la monarchie au XVIIIᵉ siècle* (Paris and The Hague, 1965). The bibliographical work will be published under the auspices of the Voltaire Foundation.

20   John Lough, *Writer and Public in France from the Middle Ages to the Present Day* (Oxford, 1978), p. 303.

21   For surveys and selections of recent German research, see Helmuth Kiesel and Paul Münch, *Gesellschaft und Literatur im 18. Jahrhundert. Voraussetzung und Entstehung des literarischen Marktes in Deutschland* (Munich, 1977); *Aufklärung, Absolutismus und Bürgertum in Deutschland*, edited by

Franklin Kopitzsch (Munich, 1976); and Herbert G. Göpfert, *Vom Autor sum Leser* (Munich 1978).

22   Marino Berengo, *Intellettuali e librai nella Milano della Restaurazione* (Turin, 1980). On the whole, however, the French version of *histoire du livre* has received a less enthusiastic reception in Italy than in Germany: see Furio Diaz, 'Metodo quantitativo e storia delle idee', *Rivista storica italiana* 78 (1966): 932–47.

23   A. S. Collins, *Authorship in the Days of Johnson* (London, 1927) and *The Profession of Letters (1780–1832)* (London, 1928). For more recent work, see John Feather, 'John Nourse and His Authors', *Studies in Bibliography* 34(1981): 205–26.

24   Robert Escarpit, *Le Littéraire et le social. Eléments pour une sociologie de la littérature* (Paris, 1970).

25   Peter John Wallis, *The Social Index: A New Technique for Measuring Social Trends* (Newcastle upon Tyne, 1978).

26   William Gilmore is now completing an extensive research project on the diffusion of books in colonial New England. On the political and economic aspects of the colonial press, see Stephen Botein, ' "Meer Mechanics" and an Open Press: The Business and Political Strategies of Colonial American Printers', *Perspectives in American History* 9 (1975): 127–225; and *The Press and the American Revolution*, edited by Bernard Bailyn and John B. Hench (Worcester, Mass., 1980), which contain ample references to work on the early history of the book in America.

27   For a general survey of work on the later history of books in this country, see Hellmut Lehmann-Haupt, *The Book in America*, rev. ed. (New York, 1952).

28   Philip Gaskell, *A New Introduction to Bibliography* (New York and Oxford, 1972), preface. Gaskell's work provides an excellent general survey of the subject.

29   D. F. McKenzie, 'Printers of the Mind: Some Notes on Bibliographical Theories and Printing House Practices', *Studies in Bibliography* 22 (1969): 1–75.

30   D. F. McKenzie, *The Cambridge University Press 1696–1712* (Cambridge, 1966), 2 volumes; Leon Voet, *The Golden Compasses* (Amsterdam, 1969 and 1972), 2 volumes; Raymond de Roover, 'The Business Organization of the Plantin Press in the Setting of Sixteenth-Century Antwerp', *De gulden passer* 24 (1956): 104–20; and Jacques Rychner, 'A l'ombre des Lumières: coup d'oeil sur la main-d'oeuvre de quelques imprimeries du XVIIIe siècle', *Studies on Voltaire and the Eighteenth Century*, 155 (1976): 1925–55, and 'Running a Printing House in Eighteenth-Century Switzerland: the Workshop of the Société typographique de Neuchâtel', *The Library*, sixth series, 1(1979): 1–24.

31   For example, see J.-P. Belin, *Le Commerce des livres prohibés à Paris de 1750 à 1789* (Paris, 1913); Jean-Jacques Darmon, *Le Colportage de librairie en France sous le second empire* (Paris, 1972); and Reinhart Siegert, *Aufklärung und Volkslektüre exemplarisch dargestellt an Rudolph Zacharias Becker und seinem 'Noth- und Hülfsbüchlein' mit einer Bibliographie zum Gesamtthema* (Frankfurt am Main, 1978).

32   H. S. Bennett, *English Books and Readers 1475 to 1557* (Cambridge, 1952) and *English Books and Readers 1558–1603* (Cambridge, 1965); L. C. Wroth, *The Colonial Printer* (Portland, 1938); Martin, *Livre, pouvoirs et société*; and Johann Goldfriedrich and Friedrich Kapp, *Geschichte des Deutschen Buchhandels* (Leipzig, 1886–1913), 4 volumes.

33   Compare Cyprian Blagden, *The Stationers' Company, A History, 1403–1959* (Cambridge, 1960); Martin, *Livre, pouvoirs et société*; and Rudolf Jentzsch, *Der deutsch-lateinische Büchermarkt nach den Leipziger Ostermesskatalogen von 1740, 1770 und 1800 in seiner Gliederung und Wandlung* (Leipzig, 1912).

34   James Barnes, *Free Trade in Books: A Study of the London Book Trade Since 1800* (Oxford, 1964); John Tebbel, *A History of Book Publishing in the United States* (New York, 1972–78), 3 volumes; and Barbier, *Trois cents ans de librairie et d'imprimerie.*

35   See, for example, Wolfgang Iser, *The Implied Reader: Patterns of Communication in Prose Fiction*

from Bunyan to Beckett (Baltimore, 1974); Stanley Fish, *Self-Consuming Artifacts: The Experience of Seventeenth-Century Literature* (Berkeley and Los Angeles, 1972) and *Is There a Text in This Class? The Authority of Interpretive Communities* (Cambridge, Mass., 1980); Walter Ong, 'The Writer's Audience Is Always a Fiction', *PMLA (Publication of the Modern Language Association of America)* 90 (1975): 9–21; and for a sampling of other variations on these themes, Susan R. Suleiman and Inge Crosman, *The Reader in the Text: Essays on Audience and Interpretation* (Princeton: Princeton University Press, 1980).

36 Carlo Ginzburg, *The Cheese and the Worms: The Cosmos of a Sixteenth-Century Miller* (Baltimore: Johns Hopkins University Press, 1980); Margaret Spufford, 'First Steps in Literacy: The Reading and Writing Experiences of the Humblest Seventeenth-Century Spiritual Autobiographers, *Social History* 4 (1979): 407–35.

37 Ong, 'The Writer's Audience Is Always a Fiction'.

38 D. F. McKenzie, 'Typography and Meaning: The Case of William Congreve', *Wolfenbütteler Schriften zur Geschichte des Buchwesens* (Hamburg: Dr. Ernst Hauswedell, 1981), IV: 81–125.

39 See Paul Saenger, 'Silent Reading: Its Impact on Late Medieval Script and Society', *Viator* 13 (1982): 367–414.

40 See *Lesegesellschaften and bürgerliche Emanzipation. Ein Europäischer Vergleich*, edited by Otto Dann (Munich: C. H. Beck, 1981), which has a thorough bibliography.

41 For examples of recent work, see *Öffentliche und Private Bibliotheken in 17. und 18. Jahrhundert: Raritätenkammern, Forschungsinstrumente oder Bildungsstätten?* edited by Paul Raabe (Bremen and Wolfenbütttel, 1977). Much of the stimulus for recent reception studies has come from the theoretical work of Hans Robert Jauss, notably *Literaturgeschichte als Provokation* (Frankfurt am Main, 1970).

42 Engelsing, *Analphabetentum und Lektüre, Zur Sozialgeschichte des Lesens in Deutschland zwischen feudaler und industrieller Gesellschaft* (Stuttgart, 1973), and *Der Burger als Leser. Lesergeschichte in Deutschland 1500–1800* (Stuttgart, 1974); Siegert, *Aufklärung und Volkslektüre*; and Martin Welke, 'Gemeinsame Lektüre und frühe Formen von Gruppenbildungen im 17. and 18. Jahrhundert: Zeitungslesen in Deutschland', in *Lesegesellschaften und bürgerliche Emanzipation*, pp. 29–53.

43 As an example of this alignment, see Rudolf Schenda, *Volk ohne Buch* (Frankfurt am Main, 1970), and for examples of more recent work, *Leser und Lesen im Achtzehnten Jahrhundert*, edited by Rainer Gruenter (Heidelberg, 1977) and *Lesen und Leben*, edited by Herbert G. Göpfert (Frankfurt am Main, 1975).

44 See François Furet and Jacques Ozouf, *Lire et écrire: L'Alphabétisation des français de Calvin à Jules Ferry* (Paris, 1978); Lawrence Stone, 'Literacy and Education in England, 1640–1900', *Past and Present* 42 (1969): 69–139; David Cressy, *Literacy and the Social Order: Reading and Writing in Tudor and Stuart England* (Cambridge, 1980); Kenneth A. Lockridge, *Literacy in Colonial New England* (New York, 1974); and Carlo Cipolla, *Literacy and Development in the West* (Harmondsworth, 1969).

45 For a survey and a synthesis of this research, see Peter Burke, *Popular Culture in Early Modern Europe* (New York, 1978).

46 As an example of the older view, in which the *bibliothéque bleue* serves as a key to the understanding of popular culture, see Robert Mandrou, *De la culture populaire aux XVIIe et XVIIIe siècles: La Bibliothèque bleue de Troyes* (Paris, 1964). For a more nuanced and up-to-date view, see Roger Chartier, *Figures de la gueuserie* (Paris, 1982).

47 Douglas Waples, Bernard Berelson, and Franklyn Bradshaw, *What Reading Does to People* (Chicago, 1940); Bernard Berelson, *The Library's Public* (New York, 1949); Elihu Katz, 'Communication Research and the Image of Society: The Convergence of Two Traditions', *American Journal of Sociology* 65 (1960): 435–40; and John Y. Cole and Carol S. Gold, eds., *Reading in America 1978* (Washington, DC, 1979). For the Gallup report, see the volume published by

the American Library Association, *Book Reading and Library Usage: A Study of Habits and Perceptions* (Chicago, 1978). Much in this older variety of sociology still seems valid, and it can be studied in conjunction with the current work of Pierre Bourdieu; see especially his *La distinction: Critique sociale du jugement* (Paris, 1979).

48   Richard D. Altick, *The English Common Reader: A Social History of the Mass Reading Public 1800–1900* (Chicago, 1957); Robert K. Webb, *The British Working Class Reader* (London, 1955); and Richard Hoggart, *The Uses of Literacy* (Harmondsworth, 1960; 1st edition, 1957).

49   Elisabeth L. Eisenstein, *The Printing Press as an Agent of Change* (Cambridge, 1979), 2 volumes. For a discussion of Eisenstein's thesis, see Anthony T. Grafton, 'The Importance of Being Printed', *Journal of Interdisciplinary History* 11(1980): 265–86; Michael Hunter, 'The Impact of Print', *The Book Collector* 28 (1979): 335–52; and Roger Chartier, 'L'Ancien Régime typographique: Réflexions sur quelques travaux récents', *Annales: Economies, sociétés, civilisations* 36 (1981): 191–209.

50   Some of these general themes are taken up in Eric Havelock, *Origins of Western Literacy* (Toronto, 1976); *Literacy in Traditional Societies*, edited by Jack Goody (Cambridge, 1968); Jack Goody, *The Domestication of the Savage Mind* (Cambridge, 1977); Walter Ong, *The Presence of the Word* (New York, 1970); and Natalie Z. Davis, *Society and Culture in Early Modern France* (Stanford, 1975).

Chapter 3

Fredson Bowers*

BIBLIOGRAPHY, PURE BIBLIOGRAPHY, AND LITERARY STUDIES

There is some value for any scholarly method periodically to examine its principles, its aims and methods, with a view to determining whether it has lost sight of its original objectives and experienced a change of values. The necessity to define, or to re-define, the methods and aims of a field of research is also useful for any individual toiler in the vineyard, for it may serve to raise him, at least momentarily, from concentration on the detailed minutiae to which he must ordinarily apply himself in his research, and by bringing an added consciousness of the purport of what he is engaged in, give to his work a fresh sense of direction. On some occasions it may enforce a recognition that routine has worn ruts which are too deep. But above all, in this specialized society of scholars today when in numerous fields we are coming to know less and less of what our fellows are doing, and why, it is almost incumbent once in a while to try to gather together certain principles of the craft of which we are members for translation into general theories of scholarship. It may be that the statement in plain terms of the objectives of a method or field of research will serve to clarify its position not only to its practitioners but also to those scholars whom it may in one manner or another affect. It may be, also, that a statement in plain terms will arouse such critical objections as to force a reconsideration of the position and thus lead to a valuable reorientation of principles.

I am not concerned with explaining or defining the validity of the bibliographical approach to appropriate literary problems. That battle was fought and won many years ago, and there is no value at this late date in adding a 'me too' to the clear expositions of Sir Walter Greg and R. B. McKerrow. It seems to me, however (or rather I should say, perhaps, it has been forcibly brought to my attention), that the almost incredibly rapid strides which have taken place of recent years in some special areas of bibliographical research have brought into being not a resistance but rather a sympathetic fear that bibliography is in process of developing into something quite different from its original intent. This is worth examining, even with an enforced brevity, for the objections come as well from within as from without the camp and are concerned with a most significant matter, whether bibliography is losing touch with literary study.
[. . .]

With some deliberate simplification, therefore, let me suggest that the major, but by no means mutually exclusive, compartments within the far too general term *bibliography* are these:

---

* Based on a paper read on May 9, 1952, before the Bibliographical Society of the University of Virginia in joint meeting with the Bibliographical Society of America.

(1) The construction of lists of books and writings on various subjects. This common and extremely useful form of bibliographical endeavor I should like to distinguish as *enumerative* or *compilative bibliography*, and thereafter to drop it from consideration since it has no bearing on our present enquiry and has not been brought into question.

(2) Enquiries into the evolution of printing (including type-founding and paper-making), binding, book ownership, and book-selling. I distinguish this as *historical bibliography* and suggest that we limit this field as much as possible according to its historical intent. That is, I take it we should include here all biographical and historical studies of printers, papermakers, binders, type-founders, engravers, publishers, booksellers, and anyone else in any way concerned with the materials and the production of the book and its subsequent dissemination. Under the history of such I should also include studies of costs and prices, methods of sale and distribution; studies of the meaning of imprints, colophons, copyright entries, and of advertisements; all aesthetic studies of printing and its materials as an art; all studies of sizes of editions from the collateral evidence of publishers' records or other external material; all investigation into the circumstances of literary composition which have any relation to the physical form of the literary work, the transmission of literary documents, and the relation of authors to the commercial process of publication. It is difficult to limit this grouping narrowly, but let us say very much in general that it concerns itself chiefly with the discovery and interpretation of external evidence.

In between this section and the next there is an intermediate group about which opinions as to the placement may well differ. I refer to such studies as Hodnett's of woodcuts, McKerrow's and Ferguson's of printer's devices, or Miller's of ornaments,[1] the purpose being to identify ownership, establish dating, and trace deterioration, recutting, and copying. Studies of watermarks, their forms, places, and dates, such as by Briquet, Churchill, Heawood, and Stevenson, are analogous, as are the type studies of Isaac. In one sense these are historical studies; in another, the investigation may verge on the analytical. But some idea of what I assume to be an essential difference, at least in their pure states, may be exhibited if one compares the largely historical and compilative study of watermarks in A. H. Stevenson's 'Watermarks are Twins'[2] with his earlier and strictly analytical investigation of the bibliographical evidence afforded by watermarks for determining the order of sheets through the press, the use of one or of two presses, and the size of an edition-sheet.[3] Another example would be the establishing of the date of a book by the historical method of aligning it with publishers' advertisements versus the more analytical method of placing its ornaments on evidence of wear or fracture within a dated series of books in which they also appear.

(3) This distinction may serve to introduce the third major grouping, covered under the term *analytical bibliography*. In general I define this as technical investigation of the printing of specific books, or of general printing practice, based exclusively on the physical evidence of the books themselves, not ignoring, however, what helpful correlation may be available with collateral evidence.[4] It is possible to give only a selection of the various lines of investigation that have developed, such as the detection and explanation of cancels and of reprinted sheets of all kinds; the detection and explanation of any departure from normal printing practice within a book; determination of the order of the formes through the press and of the number of presses engaged on a book at any one time, with an identification of the formes and sheets printed by each; the analysis of press-figures, running-titles, and watermarks as bearing on the above, as well as the evidence for different composi-torial activity; identification of the date of undated or misdated books by such internal physical evidence unrelated to the readings of the text, including the evidence of its materials (as in the Carter and Pollard study of the Wise forgeries); identification of the printers when more than one participated in a book; and so on.

It is worth emphasis that this analytical method operates only on the physical evidence of the book, and generalizes from that. It is far from true, however, that a book with blank leaves would serve as well, except for the most elementary of analytical operations. What is important is that the impressed symbols which are letters and words are treated in a physical and not in a literary way. (I think it was Sir Walter Greg who once remarked that it should make little difference to analytical studies whether a book were printed in Sanskrit or in English.) Without regard for the meaning conveyed by these symbols, the method of typesetting, punctuating, and spelling the text may provide evidence for analytical procedures, in revealing the presence of one or more compositors from spelling tests or typographical characteristics, without any consideration whatever for the meaning of the words or for their correctness.

[. . .]

(4) This pure form of analytical bibliography lies in back of and leads directly into two other divisions: *descriptive bibliography* and what I should like to distinguish as *critical* or *textual* bibliography.[5] The function of *descriptive bibliography* is to examine a book by all the methods of analytical bibliography in order to arrive at a total comprehension of the maximum physical facts as a preliminary to writing these up in set terms as a definitive physical description of the book, its external appearance, and the internal evidence bearing on the details of this external appearance. There is some need to emphasize that descriptive bibliography which is not based on analytical is practically useless, for it is as important to explain the reason for the peculiarities as it is to give the external facts about them; and, truly, the external facts often cannot be properly described until analytical bibliography has provided the reasons for their existence.[6]

(5) I shall try to define *critical* or *textual bibliography* as the application of the evidence of analytical bibliography, or at least of its pertinent methods, to textual problems where meaning of some sort is involved and where it does make a difference whether a book is printed in English or in Sanskrit. The analytical basis for critical bibliography is usually the bibliographer's experience with the details and characteristics of the printing process interpreted in terms of its specific application to text. This process can take many forms, but a few typical illustrations may serve to indicate what I mean. When Dr. Williams demonstrated on the physical evidence for the method of printing the book, chiefly its pattern of running-titles, that the cancellans fold in the 1609 *Troilus and Cressida* containing a new title-page and an added foreword was not a later substitution as commonly thought but instead that it was printed at the same time as the rest of the book, and as an integral part of the final sheet,[7] he was engaging in pure analytical bibliography. When, on another occasion, he demonstrated that the Folio used as copy an annotated 1609 quarto and not an independent manuscript,[8] he was dealing with critical bibliography since his evidence was the form of the text itself insofar as it related to common typographical features in the two editions which could be explained rationally only by the fact that one was printed from the other. A similar investigation was that of Sir Walter Greg, who demonstrated that the Folio printer's copy for *King Lear* was the Pied Bull quarto on the evidence that it followed certain uncorrected states of the quarto's press-variant formes.[9] As a further example one can cite the evidence based on the physical facts of typesetting used by Dr. Hinman (with no regard for the goodness or badness of the readings) to demonstrate that Q2 *Othello* had merely reprinted the Folio for the added lines not found in Q1 and had not utilized an independent manuscript.[10]

I have suggested some major differences elsewhere between textual criticism and analytical bibliography,[11] and therefore need not belabor the point again except by summarizing my belief that textual criticism concerns itself with words and their meanings, with stylistic and linguistic considerations, and with basic questions of authority in text both in whole and in part. Pure analytical bibliography, on the other hand, deals with books and their texts as material objects and forms manufactured by the mechanical process of printing, and therefore has no proper concern with meaning in texts. The two may join, and even become inextricably mingled, in certain reaches of textual bibliography. Again, an illustration or two may be useful. If a scholar collates a series of editions and on the basis of their readings alone decides their genetic relationship and order, I take it that he is engaging in simple textual criticism. That is, edition B is derived from edition A and not from an independent manuscript. Edition C follows various unique readings in B and therefore derives from B, not A. Edition D follows the unique readings of B, but not the unique readings of A or of C, and therefore derives from B, and so on. Ordinarily a study of this sort can be made with no bibliographical training whatsoever.[12] But when, as with Shakespeare's *King Lear* or Dryden's *Wild Gallant*, the genetic relationship is in fact indeterminate from the readings in this manner and the evidence rests on the fact that one physical state of a given variant edition was followed in certain readings rather than the readings of another physical state (again with no regard for meaning), we have a different order of evidence which is within the province of critical bibliography. . . .

The above is a most incomplete and sketchy account; but I must pass on to the main point of this paper. If the five major divisions, as I understand them, are generally valid within the field of bibliography — even though admittedly they are not watertight — then I hope that recognition of the functions of these divisions will somewhat help to clarify the relation of bibliography as a whole to literary studies. Each one of these divisions may have some ultimate application to literary problems, but the relationship is much more intimate for some than for others. It would seem, then, to be an unduly narrow view which would lump all these different disciplines together and to demand that each be as immediately applicable as the others. . . .

 . . . Let us instead try to face certain facts without self-deception. It has always been a cornerstone of belief that bibliography is the servant of the humanities. I believe this is true and demonstrable. Yet we are only confusing ourselves if we fail to see the obvious fact that certain branches of bibliography are more related to pure research than other branches which have a nearer degree of immediate and practical usefulness. If we are willing to face the truth that no knowledge or love of literature is of material assistance (except as a spur) to the solution of the technical problems which analytical bibliography in its pure state has always set itself, we shall come to the accurate conclusion that it is not itself essentially a literary study no matter how applicable its findings prove to be in the solution of literary problems. The full implications of Sir Walter Greg's remark that [analytical] bibliography is exclusively concerned with the book as a material object have never been properly recognized. If one thinks of a book as a material object, for the purposes of analytical bibliography there is not the slightest difference between a unique first-edition quarto of Shakespeare and the most worthless ephemeral pamphlet of the time.[13] In fact, for the analytical evidence it yields, the pamphlet may be much more valuable than the Shakespeare.

I am talking now in terms of absolutes, for anything less can lead only to confusion. It has been in general true in the past that those who engaged themselves to analytical investigations had earlier had a primary concern with literature, or at least busied themselves as much as possible in turning their analytical results into practical application to literary studies. So far as I can see this is still the case; moreover, I know of no analytical bibliographers who are not either professors of English literature or at least professed students and admirers of literature. But it must be emphasized that this has come about only through certain historical circumstances and need not of necessity be the rule for the future. The discipline is a technical study of a material object divorced from its content, and as such might easily fascinate anyone with a logical turn of mind no matter what his opinions about the humanities. There is nothing we can do about it, and nothing we need do, for it is not a dangerous situation so long as we have critical bibliography to translate the results of pure research into practical application to literature. No scientist would dream of fearing that pure research would become an end in itself, for by its nature it cannot do otherwise; hence I fail to see why literary men should be concerned about the natural course of analytical bibliography, which by its nature is truly written for other bibliographers and not for literary students. Moreover, I think it true that just as the advances of applied science have usually been predicated on the discoveries of pure science, so the astonishing new methods by which critical bibliography can attack problems of text have descended directly from the complex and non-literary work of the analytical bibliographers.

Why, then, has the future of analytics become disquieting even to clear-sighted scholars? There is, I think, at least a partial answer. Analytical bibliography finds its practical application in, first, descriptive bibliography and, second, critical bibliography, which is now a necessary supplement to textual criticism. By using the resources of historical and of analytical bibliography, descriptive bibliography attempts to set in order the basic materials for literary scholarship not only by the discovery of their maximum extent but also by establishing their proper relationship, their internal variants, and last by defining all these matters within the formula of a description. The major justification for this applied scholarship is undoubtedly its usefulness, indeed its necessity, for accurate results in humane studies. So far as this is true, it is certainly an obligation on the part of the bibliographer to state the immediately essential results of his findings in terms that can be understood by a literary student willing to make a reasonable attempt to comprehend them. On the other hand, if a literary student is unwilling to read his McKerrow to achieve an elementary knowledge of the basic printing processes which are being described as part of the procedure of adequately defining a volume under scrutiny, then he has no business coming to such a bibliography for this definition and should content himself with the more general information purveyed in it.

I rather imagine that the greatest uneasiness concentrates on the apparent complexities of the collational-formula system for describing the makeup of a book first proposed by Sir Walter Greg[14] and successfully used by him in his great *Bibliography of the English Drama to the Restoration*. The more immediate source of discomfort, however, may well be my own efforts, as a disciple, to fill-in and slightly elaborate certain features of this system to take account of various bibliographical peculiarities which might be met with by a descriptive bibliographer. The only question, then, is whether this system is too complex to be understood with reasonable effort by those literary students who are competent to make use of the information which it endeavors to crystallize. On this one can only say that time alone will tell. I myself feel that the apparent horrors vanish on slight acquaintance with the few logical principles and symbols underlying the system, and I will guarantee to teach any student in under two hours, no matter how slight his bibliographical knowledge, to read the most tolerably complex collational formula he is ever likely to encounter in the normal course of events. It takes rather longer, however, to teach one to write these formulas, but that is not the point of criticism. Thus I am still inclined to stand by a statement earlier made, 'In actual truth the characters employed in standard description are very few and readily learned; the various shortcuts are so clear in principle and construction that no extraordinary intelligence is needed to decipher them correctly after only the briefest acquaintance, provided the reader has a minimum knowledge of the makeup of books.'[15]

[. . .]

If, then, we may dismiss a fear of technical descriptive bibliography, which is in course of absorbing some of the lessons from its analytical progenitor long overdue, may we not bring equal confidence to charting the future of critical bibliography, the second derivative from analytical. Here I must restate my prime assumption that it is the chief purpose of critical bibliography to translate the pure end-in-itself findings of analytical bibliography into direct application to literary study. This will, of course, chiefly be in connection with problems of text both of a general and of a specific nature. It is clear that this translation can be achieved only by those among the analytics who are interested in both divisions of bibliography or else by the pure textual bibliographers constantly keeping pace with analytical methods not as an independent field of research for them but as a necessary understanding on which to develop their own method. In practice there need be little reason to fear a lack of communication. Since analytical bibliographers do not work by ratiocination in a void but instead with material books, they often cannot help solving textual problems in the simple course of analyzing the printing history of a book.[16] In fact it is almost impossible to stay away from text in pursuing evidence to its ultimate conclusions. Hence even the most arrant technicians of the future will be unable to avoid applying their findings to text on many occasions, since that often represents the most complex technical problem for ingenuity to solve. And critical biblio-graphers, since it is their only excuse for existence, will need to be peculiarly apt in picking up hints in this direction. It does not really seem that we have much to fear if analytics sometimes appears to be going off on its own. Its primary concern is not with text, but somehow it can never for long avoid the problem.

Where the danger lies, in my opinion, is in quite another direction. In my paper on bibli-ography and editorial problems I attempted to comment on this, and so shall be brief here. I have a great respect for the possibilities, still largely unexplored,[17] of applying critical bibliography to knotty textual problems, but some practical experiences as an editor have convinced me that, though it is the only basic method, it is not an invariably complete one. In other words, critical bibliography does not comprise in itself the whole of textual criticism by a long shot, and any claims that it is more than a basic approach to textual criticism should be vigorously combatted. On the other hand, pure textual criticism as such, without a basis in critical bibliography, is no longer a discipline to inspire utter confidence.

It follows that to produce the best texts critical bibliographers must learn as well as they can the highly developed methods of textual criticism to implement their own work when they turn editors. Correspondingly, textual critics must learn their essential bibliography in a manner not previously thought necessary if their results are to stand up under any searching scrutiny. There are times when after the most scrupulous bibliographical examination, only refined textual criticism can lend authority to a decision.[18] But decisions of textual criticism made without reference to bibli-ography may too often be exposed as futile guesswork. One may not unreasonably yearn to turn the clock back to simpler days, before the complexities attending the definitive treatment of a text were recognized, but to do so is to invite the dodo.

I take this view the more seriously because, though I welcome scientific method where it is applicable, I am distressed by the overweening claims which are made for it when it comes into conflict with the higher values of the humanities. The methods of critical bibliography at least parallel the scientific method and to that extent partake both of its strength and of its weakness, with the latter powerfully reinforced on occasion by the inescapable fact that critical bibliography must deal with a text which was both written and printed by a human being, and is therefore subject at every step in its path to the unknowable and aberrant human equation, no matter how material the form of the text, in a manner denied to neutrons and protons. This is where the higher values of textual criticism must not be lost if we are to avoid mechanical texts of which the best that can be said is that they do least harm. But if we are to continue to receive saving grace from the higher values of textual criticism, it must be on different terms than before, and in that respect the pressure is on textual criticism to understand and to utilize where applicable the newer semi-scientific method.

Insofar as critical bibliography, stemming from analytical, is a scientific method, it can secure good results within its natural limitations. Nevertheless, as a scientific method, if too sweepingly applied it cannot fail to ignore certain higher values which only pure textual criticism can preserve, and these are values we should not willingly forfeit. The scientific method should have its valued place in humane studies, but as a servant, not the master. The current exaltation of the scientist in other fields should not lead to his domination of the humanities. Yet the processes of logical and material demonstration which the more scientific bibliographical methods bring to literary studies cannot be idly surveyed from an ivory tower or they will eat away its foundations and topple it. A new form of scholarship is reaching its majority. Literary students must now make the necessary efforts to understand it and thus to absorb it into the larger stream of the humanities.

Notes

1   C. W. Miller, 'Thomas Newcomb: A Restoration Printer's Ornament Stock', in *Studies in Bibliography*, III (1950), 155–170.
2   *Studies in Bibliography*, IV (1951), 58–91.
3   'New Uses of Watermarks as Bibliographical Evidence', *Studies in Bibliography*, I (1948), 151–182.
4   It is a feature of bibliography that in practice the methods of its different disciplines frequently overlap. Thus *critical*, or *textual bibliography* will often call on the help of *analytical*, as will *historical*; or *analytical* will merge with *historical*, and *descriptive* with both. As an example, my recent identification of Robert Roberts as the printer of the first section of the Shakespeare Fourth Folio rested exclusively on the identification of his ornamental initial letters. The investigation was historical insofar as this was necessarily related to the records of his printing with and without his sometime partner Anne Maxwell and his relations with a certain group of publishers. But it was analytical in respect to the attempt to claim these initials exclusively for Roberts, despite the fact that they had appeared in a book with a Thomas Newcomb imprint, by showing that the book in question was printed in two sections. Analysis based on physical evidences of the printing process was also necessary to show that the Folio was also not printed as a continuous operation in the same shop, and thus to limit that part printed by Roberts, with the further object of showing that he also printed the preliminaries as well as the first section of text. See *Shakespeare Quarterly*, II (1951), 241–246.
5   *Critical* is often applied, especially in England, to what I have called *analytical* bibliography.
6   An elementary example would be the fact that a descriptive bibliographer must discover whether an odd number of leaves in a gathering is the result of excision or of addition before he can construct an accurate collational formula for the book.
7   'The Second Issue of *Troilus and Cressida*, 1609', *Studies in Bibliography*, II (1949), 25–33.
8   'Shakespeare's *Troilus and Cressida*: The Relationship of Quarto and Folio', *Studies in Bibliography*, III (1950), 131–143.
9   *The Variants in the First Quarto of* KING LEAR (London: The Bibliographical Society, 1940), pp. 18–39, expanding and confirming the earlier discovery by P. A. Daniel.
10   'The "Copy" for the Second Quarto of *Othello*', *Joseph Quincy Adams Memorial Studies* (Washington, DC, Folger Shakespeare Library, 1948), pp. 373–389.
11   *Studies in Bibliography*, III (1950), 37 ff.
12   In this statement there is, of course, a weak link, in that readings alone could never positively demonstrate that edition B derived from A and not from a manuscript. The exact demonstration must always be made on such bibliographical evidence as the fact that one is a page-for-page reprint of the other, or demonstrates precise typographical links with the other. In some complex cases readings alone, without a bibliographical explanation, may prove an uncertain guide. For instance, a late edition of Dryden's *Indian Emperour* is not clearly derived from either of its two immediate predecessors but takes over unique readings from each. The ordinary solution of pure textual criticism would be to posit a lost intermediate edition. Bibliography, however, demonstrates that two compositors alternated in setting the text, one

using one edition and the other the other. See J. S. Steck, 'Dryden's *Indian Emperour: The Early Editions and their Relation to the Text'*, *Studies in Bibliography*, II (1949), 147.

13   One must handle the first rather more carefully; of course.

14   'A Formulary of Collation', in *The Library*, 4th ser., XIV (1934), 365–382.

15   *Principles of Bibliographical Description* (Princeton, NJ, Princeton University Press, 1949), p. 28.

16   If I may be forgiven an example from my own experience, I came upon the fact in the course of investigations for a descriptive bibliography that John Banks's *Cyrus the Great*, 1696, had three sheets which existed in two quite different typesettings. Since I hold that a descriptive bibliographer must not only record but also classify, order, and explain, it was incumbent on me to demonstrate which setting was the initial one. Before I had finished doing this to the best of my ability, I was forced to run the gamut of a particularly complex and technical explanation of the printing which made use of various bibliographical arguments which could only be incomprehensible to a literary student. The end result, however, was – I hope – a determination of which setting was made from manuscript and which was a mere reprint, without which information an editor could not properly tackle the text. Any pure analytical technician – which I am not – would have been forced to follow the same course and eventually end with the text. See, for the horrid example, *Studies in Bibliography*, IV (1951), 174–182. As a similar instance, the bibliographical investigation of the evidence of running-titles, with which I have been in part connected, began purely for the technical problem they posed. Shortly, the research led in direct path to the application of the printing process they revealed to the textual question of proof-reading.

17   Some suggestions as to lines of exploration were made in my paper 'A Definitive Text of Shakespeare: Problems and Methods' recently read before the Shakespeare Conference at the University of Miami and scheduled for future publication.

18   In this class I should place the *sallied-solid flesh* crux in *Hamlet*, since the strict bibliographical argument for *sallied* may be very slightly suspect.

Chapter 4

D. F. McKenzie

THE BOOK AS AN EXPRESSIVE FORM

My purpose in these lectures – one I hope that might be thought fitting for an inaugural occasion – is simply to consider anew what bibliography is and how it relates to other disciplines. To begin that inquiry, I should like to recall a classic statement by the late Sir Walter Greg. It is this: 'what the bibliographer is concerned with is pieces of paper or parchment covered with certain written or printed signs. With these signs he is concerned merely as arbitrary marks; their meaning is no business of his'.[1] This definition of bibliography, or at least of 'pure' bibliography, is still widely accepted, and it remains in essence the basis of any claim that the procedures of bibliography are scientific.

A recent study by Mr Ross Atkinson supports that view by drawing on the work of the American semiotician, C. S. Peirce.[2] It can be argued, for example, that the signs in a book, as a bibliographer must read them, are simply iconic or indexical. Briefly, iconic signs are those which involve similarity; they represent an object, much as a portrait represents the sitter. In enumerative bibliography, and, even more so in descriptive, the entries are iconic. They represent the object they describe. Textual bibliography, too, may be said to be iconic because it seeks, as Mr Atkinson puts it, 'to reproduce the Object with maximum precision in every detail'. In that way, enumerative, descriptive, and textual bibliography may be said to constitute a class of three *referential* sign systems. Analytical bibliography, however, would form a distinct class of indexical signs. Their significance lies only in the physical differences between them as an index to the ways in which a particular document came physically to be what it is. It is their causal status that, in Peirce's terms, makes the signs *indexical*. In the words of Professor Bowers, writing of analytical bibliography, the physical features of a book are 'significant in the order and manner of their shapes but indifferent in symbolic meaning'.[3]

I must say at once that this account comes closer than any other I know to justifying Greg's definition of the discipline. I am also convinced, however, that the premise informing Greg's classic statement, and therefore this refinement of it, is no longer adequate as a definition of what bibliography is and does.

In an attempt to escape the embarrassment of such a strict definition, it is often said that bibliography is not a subject at all but only, as Mr G. Thomas Tanselle once put it, 'a related group of subjects that happen to be commonly referred to by the same term'.[4] Professor Bowers virtually concedes as much in dividing it into enumerative or systematic bibliography, and descriptive, analytical, textual, and historical bibliography.[5] The purity of the discipline which Greg aspired to is to that extent qualified by its particular applications and these in turn imply that the definition does not fully serve its uses.

The problem is, I think, that the moment we are required to explain signs in a book, as distinct from describing or copying them, they assume a symbolic status. If a medium in any sense affects a message, then bibliography cannot exclude from its own proper concerns the relation between form, function and symbolic meaning. If textual bibliography were merely iconic, it could produce only facsimiles of different versions. As for bibliographical analysis, that depends absolutely upon antecedent historical knowledge, for it can only function 'with the assistance of previously gathered information on the techniques of book production'.[6] But the most striking weakness of the definition is precisely its incapacity to accommodate history. Mr Atkinson is quite frank about this. Accepting the bibliographer's presumed lack of concern for the meaning of signs, he writes: 'we are left now only with the problem of historical bibliography'. He cites with approval the comment by Professor Bowers that the numerous fields concerned with the study of printing and its processes both as art and craft are merely 'ancillary to analytical bibliography'.[7] He is therefore obliged to argue that

> historical bibliography is not, properly speaking, bibliography at all. This is because it does not have as its Object material sign systems or documents. Its Object rather consists of certain mechanical techniques and as such it must be considered not part of bibliography but a constituent of such fields as the history of technology or, perhaps, information science.

Such comments, although recent, and indeed advanced in seeking to accommodate bibliography to semiotics as the science of signs, are oddly out of touch with such developments as, for example, the founding of The Center for the Book by the Library of Congress, the American Antiquarian Society's Programme for the History of the Book in American Culture, or proposals for publication of national histories of the book, of which the most notable so far is *L'Histoire de l'Édition Française*.

I am not bold enough to speak of paradigm shifts, but I think I am safe in saying that the vital interests of most of those known to me as bibliographers are no longer fully served by description, or even by editing, but by the historical study of the making and the use of books and other documents. But is it right that in order to accomplish such projects as, for example, a history of the book in Britain, we must cease to be bibliographers and shift to another discipline? It is here, if anywhere, that other disciplines such as history, and especially cultural history, are now making demands of bibliography. Far from accepting that 'historical bibliography is not, properly speaking, bibliography at all', it is tempting to claim, now, that all bibliography, properly speaking, is historical bibliography.

In such a world, Greg's definition of the theoretical basis of bibliography is too limited. As long as we continue to think of it as confined to the study of the non-symbolic functions of signs, the risk it runs is relegation. Rare book rooms will simply become rarer. The politics of survival, if nothing else, require a more comprehensive justification of the discipline's function in promoting new knowledge.

If, by contrast, we were to delineate the field in a merely pragmatic way, take a panoptic view and describe what we severally *do* as bibliographers, we should note, rather, that it is the only discipline which has consistently studied the composition, formal design, and transmission of texts by writers, printers, and publishers; their distribution through different communities by wholesalers, retailers, and teachers; their collection and classification by librarians; their meaning for, and – I must add – their creative regeneration by, readers. However we define it, no part of that series of human and institutional interactions is alien to bibliography as we have, traditionally, practised it.

But, like Panizzi himself, faced with everything printed in a world in change, we reach a point where the accretion of subjects, like the collection of books, demands that we also seek a new principle by which to order them. Recent changes in critical theory, subsuming linguistics, semiotics, and the psychology of reading and writing, in information theory and communications studies, in the status of texts and the forms of their transmission, represent a formidable challenge to traditional practice, but they may also, I believe, give to bibliographical principle a quite new centrality.

The principle I wish to suggest as basic is simply this: bibliography is the discipline that studies texts as recorded forms, and the processes of their transmission, including their production and reception. So stated, it will not seem very surprising. What the word 'texts' also allows, however, is the extension of present practice to include all forms of texts, not merely books or Greg's signs on pieces of parchment or paper. It also frankly accepts that bibliographers should be concerned to show that forms affect meaning. Beyond that, it allows us to describe not only the technical but the social processes of their transmission. In those quite specific ways, it accounts for non-book texts, their physical forms, textual versions, technical transmission, institutional control, their perceived meanings, and social effects. It accounts for a history of the book and, indeed, of all printed forms including all textual ephemera as a record of cultural change, whether in mass civilization or minority culture. For any history of the book which excluded study of the social, economic, and political motivations of publishing, the reasons why texts were written and read as they were, why they were rewritten and redesigned, or allowed to die, would degenerate into a feebly degressive book list and never rise to a readable history. But such a phrase also accommodates what in recent critical theory is often called text production, and it therefore opens up the application of the discipline to the service of that field too.

In terms of the range of demands now made of it and of the diverse interests of those who think of themselves as bibliographers, it seems to me that it would now be more useful to describe bibliography as the study of the sociology of texts. If the principle which makes it distinct is its concern with texts in some physical form and their transmission, then I can think of no other phrase which so aptly describes its range. Both the words 'texts' and 'sociology', however, demand further comment.

I define 'texts' to include verbal, visual, oral, and numeric data, in the form of maps, prints, and music, of archives of recorded sound, of films, videos, and any computer-stored information, everything in fact from epigraphy to the latest forms of discography. There is no evading the challenge which those new forms have created.

We can find in the origins of the word 'text' itself some support for extending its meaning from manuscripts and print to other forms. It derives, of course, from the Latin *texere*, 'to weave', and therefore refers, not to any specific material as such, but to its woven state, the web or texture of the materials. Indeed, it was not restricted to the weaving of textiles, but might be applied equally well to the interlacing or entwining of any kind of material. The Oxford Latin Dictionary suggests that it is probably cognate with the Vedic 'tāṣṭi', to 'fashion by carpentry', and consequently with the Greek τέκτων and τέχνη.

The shift from fashioning a material medium to a conceptual system, from the weaving of fabrics to the web of words, is also implicit in the Greek ὕφος 'a web or net', from ὑφαίνω 'to weave'. As with the Latin, it is only by virtue of a metaphoric shift that it applies to language, that the verb 'to weave' serves for the verb 'to write', that the web of words becomes a text. In each case, therefore, the primary sense is one which defines a process of material construction. It creates an object, but it is not peculiar to any one substance or any one form. The idea that texts are written records on parchment or paper derives only from the secondary and metaphoric sense that the writing of words is like the weaving of threads.

As much could now be said of many constructions which are not in written form, but for which the same metaphoric shift would be just as proper. Until our own times, the only textual records created in any quantity were manuscripts and books. A slight extension of the principle – it is, I believe, the same principle – to cope with the new kinds of material constructions we have in the form of the non-book texts which now surround, inform, and pleasure us, does not seem to me a radical departure from precedent.

In turning briefly now to comment on the word 'sociology', it is not perhaps impertinent to note that its early history parallels Panizzi's. A neologism coined by Auguste Comte in 1830, the year before Panizzi joined the staff of the British Museum, it made a fleeting appearance in Britain in 1843 in *Blackwood's Magazine*, which referred to 'a new Science, to be called Social Ethics, or Sociology'. Seven years later it was still struggling for admission. *Fraser's Magazine* in 1851 acknowledged its function but derided its name in a reference to 'the new science of sociology, as it is barbarously called'. Only in 1873 did it find a local habitation and a respected name. Herbert Spencer's *The Study of Sociology*, published in that year, provides a succinct description of its role: 'Sociology has to recognize truths of social development, structure and function'.

As I see it, that stress on structure and function is important, although I should resist its abstraction to the point where it lost sight of human agency. At one level, a sociology simply reminds us of the full range of social realities which the medium of print had to serve, from receipt blanks to bibles. But it also directs us to consider the human motives and interactions which texts involve at every stage of their production, transmission, and consumption. It alerts us to the roles of institutions, and their own complex structures, in affecting the forms of social discourse, past and present. Those are the realities which bibliographers and textual critics as such have, until very recently, either neglected, or by defining them as strictly non-bibliographical, have felt unable to denominate, logically and coherently, as central to what we do. Historical bibliography, we were told, was not strictly bibliography at all.

A 'sociology of texts', then, contrasts with a bibliography confined to logical inference from printed signs as arbitrary marks on parchment or paper. As I indicated earlier, claims were made for the 'scientific' status of the latter precisely because it worked only from the physical evidence of books themselves. Restricted to the non-symbolic values of the signs, it tried to exclude the distracting complexities of linguistic interpretation and historical explanation.

That orthodox view of bibliography is less compelling, and less surprising, if we note its affinities with other modes of thinking at the time when Greg was writing. These include certain formalist theories of art and literature which were concerned to exclude from the discussion of a work of art any intended or referential meaning. They were current not only in the years when Greg was formulating his definitions but were still active in the theory of the New Criticism when Professor Fredson Bowers was developing his. The congruence of bibliography and criticism lay precisely in their shared view of the self-sufficient nature of the work of art or text, and in their agreement on the significance of its every verbal detail, however small. In neither case were precedent or subsequent processes thought to be essential to critical or bibliographical practice. The New Criticism showed great ingenuity in discerning patterns in the poem-on-the-page as a self-contained verbal structure. It is not I think altogether fanciful to find a scholarly analogy in analytical bibliography. Compositor studies, for example, have shown a comparable virtuosity in discerning patterns in evidence which is entirely internal, if not wholly fictional.

I shall return to that analogy with the New Criticism, but I am more concerned for the moment to emphasize the point that this confinement of bibliography to non-symbolic meaning, in an attempt to give it some kind of objective or 'scientific' status, has seriously impeded its development as a discipline. By electing to ignore its inevitable dependence upon interpretive structures, it has obscured the role of human agents, and virtually denied the relevance to bibliography of anything we might now understand as a history of the book. Physical bibliography – the study of the signs which constitute texts and the materials on which they are recorded – is of course the starting point. But it cannot define the discipline because it has no adequate means of accounting for the processes, the technical and social dynamics, of transmission and reception, whether by one reader or a whole market of them.

In speaking of bibliography as the sociology of texts, I am not concerned to invent new names but only to draw attention to its actual nature. Derrida's 'Grammatology', the currently fashionable word 'Textuality', the French 'Textologie', or even 'Hyphologie' (a suggestion made, not altogether seriously, by Roland Barthes) would exclude more than we would wish to lose. Nor is bibliography a sub-field of semiotics, precisely because its functions are not merely synchronically descriptive. Our own word, 'Bibliography', will do. It unites us as collectors, editors, librarians, historians, makers and readers of books. It even has a new felicity in its literal meaning of 'the writing out of books', of generating new copies and therefore in time new versions. Its traditional concern with texts as recorded forms, and with the processes of their transmission, should make it hospitably open to new forms. No new names, then; but to conceive of the discipline as a sociology of texts is, I think, both to describe what the bibliography is that we actually do and to allow for its natural evolution.

Nevertheless, I must now turn to consider the special case of printed texts. In doing so, the particular inquiry I wish to pursue is whether or not the material forms of books, the non-verbal elements of the typographic notations within them, the very disposition of space itself, have an expressive function in conveying meaning, and whether or not it is, properly, a bibliographical task to discuss it.

Again, I sense that theory limps behind practice. At one end of the spectrum, we must of course recognize that Erwin Panofsky on perspective as symbolic form has long since made the theme familiar; at the other end, we find that Marshall McLuhan's *Understanding Media* has made it basic to media studies. In our own field, Mr Nicolas Barker, on 'Typography and the Meaning of Words: The Revolution in the Layout of Books in the Eighteenth Century'; Mr David Foxon on Pope's typography; Mr Giles Barber on Voltaire and the typographic presentation of *Candide*; Mr Roger Laufer on 'scripturation' or 'the material emergence of sense' are all distinguished bibliographers demonstrating in one way or another, not the iconic or indexical, but the symbolic function of typographic signs as an interpretive system.[8] Words like the 'articulation' or 'enunciation' of the book in this sense make similar assumptions. Discussions of the morphology of the book in relation to genre or to special classes of readers and markets assume a complex relation of medium to meaning. Journals like *Visible Language* and *Word & Image* were founded specifically to explore these questions. The persistent example of fine printing and the revival of the calligraphic manuscript, and numerous recent studies of the sophisticated displays of text and illumination in medieval manuscript production, also share a basic assumption that forms affect sense.[9]

Perhaps on this occasion the simplest way of exploring some of these issues as they relate to the expressive function of typography in book forms, as they bear on editing, and as they relate to critical theory, is to offer an exemplary case. I have chosen the four lines which serve as epigraph to 'The Intentional Fallacy', the distinguished essay by W. K. Wimsatt Jr. and M. C. Beardsley which was first published in *The Sewanee Review* in 1946.[10] It would, I think, be hard to name another essay which has so influenced critical theory and the teaching of literature in the past forty years. Briefly, they argued that it was pointless to use the concept of an author's intentions in trying to decide what a work of literature might mean, or if it was any good. And of course exactly the same objection must apply, if it holds at all, to the interpretation of a writer's or printer's intentions in presenting a text in a particular form, or a publisher's intentions in issuing it at all.

Let me say at once that my purpose in using an example from this essay is to show that in some cases significantly informative readings may be recovered from typographic signs as well as verbal ones, that these are relevant to editorial decisions about the manner in which one might reproduce a text, and that a reading of such bibliographical signs may seriously shape our judgement of an author's work. I think it is also possible to suggest that their own preconceptions may have led Wimsatt and Beardsley to misread a text, that their misreading may itself have been partly a function of the manner in which it was printed, and that its typographic style was in turn influenced by the culture at large. My argument therefore runs full circle from a defence of authorial meaning, on the grounds that it is in some measure recoverable, to a recognition that, for better or worse, readers inevitably make their own meanings. In other words, each reading is peculiar to its occasion, each can be at least partially recovered from the physical forms of the text, and the differences in readings constitute an informative history. What writers thought they were doing in writing texts, or printers and booksellers in designing and publishing them, or readers in making sense of them are issues which no history of the book can evade.

'The Intentional Fallacy' opens with an epigraph taken from Congreve's prologue to *The Way of the World* (1700). In it, as Wimsatt and Beardsley quote him,

He owns with toil he wrote the following scenes;
But, if they're naught, ne'er spare him for his pains:
Damn him the more; have no commiseration
For dullness on mature deliberation.
　　　　　WILLIAM CONGREVE, Prologue to
　　　　　The Way of the World

Congreve's authorized version of 1710 reads:

He owns, with Toil, he wrought the following
Scenes,
But if they're naught ne'er spare him for his Pains:
Damn him the more; have no Commiseration
For Dulness on mature Deliberation.

It has not, I think, been observed before that, if we include its epigraph, this famous essay on the interpretation of literature opens with a misquotation in its very first line. Wimsatt and Beardsley say that Congreve 'wrote' the following scenes, but Congreve was a deliberate craftsman. He said he 'wrought' them. Since the words quoted are ascribed to Congreve, I think we are clearly meant to accept them as his, even if the essay later persuades us that we cannot presume to know what Congreve might have intended them to mean. By adopting that simple change from 'wrought' to 'wrote', Wimsatt and Beardsley oblige us to make our meaning from their misreading. The epigraph thereby directs us to weaken the emphasis that Congreve placed on his labour of composition: he writes of the '*Pains*' it cost him to hammer out his meaning. The changed wording destroys the carefully created internal rhyme, the resonance between what, in the first line, Congreve said he '*wrought*' and, in the second line, its fate in being reduced to '*naught*' by those who misquote, misconstrue, and misjudge him. Congreve's prologue to *The Way of the World* put, in 1700/1710, a point of view exactly opposite to the one which the lines are cited to support.

Less noticeable perhaps are the implications of the way in which the epigraph is printed. For Congreve's precise notation of spelling, punctuation and initial capitals, the 1946 version offers a flat, even insidiously open form. Congreve wrote that '*He owns*' – comma – '*with Toil*' – comma – '*he wrought the following Scenes'*. In their performance of the line, Wimsatt and Beardsley drop the commas. By isolating and emphasizing the phrase, Congreve may be read as affirming his seriousness of purpose, the deliberation of his art. Wimsatt and Beardsley speed past it, their eyes perhaps on a phrase more proper to their purpose in the next line. What their reading emphasizes instead, surrounding it with commas where Congreve had none, is the phrase 'if they're naught'. By that slight change they highlight Congreve's ironic concession that an author's intentions have no power to save him if an audience or reader thinks he is dull. Congreve, without commas, had preferred to skip quickly past that thought. Wimsatt and Beardsley allow us to dwell on it, for in their reading it would seem to justify their rather different argument.

Those shifts of meaning which result from the variants noted are, I believe, serious, however slight the signs which make them. But there are more. In his second couplet, Congreve writes:

> *Damn him the more; have no Commiseration*
> *For Dulness on mature Deliberation.*

Again, it suits the purpose of the epigraph to remove Congreve's irony, but as irony is crucially dependent upon context, the loss is perhaps inevitable. Reading the words literally, Wimsatt and Beardsley must take them to mean: 'If you really think my scenes are dull, don't waste your pity on their author'. But you will note that Congreve gives upper-case 'D's for '*Dulness*' and '*Deliberation*'. Those personified forms allow two readings to emerge which tell us something of Congreve's experience. The first is that these abstractions have human shapes (they were sitting there in the theatre); the second alludes to the age-old combat between Dulness and Deliberation, or Stupidity and Sense. By reducing all his nouns to lower case and thereby destroying the early eighteenth-century convention, the epigraph kills off Congreve's personified forms, and by muting his irony, it reverses his meaning. Where Congreve's irony contrasts his own '*mature Deliberation*' with the '*Dulness*' of his critics, their meaning has him saying the reader knows best.

If we look again at the form and relation of the words '*Toil*', '*Scenes*' and its rhyme-word '*Pains*', we note that they, too, have initial capitals. The convention thereby gives us in print a visual, semantic and ultimately moral identity between Congreve's own description of his labours ('*Toil . . . Pains*') and their human products who people his plays. The text as printed in the epigraph breaks down those visual links by depriving the words of their capitals. One set of meanings, which stress a writer's presence in his work, is weakened in favour of a preconceived reading which would remove him from it.

Small as it is, this example is so instructive that I should like to explore it further. It bears on the most obvious concerns of textual criticism – getting the right words in the right order; on the semiotics of print and the role of typography in forming meaning; on the critical theories of authorial intention and reader response; on the relation between the past meanings and present uses of verbal texts. It offers an illustration of the transmission of texts as the creation of the new versions which form, in turn, the new books, the products of later printers, and the stuff of subsequent bibliographical control. These are the primary documents for any history of the book. By reading one form of Congreve's text (1700/1710), we may with some authority affirm certain readings as his. By reading other forms of it (1946), we can chart meanings that later readers made from it under different historical imperatives.

I may believe – as I do – that Wimsatt and Beardsley have mistaken Congreve's meaning; that they have misconceived his relation to his tradition; that they have misreported his attitude to his own audience and readers. At the same time, their misreading has become an historical document in its own right. By speaking to what they perceived in 1946 to be the needs of their own time, not Congreve's in 1700/1710, they have left a record of the taste, thought, and values of a critical school which significantly shaped our own choice of books, the way we read them and, in my own case, the way I taught them. The history of material objects as symbolic forms functions, therefore, in two ways. It can falsify certain readings; and it can demonstrate new ones.

To extend that line of argument, I should like to comment briefly on the word 'Scenes'. We recall first that Congreve's 'Scenes' cost him 'Pains'. Next, we should note that his editors and critics have, almost without exception, replaced his meaning of the word with a commoner one of their own. They have defined them by geography and carpentry, as when a scene shifts from a forest to the palace. For Congreve, by contrast, they were neoclassical scenes: not impersonal places in motion, but distinct groups of human beings in conversation. These made up his scenes. For him, it was the intrusion of another human voice, another mind, or its loss, that most changed the scene. The substance of his scenes, therefore, what he 'wrought with Toil', were men and women. Once we recover that context and follow Congreve's quite literal meaning in that sense, his rhyme of 'Scenes' with 'Pains' glows with an even subtler force. What he hints at is a serious critical judgement about all his work: beneath the rippling surface of his comedy there flows a sombre undercurrent of human pain. In a more mundane way, that perception may direct an editor to adopt a typography which divides Congreve's plays into neoclassical scenes, as he himself did in his edition of 1710.

With that last example, it could be argued that we reach the border between bibliography and textual criticism on the one hand and literary criticism and literary history on the other. My own view is that no such border exists. In the pursuit of historical meanings, we move from the most minute feature of the material form of the book to questions of authorial, literary, and social context. These all bear in turn on the ways in which texts are then re-read, re-edited, re-designed, re-printed, and re-published. If a history of readings is made possible only by a comparative history of books, it is equally true that a history of books will have no point if it fails to account for the meanings they later come to make.

Though at times they may pretend otherwise, I suspect that few authors, with the kind of investment in their work that Congreve claims, are indifferent to the ways in which their art is presented and received. There is certainly a cruel irony in the fact that Congreve's own text is reshaped and misread to support an argument against himself. Far from offering a licence for his audience and readers to discount the author's meaning, Congreve is putting, with an exasperated irony, the case for the right of authors, as he says in another line of the prologue, 'to assert their Sense' against the taste of the town. When Jeremy Collier wrenched to his own purposes the meaning of Congreve's words, Congreve replied with his *Amendments of Mr Collier's False and Imperfect Citations*. He too had a way with epigraphs and chose for that occasion one from Martial which, translated, reads: 'That book you recite, O Fidentinus, *is* mine. But your vile *re*-citation begins to make it your own'.

With that thought in mind, I should like to pursue one further dimension of the epigraph's meaning which is not in itself a matter of book form. It nevertheless puts Congreve in the tradition of authors who thought about the smallest details of their work as it might be printed, and who directed, collaborated with, or fumed against, their printers and publishers. One such author is Ben Jonson. As it happens, Wimsatt and Beardsley might with equal point have quoted him to epitomize their argument that an author's intentions are irrelevant. This, for example:

> Playes in themselues haue neither hopes, nor feares,
> Their fate is only in their hearers ears . . .[11]

It chimes in perfectly with the very end of Congreve's prologue although, here, his irony is too heavy to miss:

In short, our Play shall (with your leave to show it),
Give you one instance of a Passive Poet.
Who to your Judgments yields all Resignation;
So Save or Damn, after your own Discretion.

To link Congreve with Jonson is to place his prologue and what it says in a developing tradition of the author's presence in his printed works. In that context, Congreve's lines become a form of homage to his mentor, an acceptance of succession, and a reminder that the fight for the author's right not to be mis-read can ultimately break even the best of us. For not only had Jonson inveighed against the usurpation of his meanings by those of *his* asinine critics, but he was a dramatist who for a time virtually quit the public stage to be, as he put it, 'Safe from the wolues black iaw, and the dull asses hoofe'. Jonson's rejection of free interpretation is venomous:

Let their fastidious, vaine
Commission of the braine
Run on, rage, sweat, censure and condemn:
They were not meant for thee, lesse, thou for them.[12]

Congreve's ironies allow him a more tactful, more decorous, farewell. Less tough, more delicate, than Jonson, he did leave the stage, sensing himself expelled by the misappropriation of his works, convinced that *his* meanings would rarely survive their reception. The imminence of that decision informs his prologue to *The Way of the World*. It was to be his last play. On '*mature Deliberation*', he found he could no longer bear the deadly '*Dulness*' of his critics. By respecting not only the words Congreve uses – a simple courtesy – but also the meanings which their precise notation gives, we can, if we wish, as an act of bibliographical scholarship, recover his irony, and read his pain.

In that long series of Pyrrhic victories which records the triumphs of critics and the deaths of authors, 'The Intentional Fallacy' has earned a distinguished place for the argument which follows its feat of misprision. Its epigraph is no celebration of Congreve's perspicacity in foreseeing a new cause; it is, rather, an epitaph to his own dismembered text. A vast critical literature has been generated by this essay, but I am unaware of any mention of the textual ironies which preface it. With what seems an undue reverence for the tainted text printed by Wimsatt and Beardsley, the epigraph has been reproduced in reprint after reprint with exceptional fidelity, its errors resistant to any further reworking of a classic moment of mis-statement, resistant even to the force of the argument which follows it. It is now incorporate with Congreve's history and with that of our own time.

Yet if the fine detail of typography and layout, the material signs which constitute a text, do signify in the ways I have tried to suggest, it must follow that any history of the book – subject as books are to typographic and material change – must be a history of misreadings. This is not so strange as it might sound. Every society rewrites its past, every reader rewrites its texts, and, if they have any continuing life at all, at some point every printer redesigns them. The changes in the way Congreve's text was printed as an epigraph were themselves designed to correct a late Victorian printing style which had come to seem too fussily expressive. In 1946, 'good printing' had a clean, clear, impersonal surface. It left the text to speak for itself.

This newly preferred form of printing had conspired with shifts in critical opinion. Eliot's theory of the impersonality of the poet affected to dissociate the writer from his text. The words on the page became what Wimsatt called a 'verbal icon', a freestanding artefact with its own inner coherence, what Cleanth Brooks was to call (as it happens) a '*well-wrought Urn*', a structure complete in itself which had within it all the linguistic signs we needed for the contemplation of its meaning.

The unprecedented rise of English studies and the decline of classics made quite new demands of teachers of literature. At one level, the critical analysis of set texts was an efficient way to teach reading from what was irreducibly common to a class, the text itself laid out on the page in a kind of lapidary state. At another level, it brought into sharper focus than ever before the fact that different readers brought the text to life in different ways. If a poem *is* only what its individual readers make it in their activity of constructing meaning from it, then a good poem will be one which most compels its own destruction in the service of its readers' new construction. When the specification of meaning is one with its discovery in the critical practice of writing, the generative force of texts is most active. In that context, the misreading of Congreve in 1946 may be seen as almost a matter of historical necessity, an interesting document itself in the nature of reading and the history of the book.

And it *is* a physical document. We can date it; we can read it; we can locate it in the context of *The Sewanee Review* and the interests of its readers; we can interpret it reasonably according to the propositional intentions of the anti-intentionalist essay which lies beneath it. It is, I hope, unnecessary to multiply instances. This scrap of prologue, this fragment of text, raises most of the issues we need to address as we think about books as texts which have been given a particular physical form.

But as a dramatic text, it was originally written to be spoken, and so other questions arise. Can we hear the voice of Thomas Betterton conveying orally the ironies we now read visually? Congreve's autograph letters show no concern for the niceties I suggested in the form of the epigraph. Am I therefore reading an interpretation of Congreve's meaning by his printer, John Watts? Is Watts merely following a general set of conventions imposed at this time, with or without Congreve's assent, by Congreve's publisher, Jacob Tonson? Who, in short, 'authored' Congreve? Whose concept of the reader do these forms of the text imply: the author's, the actor's, the printer's, or the publisher's? And what of the reader? Is a knowledge of Jonson, Betterton, Congreve, Watts, and Tonson a necessary condition of a 'true' reading? Does my reading betray a personal need to prove that a technical interest in books *and* in the teaching of texts is not radically disjunctive, that bibliographical scholarship and criticism are in fact one? Visited by such questions, an author disperses into his collaborators, those who produced his texts and their meanings.

If we turn to the 1946 epigraph, similar questions insist on an answer. Does its removal from context entirely free it from irony? Do the slight changes of form alter the substance? Are they no more than a case of careless printing in a new convention? But the crucial questions for a history of reading, and the re-writing of texts, are these: did the intentions of these two authors (something extrinsic to their text) lead them to create from Congreve's lines a pre-text for their own writing; and, if so, did they do it consciously, unconsciously, or accidentally?

To venture into distinctions between conscious and unconscious intentions would be to enter upon troubled waters indeed. The probable answer is, I fear, banal, but as an illustration of the vagaries of textual transmission it should be given. The anthology of plays edited by Nettleton and Case, from which Wimsatt would almost certainly have taught, includes *The Way of the World*, the prologue to which in that edition inexplicably reads 'wrote' for '*wrought*'. We must therefore, I think, relieve Wimsatt and Beardsley of immediate responsibility, and we should certainly free them from any suggestion of deliberate contamination. But I wonder if they would have ventured to choose the lines had they been more carefully edited.[13]

The case, however, is not altered. If we think of the physical construction of Congreve's text in the quarto of 1700 or the octavo edition of 1710, and its physical re-presentation in 1946, then at least we begin by seeing two simple facts. One gives us the historical perspective of an author directing one set of meanings in a transaction with his contemporaries. The other gives us an equally historical perspective of two readers creating a reverse set of meanings for an academic – indeed, a scholarly – readership whose interests in the text were different. Each perspective can be studied distinctively in the signs of the text as printed. Those signs range in significance from the trivial to the serious, but far from importing the author's irrelevance, they take us back to human motive and intention. In Congreve's case, they reveal a man of compassion whose scenes record the human struggle they spring from as the very condition of writing.

In one sense at least, little has changed in critical theory since 1946. New Critical formalism and structuralism on the one hand, post-structuralism and deconstruction on the other, all share the same scepticism about recovering the past. One of the most impressive objections to this critical self-absorption, to the point of excluding a concern for the complexities of human agency in the production of texts, is Edward Said's *The World, the Text, and the Critic*. I can only agree with his judgement that 'As it is practised in the American academy today, literary theory has for the most part isolated textuality from the circumstances, the events, the physical senses that made it possible and render it intelligible as the result of human work'.[14] Commenting upon Said in his most recent book, *Textual Power*, Robert Scholes pursues the point: 'At the present time there are two major positions that can be taken with respect to this problem, and . . . it is extremely difficult to combine them or find any middle ground between them'.[15] Scholes describes those two positions as the hermetic and the secular.

To return now to my larger theme: Greg's definition of what bibliography is would have it entirely hermetic. By admitting history, we make it secular. The two positions are not entirely opposed, for books themselves are the middle ground. It is one bibliographers have long since explored, mapped, and tilled. Their descriptive methods far surpass other applications of semiotics as a science of signs. In the ubiquity and variety of its evidence, bibliography as a sociology of texts has an unrivalled power to resurrect authors in their own time, and their readers at any time. It enables what Michel Foucault called 'an insurrection of subjugated knowledges'.[16] One of its greatest strengths is the access it gives to social motives: by dealing with the facts of transmission and the material evidence of reception, it can make discoveries as distinct from inventing meanings. In focusing on the primary object, the text as a recorded form, it defines our common point of departure for any historical or critical enterprise. By abandoning the notion of degressive bibliography and recording *all* subsequent versions, bibliography, simply by its own comprehensive logic, its indiscriminate inclusiveness, testifies to the fact that new readers of course make new texts, and that their new meanings are a function of their new forms. The claim then is no longer for their truth as one might seek to define that by an authorial intention, but for their testimony, as defined by their historical use. There was a year 1710 in which Tonson published Congreve's *Works*, and there was a year 1946 in which some lines from the prologue to *The Way of the World* were quoted in *The Sewanee Review*. Wimsatt and Beardsley might be wrong from Congreve's point of view, but, given their published text, they indubitably *are*, and it is a very simple bibliographical function to record and to show their reading – indeed, in the interests of a history of cultural change, to show it up.

Reviewing Scholes in *The Times Literary Supplement*, Tzvetan Todorov gave a blunt appraisal of the relation of the present American literary scene to the traditions of western humanism: 'If we wish to call a spade a spade, we must conclude that the dominant tendency of American criticism is anti-humanism'.[17] Bibliography has a massive authority with which to correct that tendency. It can, in short, show the human presence in any recorded text.

Notes

1   'Bibliography – an Apologia', in *Collected Papers*, ed. J. C. Maxwell (Oxford: Clarendon Press, 1966), p. 247.

2   Ross Atkinson, 'An Application of Semiotics to the Definition of Bibliography', *Studies in Bibliography* 33 (1980), 54–73.

3   *Bibliography and Textual Criticism* (Oxford: Clarendon Press, 1964), p. 41; cited by Atkinson, p. 63.

4   'Bibliography and Science', *Studies in Bibliography* 27 (1974), 88.

5   Principally in 'Bibliography, Pure Bibliography, and Literary Studies', *Papers of the Bibliographical Society of America* 47 (1952), 186–208; also in 'Bibliography', *Encyclopaedia Britannica* (1970), III, 588–92.

6   Atkinson, p. 64.

7   *Encyclopaedia Britannica*, III, 588.

8   Nicolas Barker, 'Typography and the Meaning of Words', *Buch und Buchhandel in Europa im achtzehnten Jahrhundert*, ed. G. Barber and B. Fabian, *Wolfenbütteler Schriften zur Geschichte des Buchwesens* 4 (Hamburg, 1981), pp. 126–65; Giles Barber, 'Voltaire et la présentation typographique de *Candide*'. *Transmissione dei Testi a Stampa nel Periodo Moderno I* (Seminario Internazionale, Rome 1985), pp. 151–69; Roger Laufer, 'L'Énonciation typographique au dixhuitième siècle', *ibid.*, 113–23; 'L'Espace visuel du livre ancien', *Revue Française d'Histoire du Livre* 16 (1977), 569–81; 'L'Esprit de la lettre', *Le Débat* 22 (November 1982), 147–59; see also Barbara R. Woshinsky, 'La Bruyère's *Caractères*: A Typographical Reading', *TEXT, Transactions of the Society for Textual Scholarship* 2 (1985), 209–28. Those examples from the past, implying a consciousness of the non-verbal resources of book forms to enhance and convey meaning, may be paralleled with others from current research into text design. A useful recent summary is James Hartley, 'Current Research on Text Design', *Scholarly Publishing* 16 (1985), 355–68; see also James Hartley and Peter Burnhill, 'Explorations in Space: A Critique of the Typography of BPS Publications', *Bulletin of the British Psychological Society* 29 (1976), 97–107.

9   For an excellent example, see Michael Camille, 'The Book of Signs: Writing and visual difference in Gothic manuscript illumination', *Word & Image* I, no. 2 (April–June 1985), 133–48.

10   *The Sewanee Review* liv (Summer, 1946), 468–88; subsequently collected in *The Verbal Icon* (Lexington: University of Kentucky Press, 1954).

11   Ben Jonson, *The New Inne*, epilogue, ll. 1–2.

12   'Ode to *himselfe*', ll. 7–10.

13   I am indebted to Professor Albert Braunmuller for suggesting the probable source of the error. In fairness to Wimsatt and Beardsley, whose matching essay, 'The Subjective Fallacy', warns against readings uncontrolled by the formal limits of the words on the page, it should be said that they might well have welcomed and accepted as constituting a more acceptable text the lines as originally printed.

14   *The World, the Text, and the Critic* (London: Faber and Faber, 1984), p. 4.

15   *Textual Power* (New Haven and London: Yale University Press, 1985), p. 75.

16   Michel Foucault, 'Two Lectures: Lecture One: 7 January 1976', in *Power/Knowledge: Selected Interviews and Other Writings 1972–77*, ed. Colin Gordon (Brighton: Harvester Press, 1980), p. 81.

17   'Against all humanity', *Times Literary Supplement*, 4 October 1985, p. 1094.

Chapter 5

Thomas R. Adams and Nicolas Barker

A NEW MODEL FOR THE STUDY OF THE BOOK

I

'The History of the Book' has become a catch-phrase, adapted and half translated from the French. It is almost 30 years since *L'Apparition du Livre*, by Lucien Febvre and H.-J. Martin, from which the phrase stems, was published.[1] It is time to take stock of what has happened to bibliography as a science in that period; to consider the longer period during which 'bibliography' (in the modern sense) has addressed itself to the history of books; and finally, taking the longest period of all, the two millennia during which the book has developed in western Europe, to attempt a model for the study of books considered as historic artifacts and as a function of social history.

  L'Apparition du Livre applied the comprehensive view of social history given currency by *Annales*.[2] Unlike the German school, who saw the manufacture and trade in books as a matter for straightforward chronicle (admirably represented in English by S. H. Steinberg's *Five Centuries*[3]), Febvre (who with Marc Bloch founded *Annales*) and Martin were concerned primarily with the impact of the invention of printing on society. 'Le livre, ce ferment' had dynamically changed society: to understand the change, it was necessary to understand how the new technology worked and how the new commerce had grown; but it was also necessary to understand how it had permeated and changed habits and ways of thought, communications and the structure of society. The use of maps and graphic diagrams, the visual aids of *Annales*-istic demography, made the presentation of this thesis more vivid and intelligible.

  The seed thus sown by Febvre and Martin among historians has been slow to germinate. One important off-shoot has been Elizabeth Eisenstein's *The Printing Press as an Agent of Change*.[4] Its thesis – that large movements, the 'Renaissance' or the 'Reformation', were not so much influences on the press as products of it – is a critique of history, rather than a work of primary research; as such it has been misunderstood by bibliographers, who have seen its dependence on secondary sources as a weakness. No such criticism could be made of Robert Darnton's *The Business of Enlightenment*,[5] based on the still-preserved archives of the Société Typographique de Neuchâtel, but he too has been concerned with the larger issues of the press as agent or product of the Enlightenment.

  The bibliographer, his field of study thus unexpectedly dragged into the limelight by academic historians, has reacted to exposure on the wider stage with mingled fascination and alarm.[6] Both are evinced by the proceedings of several conferences, at Boston,[7] Wolfenbüttel,[8] Athens,[9] Paris,[10]

Geneva,[11] and at Worcester,[12] where bibliographers and historians have gathered together, not so much to resolve their differences as to explore a common path forwards. The task of blazing a trail has been approached with much enthusiasm but not a little misunderstanding. Some sort of chart would clearly help.

Why, it may be asked, should any difference exist between bibliographers and historians? A century ago bibliographers and archaeologists occupied very similar positions in the scholarly world; both would have been called 'antiquaries'. A century later, archaeology has become an accepted independent academic discipline and course of study, with departments in most universities: bibliography still hovers on the sidelines of academe. There are two primary reasons for this. First, too many books survive from all periods, compared with any other kind of artifact, from cathedrals to pins, for them to be easily susceptible of 'archaeological' treatment. However numerous, the archaeologist classifies all objects of study as unique: the bibliographer's catalogue entry still treats all the hundreds or thousands of extant copies of a book as a single entity. Secondly, in bibliography there is no line dividing the dead past from the living present. Many – most – books are still living tools, kept in libraries for use. The passage of time alters the context of use, but does not isolate the book, as an object is in a museum. Archaeologists may handle such objects, curators display them to the public. The bibliographer may treat some books in this way. But for a librarian the prime duty is to make books available to all those who wish to use them.

Bibliography meant first writing, then the listing of books. From this it grew and came to include distinguishing one book from another, or different editions of the same book, the arranging of books in order, by author, title, subject, place or date. Latterly, characterized diversely as 'analytical' or 'descriptive' bibliography, it has come to be treated as an ancillary discipline, in service to the higher goal of establishing an accurate text. Increasing sophistication has shown diminishing returns, in this respect. Hinman's *The Printing and Proof-Reading of the First Folio of Shakespeare*[13] was a major landmark in understanding early-seventeenth-century English printing house practices; it did not, as was first hoped when Hinman began comparing all the copies of the First Folio in the Folger Library, add substantially to the solution of the problem of an authoritative Shakespearean text. The mass of ancillary evidence thus amassed, however, led to a further change of direction summarized in D. F. McKenzie's celebrated statement, 'The essential task of the bibliographer is to establish the facts of transmission for a particular text, and he will use *all* relevant evidence to determine the bibliographical truth.'[14] Thus the activities of literary bibliographers shifted focus from the purity of the text to its transmission. Participants in the Boston 1980 meeting of the Rare Book and Manuscripts Section of the Association of College and Research Libraries at Boston have now taken this process still further in 'A Statement on the History of the Book'.[15] In the preamble they say that the 'history of the book' means 'all aspects of the history of production, publication and distribution, from the stage of authorship on through to the impact of books on readers and, ultimately, on society'. It is in the insertion of the word 'ultimately' that we see the influence of social historians emerging. The statement would have been just as strong an assertion of the importance of the history of the book without it. With it, bibliography again becomes ancillary to social history, again a 'hand-maiden' to another discipline.

In the largest sense, every discipline is, in certain respects, the hand-maiden of others. Is the study of books to be doomed to perpetual servitude to all others? Like jurisprudence, it demands a knowledge of all things human and divine, since the subjects of books are equally diverse. If ever there was a subject (in modern academic jargon) 'interdisciplinary', it is the study of books, since they are the most important and (next to coins) numerous of human artifacts; they are vital witnesses to the progress of civilization. The subject is important enough to be recognized as something that stands by itself. Like many 'new' areas of study, for example anthropology, it does not fit into a conventional academic framework. It does not apply a specific discipline (such as history or physics) to all events, but all disciplines to specific events, in this case books. How then to define its scope, its true function?

II

To answer this question, let us reverse the historian's point of view and consider, not the impact of the book on society, but that of society on the book. What did people imagine a book was? What was it for? The modern tendency is to assume that a book was what it is now, a tool. It is difficult to recognize how recent a concept this is, the creation of mechanical multiplication, five centuries old but still new. In one sense, a real and practical sense, it was not new in the fifteenth century. Multiple copying of texts, by a variety of means, had existed for at least two millennia: what was new was an abrupt change of scale, of volume. Books possess an earlier, greater, power, as the vehicle of knowledge or inspiration that outlives the time in which they were first conceived or written. It was a form of magic. We still acknowledge this when we say 'I couldn't put it down.' But this was not solely a factor of the text. The physical form of the book was equally important. A book can exercise its power by its outward or inward appearance, by its impressive strength and durability, by its size, large or small. Now, when all except large picture-books are easy to handle, we forget the import-ance of size: a ponderous folio was impressive, but so equally was the miniature book. A large book might indicate the power it exercised over those who handled it; a small book indicated the power of its owner over the book. Holy Writ or the law set on a great lectern was a monument to all who beheld it: a pocket-book of hours or account book added its virtues to the owner wherever he or she went.

To us, the miracle of the Stonyhurst Gospel is its beauty and (even more) the fact of its survival from the seventh century to our time. But the shape, script and binding, as well as the text, are witness to the power attributed to it when it was first created, as a mobile supplement to the miraculous tomb of St Cuthbert. Its power was acknowledged again when with other relics it was disinterred at the Translation of Saint Cuthbert's bones to the High Altar at Durham in 1104. Ellinger, Abbot of Tegernsee in the eleventh century when he had a series of near identical gospel-books and psalters made for use in his own abbey and its dependent houses, was not evincing an early interest in facsimile reproductions nor just ensuring uniformity of liturgical practice; each book was to be an image of divine authority.[16] Vespasiano da Bisticci's memoirs explain the figure cut in the world by his fifteenth-century customers who demanded the grand books he supplied. The beautifully written and illuminated copies of the works of the great jurists that Cardinal Oliviero Caraffa acquired and commissioned in the sixteenth century were not just for reading, but were part of the outward and visible splendour of his court and the canon law dispensed in it.[17] The pile of books on the coffee table today impresses on you the wealth and cultivation of the owner.

The capacity to multiply books did not diminish this power, nor society's appreciation of it, but changed it. Abbot Tritheim, asking whether the mere quantity of paper copies would prove an effective a substitute for the known durability of vellum,[18] guessed the change; but the need for the permanence of the individual copy typifies the power as well as utility of the book, not just the text. This is the 'rough magic' that Prospero abjured when 'deeper than did ever plummet sound, I'll drown my book':[19] the book meant more than the text, preserved memorially or in another text. This is why 'books are not absolutely dead things, but so contain a potency of life in them to be as active as that soul was whose progeny they are'.[20] Pope, who took so much care with the presentation of his works in print, knew why:

> Yes, I am proud, I must be proud to see
> men not afraid of God, afraid of me.[21]

Voltaire, who took equal pains to assert the power of his works, knew the force of retention: 'Le secret d'ennuyer est . . . de toute dire.'[22] The power of books is not just what strikes the eye, but what may be latent, to be disclosed in the future.

This latent power is vastly magnified by the multiplicity of copies. The successive editions of *The Pilgrim's Progress* show its growth from popular tract to classic; the changes of format, from popular chap-book in the eighteenth century to the pocket classic to edition-de-luxe, to canonical status as an 'Oxford English Text', are equally revealing of the way it has woven itself into the national, now international, consciousness. Cross-fertilization ensues, in a way that the most inter-disciplinary studies can hardly capture. How much did *On the Origin of Species* owe to the acknow-ledged influence of Lyell's *Principles of Geology*, and how much to the copy of Milton that went everywhere with Darwin on the voyage of the *Beagle*?[23] How potent was the influence of *On the Origin of Species* on the novels of George Eliot?[24]

These are questions that cannot just be answered by matching words and texts. The author's intention, the process by which it was converted into a text, the form in which the text was published, its reception, dissemination, the anatomy of its survival – all this can be related to books, vast but not infinite in number, and the supporting evidence that explains their existence and movements. The relation of intention to reception is a special aspect of this, which we consider below.

III

The fact that historians have begun to take a serious interest in the book as such is a step forward of major importance. On the other hand, there are pitfalls ahead. Overwhelmed and bemused as they have every right to be with the volume of secondary writing on the subject (let alone that of primary material), it is not surprising that historians should seek to impose some kind of order, a framework, so that the subject can be treated systematically. But, like all scholars, they have already spent all their professional life with books and so bring to the subject unconscious assumptions about the book derived from that experience. This has unexpected advantages, like M. Jourdain's discovery that all his life he has been speaking prose.[25] It also has disadvantages: the scholar who buries himself in the large secondary literature on the whale fisheries could well write a book on the assumption that a whale is a fish. Unfortunately a patronizing tone has appeared in some of the writings that have thus far appeared suggesting that the work thus far done isn't 'real' or important history.[26] No one questions the need of social historians to construct a framework which they believe will serve as the most effective way of arriving at their goals. When books and their history fall within this frame-work, the social historian must indeed make judgements and choices about those aspects that are most significant for their purpose. But that is social history: they are not writing the history of the book.

All this is not to say that social historians cannot make important contributions to it. Indeed, they are particularly well placed to do so. The history of the book has all too long suffered from fragmentation. Too many bibliographers have been content to dig their own small patch, without surveying the whole landscape beyond. There is a need for integration. The most significant recent contribution is Robert Darnton's model 'The communications circuit' [Figure 5.1] , which he offers as a possible framework for absorbing and interpreting the masses of information we have on the 'fate of books'.[27] It is a schematic structure that is well adapted to the needs of the history of the book in general, allowing as it does for the interplay between external forces and the various processes through which the book goes. The word 'publisher' is anachronistic, except for the last century, and conceals a tissue of complex relationships between the roles of patron, printer, stationer and bookseller. The 'bookbinder' is oddly placed, outside the circle in which he more often forms a link between printer and bookseller. The interposition of the shipper as a major factor seems odd: lines of communication, by sea or land, were certainly an important factor, and the necessity for barter explains some odd book-movements, but the shipper (as opposed to the wholesaler) merely provided a service, as he would for any other commodity.

However, from the point of view of serving the history of the book, the weakness of Darnton's scheme is that it deals with people, rather than the book. It is concerned with the history of communication. The principal emphasis is placed on the people who participate in the process through which the book went in providing a means of communication. For the purpose of the social historian it is a useful approach. For those who are concerned with the total significance of books (especially the printed book) it has limitations. To begin with, it ignores the sheer randomness, the speculative uncertainty of the book trade. Especially in the early day of print, those who made or sold books had no precise idea what would sell where, or how to reach that market. Books often took longer to sell, and travelled far further, than conventional lines of communication and trade would suggest.

If the printed book is an artifact that in its creation, dissemination and continued existence has had a profound influence on the history of the world, it is an influence that we still do not wholly comprehend. We have to remember that the printed book was preceded by, and long overlapped with, the manuscript book. (*The Character of a Trimmer*, written late in 1684, began to circulate in manuscript early in the new year; only in 1688, after its work was done and with the Glorious Revolution imminent, did it reach print, and in a form so corrupt as to show that many scriveners had copied and recopied the text before it reached the printer who ultimately printed it.)[28] Now the printed book in turn is being superseded by the electronic book, as print superseded the manuscript. However, for a period of roughly five hundred years the printed book reigned supreme, as a method of recording, communicating and storing all that people put on paper: knowledge, ideas, persuasion (political or religious), diversions, etc. Its influence on one or more of these areas touched almost every aspect of what we call western civilization, in ways we have still to discover.

Now comes the troublesome question of whether the term 'printed book' is really precise enough. It conjures up an image of the codex, the bound volume of printed and folded sheets sewn along the folds and usually (but not always) put between two covered boards. It takes only a moment's thought to realize that printing was used for a great deal more than producing that kind of artifact. The most obvious are broadsides and other similar printed ephemera. In the early days of the planning of the *The Eighteenth Century Short Title Catalogue* it was suggested that ephemera be omitted. This proposal was dropped when it was pointed out that that would leave out John Dunlap's broadside of the *Declaration of Independence*, the earliest official version of that document. For purposes of brevity the terms 'Printed Book' or just 'Book' will be used here, as no doubt they will in future writing on the subject. However, in the interests of clarity somewhat more precise definition should be made at this point.

The term we propose is an awkward one: bibliographical document. By this is meant something printed or written in multiple copies that its agent, be it author, stationer, printer or publisher, or any combination thereof, produces for public consumption. This can include anything from a multi-volume set to a slip of paper. The controlling factor is that the document was designed to perform a specific function, either private or public. Thus an issue of a newspaper, or magazine, or a fascicle of a book in parts, are bibliographical documents. Proofs of books, printed blank forms to be filled in, playbills, proclamations, printed pictures, business cards, even matchbox covers are all documents. The size of the audience addressed is not a factor; rather it is the fact that the agent's intention involves the process of duplication, so that more than one person can have access to what is on the paper. This need and intention was one of the important elements that led to the invention of printing, and the development of printing had an equally important (but not exclusive) reciprocal

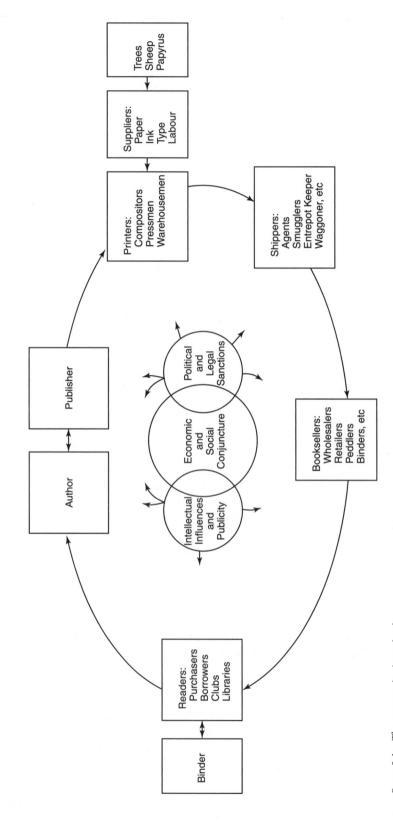

Figure 5.1 The communications circuit

influence on the process, and, while not ignoring the existence of manuscripts or documents, it is to the printed bibliographical document that we now direct our attention.

The artifact and its uses thus defined, what kind of structure can we create that will encompass all aspects of the subject in such a way that the work of those who specialize in one part of the field will not be lost to those who work in other parts, for whom it might have some bearing? The structure, or model, now to be put forward owes its inspiration to that offered by Darnton: that is, a circle of connected elements which are influenced, or can be influenced, by the forces placed in the centre. But since our theme is the book rather than the people involved in its movements, the order of Darnton's elements and forces is inverted. The cycle of the book becomes the centre: the indirect forces are seen outside it, looking and pressing inwards. Instead of the six groups of people who make the 'Communications Network' operation we have five events in the life of a book – publishing, manufacturing, distribution, reception and survival – whose sequence constitutes a system of communication and can in turn precipitate other cycles. Instead of overlapping circles of influence in the centre, indicating intellectual, socio-economic, and official pressures, there are four separate zones, enlarging the scope of outside influences, on the periphery of the circle, each influencing two or more of its stages, depending on individual circumstance. Secondary groups such as the 'binder' or 'shipper' have been omitted, because they are subsumed in one of the five categories. The text is the reason for the cycle of the book: its transmission depends on its ability to set off new cycles.

[. . .]

IV Publishing

Publishing is the name we have given to the point of departure, the initial decision to multiply a text or image for distribution. To understand it we have to balance the many factors taken into account in the decision to publish a particular book at a particular time. There are four parties to the transaction, any of whom might be identical with each other: author, patron (or financier), manufacturer and distributor. The factors in their decision can be grouped under four headings: creation, communication, profit, preservation. Creation is the desire to present a text, whether written recently or long ago, in a particular physical form. Communication is the intention to make it known and available to others. Profit is the need for the enterprise to make a return, which may be commercial (revenue from sales), indirectly commercial (an advertisement or prospectus), or non-commercial (the promotion of religion or a political cause or the enforcement of law). Preservation is to ensure its continued existence through the creation of multiple copies. Usually, but not always, all four factors were at work. The many variations in publishing practice come through the amount of emphasis placed on each of the factors in any given instance.

The most familiar kind of publishing is commercial. Here the profit is a surplus of revenue over expenditures after costs are met. Although their business is also communication, what publishers choose to communicate is contingent on the health of their business. If, on occasion, a publisher may be willing to publish something in which he has a particular interest, whether it shows a profit or not, any loss must be made up somewhere else. The function of the patron is to obviate this need by meeting the costs in advance: manufacturer and distributor will require at least a guarantee before embarking on a doubtfully saleable book. The influence of preservation varies with the opinions and wishes of the publishers. There are some works that at the outset are intended to be lasting. This is reflected in the way the book is made. Others are felt to be transitory, and this too is indicated in the way they are manufactured. Likewise some publishers take pride in the design of their books, while for others anything that is serviceable will do. An author, printer or publisher may be prepared to invest extra time and money to achieve a splendid form, hoping that others will share their view. In the end, if the venture is a commercial one, the cost must still be met, and the business as a whole must prosper.

[. . .]

The decision to publish, not the creation of a text, is, then, the first step in the creation of a book. The nature of the text and, in some but not all instances, the intention of the author are factors in this decision, but other forces control it that have little to do with the intrinsic merit of the text.

V Manufacturing

Manufacturing is primarily a matter of technology and economics. Chronologically it comes first because it was the development of the central technology, printing, that made possible the existence of the object under discussion, but the economics of the technology make it dependent on the decision to publish. The need of the printer, papermaker and binder to make a profit on their investment is a major factor in that decision, quite apart from the commercial considerations involved in publishing. The extent to which the commercial press in Venice in the fifteenth century was dependent on the non-commercial needs of German monastic houses is another typical factor, as is the desire of an author or his patron to promulgate his work, or the requirements of state or church. Besides major enterprises, a consortium set up to print a great book or a series of books, or the small but growing number of printers with established premises, equipment and workforce, there were many smaller, based on the production and sale of a single book, paid for by the author or a patron. In all this diverse and experimental activity, external influence, whether a fixed economy or state or ecclesiastical control, played little part.

The history of the technology of printing already has a large literature, but more is still to be discovered. For instance, it is often said that the printing press of 1800 was essentially the same as the printing press of 1500, yet the enormous growth in the number of books, the size of editions, the creation and development of types and formats, all brought about significant alterations, not only in the structure of the press, but also in compositional techniques, the employment of craftsmen, and industrial procedures generally, between the sixteenth and eighteenth centuries. The bare facts of the mechanical revolution of the nineteenth century are well known: the power press, stereotype plates, machine casting and composition, and illustration procedures. The broader issues remain neglected: how are these mechanical innovations related to those of earlier, industrial 'projectors', Arkwright or Jacquard, and to the general history of technology, and what questions posed by the economic pressure on manual production did mechanization answer?

Another dimension to the subject that has received a good deal of attention but in comparative isolation is type design and typographical layout. That is the process that determined how the printed page was to appear to the eye of the reader, a process that married technology with aesthetics. Even further from the centre of the subject is the whole area of illustration. The woodblock and engraved plate and other methods of reproducing images not made up of letters of the alphabet not only developed along with movable type, but became an integral part of the process we call printing. The vast majority of printed illustrations, including maps, in the last five hundred years have been issued as parts of printed books. This element has generally been discussed purely in terms of its aesthetic or subject content: its importance as a force in the communication process and as a factor in increasing its commercial effectiveness has been generally neglected.

The manufacture of paper and ink likewise have their own histories about which a good deal is known, particularly the former. The technology of both had to keep pace with that of the development of printing technology. Paper in particular underwent dramatic changes to meet the demands of the nineteenth century. These changes in turn had important consequences on the whole matter of survival, since they called in question the future of our record of the past. To a lesser extent ink has gone through the same process. The combination of paper and ink through the impact of metal type in the printing press creates an object with distinct visual and tactile qualities. These vary from place to place and time to time, as each country or locality developed its own style. A knowledgeable person can open any book from any period and, quite aside from its language, tell at a glance roughly where and when it was printed. This appreciation of the physical dimensions of the cultural and economic evidence implicit in any copy of a book deserves more attention as an aspect of the impact of printing.

For a long time binding was considered something apart from printing in the process of bookmaking. Right up to the twentieth century, it was always possible to buy a set of unbound sheets from the printer or publisher, to be bound at the cost of the purchaser (a fact emphasized in Darnton's diagram). But long before the invention of printing there were connections between stationers and binders, and in the fifteenth century it must have been as easy to buy a printed book bound or unbound. While some purchasers of books continued to commission their own binding, or even employ their own binder, the ordinary buyer increasingly expected a bound book, either properly bound or in a temporary protective wrapper. Not until the nineteenth century was binding automatically integrated into the process through which the book went on the way to the ultimate purchaser. Its original purpose was protection but from the earliest days it took on an additional symbolic function. The history of the subject thus takes place on two different levels. The first has to do with structure, the manner in which the folded sheets were attached to each other so that a protective covering could be attached. This process could be summarized as one of progressive simplification, in the interest of volume, speed and cost, with a parallel decline in durability. The second was the outward appearance of that cover. Jewels and gold, or finely embroidered cloth, as well as leather, might enhance the medieval book. Decorated leather, then cloth and now paper (another progressive decline in durability) have since been used.

Beginning with a printed label, the binding was increasingly used to advertise a book. In Anglo-American publishing this took the form, comparatively early, of colour printing and intaglio impressions of designs on thick paper boards. Now in the manufacture of the modern paperback the cover often costs as much as the text within it. The dust-jacket, which began simply as a protective cover for the book and the elegant decorative binding beneath it, has evolved into a vital instrument in publicizing and selling the book, so much so that collectors of modern books attach as much importance to its condition as to that of the rest of the book. The jacket and its close relation, the paperback cover, have reduced the binding proper to insignificance.

Structure and decoration are basic factors in understanding reception, function, influence and survival of books. . . . The place that books had in the social values of the time is expressed in the frame built to hold them. Besides its decorative function, the external appearance of the book has, with the advent of trade binding, become a function of distribution.

Throughout the whole manufacturing process the historian must take into account the essential ingredient that made it all happen, labour, particularly the place and function of labour in a new technology. The degree of literacy required to carry out the tasks and its effect on both social and economic forces have often been written about, but their interaction remains to be calculated. This involves more than counting each step in the process, how it was carried out and how it changed over time as all aspects of bookmaking (paper making, manufacture of ink, manufacture of type, setting of type, operation of the press and binding) grew from manual to mechanical operation. How these operations were brought into harmony and co-ordinated to produce a physical object – the book – is a further dimension. To appreciate how all these different kinds of labour functioned it is necessary to go beyond the economic and social status of each group and find out how each operates separately and collectively as a part of the larger society of which they were a part. The person who determined how a page was to be set, while part of the same unit as the person who operated the press, required different mechanical and intellectual skills, was paid differently, and had a different relation to the author or publisher whose text was being printed.

Labour, in one form or another, played a role in all the other aspects of the history of the book, publishing, distribution, reception and survival, but only in manufacturing does it have an overt effect, the product of its special skill. Capital, by contrast, came from a variety of sources, related to a wider and less specialized spectrum of economic progress. The emergence of an industry with a specialist work-force and supported by capital investment presents the socio-economic historian with a wealth of facts recorded in conventional form: that is, in chronicles, archives, and earlier historical writings. The history of the manufacture of books has its own story that parallels, has links with, yet remains quite separate from, that of other individual developments. The rise and fall of Robert Hoe and Company, whose printing presses were shipped all over the world from its red-brick factory on the East River in New York, the rise and fall of the red-brick mills of the Amoskeag Company on the Merrimack River in Manchester, New Hampshire, McCorquodale's quarter-mile-long printing machine room in Wolverton, and John Player & Son's industrial palace at Nottingham have much in common. Yet in detail the story of every business is different. The similarities and differences such as this must be taken into account in any study of the book and society.

VI Distribution

With distribution, the history of the book begins its dynamic phase: without it the book cannot perform its essential function, to communicate. On the most fundamental level it consists of four elements: the initial impetus, the consequent moving of books, the destination, both intentional and unintentional, and the momentum that carried the process along, which may last a long or a short time and move fast or slow.

In its simplest form the process of moving consists of moving a book or shipment of books from one place to another. It can be as straightforward as buying a book, or borrowing it, and taking it home; at the other end of the scale, it must allow for the complex financial, logistic and legal factors involved in smuggling forbidden books into a country and subsequently circulating them there. Among the people who might be involved are the bookseller, the shipper, the propagandist, or a librarian. The transportation can be across the street, within a city or country, across a border or across an ocean or sea. The vehicle can be a single person on foot, a cart or a ship. The consignment can go unwrapped, in a parcel, in barrels or cartons. The form in which the books are sent can be fully bound, folded but unbound, or in sheets. The financial cost can consist of cartage, shipping costs, customs duties, insurance, warehousing and bribes. It may be based on money or credit, or the first consignment may have a matching return, involving barter. An awareness of the presence or absence of these forces can in certain circumstances add to an understanding of the role the book has played in particular circumstances.

Movement is sometimes illusory. A student of American thought who writes on the impact of *The Education of Henry Adams* on American readers between 1907 and 1918 is likely to be misled. '1907' is the date of the first edition, and the only date given in the bibliography of the *Literary History of The United States* (1948). But the first printing was private and intended for a few friends so that they could comment. It was not until 1918 when Houghton Mifflin brought out the first trade edition that there was any significant movement of the book. The first edition was not distributed in the sense of being originally designed for that purpose.[29]

The forces that set the process of distribution in motion are probably those that chiefly interest the historian. The most obvious is the desire to communicate, but the motive can take a variety of forms: to amuse, to instruct, to convince, are among the most frequent. There is also the desire to recoup and improve on the investment, to gain storage space or to make a gift. All of these involve a variety of mixed motives. Indeed it is the mixture that helps determine the nature and extent of the distribution. Equally important is the lack or limited efficacy of some or all of the normal resources for distribution. If we are to understand the impact or role of any book in society this negative factor must be taken into equal consideration with the positive factors.

[. . .]

The most immediate destination of a book, once it is published, is that intended, the audiences to which the author and publisher addressed it; identifying those audiences is usually our first concern. The evidence that points to the intended audience includes the nature of the text, the size of the edition, the typographical format, the points of distribution, the reviews and advertisements. Of equal importance is the unintended audience: that is, the people to whom the publication found its way, unanticipated by the author and publisher. This can happen either by direct purchase or through a secondary distribution system. The latter can take various forms: it may come about through subsequent gift or loan of copies by the first acquirer, or through unauthorized reprints or translations, either in the place of origin or in other cities or countries. Libraries are an all-pervasive and continuous element in secondary distribution. There is also the second-hand market for books, which pre-dates printing and has only recently detached itself completely from the new book market. It also involves the fragmentation of the work as originally published, through the reprinting of sections, acknowledged or unacknowledged, in other writings; and, finally, its assimilation, consciously or unconsciously, into a wider area, as phrases find their way into the language, ideas into knowledge.

Distribution during the period immediately following publication is only the first part of the subject. There is also the matter of how the copies of a book which have survived until today reached their present resting place. It is here that an understanding of the second-hand book trade becomes important. People who buy second-hand books may do so for other reasons than those that impel people to buy new books; because they find the price attractive, whether less or more than it was originally; because they have already read them, rather than to read them for the first time; or not to read them at all, but to preserve them as historic or aesthetic artifacts. But they buy books and that activity is as much a part of the history of the book as the other. Here we find ourselves involved in the history not only of the second-hand and antiquarian book trade, but also in the history of building libraries, of private collecting and of the concept of 'classics', the selection and revival of works that have survived (that is, have a continuing usefulness and vitality) from a remote past.

Finally there is the nature of the movement and momentum that carries a book through its life cycle. The movement is initiated by the desires of the author and publisher when they launched the book on its way. The momentum is provided by the desire of others to possess the book. Again the most obvious of these desires is the wish to read the book, but to do so one must possess the object. Further, the desire to possess a book does not necessarily mean a desire to read it. Immediate reading is only one of the purposes for which people buy books. They may buy books to read later, an intention not always fulfilled, or for reference. But they may also buy a book because their position or function (or their view of that) demands it. Reasons for acquisition may be altruistic: so that the family, or community, whose needs and wishes may differ from the owners, may benefit from what he acquires. Books may be bought just as furniture, to garnish a room; that too is use expressing status. Finally, there is the power conveyed by the book itself, an incalculable, inarticulate, but none the less potent factor in the mixture of motives that makes people want books. There is more to the possession of books than mere utility.

[. . .]

Distribution is an important part of the historian's concern in understanding the text as text.

The number of reprintings, or lack of reprintings, immediately after publication are factors that enable us to determine the extent to which the author and publisher succeeded in achieving their immediate goals. Later reprintings and revivals, subsequent changes in the form of the book or the style of author or imprint, tell us something about the long-range impact of the text. They may come in response to new movements or a revival of interest in the text, or they may be a mechanical repetition, an enshrinement of the text: the form of publication shows whether the temperature is hot or cold, whether the work is warming to new life or freezing to death; the number and location of surviving copies is a different but equally important index.

Distribution, then, includes more than simply getting a book or text from one person to another. It also includes the extent, in time and space, to which that process takes place. It also helps to define the area or areas that were affected by the act of publication. It is a densely woven network about which we still know comparatively little.

VII Reception

Unlike the three previous themes reception is, initially, a passive thing, and for many of the recipients it remains mute since they leave no direct record of their reactions, if any. The problem of penetrating a reader's mind – to say nothing of groups of readers – makes this one of the most difficult aspects of the history of the book, and 'reception theory' has become an important branch of modern critical theory. But, however difficult to achieve, understanding reception is most important if we are to evaluate what impact the book has had. There is a certain amount of direct documentation, but to a large extent it is necessary to turn to indirect evidence. The evidence can be broken down into four groups: direct documentation, popularity, influence and use.

Direct documentation consists of two kinds, published and private responses. The public responses consist primarily of reviews and answers or commentaries which are published. In addition there is the border area of public oral responses, speeches, conversations and the like, which are reported and published at second hand. While all this evidence is direct evidence, it is, in general, evidence of a particular person's response. On occasion, of course, a commentator will endeavour to report the general response to a piece of writing, or a body of writing, but here again it is the evidence of only one person. All this is only an immediate response. Later assessment, in a historical context, of the individual work or a body of work, while in a larger sense reception, is primarily a study of reception not reception itself.

The popularity of a work can be measured in a number of ways; the most obvious is the number of times it was reprinted and the number of copies printed.[30] This may include not only the whole text but adaptations of it for various purposes and translations. It is here that the techniques of analytical bibliography come into play because of the importance – particularly in the era of hand-set type – of complex and deceptive evidence: corrections during the press-run; all the sheets of a single press-run deceptively issued with different edition statements attempting to suggest popularity, or the closely allied practice of substituting a new title-page on an old impression; close imitation in resetting for reasons of convenience or piratical deception, or even to conform with legal requirements.

Extensive reprinting of a text cannot be taken as a direct measure of popularity: it is at best an indication. What we really need to know is how many of the copies were actually read. What happened to the copies printed? What levels and areas of the reading public did they reach, and to what extent did copies not reach a reading public at all? Were they all sold by one bookseller, were they circulated through an elaborate chain from wholesaler to hawker, were they remaindered or simply given away? If remaindered, how many remained unsold and were scrapped, how many survived to attain a new distribution as valuable old books, and how many went directly to library shelves, there to remain undisturbed for many years? The number of editions and copies is, needless to say, but one measure. There is also the important question of how many people read or heard read a particular copy, and this in turn involved circulating libraries and their lending practices, the availability of printed matter in public places such as coffee houses, barber shops and railway waiting rooms, the extent to which private owners lent their books, and the number of copies available in proportion to the population of a particular community. How many books owed their popularity not to being read at all, but simply talked about? What influence did the title-page, often separately printed as a poster, have? Still another measure of popularity is the proportion of survival. This is an area which has received little attention but we must not forget that there were books that had a popularity, short or long, so intense that most or all of the copies have disappeared. Perhaps the most obvious are practical works with little 'literary' merit such as schoolbooks and manuals, but it must also be remembered that novels and plays now considered serious were once considered to be not worth preserving.

Popularity is but one, and in some sense the least important, aspect of response. There is the larger question of influence: that is the extent to which it can be demonstrated that the publication of a work made a recognizable or measurable difference in what happened after publication. Did the author or publisher see concrete results and, further, was the result what had been hoped for or was it something else? Was a poet's reputation enhanced by extolling an unpopular cause, or was he condemned as a crank? Did an instruction manual make it clear how to operate a computer or was the prospective user confused? These are short-range questions. The poet's work may be rediscovered later, indeed he may have been resigned to that in the first place. Time and events may vindicate him. The technical language of the manual may be ahead of its time, and future users find it lucid as understanding of the computer becomes widespread. Looking at the extent to which the act of publishing achieved its intended goals is only one criterion of reception and, in larger terms, a comparatively small aspect of the subject. The larger one is made up of the results that go beyond the original intention. One of the frequently neglected results of a decision to publish is the loss of control over what happens next. On the simplest level the major difference between a letter and a printed book is that to a large extent the audience for a letter can be controlled, while the audience for a printed book is beyond the control of those who originated it.

What then is the nature of the influence of distribution when it goes beyond its initial objectives, and how does it manifest itself? How can we see it and assess it?

The frequency with which a text was reprinted in some form or other during the years following its initial appearance is a starting point for gauging its indirect influence. This is particularly true of a work that lies dormant for a long period of time only to be revived when another set of circumstances calls for a new printing. There was only one edition of *Areopagitica* in 1644: it signified but did not initiate a change in public attitude. Although reprinted anonymously and digested as someone else's work in 1688,[31] the next acknowledged edition was not printed until 1750, at the same time as the London edition of the trial of John Peter Zenger appeared. Herrick's *Hesperides* (1648) achieved its second edition in Bristol in 1810. But this does not mean that either work ceased to be read or did not have an underground life paraphrased or quoted in other works.[32] While authors usually hope that their writing will have a timeless appeal, they cannot control the future, so that this kind of later dissemination is the result of forces that are quite different from those that controlled initial publication. A much more elusive, and in many ways a more important and less understood, aspect of reception is the way that the ideas, and even the actual wording of those ideas, are picked up and used with or without acknowledgement by later writers for a variety of purposes, some having nothing to do with the original intention of the author and publisher. It is worth noting that an early attempt to bring this secondary use under control was made by the

Cambridge bookseller, John Bartlett, to whom Harvard professors turned when trying to identify a quotation. His *Familiar Quotations* came out in 1855.

A change of language can effect even more startling transformation: the translator may do his work to fulfil needs differing from those that produced the text in the original language. When Joel Barlow, the Hartford Wit, in 1792, translated Brissot de Warville's *Nouveau voyage dans les Etats-Unis de l'Amérique* as *New Travels in the United States of America*, he turned it into a Federalist tract by alteration, omission and addition.[33] It is this dimension of reception that has received the smallest amount of attention.[34] It is elusive, but the process of tracing a text and its influence through other publications is a vital aspect of the role that printing and the book have played and it can only be done with a full awareness of who received what books and in turn produced what books derived in part from that experience.

There is also the question of literacy, an increasingly fashionable but rather ill-defined area of study. Who could read or write seems a simple question. Reading, however, is not easily distinguished from memorial repetition. A book may be used for show, or a prompt, rather than actual reading. To be able to sign your name does not prove that you can write. A signature does not mean that the same hand could write other words. Writing and reading are separate activities: the ability to write tells us nothing about the frequency or ease with which a writer could also read. But the diffusion of books is dependent on literacy. Where and how did people obtain them, at what price, and what were the physical circumstances under which they read them? All these questions are essential elements in assessing reception.

There are other questions, more remote but not less important. What was the influence of physical circumstances on reading? What role did illumination play? Did the variation in hours of daylight at different latitudes have any effect on patterns of reading? How did the improvement of artificial lighting, or the development of reading glasses, affect readers' habits? As the amount and complexity of reading material increased, what happened to the speed and thoroughness with which people read? Is not literacy relative and the study of it useful only in a specific context? The audience for Pope's poetry probably includes few ordinary tradesmen or master mariners. Yet to be successful the first had to be able to do accurate bookkeeping and the second to use the mathematical and astronomical tables necessary to navigating across the open ocean. In fact, the whole development of science depended as much on mathematical literacy as it did on the use of words. There is a further dimension to literacy, too, namely the impact of visual images as a form of human communication. These were manufactured by analogous processes (paper and the rolling press) and distributed by similar routes as were books and verbal documents. The links between the two were aptly demonstrated by William M. Ivins, *Prints and Visual Communication* (New York, 1953).

If, then, our understanding of reception is episodic and scattered, the width and extent of available evidence should encourage, not discourage, further research. Scarcity of documentation presents the historian with a challenge, not a limitation. Still, imagination and determination are required to identify and interpret the sources. Archaeology recreates the way people lived from what is dug out of the ground, on the land or in the sea. For later culture, including our own, it supplements documentation. McKenzie's summons to 'use *all* relevant evidence' has a special force for those who try to calculate the reception of the book. We cannot fully grasp it unless we take into account that there had to be a physical confrontation before reception could take place.

VIII Survival

The idea that survival should be treated as a separate element in the history of the book is unconventional. Yet, if we start with the premise that the book as a physical object is the point of departure, then evidence that the object existed is essential. The most conclusive such evidence is the survival of a copy or at least a fragment of a copy. The circumstances under which this survival took place then becomes as important a part of understanding the subject as are the circumstances which brought it into existence in the first place. Some books owe their survival to secondary causes, by being used as binder's waste or box linings. Like old newspapers found at the bottom of long-unopened trunks in the attic, these survivals have a curious fascination. In addition, there are also those books for which we have only circumstantial evidence of their existence. This is true of the first works printed in Latin America and in what is now the United States.[35] They present a somewhat difficult problem, but must be taken into consideration if we are to gain a full understanding of the role the book has played.

There are three stages in the life of books that have survived. The first includes its creation and initial reception: this is the period during which it is used to perform the function for which it was brought into existence. The second is the period during which it comes to rest without any use or at least intensive use. It is during this period that it is in the most danger of disappearing. If circumstances are right then it will survive until the third period. This is when it is discovered that it is a book desirable as an object, either in its own right or because of the text it contains. It documents the age that brought it into existence and thus enters the world of collecting and scholarly research.

[. . .]

The multiple forces which have worked and still work to allow books to survive for us to study so that we can have a 'history of the book' at all are little understood, or rather their interaction within themselves and with the other factors which must be taken into account is little understood. This is in part because of the great emphasis that has been placed on the inter-relationship between the text and the book with the emphasis on the text. The function of the book as text, as a vehicle carrying information within it, is obvious, but the information that it provides by virtue of its mere survival and existence is not less important because less obvious. The loss due to non-survival, even less measurable, cannot be left out of this equation.

Completing the circuit – the return from survival to publication – is the fuel of the dynamics of the book. A majority of the books in the libraries of the world are reprints, not the original edition. Remember that unless a prototype has survived no decision can be made to republish and thus start the process all over again under different circumstances. The large reprint and microform industry now testifies to the continuing importance of republication in the history of the book, a factor that dominated the circuit in the era of the invention of printing. Indeed the success of the first major microform publication, the microfilm of all the books and broadsides listed in STC published by University Microfilms International, had its origins in a need for survival. The decision by the British Museum to allow the company to bring its cameras into the Library in the 1940s was a result of a concern for their preservation in wartime. The other advantages of microform, such as saving space, which later became important were secondary then if they were considered at all.

An equally obvious publication that results from survival is the whole body of scholarly writing made possible because a copy or copies of books long forgotten are rediscovered when the progress of research gets around to asking for them. Libraries, like museums, are always amused, if mildly irritated, when a scholar makes headlines with an announcement that a lost book or manuscript has been 'discovered' in a collection when the curator knew it was there all the time. It is too often forgotten that before a question can properly be answered it must be properly asked. Survival is not merely a physical fact, but the degree to which that fact is known.

IX

After so extensive an exploration of the ramification, the outer fringes, of the book circuit, it may seem equally otiose to close the circle by pointing to the link between survival and publishing, or to explore the outer edges of the circle, the external forces that exert influence on the circuit. We will therefore be as brief as may be.

'Tout s'achève en Sorbonne', wrote Valéry: everything ends up as a PhD thesis.[36] So books, whether viewed as intellectual instruments or social documents, continue to exist because more books are written about them and thus depend on them. Valéry's pessimism might be countered with the analogy of the coral reef. Survival is a cumulative process.

The four external forces could be divided into many more (or less) categories: it is in the nature of such exercises in social anatomy that there is no right scheme. All schemes have some truth, and all are equally open to dangers of over-simplification. Our pattern has only the merit of following the sequence of the book circuit. Ideas for books, whether for printing something new or reprinting something old, spring from the intellectual climate of their time and influence the decision to publish. Sanctions imposed by society, cross-linked with the intellectual climate, moderate that decision and have a marked impact on both manufacturing and distribution. Commercial pressures, the case and cost of communications, bias both manufacturing and distribution, and have their own influence on the media of reception. The changing tastes and habits of society, which set their mark on reception, thus reach back to distribution and on to survival, and simultaneously link with the march of intellect and new decisions to publish that it engenders.

It is only in theory, in the simple context of a diagram, that these forces can be disentangled from each other, or from the special circumstances of the creation and survival of books. However, the existence of such a framework may have a purpose now. The passage of the old bibliography to the new history of the book is not simple: it is accompanied by an abrupt change from a reductionist to a maximalist philosophy. At the same time, there has been an enormous increase in secondary source material, only incidentally caused by the increase in the scope of the subject; antiquaries will always go on digging.

Our scheme is designed to encompass all the topics that would properly be included in the history of the book. It is a framework designed to fit the vast and sprawling mass of source material in such a way as to introduce it to those who are not familiar with all aspects of the subject so that it can be explored without the threat of straying outside familiar territory. What we offer is a map. It is a map not unlike Isidore of Seville's seventh-century map of the inhabited world which placed Jerusalem in the centre as a sort of prime meridian, and located other known geographical features, such as the Nile and the Mediterranean, schematically, suggesting relationships rather than exact locations. The medieval world map was a synthesis designed to show what was known and perceived about the growing welter of facts and myths relating to the geography of the earth. It is a staging-point in the process that has only recently culminated in the mapping of the world from direct observation by satellite. Our scheme for the study of the book is likewise intended only as a point of departure, a brief for a map that can encompass what we know and perceive. Fuller knowledge of the circumstances and the passage of time will change the pattern. The book will shift from its central position as other forms of communication grow in importance. But for two millennia its place has been pivotal and its prominence will continue for some time to come. So Jerusalem continued to serve as a prime meridian on some world maps until the middle of the fifteenth century, not to be finally displaced until the discovery of the New World revolutionized geography.

A map cannot save the traveller from all dangers that may beset his path. It may save him from some; it also offers him the promising opportunity of pointing out its errors when he returns home, safe and sound.

Acknowledgement

The figure 'The communications circuit' is reprinted by permission of *Daedalus*, Journal of the American Academy of Arts and Sciences, from the issue entitled 'Representations and Realities', Summer 1982, Vol. III, no. 3. p. 68.

Notes

1   Lucien Febvre and Henri-Jean Martin, *L'Apparition du Livre*, Paris, 1958; in English as *The Coming of the Book; The Impact of Printing, 1450–1800*, trans. David Gerard, London, 1976.

2   For an early assessment see Wallace Kirsop, 'Literary History and Book Trade History: the Lessons of *L'Apparition du livre*', *Australian Journal of French Studies*, 1979, 16, pp. 488–535.

3   S. H. Steinberg, *Five Hundred Years of Printing*, Harmondsworth, 1955, 2nd edn 1961.

4   Elizabeth L. Eisenstein, *The Printing Press as an Agent of Change: Communications and Cultural Transformations in Early-Modern Europe*, Cambridge, 1979. For a condensation see her *The Printing Revolution in Early Modern Europe*, Cambridge, 1983.

5   Robert Darnton, *The Business of Enlightenment: A Publishing History of the Encyclopédie 1775–1800*, Cambridge, Mass., 1979.

6   The most prominent expression is to be found in the reviews of Eisenstein's *The Printing Press as an Agent of Change*; see particularly Paul Needham in *Fine Print*, 1980, 6, pp. 23–5, 32–5. For an assessment of her achievements and failures by an historian see Anthony T. Grafton, 'The Importance of Being Printed', *Journal of Interdisciplinary History*, 1980, 11, pp. 256–86. *The Advent of Printing: Historians of Science Respond to Elizabeth Eisenstein's 'The Printing Press as an Agent of Change'*, ed. Peter F. McNally, Montreal: Graduate School of Library and Information Studies, 1987, includes a list of all the reviews of the work up to the time of publication.

7   *Books and Society in History*, Papers of the Association of College and Research Libraries Rare Books and Manuscript Preconference, 24–28 June 1980, ed. Kenneth E. Carpenter, New York and London, 1983.

8   *Buch und Buchhandel in Europa im achtzehnten Jahrhundert: the Book and Book Trade in Eighteenth-Century Europe*, proceedings of the Fifth Wolfenbütteler Symposium, 1–3 November 1977, ed. Giles Barber and Bernard Fabian, Hamburg, 1981.

9   *Le Livre dans les Sociétés Pré-Industrielles*, Colloque International du Centre de Recherches Néohelléniques, Athens, 1982.

10   *La Bibliographie Matérielle*, Giles Barber, Nicolas Barker, Jean-Daniel Candaux, Nina Catach, H. Gaston Hall, Allan Holland, Wallace Kirsop, Paule Koch, Roger Laufer, Henri-Jean Martin, Jeroom Vercruysse, Ian R. Willison, présentée par Roger Laufer, Table ronde organisée pour CNRS par Jacques Petit sous l'égide du CNRS–GRECO n°1 (Groupement de Recherche sur Textes Modernes) tenue à la Bibliothèque Nationale à Paris les 17 et 18 mai 1979, Paris, 1983.

11   *Actes du colloque international sur l'histoire de l'imprimerie à Genève*, ed. Jean-Daniel Candaux and Bernard Lescaze, 27–30 avril 1978, Geneva, Société d'histoire et d'archéologie, 1980.

12   *Printing and Society in Early America*, ed. William L. Joyce, David D. Hall, Richard D. Brown and John Hench, Worcester, Mass., 1983 (the papers of a conference held October 1980).

13   Charlton Hinman, *The Printing and Proof-Reading of the First Folio of Shakespeare*, Oxford, 1963.

14   D. F. McKenzie, 'Printers of the Mind; Some Notes on Bibliographical Theories and Printing House Practices', *Studies in Bibliography*, 1969, 22, p. 75.

15   *Books and Society in History*, pp. xi–xii.

16   Christine Elisabeth Eder, 'Die Schule des Klosters Tegernsee im frühen Mittelalter im Spiegel der Tegernseer Handschriften', *Studien und Mitteilungen zur Geschichte des Benediktiner-Ordens*, 1972, 71, pp. 6–135.

17   Diana Norman, 'The Library of Cardinal Oliviero Caraffa', *The Book Collector*, 1987, XXXVI, pp. 354–71, 471–90.

18   Letter to Abt Gerlach von Deutz (1492), quoted by W. Wattenbach, *Das Schriftmesen im Mittelalter*, 3rd edn, Leipzig, 1896, p. 452.

19   Shakespeare, *The Tempest*, Act V, Scene 1.

20   Milton, *Areopagitica*, ed. K. M. Lea, Oxford, 1973, p. 6.

21   *Epistles and Satires of Horace Imitated* (1737–8), epilogue, dialogue, 2:197–8.

22   *Sept Discours en vers sur l'homme*, VI. Sur la nature de l'homme, ll. 174–5.

23   Gillian Beer, *Darwin's Plots: Evolutionary Narrative in Darwin, George Eliot and Nineteenth-Century Fiction*, London, 1983, p. 87.

24   Ibid., pp. 149–235.

25   Molière, *Le Bourgeois Gentilhomme*, Act II, Scene 4.

26   R. Darnton, 'Reading, Writing, and Publishing in Eighteenth-Century France: A Case Study in the Sociology of Literature', *Daedalus*, Winter, 1971, pp. 214–56; id., 'What is the History of Books?', and E. L. Eisenstein, 'From Scriptoria to Printing Shops: Evolution and Revolution in the Fifteenth-Century Book Trade', *Books and Society in History*, ed. K. E. Carpenter, New York, 1983, pp. 3–42.

27   Robert Darnton, 'What is the History of Books?', *Daedalus*, 1982, 111, pp. 65–83, reprinted with slight alterations in *Books and Society in History*, pp. 3–26.

28   *The Works of George Savile, Marquis of Halifax*, ed. Mark Brown, Oxford, 1989, I, pp. 33–5, 61–8.

29   See the 'Editor's Preface' by Henry Cabot Lodge in the 1918 edition.

30   Figures are apt to be misleading, if only because the exceptional is more frequently cited than the normal. The latter was commonly 200–500 copies in the first century of printing, rising to 500–1000 by the eighteenth century and 1000–3000 after the Industrial Revolution. Ficino's translation of Plato (1491), with an edition of 3000, Gibbon's *Decline and Fall of the Roman Empire* (1776–88), also 3000 in the first printing of the later volumes, Mrs Henry Wood's *East Lynne* (1861), 500,000 copies by 1900, and Mrs Humphry Ward's *Robert Elsmere* (1888), 70,500 copies of the first three printings, were all exceptional.

31   On Blount's *A Just Vindication of Learning and of the Liberties of the Press*, London, 1693, and *Reasons humbly offered for the Liberty of Unlicensed Printing*, London, 1693, see Macaulay's *History of England* (ch. 19) and Robert Birley, *Printing and Democracy*, London, Monotype Corporation, 1964, pp. 22–4. The first edition of *Areopagitica* is by no means a scarce book. The standard authorities, NUC, Wing and the RLIN and OCLC networks list twenty-five copies in libraries in the United States. Wing lists five copies in the British Isles, the maximum number it will list. There is little doubt that there are a great many more. It appeared regularly in Anglo-American auctions until the mid 1960s, when seventeenth-century English books in general began to be in short supply. From 1902 to 1965 it was sold at auction only slightly less than once every year. Many more copies passed through the book trade during those years. To what extent, then, were these copies actually read at the time of publication?

32   John Sparrow, 'George Herbert and John Donne among the Moravians', in Martha Winburn England and John Sparrow, *Hymns Unbidden*, New York, 1966, pp. 1–28.

33   J. P. Brissot de Warville, *New Travels*, ed. Durand Echeverria, Cambridge, Mass., 1964, p. xxvii.

34   But see Kenneth E. Carpenter, 'The Bibliographical Description of Translations', *Papers of the Bibliographical Society of America*, 76, 3, pp. 253–71, which offers new hope here.

35   *Rare Americana: A Selection of One Hundred & One Books, Maps & Prints NOT IN The John Carter Brown Library*, Providence, RI, The Associates of the John Carter Brown Library, 1974, nos 10 & 41. The recent announcement of the discovery of a copy of *The Oath of a Freeman* is not

accepted by the authors. See 'A Scandal in America', *The Book Collector*, 1987, xxxvi, pp. 449–70, 1988, xxxvii.

36   Paul Valéry, *Variété* II, Paris, 1930, 50–2 ('Oraison funèbre d'une fable'); quoted by R. Birley, *Sunk Without Trace*, London, 1962, pp. 207–8.

Chapter 6

Jerome McGann

THE SOCIALIZATION OF TEXTS

I

[Several] years ago G. Thomas Tanselle published an influential essay for scholars, 'The Editing of Historical Documents'. This paper was written as a strong, if also a friendly, critique of postwar work in historical editing. Tanselle argued that historical editing had, in general, been based upon an inadequate understanding of the nature of text. In this regard, according to Tanselle, many distinguished historical editing projects lagged far behind analogous projects undertaken by literary scholars. The problem was that historical editors, in contrast to their literary counterparts, had been too 'apt to neglect the physical form in which the evidence on which they subsist has been preserved'.[1]

This judgment must have come as a surprise to most historical editors, since the nature of their principal material – its documentary character – forces them to encounter the physique of their texts in ways that many literary editors do not experience. But Tanselle showed that historical editors were making excessive interventions into the documents being edited, changing text in misguided and often contradictory efforts to deliver the material in more efficient or accessible ways.

Today few people – certainly not I – would disagree with Tanselle's plea that editors should give the greatest respect to the physical integrity of the documents. Most of what I wish to argue here will involve an extrapolation of Tanselle's plea. But to the extent that Tanselle's essay focussed on the editing of manuscript-based materials, his representation of the problems confronting literary editors can be misleading.

The heart of his theoretical argument rests in his insistence that no sharp distinction should be made in the editorial policy applied to historical and to literary texts: 'No clear line can be drawn between writing which is "literature" and writing which is not' (495), Tanselle says, and he adduces various examples, all very much – so far as they go – to the point. He then adds, however, that 'a distinction does need to be made, not between literary and historical materials [but between] works intended for publication and private papers' (496). Tanselle gives about one-third of a single page to a discussion of this important matter – his essay is fifty-six pages long – and then proceeds to say that 'this is not the place to explore' the distinction he has drawn. 'The point here', he remarks, 'is to contrast that situation [i.e., text involved in a publishing venue] with the very different one which exists for private documents' (497).

When Tanselle rejects the distinction between a historical and a literary document – between informational and aesthetic works – he sets a gulf between himself and a textual theorist like Hershel Parker. Parker is aware, I am sure, that a historical work can be pursued or considered within an aesthetic horizon. Gibbon's *Decline and Fall* is probably as much a work of art as it is a work of history. He must be equally aware that literary works always disseminate historical information. Nonetheless, Parker, like Aristotle, would not want to collapse the distinction between these two kinds of work because they epitomize the difference between a form of writing that is committed to facticity and information, and a form that is, by contrast, devoted to creation.

History and literature differ, that is to say, along the line of their intentionalities. This being the case, we find in Parker's work a passionate engagement with the issue of literary intention. Parker's insistence that editors of literary works should return to authorial manuscripts wherever possible represents his desire to position the text in as close a relation to its authoritative source as possible. For literary work, in this view, is the creative expression of an individual's quest for meaning and order. The scholarly editor's task is to clarify as much as one can the artistic process of creative activity, for it is that process which is the literary work, whether we look at the work as a carrier of meaning (informational) or as a creative event (aesthetic).

Furthermore, if Parker, in contrast to Tanselle, maintains a clear distinction between historical and literary work, he reverses Tanselle's text-theoretical distinction between private papers and public (normally; for our period, printed) texts. Tanselle takes the distinction as a sign that some texts (typically, 'creative works') seek wide dissemination and a kind of iconic perfection, whereas others (typically, private documents) do not. But for Parker, the question of dissemination through printing is secondary, if not irrelevant, to the primary issue of artistic creativity.

For this reason Parker argues that Bowers and Tanselle are confused on the issue of intentionality. Their confusion is most apparent in the value they set upon so-called eclectic editing. To proceed with an editorial process along those lines is, for Parker, at best to court and at worst to ensure an unhappy result. The eclectic edition is by definition *not* a single authorial construct but a polyglot formation imagined by the editor. Furthermore, if the eclectic edition is based on a printed version of the work rather than an authorial manuscript version, the result will be to move even further from that moment 'when the artist was most in control' of his own work.[2]

I detail these matters here in order to position my argument with respect to this seminal debate. In what follows, therefore, I shall be trying to explain why I stand with Parker (and against Tanselle) in maintaining the distinction between historical and literary work, and why I support Tanselle (as against Parker) in Tanselle's view of the distinction between private and public documents. My own view of literary work, and hence of how to go about editing it, rests on this pair of distinctions. Furthermore, the distinctions highlight the centrality of literary texts for understanding the textual condition.

II

I have no disagreement with Parker, or Bowers, or Tanselle on a great many issues of editorial procedure. I take it we all agree that no scholarly editing can take place which does not enumerate all the relevant texts and establish their genetic or collateral relations. We also agree that all such information should be made available to readers who wish to judge both the nature and the executive adequacy of the edition. On other technical matters we differ. We do not agree, for instance, on the criteria for establishing copy-text; we also differ, in various ways, on the appropriateness of copy-text editing (which is to say, 'eclectic' editing) for different kinds of text.

But these are not the subjects I mean to discuss here. Rather, I want to explore a pair of topics that expose the kind of approach I take toward editing literary works. The first deals with the question of multiple artistic intentionalities. The second concerns the aesthetic dimension of documentary materials.

Contemporary text theory, in the arena of literary scholarship, founded itself on the idea of authorial intentions. No one, of course, repudiates either the reality or the importance of authorial intentionality for the problem of text theory or editorial method. What is at issue is how absolutely the concept of authorial intention is to be understood *so far as the editing of literary works is concerned*. For Parker, the sole criterion on which a literary-editorial project ought to be based is the criterion of authorial intention. Furthermore, Parker postulates for every literary work an ideal process of creation. This process may become diverted or corrupted in many ways, by the author or by any number of other agents. The editor's task is to cut through those diversions and corruptions in order to reveal, as purely as possible, the original artist's creative intention.

Bowers and Tanselle also base their editorial theories on the concept of authorial intention. But because they discern in the production of literary works the presence of multiple authorial intentions, they seek to make compromises between the options offered by the diversity of textual witnesses. These compromises appear as the eclectic edition, which is an editorial construction built up from a copy-text. That copy-text becomes 'eclectic' when the editor, after examining the relevant documents, introduces readings from other textual witnesses which are judged to exhibit greater authority than the authority of the copy-text.

Parker criticizes the eclectic approach because it violates his notion of artistic integrity. The creative process for him is the artist's rage for order, which cannot be well approximated when an editor seeks for rationally derived compromises. It succeeds least of all if an editor grants equal authority to printed as to manuscript materials. Its this situation, Parker devalues printed texts because they cannot embody the integrity of the artist's vision – too many other agents are involved in the production of such work. The job of the editor is to rescue the work from the chaos of conflicting and secondary authorities and agents – including the author's own secondary thoughts.

Eclectic editors, for their part, observe the scene somewhat differently. Where Parker sees randomness obscuring a hidden wholeness, the eclectic editor observes a kind of textual solar system, with the famous 'copy-text' standing as the center of gravity around which many textual planets move and have their being. 'Copy-text' is the still point in the turning world of a diversity of secondary or dependent texts.

But suppose the textual condition does not correspond to either of these imaginings. Suppose, for example, that the textual condition were to appear in the likeness of D. G. Rossetti's poetic sequence *The House of Life*. This work was produced in multiple versions. Some of these versions stand in a genetic line of relation with each other, and hence could be taken for the dependencies of a primary authority. But one of the versions does not stand in such a relation, and the work breaks up into other kinds of independent units within each of the larger versions. Besides, the standard version of this work is a posthumous editorial construction made up from a decision about how to treat the heterodox amalgam of textual deposits.

Multiple versions of many Shakespeare works also come down to us – most notoriously, *King Lear* – and this situation is not merely common in the case of theatrical work, it is the rule. Today, the very concept of the famous 'bad quartos', once firmly established in editorial treatment of Shakespeare, has been undermined. Furthermore, it is equally typical that alterations in the texts of plays are the consequence of the collective efforts of the theatrical company. Texts change under the pressure of immediate events.

Charles Lamb's highly artistic essays – they are really types of prose poem – appear as one thing when they are first published in *The London Magazine*, and as quite other things when he moves to have them produced in book form. The Cuala Press editions of Yeats's poems differ sharply from the texts brought out (almost at the same time) under the Macmillan imprint.

But there is no call to multiply examples. The problem is well known. Let me just conclude with the startling case of Ezra Pound's last published installment of his *Cantos* project, the section known as *Drafts and Fragments*. Here it is not merely that an extreme indeterminacy governs the state of the texts. More difficult is the fact, now well documented, that various agents besides Pound were involved in the production of this work.[3] I should also make it clear that this case is just an extreme instance of something one discovers repeatedly in literary studies. Traditional ballads and songs typically descend to us through wildly heterodox lines of textual transmission. In such cases, trying to edit on the basis of any concept of 'authorial intention' or 'authorial control' is simply impossible.

Of course, each of these versions may be usefully studied as a singular example of a creative process, as may the two texts of *King Lear*, or the multiple versions of Stoppard's plays. Literary editing should encourage that kind of study. Nevertheless, literary work by its very nature sets in motion many kinds of creative intentionalities. These orbit in the universe of the creative work – but not around some imaginary and absolute center. Rather, they turn through many different kinds of motion, at many structural scales, and in various formal relationships. The universe of poiesis no more has an absolute center than does the stellar universe we have revealed through our astronomy. What it has are many relative centers which are brought to our attention by our own acts of observation. The universe of literature is socially generated and does not exist in a steady state. Authors themselves do not have, *as authors*, singular identities; an author is a plural identity and more resembles what William James liked to call the human world at large, a multiverse.

Literary texts differ from informational texts by being polyvocal. Whereas 'noise' is always a form of corruption for a channel of information, it can be exploited in literary texts for positive results. The thicker the description, so far as an artist is concerned, the better. (Minimalist styles of art thicken their media by processes of subtraction and absence.) A thickened text is a scene where metaphor and metonymy thrive (Coleridge's 'opposite or discordant qualities', his 'sameness with difference'). For Parker, the thickness comes from the artists' imaginative resources, who can be counted on to put into their texts far more than even they are aware of. Parker's 'intention' includes, crucially, the vast resources of the unconscious and preconscious.

But thickness is also built through the textual presence and activities of many non-authorial agents. These agencies may be the artist's contemporaries – these are the examples most often adduced – or they may not; furthermore, the agencies may hardly be imagined as 'individuals' at all. The texts of Sappho, for example, gain much of their peculiar power from their fragmented condition, and the same is true for various ballads and songs, which exploit their textual fractures and absences for poetic results.

Most important of all, however, so far as the *aesthesis* of texts is concerned, are the scholars and institutions of transmission who hand our cultural deposits down to us. Texts emerge from these workshops in ever more rich and strange forms. Indeed, readers sometimes complain that cultural transmitters interfere with the original texts too much, that they make them appear too difficult, too alien – too thick and encumbered. And no doubt there are many helpless and hopeless interventions. But who is to say for certain which they are? Besides, 'literary' work, in its textual condition, is not meant for transparency, is not designed to carry messages. Messages may be taken from such work, but always and only by acts of simplification and diminishment. So readers, in those ghostly shapes we call critics and scholars, hear many voices in the texts they study. Like Tennyson's sea, what is literary 'moans round' with many such voices. In doing and being so, texts put the features of textuality on fullest display.

III

To this point I have been taking the word 'text' to signify the linguistic text, the verbal outcome at every level (from the most elementary forms of single letters and punctuation marks up to the most complex rhetorical structures that comprise the particular linguistic event). And even if we agree, for practical purposes, to restrict the term 'text' to this linguistic signification, we cannot fail to see that literary works typically secure their effects by other than purely linguistic means. Every literary work that descends to us operates through the deployment of a double helix of perceptual codes: the linguistic codes, on one hand, and the bibliographical codes on the other.

We recognize the latter simply by *looking* at a medieval literary manuscript – or at any of William Blake's equivalent illuminated texts produced in (the teeth of) the age of mechanical reproduction. Or at Emily Dickinson's manuscript books of poetry, or her letters. In each of those cases the physique of the 'document' has been forced to play an aesthetic function, has been made part of the 'literary work'. That is to say, in these kinds of literary works the distinction between physical medium and conceptual message breaks down completely.

I could adduce scores of similar examples of works generated out of the production mechanisms developed by printing institutions. The most obvious are the ornamental texts produced, for example, by writers like William Morris, but the books published by Whitman, Yeats, W. C. Williams, and Pound – to name only the most obvious examples – make the same point. Less apparent, but no less significant, are the novels of Dickens and Thackeray, or the serial fictions produced throughout the nineteenth century – topics I shall elaborate upon in a moment. If Tanselle cannot easily draw a distinction between a historical and a literary work, it is just as difficult to distinguish, in all these cases, between that which is documentary and that which is literary. The physical presentation of these printed texts has been made to serve aesthetic ends.

Textual and editorial theory has heretofore concerned itself almost exclusively with the linguistic codes. The time has come, however, when we have to take greater theoretical account of the other coding network which operates at the documentary and bibliographical level of literary works.

Not that scholars have been unaware of the existence of these bibliographical codes. We have simply neglected to incorporate our knowledge into our theories of text. Surely no editor of Coleridge's 'The Rime of the Ancient Mariner' – if the editor chose to print the 1816 rather than the 1798 text – would consider placing the famous set of glosses anywhere except in the margin of the work. The glosses have to be *there*, and not set as either footnotes or endnotes, because their bibliographical position is in itself highly meaningful. Placed as they are, the glosses make an important historical allusion that affects the work in the most profound way. A similar kind of historical allusion operates in the ink, type-face, and paper used by William Morris in the first edition of his *The Story of the Glittering Plain* (1891). Both involve literary allusions: the one to medieval conventions of textual glossing, the other to fifteenth-century styles of typography and book production.

As Tanselle has argued, every documentary or bibliographical aspect of a literary work is meaningful, and potentially significant. But Tanselle's clear, practical sense of this matter has not led him to imagine how such materials are to be incorporated into a theory of texts and editing. On the contrary, in fact. He has neglected doing so, I believe, not because of his adherence to an eclectic model of editing, but because of his unnecessarily restricted view of the processes of literary signification.

A few more examples will clarify what I have in mind. In the current controversy over the edition of *Ulysses*, attention has been focussed on a number of specialized, and largely executive, issues (for example, the *Ulysses* editors' failure to work directly from original documents rather than from photocopies).[4] The overriding editorial question, however, has always been this: Should Gabler have chosen the 1922 *Ulysses* as copy-text instead of trying to construct as his copy-text (if that is the right term in this peculiar case) the theoretical entity he called in his edition 'the continuous manuscript text'? Without going into the technical issues involved, let me simply observe that John Kidd – Gabler's chief critic – originally took his own preference for the 1922 edition because he detected in that book an elaborate symbolism keyed to the sequence of page numbers. If Joyce's page numbering has been symbolically deployed, that fact has to be registered in the editorial reconstruction. Specifically, the 1922 pagination of *Ulysses* would have to be editorially preserved.

The example of *Ulysses* ought to remind us that many of the key works of the modernist movement in literature, especially the work produced before 1930, heavily exploit the signifying power of documentary and bibliographical materials. The first thirty of Pound's *Cantos*, published in three book installments between 1925 and 1930, are only the most outstanding examples of this fact about modernist texts. A great many similar examples could be cited from modernist writers working all across the Euro-American literary scene.

Nor does the situation change if we move back in time. The case of Thackeray is well known and typical, and the particular example of *Vanity Fair* eloquent. In the first 1848 edition Thackeray himself designed the sixty-six decorated initials and eighty-three vignettes – as well, of course, as the thirty-eight principal illustrations. His surviving manuscript of the novel with his markups shows where he wanted various cuts to appear. Yet most editions of *Vanity Fair* omit these materials altogether, even though they are clearly involved in the structure of the book's meaning. Gordon Ray has pointed out, for example, that while the verbal text 'leaves unanswered the question of whether or not Becky Sharp brought about the death of Jos Sedley[,] his etching of Becky's second appearance in the character of Clytemnestra more than hints that she did'.[5] Thackeray's decorated cover for the nineteen separate parts of the serially published text (1847–48) is an equally unmistakable case of the book's graphic materials being coded for significance. Indeed, in chapter 8 of the novel the narrator refers to that symbolic design and explicates its meaning.[6]

From a scholarly point of view, it would be difficult to justify an edition of Thackeray that omits the illustrative matter handled at the documentary level of the work. For the novel is not merely 'one of the best illustrated books in the world', it is also an important 'experiment in composite form as much as Edward Lear's *Book of Nonsense*' (1846)[7] – as much, indeed, as the more famous 'composite art' of William Blake. Indeed, Thackeray explicitly calls attention to his own composite art in the subtitle of his novel: 'Pen [i.e., linguistic] and Pencil [i.e., graphic] Sketches of English Society'.

Yet the same must be said in the case of Dickens, even though Dickens did not, like Blake, Thackeray, and Lear, design his own illustrations. For the texts of Dickens's novels were equally produced as works of composite art, though in this case Dickens supplied only the pen, while others worked with the pencil. The relevance of the illustrative material has been acknowledged throughout the editorial history of Dickens's works, both their scholarly and their commercial history.

Or what would one say of a critical edition of the Alice books that omitted the designs of Sir John Tenniel? So important was Tenniel's work for the first of the Alice books (*Alice's Adventures in Wonderland*, 1865) that his protest at the poor printing of the first edition caused the book to be cancelled altogether.

In fact, we have two distinct versions of this famous book: the version on which Carroll and Tenniel collaborated, published in 1865, and the fair manuscript copy with Carroll's own illustrations made as a Christmas gift for Alice Liddell, and eventually published in 1886. In both cases the verbal text and the documentary materials operate together to a single literary result.

Nor do I mean to isolate for importance, in the case of this work, only the marriage of illustration and text. As Tenniel's protest over the poor printing of the first edition indicates, the entire documentary level of the work must be understood as carrying significance. The fact that one version was conceived as a publishing event, and the other as a manuscript gift book, sets the bibliographical coding for each version on an entirely different footing.

The two versions of *Alice's Adventures in Wonderland* may well remind us of the variant versions of so many nineteenth-century books, especially the novels. Serial publication of one kind or another was the rule, as were the related publication mechanisms we associate with institutions like the circulating library. Writers worked within those particular sets of circulatory conventions (though they vary with place and time, such conventions always exist) and the literary results – the books issued – are coded for meaning accordingly.

Furthermore, different types of serialization were available. A novel written for weekly serial publication, like Dickens's *Hard Times* (1854),[8] is not merely *written* differently from one that is written for monthly circulation (or for no serial publication at all); it is *produced* differently and comes into the reader's view via differently defined bibliographical structures of meaning. Or consider the exemplary case of *Oliver Twist*. First issued in serial parts in the monthly magazine *Bentley's Miscellany* (1837–39), it was printed again in three volumes (1838) even before the serial run had been concluded. Then in 1846 it was published again, this time in ten serial installments (the run in *Bentley's Miscellany* had been twenty-four installments). In each of these cases the text is organized very differently. The *Bentley's* and the three-volume publications comprise fifty-one chapters, whereas the 1846 serial publication has fifty-three. *Bentley's* is divided into three 'Books', but these do not correspond exactly to the three 'volumes' of 1838. The *Bentley's* serial typically prints two, sometimes three chapters per unit, whereas the monthly numbered parts of 1846 typically contain six, sometimes five (and in one case, four) chapters.[9]

These kinds of production structures can be exploited for aesthetic effects in particular and always highly individuated ways. *Pickwick Papers* first appeared in serial parts (1836–37), as did *Little Dorrit* (1855–57), but in each case the bibliographical codes are manipulated to unique effect. The latter is one of the late novels, produced twenty years after the groundbreaking effort of *Pickwick Papers*. The early work is far more episodic than the later, so much so that many would be reluctant to call *Pickwick Papers* a novel at all. Whatever it is, the work emerged through the mutual efforts of Dickens, two illustrators (Robert Seymour and Hablot Knight Browne ['Phiz']), and the production mechanisms set in motion by the publishers Chapman and Hall, all working together in cooperative consultation.[10]

Literary works are distinct from other linguistic forms in their pursuit of extreme concrete particularity. That special feature of 'literature' has two consequences we all recognize. First, literary works tend toward textual and bibliographical dispersion (signalled at the earliest phases of the work by authorial changes of direction and revision, which may continue for protracted periods). Second, they are committed to work via the dimension of *aesthesis* (i.e., via the materiality of experience that Blake called 'the doors of perception' and that Morris named 'resistance'). In each case, literary works tend to multiply themselves through their means and modes of production. These processes of generation are executed in the most concrete and particular ways. *Oliver Twist* is produced during Dickens's lifetime in several important creative forms. But then there are equally important versions of that work – equally significant from an aesthetic point of view – that are produced later. Kathleen Tillotson's is a splendid edition of a great literary work, but perhaps we should want to argue that her edition is not the work of Charles Dickens. And perhaps we should be right in doing so.

Tillotson's edition stands in relation to Dickens's novel in the same kind of relation that (say) the Tate Gallery stands to the paintings of Turner. Both gallery and edition force us to engage with artistic work under a special kind of horizon. It is far from the horizon under which Dickens and Turner originally worked. It is nonetheless, still, an aesthetic and literary horizon, and that fact cannot be forgotten. Of course we cannot recover the earlier frame of reference; all we can do is make imaginative attempts at reconstituting or approximating it for later persons living under other skies. The vaunted immortality sought after by the poetic impulse will be achieved, if it is achieved at all, in the continuous socialization of the texts.

Notes

1   Tanselle here is quoting with approval the words of Nicolas Barker. See G. Thomas Tanselle 'The Editing of Historical Documents', reprinted from *Studies in Bibliography* (1978) in *Selected Studies in Bibliography* (Charlottesville: University Press of Virginia, 1979), 454.

2   Hershel Parker, *Flawed Texts and Verbal Icons: Literary Authority in American Fiction* (Evanston: Northwestern University Press, 1984), 49.

3   Peter Stoicheff detailed the complex history of the *Drafts and Fragments* text in a lecture at the Yale conference on editing Pound, sponsored by Yale and the Beinecke Library in October, 1989. The lecture forms part of a book which is now in press. [Peter Stoicheff, *The Hall of Mirrors: Drafts and Fragments and the End of Ezra Pound's Cantos* (Ann Arbor: University of Michigan Press, 1995).]

4   John Kidd's recently published 'An Inquiry into *Ulysses:* The Corrected Text' supplies, in great detail, the case against the edition in this respect. See *The Papers of the Bibliographical Society of America* 82 (December 1988): 412–584.

5   See Gordon N. Ray, *The Illustrator and the Book in England from 1790 to 1914* (New York and Oxford: The Pierpont Morgan Library and Oxford University Press, 1976), 75.

6   See *Vanity Fair by William Makepeace Thackeray*, edited with an introduction by Geoffrey and Kathleen Tillotson (Boston: Houghton Mifflin Co., 1963); see pp. xxii and 80.

7   Gordon Ray, op. cit., xxxix.

8   *Hard Times* was first published in weekly parts in *Household Words* over five months, beginning 1 April 1854. It was then published separately.

9   See *Charles Dickens: Oliver Twist*, ed. Kathleen Tillotson (Oxford: Oxford University Press, 1966), especially pp. 369–71.

10   For the story of these events see Robert L. Patten, *Charles Dickens and His Publishers* (Oxford: Oxford University Press, 1978), chapter 3, especially pp. 63–68.

Chapter 7

Harold Love[1]

EARLY MODERN PRINT CULTURE
Assessing the models

The concept 'print culture' has been central for many decades to the work of book historians and media theorists. The influence of Lucien Febvre and Henri-Jean Martin, supplemented by that of Elizabeth Eisenstein, has made it no less significant for mainstream historians of Renaissance and early modern Europe. It has also been important for literary scholarship, especially through recent documentation of the continued vitality of scribal transmission during print's early centuries.[2] However, the concept has never been a clearly defined one, and in recent years has come to be used in a number of, at best, semi-related senses. The aim of the present article is the methodological one of distinguishing these senses and assessing their utility for literary and historical study.

At an elementary level, 'print culture' is an umbrella term for an indiscriminate body of subject matter linked in one way or another with the printed word and image. In more specialised ways it is used to refer to: (1) a 'noetic world' or consciousness constructed through print; (2) the industrial relationships of book production and distribution; (3) a body of practices arising from the social relationships of reading and information management; and (4) a specialised field of study within the wider discipline of Communication. We will consider each of these senses in which 'print' can be seen as having founded a 'culture'. However, since 'print culture' is also used as a means by which we slice intellectual history into chronological segments, I shall begin by examining the assumption that there was an 'age of print', sharply or fuzzily distinguishable from other information ages, and the characteristics that have been attributed to it.

In the most familiar version of this sectional narrative, print culture, however defined, came on stream in Europe in the late fifteenth century, achieved primacy over oral and scribal culture around 1700 and is currently in its death throes.[3] That the invention of printing precipitated, or at least facilitated, social change, is hardly in dispute; however, there has been disagreement over which criteria might allow us to divide off the posited age of print from that of what Walter J. Ong calls chirographic culture.[4] Ong's own view, to be discussed shortly, sees this crucial development as a noetic one, residing in altered perceptions of language encouraged by the new medium, specifically through an erosion of 'presence' from the textual record and its replacement by an object-like impersonality. Others see the effect, and therefore the temporal borderland, falling elsewhere. Eisenstein lays her main emphasis on improvements in the speed and volume of information flow. Print culture, in her conception, is a series of techniques and practices that allowed the world's stock of recordable knowledge to be put to use with a fearsome new efficiency.[5] This, at the time, was also Francis Bacon's view.[6] For David Zaret, in *Origins of Democratic Culture*, coming to the matter with different priorities, the defining impact of early modern print culture lay in its overcoming of 'restrictive norms of secrecy and privilege' and the creation of a public sphere, another view with which Bacon would have agreed.[7] Less sanguinely, Jan-Dirk Müller, citing Trithemius, sees the distinguishing effect of print culture as lying in a 'trivialization of the written' arising from the perishability of the new product and a loss of selectivity in what was broadcast and preserved,[8] while Adrian Johns identifies a reduced confidence in the veracity of public information, thus reversing Ong's argument that the visuals of print create their own authority.[9] Not all the scholars I have mentioned would have viewed these developments as epiphenomena of a totalising print culture with an identifiable beginning and end, but their results are frequently used to support this notion, as is the case with James J. O'Donnell when he speaks of how 'the social order found itself wrenched, sometimes agonisingly slowly, sometimes shockingly quickly, to align itself with what technology had created'.[10] In a recent exchange with Eisenstein, Johns charged her with attributing 'a synthetic, universal character' to print culture.[11]

Another version of Müller's trivialisation thesis is given by Hobart and Schiffman's *Information Ages*, which sees the advent of print as precipitating a transition from a classical age of literacy to a modern age of numeracy.[12] Their study draws on Roger Chartier's diagnosis of an 'anxiety' arising from a surfeit of books, which Hobart and Schiffman reformulate as 'information overload'.[13] They cite Montaigne as an example of a mind drowning in the ocean of textual particulars, and then turn to Descartes as the archetypal figure of a movement to replace unmanageable bodies of verbal information with manageable analysis conducted through the symbolic notations of algebra and geometry.[14] The impact of print culture, in this view, is realised in the experience of private intellectual stress. Concerning information overload or, as others have it, 'the information explo-sion', we should note that this could also manifest itself through saturating a particular narrow interest-band with so much material that wider perspectives were neglected: Don Quixote is a famous example. Yet the human mind has always been subject to overload, beginning with sensory overload; it deals with this by creating filters, both physical ones, like the thalamus in the brain, and cultural ones, such as the humble bibliography. The question of the nature and variety of these cultural filters, and the ways in which new filters were devised to deal with the impact of print, is a much more complex one than Hobart and Schiffman concede. Chartier and Richard Yeo have both addressed this issue.[15] What we might call the Cartesian filter was far from the only one activated during the early modern period. In any case, while a Montaigne or a Robert Burton were over-whelmed by the sheer abundance of information, for others – a Pierre Bayle or an Anthony Wood – it promoted an Erysichthonian hunger for *unfiltered* fact.[16] A lot depended on one's inherent appetite for knowledge.

A further consideration is that much of the information that caused the overload was trans-mitted independently of the press: consider for a start the very considerable body of operative knowledge involved in the conduct of the printing and bookselling trades themselves, all of it transmitted orally, visually or kinaesthetically (i.e. through demonstrated expert practice). No-one ever learned to print by reading Moxon, any more than, as Johns points out, they learned to build airpumps by reading Boyle.[17] Technological expertise communicated itself through the voices, eyes and hands of its exponents. A still more important issue is that cultures of communication progress by supplementation as much as by replacement. Not only do the old media continue in existence but often they continue in an enhanced rather than depleted form. Consider the way that, in modern times, the printed codex has encountered the challenge of the phonograph, the silent cinema, the radio, the talkies, technicolour, television, colour television, the home video, the personal computer, the internet and now the e-book – all of which were announced as about to bring it to extinction –

and emerged from each encounter with overall book production still higher than before. In the same way, while we tend to think of early modern scribal culture as a survival of pre-print practices, we should remember that it was a triumphant survival, in that many times more handwritten texts were circulating in Britain in 1700 than was the case in 1600 or 1500. These included business and legal documents inscribed by a constantly growing cadre of professional clerks, and letters circulated through the rapidly expanding postal services – a huge expansion of record-keeping in every department of public and private life was predominantly the work of the pen. However, as I have shown elsewhere, many literary and informative texts also continued to circulate in manuscript as a deliberately chosen alternative to print.[18]

Likewise, early modern oral culture was much more than 'residual', as Ong would have it, or a 'preliterate residue' in Julie Stone Peters's phrase.[19] Isaac Barrow, writing in the 1670s, argued that political, religious, and judicial authority in his time were almost wholly exercised by oral means, with the role of the pen and the press insignificant by comparison, concluding 'Whatever almost great or small is done in the Court or in the Hall, in the Church or at the Exchange, in the School or in the Shop, it is the Tongue alone that doeth it'.[20] Consider too these words of a near-contemporary of Barrow:

> 1 Writing is a dead kind of Representation, and therefore not proper to Express us whilst wee are liuing. 2 Writing sticks in the paper and produces no effects outward, speech goes forth and makes impression.[21]

When this dominance of the tongue in the exercise of power yielded place it was not to print but to the dossier system of bureaucratic decision-making, originating with the court of Star Chamber and reaching its most refined form during British Imperial rule in India. Adam Fox's *Oral and Literate Culture in England 1500–1700* demonstrates that oral culture was far more deeply interpenetrated by writing than is generally recognised, but in doing this, also shows how firmly the early modern cultures he discusses remained grounded in the spoken rather than the inscribed or the printed word.[22] Even today, the Watergate and Clinton tapes testify to the survival of power executed through the spoken word without any recourse to script, print or computers. The direction of Rupert Murdoch's global communications empire is, I am informed, exercised principally through oral messages communicated by the proprietor over the telephone. Early modern print certainly sent messages to and from those who held power and would sometimes help to unseat them, but print only became an instrument for the actual exercise of power by being converted into conversation, oratory or the signed handwritten document.

Instead of a new communicative technology wholly obliterating old ones, what more commonly happens is an overall expansion of communication in which all kinds are carried forward, though there will inevitably be interactions and reallocations of cultural responsibilities of the kind analysed by Fox. James W. Carey speaks of 'ancient forms of association, politics and entertainment conducted by speech and storytelling' being 'overlaid with newer habits of literacy: reading and writing' – overlaid, but not replaced.[23] Yet 'print culture' continues to be spoken of as if it were the equivalent of intellectual culture generally. As a result of this symbiosis of communicative cultures, no reader or writer of the early modern period was ever 'within' print culture without also being within oral culture, scribal culture, a culture of symbolic images, a culture of the use of signs and graphics, a culture of physical performance and bodily self-presentation, numerous cultures of expert practice passed on through visual, tactile and kinaesthetic demonstration, and, as Bruce Smith has shown, a culture of response to ambient sound.[24] Nor can any of these be regarded as coherent and unified entities; it is obvious from the simplest inspection that we are dealing with accumulations of subcultures, some of which had more common ground in terms of method and function with their cousins in other media than with their siblings in their own. (Consider, for example, Roger L'Estrange's naturalisations of intensely colloquial speech in his *Observator*, written in dialogue and appearing as a bi- or tri-weekly newspaper. Print has several effective techniques for conveying the illusion of voice.) Each of these cultures and subcultures enforced its own particular body of what Carey calls 'habits and capacities', but it has never been difficult for individuals to accommodate multiple sets of these. The experience of early modern consumers of texts would have been one of a constant movement between 'cultures' – reading Raleigh's *History* in print or his 'A dialogue between a counsellor of state and a justice of the peace' in manuscript, seeing him represented in the theatre as Caius Silius in Jonson's *Sejanus*, hearing him denounced in a speech in parliament or defending himself at his trial, reading a printed account of his execution, coming across a manuscript of a poem supposed to have been written the night before that execution, hearing 'Walsingham' sung by a ballad-seller in the street.[25]

In many cases the same text could have been encountered in several media: a Biblical verse could be read in a printed Bible or from a handwritten harmony or commonplace book, heard aloud (either spoken or set to music) in the course of a public or a private ceremony, or seen translated into graphic form in an emblem, painting, or tapestry. A broadside ballad could be sung in a street, read aloud after dinner or, if it was of the bawdy kind, pasted for reading onto the wall of a jakes.[26] Each of these experiences may well have activated different kinds of consciousness, yielded different inflections of meaning, assisted in constructing different sets of social relationships; yet early modern people clearly had well-practised ways of integrating diverse communicative experiences and switching between them, as we do ourselves when we move between the same text read on a page, or a screen or heard from an audio tape. In the present state of our understanding of early modern textuality it seems important that we should investigate the nature of these transitions – a task for which Fox's study of the mutual interpenetrations of the written and the oral offers valuable guidance. We may well feel that we do not have the evidence to observe these transitions in action, but it could also be that – with a few noble exceptions – we have never properly tried to look for them.

Yet, while acknowledging the very real differences between the kinds of response drawn forth by different media and submedia, we also need to acknowledge that the differences could never have been as extreme as we imply when we allocate each of them to a distinct and independent consciousness or culture. As an example, there is a level at which it would have been significant for Parson Adams in Fielding's *Joseph Andrews* that he read Aeschylus in his own transcribed manuscript rather than from a Delphin classic bound in fine red turkey leather with gold tooling, and another level at which it would have been insignificant, in the sense that his engagement with certain discrete aspects of the Aeschylean text would have been unaffected by the medium through which it was encountered. Which particular aspects these were would be something that varied with the reader and the particular occasion of the reading. Cultures of inscription always share some degree of operational ground. During the events of mid-September 2001 and mid-October 2002 we went to television and radio for the unfolding narrative and to the press for analysis and interpretation; but television did some interpreting, radio more, and the papers recapitulated and amplified the narratives.

For these reasons, the notion of an Age of Print and an all-enveloping Print Culture with stable attributes becomes untenable as a way of interrogating the everyday realities of communication. By the same token, taxonomic distinctions of the kind represented by a division of history into communication ages, even if defensible on a heuristic basis for specific, carefully framed enquiries, must never be mistaken for agencies of causation. We may locate certain phenomena within something we call print culture but we are not thereby entitled to say that they were caused or determined by print culture, however we define it. This limitation arises from well-understood problems concerning the referentiality of general statements in humanities disciplines. Such statements are neither enunciations of general laws which are testable by experiment, as in the physical sciences, nor are they probabilities expressed in statistical form as in the social sciences. Often, in current practice they turn out to be deliberated hypotheses; historical scholarship is a department of rhetoric. In particular, whatever general claims we may like to make about 'The Renaissance reader' cannot be assumed in advance to apply to any given individual act of reading.[27]

In what ways is print a culture?

Our consideration of the dangers of misinterpretation that arise from an overreliance on chronologically defined conceptions of 'print culture' has led us back to the four, often confused, senses in which print culture has been understood as a culture. These will now be examined.

In the first conception, culture is a modality of consciousness, a structure of beliefs and perceptions, a socially constructed subjectivity. This view of print culture has its origins in the work of Marshall McLuhan and Walter J. Ong, drew further inspiration from structuralist anthropology and, with help from Foucault, has been deployed since by scholars such as Kernan and Peters.[28]

Insofar as we are able to inspect a generalised print consciousness as an object of study, it is by seeing it in disjunctive relation to other forms of communicative consciousness – particularly those attributed to oral culture, scribal culture, and electronic culture, all of which, however, pose the same problem of definition. This kind of comparison, which Ong performs with especial flair in *Orality and Literacy*, and its tributary studies, and that I have also attempted in a modest, epigonic way, is fascinating in itself but of limited use, for the reasons just given, in understanding particular individual acts of text production or consumption. Ong argues that certain new kinds of cognitive experience arose from the encounter with the printed page. These include 'a shift from sound to visual space' (p. 117), a sense of 'tidiness and inevitability' (p. 122), the reduction of language to a thing-like status with a consequent 'commodification of the word' (p. 118), a reduction of living knowledge to 'cold non-human facts', the imposition upon discourse of a sense of closure (p. 133 ff.), and the replacement of a speech-like sense of presence characteristic of the handwritten text with a mechanistic impersonality. The sum of these changes is the creation of a new 'noetic world' (pp. 125, 127). Let us accept these distinctions as a valuable adjunct to our study of reading and authorship in the early modern period while at the same time never losing sight of the fact that Ong's model of print subjectivity is not constructed from the recorded experience of readers or authors, but generated from a figurative remodelling of the material form of records. In other words, it is a highly speculative proceeding that moves from the nature of the artefact to assumptions about the use of that artefact, then to assumptions about the metaphors suggested by that artefact, then to assumptions about a hypothetical user's assimilation of those metaphors, and then to further assumptions about a generalised and then an individual subjectivity.

At the end of this risk-prone process we need to ask what reference it might have to a particular reader of 1605 sitting down to *Don Quixote*. The answer must surely be that Ong's modellings represent nothing more than tendencies that could as well be resisted as realised in individual cognitive performances. However, it is also necessary to register that Ong never says that the way in which the visual appearance of the printed text broadcasts Eisenstein's messages of fixity, objectivity, and veracity corresponds to any inherent quality of the text so presented. Indeed, he is aware that these qualities of what he calls the 'meaningful surface' are an illusion and in many cases a deception, a point taken further by Johns.[29] But Ong would presumably agree that naive readers often allowed the message of the media to influence their response to content. Mopsa says in *The Winter's Tale*, 'I loue a ballet in print, a life, for then we are sure they are true'.[30] Jonathan Goldberg in his influential *Writing Matter: From the Hands of the English Renaissance*[31] performs a similar figurative remodelling of the physical act of inscription; however, whereas Ong's generative metaphor is the Thomist one of the soul's progressive estrangement from an originating divine 'presence', Goldberg invokes Derridean figurings of deferral and Foucaultian ones of the circulation of power. Hobart and Schiffman's model is one of the reconceptualising of information at progressively higher, media-governed levels of abstraction, categorised as 'commemoration', taxonomy, analysis, algorithmic play, and complexity theory. In none of these cases is it legitimate to assume an explanatory capacity for purely interpretive formulations.

The study of cultures of consciousness is a legitimate and important one. Its drawback is that it is only pursued at an astronomically high level of generality. To take this study further we would need to find new, specific ways of talking about a range of cognitive capacities made possible by the coming into use of the printed surface. Yet to say that some historical phenomenon occurred in consequence of 'Print consciousness' or simply Print with a capital 'P' is nearly always to reason by a process of back-propagation in which the question is constructed out of a prefigured answer. The most any noetic model can offer is an explanatory hypothesis that still has to be tested against all other possible explanations in each particular instance. 'Print culture', configured as a consciousness independent of individual acts of apprehension, is a kind of supernatural entity which, like other supernatural entities, we are driven to invoke in times of perplexity.

Print culture as a culture of social relationships

In the second and third conceptions suggested in my second paragraph, print culture was a contexture of social and industrial relationships arising from, on one hand, the everyday activities of printing, publishing and distribution, and, on the other, the consumption of printed materials by their users. Print production has received its most searching examination for our period in Donald McKenzie's studies of the seventeenth-century and early-eigtheenth-century booktrade and has been reformulated from a different perspective by Johns, who, in rejecting 'ethereal' models of print culture, insists that we track back the effects attributed to print to the 'situated labors' that have produced them.[32] Both writers agree in this with Edward Said's comment, cited approvingly by McKenzie, that a fundamental weakness of literary theory in our time is that it has 'isolated textuality from the circumstances, the events, the physical senses that make it possible and render it intelligible as the result of human work'.[33] McKenzie was principally concerned with the ways in which the activities involved in the manufacture and distribution of printed records became productive in their own right of textual or paratextual meaning. Johns concentrates on the difficulty contemporaries experienced in defending the knowledge presented in the products of the press against perfectly valid fears of textual decay and piracy. McKenzie is more interested in printers, Johns in booksellers and authors. One might well hold that the problems of determining authorial responsibility for the print-published word identified by Johns have never been solved, and that they are as pressing today as they ever were; that is not to question his diagnosis of early modern print, but merely to extend it.[34] What is important here is that both the scholars I have mentioned are centrally concerned with the textual concomitants of what those active in the printing and publishing trades actually do.[35]

Print culture, viewed from this perspective, is a sequencing of actors and activities which can be modelled as a continuously evolving, ever-repeating cycle in which each set of events is linked sequentially to a predecessor set and a successor set, and more distantly with the predecessor's predecessor and the successor's successor. How many elements we place in the cycle is a matter of convenience; but a simple illustrative version would probably have five or six.

Any choice of a starting point has to be arbitrary, since the whole point of a cycle is that it has no starting point; but let it be the stage of production, that is the manufacture of the material record in the print-shop, and the bindery. The technology of these processes has been thoroughly studied for the early modern period but there is still much we do not understand and perhaps never will. McKenzie's famous judgement on the relationship between composition and presswork states that the norm revealed by the surviving trade records was 'patterns . . . of such an unpredictable complexity, even for such a small printing shop, that no amount of inference from what we think of as bibliographical evidence could ever have led to their reconstruction'.[36] Production practice in the printeries of early modern Europe had its constants and its variables, and we must be sure that we understand which was which.

The next stage in the cycle would be that of distribution, a more complex matter because in a sense it was a process without end. The initial movement out of the warehouse to the bookseller's shop to the customer might only be the first of many. For a considerable number of printed books, pamphlets and ephemera from the early modern period, that process continues today, in, for instance, the movement of volumes onto the shelves of research libraries, and is studied through the tracing of provenances; however we will restrict ourselves here to the earliest stage – that which took the book into a reader's bookcase, chest, or pocket. This process has a geography and a sociology; social formations emerge from the relationships of distribution in bookshops, which were also meeting places, in libraries, in learned societies, and through formal and informal book clubs. Hugh Amory has observed that 'perhaps the majority of books ever printed have rarely been read', implying that their meaning and significance must be sought in other uses.[37] This idea is echoed in Brown and Duguid's insistence that the social relationships generated by printed records are as important as the content of the records.[38] These relationships of consumption (our third category) are another aspect of the cycle of print culture, but in the tangential sense of being an element of patterns of sociability that extend beyond that culture.

This is also the point at which the economic or social means are generated that permit the persistence of the cycle – the energy source. Once books prove incapable of earning sustenance for the cycle, either the cycle itself withers or certain types of publication have to be discarded and replaced with others. So this stage is both distributive and ingestive, with the narrative of the book moving out in what we might think of as a clockwise direction while the money earned moves anticlockwise, from purchasers to booksellers, to publishers, to printers, and occasionally even as far as authors. This, at least, is the dominant model: Jason Scott-Warren's recent study of Sir John Harington explores the alternative by which printed books move in a way usually more characteristic of manuscripts as gifts, feudal dues, or thinly disguised job applications.[39]

Next comes the stage of consumption, which these days is assigned to the history of reading, a highly productive field of scholarship. However, reading is not the end of the cycle – a cycle has no end – but leads on towards authorship. Between reading and authorship I would place an additional stage of reconstitution. This is what occurs both communally and individually as the fruits of reading are digested and reformulated in personal and group experience prior to their being employed in new acts of writing. This is the point where new ideas, new experiences, new kinds of language, new instances of work are fed into the cycle, thus making it an open system, not a closed one. It is also the point in the cycle where print culture is most actively in dialogue with other media and their texts. New Historicism's exploration of oblique and long-range relationships between texts, including 'social texts', as opposed to the short-range ones that concern studies of literary influences, has enlarged our sense of the connections between media involved in the genesis of new textual formations. Print authorship cannot be accounted for from within print culture.

Print authorship, as it emerges from this fourth stage, takes its particular character from being directed towards the requirements of the press and the market served by the press; other kinds of authorship – scribal, oral and theatrical – are governed by other requirements. Martin Elsky has pointed out that to become a print author is to acquire a new kind of social identity which did not exist before Gutenberg.[40] One should add that this identity was not itself historically stable. Dryden was a different kind of print author from Ben Jonson, and Samuel Johnson from Dryden. Aphra Behn and Mary Wroth were different kinds of print authors from all three, and from each other. Jonson, Francis Bacon and Wroth were scribal authors as well as print authors, switching from one kind of authorial identity, with its attendant sets of techniques and relationships, to another as they moved between media. Shakespeare was a print author only in his poems; the plays were composed for the oral medium.

Before the process of physical production begins again, there has to be a further stage of commissioning and enabling, which in the early modern period was conducted principally by booksellers and is now the responsibility of publishers and agents. Our cycle then, in its crudest form, is one of physical production leading to distribution and sale, leading to consumption/reception, leading to reconstitution, leading to authorship, leading to enabling, leading us back to printing, but as part of a process that is evolutionary as well as repetitive. To participate as an economically active individual in sustaining the movement of texts through this cycle is to participate in print culture defined as a system of interrelated kinds of industrial work and of consumption of the products of that work.

The functioning of different parts of this cycle has attracted a great deal of excellent scholarship but I am not sure that we have ever mastered its full revolution. The closest we have to such an examination is that given, for a particular class of writing produced in a particular country over a fairly narrow span of time, by Johns's *The Nature of the Book*, and the message of his case studies is that there was an immense amount of creaking and friction in the operation of the cycle and in the interactions of its different parts. Nothing about it was effortless. The challenge now is to examine the interactions of not only the contiguous but the mutually remote parts of this cycle of industrial activity, remembering, again, that it had both its constants and its variables and that some of the variables could be very variable indeed.

Print as a culture of communication

To print culture conceived as consciousness and print culture conceived as an industrial system of text production, manufacture, distribution, and consumption, we should add a further conception in which print culture is a part of a larger informational entity which originates in a perception of relationships between transmitters and receivers. An account of this matter would involve some backtracking to McLuhan and Ong and their successors, but in order to ask different questions from those raised earlier – not about what qualities might be regarded as psychosymbolically inherent in the printed record, but how the transmissional tasks performed by print stand in relationship to those performed by speech, manual inscriptions of all kinds, pictorial signs, non-linguistic sound (including music), demonstrative gesture, the semaphore, the heliograph, the telegraph, and the entire field of messages transmitted in the form of or with the aid of electromagnetic energy. This would require an even more radical reconsideration of Eisenstein's model for the effects of the advent of print on patterns of communication, since the European perspective would now become a world one and attention would need to be directed to co-operation between media as well as competition (a matter to be considered in an eagerly awaited study by David McKitterick).[41] The most fruitful way of understanding the effect of the 'printing revolution' may well be as a reassignment of specific communicative tasks among a variety of media over a variety of geographical realms, among which we need to number the European metropolitan hinterlands and the continually enlarged frontier of European expansion.

A study of early modern print as communication would need to invoke a geography of information. This would require consideration of the ways in which information moved, by whatever channel or medium – its range, its speed, its routes, its vehicles from the carrier's cart to the post-horse and from the canalboat to the East-Indiaman, its answering of messages through countermessages and how these travelled, the establishment of informational linkages between both individuals and communities and how these helped to structure those communities, the ways in which information became corrupted during relay, and the ways in which centre–periphery and metropole–frontier transfers came into existence and were dissolved, fractured or reversed.[42] Some of these matters have been looked into by European, especially French, book historians, inspired by Braudel, and Anglophone historians of the expanding European frontier, drawing on the work of Harold Innis, James W. Carey and Geoffrey Blainey, but they still await a comprehensive overview.[43]

Three themes deserve particular attention. The first is the concentration of print production in a small number of urban centres. Despite the stress laid by Eisenstein on the proliferation of presses from small town to small town during the early decades, an overwhelming preponderance of print publication was soon localised in Paris, Amsterdam, London, Madrid, Basel, and a few other powerful cities. In the German-speaking lands, where the practice of printing was less centralised, the marketing of books was soon channelled through the annual fair held at Frankfurt. Even Italy was only relatively decentred. Not only did Rome, Florence and Venice dominate book production, but the influence of the first was felt everywhere through that of the church acting both as censor and primary customer. One obvious reason for this centralising tendency was that national governments and international churches did everything in their power to control what was issued through the press, a goal best achieved by concentrating publishing and distribution not simply into major cities but into small areas of those cities. In Britain, printing was restricted by law to London and the two university towns, and in London was largely conducted in the immediate vicinity of Paul's church-yard. It was only during periods of civil war or intense religious schism that anything approaching a modern liberty of utterance through print was briefly possible, and even then opposed parties might well have their own systems of censorship and control. But centralisation also made good commercial sense. Printing might be done anywhere, but publishing, with its reliance on the co-operative use of investment capital and access to assured pathways of distribution, was most success-fully pursued in the great port cities. Technological advance was not a factor, since the methods and materials of typefounding, composition, and presswork remained virtually unchanged during the three centuries following Gutenberg; however, methods of financing editions, techniques of distribu-tion, ways of organising literary ownership, and the social relationships of consumption were repeatedly subject to radical innovation. The career of the English bookseller/publisher Jacob Tonson (1656–1736) saw resourceful use of Stationers' copyrights to gain control of the text of *Paradise Lost*; brilliant experiments, most evident in Dryden's Virgil, in pre-selling through the subscription system; and, in one interpretation, the invention of 'English literature' as a trade category and style of material product. None of this would have been possible outside London.

This centralisation of publishing was both a strength and a weakness of early print culture – a strength because it allowed it to harness the resources of the centralising state and the new mercan-tile economies, and a weakness because it anchored a powerful technology of communication in culturally insular communities, which (as the Spanish experience shows very clearly) were often violently resistant to the new knowledge flooding in from the expanding European frontier. The printed Bible, almanac, inquisitor's manual, and government decree might be transmitted in impres-sive quantities to the newly settled lands of wide-flung empires but the return passage of knowledge arising from trade, agriculture, shipbuilding, science, and dissident politics and religion, which at its points of origin circulated orally, through manuscript, and (often overlooked among the media) through the direct transmission of expert practice from teacher to apprentice and from one settler, merchant, tradesman, or natural philosopher to another, was impeded by the centre's unshakeable conviction that its own, often deeply parochial, knowledge was up to date and universal. Opinions radiated through print from the centre were of interest on the periphery because of the prestige of the centre, and because the centre remained the point of origin of administrative and economic power; in addition, they remain visible to history because they circulated in the one medium that left an assured record of its own existence. (We should also note that it was the centre that wrote the histories.) Yet what the metropolitan publishers regarded as suitable for the periphery was often irrelevant to the periphery's own understandings of the world. Indeed, the metropolis made something of a speciality of exporting its garbled and inaccurate knowledge about the periphery to the periphery; Shakespeare's *The Tempest*, in its printed form, is an oblique example. Where knowledge from the periphery was, somewhat exceptionally, welcomed and accepted by the centre, that print should redeliver it tardily and imperfectly back to its discoverers was an exercise in redundancy. The positive role played by certain print-media, such as the scientific journal, in assessing and classifying new knowledge and then distributing it to a world-wide audience of its language community needs to be set against the far greater speed and fullness with which what was practically valuable in that knowledge travelled from point to point on the periphery itself through non-print media.

It is only with the world-wide consolidation of the local newspaper that print as a culture of communication achieved a rapidity of response that rivalled that of oral narration, expert demonstration, and the personal letter. Such newspapers were characteristically rewritten from each other. On the arrival of a ship in port, the papers it brought would be excerpted at once for the local organ. The new local number would then itself travel on and be excerpted by newspapers at the points of its arrival, whether these were in a neighbouring port or on another continent. Through this process, paragraphs or whole stories might circumnavigate the globe, perhaps to encounter each other moving in opposite directions at a point equidistant from that of their origin. This decentralisation of print-communication, which was only extinguished by the arrival of the electric telegraph and the attendant triumph of the news agency, reinscribed the local resistance to the centralised monopoly of print-information which had been supported through the oral and scribal media during the Renaissance and early modern period. Even the local newspaper, however, was never more than one part of a wider informational economy and never enjoyed that dominance over non-print ways of circulating news that is suggested by the massive survival of its products.

'Print culture', then, can mean a number of very different things, and when we speak about it we need to be clear which of these we are referring to. We should certainly abstain from invoking it as a means of dividing up history into chronological segments. We should be extremely cautious about using it as a means of historical explanation. We should be careful not to become involved in the kind of argument which approaches different models of it as if they were the same thing. Most of all, we should cease to see it as somehow isolated from the complementary and often actively co-operating media of the oral, the scribal and the physically performative.

Notes

1   This article is a revised and extended version of the opening address given to the Folger Shakespeare Library Conference, 'Transactions of the Book', 2 November 2001.

2   See in particular Lucien Febvre and Henri-Jean Martin, *L'Apparition du Livre* (Paris: Albin Michel, 1958); Elizabeth Eisenstein, *The Printing Press as an Agent of Change*, 2 vols (Cambridge: Cambridge University Press, 1979) and *The Printing Revolution in Early Modern Europe* (Cambridge: Cambridge University Press, 1983); and my own *Scribal Publication in Seventeenth-Century England* (Oxford: Clarendon Press, 1993), repr. *The Culture and Commerce of Texts:*

Scribal Publication in Seventeenth-Century England (Amherst: University of Massachusetts Press, 1998).

3   For this timetable, see in particular Alvin Kernan, *Printing Technology, Letters and Samuel Johnson* (Princeton: Princeton University Press, 1987), pp. 48–49. Others, including Eisenstein, would date the dominance of print over its sibling media almost from the invention of the art.

4   Walter J. Ong, *Orality and Literacy: The Technologizing of the Word* (London: Methuen, 1983), pp. 78–116.

5   Eisenstein, *Printing Revolution*, pp. 41–90.

6   See on this Martin Elsky, *Authorizing Words: Speech, Writing and Print in the English Renaissance* (Ithaca: Cornell University Press, 1989), p. 202.

7   David Zaret, *Origins of Democratic Culture: Printing, Petitions, and the Public Sphere in Early-Modern England* (Princeton: Princeton University Press, 2000), p. 133; for Bacon's hostility to sects and personal schools of thought see Elsky, *Authorizing Words*, pp. 198–203.

8   Jan-Dirk Müller, 'The body of the book: the media transition from manuscript to print', in *Materialities of Communication*, ed. Hans Ulrich Gumbrecht and K. Ludwig Pfeiffer (Stanford: Stanford University Press, 1994), pp. 35, 37.

9   Adrian Johns, *The Nature of the Book: Print and Knowledge in the Making* (Chicago: University of Chicago Press, 1998).

10 James J. O'Donnell, *Avatars of the Word: From Papyrus to Cyberspace* (Cambridge, Mass.: Harvard University Press, 1998), pp. 82–83.

11 Adrian Johns, 'How to acknowledge a revolution', *American Historical Review* 107 (2002), 109. Eisenstein defends herself against the charge on pp. 126–28 of the same issue.

12 Michael Hobart and Zachary Schiffman, *Information Ages: Literacy, Numeracy, and the Computer Revolution* (Baltimore: Johns Hopkins University Press, 1998).

13 Hobart and Schiffman, *Information Ages*, p. 283; see also Roger Chartier, *The Order of Books* (Stanford: Stanford University Press, 1994), p. 1 and *passim*. The phenomenon is further documented in Richard Yeo, *Encyclopaedic Visions: Scientific Dictionaries and Enlightenment Culture* (Cambridge: Cambridge University Press, 2001).

14 Cartesian physics and cosmology cannot, however, be cited in this respect, as they were not susceptible to mathematical modelling.

15 Guglielmo Cavallo and Roger Chartier in their introduction to *A History of Reading in the West*, trans. Lydia G. Cochrane (Oxford: Polity Press, 1999), pp. 1–36, emphasise the medieval origins of methods of layout and habits of extensive reading often presented as the creation of print culture. Supposedly new methods of information management such as commonplacing and the creation of epitomes, reference works, bibliographies, and library catalogues also have their medieval and ancient precedents. Yeo's *Encyclopaedic Visions: Scientific Dictionaries and Enlightenment Culture* evaluates the role of reference works in early modern information management (Cambridge: Cambridge University Press, 2001).

16 For Burton see Elsky, *Authorizing Words*, pp. 210–11. Insight into the methods and assumptions of the compilers of the vast collections of antiquarian knowledge that progressed from the presses of Europe in multi-volume folio and large-quarto format during the seventeenth century is given in David Douglas, *English Scholars 1660–1730*, 2nd edition (London: Eyre and Spottiswoode, 1951).

17 The difficulty of transmitting expert practice through written description is emphasised by Johns, *The Nature of the Book*, pp. 43–45. By contrast, a recent Japanese experiment, referred to in Ian Tattersall, 'How we came to be human', *Scientific American* 285/6 (Dec. 2001), pp. 46–47, has shown that toolmaking can be as effectively taught through silent example as by verbal explanation.

18 In *Scribal Publication in Seventeenth-Century England*.

19   Ong, *Orality and Literacy*, pp. 20, 115–16, 119–21; Julie Stone Peters, *Congreve, the Drama and the Printed Word* (Stanford: Stanford University Press, 1990), p. 4.

20   Isaac Barrow, *Several Sermons against Evil Speaking* (London: B. Aylmer, 1678), pp. 9–10. The passage is discussed in my 'Oral and Scribal Texts in Early Modern England', to appear in *The Cambridge History of the Book in Britain*, Vol. 4. Zaret, *Origins of Democratic Culture*, pp. 68–99, illustrates the dominance of oral media and public ritual in the transmission of political messages from the centre to the periphery and vice versa.

21   Hertfordshire Record Office MS D/EP 37, p. 156, as part of a collection of aphorisms copied and perhaps augmented by Sarah Cowper, there attributed to 'M. C.' (Martin Clifford) but elsewhere to George Villiers, second Duke of Buckingham.

22   Adam Fox, *Oral and Literate Culture in England 1500–1700* (Oxford: Oxford University Press, 2000).

23   James W. Carey, *Communication as Culture* (New York: Routledge, 1992), p. 3.

24   Bruce Smith, *The Cultural Life of Ambient Sound* (Chicago: University of Chicago Press, 1999).

25   For a stimulating acknowledgement of Raleigh's manysidedness as a cultural phenomenon, see Michael Rudick's introduction to *The Poems of Sir Walter Raleigh: A Historical Edition* (Tempe, Arizona: Renaissance English Text Society, 1999), pp. xii–xxix. The identification with Silius is made in Phillip J. Ayres, 'Jonson, Northampton, and the "treason" in *Sejanus*', *Modern Philology* 80 (1983), 356–63. For a fuller inventory of early modern media experiences, see Barry Reay, *Popular Cultures in England 1550–1750* (Harlow: Longman, 1998), pp. 36–70.

26   For a reference to the last-named practice, see Manchester Chetham's Library MS Mun. A. 4. 14, p. 91.

27   See further on this point Robert D. Hume, *Reconstructing Contexts: The Aims and Principles of Archaeo-Historicism* (Oxford: Oxford University Press, 1999), p. 138 and *passim*.

28   See notes 3 and 19 above.

29   Johns, *The Nature of the Book* (pp. 10–20), criticises Eisenstein for 'attributing to printed books themselves attributes of credibility and persuasion that actually took much work to sustain' (pp. 10, 19). This argument would have been more fruitfully conducted with Ong, and especially with his claim that 'One consequence of the new exactly repeatable statement was modern science' (*Orality and Literacy*, p. 127). Ong cites Eisenstein in support of this view. Johns's book makes no mention of Ong.

30   Lines 1865–66. See further on this topic, Zaret's comments on the 'probity of print', *Origins of Democratic Culture*, pp. 166–67.

31   Jonathan Goldberg, *Writing Matter: From the Hands of the English Renaissance* (Stanford: Stanford University Press, 1990)

32   Johns, *The Nature of the Book*, pp. 18, 42. McKenzie's shorter essays on this topic are now available in *Making Meaning: 'Printers of the Mind' and Other Essays*, ed. Peter D. McDonald and Michael F. Suarez, S.J. (Amherst: University of Massachusetts Press, 2002).

33   Donald McKenzie, *The World, the Text, and the Critic* (London: Vintage, 1991), p. 19. See also my 'Don McKenzie, bibliographer', *Parergon*, n.s. 17 (1999), 1–8 and 'The intellectual heritage of Donald Francis McKenzie', *The Library*, 7th ser. 2 (2001), 267–80.

34   This point is conceded by Johns himself in his concluding chapter. Print's insistence on the fiction (as it often is) of the single validating author masks a reality in which much published work is the product of greater or lesser degrees of collaboration. The issue is considered at several points of my *Attributing Authorship: An Introduction* (Cambridge: Cambridge University Press, 2002).

35   Both McKenzie and Johns also raise interesting questions concerning the hegemonic status claimed by the metropolis in presenting what is frequently local information as if it was universal. This matter is further considered below.

36   'Printers of the mind: some notes on bibliographical theories and printing-house practices', *Studies in Bibliography* 22 (1969), 7.

37   Hugh Amory, 'The trout and the milk: an ethnobiographical talk', *Harvard Library Bulletin*, n.s. 7 (1996), 51.

38   John Seely Brown and Paul Duguid, *The Social Life of Information* (Cambridge, Mass.: Harvard Business School Press, 2000), pp. 189–97.

39   Jason Scott-Warren, *Sir John Harington and the Book as Gift* (Oxford: Oxford University Press, 2001). Scott-Warren's starting point was Natalie Zemon Davis's 'Beyond the market: books as gifts in sixteenth-century France', *Transactions of the Royal Historical Society*, 5th ser., 33 (1983), 69–88. Cf. also Johns, *The Nature of the Book*, pp. 14–16.

40   Elsky, *Authorizing Words*, p. 187.

41   David McKitterick, *Print, Manuscript and the Search for Order, 1450–1830* (Cambridge: Cambridge University Press, forthcoming).

42   I give some preliminary personal thoughts on these matters in my 'Modelling centre–periphery relationships in book publication and information transfer', to appear in *Centre and Periphery in the World of the Book 1500–2000*, ed. Wallace Kirsop (Florence: Olschki, forthcoming).

43   Carey in *Communication as Culture*, pp. 142–72, gives a sympathetic account of the work of Innis on the influence of innovations in information transfer on the development of economic and political life in the early centuries of European settlement in North America. Geoffrey Blainey's *The Tyranny of Distance* (Melbourne: Melbourne University Press, 1966) traces the effect of geographical isolation on similar developments in Australia.

Chapter 8

Roger Chartier

LABOURERS AND VOYAGERS
From the text to the reader

Far from being writers – founders of their own place, heirs to the peasants of earlier ages now working on the soil of language, diggers of wells and builders of houses – readers are voyagers: they move across lands belonging to someone else, like nomads poaching their way across fields they did not write, despoiling the wealth of Egypt to enjoy it themselves. Writing accumulates, stocks up, resists time by the establishment of a place and multiplies its production through the expansionism of reproduction. Reading takes no measures against the erosion of time (one forgets oneself and also forgets), reading does not keep what it acquires, or it does so poorly, and each of the places through which it passes is a repetition of the lost paradise.

(Michel de Certeau, *The Practice of Everyday Life*)

This magnificent text by Michel de Certeau, which contrasts writing (conservative, durable, and fixed) with readings (always on the order of the ephemeral), constitutes at the same time a necessary foundation and a disquieting challenge for any history that intends to inventory and account for a practice – reading – that rarely leaves traces, is scattered into an infinity of singular acts, and purposely frees itself from all the constraints seeking to subdue it. Such a project fundamentally rests on a double assumption: that reading is not already inscribed in the text, with no conceivable difference between the sense assigned to it (by the author, usage, criticism, and so forth) and the interpretation constructable by its readers; and that, correlatively, a text does not exist except for a reader who gives it signification:

Whether it is a newspaper or Proust, the text has a meaning only through its readers; it changes along with them; it is ordered in accordance with codes of perception that it does not control. It becomes a text only in its relation to the exteriority of the reader, by an interplay of implication and ruses between two sorts of 'expectation' in combination: the expectation that organizes a readable space (a literality), and one that organizes a procedure necessary for the *actualization* of the work (a reading).

(de Certeau, *Practice*, pp. 170–1)[1]

The task of the historian is, then, to reconstruct the variations that differentiate the 'readable space' (the texts in their material and discursive forms) and those which govern the circumstances of their 'actualization' (the readings seen as concrete practices and interpretive procedures).

Based upon de Certeau's suggestions, I would like to indicate some of the stakes, problems, and conditions of possibility for such an historical project. Three poles, generally separated by academic tradition, define the space of this history: first, the analysis of texts, either canonical or ordinary, deciphered in their structures, themes, and aims; second, the history of books and, more generally, of all the objects and forms that carry out the circulation of writing; and finally, the study of practices which in various ways take hold of these objects or forms and produce usages and differentiated meanings. A fundamental question underlies this approach in associating textual criticism, bibliography, and cultural history. That is to understand how in the societies of the ancien régime between the sixteenth and eighteenth centuries the increasing circulation of printed writing transformed the modes of social interaction (*sociabilité*), permitted new ways of thinking, and modified power relations.

Hence the attention placed upon the manner in which (to use the terms of Paul Ricoeur) the encounter between 'the world of the text' and 'the world of the reader' functions (*Time and Narrative*, 3: 6). To reconstruct in its historical dimensions this process of the 'actualization' of texts above all requires us to realize that their meaning depends upon the forms through which they are received and appropriated by their readers (or listeners). Readers, in fact, never confront abstract, idealized texts detached from any materiality. They hold in their hands or perceive objects and forms whose structures and modalities govern their reading or hearing, and consequently the possible comprehension of the text read or heard. In contrast to a purely semantic definition of the text, which characterizes not only structuralist criticism in all its variants but also literary theories concerned with reconstructing the modes of reception of works, it is necessary to maintain that forms produce meaning, and that even a fixed text is invested with new meaning and being (*statut*) when the physical form through which it is presented for interpretation changes. We must also realize that reading is always a practice embodied in gestures, spaces, and habits. Far from the phenomenology of reading, which erases the concrete modality of the act of reading and character-izes it by its effects, postulated as universals, a history of modes of reading must identify the specific dispositions that distinguish communities of readers and traditions of reading. This approach sup-poses the recognition of a series of contrasts: to begin with, the distinctions between reading competencies. The fundamental but rough separation between the literate and the illiterate does not exhaust the possible differences in the relation to writing. Those who can read texts do not all read them in the same fashion. There is a wide gap between the most skillful and the least competent readers – those who are obliged to read what they read aloud in order to understand it and who are at ease only with certain textual or typographical forms. Another contrast distinguishes between the norms and conventions of reading, defining for each community of readers the legitimate uses of the book, the forms of reading, and the instruments and procedures of interpretation. Finally, we have the contrast between the expectations and diverse interests that different groups of readers invest in the practice of reading. Upon these determining factors, which govern practice, depend the ways in which texts can be read – and read differently by readers who are equipped with different intel-lectual tools and maintain quite different relations to writing.

Michel de Certeau illustrated such an approach in describing the specific characteristics of the mystical reader: 'By "mystical readers" I have in mind all the procedures of reading which were suggested or practised in the field of solitary or collective experience designated in the sixteenth and seventeenth centuries as "illuminated", "mystical", or "spiritual" ' (Certeau, 'La lecture', p. 67).[2] In the minor, marginal, and dispersed community that was mysticism's milieu, reading, determined by norms and habits, invested the book with novel functions: to replace the ecclesiastical institution considered to be inadequate; to make a certain kind of speech possible (that of the prayer, the communication with God, the *conversar*); and to indicate the practices through which spiritual experience is constructed. The mystical relation to the book can also be understood as a trajectory in which several 'moments' of reading succeed one another: the establishment of an otherness (*altérité*) which founds the subjective quest; the development of ecstasy (*jouissance*); the marking of bodies physically reacting to the digestion (*manducation*) of the text; and, at the extreme, the interruption of reading, the abandonment of the book, and detachment. Consequently to locate the network of practices and roles of reading specific to diverse communities of readers (spiritual, intellectual, professional, and so forth) is a primary task for any history concerned with understanding, in its differentiations, the pragmatic figure of the 'poaching' reader (*lecteur braconnier*) (see, for example, Jardine and Grafton).

But to read is always to read something. Certainly, to exist at all, the history of reading must be radically distinguished from the history of what is read: 'The reader emerges from the history of the book, in which he was for a long time undifferentiated or indistinct. . . . The reader was taken as the effect of the book. Today he has become detached from the books of which he had seemed no more than a shadow. Suddenly this shadow has been released, has taken on a physiognomy, has acquired an independence' (de Certeau, 'La lecture', pp. 66–7). But this founding independence is not an arbitrary license. It is confined by the codes and conventions that govern the practices of a community. It is also confined by the discursive and material forms of the texts read. 'New readers make new texts, and their new meanings are a function of their new forms' (McKenzie, *Bibliography and the Sociology of Texts*, p. 20). D. F. McKenzie thus points out with great acuity the double network of variations – variations of the dispositions of readers and variations of textual and formal devices – which must be taken into account in any history seeking to recover the shifting and plural meaning of texts. One can make use of this analysis in different ways: by locating the major contrasts distinguishing different modes of reading by characterizing the most popular reading practices; or by paying attention to the publishing changes that offered old texts to new consumers, changes that made them more numerous and of more modest condition. Such a perspective translates a double dissatisfaction with the history of the book in France over the last twenty or thirty years, which has consistently taken as its objective to measure the unequal distribution of books in the different groups composing the society of the ancien régime. This led to the indispensable construction of factors revealing cultural divisions: for example, for a given location and time, the percentage of property inventories taken after death indicating the possession of books, the classification of collections according to the number of works they contain, or the thematic characterization of private libraries according to the proportion of different bibliographic categories present in them. From this perspective, to conceptualize reading in France between the sixteenth and eighteenth centuries was, above all, to put together series of quantitative data, to establish quantitative thresholds, and to locate how social differences were culturally translated.

This approach, pursued collectively (including by the author of this essay), produced a body of knowledge without which other inquiries would have been impossible. However, it poses a problem of its own. To begin with, it rests on a strictly sociographic conception which implicitly postulates that cultural separations are necessarily organized according to a preexisting social division. I believe it is necessary to challenge the analytic model which links differences in cultural practices with social oppositions constructed *a priori* – either on the scale of macroscopic contrasts (between the dominant and the dominated, between the elite and the people) or on a scale of finer differentiations (for example, between social groups hierarchized by distinctions of status or profession and levels of wealth).

Cultural separations are not necessarily ordered only according to a single grid of social divisions, conceived as determining the unequal possession of objects and the difference between behaviors. The perspective must be reversed to outline, first of all, the social areas where each corpus of texts and each variety of printed materials circulates. To start out thus from objects, and not from classes or groups, brings us to the realization that French sociocultural history has for too long been based on an incomplete conception of the social. In privileging only socioprofessional classifications, it has forgotten that other principles of differentiation, also fully social, could explain cultural divisions with greater pertinence. Thus there are also considerations of gender or generation, religious belief, community membership, academic or group traditions, and so on.

In another register, the history of the book in its social and serial definition sought to characterize cultural configurations according to categories of texts considered specific to them. Such an operation proves to be doubly reductive. For one thing, it simply equates the identification of differences to inequalities of distribution; and for another, it ignores the process by which a text takes on meaning for those who read it. Against these claims it is necessary to propose several modifications. The first of these situates the recognition of the most deeply embedded social divisions in the contrasting uses of shared material. More than we have tended to acknowledge, in the societies of the ancien régime it is the same texts which are taken up by readers from the popular classes and by those who are not. Sometimes readers of humble conditions owned books that were not particularly aimed at them (this was the case of Menocchio, the Friulian miller; of Jamerey Duval, the shepherd from Lorraine; and of Ménétra, the Parisian glazier: see Ginzburg, Hébrard, and Ménétra). Or sometimes creative and shrewd booksellers put within the reach of a broader clientele texts that previously had not circulated except in the narrow world of the wealthy and well read (as was the case with Castilian and Catalan *pliegos sueltos*, English chapbooks, or the collection known in France under the generic term Bibliothèque Bleue). What is essential, then, is to understand how the same texts could be diversely apprehended, handled, and understood.

The second modification is to reconstruct the networks of practices that organize the historically and socially differentiated modes of access to texts. Reading is not only an abstract operation of the intellect: it puts the body into play and is inscribed within a particular space, in a relation to the self or to others. This is why attention should particularly be paid to ways of reading that have been obliterated in our contemporary world: for example reading out loud in its double function – communicating that which is written to those who do not know how to decipher it, and binding together the interconnected forms of sociability which are all figures of the private sphere (the intimacy of the family, the conviviality of social life, the cooperation of scholars: *connivence lettré*). A history of reading, then, cannot limit itself only to the genealogy of our contemporary manner of reading – in silence and by sight. It most equally, perhaps above all, take on the task of discovering forgotten gestures and habits that have now disappeared. The stakes are important because they reveal not only the remote peculiarity of traditionally shared practices, but also the specific structures of texts composed for uses that are no longer those of their readers today. Often in the sixteenth and seventeenth centuries, the implicit reading of a text, literary or not, was construed as a vocalization and its 'reader' as the auditor of read speech (*parole lectrice*). Thus addressed to the ear as much as the eye, the work played with forms and processes designed to submit the written word to the requirements of oral 'performance'. From the motifs of the *Quijote* to the structures of texts published in the Bibliothèque Bleue, there are numerous examples of this link maintained between the text and the voice (see Chartier, 'Leisure and Sociability').

'Whatever they may do, authors do not write books. Books are not written at all. They are manufactured by scribes and other artisans, by mechanics and other engineers, and by printing presses and other machines' (Stoddard, 'Morphology', p. 4). This remark introduces the third modification that I would like to propose. Against the representation developed by literature itself and repeated by the most quantitative histories of the book, according to which the text exists in itself, separated from all materiality, we must insist that there is no text outside the material structure in which it is given to be read or heard. Thus there is no comprehension of writing, whatever it may be, which does not depend in part upon the forms in which it comes to its reader. Hence the necessary distinction between two groups of apparatuses: those which reveal strategies of writing and the intentions of the author, and those which are a result of the publishers' decisions or the constraints of the printing house. Authors do not write books. Rather they write texts which become objects copied, handwritten, etched, printed, and today computerized. This gap, which is rightly the space in which meaning is constructed, has too often been forgotten not only by classical literary history, which thinks of the work in itself as an abstract text for which the typographic forms are unimportant, but even by *Rezeptionstheorie*. Despite its desire to historicize the experience that readers have with works, *Rezeptionstheorie* postulates a pure and immediate relation between the 'signals' emitted by the text (which plays with accepted literary conventions) and the 'horizon of expectation' of the public to which they are addressed. In such a perspective the 'effect produced' does not depend at all upon the material forms the text takes.[3] Yet these forms contribute fully to shaping the anticipations of the reader *vis-à-vis* the text and to the production of new publics or innovative uses for it.

We thus return to the triangle with which we began, defined by the intricate relation between text, book, and reader. The variations of this relation outline some elementary figures in the connection between 'readable space' and 'actualization' of the text. The first variation considers a linguistically stable text presented in printed forms which themselves change. In studying the innovations occurring in the publication of the plays of William Congreve at the turn of the seventeenth and eighteenth centuries, McKenzie was able to demonstrate how some apparently insignificant formal transformations – the change from quarto to octavo formats, the numbering of scenes, the presence of an ornament between each scene, the list of the dramatis personae at the beginning of them, the marginal notation of the name of the character speaking, the indication of entrances and exits – had a major effect on the status of the works. A new readability was created by a format easier to handle and by a layout that reproduced in the book something of the movement of the actual production, thus breaking with the ancient conventions of printing plays with no rendering of their theatricality. A new manner of reading the same text resulted, but also a new horizon of reception. The forms used in the octavo edition of 1710, borrowed from those used in France for the edition of plays, gave an unofficial legitimacy to Congreve's plays, which from then on were inscribed in a classic canon. This is what could induce an author to refine his style in order to make the works conform to their new 'typographic' dignity (see McKenzie, 'Typography and Meaning'). Variations of the most formal modes of textual presentation can modify the register of reference and the mode of interpretation.

The same is true on a larger scale concerning the principal alteration of the layout in which texts were presented between the sixteenth and eighteenth centuries – what Henri-Jean Martin has termed 'the definitive triumph of white over black' (see Martin and Delmas, pp. 295–9): in other words, the opening up of the page through the multiplication of paragraphs that broke the uninterrupted continuity of the text common in the Renaissance and the indentations which, through varying the left margin, make the order of discourse immediately visible. A new reading of the same works or of the same genres was consequently suggested by their new publishers – a reading that fragments texts into small and separate units, an approach that reinforces the argument, whether intellectual or discursive, by a visual articulation of the page.

This textual segmentation (*découpage*) had fundamental implications when it was applied to sacred texts. The story of Locke's anxiety regarding the practice of dividing the text of the Bible into chapter and verse is well known. For him such a division presented a considerable risk of obliterating the powerful coherence of the Word of God. Referring to the Epistle of Paul, he thus noted that 'not only Common People take the Verses usually for distinct Aphorisms but even Men of more advanc'd

Knowledge in reading them, lose very much of the strength and force of the Coherence and the Light that depends on it'. The effects of such a division he thought disastrous, authorizing each sect or religious body to found its legitimacy on the fragments of the Scriptures that supported its views:

> If a Bible was printed as it should be, and as the several Parts of it were writ, in continued Discourse where the Argument is continued, I doubt not that the several Parties would complain of it, as an Innovation, and a dangerous Change in the publishing of those holy Books. . . . He [i.e., the member of a particular sect] need but be furnished with Verses of Sacred Scriptures, containing Words and Expressions that are but flexible . . . and his System that has appropriated them to the Orthodoxie of His Church, makes them immediately strong and irrefragable Arguments for his Opinion. This is the Benefit of loose Sentences and Scripture crumbled into Verses, which quickly turn into independent Aphorism.
>
> (Quoted in McKenzie, *Bibliography and the Sociology of Texts*, pp. 46–7)

The second figure in our triangle of relations is that in which the text passes from one published form to another order, transforming the text itself and constituting a new public. This is clearly the case with the body of texts that constitute the catalogue of the Bibliothèque Bleue. If this collection has occupied French historians for a long time, it is because it seems to furnish direct access to the 'popular culture' of the ancien régime, a culture supposedly expressed and nourished by texts distributed 'en masse' to the humblest readers.[4] But such is not the case for three essential reasons. To begin with, it is clear that the texts which formed the stock of French book peddlers were almost never written for this purpose. The Bibliothèque Bleue drew from the repertoire of already published texts those which appeared to be best suited to attract a large public. Hence two necessary precautions: first, not to take the texts put into the books included in the Bibliothèque Bleue as 'popular' in themselves, because in fact they belonged to a wide variety of genres drawn from learned literature; and second, to consider that these texts generally had already had a published existence, sometimes quite lengthy, before entering the repertoire of 'popular' books (*livres pour le plus grand nombre*). The study of titles in this 'popular' catalogue has moreover permitted registering how the most formal and material arrangements can inscribe in themselves the indices of cultural differentiation. Indeed the fundamental specificity of the Bibliothèque Bleue is in the editorial interventions it imposed upon texts in order to make them readable by the large clientele at which they were aimed. All this work of adaptation – which shortened texts, simplified them, cut them up, and illustrated them – was determined according to the manner in which booksellers conceived the competencies and expectations of their customers. Thus the very structures of the book were governed by what the publishers thought to be the mode of reading of the clientele they were targeting.

Such a reading always required visible references, and this is my third assertion. Thus the anticipatory titles or the recapitulative summaries or even the wood engravings functioned as protocols of reading or sites of memory (*lieux de mémoire*). Such a reading was comfortable only with brief, self-contained sequences, separated from one another – a reading that appears to have been satisfied with only minimal coherence. This manner of reading is not at all that of the lettered elite of the time – even if certain notables did not disdain to buy books from the Bibliothèque Bleue. These texts assumed their readers' foreknowledge. By the recurrence of highly coded forms, by the repetition of similar motifs from one title to another, and by the reuse of the same images, the knowledge of texts already encountered (either read or heard) was mobilized to help in the comprehension of new readings. The catalogue of the Bibliothèque Bleue thus organized a form of reading that was more recognition or recapitulation than discovery. It is therefore in the formal particularity of the Bibliothèque Bleue publications and in the modifications they impose on texts that they possess their 'popular' character.

In proposing this re-evaluation of the Bibliothèque Bleue, my intention has been not only to better understand what was the single most powerful instrument of the acculturation to writing in ancien régime France.[5] It is also to argue that the detection of sociocultural differentiations and the study of formal and material devices, far from excluding one another, are necessarily linked. This is true not only because the forms are modeled on the expectations and competencies attributed to the public at which they are aimed, but above all because the works and objects produce the space of their social reception much more than they are produced by already concretized divisions. Recently Lawrence W. Levine provided a persuasive demonstration of this fact (see his 'William Shakespeare and the American People' and *Highbrow/Lowbrow*). Analyzing the manner in which the plays of Shakespeare were produced in America in the nineteenth century (that is to say, combined with other genres: melodrama, farce, circus, dance), he showed how this type of representation created a diverse public – 'popular' in the sense that it did not reduce down to just the lettered elite but actively participated in the production through its emotions and reactions. At the end of the century the strict separation established between genres, styles, and cultural sites dispersed this universal public, reserving a 'legitimate' Shakespeare for the few and relegating the other versions to the status of 'popular' entertainment. In establishing this 'bifurcated culture', transformations in the forms of presentation of a Shakespeare play (but also of symphony music, opera, or works of art) had a decisive role. Following a time of cultural mixing and sharing came another, in which the process of cultural distinction produced social separation. The traditional devices of representation in the American Shakespearean repertoire are thus of the same order as the 'typographic' transformations imposed by the publishers of the Bibliothèque Bleue upon the texts of which they took possession: both aim, in effect, to inscribe the text in a cultural matrix that was not its original destination, thereby permitting readings, understandings, and uses possibly disqualified by other intellectual practices.

These two cases lead us to the consideration of cultural differentiations not as the translation of already concretized and static divisions, but as the effect of a dynamic process. On the one hand, the transformation of forms and devices by which a text is presented authorizes new appropriations and consequently creates new publics for and uses of it. On the other hand, the sharing of the same objects by the whole of society gives rise to the search for new differences, suited to marking the divisions that were preserved. The trajectory of printed works in the French ancien régime bears witness to this situation. We could say that the distinctions between the manners of reading were progressively reinforced to the degree that printed works became less rare, less threatened by seizure, and more ordinary. Whereas the simple possession of a book had for a long time signified a cultural division in itself, with the conquests of printing it is, rather, specific reading attitudes and typographical objects which progressively take on this function. Against refined readings and carefully made books were henceforth counterposed hastily printed material and unskilled interpreters. But both groups, let us recall, often read the same texts, for which plural and contradictory significations were produced according to their contrasting uses. The question consequently becomes one of selection: why do certain texts lend themselves better than others to these continuing and recurrent uses (see Harlan)? Or at least, why do the makers (*faiseurs*) of books consider them capable of reaching a very diverse public? The answer lies in subtle relations between the structures of the works themselves, unequally suited to reappropriations, and the multiple determinations, as much institutional as formal, that establish their possible 'application' (in the phenomenological sense) to very different historical situations.

In the relation between the text, its printed form, and reading there is a third figure produced as soon as a text, fixed in its form and linguistically stable, is taken up by new readers who read differently from their predecessors. 'A book changes by the fact that it remains changeless while the world changes' (Bourdieu and Chartier, p. 236) – or, to make the proposition compatible with the scale of our reflection here, let us say, 'when its mode of being read changes'. The remark serves to justify the project of a history of the practices of reading, which attempts to mark the major contrasts that can give diverse meaning to the same text. It is surely time to reexamine three fundamental oppositions that have long been considered incontestable: to begin with, between a reading in which comprehension presupposes a required oral articulation, whether aloud or barely vocalized (*à basse voix*), and another species of reading that is purely visual (see Saenger, 'Silent Reading' and 'Physiologie de la lecture'). Let us recall (even if its chronology is questionable) a fundamental assertion of Michel de Certeau that associates the freedom of the reader with silent reading:

> In the last three centuries reading has become a gesture of the eye. It is no longer accompanied, as it used to be, by the murmur of vocal articulation, nor by the movement of a muscular mastication (*manducation*). To read without speaking the words or at least muttering them is a modern experience, unknown for millennia. In earlier times, the reader interiorized the text: he made his voice the body of the other; he was its actor. Today the text no longer imposes its own rhythm on the subject, it no longer manifests itself through the reader's voice. This withdrawal of the body, which is the condition of its autonomy, puts the text at a distance. It is the reader's *habeas corpus*.
>
> (*Practice of Everyday Life*, pp. 175–6; translation modified)

The second of these oppositions contrasts 'intensive' reading applied only to a few texts and sustained by hearing and memory with 'extensive' reading – consuming many texts, passing without constraint from one to another, granting little consecration (*sacralité*) to the object read (see Engelsing and Schön). Finally, the third of these oppositions is between the reading of intimacy, enclosure, and solitude – considered to be one of the essential foundations of the private sphere – and collective readings, whether orderly or unruly, in communal spaces (see Ariès, 'Introduction'; and Chartier, 'The Practical Impact of Writing').

In outlining a preliminary chronological thread, which marks as major transformations the progressive advances of silent reading in the Middle Ages and the entry into the world of extensive reading at the end of the eighteenth century, these now classic contrasts suggest several reflections. Some of these tend to complicate the oppositional pairs presented: shifting attention to the model's inaccuracies, complicating criteria that too rigidly differentiate styles of reading, reversing the image of an automatic connection between the collective and the 'popular' or between the elite and the private (see Darnton). Others invite the articulation of three series of transformations whose effects have often been imperfectly sorted out: first, the 'revolutions' that have occurred in the techniques of textual reproduction (with, most importantly, the passage from 'scribal culture' to 'print culture'); second, the changes in the forms of books themselves (the replacement of the *volumen* by the *codex* in the first centuries of the Christian era is the most fundamental; but others, certainly more subtle, alter the visual layout of the printed page between the sixteenth and eighteenth centuries – see Laufer); and finally, major alterations in reading abilities and in reading modes. These different evolutions do not proceed at the same pace and are not at all organized around the same turning points. The most interesting question posed to and by the history of reading today is without doubt that of the conjunction between these three sets of changes: technological, formal, and cultural.

The response we give to this question depends upon a reevaluation of the trajectories and cultural divisions that characterize the society of the ancien régime. More than has been recognized, these were themselves ordered according to the role played by printed works. For a long time their distribution was measured by two restricted series of criteria: one, based upon the proportion of signatures, which sought to establish percentages of literacy and hence to estimate variations in the ability to read according to period, place, gender, and social situation; and another which, by inventorying the catalogues of libraries established by notaries or booksellers, sought to establish the circulation of books and the traditions of reading. But neither in ancien régime societies nor in our own can access to printing be reduced simply to the possession of books: not all books read are privately owned, and not all privately owned printed matter is in the form of books. Moreover written material occupies the very heart of the culture of the illiterate – in rituals, in public spaces, and in workplaces (see Chartier, *The Culture of Print*). Thanks to speech which deciphers it and to images which accentuate it, it is made accessible even to those who are incapable of reading or who cannot by themselves have more than a rudimentary understanding of the text. Rates of literacy, then, do not give a fair indication of familiarity with the written – particularly because in more traditional communities, where instruction in reading and instruction in writing were dissociated and successive, there were many individuals (especially among women) who left school knowing how to read, at least a little, but not how to write (see Spufford). Similarly, the private possession of books cannot adequately indicate the frequency with which printed texts were utilized by those who were too poor to have their own 'library'.

Even if it is impossible to establish the number of the reading-literate (*lisants*) who did not know how to set their names on paper, or how many possessed not a single book (at least none worth mentioning by a notary establishing the inventory of a decedent's possessions) but could still read posters and broadsheets, pamphlets and chapbooks, it is necessary to postulate that there were many such readers in order to comprehend the impact of print on the traditional forms of a culture that was still largely oral, gestural, and iconographic. The overlaps between the two modes of expression and communication are multiple: to begin with overlaps between writing and gesture, not only was writing at the center of everyday celebrations such as religious ceremonies, but numerous texts attempt to efface themselves as discourse and to produce, in practice, behavior conforming to social or religious norms. Such is the case, for example, of conduct books (*traités de civilité*), whose aim was to help individuals internalize the rules of worldly *politesse* or Christian decency (see Patrizi and Chartier). There is equally an interweaving between speech and writing, in two ways. First, texts intended by their author and, more often, by their publisher to reach the most popular audience often contain formulas or motifs that are themselves drawn from the oral tradition of tales and recitations. The writing styles in certain occasional pieces that plagiarize the speaking style of storytellers or the variations introduced in the fairy tales in the Bibliothèque Bleue, themselves originally drawn from written compilations, are good examples of the emergence of orality in print (see Chartier, 'The Hanged Woman Miraculously Saved', and Velay-Vallantin). Second, as mentioned above, a number of 'readers' do not understand texts except through the mediation of a voice. To understand the specificity of this relation to writing thus presumes that all reading is not necessarily individual, silent, and solitary but, on the contrary, marks the importance and diversity of a practice now largely lost – reading aloud.

From this initial assertion, which registers the powerful penetration of printed culture into the societies of the ancien régime, several others follow. It allows us to understand the importance given to writing, and the objects in which it is found, by the authorities whose intentions were to regulate behavior and to shape minds. Whence the pedagogical, acculturating, and disciplinary role attributed to texts placed in circulation for broad readerships; and the surveillance exercised over printing, subjected to a censor who was supposed to eliminate all that might endanger order, religion, or morals. Concerning these constraints, Michel de Certeau urges us to recognize both their power – all the stronger because of the strength of the institution that decreed them ('The creativity of the reader grows as the institution that controls him declines': *Practice of Everyday Life*, p. 172) – and their modalities, ranging from brutal prohibition to authorized interpretation, from exterior disciplines (administrative, judicial, inquisitorial, academic, and so forth) to the mechanisms which, in the book itself, seek to restrain the freedom of the reader.

Out of practices of writing and diverse treatments of printing, traditional texts constructed representations in which we can recognize the divisions that were considered decisive by the producers of books. These perceptions are fundamental because they found the strategies of writing and printing, regulated by the competencies and expectations of the different target audiences. They thereby acquire an efficacy of which the trace can be found in the protocols of explicit reading, in the forms given to typographic objects, or in the transformations that modified a text as soon as it was offered to new readers in a new published format. It is thus from these diverse representations of reading and from the dichotomies constructed in the modern age (between the reading of a text and the reading of an image, between literate reading and unskilled reading, between intimate reading and communal reading) that an attempt must be made to understand the agency and the uses of those printed texts, more modest than the book, but also more pervasive – texts ranging from individual images and posters (always accompanied by words) to occasional pieces and pamphlets like those found in the Bibliothèque Bleue (often illustrated with images). The representations of traditional ways of reading and of their differences from each other – revealed on the practical level by the transformations of printed materials (*mises en imprimé*) or in their normative purposes (*finalité*) by their literary, pictorial, or autobiographical stagings (*mises en scène*) – constitute the essential data for an archeology of reading practices. Yet while they may articulate the contrasts most apparent to the minds of their contemporaries, they should not be allowed to mask other divisions which may have been less clearly perceived. For example, it is certain that there are many practices that reverse the very terms of the frequently described opposition between readings in bourgeois or aristocratic solitude on the one hand, and mass communal readings on the other. Indeed, reading aloud (for others to listen to) remained an enduring, unifying element in elite society, and, conversely, printing penetrated to the very heart of intimate popular culture, capturing in unpretentious objects (not all of which were books) the traces of an important moment of existence, the memory of an emotion, the sign of an identity. Contrary to classic imagery – in fact, a product of the modern age – 'the people' are not always plural, and it is necessary to rediscover in their secret solitude the modest practices of those who cut out images of occasional works, colored printed etchings, and read books from the Bibliothèque Bleue for their personal pleasure.

Attached to a particular country (France between the sixteenth and eighteenth centuries) and having chosen a specific problem (the effects of the penetration of printed works into popular culture – *la culture du plus grand nombre*), the approach suggested in this text (and at work in several others) attempts to make functional two propositions of Michel de Certeau. The first reminds us, against all the reductions that cancel out the creative and inventive force of practices, that reading is never totally constrained and that it cannot be recursively deduced from the texts to which it is applied. The second emphasizes that the tactics of readers, infiltrating the 'special space' (*lieu propre*) produced by the strategies of writing, obey certain rules, logics, and models. Thus is articulated the founding paradox of any history of reading, which must postulate the freedom of a practice of which, broadly, it can only grasp the determinations. To construct communities of readers as 'interpretive communities' (to use the expression of Stanley Fish), to detect how material forms affect meaning, to locate social difference more in real practices than in statistical distributions – such are the paths outlined in our attempt to understand historically this 'silent production' which is the activity of reading.

Notes

The translator and editors gratefully acknowledge support for the translation of this essay provided by the Center for Cultural Studies, University of California, Santa Cruz.

1   On the reading–writing duo in this book see the article by Anne-Marie Chartier and Jean Hébrard, 'L'invention du quotidien, une lecture, des usages', *Le Débat*, **49** (March–April 1988): 97–108.

2   The suggestions in this essay are reconsidered in one of Michel de Certeau's major works, *La Fable mystique* (Paris: Gallimard, 1982), in particular the third part, 'La Scène de l'énoncia-tion' (pp. 209–73). This work has recently been translated into English: *The Mystic Fable*, trans. Michael B. Smith (Chicago: University of Chicago Press, 1992).

3   For a programmatic definition of *Rezeptionstheorie*, see Hans Robert Jauss, *Literaturgeschichte als Provokation* (Frankfurt-am-Main: Suhrkamp, 1974).

4   The fundamental but contested study on this issue is by Robert Mandrou, *De la culture populaire aux XVIIe et XVIIIe siècles*. Among the criticisms addressed to this book is de Certeau, 'La beauté du mort'; reconsidered in de Certeau, *La Culture au pluriel* (pp. 49–80).

5   See Chartier, 'The Bibliothèque Bleue and Popular Reading' and 'The Literature of Roguery in the Bibliothèque Bleue' in *The Cultural Uses of Print in Early Modern France* (pp. 240–64 and pp. 265–342).

References

Ariès, Philippe 'Introduction', *Passions of the Renaissance*. Vol. 3 of *A History of Private Life*. Ed. Roger Chartier. Cambridge, Mass.: Harvard University Press, 1989, pp. 1–11.

Bourdieu, Pierre and Roger Chartier 'La Lecture: Une pratique culturelle', *Pratiques de la lecture*. Ed. Roger Chartier. Marseille: Rivages, 1985.

Certeau, Michel de *La Culture au pluriel*. 1974. 2nd edn Paris: Bourgois, 1980.

——— 'La Lecture absolue (Théorie et pratique des mystiques chrétiens: XVIe–XVIIe siècles)', *Problèmes actuels de la lecture*. Ed. Lucien Dällenbach and Jean Ricardou. Paris: Clancier-Guénaud, 1982.

——— *The Practice of Everyday Life*. Trans. Steven F. Rendall. Berkeley: University of California Press, 1984.

Certeau, Michel de, Dominique Julia and Jacques Revel 'La Beauté du mort: Le concept de "culture populaire"', *Politique aujourd'hui* (December 1970): 3–23.

Chartier, Roger (ed.) *The Culture of Print: Power and the Uses of Print in Early Modern Europe*. Cambridge: Polity; Ithaca: Cornell University Press, 1989.

——— *The Cultural Uses of Print in Early Modern France*. Princeton: Princeton University Press, 1987.

——— 'The Hanged Woman Miraculously Saved: An Occasional', *Culture of Print*, pp. 59–91.

——— 'Leisure and Sociability: Reading Aloud in Early Modern Europe', *Urban Life in the Renaissance*. Ed. S. Zimmermann and R. F. E. Weissman. Newark: University of Delaware Press; London: Associated University Press, 1989.

——— 'The Practical Impact of Writing', *Passions of the Renaissance*. Vol. 3 of *A History of Private Life*. Ed. Roger Chartier. Cambridge: Harvard University Press, 1989.

Darnton, Robert 'First Steps toward a History of Reading', *Australian Journal of French Studies*, **23**, 1 (1986): 5–30.

Engelsing, Rolf 'Die Perioden der Lesergeschichte in die Neuzeit. Das statistische Ausmass und die soziokulturelle Debeutung der Lektüre', *Archiv für Geschichte des Buchwesens*, **10** (1970): 945–1002.

Ginzburg, Carlo *The Cheese and the Worms: The Cosmos of a Sixteenth-Century Miller.* Trans. John and Anne Tedeschi. Baltimore: Johns Hopkins University Press, 1980.

Harlan, David 'Intellectual History and the Return of Literature', *American Historical Review*, **94** (June 1989): 581–609.

Hébrard, Jean 'Comment Valentin Jamerey-Duval apprit-il à lire? L'autodidaxie excemplaire?', *Pratiques de la lecture.* Ed. Roger Chartier. Marseille: Rivages, 1985.

Jardine, Lisa and Anthony Grafton ' "Studied for Actions": How Gabriel Harvey Read his Livy', *Past and Present*, **129** (November 1990): 30–78.

Laufer, Roger 'L'Espace visuel du livre ancien', Martin and Chartier, **1**, pp. 478–97.

—— 'Les Espaces du livre', Martin and Chartier, **2**: 128–39.

Levine, Lawrence W. *Highbrow/Lowbrow: The Emergence of Cultural Hierarchy in America.* Cambridge: Harvard University Press, 1988.

—— 'William Shakespeare and the American People: A Study in Cultural Transformation', *American Historical Review*, **89** (February 1984): 34–66.

Mandrou, Robert *De la culture populaire aux XVIIe et XVIIIe siècles: La bibliothèque bleue de Troyes.* 1964. Paris: Stock, 1974.

Martin, Henri-Jean and Roger Chartier (eds) *Histoire de l'édition française.* 2 vols, Paris: Promodis, 1982–84.

Martin, Henri-Jean and Bruno Delmas *Histoire et pouvoirs de l'écrit.* Paris: Perrin, 1988.

McKenzie, D. F. *Bibliography and the Sociology of Texts.* Panizzi Lectures, 1985. London: British Library, 1986.

—— 'Typography and Meaning: The Case of William Congreve', *Buch und Buchhandel in Europa im achtzehnten Jahrhundert.* Ed. Giles Barber and Bernhard Fabian. Hamburg: Ernest Hauswedell, 1981.

Ménétra, Jacques-Louis *Journal de ma vie: Jacques-Louis Ménétra, compagnon vitrier au 18e siècle.* Ed. Daniel Roche. Paris: Montalba, 1982.

Patrizi, Giorgio 'Il libro del Cortegiano e la trattatistica sul comportamento', *La prosa.* Part 2 of *Le forme del testo.* Vol. 3 of *Letteratura italiana.* Turin: Einaudi, 1984: pp. 855–90.

Patrizi, Giorgio and Roger Chartier 'From Texts to Manners: A Concept and its Books: *Civilité* between Aristocratic Distinction and Popular Appropriation', Chartier, *Cultural Uses of Print*, pp. 71–109.

Ricoeur, Paul *Time and Narrative.* Trans. Kathleen McLaughlin and David Pellauer. 3 vols. Chicago: University of Chicago Press, 1984–88.

Saenger, Paul 'Physiologie de la lecture et séparation des mots', *Annales* E.S.C. (1989): 939–52.

—— 'Silent Reading: Its Impact on Late Medieval Script and Society', *Viator*, **13** (1982): 367–414.

Schön, Erich *Der Verlust der Sinnlichkeit oder die Verwandlungen des Lesers: Mentalitätswandel um 1800.* Stuttgart: Klett-Cotta, 1987.

Spufford, Margaret 'First Steps in Literacy: The Reading and Writing Experiences of the Humblest Seventeenth-Century Autobiographers', *Social History*, **4**, 3 (1979): 407–35.

Stoddard, Roger E. 'Morphology and the Book from an American Perspective', *Printing History*, **9**, 1 (1987): 2–14.

Velay-Vallantin, Catherine 'Tales as a Mirror: Perrault in the Bibliothèque Bleue', Chartier, *Culture of Print*, pp. 92–135.

Chapter 9

Pierre Bourdieu

THE FIELD OF CULTURAL PRODUCTION

The struggle for the dominant principle of hierarchization

The literary or artistic field is at all times the site of a struggle between the two principles of hierarchization: the heteronomous principle, favourable to those who dominate the field economic-ally and politically (e.g. 'bourgeois art'), and the autonomous principle (e.g. 'art for art's sake'), which those of its advocates who are least endowed with specific capital tend to identify with a degree of independence from the economy, seeing temporal failure as a sign of election and success as a sign of compromise.[1] The state of the power relations in this struggle depends on the overall degree of autonomy possessed by the field, that is, the extent to which it manages to impose its own norms and sanctions on the whole set of producers, including those who are closest to the dominant pole of the field of power and therefore most responsive to external demands (i.e. the most heteronomous); this degree of autonomy varies considerably from one period and one national tradition to another, and affects the whole structure of the field. Everything seems to indicate that it depends on the value which the specific capital of writers and artists represents for the dominant fractions, on the one hand in the struggle to conserve the established order and, perhaps especially, in the struggle between the fractions aspiring to domination within the field of power (bourgeoisie and aristocracy, old bourgeoisie and new bourgeoisie, etc.), and on the other hand in the production and reproduction of economic capital (with the aid of experts and cadres).[2] All the evidence suggests that, at a given level of overall autonomy, intellectuals are, other things being equal, proportionately more responsive to the seduction of the powers that be, the less well endowed they are with specific capital.[3]

The struggle in the field of cultural production over the imposition of the legitimate mode of cultural production is inseparable from the struggle within the dominant class (with the opposition between 'artists' and 'bourgeois') to impose the dominant principle of domination (that is to say – ultimately – the definition of human accomplishment). In this struggle, the artists and writers who are richest in specific capital and most concerned for their autonomy are considerably weakened by the fact that some of their competitors identify their interests with the dominant principles of hierarchization and seek to impose them even within the field, with the support of the temporal powers. The most heteronomous cultural producers (i.e. those with least symbolic capital) can offer the least resistance to external demands, of whatever sort. To defend their own position, they have to produce weapons, which the dominant agents (within the field of power) can immediately turn against the cultural producers most attached to their autonomy. In endeavouring to discredit every attempt to impose an autonomous principle of hierarchization, and thus serving their own interests, they serve the interests of the dominant fractions of the dominant class, who obviously have an interest in there being only one hierarchy. In the struggle to impose the legitimate definition of art and literature, the most autonomous producers naturally tend to exclude 'bourgeois' writers and artists, whom they see as 'enemy agents'. This means, incidentally, that sampling problems cannot be resolved by one of those arbitrary decisions of positivist ignorance which are dignified by the term 'operational definition': these amount to blindly arbitrating on debates which are inscribed in reality itself, such as the question as to whether such and such a group ('bourgeois' theatre, the 'popular' novel, etc.) or such and such an individual claiming the title of writer or artist (or philosopher, or intellectual, etc.) belongs to the population of writers or artists or, more precisely, as to who is legitimately entitled to designate legitimate writers or artists.

The preliminary reflections on the definitions of the object and the boundaries of the population, which studies of writers, artists and, especially, intellectuals, often indulge in so as to give themselves an air of scientificity, ignore the fact, which is more than scientifically attested, that the definition of the writer (or artist etc.) is an issue at stake in struggles in every literary (or artistic etc.) field.[4] In other words, the field of cultural production is the site of struggles in which what is at stake is the power to impose the dominant definition of the writer and therefore to delimit the population of those entitled to take part in the struggle to define the writer. The established definition of the writer may be radically transformed by an enlargement of the set of people who have a legitimate voice in literary matters. It follows from this that every survey aimed at establishing the hierarchy of writers predetermines the hierarchy by determining the population deemed worthy of helping to establish it. In short, the fundamental stake in literary struggles is the monopoly of literary legitimacy, i.e., *inter alia*, the monopoly of the power to say with authority who are authorized to call themselves writers; or, to put it another way, it is the monopoly of the power to consecrate producers or products (we are dealing with a world of belief and the consecrated writer is the one who has the power to consecrate and to win assent when he or she consecrates an author or a work – with a preface, a favourable review, a prize, etc.).

While it is true that every literary field is the site of a struggle over the definition of the writer (a universal proposition), the fact remains that scientific analysts, if they are not to make the mistake of universalizing the particular case, need to know that they will only ever encounter historical definitions of the writer, corresponding to a particular state of the struggle to impose the legitimate definition of the writer. There is no other criterion of membership of a field than the objective fact of producing effects within it. One of the difficulties of orthodox defence against heretical transformation of the field by a redefinition of the tacit or explicit terms of entry is the fact that polemics imply a form of recognition; adversaries whom one would prefer to destroy by ignoring them cannot be combated without consecrating them. The '*Théâtre libre*' effectively entered the sub-field of drama once it came under attack from the accredited advocates of bourgeois theatre, who thus helped to produce the recognition they sought to prevent. The '*nouveaux philosophes*' came into existence as active elements in the philosophical field – and no longer just that of journalism – as soon as consecrated philosophers felt called upon to take issue with them.

The *boundary* of the field is a stake of struggles, and the social scientist's task is not to draw a dividing line between the agents involved in it by imposing a so-called operational definition, which is most likely to be imposed on him by his own prejudices or presuppositions, but to describe a *state* (long-lasting or temporary) of these struggles and therefore of the frontier delimiting the territory held by the competing agents. One could thus examine the characteristics of this boundary, which may or may not be institutionalized, that is to say, protected by conditions of entry that are tacitly and practically required (such as a certain cultural capital) or explicitly codified and legally guaranteed (e.g. all the forms of entrance examination aimed at ensuring a *numerus clausus*). It would be found that one of the most significant properties of the field of cultural production, explaining its extreme dispersion and the conflicts between rival principles of legitimacy, is the extreme permeability of its frontiers and, consequently, the extreme diversity of the 'posts' it offers, which defy any unilinear hierarchization. It is clear from comparison that the field of cultural production demands neither as much inherited economic capital as the economic field nor as much educational capital as the university sub-field or even sectors of the field of power such as the top civil service or even the field of the 'liberal professions'.[5] However, precisely because it represents one of the *indeterminate sites* in the social structure, which offer ill-defined posts, waiting to be made rather than ready made, and therefore extremely elastic and undemanding, and career paths which are themselves full of uncertainty and extremely dispersed (unlike bureaucratic careers, such as those offered by the university system), it attracts agents who differ greatly in their properties and dispositions but the most favoured of whom are sufficiently secure to be able to disdain a university career and to take on the risks of an occupation which is not a 'job' (since it is almost always combined with a private income or a 'bread-and-butter' occupation).

> The 'profession' of writer or artist is one of the least professionalized there is, despite all the efforts of 'writers' associations', 'Pen Clubs', etc. This is shown clearly by (*inter alia*) the problems which arise in classifying these agents, who are able to exercise what they regard as their main occupation only on condition that they have a secondary occupation which provides their main income (problems very similar to those encountered in classifying students).

The most disputed frontier of all is the one which separates the field of cultural production and the field of power. It may be more or less clearly marked in different periods, positions occupied in each field may be more or less totally incompatible, moves from one universe to the other more or less frequent and the overall distance between the corresponding populations more or less great (e.g. in terms of social origin, educational background, etc.).

The structure of the field

Heteronomy arises from *demand*, which may take the form of personal *commission* (formulated by a 'patron' in Haskell's sense of a protector or client) or of the sanction of an autonomous *market*, which may be *anticipated* or *ignored*. Within this logic, the *relationship to the audience* and, more exactly, economic or political interest in the sense of interest in success and in the related economic or political profit, constitute one of the bases for evaluating the producers and their products. Thus, strict application of the autonomous principle of hierarchization means that producers and products will be distinguished according to their degree of success with the audience, which, it tends to be assumed, is evidence of their interest in the economic and political profits secured by success.

The duality of the principles of hierarchization means that there are few fields (other than the field of power itself) in which the antagonism between the occupants of the polar positions is more total (within the limits of the interests linked to membership of the field of power). Perfectly illustrating the distinction between relations of interaction and the structural relations which constitute a field, the polar individuals may never meet, may even ignore each other systematically, to the extent of refusing each other membership of the same class, and yet their practice remains determined by the negative relation which unites them. It could be said that the agents involved in the literary or artistic field may, in extreme cases, have nothing in common except the fact of taking part in a struggle to impose the legitimate definition of literary or artistic production.[6]

The hierarchy by degree of real or supposed dependence on audience, success or the economy itself overlaps with another one, which reflects the degree of specific consecration of the audience, i.e. its 'cultural' quality and its supposed distance from the centre of the specific values. Thus, within the sub-field of production-for-producers, which recognizes only the specific principle of legitimacy, those who are assured of the recognition of a certain fraction of the other producers, a presumed index of posthumous recognition, are opposed to those who, again from the standpoint of the specific criteria, are relegated to an inferior position and who, in accordance with the model of heresy, contest the legitimation principle dominant within the autonomous sub-field, either in the name of a new legitimation principle or in the name of a return to an old one. Likewise, at the other pole of the field, that of the market and of economic profit, authors who manage to secure 'high-society' successes and bourgeois consecration are opposed to those who are condemned to so-called 'popular' success – the authors of rural novels, music-hall artists, *chansonniers*, etc.

The duality of literary hierarchies and genres

In the second half of the nineteenth century, the period in which the literary field attained its maximum autonomy, these two hierarchies seem to correspond, in the first place, to the specifically cultural hierarchy of the genres – poetry, the novel and drama – and secondarily to the hierarchy of ways of using them which, as is seen clearly in the case of the theatre and especially the novel, varies with the position of the audiences reached in the specifically cultural hierarchy.

> The literary field is itself defined by its position in the hierarchy of the arts, which varies from one period and one country to another. Here one can only allude to the effect of the hierarchy of the arts and in particular to the dominance which poetry, an intellectual art, exerted until the sixteenth century over painting, a manual art,[7] so that, for example, the hierarchy of pictorial genres tended to depend on their distance – as regards the subject and the more or less erudite manner of treating it – from the most elaborate model of poetic discourse. It is well known that throughout the nineteenth century, and perhaps until Duchamp, the stereotype which relegated the painter to a purely manual genre ('stupid as a painter') persisted, despite the increasing exchange of symbolic services (partly, no doubt, because the painters were generally less rich in cultural capital than the writers; we know, for example, that Monet, the son of a Le Havre grocer, and Renoir, the son of a Limoges tailor, were much intimidated in the meetings at the Café Guerbois on account of their lack of education). In the case of the field of painting, autonomy had to be won from the literary field too, with the emergence of specific criticism and above all the will to break free from the writers and their discourse by producing an intrinsically polysemic work beyond all discourse, and a discourse about the work which declares the essential inadequacy of all discourse. The history of the relations between Odilon Redon and the writers – especially Huysmans – shows in an exemplary way how the painters had to fight for autonomy from the *littérateur* who enhances the illustrator by advancing himself, and to assert the irreducibility of the pictorial work (which the professional critic is more ready to recognize).[8] The same logic can be used to analyse the relations between the composers and the poets: the concern to use without being used, to possess without being possessed, led some composers (Debussy, for example) to choose to set mediocre texts which would not eclipse them.

From the economic point of view, the hierarchy is simple and relatively stable, despite cyclical fluctuations related to the fact, for example, that the more economically profitable the various genres, the more strongly and directly they are affected by recession.[9] At the top of the hierarchy is drama, which, as all observers note, secures big profits – provided by an essentially bourgeois, Parisian, and therefore relatively restricted, audience – for a very few producers (because of the small number of theatres). At the bottom is poetry, which, with a few, very rare exceptions (such as a few successes in verse drama), secures virtually zero profit for a small number of producers. Between the two is the novel, which can secure big profits (in the case of some naturalist novels), and sometimes very big profits (some 'popular' novels), for a relatively large number of producers, from an audience which may extend far beyond the audience made up of the writers themselves, as in the case of poetry, and beyond the bourgeois audience, as in the case of theatre, into the *petite bourgeoisie* or even, especially through municipal libraries, into the 'labour aristocracy'.

From the point of view of the symbolic hierarchies, things are less simple since, as can be seen from Figure 9.1, the hierarchies according to distance from profits are intersected by hierarchies internal to each of the genres (i.e. according to the degree to which the authors and works conform to the specific demands of the genre), which correspond to the social hierarchy of the audiences. This is seen particularly clearly in the case of the novel, where the hierarchy of specialities corresponds to the hierarchy of the audiences reached and also, fairly strictly, to the hierarchy of the social universes represented.

The complex structure of this space can be explained by means of a simple model taking into account, on the one hand, the properties of the different arts and the different genres considered as economic enterprises (price of the product, size of the audience and length of the economic cycle) and, on the other hand, the negative relationship which, as the field increasingly imposes its own logic, is established between symbolic profit and economic profit, whereby discredit increases as the audience grows and its specific competence declines, together with the value of the recognition implied in the act of consumption. The different kinds of cultural enterprise vary, from an economic standpoint, in terms of the unit price of the product (a painting, a play, a concert, a book, etc.) and the cumulative number of purchasers; but they also vary according to the length of the production cycle, particularly as regards the speed with which profits are obtained (and, secondarily, the length of time during which they are secured). It can be seen that, although the opposition between the short cycle of products which sell rapidly and the long cycle of products which sell belatedly or slowly is found in each of the arts, they differ radically in terms of the mode of profit acquisition and therefore, because of the connection that is made between the size of the audience and its *social quality*, in terms of the objective and subjective relationship between the producer and the market.

There is every difference between painters who, even when they set themselves in the avant-garde, can expect to sell to a *small number of connoisseurs* (nowadays including museums) works whose value derives partly from the fact that they are produced in limited numbers, and the writer who has to sell to an audience that is as wide as possible but one which, as it grows, is no doubt less and less composed of connoisseurs. This explains why the writers are, much more than painters, condemned to have an ambivalent attitude towards sales and their audience. They tend to be torn between the internal demands of the field of production, which regard commercial successes as suspect and push them towards a heretical break with the established norms of production and consumption, and the expectations of their vast audience, which are to some degree transfigured into a populist mission (Zola, for example, endeavoured to invoke a popular legitimacy to sublimate commercial success by transforming it into popular success). As for the dramatists, they are situated between the two poles. Established

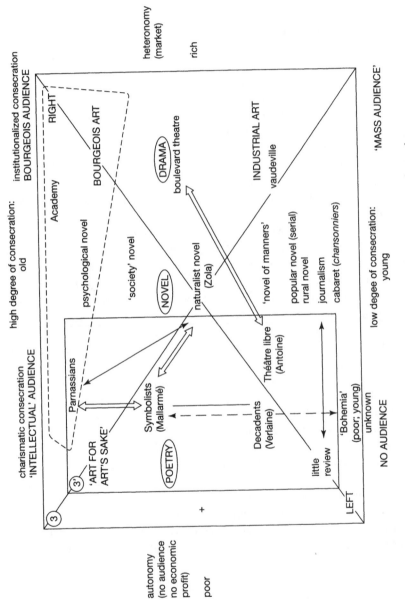

Figure 9.1 French literary field in the second half of the nineteenth century; + = positive pole, implying a dominant position, – = negative pole, implying a dominated position

playwrights can earn big profits through repeated performances of the same work; for the others, as for composers, the main difficulty is to get their work performed at all.

Thus, the relationship of mutual exclusion between material gratification and the sole legitim-ate profit (i.e. recognition by one's peers) is increasingly asserted as the exclusive principle of evaluation as one moves down the hierarchy of economic gratifications. Successful authors will not fail to see this as the logic of resentment, which makes a virtue of necessity; and they are not necessarily wrong, since the absence of audience, and of profit, may be the effect of privation as much as a refusal, or a privation converted into refusal. The question is even harder to resolve, at least summarily, since the collective bad faith which is the basis of a universe sustained by denial of the economy helps to support the effort of individual bad faith which makes it possible to experience failure in this world as election hereafter, and the incomprehension of the audience as an effect of the prophetic refusal to compromise with the demands of an audience attached to old norms of production. It is no accident that ageing, which dissolves the ambiguities, converting the elective, provisional refusals of adolescent bohemian life into the unrelieved privation of the aged, embittered bohemian, so often takes the form of an emotional crisis, marked by reversals and abjurations which often lead to the meanest tasks of 'industrial art', such as vaudeville or cabaret, and of political pamphleteering. But, at the other end of the scale of economic profits, a homologous opposition is established, through the size of the audience, which is partly responsible for the volume of profit, and its recognized social quality, which determines the value of the consecration it can bestow, between bourgeois art, which has an honoured place in society, and industrial art, which is doubly suspect, being both mercantile and 'popular'.

Thus we find three competing principles of legitimacy. First, there is the specific principle of legitimacy, i.e., the recognition granted by the set of producers who produce for other producers, their competitors, i.e. by the autonomous self-sufficient world of 'art for art's sake', meaning art for artists. Secondly, there is the principle of legitimacy corresponding to 'bourgeois' taste and to the consecration bestowed by the dominant fractions of the dominant class and by private tribunals, such as *salons*, or public, state-guaranteed ones, such as academies, which sanction the inseparably ethical and aesthetic (and therefore political) taste of the dominant. Finally, there is the principle of legitimacy which its advocates call 'popular', i.e. the consecration bestowed by the choice of ordinary consumers, the 'mass audience'. It can be seen that poetry, by virtue of its restricted audience (often only a few hundred readers), the consequent low profits, which make it the disinterested activity *par excellence*, and also its prestige, linked to the historical tradition initiated by the Romantics, is destined to charismatic legitimation which is given to only a few individuals, sometimes only one per generation and, by the same token, to a continuous struggle for the monopoly of poetic legitimacy and a succession of successful or abortive revolutions: Parnassians against Romantics, Symbolists against Parnassians, neo-classicists against the early Symbolists, neo-Symbolists against neo-classicists.

Although the break between poetry and the mass readership has been virtually total since the late nineteenth century (it is one of the sectors in which there are still many books published at the author's expense), poetry continues to represent the ideal model of literature for the least cultured consumers. As is confirmed by analysis of a dictionary of writers (such as the *Annuaire national des lettres*), members of the working and lower middle classes who write have too elevated an idea of literature to write realist novels; and their production does indeed consist essentially of poetry – very conventional in its form – and history.

The theatre, which directly experiences the immediate sanction of the bourgeois public, with its values and conformisms, can earn the institutionalized consecration of academies and official honours, as well as money. The novel, occupying a central position in both dimensions of the literary space, is the most dispersed genre in terms of its forms of consecration. It was broadly perceived as typical of the new mercantile literature, linked to the newspaper and journalism by serialization and the impact they gave to it, and above all because, unlike the theatre, it reached a 'popular' audience; with Zola and Naturalism it achieved a wide audience which, although socially inferior, provided profits equivalent to those of the theatre, without renouncing the specific demands of the art and without making any of the concessions typical of 'industrial' literature; and, with the 'society' novel [roman mondain], it was even able to win bourgeois consecrations previously reserved for the theatre. . . .

Structure and change

Changes which affect the structure of the field as a whole, such as major re-orderings of the hierarchy of genres, presuppose a concordance between internal changes, directly determined by modification of the chances of access to the literary field, and external changes which supply the new producers (the Romantics, the Naturalists, the Symbolists and the whole fin-de-siècle literary and artistic movement) and their new products with socially homologous consumers. This is not true to the same extent of changes which affect only the field of restricted production. These endless changes, which arise from the very structure of the field, i.e. the synchronic oppositions between the antagonistic positions (dominant/dominated, consecrated/novice, old/young, etc.), are largely independent of the external changes which may seem to determine them because they accompany them chronologically. This is true even when such internal changes owe their subsequent consecration mainly to a 'miraculous' encounter between (largely) independent causal series. This argument would have to be demonstrated, for example, in cases such as that of Mallarmé (or Debussy, or Fauré), in which the two opposing theses – the absolute independence of pure art, led solely by the autonomous logic of its own development, and the thesis of direct dependence on the historical situation – can both find arguments. Indeed, the coincidence between the properties of the social experience which privileged consumers may have had in a certain historical conjuncture and the properties of the work, in which are expressed the necessities inscribed in a position progressively instituted and containing a whole past and potential history, and in a disposition, itself progressively constituted through a whole social trajectory, is a sort of trap laid for those who, seeking to escape from internal reading of the work or the internal history of artistic life, condemn themselves to the short circuit of directly interrelating the period and the work. In such cases, both the period and the work are reduced to a few schematic properties, selected for the purposes of the argument, as in the Lukácsian or Goldmannian mythology of the writer as the unconscious spokesman of a group, which is simply an inversion of the Romantic myth of the poet vates. . . .

Without ever being a direct reflection of them, the internal struggles depend for their outcome on the correspondence they may have with the external struggles between the classes (or between the fractions of the dominant class) and on the reinforcement which one group or another may derive from them, through homology and the consequent synchronisms. When the newcomers are not disposed to enter the cycle of simple reproduction, based on recognition of the 'old' by the 'young' – homage, celebration, etc. – and recognition of the 'young' by the 'old' – prefaces, co-optation, consecration, etc. – but bring with them dispositions and position-takings which clash with the prevailing norms of production and the expectations of the field, they cannot succeed without the help of external changes. These may be political breaks, such as revolutionary crises, which change the power relations within the field (the 1848 revolution strengthened the dominated pole, causing writers to shift, very temporarily no doubt, to the left, i.e. towards 'social art'), or deep-seated changes in the audience of consumers who, because of their affinity with the new producers, ensure the success of their products.

> In fact, one never observes either total submission – and erudite reproduction presup-poses a form of regulated innovation, even an obligatory, limited, break with predeces-sors – or an absolute break – and a break with the immediately preceding generation (fathers) is often supported by a return to the traditions of the next generation back (grandfathers), whose influence may have persisted in a shadowy way. For example, though there is no need to emphasize how much the Parnassians maintain of the Romantic tradition, it is less obvious that they tapped a current of Hellenism which had lived on despite the Romantic break with imitations of Antiquity. Events such as the publication in 1819 of the works of Chénier, impregnated with Hellenism, the dis-covery of the Venus de Milo in 1820, the Greek War of Independence and the death of Byron, turn attention to Grecian Antiquity; Greek myths are revitalized by the prose poems of Ballanche (*Antigone*, 1814; *Orphée*, 1827), and at the height of the Romantic period, there are the works of Paul-Louis Courier and Maurice de Guérin.

In the field of restricted production, each change at any one point in the space of positions objectively defined by their difference, their *écart*, induces a generalized change – which means that one should not look for a specific site of change. It is true that the initiative of change falls almost by definition on the newcomers, i.e. the youngest, who are also those least endowed with specific capital: in a universe in which to exist is to differ, i.e. to occupy a distinct, distinctive position, they must assert their difference, get it known and recognized, get themselves known and recognized ('make a name for themselves'), by endeavouring to impose new modes of thought and expression, out of key with the prevailing modes of thought and with the doxa, and therefore bound to disconcert the orthodox by their 'obscurity' and 'pointlessness'. The fact remains that every new position, in asserting itself as such, determines a displacement of the whole structure and that, by the logic of action and reaction, it leads to all sorts of changes in the position-takings of the occupants of the other positions.

> As well as the countless labels too obviously intended to *produce* the differences they claim to express, one could point to 'manifestos', which often have no other content than the aim of distinguishing themselves from what already exists, even if they do not all go so far as the founders of the *Revue de métaphysique et de morale* and explicitly declare the aim of 'doing something different'.[10] As for the transformations induced by the effect of the structure, a characteristic example can be found in the changes which the Naturalist novelists made in their style and themes – Maupassant with *Une vie* and Zola with *Le rêve* – in response to the success of the psychological novel,[11] and one may even suspect that the effect of the field explains some aspects of the sociology of Durkheim (classified by Bouglé among the representatives of the 'spiritualist initiative', alongside Bergson and Laberthonnière), in which Bouglé sees 'an effort to underpin and justify spiritualist tendencies in a new way'.[12]

Because position-takings arise quasi-mechanically – that is, almost independently of the agents' consciousness and wills – from the relationship between positions, they take relatively invariant forms, and being determined relationally, negatively, they may remain virtually empty, amounting to little more than a *parti pris* of refusal, difference, rupture. Structurally 'young' writers, i.e. those less advanced in the process of consecration (who may be biologically almost as old as the 'old' writers they seek to oust),[13] will refuse everything their 'elders' (in terms of legitimacy) are and do, and in particular all the indices of *social ageing*, starting with the signs of consecration, internal (academies etc.) or external (success), whereas the 'old' writers will regard the social non-existence (in terms of success and consecration) and also the 'obscurity' of their young rivals as evidence of the voluntaristic, forced character of some endeavours to overtake them (as Zola puts it, 'a gigantic, empty pretension').

> The 'young' have an interest in describing every advance in the internal hierarchy of the sub-field of restricted production as an advance in the hierarchy of the field of cultural production as a whole, and therefore contest the independence of the internal hierarchy (cf. the contesting of the 'mandarins'). They may point to the fact that while 'bourgeois' consecration (academy places, prizes, etc.) is primarily awarded to writers who produce for the mass market, it also goes to the most acceptable members of the consecrated avant-garde (and the *Académie Française* has always made room, to a varying extent at different periods, for producers from the field of restricted production). It is also clear that the opposition, within the autonomous field, between professional writers, whose activity obliges them to lead an organized, regular, quasi-bourgeois life, and the 'bohemian' world of 'proletaroid intellectuals' who live on the odd jobs of journalism, publishing or teaching, may give rise to a political division, as was seen at the time of the Paris Commune.[14]

The history of the field arises from the struggle between the established figures and the young challengers. The ageing of authors, schools and works is far from being the product of a mechanical, chronological, slide into the past; it results from the struggle between those who have made their mark (*fait date* – 'made an epoch') and who are fighting to persist, and those who cannot make their own mark without pushing into the past those who have an interest in stopping the clock, eternalizing the present stage of things.[15] 'Making one's mark', initiating a new epoch, means winning recognition, in both senses, of one's difference from other producers, especially the most consecrated of them; it means, by the same token, creating a new position, ahead of the positions already occupied, in the vanguard. (Hence the importance, in this struggle for survival, of all distinctive marks, such as the names of schools or groups – words which make things, distinctive signs which produce existence.) The agents engaged in the struggle are both contemporaries – precisely by virtue of the struggle which synchronizes them – and separated by time and in respect of time: avant-garde writers have contemporaries who recognize them and whom they recognize – apart from other avant-garde writers – only in the future; consecrated writers recognize their contemporaries only in the past. The emergence of a group capable of 'making an epoch' by imposing a new, advanced position is accompanied by a displacement of the structure of temporally hierarchized positions opposed within a given field; each of them moves a step down the temporal hierarchy which is at the same time a social hierarchy; the avant-garde is separated by a generation from the consecrated avant-garde which is itself separated by another generation from the avant-garde that was already consecrated when it made its own entry into the field.[16] Each author, school or work which 'makes its mark' displaces the whole series of earlier authors, schools or works. As Shklovsky points out,[17] each period excludes certain hackneyed subjects: Tolstoy forbids mention of the 'romantic Caucasus' or moonlight, while Chekhov, in one of his juvenilia, lists the newly unacceptable commonplaces. Because the whole series of pertinent changes is present, practically, in the latest (just as the six figures already dialled on a telephone are present in the seventh), a work or an aesthetic movement is irreducible to any other situated elsewhere in the series; and *returns* to past styles (frequent in painting) are never 'the same thing', since they are separated from what they return to by negative reference to something which was itself the negation of it (or the negation of the negation, etc.).[18]

That is why, in an artistic field which has reached an advanced stage of this history, there is no place for *naïfs*; more precisely, the history is immanent to the functioning of the field, and to meet the objective demands it implies, as a producer but also as a consumer, one has to possess the whole history of the field.[19] . . .

Positions and dispositions

The meeting of two histories

To understand the practices of writers and artists, and not least their products, entails understanding that they are the result of the meeting of two histories: the history of the positions they occupy and the history of their dispositions. Although position helps to shape dispositions, the latter, in so far as they are the product of independent conditions, have an existence and efficacy of their own and can help to shape positions. In no field is the confrontation between positions and dispositions more continuous or uncertain than in the literary and artistic field. Offering positions that are relatively uninstitutionalized, never legally guaranteed, therefore open to symbolic challenge, and non-hereditary (although there are specific forms of transmission), it is the arena *par excellence* of struggles over job definition. In fact, however great the effect of position – and we have seen many examples of it – it never operates mechanically, and the relationship between positions and *position-takings* is mediated by the dispositions of the agents.

> Likewise, morphological changes never produce their effects *mechanically*. For example, the influx, in the 1850s, of a large number of writers living with precarious means on the lower edges of the field is retranslated into a redefinition of the post, i.e. of the image of the writer, his sartorial symbolism, his political attitudes, his preferred haunts (café rather than *salon*), etc. More generally, a *numerus clausus* has the effect of protecting a definition of the function, and an increase in the number of legitimate performers of the function – whether architects, doctors or teachers – is sufficient to change the function more or less radically, through the objective devaluation which automatically ensues, the struggle by the guardians of the post to preserve the rarity which previously defined it, and the endeavours of the new occupants to adapt the position to their dispositions.

The 'post' of poet as it presents itself to the young aspirant in the 1880s is the crystallized product of the whole previous history. It is a position in the hierarchy of literary crafts, which, by a sort of effect of *caste*, gives its occupants, subjectively at least, the assurance of an essential superiority over all other writers; the lowest of the poets (Symbolist, at this time) sees himself as superior to the highest of the (Naturalist) novelists.[20] It is a set of 'exemplary figures' – Hugo, Gautier, etc. – who have composed the character and assigned roles, such as, for intellectuals (after Zola), that of the intellectual as the champion of great causes. It is a cluster of representations – that of the 'pure' artist, for example, indifferent to success and to the verdicts of the market – and mechanisms which, through their sanctions, support them and give them real efficacy. In short, one would need to work out the full social history of the *long, collective labour* which leads to the progressive invention of the crafts of writing, and in particular to *awareness* of the *fundamental law* of the field, i.e. the theory of art for art's sake, which is to the field of cultural production what the axiom 'business is business' (and 'in business there's no room for feelings') is to the economic field.[21] Nor, of course, must one forget the role of the mechanism which, here as elsewhere, leads people to make a virtue of necessity, in the constitution of the field of cultural production as a space radically independent of the economy and of polities and, as such, amenable to a sort of pure theory. The work of real emancipation, of which the 'post' of artist or poet is the culmination, can be performed and pursued only if the post encounters the appropriate dispositions, such as disinterestedness and daring, and the (external) conditions of these virtues, such as a private income. In this sense, the collective invention which results in the post of writer or artist has to be endlessly repeated, even if the objectification of past discoveries and the recognition ever more widely accorded to an activity of cultural production that is an end in itself, and the will to emancipation that it implies, tend constantly to reduce the cost of this permanent reinvention. The more the autonomizing process advances, the more possible it becomes to occupy the position of producer without having the properties – or not all of them, or not to the same degree – that had to be possessed to produce the position; the more, in other words, the newcomers who head for the most 'autonomous' positions can dispense with the more or less heroic sacrifices and breaks of the past.

The position of 'pure' writer or artist, like that of intellectual, is an institution of freedom, constructed against the 'bourgeoisie' (in the artists' sense) and against institutions – in particular against the state bureaucracies, academies, salons, etc. – by a series of breaks, partly cumulative, but sometimes followed by regressions, which have often been made possible by diverting the resources of the market – and therefore the 'bourgeoisie' – and even the stage bureaucracies.[22] Owing to its objectively contradictory intention, it exists only at the lowest degree of institutionalization, in the form of words ('avant-garde', for example) or models (the avant-garde writer and his or her exemplary deeds) which constitute a tradition of freedom and criticism, and also, but above all, in the form of a field of competition, equipped with its own institutions (the paradigm of which might be the *Salon des refusés* or the little avant-garde review) and articulated by mechanisms of competition capable of providing incentives and gratification for emancipatory endeavours. For example, the acts of prophetic denunciation of which *J'accuse* is the paradigm have become, since Zola, and perhaps especially since Sartre, so intrinsic to the personage of the intellectual that anyone who aspires to a position (especially a dominant one) in the intellectual field has to perform such exemplary acts.[23] This explains why it is that the producers most freed from external constraints – Mallarmé, Proust, Joyce or Virginia Woolf – are also those who have taken most advantage of a historical heritage accumulated through collective labour against external constraints.

Having established, in spite of the illusion of the constancy of the thing designated, which is encouraged by the constancy of the words artist, writer, bohemian, academy, etc., what each of the positions is at each moment, one still has to understand how those who occupy them have been formed and, more precisely, the shaping of the dispositions which help to lead them to these positions and to define their way of operating within them and staying in them. The field, as a field of possible forces, presents itself to each agent as a *space of possibles* which is defined in the relationship between the structure of average chances of access to the different positions (measured by the 'difficulty' of attaining them and, more precisely, by the relationship between the number of positions and the number of competitors) and the dispositions of each agent, the subjective basis of the perception and appreciation of the objective chances. In other words, the objective probabilities (of economic or symbolic profit, for example) inscribed in the field at a given moment only become operative and active through 'vocations', 'aspirations' and 'expectations', i.e. in so far as they are perceived and appreciated through the schemes of perception and appreciation which constitute a habitus. These schemes, which reproduce in their own logic the fundamental divisions of the field of positions – 'pure art'/ 'commercial art', 'bohemian'/ 'bourgeois', 'left bank'/ 'right bank', etc. – are one of the mediations through which dispositions are adjusted to positions. Writers and artists, particularly newcomers, do not react to an 'objective reality' functioning as a sort of stimulus valid for every possible subject, but to a 'problem-raising situation', as Popper puts it; they help to create its intellectual and affective 'physiognomy' (horror, seduction, etc.) and therefore even the symbolic force it exerts on them. A position as it appears to the (more or less adequate) 'sense of investment' which each agent applies to it presents itself either as a sort of necessary locus which beckons those who are made for it ('vocation') or, by contrast, as an impossible destination, an unacceptable destiny or one that is acceptable only as temporary refuge or a secondary, accessory position. This sense of social direction which orients agents, according to their modesty or daring, their disinterestedness or thirst for profit, towards the risky, long-term investments of journalism, serials or the theatre, is the basis of the astonishingly close correspondence that is found between positions and dispositions, between the social characteristics of 'posts' and the social characteristics of the agents who fill them. The correspondence is such that in all cases of coincidence and concordance in which the position is in a sense materialized in the dispositions of its occupants, it would be equally wrong to impute everything solely to position or solely to dispositions.

> The mechanistic model that is, more or less consciously, put into operation when social origin, or any other variable, is made the principle of a linear series of determinations – e.g. father's occupation, more or less crudely defined, determining position, e.g. occupational position, which in turn determines opinions – totally ignores the effects of the field, in particular those which result from the way in which the influx of newcomers is quantitatively and qualitatively regulated.[24] Thus the absence of statistical relation between the agents' social origin and their *position-takings* may result from an unobserved transformation of the field and of the relationship between social origin and *position-taking*, such that, for two successive generations, the same dispositions will lead to different *position-takings*, or even opposing ones (which will tend to cancel each other out).

There is nothing mechanical about the relationship between the field and the habitus. The space of available positions does indeed help to determine the properties expected and even demanded of possible candidates, and therefore the categories of agents they can attract and above all *retain*; but the perception of the space of possible positions and trajectories and the appreciation of the value each of them derives from its location in the space depend on these dispositions. It follows as a point of method that one cannot give a full account of the relationship obtaining at a given moment between the space of positions and the space of dispositions, and, therefore, of the set of *social trajectories* (or constructed biographies),[25] unless one establishes the configuration, at the moment, and at the various critical turning-points in each career, of the space of available possibilities (in particular, the economic and symbolic hierarchy of the genres, schools, styles, manners, subjects, etc.), the social value attached to each of them, and also the meaning and value they received for the different agents or classes of agents in terms of the socially constituted categories of perception, and appreciation they applied to them.

It would be quite unjust and futile to reject this demand for complete reconstitution on the ground (which is undeniable) that it is difficult to perform in practice and in some cases impossible (for example, a special study would be required in order to determine, for each relevant period, the *critical points* in the trajectories corresponding to each field, which are often unquestioningly assumed to be situated where they are today). Scientific progress may consist, in some cases, in identifying all the presuppositions and begged questions implicitly mobilized by the seemingly most impeccable research, and in proposing programmes for fundamental research which would really raise all the questions which ordinary research treats as resolved, simply because it has failed to raise them. In fact, if we are sufficiently attentive, we find numerous testimonies to this perception of the space of possibilities. We see it for example in the image of the great predecessors, who provide the terms for self-definition, such as the complementary figures of Taine and Renan, for one generation of novelists and intellectuals, or the opposing personalities of Mallarmé and Verlaine for a whole generation of poets; more simply, we see it in the exalted vision of the writer's or artist's craft which may shape the aspirations of a whole generation: 'The new literary generation grew up thoroughly impregnated with the spirit of 1830. The verses of Hugo and Musset, the plays of Alexandre Dumas and Alfred de Vigny circulated in the schools despite the hostility of the University; an infinite number of Mediaeval novels, lyrical confessions and despairing verses were composed under cover of classroom desks'.[26] One could quote whole pages in which Cassagne evokes the adolescent enthusiasms of Maxime Ducamp and Renan, Flaubert and Baudelaire or Fromentin. But one can also quote this very significant passage from *Manette Salomon*, in which Goncourt and Goncourt show that what attracts and fascinates in the occupation of artist is not so much the art itself as the artist's lifestyle, the artist's life (the same logic nowadays governs the diffusion of the model of the intellectual): 'At heart, Anatole was called by art much less than he was attracted by the artist's life. He dreamt of the studio. He aspired to it with a schoolboy's imaginings and the appetites of his nature. He saw in it those horizons of Bohemia which enchant from a distance: the novel of Poverty, the shedding of bonds and rules, a life of freedom, indiscipline and disorder, every day filled with accident, adventure and the unexpected, an escape from the tidy, orderly household, from the family and its tedious Sundays, the jeering of the bourgeois, the voluptuous mystery of the female model, work that entails no effort, the right to wear fancy dress all year, a sort of unending carnival; such were the images and temptations which arose for him from the austere pursuit of art'.[27]

Thus, writers and artists endowed with different, even opposing dispositions can coexist, for a time at least, in the same positions. The structural constraints inscribed in the field set limits to the free play of dispositions; but there are different ways of playing within these limits. Thus, whereas the occupants of the dominant positions, especially in economic terms, such as bourgeois theatre, are strongly homogeneous, the avant-garde positions, which are defined mainly negatively, by their opposition to the dominant positions, bring together for a certain time writers and artists from very different origins, whose interests will sooner or later diverge.[28] These dominated groups, whose unity is essentially oppositional, tend to fly apart when they achieve recognition, the symbolic profits of which often go to a small number, or even to only one of them, and when the external cohesive forces weaken. As is shown by the progressive separation between the Symbolists and the Decadents (analysed below), or the break-up of the Impressionist group, the factor of division does in this case lie in dispositions, the basis of aesthetic and political position-takings whose divergencies are felt the more strongly when associated with unequal degrees of consecration.[29]

Starting out from the same, barely marked, position in the field, and defined by the same opposition to Naturalism and the Parnasse group from which Verlaine and Mallarmé, their leaders, were each excluded – the Decadents and the Symbolists diverged as they attained full social identity.[30] The latter, drawn from more comfortable social backgrounds (i.e. the middle or upper bourgeoisie or the aristocracy) and endowed with substantial educational capital, are opposed to the former, who are often the sons of craftsmen and virtually devoid of educational capital, as the *salon* (Mallarmé's 'Tuesdays') to the café, the right bank to the left bank and bohemia, audacity to prudence,[31] and, in aesthetic terms, as 'clarity' and 'simplicity' based on 'common sense' and 'naïveté' to a hermeticism based on an explicit theory which rejects all the old forms; politically, the Symbolists are indifferent and pessimistic, the Decadents committed and progressive.[32] It is clear that the field-effect which results from the opposition between the two schools, and which is intensified by the process of institutionalization that is needed to constitute a fully-fledged literary group, i.e. an instrument for accumulating and concentrating symbolic capital (with the adoption of a name, the drawing-up of manifestos and programmes and the setting-up of aggregation rites, such as regular meetings), tends to consecrate and underscore the critical differences. Verlaine, skilfully making a virtue of necessity, celebrated naïveté (just as Champfleury countered 'art for art's sake' with 'sincerity in art') whereas Mallarmé, who sets himself up as the theorist of 'the enigma in poetry', found himself pushed ever further into hermeticism by Verlaine's striving for sincerity and simplicity.[33] And as if to provide a crucial proof of the effect of dispositions, it was the richest Decadents who joined the Symbolists (Albert Aurier) or drew closer to them (Ernest Raynaud), whereas those Symbolists who were closest to the Decadents in terms of social origin, René Ghil and Ajalbert, were excluded from the Symbolist group, the former because of his faith in progress and the latter, who ended up as a realist novelist, because his works were not considered sufficiently obscure.

The habitus and the possibles

The propensity to move towards the economically most risky positions, and above all the capacity to persist in them (a condition for all avant-garde undertakings which precede the demands of the market), even when they secure no short-term economic profit, seem to depend to a large extent on possession of substantial economic and social capital. This is, first, because economic capital provides the conditions for freedom from economic necessity, a private income [*la rente*] being one of the best substitutes for sales [*la vente*], as Théophile Gautier said to Feydeau: 'Flaubert was smarter than us . . . He had the wit to come into the world with money, something that is indispensable for anyone who wants to get anywhere in art'.[34]

> Those who do manage to stay in the risky positions long enough to receive the symbolic profit they can bring are indeed mainly drawn from the most privileged categories, who have also had the advantage of not having to devote time and energy to secondary, 'bread-and-butter' activities. Thus, as Ponton shows,[35] some of the Parnassians, all from the petite bourgeoisie, either had to abandon poetry at some stage and turn to better-paid literary activities, such as the 'novel of manners', or, from the outset, devoted part of their time to complementary activities such as plays or novels (e.g. François Coppée, Catulle Mendès, Jean Aicard), whereas the wealthier Parnassians could concentrate almost exclusively on their art (and when they did change to another genre, it was only after a long poetic career). We also find that the least well-off writers resign themselves more readily to 'industrial literature', in which writing becomes a job like any other.

It is also because economic capital provides the guarantees [*assurances*] which can be the basis of self-assurance, audacity and indifference to profit – dispositions which, together with the flair associated with possession of a large social capital and the corresponding familiarity with the field, i.e. the art of sensing the new hierarchies and the new structures of the chances of profit, point towards the outposts, the most exposed positions of the avant-garde, and towards the riskiest investments, which are also, however, very often the most profitable symbolically, and in the long run, at least for the earliest investors.

The sense of investment seems to be one of the dispositions most closely linked to social and geographical origin, and, consequently, through the associated social capital, one of the mediations through which the effects of the opposition between Parisian and provincial origin make themselves felt in the logic of the field.[36] Thus we find that as a rule those richest in economic, cultural and social capital are the first to move into the new positions (and this seems to be true in all fields: economic, scientific, etc.). This is the case with the writers around Paul Bourget, who abandoned Symbolist poetry for a new form of novel which broke with Naturalism and was better adjusted to the expectations of the cultivated audience. By contrast, a faulty sense of investment, linked to social distance (among writers from the working class or the petite bourgeoisie) or geographical distance (among provincials and foreigners), inclines beginners to aim for the dominant positions at a time when, precisely because of their attractiveness (due, for example, to the economic profits they secure, in the case of the Naturalist novel, or the symbolic profits they promise, in the case of Symbolist poetry) and the intensified competition for them, the profits are tending to decline. It may also make them persist in declining or threatened positions when the best-informed agents are abandoning them. Or again, it may lead them to be drawn by the attraction of the dominant sites towards positions incompatible with the dispositions they bring to them, and to discover their 'natural place' only when it is too late, i.e. after wasting much time, through the effect of the forces of the field and in the mode of relegation. An ideal-typical example of this is Léon Cladel (1835–92), the son of a Montauban saddler, who came to Paris in 1857, joined the Parnasse movement and, after seven years of fairly impoverished bohemian existence, returned to his native Quercy and devoted himself to the regionalist novel.[37] The whole oeuvre of this eternally displaced writer is marked by the antinomy between his dispositions, linked to his starting point, to which he eventually returned, and the positions he aimed at and temporarily occupied: 'His ambition was to glorify his native Quercy, a Latin soil trodden by rustic Hercules, in a sort of ancient, barbarous "geste". In distilling the arrogant poses of village champions from furious peasant scuffles, Cladel aspired to be numbered among the modest rivals of Hugo and Leconte de Lisle. Thus were born *Ompdrailles* and *La Fête votive de Bartholomé-Porte-Glaive*, bizarre epics, pastiching the *Iliad* and the *Odyssey* in inflated or Rabelaisian language'.[38] Tension and incoherence, oscillating between parody and utter seriousness, are manifest in this project of describing the peasants of Quercy in the style of Leconte de Lisle: 'Being instinctively led', he writes in the preface to his novel *Celui-de-la-croix-aux-boeufs* (1878), 'towards the study of plebeian types and milieux, it was almost inevitable that there would sooner or later be a conflict between the coarse and the refined'.[39] Always out of step, Cladel was a peasant among the Parnassians (who, objectively and subjectively, placed him with the 'populace', like his friend Courbet),[40] and a petit-bourgeois among the peasants of his native region. Not surprisingly, the very form and content of the rustic novel to which he resigned himself, in which rehabilitation gives way to self-indulgent depiction of peasant savagery, express the contradictions of a position entirely defined by the trajectory which led to it: 'A beggar's son, a beggar dreamer, he had an innate love of village life and country people. If, from the outset, without any shilly-shallying, he had sought to render them with that holy roughness of touch which distinguishes the early manner of the master painters, perhaps he would have made a place for himself among the most sparkling young writers of his generation'.[41]

But these forced returns to the 'people' are only particular cases of a more general model. And all the evidence suggests that the confrontation, within the artistic and literary field, with bourgeois, Parisian artists and writers, which impels them towards the 'people', induces writers and artists of working-class or petit-bourgeois origin to accept themselves for what they are and, like Courbet, to mark themselves positively with what is stigmatized – their provincial accent, dialect, 'proletarian' style, etc. – but the more strongly, the less successful their initial attempts at *assimilation* have been. Thus, Champfleury, a writer from very modest provincial petit-bourgeois origins, after having for some time been 'torn between two tendencies, a realism *à la* Monnier and German-style poetry, Romantic and sentimental',[42] found himself impelled towards militant realism by the failure of his first endeavours and perhaps especially by consciousness of his difference, provoked by contact or objective competition with the Parisian writers, which sent him towards 'the people', i.e.

to realism in his manner and to objects excluded from the legitimate art of the day. And this negative return to the people is no less ambiguous, and suspect, than the regionalist writers' retreat to the peasantry. Hostility to the libertarian audacities and arbitrary populism of the bourgeois intellectuals can be the basis of an anti-intellectual populism, more or less conservative, in which 'the people are once again merely a projection in fantasy of relations internal to the intellectual field. A typical example of this field-effect can be seen in the trajectory of the same Champfleury, who, after having been the leader of the young realist writers of 1850 and the 'theorist' of the realist movement in literature and painting, was increasingly eclipsed by Flaubert and then by the Goncourts and Zola. He became a state official at the Sèvres porcelain factory and set himself up as the historian of popular imagery and literature, and, after a series of shifts and turns, the official theorist (awarded the Légion d'Honneur in 1867) of a conservatism based on exaltation of popular wisdom – in particular, of the resignation to hierarchies that is expressed in popular arts and traditions.[43]

Thus, it is within each state of the field that – as a function of the structure of the possibles which are manifested through the different positions and the properties of the occupants (particularly with respect to social origin and the corresponding dispositions), and also as a function of the positions actually and potentially occupied within the field (experienced as success or failure) – the dispositions associated with a certain social origin are specified by being enacted in structurally marked practices; and the same dispositions lead to opposite aesthetic or political positions, depending on the state of the field in relation to which they have to express themselves. One only has to consider the example of realism in literature or painting to see the futility of the attempts of some contemporary critics to relate the characteristics of this art directly to the characteristics of the social group – the peasantry – from which its inventors or advocates (Champfleury or Courbet) originate. It is only within a determinate state of an artistic field, and in the relationship with other artistic positions and their occupants, themselves socially characterized, that the dispositions of the realist painters and artists, which might have been expressed elsewhere in other forms of art, were fulfilled in a form of art which, within that structure, appeared as a form of aesthetic and political revolt against 'bourgeois' art and artists (or the spiritualist criticism which supported them) and, through them, against the 'bourgeois'.

To make this argument fully convincing, one would have to show how habitus, as systems of dispositions, are effectively realized only in relation to a determinate structure of positions socially marked by the social properties of their occupants, through which they manifest themselves. Thus, nothing would be more naïve than to endeavour to understand the differences between the *Théâtre de l'Oeuvre* and the *Théâtre libre* solely in terms of the differences of habitus between their respective founders, Lugné-Poe, the son of a Parisian bourgeois, and Antoine, a provincial petit-bourgeois.[44] Yet it seems quite impossible to understand them solely on the basis of the structural positions of the two institutions which, initially at least, seem to reproduce the opposition between the founders' dispositions. This is only to be expected, since the former are the realization of the latter in a certain state of the field, marked by the opposition between Symbolism, which is more bourgeois – not least in the characteristics of its advocates – and Naturalism, which is more petit-bourgeois. Antoine, who, like the Naturalists, and with their theoretical support, defined himself against bourgeois theatre, proposed a systematic transformation of *mise en scène*, a *specific* theatrical revolution based on a coherent thesis. Emphasizing milieu over characters, the determining context over the determined text, he made the stage 'a coherent, complete universe over which the director is sole master'.[45] By contrast, Lugné-Poe's 'scrappy but fertile' directing, which defined itself in relation to bourgeois theatre, but also in relation to Antoine's innovations, led to performances described as 'a mixture of refined invention and sloppiness'; inspired by a project that was 'sometimes demagogic, sometimes elitist', they brought together an audience in which anarchists rubbed shoulders with mystics.[46] In short, without exploring any further an opposition which appears everywhere, between the writers, newspapers or critics who support one or the other, between the authors performed and the content of the works, with, on one side, the 'slice of life', which in some ways resembles vaudeville, and, on the other, intellectual refinements inspired by the idea, enunciated by Mallarmé, of the multi-levelled work, it can be seen that the opposition between class dispositions receives its particular content in a particular space. There is every reason to think that, as this case suggests, the weight of dispositions – and the explanatory force of 'social origin' – is particularly strong when one is dealing with a position that is in the process of birth, still to be made (rather than already made, established and capable of imposing its own norms on its occupants); and, more generally, that the scope allowed to dispositions varies according to the state of the field (in particular, its autonomy), the position in the field and the degree of institutionalization of the position.

Finally, we must ask explicitly a question which is bound to be asked: what is the degree of conscious strategy, cynical calculation, in the objective strategies which observation brings to light and which ensure the correspondence between positions and dispositions? One only has to read literary testimonies, correspondence, diaries and, especially perhaps, explicit position-takings on the literary world as such (like those collected by Huret) to see that there is no simple answer to these questions and that lucidity is always partial and is, once again, a matter of position and trajectory within the field, so that it varies from one agent and one moment to another. As for awareness of the logic of the game as such, and of the *illusio* on which it is based, I had been inclined to think that it was excluded by membership of the field, which presupposes (and induces) belief in everything which depends on the existence of the field, i.e. literature, the writer, etc., because such lucidity would make the literary or artistic undertaking itself a cynical mystification, a conscious trickery. So I thought, until I came across a text by Mallarmé which provides both the programme and the balance-sheet of a rigorous science of the literary field and the recognized fictions that are engendered within it: 'We know, captives of an absolute formula that, indeed, there is only that which is. Forthwith to dismiss the cheat, however, on a pretext, would indict our inconsequence, denying the pleasure we want to take: for that *beyond* is its agent, and the engine I might say were I not loath to perform, in public, the impious dismantling of the fiction and consequently of the literary mechanism, display the principal part or nothing. But I venerate how, by a trick, we project to a height forfended – and with thunder! – the conscious lack in us of what shines up there. What is it for? A game'.[47] This quasi-Feuerbachian theory reduces beauty, which is sometimes thought of as a Platonic Idea, endowed with an objective, transcendent existence, to no more than the projection into a metaphysical beyond of what is lacking in the here-and-now of literary life. But is that how it is to be taken? Hermeticism, in this case, perfectly fulfils its function: to utter 'in public' the true nature of the field, and of its mechanisms, is sacrilege *par excellence*, the unforgivable sin which all the censorships constituting the field seek to repress. These are things that can only be said in such a way that they are not said. If Mallarmé can, without excluding himself from the field, utter the truth about a field which excludes the *publishing* of its own truth, this is because he says it in a language which is designed to be *recognized* within the field because everything, in its very *form*, that of euphemism and *Verneinung*, affirms that he recognizes its censorships. Marcel Duchamp was to do exactly the same thing when he made artistic acts out of his bluffs, demystificatory mystifications which denounce fiction as mere fiction, and with it the collective belief which is the basis of this 'legitimate' imposture (as Austin would have put it). But Mallarmé's hermeticism, which bespeaks his concern not to destroy the *illusio*, has another basis too: if the Platonic illusion is the 'agent' of a pleasure which we take only because 'we *want* to take it', if the pleasure of the love of art has its source in unawareness of producing the source of what produces it, then it is understandable that one might, by another willing suspension of disbelief, choose to 'venerate' the authorless trickery which places the fragile fetish beyond the reach of critical lucidity.

Notes

1 The status of 'social art' is, in this respect, thoroughly ambiguous. Although it relates artistic or literary production to external functions (which is what the advocates of art for art's sake object to about it), it shares with art for art's sake a radical rejection of the dominant principle of hierarchy and of the 'bourgeois' art which recognizes it.

2 The specific, and therefore autonomous, power which writers and artists possess *qua* writers and artists must be distinguished from the alienated, heteronomous power they wield *qua* experts or cadres – a share in domination, but with the status of dominated mandatories, granted to them by the dominant.

3 Thus, writers and artists who are 'second-rank' in terms of the specific criteria may invoke populism and social art to impose their reign on the 'leading intellectuals' who, as has happened in China and elsewhere, will protest against the disparity between the revolutionary ideal and the reality, i.e. the reign of functionaries devoted to the Party. See M. Godman, *Literary Dissent in Communist China* (Cambridge, Mass.: Harvard University Press, 1967).

4 Throughout this passage, 'writer' can be replaced by 'artist', 'philosopher', 'intellectual', etc. The intensity of the struggle, and the degree to which it takes visible, and therefore conscious, forms, no doubt vary according to the genre and according to the rarity of the specific competence each genre requires in different periods, i.e. according to the probability of 'unfair competition' or 'illegal exercise of the profession'. (This no doubt explains why the intellectual field, with the permanent threat of casual essayism, is one of the key areas in which to grasp the logic of the struggles which pervade all fields.)

5 Only just over a third of the writers in the sample studied by Rémy Ponton had had any higher education, whether or not it led to a degree. See R. Ponton, 'Le champ littéraire de 1865 à 1905' (Paris: École des Hautes Études en Sciences Sociales, 1977), p. 43. For the comparison between the literary field and other fields, see C. Charle, 'Situation du champ littéraire', *Littérature*, 44 (1981), pp. 8–20.

6 This struggle can be observed as much in the literary field as in the artistic field (with the opposition between 'pure' art and 'bourgeois' art) and in each genre (with, for example, the opposition between avant-garde theatre and 'middle brow' boulevard theatre).

7 See R. W. Lee, *Ut pictura poesis: The Humanistic Theory of Painting* (New York: W. W. Norton, 1967); F. Bologna, *Dalle arte minori all' industrial design: storia di un' idealogia* (Bari: Laterza, 1972).

8 See D. Gamboni, 'Redon écrivain et épistolier', *Revue d'art* (1980), pp. 68–71, and 'Remarques sur la critique d'art, l'histoire de l'art et le champ artistique à propos d'Odilon Redon', *Revue suisse d'art et d'archéologie*, 2 (1982), pp. 57–63.

9 C. Charle, *La Crise littéraire à l'époque du naturalisme* (Paris: Presses de l'École Normale Supérieure, 1979), p. 37.

10 J.-L. Fabiani, 'La crise du champ philosophique (1880–1914): contribution à l'histoire sociale du système d'enseignement', doctoral dissertation (Paris: École des Hautes Études Sciences Sociales, 1980), p. 100.

11 Ponton, 'Le champ littéraire de 1865 à 1905', p. 206. An exemplary expression of a field-effect converted into an explicit project can be seen in this declaration of Zola's: 'Anyway, if I have time, I will do what they want!' (J. Huret, *Enquête sur l'évolution littéraire* (Vanves: Thot, 1982), p. 160; first published Paris: Charpentier, 1891). In other words: I myself will perform the suppression of Naturalism, i.e. of myself, which my adversaries vainly seek to perform.

12 Cited by Fabiani, 'La crise du champ philosophique', p. 82.

13 Zola does not fail to point out this discrepancy between positional age and 'real' age: 'In their dallying with stupidities, with such futilities, at such a grave moment in the evolution of ideas, all these young people, all between thirty and forty, remind me of nutshells bobbing on

Niagara Falls! The fact is, they have nothing beneath them but a gigantic, empty pretension!'
(cited by Huret, *Enquête sur l'évolution littéraire*, p. 158).

14   See P. Lidsky, *Les Écrivains contre la commune* (Paris: Maspero, 1970), pp. 26–7.

15   In every field, the dominant have an interest in continuity, identity and reproduction, whereas
the dominated, the newcomers, are for discontinuity, rupture and subversion.

16   Divisions between generations therefore occur in accordance with the logic specific to the
struggles which characterize each field (so that oppositions formed in the literary field cannot
properly be extended to the whole social field – as was often done in late nineteenth-century
France, i.e. at a time when the opposition between the generations tended to be generalized
to the whole literary field. See R. Wohl, *The Generation of 1914* (Cambridge, Mass.: Harvard
University Press, 1979).

17   V. Shklovsky, *Sur la théorie de la prose* (Lausanne: L'Age d'Homme, 1973), p. 24.

18   On the question of returns and Duchamp's approach to it, see 'The Production of Belief' (ch.
2 in P. Bourdieu, *The Field of Cultural Production* (Cambridge: Polity Press, 1993)).

19   The perception called for by a work produced in accordance with the logic of the field is a
differential, distinctive perception, attentive to the differences, the deviations from what is
normal, usual, *modal* at the moment in question, i.e. from other works, both contemporary
and, especially, past ones – in short, a historical perception.

20   This was said in so many words by a Symbolist poet questioned by Huret: 'In all cases, I
consider the worst Symbolist poet far superior to any of the writers enrolled under the
banner of Naturalism' (Huret, *Enquête sur l'évolution littéraire*, p. 329). Another example, less
forthright but closer to the experience which really inflects choices: 'At fifteen, nature tells a
young man whether he is cut out to be a poet or should *be content with mere prose* [*la simple
prose*]' (*ibid.*, p. 299, emphasis added). It is clear what the shift from poetry to the novel means
for someone who has strongly internalized these hierarchies. (The division into castes separated by absolute frontiers which override real continuities and overlappings produces everywhere – e.g. in the relationships between disciplines, philosophy and the social sciences, the
pure and applied sciences, etc. – the same effects, *certitudo sui* and the refusal to demean
oneself, etc.)

21   The painters still had to win their autonomy with respect to the writers, without whom they
would perhaps not have succeeded in freeing themselves from the constraints of the bureaucracies and academicism.

22   To those who seek to trace a direct relationship between any producers and the group from
which they draw their economic support, it has to be pointed out that the logic of a relatively
autonomous field means that one can use the resources provided by a group or institution to
produce products deliberately or unconsciously directed against the interests or values of that
group or institution.

23   It goes without saying that freedom with respect to institutions can never be truly institutionalized. This contradiction, which every attempt to institutionalize heresy comes up
against (it is the antinomy of the Reformed Church), is seen clearly in the ambivalent image of
institutional acts of consecration, and not only those performed by the most heteronomous
institutions, such as academics (one thinks of Sartre's refusal of the Nobel Prize).

24   Although I realize that theoretical warnings count for little against the social drives which
induce simplistic, apologetic or terroristic use of more-or-less scientific-seeming reference to
'father's occupation', it seems useful to condemn the inclination – in which the worst
adversaries and acolytes too easily find common ground – to reduce the model that is
proposed to the mechanical and mechanistic mode of thinking in which inherited capital
(internalized in habitus, or objectified) determines the position occupied, which in turn
directly determines position-takings.

25   *Social trajectory or constructed biography* is defined as the set of successive movements of an agent

in a structured (hierarchized) space, itself subject to displacements and distortions, or, more precisely, in the structure of the distribution of the different kinds of capital which are at stake in the field, economic capital and the specific capital of consecration (in its different kinds). These movements, which define *social ageing*, are of two orders. They may be limited to one sector of the field and lie along the same axis of consecration, in which case ageing is marked by a positive, zero or negative accumulation of specific capital; or they may imply a change of sector and the reconversion of one kind of specific capital into another (e.g. the case of the Symbolist poets who moved into the psychological novel) or of specific capital into economic capital (in the case of shifts from poetry to the 'novel of manners' or the theatre or, still more clearly, to cabaret or serialized fiction).

26   A. Cassagne, *La Théorie de l'art pour l'art en France chez les derniers romantiques et les premiers réalistes* (Geneva: Slatkine Reprints, 1979), pp. 75ff. Originally published Paris, 1906.

27   E. de Goncourt and J. de Goncourt, *Manette Salomon* (Paris: Union générale d'éditions, 1979), p. 32.

28   The solidarity which is built up, within artistic groups, between the richest and the poorest is one of the means which enables some impecunious artists to carry on despite the absence of resources provided by the market.

29   See M. Rogers, 'The Batignolles Group: Creators of Impressionism', in M. C. Albrecht *et al.*, eds, T*he Sociology of Art and Literature* (New York: Praeger, 1970).

30   Similarity of position, especially when defined negatively, is not sufficient to found a literary or artistic group, although it tends to favour rapprochement and exchanges. This was the case, for example, with the advocates of 'art for art's sake', who were linked by relations of esteem and sympathy without actually forming a group. Gautier received Flaubert, Théodore de Banville, the Goncourt brothers and Baudelaire at his Thursday dinner parties. The rapprochement between Flaubert and Baudelaire stemmed from the near simultaneity of their early works and their trials. The Goncourts and Flaubert much appreciated each other, and the former met Bouillet at Flaubert's home. Théodore de Banville and Baudelaire were long-standing friends. Louis Ménard, a close friend of Baudelaire, Banville and Leconte de Lisle, became one of the intimates of Renan. Barbey d'Aurevilly was one of Baudelaire's most ardent advocates. Whereas they were close acquaintances, these writers were little seen in high society since their high degree of professionalization limited their social intercourse (see Cassagne, *La Théorie de l'art pour l'art*, pp. 130–4).

31   'The Decadents did not mean to sweep away the past. They urged necessary reforms, conducted *methodically* and *prudently*. By contrast, the Symbolists wanted to *keep nothing* of our old ways and aspired to create an entirely new mode of expression' (E. Reynaud, *La Mêlée symboliste*, vol. 1 (Paris: La Renaissance du livre, 1918), p. 118, cited by J. Jurt, 'Symbolistes et Décadentes, deux groupes littéraires parallèles', mimeo (1982), p. 12 (emphasis added).

32   Ponton, 'Le champ littéraire de 1865 à 1905', pp. 299ff.; Jurt, 'Symbolistes et Décadentes', p. 12.

33   The opposition between Mallarmé and Verlaine is the paradigmatic form of an opposition which was gradually constituted and more and more strongly asserted through the nineteenth century – that between the professional writer, occupied full time by his research and conscious of his mastery, and the amateur writer, a bourgeois dilettante who wrote as a pastime or hobby, or a frivolous, impoverished bohemian. At odds with the bourgeois world and its values, the professional writers, in the first rank of whom are the advocates of 'art for art's sake', are also set apart in countless ways from the bohemian sub-culture, its pretension, its incoherences and its very disorder, which is incompatible with methodical production. Flaubert must be cited: 'I maintain, and this should be a practical dogma for the artistic life, that one must divide one's existence into two parts: live like a bourgeois and think like a demigod' (*Correspondence*, cited by Cassagne, *La Théorie de l'art pour l'art*, p. 307). And the

Goncourt brothers: 'Literature is conceived only in silence and as it were in the sleep of the activity of the things and facts around one. Emotions are not good for the gestation of the imagination. One needs regular, calm days, a bourgeois state of one's whole being, a grocer's tranquillity, to give birth to the grand, the tormented, the poignant, the pathetic . . . Those who spend themselves in passion, in nervous agitation, will never write a book of passion' (*Journal*, cited by Cassagne, *La Théorie de l'art pour l'art*, p. 308). This opposition between the two categories of writers is no doubt the source of specifically political antagonisms, which were particularly manifested at the time of the Commune.

34   Cited by Cassagne, *La Théorie de l'art pour l'art*, p. 218.

35   Ponton, 'Le champ littéraire de 1865 à 1905', pp. 69–70.

36   An example of this is the case of Anatole France, whose father's unusual position as a Paris bookseller enabled him to acquire a social capital and a familiarity with the world of letters which compensated for his low economic and cultural capital.

37   Ponton, 'Le champ littéraire de 1865 à 1905', p. 57.

38   P. Vernois, 'La fin de la pastorale', in *Histoire littéraire de la France* (Paris: Éditions Sociales, 1977), p. 272.

39   Cited in *ibid.*, p. 272.

40   'As described by Champfleury (a Realist novelist, a friend of Courbet and Cladel), the Brasserie Allemande de Paris, where Realism emerged as a movement, was a Protestant village where there reigned rustic manners and a frank gaiety. The leader, Courbet, was a "journeyman", he went around shaking hands, he talked and ate a great deal, strong and stubborn as a peasant, the very opposite of the dandy of the 1830s and '40s. His behaviour in Paris was deliberately popular; he ostentatiously spoke patois, he smoked, sang and joked like a man of the people. Observers were impressed by the plebeian, domestic familiarity of his technique . . . Du Camp wrote that he painted "like a man polishing boots" ' (M. Schapiro, 'Courbet et l'imagerie populaire', in *Style, artiste et société* (Paris: Gallimard, 1982), p. 293).

41   Cladel, cited by Ponton, 'Le champ littéraire de 1865 à 1905', p. 98. To assess how much the regionalist novel, the paradigmatic expression of one of the forms of the regionalist – and, more generally, populist – enterprise, derives from being the product of a negative vocation, one would have to compare systematically all those who ended up writing populist novels after such a trajectory with those who are exceptions, such as Eugène Le Roy, a minor civil servant in the Périgord who passed through Paris, author of *Le Moulin du Frau* (1895) and *Jacquou le Croquant* (1899), etc., and especially Émile Guillaumin, a sharecropper in the Bourbonnais and author of *La Vie d'un simple* (1904).

42   Schapiro, 'Courbet et l'imagerie populaire', p. 299.

43   *Ibid.*, p. 315ff.

44   Ponton, 'Le champ littéraire de 1865 à 1905', p. 73.

45   B. Dort, 'Vers un nouveau théâtre', in *Histoire littéraire de la France*, vol. 5 (Paris: Editions Sociales, 1977) p. 615.

46   *Ibid.*, p. 617. In terms of the same logic, Ponton ('Le champ littéraire de 1865 à 1905', pp. 80–2) observes that among the boulevard playwrights, directly subjected to the financial sanction of bourgeois taste, writers from the working classes or petite bourgeoisie are very strongly underrepresented, whereas they are more strongly represented in vaudeville, a comic genre which gives more scope for the easy effects of farcical or salacious scenes and also for a sort of semi-critical freedom, and that the authors who write for both boulevard theatre and vaudeville have characteristics intermediate between those of specialists in each genre.

47   S. Mallarmé, 'La musique et les lettres', in *Oeuvres complètes* (Paris: Gallimard (Pléiade), 1945), p. 647. On this text and the reading put forward by Heinrich Merkl, see Jurt, 'Symbolistes et Décadentes'.

PART TWO

The impact of print

EDITORS' INTRODUCTION

The development of script traced back to Sumerian cuneiform and forward through the alphabet of the Phoenicians to those of the Greeks and the Romans, as discussed in Scott B. Noegel's piece, provides a fascinating history of the movement from speech to writing. Previous accounts of this development were incomplete: not in the sense of a lack of self-sufficiency, although they did contain their own lacunae and cruces, but rather in their failure to take into account the social and cultural results of the technological changes they described. Noegel's piece rectifies to a great extent this deficiency, taking what had resembled a history of printing and bringing it more in line with the ambitious programme of book history outlined in the first part of this Reader.

Walter Ong's use of the terms 'orality' and 'literacy' itself attempts to indicate the wider perspective than that encapsulated in 'speech' and 'writing'. His approach spans past and present both in the sense of looking at historical evidence relating to the transition from orality to literacy and at recent anthropological and other studies of that transition in remoter parts of the globe, on the one hand, and in the sense of employing the anthropologist's toolbox to recreate the past, on the other. In doing so, Ong acknow-ledges the greater precision of the written – 'written words sharpen analysis, for the individual words are called upon to do more' – but its greater ability, in the absence of an interlocutor, to be ambiguous or deceitful. Hence the continuing oral nature of most legal systems where the cross-examination of witnesses remains a better guarantor of justice than scrutiny of written statements. Ong is clear that not only does the transition bring change in thought as well as new modes of written expression, but this change was not always received positively. He draws parallels with reactions to the use of calculators and others can be made with the growth of computer-mediated communication, what we termed in the Introduction the third revolution.

Marcel Thomas's piece surveys the history of the production and consumption of manuscripts between the mid-thirteenth and late fifteenth centuries in Western Europe. His survey usefully draws attention to the development of sophisticated networks for the distribution of texts. In the medieval period, Roger Chartier makes similar points in discussing the spread of reading skills at a much later date than Ong's and Thomas's medieval European examples. Chartier stresses 'a persistent hostility to writing and its dissemination', a dissemination accelerated by the mass production of the printing press. The learned, and privileged, classes had a perhaps obvious antipathy to a phenomenon which challenged their status although the arguments could always be wrapped in an ersatz idealism: that printing produced multiple copies of faulty editions; that it issued heterodox works to undermine morality and society; and that knowledge spread in so facile a manner would be misunderstood and distorted. Jan-Dirk Müller adds to these objections a fifteenth-century concern for loss of interaction, 'such as had always characterized the medieval manuscript culture, even where it was not oriented toward oral forms of communication', and loss of longevity, guaranteed through the material characteristics of the individual manuscript as opposed to the decisions of printers as publishers. Antagonism came, moreover, from the unlettered classes as well, arising from the associations of writing with the law, with legally enforced duties and obligations, and with power whether legal or magical. Even a working-man's diary written as late as 1802 or 1803 can mention a work on black magic among his few references to books.

The relationship of writing to power is delineated by D. F. McKenzie in his discussion of the Treaty of Waitangi set in the context of Maori orality/literacy and British literacy/print culture. The missionaries developed a Maori alphabet so that an oral culture could read the Scriptures (while the Maoris wished to use their new tool to write letters) and encouraged printing so that copies of the Word of God could be circulated throughout New Zealand. C. A. Bayly recounts the entry of print into the rich and long-standing manuscript culture of nineteenth-century India. It is clear, from Bayly's description of the communication methods and networks available within the public sphere at that time as much as from McKenzie's analysis, that a simplistic, ameliorist model of progression from oral to literate to print has little validity. It should also make us wary of adding computer-mediated as the current culmination of such a movement.

Yet the conventional image of progress we hold in Western Europe and North America places printing at the heart of what has since been called 'the Enlightenment project' but which has its roots in the confluence of Humanism and the Reformation. Eisenstein, in the extract reproduced here, exercises some caution in claiming that 'an increase in the output of old texts contributed to the formulation of new theories' but the general thrust of her work has been to strengthen that Whiggish, and Eurocentric, view of history. More recently, Adrian Johns's work challenges Elizabeth Eisenstein's assessment of the revolutionary impact of the printing press on Western Renaissance culture, suggesting that the effect was less overwhelming than we believe. The result is a radical reworking of previously uncontested views of Western print culture history.

Chapter 10

Scott B. Noegel

TEXT, SCRIPT, AND MEDIA
New observations on scribal activity in the ancient Near East

Living in an age of microchips and monitors, one might think that the ancient eras that saw the heyday of the stylus share nothing in common with our baud-rate generation. Yet, as Edward Mendelson wrote in a report on Web sites created by Benedictine monks,

> the relations between modern Web sites and medieval scriptoria, or writing rooms, is even closer than these monks may have guessed. The technology that connects millions of pages on the World Wide Web derives ultimately from techniques invented by the scribes and scholars who copied out the Bible more than a thousand years ago.[1]

Mendelson's report focused primarily on the similarity of biblical cross-referencing systems to Web links, but it also offered new ways of looking at the role of media within the matrix of ancient scribal culture:

> The marginal references to the Bible and the hyperlinks of the World Wide Web may be the only two systems ever invented that give concrete expression to the idea that everything in the world hangs together – that every event, every fact, every datum is connected to every other. Where the two systems differ drastically is in what their connections mean.[2]

Mendelson's remark illustrates how cybermedia have forced us to rethink both modern and ancient text-related issues and suggests that these two types of issues may not be altogether dissimilar or, at least, unworthy of comparison. Indeed, I would suggest that our modern experiences as technophiles offer new insights into issues of text and context in scribal systems antedating even the Middle Ages.

In this essay, I would like to take a step in this direction by examining scribal activities in ancient Egypt, Mesopotamia, and ancient Israel from the standpoint of the following cyber-induced issues: the cultural context of, and attitudes toward, script and various textual media; the formative role of a script and the physical medium in shaping the cultural conception of language; the cultural significance of the compositional structure of various written media; and the cognitive function of images as text. My remarks will be exploratory and will remain cursory but will, I hope, suggest new avenues for research.

I begin with the general ancient Near Eastern cultural context of script and the textual medium, a context that cannot be understood without acknowledgment of the ancient widespread belief in the inherent power of words, both human and divine.[3] As Georges Contenau has written,

> Since to know and pronounce the name of an object instantly endowed it with reality, and created power over it, and since the degree of knowledge and consequently of power was strengthened by the tone of voice in which the name was uttered, writing, which was a permanent record of the name, naturally contributed to this power, as did both drawing and sculpture, since both were a means of asserting knowledge of the object and consequently of exercising over it the power that knowledge gave.[4]

The belief in the written and spoken power of words derives, ultimately, not from a courtly social matrix, where a king's word was law, but rather from religious associations attached to the very invention of writing. In the earliest texts from ancient Sumer (ca. 3300 B.C.E.), we find a pictographic cuneiform (or 'wedge-writing') system employed to record the daily activities of religious authorities who were concerned foremost with the number of sacrificial animals and foodstuffs brought to the temple. The pictographic script gradually would become syllabically oriented over the next five hundred years, but would forever retain its connection to the images that the original signs represented. By 2500 B.C.E. this system had become rich in what we would call 'literary' allusive sophistication and was employed by a variety of different language groups.[5] Throughout the more than three-thousand-year history of Mesopotamia, both writing and reciting constituted sacred acts, and the highly protected technological privilege of a select few who were not just scholars but also magicians, physicians, and priests. Thus in second-millennium documents we hear that writing is the 'cosmic bond of all things'[6] and the secret of scribes and gods. In fact, the Mesopotamian gods also kept ledgers, or 'tablets of life', on which they inscribed the destinies of individuals.[7] Moreover, the Mesopotamian creation myth Enuma Elish, which was recited during a ritual enactment of the myth on the fourth day of the new year festival, begins with an act of speaking that brings all things into existence.

Writing appeared in Egypt around 3000 B.C.E., in the form of the hieroglyphic script, a writing system that worked on phonetic, syllabic, and logographic levels. Though genetically unrelated to the Mesopotamian system, hieroglyphic Egyptian similarly expanded, over time, its repertoire of signs while retaining and multiplying their visual associations. The pictographic nature of the script permitted scribes to write in multiple directions: right to left, left to right, even top to bottom, and sometimes alternately left to right and then right to left, in 'boustrophedon' (literally, 'as the ox plows') fashion. Also, as in the Mesopotamian system, hieroglyphs were the tools of an elite priesthood expert in medicine and magic. The scribes guarded and boasted of their techno-logical secrets, with a zeal that rivals even Microsoft.[8] Writing was, to use the Egyptian expression, 'the words of the gods' (mdw-nṯr), and the scribal art was to the Egyptians an occupation without equal.[9] The ibis-headed god Thoth is credited with the invention of writing and is said to be 'excellent of magic' and 'Lord of hieroglyphs'. He appears writing the hieroglyphic feather sign representing the word Ma'at, which stands for the cosmic force of equilibrium by which kings keep their thrones and justice prevails. The link between writing and Ma'at suggests that Egyptian scribes viewed the scribal art as integral to maintaining this cosmic equilibrium.[10]

The spoken word was equally potent in Egypt. Execration and prophetic texts abound and bespeak a belief in the efficacy of spoken words. The oracular use of speech is evident in the term for the Egyptian temple's innermost sanctum or, literally, 'the Mouth of the House' (r3-pr).[11] The written and the spoken word similarly play prominent roles in the Egyptian description of creation.[12]

The Hebrew Bible displays a belief in the power of words similar to the belief evidenced in Egyptian and Mesopotamian records. This is not surprising, since Israel became a cultural conduit and receptacle for Egyptian and Mesopotamian influences, and since in Canaan (which eventually would become the land of Israel) writing first appeared in cuneiform script.[13] Even as the Israelites rejected parts of the cosmopolitan culture they inherited, the belief in the power of words prevailed. Thus, while the biblical legal code states that the Israelites rejected all forms of magical praxis and divination, the very presence of laws prohibiting such practices, and references to speech and words found elsewhere in the Bible, imply a belief in the power of words on a par with Mesopotamian and Egyptian dogmata.[14] Also, God's creation in Genesis takes place by fiat, and the Israelite holy of holies is called a *debîr*, a word derived from the Hebrew root for 'speaking'.[15] A belief in the power of words explains why the prophets often speak in the past tense about events they predict for the future. Once spoken, an event is as good as realized.[16] The written word apparently was no less important, for as the God of Israel informs Moses in Exodus 32:33, 'Whoever has sinned respecting me, him will I blot out from my text *[sepher]*.' Job, too, cries out, 'Oh that my words were written! Oh that my words were inscribed in a text *[sepher]*' (Job 19:23).

Despite their obvious differences, Mesopotamian, Egyptian, and Israelite cultures had in common a conception of words as vehicles of power, of creation by fiat, and of the oracular use of written and spoken words. This observation greatly affects how we understand the written words that these cultures have left us. What we label 'literary' or 'rhetorical' was to them a deployment of power – of divine and, in many cases, magical import – as demonstrated by the ubiquitous appearance of wordplay in these texts.[17] Since words are deemed loci of power, puns and paranomasia must have more power because they magnify meaning through association.[18] In the Mesopotamian and Egyptian scripts, wordplay often takes place purely on a visual level, suggesting that the visual dimension of the sign, like the spoken word, conveys power.[19] Drawing on technojargon, we might say that written puns provide multiple links. Other devices, such as chiasm, acrostics,[20] and parallelism, might not be mere embellishments but rather manifestations of divinity and vehicles by which scribes harnessed the power of words.

The power of images extended beyond the script to iconography and the plastic arts. In Egypt, for example, sculptures also read as hieroglyphic signs, and drawings functioned as tools of magic.[21] This is why Egyptian pharaohs wore sandals with soles that depicted the ritual annihilation of their enemies. By placing their foes beneath their feet, they could magically trample them daily. Since art was language in Egypt, drawings and sculptures also carried verbal dimensions.[22] The name, being essentially a word, was also a locus of power that could be handled in written form only by experts familiar with the dangers of this power. This is why pharaohs possessed one secret name, and why cartouches were essentially hieroglyphs bound by the magical power of a knotted rope. We also see the belief in a tie between one's name and one's existence in usurping pharaohs' blotting of their predecessors out of existence by chiseling their names from inscriptions.

The belief in the power of words, despite its importance, is seldom incorporated into studies on ancient writing and literacy, yet even a scribal error, an accidental slip of the stylus, could have devastating consequences. An accurate memory is everything, copying is sacred, and knowledge of the associative subtleties embedded in a text is tantamount to secret knowledge of the divine.[23] The richer the allusive language, the more portents embedded in the text – or, in cyberlanguage, the more links embedded in a text, the more influential it is.

Our experiences with cybermedia, especially because we are biased users of particular platforms, also urge us to explore the various physical media to which ancient scribes committed their words and their cultural attitudes. For the Mesopotamians, the medium of choice was clay.

Most of the writings that have survived, ranging from administrative and divinatory texts to poems and paeans, are in clay. There are a few documents in other materials, such as stone, but stone was not native to Mesopotamia (or to Egypt, for that matter), and so such materials were reserved for monumental inscriptions.

While clay as a writing medium might appear a mundane topic, documented religious beliefs about clay allow us to appreciate more fully the Mesopotamian scribes' approach to their material. It is of import, for example, that the Mesopotamians saw clay as the medium with which the gods mixed blood to form the first living mortal. The placental afterbirth also was called 'clay', and the expression 'baked brick' was an idiomatic term for 'newborn', similar to the vulgar English idiom 'bun in the oven', equating the womb with a heat source.[24] Clay is also the material that the Mesopotamians used to build their homes. Thus it is the material of creation, both for gods and for humans. When a scribe impressed a stylus into moist clay, he was, in a sense, participating in creation. He was giving form to language.

Several other examples can be mentioned that reveal the intimate connections among architecture, creation, and language in Mesopotamian culture. Ea, the god of magic, is said to have 'built' his words,[25] and the gods did not 'create' humans but rather 'built' them (as we find also in the book of Genesis 2:22, in connection with Eve). We also find in Mesopotamia the use of clay cones inscribed with prayers and temple dedications. These cones were driven into temple walls and sometimes buried in the cornerstones of buildings, much like modern time-capsules. They were rarely intended for human eyes, and, once set into temple walls, would become the words that magically held the temple together and gave it longevity.[26] If the medium is the message, then in ancient Mesopotamia the message was constructive; it was creation, a message reminiscent of modern technophrases like 'build a cyber-portfolio' and 'create a Web site'.

In Egypt, clay is the medium of builders, but papyrus is the preferred medium of scribes. Here, too, we find a religious attachment to the written medium, both in the script and in the Egyptian mythologies.[27] Thus the hieroglyphic sign representing a papyrus clump denotes concepts like 'flourish', 'joy', and 'life' and appears as an apotropaic symbol on magical amulets. Several deities, such as the life-giving Nile god Hapi, appear with the papyrus hieroglyph, a fact that illustrates the connection of papyrus to divinity and creation. In Egyptian belief, papyrus pillars also held up the sky, and papyriform columns architecturally supported Egyptian temples, suggesting the forces of creation. As in Mesopotamia, the architectural connection to the creative aspect of writing obtains at the linguistic level as well. In Egyptian, the term 'house' can mean a stanza of poetry, and 'bricks' and 'walls' can refer to stichs and lines.[28] With computer terminology in mind, I note that at an inscription at Edfu an unrolled papyrus scroll is referred to as 'magic spread out', thus characterizing scrolling and unscrolling as acts of magical praxis.[29] In fact, the word 'magic' (ḥk3) appears with the determinative for a scroll. Writing on papyrus, therefore, was to those who employed the materials of magic and creation much as employing clay was to the Mesopotamian scribe.

Such observations are suggestive as a backdrop when we examine scribal activity in the Hebrew Bible. The Hebrew word for writing surface, sepher, is used for a wide variety of media that include stone, clay, papyrus, parchment, and potsherds, and the verbs used for writing occur with equal variety.[30] Moreover, the words 'scroll' and 'tablet' often appear side by side, and both appear as media for containing sacred words. Yet the Israelites, unlike their superpower neighbors, evidently did not attach special religious significance to their written media (whether scroll, parchment, or tablet), even though the Hebrew Bible portrays words as loci of power and the creation of the first mortal from clay.[31] It is the writing alone that is sacred, and the medium becomes sacred by default. It is as if the conception of the text transcended the written page. Even if we look to Jewish tradition as contained in the later Talmudic tractate Sepher Torah, we find that the parchment used for the Torah scroll must come from ritually clean animals, but this attaches no religious significance to the animal from which the parchment was taken.[32]

The intimate connection between physical media and religious beliefs as reflected in these media also compels us to look anew at the composition of ancient Near Eastern texts. For example, the number of tablets and verses comprising a particular ritual text may be not so much a function of space considerations as a consequence of cultural conceptions of certain numbers. For example, the Mesopotamian creation account was neatly composed on seven tablets, and seven was a well-known sacred number in Mesopotamia.[33] I am reminded of the rabbinic observation that the first line in the biblical creation of Genesis begins with seven words, the number seven playing a prominent structural role in that composition. The Mesopotamian Epic of Gilgamesh was redacted into twelve tablets that possibly correspond to the sexigesimal system of the Mesopotamians.[34] It is of note that the scribe who redacted the epic came from a family of exorcists steeped in the magical sciences.[35] I could cite other ancient Near Eastern texts, both biblical and extrabiblical, that illustrate such numerically allusive compositional structures.[36]

In line with this observation is the use of numbers to represent words and names, a practice that appeared first in Mesopotamia and, later, in the rabbinic interpretive strategy known as Gematria. In Mesopotamia this practice was not literary whimsy; it was how divine secrets were derived from texts.[37] Many gods' names also can be read as numbers; thus the number thirty may be read as Sin the moon god; Ishtar, as fifteen; Enlil, as fifty; and so on.[38] The connection of deities to numbers is widespread and perhaps helps us to understand the numerical significance of later non-Mesopotamian divinities, such as the God of Israel, who, we are told in Deuteronomy 6:4, is One.[39] It also may explain the preoccupation that later Jewish scribes, such as the Masoretes, had in the ninth century C.E. with counting all the words and verses in the Bible. In fact, the tradition of counting letters and words must be far more ancient than the Masoretes, for it is embedded in the very word *sopher*, 'scribe' – literally 'one who counts', or who 'gives an account' as we might say.[40]

Finally, our inquiry into ancient cyberesque conceptions of media naturally leads us to an examination of images as text. Throughout the Near East we find a fascinating conceptual correspondence between pictures and writing, surpassing even the power of a Nike symbol. In Egypt, the word *t?t* means not only 'written words' or 'letters' but also an 'artistic image', 'form', or 'sign'.[41] To Egyptians, the sculpted image of a god was both an image and a living word. Thus the New Kingdom book of the dead depicts the weighing of the pharaoh's heart against the feather of truth (*Ma'at*) but would never show Pharaoh's heart tipping the scales. Had the scribe illustrated this, Pharaoh would not have entered into the afterlife, since the images enscripted Pharaoh's future.

Within the broader cultural conception of word as image and its association with creation, the Israelites appear somewhat anomalous, since the Bible's ten commandments specifically prohibit the creation of graven images but demand the transmission of divine knowledge by way of the written and spoken words. Moreover, although the Hebrew word for an alphabetic letter (*'ôt*) also means 'sign, portent', the Bible nowhere connects the two semantic ranges or attaches religious import to particular letters outside the tetragrammaton, or sacred name of God, Yahweh. I believe that this puzzle can be solved, at least in part, with acknowledgment of the generative role that the sacred script (and, in the case of the Israelites, a consonantal script) played in ancient Near Eastern religions. Although the Hebrew script evolved from pictographic signs,[42] and the Old Canaanite script that preceded it had adopted the directional flexibility of hieroglyphic Egyptian, by the time of the Israelites it had lost its pictographic associations, and its direction had become fixed. Thus its associative dimension was limited to such sound devices as paronomasia; and, by contrast with the Egyptian and Mesopotamian conceptions of writing as an act of creation, the book of Genesis reports creation as solely an oral work, even though later Jewish tradition recalls the role of the alphabet in the creative process.[43] I cannot help wondering if the nonpictographic script played a partial role in shaping the ancient Israelite conception of creation.

Since I have written at length about ancient scribes, it is only appropriate that I conclude by quoting one of them. The citation comes to us from the stylus of a nameless Egyptian master of script, and although it was written at a time and in a place wholly foreign to us, it reminds our tech-savvy world that the utility of technology depends upon the quality of its use, and that its quality provides for its own legacy. Here are the words of the sage:

> As for the erudite scribes from the time of those who lived after the gods, they could prophesy what was to come, their names have become eternal, [and though] they are no more, they finished their lives, and all their relatives have been forgotten. They did not make for themselves pyramids of metal, with coffins of iron. They were not able to leave heirs in children, pronouncing their names, but they made heirs of themselves in the writings and in [the scrolls of wisdom] which they composed.[44]

Notes

1   Edward Mendelson, 'Monastery of Christ in the Desert, New Mexico', *New York Times Book Review*, June 2, 1996.

2   Ibid.

3   Sheldon W. Greaves, 'The Power of the Word in the Ancient Near East' (Ph.D. diss., University of California, Berkeley, 1996); J. N. Lawson, 'Mesopotamian Precursors to the Stoic Concept of Logos', in R. M. Whiting, ed., *Mythology and Mythologies: Methodological Approaches to Intercultural Influences*, Melammu Symposia II (Helsinki: Neo-Assyrian Text Corpus Project, 2001), 68–91.

4   Georges Contenau, *Everyday Life in Babylon and Assyria* (London: Edward Arnold, 1955), 164.

5   For the development of writing and its relationship to 'magic', see Jean Bottéro, *Mesopotamia: Writing, Reasoning, and the Gods* (Chicago: University of Chicago Press, 1992); Jean Bottéro, 'Symptômes, signes, écritures en Mésopotamie ancienne', in J. P. Vernat et al., eds., *Divination et rationalité* (Paris: Éditions du Seuil, 1974), 70–197.

6   A. W. Sjöberg, 'In Praise of the Scribal Art', *Journal of Cuneiform Studies* 24 (1972), 126–31.

7   Shalom M. Paul, 'Heavenly Tablets and the Book of Life', *Journal of the Ancient Near Eastern Society of Columbia University* 5 (1973), 345–53.

8   See, e.g., the famous Egyptian texts known as 'The Satire on the Trades' and 'In Praise of Learned Scribes', translated in James B. Pritchard, *Ancient Near Eastern Texts Relating to the Old Testament* (Princeton, N.J.: Princeton University Press, 1950).

9   For the connections among writing, speech, and 'magic', see Robert Kriech Ritner, *The Mechanics of Ancient Egyptian Magical Practice*, Studies in Ancient Oriental Civilization, no. 54 (Chicago: Oriental Institute of the University of Chicago, 1993). The importance of writing also can be seen in the word *rh*, 'knowledge', which contains the papyrus scroll determinative.

10 On the possible origin of the deity Thoth, see Carleton T. Hodge, 'Thoth and Oral Tradition', in Mary Ritchie Key and Henry M. Hoenigswald, eds., *General and Amerindian Ethnolinguistics: In Remembrance of Stanley Newman* (Berling: Mouton de Gruyter, 1989), 407–16; for more about Thoth, see also Ritner, *Mechanics of Ancient Egyptian Magical Practice*, 35. On *Ma'at*, see Jan Assmann, *Ma'at: Gerechtikeit und Unsterblichkeit im alten Ägypten* (Munich: Verlag C. H. Beck, 1990), and, more recently, Emily Teeter, *The Presentation of Maat: Ritual and Legitimacy in Ancient Egypt*, Studies in Oriental Civilization, no. 57 (Chicago: Oriental Institute of the University of Chicago, 1997).

11   Adolf Erman and Hermann Grapow, *Ägyptisches Handwörterbuch* (Hildesheim: Georg Olms Verlag, 1995), 92.

12   Cf. the role of the scribal god Thoth in the Memphite Theology.

13   A. Leo Oppenheim, *Ancient Mesopotamia: Portrait of a Dead Civilization* (Chicago: University of Chicago Press, 1977), 236.

14   See, e.g., I. Rabinowitz, *A Witness Forever: Ancient Israel's Perception of Literature and the Resultant Hebrew Bible* (Bethesda, Md.: CDL Press, 1993).

15   Contra Francis Brown et al., eds., *A Hebrew and English Lexicon of the Old Testament* (Oxford: Clarendon Press, 1951), who propose an Arabic cognate *dabara* 'back, behind'. See also the ancient Greek and Latin translations that treat the word as if connected to the common Hebrew verb *dābar*, 'speak'.

16   E.g., Ezekiel 29:13. Compare Psalm 85, which begins by telling us that God has restored the captivity of Jacob and forgiven the iniquity of his people and then concludes with a prayer for the enactment of these very events.

17   For an accessible treatment of the subject of wordplay, see Scott B. Noegel, ed., *Puns and Pundits: Word Play in the Hebrew Bible and Ancient Near Eastern Literature* (Bethesda, Md.: CDL Press, 2000).

18   Similarly, see Scott B. Noegel, 'Atbash in Jeremiah and Its Literary Significance: Part I', *Jewish Bible Quarterly* 24:2 (1996), 82–89; Scott B. Noegel, 'Atbash in Jeremiah and Its Literary Significance: Part 2', *Jewish Bible Quarterly* 24:3 (1996), 160–66; Scott B. Noegel 'Atbash in Jeremiah and Its Literary Significance: Part 3', *Jewish Bible Quarterly* 24:4 (1996), 247–50.

19   See, e.g., Carleton T. Hodge, 'Ritual and Writing: An Inquiry into the Origin of Egyptian Script', in M. Dale Kinkade et al., eds., *Linguistics and Anthropology: In Honor of C. F. Voegelin* (Lisse, The Netherlands: Peter de Ridder Press, 1975), 331–50; Scott B. Noegel, 'Wordplay in the Tale of the Poor Man of Nippur', *Acta Sumerologica* 18 (1996), 169–86.

20   See, e.g., W. M. Soll, 'Babylonian and Biblical Acrostics', *Biblica* 69 (1988), 305–32; H. M. Stewart, 'A Crossword Hymn to Mut', *Journal of Egyptian Archaeology* 57 (1971), 87–104.

21   Ritner, *Mechanics of Ancient Egyptian Magical Practice*, 111–43.

22   See M. Étienne Droiton, 'Une figuration cryptographique sur une stèle du Moyen Empire', *Revue d'Égyptologie* I (1933), 203–29. See also Scott B. Noegel, 'Moses and Magic: Notes on the Book of Exodus', *Journal of the Ancient Near Eastern Society* 24 (1997), 45–59. Mesopotamian iconography conveying textual information also is known. See, e.g., I. L. Finkel and J. E. Reade, 'Assyrian Hieroglyphs', *Zeitschrift für Assyriologie* 86 (1996), 244–68; J. A. Scurlock, 'Assyrian Hieroglyphs Enhanced', *Nouvelles Assyriologiques Brèves et Utilitaires* (1997), 85–86.

23   Alasdair Livingstone, *Mystical and Mythological Explanatory Works of Assyrian and Babylonian Scholars* (Oxford: Clarendon Press, 1986).

24   See the important brief note in Anne Draffkorn Kilmer, 'The Brick of Birth', *Journal of Near Eastern Studies* 46 (1987), 211–13.

25   See, e.g., the remark about Ea, god of magic, in Enuma Elish XI: 175–76: *mannuma ša lā ᵈEa amatu ibann[u]* (lit.) 'Who other than Ea can build word / ideas?'

26   Oppenheim, *Ancient Mesopotamia*, 234–35.

27   Papyrus was associated with the Deltan cosmology of the god Ptah, who created all life from a primeval papyrus thicket. Some Egyptian myths did involve clay, such as the myth of Khnum, a ram-headed god responsible for making humankind on a potter's wheel. Nevertheless, it is Ptah and papyrus that concern us here.

28   Cf. the Talmud Bavli Meg 16b, Talmud Yerushalmi Meg 3:8 (74b), Sot 12:9, which refer to Moses' Song at the Sea in Exodus 15 as composed of alternating stichs of 'one-half brick over a whole brick, and a whole brick over a half-brick'.

29   Cf. Isaiah 34:4, 'All the host of heaven shall dwindle away, and the heavens shall be rolled up like a scroll *[sepher].*'

30   E.g., *kārat*, 'cut'; *hāqaq*, 'engrave'; and *kātab*, 'inscribe'. The latter covers not only writing with ink but also inscribing; see, e.g., Exodus 31:18 and Isaiah 44:5.

31   Note also the semantic range of the Hebrew word *bayit*, which means 'house' as well as 'dynasty, family'.

32   This does not rule out, of course, the possibility that the animals from which parchment was made possessed a sacred significance in the period before the Israelites began to use the material.

33   For the use of seven in ancient Near Eastern literature, see W. R. Dawson, 'The Number "Seven" in Egyptian Texts', *Aegyptus* 8 (1927), 27–107; S. E. Loewenstamm, 'The Seven-Day-Unit in Ugaritic Epic Literature', in S. E. Loewenstamm, ed., *Comparative Studies in the Bible and Ancient Near Eastern Literature, AOAT* [Alter Orient und Altes Testament] 204 (Neukirchen-Vluyn: Neukirchener Verlag 1980), 192–209; Scott B. Noegel, 'The Significance of the Seventh Plague', *Biblica* 76 (995), 532–39.

34   See, e.g., Wolfgang Heimpel, 'The Sun at Night and the Doors of Heaven in Babylonian Texts', *Journal of Cuneiform Studies* 38 (1986), 127–51.

35   See W. G. Lambert, 'A Catalogue of Texts and Authors', *Journal of Cuneiform Studies* 16 (1962), 59–77. P. A. Beaulieu, however, convincingly suggested to the American Oriental Society (March 20, 1996) that this author belongs to a family of *kalû*, 'lamentation priests'. The difference in profession matters little here, since both occupations required a knowledge of 'magic'.

36   See, e.g., the praise of Enlil, which contains fifty lines, fifty being the number of Enlil's name. This was pointed out to me by Professor Anne Kilmer of the University of California-Berkeley, who also informs me that she has collected a great deal of information on this topic and is preparing it for publication under the title 'Weaving Textual Patterns: Symmetry in Akkadian Poetic Texts'; see, provisionally, Anne Draffkorn Kilmer, 'Fugal Features of Atra-Hasis: The Birth Theme', in M. E. Vogelzang and H. L. J. Vanstiphout, eds., *Mesopotamian Poetic Language: Sumerian and Akkadian*, Cuneiform Monographs, no. 6 (Groningen: Styx Publications, 1996), 127–39. We might add to this the so-called acrostics, which are found in the Bible and in Egyptian and Mesopotamian literature (see n. 20 above). For the use of numbers in biblical and rabbinic compositions see Robert Gordis, *Poets, Prophets, and Sages: Essays in Biblical Interpretation* (Bloomington: Indiana University Press, 1971), 95–103.

37   Livingstone, *Mystical and Mythological Explanatory Works*; Laurie E. Pearce, 'The Number-Syllabary Texts', *Journal of the American Oriental Society* 116 (1996), 453–74.

38   See, e.g., Jean Bottéro, 'Les noms de Marduk, l'écriture et la "logique" en Mésopotamie ancienne', in Maria de Jong Ellis, ed., *Essays on the Ancient Near East in Memory of Jacob Joel Finkelstein*, Memoirs of the Connecticut Academy of Arts and Sciences, no. 19 (Hamden, Conn.: Hamden Books, 1977), 5–28.

39   I cautiously add here Gemini and the Trinity. The relationship between numbers and gods was first espied by K. Jaritz, 'Geheimschriftsysteme im alten Orient', *Adeva Mitteilungen* 8 (1996), 11–15, and was applied to the biblical material by Cyrus H. Gordon, 'His Name is "One"', *Journal of Near Eastern Studies* 29 (1970), 198–9.

40   It is of interest to note Z. ben Hayyim's observation that the word *masorah* is related to the tradition of scribal counting; see Z. ben Hayyim, '*mswrh wmswrt*', *Leshonenu* 21 (1957), 283–92.

41   Note that *tꜣt* is written with the determinatives *wḏꜣt*, 'magical eye of Horus', and the papyrus scroll.

42   The discovery in October 1999 at Wadi el-Hol, Egypt, of an early alphabetic script related to the inscriptional hieratic of early Middle Kingdom Egypt may shed light on this issue. Several of the letterforms discovered there relate closely to those in the so-called proto-Sinaitic script, found several centuries later in the Sinai.

43 See, e.g., the explanation of the raised letter *he-* in *bʰbrˁm* as 'with the *he* . . . he created them [the heavens and the earth]' (Midrash Rabbah 1:10).

44 I have based this rendering, with some modification, on the translation of John A. Wilson in Pritchard, *Ancient Near Eastern Texts Relating to the Old Testament*, 431.

Chapter 11

Walter Ong

ORALITY AND LITERACY
Writing restructures consciousness

The new world of autonomous discourse

A deeper understanding of pristine or primary orality enables us better to understand the new world of writing, what it truly is, and what functionally literate human beings really are: beings whose thought processes do not grow out of simply natural powers but out of these powers as structured, directly or indirectly, by the technology of writing. Without writing, the literate mind would not and could not think as it does, not only when engaged in writing but normally even when it is composing its thoughts in oral form. More than any other single invention, writing has transformed human consciousness.

Writing establishes what has been called 'context-free' language (Hirsch 1977: 21–3, 26) or 'autonomous' discourse (Olson 1980), discourse which cannot be directly questioned or contested as oral speech can be because written discourse has been detached from its author.

Oral cultures know a kind of autonomous discourse in fixed ritual formulas (Olson 1980: 187–94; Chafe 1982), as well as in vatic sayings or prophesies, for which the utterer himself or herself is considered only the channel, not the source. The Delphic oracle was not responsible for her oracular utterances, for they were held to be the voice of the god. Writing, and even more print, has some of this vatic quality. Like the oracle or the prophet, the book relays an utterance from a source, the one who really 'said' or wrote the book. The author might be challenged if only he or she could be reached, but the author cannot be reached in any book. There is no way directly to refute a text. After absolutely total and devastating refutation, it says exactly the same thing as before. This is one reason why 'the book says' is popularly tantamount to 'it is true'. It is also one reason why books have been burnt. A text stating what the whole world knows is false will state falsehood forever, so long as the text exists. Texts are inherently contumacious.

Plato, writing and computers

Most persons are surprised, and many distressed, to learn that essentially the same objections commonly urged today against computers were urged by Plato in the *Phaedrus* (Plato 1973: 274–7) and in the *Seventh Letter* against writing. Writing, Plato has Socrates say in the *Phaedrus*, is inhuman, pretending to establish outside the mind what in reality can be only in the mind. It is a thing, a manufactured product. The same of course is said of computers. Secondly, Plato's Socrates urges, writing destroys memory. Those who use writing will become forgetful, relying on an external resource for what they lack in internal resources. Writing weakens the mind. Today, parents and others fear that pocket calculators provide an external resource for what ought to be the internal resource of memorized multiplication tables. Calculators weaken the mind, relieve it of the work that keeps it strong. Thirdly, a written text is basically unresponsive. If you ask a person to explain his or her statement, you can get an explanation; if you ask a text, you get back nothing except the same, often stupid, words which called for your question in the first place. In the modern critique of the computer, the same objection is put, 'Garbage in, garbage out'. Fourthly, in keeping with the agonistic mentality of oral cultures, Plato's Socrates also holds it against writing that the written word cannot defend itself as the natural spoken word can: real speech and thought always exist essentially in a context of give-and-take between real persons. Writing is passive, out of it, in an unreal, unnatural world. So are computers.

A fortiori, print is vulnerable to these same charges. Those who are disturbed by Plato's misgivings about writing will be even more disturbed to find that print created similar misgivings when it was first introduced. Hieronimo Squarciafico, who in fact promoted the printing of the Latin classics, also argued in 1477 that already 'abundance of books makes men less studious' (quoted in Lowry 1979: 29–31): it destroys memory and enfeebles the mind by relieving it of too much work (the pocket-computer complaint once more), downgrading the wise man and wise woman in favor of the pocket compendium. Of course, others saw print as a welcome leveler: everyone becomes a wise man or woman (Lowry 1979: 31–2).

One weakness in Plato's position was that, to make his objections effective, he put them into writing, just as one weakness in anti-print positions is that their proponents, to make their objections more effective, put the objections into print. The same weakness in anti-computer positions is that, to make them effective, their proponents articulate them in articles or books printed from tapes composed on computer terminals. Writing and print and the computer are all ways of technologizing the word. Once the word is technologized, there is no effective way to criticize what technology has done with it without the aid of the highest technology available. Moreover, the new technology is not merely used to convey the critique: in fact, it brought the critique into existence. Plato's philosophically analytic thought, as has been seen (Haveloek 1963), including his critique of writing, was possible only because of the effects that writing was beginning to have on mental processes.

In fact, as Havelock has beautifully shown (1963), Plato's entire epistemology was unwittingly a programmed rejection of the old oral, mobile, warm, personally interactive lifeworld of oral culture (represented by the poets, whom he would not allow in his Republic). The term *idea*, form, is visually based, coming from the same root as the Latin *video*, I see, and such English derivatives as vision, visible, or videotape. Platonic form was form conceived of by analogy with visible form. The Platonic ideas are voiceless, immobile, devoid of all warmth, not interactive but isolated, not part of the human lifeworld at all but utterly above and beyond it. Plato of course was not at all fully aware of the unconscious forces at work in his psyche to produce this reaction, or overreaction, of the literate person to lingering, retardant orality.

Such considerations alert us to the paradoxes that beset the relationships between the original spoken word and all its technological transformations. The reason for the tantalizing involutions here is obviously that intelligence is relentlessly reflexive, so that even the external tools that it uses to implement its workings become 'internalized', that is, part of its own reflexive process.

One of the most startling paradoxes inherent in writing is its close association with death. This association is suggested in Plato's charge that writing is inhuman, thing-like, and that it destroys memory. It is also abundantly evident in countless references to writing (and/or print) traceable in printed dictionaries of quotations, from 2 Corinthians 3:6, 'The letter kills but the spirit gives life' and Horace's reference to his three books of *Odes* as a 'monument' (*Odes* iii. 30.1), presaging his own death, on to and beyond Henry Vaughan's assurance to Sir Thomas Bodley that in the Bodleian Library at Oxford 'every book is thy epitaph'. In *Pippa Passes*, Robert Browning calls attention to the still widespread practice of pressing living flowers to death between the pages of printed books, 'faded yellow blossoms/twixt page and page'. The dead flower, once alive, is the psychic equivalent of the verbal text. The paradox lies in the fact that the deadness of the text, its removal from the living human lifeworld, its rigid visual fixity, assures its endurance and its potential for being resurrected into limitless living contexts by a potentially infinite number of living readers (Ong 1977: 230–71).

Writing is a technology

Plato was thinking of writing as an external, alien technology, as many people today think of the computer. Because we have by today so deeply interiorized writing, made it so much a part of ourselves, as Plato's age had not yet made it fully a part of itself (Havelock 1963), we find it difficult to consider writing to be a technology as we commonly assume printing and the computer to be. Yet writing (and especially alphabetic writing) is a technology; calling for the use of tools and other equipment: styli or brushes or pens, carefully prepared surfaces such as paper, animal skins, strips of wood, as well as inks or paints, and much more. Clanchy (1979: 88–115) discusses the matter circumstantially, in its western medieval context, in his chapter entitled 'The technology of writing'. Writing is in a way the most drastic of the three technologies. It initiated what print and computers only continue, the reduction of dynamic sound to quiescent space, the separation of the word from the living present, where alone spoken words can exist.

By contrast with natural, oral speech, writing is completely artificial. There is no way to write 'naturally'. Oral speech is fully natural to human beings in the sense that every human being in every culture who is not physiologically or psychologically impaired learns to talk. Talk implements conscious life but it wells up into consciousness out of unconscious depths, though of course with the conscious as well as unconscious co-operation of society. Grammar rules live in the unconscious in the sense that you can know how to use the rules and even how to set up new rules without being able to state what they are.

Writing or script differs as such from speech in that it does not inevitably well up out of the unconscious. The process of putting spoken language into writing is governed by consciously contrived, articulable rules: for example, a certain pictogram will stand for a certain specific word, or *a* will represent a certain phoneme, *b* another, and so on. (This is not to deny that the writer–reader situation created by writing deeply affects unconscious processes involved in composing in writing, once one has learned the explicit, conscious rules. More about this later.)

To say writing is artificial is not to condemn it but to praise it. Like other artificial creations and indeed more than any other, it is utterly invaluable and indeed essential for the realization of fuller, interior, human potentials. Technologies are not mere exterior aids but also interior transformations of consciousness, and never more than when they affect the word. Such transformations can be uplifting. Writing heightens consciousness. Alienation from a natural milieu can be good for us and indeed is in many ways essential for full human life. To live and to understand fully, we need not only proximity but also distance. This writing provides for consciousness as nothing else does.

Technologies are artificial, but – paradox again – artificiality is natural to human beings. Technology, properly interiorized, does not degrade human life but on the contrary enhances it. The modern orchestra, for example, is the result of high technology. A violin is an instrument, which is to say a tool. An organ is a huge machine, with sources of power – pumps, bellows, electric generators – totally outside its operator. Beethoven's score for his Fifth Symphony consists of very careful directions to highly trained technicians, specifying exactly how to use their tools. *Legato*: do not take your finger off one key until you have hit the next. *Staccato*: hit the key and take your finger off immediately. And so on. As musicologists well knows it is pointless to object to electronic compositions such as Morton Subotnik's *The Wild Bull* on the grounds that the sounds come out of a mechanical contrivance. What do you think the sounds of an organ come out of? Or the sounds of a violin or even of a whistle? The fact is that by using a mechanical contrivance, a violinist or an organist can express something poignantly human that cannot be expressed without the mechanical contrivance. To achieve such expression of course the violinist or organist has to have interiorized the technology, made the tool or machine a second nature, a psychological part of himself or herself. This calls for years of 'practice', learning how to make the tool do what it can do. Such shaping of a tool to oneself, learning a technological skill, is hardly dehumanizing. The use of a technology can enrich the human psyche, enlarge the human spirit, intensify its interior life. Writing is an even more deeply interiorized technology than instrumental musical performance is. But to understand what it is, which means to understand it in relation to its past, to orality, the fact that it is a technology must be honestly faced.

What is 'writing' or 'script'?

Writing, in the strict sense of the word, the technology which has shaped and powered the intellectual activity of modern man, was a very late development in human history. *Homo sapiens* has been on earth perhaps some 50,000 years (Leakey and Lewin 1979: 141 and 168). The first script, or true writing, that we know, was developed among the Sumerians in Mesopotamia only around the year 3500 BC (Diringer 1953; Gelb 1963).

Human beings had been drawing pictures for countless millennia before this. And various recording devices or *aides-mémoire* had been used by various societies: a notched stick, rows of pebbles, other tallying devices such as the quipu of the Incas (a stick with suspended cords onto which other cords were tied), the 'winter count' calendars of the Native American Plains Indians, and so on. But a script is more than a mere memory aid. Even when it is pictographic, a script is more than pictures. Pictures represent objects. A picture of a man and a house and a tree of itself *says* nothing. (If a proper code or set of conventions is supplied, it might: but a code is not picturable, unless with the help of another unpicturable code. Codes ultimately have to be explained by something more than pictures; that is, either in words or in a total human context, humanly understood.) A script in the sense of true writing, as understood here, does not consist of mere pictures, of representations of things, but is a representation of an *utterance*, of words that someone says or is imagined to say.

It is of course possible to count as 'writing' any semiotic mark, that is, any visible or sensible mark which an individual makes and assigns a meaning to. Thus a simple scratch on a rock or a notch on a stick interpretable only by the one who makes it would be 'writing'. If this is what is meant by writing, the antiquity of writing is perhaps comparable to the antiquity of speech. However, investigations of writing which take 'writing' to mean any visible or sensible mark with an assigned meaning merge writing with purely biological behavior. When does a footprint or a deposit of feces or urine (used by many species of animals for communication – Wilson 1975: 228–9) become 'writing'? Using the term 'writing' in this extended sense to include any semiotic marking trivializes its meaning. The critical and unique breakthrough into new worlds of knowledge was achieved within human consciousness not when simple semiotic marking was devised but when a coded system of visible marks was invented whereby a writer could determine the exact words that the reader would generate from the text. This is what we usually mean today by writing in its sharply focused sense.

With writing or script in this full sense, encoded visible markings engage words fully so that the exquisitely intricate structures and references evolved in sound can be visibly recorded exactly in their specific complexity and, because visibly recorded, can implement production of still more exquisite structures and references, far surpassing the potentials of oral utterance. Writing, in this ordinary sense, was and is the most momentous of all human technological inventions. It is not a mere appendage to speech. Because it moves speech from the oral–aural to a new sensory world, that of vision, it transforms speech and thought as well. Notches on sticks and other *aides-mémoire* lead up to writing, but they do not restructure the human lifeworld as true writing does.

True writing systems can and usually do develop gradually from a cruder use of mere memory aides. Intermediate stages exist. In some coded systems the writer can predict only approximately what the reader will read off, as in the system developed by the Vai in Liberia (Scribner and Cole 1978) or even in ancient Egyptian hieroglyphics. The tightest control of all is achieved by the alphabet, although even this is never quite perfect in all instances. If I mark a document 'read', this might be a past participle (pronounced to rhyme with 'red') indicating that the document has been gone over, or it might be an imperative (pronounced to rhyme with 'reed') indicating that it is to be gone over. Even with the alphabet, extra-textual context is sometimes needed, but only in exceptional cases – how exceptional will depend on how well the alphabet has been tailored to a given language. . . .

The onset of literacy

When a fully formed script of any sort, alphabetic or other, first makes its way from outside into a particular society, it does so necessarily at first in restricted sectors and with varying effects and implications. Writing is often regarded at first as an instrument of secret and magic power (Goody 1968b: 236). Traces of this early attitude toward writing can still show etymologically: the Middle English 'grammarye' or grammar, referring to book-learning, came to mean occult or magical lore, and through one Scottish dialectical form has emerged in our present English vocabulary as 'glamor' (spell-casting power). 'Glamor girls' are really grammar girls. The futharic or runic alphabet of medieval North Europe was commonly associated with magic. Scraps of writing are used as magic amulets (Goody 1968b: 201–3), but they also can be valued simply because of the wonderful permanence they confer on words. The Nigerian novelist Chinua Achebe describes how in an Ibo village the one man who knew how to read hoarded in his house every bit of printed material that came his way – newspapers, cartons, receipts (Achebe 1961: 120–1). It all seemed too remarkable to throw away.

Some societies of limited literacy have regarded writing as dangerous to the unwary reader, demanding a guru-like figure to mediate between reader and text (Goody and Watt 1968: 13). Literacy can be restricted to special groups such as the clergy (Tambiah 1968: 113–14). Texts can be felt to have intrinsic religious value: illiterates profit from rubbing the book on their foreheads, or from whirling prayer-wheels bearing texts they cannot read (Goody 1968a: 15–16). Tibetan monks used to sit on the banks of streams 'printing pages of charms and formulas on the surface of the water with woodcut blocks' (Goody 1968a: 16, quoting R. B. Eckvall). The still flourishing 'cargo cults' of some South Pacific islands are well known: illiterates or semi-literates think that the commercial papers – orders, bills of lading, receipts, and the like – that they know figure in shipping operations are magical instruments to make ships and cargo come in from across the sea, and they elaborate various rituals manipulating written texts in the hope that cargo will turn up for their own possession and use (Meggitt 1968: 300–9). In ancient Greek culture Havelock discovers a general pattern of restricted literacy applicable to many other cultures: shortly after the introduction of writing a 'craft literacy' develops (Havelock 1963; cf. Havelock and Herschell 1978). At this stage writing is a trade practiced by craftsmen, whom others hire to write a letter or document as they might hire a stone-mason to build a house, or a shipwright to build a boat. Such was the state of affairs in West African kingdoms, such as Mali, from the Middle Ages into the twentieth century (Wilks 1968; Goody 1968b). At such a craft-literacy stage, there is no need for an individual to know reading and writing any more than any other trade. Only around Plato's time in ancient Greece, more than three centuries after the introduction of the Greek alphabet, was this stage transcended when writing was finally diffused through the Greek population and interiorized enough to affect thought processes generally (Havelock 1963).

The physical properties of early writing materials encouraged the continuance of scribal culture (see Clanchy 1979: 88–115, on 'The technology of writing'). Instead of evenly surfaced machine-made paper and relatively durable ball-point pens, the early writer had more recalcitrant technological equipment. For writing surfaces, he had wet clay bricks, animal skins (parchment, vellum) scraped free of fat and hair, often smoothed with pumice and whitened with chalk, frequently reprocessed by scraping off an earlier text (palimpsests). Or he had the bark of trees, papyrus (better than most surfaces but still rough by high-technology standards), dried leaves or other vegetation, wax layered onto wooden tables often hinged to form a diptych worn on a belt (these wax tablets were used for notes, the wax being smoothed over again for re-use), wooden rods (Clanchy 1979: 95) and other wooden and stone surfaces of various sorts. There were no corner stationery stores selling pads of paper. There was no paper. As inscribing tools the scribes had various kinds of styli, goose quills which had to be slit and sharpened over and over again with what we still call a 'pen knife', brushes (particularly in East Asia), or various other instruments for incising surfaces and/or spreading inks or paints. Fluid inks were mixed in various ways and readied for use into hollow bovine horns (inkhorns) or in other acid-resistant containers, or, commonly in East Asia, brushes were wetted and dabbed on dry ink blocks, as in watercolor painting.

Special mechanical skills were required for working with such writing materials, and not all 'writers' had such skills suitably developed for protracted composition. Paper made writing physically easier. But paper, manufactured in China probably by the second century BC and diffused by Arabs to the Middle East by the eighth century of the Christian era, was first manufactured in Europe only in the twelfth century.

Longstanding oral mental habits of thinking through one's thoughts aloud encourages dictation, but so did the state of writing technology. In the physical act of writing, the medieval Englishman Orderic Vitalis says, 'the whole body labors' (Clanchy 1979: 90). Through the Middle Ages in Europe authors often employed scribes. Composition in writing, working out one's thought pen-in-hand, particularly in briefer compositions, was, of course, practiced to some extent from antiquity, but it became widespread for literary and other prolonged composition at different times in different cultures. It was still rare in eleventh-century England, and, when it occurred, even this late, could be done in a psychological setting so oral that we find it hard to imagine. The eleventh-century Eadmer of St Albans says that, when he composed in writing, he felt he was dictating to himself (Clanchy 1979: 218). St Thomas Aquinas, who wrote his own manuscripts, organizes his *Summa theologiae* in quasi-oral format: each section or 'question' begins with a recitation of objections against the position Thomas will take, then Thomas states his position, and finally answers the objections in order. Similarly, an early poet would write down a poem by imagining himself declaiming it to an audience. Few if any novelists today write a novel by imagining themselves declaiming it aloud, though they might be exquisitely aware of the sound effects of the words. High literacy fosters truly written composition, in which the author composes a text which is precisely a text, puts his or her words together on paper. This gives thought different contours from those of orally sustained thought. More will be said (that is, written) here later about the effects of literacy on thought processes.

From memory to written records

Long after a culture has begun to use writing, it may still not give writing high ratings. A present-day literate usually assumes that written records have more force than spoken words as evidence of a long-past state of affairs, especially in court. Earlier cultures that knew literacy but had not so fully interiorized it, have often assumed quite the opposite. The amount of credence accorded to written records undoubtedly varied from culture to culture, but Clanchy's careful case history (1979) of the use of literacy for practical administrative purposes in eleventh- and twelfth-century England gives an informative sample of how much orality could linger in the presence of writing, even in an administrative milieu.

In the period he studies, Clanchy finds that 'documents did not immediately inspire trust' (Clanchy 1979: 230). People had to be persuaded that writing improved the old oral methods sufficiently to warrant all the expense and troublesome techniques it involved. Before the use of documents, collective oral testimony was commonly used to establish, for example, the age of feudal heirs. To settle a dispute in 1127 as to whether the customs dues at the port of Sandwich went to St Augustine's Abbey at Canterbury or to Christ Church, a jury was chosen consisting of twelve men from Dover and twelve from Sandwich, 'mature, wise seniors of many years, having good testimony'. Each juror then swore that, as 'I have received from my ancestors, and I have seen and heard from my youth', the tolls belong to Christ Church (Clanchy 1979: 232–3). They were publicly remembering what others before them had remembered.

Witnesses were *prima facie* more credible than texts because they could be challenged and made to defend their statements, whereas texts could not (this, it will be recalled, was exactly one of Plato's objections to writing). Notarial methods of authenticating documents undertake to build authenticating mechanisms into written texts, but notarial methods develop late in literate cultures, and much later in England than in Italy (Clanchy 1979: 235–6). Written documents themselves were often authenticated not in writing but by symbolic objects (such as a knife, attached to the document by a parchment thong – Clanchy 1979: 24). Indeed symbolic objects alone could serve as instruments transferring property. In *c.* 1130, Thomas de Muschamps conveyed his estate of Hetherslaw to the monks at Durham by offering his sword on an altar (Clanchy 1979: 25). Even after the Domesday Book (1085–6) and the accompanying increase in written documentation, the story of the Earle Warrenne shows how the old oral state of mind still persisted: before the judges in quo warranto procedures under Edward I (reigned 1272–1306), the Earle Warrenne exhibited not a charter but 'an ancient and rusty sword', protesting that his ancestors had come with William the Conqueror to take England by the sword and that he would defend his lands with the sword. Clanchy points out (1979: 21–2) that the story is somewhat questionable because of certain inconsistencies, but notes also that its persistence attests to an earlier state of mind familiar with the witness value of symbolic gifts.

Early charters conveying land in England were originally not even dated (Clanchy 1979: 231, 236–41), probably for a variety of reasons. Clanchy suggests that the most profound reason was probably that 'dating required the scribe to express an opinion about his place in time' (1979: 238), which demanded that he choose a point of reference. What point? Was he to locate this document by reference to the creation of the world? To the Crucifixion? To the birth of Christ? Popes dated documents this way, from Christ's birth, but was it presumptuous to date a secular document as popes dated theirs? In high-technology cultures today, everyone lives each day in a frame of abstract computed time enforced by millions of printed calendars, clocks, and watches. In twelfth-century England there were no clocks or watches or wall or desk calendars.

Before writing was deeply interiorized by print, people did not feel themselves situated every moment of their lives in abstract computed time of any sort. It appears unlikely that most persons in medieval or even Renaissance western Europe would ordinarily have been aware of the number of the current calendar year – from the birth of Christ or any other point in the past. Why should they be? Indecision concerning what point to compute from attested the trivialities of the issue. In a culture with no newspapers or other currently dated material to impinge on consciousness, what would be the point for most people in knowing the current calendar year? The abstract calendar number would relate to nothing in real life. Most persons did not know and never even tried to discover in what calendar year they had been born.

Moreover, charters were undoubtedly assimilated somewhat to symbolic gifts, such as knives or swords. These were identifiable by their looks. And indeed, charters were quite regularly forged to make them look like what a court (however erroneously) felt a charter should look like (Clanchy 1979: 249, citing P. H. Sawyer). 'Forgers', Clanchy points out, were not 'occasional deviants on the peripheries of legal practice' but 'experts entrenched at the centre of literary and intellectual culture in the twelfth century'. Of the 164 now extant charters of Edward the Confessor, 44 are certainly forged, only 64 certainly authentic, and the rest uncertainly one or the other.

The verifiable errors resulting from the still radically oral economic and juridical procedures that Clanchy reports were minimal because the fuller past was mostly inaccessible to consciousness. 'Remembered truth was . . . flexible and up to date' (Clanchy 1979: 233). As has been seen in instances from modern Nigeria and Ghana (Goody and Watt 1968: 31–4), in an oral economy of thought, matters from the past without any sort of present relevance commonly dropped into oblivion. Customary law, trimmed of material no longer of use, was automatically always up to date and thus youthful – a fact which, paradoxically, makes customary law seem inevitable and thus very old (cf. Clanchy 1979: 233). Persons whose world view has been formed by high literacy need to remind themselves that in functionally oral cultures the past is not felt as an itemized terrain, peppered with verifiable and disputed 'facts' or bits of information. It is the domain of the ancestors, a resonant source for renewing awareness of present existence, which itself is not an itemized terrain either. Orality knows no lists or charts or figures.

Goody (1977: 52–111) has examined in detail the noetic significance of tables and lists, of which the calendar is one example. Writing makes such apparatus possible. Indeed, writing was in a sense invented largely to make something like lists: by far most of the earliest writing we know, that in the cuneiform script of the Sumerians beginning around 3500 BC, is account-keeping. Primary oral cultures commonly situate their equivalent of lists in narrative, as in the catalogue of the ships and captains in the *Iliad* (ii. 461–879) – not an objective tally but an operational display in a story about a war. In the text of the Torah, which set down in writing thought forms still basically oral, the equivalent of geography (establishing the relationship of one place to another) is put into a formulary action narrative (Numbers 33:16 ff.): 'Setting out from the desert of Sinai, they camped at Kibroth-hattaavah. Setting out from Kibroth-hattaavah, they camped at Hazeroth. Setting out from Hazeroth, they camped at Rithmah . . .', and so on for many more verses. Even genealogies out of such orally framed tradition are in effect commonly narrative. Instead of a recitation of names, we find a sequence of 'begats', of statements of what someone did: 'Irad begat Mahajael, Mehajael begat Methusael, Methusael begat Lamech' (Genesis 4:18). This sort of aggregation derives partly from the oral drive to use formulas, partly from the oral mnemonic drive to exploit balance (recurrence of subject–predicate–object produces a swing which aids recall and which a mere sequence of names would lack), partly from the oral drive to redundancy (each person is mentioned twice, as begetter and begotten), and partly from the oral drive to narrate rather than simply to juxtapose (the persons are not immobilized as in a police line-up, but are doing something – namely, begetting).

These biblical passages obviously are written records, but they come from an orally constituted sensibility and tradition. They are not felt as thing-like, but as reconstitutions of events in time. Orally presented sequences are always occurrences in time, impossible to 'examine', because they are not presented visually but rather are utterances which are heard. In a primary oral culture or a culture with heavy oral residue, even genealogies are not 'lists' of data but rather 'memory of songs sung'. Texts are thing-like, immobilized in visual space, subject to what Goody calls 'backward scanning' (1977: 49–50). Goody shows in detail how, when anthropologists display on a written or printed surface lists of various items found in oral myths (clans, regions of the earth, kinds of winds, and so on), they actually deform the mental world in which the myths have their own existence. The satisfaction that myths provide is essentially not 'coherent' in a tabular way.

Lists of the sort Goody discusses are of course useful if we are reflectively aware of the distortion they inevitably introduce. Visual presentation of verbalized material in space has its own particular economy, its own laws of motion and structure. Texts in various scripts around the world are read variously from right to left, or left to right, or top to bottom, or all these ways at once as in boustrophedon writing, but never anywhere, so far as is known, from bottom to top. Texts assimilate utterance to the human body. They introduce a feeling for 'headings' in accumulations of knowledge: 'chapter' derives from the Latin *caput*, meaning head (as of the human body). Pages have not only 'heads' but also 'feet', for footnotes. References are given to what is 'above' and 'below' in a text when what is meant is several pages back or farther on. The significance of the vertical and the horizontal in texts deserves serious study. Kerckhove (1981: 10–11 in proofs) suggests that growth in left-hemisphere dominance governed the drift in early Greek writing from right-to-left movement, to boustrophedon movement ('ox-plowing' pattern, one line going right, then a turn around a corner into the next line going left, the letters inverted according to the direction of the line), to *stoichedon* style (vertical lines), and finally to definitive left-to-right movement on a horizontal line. All this is quite a different world of order from anything in the oral sensibility, which has no way of operating with 'headings' or verbal linearity. Across the world the alphabet, the ruthlessly efficient reducer of sound to space, is pressed into direct service for setting up the new space-defined sequences: items are marked *a*, *b*, *c*, and so on to indicate their sequences, and even poems in the early days of literacy are composed with the first letter of the first word of successive lines following the order of the alphabet. The alphabet as a simple sequence of letters is a major bridge between oral mnemonics and literate mnemonics: generally the sequence of the letters of the alphabet is memorized orally and then used for largely visual retrieval of materials, as in indexes.

Charts, which range elements of thought not simply in one line of rank but simultaneously in horizontal and various criss-cross orders, represent a frame of thought even farther removed than lists are from the oral noetic processes which such charts are supposed to represent. The extensive use of lists and particularly of charts so commonplace in our high-technology cultures is a result not simply of writing, but of the deep interiorization of print (Ong 1958: 307–18, and *passim*), which implements the use of fixed diagrammatic word-charts and other informational uses of neutral space far beyond anything feasible in any writing culture.

Some dynamics of textuality

The condition of words in a text is quite different from their condition in spoken discourse. Although they refer to sounds and are meaningless unless they can be related – externally or in the imagination – to the sounds or, more precisely, the phonemes they encode, written words are isolated from the fuller context in which spoken words come into being. The word in its natural, oral habitat is a part of a real, existential present. Spoken utterance is addressed by a real, living person to another real, living person or real, living persons, at a specific time in a real setting which includes always much more than mere words. Spoken words are always modifications of a total situation which is more than verbal. They never occur alone, in a context simply of words.

Yet words are alone in a text. Moreover, in composing a text, in 'writing' something, the one producing the written utterance is also alone. Writing is a solipsistic operation. I am writing a book which I hope will be read by hundreds of thousands of people, so I must be isolated from everyone. While writing the present book, I have left word that I am 'out' for hours and days – so that no one, including persons who will presumably read the book, can interrupt my solitude. In a text even the words that are there lack their full phonetic qualities. In oral speech, a word must have one or another intonation or tone of voice – lively, excited, quiet, incensed, resigned, or whatever. It is impossible to speak a word orally without any intonation. In a text punctuation can signal tone minimally: a question mark or a comma, for example, generally calls for the voice to be raised a bit. Literate tradition, adopted and adapted by skilled critics, can also supply some extratextual clues for intonations, but not complete ones. Actors spend hours determining how actually to utter the words in the text before them. A given passage might be delivered by one actor in a shout, by another in a whisper.

Extratextual context is missing not only for readers but also for the writer. Lack of verifiable context is what makes writing normally so much more agonizing an activity than oral presentation to a real audience. 'The writer's audience is always a fiction' (Ong 1977: 53–81). The writer must set up a role in which absent and often unknown readers can cast themselves. Even in writing to a close friend I have to fictionalize a mood for him, to which he is expected to conform. The reader must also fictionalize the writer. When my friend reads my letter, I may be in an entirely different frame of mind from when I wrote it. Indeed, I may very well be dead. For a text to convey its message, it does not matter whether the author is dead or alive. Most books extant today were written by persons now dead. Spoken utterance comes only from the living.

Even in a personal diary addressed to myself I must fictionalize the addressee. Indeed, the diary demands, in a way, the maximum fictionalizing of the utterer and the addressee. Writing is always a kind of imitation talking, and in a diary I therefore am pretending that I am talking to myself. But I never really talk this way to myself. Nor could I without writing or indeed without print. The personal diary is a very late literary form, in effect unknown until the seventeenth century (Boerner 1969). The kind of verbalized solipsistic reveries it implies are a product of consciousness as shaped by print culture. And for which self am I writing? Myself today? As I think I will be ten years from now? As I hope I will be? For myself as I imagine myself or hope others may imagine me? Questions such as this can and do fill diary writers with anxieties and often enough lead to discontinuation of diaries. The diarist can no longer live with his or her fiction.

The ways in which readers are fictionalized is the underside of literary history, of which the topside is the history of genres and the handling of character and plot. Early writing provides the reader with conspicuous helps for situating himself imaginatively. It presents philosophical material in dialogues, such as those of Plato's Socrates, which the reader can imagine himself overhearing. Or episodes are to be imagined as told to a live audience on successive days. Later, in the Middle Ages, writing will present philosophical and theological texts in objection-and-response form, so that the reader can imagine an oral disputation. Boccaccio and Chaucer will provide the reader with fictional groups of men and women telling stories to one another, that is, a 'frame story', so that the reader can pretend to be one of the listening company. But who is talking to whom in *Pride and Prejudice* or in *Le Rouge et le noir*, or in *Adam Bede*? Nineteenth-century novelists self-consciously intone, 'dear reader', over and over again to remind themselves that they are not telling a story but writing one in which both author and reader are having difficulty situating themselves. The psychodynamics of writing matured very slowly in narrative.

And what is the reader supposed to make himself out to be in *Finnegans Wake*? Only a reader. But of a special fictional sort. Most readers of English cannot or will not make themselves into the special kind of reader Joyce demands. Some take courses in universities to learn how to fictionalize themselves à la Joyce. Although Joyce's text is very oral in the sense that it reads well aloud, the voice and its hearer do not fit into any imaginable real-life setting, but only the imaginative setting of *Finnegans Wake*, which is imaginable only because of the writing and print that have gone before it. *Finnegans Wake* was composed in writing, but for print: with its idiosyncratic spelling and usages, it would be virtually impossible to multiply it accurately in handwritten copies. There is no mimesis here in Aristotle's sense, except ironically. Writing is indeed the seedbed of irony, and the longer the writing (and print) tradition endures, the heavier the ironic growth becomes (Ong 1971: 272–302).

Distance, precision, grapholects and magnavocabularies

The distancing which writing effects develops a new kind of precision in verbalization by removing it from the rich but chaotic existential context of much oral utterance. Oral performances can be impressive in their magniloquence and communal wisdom, whether they are lengthy, as in formal narrative, or brief and apophthegmatic, as in proverbs. Yet wisdom has to do with a total and relatively infrangible social context. Orally managed language and thought are not noted for analytic precision.

Of course, all language and thought is to some degree analytic: it breaks down the dense continuum of experience, William James's 'big, blooming, buzzing confusion', into more or less separate parts, meaningful segments. But written words sharpen analysis, for the individual words are called on to do more. To make yourself clear without gesture, without facial expression, without intonation, without a real hearer, you have to foresee circumspectly all possible meanings a statement may have for any possible reader in any possible situation, and you have to make your language work so as to come clear all by itself, with no existential context. The need for this exquisite circumspection makes writing the agonizing work it commonly is.

What Goody (1977: 128) calls 'backward scanning' makes it possible in writing to eliminate inconsistencies (Goody 1977: 49–50), to choose between words with a reflective selectivity that invests thought and words with new discriminatory powers. In an oral culture, the flow of words, the corresponding flood of thought, the *copia* advocated in Europe by rhetoricians from classical antiquity through the Renaissance, tends to manage discrepancies by glossing them over – the etymology here is telling, *glossa*, tongue, by 'tonguing' them over. With writing, words once 'uttered', outered, put down on the surface, can be eliminated, erased, changed. There is no equivalent for this in an oral performance, no way to erase a spoken word: corrections do not remove an infelicity or an error, they merely supplement it with denial and patchwork. The *bricolage* or patchwork that Lévi-Strauss (1966, 1970) finds characteristic of 'primitive' or 'savage' thought patterns can be seen here to be due to the oral noetic situation. Corrections in oral performance tend to be counterproductive, to render the speaker unconvincing. So you keep them to a minimum or avoid them altogether. In writing, corrections can be tremendously productive, for how can the reader know they have even been made?

Of course, once the chirographically initiated feel for precision and analytic exactitude is interiorized, it can feed back into speech, and does. Although Plato's thought is couched in dialogue form, its exquisite precision is due to the effects of writing on the noetic processes, for the dialogues are in fact written texts. Through a chirographically managed text couched in dialogue form, they move dialectically toward the analytic clarification of issues which Socrates and Plato had inherited in more 'totalized', non-analytic, narratized, oral form.

In *The Greek Concept of Justice: From Its Shadow in Homer to Its Substance in Plato* (1978), Havelock has treated the movement which Plato's work brought to a head. Nothing of Plato's analytic targeting on an abstract concept of justice is to be found in any known purely oral cultures. Similarly, the deadly targeting on issues and on adversaries' weaknesses in Cicero's orations is the work of a literate mind, although we know that Cicero did not compose his orations in script before he gave them but wrote down afterwards the texts that we now have (Ong 1967: 56–7). The exquisitely analytic oral disputations in medieval universities and in later scholastic tradition into the present century (Ong 1981: 137–8) were the work of minds honed by writing texts and by reading and commenting on texts, orally and in writing.

By separating the knower from the known (Havelock 1963), writing makes possible increasingly articulate introspectivity, opening the psyche as never before not only to the external objective world quite distinct from itself but also to the interior self against whom the objective world is set. Writing makes possible the great introspective religious traditions such as Buddhism, Judaism, Christianity, and Islam. All these have sacred texts. The ancient Greeks and Romans knew writing and used it, particularly the Greeks, to elaborate philosophical and scientific knowledge. But they developed no sacred texts comparable to the Vedas or the Bible or the Koran, and their religion failed to establish itself in the recesses of the psyche which writing had opened for them. It became only a genteel, archaic literary resource for writers such as Ovid and a framework of external observances, lacking urgent personal meaning.

Writing develops codes in a language different from oral codes in the same language. Basil Bernstein (1974: 134–5, 176, 181, 197–8) distinguishes the 'restricted linguistic code' or 'public language' of the lower-class English dialects in Britain and the 'elaborated linguistic code' or 'private language' of the middle- and upper-class dialects. Walt Wolfram (1972) had earlier noted distinctions like Bernstein's between Black American English and standard American English. The restricted linguistic code can be at least as expressive and precise as the elaborated code in contexts which are familiar and shared by speaker and hearer. For dealing with the unfamiliar expressively and precisely, however, the restricted linguistic code will not do; an elaborated linguistic code is absolutely needed. The restricted linguistic code is evidently largely oral in origin and use and, like oral thought and expression generally, operates contextually, close to the human lifeworld: the group whom Bernstein found using this code were messenger boys with no grammar school education. Their expression has a formula-like quality and strings thoughts together not in careful subordination but 'like beads on a frame' (1974: 134) – recognizably the formulaic and aggregative mode of oral culture. The elaborated code is one which is formed with the necessary aid of writing, and, for full elaboration, of print. The group Bernstein found using this code were from the six major public schools that provide the most intensive education in reading and writing in Britain (1974: 83). Bernstein's 'restricted' and 'elaborated' linguistic codes could be relabeled 'oral-based' and 'text-based' codes respectively. Olson (1977) has shown how orality relegates meaning largely to context whereas writing concentrates meaning in language itself.

Writing and print develop special kinds of dialects. Most languages have never been committed to writing at all. But certain languages, or more properly dialects, have invested massively in writing. Often, as in England or Germany or Italy, where a cluster of dialects are found, one regional dialectic has developed chirographically beyond all others, for economic, political, religious, or other reasons, and has eventually become a national language. In England this happened to the upper-class London English dialect, in Germany, to High German (the German of the highlands to the south), in Italy to Tuscan. While it is true that these were all at root regional and/or class dialects, their status as chirographically controlled national languages has made them different kinds of dialects or language from those which are not written on a large scale. As Guxman has pointed out (1970: 773–6), a national written language has had to be isolated from its original dialect base, has discarded certain dialectal forms, has developed various layers of vocabulary from sources not dialectal at all, and has developed also certain syntactical peculiarities. This kind of established written language Haugen (1966: 50–71) has aptly styled a 'grapholect'.

A modern grapholect such as 'English', to use the simple term which is commonly used to refer to this grapholect, has been worked over for centuries, first and most intensively, it seems, by the chancery of Henry V (Richardson 1980), then by normative theorists, grammarians, lexicographers, and others. It has been recorded massively in writing and print and now on computers so that those competent in the grapholect today can establish easy contact not only with millions of other persons but also with the thought of centuries past, for the other dialects of English as well as thousands of foreign languages are interpreted in the grapholect. In this sense, the grapholect includes all the other dialects: it explains them as they cannot explain themselves. The grapholect bears the marks of the millions of minds which have used it to share their consciousnesses with one another. Into it has been hammered a massive vocabulary of an order of magnitude impossible for an oral tongue. *Webster's Third New International Dictionary* (1971) states in its Preface that it could have included 'many times' more than the 450,000 words it does include. Assuming that 'many times' must mean at least three times, and rounding out the figures, we can understand that the editors have on hand a record of some million and a half words used in print in English. Oral languages and oral dialects can get along with a small fraction of this number.

The lexical richness of grapholects begins with writing, but its fullness is due to print, for the resources of a modern grapholect are available largely through dictionaries. There are limited word lists of various sorts from very early in the history of writing (Goody 1977: 74–111), but until print is well established there are no dictionaries that undertake generalized comprehensive accounts of the words in use in any language. It is easy to understand why this is so if you think of what it would mean to make even a few dozen relatively accurate hand-written copies of *Webster's Third* or even of the much smaller *Webster's New Collegiate Dictionary*. Dictionaries such as these are light-years away from the world of oral cultures. Nothing illustrates more strikingly how it is that writing and print alter states of consciousness.

Where grapholects exist, 'correct' grammar and usage are popularly interpreted as the grammar and usage of the grapholect itself to the exclusion of the grammar and usage of other dialects. The sensory bases of the very concept of order are largely visual (Ong 1967: 108, 136–7), and the fact that the grapholect is written or, *a fortiori*, printed encourages attributing to it a special normative power for keeping language in order. But when other dialects of a given language besides the grapholect vary from the grammar of the grapholect, they are not ungrammatical: they are simply using a different grammar, for language is structure, and it is impossible to use language without a grammar. In the light of this fact, linguists today commonly make the point that all dialects are equal in the sense that none has a grammar intrinsically more 'correct' than that of others. But Hirsch (1977: 43–50) makes the further point that in a profound sense no other dialect, for example in English or German or Italian, has anything remotely like the resources of the grapholect. It is bad pedagogy to insist that because there is nothing 'wrong' with other dialects, it makes no difference whether or not speakers of another dialect learn the grapholect, which has resources of a totally different order of magnitude.

Chapter 12

Marcel Thomas

MANUSCRIPTS

Historians have long divided the evolution of the manuscript in western Europe into two main periods, the 'Monastic Age', and the 'Secular Age'. These terms, long current in the field, and familiar to anyone who knows something of the subject, may be somewhat lacking in precision, but nevertheless they do express an undoubted reality. In the 700 years between the Fall of Rome and the 12th century, it was the monasteries and other ecclesiastical establishments associated with them which enjoyed an almost complete monopoly of book production and so of book culture. It is also true that from the end of the 12th century a profound transformation took place. The social and intellectual changes which are particularly clearly reflected in the founding of the universities and the development of learning among the laity, and which occurred at the same time as the bourgeoisie emerges as a class, had profound repercussions on the ways in which books came to be written, copied and distributed.

In this short survey we will ignore the Monastic Age which has been the subject of many recent and excellent studies.[1] Our intention is to show (in so far as the surviving evidence makes it possible, for many of the problems relating to our subject are still far from being solved) how, from the 13th century onwards, new organisational structures made it possible to satisfy, more or less, the new requirements for books expressed by a steadily growing number of clients.

Although it is impossible to draw up an accurate list of centres of manuscript book production or furnish details of the output of a particular region at a particular time, we can at least give a reasonably accurate impression of the conditions under which books were made and disseminated in the 13th, 14th and 15th centuries. We will not summarise here even the most important features in the evolution of the manuscript book, we will only describe the situation that had developed at the time when printers placed their new techniques of manufacture at the disposal of book producers.

In the Secular Period, if we leave aside changes in the presentation and decoration of books, only small technical improvements can be said to have taken place. But one innovation must be mentioned because it had important effects both upon their manufacture and upon their price, namely the introduction of paper. It did not replace parchment, but supplemented it and made possible the production of less expensive books alongside the traditional luxury manuscripts, though the difference in price was not as great as is sometimes thought. It also made possible the production of books in greater numbers than before.

As far as the manuscript goes, paper did not offer advantages over parchment apart from its lower price and the possibility of producing it in unlimited quantity, in theory at least. Medieval paper was more fragile than parchment, had a rougher surface, and was less impervious to ink and less amenable to the pigments used by the illuminators. On the other hand it was lighter in weight. But less than might be imagined, since parchment of great delicacy was being produced in the 13th century, even thinner than the paper of the same period. For example many small Bibles of that date were, thanks to the joint skills of parchmeter and copyist, actually less bulky than the two-volume modern translation by Lemaistre de Sac. Admittedly it requires keen eyesight to read them now, and the eyes need to be accustomed to the handwriting. But there is no doubt that these small Bibles were less cumbersome than the more famous early printed Bibles, and in fact portable printed Bibles were not produced until the 16th century.

Although the main advantage of paper was its low cost and, by the 15th century, its relative abundance, it is not easy to make exact comparisons with parchment or vellum. While we possess many manuscripts which mention the price of vellum, and accounts (usually royal accounts) which record the purchase of vellum and paper,[2] the significance of the terms used is not always clear. Vellum was generally bought by the bundle (usually a dozen and a half whole skins), or by the dozen skins, or by the individual whole skin, or by the *cahier*, that is, already cut and folded into booklets of six or eight leaves. When *cahiers* are mentioned in accounts we have no way of knowing their dimensions or even the number of pages, and so we can draw no firm conclusions about costs.

At the end of the 14th century the price of skins varied between 12 and 20 deniers in Paris. The average area of a skin being about 1/2 a square metre, ten to twelve were needed to make a volume of 150 leaves measuring 24 cm × 16 cm, typical dimensions of a manuscript book in the 14th–15th centuries. The raw material from which such a book was made could thus be worth anything from 10 to 20 sous in its crude state, and to this we would have to add 4 to 6 deniers for preparing it, i.e. clearing the surface of the remaining bristles and of other blemishes to render it fit to write on. Even these figures are only an indication, since prices varied so much depending on the quality of the skin, the supplies available, and the region in which it was sold. At Paris, the Lendit Fair was an important centre for the sale of vellum.

A simple calculation will be sufficient to demolish the stories so often told about the fabulous numbers of sheep and calves required to make a single book. Even modern works of scholarship continue to repeat these old errors. Thompson, for example,[3] quotes an order by the Countess of Clare in England in 1324 for a copy of the *Vitae Patrum*, for which no fewer than 1,000 skins were allegedly required. At the current price of 2 pennies per skin, the vellum alone would have cost the fabulous sum of £6. In fact an examination of the *Vitae Patrum*, whether in Latin or in one of the contemporary French versions, quickly shows that when written in two columns the text generally fills about 150–160 leaves of 25 cm × 16 cm, or a total area amounting to no more than 6 square metres – a dozen skins at the most.

At about the same time Treasury accounts[4] show that the price of paper was 2 sols 6 deniers for a quire of 'petite forme' (i.e. about 50 cm × 30 cm), which would be a denier and a half for a leaf measuring 0.15 metres square, while vellum, as we have seen, was worth a maximum of 24–26 deniers for a skin measuring 0.5–0.6 metres square, including the cost of shaving and preparation. While the difference is certainly appreciable, it is far from attaining the importance once assigned to it. In fact, until the century paper did not seem to possess sufficient advantages, or perhaps was not marketed in large enough quantities, to supplant parchment.[5]

But was there an abundant supply of parchment? In France as in England its price remained reasonably stable from the second half of the 14th to the first half of the century, when book production was increasing rapidly, and this seems to prove that it was not such a rare commodity. It would be interesting to study the number of livestock, and of sheep in particular, to see if there was a corresponding increase over the same period. We do know that 300 years later, when vellum was no longer in general use, except in the copying of legal documents and for some industrial purposes, more than 100,000 bundles a year, each containing 40 skins, were sold in France.

All of which does not mean, of course, that printing could have developed the way it did without paper. Even if a leaf of vellum would have passed through the press easily, the smallest edition of a work would have consumed several hundred skins, even for a book of small format. For larger sizes, thousands of skins would have been required. Aloys Ruppel[6] calculated that each volume of the Gutenberg Bible that was printed on vellum must have required 170 skins (340 leaves measuring 42 cm × 62 cm). The 30 or so copies produced in this way, therefore, would have needed 5,000 skins. For the 100 copies printed on paper the equivalent on vellum would have used up 15,000 skins. Under such circumstances we can only wonder that so many luxury editions were printed on vellum in the 15th and 16th centuries, even though many were Books of Hours of small size.

Monasteries in the Secular Period continued to copy the manuscripts they needed for their own use, just as they had done in the 'monastic' period. The rules of the monastic orders prescribed a certain number of hours each day for intellectual work, and copying was an important part of this. Organised on traditional lines, the scriptoria[7] produced works of learning and service books, and went on doing so until printing finally relegated the manuscript to the past – and indeed beyond, for, as much from tradition as necessity, monasteries still continued to copy missals, antiphonaries and breviaries until well into the 16th century. The predominant feature of the new period which began at the beginning of the 13th century was that the monasteries were no longer the sole producers of books of all kinds and thenceforth scarcely produced more than were needed for their own use.

Intellectual life was now centred outside the monasteries, and it was in the universities that scholars, teachers and students, working in co-operation with artisans and craftsmen, organised an active book trade.

Occasionally, and up until a later date in England than in France, a monastery where the art of calligraphy or illumination was particularly well preserved would still be approached by a monarch or nobleman with a request for a de luxe manuscript. The sale of these was a source of income to the abbeys, but the practice grew rarer and rarer. John Lydgate, poet and monk of Bury St. Edmunds, who composed and copied texts in English which he sold to laymen until his death in 1446, was an exceptional case.[8]

From the early 13th century, and even from the end of the 12th, the foundation of the new universities gave rise to a new reading public. The new readers were, it is true, still chiefly clerics; but for as long as they were at university they were closely attached only to their college, their *alma mater*, and not to any other religious community.

The professors needed texts for their courses, along with works of reference, and commentaries. In medieval education the gloss or commentary on well-established authorities was all important in every field of learning. It was therefore indispensable for them to have these works conveniently to hand, and the university would have to provide a library where they could consult them. But it was not always possible to secure texts already in existence, and so the need arose for the establishment of workshops where professional craftsmen, employed by the university, could copy essential texts expeditiously and cheaply.

This did not exclude the use of libraries which existed outside the university, where many rare and useful works could often be found. The loan of books had long been an established practice in the Middle Ages, and various church foundations, such as monasteries and chapters, loaned out works which they would not have agreed definitively to relinquish by selling them to the new university libraries.

Despite the importance of oral instruction, the students too required a few essential books. Even if, for much of the time, they took notes at lectures and trusted to their memory, which medieval methods of education must have served to develop considerably, they still needed some basic books. If they had no time to copy them for themselves and were rich enough to have it done for them, they could order them from professional copyists, who appeared in increasing numbers around the universities. In each university town a Guild of Scriveners or Stationers came to be formed, consisting of clerks in holy orders and also often of laymen: the booksellers were laymen, while the scriveners were usually clerks. Both were assimilated into the university as a clerical branch and enjoyed certain privileges: in particular exemption from some taxes and from duties of watch and ward, together with the right to be tried by the university courts (this being the privilege of *committimus* which goes back in their case to the beginning of the 13th century).[9]

As the price for their privileges, the booksellers, copyists and 'stationers' (the term dates back to classical antiquity and was first revived in the Italian universities) had to accept strict control by the university. As the servants of a body of scholars which extended its protection over them, they were not free, as ordinary craftsmen were, to work for themselves. The way their work was organised was a constant reminder that they were carrying out what we should call a 'service'.

Numerous documents,[10] the chief ones dated 1275, 1302, 1316, 1323 and 1342, give us a fairly precise idea of their duties. They were appointed after a preliminary enquiry to confirm their good standing and professional ability, and they had to furnish guarantees and take an oath in the presence of the university authorities. Once installed, their duties were strictly laid down and their activities controlled. The booksellers were not so much retailers as custodians of books. Because of their scarcity, manuscripts were sold and resold through successive generations of students and teachers. This second-hand market employed the bookseller, who was usually no more than an agent for the vendor, as an intermediary. The security he had to pledge to get his appointment guaranteed his solvency. He could buy and sell only under certain conditions. He had to advertise publicly the titles he held in stock to prevent his making a profit out of an artificial scarcity. And he was remunerated for his labours according to a fixed rate of commission, not being allowed to charge more than 4 deniers for the sale of a volume if the purchaser was a student or teacher at the university, 6 deniers if he was not.

Alongside the booksellers who simply sold books or acted as intermediaries in the sale of books, there were the 'stationers', whose role was more complicated and whose functions have recently been made clearer by the remarkable work of Father Destrez. Thanks to him we now know in some detail the mechanism of the 'taxation' of copies and of the circulation of the 'exemplaria' and, in general, of the institution of the *pecia* or the loan of sections of books.[11]

To keep proper intellectual as well as economic control over the use of books, the authorities required all essential works to be scrupulously checked for textual correctness so that no errors might slip in, distorting the sense. To assure the reproduction of copies under the best conditions, so that the text would be unaltered and the copyists could not make unjustified profits, the universities devised an ingenious system. Manuscripts were loaned which had been carefully checked and revised. From them copies could be made and charged for according to a fixed tariff or 'tax'. The original text (the 'exemplar') was returned to the stationer after copying, and he could hire it out again. This method prevented the corruption of the text, which could otherwise become worse with every copy made, since by this method each copy was made from the same original. Anyone who has had to study the transmission of ancient texts will understand what a good idea this was.

The stationers, apart from multiplying copies themselves, loaned the copy-text or exemplar to students who either wished to copy it or have it copied by the authorised copyists. It did not go out as one book, but in quires (*peciae*), so that several copyists could be making copies from the same manuscript simultaneously. The hiring charge for each quire was determined by the university, and stationers were forbidden to increase it. Moreover they had to loan them to anyone wanting to copy them. If an exemplar was known to be imperfect it was withdrawn from circulation. A number of exemplars have come down to us, often written in a large hand and very worn because of constant use. Since they were made to a consistent standard they had the added advantage of providing a reliable measurement of the quantity of text that a copyist had transcribed, and so made it easier for clients and authorised copyists to agree on a price.

The system thus established for the multiplication of texts lasted until the close of the Middle Ages. In Paris, for example, it was within the framework of such an organisation that printing was introduced, under the auspices of the university. As far as the authorities were concerned, the printing press simply represented a handy means of multiplying indispensable texts even more rapidly and accurately than was possible under the *pecia* system.

The first Paris presses, as we shall see, were set up not so much to turn out the basic university texts of the Schoolmen as to produce a plentiful supply of the classical authors, and the examples of a pure Latin prose style which were particularly in demand. The *pecia* system seems to have answered most normal requirements quite easily. Even before scribal workshops were fully developed in the late 12th and early 13th centuries, Latin texts of Aristotle had spread across Europe:[12] more than 2,000 copies of Aristotle's works have come down to us from the and 14th centuries. If we include those that have disappeared, it is evident that the works of an author of his standing were widely known and that, if the spread of ideas was slow, it was nonetheless effective. The role of memory must not be underestimated in all this. Teaching was conceived in such a way that it could not but develop the memory. Remember that even now a Muslim child of 12 is supposed to be able to recite the whole of the Koran by heart, surprising though it might seem to us.

Still, it was difficult to assemble all the books needed for research. While Raoul de Presles was preparing his translation of *The City of God*, he collated no fewer than 30 manuscripts and 200 different works to compose his commentaries, in order to make his edition as 'critical' as possible.[13] But a note found in a manuscript of the century testifies to the difficulties encountered in the search for a given text: 'I have handed over 14 sols to the scribe who wrote this and 10 deniers to the inn-keeper, and to the person who found the exemplar for me in the inn, 2 sols'. This tip for the person who told him of a copy to be found in an unexpected place recalls the book expeditions of Richard de Bury, author of the *Philobiblion*. We need not exaggerate, however, the difficulties of scholars in the 14th or 15th century; it was simply that texts were much scarcer than they were to be after printing took over. The information we have about libraries in the 15th and 16th centuries gives us an idea of how the situation improved.

While new methods were being used in the universities to supply as many of the required 'learned' works as possible, there remained the problem of producing popular or recreational literature. A new reading public emerged in the late century, with the slow and gradual change from feudalism. A bourgeois class was appearing alongside the nobility and the clergy, equally capable of developing a literary culture. Lawyers, lay advisers at Court, state officials and, later on, rich merchants and town citizens – all needed books, not only in their own subjects like law, politics or science, but also works of literature, edifying moral treatises, romances and translations. This kind of material was not intended for clerics, although they were sometimes the authors, and usually it was in the vernacular. Original works, at first in verse, then prose, adaptations of out-dated works and translations of Latin or medieval classics were soon produced. To distribute them, and satisfy the demands of a growing reading public, required a reorganisation of the book trade.

Any history of French literature will confirm that writings in the French language were already extant by the 12th century. But the means of dissemination were a different matter. The literature of the day was meant above all to be recited or read aloud to an audience, since the reading public was not large enough to warrant any other form of publication. It may seem surprising that a large body of traditional literature could develop in such conditions. We are so permeated by our written culture that it is not easy to make the effort of imagination needed to understand the manner in which oral culture perpetuates itself, despite the fact that we have evidence on the subject from many contemporary cultures. Perhaps the new media of our age, broadcasting and the cinema, may help us grasp how ideas and works can be transmitted without passing through the medium of print.

In the 11th and 12th centuries little was read in the vernacular but many texts were composed in it. M. Faral[14] has shown convincingly how the *jongleurs* on their travels from château to château singing and reciting their poems, romances and lives of the saints — in verse because it was easier to memorise — often composed their own material. The names 'trouvères' and 'troubadours' give us an indication of their roles as creators of literature; the minstrel, on the other hand, attached to a great household, worked only for the lord and his household, to whom he addressed the poems which he either recited from stock or composed himself. The circumstances in which the early men of letters were constrained to practise their craft posed some delicate problems. It was impossible for these writers to retain any literary rights in their work unless they jealously kept the text of their compositions to themselves. But if they did that it was impossible for them to enjoy the satisfaction every artist seeks by broadcasting his work to as large an audience as possible. The two conflicting demands had to be reconciled according to the author's material needs. The best solution was to find a patron, as writers had done in ancient Rome. To him the author could offer his work, in which he included, if need be, flattery of the benefactor and his family. Failing that he could teach the words of his poems and songs to other *jongleurs* for a fee, or sell them copies.

By the late 13th and early 14th centuries we become aware of a more specialised audience, of the emergence of a large public of readers as well as listeners. Henceforward authors could write (or compile) their works without worrying about how they would be communicated to their public. The surest way to success was still through the patron. By getting a king, prince or great nobleman to accept a dedication, and presenting him with a de luxe edition, the writer secured not only the virtual certainty of material reward for his pains, but a good chance of seeing his composition becoming a popular success. Fashion is set at the top and snobbery is a feature of every age. If the public knows a translation has not only been accepted but requested by the king of France, it is almost inevitable that the translation will be widely in demand and that more copies will be requested from the author. He can then have another copy made by a scribe from his own master copy and thus become his own publisher. Boccaccio, for example,[15] in a letter to his friend Maghinardo dei Cavalcanti, which accompanied his gift of a de luxe copy of his latest works, explains how it stayed in his hands a long time after completion because he did not know to whom he might offer it. Finally, he sends it to his friend so that he may let his relations have the pleasure of reading it after him, and after that may 'publish' it abroad (*emittat in publicum*). In fact, this seems to have been one of the tacitly understood functions of the patron, because in the dedication of his *De claris mulieribus* (*On Famous Women*) to Andreina Acciajuoli, Boccaccio writes: 'If you think it good to give my book courage enough to appear in public (*procedendi in publicum*) then, once it is spread abroad (*emissus*) under your auspices, it will, I believe, rise above all the insults of ill-wishers.'

For authors more concerned about material benefits, there was always the possibility of keeping a copy-text of their book and selling further copies made from it, and sometimes we hear of authors running what amounts to their own publishing concern, as did Jean Wauquelin of Mons.[16] Sometimes they used an agent or bookseller, as when Jean Golein sent a copy-text of his translation of Guillaume Durand's *Rational* to the bookseller Henri de Trévou, who sold it in 1395 to the Duke of Orleans' valet for his master 'in his name and on behalf of M. Jean Golein'. This translation had been made by Jean Golein for Charles V twenty years earlier.[17]

The system of patronage was widespread in the 14th and 15th centuries, at least as a method of launching a new work. This explains the difference between the sometimes considerable sum paid out by a king or prince to an author for a first edition or presentation copy of a recent work, and the much lower price which later copies fetched, even if de luxe. From the economic viewpoint the author's rights may be considered to be vested in that first edition, even if it only consisted of a single copy, since thereafter he had no rights in his work. Hence to some extent the patronage system allowed literary men to live by the pen; the price paid by the author was his obligation not to say anything displeasing to his patron, while at the same time trying to write to please a growing public.[18] Books were even quite frequently produced by express command. Charles V, for example, rewarded a number of translators. When, in the hope of encouraging certain political reforms, he wanted to have his advisers and state officials read Aristotle's *Politics*, *Economics* and *Ethics*, he had them translated for that purpose by Nicole Oresme between 1369 and 1372.[19]

Once the work had been completed and offered in its 'first edition' to the patron who had ordered it, or at least accepted it as a gift, later publication was arranged through the copyists and booksellers. The author participated in the process at least in the early stages, though under conditions that are still rather obscure. He appears to have had no greater financial interest in ensuring the speedy circulation of his work than the troubadours had in the previous century, because once it had left him it was out of his hands. Yet he had no desire to remain in total obscurity. He had to find a balance between these two opposing interests.

We are ill-informed about the organisation of the book trade outside the universities, but we know that book dealers who were appointed by the university could do business with private individuals, and that they were not then subject to the same regulations (this we deduce from the regulations' silence on the subject). It is quite certain that, from the end of the century in France and the early century in England,[20] workshops were in existence employing copyists to produce books in the vernacular to be sold just as printed books are today.

Even members of the aristocracy who maintained their own scriptoria were willing to make use of such sources. The Duc de Berry, for example, who frequently ordered de luxe editions from the artists domiciled with him and in his pay, also purchased equally fine copies of manuscripts from booksellers. We know for example that in 1403 he acquired a manuscript of the Arthurian tales in prose from a bookseller called Raoul du Montet.[21] The surviving records reveal that the book was bought from a bookseller and not executed by command: proof that the clientele with a taste for de luxe editions was large enough for a stationer to order a manuscript to be prepared at considerable expense (it was sold for 300 gold écus) without a definite buyer in view. With an increase in this kind of clientele producing an increase in demand, copyists and associated craftsmen concerned in the making of books were prompted to rationalise their production methods to improve productivity.

Long before this, a degree of specialisation had developed in the monastic scriptoria. Some monks specialised in copying, others in illumination, according to their talents. But scribe and illuminator still worked side by side in constant collaboration. In the secular age, however, it became more and more common for separate workshops to be set up, with copyists in one shop, rubricators perhaps in another, and illuminators in another. Thus quite recognisable production lines slowly came into being, involving a large number of artisans, each of whom had his specific task.

By then, the raw material on which everything else depended was rarely prepared in the workshops of the copyists. Treasury accounts show that the vellum, which was usually bought in the crude state (*parchemin froutin*), passed through the hands of specialist craftsmen whose job was to thin it, shave it and bleach it. The payment of each is usually listed separately. When one artisan had written the text, another (the rubricator) added the initial letters or the chapter headings. A further specialist would do any fine capitals that might be required, whether they were coloured, illuminated or historiated. He would not even read the text, and so, in order to avoid any delay or doubt, the copyist would inscribe a small guide letter in the blank space reserved for the initial, a letter known as the *lettre d'attente* (literally the 'waiting letter'). Thus we have proof that the work was done in stages. The illumination, if it was required, came next. This art has been studied in some depth and thanks to the work of Henri Martin we have long had considerable knowledge of its craft organisation;[22] but here we will confine our account to a demonstration of how, in this field as well, attempts were made to introduce serial production.

The illuminator's atelier was separate from the copyist's, though the latter supplied the artist with an indication of the illustrations he wanted. The instructions he placed in the margin have generally disappeared in our surviving manuscripts, though Léopold Delisle[23] has tracked down numerous examples. They seem to have been very brief – for example: 'a Pope on his throne'; 'two monks'; 'a lady on horseback'. The chief artist would first take charge and decide in greater detail what scenes and portraits were to be drawn.[24] If the manuscript was not too expensive he would be content to do a rapid sketch in pencil to help his pupils compose their pictures, according to rules which were well understood and which they had put into practice a thousand times before. Thus an illuminator's atelier at the beginning of the 15th century could produce both a masterpiece like the great Book of Hours known as the 'de Rohan' and mass-produced works in which the general style of the master is recognisable but which are obviously hack copies. And, once the main work was completed, still more specialists might be required to do the backgrounds if the style employed demanded the use of special techniques – if, for example, it called for backgrounds of burnished gold, with or without scrollwork or stippling, or of chequerboard patterns.

Given this multiplicity and complexity of operations, it has frequently been emphasised that the production of a single book involved a colossal amount of work. Such a view is justified, but we must not generalise too readily. The supreme luxury article, a work of art in itself, designed for admiration rather than use – like the sumptuous books belonging to the Duc de Berry, the greatest bibliophile of his day – took months if not years of work and cost a fortune. But many other books were also being turned out (editions of the Book of Hours, for example, whose use spread everywhere in Europe in the 14th and 15th centuries) which were within reach of clients of modest means, and yet were illuminated and decorated. The trade in these Books of Hours was the virtual monopoly of certain specialist workshops, and in these, above all, an ingenious division of labour allowed time to be saved and made possible proper mass production. Ateliers of this kind existed in Flanders, and M. Delaissé has shown how illuminators would produce identical stock scenes for each of the main religious festivals (the Nativity, the Annunciation, etc.), while scribes copied out the different calendars of the various dioceses, so that they could then be joined on to those sections of the Book of Hours which did not vary from diocese to diocese.

Illuminators even perfected a process which permitted them to make several copies from one original. As Henri Martin has shown, a kind of tracing paper (*carta lustra*) with a resin base was in use from the 14th century which allowed identical copies to be made of a single 'cartoon' or design. There were frequent cases of quarrels and even brawls between illuminators accusing each other of stealing the original cartoon, a priceless resource. Nor were methods like this confined to Books of Hours. Manuscript 117/120 in the Bibliothèque Nationale, which contains tales from the Arthurian cycle, is an exact replica of a manuscript in the Library of the Arsenal. Foliation, the subjects of the illustrations, the breaks in the text to leave space for illustrations are all identical. A discovery made in Holland by M. Lieftinck and announced at the *Congrès des Sciences Historiques* by M. Samaran in 1955[25] gives us an idea of the productive capacity of the workshops using methods like this. In a manuscript at the University of Leyden (B.P.L. 138), which contains a collection of texts known as the *Auctores Octo* and was written in 1437, there is a reference in Flemish to an order from someone who was almost certainly a wholesale bookseller to the chief copyist in a workshop. The order is for a large number of copies of different texts which went to make up a little manual used in the Faculty of Arts: 200 copies of the Seven Penitential Psalms, 200 copies of Cato's *Disticha* in Flemish, 400 copies of a small prayerbook. Figures as large as this amount to true editions.

So, from the mid-13th century, copyists were forced to improve their methods to meet the growing demand, and this in turn led in some workshops to something very like standardised mass production. By using the *pecia* system they succeeded in multiplying university textbooks while avoiding the dangers of reproducing copying mistakes in manuscript after manuscript. Through the rationalisation of work in the large ateliers they were able to produce great quantities of manuals, elementary textbooks and literary works (translations, prose adaptations of the chivalric epics, courtly romances). Most frequent of all were those devotional works without which no bourgeois household was complete, since they were commonly offered as a marriage gift. Even before it was printed in so many editions, the *Travels of Sir John Mandeville*, completed in 1356, was widely reproduced in manuscript. 250 copies survive to this day in many languages: 73 in German and Dutch, 37 in French, 40 in English, 50 in Latin, not to speak of Spanish, Italian, Danish, Czech and Irish translations. All were circulating in the early 15th century.[26]

All things considered, the work of copyists and scriveners paved the way for the printers. On the eve of the appearance of the first printed texts a growing demand for books was obvious, particularly among the emergent social classes, the merchants and the bourgeoisie, who were themselves, in the first half of the 15th century, the inventors and the beneficiaries of many radical new techniques (for example, the blast furnace). Printing, which was essentially a technical development, was to have repercussions which could not have been foreseen in its early stages. The aim of the pages that follow is to show how printing came into being and what were its effects, both immediate and unforeseen.

Notes

1   W. Wattenbach, *Das Schriftwesen im Mittelalter*, 3rd edition, Leipzig, 1896; J. W. Thompson, *The Medieval Library*, Chicago, 1939 (Bibliography); Mgr Lesne, *Les Livres: scriptoria et bibliothèques du début du VIII à la fin du XI siècle*, in Vol. 4 of the *Histoire de la Propriété Ecclésiastique*, Lille, 1938.

2   Douet D'Arcq, *Comptes de l'Hôtel des Rois de France aux XIV et XV Siècles*, Paris, 1865 (*Société de l'Histoire de France*, pp. 64, 67, 97, 101ff., 151, 160, 162, 183, 224, 231, 233, 332 and 334.

3   J. W. Thompson, op. cit.

4   Douet D'Arcq, op. cit.

5   J. de la Lande, *L'Art de Faire le Parchemin*, Paris, 1761.

6   A. Ruppel, *Johannes Gutenberg, sein Leben und sein Werk*, Berlin, 1947, p. 141.

7   On this, see Mgr Lesne, op. cit., and J. W. Thompson, op. cit.

8   R. R. Root, 'Publication before Printing', in *Publications of the Modern Language Association* (PMLA), XXVIII, 1913, p. 417.

9   P. Delalain, *Étude sur le Libraire Parisien du XIII au XV Siècle*, Paris, 1891.

10   Ibid.; and *Chartularium Universitatis Parisiensis*, ed. H. Denifle and E. Chatelain, Vol. 1 (1889), Vol. 2 (1891), Paris, 1889–97, 4 vols.

11   J. Destrez, *La 'Pecia' dans les Manuscrits Universitaires du XIII et du XIV Siècle*, Paris, 1935.

12   D. A. Callus, 'Introduction of Aristotelian Learning to Oxford', in *Proceedings of the British Academy*, Vol. XXIX, 1943. St Bernard complained about the popularity of Abelard's ideas,

altogether too hasty in his view. When Abelard was expelled from the university, students paid for private lessons from him. Cf. *Patres Latini*, CLXXXII.

13   L. Delisle, *Recherches sur la Librairie de Charles V*, Paris, 1907, 3 volumes, one of plates.

14   E. Faral, *Les Jongleurs en France au Moyen Age*, Paris, 1910 (*Bibliothèque de l'École des Hautes Études. Sciences Historiques et Philologiques*, fascicule 187).

15   R. R. Root, op. cit., p. 417.

16   L. Delaissé, 'Les Chroniques de Hainault et l'Atelier de Jean Wauquelin à Mons', in the *Bulletin des Musées Royaux des Beaux-Arts*, Brussels, 1955.

17   L. Delisle, *Le Cabinet des Manuscrits*, Paris, 1868–81, 3 Vols. Vol. 1, p. 102.

18   On royal patronage in the 15th century, see Doutrepont, *La Littérature Française à la Cour des Ducs de Bourgogne*, Paris, 1909, and A. Coville, *La Vie Intellectuelle dans la Domaine d'Anjou-Provence de 1380 à 1435*, Paris, 1941.

19   Nicole Oresme, *Le Livre des Éthiques d'Aristote*, published from the text of MS. 2902 in the Belgian Royal Library, by A. D. Menut, New York, 1940.

20   H. Loomis, 'The Auchinleck Manuscript and a Possible London Bookshop of 1330–1340', in *Publications of the Modern Language Association*, LVIII, 1942, pp. 595–627.

21   J. J. Guiffrey, *Inventaires de Jean, Duc de Berry, 1401–1416*, Paris, 1894–96; M. Thomas, 'Recherches sur un Groupe de Manuscrits à Peinture du Début du XV Siècle', in *Bulletin Bibliographique de la Société Internationale Arthurienne*, 4, 1952, pp. 81–89.

22   H. Martin, *Les Miniaturistes Français*, Paris, 1906.

23   L. Delisle, *Le Cabinet des Manuscrits*, passim.

24   On illuminators' workshops in the early part of the 15th century, see the catalogue of the exhibition, *Manuscrits à Peinture du XIII au XVI Siècle*, Paris, Bibliothèque Nationale, 1955. Reviews of this have been compiled by Jean Porcher, with an extensive bibliography.

25   The Tenth Congress, Rome, 4–11 September, 1955, in *Atti*, Florence, 1955, p. 152 ff.

26   H. S. Bennett, 'The Author and his Public in the 14th and 15th Century', in *Essays and Studies by Members of the English Association*, XXIII, 1938, p. 7 ff.

Chapter 13

Roger Chartier

THE PRACTICAL IMPACT OF WRITING

One of the most important developments of the modern era, according to Philippe Ariès, was the advent of written culture in Western society. The spread of literacy, the widespread circulation of written materials whether in printed or manuscript form, and the increasingly common practice of silent reading, which fostered a solitary and private relation between the reader and his book, were crucial changes, which redrew the boundary between the inner life and life in the community.

Between 1500 and 1800 man's altered relation to the written word helped to create a new private sphere into which the individual could retreat, seeking refuge from the community.

This development, however, as I will show, did not totally obliterate earlier practices, nor did it affect everyone who dealt with printed materials. Reading aloud, reading in groups for work or pleasure, did not cease with the arrival of silent and private reading. Different kinds of reading overlapped. But this should not cause us to lose sight of the fact that new models of behavior were being established, models that tell us a great deal about the process of privatization in the early modern period.

Measuring literacy

Can the extent to which the written word penetrated Western societies in the early modern period be measured? Attempting to do so, historians have counted signatures on documents from parish records, notarial archives, the courts, and tax authorities; using these data they have estimated what proportion of the population consisted of people able to sign their own names. After lengthy debate, it is now widely accepted that, although this figure can be taken as a very rough estimate of a society's familiarity with writing, it cannot be interpreted directly as a measure of cultural advancement. In early modern societies, where the small fraction of children who attended school learned first to read and then to write, everyone who could sign his name could also read, but not everyone who knew how to read could sign his name.

Furthermore, not all signers could actually write. For some, instruction in writing never went

Reprinted by permission of the Publisher from *A History of Private Life, Volume 3: Passions of die Renaissance*, Roger Chartier, translated by Arthur Goldhammer, Cambridge, Mass.: The Belknap Press of Harvard University Press, © 1989 the President and Fellows of Harvard College.

beyond learning how to sign their names; for others writing was a skill lost for want of practice, and the ability to sign was merely a relic of that lost skill. Paradoxically, the signature is the mark of a population that knows how to read but not necessarily how to write. It is impossible to estimate what fraction of the signers could actually write, and some people who could read never learned to sign their names. This does not mean that all the data concerning percentages of signers at different times and in different places are worthless. The figures constitute a kind of rough, composite index, which does not precisely measure the diffusion of either writing skills (which the percentages exaggerate) or reading skills (which they underestimate).[1]

Numbers of readers

With this caveat in mind, it is clear from all the data that between 1500 and 1800 the percentage of signers rose sharply throughout Europe. (For convenience, we may refer to this percentage as the 'literacy rate', bearing in mind that it does not necessarily indicate the percentage of the population that could both read and write.) We possess sufficient data about three countries to permit generalizations on a national scale. In Scotland signatures collected for the National Covenant of 1638 (which affirmed the unity of the Presbyterian churches) and for the Solemn League and Covenant of 1643 (which promised Scottish support to the English Parliament, provided that it established the Presbyterian religion) reveal a literacy rate among males of 25 percent. A century later, signatures collected in the 1750s before the High Court of the Judiciary reveal rates of 78 percent for men and 23 percent for women; corrected to reflect differences between the social composition of the witness group and the general population, these figures suggest literacy rates of 65 and 15 percent, respectively.[2] In England signatures collected for the Protestation Oath of 1641 (an oath of allegiance to the 'true religion, reformed and Protestant') for the Vow and Covenant of 1643 (an oath of loyalty to Parliament), and for the Solemn League and Covenant of 1644 (which introduced Presbyterianism) indicate a male literacy rate of 30 percent. In the second half of the eighteenth century the marriage registers of the Church of England, which after 1754 required the signatures of both bride and groom, reflect the progress of the written word: 60 percent of the men signed in 1755 and in 1790, compared with 35 percent of the women in 1755 and 40 percent in 1790.[3] In France, finally, signatures of brides and grooms in the parish registers (recorded in almost all départements by schoolteachers enlisted for the purpose by Rector Maggiolo in 1877) reflect a century of progress: in 1686–1690, only 29 percent of men and 14 percent of women signed; in 1786–1790, 48 percent of men and 27 percent of women did.[4] Thus, over a period of a century and a half, male literacy rates rose by 40 percent in Scotland, 30 percent in England, and 19 percent in France.

In other countries, for which we lack the data to determine the national literacy rate, we find evidence of similar progress in specific cities or regions. In Amsterdam, for example, notarized betrothal agreements were signed by 85 percent of men and 64 percent of women in 1780, compared with 57 percent of men and 32 percent of women in 1630.[5] In Turin 83 percent of husbands and 63 percent of wives signed their marriage contracts in 1790, compared with 70 and 43 percent, respectively, in 1710. And in the province of Turin – that is, in the rural region governed by the city – progress was even more spectacular: the percentage of male signatories rose from 21 to 65, and of female signatories from 6 to 30.[6] In New Castile, in the jurisdiction of the inquisitorial court of Toledo, witnesses and accused (eight out of ten of whom were men and nearly one out of two a notable), 49 percent could sign their names, more or less, between 1515 and 1600, 54 percent between 1651 and 1700, and 76 percent between 1751 and 1817. The nature of the sample precludes using these figures as an indication of the literacy of the Castilian population as a whole, but the rising percentages suggest that literacy was making steady progress.[7]

The trend was similar in the American colonies. In New England, 61 percent of men signed their wills in 1650–1670, 69 percent in 1705–1715, 84 percent in 1758–1762, and 88 percent in 1787–1795.[8] For women, the comparable figures for the first three dates were 31, 41, and 46 percent, respectively. In Virginia, 50 percent of men signed their wills between 1640 and 1680, compared with 65 percent between 1705 and 1715 and 70 percent between 1787 and 1797.[9]

Thus, there was a widespread and often marked increase in the percentage of men and women able to sign their names, an increase that occurred regardless of the absolute level of literacy. In Protestant as well as Catholic countries, in countryside as well as cities, and in the New World as well as the Old, more and more people were familiar with writing. Large numbers of people acquired cultural skills that previously had been the exclusive possession of a minority. This is not to say that progress was uninterrupted. Although the literacy rate reveals a marked trend upward stretching over centuries, it was not without setbacks and recessions. In England the percentage of signers among witnesses before the ecclesiastical court of the diocese of Norwich shows temporary but significant declines. They affected those who reached their tenth year between 1580 and 1610, especially merchants, husbandmen, and yeomen; as well as the civil war generation, educated in the 1640s, where the decline among yeomen reached 20 percent; or in the period 1690–1710, which saw a particularly sharp decline in peasant literacy, especially among husbandmen.[10]

In Madrid the second half of the seventeenth century witnessed a similar decline in literacy: in 1650, 45 percent of testators signed their wills or declarations of poverty; between 1651 and 1700, this figure dropped to 37 percent.[11] The decline was more marked among men (68 to 54 percent) than among women (26 to 22 percent). Finally, in Provence the generations educated between 1690 and 1740 show no progress in literacy and in some areas suffered a sharp decline, to judge by the percentages of signatures on wills and marriage documents.[12] In general, literacy in Provence increased as it did everywhere else: between the end of the seventeenth century and the beginning of the nineteenth century, thirteen out of a sample of twenty communities doubled the percentage of signers. Yet this overall progress came in spite of lack of progress or even decline in the intervals between periods of significant advance, which in the case of Provence came between 1650 and 1680 and in the fifty or sixty years after 1740.

Reasons for the lack of progress, which varied from place to place, included deterioration of the schools, influx of less literate immigrants, or setbacks in the economy. The important point is that between 1500 and 1800 the progress of literacy was neither steady nor uninterrupted. It is this, perhaps, which distinguishes our period most sharply from the nineteenth century, when the advent of mass education inaugurated an era of steady improvement.

Unequal skills

Although familiarity with writing increased, it was not shared equally. Certain inequalities stand out, probably the most glaring of all being the inequality between men and women. Everywhere the male literacy rate is higher than the female, with a gap between the two as high as 25 or 30 percent. Obviously women had less of a role to play in the world of the written word. But the figures do not give an accurate idea of differences in reading ability. In early modern societies learning to read was long considered a part of a girl's education; learning to write was not, for writing was held to be a useless and dangerous skill for women to acquire. In Molière's Ecole des femmes, Arnolphe is eager for Agnès to read so that she can absorb his 'Maxims for Marriage', but he succumbs to despair when he discovers that she knows how to write, especially to her beloved Horace. Thus, for women even more than for men, the percentage of signers is an inadequate measure of the percentage of readers (especially in the lower classes).

Inequalities existed between people in different occupations and estates. In seventeenth-century rural England the ability to sign (measured by signatures of witnesses before the ecclesiastical courts) was closely correlated with work and social status. Nearly all clerics, notables, and important merchants knew how to write. Skilled artisans (goldsmiths, harness-makers, drapers) and yeomen could write in seven or eight out of ten cases. In most other trades, especially textiles and clothing, only about one in two could sign their names. Next came the village artisans and merchants (blacksmiths, carpenters, millers, butchers, and so forth), of whom only 30 to 40 percent could sign. At the bottom of the scale were building laborers, fishermen, shepherds, husbandmen, and agricultural workers, of whom at most one in four could sign their names.[13] With minor variations this example holds good throughout rural Europe, where the ability to sign one's name was largely determined by such factors as the degree of skill required by one's work and the degree of involvement in nonlocal markets.

In cities too the ability to write depended largely on occupation and status, but city dwellers were far in advance of their rural counterparts in absolute percentages. Consider early-nineteenth-century marriage records from the Emilia region of Italy.[14] In the five cities Piacenza, Parma, Reggio, Modena, and Bologna we find that 42 percent of grooms and 21 percent of brides were able to sign their names, whereas in the surrounding countryside the corresponding figures were, respectively, just 17 and 5 percent. The same is true in northern Europe: seventeenth-century London artisans and merchants were two to three times as literate as their rural counterparts, and domestic servants were two-and-a-half times as literate (in London, 69 percent signed, compared with only 24 percent in rural England).[15] This is one reason why the culture of the modern city was unique: large numbers of city dwellers knew how to write, and the ability to read and write was less unequally distributed than in the countryside.

All of these differences in access to the written word affected the process of privatization in the sixteenth, seventeenth, and eighteenth centuries. The ability to read was an essential prerequisite for certain new practices around which people built their private lives. Personal communion with a read or written text liberated the individual from the old mediators, freed him or her from the control of the group, and made it possible to cultivate an inner life. Solitary reading permitted the development of new forms of piety, which radically altered man's relation to the divine. The ability to read and write enabled people to relate to others and to the authorities in new ways. The greater a person's familiarity with writing, the more emancipated he was from traditional ways of life, which bound the individual tightly to his community and made him dependent on others to read and interpret the divine word and the commandments of his sovereign.

The geography of literacy

Increasingly private ways of reading and relating changed the nature of European society, but at a different pace in each country. Broadly speaking, northern and northwestern Europe enjoyed higher rates of literacy than other areas. By the end of the eighteenth century 60 to 70 percent of the men in the more literate regions could sign their name: 71 percent in France north of the Saint-Malo–Geneva line, 61 percent in Austrian-dominated parts of the Low Countries,[16] 60 percent in England, 65 percent in Scotland. For women, the figures are 44 percent for northern and northeastern France, 37 percent in the Low Countries, and 40 percent in England. It is harder to gauge the literacy rate in other parts of Europe, where historians have done less research, but various signs indicate that it lagged well behind the rate of the more advanced regions. In Emilia, for instance, the urban signature rates were no higher than 45 percent for men and 26 percent for women in the early nineteenth century – a very late date. Hence there is every reason to believe that the literacy rate of the Italian population as a whole, counting peasants as well as city dwellers and the Mezzogiorno as well as the relatively advanced north, most have been lower, probably much lower, than that in northern Europe. In Hungary, in 1768, only 14 percent of the municipal magistrates in villages and towns could sign their names, and the percentage for the peasant population must have been even lower.[17] Finally, in Sweden, only 35 percent of conscripts in the 1870s knew how to write, which suggests that the literacy rate in the late eighteenth century must have been very low.

On the whole, however, northern and northwestern Europe was culturally more advanced than the rest of the continent: a crude contrast, but undoubtedly correct as far as it goes. Some corrections are called for, however. Between regions where the signature rate was as high as 30 percent in the late eighteenth century and regions where it was as low as 10 or 20 percent, there were transitional zones. Southern France, below the Saint-Malo–Geneva line, was one: on the eve of the Revolution, 44 percent of men and 17 percent of women signed their marriage papers.

Furthermore, even within the relatively backward zone, we can distinguish between areas where people could neither read nor write (as may have been the case in Italy and Hungary) and those where many people who could read were unable to write. In mid-eighteenth-century Sweden, for example, few people could write but 80 percent could read. With the promulgation of the Church Law of 1686, the Lutheran Church, backed by the state, had launched a campaign to teach people to read and see with their own eyes what God ordered and commanded through his sacred word. The parish clergy subsequently took charge of teaching reading. Periodically, parishioners were examined to test their reading skills and knowledge of the catechism, and those who could not read and did not know their catechism were prevented from receiving communion and marrying in the church. The campaign, which reached a peak of intensity between 1690 and 1720, left an enduring mark on the populations of Sweden and Finland, where everyone knew how to read (having been trained to do so by the clergy for religious purposes) but only a narrow elite knew how to write.[18]

Such a situation was probably not peculiar to Sweden. It may also have been true of Denmark, where the gap between reading and writing at the end of the eighteenth century seems to have been quite marked. It was surely true of Scotland, one of the most literate countries in Europe. According to evidence gathered in 1742 by the evangelical pastor of Cambuslang, a parish at the center of the religious revival then shaking the Church of Scotland, every man and woman in the parish claimed to be able to read, but only 60 percent of the men and 10 percent of the women said that they knew how to write.[19] Many said that they had learned to read in order to avoid the 'shame' of not being able to participate fully in religious assemblies. Thus, in some Protestant countries, the ability to read was universal, regardless of the 'literacy rate' measured by counting signatures.

Writing and the Reformation

A high rate of literacy was not a necessary effect of Protestantism, however. In Germany, as early as the third decade of the sixteenth century, Luther abandoned his insistence that every Christian should know how to read the Bible. Instead he emphasized the importance of preaching and catechism, that is, the role of the pastor as teacher and interpreter of the holy text. In Lutheran states there was a marked difference between the education offered to the pastoral and administrative elites and popular religious instruction, which, being mainly oral and based on memorization, was quite compatible with illiteracy.[20] In the Rhineland, in the second half of the sixteenth century, religious examiners found that many people could recite texts that they did not understand and that they responded to questions with answers learned by heart and not always appropriate, proving that catechism classes taught formulas by rote and did not seek to foster a personal interpretation of the Bible.[21]

It was not until the so-called Second Reformation initiated by Pietism at the end of the seventeenth century that all the faithful were expected to learn what was in the Bible and develop a personal interpretation. To that end, Protestants first taught one another in religious conventicles. Later the government issued ordinances governing the course of instruction to be offered in the elementary schools. This changed the very status of the Bible. In sixteenth-century Germany it had been a book for pastors, students studying for the ministry, and parish libraries; by the early eighteenth century it had become a book for everyone, mass-produced and sold at a low price. This may account for the steep increase of literacy among German Pietists: in eastern Prussia the percentage of peasants capable of signing their name rose from 10 percent in 1750 to 25 percent in 1756 and to 40 percent by the end of the century.[22] Pietism, not Lutheranism, spread the ability to read in Germany.

Medieval advances

The progress of literacy and diffusion of reading were major factors contributing to change in Western man's idea of himself and his relation to others. The magnitude of the phenomenon can be measured, however, only for the seventeenth and eighteenth centuries, because series of documents suitable for such techniques as counting signatures did not become available until the very end of the sixteenth century, and often much later. The cultural state of Europe in the late Middle Ages and even in the sixteenth century therefore remains largely unknown, and it is probably incorrect to assume that literacy rates were low everywhere and that only the clergy knew how to write. In Flanders, for example, various signs suggest that ordinary people could read, write, and count. In the cities 'Latinless' schools taught the basics to common folk. There were probably more than twenty of them in Saint-Omer in 1468, and Valenciennes, a town of 10,000 inhabitants, had twenty-four such schools in 1497. Another sign is the presence of texts on church frescoes and paintings. Still another is the high percentage of signatures – of the order of 70 percent – found in receipts of all sorts (for rents, supplies, and labor) collected by the accountants of the aldermen and hospitals of Saint-Omer in the fifteenth century. Many merchants and artisans seem to have been literate, and only laborers and haulers appear in the majority to have been unable to sign their names. In the countryside the situation was no doubt different, but the keeping of poor-table records, community and charity registers, and tax rolls suggests that writing was a widely shared ability, and the posting of tax rates suggests that at least some people could read them.[23]

Medieval Flanders was by no means unique in its ability to read and write. In Italian cities, as early as the fourteenth century, many people, even among the lower orders, were able to write. In Florence, in 1340, 45 to 60 percent of children between the ages of six and thirteen attended city elementary schools; since far more boys than girls attended school, the percentage of boys receiving an elementary education must have been very high.[24] In some places the ability to write was an accomplished fact by the end of the Middle Ages. Accordingly, the spectacular and widespread advances that occurred in the period 1600–1800 should not be taken to indicate that only a very few people knew how to read and write between 1400 and 1500.

The rejection of writing

The progress made should not be allowed to obscure a persistent hostility to writing and its dissemination. Shakespeare dramatizes this resistance in *Henry VI, Part 2* (whose quarto edition dates from 1594), in the treatment of Jack Cade's rebellion. In scene 2 of act 4 Cade and his men decide to kill 'all the lawyers' and for their first victim choose the clerk of Chatham. Their social animosity is fed by a threefold rejection of writing. First, writing is the medium in which the decisions of the authorities are couched. Cade's reference to 'parchment scribbled o'er' and sealed undoubtedly alludes to royal writs, which since the twelfth century had been used to record complaints submitted to the king and to convey decisions of the royal courts to local sheriffs. (Cade had been sentenced to having his hand burned for stealing livestock.) Second, writing was used to record the obligations of the poor, whence the reproach leveled against the clerk of Chatham: 'He can make obligations and write court-hand', which is to say, he records debts in the cursive script used in notarized documents. Third, writing was thought to have magic and evil powers. The clerk of Chatham has 'a book in his pocket with red letters in't', in other words, a book of witchcraft with rubrics or titles in red ink, possibly associated with his Jewishness, as indicated by his name, Emmanuel, whose epistolary significance is understood by Dick, one of the rebels: 'They use to write it on top of the letters.' The ability to write is thus a tool of the authorities, a method of domination, whether by law or magic, employed by the strong against the weak, hence the sign of a rejection of communal equality. Thus, Cade asks the clerk: 'Dost thou use to write thy name, or hast thou a mark to thyself, like an honest plain-dealing man?' The mark, which anyone can make, is proof of respect for man's original equality, whereas the signature, which sets apart those who know how to write, indicates rejection of the common rule.

In scene 7 the rebels, having gained control of London, give free rein to their hatred of written culture. They attempt to destroy the places where that culture is transmitted ('others to th'Inns of Court: down with them all'), its ancient monuments ('burn all the records of the realm'), its techniques of reproduction (Lord Say is accused of having constructed a paper mill and introduced printing), and its lexicon of description (another charge against Lord Say being that he is surrounded by men 'that usually talk of a noun and a verb, and such abominable words'). Against these oppressive and corrupting innovations Cade sets forth the claims of a traditional culture, based on speech and signs: 'My mouth shall be the parliament of England'. He thus alludes to the ancient conception of law, according to which its force stems from its oral proclamation. Instead of books and printed materials, Cade prefers the ancient practice of recording private debts by making notches on pieces of wood: 'the score and the tally'. In fact, Jack Cade's rebellion took place in 1449, twenty-seven years before the introduction of printing into England. In writing about a rebellion that occurred a century and a half earlier, Shakespeare was able to incorporate into his play the fundamental tension between two cultures: one increasingly based on recourse to the written word in both the public and the private spheres; the other based on nostalgic and utopian esteem for a society without writing, governed by words that everyone could hear and signs that everyone could understand. Whatever his intention in depicting a popular uprising as foolish and bloody and the rebels as dupes manipulated by others, it is clear that the underlying cause of the rebellion is hostility to writing, which is blamed for the upheavals that are transforming the society.

If Shakespeare depicted hostility to writing as a sentiment of the lower classes, that sentiment had a more literate counterpart in the rejection by the educated of printed books, a common reaction around the turn of the sixteenth century. In Venice, for example, a Dominican named Filippo di Strata proposed an argument against Gutenberg's invention that was accepted by a large part of the Venetian Senate. Printing, he maintained, was guilty on several counts: it corrupted texts, which were circulated in hastily manufactured, faulty editions composed solely for profit; it corrupted minds by making available immoral and heterodox works over which the ecclesiastical authorities had no control; and it corrupted knowledge, which was debased by being divulged to the ignorant. Whence the judgment: '*Est virgo hec penna, meretrix eat stompificata*' (The pen is a virgin, the printing press a whore).[25]

More than a century later echoes of di Strata's argument can be heard in Lope de Vega's *Fuenteovejuna*, published in Madrid in 1619. In act 2, lines 892–930, a peasant, Barrildo, and a licentiate of the University of Salamanca, Leonelo, discuss the merits of printing. The learned Leonelo reveals his doubts about the usefulness of Gutenberg's invention. To be sure, it preserves valuable works and assures their wide distribution, but it also causes errors and absurdities to circulate, allows those who would ruin an author's reputation to usurp his identity and distribute nonsense in his name, and confuses people's minds with an overabundance of texts. Far from contributing to the progress of knowledge, printing may well have added to the sum of ignorance. When Barrildo says that the growing number of printed books has made it possible for every man to think of himself as a scholar, Leonelo curtly replies: '*Antes que ignoran màs*' (No, they are more ignorant than before).

The advent of written culture in the West had to contend with the persistent notion that dissemination of knowledge was tantamount to profanation. The growing number of those who could read and write and the proliferation of printed matter caused disarray among 'clerks' (lay as well as ecclesiastical), who had hitherto enjoyed a monopoly of the production and discussion of knowledge. In the Christian tradition, only clerics were authorized to interpret the secrets of God, nature, and the state. With the scientific revolution of the seventeenth century, the ancient taboos and limitations on access to knowledge were lifted, but only for a small minority, the *respublica litteratorum*, whose members were held to be the only people capable of pursuing knowledge without danger to religion, law, and order. At a time when Icarus and Prometheus became emblems of a knowledge without limits, people were also reminded that knowledge must remain the exclusive province of the new clerks: the intellectuals.[26]

Two motifs were indissolubly linked: the idea that the lower orders rejected written culture because they saw it as an instrument of domination and a threat to the social fabric, and the idea that the educated resisted appropriation by the vulgar of knowledge that had been theirs exclusively, hence also of the keys that gave access to that knowledge. Before the written word could find a place in Western society, it had to overcome both of these representations.

Reading practices

Silent reading

Between the sixteenth and eighteenth centuries, as growing numbers of people learned to read, new ways of reading became popular. The most novel of these, as Philippe Ariès has noted, was private reading in a quiet place away from other people, which allowed the reader to engage in solitary reflection on what he or she read. This 'privatization' of reading is undeniably one of the major cultural developments of the early modern era.

What conditions made it possible? First of all, people needed to acquire a new skill: the ability to read without pronouncing the words as they were read. Otherwise the reader remained subject to communal constraints while reading in a library, say, or a room where others were present. Silent reading also made possible the immediate internalization of what the reader read. Reading aloud was slow, laborious, and externalized; silent reading was faster, easier, and more immediate in its impact on the inner self. Apparently, during the Middle Ages, one group of readers after another mastered the technique of silent reading. The first were the copyists working in the monastic scriptoria. Then, around the middle of the twelfth century, scholars in the universities acquired the ability. Two centuries later the lay aristocracy learned to read silently. By the fifteenth century silent reading was the norm, at least for readers who also knew how to write and who belonged to segments of society that had long been literate. For others, who belonged to groups that slowly learned to read and for whom books remained strange, rare objects, the old way of reading no doubt remained a necessity. As late as the nineteenth century, neophytes and maladroit readers could be identified by their inability to read silently. In Labiche's play *La Cagnotte* (1864), the farmer Colladan replies to a person who loses patience when he reads a very private letter out loud: 'If I read out loud, it's not for you, it's for me . . . Whenever I don't read out loud . . . I don't understand what I'm reading.'

Silent reading opened new horizons for those who mastered it. It radically transformed intellectual work, which in essence became an intimate activity, a personal confrontation with an ever-growing number of texts, a question of memorization and cross-referencing. It made possible a more personal form of piety, a more private devotion, a relation with the sacred not subject to the discipline and mediation of the Church. The spirituality of the mendicant orders, the *devotio moderna*, and even Protestantism, all of which presuppose a direct relation between the individual and God, relied heavily on silent reading, which enabled at least some people to nurture their faith on private reading of spiritual books or the Bible itself. Finally, silent, secret, private reading paved the way for previously unthinkable audacities. In the late Middle Ages, even before the invention of the printing press, heretical texts circulated in manuscript form, critical ideas were expressed, and erotic books, suitably illuminated, enjoyed considerable success.[27]

Although the invention of printing was indeed a 'revolution' in that it made it possible to produce a large number of identical copies at a cost much lower than that of copying by hand (even at a time when print runs were small and printing costs quite high), it should not be credited with intellectual and psychological changes that were really the result of a new method of reading, regardless of whether the text was printed or manuscript. By the sixteenth century, the 'other revolution' – the revolution in reading – was already accomplished, although it had only recently made its impact felt on laymen and remained incomplete, since large numbers of readers who had not yet mastered writing were incapable of reading silently. There seems to have been a clear division between those for whom reading was a private act and those for whom it remained a communal act, perhaps even an act of class solidarity.

More books for more readers

Did silent reading result in greater familiarity with books and a more prominent place for them in the home? The evidence is unfortunately imperfect, incomplete, and much criticized; we must rely primarily on inventories, generally compiled after a death, which described (to a limited extent) and estimated the value of an individual's possessions, including his books. One problem is that the presence of a book in an estate inventory does not imply that the book was read or even purchased by the deceased. Inventories also failed to include printed materials of little value, even though these might constitute the bulk of a person's reading, and of course omitted any valuable or dangerous books that might have been removed from the library beforehand. Such evidence, therefore, should not be relied upon for anything more than very general indications concerning, for instance, the presence of a particular book in the libraries of a particular class of society. Even more than in the case of signature rates, we must be very cautious in comparing data from different places, for the figures may be influenced by differences in notarial practices and in the composition of the populations for which estate inventories were compiled.

By the sixteenth century the evidence suggests that private individuals owned more books than ever before. In some places the percentage of book owners, both overall and by social class, remained constant, but the number of books owned increased. In Valencia, for example, books are mentioned in one out of three inventories between 1474 and 1550. The hierarchy of ownership remained stable: nine out of ten clerics owned books, as did three out of four members of the liberal professions, one out of two nobles, one out of three merchants, and only one out of ten manual laborers. Within each group the number of books in the average library increased. Between the end of the fifteenth century and the second quarter of the sixteenth century, the average physician's collection increased from 26 to 62 books; the average jurist's from 25 to 55; and the average merchant's from 4 to 10. As for artisans in the textile trade, who had generally owned only one book, the average 'library' now increased to four volumes.[28]

In sixteenth-century Florence the percentage of inventories compiled by the Magistrato de'pupilli in which books are mentioned remained quite low: 4.6 percent between 1531 and 1569, 5.2 percent between 1570 and 1608. (It had reached 3.3 percent between 1413 and 1453 but fell to 1.4 percent in the second half of the fifteenth century.) This percentage is much lower than that found in Valencia or Amiens (where, between 1503 and 1576, 20 percent of inventories mentioned books).[29] Was Italy backward in this respect? It is hard to say. We can, however, assert with confidence that, while the percentage of book owners increased very little, the proportion of books belonging to the largest libraries increased substantially. Libraries containing fewer than six volumes accounted for 55 percent of the total before 1570, but for only 31 percent after that date. Conversely, libraries with 51 to 100 volumes increased from 4.5 to 9 percent, and those with 101 to 200 volumes from 1 to 8 percent. Libraries with from 6 to 50 volumes, which had accounted for 38 percent of the total before 1570, rose to 47 percent afterward.[30]

A third possibility was an increase in the percentage of the population that owned books. In Canterbury, around the turn of the seventeenth century, inventories of men's estates indicate ownership of books in one out of ten cases in 1560, one out of four cases in 1580, one out of three cases in 1590, and nearly one out of two cases in 1620. A similar pattern has been noted in two smaller cities in Kent: Faversham and Maidstone. Here again, ownership of books depends strongly on social rank: between 1620 and 1640 in Canterbury 90 percent of men in the professions and 73 percent of nobles owned books, compared with only 45 percent of textile artisans, 36 percent of construction workers, and 31 percent of the city's yeomen. With such high percentages the three cities in Kent are not typical of England as a whole. In rural parishes books remained rare, even in the seventeenth century. Only 13 percent of inventories in Bedfordshire at the end of the second decade of the century and 14 percent of those from Middlesex between 1630 and 1690 mention the presence of books.[31]

Did private ownership of books increase between 1500 and 1800? Did growing familiarity with books contribute to the privatization characteristic of the period? The answers to these questions depend on location. Leading Europe in book ownership were the cities of the Protestant countries. In the middle of the eighteenth century, in the German Lutheran cities of Tübingen, Spire, and Frankfurt, books are mentioned in, respectively, 89, 88, and 77 percent of all inventories.[32] Compare this with Catholic France, whether in Paris, where only 22 percent of inventories in the 1750s mention books, or in provincial cities. (In nine cities of western France, the figure for 1757–1758 was 36 percent, and in Lyons in the second half of the eighteenth century it was 35 percent.)[33] Other Protestant countries were more like Germany, even largely rural countries like the United States. At the end of the eighteenth century, 75 percent of the inventories in Worcester County, Massachusetts, 63 percent in Maryland, and 63 percent in Virginia mention the presence of books.[34] These figures indicate marked progress compared with the previous century, where the figure in these same regions was about 40 percent.

Protestant reading

Religion established an important difference with respect to book ownership. There is no more striking proof of this than a comparison of Catholic and Protestant libraries in the same city. In Metz, between 1645 and 1672, 70 percent of Protestant inventories mention books, compared with only 25 percent of Catholic ones. The gap remains wide, regardless of occupation: 75 percent of Protestant nobles owned books compared with only 22 percent of Catholic nobles; in the legal professions the figures are 86 and 29 percent; in the medical professions, 88 and 50 percent; for minor officers, 100 and 18 percent; for merchants, 85 and 33 percent; for artisans, 52 and 17 percent; for 'bourgeois', 73 and 5 percent; and for manual and agricultural laborers, 25 and 9 percent. Protestants owned more books than Catholics. Protestant professionals owned on the average three times as many books as their Catholic counterparts, and the ratio was the same for merchants, artisans, and minor officers. As for those classed as 'bourgeois', the libraries of the Calvinists were ten times as large as those of the Catholics.[35]

There were differences in the composition of libraries and in reading practices. In Lutheran countries all libraries, regardless of the social rank of the owner, were organized around a common set of religious books. In Rhenish cities this consisted of the Bible, pious books, manuals of preparation for communion and confession, and hymnals or *Gesangbücher*. The larger libraries had more titles and more different editions, but basically the same kinds of books. Differences in wealth and education were reflected not in these religious works but in the number and nature of profane books (which are found in just over a quarter of the libraries in the second half of the eighteenth century). Protestants thus developed a religious and cultural identity around a common set of books, used in connection with various religious exercises: Bible-reading, prayer, hymns, sermons, communion. Not all Protestant libraries were as homogeneous as these Lutheran ones, however. In seventeenth-century Metz, for example, apart from the Bible and psalms, titles and genres of books varied widely. The more puritanical Calvinist libraries resembled Lutheran ones, however, although they usually contained a smaller number of books.

In America reading and religion were inextricably intertwined, defining a culture based entirely on familiarity with the Bible.[36] Biblical stories were heard before they were read, since fathers or servants often read aloud to the entire family. In memoirs published in 1852, Joseph T. Buckingham, editor of Boston's first daily newspaper, recalls:

> For a number of years . . . I read every day [in the presence of his master and mistress] at least one chapter, and often two or three chapters in the Bible . . . I have no doubt that I read the Bible through *in course* at least a dozen times before I was sixteen years old, with no other omissions than the jaw-breaking chapters of the Chronicles. The historical parts I had read much oftener, and the incidents and the language became almost as familiar as the grace . . . said before and after meals – neither of which ever varied a word during . . . nine years.

In this culture the ability to read was taken for granted; from the moment the child first confronted the written word, he recognized texts that he had heard before and often memorized. Buckingham says:

> I have no recollection of any time when I could not read . . . In December, 1784, the month in which I was five years old, I went to a master's school, and, on being asked if I could read, I said I could read in the Bible. The master placed me on his chair and presented a Bible opened at the fifth chapter of Acts. I read the story of Ananias and Sapphira falling down dead for telling a lie. He patted me on the head and commended my reading.

Reading meant returning again and again to the same books – the Bible and a few others – which were transmitted from generation to generation. This practice, sometimes termed 'intensive' reading, had its radical exponents, such as the Quaker William Penn: 'Keep but few books, well chosen and well read, whether concerned with religious or civil subjects. Reading many books only takes the mind away from meditation. Much reading is an oppression of the mind'. The practice also had its methodological treatises. A sermon published in Boston in 1767 contains these recommendations:

> Be diligent in reading holy scripture. Every morning and every evening you must read a chapter of your Bible or a passage from a pious sermon, and when you read you must not scan the text and then set it aside. Better not to read at all than to read in that way. When you read, you must pay close attention to what you are reading, and when you have finished you must mull over what you have just read.[37]

Repeated reading of the same texts was the norm for American Protestants. In memoirs published in 1857, Samuel Goodrich, a writer and editor, says: 'In our family Bible it is recorded that he [my father] thus read that holy book through, in course, thirteen times, in the space of about five and twenty years.' The Bostonian Robert Keayne declared in his will: 'As my special gift to him [my son] my little written book in my closet upon I Cor. II, 27, 28, which is a treatise of the sacrament of the Lord's Supper . . . [It is] a little thin pocket book bound in leather, all written in my own hand, which I esteem more precious than gold, and which I have read over I think 100 and 100 times . . . I desire him and hope that he will never part with it as long as he lives'. Read and reread, religious texts inhabited the minds of the faithful, who drew from them not only spiritual comfort but a manner of speaking and writing and ways of organizing individual and communal life in accordance with the divine word. Consider the experiences of Joseph Crosswell, an itinerant preacher born in 1712 and converted during the Great Awakening:

> I know not when I have experienced greater consolation in reading the word of God. Blessed be its glorious and gracious Author. Sweetly regaled in the afternoon by the heavenly south breezes of the divine Spirit, whilst repeating scripture passages . . . I have this day repeated the whole book of Canticles by heart . . . Some enlivening about noon while passing through woods and repeating the last three chapters in the Canticles.

In America's Puritan culture we find the most radical privatization of reading. The book became the center of family life. People read for themselves and for others. They memorized passages, which by dint of frequent repetition became part of their everyday language. No doubt such diligence was quite rare, but practices were similar in other Protestant areas, even where the Calvinist and Puritan influence was small.[38]

The library, retreat from the world

The book thus became the companion of choice in a new kind of intimacy. And the library, for those who could afford one, became the ideal place for retreat, study, and meditation. Consider, as one of many possible examples, the case of Montaigne. In 1579 he sold his post as *conseiller* with the Bordeaux parlement and went to Paris to oversee the printing of the works of his friend Etienne de La Boétie. The following year, upon returning to his château, he had painted on the walls of his library, 'a beauty among village libraries', this Latin inscription:

> In the year of Christ 1571, at the age of thirty-eight, Michel de Montaigne, long since bored with the slavery of parlement and public office but still vigorous, withdrew to lay his head on the breast of the learned Virgins in calm and security; he shall pass the remaining days of his life there. Hoping that fate will allow him to perfect this dwelling, this sweet paternal retreat, he has consecrated it to his freedom, tranquillity, and leisure.

In the first place, then, the library was a retreat from the world, freedom enjoyed out of the public eye. Montaigne's description in the *Essays* (III:3) emphasizes its role as refuge: 'When at home I turn aside a little more often to my library', the most exposed room in the castle, 'which I like for being a little hard to reach and out of the way, for the benefit of the exercise as much as to keep the crowds away'.[39] Separated from the main building by a courtyard, the library is where he engages in the best of the 'three kinds of commerce', that of a man with his books, which is to say, with himself. Retreat does not mean seclusion or rejection of the world, however. Montaigne's library is a place from which one can see without being seen, which gives a kind of power to the person who retires there. Power over the household and its inhabitants: 'I turn aside a little more often to my library, from which at one sweep I command a view of my household. I am over the entrance and see below me my garden, my farmyard, my courtyard, and into most of the parts of my house.' Power over nature, which offers itself up to the eye: 'It offers rich and free views in three directions.' Power over the knowledge accumulated in the books that the eye takes in at a glance: 'The shape of my library is round, the only flat side being the part needed for my table and chair; and curving round me it presents at a glance all my books, arranged in five rows of shelves on all sides.' At a glance too Montaigne can take in the Greek and Latin sayings that have been painted on the beams, those taken from Stobaeus at the beginning of the retreat having been covered over later, in 1575 or 1576, by others taken from Sextus Empiricus and the Bible.

The tension between the desire to withdraw from the crowd while at the same time maintaining control over the world is probably symbolic of the absolute liberty made possible by commerce with books, hence of the possibility of complete self-mastery without constraint or supervision: 'There is my throne. I try to make my authority over it absolute, and to withdraw this one corner from all society, conjugal, filial, and civil.' The hours spent in the library are hours of withdrawal in two senses, which define the essence of privacy in the modern era: withdrawal from the public sphere, from civic responsibility, from the affairs of city and state; and withdrawal from the family, from the household, from the social responsibilities of domestic intimacy. In retreat, the individual is free, master of his time, of his leisure or study: 'There I leaf through now one book, now another, without order and without plan, by disconnected fragments. One moment I muse, another moment I set down or dictate, walking back and forth, these fancies of mine that you see here.' And dictate: note that the ancient method of composition, the writer speaking his words out loud as he walks and requiring the presence of a scribe, is not thought to be in contradiction with the sense of intimacy that comes from familiarity with the books of the library, which are close by and easy to leaf through.

The sense of power conferred by withdrawal into a library is depicted in other texts, such as Shakespeare's *The Tempest*, probably written between 1610 and 1613. Like Montaigne, Prospero preferred the privacy of his study to public affairs: 'Me, poor man, my library / Was dukedom large enough' (act I, scene 2, ll. 109–110). In exile, he thanks the person who allowed him to take some of his precious books: 'Knowing I lov'd my books, he furnish'd me, / From my own library, with volumes that / I prize above my dukedom' (act I, scene 2, ll. 166–168). But these familiar, cherished books, companions in solitude and misery, are also the instruments of a secret power, feared and fearsome. Knowing this, Caliban thinks that Prospero's power can be destroyed if his books are seized and burned: 'Remember, / First to possess his books; for without them / He's but a sot, as I am' (act 3, scene 2, ll. 83–85), and 'Burn but his books' (l. 87). Prospero himself associates books with his power: 'I'll to my book; / For yet, ere supper-time, I must perform / Much business appertaining' (act 3, scene 1, ll. 92–94). He also repudiates that power: 'And, deeper than did ever plummet sound, / I'll drown my book' (act 5, scene 1, ll. 56–57).

Thus there emerges a strange alliance between reading, that most private and hidden practice, and true, effective power, power far more effective than that of public office. The reading of books of magic (such as the *Books of Experiments* in sixteenth-century England or the nameless book of magic widely read in rural Aragon and Languedoc in the nineteenth century) became the paradigm for all reading, which had to be done in secret and which conferred upon the reader a dangerous power.[40]

Reading becomes private

'Study: a place of retirement in ordinary homes where one can go to study or to find seclusion and where one keeps one's most precious goods. A room that contains a library is also called a study.' This definition, from Furetière's *Dictionary*, reveals the library's new status. It is no longer, or at any rate not always, an ostentatious room for receiving visitors, for 'show' as Pascal put it, but a place for keeping 'one's most precious goods', not only useful and rare books but one's own self. Privately owned books and the place where they were kept and consulted therefore commanded special attention.

Consider two contemporaries, Samuel Pepys (1633–1703) and John Locke (1632–1704). In the diary he kept from 1660 to 1669, Pepys, then Clerk of the Acts of the Navy Board and living in an apartment adjoining the offices of the Royal Navy, tells of his efforts to acquire, bind, and store books.[41] An assiduous client of bookstores (and not only so as to make free with the bookseller's wife) as well as an avid reader ('I know not how in the world to abstain from reading', he wrote on 18 March 1668, at a time when his eyesight had already suffered serious deterioration), he took upon himself the task of arranging his books (13 October 1660: 'Within all the afternoon, setting up shelfes in my study'), preparing a catalogue (4 February 1667: 'A little to the office and then to my chamber and there finished my catalogue of my books with my own hand, and so to supper and to bed, and had a good night's rest'), until, his eyesight almost gone, he asked his brother to finish the job (24 May 1669: 'To White Hall, and there all the morning, and thence home, and giving order for some business and setting my brother to making a catalogue of my books'). Wanting his books to look good, he made frequent trips to the binder (3 February 1665: 'My bill for the rebinding of some old books to make them suit with my study cost me, besides other new books in the same bill, £3; but it will be very handsome'). Pepys kept his money in his study and did business there, suggesting that this was one of the most private rooms in his house. On 11 December 1660, having discussed at the tavern the best ways to invest his money, he wrote: 'Up to my study, and there did make up an even 100 l and sealed it to lie by. After that to bed.' On 18 July 1664 he returned home with a man who owed him money, 'and there he took occasion to owne his obligations to me, and did lay down twenty pieces in gold upon my shelf in my closett'.

John Locke, collector and scholar, marked each of his books with his personal stamp and organized his library so as to facilitate research. In 1691, after years of exile in the United Provinces, Locke returned to England and installed his library in two rented rooms in Sir Francis Masham's castle at Otes in Essex, twenty miles from London. With the aid of an assistant, he numbered each work (with a tag glued to the back of the binding and reproduced on the top plate inside). He then marked each number on sheets inserted into the *Catalogus impressorum* of the Bodleian, published by Hyde, which served as both an annotated bibliography and a catalogue of his own library; later he pasted his numbers in two somewhat less cumbersome catalogues. This effort made his library more usable, the catalogue numbers facilitating the task of finding books on the shelves, where they were arranged according to size in two ranks, with no order by subject.

Every book that came into Locke's library was carefully marked as his personal property. He placed his signature on the top plate of the binding, alongside the book's number. He underlined the final figures of the date on the title page, placed a line over the page number on the final page, marked the price he had paid for the book, usually on the eleventh page, and recorded the number, date, and pagination in his catalogues. While reading he made additional marks in at least some of his books. Pages were noted on the lower plate of the binding, and notes were sometimes written on inserted sheets. Locke also made symbolic notations (letters in italics, dots, dashes, plus and minus signs, initials) whose meaning is for the most part unclear. (Some of these signs seem to refer to the merits of the edition or text or to the presence of a second copy in the library.)

Locke's commerce with his books was thus a time-consuming occupation. He respected them, never writing or underlining on pages that contained text. They were his most intimate possessions and therefore demanded to be passed on to someone who would know how to make good use of them. In his will, Locke specified what was to become of his books: some were to go to Dame Damaris Masham, his host's second wife ('four folios, eight quartos, and twenty small books which she may choose among the books of my library'); others to Mr. Anthony Collins of the Middle Temple, a free-thinker and recent friend of Locke's; the bulk of the library, some 3,641 titles, was to be divided between his cousin Peter King and Francis C. Masham, Damaris Masham's only son, 'when he shall have attained the age of twenty-one years'.[42]

The presence of books became firmly linked to the habit of reading and privacy in seventeenth-century England. Estate inventories from Kentish towns show that they were less likely to be found in the hall, the most open room in the house, where guests were received, and more likely to be found in private areas such as the study (closet) or bedroom. (Between 1560 and 1600, 48 percent of books were found in the hall, compared with 39 percent between 1601 and 1640; the proportion of books found in more private rooms rose from 9 percent to 23 percent during the same interval.)

Books were found more often in the bedroom than in the 'study' or 'parlor', probably because it had become common to read before going to sleep. In Kent, for example, the wife of one yeoman in Otham was described by her maid in court documents as 'reading her book as she often did before going to bed'. This was Pepys's habit too, and in his diary we find frequent notations such as these from 1667: 'and so after supper to read, and then to bed' (1 May), and 'I to my book again, and made an end of Mr. Hooker's Life, and so to bed' (19 May).

Evening reading was not necessarily solitary. A couple might read together or to each other: 'I fell a-reading in Fuller's *History of Abbys* and my wife in *Grand Cyrus* till 12 at night; and so to bed' (7 December 1660). Sometimes they read the same books (poems of Du Bartas on 2 November 1662, Aesop's *Fables* on 24 May 1663), and sometimes (as on 2 November 1660) one read aloud to the other: 'In Paul's church-yard I called at Kirton's, and there they had got a mass book for me, which I bought and cost me twelve shillings; and, when I came home, sat up late and read in it with great pleasure to my wife, to hear that she was long ago so well acquainted with.' (Pepys's wife, Elisabeth Marchand, was the daughter of an exiled Huguenot and for a time had been a student at the Ursulines' school in Paris.)

Frequently Pepys ordered his valet to read to him, even before his eyesight had begun to deteriorate: 'I had the boy up tonight for his sister to teach him to put me to bed, and I heard him read, which he doth pretty well' (22 September 1660). Or again, on 9 September 1666: 'Anon to Sir W. Pen's to bed [after the London fire, Pepys had had to leave his damaged apartment], and made my boy Tom to read me asleep.' And on 25 December 1668: 'So home and to dinner alone with my wife, who, poor wretch! sat undressed all day till ten at night, altering and lacing of a noble petticoat: while I by her, making the boy read to me the Life of Julius Caesar, and Des Cartes' book of Musick, the latter of which I understand not . . . Then after supper I made the boy play upon his lute, which I have not done twice before since he come to me; and so, my mind in mighty content, we to bed.' Like the presence of the scribe in Montaigne's library, the presence of the 'boy' in Pepys's bedroom by no means spoils his intimacy with his book; reading could be a private without necessarily being a solitary pursuit.

By contrast, a person could enjoy a strictly private relation with his book outside the confines of the home. Pepys read at home in the evening, but he also read a great deal in various places around London. Sometimes he read while walking. On 18 November 1663: 'And so I walked to Deptford, where I have not been a very great while, and there paid off the Milford in very good order . . . After dinner came Sir W. Batten, and I left him to pay off another ship, and I walked home again reading of a little book of new poems of Cowley's, given my by his brother.' On 9 May 1666 he again went to Deptford: 'Walked back again reading of my Civill Law Book.' Then, on 17 August 1666: 'Down by water to Woolwich, I walking alone from Greenwich thither, making an end of the "Adventures of Five Hours", which when all is done is the best play that ever I read in my life.' Reading whiled away the hours while traveling the Thames by boat, as on 1 May 1666: 'Thence by water to Redriffe, reading a new French book my Lord Brouncker did give me today, L'histoire amoureuse des Gaules, being a pretty Libell against the amours of the Court of France.' Or, on 10 June 1667, as Pepys returns from Gravesend: 'So I homeward, as long as it was light reading Mr. Boyles book of Hydrostatickes, which is a most excellent book as ever I read . . . When it grew too dark to read, I lay down and took a nap, it being a most excellent fine evening.'

Silent reading created an air of intimacy that separated the reader from the outside world. Thus, even in the middle of the city, in the presence of other people, he might be alone with his book and his thoughts. Certain kinds of reading demanded more privacy, however. On 13 January 1668 Pepys 'stopped at Martins my bookseller, where I saw the French book which I did think to have had for my wife to translate, called L'escholle des Filles [attributed to Michel Millot and Jean l'Ange], but when I came to look into it, it is the most bawdy, lewd book that ever I saw, rather worse than putana errante [by Aretino], so that I was ashamed of reading in it'. His shame seems not to have lasted very long, since on 8 February he revisited the bookshop 'and bought that idle, roguish book, L'escholle des Filles; which I have bought in plain binding (avoiding the buying of a better bound) because I resolve, as soon as I have read it, to burn it, that it may not stand in the list of books, nor among them, to disgrace them if it should be found'. The next day finds him impatient to read this promising work: 'Up, and at my chamber all the morning and the office, doing business and also reading a little of L'escholle des Filles, which is a mighty lewd book, but yet not amiss for a sober man once to read over to inform himself in the villainy of the world.' And that evening, after dinner and an afternoon spent with friends and well lubricated by drink, he says: 'And then they parted and I to my chamber, where I did read through L'escholle des Filles; and after I had done it, I burned it, that it might not be among my books to my shame; and so at night to supper and then to bed.' In the pidgin he reserves for such occasions, he describes the effects of his reading: 'It did hazer my prick para stand all the while, and una vez to décharger.' Licentious reading material cannot be exposed to public view.

Reading attire

The example of this seventeenth-century English reader shows that reading did indeed become a private activity, but in a variety of ways. By the eighteenth century the correlation of reading with privacy was firmly established, as though reading defined the limits of the inner life. Evidence for this can be seen in Chardin's painting The Amusements of Private Life. Commissioned in 1745 by Louise Ulrique of Sweden to paint two works, one on 'Strict Education' and the other on 'Gentle, Insinuating Education', Chardin chose to paint two different subjects: a woman surprised while reading a book covered with colored paper resting on her knees, and a woman recording her household expenses. The diptych thus contrasts leisure time with time spent in the chore of family administration. The second painting was called The Administrator and the first, The Amusements of Private Life. The latter name was acquired early in the history of the work, because the Swedish ambassador to Paris used it in a letter dated October 1746, after the work was shown at the Salon;

an engraving made in 1747 used the same name.[43] This is, so to speak, a pictorial synecdoche: the part (reading) stands for the whole (private life). A single practice, that of reading, stands for the whole range of private pleasures in the time left free after family chores and obligations.

In this portrait of a woman reading, contemporaries recognized a classic theme: the reading of romantic fiction. Consider two descriptions of the painting. In his *Reflections on Some Causes of the Present State of Painting in France* (1747), Lafont de Saint-Yenne saw it this way:

> He [Chardin] has given this year a piece that represents a pleasant but idle woman in the guise of a lady casually if fashionably dressed, with a rather striking face wrapped in a white bonnet tied under the chin, which hides the sides of her face. One arm lies on her lap, and her hand casually holds a brochure. Beside her, a little to the rear, is a spinning wheel set on a little table.

One year later, the painting, now referred to as *Amusements of the Tranquil Life*, was described in these terms in *Observations on the Arts and Some Paintings Shown at the Louvre in 1748*:

> It represents a woman nonchalantly seated in an armchair and holding in one hand, which rests on her lap, a brochure. From a sort of languor in her eyes, which gaze out toward a corner of the painting, we divine that she is reading a novel, and that the tender impressions it has made on her have set her dreaming of someone whom she would like to see arrive at any moment.

Thus, Chardin's painted act of reading is characterized in two ways: in terms of objects and in terms of postures. The objects situate the reader in a comfortable apartment, a setting of some wealth. The reader's armchair is a high-backed bergère with a thick cushion and stuffed armrests, which allow the chair's occupant to relax with feet raised on a small footstool. Other styles of furniture – the chaise longue and the duchesse – permitted the reader to stretch out and relax even more. The casual if fashionable clothing worn by the woman is a warm but lightweight indoor garment known as a *liseuse* – a dress for reading rather than for show or seduction. The book she holds in her hand is a 'brochure', a book that is not bound but held together by a paper cover. On a low cabinet in a corner of the room, several bound books, larger in size than this brochure, are ranged against the wall.

For the commentators, the woman's posture is one of abandonment: she sits 'nonchalantly' and 'casually' holds the brochure; her gaze is languorous. These signs suggest that she is reading a novel, which fills her mind with disturbing images and sentiments and arouses her senses. From this description a modern spectator has some difficulty recognizing Chardin's painting, which shows, seated in a comfortable but austere room, a woman who is not languid at all and whose eyes by no means convey emotional turmoil. In fact, the descriptions seem to refer to other paintings, to Baudoin's *Reading*, for instance, which depicts, in a highly eroticized representation, a young woman in a state of total abandonment. The comments reveal the power of an association between female reading and idleness, sensual pleasure, and secret intimacy. More than the painting, which is deliberately estranged from the *topos*, the commentators' remarks reveal how eighteenth-century men imagined the act of reading by women, which by then had become the quintessence of private activity. Without the painter's intrusion it would have remained shrouded in silence.

The spoken text

In the eighteenth century the iconography of reading is exclusively female and secular, whereas previously it had been almost entirely male and religious – think of Rembrandt's readers, hermits and philosophers who have withdrawn from society in order to meditate over a book. Yet painting does not yield an exhaustive catalogue of early modern reading practices. Between 1500 and 1800 reading aloud, whether among friends or chance companions, was an essential ingredient of social life, even among the elite. Thus, the *corrector de la impresión* (editor of the revised edition) of *La Celestina*, published in Toledo in 1500 as *La Comedia de Calisto y Melibea*, specifies how it ought to be read in an octet that he appends to the work. It is entitled *Dice el modo que se ha de tener leyendo esta tragicomedia* (he indicates the manner in which this tragicomedy should be read). The *lector* (reader) to whom these instructions are addressed is advised to vary his tone, assume the part of every character, speak asides between clenched teeth (*cumple que sepas hablar entre dientes*), and make use of the *mil artes y modos*, the thousand ways and means of reading so as to capture the attention of his listeners, *los oyentes*.

Like the Latin and Humanist comedies, *La Celestina* was written to be read 'theatrically' but by a single voice before a limited if select audience. In a prologue added to the Saragossa edition of 1507, which alludes to contradictory opinions about the work, the author accounts for the diversity of opinions by invoking the conditions under which the work was read: 'So, when ten people gather to hear this comedy, in which, as is always the case, there are so many different humors, would anyone deny that there are grounds for disagreement about things that can be heard in so many different ways?' Ten listeners choose to come together to hear a text read aloud; the book becomes the center of a cultivated society of friends or acquaintances.

Along with *La Celestina*, other texts, particularly pastorals and novels, were favored for such gatherings, in which the written word was mediated by the spoken voice. Cervantes refers to this practice in *Don Quixote*, first by dramatizing, in chapter 32 of part 1, the reading of the *Curioso impertinente* by a priest to a small group of avid listeners gathered at an inn. And as title for chapter 66 of part 2 he chose: 'Which treats of that which he who reads will see and that which he will hear who listens to a reading of it.'[44]

In the seventeenth century people frequently listened to books read aloud. In the army in the field, such activity whiled away the time, strengthened friendships, and provided food for thought. As an ensign and, later, lieutenant in the Normandy Regiment between 1635 and 1642, Henri de Campion described in his *Memoirs* reading in the military:

> I had my books, which took up a portion of my wagon's load, and frequently spent time with them, sometimes alone but most of the time with three friends from the regiment, intelligent and studious men. The Chevalier de Sévigné, a Breton and captain of the corps, was one. He was by nature a studious man, had read widely, and from birth had always been at war or at court. Le Breuil-Marcillac, a Gascon, brother of the lieutenant colonel and my captain, was the third member of our group. He had studied until the age of twenty-eight, his parents having destined him for the Church, which he quit in order to take up the sword, having spent well his time in school and later at the Sorbonne. He was a mild man, accommodating, with nothing of the rudeness of military men. D'Almivar, from Paris, a lieutenant and my close friend, was the fourth party to our studious commerce. He had a polished wit, was agreeable in conversations of all sorts, and quite sociable.

Reading, listening to, and arguing about books established a strong and lasting friendship among the four men:

Those were the three men with whom I spent my hours of leisure. After reasoning together about the subjects that came up, without bitter dispute or desire on the part of one to shine at the expense of the others, one of us would read some good book aloud, and we would examine the finest passages in order to learn to live well and to die well, in accordance with morality, which was the principal subject of our study. Many people enjoyed listening to our discussions, which, I believe, were useful to them, for nothing was said that was not conducive to virtue. Since then I have found no society so comfortable or reasonable; it lasted seven years, during which I served in the Normandy Regiment.[45]

Thus, different ways of reading defined different but related social practices: solitary reading encouraged personal study and intellectual interchange; reading aloud, combined with interpretation and discussion of what was read, fostered friendship; and these friendly study groups could attract a wider audience, which benefited by hearing the texts read and discussed.

Similar 'convenient' and 'reasonable' societies existed in the cities. Before official academies came into being, people came together over books, which they lent to one another, discussed, examined, and read aloud. In 1700 a *petite académie* was founded in Lyons. Seven scholars and friends met in the home of one of their number: 'The place where we hold our meetings is the study of one of our academicians. There we gather amid five or six thousand volumes, which constitute a library as choice as it is large. That alone provides ready and agreeable assistance to our scholarly conferences' (letter from Brossette, one of the founders and an *avocat* at the court known as the *présidial*, to Boileau, 16 July 1700). Sometimes a friendly visit could lead to discussion of books. Laurent Dugas, president of the Cour des monnaies and one of the seven 'academicians', gives a number of examples of this in his correspondence. On 12 January 1719: 'Yesterday in my study I spent a good part of the evening with Father de Vitry and Father Follard, regent of rhetoric. I gave them chocolate. We spoke of M. de Cambrai and we argued about literature. Father de Vitry wanted to look at the new edition of Saint Clement of Alexandria, which the bishop of Oxford has published and which I own, to see if the editor remarked upon passages he had noted.' 27 March 1731: 'Cheinet spent the evening and had supper with me. We read some letters of Cicero and complained about the ignorance of the public, by which I mean the want of taste on the part of our young people, who amuse themselves reading new and often frivolous or superficial books and neglect the great models that might teach them to think well.' 23 March 1733: 'M. de La Font, gentleman-in-waiting to the queen, arrived and told me that he thought I would enjoy hearing a reading of a new work by M. de Voltaire entitled *The Temple of Taste*. If I were agreeable, however, we would await the return of my son who had gone that morning to Brignais and was expected at any moment. He arrived a half-hour later and took the role of reader. The reading lasted an hour and a half. My wife who came in at seven o'clock, heard three-quarters of it.' Thus, people listened to readings, read to each other, talked about books, and conversed in their libraries: all were common practices, which depended on the existence of readers who often read alone but who sometimes used books as the basis of social occasions.[46]

Travel provided another opportunity for reading. On 26 May 1668 Samuel Pepys returned from Cambridge to London:

Up by 4 a-clock; and by the time we were ready and had eat, we were called to the coach; where about 6 a-clock we set out, there being a man and two women of one company, ordinary people, and one lady alone that is tolerable handsome, but mighty well spoken, whom I took great pleasure in talking to, and did get her to read aloud in a book she was reading in the coach, being the King's Meditations [the meditations of Charles I prior to his execution]; and the boy and I to sing.

Here, reading is a way of establishing a temporary and friendly bond between traveling companions who had not known each other previously. An anonymous, ephemeral community is bound together by reading, conversation, and song, helping make the journey more agreeable for all. 'We dining all together and pretty merry', Pepys notes, recording the felicitous consequence of his initiatives.

Reading influenced privatization in several ways. It contributed to the emergence of a sense of self, as the reader scrutinized his own thoughts and emotions in solitude and secrecy. It was also a group activity, which made it possible 'to avoid both the boredom of solitude and the crush of the multitude', as Fortin de La Hoguette put it in his treatise *On Conversation*. There are numerous eighteenth-century images of these small groups bound together by reading. In 1728 Jean-François de Troy painted *Reading Molière*. In a rococo salon, at 3:30 according to the clock, five women and two men, comfortably seated on low armchairs, listen to one of the company reading a bound book, which he holds in his hands. The door is closed and a screen has been opened to protect the little group, gathered in a circle around the reader, from the rest of the world.

A year earlier Marivaux had written for the stage a play entitled *Love's Second Surprise*. One of the characters, Hortensius, is presented as a 'pedant' who has been hired by the marquise to direct her reading and read to her: 'Two weeks ago I took on a man to whom I have entrusted my library. I do not flatter myself that I will become a scholar, but I am eager to occupy my time. He reads me something every evening. Our readings are serious and reasonable. He establishes an order that instructs as it amuses me' (act 1, scene 7). But Hortensius' readings are not reserved for his mistress alone. The marquise invites her visitors, such as the chevalier in scene 8 of act 2: 'Chevalier, you are master if you wish to remain, if my reading pleases you.' In both the painting and the play, listening together by no means precludes private sentiments. De Troy suggests them through the play of glances: eyes meet, glances are averted, people avoid looking at one another. Marivaux has the chevalier react strongly against what he hears being read, which is a way of stating his incipient love for the ironic and flirtatious marquise.

Family reading

Reading aloud was a way of structuring family life. Husband and wife read to each other. On 22 December 1667 Pepys's wife had taken to her bed: 'After dinner, up to my wife again, and who is in great pain still with her tooth and cheek; and there, they gone, I spent the most of the afternoon and night reading and talking to bear her company, and so to supper and to bed.' Three days later, on Christmas Day, she does the reading: 'And all the afternoon at home, my wife reading to me the history of the Drummer, of Mr. Monpesson, which is a strange story of spirits, and worth reading indeed.' Fathers and sons read to each other. Dugas of Lyons gives several examples: 'I spent considerable time with my son reading Greek and some odes of Horace' (22 July 1718); 'I read with my eldest son Cicero's *Treatise on Laws*, and with my second son I read Sallust' (14 September 1719); 'At night I play chess with my son. We start by reading a good book, that is, a book of piety, for half an hour' (19 December 1732).

Sometimes the entire family gathered around the reader, especially when the family was Protestant and the book the Bible. Protestant books of domestic instruction often described such compulsory reading. Justus Menius' *Oeconomia Christiana* shows, on the title page of the 1554 Regensburg edition, a father reading to his wife and children on his right and his servants in another corner of the room. On the table we see a heavy Bible, another, smaller book (perhaps the *Oeconomia* itself), a pair of eyeglasses, and a sandglass.[47] Although such Bible-reading was not always practiced in Protestant families, it is attested in a number of places from sixteenth-century Switzerland (where Felix Platter remembered from his youth that 'my father was in the habit, before we went to church, of reading the holy Bible and preaching from it') to eighteenth-century New England.

Popular customs

Conviviality, family and domestic intimacy, and individual retirement were the three aspects of life in which books and reading played a major role — and not only for the educated elite. Among the lower classes too printed materials fulfilled a variety of functions, but those materials were seldom books. Those who could read well usually read aloud to others who read less well or not at all. This was true in the cities and in the fields, at work and at leisure, among strangers or fellow workers. Reading matter ranged from 'books of portraiture', that is, collections of models and patterns used in sixteenth-century workshops, to placards posted on city walls, from religious texts (as in Swabia, where peasants gathered in the late eighteenth century to listen to the reading of the Bible) to mass-circulation books such as those in France's 'Bibliothèque bleue' or Blue Library, which were read in family gatherings or by people who shared a common life, such as early eighteenth-century shepherds in Lorraine, according to the testimony of Jamerey-Duval.[48]

In sixteenth- and seventeenth-century Spain, popular audiences gathered to hear a variety of works read aloud, novels of chivalry foremost among them. They were listened to by the common folk in the cities, according to Juan Arce de Otalora (1560): 'In Seville they say that there are artisans who, on holidays and in the evening bring a book and read it on the *Grades*', that is, in front of the cathedral.[49] Peasants also listened, at least in *Don Quixote*, according to the chapter cited earlier (part 1, chapter 32). In describing the novels of chivalry that he keeps in his inn, the innkeeper says: 'As far as I can see, there is no better reading in the world. I myself have two or three of them along with some manuscripts, and they have been the very breath of life, not only to me, but to many others as well. For in harvest time the reapers gather here in large numbers on feast days, and there are always some among them who can read. One of them will take a book in his hands and thirty or more of us will crowd around and listen to him with so much pleasure that we lose a thousand gray hairs.'[50] Gathered to hear *Don Circongilio of Thrace or Felixmarte of Hircania*, the peasants and the innkeeper's family, including his daughters, never tire of listening: 'We could go on listening day and night', says the master of the house. Other texts suitable for reading aloud included the *pliegos sueltos* or *pliegos de cordel*. Related by format (quarto volumes of two to sixteen sheets) and poetic form (generally octosyllabic, assonant *romances*), these plays were written to be read aloud. Their titles, always similar in structure, could be shouted out by those who sold them, usually blind hawkers who belonged to confraternities; the texts lent themselves to being spoken or sung to a public that related to the written word by way of the ear rather than the eye.

The common folk also had other access to written literature. Between 1500 and 1800 writing insinuated itself into the majority of households in the form of printed materials on which people set a high emotional value because they were associated with important moments in the life of the family or individual. In certain dioceses marriage charters were part of the marriage ritual; the husband handed the charter to the wife, and its text and images served as reminders of the ceremony. Certificates were distributed to pilgrims as proof that they had completed their journey and accomplished their religious duty. Confraternities gave certificates attesting to membership and fidelity to a heavenly protector. Whether displayed on a wall or kept in a safe place, such documents, which always included images along with the text, could be deciphered in a variety of ways. They played a fundamental role as aids to memory and self-affirmation, thus helping to constitute a private life that was at once intimate and on exhibit.

From reading to writing

Some common folk used their ability to write about themselves. The practice may have been more widespread than is suggested by the few surviving autobiographies, such as Jacques-Louis Ménétra's *Journal of My Life* and the writings of Louis Simon.[51] Ménétra, a Parisian glazier, began writing his journal in 1802 or 1803, based on fragments he had been accumulating since 1764. Simon in 1809 began writing 'the principal Events that happened in the Course of my life' in a 'book' (that is, a handwritten journal) inherited twenty-one years earlier from an uncle by marriage. The book opens with the century-old accounts of the uncle's uncle, who had been a wine merchant at La Flèche.

Ménétra and Simon had acquired the habit of writing long before beginning their memoirs. While touring France as a journeyman glazier, Ménétra used his writing skills for a variety of purposes, including keeping records for an organization of fellow journeymen known as the Devoir: 'I was accepted as a companion of the Devoir, and my fellow members asked me to recopy the roll of what they call Maître Jacques or the Devoir, and I was named Parisien le Bienvenu' [companions called one another by secret names]. He wrote to his family in Paris, especially his grandmother, asking for financial assistance. He dealt with the correspondence and kept the books for the widows who hired him. And he acted as secretary for his comrades in a dispute with the intendant of Bordeaux over the drawing of lots for the militia: 'They cast about for one of their number who could write. The Guyennois came looking for me, and I was the thirty-first companion [that is, he was added to the delegation of thirty chosen to negotiate with the authorities]. Thereafter I wrote the rules and counted up my fellow journeymen.' Through frequent letters he nourished the hopes of the widow in Nîmes who expected that he would return to marry her when his tour of France was complete and who in the meantime treated him most generously.

Louis Simon, a clothmaker from the village of La Fontaine, was esteemed for his ability to write. He was called upon to keep the books of the fabric and the town government and to draft the parish's grievances against the government. For him, the French Revolution was time spent – and wasted – writing: 'For I went three years without working because of the disturbances, and here they could only turn to me since I was the only one who knew how to write and who understood a little of affairs'.

In writing their accounts of their lives, both men made perhaps unwitting use of books they had read in the past. Young Louis Simon came to know the books in the local priest's library as well as those (no doubt from the Blue Library) sold by a hawker who had returned to the area: 'I spent my time enjoying the pleasure of playing instruments and reading all the books that I could obtain on ancient history, wars, geography, the lives of saints, the Old and New Testament, and other books sacred and profane. I also loved songs and psalms'. His writing bears traces of this half-scholarly, half-popular background.

Ménétra mentions few books (only the Bible, the *Petit Albert* [a book of black magic], and the works of Rousseau), but his reading and knowledge of contemporary literary forms shaped the retelling of his life, part real and part imaginary. Erotic novels had provided him with a repertory of ribald plots and characters (the nun who violates her vows, the noblewoman whose lust is insatiable, the girl who succumbs against her will but to her great satisfaction, and so on). The theater, which he loved, had taught him how to arrange the players in his little dramas so as to give himself the leading role, as in his encounter with Rousseau. Stories borrowed from widely circulated books give relief to his more commonplace adventures. Though not cited in the *Journal*, these texts served as so many mirrors, or rather prisms, by means of which Ménétra observed his own life and then recomposed it to suit his desires, creating an embellished, idealized version. The two men were very different. Simon sought to recapture through writing his beloved wife, who had died five years earlier, whereas Ménétra gazed admiringly upon his own past and attempted to assert his own culture, reflected in his deliberate refusal to abide by the ordinary rules of punctuation and spelling. The writings of both show that ordinary folk were familiar with writing, the written word, and books.

Notes

1   My interpretation of signature rates therefore differs from that of Françoise Furet and Jacques Ozouf, *Lire et Ecrire. L'alphabétisation des Français de Calvin à Jules Ferry* (Paris: Minuit, 1977), I, 27. After examining, for 1866, signatures on marriage documents, conscripts' educational documents, and cultural data, they conclude that 'the ability to sign one's name corresponds to what we now call literacy, meaning the ability to read and write' and that 'there is a presumption in favor' of the hypothesis that the correlation between ability to sign and complete literacy is valid 'for earlier periods'.

2   Robert Allan Houston, 'The Literacy Myth? Illiteracy in Scotland, 1630–1760', *Past and Present* 96 (1982): 81–102.

3   See David Cressy, *Literacy and the Social Order. Reading and Writing in Tudor and Stuart England* (Cambridge: Cambridge University Press, 1980), pp. 62–103, for the oaths of 1641–1644, and R. S. Schofield, 'Dimensions of Illiteracy, 1750–1850', *Explorations in Economic History* 10 (1973): 437–454.

4   Michel Fleury and Pierre Valmary, 'Les progress de l'instruction élémentaire de Louis XIV à Napoleon III d'après l'enquête de Louis Maggiolo (1877–1879)', *Population* 12 (1957): 71–93, and Furet and Ozouf, *Lire et Ecrire*.

5   Simon Hart, 'Onderzoek naar de samenstelling van de bevolking van Amsterdam in de 17e en 18e eeuw, op grond van gegevnes over migratie, huwelijk, beroep en alfabetisme', *Geschrift ien Getal. Een keuze uit de demografisch-economisch en sociall-historische studiën op grond van Amsterdamse en Azzanse archivalia, 1600–1800* (Dordrecht, 1976), pp. 130–132.

6   M. R. Duglion, 'Alfabetismo e società a Torino nel secolo XVIII', *Quaderni Storici* 17 (May–August 1971): 485–509.

7   M.-C. Rodriguez and Bartolomé Bennassar, 'Signatures et niveau culturel des témoins et accusés dans les procès d'Inquisition du ressort du tribunal de Cordoue (1595–1632)', *Caravelle* 31 (1978): 19–46.

8   Kenneth A. Lockridge, *Literacy in Colonial New England: An Inquiry into the Social Context of Literacy in the Early Modern West* (New York: Norton, 1974).

9   Kenneth A. Lockridge, 'L'alphabétisation en Amérique, 1650–1800', *Annales ESC*, 1977, pp. 503–518.

10   Cressy, *Literacy*, pp. 157–174.

11   André Larquié, 'L'alphabétisation à Madrid en 1680', *Revue d'histoire moderne et contemporaine* (1981): 132–157, and 'L'alphabétisation des Madrilènes dans la seconde moitié du XVIIe siècle: stagnation ou évolution?', *Colloque 'Instruction, lecture, écriture en Espagne (XVIe–XIXe siècle.)'* (Colloquium on Teaching, Reading, and Writing in Spain [16th–19th century]), Toulouse, 1982, mimeographed.

12   Michel Vovelle, 'Y a-t-il eu une révolution culturelle au XVIIIe siècle? A propos de l'éduca-tion en Provence', *Revue d'histoire moderne et contemporaine* (1975): 89–141.

13   Cressy, *Literacy*, pp. 130–137, esp. table 6.8, p. 136.

14   Daniele Marchesini, 'La fatica di scrivere. Alfabetismo e sottoscrizioni matrimoniali in Emilia, Sette et Ottocento', in Gian-Paolo Brizzi, *Il Catechismo e la Grammatica* (Bologna: Il Mulino, 1985), II, 83–169.

15   Cressy, *Literacy*, pp. 124–125, 128.

16   Joseph Ruwet and Yves Wellemans, *L'Analphabétisme en Belgique (XVIII–XIXe siècle)* (Louvain, 1978), p. 22.

17   Kalman Benda, 'Les Lumières et la culture paysanne dans la Hongrie du XVIIIe siècle', *Les*

Lumières en Hongrie, en Europe centrale et en Europe orientale, proceedings of the 3rd Colloquium of Matrafüred (1975) (Budapest, 1977), pp. 97–109.

18   Egil Johansson, 'The History of Literacy in Sweden', in H. J. Graff, ed., *Literacy and Social Development in the West: A Reader* (Cambridge: Cambridge University Press, 1981), pp. 151–182.

19   T. C. Smout, 'Born Again at Cambuslang: New Evidence on Popular Religion and Literacy in Eighteenth-Century Scotland', *Past and Present* 97 (1982): 114–127 (which cites Markussen and Skovgaard-Petersen's study on Denmark).

20   Richard Gawthrop and Gerald Strauss, 'Protestanism and Literacy in Early Modern Germany', *Past and Present* 104 (1984): 31–35.

21   Bernard Vogler, *Vie religieuse en pays rhénan dans la seconde moitié du XVIe siècle (1556–1619)* (Lille, 1974), II, 796–799.

22   Rolf Engelsing, *Analphabentum und Lektüre. Zur Sozialgeschiehte des Lesens in Deutschland zwischen feudaler und industrieller Gesellschaft* (Stuttgart, 1973), p. 62.

23   André Derville, 'L'analphabétisation du peuple à la fin du Moyen Age', *Revue du Nord*, special issue, *Liber amicorum. Mélanges offerts à Louis Trénard* nos 261–262 (April–September 1984): 761–776.

24   Christiane Klapisch-Zuber, 'Le chiavi fiorentine di Barbalù: l'apprendimento della lettura a Firenze nel XV secolo', *Quaderni Storici* 57 (1984): 765–792. The reason for the variation in the percentage of children in school has to do with varying estimates of the Florentine population in the period 1330–1340.

25   M. J. Lowry, *The World of Aldus Manutius. Business and Scholarship in Renaissance Venice* (Oxford: Basil Blackwell, 1979), pp. 26–41.

26   Carlo Ginzburg, 'High and Low: The Theme of Forbidden Knowledge in the Sixteenth and Seventeenth Centuries', *Past and Present* 73 (1976): 28–41.

27   Paul Saenger, 'Silent Reading: Its Impact on Late Medieval Script and Society', *Viator Medieval and Renaissance Studies*, 13 (1982): 367–414.

28   Philippe Berger, 'La lecture à Valence de 1747 à 1560. Evolution des comportements en fonction des milieux sociaux', *Livre et Lecture en Espagne et en France sous l'Ancien Régime*, Colloquium of the Casa de Velázquez, ADPF, 1981, pp. 97–107.

29   André Labarre, *Le Livre dans la vie amiénoise du XVIe siècle. L'enseignement des inventaires après décès, 1503–1576* (Paris-Louvain: Nauwelaerts, 1971).

30   Christian Bec, *Les Livres des Florentins (1413–1608)*, ed. Leo S. Olschki (Florence, 1984), esp. pp. 91–96.

31   Peter Clark, 'The Ownership of Books in England, 1560–1640: The Example of Some Kentish Townfolk', in Lawrence Stone, ed., *Schooling and Society. Studies in the History of Education* (Baltimore: Johns Hopkins University Press, 1976), pp. 95–111.

32   Etienne Françoise, 'Livre, confession, et société urbaine en Allemagne au XVIIIe siècle: l'exemple de Spire', *Revue d'histoire moderne et contemporaine* (July–September 1982): 353–375.

33   For an overview of the French data, see Roger Chartier and Daniel Roche, 'Les pratiques urbaines de l'imprimé', in H.-J. Martin and Roger Chartier, eds., *Histoire de l'édition française* (Paris: Promodis, 1984), vol. 2, *Le Livre triomphant, 1660–1830*, pp. 402–429, which uses, among other things, the work of Jean Quéniart on the cities of western France and that of Michel Marion on Paris.

34   R. A. Gross, 'The Authority of the Word: Print and Social Change in America, 1607–1880', paper presented to the colloquium Needs and Opportunities in the History of the Book in American Culture, Worcester, Mass., 1984, mimeographed.

35   Philip Benedict, 'Bibliothèques protestantes et catholiques à Metz au XVIIe siècle', *Annales ESC*, 1985, pp. 343–370.

36   David D. Hall, 'Introduction: The Uses of Literacy in New England, 1600–1850', in William L. Joyce et al., eds., *Printing and Society in Early America* (Worcester, Mass.: American Antiquarian Society, 1983), pp. 1–47, from which the quotations that follow are taken.

37   The quotations in this paragraph have been retranslated from the French.

38   Rolf Engelsing, 'Die Perioden der Lesforschung in der Neuzeit. Das statistische Ausmass und die soziokulturelle Bedeutung der Lektüre', *Archiv für Geschichte des Buchwesens* 10 (1969): 945–1002, and *Der Bürger als Leser. Lesergeschichte in Deutschland, 1500–1800* (Stuttgart, 1974).

39   Michel Eyquem de Montaigne, *The Complete Essays of Montaigne*, trans. Donald M. Frame (Stanford: Stanford University Press, 1957), p. 629.

40   Daniel Fabre, 'Le livre et sa magie', in Roger Chartier, ed., *Pratiques de la lecture* (Marseilles: Rivages, 1985), pp. 182–206.

41   *The Diary of Samuel Pepys*, ed. Robert C. Latham and William Matthews, 9 vols (Berkeley: University of California Press, 1970–1976).

42   John Harrison and Peter Laslett, *The Library of John Locke* (Oxford: Clarendon, 1971), 2nd ed., esp. Laslett, 'John Locke and His Books', pp. 1–65.

43   Concerning these two paintings, see the notices in the catalogue *Chardin, 1699–1779* (Paris: Editions de la Réunion des Musées Nationaux, 1979), pp. 278–283.

44   Miguel de Cervantes Saavedra, *Don Quixote de la Mancha*, trans. Samuel Putnam (New York: Modern Library, 1949), p. 943.

45   *Mémoires d'Henri de Campion* (Paris: Mercure de France, 1967), pp. 95–96.

46   See *Correspondance littéraire et anecdotique entre M. de Saint-Fonds et le président Dugas* (Lyons, 1900), and Roger Chartier, 'Une académie avant les lettres patentes. Une approche de la sociabilité des notables lyonnais à la fin du règne de Louis XIV', *Marseille*, no. 101, *Les Provinciaux sous Louis XIV* (1975): 115–120.

47   Gerald Strauss, *Luther's House of Learning: Indoctrination of the Young in the German Reformation* (Baltimore: Johns Hopkins University Press, 1979), pp. 108–131, engraving p. 114.

48   David Sabean, 'Small Peasant Agriculture in Germany at the Beginning of the Nineteenth Century: Changing Work Patterns', *Peasant Studies* 7 (1978): 222–223. Valentin Jamerey-Duval, *Mémoires. Enfance et Education d'un paysan au XVIIIe siècle* (Paris: Le Sycomore, 1981), pp. 191–193. On the reading of Blue books, see Roger Chartier, 'Livres bleus et lectures populaires', *Histoire de l'édition française*, II, 498–511.

49   Cited by Maxime Chevalier, *Lectura y Lectores en la España de los siglos XVI y XVII* (Madrid: Turner, 1976), p. 91.

50   Cervantes, *Don Quixote*, trans. Putnam, p. 275.

51   Jacques-Louis Ménétra, *Journal de ma vie* (Paris: Montalba, 1982); trans. by Arthur Goldhammer as *Journal of My Life* (New York: Columbia University Press, 1986). Anne Fillon, 'Louis Simon, étaminier 1741–1820 dans son village du haut Maine au siècle des Lumières', thesis, Université du Maine, 1982.

Chapter 14

Jan-Dirk Müller

THE BODY OF THE BOOK
The media transition from manuscript to print

More durable than bronze

'Now I have created your image in marble, if you deign to receive favorably the verses already begun. Soon I will fix it in gold, in the Temple of Minerva, that is to say, in the pure hearts of scholars' (from a leaflet concerning the victory of Charles V over France (1525)). With these words, Viennese professor of rhetoric Johann Alexander Brassican recommended epigrams praising the government bureaucrats of Lower Austria in 1525. Verses, as hard as marble statues and eventually as valuable as gold, would recall the secretaries and councillors for all time, not only in a temple but everywhere in the hearts of the scholarly world. It is an old argument that memory preserved in writing is more permanent than any other monument. The elder Pliny already knew that immortality depended on the use of papyrus (*Nat. hist.* XIII, 21). The humanist panegyrists around 1500 believed they had immediate proof: the rediscovered writings of antiquity preserved the names of kings and senators, of generals and artists. Was it not reasonable to promise the same to one's own patron, especially insofar as he was only willing to support scholarly verses (and their authors) that immortalized his name?

The argument seemed convincing, and yet one important difference escaped notice: the altered communications situation and the change of the medium. The appeal of advertisements like Brassican's depended on a history in which select texts in single manuscripts were brought back to life after the passage of time. But what would happen if suddenly everywhere an army of writers engaged in the business of immortality? What if their texts no longer circulated in small groups as manuscripts, but were suddenly available everywhere in great numbers as printed leaflets? Technical reproduction might have seemed at first a chance to preserve writing for everyone and for all time, but it abolished traditional selection mechanisms that established what is worth knowing and preserving. Written and printed monuments ceased to be monuments capable of recalling memories.

Brassican promises monuments of solid materials, marble and gold, but delivers a few pages of printed paper, a material that is, as we know, perishable and hardly permanent. He promises a precious and desirable object, but his leaflet was of little value, and almost no one held on to it. He promises a work of art that is unique or nearly so, having only a few replicas in a sacred site; but this kind of broadsheet has no particular place. Addressing virtually everyone, it concerns no one in particular. The place in the hearts of the scholarly world that was promised the Austrian bureaucrats was none too certain. Verses of praise and those praised were both fairly soon forgotten.

It is worthwhile to look from today's standpoint at the deep rift in the writing culture during the time of early print. The change wrought by the advent of print in the organization of knowledge and the social function of writing of that time was as drastic as the change wrought by the advent of electronic media today. I will not discuss the complex assumptions and consequences of book printing (see Eisenstein 1979) but will deal instead with a particular problem, the materiality of writing and its medium (marble, paper) and, along with this, the change in attitude toward time and duration and the change in perception of text and tradition. All these concepts are topics of contemporary discussion, yet in an entirely different sense. Classifieds announce the 'dematerialized' newspaper of the twenty-first century, and funeral orations are held in public for the book, that cumbersome object of information conveyance. The networking of all pieces of knowledge promises an immense acceleration of progress, that is to say, the irrelevance of anything that is old. Text is only the transitory product of the personal computer, between one proof and another. We cannot yet predict the continuing course of the process that was put in motion with the first technical revolution of writing culture. One should be cautious regarding historical parallels between the advent of printing and that of electronic media, and teleological assumptions proved to be wrong anyway, but the reactions of that time are telling insofar as they reflect certain conditions of modern writing culture in terms of resentments and exaggerated expectations, as well as the difficulty the established cultural system had in adjusting to these conditions.

Reproduction and aura

Multiplication (*multiplicatio*) was one of the main points in the praise of the new invention (Widmann 1972: 253). But very soon the other side of the coin was discovered, the 'overabundance of writing' (*vile der gschrifft*), the fact that everything was printed with little concern for selection and correctness, 'for profit alone' (*alleyn vff getwnn*), and as a 'great scam' (*groß beschiß*). Books lost value everywhere (*nütz gelten überal*), and along with them scholars, who were now replaced by 'rude people' (*geburen*) (Brant 1968: chap. 103, vv. 77–78, 98–104). According to Brant, selection and refinement of the written tradition are taken away from the only competent faculty, scholars. Ecclesiastical and governmental control of writing grows more and more difficult (Schreiner 1984). If it were true, as the Parisian theologian Guillaume Fichet claimed around 1470, that everything that can be said or thought can be immediately written and preserved for posterity by movable type (Swierk 1972: 81), then the memory capacity of the cultural system would be overstressed and oblivion would be the result. Conrad Gesner asserts in 1545, after almost a hundred years of printing, that books disappear as quickly as they are produced. He demands the establishment of public libraries at least for the valuable old manuscripts, as the apparently unlimited possibilities of reproduction by print lead to arbitrariness and uselessness (Gesner 1966: 3r). The written word loses the 'aura' that it possessed in medieval culture as a guarantor of truth, as a vessel of arcane knowledge, even as a component of magical practices.

This trivialization of the written was counteracted from the beginning by the attempt to save the aura of the medium, artificial writing (*artificialiter scribere*). God Himself gave humankind the new invention, because the requirement for writing had surpassed the work capacity of the scribe to the point that science and the handing down of sacred truth were endangered. Now a printer could produce more pages in a single day than could a scribe in a whole year (see Swierk 1972: 81, for further examples). Early on the new art was called 'divina ars'. The colophon of Justinian's *Institutions* (1468) compares the inventors with the greatest artisans of the Old Testament, who built the tabernacle and the temple furnishings. 'Moses cannot complete the plan of the tabernacle, nor can Salomon complete the temple, without ingenious craftsmen. Thus, the one who is greater than Salomon (= Christ) creates anew Bezaleel and Hyram (i.e., Gutenberg) wishing to renew the Church' (Heidenheimer 1925: 109). What Bezaleel and Hyram contributed to the cult of Jehovah was accomplished by Gutenberg and Fust for the renewal of the Church by Christ. Books are tabernacles of God's truth: 'In libris posuisti procul dubio tabernaculum tuum' (Bury 1960: 16). If God is not Himself claimed to be the inventor, print is at least placed among the cultural technologies that humanity owes to mythical heroes (cf. Polidorus Vergilius 1502: xxxvii r/v). And if the product of the press is fleeting and subject to rapid deterioration, at least the more solid quality of the writing material is emphasized: not the brittle reed, stylus, or quill but brazen letters made for longevity (see Swierk 1972: 82, for further examples). In any case, such arguments could not conceal the fact that book printing did not create a new temple as a center of Christianity but instead decentralized the Christian world. Nor could they conceal that ordinary means of control of writing and criteria of relevance were shoved aside or subjected to the needs of the market.

Very early on, print separated itself from traditional centers of writing (bishops' seats, religious convents, and universities). It became a profit-oriented commerce that had to meet the varied and growing demand of a diverse and predominantly urban society with its antagonistic interests. Although at the end of the fifteenth century it was still possible for a bishop of Mainz to oblige the printers of a town like Frankfurt to subject themselves to censorship, in the long run an effective control of all production sites, not to mention those prints that could be exported, was far beyond the capabilities of any political institutions of the time. And no matter what was written about the durability of the press in comparison with the pen, its product was no longer the costly treasure that was preserved with care and passed on from generation to generation.

Longevity of the codex versus longevity of the text

The notorious and curious words of Abbot Johannes Trithemius (1462–1516) in his *Praise of the Scribe* (*De laude scriptorum*, 1494) express how the nature of the written tradition changed along with the material characteristics of the medium. He reminds his Benedictine brethren of their duty to copy sacred books:

> The devotion of the scribe is more valuable than the office of the preacher because the admonition of the preacher disappears in time, but the message of the scribe lasts for many years. The preacher only speaks to those present, whereas the scribe also preaches to those in the future. . . . When the preacher dies, his work is finished; the scribe continues to be a teacher of morality even after his death.
>
> (Trithemius 1973: 58)

These are well-known arguments supported by quotations from Church Fathers and theologians. But are they not rendered obsolete by printing, which reproduces the sacred text much faster and for many more readers? The answer:

> Who is ignorant of the difference between writing [*scriptura*] and printing [*impressura*]? A manuscript, written on parchment, can last a thousand years. How long will print, this thing of paper [*res papirea*] last? It is quite a lot if it can last two hundred years in a volume of paper [*in volumine papireo*]. . . . Actually, no matter how many books are printed, there will never be so many printed that one couldn't find something to copy that hasn't yet been printed. Hardly anyone will have access to all books or be able to buy them. But even if all the books in the world were printed, the devout scribe should

never lessen his zeal. He should copy the usable prints and thereby give them longevity, since otherwise they would not last long. In so doing, the scribe grants stability to instable writings [*scripturis mutantibus*]. He gives value to those of little worth and longevity to those subject to deterioration. The devout scribe will always find a task by which he will do a great service. He is not restrained by external conditions like the printer. He is free and rejoices in his freely performed task. He is in no way inferior to the printer, and his zeal must not weaken because the other prints.

(Trithemius 1973: 62, 64)

D. Mertens (1983) has elucidated the background of this strange admonition. Trithemius is concerned with the reform of his order. It is therefore not a contradiction when elsewhere he praises printing and when he even benefits from its potential by giving his *Praise of the Scribe* to the press. He recognizes two main problems: selection and longevity. Not all manuscripts are printed and especially few from the Benedictine tradition (Mertens 1983: 92). Printing therefore does not encompass the entire stock of writing. Whatever is excluded has little chance of being passed on. A sufficient and standard demand must first exist in order for the effort to pay off. The rapid rise and fall of some shops and the number of business failures (see Chrisman 1982) testify to how the market corrects a publisher's bad decisions with brutal efficiency. The considerations that the printer must take into account are summarized by Trithemius as 'restrictive conditions' (*constringi sub conditione impressoris*). This he juxtaposes with the 'freedom' of the scribe. The opposition between the 'seven liberal arts' of the noble and the bound *artes mechanicae* of the artisan earning his living may be the background of this assertion. However, Trithemius also describes two ways in which texts of a past culture are handed down: extraneous conditions, and free and responsible decisions (the latter assuring results of a more durable nature). Above all, the longevity of the text is linked to writing material. 'Printing is a matter of paper and deteriorates quickly' (Trithemius 1973: 34). This is obviously a weak argument; it is based on false assumptions concerning the longevity of paper and disregards the possibility of printing on parchment – even if it is true that printing was done primarily on paper, that only the mass production of paper had allowed the development of the new technology, and that only texts of extraordinary subject matter sometimes were done on parchment (Mertens 1983). It is striking, however, that Trithemius is concerned less with the life of the text than with the life of the body of the text, that is, the individual codex. He therefore advocates the copying of prints, including his own *Praise of the Scribe*, onto parchment. This can only be understood in the framework of the manuscript culture. Jean Gerson, chancellor of the Sorbonne, made similar arguments around 1400: 'A piece of writing can last not just for a short time, but for 10, 100, or 1,000 years, and this not only by itself [*in se*] but also by the multiplication of the exemplars [*per multiplicationem exemplariorum*] that are copied from the original' (Gerson 1973: 425). Reproduction is the worse alternative because every copy is a variation if not a change of the original. A reduction of the steps of reproduction ensures the integrity of the text. Gerson criticizes the many incapable scribes and the many corruptions of texts. He recommends 'drinking' as closely to the 'source' of truth as possible, at the 'scripta veterum', this being the works of the ancients as well as the written texts. Hence, a text on parchment lasting a thousand years is more trustworthy than a chain of ten texts on paper, copied from each other, but each enduring only a short time (Gerson 1973: 428). Only the sound body of his book can guarantee the author a life after death. Otherwise the costs and labors of writing are lost.

The book as body

Writing survives as a physically present object in the body of a book. If medieval culture is performance, the interaction of voice and bodies, as P. Zumthor (1987) demonstrates, then that culture also had a far more corporeal conception of writing than the age of the early print had. The comparison holds all the more true for the age of the ubiquitously available writing of electronic media. Writing not only is more permanent than speech, but also, strangely enough, has a stronger effect on the senses. This is in any case the opinion of Richard de Bury (1287–1345) in his famous *Philobiblon* (1345). Truth that appears – with Boethius – in thoughts, speech, or writing is most profitable in books:

> For the meaning of the voice [*virtus vocis*] perishes with the sound; truth latent in the mind [*mente latens*] is wisdom that is hid and treasure that is not seen; but truth which shines forth in books desires to manifest itself to every impressionable sense [*omni disciplinabili sensui*]. It commends itself to the sight when it is read, to the hearing when it is heard, and moreover in a manner to the touch, when it suffers itself to be transcribed, bound, corrected, and preserved.
>
> (de Bury 1960: 19)

Others add the sense of taste in the sampling and rumination of what is read. Compared with writing, thoughts lack a discursive partner (*socius*) and oral instruction does not affect the sense of sight. The written word, on the other hand, is the perfect teacher, a living partner, but without the failings of a person such as bad moods, tiredness, or infirmity and death. Always friendly and available to provide information, books 'are masters [*magistri*], who instruct us without rod or ferule, without angry words, without clothes or money. If you come to them they are not asleep; if you ask and inquire of them, they do not withdraw themselves; they do not chide if you make mistakes; they do not laugh at you if you are ignorant' (de Bury 1960: 21). Books are the teachers, not their authors. The conversation is held with books, not their authors. In them the author is present. This apparent presence is expressed in pictures of authors common in medieval manuscripts. The metaphor *accessus ad auctorem*, used as a typical medieval formula of introduction, expresses the same concept. That the author is conceived as present is shown in translations of Latin texts into the vernacular. Often the author does not appear as the speaker, as in modern translations, but the translator defers to the one to whom he gives a voice: 'Here Master X speaks and says . . .'

The metaphor of tradition or its loss speaks of books in terms of living beings. They, or actually the authors embodied in them, suffer in unworthy captivity, rot in cellars subjected to the bites of moths and roaches. Since the transmission of truth depends on the survival of the codices, they must be protected from decay. Nevertheless, they are mortal: 'But because all the appliances of mortal men with the lapse of time suffer the decay of mortality, it is needful to replace the volumes that are worn out with age by fresh successors, that the perpetuity of which the individual is by its nature incapable may be secured to the species' (de Bury 1960: 147). Longevity (*perpetuitas*) means a never-ending chain of mortal individuals – the books – in whom the species survives:

> For as the bodies of books [*librorum corpora*], seeing that they are formed of a combination of contrary elements, undergo a continual dissolution of their structure [*suae compositionis*], so by the forethought of the clergy a remedy should be found, by means of which the sacred book paying the debt of nature may obtain a natural heir and may raise up like seed to its dead brother, and thus may be verified that saying of

Ecclesiasticus: His father is dead, and he is as if he were not dead; for he hath left one behind him that is like himself.

(de Bury 1960: 147. Cf. Eccles. 30: 4)

To copy the ancients means to produce sons (*propagationes recentium filiorum*), to whom the office of the fathers (*paternum officium*) is transferred. The metaphors don't seem totally convincing: a procreation by clerics, with dark relationships (brother? son?). The understanding of tradition is nonetheless clear. Ecclesiasticus speaks of permanence and change in a traditional society. Such a society is made all the more stable as the elders successfully transmit their knowledge to their sons. The heritage of the past changes constantly because it must be passed on from one individual to another. Yet everything remains basically the same as it was and always has been, because the father lives on in the son and in the son's son. Likewise the author lives on in his descendants, his books (de Bury 1960: 18). Tradition seems to be a chain of generations. Communication with tradition is therefore not a hermeneutic problem because the substance of the old remains present in the descendant.

This concept of tradition begins to break apart in early humanism. It is one of the main points that the Reformation attacks. Of course, it was recognized before this that traditions can be distorted. This is not seen, however, as a historical–philological problem (as in the *ad fontes* principle of the humanists). Whatever changes also degenerates. Poor copies are bastards. Their nobility (Richard de Bury uses *generositas*, the English translation has 'purity of race') is ruined, as in a chain of mésalliances, by compilers, revisers, and (worst of all) translators for the laity. Reborn again from generation to generation they finally degenerate completely (*regeneratione multiplici renascentes degeneramus omnino*). Their true heritage is distorted: 'Ah! how often ye pretend that we who are ancient are but lately born, and try to pass us off as sons who are really fathers, calling us who have made you clerks the production of your studies' (de Bury 1960: 46, 47). The place in the chain of generations establishes nobility and the claim to truth: the authority of age.

The chain of generations and the authentic text

Brother resembles brother and the son the father, but having a family resemblance is not the same as being identical. It is a fact that, in a manuscript culture, one copy will never be exactly the same as another. But this did not present problems as long as the authenticity of truth was granted by the 'purity' of the 'genetic heritage'. Transmission is therefore above all a moral problem. The permanence of truth depends on the scrupulous scribe and his care and not on a philological reconstruction of a corrupted text or on hermeneutic efforts to regain an obscured meaning. The truth remains the same in the generations and branches of the written text if the scribe is not lazy or a counterfeiter (and that means: an adulterer).

Textual corruption and textual variants, however, could be ignored less and less the more widespread the practice of copying became. The reform movements of the fifteenth century are not the last to criticize variants in sacred texts since they bring forth conflicts about articles of faith, differences in ecclesiastical discipline, and the religious cult. It therefore seemed necessary to Nicholas of Cusa to produce identical missals for all parishes of his diocese. This plan could have hardly been realized in the age of writing and was perhaps, as has been conjectured, based on ties between Cusa and early printers, since now liturgical books no longer needed to be renewed copy for copy but thanks to the new technology could be replaced all at once.

Yet the idea of the book as an individual within a family did not disappear right away. F. Geldner, an expert on early printing, has described an amazing example. In 1482/84, the bishop of Freising ordered liturgical texts to be meticulously proofread by a Bamberg printer. Evidently this was not done by comparing a sample with the written originals and then making the necessary corrections in the master form or transferring them from the sample to each other copy. Instead, it seems that each copy was compared individually with the written original. Only in this way, according to Geldner (1961: 102), do the payments for the proofreading make sense: 91 florins for 91 breviaries on parchment; 206 florins for 206 obsequies; 400 florins for 400 missals, and so on. The enormous sums as well as the exact correspondence between the numbers of copies and the numbers of forms paid support Geldner's thesis. Otherwise, the proofreading of the sample should have been much more expensive than each transferal of the (few) corrections onto the several copies, an operation requiring far less time. This odd investment is due to the old manuscript culture that required such individual proof, copy after copy. The result of a similar procedure, the proof-reading of a printed missal 'word for word', seemed like a miracle to the bishop of Regensburg: 'And see, it was as if by a miracle of God that the text was found to correspond in order and arrangement in each letter, syllable, word, parts of speech [*orationibus*], punctuation [*punctis*], head-ings, and everything else that is necessary, in every copy [*in omnibus et per omnia*] to the originals of our church' (Geldner 1961: 104). Correspondence in every detail of every copy (!) was discovered where family resemblance was expected. Now an identical text existed beyond its material realiza-tions. These curious cases, if Geldner has correctly interpreted them, show in an exemplary way how written communication can now be centrally controlled and how it detaches itself from a model of interaction between individuals.

The chain of generations and the *Bibliotheca universalis*

Concerning missals, the authoritative text is the result of careful selection and the decisions of the bishop. Such care was never granted in early printing. On the contrary, whatever manuscript happened to be available was chosen for print, and it was therefore left to chance what kinds of texts would experience the greatest distribution. As before, the chain of texts was simply expanded by one link that replaced the preceding one. The original was often destroyed for technical reasons; no matter: it had been replaced (Schottenloher 1931: 94). Humanist scholars and printers eventually opposed this practice (Widmann 1970: xliii). It was no longer sufficient simply to expand the chain; instead, the ever-growing inventory had to be looked through in order to produce the best text from the greatest number of prototypes. For the new philology, the single copies are but steps on the way to the ideal 'correct text', which is actually never attainable but must at least be attempted in some way by comparison and combination. Meaning is not eternally present in the materiality of the book but must first be reconstructed beyond the distance of tradition. If writing must now be collected and deciphered as a clue to a dim past, then historical understanding becomes a never-ending task for the future. Gesner discovers that the newer text, insofar as it is the result of careful philological efforts, is often better than the older text (the 'father'), in which the past seems to be present in its natural state (Gesner 1966: 4v). Historical perspective is inscribed in the new culture of writing from the beginning, even though reflection on it lags behind for two centuries.

   The generation around 1550 realized a loss of tradition, even though printing seemed at first to secure everything that had been transmitted and was worthy of transmission (*quamuis enim ars typographica librorum conseruationi nata uideatur*; Gesner 1966: 3r). The loss of tradition manifests itself in the destruction of manuscripts. Nicolaus Mameranus states in 1550 that everybody stupidly trusts the first, best print, that is, the son who replaces the father, and hence accepts that old manuscripts, once printed, are sold, cut up, scraped clean, and then used for other purposes: 'The books are printed,' they say; 'isn't that enough?' Not at all, if one wants to establish the word of the author in its original state (*pristinam suam et nativam integritatem*), as Mameranus himself says in his edition of Paschasius Radpertus. To reestablish it, all available copies must be collected; 'the old exemplars must be preserved with holy zeal, and guarded as a treasure, even if they are printed a thousand times over' (Schottenloher 1931: 93–94).

Tradition is no longer considered as this or that codex, but as a whole. Its preservation requires new institutions, Mameranus demands, as do Conrad Gesner and Conrad Lycosthenes, that libraries be placed under public oversight via the nobility and government. The private availability of books, although a highly praised achievement of print (Lycosthenes 1551: p. b 1r), does not ensure survival (Gesner 1966: 3r). Gesner's endeavors aim beyond the simple preservation of manuscripts. His *Bibliotheca universalis* is no longer concerned with individual books but with the transmission of all writing, and it makes little difference to him if the listed titles are still extant or not since, if they are lost now, they could be rediscovered later. Like the more limited catalogues of Trithemius, his *Bibliotheca* is of an imaginary extension, no longer a stock placed here or there. Its place is the literary public as a whole. Scientific interests are no longer concerned with the individually available manuscript or print but with the abstract unity of text or tradition. The idea of a corporeal presence of books is no longer appropriate to such a concept. Writing finally loses any analogy to face-to-face interaction, such as had always characterized the medieval manuscript culture, even where it was not oriented toward oral forms of communication. Books can come to everyone, but they are no longer individuals in which the absent speaker is embodied. Their longevity is no longer dependent on their material characteristics but on the mechanisms of selection of society's new institutions that keep public and present what is fixed in writing.

Final comment

The body of the book, in fact a metaphor, was in the manuscript culture a guarantor of the longevity of the word and of the presence of author and meaning. Writing naturally depends on material conditions even after the invention of print. But longevity is guaranteed no longer by the written 'monument' itself but rather by the numerous institutions that select the constantly growing reservoir of writings and allow them to become effective. Text and tradition are phenomena beyond the present available stock of books. The author and the meaning he is supposed to intend are sought behind what is written. The ties and analogies to situations involving oral communication are severed. How this process affects modern writing cannot be dealt with here. Today writing seems in any case to be losing its eminent position. The pictures, gestures, and sounds that supplement and replace it do not show a return to the medieval culture of performance (Zumthor 1987). Technically produced and disseminated, they only simulate the sensual presence that the medieval scribe still experienced in the book.

Chapter 15

C. A. Bayly

THE INDIAN ECUMENE
An indigenous public sphere

The appearance of print added a powerful new weapon to the arsenal of debate within the ecumene. When Christian missionaries began to pour printed propaganda into north India, its guardians responded vigorously, initiating formal logical contests and written refutations.[1] Missionaries were often surprised by the vehemence with which not only the religious teachers, but also local officers, *thanadars* (superintendents) and kotwals,[2] engaged them in debate. These were not cowed victims of colonial power. These were trustees of a public doctrine which seemed under threat. Rev. C. B. Leupolt, for example, noted of a tour in the vicinity of Lucknow in 1837: 'The Molwee came according to appointment, with an immense retinue of Mussulmans, learned as well as unlearned, and sat outside the tent. He brought a man with pen, ink and paper to note down what was said.'[3] Vigorous responses in pamphlet and placard form often followed Christian attacks on the Prophet. Such works often contained covert critiques of the Company as a secular ruler and were not limited to doctrinal arguments over the veracity of the Koran and Bible. In the 1830s the Muslim police chief of Buxar, for example, revealed to a passing missionary that he had often put a stop to widow burnings within his jurisdiction and denounced the Company for cowardice in failing to confront the issue.[4]

In the Hindu world, too, the activities of Brahmins and ruling-caste men had long transcended their ascribed functions as priests and warriors. Brahmins filled a similar role to Sheikhs and Sayyids as local justiciars, counsellors, literary arbiters, astronomers and doctors. The late eighteenth and early nineteenth centuries saw continuing formal debates between different schools of the Hindu learned about scripture and philosophy.[5] But, faced with direct attacks on their spiritual clienteles by Christians, priestly Brahmins had now to defend, to rationalise, to preach and to grasp the new tools of publicity. Some missionaries resorted to physical violence and coercion, such as 'shaking' the fakirs out of their spiritual trance.[6] More often, they found themselves drawn into complex and inconclusive debates which raged around the nature of godhead, the age of the universe and the qualities of good kingship, so touching directly on the political realm and claims to truth of western science. In missionary memoirs we glimpse two Hindu philosophical traditions which engaged the spiritual invader with particular force. First, Advaita Vedantists vigorously asserted the oneness of creation, directly challenging the Christian assumption of the separation of God and his creatures. Secondly, the devotional bhakti tradition afforded ample resources for arguing back against the white man in an idiom which seemed superficially similar. When a missionary advanced on a Hindu priest affirming 'God is love', the priest put his hands on the missionary and responded – to the Christian's irritation – 'I love you.'[7] Hindu devotional love (*prem*) was here used against Christian love, to diminish the moral, physical and political distance between sahib and 'native'. A generation before the modernist Arya Samaj stepped in to defend ancient religion with print, north Indian Hindu scholars were employing their skills of logical debate to refute, rebuff or incorporate the missionaries. This was no simple Hindu 'reaction' to western 'impact'; instead, the headstrong westerners plunged into a torrent of controversy which had for centuries pitted Vaishnavite scholars against Buddhists and Jains, Siddhantists against the Puranas and devotional gurus against the orthodox. All these formally doctrinal issues, however, bore on the question of good kingship and social propriety.

Speech and critical aesthetic comment

An important precondition for the development of this widespread debate on religion and politics was the flexibility and accessibility of the Hindustani or Urdu language itself (Urdu is used here to mean the more refined and Persianised form of the common north Indian language, Hindustani). Urdu came to impart to the discussions of the ecumene a popular character which was difficult when Arabic and Persian totally dominated them. The turn towards Urdu in the courts and camps of north India in the eighteenth and nineteenth centuries represented a deliberate populist strategy on the part of the elite. The emergence of Urdu was attested to by the work of indigenous grammarians as much as by the excellence of its poets. In the late eighteenth century Sirajuddin Ali Arzu, for instance, had critically edited earlier Persian works on Urdu. He argued that this was a true language and proposed a typology which ran from pure Sanskrit, through popular and regional variations of Hindustani to Urdu, which incorporated many loan words from Persian and Arabic.[8] His emphasis on the unity of languages reflected the view of the Sanskrit grammarians and also affirmed the linguistic unity of the north Indian ecumene. What emerged was a kind of register of language types which were appropriate to different conditions of man and society, and even to different times of the day and season.[9] There was a particular variant for the use of women, for court camp and army, for local officials and village registrar. Particular professions, sub-castes and even bands of criminals had their own argot. Sometimes the specific blend of language forms could be used to exclude and monopolise. This, for instance, was a claim commonly made about court and bazaar writers. But the abiding impression is of linguistic plurality running through the whole society and an easier adaptation to circumstances in both spoken and written speech.

Urdu/Hindustani itself had now taken on the character of the public tongue of the ecumene. It was a popular language spread by Sufi saints and Hindu devotees and a language of the court and discerning literati. The best Urdu could be heard, it was said, at three places: in the court and army bazaar at Delhi, at the flower-sellers' market on the river Jumna, and at the tomb of the saint Shah Madar in Etah district, a resort of horse-sellers, harkaras, palankin-bearers and other common people.[10] Outside centres of high Urdu court culture some Muslims continued to use the Devanagari character. The devotional poetry of the fifteenth- and sixteenth-century Sufi teachers was as likely to be found in the Devanagari as in the Persian script. In the eighteenth century a Sufi teacher of Bihar, writing to the governor of Malwa on the duties of rulers, remarked that 'a king's familiarity with Hindi verses is also very necessary'.[11] According to the writer, the king should consult with 'saintly ascetics', not with 'worldly ulama [doctors of law]', and should espouse 'universal toleration'. Thus regional versions of Hindustani appear to have carried overtones of community and harmony.

The learned reached down to incorporate these more localised language cultures in order to broaden cultural community. Several sources remark on the difficulty of teaching in Arabic or even Persian. Mullahs had to resort to exaggerated mimes of the action when they read out passages from the Arabic or Persian scriptures. One British observer noticed that at Muslim assemblies in which the Fateha or declaration of faith and Arabic prayers were offered, 'the mullah gave the history of the saints', presumably the Shia martyrs, in Urdu 'to enable those present the better to understand it'.[12]

Poetic assemblies held in the court, in the houses of notables and in the shops of bazaar people, spread common standards of aesthetic judgement and common forms of language across the country. Urdu writing was not confined to a self-conscious realm of literature. Instead, it was a discourse among men of weight on matters of aesthetics, health, religion and politics. Aristocratic writers were honoured in this world, but their rank did not exempt their ideas, their forms of letter-writing or their calligraphy, from critical scrutiny.[13] The poet Mir is alleged to have ridiculed the Emperor Shah Alam for his poetry. The Emperor had claimed that he was such a good poet that he could dash off several poems while he was doing his ablutions in the morning; 'Yes, and they smell like it', said Mir.[14] Aesthetic issues could become more directly political. The debate between the advocates of Persian and those of Urdu had ethnic, class, and religious undertones.[15] Though they enjoyed the patronage of the royal family, by the 1840s the proponents of Urdu were often less consciously aristocratic than the champions of Persian and were more influenced by Indian forms.[16]

One literary form which reflected and perpetuated the memory of the ecumene was the *tazkirah*, or collective literary biography. Literature here went beyond poetry to topics as diverse as medicine and topography. Through such works literary lineages and styles of endeavour could be traced over many generations. Having one's dame entered in a major tazkirah guaranteed some degree of literary immortality, and individuality. These collective biographies demonstrate the diverse origins of the people who were known to the Indian critical public. The models were Persian or central Asian forerunners, such as the biographies of the literary men and wits of Kashan, many of whom migrated to India in the thirteenth and fourteenth centuries.[17] Among the noted poets were sons of washermen, water-carriers, tailors, an 'occulist and chess-player', a 'talented man who gave himself up to profligacy', 'a great drunkard', and so on. Just as Islam was supposed to pay no attention to class in matters of faith, so in matters of style and literary excellence, men from humble backgrounds could achieve great fame.

In the 1840s Alois Sprenger carried out a detailed analysis of a number of literary biographies, including one of the Persian poets of Calcutta and Banaras, which paints a complex picture of social communication and the geography of the ecumene.[18] The literary men were often drawn from the old officers of the towns and qasbahs, such as the kazi and the King of Awadh's newswriter at Banaras.[19] As we have seen, the connection between political information systems and literary endeavour was very close. Others were dispersed remnants of the Delhi royal house, the Shahzadas of Banaras. Imperial family members who had been exiled or who had fled to Lucknow and Patna became the hubs of patterns of cultural patronage. Many of the people honoured worked in British government offices. They included residency munshis, clerks to the Calcutta Court of Appeal, clerks of the customs department at Banaras, and others in more lowly official positions who still cultivated Persian and Hindustani letters. The previously mentioned informant of the British, Ali Ibrahim Khan, was a prominent member of this group, and had written a collective biography of Persian poets.

People of poor background were not as evident here as in the Kashan list. Sprenger, however, listed many humbler authors in a comprehensive listing of tazkirahs, accounting for more than 1,800 literary people. Here, for instance, there were druggists,[20] a serving woman,[21] a Hazrat (one who had memorised the Koran) who kept an apothecary's shop in the Nakhas cattle market of Banaras,[22] a common writer,[23] a tailor skilled in *marsiyas* (lamentations on the Shia martyrs),[24] a Hyderabad 'dancing woman'[25] and many others. Hindus accounted for a small but significant percentage of the list. Most of these were from the Kashmiri Brahmin, Khattri or Kayastha communities and were traditionally associated with Persian and Urdu through Mughal service. There were, however, occasional entries for men of the Hindu commercial castes. One Eurasian even appeared: John Thomas, a 'soldier-like man',[26] son of George Thomas, who had founded a small state in Hariana at the end of the eighteenth century.

So it was not only men of power who participated in the literary activities of the ecumene. The egalitarian traditions of the Islamic lands and the community sensibilities of Indian cities encouraged ordinary artisans and people of the bazaars to aspire to eminence as poets or commentators. The form of the language was inclusive; it mirrored and even helped to stimulate the rapid social mobility which was characteristic of post-Mughal north India. Even women wrote and circulated poems.[27] In Lucknow, noblewomen, courtesans, musicians, dancers and other cultural performers from poor backgrounds achieved power in court and urban politics. This gravely offended evangelical Christian commentators and some later Indian purists, who saw corruption and decadence in what was actually striking social mobility.

History, libraries and social memory

Alongside questions of public doctrine and literary aesthetics, 'history' and topography played an important role in maintaining the identity of the ecumene. History in the Indo-Muslim tradition was, as Peter Hardy has written, a protean form which merged into poetry, moral and political instruction, and theology.[28] Amir Khusrau's poetic and panegyric history of the fourteenth century began a tradition which still had its imitators in the eighteenth century when court historians rendered the deeds of the founders of the successor states into ornate Persian. More influential yet in our period was the historical work of Abul Fazl. The 'Ain' and the 'Akbarnamah' were read and discussed extensively by the literati of the successor states and the munshis of the British offices. Besides legitimating the divinely gifted status of the house of Timur, Abul Fazl's history was the philosophy of religious insight teaching by example. Valuing the divine revelation in all mature creeds, his picture of universal harmony must have seemed particularly apposite to Muslim juris-consults practising in an age when the 'tribe of Hindus' had achieved much influence in the state. Akbar's debates with his Hindu, Jain, Christian and Parsi subjects were viewed as a template of good government in the eighteenth century. They represented the strain of historical and moral phil-osophy which inspired Mirza Jan-i Janan to reaffirm the theology of Ibn-i Arabi, and the doctrine of the immanence of God, against the more exclusive doctrines of the Delhi theologians, Shah Waliul-lah and Shah Abdul Aziz. It inspired that archetypical denizen of the ecumene, Ghalib, to describe ecstatically the sight of the festival of lights, Diwah, at Banaras, 'the Mecca of India'.[29] Despite his earlier adherence to a purist creed, Sayyid Ahmad's description of Delhi displays similar affection for the Hindu and Jain temples which had arisen in the city.[30]

This sense of the luminosity of place, and of the pleasures and ease of the erstwhile great and culturally diverse empire of Hindustan, was a compelling motif for much of the poetic-cum-historical work of the eighteenth and early nineteenth centuries. Hindus and Muslims, peasant and poet, were united in a wistful remembrance of what was and what might have been. This mode of elegiac historiography reached its fullest expression in the works of 'social poets' such as Sauda and Nazir who elaborated the form called *ashob sheher*,[31] 'bewailing the fallen greatness of the city', that is the civilisation of Mughal India. It also expressed itself in what is conventionally called 'history' (though the word *tarikh* does not quite mean history). A good example was the 'Araish-i-Mehfil' of Mir Sher Ali of Narnaul.[32] This writer had a family history typical of the military nobility of the eighteenth century. His father had been commander of the Nawab's Arsenal in Bengal. He himself moved between Delhi, Lucknow and Hyderabad, writing in Urdu under the patronage of Jawan Bakht, son of the Emperor Shah Alam. Late in his life he was introduced by Wellesley to Hasan Reza Khan and settled in Fort William College where he translated the Persian classic, 'Gulistan', under the superintendence of John Gilchrist. Drawing on the work of predecessors, notably Sujan Rai, Sher Ali wrote the history of the kings of Delhi from the Hindu period, described the customs of India's inhabitants, and the topography of each province. Though he recognised distress and decline, the overall tone seems to have been panegyric: 'All the inhabitants of Hindustan are capable, learned and clever and know merit'; the 'majority of grains have a delicious taste . . . rice is produced in a paradise on earth'.[33] There are descriptions of the excellence of palankins and other conveyances. He praises the beauty of Hindu women. He dilates on the feelings appropriate to the cycle of the Hindu months in a clear reference to the theory of *rasas* or essences which underlies Hindu aesthetics. But this was no more; after the Emperor Farrukhsiyar, corruption spread, Muhammad Shah became addicted to pleasure and 'the Empire became a sort of market'.[34] Poetry and panegyric in this tone persisted well into the nineteenth century. In 1849, for instance, Maharaja Apurva Krishna Bahadur wrote a historical epic 'The Conquerors of Hindustan' which praised the later Mughals.[35] The Empire had survived the wreck of its sister states, the Safavids and central Asian kingdoms, and even now, this work claimed, the Empire cast a glow like the setting sun. The writer apparently belonged to a family of the Sobha Bazaar, Calcutta, which had acquired its title by giving offerings to an indigent prince who was travelling around India with two mangy elephants.[36] The Anglo-Indian press ridiculed these poetic effusions, but they represent a continuing sense of cultural and political community and of criticism of the ruling powers, which remained strong until it was brutally terminated by the sack of Delhi in November 1857.

Libraries, or rather 'book houses', provided the resources from which this social memory in the fields of history, literature and theology was drawn. Indian libraries were no doubt highly unstable by European standards. Often they were built up out of patterns of princely gift-exchange[37] or plunder,[38] as annexes to royal treasuries. Royal and noble libraries were looted by their guardians as well as by external enemies.[39] Many Indian libraries were also exclusive. Temple libraries among Hindus and Jains were generally available only to priests; sacred knowledge was dangerous and had to be stored in safe places.[40] This literary memory, however, was neither negligible nor sealed off from the debates of the ecumene. The largest libraries comprised tens of thousands of volumes,[41] while many thousands of families had smaller collections amounting to a handful of manuscripts. There is some evidence, too, that a more specialist understanding of the library was developing among the elites even before the colonial period; in Jaipur, for example, Raja Jai Singh separated off a study collection from his treasury and this was used by the king and his officials in adjudications on religious and social issues.[42] Though never public, these collections could sometimes serve as a resource for the wider learned community. On occasion the Lucknow Royal Library was asked to produce a text when a controversy between the Muslim learned and Christian missionaries took place.[43] Scholars from outside princely families were allowed to see and copy texts. Sayyid Ahmad Khan, for example, was one person who was allowed to work in the Delhi Royal Library.[44]

Communications and political debate

Historians agree that in the West the public sphere was a domain of communication given form by printed media and the market.[45] Evidently, this key component was lacking from the north Indian scene before the introduction of lithography in the 1830s and 1840s, but the reasons for this remain obscure. Polities may have played a part; several Indian rulers at the turn of the nineteenth century continued to discourage the use of the printing press because it threatened their authority.[46] Rather than being testimony to passivity and the absence of political debate, however, our evidence suggests exactly the opposite conclusion: that royal authority was already too fragile to support this further dissemination of ridicule and *lèse majesté*. This in turn points to a wider reason for the late start of printing. Indians had created a highly effective information order in which strategically placed written media reinforced a powerful culture of oral communication; printing in this sense was not needed until society itself began to change more radically under colonial rule. In the ecumene written media and oral communication complemented each other. Francis Robinson[47] has made a strong case for the dominance of oral exposition and importance of the physical presence of the reputed teacher within the pre-print culture of Islamic north India. Oral exposition, presence and memory were no doubt critical in philosophical debate, and among Hindus and Jains no less than among Muslims. They were also important in poetic and aesthetic discussion. Ghalib, for instance, is said rarely to have purchased a manuscript or book, as he committed to memory anything that he needed.[48] Written media were, nevertheless, an essential part of north Indian critical debate, and could create eddies and flurries of opinion distant from the immediate presence of their authors. Ghalib's proficiency as a letter-writer was as striking as his memory.

While the dismal picture conveyed by Europeans and by Indian reformers was of a society where the communication of knowledge was stunted by hierarchy, there is much evidence to the contrary. We have already noted the speed with which information from the northwest or from Persia was conveyed to Banaras. The combination of harkara information, newsletters and public recitations in bazaars or near the platform of the kotwal's station spread news very quickly across country. During the Nepal and Burma wars, during the Afghan and Sikh campaigns of 1838–52, and during the Multan revolt of 1848 anti-British information and rumour were determinedly spread by these means.[49] At the height of the Burma War, Malcolm warned that 'there was a dangerous species of secret war against our authority carried on by numerous tho' unseen hands – the spirit of which is kept up by letters, by exaggerated reports, by pretended prophecies, etc.'[50] Though, as late as 1836, Auckland discounted the influence of the indigenous press itself, he believed that news was still widely disseminated by newswriters and agents of powerful people in whose newsletters 'anything may be inserted . . . without scruple'.

The north Indian case indicates that critical debate within a broad political class could be spread through personal and institutional letter-writing, through placarding and public congregation. In Rajasthan and adjoining areas the bardic tradition and the written stories to which it gave rise also proved capable of carrying subversive political messages. James Tod noted the prevalence of 'licence' and satire, the dissemination of 'truths unpalatable' and 'the absence of all mystery and reserve with regard to public affairs'[51] in the Rajput principalities. All this gives a picture of a lively social and political debate whose existence was reluctantly acknowledged when colonial officials made disparaging references to 'bazaar rumour'.

A similar point was made by Garcin de Tassy on the basis of a lifetime's study of Hindustani literature. It was common to argue that politics and rational discourse had no part in a society dominated by fable. On the contrary, he argued, the western distinctions between politics, literature and history did not really apply. Many so-called 'fables' were strongly political in tone and 'Nous voyons, en effet, que la politique occupe le premier rang dans les fables orientales, et en forme la portion la plus importante . . .'.[52] Here he mentions the famous 'Tota Kahani' or 'Tale of a Parrot'. Fables such as this, or the Panchatantra in its various forms, were highly pointed in their characterisation of human types and could be modified in oral presentations to refer to particular political situations. For instance one such story is a fable about diplomacy. A herd of deer hired a jackal to make a compact with a lion, but the jackal betrayed the deer to be eaten because he was the usual recipient of the lion's pickings.[53] This story must have seemed particularly timely in the savage politics of eighteenth-century India.

In contemporary west Asia, political debate was carried on in smoking dens and coffee shops.[54] The same was true in India, though here druggists' stalls, selling betel nut, tobacco or medicaments,[55] and sweetshops[56] served as more important forums of gossip and news. In west Asia, again, more resolute protests were made by seizing control of that pre-eminently public place, the mosque, at a time just before the muezzin's call to prayer and making statements critical of the authorities from the minaret. The regularity of this procedure suggests that it was sanctioned by the community, and even reluctantly tolerated by rulers. In India, too, political demonstrations were made at or near mosques. The shrines of saints, or of deceased rulers popularly revered as just men, were also the venue of demonstrations – an indication of the relative importance for the subcontinent of tomb worship and Sufism in both elite and popular life. In Lucknow at the beginning of the nineteenth century, for example, 'oppressions' by the police chief of the city brought together thousands in the garden of the tomb of the late ruler, Shuja-ud Daulah. The crowd called out 'andhera! andhera!' 'darkness!, darkness!', that is 'tyranny!'[57] In other incidents, people affixed handbills to points on or near the Friday mosque or royal temple. We have already noticed the use of placards during the celebrated affair of the British Resident, James Achilles Kirkpatrick, and the Hyderabad lady. Placards similarly denounced unpopular local Shia officials in Hyderabad,[58] announced changes of regime in Kathmandu,[59] and the onset of the Rebellion of 1857 in Lucknow. Pinning up critical poems in a mordant style, as well as passing them by word of mouth through the bazaar, appears to have been a political form as common as the pasquinade of Baroque Rome. Pasquino was the name given to a 'talking' classical statue near to the church of San Andrea della Valle. It has long been the practice to affix to it lampoons against the Pope or the authorities. Whereas in Rome, pasquinades were afforded legitimacy by the statuesque memorabilia of classical republicanism and ciceronian polemic, in India the tombs of just rulers or those Muslim saints who had been appropriately unimpressed by the powers that be served a similar purpose.

Political debates over a wider geographical area were carried on by the Indo-Muslim literati through recognised newsletters and also by private correspondence, still often delivered by covert indigenous postal systems. The literature associated with popular Sufi teachers sometimes contained critical comment on rulers, or on various ethnic groups.[60] Hindu sages crafted similar comments on contemporary politics. The poet Kavindracarya wrote verses in honour of the Emperor Shahjahan who had facilitated pilgrimage to Banaras.[61] They were recorded and used on later occasions when pilgrimage rights came under pressure. Shah Waliullah wrote letters to contemporary rulers urging a more strenuously Islamic policy.[62] Such epistles were, of course, destined for the readers of the wider critical ecumene; they were not 'private' letters.[63]

The practice of personal letter-writing also kept the ecumene informed. Figures for the early nineteenth century produced by the nascent British postal authorities suggest that even quite small towns produced a surprisingly large number of letters, perhaps as many as two hundred per annum per head for the literates and people who could afford to have letters written.[64] For men of the pen such as the poet Ghalib, letter-writing was viewed as a necessity of life. This was almost literally the case, because as much paper was spent by Ghalib and his correspondents discussing new remedies and the excellence of various physicians as on the diseases of the body politic.[65] Outside scholarly circles, most towns had substantial communities of bazaar writers acting for ordinary people who could pay them. Village schoolmasters also helped people communicate with their folk 'in distant parts'.[66] Most cities, again, supported large bodies of runners employed by private daks. After 1836, the British tried to suppress these in order to maximise postal revenue, but the impression is that many persisted clandestinely. 'Native intelligence' continued to move vigorously, transported by runners 'who shift their parcels at every sixteen or twenty miles' and never made unnecessary stops.[67]

As we have seen, the newsletters written from the courts of rulers all across the country were copied by hand in relatively limited numbers. As in the case of later printed newspapers which were read to large groups of people and handed around in the bazaar for several days, the information they purveyed seems to have become public property very quickly. Pages of newspapers were lent by one family to another.[68] Whole copies of newspapers were read out to crowds in the streets in the evening.[69] Professional newswriters moved between the world of the written newsletter and the printed newspaper. Some of these writers also kept lists of subscribers to whose houses they would repair daily in order to read the news from their own manuscript compilations.[70] A combination of these instruments could create a formidable blast of publicity even before the rise of the press. When in the early 1850s, the King of Delhi was maliciously reported to have become a Shia, a whole arsenal of written, lithographed and memorised refutations cannoned back. Ghalib, then poet laureate, was himself asked to write an ode in refutation.[71]

The ecumene was led by respectable men who could draw limits to the actions of government and also seek to impose their standards of belief and practice on the populace. Meanwhile, dense networks of social communication could bring butchers, flower-sellers, bazaar merchants and artisans into political debates and demonstrations. This has been thoroughly demonstrated by the many studies of the taxation riots and religious disputes of the early nineteenth century.[72] These events, however, are evidence of a continuing ecumenical critique; they should not be seen as sudden upsurges of resistance from tyrannised and voiceless subalterns. In 1779 in Lucknow, for instance, there was a celebrated debate between learned physicians who had newly arrived in town,[73] and resident savants who were trying to protect their livelihoods against the newcomers. The invasion of the new men was announced, according to the historian Mahomed Faiz Baksh, by a careful campaign of slander against existing 'doctors' in the city[74] (slander, of course, itself represents a kind of 'black public'). The conflict came to a head in a public debate. The ostensible subjects of the disputation were rival interpretations of an incident in early Islamic history – a revolt in AD 740 led by Ali Zaid. In fact, the two sides partly represented ethnic divisions, with Persians ranged against Indians. Alongside this there were political divisions, with the supporters of the Nawab and Warren Hastings ranged against partisans of the Begams of Awadh and other groups resisting the Awadh court and the British. The authority of texts and the spoken word were both in contention here.[75] Professional clerics contended with lay literati. Perhaps the most important aspect was the way in which the debate attracted the attention of the whole city with huge throngs of people of all persuasions, numbering more than 1,500, clustering around the house where the contest took place. Finally, order broke down amid Hogarthian scenes of rioting and revelry. As the chronicler wrote, 'It was a marvellous tumult and no-one knew what it was about . . . it ended at last, but for some time after it was much talked about and people composed ballads and wrote narratives about it'.[76]

Another example from the first months of British rule at Bareilly in 1804 revealed similar patterns. Fitzroy, a demented magistrate, had struck a Sayyid in a dispute over a garden. The cry went up: 'A Seyud has been insulted and struck; our houses are about to be demolished . . .'. The Governor-General's agent, Archibald Seton, a prolix and learned Scotsman, feared that the 'Green Banner' was about to be raised and the paltry British occupying force in the city would be overwhelmed. To compromise the dispute, 'he went to the Mosque of Moftee Mahomed Ewuz, the most popular and respected Seyud at Barelli, from the purity of his conduct and the sanctity of his manners'.[77] As he entered the mosque, Seton took off his shoes and said to the swordsmen barring his way, 'Do you not see, my friends, that I am prepared to approach a sacred place and meet a holy man'. They respectfully parted and, according to Seton, 'I distinctly heard one of them say to the other "This gentleman is one of us."'[78] The honour of the community was restored by this act of contrition on the part of the Sahib, and, with the aid of two Muslim physicians and the Mufti, the wrong was compromised. The crowds retreated and Fitzroy was bundled out of town under restraint. This story illustrates the ecumene in action, its leading men acting to quell disputes in the same way as the Prophet had compromised the quarrels of the tribes of Arabia. Here the practice of politics and jurisconsultation was more striking than the 'resistance', for which some historians perennially search. However, resistance was indeed to come when the same Mahomed Ewuz took part in the house tax disturbances of 1816, and fled the city.[79] Faced with open resistance, the British authorities had a tendency to shoot first and consult the ecumene later.

Such standard patterns of political representation and debate embraced Hindus as well as Muslims. Several historians have given us analyses of the political movement at Banaras in 1810 against the new British system of house taxation, emphasising its popular character.[80] From our perspective what is striking is that a vigorous and effective public opinion could express itself in the public arena across the boundaries of caste and religion. Here the ecumene spoke in a Hindu idiom, though Muslims were also active. The protesters presented petitions against the asssessment as discrete communities. One particular market-gardener caste leadership sent a 'letter of righteous-ness' (dharmapatra) to mobilise its rural supporters, in what was probably an adaptation of the normal method of raising temple funds or seeking adjudication in cases of infringements of caste rules.[81] The action of the Banaras citizens was, however, carefully coordinated between groups. The demonstrators all took a common oath of resistance and congregated in a single spot. Petitions argued the case against taxation in terms of the sanctity of Banaras but also the past and present usage of 'the country of Hindoostan, preferable to the kingdom of the seven climes', acknowledging a sense both of charismatic place and of wider patria.[82] Ultimately, too, they accepted the good offices of the Maharaja of Banaras as an intermediary with the British. Abdul Kadir Khan and another 'faithful old government servant', Akbar Ali Khan, also played the part of intermediaries. Although one historian has denounced them as 'spies' for the British,[83] and they certainly worked to end the uprising, these men had high status within both communities. They continued to resemble the munshis and advisers of the eighteenth century rather than the police informers of the nationalist period.

Finally, one should beware of the assumption that, even in cases where religious communities were pitted against each other, rational argument and social communication were totally abandoned. A few months earlier than the house tax affair, Banaras had been convulsed by a riot between Hindus and Muslims over the status of a holy place. In this case the petitioners on the part of the Hindus argued from history and current information. All had been well in Banaras, they said, until the Emperor Aurangzeb had destroyed the harmony between the communities by demolishing a temple; but the Emperor was so powerful that the Hindus had 'necessarily submitted with patience'.[84] Now the Muslim weavers had become 'more bigotted' than Aurangzeb, and the Hindus were forced to respond. Showing an acute awareness of current affairs, they argued that Muslims should concentrate on protecting the holy places of the Middle East against the Arabian Wahhabis who had recently sacked them, killing, it appears, the agent in Iraq of the late Ali Ibrahim Khan.[85]

Elite and mass in cultural performance

In addition to these set-piece demonstrations of discontent, strong political messages could be conveyed through cultural performance which linked elite and populace in enjoyment. Historians have been interested in recent years in the symbolism of festivals such as Ramlila, Holi or, amongst Muslims, Mohurrum and Id.[86] Well before the intervention of nationalist politicians at the end of the nineteenth century, these festivals had become the scene of attempts by magnates to claim new status or bodies of people attempting to assert cohesion or identity. In this sense, the Ramlila festival, which increased in importance and size in most parts of north India in the eighteenth and nineteenth centuries, should itself be seen as a widening arena of public communication.[87] Garcin de Tassy listed many different types of popular literature for recitation at these festivals, including songs, chants, homilies and prayers, all of which could be used to promote cohesion and mutual knowledge.[88] These ranged from laments on the death of the Shia martyrs, through didactic treatises (risalas) to what he called, as early as the 1840s, 'national-musical' performances in Indian-owned premises in Calcutta and other cities.[89] This flexible range of media, part-written and part-oral, added up to a wide array of procedures for spreading information, subversion, parody and biting political comment.

A number of different styles stand out. The heroic ballads of warrior heroes conveyed not only tales of ancient valour but observations on right kingship and religious conduct. The 'Prithvi Raja ki Kahani' which told of the last Hindu king of Delhi was a kind of foundation-legend for the high-caste warrior communities. In its full version the story contained not only genealogical and epic material but observations on grammar, diplomacy and other useful arts. Peasants could sometimes be found who had exactly mastered the whole ballad.[90] These legends had a definite reactive and community dimension. The epic of Pabuji, for instance, was circulated throughout Rajasthan by travelling story-tellers with elaborate cloth panels depicting the hero's exploits. In it the Muslim ('Turk') Mirza Khan is anathematised as a cow-killer: 'Oh king of Patan, in your kingdom calves and white cows are slain; at daybreak are slain the frogs and peacocks of the gardens'.[91] Another type of popular story was the social comedy in which stereotyped members of different communities fall into conflict and farce. One typical version was the Punjabi *jhaggra* or *jhannau* in one of which an argument develops between a Khattri woman and a Jat woman.[92] They embody respectively the merits of an acute businesswoman and a sturdy peasant. The Jat woman constantly ridicules the Khattri's assertion of caste superiority. Another version of popular communication was the didactic debate between pupil and master which was found both in the Sufi tradition and in its Hindu form. All these written media and their 'shadow' verbal forms could be used to propagate critical comment and debates on the conduct of both the rulers and society as a whole.

Alongside these, finally, should be placed the performances of wandering cultural specialists: bards, puppeteers, actors and jugglers. Bands of these artistes moved rapidly around India often from bases at the major pilgrimage places. They conveyed political and social messages which might originate in either the literate or the non-literate spheres. In Rajasthan and adjoining areas of the Agra Province, for instance, traditional bards (Bhats and Charans), singers of family pride and the heroic exploits of the Rajput rulers, introduced into their repertoire tales of the resistance of the Jats of Bharatpur against Mughal and British. Rather lower down the social scale, courtesans and prostitutes were famous purveyors of music and popular song. Some of their stock in trade were *ghazals*[93] or musical versions of poems which had been written by noted satirists, or even by popular and munificent rulers such as Nawab Asaf-ud Daulah of Awadh.[94] While the British garnered their fair share of sycophantic ditties, they were often the target of attack too. For decades after 1799, any European traveller who wandered into the red light district of Banaras was serenaded from the roof gardens of the courtesans' houses by songs praising the exploits of the deposed Nawab Vazir Ali, who had killed the British judge of Banaras and chief intelligence expert, George Cherry, during the abortive uprising of that year.[95]

Travelling puppet shows and theatrical performances also helped spread subversive political ideas. Thus, in the months before the Vellore mutiny of 1806, it was puppeteers who carried the message that Tipu Sultan's sons were about to regain their power, aided by the French. Several decades later an observer investigated the bodies of actors who took improvised comedies around north India to all the major festivals. Their plays were usually derived from Sanskrit originals but were burlesqued to include contemporary references. The Indians 'are devoted to the type of comedy which the *bazigars* [jugglers] perform at the great occasions, and which often contain political allusions'.[96] One group was attached to a body of irregular Indian cavalry, but was hired from time to time by rich magnates who wanted to entertain their guests. Captain Bevan recorded one such performance which satirised the proceedings in a British criminal court. In the drama the magistrate appeared whistling and striking his riding boots with a cane. The prisoner was brought in, but the magistrate paid no attention to him as he was flirting with a young Indian woman among the witnesses.[97] During the deposition he continued to make signs and leer at her. Finally, the bearer appeared saying '*tiffin taiyar hai*' ('tea is ready') and the magistrate got up. When the officers of the court asked what to do with the prisoner, he replied 'Dam [*sic*] his eyes, hang him!' This subversive assault on the white man's justice and lecherousness was, Bevan reported, greatly enjoyed by both the Indian troops and the British army officers present.

The limits of the ecumene

The north Indian critical ecumene as we have described it spilled over the bounds of caste, community and sect; it encompassed a dialogue between elite and popular political culture. It stands as a reminder that Indian minds and Indian social life cannot be reduced to the behaviourist simplicities of hierarchy and segmentation. It takes us beyond the limited and monolithic concept of 'resistance' to the realm of political critique and intellectual history. Yet this is not to say that the ecumene was a seamless web. On the contrary, there were significant breaks and discontinuities in it. For example, while Hindu noblemen, poets and specialists took part in the wider debate and wrote in its languages, Persian and Urdu, the Brahmin establishments stood relatively aloof.[98] Ghalib could say that 'Benares was the Mecca of India', but it is difficult to imagine him participating in the pandits' ritual debates (*shastrarthas*) in the same way that Khattri Hindus participated in the Persian poetry circles. Even Ghalib had relatively few Hindu literary correspondents. In the case of one of the most prominent, Munshi Hargopal Tafta, it seems that the poet hoped to touch him for money;[99] elsewhere he says he employed 'bunya-language' (shopkeeper talk) with a leading Delhi banker.[100] As a token of the assimilative power of public doctrinal debate, some learned Hindus became Muslims, but the process did not take place in reverse even though poor and unlettered Muslims sometimes venerated Hindu deities.[101] Muslim scholars showed interest in the Hindu classics and literature, but learned Hindus do not seem to have analysed and critiqued the Islamic corpus until Dayananda Saraswati set out to ridicule it. Khairuddin Khan's debate with the Banaras pandits in the 1770s occurred precisely because he had heard that a rich Bengali 'held no communication whatever with Mussulmans, and avoided even the shadow of a Mahomedan'.[102] Ritual pollution created hairline fractures in cross-community debate. Khairuddin tried to reconcile the genealogy of Adam with the story of the Pandavas of the Hindu epics and some of the Brahmins went along with this. Even so, he asked in irritation, 'what do you know of the Mahomedan religion?'[103] An overlapping debate did not mean equal participation. In fact, when a critical public sphere using the newspaper finally emerged, these inequalities of participation were reinforced by the desire of editors to grasp and hold abstract constituencies of readers' opinions, now more distant from the face-to-face, or pen-to-pen, relations of the ecumene.

Amongst the less privileged, too, social and even economic discourse was still to some extent constricted within what was called the 'opinion of the caste', even if, as in the Peshwa's territories, the authorities intervened to adjudicate and advise.[104] Among the upper castes, extra-caste opinion and debate appear to have influenced these insider debates. So, for instance, social transgressions by an Agarwal banker might have been dealt with by the caste assembly, but it had severe repercussions within the wider multi-caste arena of the market and its rumours, since social and commercial credit were closely bound up. But nobody worried much about what went on amongst the leather workers or liquor distillers. Only bhakti devotion bridged these divides of status, and the sects were becoming increasingly respectable and market-centred in the eighteenth and nineteenth centuries.[105] The ecumene had always worked unevenly beneath the network of the most enlightened intelligentsia. In this, India was not qualitatively different from other societies with emergent public spheres.[106] Nevertheless, the ecumene did display a range of fractures which were widened by the powerful pressures of later colonial politics.

Notes

1   Avril Powell, *Muslims and Missionaries in Pre-mutiny India* (Richmond, 1993), pp. 43–75; *Church Missionary Record* [*CMR*], 1, 3, 1830, 59, 62; 1, 6, 1830, 120–2, 133, 137; 1, 10, 1830, 217–19.

2   e.g., the Sadr Amin and 'The chief native judge' near Lucknow refutes Christianity, *CMR*, 6, 7, 1836, 137–8; ditto, the office manager of the Collector of Ghazipur, *ibid.*, 9, 1, 1838, 15.

3   *CMR*, 7, 6, 1836, 139.

4   *The Missionary Register for MDCCCXXIV* (London, 1824), April 1824, p. 195.

5   See, e.g., the description of a western Indian debate between Advaita Vedantists and their opponents, J. Howison, *European Colonies in Various Parts of the World* (London, 1834), II, 52–4.

6   C. B. Leupolt, *Recollections of an Indian Missionary* (London, 1856), p. 56.

7   e.g., *CMR*, 1, 6, 1830, 128; cf. *ibid.*, 1, 131, 133; *ibid.*, 1, 10, 1830, 243; Leupolt, *Recollections*, p. 82; the missionaries displayed particular interest in Sadhs and Kabirpanthis, *CMR*, 2, 8, 1831, 178–80; *Miss. Reg.*, April 1824, p. 314.

8   S. Kidwai, *Gilchrist and the 'Language of Hindostan'* (Delhi, 1972), pp. 88–9.

9   J. Majeed, 'The jargon of Indostan – an exploration of jargon in Urdu and East India Company English', in P. Burke and R. Porter (eds) *Languages and Jargons* (Cambridge, Mass., forthcoming); D. Lelyveld, 'The fate of Hindustani: colonial knowledge and the project of a national language', in C. Breckenridge and P. van der Veer, *Orientalism and the Postcolonial Predicament* (New York, 1993), pp. 189–215.

10 E. B. Eastwick, tr., *The Bagh o Bahar* (Hertford, 1852), pp. 7–8, Munshi's preface; cf. W. Crooke, *Ethnographic Handbook of the North-western Provinces and Oudh* (Allahabad, 1887), p. 84, on 'Madari' palankin-bearers. But see also A. Rai, *A House Divided. The origins and development of Hindi-Urdu* (Delhi, 1984), pp. 246–54, which notes the precolonial attempts to 'purify' Urdu of Sanskritic words; Surendra Gopal, *Patna in the Nineteenth Century. A socio-cultural profile* (Calcutta, 1982), pp. 60–79.

11 Askari, 'Mirat-ul-Muluk', *Indica* (Bombay, 1953), p. 31.

12 Westmacott, 'Travels', Westmacott Papers, Oriental and India Offices Collections, British Library, Ms. Eur C29 f. 183; *Friend of India*, 28 Feb. 1839.

13 A vivid picture of the world of the mushairah is given in Akhtar Qamber, *The Last Mushairah of Delhi* (Delhi, 1979).

14 R. Russell and K. Islam, *Three Mughal Poets. Mir, Sauda, Mir Hasan* (London, 1969), p. 6; cf. pp. 55–8; S. A. I. Tirmizi, *Persian Letters of Ghalib* (Delhi, 1969), p. xxiii.

15 Daud Rahbar (tr., ed.), *Urdu Letters of Mirza Asadu'lluh Khan Ghalib* (Albany, New York, 1987), p. xxvii; Tirmizi, *Persian Letters of Ghalib*, pp. xxviii–xxx.

16 cf. R. Russell and K. Islam, *Ghalib, 1797–1969*, I, *Life and Letters* (London, 1969), pp. 79–81.

17 A. Sprenger, *A Catalogue of the Arabic, Persian and Hindustani Manuscripts of the Libraries of the King of Oudh* (Calcutta, 1854), pp. 23ff.

18 *ibid.*, pp. 195–306; we have used the term ecumene to describe a style of communication but tazkirahs could be used to demonstrate the geography of social communication in the sense used by Deutsch. The relative decline of literary and social comment in the western cities, Lahore, Delhi, etc., would be matched in the late eighteenth century by the rise of Lucknow, Banaras, Patna, Hyderabad and their associated qasbahs. Calcutta would become significant for Persian and Urdu scholarship.

19 *ibid.*, pp. 165–75.

20 *ibid.*, p. 207.

21 *ibid.*, p. 217.

22 *ibid.*, p. 234.

23 *ibid.*, p. 282.

24 *ibid.*, p. 289.

25   *ibid.*, p. 217.

26   *ibid.*, p. 299.

27   *LH* (J. H. Garcin de Tassy, *Histoire de la Littérature Hindoue et Hindoustanie*, 4 vols, reprint New York, 1970), I, 69–72; cf. Garcin de Tassy, 'Les femmes poètes de l'Inde', *Revue de l'Orient*, May 1854; Sprenger, *Catalogue of Libraries of Oudh*, p. 11.

28   P. Hardy, *Historians of Medieval India. Studies in Indo-Muslim Historical Writing* (London, 1960), pp. 122–31.

29   Tirmizi, *Persian Letters of Ghalib*, p. xxiii.

30   Sayyid Ahmad Khan, 'Asar-us Sanadid', trans. as 'Description des monuments de Delhi en 1852', *Journal Asiatique*, Jan. 1861, 80, 87, 91, *passim*.

31   Fritz Lehman, 'Urdu literature and Mughal decline', *Mahfil*, 6, 2, 1970, pp. 125–31; Russell and Islam, *Three Mughal Poets*, pp. 1–68.

32   *LH*, I, 120–1.

33   *ibid.*, 127.

34   *ibid.*, 136.

35   'The conquerors of Hindustan in Persian and English', *Delhi Gazette* cited *Friend of India*, 16 Dec. 1847; *ibid.*, 3 May 1849.

36   *Friend of India*, 3 May 1849.

37   I. A. Arshi, *Catalogue of the Arabic Manuscripts in Raza Library, Rampur*, 6 vols (Rampur, 1963–77).

38   B. K. Datta, *Libraries and Librarianship of Ancient and Medieval India* (Delhi, 1970), p. 84.

39   Also note the lack of catalogues, A. Sprenger to H. Elliot, 25 Jun. 1847, Elliot Papers, Add 30, 789, BL.

40   D. C. Dasgupta, *The Jaina System of Education* (Calcutta, 1944), pp. 36–40; John E. Cort, 'The Jain knowledge warehouses: traditional libraries in India', *Journal of the American Oriental Society*, 115,1,1995,77–88.

41   Sprenger to Elliot, 25 Jun. 1847, Elliot Papers, Add. 30,789; cf. Sprenger, *Report of the Researches into the Muhammadan Libraries of Lucknow. Selections from the records of the government of India*, no. 28 (Calcutta, 1896), which records 6,000 volumes in the Topkhana Library and about 1,000 in the Farah Baksh; the private library of Sheikh Mahomed Hazin's family had 5,000 volumes, F. C. Belfour tr., *The Life of Sheikh Mohammed Au Hayin Written by Himself* (London, 1830), p. 10; Datta, *Libraries*, pp. 69, 73, 85.

42   G. N. Bahura, 'Glimpses of historical information from manuscripts in the Pothikhana of Jaipur', in J. N. Asopa (ed.), *Cultural Heritage of Jaipur* (Jodhpur, 1982), pp. 104–5; cf. Arshi, *Rampur*, I, preface p. 1.

43   *Miss. Reg.*, Aug. 1826, p. 395.

44   C. W. Troll, *Sayyid Ahmad Khan. A reinterpretation of Muslim theology* (Delhi, 1978), p. 104.

45   Jürgen Habermas, *The Structured Transformation of the Public Sphere*, tr. T. Burgen (Cambridge, Mass.: Harvard University Press, 1992), pp. 57ff.

46   e.g. the case in 1849 where the King of Awadh destroyed the Lucknow presses because they had displeased him, Sprenger, *A Catalogue of the Arabic, Persian and Hindustani Manuscripts in the Libraries of the King of Oudh*, p. vi, or an equivalent case in Punjab, Emmet Davis, *The Press and Politics in British West Punjab, 1836–47* (Delhi, 1983), p. 184.

47   F. Robinson, 'Technology and religious change. Islam and the impact of print', *Modern Asian Studies*, 27, i, 1993, 229–51.

48   Russell and Islam, *Ghalib*, I, 38.

49   *Englishman*, 12 Jan. 1835; material on Burma etc.; Banaras 1852, E. A. Reade, *Contributions to the Banaras Recorder in 1852* (Banaras, 1858), fn., pp. 67–8.

50   Marginal note to Auckland's minute on the press, 8 Aug. 1836, Auckland Papers, Add. Mss. 37, 709, f. 91b, BL.

51   J. Tod, *Annals and Antiquities of Rajast'han, or the central and western Rajpoot states of India* (London, 1829–32, repr., 1950), Introduction, p. 16; cf. V. N. Rao, D. Shulman and S. Subrahmanyam, *Symbols of Substance. Court and state in Nayaka period Tamilnadu* (Delhi, 1992), pp. 1–22 and passim.

52   *LH*, I, 10.

53   C. Bendall, 'The Tantrakhyana. A collection of Indian tales', *Journal of the Royal Asiatic Society*, 2, 4, 1890, 484; cf. *The Panchatantra*.

54   Note by Prof. Hall Inalcik in author's possession.

55   An observation of Prof. Ravinder Kumar.

56   'Bankas and swindlers', *Delhi Gazette*, 18 Dec. 1839.

57   Muhammad Faiz Baksh, 'Tarikh-i Farah Baksh' entitled *Memoirs of Delhi and Faiyabad*, tr. W. Hoey, 2 vols (Allahabad, 1889), II, 285–7.

58   Mofussilite, 11 Feb. 1848, on 'Sunni–Shia disturbances at Hyderabad'.

59   'placards have been posted at Cathmandoo threatening destruction to several prominent chiefs and the Resident': the information was sent immediately to Banaras, 'the centre of information about Nepaul', *Delhi Gazette*, 20 Jan. 1841.

60   Askari, 'Mirat-ul-Muluk', *Indica*, pp. 44ff.

61   V. Raghavan, 'The Kavindrakalpalatika of Kavindracarya Sarasvati', *ibid.*, pp. 336–7.

62   S. A. A. Rizvi, *Shah Walli-allah and his Times* (Canberra, 1980), pp. 302–3.

63   cf. David Lelyveld, reported by S. Freitag, 'Introduction' *South Asia*, n.s., 14, 1, 1991, p. 9 and fn. 19.

64   'District Dawks', *Friend of India*, 18 Jul. 1850.

65   e.g., Ghalib to Nawab Alauddin Ahmad Khan, 15 Shaban 1298 (Feb. 1862), Rahbar, *Persian Letters of Ghalib*, pp. 25–6; same to Munshi Hargopal Tafta, n.d. May (?) 1848, p. 57; same to Mirza Shahabuddin Abmad Khan, 24 Sept. 1861, p. 51; for the social networks in Ghalib's earlier correspondence, Tirmizi, *Ghalib*, pp. xiv, xxiii.

66   e.g., the case in Westmacott, 'Travels', Mss. Fur. C26, f. 173.

67   *Mofussilite*, 30 May 1848.

68   Rahbar, *Ghalib*, pp. 94, 205.

69   *Friend of India*, 4 April 1850.

70   Evidence of Chuni Lal, newswriter 'for the public', 'Trial of the King of Delhi', *Past and Present*, 1859, 1st session, xviii, 84.

71   Rahbar, *Ghalib*, p. xxxiii.

72   See K. H. Prior, 'The British administration of Hinduism in north India, 1780–1900', unpub. PhD thesis Cambridge University, 1990.

73   Juan R. I. Cole, *The Roots of North Indian Shi'ism in Iran and Iraq. Religion and state in Auradh, 1772–1859* (Berkeley, 1988), pp. 55–8.

74   Faiz Baksh, *Memoirs*, II, 44.

75   *ibid.*

76   *ibid.*

77   Seton to Wellesley, 22 Jan. 1804, Wellesley, Add. 13, 577, BL.

78   *ibid.*, cf. Seton to Merrick Shawe, 10 Feb. 1804, Wellesley, Add. 13, 577, BL.

79   Committee at Bareilly to Commrs, *Native Newspaper Reports*, 3 July 1816, 27 and encls., *Bengal Criminal Judicial Consultations*, 25 Oct. 1816, 3, 132/48, Oriental and India Office Collections, British Library; Rahman Ali, *Taskirah-i Ulama-i Hind* (Lucknow, 1914), pp. 24–5.

80   R. Heitler, 'The Varanasi house-tax hartal of 1810–11', *Indian Economic and Social History Review*, 9, 3, 1972, 239–57; G. Pandey, *The Construction of Communalism in Colonial North India* (Delhi, 1990), pp. 24–50; S. Freitag, *Collective Action and Community. Public arenas and the emergence of communalism in north India* (Berkeley, 1989), pp. 19–52.

81   Actg Magt. to Govt, 8 Jan. 1811, Bengal Criminal Judl Procs., 8 Feb. 1811, 1, 130/28, Oriental and India Office Collections, British Library.

82   Petition of Mohulla Seedhesree, Bengal Criminal Judl Procs., 5 Jan. 1811, 25, 130/27, Oriental and India Office Collections, British Library.

83   Heitler, 'Hartal', p. 251; cf. Actg Magt. to Govt, 28 Jan. 1811, Bengal Criminal Judl Procs, 8 Feb. 1811, 5, 130/28, Oriental and India Office Collections, British Library.

84   'Memorial of the Hindoos of the City of Benares', 20 Nov. 1809, 'Disturbances at Benares', BC 365, Oriental and India Office Collections, British Library; the British were peeved that another important old 'native informant', Bishambhar Pandit, had been involved in fomenting the Hindus.

85   ibid.

86   S. Freitag, *Culture and Power in Banaras. Community, performance and environment, 1800–1980* (Berkeley, 1989).

87   S. Pollock, 'Ramayana and political imagination in India', *Journal of Asian Studies*, 52, 2, 1993, 261–97.

88   *LH*, I, 24–50.

89   *LH*, I, 41.

90   *LH*, I, 382–5; *Journal of the Royal Asiatic Society*, Aug. 1851, 192; this was a source for Tod, *Annals and Antiquities*.

91   J. D. Smith, *The Epic Pabuji. A study in transcription and translation* (Cambridge, 1991), pp. 290–1.

92   D. J. Singh Johal, 'Historical significance of *Jhaggra Jatti te Katrani da*', in F. Singh and A. C. Arora (eds), *Maharaja Ranjit Singh. Politics, society, economics* (Patiala, 1984), pp. 289–91; cf. S. Sagar, 'Social change and the *kissas* of the first half of the nineteenth century', *ibid.*, 292–301.

93   see A. Bansani, 'Ghazal', *Encyclopaedia of Islam*, 2nd edn, II, 1036.

94   *LH*, I, 103–4.

95   Bholanauth Chunder, *The Travels of a Hindoo to Various Parts of Bengal and Upper India* (London, 1869), pp. i, 283; cf. *LH*, I, 103–4, on Asaf-ud Daulab; for the use of another *ghazal* in a contemporary dispute, Judge Banaras to Register Nizamat Adalat, 12 January 1813, Bengal Criminal Judicial, 12 July 1816, 18, 132/43, OIOC; for use of popular theatre in a political cause, de Tassy, *LH*, I, 24–5.

96   *LH*, I, 24; cf. 'Dramatic amusements of the natives of India', *Asiatic Journal*, n.s., 22, 1837, 25–34.

97   *ibid.*, 27.

98   'Mahommedan festivals in India', *ibid.*, 16, 1835, 52.

99   Rahbar, *Ghalib*, p. 380, n. 1.

100   Ghalib to Nawab Husain Mirza, 29 Oct. 1859, *ibid.*, p. 207.

101   *LH*, I, 63–4.

102   Khairuddin Khan Illahabadi 'Tuhfa-i-Taza', entitled *The Balwantnamah*, trans. F. C. Curwen (Allababad, 1875), p. 87.

103   *ibid.*, p. 88. The Bengali eventually shook Khairuddin's hand and said, 'You are a pandit of my religion', but the author clearly took it as the victory of Muhammadan learning!

104   G. C. Vad (ed.), *Selections from the Satara Rajas' and the Peshwas' Diaries* (Bombay, 1907–11), makes it clear that the rulers' courts acted a role as a kind of 'public tribunal' for intra-caste disputes.

105   D. Gold, 'What the merchant-guru sold; social and literary types in Hindi devotional verse', *Journal of the American Oriental Society*, 112, 1, 1992, 22–36.

106   As is made clear by C. Calhoun (ed.), *Habermas and the Public Sphere* (Cambridge, Mass., 1992).

Chapter 16

D. F. McKenzie

THE SOCIOLOGY OF A TEXT
Orality, literacy and print in early New Zealand

As I am sure most of us have now come to understand, the discipline of bibliography cannot be limited to 'the study of books as physical objects', whether manuscript or printed. In at least three ways our subject is, ineluctably, evolving.

First, what it is now fashionable to call 'the impact of print' can only be measured of course in relation to a far older manuscript culture which print parallels and only in part displaces. But a serious historical concern with any manuscript culture, in its fullest ramifications, cannot be divorced from questions about the origins, social range, and different levels of literacy in that culture. And literacy, both as a concept and as an historically traceable phenomenon, is inseparable from a concern (both precedent and concurrent) with orality and the recording function of memory. We have only to think of, say, Homer, as an oral-memorial text, later made incarnate in manuscript and print, to see at once the impossibility of denying to bibliography any stage of the composition, dissemination, reception and descent of that text.

Orality, literacy and print can of course be so ordered as the primary, secondary and tertiary stages of a (perhaps misleadingly) progressive sequence in the history of civilization; and we may as bibliographers study them as distinct phases – each with its own 'impact' and forms of record – in the evolution of western society. But we must also, I think, recognize more frankly the diverse nature of each of those stages and their persistive interaction. There is nothing new in the observation that the words I am 'saying' to you now are written, indeed 'type'-written. I therefore 'speak' my 'book'. You 'hear' these letter-forms which only this 'I' can see – at least until they resurface in the silence of a reprint.

In other words, what we much too readily call 'the book' is a friskier and therefore more elusive animal than the words 'physical object' will allow. In such matters, social anthropologists have shown a lively interest in forms of evidence which we should all, I think, call 'bibliographical', since they relate to the telling, writing, reception and distribution of 'texts'. In extending the definition of the word 'book' to include oral literature and quite elementary forms of written record, and in taking a more dynamic view of the social origin and functions of such texts, anthropologists working in non-European societies have much to teach us. As they well know, orality and literacy are not, after all, artefacts, but highly variable human conditions whose shaping force on the form and efficacy of 'texts' we cannot ignore. What, fundamentally, we study therefore is not so much the history of the book as the sociology of texts.

The second way in which I think bibliography must expand is, paradoxically, by heightening our sensitivity to the printed book as a physical form in order to refine our notions of the historicity of printed texts and our function in editing them. Specialists of type, paper, bindings and so on acknowledge the intrinsic interest for them of every physical element that goes to construct a book, yet few editors grant those physicalities of the book any textual or even contextual meaning. We practise 'textual criticism' as the meanings of words, and we study, discretely, 'book-trade history'. Occasionally a Charlton Hinman or a Peter Blayney will show how the deficiencies of a mechanical process negatively affect the choice or sequence (and therefore the symbolic import) of words. And so we seek to eliminate 'error' in the 'transmission' of 'texts'. Marshall McLuhan's catch-phrase 'the medium is the massage' makes the point in an equally negative way: the ideal (message) is *de*-formed (massage) in the process of being made manifest.

By contrast, once we acknowledge that the physical book as a whole is a rich complex of signs, each of which has its own human history and all of which unite to *create* the 'finished' book as a palpably articulated 'text' (to *form* it, not *de*-form it), then we enter an entirely new, more positive and, for me at least, more exciting phase of textual criticism. One thinks of Stanley Morison's *Politics and script* for the meanings he could give to letter forms as cultural witnesses. That example of a creatively interpretative mind addressing itself to the physical evidence makes it clear how the book as physical object becomes the book as expressive form. The inert materials of bark, clay, vellum or paper, script or type, ink, decoration, illustration, binding – we discover – were never really inert, never merely physical. For each and every one shared in a creative act, an expressive decision, within a definable historical context, to serve an author's intention, a bookseller's pocket, or an implied reader's comprehension of the 'text'. The book as physical object put together by craftsmen – as we all know – is in fact alive with the human judgements of its makers. It is not even in any sense 'finished' until it is read. And since it is re-creatively read in different ways by different people at different times, its so-called objectivity, its simple physicality, is really an illusion. But it is more directly the bibliographer's job to show editors (and historians) how rich an account of human behaviour the physical elements of a book may yield to those who *can* read all its signs and so recreate the historical dynamics of its making and reading. As such, even the book in its narrowest sense is evidence unrivalled in its complexity, its sharpness of focus, its ubiquity, and its capacity for successive reincarnations in response to changing human needs.

I turn now to my third and last general comment on the ways in which bibliography is bound to expand as a discipline. Until this century its restriction to the study of books as marks on paper or some other physical medium – stable, visible, palpable – was unavoidable. Its limitation to letter forms, singly and in combination, mental and scribal or metal and printed, their design and production, packaging, dissemination, sale, resale, collection, counterfeiting, conservation or dismemberment, merely expressed the limited technology we then commanded to record and recover human behaviour. We now have a newer technology which permits us to record the sounds of words and music and images in motion. As these in turn parallel and in part displace the manuscript letter, printed book, and the static graphics of illuminator and engraver, our visible words must interact with the kinetic image and what W. J. Ong has called the 'secondary orality' of our electronic world.[1] If one thinks of the mutability of computer-stored information, it is clear that even some of our visible word-hoards share, by chance or design, the ephemerality of speech. Or to put it another (and in present company perhaps more acceptable) way, we as bibliographers must impart our skills to those whose professional concerns lie in sounds and moving images so that their work too shows the insights and affirms the values of the older discipline which we profess, in order responsibly to conserve the 'texts' of our own culture.

A future synthesis of bibliography as the study of the conception, mediation and reception of texts must enhance its power to interpret the past and expand its role in collecting, preserving, authenticating, accessing and interpreting the polymorphous texts of today and tomorrow. The new orthodoxy of '*histoire du livre*', as phrase and concept, describes much too limited a field but it is moving historians at least towards acknowledging a quite new centrality and status for the discipline of bibliography and its principal practitioner, the scholar-librarian as archivist, whether of manuscripts, print, film, disc or recorded sound.

Those points are not so remote as you might think from the topic I originally proposed, 'Two early New Zealand printers: William Colenso and R. Coupland Harding', for the careers of those two men span the movement in New Zealand from orality, through manuscript literacy to the introduction of printing and a full consciousness of the expressive resources of typography. Together with one crucial document, they offer a model from which to exemplify my larger argument.[2]

One hundred and forty-three years ago this month – on 6 February 1840 – forty-six Maori chiefs from the northern regions of New Zealand 'signed' a document written in Maori called '*Te Tiriti o Waitangi*', 'The Treaty of Waitangi'. In doing so, according to the English versions of that document, they ceded to Her Majesty the Queen of England 'absolutely and without reservation all the rights and powers of Sovereignty' which they themselves individually exercised over their respective territories. That act of assent became the substantive ground of British sovereignty over New Zealand.[3] Beneath a statue of Queen Victoria in my own city of Wellington, the European literacy myth implicit in that event of 1840 is complacently enshrined in the image of a Maori chief – as I say – 'signing' the treaty with quill pen. The reality, as William Colenso knew, and as we shall see as we meditate the sociology of that text, was different.

Twenty-five years earlier, the indigenous New Zealanders had been completely illiterate. They were a neolithic race with a wholly oral culture and their own body of myths. Not one of their myths, however, was so absurd as the European myth of the technologies of literacy and print as agents of change and the missionaries' conviction that what took Europe over two millennia to accomplish could be achieved – *had* been achieved – in New Zealand in a mere twenty-five years: the reduction of speech to alphabetic forms, an ability to read and write them, a readiness to shift from memory to written record, to accept a signature as a sign of full comprehension and legal commitment, to surrender the relativities of time, place and person in an oral culture to the presumed fixities of the written or printed word.[4] When Samuel Marsden bought 200 acres of land at Rangihoua in 1814 for the first mission station, he drew up a deed of conveyance and solemnly had the Maori chief 'sign' it by drawing on it a copy of his *moko* or facial tattoo pattern. The price was twelve axes, itself a potent symbol of the shift from a neolithic culture to the iron age, the deforestation of New Zealand and the pastoral economy to come. But the subtler, much more elusive and indeterminate technology was literacy.

Consider its stages. In 1815 Thomas Kendall, the first resident missionary, faced the problem of re-enacting one of the most momentous transitions in human history, the reduction of speech to its record in alphabetic form. Put like that, it sounds portentous, as in a literal sense it was. But just imagine the problems of trying to capture strange sounds alphabetically, the miracle that underlies all our printed books. When one early traveller recorded what he thought he heard as the Maori word for a paradise duck, he wrote *pooadugghiedugghie* (for *putangitangi*) and for the fantail *diggowaghwagh* (for *piwakawaka*), neither of which forms translates visually the aural beauty of the originals. The place-name *Hokianga* was rendered *Showkianga, Sukyanna, Jokeeangar, Chokahanga*. Another village, *Kerikeri*, was heard and rendered as *Kiddeekiddee, Muketa* as *Muckeytoo*. Those spellings are not only aurally inefficient, but to the English eye they appear crude and culturally primitive, thus reinforcing other such attitudes.[5]

The absence of a philology (let alone a grammar and syntax for a non-European language) made a rational orthography hard to devise. Yet until there was an orthography, the teaching of reading and writing was obviously impossible, and printing of course depended upon a standard set of letter forms. Kendall's first rough list of 1815 was revised and sent off to Samuel Lee, Professor of Arabic at Cambridge. Kendall and two Maori chiefs, Hongi and Waikato, joined him there in 1820, and together they produced *A grammar and vocabulary of the language of New Zealand*. It was printed later that year by R. Watts, printer to the Church Missionary Society in London. Kendall, unlike Marsden, was determined that Maori should not be anglicized; *c, q* and *x* were dropped for a start, but the *Grammar* at that stage still included letters for non-Maori sounds thought necessary for foreign words – *f*, hard *g, j, v, z* – and so it still ran to five vowels, eighteen consonants, and one digraph *ng* (as in Ngaio Marsh). It included sample sentences such as 'the performance of the white man is good, the performance of the white man is exceeding good', but linguistically at least the performance of the white man still left room for improvement. Should stress marks be included, how should long vowels be distinguished (by macron or doubling?),[6] were all remaining letters really needed (since greater simplicity would enhance its efficacy)?

In the next ten years – by 1830 – the alphabet was in fact reduced to five vowels and nine consonants, with only two forms remaining unsettled, *h* and *w*. There were attempts to indicate a palatal *h* by adding an apostrophe (as in *H'ongi*) and the voiced *w* (pronounced rather like *f*), again by an apostrophe or by the combination *wh*. Colenso, as printer, argued for the doubling of long vowels (to avoid special sorts), the simple *h* (to avoid the troublesome Greek-style apostrophe), and a digammic *v* for *wh* (to avoid setting two letters where one would do) although *wh* was confirmed in 1842.[7] By then the foreign consonants plus *b, d, l, s* and *y* had been dropped and foreign words were rendered in Maori forms: so 'missionary' became *mihanere*, 'governor' *kawana*; I leave you to guess *komite*. Those decisions about letter forms were typographically efficient but culturally explosive, for by giving English words a Maori semblance they disguised their quite different conceptual import. But, clearly, the first great book printed in New Zealand, Colenso's Maori New Testament of 1837, is inconceivable without this prior shift from acoustics to optics, the visualization of sound in a simplified and standardized alphabet, and the human motivations at work in bringing it about. Today the Maori language is written with the five vowels, and ten consonants *h, k, m, n, p, r, t, w, g, wh*.

The pre-print years of its evolution (1815–30) were also those in which the missionaries made a tentative start to teach reading and writing. The decision to teach those skills in the vernacular had long since been settled elsewhere; in Bengal, for example, it generated a remarkable renaissance in the indigenous culture.[8] It also seemed an efficient policy. English was difficult to master and would have split the population; a universal conversion of parent and child, of old and young, was only conceivable if they were bound together by a common speech within which the new learning could pass quickly, unimpeded by language barriers. More than that, the missionaries were all too well aware that English would give the Maori access to the worst aspects of European experience. By containing them culturally within their own language, they hoped to keep them innocent of imported evils. By restricting them further to the reading of biblical texts and vocabulary, they limited the Maori to knowledge of an ancient middle-eastern culture; at the same time the missionaries enhanced their familiar pastoral role morally and politically as interpretative guides, a point I shall come back to when discussing the Treaty of Waitangi. In 1833 William Williams wrote that 'A reading population, whose only book is the Word of God, cannot fail to make a great moral change in the face of the country, as soon as that Word begins to take effect'.[9] And in 1842, when he should have known better, William Puckey rejoiced that the Maori, 'having no other books to read but Scripture and productions from Scripture, their pursuits must all be of a sacred nature'.[10] Such a vision implied that priority be given to the translation of the Scriptures into Maori. This ideological bias was reinforced by doctrinal strife in 1839–40, just when the policy should have been relaxed but when the Church Missionary Society faced competition from Bishop Pompallier's Catholic mission and press.[11] To study Colenso's printed output is simply to look at the expression of those policies.

The naivety there is now patent, but is also present in the programme to teach reading and writing in the mission schools. The enthusiastic reports back to London of the remarkable desire of the Maori to learn to read, the further stimulation of that interest through native teachers, the intense and apparently insatiable demand so created for books, formed the cumulative pressure to supply the one instrument thought essential to give instant and local effect to universal literacy as the principal means to personal salvation. I mean of course printing.

But what was the reality? Kendall set up the first school with thirty-three pupils in 1816, but it was not until the early 1830s that numbers were at all significant. There is almost complete accord in the reports, not only that the schools were effective but that the Maori achieved literacy with the greatest of ease. Of another school it was said in 1829: 'Not six years ago they commenced the very rudiments of learning: now, many of them can read and write their own language, with propriety, and are complete masters of the First Rules of Arithmetic'.[12] A visitor to one mission in 1833 noted:

> I was not prepared to find, among a people who had previously no written language, so many who had benefitted from the instruction given in our Mission Schools . . . [In the Boys' School] I observed all ranks and ages, Chiefs and subjects, old and young, bound and free, receiving and communicating instruction, with a degree of decorum and regularity which would have reflected credit on a school of the same kind in England. Catechisms, reading, spelling, writing on slates from dictation, and cyphering, formed the employment of the upper classes, while the lowest were engaged in learning the alphabet and forming letters . . . [In the Girls' School] The senior classes read remarkably well, and write equally from dictation on slates . . . Men of hostile tribes, even, now lay aside their antipathies, and unite for instruction, disregarding the person of a teacher, even if a slave, and valuing instruction even from a child.[13]

The highly literate rhetoric of that description is itself revealing: the writer, a Captain Jacob, transforms the school's routines into a vision of the society he wishes to see evolving, one indeed better than his own. Of the mission station at Waimate he remarked:

> The writing of the senior classes was really better than that of most school-boys in England; and what struck me much, it was remarkably free from orthographical mistakes; which can only be accounted for from the simplicity of their language, each letter of which admits but one simple sound. Here also I observed Chiefs and subjects, freemen and slaves, all incorporated into classes.[14]

Hobbs, writing in January 1833, noted:

> For this long time past it has become fashionable for the young people to try to learn to read . . . Such is the wish of many of the Natives to learn to read, that on several occasions they have brought pigs, which would weigh from fifty to an hundred pounds, and offered them as payment for a book, consisting of sacred portions of the Scriptures, and the Liturgy of the Church of England.[15]

The impression is also given by the missionary reports that once the rudiments were known, many a Maori pupil would go off and teach others:

> In every village there are several of the Natives who can read and write: and a School is established among them by the Natives themselves, where a number are taught to read

and write; and old and young are taught their Catechism. Their desire for books is very great.[16]

... many of the Natives, who are living at a distance, manifest a great desire for instruction; and with very little assistance from us, they are learning to read and write; and their efforts have so far been crowned with success that they know some of the letters of the alphabet and can write them.[17]

... there are many villages where Schools are conducted entirely by the Natives, and some of them making considerable proficiency in reading and writing. The day is not far distant, when the people generally will be able to read for themselves, in their own tongue, the wonderful works of God.[18]

But such reports are essentially anecdotal and less informative as objective accounts (though historians have treated them as such) than they are as expressions, at worst, of wishful thinking or, at best, of a readiness to define literacy, and therefore later the effective impact of printed texts, at a level far below that demanded by the social changes to which the Maori were being exposed.[19] It is as if the very notion of literacy itself compelled a heightened language of self-approval and infinite promise. Victims of their own myths, the missionaries found what they wanted to find, and reported what they knew their London committee wished to hear. Marsden, Williams, Hadfield and Pompallier were intelligent men, but what could they have understood by the words 'reading' and 'writing' for them to say:

The natives ... were carrying in their hands, the Litany, and the greater part of the Church Service, with their Hymns, written in their own language. The Church Service, as far as it has been translated, they can both read and write with greatest ease.[20]

I was much pleased to find, that wherever I went I found some who could read and write. The Church Service had been translated into the Native language, with the Catechism, Hymns, and some other useful pieces. They are all fond of reading; and there are many who have never had an opportunity of attending the schools who, nevertheless, can read. They teach one another in all parts of the country.[21]

What 'teaching one another' might have meant is suggested by Henry Williams:

One young man began to ask the meaning of letters. I wrote them down for him, and in half an hour he knew them all, and was teaching several outside. Numbers of others came until I had no paper left of any description on which to write a copy. At length they brought small pieces, to have the letters written for them, and about 200, old and young, were soon employed teaching and learning the letters with the greatest possible interest. [Next morning] the boys brought their papers for me to hear them their letters and asked what they were to learn next.[22]

Vast numbers learn to read and write who do not attend school, by possessing themselves of a book or part of a book, and spelling it over until they are fully acquainted with every word in it.[23]

They easily learn to read and write without the necessity of constant teaching. It is only necessary to give them a few leaflets of easy reading, and to write some characters on bits of slate to enable them to read and write their own language within three months.[24]

By comparison, R. K. Webb, in *The British working-class reader*, says that at the Borough Road School, London, in the early nineteenth century, it took twelve months to teach a child to read, and between three and four years to write well and calculate.[25] A more realistic account of the nature of Maori literacy is that given by Fairburn in 1838:

There is scarcely a petty tribe now to be met with, where there are not some who can write and read. I mention this more particularly, as it must sound strange to an English ear to be told that we have met with many of the self-taught Natives who could write on a slate or paper so as to make their wants known, while they could not read a single line from the book. Their habits of idleness . . . are in some respects favourable to their learning to read. Since they have got books among them, they make use of them, I have not the smallest doubt, in the way of amusement, in teaching each other; it seems to have superseded their once favourite game of Draughts.[26]

That at least suggests the minimal competence achieved by many so-called 'readers'.

If we reflect that the teaching of elementary reading is primarily oral/aural, not visual, because it involves the pronouncing and repetition of letters, syllables and words (a practice reinforced where there are few books, fewer texts, and group teaching), we can appreciate how oral repetition from memory might masquerade as reading; and the Maori – used to an oral tradition – had a most retentive memory.[27] The interconnection is evident in Kemp's report of 1832: 'For want of more Translations of the Scriptures, the Natives are almost at a stand: some have committed to memory all that has been printed: I hope this will soon be remedied by more being printed'.[28] Or Williams in 1832: 'We feel the want of books for the Natives very greatly: what they at present possess, they, generally, know by heart'.[29] Other specific reports have their general interest:

The Natives manifest a strong desire to learn to read the Scriptures . . . Wherever I go amongst the Natives, I hear portions of the Catechism repeated. One Native, who, though he cannot read, has learned a considerable part of the Catechisms, puts the Questions to those around him; and then he and the others repeat the answers.[30]

[I] visited a tribe in which the only teaching was done by a Maori who had learned to read at Paihia and, returning to his village, read the Scriptures to his countrymen. Before this time they were in the habit of meeting, and repeating from memory, the Confession and Lord's Prayer, not any one being able to read.[31]

My attention was called . . . to a blind man reading the Scriptures . . . He came to me some time since, and requested that I would let him have a complete book. I asked of what use a book would be to him, as he was blind. He replied that it would be of great use; for though he could not see, he could hear; and by possessing one he could let others read to him, until he should see it with his heart . . . I [later] saw the poor fellow lying on the ground with his book open before him, as though he was pondering over its contents, repeating aloud verse by verse.[32]

'Poor fellow'? The memorized text of course makes one a living library in a way the read book cannot. Repetition of the catechism – known by *heart*, not read by *eye* – was after all the higher proof of conversion. Simply to illustrate the illusory nature of the presumed shift from orality to literacy, I quote Sir Apirana Ngata, writing on 'The Maori and printed matter' as late as 1940:

> The people preferred to hear the matter, whether written or printed, read to them. Not only did this relieve the labour of spelling out words, syllable by syllable, but it was closer than mute transference through the eye to what they had been accustomed to: it was nearer the old-time narrative of adept raconteurs, or of poetical and priestly reciters. More than that, the genius of the race preferred education through the ear, conveyed by artists in intonation and gesticulation . . . The printed matter indeed achieved a limited popularity, but for every one who owned a copy of the Scriptures and Church Liturgy or Rawiri, there were in my boyhood days still fifty or more content to listen to and memorize the words which were read out of the printed books by the ministers, teachers, or lay-readers.[33]

If reading, the passively receptive and more easily acquired art, could be so easily evaded, what of writing? This was the active counterpart of reading, a personally expressive skill, but one much harder to acquire and inhibited by the primitive nature, cost and scarcity of quills, ink and paper. Just as the oral element in reading persisted to limit the full and easy visual perception of texts, so too a reliance on writing and readiness to use it could only grow slowly from a long acquaintance with documents.[34] Oral witness held its primacy over written evidence for centuries in Europe; to have expected a non-literate people to reverse that disposition within a decade was unrealistic, and to presume that it has yet happened would be a mistake.[35]

The main use of literacy to the Maori was not reading books for their ideas, much less for the access they gave to divine truths, but letter writing. For them, the really miraculous point about writing was its portability; by annihilating distance, a letter allowed the person who wrote it to be in two places at once, his body in one, his thoughts in another. It was the spatial extension, not the temporal permanence, of writing that became politically potent in gathering the tribes and planning a war a decade and more later.[36] Historical time, defined by dated and legally binding documents, represented a much more profound challenge to an oral culture used to reshaping its past traditions to accord with present needs. It is a challenge that is still resisted.

On a journey in 1833 Williams received several letters which had been sent on to him and his Maori attendants and he records the reaction of other Maori who had not seen letters before:

> This was an interesting particular for the people of the place, as they were thus enabled to see the nature and value of written characters, by the testimony of these their countrymen. Our boys seemed to look for, and read over *their* letters, with as much pleasure as we did *ours*, to the delight of all around; they repeated them aloud, to the admiration of their auditors, who were struck with wonder at hearing, as they described it, 'a book speak': for though they expect that a European can perform an extraordinary thing, yet they cannot understand how it is that a New Zealand youth can possess the same power.[37]

In the early 1830s we see the hesitant beginnings of letter writing in written requests for baptism, proving (as William Yate put it) that 'the heart of the sanguinary and untutored New Zealander is as the heart of the civilized and polished Englishman'.[38] The originals of course were in Maori.

I, Pahau, am now writing a Letter to you. Perhaps you will not be pleased with it, and send it back; and then, perhaps, my heart will be sad, and I shall cry. Now, then, I am going to write to you. Read it first, from the top to the bottom, on this side and on that side, before you say 'Nonsense', and throw it away from you and tear it to pieces. Now, Mr Yate, listen to what I am going to say upon this paper. I have been thinking and thinking about what I am going to write; and now I am thinking you will shut your ears, and will not listen to me. This is what I am going to write: – Remember, that if you say 'Nonsense', it was you who said we were to put down our wishes in a book.[39]

Another letter begins, in a vein reminiscent of Caxton: 'My ink is not good, my paper dirty, and I am altogether ashamed'.[40] Yet another, from husband and wife: 'There are many mistakes in our two's Letter: and Mary says, "Do not send it: wait and talk when he comes to Kerikeri"'.[41]

Untutored New Zealanders? These writers – the manuscript makers – were the literate elite in Maori, not draught-players turned scribblers but those trained to readiness for baptism. The effective use of letters for political purposes was many years away. Nor did printing of itself become a re-expressive tool for the Maori until the late 1850s.[42] When it did so – in Maori newspapers – the essential motives, the effective contextual forces, were economic, political and military, not religious. *He wahine, he whenua, e ngaro ai te tangata* – by women, and by land, men perish. The forcing issue for the Maori, then as now, was land. Only when literacy began to serve that supreme social interest could it be significantly achieved. Its roots in the texts of an alien religion were inevitably shallow, despite the technology of printing.

But for the missionaries, printing was the great hope. 'We feel very much the want of a Printing Press, to work off some copies of portions of Scripture, which could be read by several natives now with us', Davis had written to the Church Missionary Society in 1827.[43] In 1828 Williams wrote: 'We want a printer, and a printer we must have'.[44] The plea to the Church Missionary Society was twice repeated in 1829. When the long-sought-after press did arrive, it was an anticlimax, proving that technology in itself is nothing without a human mind and dedicated skill to make it work in a context where it matters. In 1830, William Yate brought a small press from Sydney, and a fifteen-year-old James Smith to help him. Neither Yate nor Smith had any professional competence.

In his journal for September 1830 Yate noted that, in printing off a few hymns in the native language, 'we succeeded beyond our most sanguine expectations'. These were the first items ever printed in New Zealand. 'We thank you for the Press', he wrote back to London, 'and have no doubt but that, with the blessing of God, it will be an instrument of great good in this Land. You will perceive by a copy of a Hymn forwarded by this conveyance, that we shall be able, in a short time, to manage it'.[45] Others took his tone. Kemp reported that 'The Schools will receive great benefit from the Press, for we shall be able to get portions of the Scriptures printed, as they are wanted'.[46] No copy of their Hymns is known to survive but Yate and Smith also printed a small catechism in Maori, both extant copies of which testify to the printers' gross incompetence in planing the type, locking the forme, and making ready. Writing of a new translation a year later, Yate faced facts: 'We shall not . . . be able to print it here'.[47]

Henry Williams, two years after that first experiment, told his masters:

You have sent us out a Printing Press of a certain description and a specimen of its production has been sent to you, accompanied with many expressions of delight – but these were first feelings excited by the novelty of the work: there stands the poor thing enshrined in cobwebs as an exciter for further expectations and desires. It has been examined by a printer of some experience who said he would not possess it as a gift . . . Had we something respectable, our work would be more so than it is at present.[48]

As the Maori proverb says (one later recorded by Colenso), 'even a little axe, well used, brings plenty of food'. But with Yate as food gatherer, the missionaries starved. Defeated in his own efforts, Yate returned to Sydney the following year to supervise the printing of what, when it arrived, he described as 'the most valuable cargo that ever reached the shores of New Zealand' – 1800 copies of a book containing eight chapters of Genesis and almost half the New Testament.[49] On receiving these books in 1833, Williams wrote home: 'I hope our good friends in London will see in time the necessity of allowing a press and a printer. The book contains 250 pages and abounds in typographical errors, not less . . . than two to a page. It must not be offered without correction. So much for colonial work'.[50] In 1836 Colenso was even less complimentary about this early Australian export to New Zealand: 'poor things, they reflect no credit on the printer, less on the binder, and still less on the editor – it has been computed that there are not less than 1000 errors in the work'.[51] Yate's ignominious effort in 1830 deprived William Colenso of the honour of being literally New Zealand's first printer, a New Zealand Caxton, as Coupland Harding was later to call him.

William Colenso, a cousin of the bishop of that name, was born in Penzance in 1811 and on 3 September 1826 was bound for six years to a local printer, John Thomas.[52] While still in his time he read his first paper to the Penzance Natural History and Antiquarian Society (on Phoenician trade with west Cornwall) and compiled a history of Penzance, *The ancient and modern history of the Mounts*, which was printed and published by Thomas in 1831. In October 1833 he moved to London and found work with Richard Watts and Son, Crown Court, Temple Bar, printers to the Church Missionary Society and the British and Foreign Bible Society.[53] Some anonymous articles he wrote for the religious serial *The Pilot* came for printing to Watts who recognized Colenso's handwriting. This led to an introduction to Dandeson Coates, lay secretary to the Society, just as the New Zealand missionaries were again supplicating for a press. Commissioned as printer by the Society and preparing to leave for New Zealand in 1834, Colenso wrote in his diary: 'In addition to Satan's temptations at having no interest in Jesus he assails me with "You are going abroad, and are unfit for the work" '. In fact there was none fitter. Colenso arrived at Paihia in the north of New Zealand on 30 December 1834. The next day, he records, 'Numbers of Natives came to see me – and when they found I was a Printer were quite enraptured – crying out *Pukapuka*'. Saturday 3 January 1835 was, as he wrote to Coates,

> A memorable epoch in the annals of New Zealand – I succeeded in getting the Printing Press landed. I was obliged to unpack it on board, but, I am happy to say, it is all safe on shore. Could you, my dear Sir, but have witnessed the Natives when it was landed, they danced, shouted, and capered about in the water, giving vent to the wildest effusions of joy. Enquiring the use of this, and the place of that, with all the eagerness for which uncivilized nature is celebrated. Certes, they had never seen such a thing before! I trust soon to be able to get it to work. May the father of Mercies . . . grant me strength and ability to work it for His Glory! May it be instrumental, under His blessing, in bringing thousands to the Cross of our Immanuel! – and of sending away that Sombre pall of darkness and gloom, which 'the Prince of the power of the Air' has so long successfully wrapped around the inhabitants of these islands.[54]

In fact, getting the Stanhope ashore had been far from easy and lest the parcels of type be seized for making musket balls it could not be unpacked until safely landed. Most revealing, however, for what it implies about the symbolic power of 'the press' as distinct from the realities of using one, is Colenso's list of necessary articles which he found to be absolutely wanting:

For the information of Printers I will just set down a few of them; though I almost fear my relation will scarcely be believed. There was no wooden furniture of any kind, nor quoins, . . . no galleys, no cases, no leads of any size, no brass rule, no composing sticks, (save a private one of my own that I had bought two years before in London, a most fortunate circumstance!) no inking table, no potash, no lye-brushes, no mallet and shooter, no roller-irons and stock, though there was a massy cast-iron roller mould, and . . . no imposing-stone nor page-cord; and, worst of all, actually *no printing paper!!*[55]

Colenso found a local joiner who made him a few galleys, a small inking table, some furniture and quoins, although he complained that these last 'were wretched things (partly owing to the want of proper and seasoned wood,)' and gave him 'an enormous amount of labour, vexation and trouble'. The joiner also made him

two or three pairs of type-cases for the printing office after a plan of my own. For as the Maori language contained only 13 letters (half the number in the English alphabet), I contrived my cases so, as to have both Roman and Italic characters in the one pair of cases; not distributing the remaining 13 letters (consonants) used in the compositing of English, such not being wanted . . . Such an arrangement proved to be a very good one while my compositing was confined to the Maori language only; but when I had any English copy to compose it was altogether the reverse! then I had to pick out the discarded English consonants as required from their lots put up in paper parcels. Fortunately this occurred but rarely; except at the time of the Treaty of Waitangi (1840), when I had necessarily much printing work to do for the Government of the Colony; and having no extra cases, was obliged to place the letters required in little lots on tables, and on the floor![56]

With the press in place and the type disposed, it was agreed that as all parties, European and Maori, wished to see something printed, the missionaries should supply some writing paper, that the first sheet from the press should be in Maori from the New Testament, and that it should be small. The Epistles to the Ephesians and Philippians were chosen. Colenso set it up, and on 17 February 1835 pulled proofs of what he then thought was the first book printed in New Zealand, 'the printing office being filled with spectators to witness the performance'. On 21 February,

twenty-five corrected copies were printed and stitched and cut round for the Mission-aries; their wives kindly furnishing a few sheets of pink blotting-paper from their desks wherewith to form coloured paper covers for these tracts; which, of course, had first to be pasted on to stronger paper. This little book was in post 8vo., Long-Primer type, and consisted of 16 pages in double columns. For leads I was driven to the miserable substitute of pasting paper together, and drying and cutting it up! . . . And not being able to manufacture a roller, I was obliged to do my best with a small makeshift 'ball' of my own contriving.[57]

Knowing nothing of Yate's earlier efforts, Colenso wrote home to Coates:

This 'first fruits' of the New Zealand Press, which the Lord hath pleased to allow me to begin and complete, is very much liked by the Natives. – May it, being the 'Word of God', be the means of making thousands 'wise unto Salvation' – and the preface, as it were, to a more glorious diffusion of Gospel light over these benighted lands.[58]

On 19 May he printed what was indeed the first English book, eight pages octavo, a report of the New Zealand Temperance Society. Given the later history of New Zealand's licensing laws, it was a prophetic start.

Earlier that year, on 23 March, having heard that supplies of paper and more equipment for him had reached Sydney, he began setting his one great work, the complete Maori New Testament. It was a demy-octavo, set in small Pica, and running to 356 pages. He pulled the first sheets of a run of 5,000 copies on 23 June 1836. The Maori pressmen he later employed and paid 3s. a week were soon disenchanted by 'the many disagreeables inseparable from this new and wonderful art of printing', as Colenso put it, but on two subsequent occasions he was able to secure the help of some American sailors who had trained as pressmen before going to sea. Of the second pair he wrote:

> The wages I paid these two men were, at first, the same as to the two former pressmen, 5/- per day; but after a short time, at their own request, their pay was altered to 25 cents, or 1/- each per 'token', (10 quires = ½-ream,) besides which, as they could not be always at press-work, they were paid 12 cents, or 6d per hour for other work connected with the Printing-office and Binding-room, and Warehouse, – as, in drying, and pressing, and folding the sheets, &c.; but would never do anything in the way of distributing type, and even if a letter should be drawn out, or be broken in their working-off the forms, (which sometimes though rarely did happen,) they would not, or more properly could not well, replace it; and spoiled paper (if any) they had to pay for, – which, however, did not amount to much. Upham worked alone at Press for a period of six months, after his companion left, (always a disagreeable and slow process for *one* person,) and, of course, from that time he was paid 2/- per 'token'. He was a very good and trusty pressman, and kept the 'colour' well up, and his rollers, &c., in nice working order.[59]

Colenso records that when the book was finished, in December 1837, 'the demand for copies became great beyond expression, from all parts of New Zealand, and finding it impossible to bind them fast enough he sent off lots of 500 at a time to Sydney to have them done (poorly done, as he later complained). Since the Maori were said to value more highly any article they paid for than one given to them free, the books were sold at 4s. each. As evidence of interest and demand, Colenso makes the incidentally valuable point (distinguishing reading from writing) that 'as not many of the principal Maori Chiefs or their sons could then write, many of them travelled on foot and barefooted to Paihia, from very great distances, to obtain a copy'. William Jowett, responding as clerical secretary of the Church Missionary Society to Colenso's expressed wish for ordination, advised him to turn his thoughts

> to the peculiarly useful (and therefore honourable) department which you *do* occupy. The sight of that New Testament in the Native language, which you have been privileged to carry through the Press, is such a sight as fills my heart with indescribable joy. Think now to what great ends it is capable of becoming instrumental . . . it will, moreover, help the fixing of the language; and schoolbooks, and many other books, will grow out of it. No doubt the spirit of GOD will use this sword.[60]

There is one excellent point in Jowett's response to which I shall return, but here I just wish to note again the ecstatic tone which belies both the actual achievement and the future promise of literacy.

How many Maori could read before Colenso arrived? In 1833 Yate had estimated that some 500 in the north could do so. In 1834, Edward Markham ventured 'not less then ten Thousand people that can Read, write and do sums in the Northern end of the Island'.[61] Refining such impressionism by apparently objective fact, one historian turns to the presumed demand for and effects of printing: between January 1835 and January 1840 Colenso printed 3,500,000 pages of religious material, and in 1840 produced over 2,000,000 more – figures as ignorantly impressionistic (though true) as Yates and Markham's.[62] Added to the further information that Colenso's New Testament was reprinted in London in 1841, 1843 and 1845 (each time in 20,000 copies), it reinforces the missionary notion of widespread literacy and the immense impact of print. On those figures, by 1845 there was at least one Maori New Testament for every two Maori people in New Zealand. Colenso felt confident to write in his journal in 1840:

> Here I may be permitted to remark the Press has been an inst[rument] of very great good in this land . . . Howr. partial it may be supposed I am in my opinion, I believe (and that belief too is deduced from what I have seen and heard on the spot) that the press has been more effective (under God) as an instr[ument] of good among this people during the last 5 yrs. than the whole body of miss[ionaries] put together.

As Colenso's Day- and Waste-Book, paper-book, and ledger all survive, we can detail everything he printed for the years 1836–43. In terms of *histoire-du-livre* econometrics we can say exactly what his output was; but instead of using figures like three and a half million and two million *pages*, we as bibliographers would see that from January 1835 to January 1840 he printed only 16 items, set up in type only 34.15 sheets, and printed in all only 145,775 perfected sheets in five years. The New Testament alone accounted for 22.5 of those 34.15 sheets and 122,500 of the 145,775 perfected sheets. In 1840, he printed 11 items, involving 18.875 sheets and 89,313 perfected sheets. One book, the Psalms, accounted for a third of the setting and two-thirds of the presswork.

If this technical view of Colenso's output checks us slightly, what other evidence is there of reception? It is well known that people in an oral society, seeing books for the first time, often treat them as ritual objects.

> Many people who know not a letter wish to possess themselves of a copy of the translated Scriptures because they consider it possesses a peculiar virtue of protecting them from the power of evil spirits.[63]

At an early church service,

> Many of [the Maori] thought it highly proper that they should be armed with books. It might be an old ship's almanac, or a cast-away novel, or even a few stitched leaves of old newspapers.[64]

The book was given a totemic power of warding off not only evil spirits: in 1836 it was said that a Maori fighting party had refused to storm a *pa* (a fortified village) because of a printed Bible inside it and contented themselves with a blockade.[65] In 1839 Taylor recorded seeing Maori with mission books (or at least odd leaves from them) rolled up and thrust through holes in the lobes of their ears.[66] Books were also useful for making roll-your-own cartridges. One book so used was Milner's *Church history*, thus giving a slightly different sense to the phrase 'the church militant'.[67] Colenso picked up such a cartridge in which the paper came from II Samuel and bore the words from chapter 19, v. 34: 'How long have I to live?'[68] Markham said his servants melted down his pewter spoons in 1834 to make musket balls of them, 'and the first Volume of my Voltaires, "Louis 14. et 15." torn up and made Cartridges of them'.[69] A proper use, perhaps, in Voltaire's view?

As the number of New Testaments disseminated was reaching saturation point (one to every two Maori) in the early 1840s – just when the impact of printing should have been at its height – we find Selwyn noting 'A general complaint in all parts of the country, that the schools are not so well attended as heretofore'. He remarked 'a growing indifference to religion, and a neglect of the opportunities for instruction'.[70] Another missionary comments that 'We have gained a very large portion of this people but we have no hold on their children'.[71] By 1844, Hadfield could say at last

It appears every year more evident that our present system of conveying instruction to these people is wholly inadequate to their present wants; they have been brought to a certain point, and we have no means of bringing them beyond that.[72]

What we have here is not only disillusionment about the actual extent to which literacy of the most elementary kind had been achieved, but a clear example of the way in which even the most sophisticated technology (print) will fail to serve an irrelevant ideology (an alien religion).[73] For the missionaries and their great instrument of truth had failed lamentably to equip the Maori to negotiate their rights with the Pakeha in the one area that really mattered to them – land. Nor was it merely a failure in creating literacy in Maori. In 1844 almost no Maori spoke (let alone read) English. In that year a settler said he had met only two who did so.[74] Selwyn had recognized the need to break away from the old policy and in 1843 produced the first primer to help Maori read English. Colenso followed up in 1872 on a Government commission with *Willie's first English book*, 'Written for young Maoris who can read their own Maori Tongue and who wish to learn to read the English Language'. For all his piety, however, Colenso saw the need for another innovation too: 'in order to the greater and more general use of the work, all words and sentences of a strictly religious nature have been purposely omitted'.

Historians have too readily and optimistically affirmed extensive and high levels of Maori literacy in the early years of settlement, and the role of printing in establishing it. Protestant missionary faith in the power of the written word, and modern assumptions about the impact of the press in propagating it, are not self-evidently valid, and they all too easily distort our understanding of the different and competitively powerful realities of societies whose cultures are still primarily oral. Yet, as Jowett told Colenso when congratulating him on completion of the Maori New Testament, printing had helped to fix the Maori language – albeit in one dialect and with some dangerous neologisms. Colenso himself was later to make the point that the oral memory, as a faculty, too easily absorbed and perpetuated the new and corrupt words born of settlement and trade, taking up the simpler and degenerate forms used by the settlers.[75] Had it not been for the missionaries and Colenso's printing, the language as it was at an early stage of European contact might well have been irretrievably lost.

I wish now to focus on one test of the missionaries' efforts to teach literacy in the 1830s, one test of Colenso's effect after five years' printing, one example of a 'text' which offers textual and contextual problems, one case-study to prove that bibliography is an explosive subject. I return to the Treaty of Waitangi. (The name, by the way, means 'the waters of lamentation'.) *An authentic and genuine history of the signing of the Treaty of Waitangi* was written at the time by Colenso although it was not printed until 1890.

On the morning of 30 January 1840 Colenso printed in Maori one hundred copies of a circular letter inviting Maori chiefs in the northern area to meet at Waitangi on 5 February. An English draft of the treaty (a composite version by three men, Governor Hobson, Freeman and Busby) had been cobbled together by the 3rd and was given to Henry Williams on the 4th to translate into Maori. The first English draft, the foul papers as it were, has not survived.[76] Williams's translation was discussed with the chiefs on 5 February; alterations were made and the revised Maori version copied on to parchment that night by Richard Taylor. The original copy of that revised Maori version has not survived. The fair copy of it, made on parchment the previous night, was presented to the chiefs next day, 6 February, for their signatures. It is this document in Maori, a revised version of a translation into Maori made from a composite English draft no longer extant, which is the Treaty of Waitangi. But its textual complexities do not end there.

Governor Hobson also sent abroad, either to Sydney or London, five English versions of the Treaty. There are minor differences in three of them, but the other two bear a different date, differ from the others in the wording of their preamble, and differ critically from each other in the second article. Comparison shows that the extant Maori version, the actual Treaty as signed by the chiefs on 6 February, is not a translation of any one of these five English versions, nor is any of the English ones a translation from the Maori. They must therefore descend, with greater or less accuracy and no authority, from the first full English draft, now lost, and made before the Maori translation in its first and revised forms. One English version sent to the Secretary of State was endorsed by Williams, who said it was 'as Literal a translation of the Treaty of Waitangi as the Idiom of the Language will admit of'. This cannot have been true, but a comparable disregard for strict textual accuracy in our own day has led to the inclusion of one of the unauthoritative English versions as a Schedule to the Waitangi Day Act (1960).[77] There are other complications of textual authority deriving from the fact that names were added to the Treaty over the next seven months, thirty-nine such names being found on an English copy which the signatories, being illiterate, could not have read even if they had known the language.

That last example puts at its most extreme my argument about the non-literate state of the nation in 1840 after ten years of intensive teaching and five years of proselytic printing. But even if we confine ourselves to the Maori text, how literate were the signatories? As Cressy has said, 'only one type of literacy is directly measurable – the ability or inability to write a signature' and because the evidence of signatures or marks is, in Schofield's words, 'universal, standard and direct', it has come to displace the merely anecdotal, subjective, inescapably impressionistic evidence hitherto accepted by historians.[78] Applying this test to the Treaty of Waitangi, what do we find? The number of signatories is in fact uncertain; estimates vary from 512 to 541 and, in the manner common to many societies with mass illiteracy, many of the names given were written out by the government clerk on behalf of the chief concerned. On my count the highest possible number of personal signatures, as distinct from crosses or *moko*-patterns, is seventy-two.[79] Could the Maori in the commemorative plaque *read* what he was signing in even the most literal way? Even if he could do that, the odds are heavily loaded against his knowing how to *write* even his own name.

In any case, whose 'Maori' was it? Of course it was not indigenous Maori but missionary Maori, specifically Williams's English Protestant missionary Maori, learnt from the distinctive dialect of the Ngapuhi tribe. Not only the concepts but many of the words, for all their Maori form, were English.

Before the document was signed, Hobson explained, with Williams translating, that if the chiefs did sign the Queen would protect them. In an important sense this was true: many Maori wanted the British to establish some legal authority over their own unruly European settlers and traders and incidentally by their authority to inhibit inter-tribal strife. Busby, in a half truth, said the Governor had not come to take away their land but to secure them in the possession of what they held. But Te Kemara called his bluff and asked for the return to him of the very land on which they were standing. Rewa, eloquent but sad, added, 'I have no lands now – only a name, only a name!' Kawiti rejected Hobson's plan: 'We are free'. Hakiro supported him: 'We are not thy people. We are free'. Tareha: 'No, we only are the chiefs, the rulers. We will not be ruled over. What, thou a foreigner up, and I down! Thou high, and I, Tareha, the great chief of the Ngapuhi tribes, low! No, never, never'. With a flair for the dramatic, he held a canoe paddle high in the air to deride Hobson's intolerable ambition. Tareha, says Colenso, was also clothed in a filthy piece of coarse old floor matting simply to ridicule Hobson's supposition that New Zealanders needed the extraneous aid of clothing, &c, from foreign nations.[80]

For the Maori present, the very form of public discourse and decision-making was oral and confirmed in the consensus not in the document. In signing the treaty, many chiefs made complementary oral conditions which were more important than (and certainly in their own way modified) the words on the page. For the illiterate, the document and its implications were meaningless; for the merely literate, the ability to sign one's name was a trap. At the end of the first day, as Hobson went to his boat, an elderly chief rushed in front of him and looked staringly and scrutinizingly, says Colenso, into the Governor's face. Having surveyed it, he exclaimed in a shrill, loud and mournful voice, '*Auee! he koroheke! Ekore e roa kua mate*'. Colenso was reluctant to translate but on being pressed did so: 'He says, "Alas! an old man. *He* will soon be dead!" ' – and he was, but the document lived on.

The next day, 6 February (now celebrated as a public holiday), some three to four hundred Maori were, in Colenso's words, 'scattered in small parties according to their tribes, talking about the treaty, but evidently not understanding it'. But Hobson wanted to make an end. Colenso's report runs:

> The Native chiefs were called on in a body to come forward and sign the document. Not one, however, made any move nor seemed desirous of doing so till Mr. Busby, hitting on an expedient, proposed calling them singly by their names as they stood in his (private) list, in which list the name of Hoani Heke (known, too, to be the most favourable towards the treaty) happened to be the first – at least, of those who were this day present. On his being called by name to come and sign, he advanced to the table on which the treaty lay. At this moment I, addressing myself to the Governor, said, –
>
> 'Will your Excellency allow me to make a remark or two before that chief signs the treaty'?
>
> The Governor: 'Certainly, sir'.
>
> Mr. Colenso: 'May I ask your excellency whether it is your opinion that these Natives understand the articles of the treaty which they are now called upon to sign? I this morning' –
>
> The Governor: 'If the Native chiefs do not know the contents of this treaty it is no fault of mine. I wish them fully to understand it . . . They have heard the treaty read by Mr. Williams'.
>
> Mr. Colenso: 'True, your Excellency; but the Natives are quite children in their ideas. It is no easy matter, I well know, to get them to understand – fully to comprehend a document of this kind; still, I think they ought to know somewhat of it to constitute its legality . . . I have spoken to some chiefs concerning it, who had no idea whatever as to the purport of the treaty'.
>
> Mr. Busby here said, 'The best answer that could be given to that observation would be found in the speech made yesterday by the very chief about to sign, Hoani Heke, who said, "The Native mind could not comprehend these things: they must trust to the advice of their missionaries" '.
>
> Mr. Colenso: 'Yes; and that is the very thing to which I was going to allude. The missionaries should do so; but at the same time the missionaries should explain the thing in all its bearings to the Natives, so that it should be their very own act and deed. Then, in case of a reaction taking place, the Natives could not turn round on the

missionary and say, "You advised me to sign that paper, but never told me what were the contents thereof" '.

The Governor: 'I am in hopes that no such reaction will take place'.

So Colenso gave up, having expressed his conscientious feeling and discharged what he felt strongly to be his duty. Then forty-six chiefs, anxious to get home, played this new game and put their marks on the parchment. They included chiefs who had declaimed *against* signing; but (as Colenso records of one of them) 'Marupu, having made his mark (as he could neither read nor write) shook hands heartily with the Governor' and left.

To pursue the sociology of that text one stage further: in all the English versions of the treaty the chiefs 'cede to Her Majesty the Queen of England, absolutely and without reservation, all the rights and powers of Sovereignty'. The question here is what the English meant and the Maori understood by the word 'Sovereignty'. Did it mean that the chiefs gave up to the Crown their personal power and supreme status within their own tribes, or was it only something more mundanely administrative, like 'governorship'? In fact the word used by Henry Williams to translate 'Sovereignty' was precisely that: *kawanatanga*, a transliteration of 'Governor' (*kawana*) with a suffix to make it abstract. Such was his translation for the order of morning service: 'that all our doings may be ordered by thy governance'. What he significantly omitted in translating the 'Sovereignty' which the Maori were being asked to surrender was the genuine Maori word *mana*, meaning personal prestige and the power that flowed from it, or even the word *rangatiratanga*, meaning chieftainship. He had used both words in translating Corinthians chapter 15, v. 24 with its references to the 'kingdom of God' and 'all authority and power'. By choosing not to use either *mana* or *rangatiratanga* to indicate what the Maori would exchange for 'all the Rights and Privileges of British subjects', Williams muted the sense, plain in English, of the treaty as a document of political appropriation.[81] The status of their assent is already questionable enough, but had any Maori heard that he was giving up his *mana* or *rangatiratanga* he could never have agreed to the treaty's terms. Williams's Maori version of Hobson's composite English one set the trap which King Lear fell into when (in a version published in 1608) he said to Albany and Cornwall:

> I doe inuest you iointly in my powre,
> Preheminence, and all the large effects
> That troope with Maiestie, . . . onely we still retaine
> The name and all the addicions to a King

where 'addicions' implies the attributes of ultimate personal prestige and authority.

There are other textual problems created by the versions. In the second article the word *rangatiratanga* does appear in a context which (in Maori) seeks to assure the chiefs of the *rangatiratanga* or 'full possession of their lands, their homes and all their possessions'. Four of the five English versions, however, spell out that provision to read 'full, exclusive and undisturbed possession of their Lands and Estates, Forests, Fisheries and other properties which they may collectively or individually possess'. Although technically the English version has no textual authority, its explicit references to forests and fisheries have become a matter of great import and Maori today have found good reason to plead the intention of the English versions against the more limited wording of the Maori one.[82] Even more significantly, indeed tragically, the English versions of the second article also require the chiefs to 'yield to Her Majesty the exclusive right of Pre-emption over such lands as the proprietors thereof may be disposed to alienate, at such prices as may be agreed upon'. Williams's Maori version omitted to spell out and thereby legitimate under the treaty the Crown's *pre-emptive* right to purchase Maori land. As a consequence, the English versions have been taken to bestow legality on the actions of successive Governments, while the Maori version seems morally to justify the deep sense of grievance still widely suffered over Maori land issues.[83] Once more, Colenso, writing to the Church Missionary Society, did not 'for a moment' suppose that the chiefs were aware that 'by signing the Treaty they had restrained themselves from selling their land to whomsoever they will', and cited one Maori who, although he had signed the treaty, had since offered land for sale privately. On being told that he could not do that, he replied: 'What? Do you think I won't do what I like with my own'?[84]

From a European point of view, one conditioned to accept and apply evidence as 'literally' true or false, the English versions of the treaty have proved a potent political weapon in legitimating government of the Maori, even though standards of textual and historical truth also deriving from European traditions oblige us to acknowledge the Maori one as the only authoritative document, that which states the terms and bears the written marks of assent. From a Maori point of view, the truth is not so confined, and signatures bear no absolute authority. For the Maori, as I have already indicated, the 'text' was the consensus arrived at through discussion, something much more comprehensive than the base document or any one of its extant versions. Williams later defended himself, saying that he had explained the text *orally*; but only the documents survive, and successive Governments have chosen the English ones to act on when these best served their ends. At a later treaty meeting, Mohi Tawhai said that 'the sayings of the Pakeha float light, like the wood of the *whau* tree, and always remain to be seen, but the sayings of the Maori sink to the bottom like stone'.[85] Manuscript and print, the tools of the Pakeha, persist, but words which are spoken fade as they fall.

Print is still too recent for the Maori. Oral traditions live on in a distrust of the mere document, and in a refusal by many young Maori to accept political decisions based on it. Pakeha and Maori versions of the past continue to collide. During a Russian scare in the 1880s the Government of the day pre-empted the purchase of Maori land at Bastion Point, a fine site overlooking Auckland harbour. When a more recent Government proposed to resell it for luxury housing, it was occupied for several months by Maori protesters. In my mind's eye, I can still read the vivid television news pictures of police and military vehicles as they moved in to evict the squatters. To bring my own report right up to date, and allow print its complementary role, I cite an item from a Wellington newspaper of 7 February 1983:

> 99 protesters were arrested as riot-equipped police took strong precautions at the Waitangi Day celebrations at Waitangi to prevent recurrence of last year's violence and fire-bombing.

At such moments literacy defines itself for many as a concordat of sword and pen, of politics and script indeed.

In the reports Colenso has left us, he shows his perception of the complex relationships of oral witness, text, print and political and economic power. For us, the texts in context quickly deconstruct and lose their 'literal' authority – no book was ever bound by its covers. Pakeha [i.e. Europeans] continue to assume 'Sovereignty' where radical Maori persist in believing that nothing so sacred as *mana* has ever been ceded under the treaty, that Maori sovereignty was, and is, intact.

But must the story end there, in a conflict of irreconcilable versions? In terms of a sociology of the text, it is impossible to regard the Maori version as complete, although it carries the highest authority, nor the English ones as authoritative, although they are far more explicit. Like many dramatic texts, each has been born, here maimed and deformed, of the pressures of context. In the rarefied world of textual scholarship, it would now be commendably scholarly to deny any possibility of conflation, any notion that 'the text' of the Treaty of Waitangi is anything other than its distinct historical versions. And yet, as the Maori always knew, there is a real world beyond the niceties of the literal text and in that world there is *in fact* a providential version now editing itself into the status of a social and political document of power and purpose. The physical versions and their fortuitous forms are not the only testimonies to intent: implicit in the accidents of history is an ideal text which history has begun to discover, a reconciliation of readings which is also a meeting of minds. The concept of an ideal text as a cultural and political imperative is not imposed on history but derives *from* it and from an understanding of the dynamics of bibliography as a study of the meanings 'books' make.

Lest that seem too dangerous, too messianic a mission, let me call W. W. Greg back from the shades to which he has latterly been consigned and ask him to repeat his crisply perceptive comment that many editors, declining to conflate, abdicate and 'produce, not editions of their author's works at all, but only editions of particular authorities for those works'.[86] To illustrate a principle of textual criticism operative in the real world which implies the concept of an ideal text that the versions have failed fully to express, one might cite legal opinion on the interpretation of treaties. For example, there is recent judicial authority that treaties and other judicial documents should be interpreted in the spirit in which they are drawn and taking into account the surrounding circumstances. In the case of bilingual treaties, there is ample authority for the view that the two or more versions should help one another, so that one may be interpreted by reference to another. In New Zealand, under the Treaty of Waitangi Act, an advisory tribunal was recently set up and directed by Government 'to determine the meaning and effect of the Treaty as embodied in the two [*sic*] texts' and 'to *decide* issues raised by differences between them'. As a motion towards the higher criticism it recognizes clearly the *social* inutility of a clutter of versions as distinct from the social value of a harmonized text. The Waitangi Tribunal, however, affirmed an even higher principle:

> A Maori approach to the Treaty would imply that its *wairua* or spirit is something more than a literal construction of the actual words used can provide. The spirit of the Treaty transcends the sum total of its component written words and puts narrow or literal interpretations out of place.[87]

I myself cannot help but see texts, their distinct versions, their different physical modes, and their comprehension in social contexts – in a word, the sociology of texts – as the substance of bibliography. The book, in all its forms, enters history only as an evidence of human behaviour, and it remains active only in the service of human needs.

Colenso died in 1899 at the ripe old age of eighty-eight, thirty-six hours after penning his last letter to Coupland Harding, the man who might have completed our model by transplanting us from the level of mere printing to the fine controls of typography and the book as an expressive form. Colenso left to Harding two hundred pounds for his son, William Colenso Harding, and all his printing materials, including 'my sole composing-stick – with which I did so much work both in England and in New Zealand'. Harding was a worthy recipient and was later to note: 'It was in this stick that the Maori New Testament of 1837 was set, and also the Treaty of Waitangi – Truly, a venerable relic'.[88]

Notes

Presidential address to The Bibliographical Society 15 February 1983. This paper was originally announced as 'Two early New Zealand printers: William Colenso and R. Coupland Harding', but the range of material precluded all but a brief reference (and that mainly a succession of slides) to Harding's work. A few passages omitted when the paper was first read have been restored and the final section revised. The endnotes, a literal subtext, embody suggestions made both before and after its delivery. I am particularly indebted to A. G. Bagnall,

Alexandra Barratt, Simon Cauchi, Barney Cohn, Kathleen Coleridge, Tamsin Donaldson, Penelope Griffith, Harvey Graff, Ross Harvey, Michael Jackson, Dorothy V. Jones, Iain Lonie, Jane McRae, Paul McHugh, David and Rosamond McKitterick, Robert Rosenthal, Marshall Sahlins and Ian Willison.

1   See Walter J. Ong, *Orality and literacy: the technologizing of the word* (London, 1982).

2   Denis McQuail and Sven Windahl, *Communication models* (London, 1982), p. 2, have a useful summary of the advantages of models.

3   I have consulted the treaty documents as reproduced in *Facsimiles of the Declaration of Independence and the Treaty of Waitangi*, edited by H. H. Turton (Wellington, 1877; reprinted 1960). I am most grateful to Paul McHugh for his legally informed endorsement of my claim that Maori assent to the treaty became the substantive ground of British sovereignty over New Zealand. There is, however, a body of opinion which regards the treaty as having had no effect and British sovereignty as arising rather from the occupation and settlements of lands inhabited by uncivilized native peoples.

4   The phrases 'European myth of . . . literacy and print as agents of change' and 'from memory to written record' allude to Harvey Graff's *The literacy myth: literacy and social structure in the nineteenth-century city* (New York, 1979), to Elizabeth L. Eisenstein's *The printing press as an agent of change: communications and cultural transformations in early modern Europe*, 2 vols (Cambridge, 1979), and to M. T. Clanchy's *From memory to written record: England 1066–1307* (London, 1979).

5   William Colenso, *Fifty years ago in New Zealand. A commemoration; a jubilee paper; a retrospect: a plain and true story* (Napier, 1888), p. 27. Edward Markham, writing in 1834, took a different view, criticizing what he saw as an oversimplified orthography because it obscured regional and dialect differences, 'Thus making the Language poorer instead of enriching it': *New Zealand or reminiscences of it*, edited by E. H. McCormick (Wellington, 1963), p. 62. The circumstances surrounding the reduction of spoken languages to their first alphabetic or syllabic forms seem to have received little attention. Judith Binney, *The legacy of guilt* (Auckland, 1968), pp. 177–85, discusses Kendall's work in the Maori language; see also Johannes Andersen, 'The Maori alphabet', in *A history of printing in New Zealand 1830–1940*, edited by R. A. McKay (Wellington, 1940), pp. 57–74. Joyce Banks, of the National Library of Canada, is currently working on the Cree syllabary (which is still in use). Tamsin Donaldson, 'Hearing the first Australians', in *Seeing the first Australians*, edited by Ian Donaldson and Tamsin Donaldson (Sydney, 1984), looks at the motives underlying nineteenth-century attempts at writing down two Australian languages, Ngiyampaa and Wiradjuri, and at the effects of European assumptions on the forms these writings took.

6   The length of vowels is an important discriminator of meanings in Maori: *kākā* is a parrot; *kăkă* a garment, fibre or stalk; *kăkā* is red-hot; *kākă* a bittern or, as adjective, poisoned-by-the-*tutu*. Practice in indicating long vowels still varies.

7   *Fifty years ago*, pp. 24–27, 47–49.

8   See David Kopf, *British orientalism and the Bengal renaissance: the dynamics of Indian modernization 1773–1833* (Berkeley and Los Angeles, 1969). A distinction must be drawn, of course, between reviving in print an already literate culture, as in Bengal, and capturing the current forms of an oral culture in all its diversity and levels of textual authority: see Bruce Biggs, 'The translation and publishing of Maori material in the Auckland Public Library', *Journal of the Polynesian Society*, 61 (1952), 177–91.

9   Letter of 1 October 1833, *Missionary Register* (November 1834), 513. William Brown, *New Zealand and its aborigines* (London, 1845), p. 101, had been told 'the natives would only learn every species of vice through the medium of the English language'.

10   Letter of 6 June 1842, cited by C. J. Parr, 'A missionary library, printed attempts to instruct the Maori, 1815–1843', *Journal of the Polynesian Society*, 70 (1961), 429–50 (p. 445).

11   Woon to the Wesleyan Mission Society 24 November 1838: 'The press will be a mighty engine in exposing the errors [of the Papists'] system', *Wesleyan Mission Notices*, n.s. 9 (September 1839), 142. Henry Williams 2 December 1840: '[we need] a vigorous effort at this time to meet the present demand for books before the Papists come forward with their trash', cited by Parr, 'A missionary library', p. 447. The Roman Catholic mission arrived in 1838, its main press (a Gaveau) on 15 June 1841.

12   C. Clarke, *Missionary Register* (December 1829), 372.

13   William Jacob, 13 March 1833, *Missionary Register* (January 1834), 60.

14   *Ibid.*, p.61.

15   *Missionary Register* (February 1834), 119.

16   G. Clarke, 4 June 1833, *Missionary Register* (December 1833), 550.

17   William Puckey, 6 January 1835, *Missionary Register* (July 1836), 155.

18   G. Clarke, 12 February 1833, *Missionary Register* (October 1833), 468.

19   The most useful accounts of literacy among Maori in the early period are C. J. Parr, 'A missionary library', loc. cit., and 'Maori literacy 1843–1867', *Journal of the Polynesian Society*, 72 (1963), 211–34; and Michael D. Jackson, 'Literacy, communications and social change', in *Conflict and compromise: essays on the Maori since colonization*, edited by I. H. Kawharu (Wellington, 1975), pp. 27–54. Related studies are G. S. Parsonson, 'The literate revolution in Polynesia', *Journal of Pacific History*, II (1967), 39–57, and Gérald Duverdier, 'La pénétration du livre dans une société de culture orale: le cas de Tahiti', *Revue Française d'Histoire du Livre* n.s. 1 (1972), 27–51. Parr's thoroughness in noting so many primary references to Maori reading and writing in the 1830s and 1840s has greatly eased my own search, and I have found Jackson's admirable discussion most pertinent to my own because it is specifically concerned to examine Maori social change from the useful vantage point of literacy (p. 28). Michael Jackson also directed me to Manfred Stanley's 'Technicism, liberalism, and development: a study in irony as social theory', in *Social development: critical perspectives* (New York, 1972), 274–325, a suggestive discussion of the philosophical implications of technology for social structure and (if proleptically and only implicitly) *histoire du livre*.

      Nevertheless I argue that early missionaries and recent historians have alike misread the evidence for Maori literacy. If it ceases to be true of the 1840s, the conventional view of the rapid attainment of literacy by the Maori in the 1830s must be wrong: a literacy with any potency for social change is not skin-deep. Having accepted the missionaries' euphoric accounts of the 1830s, Parr asks of the 1840s: 'What happened? Where were the self-appointed teachers, the hundred mile journeys to obtain books and instruction, the eager learners of letters, the crowded day schools of only a dozen years before'? ('Maori literacy', p. 221). The answer is at least partly that Maori 'literacy' of the 1830s is a chimera, a fantasy creation of the European mind. Although few Maori are today, in the simplest functional sense, illiterate, the written and printed word is not the mode which they habitually use. The question is therefore an even more fundamental one than whether or not the Maori failed to become fully literate in the 1830s, or why the missionaries failed to teach them full literacy. It is, rather, why have the Maori 'failed' to become literate at all? Or, to shift the burden of guilt, what is it about literacy and books that makes these technologies so inadequate to cope with the complex realities of a highly civilized social experience which the Maori know but which the literate mind too readily and reductively perhaps tries to capture in the book?

20   Marsden, 14 March 1830, *Missionary Register* (January 1831), 58.

21   Marsden, February 1837, *Missionary Register* (April 1838), 137.

22   *The life of Henry Williams*, edited by H. Carleton (Wellington, 1948), p. 137.

23   Hadfield, 22 July 1840, cited by Parr, 'A missionary library', p. 438.

24   J. F. B. Pompallier, *Early history of the Catholic Church in Oceana* (Auckland, 1888), p. 47.

25   (London, 1955), p. 17. Illiteracy was probably high among British working-class settlers. My own paternal grandfather was illiterate, signing both his marriage certificate and his will with a cross; and my paternal grandmother, like many a Maori chief and medieval king, 'wrote' her letters by dictation.

26   30 April 1836, *Missionary Register* (July 1839), 348.

27   See Duverdier, 'La pénétration', pp. 41–42, and William Ellis, *Polynesian researches, during a residence of nearly eight years in the Society and Sandwich Islands*, 2 vols (London, 1829), I, 492–93, II, 20. Duverdier draws most of his material from Ellis.

28   January 1832, *Missionary Register* (September 1832), 406.

29   6 July 1832, *ibid.* (May 1833), 243.

30   C. Baker, 26 December 1831, *ibid.* (September 1832), 407.

31   Fairburn, 30 April 1838, *ibid.* (July 1839), 348.

32   Henry Williams, 29 August 1834, *ibid.* (November 1835), 258.

33   In McKay, *A history of printing in New Zealand*, pp. 48–49.

34   This point is well made by Clanchy, *From memory to written record.*

35   Among those who currently affirm Maori rights and protect Maori *mana*, those more conciliatory towards European attitudes stress the complimentary ease and speed with which Maori are said to have become literate, those less conciliatory and more radical the supreme importance of the oral tradition and virtual irrelevance of the European 'book'. In practice, the oral mode rules. By compelling those who speak eloquently to substitute a mode in which they are less fluent, literacy can function insidiously as a culturally *regressive* force. Such at least is how many Maori experience it.

    As Jane McRae reminds me, there are few Maori writers and very few who write in Maori, but the tradition of oral composition and exposition continues; it is the only tradition with 'literary structures or styles', and the 'sound' text is usually all there is to be read. Even within University Departments of Maori Studies, the book is suspect. Manuscripts and printed texts in libraries, publications by Europeans on Maoridom, are seldom consulted; oral etiquette, debate and transfer of knowledge on the *marae* or meeting ground are what matter. Such conditions encourage the spontaneous, orally improvised, dramatic recreation of shared stories or themes and an evolutionary concept of texts; the fixed text, catching in print an arbitrary moment in the continuum of social exchange, demands a different sense of history and its own literal re-play.

36   Jackson, 'Literacy, communications, and social change', p. 38; see also A. Buzacott, *Mission life in the islands of the Pacific* (London, 1866), pp. 66–67.

37   *Missionary Register* (September 1834), 418–19.

38   *Ibid.* (April 1832), 192.

39   *Ibid.*, Letter 6.

40   *Ibid.*, Letter 7.

41   *Ibid.* (October 1834), 460. See also *Letters to the Rev. William Yate from natives of New Zealand converted to Christianity* (London, 1836).

42   See W. J. Cameron, 'A printing press for the Maori people', *Journal of the Polynesian Society*, 67 (1958), 204–10; and Johannes Andersen, 'Maori printers and translators', in McKay, *A history of printing in New Zealand*, pp. 33–47. An official Government newspaper, *Te Karere o Nui Tireni*, later *Te Karere Maori*, had been printed in Maori from 1842 to 1846 and doubtless established an early role for this medium.

43   Cited by Parr, 'A missionary library', p. 432.

44   *Ibid.*

45   July and September 1830, *Missionary Register* (January 1831), 67.

46   *Ibid.*

47   28 April 1831, *ibid.* (March 1832), 150.

48   6 July 1832, Letters of Henry Williams, vol. II (1830–38), typescript in the Auckland Institute and Museum.

49   *An account of New Zealand* (London, 1835), p. 232.

50   *Life of Henry Williams*, p. 185.

51   Letter to Dandeson Coates, 9 January 1836.

52   A. C. Bagnall and G. S. Petersen, *William Colenso; printer, missionary, botanist, explorer, politician; his life and journeys* (Wellington, 1948) is the standard life. Colenso's journals and his correspondence with the Church Missionary Society are in the Hocken Library, Dunedin; his Day- and Waste-book, Paper-book and printing-house ledger are in the Alexander Turnbull Library, Wellington; his correspondence with Coupland Harding is in the Mitchell Library, Sydney; his personal memorandum book, kept while he worked for Watts and travelled to New Zealand, and his will, are in the Hawkes Bay Museum and Art Gallery. An edition of his printing-house records and a thorough study of his work as a printer remain to be done. R. Coupland Harding has written three brief accounts: 'New Zealand's first printer', *The Inland Printer*, 7 (1889–90), 504–06; 'Relics of the first New Zealand press', *Transactions and Proceedings of the New Zealand Institute*, 32 (1900), 400–04; 'William Colenso: some personal reminiscences', *The Press* (Christchurch), 27 February 1899. Harding also printed several of Colenso's papers, including *Fifty years ago in New Zealand*. See also H. Hill, 'The early days of printing in New Zealand: a chapter of interesting history', *Transactions and Proceedings of the New Zealand Institute*, 33 (1901), 407–26; and Johannes Andersen, 'Early printing in New Zealand', in McKay, *A history of printing in New Zealand*, pp. 1–31. The fate of Colenso's Stanhope press is unknown; his Colombian is probably that now in the Dominion Museum, Wellington; his table model foolscap Albion (Hopkinson and Cope No. 1964, dated 1845) is in the Hawkes Bay Museum and Art Gallery.

53   Colenso's memorandum book for this time details his wages and the way in which they were made up for composing, correction, altering heads, share of 'fat', or reduced by candle fine and error in casting (the last cost him 16*s.* 4*d.*), along with other sharply observed features of an early nineteenth-century printing house.

54   Colenso Papers, Hocken Library.

55   *Fifty years ago*, p. 6. Writing to Coupland Harding on 31 December 1890, Colenso recalled Williams's first encounter with practical printing: 'Mr. W., evidently, had never seen Typesetting before: he was often in the Pg. Office, & well do I remember his Exclamation of pleasing surprize on seeing a line spaced out in cpg. stick – "he had often wondered how is was done to have all the lines of equal length"'.

56   *Fifty years ago*, p. 7.

57   *Ibid.*, p. 9.

58   16 March 1835, Colenso Papers, Hocken Library; also *Missionary Register* (July 1836), 164.

59   *Fifty years ago*, p. 19.

60   17 December 1838, reprinted in *Fifty years ago*, pp. 21–22.

61   For Yate, see Eric Ramsden, *Marsden and the missions* (Sydney, 1936), p. 28; for Markham, *New Zealand or recollections of it*, p. 55. Sensing that the figure he had heard might be optimistic, Markham qualified it in a note: 'For fear of exageration [sic] say 8000'.

62   Harrison M. Wright, *New Zealand, 1769–1840: early years of western contact* (Cambridge, Mass., 1959),p. 53. Wright's figures are calculated from the tables (titles, formats, edition quantities) supplied by Colenso in *The Missionary Register* (1840), p. 512, and (1841), p. 519. To keep the comparative base I have used the same source, but a more exact calculation would have to include a few jobbing items excluded from Colenso's reports but included in his ledger.

63   Richard Davis, 10 November 1832, cited by Wright, *New Zealand*, p. 176.

64   G. Clarke, *Early life in New Zealand* (Hobart, 1903), p. 31.

65   Whiteley, 22 December 1836, cited by Parr, 'A missionary library', p. 445.

66   28 April 1839, *ibid.*

67   *Life of Henry Williams*, p. 60.

68   *Fifty years ago*, p.42.

69   *New Zealand or recollections of it*, p. 32.

70   15 June 1843, cited by Parr, 'Maori literacy', p. 212.

71   Thomas Chapman, 28 March 1846, *ibid.*, p. 213.

72   Cited by Parr, 'A missionary library', p. 446.

73   As Stanley writes, 'Physical machinery [sc. books?] cannot "make" men do anything. People act or fail to act on the basis of their interpretations of the world around them, interpretations embodied in language, institutions, and social organization. The physical world created by human innovative effort reflects – in the forms of material objects – human assumptions, values, desires, and aspirations' ('Technicism, liberalism, and development', p. 279). The first part is true of Maori resistance to literacy, the second of the missionaries in the value they imparted and imputed to the book. Paradoxically the Maori is very sensitive to (because suspicious of) the very form of a book, and gives an expressive intention to features which a European takes for granted as mere 'accidentals' and has virtually ceased to see. For example, in a review of Michael King's *Maori – a photographic and social history* (Auckland, 1983), Keri Kaa questions the very depiction of corpses: 'The pictures of the tupapaku (corpses) I found most disturbing . . . My initial reaction was to ask: Whose Nanny is that? Whose Mother is that? Do their mokopuna [children] mind about their taonga [precious heirlooms] being displayed for all the world to see?' And again 'There is a strange combination of pictures on page 35. At the top of the page is a picture of a tangi [funeral], underneath is one of a woman cooking. Anyone who understands the concepts of tapu and noa [lifting of tapu] would appreciate that the two should never be mixed by being placed together *on a page*' (my italics), *The New Zealand Listener*, 24 September 1983, p. 99.

74   Brown, *New Zealand and its aborigines*, p. 99. Augustus Earle, *Narrative of a residence in New Zealand*, edited by E. H. McCormick (Oxford, 1966), pp. 133–34, wrote: 'I cannot forbear censuring the missionaries, inasmuch as they prevent the natives, by every means in their power, from acquiring the English language'. See also J. S. Polack, *Manners and customs of the New Zealanders*, 2 vols (London, 1840), II, 147: '[The Maori] take much delight in speaking the English language, and had the Missionaries chosen to have taught the children this tongue, what an immense store of able works could at once have been put into the hands of the native youth, instead of a few imperfect translations on one subject, that may teach mechanical devotion, but can never mentally illuminate the native mind'.

75   'On nomenclature', in *Three literary papers* (Napier, 1883), p. 9. In this paper Colenso also discusses the orthography of place names on maps and in school geographies, raising many of the issues recently dramatized by Brian Friel in his play *Translations* (1981). See also H. W. Williams, 'Reaction of the Maori to the impact of civilization', *Journal of the Polynesian Society*, 44 (1935), 216–43, esp. 234–35.

76   Some drafts survive: one by Hobson of the preamble; one in the hand of Freeman, Hobson's secretary, of the three articles and another version of the preamble; a fair copy of a draft by James Busby. But they do not themselves constitute the English text given to Williams to translate. Although Colenso provides an unrivalled account of the treaty occasion, by far the most perceptive analysis of the texts and their implications is that of R. M. Ross, 'Te Tiriti o Waitangi: texts and translations', *New Zealand Journal of History*, 6 (1972), 129–67. The account I give of the relationship of the texts is based wholly on Ross.

77   To add insult to injury, the Maori text printed as the first schedule to the Act contains, in the second article, numerous misprints.

78   It is also the most reductive form of 'literacy' test. See David Cressy, *Literacy and the social*

order: reading and writing in Tudor England (Cambridge, 1980), p. 53; and R. S. Schofield, 'The measurement of literacy in pre-industrial England', in *Literacy in traditional societies*, edited by Jack Goody (Cambridge, 1968), p. 319.

79   The treaty is supplemented and ultimately constituted by a collection of sheets subscribed in different parts of the country between 6 February and 3 September 1840. Fig. 2(a) [omitted] shows part of a declaration of their independence of all foreign powers that had been subscribed on 28 October 1835 by thirty-four chiefs, of whom only four signed their own name. In the next four years a further eighteen chiefs subscribed, of whom only three signed their own names. Most such signatures appear to have been written with difficulty. In later times some Maori who could in fact write their names preferred to use their *moko* as giving documents a more sacred sign of approval.

80   Graphic as it is, Colenso's account of the Maori speeches understandably does scant justice to the originals. As he wrote much later, 'Some of the New Zealanders were truly natural orators, and consequently possessed in their large assemblies great power and influence. This was mainly owing to their tenacious memories, to their proper selection from their copious and expressive language; skilfully choosing the very word, sentence, theme, or natural image best fitted to make an impression on the lively impulsive minds of their countrymen . . . the orator's knowledge of their traditions and myths, songs, proverbs and fables was ever to him an inexhaustible mine of wealth . . . All the people well knew the power of persuasion – particularly of that done in the open air – before the multitude' (*The New Zealand Exhibition* (Wellington, 1865); section on 'Ethnology: On the Maori races of New Zealand', pp. 70–71). What Hobson was up against may be judged from his letter of 17 February 1840, reporting the Hokianga meeting at which he had sought further subscriptions to the treaty: 'The New Zealanders are passionately fond of declamation, and they possess considerable ingenuity in exciting the passions of the people. On this occasion all their best orators were against me, and every argument they could devise was used to defeat my object' (Facsimiles, p. [x]). Maori orators, it should be noted, often enjoyed playing devil's advocate. Colenso vividly recounts the anger of Te Kemara ('eyes rolling . . . extravagant gestures and grimace'), but adds: 'And yet it was all mere show – not really intended; as was not long after fully shown, when they gave their evidence as to the fair sale, &c., of their lands before the Land Commissioners, I myself acting as interpreter'.

        All quotations here and below relating to the discussion and signing of the treaty on 5 and 6 February are taken from Colenso's own eye- and ear-witness report, *The authentic and genuine history of the signing of the Treaty of Waitangi* (Wellington, 1890), principally pp. 32–33. Written immediately after the events described, it was read and its accuracy confirmed by James Busby who was also present.

81   I do not impute to Williams any will to deceive the Maori by his choice of terms. Attempts to establish a legal basis for the control of British subjects in New Zealand by extraterritorial jurisdiction had proved unsuccessful. Furthermore, unless Britain formally secured sovereignty, neither Britain nor the Maori could establish an exclusive claim to the islands as against claims that might be made by other European powers. (The Declaration of Independence of 1835 was a device to establish the chiefs' collective territorial rights and forestall an imminent French claim.) In furthering both concerns, however dubious the exact legal status of the treaty, the British Government was anxious to secure Maori assent and genuinely hopeful that British sovereignty would not disrupt Maori life. Nevertheless, cultural and linguistic suppositions on both sides, compounded by European assumptions about literacy and the status of documents, frustrated that hope and later (if then still unforeseen) patterns of immigration destroyed it. Williams certainly shows himself, at that critical time, to have been less sensitive than Colenso to Maori modes of understanding. As Claudia Orange has made clear to me, Maori understanding of the Treaty was undoubtedly formed by their sense

that the independence (the *rangatiratanga*) they had affirmed in 1835 and reaffirmed by further subscriptions as late as 1839, was not nullified by the Treaty. One document did not supersede the other: they lived together, one complementing the other.

82   Fishing rights have again become a matter of contention in this century, most recently in 1983 when the then Government proposed to direct into the sea effluent from a synthetic petrol plant at Motunui. The subsequent *Report, findings and recommendations of the Waitangi Tribunal on an application . . . on behalf of the Te Atiawa Tribe in relation to fishing grounds in the Waitara district* (Wellington, 1983) includes a valuable résumé of many textual issues raised by the present paper.

83   Sir Apirana Ngata's literal translation from the Maori of the second article reads: 'The Queen of England confirms and guarantees to the Chiefs and Tribes and to all the people of New Zealand the full possession of their lands, their homes and all their possessions, but the chiefs assembled and all other chiefs yield to the Queen the right to alienate such lands which the owners desire to dispose of at a price agreed upon between the owners and person or persons appointed by the Queen to purchase on her behalf' (*The Treaty of Waitangi: an explanation*, Christchurch, 1950, p. 7).

84   Letter begun 24 January 1840, cited by Bagnall and Petersen, *William Colenso*, pp. 93–94. Again I acknowledge the kind help of Paul McHugh. The Crown's pre-emptive right to extinguish the native title had been long practised in colonizing overseas territories and was most vigorously affirmed in the Royal Proclamation of 1763 which was seen as protecting North American Indian lands from unscrupulous appropriation. The English land law assumption that all rights to land derive from a grant by the Crown clearly did not apply to new territories, where the aboriginal title rested at law, not upon a grant from the Crown, but (exceptionally) upon the Crown's recognition of aboriginal rights. To the British mind, however, it was unthinkable that aboriginal and heathen notions of title should control the form of land transfers to British settlers, and so the pre-emptive right was adopted as a way of converting Crown-recognized title into Crown-derived title. From the British point of view, it was undoubtedly seen as preventing the chaos which must have followed from the operation of a mixed system, and at the same time (if fairly administered) as protecting the Maori from land-jobbers. One has to concede that neither Hobson nor Williams could have communicated the full import of 'pre-emptive' to those who were asked to assent to the treaty, but by so simplifying the issue in his translation of the second article into Maori, Williams again showed less readiness than did Colenso to penetrate 'the Native mind' and 'explain the thing in all its bearings . . . so that it should be their very own act and deed'. One might be accused of arguing from hindsight were it not for Colenso's contemporary insight.

85   Cited by Ross 'Te Tiriti o Waitangi', p. 152, from British Parliamentary Papers, 1845, XXXIII, 108, p. 10. Despite the transience of the spoken word, there is a wealth of Maori speech in manuscripts still to be studied. Some are *tapu* and unable to be consulted, but the written transcripts of evidence delivered in Maori land courts are a rich source of information about language and forms of oral witness to land rights as declaimed in court. Elsdon Best records that when he was secretary to the Land Commission, an old man recited 406 songs for him from memory, a genealogy which took three days to recite and included over 1400 persons in proper sequence, and much other evidence on the occupation of certain lands: *The Maori school of learning: its objects, methods and ceremonies* (Wellington, 1923), p. 5.

86   'The rationale of copy-text', in *Collected papers*, edited by J. C. Maxwell (Oxford, 1966), p. 384.

87   *Report*, pp. 52–63; the immediate quotation is on p. 55. As indicated in note 35 above, an oral culture will generate, not a fixed text, but a variety of versions which have their local and topical value in giving life to the *wairua* of the 'text' which comprehends and transcends them all. As it is so pertinent to my larger argument, I have here incorporated opinion from the

Waitangi Tribunal's report, although neither the report nor the circumstances which occasioned it existed when this paper was delivered. Treaties are likely to become a more frequently used resource, not only for ethnohistorical studies, but for concepts of text in complex political, linguistic and cultural contexts, for their mixed modes of oral and written discourse, for their synchronic and diachronic dimensions, for their continuing human implications (they are not exactly dramatic fictions), and for the forcing circumstances which compel the law to offer what are essentially editorial judgements. David R. Miller of the Newberry Library tells me that the microfilming of 9,552 Iroquois treaty documents has been almost completed and that an associated study has just been published: *The history and culture of Iroquois diplomacy: an interdisciplinary guide to the treaties of the Six Nations and League* (Syracuse, 1983). The value of treaties as texts for analysis of diplomacy as a matter of cultural as well as political contact is well demonstrated in Dorothy V. Jones's *Licence for empire: colonisation by treaty* (Chicago, 1983). A. S. Keller, O. J. Lissitzyn, and F. J. Mann, *Creation of rights of sovereignty through symbolic acts, 1400–1800* (New York, 1938), remains a convenient historical summary of European attitudes and practice.

88   Letter to G. Robertson, 1 March 1899: Mitchell MS AC 83/4.

Chapter 17

Elizabeth Eisenstein

DEFINING THE INITIAL SHIFT
Some features of print culture

We should note the force, effect, and consequences of inventions which are nowhere more conspicuous than in those three which were unknown to the ancients, namely, printing, gunpowder, and the compass. For these three have changed the appearance and state of the whole world . . .

(Francis Bacon, Novum Organum, Aphorism 129)

To dwell on the reasons why Bacon's advice ought to be followed by others is probably less helpful than trying to follow it oneself. This task clearly outstrips the competence of any single individual. It calls for the pooling of many talents and the writing of many books. Collaboration is difficult to obtain as long as the relevance of the topic to different fields of study remains obscure. Before aid can be enlisted, it seems necessary to develop some tentative hypotheses relating the shift from script to print to significant historical developments.

This task, in turn, seems to call for a somewhat unconventional point of departure and for a reformulation of Bacon's advice. Instead of trying to deal with 'the force, effect, and consequences' of a single post-classical invention that is coupled with others, I will be concerned with a major transformation that constituted a large cluster of changes in itself. Indecision about what is meant by the advent of printing has, I think, helped to muffle concern about its possible consequences and made them more difficult to track down. It is difficult to find out what happened in a particular Mainz workshop in the 1450s. When pursuing other inquiries, it seems almost prudent to bypass so problematic an event. This does not apply to the appearance of new occupational groups who employed new techniques and installed new equipment in new kinds of workshops while extending trade networks and seeking new markets to increase profits made from sales. Unknown anywhere in Europe before the mid-fifteenth century, printers' workshops would be found in every important municipal center by 1500. They added a new element to urban culture in hundreds of towns.[1] To pass by all that, when dealing with other problems, would seem to be incautious. For this reason, among others, I am skipping over the perfection of a new process for printing with movable types and will not pause over the massive literature devoted to explanations of Gutenberg's invention.[2] Instead, I will begin where many studies end, after the first dated printed products had been issued and the inventor's immediate successors had set to work.

By the advent of printing then, I mean the establishment of presses in urban centers beyond the Rhineland during an interval that begins in the 1460s and coincides, very roughly, with the era of incunabula.[3] So few studies have been devoted to this point of departure that no conventional label has yet been attached to it. One might talk about a basic change in a mode of production, about a book revolution, or a media revolution, or perhaps, most simply and explicitly, about a shift from script to print. Will Durant refers to a 'typographical revolution'. Partly because it can be neatly coupled with the already well-entrenched commercial revolution and also because it points to a major dimension of history which needs more attention, I believe 'communications revolution' best suits my purposes in this book. Whatever label is used, it should be understood to cover a large cluster of relatively simultaneous, closely interrelated changes, each of which needs closer study and more explicit treatment – as the following quick sketch may suggest.

First of all, the marked increase in the output of books and the drastic reduction in the number of man-hours required to turn them out deserve stronger emphasis. At present there is a tendency to think of a steady increase in book production during the first century of printing. An evolutionary model of change is applied to a situation that seems to call for a revolutionary one.

A man born in 1453, the year of the fall of Constantinople, could look back from his fiftieth year on a lifetime in which about eight million books had been printed, more perhaps than all the scribes of Europe had produced since Constantine founded his city in A.D. 330.[4]

The actual production of 'all the scribes of Europe' is inevitably open to dispute. Even apart from the problem of trying to estimate numbers of books that went uncatalogued and then were destroyed, contemporary evidence must be handled with caution, for it often yields false clues to the numbers of books involved. Since it was customary to register many texts bound within one set of covers as but one book, the actual number of texts in a given manuscript collection is not easily ascertained.[5] That objects counted as one book often contained a varying combination of many provides yet another example of the difficulty of quantifying data provided in the age of scribes. The situation is similar when we turn to the problem of counting the man-hours required to copy manuscript books. Old estimates based on the number of months it took forty-five scribes working for Vespasiano da Bisticci to produce 200 books for Cosimo de Medici's Badia library have been rendered virtually worthless by recent intensive research.[6]

Thus the total number of books produced by 'all the scribes of Europe' since 330 or even since 1400, is likely to remain elusive. Nevertheless, some comparisons are possible and they place the output of printers in sharp contrast to preceding trends. 'In 1483, the Ripoli Press charged three florins per quinterno for setting up and printing Ficino's translation of Plato's *Dialogues*. A scribe might have charged one florin per quinterno for duplicating the same work. The Ripoli Press produced 1,025 copies; the scribe would have turned out one'.[7] Given this kind of comparison, it seems misguided to suggest that 'the multiplication of identical copies' was merely 'intensified' by the press.[8] Doubtless, hand-copying could be quite efficient for the purpose of duplicating a royal edict or papal bull.[9] Sufficient numbers of copies of a newly edited Bible were produced in the thirteenth century for some scholars to feel justified in referring to a Paris 'edition' of a manuscript Bible. To turn out one single whole 'edition' of any text was no mean feat in the thirteenth century, however. The one thirteenth-century scribal 'edition' might be compared with the large number of Bible editions turned out in the half century between Gutenberg and Luther. When scribal labor was employed for multiplying edicts or producing a whole 'edition' of scripture, moreover, it was diverted from other tasks.

Many valued texts were barely preserved from extinction; untold numbers failed to survive. Survival often hinged on the occasional copy being made by an interested scholar who acted as his own scribe. In view of the proliferation of 'unique' texts and of the accumulation of variants, it is doubtful whether one should refer to 'identical copies' being 'multiplied' before print. This point is especially important when considering technical literature. The difficulty of making even one 'identical' copy of a significant technical work was such that the task could not be trusted to any hired hands. Men of learning had to engage in 'slavish copying' of tables, diagrams and unfamiliar terms. The output of whole editions of sets of astronomical tables did not 'intensify' previous trends. It reversed them, producing a new situation which released time for observation and research.

The previous introduction of paper, it should be noted, did not have anything like a 'similar' effect, any more than did 'the organization of a regular trade in manuscript books'.[10] Paper production served the needs of merchants, bureaucrats, preachers and literati; it quickened the pace of correspondence and enabled more men of letters to act as their own scribes. But since the same number of man-hours was still required to turn out a given text, the increase in book production was sluggish and copies continued to be made at an irregular rate. Shops run by stationers or *cartolai* multiplied in response to an increasing demand for tablets, notebooks, prepared sheets and other supplies.[11] In addition to selling writing materials and school books as well as book-binding materials and services, some merchants also helped book-hunting patrons by locating valued works. They had copies made on commission and kept some for sale in their shops. But their involvement in the book-trade was more casual than one might think.

> The activities of the *cartolai* were multifarious, although they usually specialized in one or another branch of their trade. The preparation and selling of book materials and binding were probably their commonest occupations. Some *cartolai* were also illuminators or employed illuminators in their shops . . . Scribes who mostly had other occupations (they were often notaries or priests) seem usually to have worked at home or in their shops, on commission . . . Many of the *cartolai* especially those who specialized in the sale and preparation of book materials or in bindings were probably concerned little if at all, with the production or sale of manuscripts and (later) printed books, either new or secondhand . . .[12]

Even the retail book-trade that was conducted by Vespasiano da Bisticci, the most celebrated Florentine book merchant, who served prelates and princes and 'did everything possible' to attract patrons and make sales, never verged on becoming a wholesale business. Despite Vespasiano's unusually aggressive tactics in promoting sales and matching books with clients, he showed no signs of ever 'having made much money' from all his transactions.[13] He did win notable patrons, however, and achieved considerable celebrity as 'prince of publishers'. His shop was praised by humanist poets along lines which were similar to those used in later tributes to Gutenberg and Aldus Manutius.[14] His posthumous fame – achieved only in the nineteenth century after the publication of his memoirs and their use by Jacob Burckhardt – is perhaps even more noteworthy. Vespasiano's *Lives of Illustrious Men* contains a reference to the beautifully bound manuscript books in the Duke of Urbino's library and snobbishly implies that a printed book would have been 'ashamed' in such elegant company. This one reference by an atypical and obviously prejudiced bookdealer has ballooned into many misleading comments about the disdain of Renaissance humanists for vulgar machine-made objects. Thus the catalogue to the beautiful Morgan Library 1973 Exhibition on 'The Art of the Printed Book' asserts that the Medici [*sic*] 'considered newly printed books a degradation and would not allow them in their libraries'.[15] The same error was amplified by an article in *The New York Times*: 'The Medici and other Florentine Princes [*sic*] considered printing a degradation and barred it from their sacred manuscript libraries'.[16] Similar distortions, all emanating from Burckhardt's use of

Vespasiano's *Lives*, have been multiplied and amplified in so many varying contexts that scholarly disclaimers cannot catch up with them.[17]

The need to make Renaissance bibliophiles and patrons into snobbish enemies of machine-made objects seems oddly compelling. Why else is the story so often told with no real hard evidence to support it and expanded to Florence with no supporting evidence at all? Actually, Florentine bibliophiles were sending to Rome for printed books as early as 1470. Under Guidobaldo da Montefeltro, the ducal library at Urbino acquired printed editions and (shamelessly or not) had them bound with the same magnificent covers as manuscripts. The same court also sponsored the establishment of an early press in 1482.[18] That Vespasiano was indulging in wishful and nostalgic thinking is suggested by his own inability to find sufficient support from princely patrons to persist in his exclusive trade. His chief rival in Florence, Zanobi di Mariano, managed to stay in business right down to his death in 1495. 'Zanobi's readiness to sell printed books – a trade which Vespasiano spurned – explains his survival as a bookseller in the tricky years of the late fifteenth century. Vespasiano dealing exclusively in manuscripts was forced out of business in 1478'.[19]

One must wait for Vespasiano to close shop before one can say that a genuine wholesale book-trade was launched.

> As soon as Gutenberg and Schoeffer had finished the last sheet of their monumental Bible, the financier of the firm, John Fust, set out with a dozen copies or so to see for himself how he could best reap the harvest of his patient investments. And where did he turn first of all to convert his Bibles into money? He went to the biggest university town in Europe, to Paris, where ten thousand or more students were filling the Sorbonne and the colleges. And what did he, to his bitter discomfiture, find there? A well organized and powerful guild of the book-trade, the Confrérie des Libraires, Relieurs, Enlumineurs, Ecrivains et Parcheminiers . . . founded in 1401 . . . Alarmed at the appearance of an outsider with such an unheard of treasure of books; when he was found to be selling one Bible after another, they soon shouted for the police, giving their expert opinion that such a store of valuable books could be in one man's possession through the help of the devil himself and Fust had to run for his life or his first business trip would have ended in a nasty bonfire.[20]

The story may be just as unfounded as the legend that linked the figure of Johann Fust with that of Dr Faustus.[21] The adverse reaction it depicts should not be taken as typical; many early references were at worst ambivalent.[22] The ones that are most frequently cited associate printing with divine rather than diabolic powers. But then the most familiar references come either from the blurbs and prefaces composed by early printers themselves or from editors and authors who found employment in print shops.[23] Such men were likely to take a more favorable view than were the guildsmen who had made a livelihood from manuscript books. The Parisian *libraires* may have had good reason to be alarmed, although they were somewhat ahead of the game; the market value of hand-copied books did not drop until after Fust was dead.[24] Other members of the *confrérie* could not foresee that most 'book-binders, rubricators, illuminators, and calligraphers would be kept busier than ever after early printers set up shop'.[25] Whether the new art was considered a blessing or a curse; whether it was consigned to the Devil or attributed to God; the fact remains, that the initial increase in output did strike contemporary observers as sufficiently remarkable to suggest supernatural intervention. Even incredulous modern scholars may be troubled by trying to calculate the number of calves required to supply enough skins for Gutenberg's Bible.[26] It should not be too difficult to obtain agreement that an abrupt rather than a gradual increase did occur in the second half of the fifteenth century.

Scepticism is much more difficult to overcome when we turn from consideration of quantity to that of quality. If one holds a late manuscript copy of a given text next to an early printed one, one is likely to doubt that any change at all has taken place, let alone an abrupt or revolutionary one.

> Behind every book which Peter Schoeffer printed stands a published manuscript . . .
> The decision on the kind of letter to use, the selection of initials and decoration of
> rubrications, the determination of the length and width of the column, planning for
> margins . . . all were prescribed by the manuscript copy before him.[27]

Not only did early printers such as Schoeffer try to copy a given manuscript as faithfully as possible, but fifteenth-century scribes returned the compliment. As Curt Bühler has shown, a large number of the manuscripts made during the late fifteenth century were copied from early printed books.[28] Thus handwork and presswork continued to appear almost indistinguishable, even after the printer had begun to depart from scribal conventions and to exploit some of the new features inherent in his art.

That there were new features and they were exploited needs to be given due weight. Despite his efforts to duplicate manuscripts as faithfully as possible, the fact remains that Peter Schoeffer, printer, was following different procedures than had Peter Schoeffer, scribe. The absence of any apparent change in product was combined with a complete change in methods of production, giving rise to the paradoxical combination, noted above, of seeming continuity with radical change. Thus the temporary resemblance between handwork and presswork seems to support the thesis of a very gradual evolutionary change; yet the opposite thesis may also be supported by underlining the marked difference between the two different modes of production and noting the new features that began to appear before the fifteenth century had come to an end.

Concern with surface appearance necessarily governed the handwork of the scribe. He was fully preoccupied trying to shape evenly spaced uniform letters in a pleasing symmetrical design. An altogether different procedure was required to give directions to compositors. To do this, one had to mark up a manuscript while scrutinizing its contents.[29] Every manuscript that came into the printer's hands, thus, had to be reviewed in a new way – one which encouraged more editing, correcting and collating than had the hand-copied text.[30] Within a generation the results of this review were being aimed in a new direction – away from fidelity to scribal conventions and toward serving the convenience of the reader. The highly competitive commercial character of the new mode of book production encouraged the relatively rapid adoption of any innovation that commended a given edition to purchasers.[31] Well before 1500, printers had begun to experiment with the use 'of graduated types, running heads . . . footnotes . . . tables of contents . . . superior figures, cross references . . . and other devices available to the compositor' – all registering 'the victory of the punch cutter over the scribe'.[32] Title pages became increasingly common, facilitating the production of book lists and catalogues, while acting as advertisements in themselves.[33] Hand-drawn illustrations were replaced by more easily duplicated woodcuts and engravings – an innovation which eventually helped to revolutionize technical literature by introducing 'exactly repeatable pictorial statements' into all kinds of reference works.

The fact that identical images, maps and diagrams could be viewed simultaneously by scattered readers constituted a kind of communications revolution in itself. This point has been made most forcefully by William Ivins, a former curator of prints at the Metropolitan Museum.[34] Although Ivins' special emphasis on 'the exactly repeatable pictorial statement' has found favor among historians of cartography,[35] his propensity for overstatement has provoked objections from other specialists. Repeatable images, they argue, go back to ancient seals and coins; while exact replication was scarcely fostered by woodblocks which got worn and broken after repeated use. Here as elsewhere one must be wary of underrating as well as of overestimating the advantages of the new technology. Even while noting that woodcuts did get corrupted when copied for insertion in diverse kinds of texts, one should also consider the corruption that occurred when hand-drawn images had to be copied into hundreds of books. Although pattern books and 'pouncing' techniques were available to some medieval illuminators, the precise reproduction of fine detail remained elusive until the advent of woodcarving and engraving. Blocks and plates did make repeatable visual aids feasible for the first time. In the hands of expert craftsmen using good materials and working under supervision, even problems of wear and tear could be circumvented; worn places could be sharpened; blurred details refined and a truly remarkable durability achieved.[36]

It is not so much in his special emphasis on the printed image but rather in his underrating the significance of the printed text that Ivins seems to go astray. In his work the use of movable type is oddly described as 'little more than a way to do with a smaller number of proof readings'. A reference by Pliny the Younger to one thousand copies of a book being made in the second century A.D. is cited repeatedly as evidence that the duplicative powers of print were relatively feeble.[37] The incapacity of any two scribes (let alone one thousand) to produce identical copies while taking dictation is overlooked. Although he mentions in passing that 'the history of prints as an integrated series' begins with their use 'as illustrations in books printed from movable types',[38] Ivins' analysis elsewhere tends to detach the fate of printed pictures from that of printed books. His treatment implies that the novel effects of repeatability were confined to pictorial statements. Yet these effects were by no means confined to pictures or, for that matter, to pictures and words. Mathematical tables, for example, were also transformed. For scholars concerned with scientific change, what happened to numbers and equations is surely just as significant as what happened to either images or words. Furthermore, many of the most important pictorial statements produced during the first century of printing employed various devices – banderoles, letter-number keys, indication lines – to relate images to texts.[39] To treat the visual aid as a discrete unit is to lose sight of the connecting links which were especially important for technical literature because they expressed the relationship between words and things.

Even though block-print and letterpress may have originated as separate innovations and were initially used for diverse purposes (so that playing cards and saints' images, for example, were being stamped from blocks at the same time that hand illumination continued to decorate many early printed books), the two techniques soon became intertwined. The use of typography for texts led to that of xylography for illustration, sealing the fate of illuminator along with that of the scribe.[40] When considering how technical literature was affected by the shift from script to print, it seems reasonable to adopt George Sarton's strategy of envisaging a 'double invention; typography for the text, engraving for the images'.[41] The fact that letters, numbers and pictures were *all* alike subject to repeatability by the end of the fifteenth century needs more emphasis. That the printed book made possible new forms of interplay between these diverse elements is perhaps even more significant than the change undergone by picture, number or letter alone.

Intellectual historians may find the new interplay between 'literate, figurative and numerate' forms of expression of particular interest.[42] Social historians also need to be alerted to the new interplay between diverse occupational groups which occurred within the new workshops that were set up by early printers. The preparation of copy and illustrative material for printed editions led to a rearrangement of all book-making arts and routines. Not only did new skills, such as typefounding and presswork, involve veritable occupational mutations;[43] but the production of printed books also gathered together in one place more traditional variegated skills. In the age of scribes, book-making had occurred under the diverse auspices represented by stationers and lay copyists in university towns; illuminators and miniaturists trained in special ateliers; goldsmiths and leather workers belonging to special guilds; monks and lay brothers gathered in scriptoria; royal clerks and papal secretaries working in chanceries and courts; preachers compiling books of sermons on their own;

humanist poets serving as their own scribes. The advent of printing led to the creation of a new kind of shop structure; to a regrouping which entailed closer contacts among diversely skilled workers and encouraged new forms of cross-cultural interchange.

Thus it is not uncommon to find former priests among early printers or former abbots serving as editors and correctors.[44] University professors also often served in similar capacities and thus came into closer contact with metal workers and mechanics. Other fruitful forms of collaboration brought astronomers and engravers, physicians and painters together, dissolving older divisions of intellectual labor and encouraging new ways of coordinating the work of brains, eyes and hands. Problems of financing the publication of the large Latin volumes that were used by late medieval faculties of theology, law, and medicine also led to the formation of partnerships that brought rich merchants and local scholars into closer contact. The new financial syndicates that were formed to provide master printers with needed labor and supplies brought together representatives of town and gown.[45] As the key figure around whom all arrangements revolved, the master printer himself bridged many worlds.[46] He was responsible for obtaining money, supplies and labor, while developing complex production schedules, coping with strikes, trying to estimate book markets and lining up learned assistants.[47] He had to keep on good terms with officials who provided protection and lucrative jobs, while cultivating and promoting talented authors and artists who might bring his firm profits or prestige. In those places where his enterprise prospered and he achieved a position of influence with fellow townsmen, his workshop became a veritable cultural center attracting local literati and celebrated foreigners; providing both a meeting place and message center for an expanding cosmopolitan Commonwealth of Learning.

Some manuscript bookdealers, to be sure, had served rather similar functions before the advent of printing. That Italian humanists were grateful to Vespasiano da Bisticci for many of the same services that were later rendered by Aldus Manutius has already been noted. Nevertheless, the shop structure over which Aldus presided differed markedly from that known to Vespasiano. As the prototype of the early capitalist as well as the heir to Atticus and his successors, the printer embraced an even wider repertoire of roles. Aldus' household in Venice, which contained some thirty members, has recently been described as an 'almost incredible mixture of the sweat shop, the boarding house and the research institute'.[48] A most interesting study might be devoted to a comparison of the talents mobilized by early printers with those previously employed by stationers or manuscript bookdealers. Of equal interest would be a comparison of the occupational culture of Peter Schoeffer, printer, with that of Peter Schoeffer, scribe. The two seem to work in contrasting milieux, subject to different pressures and aiming at different goals. Unlike the shift from stationer to publisher, the shift from scribe to printer represented a genuine occupational mutation. Although Schoeffer was the first to make the leap, many others took the same route before the century's end.[49]

Judging by Lehmann-Haupt's fine monograph, many of Schoeffer's pioneering activities were associated with the shift from a retail trade to a wholesale industry which led the printer to turn peddler and to launch what soon became an annual book fair at Frankfurt. 'For a while the trade in printed books flowed within the narrow channels of the manuscript book market. But soon the stream could no longer be contained'. New distribution outlets were located; handbills, circulars and sales catalogues were printed and the books themselves were carried down the Rhine, across the Elbe, west to Paris, south to Switzerland. The drive to tap markets went together with efforts to hold competitors at bay by offering better products or, at least, by printing a prospectus advertising the firm's 'more readable' texts, 'more complete and better arranged' indexes, 'more careful proof reading' and editing. Officials serving archbishops and emperors were cultivated, not so much as potential bibliophiles, nor even as potential censors, but rather as potential customers, who issued a steady flow of orders for the printing of ordinances, edicts, bulls, indulgences, broadsides and tracts. By the end of the century, Schoeffer had risen to a position of eminence in the city of Mainz. He commanded a 'far-flung sales organization', had become a partner in a joint mining enterprise, and had founded a printing dynasty. His supply of types went to his sons upon his death and the Schoeffer firm continued in operation, expanding to encompass music printing, through the next generation.[50]

As the foregoing may suggest, there are many points of possible contrast between the activities of the Mainz printer and those of the Paris scribe. All need to be brought out more clearly when considering fifteenth-century trends. The movement of centers of book production from university towns, princely courts, patrician villas and monasteries to commercial centers; the organization of new trade networks and fairs; the new competition over lucrative privileges and monopolies; the new restraints imposed by official censors have been covered in special accounts.[51] But the implications of such changes need to be underlined so that they may be related to other concurrent developments. Competitive and commercial drives were not entirely absent among the stationers who served university faculties, the lay scribes who were hired by mendicant orders, or the semi-lay copyists who belonged to communities founded by the Brethren of the Common Life. But they were muted in comparison with the later efforts of Schoeffer and his competitors to recoup initial investments, pay oil creditors, use up reams of paper, and keep pressmen employed. The manuscript bookdealer did not have to worry about idle machines or striking workmen as did the printer. It has been suggested indeed that the mere act of setting up a press in a monastery or in affiliation with a religious order was a source of disturbance, bringing 'a multitude of worries about money and property' into space previously reserved for meditation and good works. When one considers that such an event occurred in several places in the late fifteenth century, it seems to warrant more attention in studies of changes affecting late medieval religious life.[52]

We also need to hear more about the job-printing that accompanied book-printing. It lent itself to commercial advertising, official propaganda, seditious agitations and bureaucratic red tape as no scribal procedure ever had.[53] The very term 'avertissement' underwent an intriguing change. In the Low Countries, books copied during holy days in medieval scriptoria were regarded as specially consecrated. A note placed in the colophon designating holy-day work served as a warning (or 'avertissement') against sale.[54] Of course such a warning can be interpreted as indicating the commercialization of the manuscript book-trade. Books were being copied not just for the love of God but for sale, on all save holy days. But a different, more muted commercial theme was sounded by this kind of 'avertissement' than would be the case after presses were established.

As self-serving publicists, early printers issued book lists, circulars and broadsides. They put their firm's name, emblem and shop address on the front page of their books. Indeed, their use of title pages entailed a significant reversal of scribal procedures; they put themselves first. Scribal colophons had come last. They also extended their new promotional techniques to the authors and artists whose work they published, thus contributing to the celebration of lay culture-heroes and to their achievement of personal celebrity and eponymous fame. Reckon masters and instrument makers along with professors and preachers also profited from book advertisements that spread their fame beyond shops and lecture halls.[55] Studies concerned with the rise of a lay intelligentsia, with the new dignity assigned to artisan crafts or with the heightened visibility achieved by the 'capitalist spirit' might well devote more attention to these early practitioners of the advertising arts.

Their control of a new publicity apparatus, moreover, placed early printers in an exceptional position with regard to other enterprises. They not only sought ever larger markets for their own products; but they also contributed to, and profited from, the expansion of other commercial enterprises. What effects did the appearance of new advertising techniques have on sixteenth-century commerce and industry? Possibly some answers to this question are known. Probably others can still be found. Many other aspects of job printing and the changes it entailed clearly need further study. The printed calendars and indulgences that were first issued from the Mainz workshops of Gutenberg and Fust, for example, warrant at least as much attention as the more celebrated Bibles. Indeed the mass production of indulgences illustrates rather neatly the sort of change that often goes overlooked, so that its consequences are more difficult to reckon with than perhaps they need be.

In contrast to the changes sketched above, those that were associated with the consumption of new printed products are more intangible, indirect, and difficult to handle. A large margin for uncertainty must be left when dealing with such changes. Many of them also have to be left for later discussion because they involved prolonged, unevenly phased transformations which occurred over the course of several centuries. This seems especially true of those changes which are most commonly associated with the impact of printing: changes, that is, which hinge on the spread of literacy and which entail a variety of popularizing trends.

On the difficult problem of estimating literacy rates before and after printing, the comments of Carlo Cipolla seem cogent:

> It is not easy to draw a general conclusion from the scattered evidence that I have quoted and from the similarly scattered evidence that I have not quoted . . . I could go on to conclude that at the end of the sixteenth century 'there were more literate people than we generally believe' . . . I could equally conclude that 'there were less literate people than we generally believe' for in all truth one never knows what is it that 'we generally believe' . . . one could venture to say that at the end of the sixteenth century the rate of illiteracy for the adult population in Western Europe was below 50 percent in the towns of the relatively more advanced areas and above 50 percent in all rural areas as well as in the towns of the backward areas. This is a frightfully vague statement . . . but the available evidence does not permit more precision.[56]

Statements about literacy rates during the fourteenth and early fifteenth centuries are likely to be just as vague – perhaps even more so. In the absence of hard data, plausible arguments may be developed to support sharply divergent opinions and there is no way of settling the inevitable conflict between revolutionary and evolutionary models of change. Thus one may envisage a relatively swift 'educational revolution' in the sixteenth century, in which case the effects produced by printing will loom large; or one may instead describe a 'long revolution' which unfolds so slowly that these effects are completely flattened out.[57]

In view of the fragmentary evidence that is available and the prolonged fluctuations that were entailed, it would seem prudent to bypass vexed problems associated with the spread of literacy until other issues have been explored with more care. That there are other issues worth exploring – apart from the expansion of the reading public or the 'spread' of new ideas – is in itself a point that needs underlining (and that will be repeatedly underscored). When considering the *initial* transformations wrought by print, at all events, changes undergone by groups who were already literate ought to receive priority over the undeniably fascinating problem of how rapidly such groups were enlarged.

Once attention has been focused on already literate sectors, it becomes clear that their social composition calls for further thought. Did printing at first serve prelates and patricians as a 'divine art' or should one think of it rather as the 'poor man's friend'? It was described in both ways by contemporaries, and probably served in both ways as well. When one recalls scribal functions performed by Roman slaves or later by monks, lay brothers, clerks and notaries, one may conclude that literacy had never been congruent with élite social status.[58] One may also guess that it was more compatible with sedentary occupations than with the riding and hunting favored by many squires and lords.[59] In this light, it may be misguided to envisage the new presses as making available to low-born men products previously used only by the high born. That many rural areas remained untouched until after the coming of the railway age seems likely. Given the large peasant population in early-modern Europe and the persistence of local dialects which imposed an additional language barrier between spoken and written words, it is probable that only a very small portion of the entire population was affected by the initial shift. Nevertheless within this relatively small and largely urban population, a fairly wide social spectrum may have been involved. In fifteenth-century England, for example, mercers and scriveners engaged in a manuscript book-trade were already catering to the needs of lowly bakers and merchants as well as to those of lawyers, aldermen, or knights.[60] The proliferation of literate merchants in fourteenth-century Italian cities is no less notable than the presence of an illiterate army commander in late sixteenth-century France.[61]

It would he a mistake, however, to assume that a distaste for reading was especially character-istic of the nobility, although it seems plausible that a distaste for Latin pedantry was shared by lay aristocrat and commoner alike. It also remains uncertain whether one ought to describe the early reading public as being 'middle class'. Certainly extreme caution is needed when matching genres of books with groups of readers. All too often it is taken for granted that 'low-brow' or 'vulgar' works reflect 'lower class' tastes, despite contrary evidence offered by authorship and library catalogues.[62] Before the advent of mass literacy the most 'popular' works were those which appealed to diverse groups of readers and not just to the plebes.

Divisions between Latin and vernacular reading publics are also much more difficult to correlate with social status than many accounts suggest. It is true that the sixteenth-century phys-ician who used Latin was regarded as superior to the surgeon who did not, but also true that neither man was likely to belong to the highest estates of the realm. Insofar as the vernacular translation movement was aimed at readers who were unlearned in Latin, it was often designed to appeal to pages as well as apprentices; to landed gentry, cavaliers and courtiers as well as to shopkeepers and clerks. In the Netherlands, a translation from Latin into French often pointed away from the urban laity who knew only Lower Rhenish dialects and toward relatively exclusive courtly circles. At the same time, a translation into 'Dutch' might be aimed at preachers who needed to cite scriptural passages in sermons rather than at the laity (which is too often assumed to be the only target for 'vernacular' devotional works). Tutors trying to educate young princes; instructors in court or church schools; and chaplains translating from Latin in response to royal requests had pioneered in 'popularizing' techniques even before the printer set to work.

But the most vigorous impetus given to popularization before printing came from the felt need of preachers to keep their congregations awake and also to hold the attention of diverse outdoor crowds.[63] Unlike the preacher, the printer could only guess at the nature of the audience to which his work appealed. Accordingly, one must be especially careful when taking the titles of early printed books as trustworthy guides to readership. A case in point is the frequent description of the fifteenth-century picture Bible, which was issued in both manuscript and then blockbook form, as the 'poor man's' Bible. The description may well be anachronistic, based on abbreviating the full Latin title given to such books. The *Biblia Pauperum Praedicatorum* was not aimed at poor men but at poor preachers who had a mere smattering of Latin and found scriptural exposition easier when given picture books as guides.[64] Sophisticated analysts have suggested the need to discriminate between 'audiences' – that is, actual readership as determined by library catalogues, subscription lists and other objective data – and 'publics', the more hypothetical targets envisaged by authors and publishers, those to whom they address their works.[65] Given the tendency to cite titles or prefaces as evidence of actual readership, this distinction is worth keeping in mind.

> To arrive at valid conclusions . . . we must proceed with care and caution. Information on the spread of reading and writing . . . is limited and must be supplemented by analysis of the subject contents of the total production (in itself not an easy task); this in turn provides circumstantial evidence on the composition of the reading public: a cookbook . . . reprinted eight or more times in the xvth century was obviously read by

people concerned with the preparation of food, the *Doctrinal des Filles . . .* a booklet on the behavior of young women, primarily by 'files' and 'mesdames'.[66]

Such 'circumstantial evidence', however, is highly suspect. Without passing judgment on the audience for early cookbooks (its character seems far from obvious to me), booklets pertaining to the behavior of young ladies did not necessarily attract feminine readers and were probably also of interest to male tutors, or confessors, or guardians. As a later chapter suggests, the circulation of printed etiquette books had wide-ranging psychological ramifications; their capacity to heighten the anxiety of parents should not go ignored. Furthermore such works were probably also read by authors, translators and publishers of other etiquette books. That authors and publishers were wide-ranging readers needs to be perpetually kept in mind. Even those sixteenth-century court poets who shunned printers and circulated their verse in manuscript form[67] took advantage of their own access to printed materials. It has been suggested that books describing double entry bookkeeping were read less by merchants than by the writers of accountancy books and teachers of accountancy. One wonders whether there were not more playwrights and poets than shepherds who studied so-called *Shepherd's Almanacks*. Given the corruption of data transmitted over the centuries, given the false remedies and impossible recipes contained in medical treatises, one hopes that they were studied more by poets than by physicians. Given the exotic ingredients described, one may assume that few apothecaries actually tried to concoct all the recipes contained in early printed pharmacopeia, although they may have felt impelled to stock their shelves with bizarre items just in case the new publicity might bring such items into demand.[68] The purposes, whether intended or actual, served by some early printed handbooks offer puzzles that permit no easy solution. What was the point of publishing vernacular manuals outlining procedures that were already familiar to all skilled practitioners of certain crafts?[69] It is worth remembering, at all events, that the gap between shoproom practice and classroom theory was just becoming visible during the first century of printing and that many so-called 'practical' handbooks and manuals contained impractical, even injurious, advice.

While postponing conjectures about social and psychological transformations, certain points should be noted here. One must distinguish, as Altick suggests, between literacy and habitual book reading. By no means all who mastered the written word have, down to the present, become members of a book-reading public.[70] Learning to *read* is different, moreover, from learning by reading. Reliance on apprenticeship training, oral communication and special mnemonic devices had gone together with mastering letters in the age of scribes. After the advent of printing, however, the transmission of written information became much more efficient. It was not only the craftsman outside universities who profited from the new opportunities to teach himself. Of equal importance was the chance extended to bright undergraduates to reach beyond their teachers' grasp. Gifted students no longer needed to sit at the feet of a given master in order to learn a language or academic skill. Instead they could swiftly achieve mastery on their own, even by sneaking books past their tutors – as did the young would-be astronomer, Tycho Brahe. 'Why should old men be preferred to their juniors now that it is possible for the young by diligent study to acquire the same knowledge?' asked the author of a fifteenth-century outline of history.[71]

As learning by reading took on new importance, the role played by mnemonic aids was diminished. Rhyme and cadence were no longer required to preserve certain formulas and recipes. The nature of the collective memory was transformed.

In Victor Hugo's *Notre Dame de Paris* a scholar, deep in meditation in his study . . . gazes at the first printed book which has come to disturb his collection of manuscripts. Then . . . he gazes at the vast cathedral, silhouetted against the starry sky . . . 'Ceci tuera cela', he says. The printed book will destroy the building. The parable which Hugo develops out of the comparison of the building, crowded with images, with the arrival in his library of a printed book might be applied to the effect on the invisible cathedrals of memory of the past of the spread of printing. The printed book will make such huge built-up memories, crowded with images, unnecessary. It will do away with habits of immemorial antiquity whereby a 'thing' is immediately invested with an image and stored in the places of memory.[72]

To the familiar romantic theme of the Gothic cathedral as an 'encyclopedia in stone', Frances Yates has added a fascinating sequel. Not only did printing eliminate many functions previously performed by stone figures over portals and stained glass in windows but it also affected less tangible images by eliminating the need for placing figures and objects in imaginary niches located in memory theatres. The way was paved for a more thorough-going iconoclasm than any Christian church had ever known. 'The "Ramist man" must smash the images both within and without, must substitute for the old idolatrous art, the new image-less way of remembering through abstract dialectical order'.[73]

This line of argument dovetails neatly with Walter Ong's earlier studies of Ramism and print culture – perhaps too neatly in the judgment of some medieval scholars who see evidence in medieval manuscripts of those diagrammatic features which Ong reserves for the printed page.[74] But even if all parts of the argument are not deemed equally acceptable, the basic point still seems valid. Printing made it possible to dispense with the use of images for mnemonic purposes and thus reinforced iconoclastic tendencies already present among many Christians. Successive editions of Calvin's *Institutes* elaborated on the need to observe the Second Commandment. The favorite text of the defenders of images was the dictum of Gregory the Great that statues served as 'the books of the illiterate'.[75] Although Calvin's scornful dismissal of this dictum made no mention of printing, the new medium did underlie the Calvinist assumption that the illiterate should not be given graven images but should be taught to read. In this light it may seem plausible to suggest that printing fostered a movement 'from image culture to word culture', a movement which was more compatible with Protestant bibliolatry and pamphleteering than with the Baroque statues and paintings sponsored by the post-Tridentine Catholic Church.

Yet the cultural metamorphosis produced by printing was really much more complicated than any single formula can possibly express.[76] For one thing, the graven image became more, rather than less, ubiquitous after the establishment of print shops throughout Western Europe. For another thing, Protestant propaganda exploited printed image no less than printed word – as numerous caricatures and cartoons may suggest. Even religious imagery was defended by some Protestants, and on the very grounds of its compatibility with print culture. 'If graving were taken away we could have not printing', wrote Stephen Gardiner, putting the case for images against Nicholas Ridley in 1547. 'And therefore they that press so much the words of *Non facies tibi sculptile* . . . they condemn printed books, the original whereof is graving to make *matrices literarum*'.[77] A close study of two versions of sixteenth-century Dutch Bibles, one Protestant, the other Catholic, suggests that there was indeed a tendency for Protestants to deemphasize pictures and stress words; yet at the same time, they did engage in illustrating Bibles – a movement which Lutherans, at least, encouraged.[78] Luther himself commented on the inconsistency of iconoclasts who tore pictures off walls while handling the illustrations in Bibles reverently. Pictures 'do no more harm on walls than in books', he commented and then, somewhat sarcastically, stopped short of pursuing this line of thought: 'I must cease lest I give occasion to the image breakers never to read the Bible or to burn it'.[79]

If we accept the idea of a movement from image to word, furthermore, we will be somewhat at a loss to account for the work of Northern artists, such as Dürer or Cranach or Holbein, who were affiliated with Protestantism and yet owed much to print. As Dürer's career may suggest, the new arts of printing and engraving, far from reducing the importance of images, increased opportunities for image makers and helped to launch art history down its present path. Even the imaginary figures and memory theatres described by Frances Yates did not vanish when their mnemonic functions were outmoded, but received a 'strange new lease on life'. They provided the content for magnificent emblem books and for elaborate Baroque illustrations to Rosicrucian and occult works in the seventeenth century. They also helped to inspire an entirely new genre of printed literature – tile didactic picture book for children. Leipzig boys in Leibniz' day 'were brought up on Comenius' picture book and Luther's Catechism'.[80] In this form, the ancient memory images re-entered the imagination of Protestant children, ultimately supplying Jung and his followers with evidence that suggested the hypothesis of a collective Unconscious. Surely the new vogue for image-packed emblem books was no less a product of sixteenth-century print culture than was the imageless 'Ramist' textbook.

Furthermore, in certain fields of learning such as architecture, geometry or geography and many of the life sciences as well, print culture was not merely incompatible with the formula offered above; it actually increased the functions performed by images while reducing those performed by words. Many fundamental texts of Ptolemy, Vitruvius, Galen and other ancients had lost their illustrations in the course of being copied for centuries and regained them only after script was replaced by print. To think in terms of a movement going from image to word points technical literature in the wrong direction. It was not the 'printed word' but the 'printed image' which acted as a 'savior for Western science' in George Sarton's view. Within the Commonwealth of Learning it became increasingly fashionable to adopt the ancient Chinese maxim that a single picture was more valuable than many words.[81] In early Tudor England, Thomas Elyot expressed a preference for 'figures and charts' over 'hearing the rules of a science'[82] which seems worth further thought. Although images were indispensable for prodding memory, a heavy reliance on verbal instruction had also been characteristic of communications in the age of scribes. To be sure, academic lectures were sometimes supplemented by drawing pictures on walls; verbal instructions to apprentices were accompanied by demonstrations; the use of blocks and boards, fingers and knuckles were common in teaching reckoning and gestures usually went with the recitation of key mnemonics. Nevertheless, when seeking rapid duplication of a given set of instructions, words simply had to take precedence over other forms of communication. How else save by using words could one dictate a text to assembled scribes? After the advent of printing, visual aids multiplied, signs and symbols were codified; different kinds of iconographic and non-phonetic communication were rapidly developed. The fact that printed picture books were newly designed by educational reformers for the purpose of instructing children and that drawing was considered an increasingly useful accomplishment by pedagogues also points to the need to think beyond the simple formula: image to word.

As these comments may suggest, efforts to summarize changes wrought by printing in any one statement or neat formula are likely to lead us astray. Even while acknowledging that there was an increased reliance on rule books and less on rules of thumb, or that learning by reading gained at the expense of hearing or doing; one must also consider how printing encouraged new objections to bookish knowledge based on 'slavish' copying and how it enabled many observers to check freshly recorded data against received rules. Similarly, one must be cautious about assuming that the spoken word was gradually silenced as printed words multiplied or that the faculty of hearing was increasingly neglected in favor of that of sight. Surely the history of Western music after Gutenberg argues against the latter suggestion. As for the many questions raised by the assertion that print silenced the spoken word, a few are noted elsewhere in this chapter; all must be passed over here.

The purpose of this preliminary section has been simply to demonstrate that the shift from script to print entailed a large ensemble of changes, each of which needs more investigation and all of which are too complicated to be encapsulated in any single formula. But to say that there is no simple way of summarizing the complex ensemble is not the same thing as saying that nothing had changed. To the contrary!

Granted that some sort of communications revolution did occur during the late fifteenth century, how did this affect other historical developments? Since the consequences of printing have not been thoroughly explored, guidance is hard to come by. Most conventional surveys stop short after a few remarks about the wider dissemination of humanist tomes or Protestant tracts. Several helpful suggestions – about the effects of standardization on scholarship and science, for example – are offered in works devoted to the era of the Renaissance or the history of science. By and large, the effects of the new process are vaguely implied rather than explicitly defined and are also drastically minimized. One example may illustrate this point. During the first centuries of printing, old texts were duplicated more rapidly than new ones. On this basis we are told that 'printing did not speed up the adoption of new theories'.[83] But where did these new theories come from? Must we invoke some spirit of the times, or is it possible that an increase in the output of old texts contributed to the formulation of new theories? Maybe other features that distinguished the new mode of book production from the old one also contributed to such theories. We need to take stock of these features before we can relate the advent of printing to other historical developments.

Notes

1   For estimate of numbers of printing offices and places of printing, see Lenhart, *Pre-Reformation Printed Books*, p. 7. For graphic presentation, see maps in Febvre and Martin, *L'Apparition*, p. 273, covering the two intervals: 1471 to 1480 and 1481 to 1500, and discussion in Hirsch's 1974 edition of *Printing, Selling*, p. x, concerning the updating of R. Teichl's more detailed rendering, 'Der Wiegendruck im Kartenbild'. Uhlendorf's 1932 article, 'The Invention and Spread of Printing', has not been superseded as a brief suggestive treatment of possible socioeconomic factors contributing to the rapid spread of printing, and the clustering of early presses in certain centers. When one considers the massive literature devoted to shifts in trade routes during the early-modern era, it is remarkable how little work has been done on shifts in communications centers.

2   Stillwell, *The Beginning of the World of Books*, offers useful guidance. See especially appendix A, pp. 75–87. Stillwell selects 1470 as a take-off point for the rapid spread of the new art (p. x).

3   That the age of incunabula should be extended to encompass the life-spans of the founders of early firms and hence to embrace the first few decades of the sixteenth century is persuasively argued by Steinberg, *Five Hundred Years*, pp. 15–17.

4   Clapham, 'Printing', p. 37. It is not clear whether Clapham takes 'all the scribes of Europe' to include those of Byzantium or not. If not, the statement becomes much more plausible.

5   The problematic and often composite nature of the medieval 'book' and the absence of any uniform conventions among medieval cataloguers who recorded them is discussed with many pertinent examples by E. P. Goldschmidt, *Medieval Texts*, pp. 95–101.

6   On the classic version derived from Vespasiano's *Lives*, see Burckhardt, *The Civilization of the Renaissance* I, part 3, chap. 3, p. 201. Doubts expressed by Ullman, *The Origin*, p. 132, have been thoroughly documented from surviving Fiesole accounts and mss. by de la Mare, 'Vespasiano', pp. 74–76 and appendix. (Her forthcoming study on 'Vespasiano and the Library of the Badia at Fiesole' to be published by the Warburg Institute will supply additional data.) She shows that Vespasiano obtained the books that filled the library by diverse methods, including the purchase of second-hand copies and reliance on other *cartolai*, and that the work took more than two years, encompassing an interval from 1461 until at least 1466–7. For recent use of the now discredited figures to estimate 'average' scribal output, see Burke, *Culture and Society*, p. 59.

7   De la Mare, 'Vespasiano', p. 207. The remarkable success of this 'uncommonly large edition' which was 'sold out in six years' when another printing took place is noted by Reynolds and Wilson, *Scribes and Scholars*, p. 130. According to Kristeller, 'Contribution of Religious Orders', p. 99, the Ripoli Press was 'one of the chief early presses in Florence'. In addition to the first edition of Ficino's Plato, which appeared in 1484, a 'Donatus' of 1476 and a *Book of Revelations* of 1478 are also noteworthy. The nuns of the Convent of San Jacopo di Ripoli, who ran the press, were 'the first women actually to print', according to Giles, 'Some Early Ladies', p. 1421. For basic work, see Nesi, *Il Diario della Stamperia di Ripoli*.

8   Harrington, 'The Production and Distribution', p. 3. This seems especially true when considering the fifty years before Gutenberg, when the system of the 'pecia' which had helped to speed duplication of large academic texts was no longer employed.

9   From conversation with Joseph Strayer, I learned that fourteenth-century French royal edicts were rapidly multiplied and distributed by a kind of 'chain letter' technique. At court, ten scribes were put to work producing ten copies each, some of which were carried by couriers to numerous provincial centers where the same procedure was repeated so that thousands of copies were quickly produced. See also evidence on Burgundian propaganda offered by Willard, 'The Manuscripts of Jean Petit'.

10   The 'enormous number' of manuscript copies of the Latin classics produced after the advent of paper is stressed by Kristeller, *Renaissance Thought*, pp. 14–15, who writes as a scholar concerned about the neglect of later Latin works and as an assiduous energetic investigator of Renaissance manuscript book lists. The compiler of *Iter Italicum* and *Latin Manuscript Books before 1600* is bound to be impressed by the remarkable output of copyists before print. Nevertheless, one must also make allowance for the fact that handmade copies, however enormous their number may seem, were still in very short supply compared to the number issued after printing. Paper was incapable of reducing the man-hours required for copying and hence could not achieve effects 'similar' to those produced by the press.

11   For a close-up view of the shop of an ordinary Florentine *cartolaio* who was engaged in binding books and selling writing materials rather than in procuring or producing books (although he kept some texts on hand for sale), see de la Mare, 'The Shop of a Florentine "Cartolaio" in 1426'.

12   De la Mare, 'Bartolomeo Scala's Dealings', p. 240.

13   De la Mare, 'Vespasiano', pp. 95–7; 226.

14   See de la Mare, 'Vespasiano', pp. 108–9 for laudatory verses.

15   *Art of the Printed Book 1455–1955*, introduction by Joseph Blumenthal, p. 9. The same assertion was made on the label attached to entry no. 55 in this exhibition.

16   Shenker, 'Books as an Art Form Through Five Centuries', *The New York Times* (10 Sept., 19731), 2nd sect., p. 1.

17   See Burckhardt, *The Civilization of the Renaissance in Italy* I, p. 204 where Duke Federigo's shame is attributed to the idea of owning a printed book and Cardinal Bessarion's envoys when seeing a printed book in the house of Constantine Lascaris 'laughed at the discovery made among the barbarians in some German city'. Burckhardt's use of Vespasiano is discussed by Wieruszowski, 'Burckhardt and Vespasiano'.

18   Bühler, *Fifteenth Century Book*, p. 62; de la Mare, 'Vespasiano', p. 112; Moranti, *L'Arte Tipografia in Urbino*, p. 9.

19   De la Mare, 'Bartolomeo Scala's Dealings', p. 241.

20   Goldschmidt, *Gothic and Renaissance Bookbindings* I, 43–4.

21   By 1910, when the article for the eleventh edition of the *Britannica* was written, Phillips's 'Faust', *Encyclopedia Britannica* X, 210, n. 1, could assert that 'the opinion, long maintained' of Faust and Fust being identical was 'now universally rejected'. Evidence showing that Fust was

in Paris selling books in 1466 when he was killed by the plague suggests that the outcome of his first business trip did not discourage him from making a later one.

22   The ambivalence of scholars who cursed the errors made by careless printers much as earlier authors had cursed careless scribes is brought out by Bühler, *Fifteenth Century Book*, pp. 50–1, and by Hirsch, *Printing, Selling*, p. 48, n. 20. Early tributes to the 'divine' art are conveniently collected by Stillwell, *The Beginning of the World of Books*, appendix A: 2, pp. 88 ff. They often echo tributes to the labors of scribes – a topos that goes back at least to Cassiodorus and which was publicized by early printings of both Gerson's and Trithemius' *De Laude Scriptorum*.

23   Gianandrea de' Bussi, a minor cleric, one-time private secretary to Nicholas of Cues and later Bishop of Aleria, helped to edit texts for Sweynheim and Pannartz (after they established the first press in Rome). In his dedicatory letter to Pope Paul II which appeared in the 1469 Roman edition of Saint Jerome's *Epistles* de' Bussi attributes the phrase 'divine art' ('Haec sancta ars') to Cusanus. Needless to say, early printers saw to it that the phrase received maximum exposure. A thoughtful essay on less well-publicized reactions – particularly some unpublished diatribes against early printing by a Dominican friar who had served as a copyist and reacted unfavorably to the Venetian press in the late fifteenth century – is contained in an article by Martin Lowry, 'Intellectuals and the Press in Fifteenth Century Venice' to appear in a forthcoming issue of the *Bulletin of the John Rylands University Library*.

24   De la Mare, 'Vespasiano', p. 113. On prices, see also Hirsch, *Printing, Selling*, pp. 68–73; Febvre and Martin, *L'Apparition*, chap. 4; Pettas, 'The Cost of Printing a Florentine Incunable'.

25   Of course, hindsight is required to show that technological unemployment was not severe, and fears, whether ultimately justified or not, may well have been aroused. On the new jobs created by printing, see Bühler, *Fifteenth Century Book*, pp. 25–7; Hirsch, *Printing, Selling*, pp. 48–9. In Florence the number of stationers' shops rose from twelve to thirty during the first half-century after the advent of the press. De la Mare, 'Vespasiano', p. 44.

26   See amusing speculations on sales of veal by Bühler, *Fifteenth Century Book*, p. 41.

27   Lehmann-Haupt, *Peter Schoeffer*, pp. 37–8.

28   Bühler, *Fifteenth Century Book*, p. 16. A detailed description of particular cases found in the Beinecke Library at Yale is offered by Lutz, 'Manuscripts Copied from Printed Books'.

29   Some Yale mss. marked up by early printers to be used as copy are noted by Lutz, 'Manuscripts Copied', p. 262, who also offers evidence of the irritation of a thirteenth-century scribe at a correction made by a bookdealer which destroyed the surface symmetry of two pages of a copy of a commentary by Thomas Aquinas.

30   For a pertinent example, see the account of the procedure used by Aldus Manutius' chief editor, Marcus Musurus, when preparing the printer's copy for the 1498 edition of Aristophanes' works. Reynolds and Wilson, *Scribes and Scholars*, pp. 132–3.

31   Lehmann-Haupt, *Peter Schoeffer*, pp. 53–4 contains relevant data.

32   Steinberg, *Five Hundred Years*, p. 28.

33   Steinberg, *Five Hundred Years*, p. 145. Along with many other authorities, both Steinberg (pp. 145 ff.) and Hirsch, *Printing, Selling*, p. 25, overstate the novelty of the title page when describing it as a purely post-print phenomenon. The Folger Library has a copy of Lorenzo Valla's *De Elegantiis Linguae Latinae* – Phillipps Ms 2966 (Folger 'v.a. 102') which is identified by A. M. de la Mare as being by the hand of a Veronese scribe: Cristoforo Schioppo. The name of the book's author, 'Lauretii Vallae', and part of the title are clearly placed on a single page as if engraved on a stone tablet. That this is by no means the only ms. 'title page' of its kind is attested to by Dr de la Mare. But the basic points made by Steinberg in his section on the title page are not really invalidated by his overlooking quattrocento humanist manuscripts and

taking Northern ms. styles for his norm. Title pages did not become common and information contained in colophons did not get shifted until after print.

34   Ivins, *Prints and Visual Communication*. Sonic specific examples discussed by Ivins are treated in later discussion of scientific data collection and early field trips.

35   See e.g., Bagrow, *History of Cartography*, p. 89; Skelton, *Maps*, p. 12; Robinson, 'Map Making', *Five Centuries of Map Printing*, p. 1. The illustrations (in this last mentioned work) of relevant tools and techniques are unusually clear and helpful.

36   Thus the second edition of Vesalius' *De Fabrica* profited from the sharpening of indistinct letters and lines by a Basel woodcarver using a fine knife. Woodblocks impressed only on moist paper and made of birchwood treated with hot linseed oil can remain unspoiled even after running off 3,000 to 4,000 copies, according to Willy Wiegand (who printed an edition of Vesalius' *Icones anatomicae* from old woodblocks in 1935). See Herrlinger, *History of Medical Illustration*, p. 113.

37   Ivins, *Prints and Visual Communication*, pp. 2, 11, 163.

38   Ivins, *Prints and Visual Communication*, p. 27.

39   See fascinating section on 'indication lines' in Herrlinger, *History of Medical Illustration*, pp. 54–60. I owe thanks to Karen Reeds for bringing this to my attention.

40   Questions pertaining to the relationship between block-printing and book-printing and to whether the block book preceded the invention and use of movable type have given rise to a massive controversial literature that cannot be examined here. To sample recent arguments see Musper, 'Xylographic Books', pp. 345–7 (esp. bibliography p. 347), and Lehmann-Haupt, *Gutenberg and the Master of the Playing Cards*. A close-up view of the overlap between hand illumination and early Mainz printing is offered by Vaassen, *Die Werkstatt der Mainzer Riesenbibel in Würzburg und Ihr Umkreis*. See review article by Labarre, 'Un Atelier Mayençais d'Enluminure vers 1450–1500'. For stimulating speculation relating changes in shop structure to new handbooks for illuminators, see Bober's review of *The Göttingen Model Book*.

41   Sarton, *Appreciation of Ancient and Medieval Science During the Renaissance 1450–1600*, p. xi.

42   I borrow these terms from Derek de Solla Price's article, 'Geometrical and Scientific Talismans'.

43   How the diverse skills of the punchcutter, matrix-maker and mold-maker got lumped under the heading of 'typefounder' is discussed by Harry Carter, *A View of Early Typography*, p. 92.

44   The widely varying social and occupational origins of early printers, extracted from biographical dictionaries such as those compiled by E. Voullième and Joseph Benzing for German-speaking regions, are indicated by Hirsch, *Printing, Selling*, pp. 18–23. A 'flocking of priests into printing' is noted on p. 22 and the numbers of priests and bishops involved in proof-reading, on p. 47. How a former monk and abbot abandoned his monastery to work full-time as an editor for Peter Schoeffer's early firm is noted by Lehmann-Haupt, *Peter Schoeffer*, p. 83, n. 6. A recent finely detailed study of the Paris book-trade in the mid-sixteenth century confirms the impression of diverse backgrounds among those entering the trade: Parent, *Les Métiers du Livre*, pp. 175 ff. Parent also notes that publication of devotional literature was often supervised by a priest who was sent by a bishop to receive room and board from the printer (p. 122).

45   References to pertinent studies are given by Hirsch, *Printing, Selling*, p. 51. Bühler, *The University and the Press in 15th Century Bologna*, pp. 15–16, gives an example of a contract drawn up in 1470 to build and run a press for academic purposes. The complex arrangements that went into the printing for academic purposes of a massive commentary on Avicenna's *Canon* (comprising over a thousand double column large folio-sized pages of text) are described by Mardersteig, *Remarkable Story*.

46   He was such a protean figure that no one label such as 'printer' adequately designates his many-faceted role.

47   Mardersteig's *Remarkable Story* shows the printer, Petrus Maufer, coping with strikes and many
      other complications before triumphantly concluding the actual printing which began in May
      1477 when the first reams of paper were delivered. From then until December 1, 1477 when
      the last sheet came off the press, 'not a working day was wasted'. Four hand presses had been
      in operation from daybreak to night-time without interruption, and 6,800,000 separate
      pieces of type had been procured and used. For general description of the complex working
      routines observed in most print shops during the first centuries after Gutenberg, McKenzie's
      article, 'Printers of the Mind', is unexcelled. A useful glimpse of Plantin's operational plan is
      given by Lotte and Wytze Hellinga, 'Regulations'. That routines were somewhat more
      orderly than either McKenzie or the Hellingas imply is suggested by K. I. D. Maslen and John
      Gerritsen, correspondence in *The Library* (June, 1975).

48   Martin Lowry, *The World of Aldus Manutius* (Oxford: Blackwell, 1979).

49   In sustaining a gradual evolutionary approach to the impact of printing, authorities on the
      history of the book naturally emphasize the stationer as the true precursor of the printer. Yet
      use of the term *scriptor* for *impressor* by printers showed that they considered themselves the
      successors not of stationers but of copyists. (See Hirsch, *Printing, Selling*, p. 19, n. 21.) It
      seems fair to say that early printers took over functions performed both by copyists and by
      stationers (or 'publishers') while diverging from both in significant ways.

50   See Lehmann-Haupt, *Peter Schoeffer, passim*.

51   Much of this is covered in detail by Febvre and Martin, *L'Apparition*, chap. 6, and is also well
      documented by Pollard and Ehrman, *The Distribution of Books*. Hirsch, *Printing, Selling*, pp. 63–
      4 points out how Schirokauer's (1951) study drastically underestimates the size of markets
      tapped by early printers.

52   Wytze Hellinga, 'Thomas à Kempis', pp. 4–5.

53   Although Steinberg, *Five Hundred Years* (p. 22) stresses this aspect of Gutenberg's invention as
      the most far-reaching, it receives little attention from Febvre and Martin, *L'Apparition*, because
      of their focus on 'the book'. 'Jobbing printing' was also, with one exception, omitted from
      the exhibition on 'Printing and the Mind of Man' assembled at the British Museum and at
      Earl's Court, July 16–27, 1963. See British Museum Catalogue (London, 1963) p. 8. Official
      printing for ecclesiastical and secular governments is discussed by Hirsch, *Printing, Selling*,
      pp. 52–3. It furnished an important part of Peter Schoeffer's output, according to
      Lehmann-Haupt, *Peter Schoeffer*, pp. 78–9.

54   See item 7, Catalogue of Exhibition held in the Royal Library of Brussels (Sept.–Oct. 1973):
      Le Cinquième Centenaire de L'Imprimerie dans les Anciens Pays-Bas (Brussels, 1973), pp. 11–12, and
      footnote reference to B. Kruitwagen, 'Her Schrijven op Feestdagen in de Middeleeuwen'. One
      might compare this medieval approach to holy-day book making with the indignation of a
      member of the Royal Society at printing delays caused by 'the holy days sticking in the
      workman's hands', cited by Hill, book review, *English Historical Review* (1973).

55   Printed announcements of university lectures containing blurbs for pertinent books on sale
      are described by Hirsch, *Printing, Selling*, p. 51, and Parent, *Les Métiers*, p. 142.

56   Cipolla, *Literacy*, p. 60.

57   See Cipolla, *Literacy*, p. 52, where he discusses whether Lawrence Stone's concept of an
      'educational revolution' in England is relevant to continental trends. In his article on 'Literacy
      and Education', p. 78, Stone underlines the importance of cheap paper and movable type
      whereas Williams, *The Long Revolution*, pp. 132–3, discusses the interval encompassed by
      Stone's 'educational revolution' without mentioning printing at all. On pp. 156–7, Williams
      mentions printing but traces the growth of the reading public back to the eighth century and
      beyond to Rome. When this approach is coupled with emphasis on the advent of a mass
      reading public after the steam press, the fifteenth-century typographical revolution is bound
      to recede. Williams does bring out the importance of printing as against writing in his brief

study of *Communications*, p. 22. The topic is especially likely to be underplayed in connection with the history of education. See e.g. Talbott, 'The History of Education', where a survey of the literature shows printing to be omitted from among factors which 'triggered educational expansion' in early-modern England (p. 136).

58   The very term 'poor man's book' ('Liber Pauperum') goes back at least as far as the twelfth century in England where a Lombard master arranged a compilation of the Code and Digest for poor law clerks. Cf. Haskins, *The Renaissance of the Twelfth Century*, p. 211.

59   Thus in Richard Pace's celebrated anecdote about the early Tudor squire who questioned the need to teach his sons how to read, hunting and hawking are opposed to armchair study.

60   Jacob, *The Fifteenth Century*, pp. 663–7. See also Adamson, 'The Extent of Literacy in England', pp. 163–93; Bennett, *English Books and Readers 1457–1557*, p. 20; Parkes, 'The Literacy of the Laity'. Thrupp, *The Merchant Class*, p. 157, provides a useful table as well as relevant data.

61   See Renouard, *Etudes d'Histoire Médiévale*, I, pp. 419–26; Jeannin, *Merchants of the Sixteenth Century*, pp. 80–6; Sapori, *The Italian Merchant, passim*. Bec, *Les Marchands Ecrivains, passim*, has data on the numerous merchants who kept diaries as well as accounts.

62   Useful warnings on this point are offered by Natalie Z. Davis, 'Printing and the People'.

63   A thirteenth-century Dominican manual: *De Arte Predicandi* issued on 'how to sew a sermon together quickly' and how to appeal to special interest groups such as 'rich women in towns' or 'crowds at fairs' or 'young girls' is described by Murray, 'Religion among the Poor'.

64   James Strachan, *Early Bible Illustrations*, p. 7, raises the question of whether the abbreviated title *Biblia Pauperum* is appropriate or not.

65   This distinction, suggested by T. J. Clark in his study of Courbet, is discussed in connection with problems posed by sixteenth-century 'popular' culture by Natalie Davis, 'Printing and the People'. It seems futile to try to restrict usage of terms already employed interchangeably in a large literature. I prefer the phrase: 'assumed public' (which is used by Davis elsewhere in the same article) since it is less likely to be misinterpreted.

66   Hirsch, *Printing, Selling*, p. 7.

67   Saunders, 'From Manuscript to Print', pp. 507–28.

68   On accountancy books, almanacs, pharmacopeia and other 'practical' guide-books see Natalie Davis, 'Printing and the People'.

69   In his *Speculum* review of *The Göttingen Model Book*, Harry Bober suggests that the detailed instructions for illumination contained therein (which included sixteen separate steps for painting one acanthus leaf) must have been aimed at a new group of untrained craftsmen mobilized by printers since scribal illuminators had no need of such a manual – any more than 'an experienced chef needs the numbered instructions on soup cans'. Even if this argument holds good for book-making, it still leaves open questions raised by other craft manuals in trades where there was no dramatic change in shop structure or influx of neophytes. The purposes served by the early publication of vernacular booklets by the two German master masons: Matthias Roriczer and Hans Schmuttermayer, for example, remain somewhat baffling, as I have learned from two articles by Shelby, 'The Education of Medieval English Master Masons', pp. 1–26; 'The Geometrical Knowledge', pp. 395–421, and correspondence with their author.

70   Altick, *The English Common Reader*, p. 31.

71   Jacobo Filippo Foresti, *Supplementum Chronicarum* (Venice, 1483), cited by Martin Lowry in his biography of Aldus.

72   Yates, *Art of Memory*, p. 131.

73   Yates, *Art of Memory*, p. 271.

74   In slide lectures given at Catholic University during the 1974 Medieval Academy Summer Institute program on 'The Archeology of the Book', Professor Richard H. Rouse of U.C.L.A. demonstrated graphically the frequent use of diagrams, brackets, cross-references, marginal

guides and other devices in scribal compilations (especially in concordances and guides to patristic works) produced by medieval teachers and preachers.

75   Myron Gilmore, 'Italian Reactions to Erasmian Humanism', pp. 87–8.

76   Although Stone, 'Literacy and Education', p. 76, cites my preliminary 'Conjectures' as suggesting that the printed book caused Europe to move 'decisively from image culture to word culture' I am not convinced that this formulation is valid and regret any inadvertent implication that such a movement occurred. That Protestant bibliolatry and iconoclasm were more compatible with early print culture than Tridentine Catholicism was suggested in my article but that is a different matter than suggesting that European culture moved from image to word. For objections to the latter formulation, see paragraphs following this note in text above.

77   *The Letters of Stephen Gardiner*, pp. 258–9. I owe this reference and the one from Luther below to Margaret Aston, who is completing a major study of iconoclasm in Tudor England.

78   Hindman, 'The Transition from Manuscripts'. See esp. p. 205.

79   'Against the Heavenly Prophets in the Matter of Images and Sacraments' (1525), *Luther's Works*, XL 99–400. On Lutheran Bible illustration, see Ph. Schmidt, *Die Illustration der Lutherbibel 1522–1700*.

80   Yates, *Art of Memory*, pp. 134; 377. The magnificent Baroque engravings that made visible the elaborate memory systems developed in the sixteenth and seventeenth centuries may be sampled by examining almost any work by Robert Fludd. How much Comenius' *Orbis Pictus* (1658) owed to Campanella's *City of the Son* and Rosicrucian manifestos is noted by Yates, p. 377.

81   Sarton, *Appreciation*, pp. 91; 95. As is noted, the notion that the ancient Egyptians had compressed valuable data in each hieroglyph was believed by would-be decipherers of hieroglyphs until the nineteenth-century discovery of the Rosetta Stone.

82   See citation from the *Boke Called the Gouvernour* (1531) in Watson, *The Beginning of the Teaching of Modern Subjects in England*, p. 136.

83   Febvre and Martin, *L'Apparition*, pp. 420–1.

References

Adamson, J. W. 'The Extent of Literacy in England in the Fifteenth and Sixteenth Centuries: Notes and Conjectures', *The Library*, 4th ser. x (1929) 163–93.

Altick, R. *The English Common Reader. A Social History of the Mass Reading Public 1800–1900* (Chicago, 1963).

Bagrow, Leo. *History of Cartography*, rev. and ed. R. A. Skelton (Cambridge, Mass., 1964).

Bec, Christian (1967) *Les Marchands Ecrivains; Affaires et Humanisme à Florence 1375–1434* (Paris: Mouton).

Bennett, H. S. *English Books and Readers 1475–1557* (Cambridge, 1952).

Blumenthal, Joseph. Introduction. *Art of the Printed Book 1455–1955* (New York, 1973).

Bober, Harry. *Review of The Göttingen Model Book*, ed. H. Lehmann-Haupt, *Speculum* XLIX (April 1974) 354–8.

Bühler, Curt. *The Fifteenth Century Book, the Scribes, the Printers, the Decorators* (Philadelphia, 1960).

—— *The University and the Press in 15th Century Bologna*, Texts and Studies in the History of Medieval Education, vol. VII (South Bend, Indiana, 1958).

Burckhardt, Jacob. *The Civilization of the Renaissance in Italy*, tr. S. C. C. Middlemore, ed. B. Nelson and C. Trinkaus (2 vol. New York, 1958).

Burke, Peter. *Culture and Society in Renaissance Italy 1420–1540* (London, 1972).

Cipolla, Carlo M. *Literacy and Development in the West* (London, 1969).

Clapham, Michael. 'Printing', *A History of Technology*: II *From the Renaissance to the Industrial Revolution*, ed. Charles Singer, F. J. Holmyard, A. R. Hall and Trevor Williams (4 vol. Oxford, 1957) 377–411.

Davis, Natalie Zemon. 'Printing and the People', *Society and Culture in Early Modern France: Eight Essays* (Palo Alto, California, 1975).

De la Mare, Albinia. 'Bartolomeo Scala's Dealings with Booksellers, Scribes and Illuminators, 1459–63', *Journal of the Warburg and Courtauld Institutes* XXXIX (1976) 237–45.

—— 'The Shop of a Florentine "Cartolaio" in 1426', *Studi Offerti a Roberto Ridolfi* (Florence, 1973) 237–48.

—— 'Vespasiano and the Library of the Badia at Fiesole' to be published by the Warburg Institute. Forthcoming.

—— 'Vespasiano da Bisticci Historian and Bookseller' (unpublished doctoral dissertation, London University, 1965).

Ehrman, Albert and Pollard, Graham (1965) *The Distribution of Books by Catalogue from the Invention of Printing to A.D. 1800*, (Cambridge: Roxburghe Club).

Febvre, Lucien and Martin, H.-J. *L'Apparition du Livre* (Paris, 1958).

Gardiner, Stephen. *The Letters of Stephen Gardiner*, ed. J. A. Muller (Cambridge, UK, 1933).

Giles, Dorothy. 'Some Early Ladies of the Book Trade', *The Publishers Weekly* (Oct. 5, 1940).

Gilmore, Myron P. 'Italian Reactions to Erasmian Humanism', *Itinerarium Italicum*, ed. H. Oberman (Leiden, 1975) 61–115.

Goldschmidt, E. P. *Gothic and Renaissance Bookbindings* (2 vol. Amsterdam, 1967).

—— *Medieval Texts and Their First Appearance in Print* (London, 1943).

Harrington, J. H. 'The Production and Distribution of Books in Western Europe to the Year 1500' (unpublished dissertation, Columbia University, 1956).

Haskins, C. H. *The Renaissance of the Twelfth Century* (Cambridge, Mass., 1939).

Hellinga, Wytze. 'Thomas à Kempis – The First Printed Editions', *Quaerendo* IV (1974) 3–30.

Hellinga, Lotte and Wytze. 'Regulations Relating to the Planning and Organization of Work by the Master Printer in the Ordinances of Christopher Plantin', *The Library*, 5th ser. XXIX (March 1974) 52–61.

Herrlinger, Robert. *History of Medical Illustration from Antiquity to 1600*, tr. G. Fulton-Smith (New York, 1970).

Hill, Christopher. Book review, *English Historical Review* LXXXVIII (April 1973) 383–5.

Hindman, Sandra. 'The Transition from Manuscripts to Printed Books in the Netherlands: Illustrated Dutch Bibles', In *Navolging, Een bundel studies aangeboden ann C. C. de Bruin* (Leiden, 1975) 189–209.

Hirsch, Rudolf. *Printing, Selling, and Reading 1450–1550* (Wiesbaden, 1967; rev. edn, 1974).

Ivins, Jr., William M. *Prints and Visual Communication* (Cambridge, Mass., 1953).

Jacob, E. F. *The Fifteenth Century 1399–1485* (Oxford History of England) (Oxford, 1961).

Jeannin, Pierre. *Merchants of the Sixteenth Century*, tr. P. Fittingoff (New York, 1972).

Kristeller, Paul Oskar. *Iter Italicum: A Finding List of Uncatalogued Humanistic Mss* (2 vol. London and Leiden, 1963–67) I, preface, xi–xxviii.

—— *Latin Manuscript Books before 1600* (New York, 1965).

—— *Renaissance Thought: The Classic, Scholastic and Humanist Strains* (New York, 1961).

—— 'The Contribution of Religious Orders to Thought and Learning', *Medieval Aspects of Renaissance Learning: Three Essays*, ed. E. P. Mahoney (Durham, N.C., 1974) 95–159.

Kruitwagen, B. 'Het Schrijven op Feestdagen in de Middeleuwen', *Tijdschrift voor Boek en Bibliotheek Wezen* V (1907) 97–120.

Labarre, A. 'Un Atelier Mayençais d'Enluminure vers 1450–1500', *Revue Française d'Histoire du Livre* IV (1974) 127–31.

Lehmann-Haupt, Hellmut. *Gutenberg and the Master of the Playing Cards* (New Haven, 1966).

—— *Peter Schoeffer of Gernsheim and Mainz* (Rochester, New York, 1950).

Lenhart, John M. *Pre-Reformation Printed Books: A Study in Statistical and Applied Bibliography* (Franciscan Studies no. 14) (New York, 1935).

Luther, Martin. 'Against the Heavenly Prophets in the Matter of Images and Sacraments' (1525), *Luther's Works*, ed. C. Bergendorff and H. J. Lehmann, XL (Philadelphia, 1958) 99–100.

Lutz, Cora E. 'Manuscripts Copied from Printed Books', *Essays on Manuscripts and Rare Books* (Hamden, Conn., 1975) 129–39.

McKenzie, D. F. 'Printers of the Mind: Some Notes on Bibliographical Theories and Printing House Practices', *Studies in Bibliography* XXII (Charlottesville, Va., 1969) 1–75.

Mardersteig, Giovanni. *The Remarkable Story of a Book Made in Padua in 1477*, tr. H. Schmoller (London, 1967).

Maslen, K. I. D. and Gerritsen, John. Correspondence, *The Library* XXX (June 1975) 81–94, 134–6.

Moranti, Luigi. *L'Arte Tipografia in Urbino* (Florence, 1967).

Murray, Alexander. 'Religion among the Poor in Thirteenth-century France', *Traditio* XXX (1974) 287–324.

Musper, Heinrich T. 'Xylographic Books', *The Book Through Five Thousand Years*, ed. H. D. L. Vervliet (Brussels, 1972) 341–8.

Nesi, Emilia. *Il Diario della Stamperia di Ripoli* (Florence, 1903).

Parent, Annie. *Les Métiers du Livre à Paris au XVIe Siècle (1535–1560)* (Geneva, 1974).

Parkes, Malcolm B. 'The Literacy of the Laity', *The Medieval World*, ed. D. Daiches and A. Thorlby (*Literature and Western Civilization*, Vol. II) (London, 1972–6) 555–76.

Pettas, William. 'The Cost of Printing a Florentine Incunable', *La Bibliofila* LXXV (1973) 67–85.

Phillips, W. A. 'Faust', *Encyclopedia Britannica* X (28 vol. 11 edn, London, 1910–11) 210–11.

Price, Derek de Solla. 'Geometrical and Scientific Talismans', *Changing Perspectives in the History of Science: Essays in Honor of Joseph Needham*, ed. M. Teich and R. Young (London, 1973) 250–64.

Renouard, Yves. *Etudes d'Histoire Médiévale* (2 vol. Paris, 1968).

Reynolds, L. D. and Wilson, N. G. *Scribes and Scholars* (Oxford, 1968).

Robinson, Arthur H. 'Map Making and Map Printing', *Five Centuries of Map Printing*, ed. David Woodward (Chicago, 1975) 1–25.

Sapori, Armando. *The Italian Merchant in the Middle Ages*, tr. P. A. Kennen (New York, 1970).

Sarton, George. *Appreciation of Ancient and Medieval Science During the Renaissance 1450–1600* (New York, 1958, 2nd edn).

Saunders, J. W. 'From Manuscript to Print: A Note on the Circulation of Poetic Manuscripts in the Sixteenth Century', *Proceedings of the Leeds Philosophical and Literary Society* VI (May 1951) 507–28.

Schmidt, Ph. *Die Illustration der Lutherbibel 1522–1700* (Basel, 1962).

Shelby, Lon R. 'The Education of Medieval English Master Masons', *Medieval Studies* (Toronto) XXXII (1970) 1–26.

—— 'The Geometrical Knowledge of Medieval Master Masons', *Speculum* XLVII (July 1972) 395–421.

Shenker, Israel. 'Books as an Art Form Through Five Centuries', *The New York Times* (Sept. 10, 1973).

Skelton, R. A. *Maps: A Historical Survey* (Chicago, 1972).

Steinberg, S. H. *Five Hundred Years of Printing* (rev. edn, Bristol, 1961).

Stillwell, Margaret Bingham. *The Beginning of the World of Books 1450 to 1470. A Chronological Survey of the Texts Chosen for Printing . . . With a Synopsis of the Gutenberg Documents* (New York, 1972).

Stone, Lawrence. 'Literacy and Education in England 1640–1900', *Past and Present* 42 (Feb. 1969) 69–139.

Strachan, James. *Early Bible Illustrations: A Short Study* (Cambridge, 1957).

Talbott, John E. 'The History of Education', *Daedalus* 100 (Winter 1971) 133–51.

Teichl, R. 'Der Wiegendruck im Kartenbild', *Bibliothek und Wissenschaft* I (1964) 210–65.

Thrupp, Sylvia, *The Merchant Class of Medieval London (1300–1500* (Ann Arbor, 1962).

Uhlendorf, B. A. 'The Invention and Spread of Printing till 1470 with Special Reference to Social and Economic Factors', *The Library Quarterly* II (1932) 179–231.

Ullman, B. L. *The Origin and Development of Humanistic Script* (Rome, 1960).

Watson, Foster. *The Beginning of the Teaching of Modern Subjects in England* (London, 1909).

Wieruszowski, Helen. 'Burckhardt and Vespasiano', *Philosophy and Humanism: Essays in Honor of P. O. Kristeller*, ed. E. P. Mahoney (New York, 1976) 387–405.

Willard, C. C. 'The Manuscripts of Jean Petit's Justification: Some Burgundian Propaganda Methods of the Early Fifteenth Century', *Studi Francesi* 38 (1969) 271–80.

Williams, Raymond. *Communications* (London, 1962).

—— *The Long Revolution* (New York, 1966).

Yates, Frances. *The Art of Memory* (London, 1966).

Chapter 18

Adrian Johns

THE BOOK OF NATURE AND THE NATURE OF THE BOOK

Pick up a modern book. This one will do: the one you are looking at right now. What sort of object is this? There are certain features about it of which you can be reasonably confident. Its professed author does indeed exist and did indeed write it. It contains information believed to be accurate, and it professes to impart knowledge to readers like you. It is produced with its author's consent, and it is indeed the edition it claims to be. If the dust jacket announces that it is the product of a given organization – for example the University of Chicago Press – then this too may be believed. Perhaps you may even say to yourself that that fact vouches for the quality of its content. You may safely assume that the book you now hold will have been printed in many copies, and a copy of the same book bought in Australia, say, will be identical in all relevant respects to one bought in the United States or in Great Britain.

Begin to use this object. It should immediately become clear that there are things about its proper utilization of which a reader like you can be equally confident. This book has not been produced with a specific, individual reader in mind. To some extent, at least, it is a commercial product, designed to appeal to purchasers. Its cost may have limited its readership somewhat, but its distribution will still have been fairly widespread, and it may be available for consultation in a number of libraries. Readers will not have to endure any formal vetting or approval process before being permitted to read this book. You yourself are free to carry it around and to lend it to others. You are not free, however – beyond certain legal limits – to reproduce its contents in your own right for commercial gain. Nor may you now proceed to issue translations, epitomes, or abridgments of those contents. It is improbable (but not impossible) that you will choose to declaim the text of this book aloud in a public place, and it is even more unlikely that you will make it the focus of a collective act of commemoration, worship, or similar ritual. Some books are indeed used in these ways, incidentally, but this is probably not going to be one of them. In short, while in some respects this book's usage is up to you, in others it appears to be quite closely constrained.

That we can assume all these things of such an object – that such an object actually exists – derives from our living in what many people call 'print culture'. Such phenomena, we say, are due to printing. Or rather, we would say this, but so infallibly reliable are they that we rarely even have to articulate the relation. It is obvious, self-evident, even necessary. The practical consequence is that we do not have to agonize over the reliability of a published book before we can put it to use. We do not need to undertake investigatory work to confirm that its author does exist and that its text is authorized. No literary spy need be hired to ascertain that it was indeed made by its stated publisher and that its contents will be the same as those of another copy of the same book found in any other place. In our world, all these characteristics are inherent in virtually any published book (and the duties of a 'literary agent' are comparatively mundane). We take them for granted, every day of our lives. We depend on them, and our reliance is, by and large, justified.

It is this very self-evidence that encourages us to ascribe all these characteristics to a technological order of reality. If called upon, we may assert that printed texts are identical and reliable because that is simply what printing *is*. The identification is as momentous as it is straightforward. It has become the point of departure for all current interpretations of print and its cultural consequences, and is the root from which the very concept of 'print culture' has grown.[1] It is thereby also the foundation of a conviction that that culture has rendered possible the establishment of veracious knowledge in modern society. Yet this book [i.e. Johns's book] argues that it is substantially false. Not only that: *The Nature of the Book* maintains that it is probably the most powerful force resisting the acceptance of a truly historical understanding of print and any cultural consequences it may foster.

This book contends that what we often regard as essential elements and necessary concomitants of print are in fact rather more contingent than generally acknowledged. Veracity in particular is, it argues, extrinsic to the press itself, and has had to be grafted onto it. The same may be said of other cognate attributes associated with printing. In short, *The Nature of the Book* claims that the very identity of print itself has had to be *made*. It came to be as we now experience it only by virtue of hard work, exercised over generations and across nations. That labor has long been overlooked, and is not now evident. But its very obscurity is revealing. It was dedicated to effacing its own traces, and necessarily so: only if such efforts disappeared could printing gain the air of intrinsic reliability on which its cultural and commercial success could be built. Recovering it is therefore a difficult task, but one well worth attempting. This book tries accordingly to excavate the complex issues involved in the historical shaping of print – issues that our conventional notion of print culture obscures with all the authority of a categorical definition. *The Nature of the Book* is the first real attempt to portray print culture in the making.

Yet how could print conceivably be anything else? If it were really the result of a significant process of historical construction, then surely we could not now find it so obvious, universal, and undeniable. If it could have developed differently, then surely it would now differ noticeably from place to place, and in any one place it would still bear the traces of its development. We would see the wreckage of failed alternatives all about us. In practical terms, we would indeed have to worry about the specific status of a given printed book in order to use it. Questions of where it had come from, who had made it, and whether or not its putative author acknowledged its content would all need to be posed and answered before we could safely trust any printed book. That they do not constitutes a powerful reason to accept the obvious.

Even a little reflection suggests that there is greater complexity to the subject than this. Any printed book is, as a matter of fact, both the product of one complex set of social and technological processes and also the starting point for another. In the first place, a large number of people, machines, and materials must converge and act together for it to come into existence at all. How exactly they do so will inevitably affect its finished character in a number of ways. In that sense a book is the material embodiment of, if not a consensus, then at least a collective consent. Its identity can be understood accordingly, in terms of these intricate processes. But the story of a book evidently does not end with its creation. How it is then put to use, by whom, in what circumstances, and to what effect are all equally complex issues. Each is worthy of attention in its own right. So a printed book can be seen as a nexus conjoining a wide range of worlds of work. Look closely and you are likely to find simplicity and inevitability in neither the manufacture of an object like this nor its subsequent construal. The processes leading to the deployment of a book and those consequent upon its use both depend on too many contingencies. That in turn means that print cannot be as straightforward as it seems.

One way to appreciate the implications is to examine more closely places where printing exists, but where its cultural consequences seem very different from those familiar to us. There are two such places, separated from us by space and by time. The first may be found in certain regions of the world where, to international publishers' disgust, so-called 'piracy' has become a prevalent commercial practice. You could not be so sure of all those 'self-evident' facts about this book if you had bought your copy in such a place. It might indeed prove reliable. But it might also have been produced by an anonymous manufacturer, and have different contents. Its purported author might have no idea of the claims it contained. Some such companies produce not just unauthorized reprints of existing books, but wholly new texts claiming to be written by bestselling authors. Their products threaten to compromise both the economic production of authorized works and, by generating correspondingly divergent readings, their reception. The potential effects are suggested by the most notorious of all recent controversies to arise from publishing. The author Salman Rushdie was complaining of piracy of his works in Pakistan and India long before the appearance of his *Satanic Verses*. When it did appear, the book was properly published in neither country; the protests that occurred in Lahore and elsewhere, and that first set in train the events leading eventually to Khomeini's fatwa, centered on the public reading of unauthorized copies and photocopied extracts. A Penguin representative even noted that piracy would permit readers to circumvent the Indian government's subsequent ban on the book.[2]

Rushdie's is admittedly an extreme case. But for good or ill, countless authors and publishers have encountered to some degree the loss of control induced by piracy. It means that the experiences associated with print are indeed different from those familiar to most Western readers. And any suggestion that the intrinsic cultural consequences of technology have simply been inadequately realized in such settings would be difficult to endorse. The evidence of recent international trade disputes indicates that modern technology, far from eliminating such practices, may even be facilitating them. The arguments currently raging over such matters are intense and important. Few claim to know how they will end.[3]

The alternative is to look not to other places in our own time, but to other times in our own place. It is possible to argue not only that print may differ from place to place, but also that its nature has changed over time even in our own society. If this is so, the implications are again substantial, but in rather different ways. Such an argument compels us to reappraise where our own concept of print culture comes from, how it developed, when it took hold, and why its sway continues to seem secure.

If an early modern reader picked up a printed book – *De Natura Libri*, perhaps – then he or she could not be immediately certain that it was what it claimed to be, and its proper use might not be so self-evident. Piracy was again one reason: illicit uses of the press threatened the credibility of all printed products. More broadly, ideas about the correct ways to make and use books varied markedly from place to place and time to time. But whatever the cause, it is not easy for us to imagine such a realm, in which printed records were not necessarily authorized or faithful. What could one know in such a realm, and how could one know it? We ourselves routinely rely on stable communications in our making and maintenance of knowledge, whether of the people around us or of the world in which we live. That stability helps to underpin the confidence we feel in our impressions and beliefs. Even the brisk skepticism we may express about certain printed materials – tabloid newspapers, say – rests on it, inasmuch as we feel confident that we can readily and consistently identify what it is that we are scorning. Instability in records would equally rapidly translate into uncertainty of judgment. The most immediate implication, then, would be epistemic.

In a sense, the point is a well-entrenched one. It has been made at least since the sixteenth century, when printers and others took to lauding their craft for its power to preserve. The contrast they drew was with previous scribal forms of reproduction, which they delineated as intrinsically corruptive. It now seems almost indisputable. We should recognize, however, that the first identification of that contrast was partly a product of interest. Printers stood to gain from what was originally a contentious argument, not a straightforward observation. If, on the other hand, it is not printing *per se* that possesses preservative power, but printing put to use in particular ways, then we ourselves may usefully draw some rather different distinctions. We may look not just for differences between print and manuscript reproduction, but for different ways in which the press itself and its products have been (and continue to be) employed. The roots of textual stability may be sought as much in these practices as in the press itself. And knowledge, such as it is, has come to depend on that stability. Here, then, is one way in which a social history of print can prove not just interesting, but consequential. A reappraisal of print in the making can contribute to our historical understanding of the conditions of knowledge itself.

Tycho Brahe, Galileo Galilei, and the problems of 'print culture'

In 1576 the king of Denmark granted Tycho feudal powers over a small island named Hven, lying in the sound just north of Copenhagen. Here Tycho erected a remarkable castle-observatory, in which he lived and worked for the next two decades. His work at this palatial observatory, which he called Uraniborg, resulted in an unequaled series of observations and interpretations of the heavens. They secured for him a reputation as the greatest of all astronomers. Almost immediately, Tycho himself became an icon of the very enterprise of astronomy. Mathematical practitioners in succeeding generations came to see in him an unimpugnable model of the harmony of nobility and 'mechanic' skill. In the hands of modern historians, moreover, Tycho has again proved a powerful emblem, in two important and revealingly paradoxical respects. First, Uraniborg has become the outstanding Renaissance exemplar of the importance of locale in the making of knowledge.[4] This is an important issue, to be addressed later in this chapter. At the same time, however, Tycho has come to personify the role of print in transcending place and rendering natural knowledge universal. He has thus become emblematic of the transformation of local craft into global science. This latter apotheosis has been due above all to Elizabeth Eisenstein's *The Printing Press as an Agent of Change*. Published in 1979, this is still probably the most influential anglophonic interpretation of the cultural effects of printing. Yet *The Nature of the Book* pursues for the most part a quite different approach from hers. A consideration of Tycho Brahe provides the ideal opportunity to specify how and why it does so.[5]

The unifying concept of Eisenstein's argument is that of 'print culture'. This 'culture' is characterized primarily in terms of certain traits that print is taken to endow on texts. Specifically, those produced in such an environment are subject to conditions of *standardization*, *dissemination*, and *fixity*. The last of these is perhaps the most important. According to Eisenstein, printing meant the mass reproduction of precisely the same text, repeatable on subsequent occasions and in different locations. No longer need any work suffer the increasing corruption that Eisenstein assumes to be endemic to any 'script culture'. She focuses on this attribute of fixity as the most important corollary of the press, seeing it as central to most of the effects of print culture.[6] For example, in conditions of fixity the simple practice of juxtaposing texts became immensely significant. Newly available printed representations of opposing astronomical, anatomical, or other knowledge could be placed side by side, and their viewer could now be confident that conclusions drawn from comparing such reliable texts would be worthwhile. Correspondents on the other side of Europe could do the same, with representations that could be supposed identical.[7] Such scholars no longer needed to concern themselves primarily with the fidelity of their representations, and were freed from spending their lives eradicating scribal mistakes. It was fixity that liberated them from such labor and thus made possible the progressive improvement of knowledge. This is the basis on which Eisenstein's main claim that the Renaissance and Reformation were rendered permanent by the very permanence of their canonical texts, that nationalism developed thanks to the stabilization of laws and languages, and that science itself became possible on the basis of phenomena and theories reliably recorded.[8] With this new foundation of certainty at their disposal, 'scientists' (as Eisenstein insists on calling them) could begin to develop new doubts about their previous authority, namely antiquity. The 'Scientific Revolution' was thus inconceivable without a preceding printing revolution.[9] And for Eisenstein Tycho Brahe personifies both.

Eisenstein's Tycho was an autodidact. This in itself was remarkable: before the printing revolution, not enough faithful editions could have been amassed in one place to enable him to teach himself. But while he was doing this, Tycho was able to place authoritative printed representations of the Copernican and Ptolemaic systems of the heavens side by side before his eyes. By this simple process of juxtaposition, he could immediately see that there were serious discrepancies. Later, working on Hven, he instigated a program to rectify the data and theories on which astronomy was based. He and his assistants labored for years to produce a systematic corpus of recorded observations of the heavenly bodies, using not only Tycho's own careful observations but those sent to him by astronomers across central Europe. When ready, Tycho could then supervise the correct printing of this vital material in his own printing house, using paper made in his own paper mill. As a result, one nova – 'Tycho's star', as it came to be called – became 'fixed' to the extent that it continued to be shown on celestial globes long after it had disappeared from the sky.[10]

In this guise has Eisenstein's Tycho entered a current debate over science itself. Bruno Latour has built an account of the making and power of science on her representation of a print culture, first in his concept of 'immutable mobiles'[11] and more recently in that of 'mediators'.[12] Latour identifies the collection and deployment of durable paper entities as the foundation of science's success. The creation and circulation of such objects, Latour maintains, enabled Tycho to master natural and social entities that were otherwise beyond reach. He could use print both to capture heavenly bodies, as Eisenstein claimed, and, furthermore, effectively to turn every observatory in Europe into an extension of Uraniborg. This he achieved by distributing printed forms on which astronomers could enter their observations before returning them to the central site of Hven.[13] In doing so, he pioneered a practice central to the development of modern science. For this, Latour thinks, is essentially how the modern laboratory sustains its authority too. The Latourian laboratory is an inscription engine, dedicated to the construction, collation, dispersal, and accommodation of such materials. It is a compelling and enormously influential argument. And it is consonant not only with Eisenstein herself, but more extensively still with her inspiration and *bête noire*, Marshall McLuhan.[14] Latour's vision of science in action depends on Eisenstein's 'print culture' – and thereby implicitly on McLuhan's 'Gutenberg Galaxy' – to underwrite the stability of both knowledge and society.[15]

The Tycho of Eisenstein and Latour has become the incarnation of textual, social, and epistemic order. But just how credible is this Tycho? There is something altogether too neat, too immaculate, about the figure and his achievements. As Philip Marlowe put it in *The Big Sleep*, such testimony displays 'the austere simplicity of fiction rather than the tangled woof of fact'.[16] Maybe the Tycho so far portrayed will change somewhat if we investigate more closely how his 'mediators' actually came into being and were put to use. For Tycho does indeed represent perhaps the purest example of a particular kind of printing, and a particular way of using the products of the press. Like Regiomontanus before him, and Hevelius after, he controlled his own printing operation. His was a singular printing house, however. It was as geographically isolated on the island of Hven as it was socially isolated from the companies of the European book trade. It was even physically embedded in the five-meter high, five-meter thick wall that enclosed his entire estate. Such isolation meant, at least in principle, that Tycho could produce books when, for whom, and in whatever form he liked.[17] Works like his *Astronomiae Instauratae Mechanica*, which described Uraniborg in all its glory, were scarcely intended to be *published* at all, but were to be distributed as gifts to patrons at courts and universities. The more prestigious were not just printed books, but hybrids – hand-colored, individualized tributes, presented to their intended recipients on specific dates.[18] Tycho meant to bypass the structures of the international book trade altogether.

The recipient of a book like Tycho's *Astronomiae Instauratae Mechanica* was thus likely to be found in a distinctive place: a royal court or a university. Here a book took its place and gained its meaning only amid a vast arsenal of other objects directed to similar ends. It would be encountered alongside natural curiosities, thaumaturgical wonders, mathematical devices, paintings, musical compositions, alchemical medallions, magical machines, and other books. In such surroundings, every aspect of appearance and handling mattered for creating an impact. The reader of such a work, in such a place, would be consciously engaging in a distinctive system of practices and ideas – in Tycho's case, feudal ones. The giving and receiving of such gifts was an important part of court culture, enmeshed in conventions of status recognition, reciprocation, and reward. This could not fail to affect the way in which that reader regarded the book. It was invested with enhanced credit, being untainted by 'mechanick' influence, and it was accorded the privileged reception due to such a noble gesture.[19] The veracity of its contents warranted respect. They could not be dismissed without cost. Yet at the same time such a gesture all but commanded creative responses – including challenges from suitably prestigious interlocutors. Tycho's book would now fall subject to the conventions surrounding philosophical and mathematical disputes in these settings. The variables that determined both whether a 'scientific' debate would even take place, and, once battle had been joined, how it would proceed, were local ones: to whom one presented the book, through which channels it was distributed, with which patron it was identified. Disputes like this were affairs of honor, conducted through appropriate intermediaries and champions. Printed books were their vehicles. That was what they were *for*.[20]

When, therefore, Tycho found himself attacked by Nicolai Reymers Baer (or Ursus), a recognized mathematician but a man of low birth whom he himself had accused of plagiarism, a scientific debate was not the principal outcome. Rather unusually, Tycho did in fact deign to reply himself. But he did so with a series of elaborately indignant letters to his fellows across Europe, which he had printed on his press at Uraniborg and circulated in 1596. In this correspondence he recited the tale of Ursus's alleged theft and argued that, whatever the date of Ursus's publication, Tycho had *printed* the cosmology first. Ever willing to recall his opponent's low birth, he even seems to have suggested that Ursus be executed for his presumption. But the more philosophical side of the dispute he delegated to a second, the relatively humble Kepler. The result was Kepler's 'Defense of Tycho against Ursus', a remarkably sophisticated historical argument for the status of astronomical hypotheses and their creators. It was never printed.[21]

Much even of this story could be taken as reinforcing Eisenstein's image. However, two elements make it less confirmatory. The first is that Tycho was extremely atypical in his successful use of print. Other writers regarded him not as representative of their own situation, but as a model that they sought, with widely varying degrees of success, to emulate. Like most icons, he stood for an ideal that was unrealizable. The second is that, as his argument against Ursus implies, even Tycho himself found the ideal impossible to achieve. That was why he built his own printing house and paper mill: he discovered that he could not otherwise obtain acceptable materials and workman-ship.[22] Even with these in place, moreover, most of his work remained unprinted until after his death.[23] Latour's preprinted forms, for example, seem to be mythical; Tycho did correspond extensively, but left no trace of having used such objects.[24] And while he began producing the images and descriptions for the *Astronomiae Instauratae Mechanica* as early as 1585, soon after building his printing house, the volume was not completed until thirteen years later. By that time he was in exile in Hamburg – the only place he could find with printers capable of finishing the book, even though he had brought his own press with him from Hven. Taken by his son to the Holy Roman Emperor, the book now became an instrument in Tycho's attempt to secure imperial patronage.[25] This proved successful, and he removed to Prague. But he soon discovered that even here, in the center of the empire, no printer able to undertake his prized star catalogue could be found. He was reduced to circulating hand-copied versions, and the catalogue remained unprinted on his death.[26]

At that point his works began to fall out of court circles altogether. They descended into the hands of the book trade. Even the *Astronomiae Instauratae Mechanica* was reprinted commercially. Such books were likely to be produced to different standards. They stood at risk of piracy and imitation, despite Rudolf II's stern commands forbidding such 'printers' frauds'. They were also likely to be read in different ways, by different people, in different places and for different reasons. Their accreditation became far more insecure. So, for example, the English astronomer royal, John Flamsteed – who, as we shall see, identified himself profoundly with Tycho – dismissed the post-humous printing of his star tables as, quite simply, a 'fraud'.[27] Tycho's inscriptions appear to have become distinctly mutable once they fell out of his control and left the courtly matrix.

If even Tycho Brahe found it so difficult to maintain his printed materials as mobile and immutable, what hope is there of explaining the achievements of less powerful figures in Eisenstein's terms? Attempting to do so would mean attributing to printed books themselves attributes of credibility and persuasion that actually took much work to maintain. It would thereby draw our attention away from important problems that any individual, even Tycho, had to overcome.[28] Talk of 'print culture' is strangely ethereal when compared to Tycho's struggles. It stands oddly discon-nected from the professed experiences of real historical figures. For example, who actually printed (and reprinted) Tycho's pages? It is a question worth asking, since Tycho himself spent many frustrating years seeking suitable printers – and the astronomer Christoph Rothmann, at least, believed that Ursus had been able to plagiarize his world system because he had been employed in Tycho's printing house.[29] And how were those pages employed by their recipients? Of what use were they to *them*? How did Tycho ensure that such distant readers took them as authoritative, especially when, as was often the ease in early modern testimony about celestial observations, they conflicted with figures produced locally? Eisenstein and Latour begin by decreeing such issues peripheral. *The Nature of the Book* does the opposite. If we are to understand how and why printed texts became trustworthy, it argues, we need to appreciate all of them, in something approaching their full 'woof'.

The disconnected air exhibited by Eisenstein's account is not accidental. In her work, printing itself stands outside history. The press is something '*sui generis*', we are told, lying beyond the reach of conventional historical analysis. Its 'culture' is correspondingly placeless and timeless. It is deemed to exist inasmuch as printed texts *possess* some key characteristic, fixity being the best candidate, and carry it with them as they are transported from place to place. The origins of this property are not analyzed. In fact, the accusations of technological determinism sometimes leveled against Eisenstein may even be wide of the mark, since she consistently declines to specify *any* position on the question of how print culture might emerge from print.[30] But the example of Tycho does suggest that the focus of her approach is *in practice* highly selective. The portrait it generates identifies as significant only the clearest instances of fixity. It regards instances when fixity was not manifested as exceptional failures, and even in the successful cases it neglects the labors through which success was achieved. It identifies the results of those labors instead as powers intrinsic to texts. Readers consequently suffer the fate of obliteration: their intelligence and skill is reattributed to the printed page. Tycho's labors deserve better. To put it brutally, what those labors really tell us is that Eisenstein's print culture does not exist.

There is an alternative. We may consider fixity not as an *inherent* quality, but as a *transitive* one. That is, it may be more useful to reverse our commonsense assumption. We may adopt the principle that fixity exists only inasmuch as it is recognized and acted upon by people – and not otherwise. The consequence of this change in perspective is that print culture itself is immediately laid open to analysis. It becomes a *result* of manifold representations, practices and conflicts, rather than just the monolithic *cause* with which we are often presented.[31] In contrast to talk of a 'print logic' imposed on humanity,[32] this approach allows us to recover the construction of different print cultures in particular historical circumstances. It recognizes that texts, printed or not, cannot compel readers to react in specific ways, but that they must be interpreted in cultural spaces the character of which helps to decide what counts as a proper reading. In short, this recasting has the advantage of positioning the cultural and the social where they should be: at the center of our attention. . . .

From fixity to credit

A new historical understanding of print is needed. What will it look like? One immediately evident feature will be its regard for the labors of those actually involved in printing, publishing, and reading. Another will be its respect for their own representations of printing, embracing both its prospects and its dangers. The dangers in particular will loom larger and more substantial than they have hitherto. Historians tend to disregard such perils as accidental; early modern readers and writers knew otherwise. . . . Increasingly they articulated responses by which the culture of the learned gentleman could be saved from this 'mechanick art'. Perhaps we should remind ourselves of the extent to which those responses appeared to fail – of the extent to which the print culture of the eighteenth century could be perceived by contemporaries, not as a realization of the rationalizing effects now so often ascribed to the press, but as destabilizing and threatening to civility. Such a stance, artificial though it would be, might help us to distance ourselves from the apparent stability of our own print culture, with its uniform editions, mass reproduction, and typographical fixity. Early modern fears would then begin to appear not as incidental lapses, defined a priori as marginal, but as credible statements of experience. They would finally be recognized as no less substantial than the phenomenon of fixity itself.

The Nature of the Book tries to treat all sides of the world of print with equal historiographical respect. In so doing, it inherits and attempts to develop initiatives central to the current state of cultural history. In particular, it reflects the important French field of *histoire du livre*. This field, at first associated with the *Annales* movement, has since the 1950s developed into an academic industry in its own right.[33] At the same time, its approaches have changed substantially. Its original practitioners dedicated themselves to accounting for the effects of printing in terms of quantitative measures of manufacture and distribution. They divided up the realm of print by subject matter and by the social character of purchasers, hoping to arrive at objective indices of cultural change. In fact, fewer useful figures emerged than had been hoped for. But the approach, so representative of *Annales* historiography, nonetheless had – and still has – substantial advantages. Above all, it suited commonsense perceptions of what it is that most properly characterizes print: the large-scale reproduction and distribution of precisely the same objects. Eisenstein's representation of print culture effectively embodies those same perceptions, albeit without the quantification. However, as illustrated by the examples of Galileo and Tycho, there were also costs to such a strategy. One was that it was effectively 'indifferent to the objects themselves'. It assumed that successive editions of a work were essentially the same, whatever their variations in text, format, or appearance. . . . Another, equally serious, disadvantage was that it remained silent about how the objects being counted were employed by readers such that they could have divergent cultural consequences. It could not have explained the different receptions accorded Galileo's *Dialogo*, because it ignored what Roger Chartier calls the 'intellectual "labor" ' required to put a book or paper to use.[34]

Chartier himself has been central to efforts to address these costs. He has worked to recover the different modes of labor surrounding printed materials, revealing how readers in local settings could 'appropriate' in different ways the books they read. From this perspective, ways of reading are recognized as 'social and cultural practices'. Like other such practices, they have a history, and one that can be reconstructed. The practical implications prove substantial. Sensitivity to the historical character of these practices often shows that an apparently authoritative text, however 'fixed', could not compel uniformity in the cultures of its reception. In practice, rather the reverse seems to have happened. Local cultures created their own meanings with and for such objects. For example, during the Counter-Reformation, printed images issued in large numbers in an attempt to standardize religious practice instead frequently served as vehicles for continued differentiation. The elements of a printed book – its format, layout, and typography – acted as no more than elements in an instrument, the book itself, that was useful for constructing knowledge. They were the tools, among others, with which users forged readings. In general, we may conclude that print entailed not one but many cultures, and that these cultures of the book were themselves local in character.[35]

As the opening pages of this chapter implied, there was one concern in particular that possessed early modern readers, and that may be used as a key to the rest. Could a printed book be trusted to be what it claimed? Perhaps a reader would be prudent to reserve judgment. On the most obvious level, whether a *Sidereus Nuncius* printed in Frankfurt was really Galileo's text, or an *Astronomiae Instauratae Mechanica* produced in Nuremburg was really Tycho's, could justifiably be doubted. More broadly, the very apprehension that printed books might not be self-evidently creditable was enough to rule out any possibility of their bearing the power attributed to them by most modern historians. And that apprehension was widespread. Piracy and plagiarism occupied readers' minds just as prominently as fixity and enlightenment. Unauthorized translations, epitomes, imitations, and other varieties of 'impropriety' were, they believed, routine hazards. Very few noteworthy publications seemed to escape altogether from such practices, and none at all could safely be regarded as immune a priori. It was regarded as extremely unusual for a book professing knowledge – from lowly almanacs to costly folios – to be published in the relatively unproblematic manner we now assume. Contemporaries had good reason to be wary. Their editions of Shakespeare, Donne, and Sir Thomas Browne were liable to be dubious. So were those of Robert Boyle, not to mention the first 'scientific' journal, the *Philosophical Transactions*. Even Isaac Newton's *Principia* suffered from unauthorized reprinting. From Galileo and Tycho to Newton and John Flamsteed, no significant learned author seemed to escape the kinds of practices soon colloquially subsumed under the label of piracy. This meant that even when a book was not so treated, the possibility that it might be still permeated the negotiations, practices, and conventions by which it was made, distributed, exchanged, and used. If piracy was as widespread as commonly feared, then trusting any printed report without knowledge of those processes could be rash. Profound problems of credit thus attended printed materials of all kinds. Without solutions there could be few meaningful uses for books – and perhaps no durable reasoning from them.

It should not be surprising, then, that contemporaries did not always identify fixity as a central characteristic of print. Surveying the books available to aid ocean navigators, Edmond Halley, for one, noted that 'the first Editions have generally been the best; frequent Copying most commonly vitiating the Originals'.[36] Even when people did refer to enhanced reliability, it was often in the face of direct evidence to the contrary. Textual corruption of even such closely monitored texts as the Bible actually increased with the advent of print, due to various combinations of piracy and careless printing.[37] The first book reputed to have been printed without any errors appeared only in 1760. Before then, variety was the rule, even within single editions. Martin Luther's German translation of Scripture was actually beaten into print by its first piracy, and in succeeding years the proportion of unauthorized to authorized texts was roughly ninety to one; these included Luther's own translation, newly ascribed to others (including Catholics), and others' work reattributed to him. A century later, the first folio of Shakespeare boasted some six hundred different typefaces, along with non-uniform spelling and punctuation, erratic divisions and arrangement, mispaging, and irregular proofing. No two copies were identical. It is impossible to decide even that any one is 'typical'.[38] In such a world, questions of credit took the place of assumptions of fixity. . . .

When early modern readers determined a book not to be worthy of credit, they could do so on a number of grounds. It was in the attribution of 'piracy', however, that the issues of credibility and print particularly converged. The term seems to have been coined by John Fell, bishop of Oxford, to describe the rapacious practices of London printers and booksellers. It had a technical meaning: a pirate was someone who indulged in the unauthorized reprinting of a title recognized to belong to someone else by the formal conventions of the printing and bookselling community. But it so on came to stand for a wide range of perceived transgressions of civility emanating from print's practitioners. As such, almost any book could, in principle, find itself accounted a piracy, whatever its actual circumstances of production and distribution. Historians of printing have therefore mis-construed instances of alleged piracy in at least two senses. First, they have seen piracy, like fixity, as inherent in the object, and not as a contestable attribution. Second, furthermore, they have assumed cases of piracy to be exceptions, accidental (in the philosophical sense of the word) to the essentially stabilizing character of print. Contemporaries were not so sure of this. Incidents that have been retrospectively dismissed as isolated and exceptional often seemed to them commonplace and representative. They might even be seen as attempts to undermine, and thereby to reform, the whole structure of the book trade. Even when conducted in more humdrum circumstances, more-over, and with less ambitious ends in sight, piracy still had powerful implications. Its apparent prevalence affected the economic and cultural conditions of all printed and written communication. It conditioned the accreditation of printed materials of all sorts, from the humblest ABC to the most elaborate encyclopedia.[39]

For the learned, and for natural philosophers in particular, this had peculiarly important consequences. In the agonistic field of early modern natural knowledge, allegations of piracy readily shaded into charges of plagiarism. Such allegations therefore extended to the reputation of authors. That is, unauthorized printing threatened to 'unauthorize' authors themselves. Even more import-ant, it threatened the credibility to be attributed to their ideas. Like print itself, piracy therefore had *epistemic* as well as *economic* implications: it affected the structure and content of knowledge. For an enterprise like experimental philosophy, in particular, which depended implicitly on the trust accorded to the printed reports issued by its protagonists, the consequences threatened to be nothing short of devastating. . . .

Printers and booksellers were manufacturers of credit. They had to be. The skills of those producing and trading in books, and the perceptions of those using them in learned work, might not intersect harmoniously. Whether or not they did at the moment of publication, moreover, accounts of printers' and booksellers' actions might still be drawn upon later by critics and rivals to challenge the value of any particular book, for example by alleging piracy. When they did succeed in remaining in the background – a rarer achievement than we might suppose – it was likely to be the result of hard and continuing work carried out 'behind the scenes'. . . .

The indispensable agency of printers and booksellers might remain unnoticed, for example, since the credit of their products depended on its being so. They themselves developed sophisticated ways of ensuring that they stayed just sufficiently in the background to avoid suspicion of either subterfuge or authorship. But in disputes the character of a bookseller or printer mattered. For readers attuned to its significance, anonymity itself might then become a source of suspicion.[40]

Historians can put the resulting allegations to use as evidence. They need no longer be complicit in the cabal by their own silence. . . .

The sources of print culture are therefore to be sought in civility as much as in technology, and in historical labors as much as in immediate cause and effect. The 'printing revolution', if there was one, consisted of changes in the conventions of handling and investing credit in textual materials, as much as in transformations in their manufacture. The point deserves to be stressed explicitly. I do not question that print enabled the stabilization of texts, to some extent, although fixity was far rarer and harder to discern in early modern Europe than most modern historians assume. I do, however, question the character of the link between the two. Printed texts were not intrinsically trustworthy. When they were in fact trusted, it was only as a result of hard work. Fixity was in the eye of the beholder, and its recognition could not be maintained without continuing effort. At no point could it be counted on to reside irremissibly in the object itself, and it was always liable to contradiction. Those faced with using the press to create and sustain knowledge thus found themselves confronting a culture characterized by nothing so much as indeterminacy. If printing held no necessary bond to truth, neither did it show a necessary bond to falsity or corruption. Each link remained vulnerable to dispute. It is this epistemic indeterminacy that lends the history of the book its powerful impact on cultural history. Understanding how it could be overcome to make knowledge and hence cultural change is what the history of the book is for.

Notes

1   For this term, see Eisenstein, *Printing Press*, I, 43–159. I am not sure of its genesis; Eisenstein, its prime recent exponent, seems to take it from McLuhan (e.g., *Gutenberg Galaxy*, 146–9).

2   *The Times*, 24 November 1984; Appignanesi and Maitland, *Rushdie File*, 42; Pipes, *Rushdie Affair*, 24, 85, 113, 201–2.

3   These disputes extend far beyond 'copyright' as conventionally understood, and include conventions now being forged to cover the 'inventions' and 'texts' produced in areas such as biotechnology and genome research. The economic, cultural, and moral implications at stake in these, as in the battles raging over computer and music software, are truly massive. For confrontations between the USA and China over the latter, see Faison, 'Copyright Pirates'.

4   Hannaway, 'Laboratory Design'. Shackelford has responded to Hannaway, with more heat than really necessary, in 'Tycho Brahe'.

5   Eisenstein, *Printing Press*, abridged as *Printing Revolution*. For examples of Eisenstein's influence in a range of fields, see Tribble, *Margins and Marginality*, 3–4; Neuschel, *Word of Honor*, chap. 6; Olson, *World an Paper*, 37 and passim; Rose, *Authors and Owners*, 3–4; Sommerville, *Secularization*, 48, 70, 79, 178, 180, 219 n. 1; Anderson, *Imagined Communities*, 30–49; Eamon, *Science and the Secrets of Nature*, 6–9, 94–6; Lowood and Rider, 'Literary Technology and Typographic Culture' (where 'typographic culture' and 'print culture' are indistinguisable). Many more could be cited. It is difficult to be sure, but I would estimate that Tycho Brahe is referred to at least as frequently in *Printing Press* as any other Renaissance figure.

6   Eisenstein, *Printing Press*, 71–88, 113, 26.

7   Eisenstein, *Printing Press*, 74–5, 597; *Printing Revolution*, 42–88. It is worth pointing out that these phenomena are similar to those attributed by anthropologists to the invention of writing, e.g., in Goody, *Logic of Writing*, 134–8, 174.

8   Eisenstein, *Printing Press*, 80, 117, 180–2, 200–10, 212, 646. The argument about nationalism has since been developed more thoroughly by Anderson in *Imagined Communities*, esp. 41–9.

9   Eisenstein, *Printing Press*, 107, 186, 193–4, 197, 640; Hunter, 'Impact of Print'; Leed, 'Elizabeth Eisenstein's *The Printing Press as on Agent of Change*'.

10   Eisenstein, *Printing Press*, 377, 583–4, 593, 596–603, 623–5, 629–30, 640, 699.

11   Latour, *Science in Action*, 52, 132–44, 226; Latour, 'On the Powers of Association'; Latour, 'Visualization and Cognition'. Compare also Latour, 'Give Me a Laboratory'; Latour and Woolgar, *Laboratory Life*, 45–53, 69–88; and Callon, Law, and Rip, *Mopping the Dynamics of Science and Technology*, 7–14, 35–99.

12   Latour, *We Have Never Been Modern*, 77–82, 128–9, 138; Latour, 'Technology Is Society Made Durable', 104–6, 127; Latour, 'Where Are the Missing Masses?', 237.

13   Latour, *Science in Action*, 32, 132–44, 226–7; Latour, 'Drawing Things Together'; Latour, 'Visualization and Cognition', 11–14; Latour, 'Politics of Explanation', 159; Callon, Law, and Rip, 'Putting Texts in Their Place', 223, 228–9.

14   A plausible summary of McLuhan's views in relation to Latour's might run as follows. Like Latour, McLuhan urged the importance of what he called the 'network' as a category of analysis, important in deciding ways of perceiving the world. He too identified a railway system as the representative network par excellence (compare Latour, *We Have Never Been Modern*, 117; and Latour, *Aramis*). What McLuhan's networks achieve – what lends them their power – is their ability to produce changes in scale. They permit individuals and organizations to localize and universalize by allowing them to magnify and reduce traces of the things on which they wish to operate to roughly the same size without destroying them. The 'message' of his networks is that they permit such control; and what is perceived as reality is in fact the current state of competing networks in dynamic interaction. The boundary between natural and social must therefore be forgotten when considering them. In such a world of natural/social hybrids, power comes from 'translation'. This is the agency by which we 'enlarge the scope of [our] action' and affect sites distant from ourselves. See McLuhan, *Understanding Media*, 3–21, 56–61, 89–105, 338–43, 346–59; compare Latour, *Science in Action*, 108–21, 223–32, 247–37, and *We Have Never Been Modern*, 10–12, 49–142. A reassessment of McLuhan is, I think, overdue, though attention to his work is currently reviving. Eisenstein herself roundly denied following him, but with an insistence and a perseverance that almost amounted to protesting too much: e.g., *Printing Press*, ix–xi, xvii, 40–1, 88, 129, 171.

15   Compare Shapin, 'Following Scientists Around', 541, 545–6.

16   Chandler, *Chandler Collection*, I, 143.

17   Thoren, *Lord of Uraniborg*, 144.

18   Brahe, *Astronomiae Instauratae Mechanica* (1598); Brahe, *Opera Omnia*, V, 317–18. A list of known copies with their recipients is in Norlind, *Tycho Brahe*, 286–93.

19   Westman, 'Astronomer's Role'. See also Hannaway, 'Laboratory Design'; and compare Eamon, 'Court, Academy and Printing House', 41.

20   In addition to the works of Biagioli and Hannaway cited here, see Findlen, 'Economy of Exchange'; Findlen, 'Courting Nature', esp. 61; Moran, *Alchemical World*, esp. 9, 93–4, 97, 110–12; Smith, *Business of Alchemy*, 49–50; Daston, 'Factual Sensibility'; and Davis, 'Beyond the Market'. Compare also the difficulties experienced by Becher in translating commercial documents for courtly readers: Smith, *Business of Alchemy*, 139.

21   Brahe, *Epistolarum Astronomicarum Libri*, 33–4, 148–51; Brahe, *Opera Omnia*, VI, 61–2, 179; Jardine, *Birth of History and Philosophy of Science*, 9–28 and *passim* (15 for Ursus's peasant background); Dreyer, *Tycho Brahe*, 183; Rosen, *Three Imperial Mathematicians*. Tycho's decision to strike at Ursus personally (which Kepler, for one, found surprising) may well be related to the fact that, as Hannaway points out, his status was feudal in origin; Tycho was not a courtier. See Hannaway, 'Laboratory Design', 589 n. II. For Tycho's conflicts see also Gingerich and Westman, *Wittich Connection* (which contrasts Tycho's treatment of Ursus to his response to the relatively well-born Wittich), and Thoren, *Lord of Uraniborg*. I am grateful to Robert Westman for conversations about this affair, which remains one of the more controversial among scholars of early modern astronomy.

22 Brahe, *Opera*, VI, 224, 365 n; VII, 214, 274; IX, 175; X, 302. Even with the mill in working order, he remained reliant on the cooperation of nearby parishioners to provide raw materials, as they were exhorted to do in regular 'rag sermons'.

23 In particular, the star catalogue (circulated only in manuscript until years after Tycho's death, and then inaccurately printed) and the *Astronomiae Instauratae Progymnasmata* (begun at Uraniborg, but completed only under the aegis of his heirs in 1602).

24 I have found no trace of these preprinted forms in Tycho's *Opera Omnia*, nor in any relevant secondary authority. I am also unable to find Latour's source for this central claim; it may well derive from an imaginative reading of certain passages in Einenstein's *Printing Press*, e.g., 626–7.

25 Brahe, *Opera*, V, 317–8; VIII, 166, 177, 388.

26 Thoren, *Lord of Uraniborg*, 150, 185–7, 367, 381–97, 414–15, 421, 478. Tycho had planned to present the catalogue to Rudolf II on New Year's Day, apparently a customary occasion for gift-giving: Kaufmann, *Mastery of Nature*, 106. For Rudolf II's undertaking to provide a 'new Uraniborg', see Brahe, *Opera*, VIII, 178, 188. It is also likely, of course, that Tycho's circulation of the catalogue in manuscript was intended to enhance its status as a collectible object.

27 Brahe, *Astronomiae Instauratae Mechanica* (1602); Curtius, *Historia Cœlestis*; Flamsteed, *Preface to John Flamsteed's 'Historia Cœlestis Britannica'*, 99–100. For Rudolf's condemnation of 'Typographorum fraudem', see Brahe, *Opera*, II, 9.

28 Compare Schaffer, 'Eighteenth Brumaire', 178–92, on the concept of the 'ideal reader'.

29 Dreyer, *Tycho Brahe*, 184 n. 1.

30 Eisenstein, *Printing Press*, e.g., 159, 166–8, 609 n, 89–90, 702–3. See also Grafton, 'Importance of Being Printed'. The fact that Eisenstein is simultaneously too provincial (thus missing the contingent elements of print culture by her lack of a comparative perspective) and not local enough (thus missing the work needed to make print culture at all) may be inferred from Cohen's discussion in *Scientific Revolution*, 357–67.

31 Compare the discussions of power in Latour, 'On the Powers of Association', and Latour, 'Technology Is Society Made Durable'. This suggestion has obvious resonances with certain works in critical theory, such as Fish, *Is There a Text in This Class?*. Since my aim is primarily historical I shall not be making many explicit links with such material, though the parallel deserves to be noted. Compare also McKenzie, *Bibliography and the Sociology of Texts*.

32 E.g., Kernan, *Printing Technology, Letters and Samuel Johnson*, 48 ff.

33 Its origin is conventionally dated to the appearance in 1958 of Febvre and Martin's *L'Apparition du Livre* (which has appeared in English translation as *The Coming of the Book*). Perhaps its most ambitious recent product has been Martin, *History and Power of Writing*. I have surveyed the field and its implications at greater length in Johns, 'Science and the Book'.

34 Chartier, *Cultural History*, 33–4.

35 These and similar points have been made in many contexts: Chartier, *Order of Books*, 16–17; Chartier, 'Culture as Appropriation'; Chartier, 'Publishing Strategies', 155–60; Chartier, 'Practical Impact of Writing', 122–6; Chartier, *Culture of Print*, 1–5; Chartier, 'Du Livre au Lire'; Chartier, *Cultural Uses of Print*, 3–12, 70; Chartier, *Lectures et Lecteurs*; Chartier, 'Texts, Printings, Readings'; Chartier, *Passions of the Renaissance*, 1–11, 110–59, 326–61, 362–95; Bourdieu and Chartier, 'La Lecture'; Martin, 'Pour une Histoire de la Lecture'; de Certeau, 'Reading as Poaching'; Darnton, 'History of Reading'; McKenzie, 'Typography and Meaning'; McKenzie, *Bibliography and the Sociology of Texts*; Martin and Vezin, *Mise en Page*. On the specific theme of *mise en page* see also Laufer, 'L'Espace Visuel du Livre Ancien'; Laufer, 'Espaces du Livre'; Pastoureau, 'L'Illustration du Livre'. Compare also the fascinating discussion of 'kitsch' in Clark, 'Scientific Revolution in the German Nations', 97–8.

36 *Atlas Maritimus & Commercialis*, i–iii.

37 Black, 'Printed Bible'. Eisenstein dismisses Black's argument out of hand: *Printing Press*, 80.

38   Newman, 'Word Made Print', 106–7 and *passim*; de Grazia, *Shakespeare Verbatim*, 15–19, 42; Kernan, *Printing Technology*, 48.

39   An inspiration for this treatment, as for other aspects of this book, has come from medieval history. Medievalists have devoted much attention to activities of 'forgery' and 'plagiarism'. They have constructed a sophisticated historiography addressing the diversity of sets since subsumed under such labels, immersing the subject in a detailed and authoritative treatment of the cultural uses of writing and reading in general. Medieval 'forgery' is appropriately seen as a form of truth-creation, justified (and perhaps even determined) by contemporary ideas about the nature and purposes of writing. It was also extraordinarily common. Perhaps half the documents known from Merovingian times are by our lights fake, and two-thirds of the documents known to have been issued to ecclesiastics before 1100 would now be reckoned forgeries. See Grafton, *Forgers and Critics*, 24–5, 30–32; Clanchy, *From Memory to Written Record*, 118–20, 231–57; Stock, *Implications of Literacy*, 59–87; Constable, 'Forgery and Plagiarism'. For a robust contrasting view, see Brown, '*Falsitas pia sive Reprehensibilis*'. For these medievalists' perspectives on print – which deserve more attention than they have received – see Clanchy, 'Looking Back', and Rouse and Rouse, *Authentic Witnesses*, 449–66.

40   For example, in his attacks on Ursus, Tycho Brahe was given to remarking upon his antagonist's books having been published without a printer's name, as was customary for 'notorious libels': Jardine, *Birth of History and Philosophy of Science*, 16.

References

Primary sources

Atlas Maritimus & Commercalis; Or, a General View of the World, so far as relates to Trade and Navigation. London: printed for J. and J. Knapton, W. and J. Innys, J. Darby, A. Bettesworth, J. Osborn, T. Longman, J. Senex, E. Symon, A. Johnston, and the executors of W. Taylor, 1728.

Brahe, Tycho. *Astronomiae Instauratae Mechanica*. Wandesbek: n.p., 1598.

Brahe, Tycho. *Astronomiae Instauratae Mechanica*. Nuremburg: Levinus Hulsius, 1602.

Brahe, Tycho. *Epistolarum Astronomicarum Libri*. Vol. 1. Uraniborg: from the author's printing house, 1596.

Brahe, Tycho. *Opera Omnia*, 15 vols. Edited by J. L. E. Dreyer. Copenhagen: Gyldendal.

Curtius, A. [Lucius Barettus, pseud.]. *Historia Cœlestis*. Augsburg: S. Utzschneider, 1666; reissue Ratisbon: J. C. Emmrich, 1672.

Flamsteed, J. *The Preface to John Flamsteed's 'Historia Cœlestis Britannica'* (1725). Translated and edited by A. D. Johnson and A. Chapman. London: National Maritime Museum, 1982.

Secondary sources

Anderson, B. *Imagined Communities: Reflections on the Origin and Spread of Nationalism*. Rev. ed. London: Verso, 1983.

Appignanesi, L., and S. Maitland, eds. *The Rushdie File*. London: Fourth Estate, 1989.

Barber, G., and B. Fabian, eds. *Buch und Buchhandel in Europa im Achtzehnten Jahrhundert*. Hamburg: Hauswedell, 1981.

Biagioli, M. *Galileo, Courtier: The Practice of Science in the Culture of Absolutism*. Chicago: University of Chicago Press, 1993.

Biagioli, M. 'Galileo the Emblem Maker'. *Isis* 81(1990): 230–58.

Biagioli, M. 'Galileo's System of Patronage'. *History of Science* 28 (1990): 1–62.

Biagioli, M. 'Playing with the Evidence'. *Early Science and Medicine* 1 (1996): 70–105.

Bijker, W. E., and J. Law, eds. *Shaping Technology/Building Society: Studies in Sociotechnical Change.* Cambridge, Mass.: MIT Press, 1992.

Black, M. H. 'The Printed Bible'. In Greenslade, *Cambridge History of the Bible*, 408–75.

Bourdieu, P., and R. Chartier, 'La Lecture: Une Pratique Culturelle'. In Chartier, *Pratiques de la Lecture*, 218–39.

Brown, E. A. R. '*Falsitas pia sive Reprehensibilis*: Medieval Forgers and their Intentions'. In *Fälschungen in Mittelalter: Internationaler Kongress der Monumenta Germaniae Historica München, 16–19 September 1986. Teil I: Kongressdaten und Festvortäge Literatur und Fälschung*, 101–19. Hanover: Hahnsche Buchhandlung, 1988.

Burke, P., ed. *New Perspectives on Historical Writing.* Cambridge: Polity, 1991.

Callow, M., J. Law, and A. Rip. 'Putting Texts in Their Place'. In Callow, Law, and Rip, *Mapping the Dynamics of Science and Technology*, 221–30.

Callow, M., J. Law, and A. Rip, eds. *Mapping the Dynamics of Science and Technology: Sociology of Science in the Real World.* Basingstoke: Macmillan, 1986.

Chandler, R. *The Chandler Collection.* 3 vols. London: Picador, 1983–4.

Chartier, R. *Cultural History: Between Practices and Representations.* Translated by L. G. Cochrane. Cambridge: Polity, 1988.

Chartier, R. *The Cultural Uses of Print in Early Modern France.* Translated by L. G. Cochrane. Princeton: Princeton University Press, 1987.

Chartier, R. 'Culture as Appropriation: Popular Cultural Uses in Early Modern France'. In Kaplan, *Understanding Popular Culture*, 229–53.

Chartier, R. 'Du Livre au Lire'. In Chartier, *Pratiques de la Lecture*, 62–88.

Chartier, R. *Lectures et Lecteurs dans la France d'Ancien Régime.* Paris: Editions du Seuil, 1987.

Chartier, R. *The Order of Books: Readers, Authors, and Libraries in Europe between the Fourteenth and Eighteenth Centuries.* Translated by L. G. Cochrane. Cambridge: Polity Press, 1994.

Chartier, R. 'The Practical Impact of Writing'. In Chartier, *Passions of the Renaissance*, 111–59.

Chartier, R. 'Publishing Strategies and What the People Read, 1530–1660'. In Chartier, *Cultural Uses of Print in Early Modern France*, 145–82.

Chartier, R., 'Texts, Printings, Readings'. In Hunt, *The New Cultural History*, 154–75.

Chartier, R., ed. *The Culture of Print: Power and the Uses of Print in Early Modern Europe.* Translated by L. G. Cochrane. Cambridge: Polity Press, 1989.

Chartier, R., ed. *Passions of the Renaissance.* Vol. III of *A History of Private Life.* Edited by P. Ariès and G. Duby. Translated by A. Goldhammer. Cambridge, Mass.: Belknap, 1989.

Chartier, R., ed. *Pratiques de la Lecture.* Marseille: Editions Rivages, 1985.

Chartier, R., and H.-J. Martin, eds. *Histoire de l'Edition Française.* 2d ed. 4 vols. Paris: Fayard, 1989–91.

Clanchy, M. T. *From Memory to Written Record: England 1066–1307.* London: Edward Arnold, 1979.

Clanchy, M. T. 'Looking Back from the Invention of Printing'. In Resnick, *Literacy in Historical Perspective*, 7–22.

Clark, W. 'The Scientific Revolution in the German Nations'. In Porter and Teich, *Scientific Revolution in National Context*, 90–114.

Cohen, H. F. *The Scientific Revolution: A Historiographical Inquiry.* Chicago: University of Chicago Press, 1994.

Constable, G. 'Forgery and Plagiarism in the Middle Ages'. *Archiv für Diplomatik* 29 (1983): 1–41.

Darnton, R. *The Great Cat Massacre, and Other Episodes in French Cultural History.* London: Allen Lane, 1984.

Darnton, R. 'History of Reading'. In Burke, *New Perspectives*, 140–67.

Daston, L. 'The Factual Sensibility'. *Isis* 79 (1988): 452–70.

Davis, N. Z. 'Beyond the Market: Books as Gifts in Sixteenth-Century France'. *Transactions of the Royal Historical Society*, 5th ser., 33 (1983): 69–88.

De Certeau, M. *The Practice of Everyday Life*. Translated by S. Rendall. Berkeley and Los Angeles: University of California Press, 1984.

De Certeau, M. 'Reading as Poaching'. In de Certeau, *The Practice of Everyday Life*, 165–76.

De Grazia, M. *Shakespeare Verbatim: The Reproduction of Authenticity and the 1790 Apparatus*. Oxford: Oxford University Press, 1991.

Dreyer, J. L. E. *Tycho Brahe: A Picture of Scientific Life and Work in the Sixteenth Century*. Edinburgh: A. and C. Black, 1890.

Eamon, W. 'Court, Academy and Printing House: Patronage and Scientific Careers in Late Renaissance Italy'. In Moran, *Patronage and Institutions*, 25–50.

Eamon, W. *Science and the Secrets of Nature: Books of Secrets in Medieval and Early Modern Culture*. Princeton: Princeton University Press, 1994.

Eisenstein, E. L. *The Printing Press as an Agent of Change: Communications and Cultural Transformations in Early-Modern Europe*. 2 vols. Cambridge: Cambridge University Press, 1979.

Eisenstein, E. L. *The Printing Revolution in Early Modern Europe*. Cambridge: Cambridge University Press, 1983.

Faison, S. 'Copyright Pirates Prosper in China Despite Promises'. *New York Times*, 20 February 1996, 1, 4.

Febvre, L., and H.-J. Martin. *The Coming of the Book: The Impact of Printing 1450–1800*. Translated by D. Gerard. London: Verso, 1984. Originally published as *L'Apparition du Livre* (Paris: Albin Michel, 1958).

Findlen, P. 'The Economy of Exchange in Early Modern Italy'. In Moran, *Patronage and Institutions*, 5–24.

Findlen, P. 'Courting Nature'. In N. Jardine, J. A. Secord and E. C. Spary, eds. *Cultures of Natural History*. Cambridge: Cambridge University Press, 1996, 57–74.

Fish, S. *Is There a Text in This Class? The Authority of Interpretive Communities*. Cambridge, Mass.: Harvard University Press, 1980.

Gingerich, O., and R. S. Westman. *The Wittich Connection: Conflict and Priority in Late Sixteenth-Century Cosmology*. Philadelphia: American Philosophical Society, 1988. Vol. 78, no. 7 of *Transactions of the American Philosophical Society*.

Goody, J. *The Logic of Writing and the Organization of Society*. Cambridge: Cambridge University Press, 1986.

Grafton, A. *Forgers and Critics: Creativity and Duplicity in Western Scholarship*. London: Collins and Brown, 1990.

Grafton, A. 'The Importance of Being Printed'. *Journal of Interdisciplinary History* 11 (1980): 265–86.

Greenslade, S. L., ed. *The Cambridge History of the Bible*, vol. 3. Cambridge: Cambridge University Press, 1963.

Hannaway, O. 'Laboratory Design and the Aim of Science: Andreas Libavius versus Tycho Brahe'. *Isis* 77 (1986): 585–610.

Hunt, L., ed. *The New Cultural History*. Berkeley and Los Angeles: University of California Press, 1989.

Hunter, M. 'The Impact of Print'. *The Book Collector* 28 (1979): 335–52.

Jardine, N. *The Birth of History and Philosophy of Science: Kepler's 'A Defence of Tycho Against Ursus' with Essays on Its Provenance and Significance*. Cambridge: Cambridge University Press, 1984.

Johns, A. 'Science and the Book in Modern Cultural Historiography'. *Studies in History and Philosophy of Science* 35 (1997): 23–59.

Kaplan, S. L., ed. *Understanding Popular Culture: Europe from the Middle Ages to the Nineteenth Century*. Berlin: Mouton, 1984.

Kaufmann, T. D. *The Mastery of Nature: Aspects of Art, Science, and Humanism in the Renaissance*. Princeton: Princeton University Press, 1993.

Kernan, A. *Printing Technology, Letters and Samuel Johnson*, Princeton: Princeton University Press, 1987.

Knorr-Cetina, K. D., and M. Mulkay, eds. *Science Observed: Perspectives on the Social Study of Science*. London: Sage, 1983.

Latour, B. *Aramis, ou l'Amour des Techniques*. Paris: Découverte, 1992.

Latour, B. 'Drawing Things Together'. In Lynch and Woolgar, *Representation in Scientific Practice*, 19–68.

Latour, B. 'Give Me a Laboratory and I Will Raise the World'. In Knorr-Cetina and Mulkay, *Science Observed*, 141–70.

Latour, B. 'On the Powers of Association'. In Law, *Power, Action and Belief*, 264–80.

Latour, B. 'The Politics of Explanation: An Alternative'. In Woolgar, *Knowledge and Reflexivity*, 155–76.

Latour, B. *Science in Action: How to Follow Scientists and Engineers through Society*. Milton Keynes: Open University Press, 1987.

Latour, B. 'Technology Is Society Made Durable'. In Law, *A Sociology of Monsters*, 103–31.

Latour, B. 'Visualization and Cognition: Thinking with Eyes and Hands'. *Knowledge and Society* 6 (1986): 1–40.

Latour, B. *We Have Never Been Modern*. Translated by C. Porter. New York: Harvester Wheatsheaf, 1993.

Latour, B. 'Where Are the Missing Masses? The Sociology of a Few Mundane Artifacts'. In Bijker and Law, *Shaping Technology/Building Society*, 225–58.

Latour, B., and S. Woolgar. *Laboratory Life: The Social Construction of Scientific Facts*. London: Sage, 1979.

Laufer, R. 'Les Espaces du Livre'. In Chartier and Martin, *Histoire de l'Edition Française*, II, 156–72.

Laufer, R. 'L'Espace Visuel du Livre Ancien'. In Chartier and Martin, *Histoire de l'Edition Française*, I, 579–601.

Law, J., ed. *Power, Action and Belief: A New Sociology of Knowledge?* London: Routledge and Kegan Paul, 1986.

Law, J., ed. *A Sociology of Monsters: Essays on Power, Technology and Domination*. London: Routledge, 1991.

Leed, E. J. 'Elizabeth Eisenstein's *The Printing Press as an Agent of Change* and the Structure of Communications Revolutions'. *American Journal of Sociology* 88 (1982): 413–29.

Lowood, H. E., and R. E. Rider. 'Literary Technology and Typographic Culture: The Instrument of Print in Early Modern Science'. *Perspectives on Science* 2 (1994): 1–37.

Lynch, M., and S. Woolgar, eds. *Representation in Scientific Practice*. Cambridge, Mass.: MIT Press, 1990.

Martin, H.-J. *The History and Power of Writing*. Translated by L. C. Cochrane. Chicago: University of Chicago Press, 1994.

Martin, H.-J. *Le Livre Français sous l'Ancien Régime*. Paris: Promodis, 1987.

Martin, H.-J. 'Pour une Histoire de la Lecture'. In Martin, *Le Livre Français*, 227–46.

Martin, H.-J., and J. Vezin, eds. *Mise en Page et Mise en Texte du Livre Manuscrit*. Paris: Promodis, 1990.

McKenzie, D. F. *Bibliography and the Sociology of Texts*. London: British Library, 1985.

McKenzie, D. F. 'Typography and Meaning: The Case of William Congreve'. In Barber and Fabian, *Buch und Buchhandel*, 81–123.

McLuhan, M. *The Gutenberg Galaxy*. London: Routledge and Kegan Paul, 1962.

McLuhan, M. *Understanding Media: The Extension of Man*. 1964. Reprint, London: Ark, 1987.

Moran, B. T. *The Alchemical World of the German Court: Occult Philosophy and Chemical Medicine in the Circle of Moritz of Hessen (1572–1632)*. Stuttgart: F. Steiner, 1991.

Moran, B. T., ed. *Patronage and Institutions: Science, Technology and Medicine at the European Court 1500–1700*. Woodbridge: Boydell, 1991.

Neuschel, K. B. *Word of Honor: Interpreting Noble Culture in Sixteenth-Century France*. Ithaca: Cornell University Press, 1989.

Newman, J. O. 'The Word Made Print: Luther's 1522 *New Testament* in an Age of Mechanical Reproduction'. *Representations* 11 (1985): 95–133.

Norlind, W. *Tycho Brahe: En levnadsteckning med nya bidrag belysande hans liv och verk.* Lund, Sweden: C. W. K. Gleerup, 1970.

Olson, D. R. *The World on Paper: The Conceptual and Cognitive Implications of Writing and Reading.* Cambridge: Cambridge University Press, 1994.

Pastoureau, M. 'L'Illustration du Livre: Comprendre ou Rêver?' In Chartier and Martin, *Histoire de l'Edition Française*, 1, 602–28.

Pipes, D. *The Rushdie Affair: The Novel, the Ayatollah, and the West.* London: Carol Publishing, 1990.

Porter, R., and M. Teich, eds. *The Scientific Revolution in National Context.* Cambridge: Cambridge University Press, 1992.

Resnick, D. P., ed. *Literacy in Historical Perspective.* Washington: Library of Congress, 1983.

Rose, M. *Authors and Owners: The Invention of Copyright.* Cambridge, Mass.: Harvard University Press, 1993.

Rosen, E. *Three Imperial Mathematicians: Kepler Trapped between Tycho Brahe and Ursus.* New York: Abaris, 1986.

Rouse, M. A., and R. H. Rouse. *Authentic Witnesses: Approaches to Medieval Texts and Manuscripts.* Notre Dame, Ind.: University of Notre Dame Press, 1991.

Schaffer, S. J. 'The Eighteenth Brumaire of Bruno Latour'. *Studies in History and Philosophy of Science* 22 (1991): 174–92.

Shackelford, J. (1993) 'Tycho Brahe, Laboratory Design, and the aims of Science', *Isis* 84: 211–30.

Shapin, S. 'Following Scientists Around'. *Social Studies of Science* 18 (1988): 533–50.

Smith, P. H. *The Business of Alchemy: Science and Culture in the Holy Roman Empire.* Princeton: Princeton University Press, 1994.

Sommerville, C. J. *The Secularization of Early Modern England: From Religious Culture to Religious Faith.* New York: Oxford University Press, 1992.

Stock, B. *The Implications of Literacy: Written Language and Models of Interpretation in the Eleventh and Twelfth Centuries.* Princeton: Princeton University Press, 1983.

Thoren, V. E. *The Lord of Uraniborg: A Biography of Tycho Brahe.* Cambridge: Cambridge University Press, 1990.

Tribble, E. B. *Margins and Marginality: The Printed Page in Early Modern England.* Charlottesville: University Press of Virginia, 1993.

Westman, R. S. 'The Astronomer's Role in the Sixteenth Century: A Preliminary Study'. *History of Science* 18 (1980): 105–47.

Woolgar, S., ed. *Knowledge and Reflexivity: New Frontiers in the Sociology of Knowledge.* London: Sage, 1988.

PART THREE

Texts and authors

EDITORS' INTRODUCTION

The establishment of print as a major form of social communication in the centuries following the Gutenberg print revolution meant also the development of print as a commodity and textual production as a profession. Demands for books created a demand for authors to write and produce them. But what exactly is meant by 'authorship' has been subject to debate and changing interpretation in critical circles over recent years. Questions about and examinations of the notion of the author are at the heart of this part's extracts. Roland Barthes's oft-quoted 'Death of the Author' set the tone in the 1960s for upturning previous assumptions about the role of the author in the formation of texts. His point, as of that in Michel Foucault's response, was to attempt to shift critical emphasis from author-centred enquiry to reader-based analysis.

Decentring and decoupling the author from texts was not a new concept: elevating the common reader to ultimate creator of textual meaning was. But as Foucault was clear to point out, eliminating the authorial role completely from the textual production equation was not satisfactory. 'Authorship' was a cultural formation inseparable from the commodification of literature: literary reputation could and did shape cultural responses to texts in a manner not accounted for by Barthesian analysis. Subsequent developments in book history studies have expanded and developed critical thinking regarding these matters, as seen in Paula McDowell's discussion of the links between oral culture, religio-political activism and the production of texts under the auspices of the Quaker communities in seventeenth-century Britain. Her piece offers an insightful case study into the manner in which female polemicists and preachers in particular utilised oral and textual means to influence public opinion and 'authenticate' their activities.

Mark Rose's empirically situated piece draws attention to the struggle over authorship as a legal concept, located in the creation of literary property under copyright legislation in Britain in the eighteenth century, itself a product of national struggle between the Scots and the English. Copyright legislation allowed authors' legal rights to be recognised as originators and therefore owners of a specific commodity (in this case text). It formed the basis for a new profession and industry to develop exponentially in the eighteenth century, one that combined the manufacture and distribution of cultural commodities with an affirmation of the author (rather than as before the printer/

bookseller) as the original source of such material. John Brewer's piece traces the resulting development of the literary marketplace in eighteenth-century Britain. These changes in social and cultural networks of literary production laid the groundwork for the full-fledged emergence of authorship as a respected and lucrative profession in the industrially driven and print-literate world of nineteenth-century Western Europe and North America. How this applied to didactic material is the subject of Leah Price's investigation of the development of the anthology in late eighteenth-century British culture. Copyright allowed such collections to flourish for a period, establish the contents of the literary canon for years to come, and determine the rules by which future collections would align themselves.

An example of the incorporation of such matters into revisionist analyses of authorial concepts is Jane Tompkins's 1985 *Sensational Designs: The Cultural Work of American Fiction: 1790–1860*, a portion of which is reproduced here. Tompkins's contrast of the New York-based Sophie Warner's waning cultural significance with Nathaniel Hawthorne's emerging literary reputation (the latter achieved as a result of cultural and social networks embedded in mid-nineteenth-century New England) very clearly illustrates the manner in which authorial reputation and textual readings could shift according to changing cultural conditions. As Tompkins points out, how both authors emerged into or disappeared from cultural visibility and the literary marketplace can be traced to the specific social, literary and economic circumstances in which they were read and produced. John Sutherland's piece provides a contrasting view of authorial identity and activity in Victorian Britain. His detailed empirical study of 878 novelists offers insight into the vastness of the infrastructure which by the late nineteenth century had developed to support and produce textual material for cultural consumption.

Robert L. Patten's study of *Oliver Twist* draws out links between genre, authorial expectations and paratext in reader interpretations. More specifically, he demonstrates how the planning and textual production of Charles Dickens's work was materially shaped by the generic protocols operating within the literary periodical field, as well as reshaped when reproduced in novel form. With such appraisals has come recognition that book history studies now needs to take into account the economic imperatives governing textual production. The work of James L. W. West III illustrates, for example, the manner in which twentieth-century American authors such as F. Scott Fitzgerald maximised earnings through manipulation of literary markets and diverse print outlets such as modern mass-circulation magazines and film and radio. Jayne Marek's piece rounds off the section with a more detailed examination of literary editing and publishing during the rise of Modernism. She focuses on the work of H.D. and Bryher for the small magazines of the period, particularly the *Egoist*, and draws attention to the role of women and their social relationships in the creation of canonical texts.

Chapter 19

Roland Barthes

THE DEATH OF THE AUTHOR

In his story *Sarrasine* Balzac, describing a castrato disguised as a woman, writes the following sentence: '*This was woman herself with her sudden fears, her irrational whims, her instinctive worries, her impetuous boldness, her fussings, and her delicious sensibility.*' Who is speaking thus? Is it the hero of the story bent on remaining ignorant of the castrato hidden beneath the woman? Is it Balzac the individual, furnished by his personal experience with a philosophy of Woman? Is it Balzac the author professing 'literary' ideas on femininity? Is it universal wisdom? Romantic psychology? We shall never know, for the good reason that writing is the destruction of every voice, of every point of origin. Writing is that neutral, composite, oblique space where our subject slips away, the negative where all identity is lost, starting with the very identity of the body writing.

No doubt it has always been that way. As soon as a fact is *narrated* no longer with a view to acting directly on reality but intransitively, that is to say, finally outside of any function other than that of the very practice of the symbol itself, this disconnection occurs, the voice loses its origin, the author enters into his own death, writing begins. The sense of this phenomenon, however, has varied; in ethnographic societies the responsibility for a narrative is never assumed by a person but by a mediator, shaman or relator whose 'performance' – the mastery of the narrative code – may possibly be admired but never his 'genius'. The author is a modern figure, a product, of our society insofar as, emerging from the Middle Ages with English empiricism, French rationalism and the personal faith of the Reformation, it discovered the prestige of the individual, of, as it is more nobly put, the 'human person'. It is thus logical that in literature it should be this positivism, the epitome and culmination of capitalist ideology, which has attached the greatest importance to the 'person' of the author. The *author* still reigns in histories of literature, biographies of writers, interviews, magazines, as in the very consciousness of men of letters anxious to unite their person and their work through diaries and memoirs. The image of literature to be found in ordinary culture is tyrannically centred on the author, his person, his life, his tastes, his passions, while criticism still consists for the most part in saying that Baudelaire's work is the failure of Baudelaire the man, Van Gogh's his madness, Tchaikovsky's his vice. The *explanation* of a work is always sought in the man or woman who produced it, as if it were always in the end, through the more or less transparent allegory of the fiction, the voice of a single person, the *author* 'confiding' in us.

Though the sway of the Author remains powerful (the new criticism has often done no more than consolidate it), it goes without saying that certain writers have long since attempted to loosen it. In France, Mallarmé was doubtless the first to see and to foresee in its full extent the necessity to substitute language itself for the person who until then had been supposed to be its owner. For him, for us too, it is language which speaks, not the author; to write is, through a prerequisite impersonality (not at all to be confused with the castrating objectivity of the realist novelist), to reach that point where only language acts, 'performs', and not 'me'. Mallarmé's entire poetics consists in suppressing the author in the interests of writing (which is, as will be seen, to restore the place of the reader). Valéry, encumbered by a psychology of the Ego, considerably diluted Mallarmé's theory but, his taste for classicism leading him to turn to the lessons of rhetoric, he never stopped calling into question and deriding the Author; he stressed the linguistic and, as it were, 'hazardous' nature of his activity, and throughout his prose works he militated in favour of the essentially verbal condition of literature, in the face of which all recourse to the writer's interiority seemed to him pure superstition. Proust himself, despite the apparently psychological character of what are called his *analyses*, was visibly concerned with the task of inexorably blurring, by an extreme subtilization, the relation between the writer and his characters; by making of the narrator not he who has seen and felt nor even he who is writing, but he who *is going to write* (the young man in the novel – but, in fact, how old is he and who is he? – wants to write but cannot; the novel ends when writing at last becomes possible). Proust gave modern writing its epic. By a radical reversal, instead of putting his life into his novel, as is so often maintained, he made of his very life a work for which his own book was the model; so that it is clear to us that Charlus does not imitate Montesquiou but that Montesquiou – in his anecdotal, historical reality – is no more than a secondary fragment, derived from Charlus. Lastly, to go no further than this prehistory of modernity, Surrealism, though unable to accord language a supreme place (language being system and the aim of the movement being, romantically, a direct subversion of codes – itself moreover illusory: a code cannot be destroyed, only 'played off'), contributed to the desacrilization of the image of the Author by ceaselessly recommending the abrupt disappointment of expectations of meaning (the famous surrealist 'jolt'), by entrusting the hand with the task of writing as quickly as possible what the head itself is unaware of (automatic writing), by accepting the principle and the experience of several people writing together. Leaving aside literature itself (such distinctions really becoming invalid), linguistics has recently provided the destruction of the Author with a valuable analytical tool by showing that the whole of the enunciation is an empty process, functioning perfectly without there being any need for it to be filled with the person of the interlocutors. Linguistically, the author is never more than the instance writing, just as *I* is nothing other than the instance saying *I*: language knows a 'subject', not a 'person', and this subject, empty outside of the very enunciation which defines it, suffices to make language 'hold together', suffices, that is to say, to exhaust it.

The removal of the Author (one could talk here with Brecht of a veritable 'distancing', the Author diminishing like a figurine at the far end of the literary stage) is not merely an historical fact or an act of writing; it utterly transforms the modern text (or – which is the same thing – the text is henceforth made and read in such a way that at all its levels the author is absent). The temporality is different. The Author, when believed in, is always conceived of as the past of his own book: book and author stand automatically on a single line divided into a *before* and an *after*. The Author is thought to *nourish* the book, which is to say that he exists before it, thinks, suffers, lives for it, is in the same relation of antecedence to his work as a father to his child. In complete contrast, the modern scriptor is born simultaneously with the text, is in no way equipped with a being preceding or exceeding the writing, is not the subject with the book as predicate; there is no other time than that of the enunciation and every text is eternally written *here and now*. The fact is (or, it follows) that *writing* can no longer designate an operation of recording, notation, representation, 'depiction' (as the Classics would say); rather, it designates exactly what linguists, referring to Oxford philosophy, call a performative, a rare verbal form (exclusively given in the first person and in the present tense) in which the enunciation has no other content (contains no other proposition) than the act by which it is uttered – something like the *I declare* of kings or the *I sing* of very ancient poets. Having buried the Author, the modern scriptor can thus no longer believe, as according to the pathetic view of his predecessors, that this hand is too slow for his thought or passion and that consequently, making a law of necessity, he must emphasize this delay and indefinitely 'polish' his form. For him, on the contrary, the hand, cut off from any voice, borne by a pure gesture of inscription (and not of expression), traces a field without origin – or which, at least, has no other origin than language itself, language which ceaselessly calls into question all origins.

We know now that a text is not a line of words releasing a single 'theological' meaning (the 'message' of the Author-God) but a multi-dimensional space in which a variety of writings, none of them original, blend and clash. The text is a tissue of quotations drawn from the innumerable centres of culture. Similar to Bouvard and Pécuchet, those eternal copyists, at once sublime and comic and whose profound ridiculousness indicates precisely the truth of writing, the writer can only imitate a gesture that is always anterior, never original. His only power is to mix writings, to counter the ones with the others, in such a way as never to rest on any one of them. Did he wish to *express himself*, he ought at least to know that the inner 'thing' he thinks to 'translate' is itself only a ready-formed dictionary, its words only explainable through other words, and so on indefinitely; something experienced in exemplary fashion by the young Thomas de Quincey, he who was so good at Greek that in order to translate absolutely modern ideas and images into that dead language, he had, so Baudelaire tells us (in *Paradis Artificiels*), 'created for himself an unfailing dictionary, vastly more extensive and complex than those resulting from the ordinary patience of purely literary themes'. Succeeding the Author, the scriptor no longer bears within him passions, humours, feelings, impressions, but rather this immense dictionary from which he draws a writing that can know no halt: life never does more than imitate the book, and the book itself is only a tissue of signs, an imitation that is lost, infinitely deferred.

Once the Author is removed, the claim to decipher a text becomes quite futile. To give a text an Author is to impose a limit on that text, to furnish it with a final signified, to close the writing. Such a conception suits criticism very well, the latter then allotting itself the important task of discovering the Author (or its hypostases: society, history, psyché, liberty) beneath the work: when the Author has been found, the text is 'explained' – victory to the critic. Hence there is no surprise in the fact that, historically, the reign of the Author has also been that of the Critic, nor again in the fact that criticism (be it new) is today undermined along with the Author. In the multiplicity of writing, everything is to be *disentangled*, nothing *deciphered*; the structure can be followed, 'run' (like the thread of a stocking) at every point and at every level, but there is nothing beneath: the space of writing is to be ranged over, not pierced; writing ceaselessly posits meaning ceaselessly to evaporate it, carrying out a systematic exemption of meaning. In precisely this way literature (it would be better from now on to say *writing*), by refusing to assign a 'secret', ultimate meaning, to the text (and to the world as text), liberates what may be called an anti-theological activity, an activity that is truly revolutionary since to refuse to fix meaning is, in the end, to refuse God and his hypostases – reason, science, law.

Let us come back to the Balzac sentence. No one, no 'person', says it: its source, its voice, is not the true place of the writing, which is reading. Another – very precise – example will help to make this clear: recent research (J.-P. Vernant[1]) has demonstrated the constitutively ambiguous nature of Greek tragedy, its texts being woven from words with double meanings that each character understands unilaterally (this perpetual misunderstanding is exactly the 'tragic'); there is, however, someone who understands each word in its duplicity and who, in addition, hears the very deafness of the characters speaking in front of him – this someone being precisely the reader (or here, the listener). Thus is revealed the total existence of writing: a text is made of multiple writings, drawn from many cultures and entering into mutual relations of dialogue, parody, contestation, but there is one place where this multiplicity is focused and that place is the reader, not, as was hitherto said, the author. The reader is the space on which all the quotations that make up a writing are inscribed without any of them being lost; a text's unity lies not in its origin but in its destination. Yet this destination cannot any longer be personal: the reader is without history, biography, psychology; he is simply that *someone* who holds together in a single field all the traces by which the written text is constituted. Which is why it is derisory to condemn the new writing in the name of a humanism hypocritically turned champion of the reader's rights. Classic criticism has never paid any attention to the reader; for it, the writer is the only person in literature. We are now beginning to let ourselves be fooled no longer by the arrogant antiphrastical recriminations of good society in favour of the very thing it sets aside, ignores, smothers, or destroys; we know that to give writing its future, it is necessary to overthrow the myth: the birth of the reader must be at the cost of the death of the Author.

Note

1   Cf. Jean-Pierre Vernant (with Pierre Vidal-Naquet), *Mythe et tragédie en Grèce ancienne*, Paris 1972, esp. pp. 19–40, 99–131.

Chapter 20

Michel Foucault

WHAT IS AN AUTHOR?

The coming into being of the notion of 'author' constitutes the privileged moment of *individualiza-tion* in the history of ideas, knowledge, literature, philosophy, and the sciences. Even today, when we reconstruct the history of a concept, literary genre, or school of philosophy, such categories seem relatively weak, secondary, and superimposed scansions in comparison with the solid and funda-mental unit of the author and the work.

I shall not offer here a sociohistorical analysis of the author's persona. Certainly it would be worth examining how the author became individualized in a culture like ours, what status he has been given, at what moment studies of authenticity and attribution began, in what kind of system of valorization the author was involved, at what point we began to recount the lives of authors rather than of heroes, and how this fundamental category of 'the-man-and-his-work criticism' began. For the moment, however, I want to deal solely with the relationship between text and author and with the manner in which the text points to this 'figure' that, at least in appearance, is outside it and antecedes it.

Beckett nicely formulates the theme with which I would like to begin: ' "What does it matter who is speaking," someone said, "what does it matter who is speaking." ' In this indifference appears one of the fundamental ethical principles of contemporary writing (*écriture*). I say 'ethical' because this indifference is not really a trait characterizing the manner in which one speaks and writes, but rather a kind of immanent rule, taken up over and over again, never fully applied, not designating writing as something completed, but dominating it as a practice. Since it is too familiar to require a lengthy analysis, this immanent rule can be adequately illustrated here by tracing two of its major themes.

First of all, we can say that today's writing has freed itself from the dimension of expression. Referring only to itself, but without being restricted to the confines of its interiority, writing is identified with its own unfolded exteriority. This means that it is an interplay of signs arranged less according to its signified content than according to the very nature of the signifier. Writing unfolds like a game (*jeu*) that invariably goes beyond its own rules and transgresses its limits. In writing, the point is not to manifest or exalt the act of writing, nor is it to pin a subject within language; it is, rather, a question of creating a space into which the writing subject constantly disappears.

The second theme, writing's relationship with death, is even more familiar. This link subverts an old tradition exemplified by the Greek epic, which was intended to perpetuate the immortality of the hero: if he was willing to die young, it was so that his life, consecrated and magnified by death, might pass into immortality; the narrative then redeemed this accepted death. In another way, the motivation, as well as the theme and the pretext of Arabian narratives – such as *The Thousand and One Nights* – was also the eluding of death: one spoke, telling stories into the early morning, in order to forestall death, to postpone the day of reckoning that would silence the narrator. Scheherazade's narrative is an effort, renewed each night, to keep death outside the circle of life.

Our culture has metamorphosed this idea of narrative, or writing, as something designed to ward off death. Writing has become linked to sacrifice, even to the sacrifice of life: it is now a voluntary effacement which does not need to be represented in books, since it is brought about in the writer's very existence. The work, which once had the duty of providing immortality, now possesses the right to kill, to be its author's murderer, as in the cases of Flaubert, Proust, and Kafka. That is not all, however: this relationship between writing and death is also manifested in the effacement of the writing subject's individual characteristics. Using all the contrivances that he sets up between himself and what he writes, the writing subject cancels out the signs of his particular individuality. As a result, the mark of the writer is reduced to nothing more than the singularity of his absence; he must assume the role of the dead man in the game of writing.

None of this is recent; criticism and philosophy took note of the disappearance – or death – of the author some time ago. But the consequences of their discovery of it have not been sufficiently examined, nor has its import been accurately measured. A certain number of notions that are intended to replace the privileged position of the author actually seem to preserve that privilege and suppress the real meaning of his disappearance. I shall examine two of these notions, both of great importance today.

The first is the idea of the work. It is a very familiar thesis that the task of criticism is not to bring out the work's relationships with the author, nor to reconstruct through the text a thought or experience, but rather to analyze the work through its structure, its architecture, its intrinsic form, and the play of its internal relationships. At this point, however, a problem arises: What is a work? What is this curious unity which we designate as a work? Of what elements is it composed? Is it not what an author has written? Difficulties appear immediately. If an individual were not an author, could we say that what he wrote, said, left behind in his papers, or what has been collected of his remarks, could be called a 'work'? When Sade was not considered an author, what was the status of his papers? Were they simply rolls of paper onto which he ceaselessly uncoiled his fantasies during his imprisonment?

Even when an individual has been accepted as an author, we must still ask whether everything that he wrote, said, or left behind is part of his work. The problem is both theoretical and technical. When undertaking the publication of Nietzsche's works, for example, where should one stop? Surely everything must be published, but what is 'everything'? Everything that Nietzsche himself published, certainly. And what about the rough drafts for his works? Obviously. The plans for his aphorisms? Yes. The deleted passages and the notes at the bottom of the page? Yes. What if, within a workbook filled with aphorisms, one finds a reference, the notation of a meeting or of an address, or a laundry list: Is it a work, or not? Why not? And so on, ad infinitum. How can one define a work amid the millions of traces left by someone after his death? A theory of the work does not exist, and the empirical task of those who naively undertake the editing of works often suffers in the absence of such a theory.

We could go even further: Does *The Thousand and One Nights* constitute a work? What about Clement of Alexandria's *Miscellanies* or Diogenes Laertius's *Lives*? A multitude of questions arises with regard to this notion of the work. Consequently, it is not enough to declare that we should do without the writer (the author) and study the work itself. The word *work* and the unity that it designates are probably as problematic as the status of the author's individuality.

Another notion which has hindered us from taking full measure of the author's disappearance, blurring and concealing the moment of this effacement and subtly preserving the author's existence, is the notion of writing (*écriture*). When rigorously applied, this notion should allow us not only to circumvent references to the author, but also to situate his recent absence. The notion of writing, as currently employed, is concerned with neither the act of writing nor the indication – be it symptom or sign – of a meaning which someone might have wanted to express. We try, with great effort, to imagine the general condition of each text, the condition of both the space in which it is dispersed and the time in which it unfolds.

In current usage, however, the notion of writing seems to transpose the empirical characteristics of the author into a transcendental anonymity. We are content to efface the more visible marks of the author's empiricity by playing off, one against the other, two ways of characterizing writing, namely, the critical and the religious approaches. Giving writing a primal status seems to be a way of retranslating, in transcendental terms, both the theological affirmation of its sacred character and the critical affirmation of its creative character. To admit that writing is, because of the very history that it made possible, subject to the test of oblivion and repression, seems to represent, in transcendental terms, the religious principle of the hidden meaning (which requires interpretation) and the critical principle of implicit significations, silent determinations, and obscured contents (which gives rise to commentary). To imagine writing as absence seems to be a simple repetition, in transcendental terms, of both the religious principle of inalterable and yet never fulfilled tradition, and the aesthetic principle of the work's survival, its perpetuation beyond the author's death, and its enigmatic *excess* in relation to him.

This usage of the notion of writing runs the risk of maintaining the author's privileges under the protection of writing's *a priori* status: it keeps alive, in the gray light of neutralization, the interplay of those representations that formed a particular image of the author. The author's disappearance, which, since Mallarmé, has been a constantly recurring event, is subject to a series of transcendental barriers. There seems to be an important dividing line between those who believe that they can still locate today's discontinuities (*ruptures*) in the historico-transcendental tradition of the nineteenth century, and those who try to free themselves once and for all from that tradition.

It is not enough, however, to repeat the empty affirmation that the author has disappeared. For the same reason, it is not enough to keep repeating (after Nietzsche) that God and man have died a common death. Instead, we must locate the space left empty by the author's disappearance, follow the distribution of gaps and breaches, and watch for the openings that this disappearance uncovers.

First, we need to clarify briefly the problems arising from the use of the author's name. What is an author's name? How does it function? Far from offering a solution, I shall only indicate some of the difficulties that it presents.

The author's name is a proper name, and therefore it raises the problems common to all proper names. (Here I refer to Searle's analyses, among others.[1]) Obviously, one cannot turn a proper name into a pure and simple reference. It has other than indicative functions: more than an indication, a gesture, a finger pointed at someone, it is the equivalent of a description. When one says 'Aristotle', one employs a word that is the equivalent of one, or a series, of definite descriptions, such as 'the author of the *Analytics*', 'the founder of ontology', and so forth. One cannot stop there, however, because a proper name does not have just one signification. When we discover that Rimbaud did not write *La Chasse spirituelle*, we cannot pretend that the meaning of this proper name, or that of the author, has been altered. The proper name and the author's name are situated between the two poles of description and designation: they must have a certain link with what they name, but one that is neither entirely in the mode of designation nor in that of description; it must be a *specific* link. However – and it is here that the particular difficulties of the author's name arise – the links between the proper name and the individual named and between the author's name and what it names are not isomorphic and do not function in the same way. There are several differences.

If, for example, Pierre Dupont does not have blue eyes, or was not born in Paris, or is not a doctor, the name Pierre Dupont will still always refer to the same person; such things do not modify the link of designation. The problems raised by the author's name are much more complex, however. If I discover that Shakespeare was not born in the house that we visit today, this is a modification which, obviously, will not alter the functioning of the author's name. But if we proved that Shakespeare did not write those sonnets which pass for his, that would constitute a significant change and affect the manner in which the author's name functions. If we proved that Shakespeare wrote Bacon's *Organon* by showing that the same author wrote both the works of Bacon and those of Shakespeare, that would be a third type of change which would entirely modify the functioning of the author's name. The author's name is not, therefore, just a proper name like the rest.

Many other facts point out the paradoxical singularity of the author's name. To say that Pierre Dupont does not exist is not at all the same as saying that Homer or Hermes Trismegistus did not exist. In the first case, it means that no one has the name Pierre Dupont; in the second, it means that several people were mixed together under one name, or that the true author had none of the traits traditionally ascribed to the personae of Homer or Hermes. To say that X's real name is actually Jacques Durand instead of Pierre Dupont is not the same as saying that Stendhal's name was Henri Beyle. One could also question the meaning and functioning of propositions like 'Bourbaki is so-and-so, so-and-so, etc.' and 'Victor Eremita, Climacus, Anticlimacus, Frater Taciturnus, Constantine Constantius, all of these are Kierkegaard.'

These differences may result from the fact that an author's name is not simply an element in a discourse (capable of being either subject or object, of being replaced by a pronoun, and the like); it performs a certain role with regard to narrative discourse, assuring a classificatory function. Such a name permits one to group together a certain number of texts, define them, differentiate them from and contrast them to others. In addition, it establishes a relationship among the texts. Hermes Trismegistus did not exist, nor did Hippocrates – in the sense that Balzac existed – but the fact that several texts have been placed under the same name indicates that there has been established among them a relationship of homogeneity, filiation, authentication of some texts by the use of others, reciprocal explication, or concomitant utilization. The author's name serves to characterize a certain mode of being of discourse: the fact that the discourse has an author's name, that one can say 'this was written by so-and-so' or 'so-and-so is its author', shows that this discourse is not ordinary everyday speech that merely comes and goes, not something that is immediately consumable. On the contrary, it is a speech that must be received in a certain mode and that, in a given culture, must receive a certain status.

It would seem that the author's name, unlike other proper names, does not pass from the interior of a discourse to the real and exterior individual who produced it; instead, the name seems always to be present, marking off the edges of the text, revealing, or at least characterizing, its mode of being. The author's name manifests the appearance of a certain discursive set and indicates the status of this discourse within a society and a culture. It has no legal status, nor is it located in the fiction of the work; rather, it is located in the break that founds a certain discursive construct and its very particular mode of being. As a result, we could say that in a civilization like our own there are a certain number of discourses that are endowed with the 'author function', while others are deprived of it. A private letter may well have a signer – it does not have an author; a contract may well have a guarantor – it does not have an author. An anonymous text posted on a wall probably has a writer – but not an author. The author function is therefore characteristic of the mode of existence, circulation, and functioning of certain discourses within a society.

Let us analyze this 'author function' as we have just described it. In our culture, how does one characterize a discourse containing the author function? In what way is this discourse different from other discourses? If we limit our remarks to the author of a book or a text, we can isolate four different characteristics.

First of all, discourses are objects of appropriation. The form of ownership from which they spring is of a rather particular type, one that has been codified for many years. We should note that, historically, this type of ownership has always been subsequent to what one might call penal appropriation. Texts, books, and discourses really began to have authors (other than mythical, 'sacralized' and 'sacralizing' figures) to the extent that authors became subject to punishment, that is, to the extent that discourses could be transgressive. In our culture (and doubtless in many others), discourse was not originally a product, a thing, a kind of goods; it was essentially an act – an act placed in the bipolar field of the sacred and the profane, the licit and the illicit, the religious and the blasphemous. Historically, it was a gesture fraught with risks before becoming goods caught up in a circuit of ownership.

Once a system of ownership for texts came into being, once strict rules concerning authors' rights, author–publisher relations, rights of reproduction, and related matters were enacted – at the end of the eighteenth and the beginning of the nineteenth century – the possibility of transgression attached to the act of writing took on, more and more, the form of an imperative peculiar to literature. It is as if the author, beginning with the moment at which he was placed in the system of property that characterizes our society, compensated for the status that he thus acquired by rediscovering the old bipolar field of discourse, systematically practicing transgression and thereby restoring danger to a writing which was now guaranteed the benefits of ownership.

The author function does not affect all discourses in a universal and constant way, however. This is its second characteristic. In our civilization, it has not always been the same types of texts which have required attribution to an author. There was a time when the texts that we today call 'literary' (narratives, stories, epics, tragedies, comedies) were accepted, put into circulation, and valorized without any question about the identity of their author; their anonymity caused no difficulties since their ancientness, whether real or imagined, was regarded as a sufficient guarantee of their status. On the other hand, those texts that we now would call scientific – those dealing with cosmology and the heavens, medicine and illnesses, natural sciences and geography – were accepted in the Middle Ages, and accepted as 'true', only when marked with the name of their author. 'Hippocrates said', 'Pliny recounts', were not really formulas of an argument based on authority; they were the markers inserted in discourses that were supported to be received as statements of demonstrated truth.

A reversal occurred in the seventeenth or eighteenth century. Scientific discourses began to be received for themselves, in the anonymity of an established or always redemonstrable truth; their membership in a systematic ensemble, and not the reference to the individual who produced them, stood as their guarantee. The author function faded away, and the inventor's name served only to christen a theorem, proposition, particular effect, property, body, group of elements, or pathological syndrome. By the same token, literary discourses came to be accepted only when endowed with the author function. We now ask of each poetic or fictional text: From where does it come, who wrote it, when, under what circumstances, or beginning with what design? The meaning ascribed to it and the status or value accorded it depend on the manner in which we answer these questions. And if a text should be discovered in a state of anonymity – whether as a consequence of an accident or the author's explicit wish – the game becomes one of rediscovering the author. Since literary anonymity is not tolerable, we can accept it only in the guise of an enigma. As a result, the author function today plays an important role in our view of literary works. (These are obviously generalizations that would have to be refined insofar as recent critical practice is concerned.)

The third characteristic of this author function is that it does not develop spontaneously as the attribution of a discourse to an individual. It is, rather, the result of a complex operation which constructs a certain rational being that we call 'author'. Critics doubtless try to give this intelligible being a realistic status, by discerning, in the individual, a 'deep' motive, a 'creative' power, or a 'design', the milieu in which writing originates. Nevertheless, these aspects of an individual which we designate as making him an author are only a projection, in more or less psychologizing terms, of the operations that we force texts to undergo, the connections that we make, the traits that we establish as pertinent, the continuities that we recognize, or the exclusions that we practice. All these operations vary according to periods and types of discourse. We do not construct a 'philosophical author' as we do a 'poet', just as, in the eighteenth century, one did not construct a novelist as we do today. Still, we can find through the ages certain constants in the rules of author construction.

It seems, for example, that the manner in which literary criticism once defined the author – or, rather, constructed the figure of the author beginning with existing texts and discourses – is directly derived from the manner in which Christian tradition authenticated (or rejected) the texts at its disposal. In order to 'rediscover' an author in a work, modern criticism uses methods similar to those that Christian exegesis employed when trying to prove the value of a text by its author's saintliness. In *De viris illustribus*, Saint Jerome explains that homonymy is not sufficient to identify legitimately authors of more than one work: different individuals could have had the same name, or one man could have, illegitimately, borrowed another's patronymic. The name as an individual trademark is not enough when one works within a textual tradition.

How, then, can one attribute several discourses to one and the same author? How can one use the author function to determine if one is dealing with one or several individuals? Saint Jerome proposes four criteria: (1) if among several books attributed to an author one is inferior to the others, it must be withdrawn from the list of the author's works (the author is therefore defined as a constant level of value); (2) the same should be done if certain texts contradict the doctrine expounded in the author's other works (the author is thus defined as a field of conceptual or theoretical coherence); (3) one must also exclude works that are written in a different style, containing words and expressions not ordinarily found in the writer's production (the author is here conceived as a stylistic unity); (4) finally, passages quoting statements that were made or mentioning events that occurred after the author's death must be regarded as interpolated texts (the author is here seen as a historical figure at the crossroads of a certain number of events).

Modern literary criticism, even when – as is now customary – it is not concerned with questions of authentication, still defines the author the same way: the author provides the basis for explaining not only the presence of certain events in a work, but also their transformations, distortions, and diverse modifications (through his biography, the determination of his individual perspective, the analysis of his social position, and the revelation of his basic design). The author is also the principle of a certain unity of writing – all differences having to be resolved, at least in part, by the principles of evolution, maturation, or influence. The author also serves to neutralize the contradictions that may emerge in a series of texts: there must be – at a certain level of his thought or desire, of his consciousness or unconscious – a point where contradictions are resolved, where incompatible elements are at last tied together or organized around a fundamental or originating contradiction. Finally, the author is a particular source of expression that, in more or less completed forms, is manifested equally well, and with similar validity, in works, sketches, letters, fragments, and so on. Clearly, Saint Jerome's four criteria of authenticity (criteria which seem totally insufficient for today's exegetes) do define the four modalities according to which modern criticism brings the author function into play.

But the author function is not a pure and simple reconstruction made secondhand from a text given as passive material. The text always contains a certain number of signs referring to the author. These signs, well known to grammarians, are personal pronouns, adverbs of time and place, and verb conjugation. Such elements do not play the same role in discourses provided with the author function as in those lacking it. In the latter, such 'shifters' refer to the real speaker and to the spatiotemporal coordinates of his discourse (although certain modifications can occur, as in the operation of relating discourses in the first person). In the former, however, their role is more complex and variable. Everyone knows that, in a novel narrated in the first person, neither the first-person pronoun nor the present indicative refers exactly either to the writer or to the moment in which he writes, but rather to an alter ego whose distance from the author varies, often changing in the course of the work. It would be just as wrong to equate the author with the real writer as to equate him with the fictitious speaker; the author function is carried out and operates in the scission itself, in this division and this distance.

One might object that this is a characteristic peculiar to novelistic or poetic discourse, a 'game' in which only 'quasi-discourses' participate. In fact, however, all discourses endowed with the author function do possess this plurality of self. The self that speaks in the preface to a treatise on mathematics – and that indicates the circumstances of the treatise's composition – is identical neither in its position nor in its functioning to the self that speaks in the course of a demonstration, and that appears in the form of 'I conclude' or 'I suppose'. In the first case, the 'I' refers to an individual without an equivalent who, in a determined place and time, completed a certain task; in the second, the 'I' indicates an instance and a level of demonstration which any individual could perform provided that he accepted the same system of symbols, play of axioms, and set of previous demonstrations. We could also, in the same treatise, locate a third self, one that speaks to tell the work's meaning, the obstacles encountered, the results obtained, and the remaining problems; this self is situated in the field of already existing or yet-to-appear mathematical discourses. The author function is not assumed by the first of these selves at the expense of the other two, which would then be nothing more than a fictitious splitting in two of the first one. On the contrary, in these discourses the author function operates so as to effect the dispersion of these three simultaneous selves.

No doubt analysis could discover still more characteristic traits of the author function. I will limit myself to these four, however, because they seem both the most visible and the most important. They can be summarized as follows: (1) the author function is linked to the juridical and institutional system that encompasses, determines, and articulates the universe of discourses; (2) it does not affect all discourses in the same way at all times and in all types of civilization; (3) it is not defined by the spontaneous attribution of a discourse to its producer, but rather by a series of specific and complex operations; (4) it does not refer purely and simply to a real individual, since it can give rise simultaneously to several selves, to several subjects – positions that can be occupied by different classes of individuals.

Up to this point I have unjustifiably limited my subject. Certainly the author function in painting, music, and other arts should have been discussed, but even supposing that we remain within the world of discourse, as I want to do, I seem to have given the term 'author' much too narrow a meaning. I have discussed the author only in the limited sense of a person to whom the production of a text, a book, or a work can be legitimately attributed. It is easy to see that in the sphere of discourse one can be the author of much more than a book – one can be the author of a theory, tradition, or discipline in which other books and authors will in their turn find a place. These authors are in a position which we shall call 'transdiscursive'. This is a recurring phenomenon – certainly as old as our civilization. Homer, Aristotle, and the Church Fathers, as well as the first mathematicians and the originators of the Hippocratic tradition, all played this role.

Furthermore, in the course of the nineteenth century, there appeared in Europe another, more uncommon, kind of author, whom one should confuse with neither the 'great' literary authors, nor the authors of religious texts, nor the founders of science. In a somewhat arbitrary way we shall call those who belong in this last group 'founders of discursivity'. They are unique in that they are not just the authors of their own works. They have produced something else: the possibilities and the rules for the formation of other texts. In this sense, they are very different, for example, from a novelist, who is, in fact, nothing more than the author of his own text. Freud is not just the author of *The Interpretation of Dreams* or *Jokes and Their Relation to the Unconscious*; Marx is not just the author of the *Communist Manifesto* or *Das Kapital*: they both have established an endless possibility of discourse.

Obviously, it is easy to object. One might say that it is not true that the author of a novel is only the author of his own text; in a sense, he also, provided that he acquires some 'importance', governs and commands more than that. To take a very simple example, one could say that Ann Radcliffe not only wrote *The Castles of Athlin and Dunbayne* and several other novels, but also made possible the appearance of the Gothic horror novel at the beginning of the nineteenth century; in that respect, her author function exceeds her own work. But I think there is an answer to this objection. These founders of discursivity (I use Marx and Freud as examples, because I believe them to be both the first and the most important cases) make possible something altogether different from what a novelist makes possible. Ann Radcliffe's texts opened the way for a certain number of resemblances and analogies which have their model or principle in her work. The latter contains characteristic signs, figures, relationships, and structures which could be reused by others. In other words, to say that Ann Radcliffe founded the Gothic horror novel means that in the nineteenth-century Gothic novel one will find, as in Ann Radcliffe's works, the theme of the heroine caught in the trap of her own innocence, the hidden castle, the character of the black, cursed hero devoted to making the world expiate the evil done to him, and all the rest of it.

On the other hand, when I speak of Marx or Freud as founders of discursivity, I mean that they made possible not only a certain number of analogies, but also (and equally important) a certain number of differences. They have created a possibility for something other than their discourse, yet something belonging to what they founded. To say that Freud founded psychoanalysis does not (simply) mean that we find the concept of the libido or the technique of dream analysis in the works of Karl Abraham or Melanie Klein; it means that Freud made possible a certain number of divergences – with respect to his own texts, concepts, and hypotheses – that all arise from the psychoanalytic discourse itself.

This would seem to present a new difficulty, however: is the above not true, after all, of any founder of a science, or of any author who has introduced some important transformation into a science? After all, Galileo made possible not only those discourses that repeated the laws that he had formulated, but also statements very different from what he himself had said. If Cuvier is the founder of biology or Saussure the founder of linguistics, it is not because they were imitated, nor because people have since taken up again the concept of organism or sign; it is because Cuvier made possible, to a certain extent, a theory of evolution diametrically opposed to his own fixism; it is because Saussure made possible a generative grammar radically different from his structural analyses. Superficially, then, the initiation of discursive practices appears similar to the founding of any scientific endeavor.

Still, there is a difference, and a notable one. In the case of a science, the act that founds it is on an equal footing with its future transformations; this act becomes in some respects part of the set of modifications that it makes possible. Of course, this belonging can take several forms. In the future development of a science, the founding act may appear as little more than a particular instance of a more general phenomenon which unveils itself in the process. It can also turn out to be marred by intuition and empirical bias; one must then reformulate it, making it the object of a certain number of supplementary theoretical operations which establish it more rigorously, etc. Finally, it can seem to be a hasty generalization which must be limited, and whose restricted domain of validity must be retraced. In other words, the founding act of a science can always be reintroduced within the machinery of those transformations that derive from it.

In contrast, the initiation of a discursive practice is heterogeneous to its subsequent transformations. To expand a type of discursivity, such as psychoanalysis as founded by Freud, is not to give it a formal generality that it would not have permitted at the outset, but rather to open it up to a certain number of possible applications. To limit psychoanalysis as a type of discursivity is, in reality, to try to isolate in the founding act an eventually restricted number of propositions or statements to which, alone, one grants a founding value, and in relation to which certain concepts or theories accepted by Freud might be considered as derived, secondary, and accessory. In addition, one does not declare certain propositions in the work of these founders to be false: instead, when trying to seize the act of founding, one sets aside those statements that are not pertinent, either because they are deemed inessential, or because they are considered 'prehistoric' and derived from another type of discursivity. In other words, unlike the founding of a science, the initiation of a discursive practice does not participate in its later transformations.

As a result, one defines a proposition's theoretical validity in relation to the work of the founders – while, in the case of Galileo and Newton, it is in relation to what physics or cosmology *is* (in its intrinsic structure and 'normativity') that one affirms the validity of any proposition that those men may have put forth. To phrase it very schematically: the work of initiators of discursivity is not situated in the space that science defines; rather, it is the science or the discursivity which refers back to their work as primary coordinates.

In this way we can understand the inevitable necessity, within these fields of discursivity, for a 'return to the origin'. This return, which is part of the discursive field itself, never stops modifying it. The return is not a historical supplement which would be added to the discursivity, or merely an ornament; on the contrary, it constitutes an effective and necessary task of transforming the discursive practice itself. Reexamination of Galileo's text may well change our knowledge of the history of mechanics, but it will never be able to change mechanics itself. On the other hand, reexamining Freud's texts modifies psychoanalysis itself, just as a reexamination of Marx's would modify Marxism.

What I have just outlined regarding the initiation of discursive practices is, of course, very schematic; this is true, in particular, of the opposition that I have tried to draw between discursive initiation and scientific founding. It is not always easy to distinguish between the two; moreover, nothing proves that they are two mutually exclusive procedures. I have attempted the distinction for only one reason: to show that the author function, which is complex enough when one tries to situate it at the level of a book or a series of texts that carry a given signature, involves still more determining factors when one tries to analyze it in larger units, such as groups of works or entire disciplines.

To conclude, I would like to review the reasons why I attach a certain importance to what I have said.

First, there are theoretical reasons. On the one hand, an analysis in the direction that I have outlined might provide for an approach to a typology of discourse. It seems to me, at least at first glance, that such a typology cannot be constructed solely from the grammatical features, formal structures, and objects of discourse: more likely there exist properties or relationships peculiar to discourse (not reducible to the rules of grammar and logic), and one must use these to distinguish the major categories of discourse. The relationship (or nonrelationship) with an author, and the different forms this relationship takes, constitute – in a quite visible manner – one of these discursive properties.

On the other hand, I believe that one could find here an introduction to the historical analysis of discourse. Perhaps it is time to study discourses not only in terms of their expressive value or formal transformations, but according to their modes of existence. The modes of circulation, valorization, attribution, and appropriation of discourses vary with each culture and are modified within each. The manner in which they are articulated according to social relationships can be more readily understood, I believe, in the activity of the author function and in its modifications than in the themes or concepts that discourses set in motion.

It would seem that one could also, beginning with analyses of this type, reexamine the privileges of the subject. I realize that in undertaking the internal and architectonic analysis of a work (be it a literary text, philosophical system, or scientific work), in setting aside biographical and psychological references, one has already called back into question the absolute character and founding role of the subject. Still, perhaps one must return to this question, not in order to reestablish the theme of an originating subject, but to grasp the subject's points of insertion, modes of functioning, and system of dependencies. Doing so means overturning the traditional problem, no longer raising the questions: How can a free subject penetrate the substance of things and give it meaning? How can it activate the rules of a language from within and thus give rise to the designs which are properly its own? Instead, these questions will be raised: How, under what conditions, and in what forms can something like a subject appear in the order of discourse? What place can it occupy in each type of discourse, what functions can it assume, and by obeying what rules? In short, it is a matter of depriving the subject (or its substitute) of its role as originator, and of analyzing the subject as a variable and complex function of discourse.

Second, there are reasons dealing with the 'ideological' status of the author. The question then becomes: How can one reduce the great peril, the great danger with which fiction threatens our world? The answer is: one can reduce it with the author. The author allows a limitation of the cancerous and dangerous proliferation of significations within a world where one is thrifty not only with one's resources and riches, but also with one's discourses and their significations. The author is the principle of thrift in the proliferation of meaning. As a result, we must entirely reverse the traditional idea of the author. We are accustomed, as we have seen earlier, to saying that the author is the genial creator of a work in which he deposits, with infinite wealth and generosity, an inexhaustible world of significations. We are used to thinking that the author is so different from all other men, and so transcendent with regard to all languages that, as soon as he speaks, meaning begins to proliferate, to proliferate indefinitely.

The truth is quite the contrary: the author is not an indefinite source of significations which fill a work; the author does not precede the works; he is a certain functional principle by which, in our culture, one limits, excludes, and chooses; in short, by which one impedes the free circulation, the free manipulation, the free composition, decomposition, and recomposition of fiction. In fact, if we are accustomed to presenting the author as a genius, as a perpetual surging of invention, it is because, in reality, we make him function in exactly the opposite fashion. One can say that the author is an ideological product, since we represent him as the opposite of his historically real function. (When a historically given function is represented in a figure that inverts it, one has an ideological production.) The author is therefore the ideological figure by which one marks the manner in which we fear the proliferation of meaning.

In saying this, I seem to call for a form of culture in which fiction would not be limited by the figure of the author. It would be pure romanticism, however, to imagine a culture in which the fictive would operate in an absolutely free state, in which fiction would be put at the disposal of everyone and would develop without passing through something like a necessary or constraining figure.

Although, since the eighteenth century, the author has played the role of the regulator of the fictive, a role quite characteristic of our era of industrial and bourgeois society, of individualism and private property, still, given the historical modifications that are taking place, it does not seem necessary that the author function remain constant in form, complexity, and even in existence. I think that, as our society changes, at the very moment when it is in the process of changing, the author function will disappear, and in such a manner that fiction and its polysemous texts will once again function according to another mode, but still with a system of constraint – one which will no longer be the author, but which will have to be determined or, perhaps, experienced.

All discourses, whatever their status, form, value, and whatever the treatment to which they will be subjected, would then develop in the anonymity of a murmur. We would no longer hear the questions that have been rehashed for so long: Who really spoke? Is it really he and not someone else? With what authenticity or originality? And what part of his deepest self did he express in his discourse? Instead, there would be other questions, like these: What are the modes of existence of this discourse? Where has it been used, how can it circulate, and who can appropriate it for himself? What are the places in it where there is room for possible subjects? Who can assume these various subject functions? And behind all these questions, we would hear hardly anything but the stirring of an indifference: What difference does it make who is speaking?

Note

1   *Ed.*: John Searle, *Speech Acts: An Essay in the Philosophy of Language* (Cambridge, Eng.: Cambridge University Press, 1969), pp. 162–74.

Chapter 21

Paula McDowell

ORAL RELIGIO-POLITICAL ACTIVISM
AND TEXTUAL PRODUCTION

> For all my Labours and Travels, this Paper will not contain them.
> (Elinor James, *Mrs. Jame's* [sic] *Apology because of Unbelievers*, c.1694)

What did print mean to early female polemicists and preachers, and especially to those women whose lack of access to printed texts – or lack of time to read them – ensured that they remained rooted in a still fundamentally oral world? 'I wish well to the Readers, whoever they be,' Elinor James declared at the head of one of her earliest broadsides. James's headnote sounds a tone of regret, as if she recognized that to print her ideas was to lose control over how her audience would respond to them. '*I have given so many, that I can give no more,*' she lamented, '*and therefore through the earnest desires of some, I have yielded to Publish them, contrary to my Intentions.*' Unable to chastise her addressees in person, or to correct their mistaken interpretations, she could only ask God to 'bless this Paper, that the Reader may be the better'. Even with God's help, print could be a strangely distancing mode of communication.[1]

  In turning to the newly available tool of print to supplement their ongoing oral efforts to influence public opinion, Elinor James, Anne Docwra, Joan Whitrowe, and Jane Lead were not trying to avoid more public polemical encounters. These women used print not to 'cover' themselves but rather to expand the public oral audience that they already had. These women typically signed their papers and books, and provided readers and hearers with their own personal addresses.[2] They did this to 'authenticate' their works and of course to maximize the sales of their texts. But they also provided their personal addresses so that readers and hearers who disagreed with their opinions could come and debate issues further with them in person. . . . The broadsides, pamphlets, and books written by these polemicists must be read as the products – and agents – of oral discussion and debate: voicings of specific speech communities which may be inferred by listening between the lines of the texts themselves. They are utterances responding to specific other utterances, and in them, their authors' anticipation of readers' rejoinders can be heard.

[. . .]

  . . . In late seventeenth- and early eighteenth-century London, the religio-political culture of ordinary women was still fundamentally an oral culture. Furthermore, this chapter will show, this oral polemical culture informed not only the content, but also the format and other aspects of the material production and circulation of these women's printed texts. A consideration of these authors' diverse modes of publishing their religious and political ideas, of their intended audiences, and of the ways that these conditions of publication influenced the external format and internal characteristics of their texts will help to reduce the opaqueness of these women's writings for the modern reader, and enable us to move on to a consideration of their religious and political world views and ideas.

[. . .]

. . . Quaker Anne Docwra (c.1624–1710) had access to a remarkably sophisticated alternative publishing formation: a network and support system designed to spread the Word, and lend the Society of Friends crucial coherence from within. As their name 'Publishers of Truth' suggests, early Quakers made extensive use of the power of the printed word to shape public opinion and foment sociopolitical change. Quaker commitment to the use of the press may be inferred from the fact that in the years 1659 and 1660 the Friends published about 10 per cent of the total extant titles published in England, despite comprising less than 1 per cent of the population.[3] According to one historian of Quakerism, between the beginnings of the movement in the early 1650s and the appearance of the first Quaker bibliography in 1708, 440 Quaker writers printed 2,678 different publications.[4] At this time of harsh prosecution and strict press licensing, this illegal nonconformist sect produced not less than two and a quarter million books and tracts.[5]

For Quaker women in particular the practical and psychological benefits of access to this publishing support system may be surmised from the fact that seventeenth-century Quaker women produced twice as many extant printed editions as any other female group.[6] Anne Docwra published at least seven tracts between 1682 and 1700, and was an ardent polemicist for religious toleration, the separation of church and state, and women's right to prophesy and testify in public.[7] The benefits of the Quaker publishing system may also be surmised from the many jealous observations of Docwra's chief polemical opponent, apostate Quaker Francis Bugg. Bugg remarked, for instance, that Docwra's books were printed and 'Sold by *Tacy Sowle*, the Quakers Bookseller, as a Sign both of their Approbation, and Unity'.[8] Tace Sowle served as primary printer and publisher for the Friends, and her press was the primary channel through which Quaker works were issued. In addition to Anne Docwra's pamphlets, Tace Sowle printed books and tracts by more than a dozen women writers. These women, not all of them Quakers, include Elizabeth Bathurst, Sarah Cheevers, Elizabeth Chester, Mary Edwards, Alice Ellis, Katharine Evans, Jane Fearon, Alice Hayes, Elizabeth Jacob, Jane Lead, Mary Mollineaux, Elizabeth Stirredge, Jane Truswell, and the 'mother of Quakerism' Margaret Askew Fell Fox.

From its beginnings, then, Quakerism was a religion of the book. As part of her ongoing efforts to educate the public as to who Quakers were and what they believed, Anne Docwra engaged in an ongoing battle-in-print with apostate Quaker Francis Bugg. In addition to their other religio-political writings Docwra and Bugg produced a total of at least one dozen works slandering each other's beliefs, backgrounds, and personal characters. Their exceedingly public dispute is worth considering in detail for the insights it provides into the character and rhetorical and commercial strategies of early modern popular religio-political print culture.[9]

Remembering that theological discourse was in fact the 'bestselling' form of print material in the early modern literary marketplace does much to help decode the 'otherness' for twentieth-century readers of debates such as Docwra and Bugg's. As a Quaker, Docwra did not need to concern herself with printing costs as much as Bugg did; Quaker central organization did this for her.[10] Quaker texts also had a ready-made readership. Quaker Monthly Meetings throughout Great Britain and Ireland were required to take copies of all Quaker books authorized and published by central organization. Bugg, by way of contrast, had to rely on a general audience to purchase his books for their educational and entertainment value. To some extent, the extraordinary mudslinging of his exchange with Docwra can be explained by this simple fact. In the increasingly competitive literary marketplace in which these authors wrote, even religious books had to entertain as well as edify. Then as now, there were potential 'sales advantages in calculated eccentricity'.[11] The outrageous rudeness of these religious-tracts-cum-jestbooks is to some degree the textual equivalent of 'going naked as a sign'. The taunting jests, breathless rant, and verbal jousting to be found there are a form of rhetorical entrepreneurism. Theological arguments and gossipy, personal squabbling interanimate one another, and satisfy a public need for 'news' as well as intellectual debate.[12] In addition, while from their beginnings the 'Publishers of Truth' were a well-organized 'religion of the book', at the same time the traces of contemporary oral culture are everywhere evident in their writings. The magnificent series of insults bandied back and forth between Docwra and Bugg, and the statement and rebuttal form of their pamphlets, are the textual equivalents of a verbal street fight. Criticism, no matter how outrageous, is responded to point by point, and name-calling and derogatory remarks are standard (rather like the verbal phenomenon oral theorists refer to as 'flyting').

Francis Bugg's concern with expenses is certainly one unrelenting reminder that religious books are commodities as well as vehicles of ideas. Bugg frequently complained of the expense of engaging in public debate with Docwra, and this is not surprising, for while indebted to contemporary oral culture, theirs was a text-based, as well as text-focused, confrontation. Docwra and Bugg fought against one another's books, responded to each other's printed texts with more printed texts, and referred to printed texts as evidence for their charges. Bugg printed Docwra's letters and concerned himself largely with what Docwra had or had not written. Docwra repeatedly referred to 'my book' and provided her readers with specific page numbers and citations. Nor, as Docwra herself pointed out, was Bugg the only polemical opponent to find her threatening enough to attack by name in print. As she explained, one of her papers which Bugg had tried to use against her was itself written in response to 'a Book that came out in Print, written against me, printed 1685'.[13] As with Docwra's pamphlets, so Bugg's were published by a woman: 'Mrs. *Janeway*, Bookbinder, in *London*-house Yard, next door to *Child's Coffee-House* in St. Paul's churchyard.' By 1701, Bugg claimed to have published '17800 Books, Small and Great', and to be 'indebted for Paper, Printing, and Binding, near 100 pounds'. Bugg also provides us with the information that his *Jezebel Withstood, and Her Daughter Anne Docwra, Publickly Reprov'd* (1699) was printed in a substantial edition of 1,000 copies, while his *A Winding-Sheet for Ann Dockwra* was printed in an edition of 500.[14] There is a strong sense of the materiality of literary production throughout Bugg's religious writings, for he constantly lamented print's expense. He claimed to have irrefutable evidence against Docwra's claims in his possession, but that to print these materials would be to 'fill another Half Sheet'. This expense was too much to 'bestow . . . upon this craz'd old piece which is now creeping into the Unity of the Quakers' (*Jezebel Withstood* (1699), 4).

While Bugg jealously noted Docwra's indebtedness to the Quaker system of textual financing, Docwra argued that Bugg was a Grub Street hack writing in the pay of the established church. Docwra's works represent the Anglican church as a propaganda machine: a state-sponsored publishing system which encouraged malcontents like Bugg to slander dissenters for pay. Bugg was a 'Mercenary Agent, belonging to such of the Clergy, as are uneasie under the Liberty granted to Protestant Dissenters' (*Second Part of an Apostate-Conscience Exposed* (1700), 3). He turned to religious hackwork due to his 'Seared Conscience', his 'Shatter'd Head', and above all his 'Desperate Fortunes' (*Second Part of an Apostate-Conscience Exposed* (1700), 7). His pious tracts were in fact nothing but 'Lyes and Deceit', written 'to cheat the *Clergy* of their Money' (*Second Part of an Apostate-Conscience Exposed* (1700), 40 (sic; recte 16)). We have seen how, in the *Dunciad*, Alexander Pope pronounced that 'Law can pronounce judgment only on open Facts' and called for 'good writer[s]' to step in to supply the deficiencies of the government. In her own writings, Anne Docwra also recognized the power of writers to influence public opinion, but she also recognized government-sponsored print propaganda as a powerful new form of 'positive censorship' in her society. She argued that the legal slander of nonconformists was in fact an increasingly central form of state persecution of oppositional voices: 'F. Bugg, and his Abettors of the Clergy, have raised a New Persecution, with Tongue and Pen' (*Second Part of an Apostate-Conscience Exposed* (1700), 5). A propagandist such as Bugg might publish 'Lyes and Deceit', but once those 'Lyes and Deceit' were printed they were powerful weapons. Playing on the meaning of 'magazine' as a place where ammunition is stored, she observed, 'I perceive by [Bugg's] Writing, that he hath prepared a large *Magazine of Forgery* against me, if his Clergy will pay for printing it' (*Second Part of an Apostate-Conscience Exposed* (1700), 33).

Bugg rallied back against Docwra's charges that he was in the pay of the established church. He declared, 'I never Wrot for Money, nor was I ever a Beggar, nor have I wanted a sufficient support to this Day.' But he contradicted his claim that he 'never Wrot for Money' when he then went on to admit to having accepted support for his writing from the church, and sought to justify his financial strategies by comparing them to what appeared to him the well-funded publishing programme of the Quakers. 'If I have Applyld my self to the Clergy,' he explained, 'that thereby, I might be Inabled to Defend my Christian Profession, against the Powerful Fund of the Quakers; it is no more than *Fox, Whitehead*, and others of the Quakers have done, who at first were not able to Print a Book at their own Charge' (*William Penn, the Pretended Quaker* (1700), 15). In *An Apostate-Conscience Exposed, And The Miserable Consequences thereof Disclosed, For Information and Caution* (1699), Docwra attacked Bugg's services as a 'Mercenary Agent', and attempted to counter his church-subsidized propaganda. In *Jezebel Withstood, and Her Daughter Anne Docwra, Publickly Reprov'd; For Her Lies and Lightness in Her Book, stiled, An Apostate Conscience &c.* (1699) Bugg responded to Docwra's charges, systematically quoting each one of Docwra's 'Lies' and printing replies. In *The Second Part of an Apostate-Conscience Exposed* (1700) Docwra responded to Bugg's response, and provided further evidence for her own case against him. Referring to the Act of Toleration granting freedom of worship to Protestant subjects, she accused her opponent of being 'uneasie under the Liberty granted to Protestant Dissenters' (3).

In opposition to the rising tide of Augustan polemics against religious enthusiasm, Docwra appended to this pamphlet a defence of inspiration, a 'Treatise concerning Enthusiasm' by 'A. D.' By the eighteenth century, religious enthusiasm was associated with the political upheaval of the Civil War period, and increasingly became 'the bugbear . . . of polite and scholarly . . . society'.[15] Jonathan Swift's satire *A Tale of a Tub* (wr. 1696; pub. 1704), written and published during the same years that Anne Docwra was publishing her works, exposes 'Enthusiasts and Phanaticks among us' and specifically links religious enthusiasm to women.[16] Section VIII is devoted to 'the Learned *Æolists*' ('All Pretenders to Inspiration whatsoever' (95 n.)) and notes that the practices of 'our *Modern Æolists*' are encouraged in '*Female* Priests . . . who are agreed to receive their Inspiration . . . like their Ancestors, the *Sybils*' (99). ('*Female* Priests' is glossed 'Quakers who suffer their Women to preach and pray' (99 n.).) Docwra, by way of contrast, argued that the motives of those who would represent marginalized and persecuted religious groups as 'fanaticks' were fundamentally political ones. She worked to 'shew the Legerdemain that hath been used in this Nation, by some of the Learned, concerning this strange word *Enthusiasm*, which they have frighted the Ignorant People with, making them believe that there is dangerous matter contained in it' (*Second Part*, 39). (Swift for instance specifically links religious enthusiasm with 'revolutions of government'.) By means of her word choice 'Legerdemain', Docwra suggested that the leaders of the Church of England, rather than the dissenters, were the purveyors of deception and 'black arts'. In the case of enthusiasm, Docwra argued, it was in fact the 'Learned' rather than the simple folk who were 'superstitious' and 'irrational'. She pointed out that 'the strange word *Enthusiasm*, is from a Greek word, and signifies in *English, Inspiration*' (*Second Part*, 39) and noted that English dictionaries confused '*Divine Motions* with

Poetical Fury'. She concluded her treatise by emphasizing that in all such matters, it was not ordinary folks but 'learned Men [who] are most subject to Error' (*Second Part*, 46).

Docwra came to believe that the new public forum of print was in fact the safest place to do battle with one's enemies. Oral debates could be misrepresented to those who did not hear them, and manuscript letters could be misquoted or forged. Docwra claimed to have received personal letters from Bugg full of 'Clamour and Threats, if I will not Retract my Book, which I do not intend' (*Second Part of an Apostate-Conscience Exposed* (1700), preface, 31). She claimed too that her opponent had 'forged letters, as from me to him, and printed them with my name to them'. Docwra believed that she was no longer 'free to answer F. Bugg, or any of his Cabal, but in Print, least they should put false Constructions of them, or add some Forgery to them' (*Second Part*, 9, 31). While Docwra increasingly saw print as one of the safest places to conduct an argument, Francis Bugg fundamentally distrusted this new mode of communication. Despite a John Dunton-like obsession with print, Bugg still appears to have felt most comfortable with oral modes of debate. In his *Seasonable Caveat Against the Prevalency of Quakerism* (1701) Bugg questioned why 'this *Ann Docwra*, whose Books they [the Quakers] sell, disperse, and spread for the Service of Truth . . . does she not come forth and prove what she says' (75). In *William Penn, the Pretended Quaker, Discovered to hold a Correspondence with the Jesuite's* [sic] *at Rome. To which is Added, A Winding-Sheet for Ann Dockwra* (1700), he went further, actually challenging Docwra to a public trial. He listed the names of four people – including a son – who would witness that he was not as Docwra claimed 'distracted'. He dared Docwra to abandon the 'shelter' of print and dispute religio-political matters with him in person. He suggested that she choose six men to serve on an ad hoc 'jury', along with six men of his own choice. And he added that if this supposedly neutral jury could not decide who made the better argument, he was willing to stand before two more supposedly neutral judges, the Vice-Chancellor and Mayor of Cambridge. In the 1640s, the Brownist pamphleteer and preacher Katherine Chidley carried on a pamphlet war with Thomas Edwards, and challenged her opponent to an oral parley much like this one that Bugg proposed to Docwra. Each opponent was to choose six persons who, in the presence of an impartial moderator, would listen to the details of the oral debate, then decide upon a verbal 'victor'.[17] In stylistic terms, as well as in actuality, oral parleys such as the Chidley–Edwards and Docwra–Bugg debates are at the heart of early modern religio-political print polemic. They are another example of the fundamentally oral underpinnings of late Stuart and early Hanoverian literary life.

Obsessed with print and yet afraid of it, Francis Bugg complained of his polemical opponent that the Friends 'now cry her up, *Oh, a brave Woman!* and she cries up them, *Oh G.* Whitehead *is a Gentleman Quaker*' (*Seasonable Caveat*, 62–3). Bugg dedicated his career as a polemicist-hack to alerting the nation to the powerful new combination of dissent and print, and to pointing out the dangerous 'Effects such Books have amongst . . . credulous People' (71).

Other than Francis Bugg, what were some of Anne Docwra's most pressing concerns as a Quaker? Docwra's first publication, *A Looking-Glass for the Recorder and Justices of the Peace, And Grand Juries for the Town and County of Cambridge* (1682), was written in response to the intensified persecution of dissenters during the Popish Plot and Exclusion Crisis (1678–83). In December 1681, the Privy Council had attempted to enforce the Clarendon Code to the fullest. Local magistrates had been ordered to enforce the Corporation Act of 1661, excluding Quakers and other nonconformists from any share in government or administration, and subjecting them to disabling fines and imprisonment. Docwra's *Looking-Glass* was written to chastise what she saw as a corrupt local government. Two of her other pamphlets of the 1680s were also responses to intensified persecution: *An Epistle of Love and Good Advice to My Old Friends and Fellow-Sufferers in the Late Times, The Old Royalists And their Posterity* (1683) and *Spiritual Community, vindicated amongst people of different perswasions in some things* (1687). These pamphlets, however, are directed not to corrupt magistrates and governors but to 'Old Friends and Fellow-Sufferers', and are aimed primarily at enhancing internal cohesion among the Quaker movement.

In her address to local magistrates in *A Looking-Glass for the Recorder* (1682), Docwra used unwritten collective oral memory, written and printed texts, and a subtext of prophetic threat to condemn the hypocrisy and corruption of local governments. Demonstrating typical Quaker familiarity with English statute law,[18] she pointed to specific laws pertaining to dissent. More generally, she boldly demanded that justices and juries might 'understand so much of Religion as is declared in the Laws and Statutes of this Land, and that the Oyer of the Law may be observed and allowed in all points, which is no more than the undoubted Right of every Free-Born Subject of this Nation' (1). Barely disguising her contempt for local magistrates and clergymen, she pointed out that these spiritual and political leaders were paid to uphold the law, not abuse it by fining dissenters and confiscating their property for their own gain. 'I pray let us have Law for our Money, ye are paid for it before-hand,' Docwra wrote. 'It is hard to find in the Histories of former Ages such a Money-Trade made of Religion, as hath been made in *England* within this two and Forty Years' (*Looking-Glass*, 2).

Docwra believed that the ideological notion of a national church of which all British subjects were members was a pernicious myth likely to cause England's downfall if left unchallenged. At the very least, those who did not choose to participate in Church of England services should be left to the censure of the parish church, rather than be punished by secular authorities. Relying on personal memory as well as on the collective oral memory of her audience, she illustrated the evils of forced conformity, warning that the persecution of dissenters would bring on another civil war:

> Force makes Hypocrites, which is the same Spirit that appeared in many of those that were concerned in the War against King *Charles* the first, which were the conforming Party mostly: *I very well remember that* [my emphasis], and the Bishops Severity also; they were very Officious in their Offices, to make them Church-men with their Church-Policy, so called, which proved to be the same nature in effect with that of the *Spaniards* with the *West-Indians*.
>
> (*Looking-Glass*, 3–4)

She argued that recent Acts of Parliament were directed primarily against Catholics, not Protestant dissenters. And she pointed out that if the justices of the peace were genuinely concerned that Quakers harboured Catholic affiliations, there was a Test Act in force which made it easy for those in power to determine who was Catholic. She herself, she claimed, had nearly been made subject to the penalties of 'the 32nd and 29th of *Elizabeth*', but was later discharged – presumably the best evidence that she was not a Papist. Employing the 'I was there' mode of argument of a residual oral culture even as she referred to printed statute law, she referred to a document that she herself had signed as evidence of her fundamental harmony with the government: 'I my self, with several others, subscribed to the Declaration contained in the said Act, before Judge *Montegue*, a Record thereof is in the Exchequer, and a Copy of it in the Sheriffs hand, whereby we are discharged of the Penalties of the Statutes of the 32nd and 29th of *Elizabeth*, aforesaid' (*Looking-Glass*, 6). Notwithstanding her subscription to this act, she and fellow Quakers had been robbed of their goods, though 'restored again upon Complaint' (6). This was illegal, for 'there is no Law to compel People to Conform, if they can shew a lawful or reasonable excuse' (7). The Scriptures provided examples of ordinary people like herself who dissented not against the faith but against the corruption of clergymen and princes (5). Finally, Docwra argued, imprisoning the people of England in filthy gaols and confiscating their property was not an effective way to promote Christ's gospel.

For Docwra, as for so many early religio-political polemicists, the notion of historical inevitability served as a crucial enabling presupposition. The 'legal Tyranny' of those in power would certainly bring on another civil war, for the 'poor People' of England could endure their wretched circumstances no longer. 'Vipers' might flourish now, Docwra warned,

> But Storms will come to make them Creep
> Into their Holes, in hopes of Sleep;
> Instead of Rest, with Sorrow Weep
> This is the Portion that will be
> Due to so great Hypocrisie.
> Anne Docwra.
>
> (*Looking-Glass*, 10)

Recalling the 'late Experience' of the Civil War, as well as the continuing instability of recent years, Docwra deployed unwritten oral memories to support her political prophecies for the future: 'There is nothing but Truth and Righteousness will stand in this Land of our Nativity, all things else stand but as a tottering Wall in *England*, as late Experience hath shown, whether they be Laws against Dissenters, flattering Addresses, Abhorrences, forced Oaths, contrived Covenants and Engagements for or against this or that Government' (*Looking-Glass*, 7). As an appendix to her argument for religious freedom, she affixed an advertisement informing those in power that the warrants they had had drawn up against local dissenters were unlawful and unlikely to be profitable: 'Those People that the warrants are out against are mostly poor People, and but few, if any at all (that I can hear of) that can or will provide the Money for to pay such an illegal Debt.' As in the body of her pamphlet, so in the appended advertisement she concluded her appeal with a prophetic curse: 'Disappointment will be the portion of all those that carry on such Designs as this: The Lord God Everlasting hasten the Confirmation of it that men may see where they are, and what they are doing. A.D.' (*Looking-Glass*, 11). If nothing else could authorize her public political critique of the government, the end of the world made it not only possible, but urgent for her to write.

Polemicist and preacher Joan Whitrowe published at least eight tracts over a period of twenty years from 1677 to 1697.[19] Most active in the immediate post-revolutionary period, she addressed most of her pamphlets specifically to William and Mary, expressing a sense of disillusionment that these professed saviours of the church had not lived up to her own and the nation's expectations. Whitrowe's relentless threats and advice are distinctive in their tone and in the specificity of their demands for social change. More than any of the other women political writers considered here, Whitrowe was motivated to write by her anger at the indifference of the propertied classes to the ubiquitous suffering of the poor. Concerned with immediate social problems rather than abstract constitutional issues, her pamphlets are rich in social observation, and her critique of property is sustained. Her papers are informed by an intensive, primary concern with what we might call class relationships, and serve as a reminder of the importance of class hostilities to seventeenth-century religious and political upheaval. They should also serve to caution those modern scholars who see sectarian radicals as having been 'reduced to silence and inertia' after the Restoration.[20]

Initially united with the Quakers but later separated from them, Joan Whitrowe may have been one casualty of the Quakers' own intensified internal press controls during the later years of the Restoration. Mysterious references to Whitrowe in Francis Bugg's polemics against Anne Docwra suggest that at one point the Society of Friends tried to put an end to Whitrowe's radical (and exceptionally dangerous) writings by withdrawing support for their publication. In denigrating Anne Docwra, Francis Bugg made a vague and chilling allusion to Joan Whitrowe's books being 'stopt'. Anne Docwra's books, Francis Bugg complained, were still 'sold by [the Quakers], and not stopt, as *Joan Whitrow's*'. Bugg implied that Joan Whitrowe was 'rebuked as an Incendiary', and suffered pre-publication censorship of her writings not by the government but rather by her own persecuted group. Joan Whitrowe's censorship by her peers, and difficulty in publishing her 'too-radical' writings, presents an interesting case study of one woman political writer's access to the means of material literary production. It should also serve to caution twentieth-century readers against idealizing the mutual support systems and collaborative publishing programmes of early sectarian groups.

Early Quakers suffered relentless persecution from dominant religious institutions, and it is not surprising that the leaders of the movement sought to minimize divisive criticism from within. After 1672, Quaker central organization acted in the capacity of a modern 'publisher', financing production, supplying printers with copy, and overseeing national and international distribution. But the executive bodies of 'antient men Friends' which made up Quaker central organization also served as a complex board of review for all Quaker publications. The Morning Meeting read over even the works of their founder George Fox line by line with meticulous care, and decided which passages must be altered or omitted. Like any alternative social formation for which survival is dependent on internal cohesion, the embattled Quaker community of the late seventeenth and early eighteenth centuries was a powerful force for internal censorship. By the 1700s, the Quaker press was 'characterised by caution and extreme political sensitivity, which had been absent in the 1650s'.[21]

Minutes of the meetings of Quaker central organization reveal that Joan Whitrowe's writings were censored by the Friends on at least one occasion. On 23 July 1677, meeting minutes record Quaker leaders' concern that Whitrowe had not yet submitted a book that she was writing to the Morning Meeting for approval. Rebecca Travers, a prominent Quaker at whose house meetings were held, was nominated by the group to speak to Whitrowe about submitting her manuscript 'book' for pre-publication review:

> Rebecca Travers is desired to speake or write to Joane Whitrow that shee submit the book (conteyning A Relation of what her daughter spoke at the time of her death) to friends as others doe that send books that friends may Leave out what they see not of service to the Truth, which friends are dissatisfied with.
>
> (MMM (Morning Meeting Minutes), vol. i (1673–92))

One week later, meeting minutes record that Whitrowe did submit this particular book to Quaker leaders as requested. The appropriate reviewers, however, found certain passages to be unacceptable: 'the book brought by Joane Whitrow [to] be left to J. Claypoole and Rebecca Travers to consider and Tis desired by this meeting that what is chiefly to her owne praise be left out' (MMM, vol. i (1673–92), 30 July 1677). The manuscript 'book' in question was *The Work of God in a dying Maid, being a short account of the dealings of the Lord with one Susanna Whitrow about the age of fifteen years and daughter of Robert Whitrow inhabiting in Covent-garden in the county of Middlesex; together with her experimental confessions to the power and work of the Lord God both in his judgments and mercy to her soul.* The first of her books that the Quakers censored, then, was Joan Whitrowe's too-personal account of the death of her daughter Susanna.[22]

By 1689, Joan Whitrowe wrote, 'I walk alone as a Woman forsaken.'[23] A marginal figure even within the Quaker movement, Whitrowe's far more radical writings after the Revolution of 1688 may have been considered too dangerous to publish. Whitrowe's post-revolutionary polemics are extremely aggressive. She had specific suggestions for social change and argued at length for a more just distribution of available resources. By 1692, she signed herself '*one that is of no Sect or gathered People*', suggesting that by this time she no longer saw herself as part of the Quaker community or any other.[24] And by 1694, her outspoken criticism of the disparities of wealth and poverty in her society was addressed to dissenters as well as to members of the Church of England. If Whitrowe's writings were 'stopt' by the Quakers, she was effectively silenced. After a flurry of activity, her publications ceased abruptly in 1697.[25] For many female polemicists, the Quaker press was the only practical avenue to print. How many women (and men) must have been silenced by the movement's understandable 'concern with uniformity and caution'?[26]

Whitrowe's printed books and papers were but a small part of her public activism. Both before and after her separation from the Quakers, she travelled enormous distances on foot, praying, preaching, and displaying her abused body as a sign of God's wrath. Just before the Great Plague, the Lord commanded her to go to Bristol. Accordingly, she undertook one of her first major journeys. With 'a Sack-Cloth on my Body, and Ashes on my Head', she travelled to Bristol to deliver her call to repentance, then returned home to London

> where I came to my Husband and Family in ten Days time, or the tenth Day of my parting from them, leaving a young Child of a Year old that suck'd at my Breast,[27] and found all things well, my-self also, so well as if I had not gon one Mile, although a weak Woman of Body, and not able to go two Miles without Pain, yet in the strength of the LORD I went almost two hundred Miles a Foot.
>
> (*Humble Address,* 9)

Shortly thereafter, the plague began, and she was once again 'commanded to go out of my own House Sack-cloth and Ashes, and proclaim the terrible Day of the LORD' (*Humble Address,* 10). Herself gravely ill, she prayed to God to remove her own burden. But the Lord explained:

> It is the burden of the Iniquities of the Nation I have laid upon thee, and thou must bear my Indignation, for thou art their Sign of the Repentance and Humiliation I require of them: then I knew what the Prophet *Habakkuk* meant when his Lips quivered, his Belly trembled, and rottenness had entered his Bones.
>
> (10)

Whitrowe saw her physical body as 'a sign to the Multitude' (12), and the illnesses to which it was liable as marks of God's wrath. Sustained fasting, sackcloth and ashes, and the discomforts of long-distance foot travel were in themselves modes of religio-political activism. They were part of a signifying system of the body, aimed at encouraging all who saw her to 'humble themselves in the dust'. When the Lord commanded Whitrowe 'to wear Sackcloth three years', she did, 'till after the death of King *Charles*' (12). And when he told her to 'depart from the Multitude . . . to give up Name and Fame, and whatsoever was dear to me in this Life', she did that too – to the point where she eventually came to see herself as 'one that is of no Sect or gathered People whatsoever' (*To King William and Queen Mary,* 16).

Upon the death of Queen Mary in 1694, God commanded Whitrowe to travel to the City of London from Putney. ('I knew not for what, for I had been there a little before, therefore had no Business of my own.'[28]) Once she had arrived in the City, the Lord commanded her to call the people of London to fasting. Caught up in a crowd somewhere between Cheapside and Cornhill, Whitrowe 'opened [her] Mouth to them, and said, *The Lord calls for Fasting, and you go to Feasting*'. She moved with the crowd through the streets, 'declaring the Word of the Lord throughout *Cornhill*, and part of the next Street'. Once she had delivered her public testimony to her own (and the Lord's) satisfaction, she 'left them, and Returned that Day to *Putney*' ('To the King', 109–10).

On another occasion, Whitrowe received a similar call to oral activism immediately after dropping off a book manuscript at the printer's:

> as I was going from the Printers, conversing with the Lord, and contemplating of his Glorious Power, being fill'd with Harmonious Praises in Melodious Sounds; yet as it were in deep Conflict of Spirit; and this going on till I came about the middle of *Paternoster-Row*, where I stood still and beheld; and, as I *looked* with Admiration, these Words, in great Power, spoke aloud in my Ears, *This is* London, *the City of Abomination, this is the Abominable City*: And these words were Repeated over and over, till I came about the middle of *Cheapside*.

> ('To the King', 187–8)

She continued walking through this central commercial area of London until she came to Bishopsgate, where, filled with a sense of despair for the 'Abominable City', she fell on her knees and prostrated herself before the Lord — as well as, no doubt, before many onlookers in this busy part of working London.

Whitrowe's writing and publishing, then, should be understood as an extension of an ongoing mode of religio-political activism which was oral and 'bodily'. As Phyllis Mack has pointed out, 'the acts of writing and public prophecy were actually more similar than one might suppose; writing involved public confrontation as well, since works were hawked by their authors on street corners or in front of taverns, or handed to magistrates like a modern summons'.[29] Whitrowe, too, was willing to endure a long journey on foot and a long wait for a fleeting opportunity to hand over her papers to the King. One of her pamphlets is signed '*Putney April* the 11th, 1696. This I delivered into the King's Own Hands, the 11th Instant. *Jone Whitrow*' — as if even the touch of a king she disapproved of gave a powerful talismanic quality to other copies of the paper.[30]

Like all of the polemicists discussed here, Whitrowe appears to have found print a challenging and sometimes awkward mode of communication. Whitrowe's printed texts paint a portrait of a zealous activist plagued not only by material hardships and loneliness, but also by the mental and material struggles of authorship. Whitrowe wrote of her depression and frustration when work was not going fast enough, and of her desire to start new projects before current ones were in press. Most poignantly, she expressed a sense of despair that she could not address all the injustices of her society at once. By 1694 she thought that she 'could write a Volume of Sights, Visions and Revelations which she hath had above for these thirty Years'. But it was not that easy. 'Had it stood with my will,' she explained,

> I had never been concern'd more with this Generation, after having delivered the three first books to the King and Queen, but having delivered the last of the three, Titled to Queen *Mary* . . . a strong powerful Voice Said, *Arise and thrash, Oh Daughter of Sion*. . . . Then after this I wrote another Printed-book to the King and Queen, and four Papers in writing at several times, which I delivered into their own hands; and then after I had delivered those Writings, I wrote another Book, which I had almost finished, but this coming so forceable upon me, I laid that by, and this hath been longer in hand than I expected when I begun it, for indeed all things looking so dark and dismal, I rather expected some dreadful Judgment would break forth before this Book would be finished.[31]

Lying in her bed feeling low in spirits, Whitrowe threw her book manuscript out of her hand, 'as Moses threw the Tables of Stone'. But 'a powerful voice' charged her with neglecting her duty, and told her to '*Write down thy Poverty*, which I immediately did'. And 'now', Whitrowe concluded of her latest publication, 'I have given you an Account why it was not committed to the Press before now' (*Widow Whiterow's* [sic] *Humble Thanksgiving* (1694), 35–7).

In this instance, Whitrowe related how she experienced a particularly dreadful form of writing-induced melancholy and 'writer's block' – a strong sense of impending 'Judgment' preventing her from putting quill to paper. On another occasion, Whitrowe was prevented not from completing a manuscript, but rather from taking it to a printer. Despite her strong dislike of William III's personal behaviour and political policies, Whitrowe claimed to have held back one of her manuscripts out of concern lest she add to the King's grief upon the death of his wife. She had originally, she claimed, written a paper to the Queen, 'telling her therein, that the Sword of the Lord was drawn and Furbished, two-Edged, yea three Edged, and only wants Commission'. But in this same paper, she had also prophesied Queen Mary's death – a prediction whose fulfilment put her on guard against printing the paper: 'And so [I] went on, declaring to [the Queen] the very thing that came to pass to my unspeakable Grief, which Paper I had Printed at this time, but for fear of renewing the *King*'s Sorrows' ('To the King, and Both Houses of Parliament', Prefatory Epistle to *Faithful Warnings* (1697), 188).

Despite her apparent concern for William's feelings upon the death of his wife, Whitrowe was in fact deeply disturbed by William and Mary, and addressed the majority of her pamphlets explicitly to them. As for so many late Stuart women writers, the Revolution of 1688 was for her a momentous occasion: a series of events of enduring spiritual and political importance. The bloodless coup was irrefutable evidence of divine intervention in state affairs: the strength of 'the Lord's own Arm which HE made bare in the sight of all' (*Humble Address of the Widow Whitrow to King William* (1689), 4). The new King and Queen were irredeemably indebted to God for their earthly crown, yet they gravely endangered their already precarious positions as heads of state by flouting God's will. Whitrowe spent the better part of her career as a polemicist and preacher urging William and Mary to fulfil their promises as professed champions of the Protestant faith, and advising the 'Church and People of *England*' to 'put into practice what you have promised the Lord' (*Humble Address*, 14). Among many other requirements, William III was to 'visit the Widow and Fatherless in their Afflictions', give up his hunting, and stop playing with his dogs in church:

> I saw thee upon *East-Sheen-Common*, where thou wast taking thy pleasure in Hunting: I was much grieved to see the King spending his precious time in such a vain Exercise, in such a day as this, when the Nation lies bleeding. . . . Oh King! is this a day for Pleasure . . .? I beseech thee consider the end of the LORD, in bringing thee into the Nation, was it to do thy own Will, or the Will of Him that sent thee? . . . thou, O King, art a witness, that it was not thy Sword, nor thy Might that brought thee hither, but the Lord's own Arm which HE made bare in the sight of all. And now I beseech thee consider how highly thou art ingaged to the LORD for all his Goodness; and what thou wilt return to the KING of Eternal Glory.
>
> (*Humble Address*, 4–5)

Queen Mary was to abandon her vain and worldly pursuits, while the people of England were to reflect:

> What did you send for King *William* out of his own Country, and turn out King *James*? You said it was to set up the *Christian Religion*, and to Establish it: why is it not done? . . . put into practice what you have promised the Lord; but if you will not, then it will appear to all the World, that you did not all this to set up the *Christian Religion*, but to set up your selves.[32]

Whitrowe repeatedly warned the King to bow down before the Lord, for 'without Him you can do nothing'.[33] Many religious polemicists of the post-revolutionary period appear to have taken special pleasure in reminding William III what little power he had in comparison to his predecessors, and in pointing out that even that mite was given to him by the Lord (and so could be taken away again). Whitrowe urged William and Mary to remember that they were God's 'Vice-Gerents here on Earth', and prayed that they would 'joyn unanimously together in Heart and Soul to humble themselves in the dust before Thee the Almighty GOD'.[34] Whitrowe's radically levelling image of the King and Queen humbling themselves in the dust was a personal favourite. She repeatedly warned William and Mary to 'come down from your Thrones, and humble yourselves in the dust by Fastings and Prayers, and deep Humiliation, crying mightily to GOD the Father' (*Widow Whiterow's Humble Thanksgiving*, 5). She also exercised considerable aggression by means of the ostensibly dutiful act of biblical quotation. In the headnote to her *Humble Thanksgiving* (1694) she highlighted Jeremiah 13: 18: 'Say unto the KING and to the QUEEN humble your Selves, sit down.'

Religious conviction afforded women such as Whitrowe an outlet for aggression in the form of a desire for millenarian 'revenge'. As in Anne Docwra's polemics, so in Joan Whitrowe's pamphlets there is a powerful subtext of prophetic threat. These women's writings contain powerful subversive 'visions' characteristic of millenarian writings. In these futuristic fictions, existing social hierarchies are dissolved, and widows and children have enough to eat. (And, of course, rulers like William and Mary are 'humbled in the dust'.) Like these millenarian visions, the curse-poem was another important subgenre in women's religio-political polemicism. Whitrowe prophesied that neither force nor the rule of law could prevent the eventual inevitable destruction of the 'great ones': 'There's neither Strength nor Policy shall stand, | Against what GOD's a bringing on this Land. | The Youth shall howl, the Aged shall weep sore, | Yet there's glad tidings for the Meek and Poor' (*Widow Whiterow's Humble Thanksgiving*, 4). In another pamphlet Whitrowe expressed her gratitude for King William's safe return from the battle at La Hogue, but recorded her disgust at the wood wasted in bonfires to celebrate his victory:

> How many poor destressed Families both in City and Country would be glad and rejoyce to have that Firing to warm and refresh them and theirs in cold and bitter Weather; that was spent in waste when the KING came home to gratifie the humors of an ungodly Crew, who one day cries *Hosana, Hosana*; and the next day with a louder vote, *Crucifie, Crucifie*.
>
> (*To King William and Queen Mary* (1692), 6)

Whitrowe's critique of the conspicuous consumption and waste of state rituals is in fact more subversive than it might initially appear. While directed ostensibly not at William III but at those 'Judges, Justices, and Officers of all sorts, that do not fulfill the Will of GOD' (5), her complaint was graphically illustrated with a powerful image of mob violence. In 1692, the image of a crowd chanting '*Crucifie, Crucifie*' would immediately bring to mind the execution of Charles I and the recent forced abdication of James II. By implicitly reminding William III of England's willingness to 'crucifie' his predecessors, Whitrowe effectively hinted that this professed saviour of the church was no more secure than they.

Whitrowe's critique of conspicuous consumption was characteristic of her increasing solidarity not with any particular faith but rather with the working poor: 'many hundreds in City and Coun-ty, [that] sits in their Houses with hungry Bellies, both of Wea-vers and others, that knows not which way to shift for Bread for their Children' (*Widow Whiterow's Humble Thanksgiving*, 21). Whitrowe was intensely aware of what the aristocracy and gentry did and did not do with their money; almost without exception, her writings contrast the subsistence-level existence of the labouring poor with the privileged lives of the propertied classes. She criticized the upper ranks' excessive attention to things of the flesh, especially fine food and apparel, and she consistently referred to élites rather than to working people as 'the drunkards, the feasters, the swearers, gamesters, whoremongers, the proud'.[35] She attacked colonialism and rapacious overseas trade, the amassing of excess wealth and estates, and especially disregard for the poor. Above all, she argued that the endless accumulation of capital in the hands of a few must be curbed:

> The next to your Habit is your Houses, which are deck'd with all manner of Curiosity, Richness and Delicacy, as your sinful Persons are: Your great spacious Lordly Houses, furnished with all manner of costly, rich and sumptuous Furniture, which would be too tedious, and fill up much Paper to insist upon; but your voluptuous Feeding, and excessive Feasting one another, in so much that you run out great Estates, both of your own and other Men's; but in your own Families, that is, among your Servants, many of you are very pinching and sparing, and to the Poor little or nothing, but what you are compell'd to in your Parish Duties; and your poor Neighbours, many hundreds in City and County, sits in their Houses with hungry Bellies, both of Weavers and others, that knows not which way to shift for Bread for their Children; some eating Bread sparingly, and drink Water, Others getting Garden stuff, as Cabbage, and such like for their Children to feed on; whilst you feed, *Dives* like, lying at your Ease, stretching your selves upon your rich Sattin Beds and Couches, wallowing in all your sinful Pleasures, not knowing what to Eat, Drink, or put on for Richness and Dainties; and others of you Hoards up Treasure as Sand, and are never satisfied, compelling Sea and Land to get Riches, adding House to House, and Land to Land, and all for Portions for our Children, say they; and thus the Fathers eat sowre Grapes, and the Childrens Teeth are set an edge.
>
> (*Widow Whiterow's Humble Thanksgiving*, 21–2)

It was the immediate duty of the substantially propertied of all faiths to make 'plentiful Provision, not only for them of your own Judgment, but for all sorts, that the Widow, Fatherless, and Strangers may have no want' (*Widow Whiterow's Humble Thanksgiving*, 23). Such stop-gap solutions to desperate poverty, however, were only the first step on the agenda for social change. Petty charity 'compell'd . . . [by] Parish Duties' was a sop to the poor rather than a commitment to social justice. For the problem of inequality was inherent in the mode of production and distribution itself:

> But you Covetous, Earthly minded Professors of all sorts, your niggardly pinching the Poor, your giving five, ten, twenty or forty Shillings, nay five, ten, twenty Pounds; (though who is so liberal) will not excuse you that have Hundreds, and Thousands, and many Thousands lying by a year will not excuse you . . . when His Majesty calls you to an account what you have done with his Treasure . . . will you say, we hoarded it up by us; or will you say, we gave it our Children for their Portions, to live in Pride and Luxury.
>
> (*Widow Whiterow's Humble Thanksgiving*, 23)

Not only the landowners and capitalists but also the 'Teachers and Rulers of this Generation' were hypocritical and covetous, concerned only 'for their Self-Interest in one kind or other; some for yearly maintenance, others for Name and Fame, or to be highly esteemed for their Gifts and Parts' (*Widow Whiterow's Humble Thanksgiving*, 12). The 'Professors of Religion' in fact 'outstrip the Prophane', striving for 'Honours and Preferments into great Places' (*Humble Address*, 6). Given insights into the relation of religion, politics, and property in this period such as these, it is perhaps not surprising that by 1689 Whitrowe declared: 'I walk alone as a Woman forsaken; I have fellowship with them that lived in Caves, and in Dens, and desolate places of the Earth, of whom the World was not worthy' (*Humble Address*, 13). For by that time, her sweeping social critique was directed at members of the Church of England and dissenters alike.

[. . .]

Notes

1   Elinor James, *Mrs.* James's *Vindication of the Church of England, In An Answer to a Pamphlet Entituled, A New Test of the Church of England's Loyalty* (1687), 1, and *Mrs. James Prayer for the Queen and Parliament, and Kingdom too* (1710). After each broadside is cited once, all further references are cited parenthetically in the text.

2   Joan Whitrowe was an exception to this rule. While she did typically sign her works, her later pamphlets were too outspoken to show either her own address or a publisher's name or address in imprints.

3   Thomas O'Malley, ' "Defying the Powers and Tempering the Spirit": A Review of Quaker Control over their Publications 1672–1689', *Journal of Ecclesiastical History*, 33 (1982), 74. The word 'extant' here is important. After 1672, the Quakers had a very thorough policy for collecting their own works; thus proportionately more of their publications survive.

4   Nathan Kite, *Antiquarian Researches among the Early Printers and Publishers of Friends' Books* (Manchester: John Harrison, 1844), 60–1.

5   Luella M. Wright, *The Literary Life of the Early Friends 1650–1725* (New York: Columbia University Press, 1932), 8. See also William C. Braithwaite, *The Beginnings of Quakerism* (1912), 2nd edn. rev. Henry J. Cadbury (York: William Sessions, 1981) and *The Second Period of Quakerism* (1919), 2nd edn. prep. Henry J. Cadbury (York: William Sessions, 1979), and Paula Joanne McDowell, 'Tace Sowle', in James K. Brachen and Joel Silver; eds., *The British Literary Trade, 1475–1700* (Columbia, SC: Bruccoli Clark Layman, 1976), 249–70.

6   Patricia Crawford, 'Women's Published Writings 1600–1700', in Mary Prior ed., *Women in English Society, 1500–1800* (New York Methuen, 1985), 211–82.

7   According to her own account, Docwra was 'the eldest daughter of William Waldegrave, of Buers, in the County of Suffolk' (*An Apostate-Conscience Exposed* (1699), 64). In about 1647, she married James Docwra of Fulborne near Cambridge, and in about 1664 she became a Quaker. Her husband died in 1672, and after about 1681 she dwelt in Cambridge. For further biographical information on Docwra, possibly of mixed value, see her works, as well as the many biographical claims made by Francis Bugg in his *Jezebel Withstood, and Her Daughter Anne Docwra, Publickly Reprov'd; For Her Lies and Lightness in Her Book, stiled, An Apostate Conscience, &c.* (1699) and *A Seasonable Caveat Against the Prevalency of Quakerism* (1701), 57.

8   Francis Bugg, *William Penn, the Pretended Quaker, Discovered to hold a Correspondence with the Jesuite's* [sic] . . . *To which is Added, A Winding-Sheet for Ann Dockwra* (1700), 3.

9   This kind of virulent personal-public debate is an understudied though central aspect of seventeenth-century popular religious controversy. For a study of nonconformist literary culture which touches on some aspects of these debates see N. H. Keeble's *The Literary Culture of Nonconformity in Later Seventeenth-Century England* (Athens: University of Georgia Press, 1987).

10   On Quaker central organization see McDowell, 'Tace Sowle'.

11   Christopher Hill, *The World Turned Upside Down: Radical Ideas during the English Revolution* (1972; Harmondsworth: Penguin-Peregrine, 1985), 17.

2   At almost the same time that Docwra and Bugg were attacking one another in print, Delarivier Manley was publishing her gossipy political allegories, satisfying a similar public desire for entertainment, 'news', and edifying intellectual debate.

13   Anne Docwra, *The Second Part of an Apostate-Conscience Exposed: Being an Answer to a Scurrilou Pamphlet . . . Written and Published, by F. Bugg, intituled, Jezebel withstood, and her Daughter An Docwra reproved for her Lies and Lightness, in her Book, stiled, An Apostate-Conscience Exposed, Etc* (1700), 29.

14   Advertisement for Francis Bugg, *News from New Rome, occasioned by the Quakers challenging ç Francis Bugg, whereby their errors are farther exposed* (1701), 13, 17, 15, 16.

15   Hill, *The World Turned Upside Down*, 355.

16   Jonathan Swift, *A Tale of a Tub with Other Early Works 1696–1707*, ed. Herbert Davis (Oxford Basil Blackwell, 1965), vol. i of *The Prose Works of Jonathan Swift*, 124 n.

17   On Katherine Chidley, see Ethyn Morgan Williams, 'Women Preachers in the Civil War' *Journal of Modern History*, 1 (1929), 561–9.

18   See Craig W. Horle, *The Quakers and the English Legal System 1660–1688* (Philadelphia: Uni versity of Pennsylvania Press, 1988). Docwra cites Michael Dalton's *The Countrey Justice Conteyning The Practise of the Justices of the Peace out of their Sessions* (London, 1618), a standar lawbook consulted by the Quakers throughout the seventeenth century. She also claims tha her father bid her read 'the great Statute Book', saying that 'it was as proper for a Woman as Man to understand the Laws' (*An Apostate-Conscience Exposed* (1699), 24–5).

19   She refers to more which apparently have not survived. Her tombstone refers to 'severa pious Books', probably her pamphlets (BL Add. MS 5841, 'Epitaph of Joan Whitrowe').

20   Even Elaine Hobby writes that 'After the Restoration, as persecution of radicals increase under the workings of the Clarendon Code, sectaries were gradually reduced to silence an inertia'. Elaine Hobby, *Virtues of Necessity: English Women's Writing 1649–1688* (Ann Arbor University of Michigan Press, 1989).

21   O'Malley, ' "Defying the Powers and Tempering the Spirit" ', 85.

22   The work also records the recent death of her 6-year-old son Jason.

23   Joan Whitrowe, *The Humble Address of the Widow Whitrow to King William: With a Faithful Warnin to the Inhabitants of England, To Haste and Prepare by True Repentance, and Deep Humiliation, to mee the Lord, Before His Indignation burns like Fire, and breaks forth into a mighty Flame, so that none ca quench it (1689)*, 13.

24   Joan Whitrowe, *To King William and Queen Mary, Grace and Peace. The Widow Whitrow's Humbl Thanksgiving . . . for the King's safe Return to England* (1692), 7.

25   It is not yet known how Whitrowe got her works into print after she left the Quakers. Onl three of her works show printers' or publishers' names in imprints. The imprint of *The Wido Whitrow's Humble Thanksgiving*, which was apparently licensed, reads: '*Printed by* D. Edwards i Nevel's Alley in Fetter-Lane, for J. B. 1694.' Two other works, *Faithful Warnings* and 'To th King and Both Houses of Parliament', show Elizabeth Whitlock's name in imprints. *Faithf Warnings* shows: 'Printed, and are to be Sold by E. Whitlock, in *Stationers-Court* near *Stationers Hall*. 1697.'

26   O'Malley, ' "Defying the Powers and Tempering the Spirit" ', 84.

27   The 'young Child of a Year old' was probably Whitrowe's daughter Susanna, who died i 1677 at the age of 15.

28   Joan Whitrowe, 'To the King, and Both Houses of Parliament', Prefatory Epistle to *Faithf Warnings, Expostulations and Exhortations, To The several Professors of Christianity in England, as we as those of the Highest as the Lowest Quality* (1697), 109.

29   Phyllis Mack, 'Gender and Spirituality in Early English Quakerism, 1650–1665', in Elisabet Potts Brown and Susan Mosher Stuard, eds., *Witnesses for Change: Quaker Women over Thre Centuries* (New Brunswick, NJ: Rutgers University Press, 1989), 59 n. 31. See also Phylli Mack, *Visionary Women: Ecstatic Prophecy in Seventeenth-Century England* (Berkeley and Lo Angeles: University of California Press, 1992).

30   Joan Whitrowe, *To the King, And Both Houses of Parliament* (1696).

31   Joan Whitrowe, *The Widow Whiterow's Humble Thanksgiving for the Kings Safe Return* (1694), 33.

32   *To Queen Mary: The Humble Salutation and Faithful Greeting of the Widow Whitrowe. With a Warning to the Rulers of the Earth* (1690) and *The Humble Address of the Widow Whitrowe to King William* (1689), 13–14.

33   Joan Whitrowe, *To the King, and Both Houses of Parliament* (1696).

34   Joan Whitrowe, *To King William and Queen Mary* (1692), 7 and *Widow Whiterow's Humble Thanksgiving* (1694), 4.

35   Joan Whitrowe, *To Queen Mary: The Humble Salutation and Faithful Greeting of the Widow Whitrowe* (14 Dec. 1690), 18.

Chapter 22

Mark Rose

LITERARY PROPERTY DETERMINED

At one level, the literary-property question was a legal struggle about the nature of property and how the law might adapt itself to the changed circumstances of an economy based on trade. At another, it was a contest about how far the ideology of possessive individualism should be extended into the realm of cultural production. At still another, it was a commercial encounter, played out in the form of a national contest between England and Scotland, in which a deeply entrenched business establishment was challenged by outsiders. The complex layering of the literary-property struggle generated a number of intriguing contradictions, among them that it was in the name of the liberal value of 'property' – and authorial property no less – that the London booksellers were defending a monopolistic system with roots in the medieval guild culture. Their principal challenger was a scrappy and determined Scottish businessman, 'who saw a new and lucrative opening in the book-selling trade, and availed himself of it' (Gray 182).

Alexander Donaldson's career as a bookseller began in 1750 in Edinburgh shortly after the determination of *Millar v. Kinkaid* in the Court of Session. After this decision was announced, Donaldson, according to his own account, took counsel from both Scottish and English lawyers who confirmed him in his opinion that copyright was limited to the statutory term. Thereupon he went into the bookselling business in a large way, specializing in inexpensive reprints of standard works whose copyright term had expired, including, according to the *Eighteenth-Century Short Title Catalogue*, works by Defoe, Fielding, Gay, Locke, Milton, Pope, Shakespeare, Swift, Thomson, and Young. Donaldson prospered, and his house and shop became something of a center for literary Scotsmen, among them the young James Boswell who, together with his friend Andrew Erskine, published an anthology of contemporary Scottish poems with Donaldson. Eventually Donaldson started a journal, the biweekly *Edinburgh Advertiser*, which also did very well.

For many years after their unsuccessful appeal of *Millar v. Kinkaid*, the great London booksellers ignored Donaldson and the other Scots. But then in the late 1750s and early 1760s they took up their campaign to establish the common-law copyright and to drive the Scottish reprint business out of England. In 1763 Donaldson responded by boldly opening his own shop in London, where he sold

Reprinted by permission of the publisher from *Authors and Owners: The Invention of Copyright* by Mark Rose Cambridge, Mass.: Harvard University Press, Copyright © 1993 by the President and Fellows of Harvard College.

his books at 30–50 percent under the usual London prices. Samuel Johnson, for one, was incensed. Boswell reports that Johnson, who held the London booksellers in high regard, 'was loud and violent against Mr. Donaldson', saying that it had always been understood by the trade that 'he, who buys the copy-right of a book from the authour, obtains a perpetual property' (*Life* 1:438, 439). A barrage of harassing Chancery lawsuits followed the opening of the shop. Donaldson retaliated by publishing *Some Thoughts on the State of Literary Property Humbly Submitted to the Consideration of the Public* in which he threatened to sue for damages caused by 'unlawful combination, whereby the London booksellers have conspired to beat down all opposition, and to suppress the sale of every book reprinted in the other parts of the united kingdom' (10).

Despite having to contend with what he later, in his petition against the Bookseller's Relief Bill of 1774, termed 'the united force of almost all the eminent booksellers of London and Westminster' (*Petitions and Papers* 10), Donaldson was determined to keep his reprint business – from which he was making a fortune, despite his legal expenses. In 1765, after the aborted decision in *Tonson v. Collins*, Donaldson succeeded in getting dissolved two injunctions against him for publication of James Thomson's poems. Sounding much like his predecessor Lord Hardwicke in *Tonson v. Walker* a dozen years earlier, Lord Chancellor Northington, who heard the arguments in *Osborne v. Donaldson* (1765) and *Millar v. Donaldson* (1765), remarked that the issue of the common-law right was 'a point of so much difficulty and consequence, that he should not determine it at the hearing, but should send it to law for the opinion of the judges'. Northington said that 'he desired to be understood as giving no opinion on the subject'. He added, however, that he thought it might be 'dangerous to determine that the author has a perpetual property in his books, for such a property would give him not only a right to publish, but to suppress too' (*ER* 28:924). Probably Donaldson would have welcomed taking the question further, as Northington invited – it was, he said, 'his fixed purpose that the law should be finally settled in the Supreme Court of the kingdom' (*Petitions and Papers* 10) but neither Osborne nor Millar wished to pursue the issue. Instead, Millar took action against Robert Taylor of Berwick upon Tweed, again in connection with Thomson's *The Seasons*, and thus began the landmark case of *Millar v. Taylor*.[1] . . .

Andrew Millar died in June 1768 while *Millar v. Taylor* was pending. A year later, after the momentous King's Bench decision, Millar's copyrights were put up for sale by his estate, and Thomas Becket and a group of other London printers and stationers purchased the rights in *The Seasons* and a number of other Thomson poems for £505. In January 1771 the new proprietors of Thomson, armed with the King's Bench decision, filed a bill in Chancery against Donaldson and his brother John, with whom he was associated in connection with the 1768 edition of *The Seasons*. An injunction was granted, and in November 1772 it was made perpetual in a hearing before Lord Chancellor Apsley who, as he explained later at the time of Donaldson's appeal, was merely affirming the decree as a matter of course, pursuant to the decision in *Millar v. Taylor*. Simultaneously, John Hinton's case against Donaldson over *Stackhouse's Bible*, initiated in the Court of Session just before the start of Becket's action in Chancery, was making its way to a decision. On 27 July 1773 the Court of Session rendered its decision in favor of Donaldson, and with this precedent in hand to offset *Millar v. Taylor*, Donaldson appealed the Chancery injunction to the House of Lords. It was time to achieve his 'fixed purpose' of seeing the law of literary property settled by Britain's highest court.

Donaldson v. Becket, then, represented both an appeal of *Millar v. Taylor*, to which Donaldson was not a party, and an attempt to secure a confirmation of the Court of Session's decision in *Hinton v. Donaldson*. Sir James Burrow's report of *Millar v. Taylor*, entitled *The Question Concerning Literary Property Determined by the Court of King's Bench*, had been brought out the previous spring while the Scottish case was impending.[2] In order to make available a comparable account of *Hinton v. Donaldson*, Donaldson's old friend James Boswell, who was one of the junior counselors in the case, 'worked up his notes' and persuaded 'several of the judges to revise their opinions freely for the benefit of peers and posterity' (Brady 88). Boswell's *Decision of the Court of Session upon the Question of Literary Property*, published by Donaldson in an elegant edition, appeared according to an advertisement in the *Morning Chronicle* in February 1774, just in time for the opening of the appeal three days later. . . .

On 22 February the peers voted to overturn the Chancery injunction, and in Scotland the reaction was tumultuous: 'Great rejoicing in Edinburgh upon victory over literary property: bonfires and illuminations' (Ross 143). In England, at least among those connected with the London book trade, the reaction was also intense. A paragraph that appeared in the *Morning Chronicle* and in a number of other places after the decision claimed that a vast amount of property had been annihilated:

> By the above decision of the important question respecting copy-right in books, near 200,000 l. worth of what was honestly purchased at public sale, and which was yesterday thought property is now reduced to nothing. The Booksellers of London and Westminster, many of whom sold estates and houses to purchase Copy-right, are in a manner ruined, and those who after many years industry thought they had acquired a competency to provide for their families now find themselves without a shilling to devise to their successors.
>
> (*Morning Chronicle* 23 Feb. 1774)

Whether the London booksellers' panic was justified is doubtful – they were by no means ruined by the decision – but the note of desperation that marks their utterances is probably sincere enough. The works of Shakespeare, Bacon, Milton, Bunyan, and others, all the great properties of the trade that the booksellers had been accustomed to treat as private landed estates, were suddenly declared open commons.

In 1774 the House of Lords decided cases by a general vote of the peers, lawyers and laymen alike. Great weight was usually given to the opinions of the lawyers, but the practice of lay peers not being recognized when the House of Lords sat as a court had not yet been instituted. In important cases such as *Donaldson v. Becket*, however, the twelve common-law judges of the realm – the judges of King's Bench, Common Pleas, and the Exchequer – would be summoned to the House to hear the arguments of counsel and to give their advice on matters of law, after which the peers would debate the issue and vote.

The arguments in *Donaldson* were made by lawyers who had been involved in the literary-property question for years. . . . After the arguments, which added little of substance to what Sir James Burrow called this 'old and often-litigated question' (*ER* 98:201), Lord Chancellor Apsley put three questions to the judges. First, did the author have a common-law right to control the first publication of his work? Second, did the author's right, if it existed, survive publication? Third, if the right survived publication, was it taken away by the statute? To these questions Charles Pratt, Lord Camden, who was a former chief justice of Common Pleas, a lord chancellor, and the major opponent of perpetual copyright in the House of Lords, added two more. Did the author or his assigns have the sole right to a composition in perpetuity by the common law? Was this right in any way restrained or taken away by the statute? Insofar as they repeat the substance of the second and third of the original questions, Camden's questions were redundant, but he was trying to remind the judges and peers that the case was not just one of authors' rights but of booksellers', and that the issue was copyright in perpetuity.

The opinions of the judges, delivered one by one over the course of three days, were divided. On the first question, the judges divided 8 to 3 in support of the author's right. On the second, the vote was 7 to 4, again in support of the author's right. There is, however, a puzzle connected with the vote on the third question. According to both the *Journal of the House of Lords* and the standard legal and historical references, the vote on this question was 6 to 5 against the author's right – that is, the majority of the judges were of the opinion that the statute took away the author's right. But contemporary newspaper and other accounts give good reason to believe that the clerk of the House of Lords made an honest error in recording the opinion of one of the judges. Most likely the tally was 6 to 5 in favor of the common-law right surviving the statute. Note that only eleven judges voted: Lord Mansfield remained silent. James Burrow explained that Mansfield, whose opinion was well known, abstained 'from reasons of delicacy' since the case was in effect an appeal from his own court (*ER* 98:262). Had Mansfield voted, the tally would have been a substantial seven to five in favor of the common-law right surviving the statute. But the judges' opinions were only advisory; the final decision would be made by vote of the entire House; and in *Donaldson* the floor debate appears to have been very important.

Any issue thrown into the House of Lords was always in danger of becoming entangled in a network of personal and political rivalries. Lord Mansfield was the acknowledged champion of the common-law right. Lord Camden, who opened the debate with a speech of an hour and a half together with a motion that the Chancery decree against Donaldson be reversed, was Mansfield's 'lifelong political opponent' (Holdsworth, *History* 12:306). Camden, a Chathamite Whig, differed from Mansfield on most matters and had clashed with him many times before, most recently and bitterly in December 1770 when the issue was the rights of juries in cases of seditious libel. In that affair Camden directly challenged Mansfield to defend his opinion in a debate in the House of Lords, but Mansfield, to the dismay of some, refused.[3] Before the *Donaldson* appeal came on for debate, Camden had been inactive in the House of Lords for several years, but now he rose to challenge his old antagonist. Given their acrimonious history, it is hard to avoid the suspicion that part of Camden's purpose in leading the attack on the common-law right was a desire to embarrass Mansfield by having the peers repudiate his determination in *Millar v. Taylor*.

As early as 16 February, after the first group of four judges had read their opinions, the *Public Advertiser* reported that Mansfield would not give his opinion as a judge but would speak later as a peer. On 22 February, after all the judges had spoken, the *Advertiser* repeated that Mansfield would speak as a peer. Camden's speech plainly called for a response, but, contrary to all expectation, Mansfield was silent. 'As Lord Mansfield had so warmly taken the Respondents side of the question on the determination in the Court of King's Bench between Miller and Taylor in 1769, it was yesterday much wondered at that his Lordship did not support his opinion in the H. of Peers'. So reported the *Morning Chronicle* on 23 February. The London booksellers, who had counted on Mansfield as their strongest bulwark in the House of Lords, felt betrayed and they were furious:

> It was his duty to have given an opinion on one side or other, and the neglecting to do so, was a manifest breach of his duty. Judges are paid by the public, and should render those services attendant on their office; and I should be glad to see a law passed to oblige them to a strict performance of their duty.
>
> (*Edinburgh Advertiser* 29 April 1774)

Why was Mansfield silent? The situation was reminiscent of Camden's challenge over jury rights four years earlier. Whatever it was that impelled him to keep his peace then — lack of courage or, more likely, lack of spirit for further bruising conflict — perhaps restrained him again. His opinion on literary property was a matter of public record, and it had been supported by a majority of the judges. If the House of Lords were inclined to overturn the Chancery decree and thereby declare that literary property was not perpetual, probably nothing he could say would materially affect the outcome.

Lord Camden was followed in the debate by Lord Chancellor Apsley, who had issued the original injunction and now delivered the *coup de grâce* to perpetual copyright by seconding the motion to overturn his own decree. He had made the decree, Apsley said, entirely as a matter of course pursuant to the judgement in *Millar v. Taylor*, and he viewed the action merely as a step toward a final determination of the copyright question in the House of Lords. As for the substance of the matter, he saw no precedents that could support the respondents in their argument. Moreover, he said he had evidence in the form of original letters from Dean Swift showing that the sense of Parliament was against the common-law right at the time of the Statute of Anne.[4] So his opinion was with the appellants. Three other peers spoke – Lord Lyttleton, who supported perpetual copyright as an encouragement to authors; the Bishop of Carlisle, who believed that literary property was limited to the statutory term, though the statute was defective and needed revision; and Lord Effingham, who thought perpetual copyright a danger to constitutional rights – and then the question was called. Eighty-four peers were present for the vote, an extraordinary show of interest (*Journal for the House of Lords* 34:33).[5] Although Cobbett reports that the vote was 22 to 11 in favor of reversing the Chancery decree (17:1003), neither the *Journal of the House of Lords* nor the contemporary newspapers indicate a formal division of the House, and the *Public Advertiser* explicitly says there was no division (23 Feb. 1774). Most likely the decision was by simple voice vote. As Donaldson's newspaper reported, undoubtedly with some exaggeration about the unanimity of the House, Lord Chancellor Apsley desired 'all who were for reversing the judgment, to say Content, and such as were of a different opinion to say, Not: Nothing was heard but the word Content' (*Edinburgh Advertiser* 1 March 1774).

In voting as they did against the perpetual right, the Lords went against the judges, whose vote on the third question was 6 to 5 – 7 to 5 if Mansfield were counted – in favor of the common-law right surviving the statute. There is no great mystery about why they did so: the House of Lords had long been antipathetic to the London booksellers' monopolies, and the outcome in *Donaldson v. Becket* was consistent with the House's previous treatment of copyright questions. But on what basis did the peers make their determination? What understanding of the nature of copyright did they adopt? Were they persuaded that there never was a common-law right? Or did they believe that there was but that it ended with publication? Or that it was taken away by the statute? Were they persuaded by Lord Camden's argument that common-law determinations had to be founded on solid written authorities, or were they more influenced by the position associated with Joseph Yates that ideas could not in the nature of things be treated as property? Some peers may have voted on the basis of a legal theory, but many others, I suspect, were less concerned with the basis than with the result. Thus the peers gave an answer to the literary-property question, but they did not provide a rationale. 'It is more satisfactory . . . to convince by reason, than merely to silence by authority' Blackstone had said in the course of arguments in *Tonson v. Collins* (*ER* 96:182). But what the House of Lords did in *Donaldson v. Becket* was finally no more than to declare by authority that copyright henceforth would be limited in term.[6] . . .

A year before the decision in *Donaldson v. Becket*, Samuel Johnson, we recall, 'descanted on the subject of Literary Property' at dinner, coming down on the side of limited copyright. So he was reasonably satisfied with the result in *Donaldson*, though he thought the present copyright term too short. In a letter dated 7 March 1774, probably written at the request of the bookseller William Strahan to use in lobbying for the booksellers' relief bill, Johnson called the Lords' decision 'legally and politically right'. On the one hand, the author had a natural right to the profits of his work; on the other, it was wrong that a useful book should become 'perpetual and exclusive property' therefore the author must purchase the protection of society by resigning 'so much of his claim as shall be deemed injurious or inconvenient to Society'. Johnson recommended an extension of the present two fourteen-year terms to a single one of the author's lifetime plus thirty years. This would in most cases yield a total term of about fifty years, which would be 'sufficient to reward the writer without any loss to the publick' (*Johnsonian Miscellanies* 2:444–445).

Johnson understood the decision in Donaldson as a compromise between the author's claim and the broader needs of society, but the peers themselves had articulated no such theory. As we have seen, they simply resolved the practical question of perpetuity. This was sufficient for the needs of the moment, but in the longer run it was necessary to make some sense of their vote, to reach some understanding as to the theory of copyright behind the limited term. What developed in the years after 1774 was a belief that Donaldson represented a compromise along lines similar to those that Johnson articulated, a belief that the decision curtailed the author's right without rejecting it entirely.

This understanding of Donaldson was made possible by the way the case was reported by James Burrow, whose excellent law reports were, and still are, regarded as authoritative. At the time of Donaldson it was technically a crime to print an account of a case on appeal in the House of Lords. Donaldson had of course been widely reported in the press, and in fact shortly after the decision two full reports were published as pamphlets under the titles The Cases of the Appellants and Respondents in the Cause of Literary Property and The Pleadings of the Counsel Before the House of Lords in the Great Cause Concerning Literary Property. But Burrow held an official position as Master of the Crown Office; so when he gave notice of Donaldson as part of his account of Millar v. Taylor in his 1776 collection of King's Bench reports, he discreetly limited himself to printing the record as it appeared in the Minute Book of the House of Lords. Like the Minute Book, Burrow gave the questions and the judges' votes, but no account of their speeches. At the conclusion he added a tally, a comment about Lord Mansfield, and a note about the reversal:

> So that of the eleven judges, there were eight to three, upon the first question; seven to four, upon the second; and five to six, upon the third.
>
> It was notorious, that Lord Mansfield adhered to his opinion; and therefore concurred with the eight, upon the first question; with the seven, upon the second; and with the five, upon the third. But it being very unusual, (from reasons of delicacy,) for a peer to support his own judgment, upon an appeal to the House of Lords, he did not speak.
>
> And the Lord Chancellor seconding Lord Camden's motion 'to reverse; the decree was reversed.'
>
> (ER 98:262)

In presenting the tally for the third question as 5 to 6 against the author's right, Burrow perpetuated the error of the clerk of the House and made it appear as if the reversal followed as a matter of course from the judges' vote. Moreover, his suppression of Lord Camden's and Lord Chancellor Apsley's speeches made it seem as if the author's common-law right was not seriously challenged; on the contrary, he conveyed the impression that the determination in Donaldson consisted of a solid affirmation of the author's right, followed by a narrow decision that perpetuity was taken away by the statute.[7] This representation was a distortion in a number of respects. In fact only a single judge, Henry Gould of Common Pleas, had held that there was a common-law right impeached by the statute. (The others had either held that there was no common-law right – or at any rate none that survived publication or that it was not taken away by the statute.) But even so it had much to recommend it, for it made it possible to suppose that, even if perpetual copyright had been rejected, still an author had a natural right to property in his work. Thus some years later in Beckford v. Hood (1798), the King's Bench found that Donaldson did not take away a plaintiff's right to sue at common law during the statutory term (ER 101:1164–1168), and by the early nineteenth century Robert Maugham was able to state bluntly in his important Treatise on the Laws of Literary Property (1828) that in Donaldson 'it was determined by the House of Lords that the common law right was merged in the statute' (27).[8]

In the eighteenth-century debates themselves, the copyright issue had nearly always been framed in terms of absolutes: either authors had a common-law right or they did not. But if copyright was seen as a kind of compromise, then it became possible to reconsider the length of the copyright term, as Johnson had done. In 1814 a revised statute extended the copyright term to twenty-eight years after publication or the author's lifetime, whichever was longer, but this seemed paltry to those such as Robert Southey or William Wordsworth, who objected to any limitation. 'The question is simply this,' Southey said in his 1819 *Quarterly Review* essay: 'upon what principle, with what justice, or under what pretext of public good, are men of letters deprived of a perpetual property in the produce of their own labours, when all other persons enjoy it as their indefeasible right – a right beyond the power of any earthly authority to take away?' (211–212). And in a letter to J. Forbes Mitchell dated 21 April 1819, Wordsworth asked 'why the laws should interfere to take away those pecuniary emoluments which are the natural Inheritance of the posterity of Authors' (*Letters* 3:535).

In 1837 Thomas Noon Talfourd, a friend of Wordsworth's and an author as well as a member of Parliament, opened a campaign for revision of the copyright act. Talfourd reminded Parliament that a majority of the judges in *Donaldson* determined that an author had a perpetual common-law right. In principle, he saw 'no reason why authors should not be restored to that inheritance which, under the name of protection and encouragement, has been taken from them'. Nevertheless, because copyright had long been treated as a matter of compromise between those who denied the author's right altogether and 'those who think the property should last as long as the works which contain truth and beauty live', he would 'rest satisfied with a fairer adjustment of the difference than the last act of Parliament affords' (8).

The term that Talfourd proposed – the author's lifetime plus sixty years – drew opposition from the book trade, most notably from Thomas Tegg, who specialized in cheap reprints, and this roused Wordsworth to action.[9] The poet addressed some fifty letters to individual members of Parliament urging them to support Talfourd's bill. He declined to present his own petition. 'I am loth to think so unfavourably of Parliament as to deem that it requires petitions from authors as a ground for granting them a privilege, the justice of which is so obvious', he wrote to Talfourd on 18 April 1838 in a letter intended as a 'public declaration' of his sentiments on the copyright bill and in which he reasserted his conviction that the author's right should be perpetual (*Prose Works* 3:313). But, in fact, personal petitions from authors were necessary to overcome the opposition. In 1839 Wordsworth, Southey, Thomas Carlyle, and Hartley Coleridge as well as other literary figures submitted petitions to Parliament (*CJ* 94:237); finally, under the stewardship of Lord Mahon, Parliament passed the Copyright Act of 1842, which lasted until the twentieth century. This provided a term of the author's lifetime plus seven years or forty-two years from publication, whichever was longer – a resolution not far off from what Johnson had proposed in 1774.

Let us note a striking reversal. In the eighteenth century the proponents of perpetual copyright were the booksellers. By the early nineteenth century, however, the trade had adjusted to the limited copyright term, and many had a vested interest in it; it was authors such as Southey and Wordsworth who were now claiming that their rights should be perpetual.[10] *Donaldson v. Becket* is conventionally regarded as having established the statutory basis of copyright, and of course it did. But given the way Donaldson came to be understood, perhaps it should be simultaneously regarded as confirming the notion of the author's common-law right put forward by Mansfield and Blackstone.

Notes

1   Millar did not charge Taylor with printing the books, only with publishing, exposing them to sale, and selling them in England, and indeed the *Eighteenth-Century Short Title Catalogue* lists

no editions of *The Seasons* with Taylor's imprint. Possibly the books involved were printed by Donaldson, who had issued *The Seasons* in 1761 shortly after the statutory copyright expired, and a two-volume set of Thomson's complete *Poetical Works* in 1763.

2   In the preface to *The Question Concerning Literary Property* Burrow notes that the Scottish account of *Millar v. Taylor — Speeches or Arguments of the Judges of the Court of King's Bench in the Cause of Millar against Taylor —* was both 'full of Faults' and 'in Every Body's Hands' and that therefore 'Some whom I have long known, and whose Friendship I am proud of' urged him to prepare his own report as a separate publication. Burrow's 'Preface', dated 5 April 1773, suggests that his book was published in time for the Court of Session to read before ruling on *Hinton v. Donaldson* in July. In any event, the book was available and widely advertised the following winter at the time of the appeal to the House of Lords.

3   This famous episode involved Mansfield's instructions to the jury in *Rex v. Woodfall*, which concerned the Junius letters. Mansfield had instructed the jury only to consider whether Woodfall had printed the letters, not whether the letters themselves were libelous, which he reserved as a point of law. According to one opinion, Mansfield in not responding to Camden's challenge showed an 'equal want of courage and of self-possession' (Fifoot 46). But perhaps Mansfield, as Holdsworth suggests, refused to rise to the bait because he was beginning to weary of political strife (*History* 12:475). The episode is recounted in Cobbett 16:1302–22, as well as in Eeles 113–114.

4   I have not been able to identify any such letters.

5   For comparison, sixty-eight peers heard the king's speech from the throne on 13 January 1774, the opening day of the session. Fifty-six peers were present on 4 February, the opening day of the arguments of counsel, and approximately the same number for the later days of argument. Seventy-four peers were present on 15 February, the first day that the judges' opinions were heard, and sixty-five on the two later days of opinions, 17 and 21 February.

6   Howard Abrams suggests that the lords 'grounded their decision on the position that copyright had never existed as a right at common law' (1157). This was the position both of Lord Camden, who made the motion to reverse the decree, and of Lord Chancellor Apsley, who seconded it. But Camden's and Apsley's speeches, important as they were, cannot be regarded as the equivalent of a modern majority opinion. Many lay peers perhaps deferred to Camden and Apsley on the technical legal issues, though there was always the contrary opinion of Lord Mansfield to give pause to any lay peer who was seeking a legal authority to follow. As Whicher remarked some years ago, the House of Lords overturned the ruling in *Millar v. Taylor*, but 'when we ask what doctrine, precisely, the lords preferred to that which they thus cast aside, Clio (that coy muse) simply shrugs' (126).

7   Josiah Brown's subsequent account in the seventh volume of his *Reports of Cases, Upon Appeals and Writs of Error, in the High Court of Parliament* (1783) would not correct this impression. Brown's report includes a summary of the cases of the appellants and respondents as well as the questions put to the judges, but it does not give the substance of the judges' opinions or say anything about the floor debate. Unlike Burrow, Brown gives only the vote on the question of whether the statute impeached the common-law right. Five of the judges were in favor of the perpetuity or common-law right, he reports, and six were opposed whereupon it was ordered that the decree be reversed (*ER* 1:837–849). The fuller report of the case in the seventeenth volume of Cobbett's *Parliamentary History* was not published until 1813 and was less cited than Burrow and Brown. On the development of the interpretation of *Donaldson v. Becket* see Whicher, esp. 130, and Howard Abrams, esp. 1164–66. Both Whicher and Abrams emphasize the crucial role of Burrow's and Brown's reports.

8   This tradition of interpretation continues to the present day. In *Copinger and Skone James on Copyright*, the standard modern British treatise, Burrow's report is cited and we are told in

terms similar to those in Maugham that it was 'held by the majority of the judges that the common law right which an author had to copyright in his works became merged in the statutory right conferred by the Copyright Act' (5).

9   On Wordsworth's involvement in the campaign that led to the copyright act of 1842, see Zall Moorman 551–555, and Owen and Smyser's commentary in Wordsworth, *Prose Works* 3 303–306. On Tegg and the resistance to Talfourd's proposal, see Zall 134–135, and Feather 'Publishers and Politicians, Part II' 48–50.

10   Moreover by the nineteenth century the notion of the author's right might be internalized by a writer. Susan Eilenberg points out the frugality of Wordsworth's style, his characteristic blurring of the distinction between the verbal and the material, his literary territoriality and resentment of plagiarism and remarks that Wordsworth's 'attitude towards his poems some times resembled that of a landowner towards his lands' (357). Part of Wordsworth's concern with copyright was his interest in providing an estate for his family, but the obsessiveness of his concern suggests that psychological factors were also at work. The length of the copyright term was linked to the length of an author's life. Eilenberg argues, then, that Wordsworth' campaign can also be understood as associated with a fear of death and annihilation: to reform copyright was for him 'to secure a refuge from oblivion' (369).

References

Abrams, Howard B. 'The Historic Foundation of American Copyright Law: Exploding the Myth of Common Law Copyright', *Wayne Law Review* 29 (1983): 1119–91.

Forbes, Gray, W. 'Alexander Donaldson and His Fight for Cheap Books', *Juridical Review* 38 (1926) 180–202.

Boswell, James. *The Life of Johnson*. 1799. Ed. George Birkbeck Hill, rev. L. E. Powell. Oxford Clarendon, 1934–1964. 6 vols.

Brady, Frank. *James Boswell: The Later Years 1769–1795*. New York: McGraw, 1984.

Cobbett, William. *Parliamentary History of England*. London, 1806–1820. 36 vols.

Copinger, Walter Arthur, and E. P. Skone James. *Copinger and Skone James on Copyright*. 12th ed London: Sweet, 1980.

Eeles, Henry S. *Lord Chancellor Camden and His Family*. London: Philip Allan. 1934.

Eilenberg, Susan. 'Mortal Pages: Wordsworth and the Reform of Copyright'. *ELH* 56 (1989) 351–374.

English Reports [ER]. Ed A. Wood Renton. London: Stevens, 1900–1932. 178 vols.

Feather, John. 'Publishers and Politicians: The Remaking of the Law of Copyright in Britain, 1775–1842. Part I: Legal Deposit and the Battle of the Library Tax. Part II: The Rights of Authors' *Publishing History* 24 (1988): 49–76; 25 (1989): 45–72.

Fifoot, C. H. S. *Lord Mansfield*. Oxford: Clarendon, 1936.

Gray, W. Forbes. 'Alexander Donaldson and His Fight for Cheap Books'. *Juridical Review* 38 (1926) 180–202.

Holdsworth, Sir William. *A History of English Law*. 1938. London: Methuen and Sweet & Maxwell 1966. 16 vols.

Johnson, Samuel. *Johnsonian Miscellanies*. Ed. George Birkbeck Hill. Oxford: Clarendon, 1907. vols.

Journal of the House of Commons [CJ].

Journal of the House of Lords [CH].

Maugham, Robert. *A Treatise of the Laws of Literary Property*. London, 1828.

Moorman, Mary. *William Wordsworth: The Later Years*. Oxford: Clarendon, 1965.

Petitions and Papers Relating to the Bill of the Booksellers Now Before the House of Commons. London, 1774

Rpt. *The Literary Property Debate: Eight Tracts 1764–1774*. Ed. Stephen Parks. New York: Garland, 1975.

Ross, Ian Simpson. *Lord Kames and the Scotland of his Day*. Oxford: Clarendon, 1972.

Some Thoughts on the State of Literary Property Humbly Submitted to the Consideration of the Public. London, 1764. Rpt. *The Literary Property Debate: Eight Tracts 1764–1774*. Ed. Stephen Parks. New York: Garland, 1975.

Southey, Robert. 'Inquiry into the Copyright Act'. *Quarterly Review* 21 (Jan. 1819): 196–213.

Talfourd, Thomas Noon. *A Speech Delivered by Thomas Noon Talfourd, Sergeant at Law, in the House of Commons*. London, 1837.

Whicher, John F. 'The Ghost of *Donaldson v. Beckett*'. *Bulletin of the Copyright Society of the U.S.A.* 9 (1961–1962): 102–151, 194–229.

Wordsworth, William. *Letters of William and Dorothy Wordsworth*. 2nd ed. Ed. E. de Selincourt. Oxford: Clarendon, 1967–1988. 7 vols.

Wordsworth, William. *The Prose Works of William Wordsworth*. Ed. W. J. B. Owen and Jane Worthington Smyser. Oxford: Clarendon, 1974. 3 vols.

Zall, Paul M. 'Wordsworth and the Copyright Act of 1842'. *PMLA* 70 (1955): 132–144.

Chapter 23

John Brewer

AUTHORS, PUBLISHERS AND THE
MAKING OF LITERARY CULTURE

Samuel Richardson (1689–1761), printer, sometime publisher and best-selling novelist, is best remembered as the author of three extremely long epistolary novels – *Pamela* (1740), *Clarissa* (1747–8) and *Sir Charles Grandison* (1753–4) – which brought him international fame and fortune in his middle age. Somewhat improbably, this pious, sober and sententious man, who travelled little and could hardly have been more English, was inundated with praise from French *philosophes* and German critics. Denis Diderot, in his hyperbolic *Éloge de Richardson* (1761), compared Richardson to Moses, Homer, Euripides and Sophocles, composing the most effulgent of the many panegyrics which sprang from the European press.

Richardson rose to literary splendour from the humblest beginnings. The son of a rural joiner, he was able by dint of hard work, good luck and astute connections, to make a comfortable fortune in the printing trade. Even before fame was thrust upon him in the 1740s he had attained a prosperity that contrasted with the poverty of his youth. He was the beneficiary, as both printer and author, of the remarkable transformation in British publishing that occurred between the late seventeenth and late eighteenth centuries.

When Richardson published his first novel, *Pamela*, he was more than fifty years old; by then there were few byways of publishing he did not know. He had worked as a proof corrector and as a hack, writing prefaces and compiling indexes; he had printed newspapers and conduct books and won the lucrative contract to be official printer to the House of Commons. He had worked for booksellers and published books on his own account. From his presses had rolled not only the finely printed folio *Journals of the House of Commons*, weighty tomes that only a successful printer at the peak of his trade could produce, but also the ephemera – handbills, advertisements and trade cards – that earned the daily bread of the humble jobbing printer.

In his early years, when he had little capital or clout, Richardson was often hired by a bookseller to print part of a work. He was a craftsman for hire, a cog in the publishing machine. To act on his own behalf, to escape the control of the booksellers who dominated publishing, he had to take risks. Printing the work of such government opponents and Jacobites as Francis Atterbury, the banished former Bishop of London, and Philip, Duke of Wharton, the mad-cap rake and sometime drinking companion of the exiled Stuart Pretender, invited the hostility of the authorities and the threat of arrest; but it was also profitable and helped the young printer to make his mark.

But as Richardson prospered in the 1730s, he grew more prudent, avoiding controversy and diversifying his business to include newspaper and government work. He bought a share in the *Daily Gazetteer*, a paper which he printed, and began the profitable business of printing parliamentary bills and reports, work that in its best year grossed him nearly £600. He also printed literary works, including James Thomson's famous poem *The Seasons* and several editions of Daniel Defoe's *Tour Through the Whole Island of Great Britain*, which he re-edited to include his own material.

Richardson's career as a printer followed the path laid down in his first published work, the advice book *The Apprentice's Vade Mecum: or, Young Man's Pocket Companion*: it took him by dint of industry and virtue from the margins of his trade to the centre of his profession. Like Hogarth's Tom Goodchild in *The Industrious and Idle Apprentice*, Richardson married his master's daughter; and though, unlike Tom, he never became Lord Mayor, he did achieve high office, being elected Master of the Company of Stationers in 1753.

Yet none of Richardson's experience and success prepared him for the remarkable chain of events that followed the publication of his first novel. *Pamela*, the moralistic story of a servant girl whose determined defence of her sexual virtue is rewarded by genteel marriage, was a runaway best-seller in 1740. Within a year of its appearance it had gone through five editions, been pirated and parodied, notably in Henry Fielding's *Shamela*, dramatized on the London stage by Henry Giffard and put into verse by George Bennett.

Pamela's popularity was not confined to Britain. North American editions appeared in New York, Philadelphia and Boston. The novel swept Europe, being translated into French, Italian, Dutch, German, Swedish, Russian, Spanish and Portuguese. Voltaire and the Italian dramatist Carlo Goldoni wrote plays based on *Pamela*'s plot. Today when we think of an eighteenth-century novelist we think of Daniel Defoe and Henry Fielding, perhaps of Tobias Smollett or Laurence Sterne; in eighteenth-century Europe the English novelist was almost synonymous with Samuel Richardson.

Richardson's second novel was also a blockbuster. *Clarissa* appeared in seven volumes, devoting more than a million words to the conflict between the rake Lovelace and the virtuous heroine Clarissa Harlowe, a struggle which ends with their deaths. It was not a book for plot lovers – as Dr Johnson remarked, 'if you would read Richardson for the story, your impatience would be so much fretted that you would hang yourself. But you must read him for the sentiment' – nor was it a quick read. But *Clarissa* followed its predecessor on to the bookshelves of Europe, being translated into German, French, Russian, Italian and Portuguese.

The success of Richardson's first two novels lay in his portrayal of female virtue under duress. His growing band of admirers – which included a coterie of literary and genteel women – urged him to create a comparable male portrait. Richardson complied in his last novel *Sir Charles Grandison*. Though *Grandison* never achieved the success of his earlier fiction, male virtue proving less popular than its female equivalent, the novel was such a hot publisher's item that copies of its sheets were stolen from Richardson's press and spirited off to Dublin; an Irish edition appeared before its author and printer had published his own in London. . . .

The success of his epistolary fiction transformed Richardson from a prosperous printer into a literary lion. He was inundated with fan mail, flooded with suggestions for his plots, and deluged with praise and criticism. His circle of acquaintance grew to include the bluestockings Mrs Mary Delany, Hester Chapone and Elizabeth Carter. Dr Johnson became a good friend, who may have borrowed money from Richardson but more than paid back his debt in the hard currency of critical acclaim. Johnson repeatedly lauded Richardson at the expense of Henry Fielding – 'Sir, there is more knowledge of the heart in one letter of Richardson's, than in all "Tom Jones" ' – and enshrined the novelist's prose in his *Dictionary*, including ninety-seven citations from *Clarissa*, almost double that of any other work by a living author.

In the 1750s Richardson looked back on his life and proudly remarked, 'Twenty years ago I was the most obscure man in Great Britain, and now I am admitted to the company of the first characters of the Kingdom'. If he had chosen to travel, he would have also graced the drawing rooms of Europe. The publishing industry had served him well; when he died in 1761 he left an enviable literary legacy and a comfortable fortune of £14,000. Richardson liked to imagine that his success as printer and author was the result of his exceptional moral probity and ferocious industry. But it was also a sign of the remarkable transformation of the publishing business that had taken place in his lifetime and was to continue into the nineteenth century.

In 1689, the year of Richardson's birth and the first year after the Glorious Revolution had toppled James II, the English press was still far from free. Controls, enshrined in the Licensing Act of 1662 and reinforced in the new charter that the Stationers' Company had been granted in 1684, were designed to ensure that the government could monitor publications and that the Stationers' Company could maintain a monopoly of commercial publishing throughout England. This compact between a government anxious to suppress dissent and a guild determined to retain control of the book trade was secured by three provisions that tightly bound the press: prior government censorship of all publications; mandatory entry of all published works in the Registers of the Stationers' Company; and limitation of the printing trade to twenty master printers. . . .

The lapse of the Licensing Act in 1695 – something of a legislative accident – finally removed the major legal constraints on the expansion of the press, but it did not entirely eliminate government control or create a completely free market. Censorship before publication ended, but laws against blasphemy, obscenity and seditious libel were frequently enforced. . . .

Numerous taxes, including duties on paper, printed matter and advertisements, created a system of fiscal regulation that could also be used against printers and publishers. And periodic though not very effective attempts were made to regulate the distribution of the press. In 1782, for instance, hawkers and street vendors were prevented from hiring out newspapers rather than selling them, a common means of increasing their circulation. But with the lapse of the Licensing Act and the consequent end of the system that registered all printed material with the Stationers' Company, and in the absence of a registry of printing presses (not required until 1799 in reaction to the French Revolution), it was impossible for the government to exercise any systematic control of publishing. Sporadic intervention, no matter how heavy-handed, was not the same as continuous policing. . . .

In the year of Richardson's birth printing and publishing had been a collection of trades, dominated by a powerful guild and confined to a few streets and lanes in the city of London. Printing presses clattered in Aldersgate Street, Bartholomew Close, Whitefriars and St John's Lane; book- and printsellers displayed their wares on stands and in shops that clustered in Little Britain, around St Paul's Churchyard and near Temple Bar; and trade publishers' premises were concentrated near Stationers' Hall on Warwick Lane and Paternoster Row. Business thrived but was confined to a community in which nearly everyone was personally acquainted and in which a short walk was all that was necessary to complete a deal.

Nearly 100 years later the publishing industry was so diverse, complex and dispersed that the bookseller John Pendred brought out the first guide to English publishing, *The London and Country Printers, Booksellers and Stationers Vade Mecum* (1785). Pendred's world extends far beyond the confines of St Paul's Churchyard and Paternoster Row. His account of the metropolitan trade lists nearly 650 businesses engaged in thirty-two different occupations. In this highly specialized world, stationers and booksellers outnumbered printers, who were enumerated alongside engravers, map-, music- and printsellers, bookbinders, paper-, card- and board-makers, typefounders and warehousemen. Fancy booksellers listed their premises in Oxford Street, Piccadilly, Berkeley Square and on Pall Mall; engravers worked in the artists' quarter of Covent Garden as well as in the fashionable West End, and printers and publishers were scattered all over the city.

But the most important part of the guide was concerned not with London at all but with the provinces. For one of Pendred's main purposes was to provide the London trade with valuable information about how to exploit provincial advertising and distribution networks. When he listed the forty-nine country newspapers printed in thirty-four towns, he gave two crucial pieces of information: the names of newspaper owners and the addresses of their London agents. Booksellers could thus place advertisements in the provincial press through London agents, or they could contact the proprietors directly in order to exploit the distribution network they had established. What had begun as a London trade had become a national business.

The world of eighteenth-century publishing is best understood as an expanding maze or labyrinth, and it offered the potential author many entrances and numerous routes to eventual publication, each full of hazards, pitfalls and dead ends. Presided over by the Cerberus-like figure of the bookseller, the maze was not difficult to enter but easy to get lost in, and the author needed both guides and a map. Richardson was an exception, for he knew the ways of publishing intimately, could print his books himself, and had good working relations with the booksellers, notably John Osborn and Charles Rivington, whose request that he write a book of morally instructive letters was the inspiration for his first novel. But few authors were either so fortunate or so well informed.

Still, the number and variety of authors who embarked on the journey into print was quite remarkable. . . .

The crucial vehicle was the periodical press. Any aspiring author seeking fame, fortune or just the pleasure of seeing their words in print could send their work to a magazine proprietor, and many a career began with such an unsolicited contribution. Elizabeth Rowe, who became a successful author of pious verse much admired by Protestant Nonconformists, had her earliest poems published anonymously in John Dunton's *Athenian Mercury* in the 1690s. Lady Wortley Montagu's first publication was an essay in Addison and Steele's *Spectator*. And *Felix Farley's Bristol Journal* was the means by which Thomas Chatterton launched his brief, tragic career as poet and forger of medieval documents. . . . What brought them all to the periodical press was the unparalleled opportunity it offered to get into print. . . .

Periodicals also made possible a career dedicated solely to writing. Magazine proprietors were inundated with unsolicited material, some of which came gratis, and the growing competition among the magazines meant that the demand for material exceeded supply. The professional author stepped into the breach with essays, reviews, poems and criticism that enlivened and enlightened the public; publication enabled him to earn a living. By the 1760s he could contribute to more than thirty London periodicals; by the end of the century there were more than eighty. . . .

By the middle of the century, in large part because of the expansion of this periodical press, a small but growing band of professional writers was established in London. These authors, personified in the shambling, eccentric but indomitable figure of Samuel Johnson, were still outnumbered by amateur and occasional writers from every walk of life, for the very circumstances that had made professional authorship possible had also enormously increased the number of dilettante writers in print. But the inconspicuousness of professional authors was not entirely attributable to their low numbers. They laboured under a more severe handicap, often suffered by new figures on the social landscape: they did not fit into prevailing ideas about how the literary world was constructed.

Fifty years earlier the tribe of authors had been conventionally divided into two radically different camps. There were those who wrote to edify, amuse and instruct but who shunned monetary reward and there were those who wrote for money. In the former view writing was a 'liberal' pursuit, the occupation of persons of enlarged views and unbiased vision. Writing for money not only reduced authorship to a mechanical trade but subverted the value of the work. . . .

Commentators considered these authors as shackled and imprisoned by their trade. As James

Ralph put it in his eloquent defence in 1758, 'there is no Difference between the Writer in his Garret, and the Slave in his Mines; but that the former has his Situation in the Air, and the latter in the Bowels of the Earth: Both have their Tasks assigned them alike: Both must drudge *and* Starve; neither can hope for Deliverance. The compiler must compile; the Composer must compose on; sick or well; in spirit or out'. Hack work provided only enough to avoid destitution. Pay was poor. A reviewer at mid-century, for example, would receive a standard fee of two guineas for writing eighty pages of reviews. . . .

How was the author to escape the double-bind which James Ralph so clearly identified? The author's dilemma, Ralph pointed out, was that he was damned if he did take the money, and poor if he didn't:

> A Man may plead for Money, prescribe or quack for Money, preach and pray for Money, marry for Money, fight for Money, do any thing within the Law for Money, provided the Expedient answers, without the least imputation.
>
> But if he writes like one inspired from Heaven, and writes for Money, the Man of *Touch*, in the right of *Midas* his great Ancestor, enters his Caveat against him as a Man of *Taste*; declares the two Provinces to be incompatible; that he who aims at Praise ought to be starved; and that there ought to be so much draw-back upon Character for Every Acquisition in Coin . . . [The author] is laugh'd at if poor; if, to avoid that curse, he endeavours to turn his Wit to Profit, he is branded as a Mercenary.

Ralph's dyspeptic diatribe against professions that purported to be liberal but that were tainted with mammon reveals his frustration; he has no alternative vision that would place the professional author in a new setting. How could the writer be paid but respectable? This was the essential question.

The answer was slow in formulation and grew out of two related debates, one about artistic value, the other about intellectual property. The former focused on the high-minded issue of creativity, the latter on the prosaic question of copyright; both helped to formulate and clarify the notion of the author as creator of a unique property which he owned by virtue of a singular, imaginative act.

The liberal criterion of what made authorship legitimate was social. Financial independence, the eighteenth-century equivalent of Virginia Woolf's '£500 a year and a room of one's own', produced good writing; the marketplace produced trash. Against this claim, Johnson and his allies argued that the ability to produce valuable literature was not determined by economic conditions but was rather a matter of individual ingenuity and originality. Literature was less a matter of uncovering and revealing traditional 'natural' truths than of creating an original – that is, new – literary artifact. This emphasis on creativity was not novel – it can be found in the work of the classical critic Longinus, and the notion of originality had a long history. But the association of creative genius with originality had never before been made so forcefully. 'The highest praise of genius', wrote Johnson in his *Life of Milton*, 'is original invention'.

Originality distinguished the true author from the hack. Both might be paid, both embark on projects suggested and financed by booksellers, like most of Johnson's major works, but an author had creative powers that the compiler and pastiche writer lacked. Above 'the drudges of the pen' and the 'manufacturers of literature' Johnson identified the few who 'can be said to produce, or endeavour to produce, new ideas, to extend any principle of science, or gratify the imagination with any uncommon train of images or contexture of events'.

The emphasis on originality and novelty, introducing as it did a new hierarchy of literary endeavour, underscored the special relationship that the author bore to his text. If a work was original it was also unique, the distinctive consequence of a writer's imagination. Each text bore the distinctive impress of its author's mind. In emphasizing the singularity of literary work, writers like Johnson threw the personality and character of the author into sharp relief. Literary criticism became more than an assessment of a work's conformity to a set of conventions and rules; it also set out to show how each individual author shaped a particular work. . . .

By the late eighteenth century the professional author, the creator of unique works of literature, had become a recognizable type, distinguishable from both the liberal writer and the hack. His creativity not only shaped what he wrote but conferred on him a public authority to explain how it should be interpreted and how it differed from earlier writing. As in Johnson's case, the creative author was inclined to become the historical critic, concerned to reveal literary tradition in order to establish his own place in literary history.

Even if the author fabricated and fashioned literary works, there was still the question of what right he had to own them. It is one of the great ironies of this period that the establishment of an author's rights in his literary property should have been achieved largely with the help his old enemy, the bookseller. . . .

How then was a writer to be ennobled and how was he or she to retain the title? Establishing the legitimacy of the idea of professional authorship did not secure the careers and status of *individual* writers, which depended on how effectively each could exploit the resources and opportunities of the literary system. The author's first task was to seek entry into the labyrinth of publishing. Without the resources of a Horace Walpole and despite the opportunities afforded by the periodical press, the writer almost certainly needed to procure the services of a bookseller. Only such a commercial middleman had the resources necessary to produce and distribute books. . . .

Whether the writer approached a bookseller in person or solicited support through importunate correspondence, the author's reception was rarely warm, occasionally tepid and often cold. The arrogance and hauteur of the bookseller, brilliantly captured in Thomas Rowlandson's pen and wash drawing *The Bookseller and the Author* (1780–4) was an authorial cliché and longstanding grievance. Still, Rowlandson's sneering bookseller, whose corpulent prosperity contrasts with the cringing emaciated figure of the imploring author, is a caricature. Though there were booksellers like Edmund Curll who abused their position and the writers they employed, most members of the trade were prudent, honest and conservative men of business who faced problems that many authors were eager to avoid. The bookseller bore the risk of publication and needed to make a profit. He was inundated with manuscripts, many of which lacked merit or commercial value. The sheer volume of material made it hard for him to discriminate, to pick out the work that would prove a success. He might claim, as James Ralph put it, to know 'best what Assortment of Wares will best suit the Market', but he knew that literary innovation was exceptionally chancy. It was much less risky to publish and trade in the copyrights of established figures. Only the most adventurous booksellers preferred an unknown living author to a dead literary monument.

How, then, was the hapless writer to overcome the bookseller's reluctance to help him into print? One of the best stratagems was to appeal to the personal interests and sympathies of the publisher. Though Rowlandson, like many embittered authors, depicted booksellers as venal monsters and ruthless profit-seeking entrepreneurs, most held certain subjects and certain causes close to their heart. Jacob Tonson loved Whiggery and *belles-lettres*; John Wilkie admired conservative works on politics and religion; John Newbery and William Darton specialized in children's literature and Robert Dodsley in poetry. Authors needed to know booksellers. The more specialized or controversial the work, the more important it was to find the right publisher. John Millan would have been delighted to publish a manuscript on British antiquities that would have made most booksellers blanch, while the radical bookseller Joseph Johnson was willing to publish tracts that many others thought too hot to handle.

Such booksellers were intent not upon the ruthless maximization of profit but upon combining their cultural, social, religious and political interests with making a respectable living. They saw themselves, as Johnson, a man not prone to flattery, described them, as 'modern patrons of literature'. For though the historical cliché has emphasized their exploitation of authors, the historical record reveals many of them to have treated their clients and employees with a patience and charity which some writers barely deserved. . . .

The bookseller was first and foremost a businessman, but this did not mean that he had no regard for authors and their works, any more than the professional author had no regard for the content of his work as long as it turned a profit. Both bookseller and author shared in the balancing act between pecuniary reward and intellectual interest that gave eighteenth-century publishing much of its energy. Yet the liberal tradition of writing, which was so concerned to deny the legitimacy of writing for money, died hard, even amongst those who became professional authors. In their eyes the bookseller remained a dangerous and dubious figure, essential to their livelihood but a constant reminder of the pact they had made with mammon.

When the would-be author approached a bookseller he still needed to allay the understandable anxieties of someone who knew how risky it was to back a literary tyro. Reassurance took two forms. First, the author could secure the support of someone whose critical acumen would vouch for the value of the work and whose public endorsement would help its sales. The best friend an aspiring author could have was someone already experienced in the ways of Grub Street. For all the personal rivalries and bitter quarrels that rent the community of authors, many of their number heeded the advice of Johnson and of James Ralph that writers should stand together, going to considerable lengths to help their brother scribblers. . . .

Johnson enjoyed his role as literary patron and played it with gusto. Though, as Hester Piozzi complained, he said 'very contemptuous things of our sex', he helped a number of female poets and novelists into print, notably Anna Williams, Frances Burney and Charlotte Lennox. Such was his enthusiasm for Lennox's writing that he induced fellow members of the Ivy Lane Club to throw an all-night party to celebrate the birth of her 'first literary child'. At times passion got the better of his judgement. Johnson was an early and ardent supporter of William Lauder's attacks on Milton. Lauder, a Scottish classicist and Jacobite schoolmaster who had lost a leg after being hit by a golfball, castigated Milton as a feeble and politically misdirected plagiarist. Johnson, who had little sympathy for Milton's politics, wrote prefaces for Lauder's work and urged it on the booksellers.

But how was an unknown writer to meet the likes of Johnson? It was best to join one of the many informal coteries and circles which made up literary London. Some of these associations, like Johnson's Club, were only open to members and the occasional guest. But, as we have seen, throughout the period writers frequented coffee houses and taverns which were open to anyone who could pay the reckoning. In these informal surroundings an introduction or witty remark could lead to acquaintance, and acquaintance to friendship with an established author or critic whose circle of influence might include booksellers, newspaper proprietors and the literary managers of magazines. Fellow authors could rarely offer financial support (except, perhaps, for the occasional short-term loan) but had something far more valuable – influence and connections, the power to mobilize the resources that the aspiring author so desperately needed. Authors, then, were not only producers of literature but also among its most important patrons.

The support of a colleague made an author's work more credible to a bookseller, but it only marginally reduced the latter's financial risk. Risk reduction could be achieved in one of two ways: by getting someone else to bear the costs of publication, or by guaranteeing a number of sales by organizing a subscription of purchasers prior to publication. Both methods required the support of literary patrons.

The question of patronage was and remains a vexed one. For much of the eighteenth century authors had two contradictory complaints about the patronage of literature. On the one hand, they regretted the demise of what was vaguely imagined as an ideal past in which kings, nobles and gentlemen supported literary endeavour of the highest quality. Such nostalgia, rampant early in the century, was a hankering for a world that authors never had, and was in large part a hostile reaction to the growth of commercial publishing and a political response to the Hanoverian regime. Many writers, especially those who aspired to gentility and literary high-mindedness, were appalled by the growing trade in literary commodities. And many of them – notably the Scriblerian circle that included Pope, Swift, Arbuthnot and Gay – were also politically opposed to George I and George II, resentful of their exclusion from royal patronage, and conscious of the court's declining importance as a centre of literary largesse.

Other authors were happy to see patrons fade away, however, and wished good-riddance to a putative golden age of patronage. The old relations between patron and client had, in the eyes of many, created a form of literary prostitution. Gentlemen, wrote the poet Charles Churchill, 'kept a bard, just as they keep a whore'. Henry Fielding's use of the whoring metaphor in his *Author's Farce* differed only slightly: 'Get a patron,' one of his characters advises, 'be pimp to some worthless man of quality, write panegyrics on him, flatter him with as many virtues as he has vices.' In the politically charged climate of eighteenth-century England, reliance on a private individual, even the patronage of the monarch, was deemed incompatible with the independent requirements of modern authorship. A professional writer, it was felt, should be servant to no one but the public. His work should not reflect the aetiolated taste of a sybaritic aristocrat but rest on the firmer foundation of public approval. . . .

In the complex and often fraught relations between patron and authorial client the balance of power slowly but irreversibly shifted in favour of the writer. Because authors increasingly had the alternative resources of a commercial literary world, they became less dependent on individual largesse. This did not make them any less eager to secure aristocratic support, but what they wanted was not, on the whole, the rather demeaning place of the household servant, but money – under-writing an edition, paying for its production costs – and, most important of all, someone to talk up their books in polite society. The influential cleric who 'went from Coffee-house to Coffee-house, calling upon all men of taste to exert themselves in rescuing one of the greatest geniuses that ever appeared from obscurity' helped James Thomson every bit as much as Lords Talbot and Lyttelton. For what a writer most needed was reputation; from this all else, including financial independence, followed.

The greatest service, then, that a patron, whether aristocratic or not, could render an author was to laud his or her abilities, to praise the writer's work in fashionable society. Johnson's famous denunciation of Lord Chesterfield – 'Is not a Patron, my Lord, one who looks with unconcern on a Man struggling for Life in the water, and when he has reached ground encumbers him with help' – complained not about the noble lord's failure to fund the *Dictionary* (which was financed, after all, by the booksellers) or about his financial niggardliness to its author, who received a meagre £10 for dedicating its plan to him. What irked Johnson was Chesterfield's failure during the *Dictionary's* seven-year gestation to provide 'one Act of assistance, one word of encouragement, or one smile of favour'. He should have been supporting the project, praising its aim and author in the literary circles and genteel drawing rooms he frequented. His job was not to commission a work nor to house and feed its author – acts that would have compromised authorial independence – but to encourage and orchestrate its praise. Chesterfield's meagre contribution to Johnson's enterprise showed that he knew what he was supposed to do. He wrote two short letters puffing the *Dictionary* in the newspaper *The World* in November and December 1754. It was a gesture, but Johnson felt that for seven years' labour it was not enough.

The shifting role of the patron from commissioner and controller of literary work to its promoter, consumer and distributor was best epitomized by the practice of book subscription which increased as the nature of patronage changed. The number of subscription volumes rose rapidly between the late seventeenth century and the 1730s, levelled off until the 1760s, and spurted again during the last two decades of the century. Poems, sermons, music, histories, medical and advice manuals, biography, theology, mathematics, husbandry and, by the end of the century, even novels and plays were published in this way.

The object of subscription was to secure down-payments on and promises to purchase a book before its publication. This ensured that production and distribution costs were covered before a work went to press, an arrangement that pleased the booksellers because it cut risks and could promise large profits. Authors solicited some subscribers by getting job printers to produce pro-posals and by hawking their wares in the drawing rooms and at the assemblies of the great. But the booksellers and authors' friends handled many more. Richardson printed numerous subscription editions and helped to organize the 1730 subscription editions of James Thomson's *The Seasons*, printing proposals and taking down-payments and orders at his shop. Johnson was an inveterate organizer of subscriptions for those he admired or whom he found in distress. He spent more than fifteen years helping to organize a subscription to Anna Williams's *Miscellanies in Prose and Verse*, which eventually appeared in 1766. The blind Miss Williams, who for many years lived in Johnson's house, earned over £300 as a result of Johnson's benevolence. His efforts on behalf of Charlotte Lennox, the success of whose novel, *The Female Quixote*, did not prevent her from falling into penury, were no less assiduous though much less successful. Numerous proposals he wrote for her in the 1770s all came to nothing. . . .

Subscription publication brought together the interests of author, patron and bookseller. For the author it helped to get into print works such as expensive and scholarly tomes which might otherwise never have been published. It was the main means of publishing a collected volume or volumes of a single author's works in either prose or verse. A well-managed subscription could also prove sufficiently popular and profitable to secure an author's financial independence. The subscrip-tions to Pope's works freed him from what he viewed as the clutches of the booksellers; the 1,200 subscribers to Elizabeth Carter's *All the Works of Epictetus* earned her almost £1,000, enabling her to devote the rest of her life to her bluestocking literary interests. From the subscriber's point of view it was an opportunity to patronize and to be seen to support an author without the difficulties that attended a more personal relationship between patron and client. For the publisher, not only was there a reduced risk but the chance of additional sales through the network of retail booksellers, encouraged by the publicity provided by a list of distinguished subscribers.

Chapter 24

Leah Price

CULTURES OF THE COMMONPLACE

The kind of anthology most familiar to academic literary critics today – delimited by nationality, arranged by chronology – was unknown in Richardson's lifetime. The anthology itself is much older, as we have seen. But the defeat of perpetual copyright in 1774 changed the use to which the form was put. Only once the legal status of earlier works came to diverge from that of new ones did English-language anthologies take on the retrospective function (and the academic audience) that they maintain today. Timely miscellanies of new works gave way to timeless gleanings from the backlist. On or about 1774, as the research of Barbara Benedict and Trevor Ross has shown, literary history became anthologists' job.[1]

A generation of late-eighteenth-century anthologies established not only the content of the canon to date, but also the rules by which future literature would be transmitted, notably the expectation that every anthology-piece bear a signature and that its signatory be dead.[2] Even more important than their ambition to consolidate a national tradition, however, was the near-monopoly that a few school anthologies achieved by the end of the century, allowing large numbers of schoolchildren to share the experience of reading not just the same anthology-pieces but the same anthologies. Looking back on the *Elegant Extracts: or Useful and Entertaining Passages in Prose Selected for the Improvement of Scholars in Classical and other Schools* first published by Vicesimus Knox in 1784, an 1816 edition could boast that the '*uniformity of English books*, in schools' which enabled '*all the students of the same class*, provided with copies of the same book, . . . to read it together' would have been logistically unthinkable a few generations ago. The class reciting in unison provided an image for a culture cemented not only by the affordability but by the ubiquity of a few standard collections.[3]

Like other late-eighteenth-century traditions, however, those anthologies backdated their own invention. A companion volume of *Elegant Extracts: or Useful and Entertaining Pieces of Poetry, Selected for the Improvement of Youth in Speaking, Reading, Thinking, Composing; and in the Conduct of Life* (1784) vests editorial responsibility with everybody and nobody, displacing Knox's originality at once by the anthologists who preceded him and by the readers forced to ratify his decisions. 'There was no occasion for singular acuteness of vision, or of optical glasses,' the preface intones heavily, 'to discover a brightness which obtruded itself on the eye.'

> The best pieces are usually the most popular. They are loudly recommended by the voice of fame, and indeed have already been selected in a variety of volumes of preceding collections . . . Almost any man, willing to incur a considerable expense, and undergo a little trouble, might have furnished as good a collection . . . It was the business of the Editor of a school-book like this, not to insert scarce and curious works . . . but to collect such as were publicly known and universally celebrated . . . Private judgement, in a work like this, must often give way to public.[4]

An anthology that reproduces the words of poets also records the voice of fame. An amanuensis rather than a creator, its editor represents a community instead of expressing a self. In the same way that each anthology-piece functions (at least in theory) as a representative synecdoche for the longer text from which it is excerpted, the anthologist claims to stand within – and for – the same audience that he addresses. Samuel Johnson had positioned himself within that public when he professed in the *Life of Gray* (itself prefaced to one of the volumes which together make up an anthology writ large of *Works of the English Poets*) to 'rejoice to concur with the common reader; for by the common sense of readers uncorrupted with literary prejudices . . . must be finally decided all claim to poetical honours'.[5] Johnson's 'common sense' anticipates Knox's 'public judgement' as closely as the latter's lumbering antitheses imitate the former's measured periods, but the *Extracts* go farther to silence Johnson's critical 'I' altogether. Caught between the readers for whom he speaks and the writers from whom he copies, the editor dwindles to a vanishing point. In the last moment of the book marked as Knox's own – since the 'extracts' themselves change him from author to compiler – the speaker writes himself out of existence. The preface ends with a quotation: 'I will, therefore, conclude my preface with the ideas of Montaigne: – "*I have here only made a nosegay of culled flowers, and have brought nothing of my own but the thread that ties them.*" '[6] By substituting Montaigne's signature for Knox's, this conclusion prefigures the transition from the preface where the editor speaks to the body of the text where other authors' voices displace his. The editor abdicates his individuality as a reader together with his originality as a writer. Far from standing above the undifferentiated passivity of the reading public, the anthologist exemplifies it.[7]

Knox's self-conscious sacrifice of 'private' or 'singular' to 'public' or 'popular' taste erases not only the editor's superiority to his audience but any difference between one reader and another. The only readers whom his ostentatiously inclusive public excludes are precisely those who try to distinguish themselves: antiquarians whose expertise on what he calls 'scarce and curious works' challenges the cohesion of his audience. The *Elegant Extracts* record a double series of discriminations – texts to be represented from texts to be ignored and, within the former, passages to be reproduced from passages to be excised. Yet Knox keeps the act of evaluation decorously offstage. His preface alternately banishes from the 'public' those readers who attempt to act upon their 'private' judgments and displaces his own editorial responsibility onto the 'preceding collections' to which he defers. That precedent itself recedes endlessly, since the preface accuses earlier anthologies of borrowing in turn: 'the freedom of borrowing [from other anthologies], it is hoped, will be pardoned, as the collectors, with whom it has been used, first set the example of it.'[8] Knox's deference to tradition lends moral significance to the longstanding tension between the demand for new editions to edge older ones out of the market, on the one hand, and the economic incentives to recycle earlier editorial principles or even to re-use old plates, on the other. Indeed, the *Extracts* exclude not only living authors, but new assessments of dead ones. In a characteristically negative formulation, the tenth edition promises that its contents will be 'selected from writers whose characters are established without controversy'.[9] With what their characters are established remains unspecified, for the anthology defines not only the production but the evaluation of literature as *faits accomplis*.

Knox's disclaimer of originality kept his anthology in print, his selection plagiarized, and his impersonal persona imitated long after more polemical competitors like Hazlitt's ephemeral *Select British Poets, or New Elegant Extracts from Chaucer to the Present Time* (1824) disappeared from sight. . . . His invocation of an already established consensus has remained formulaic from Kearsley's *Beauties of Shakespeare* (published in the same year as the first volume of the *Extracts*), which apologizes for 'dwell[ing] on perfections which every one confesses', to Francis Turner Palgrave's *Golden Treasury* (1861), which calls 'its fittest readers those who already love Poetry so well, that [the editor] can offer them nothing not already known and valued', through to Cleanth Brooks and Robert Penn Warren's influential American textbook *Understanding Fiction* (1943), which promises to include only 'stories which are popular and widely anthologized'. Knox's fantasy of editing by plebiscite was realized two centuries later in Columbia University Press's anomalously explicit *The Classic Hundred: All-Time Favorite Poems* (1990) and *Top 500 Poems* (1992), which select their contents by frequency of appearance in earlier US anthologies as measured by *Granger's Index to Poetry*. When a US Education Secretary's neoconservative *Book of Virtues* (1993) made hackneyed anthology-pieces the vehicle to bring a reluctant public 'back' to basics, his declaration that 'we don't have to reinvent the wheel' lent political point to the reinvention of tradition that has become traditional among anthologists.[10] Repeated with the same unanimity that they describe, these editorial disclaimers not only imply that texts transmit themselves – that as John Hollander and Frank Kermode's preface to the *Oxford Anthology of English Literature* put it more thoughtfully in 1973, 'English literature has generated its own history' – but present the anthology as the effect of an audience's cohesion rather than its cause.[11]

Knox's scissor-doings

Knox's disclaimers of novelty obscure the role of his *Extracts* in defining a specifically middle-class public which owes more to the endurance of the anthology than to the rise of the novel. By dismissing as 'private' the elite that prizes authorial obscurity and critical originality, Knox reduces the 'public' to the anthology-reading classes. Yet the relation of that audience to its classically educated betters remains strategically ambiguous. Where the first edition of Knox's *Elegant Extracts* (1783) addresses 'school-boys', the tenth (1816), advertised 'for the use of both sexes', presents itself as a corrective to the gender gap embodied in the absence of the 'mother tongue' from the schoolbooks of 'our fathers'. 'What ENGLISH book similar to this volume, calculated entirely for the use of young students at schools, and under private tuition, was to be found in the days of our fathers?' the preface asks. 'None, certainly. The consequence was . . . neglect [of] that mother tongue, which is in daily and hourly requisition.'[12] Knox's claim for the novelty of an 'ENGLISH' anthology (like his announcement that 'this collection may be usefully read at ENGLISH SCHOOLS, just as the Latin and Greek authors are read at the *grammar-schools*') at once acknowledges and dismisses his debt to the centuries-old machinery developed to teach ancient languages to boys.[13]

Collections of classical excerpts designed to exemplify grammatical principles, such as the *Gradus ad Parnassum*, provided a model for the more androgynous vernacular anthologies which began to supplement them in this period. William Enfield, whose academy in Warrington helped institutionalize that shift, uses the preface of his *Speaker* (1774) to reassign the pedagogical function of ancient literature to the moderns: 'Without having recourse to the ancients, it is possible to find in modern languages valuable specimens of every species of polite literature.'[14] The title's invocation of an oratorical training specific to boys overcompensates for the *Speaker*'s attack on the ancient/ modern opposition which had traditionally helped shape children's gender identity. Indeed, Anna Laetitia Barbauld's *Female Speaker* (published thirty-seven years later) opens by regretting the disappearance of that difference between women's education and men's: 'It is, perhaps, an error in modern education, liberally conducted as at present it is toward females, that . . . when they have gone through their course of education, they have a general acquaintance with, perhaps, three or four languages, and know little of the best productions of their own.'[15] Barbauld's fear that women's eagerness for the prestige of masculine learning would eliminate students' 'own' literature from the curriculum reverses Enfield's attempt to construct a national canon by teaching men to read like women. Yet both locate gender difference among consumers, rather than, like Sandra Gilbert and Susan Gubar's *Norton Anthology of Literature by Women* two centuries later, among producers. Even the inclusion of seven token women – Catherine Talbot, Frances Brooke, Lady Mary Wortley Montagu, Lucy Aiken, Hannah More, Hester Chapone, and Maria Edgeworth – fails to make *The Female Speaker* significantly more gender-balanced than Enfield's collection, which had already included one in the person of Barbauld herself. Barbauld's interpellation of readers differs sharply from Gilbert and Gubar's representation of writers; the limits of her anthology depend not on who wrote its contents, but who edits and reads them. By making clear that the 'Female Speaker' of her title refers only to the audience who recites from it, Barbauld rules out the possibility that speech might encompass original self-expression.

The *Extracts'* bid to replace the classical curriculum of 'our fathers' by its equivalent in the 'mother tongue' reinforces the feminization of bourgeois culture that Knox exploits in his equally assonant *Elegant Epistles*, whose preface reassures readers that 'merchants, men of business, and particularly the ladies' write better letters than scholars.[16] In the *Extracts*, too, the language of gender slips easily into commercial metaphors. The 1816 preface's description of 'the days of our fathers' concludes:

> Persons who had never extended their views to ancient and classic lore, but had been confined in their education to English, triumphed in the common intercourse of society, over the academical scholar . . . It became highly expedient therefore to introduce more of English reading into our classical schools; that those who went into the world with their coffers richly stored with the golden medals of antiquity, might at the same time be furnished with a sufficiency of coin from the modern mint, for the commerce of ordinary life.[17]

While adjectives like 'common' and 'ordinary' describe the same community that earlier editions invoke, the 1816 preface transposes them from words denoting evaluation ('universal celebration', 'public judgement') to terms of exchange ('common intercourse', 'the commerce of ordinary life'). Knox had already defended his lack of originality by analogy with the circulation of coins: 'the stamp of experience gave ["whatever was found in previous collections"] currency.' Here, too, the scholar's 'scarce and curious works' are to the anthology-reader's 'commerce of ordinary life' what ancestral 'stores' are to the exchange of 'coins'. Aristocratic inheritance and bourgeois commerce stand for two competing models of literature: one compares it with heirlooms valuable for their rarity, the other with a currency whose worth depends on its circulation.[18]

Knox makes even more global claims for the circulation of literature in his later essay collection, *Winter Evenings: or Lucubrations on Life and Letters* (1788), which amplifies the *Extracts'* concern with the relation of culture to commerce. The introduction to the *Evenings* defends the proliferation of new publications by describing the widening social and geographical field through which popular English literature 'flows':

> The world is wide, and readers more numerous at present than in any preceding age. A liberal education is more general, and is likely to be still more extensively diffused . . . The English language is the language of a vast continent of people . . . connecting themselves in commercial and other engagements with all nations. English literature is

of course the literature of America. The learning of England has long been flowing from the Thames to the Ganges. The late amicable connection with our neighbours, which reflects so much honour on the liberality and wisdom of the present times, will contribute greatly to extend the language and learning of Great Britain.

The new audience to which Knox appeals here is not only English but British, not only commercial but colonial or post-colonial. Like the audience of the *Extracts*, it derives authority from shared ignorance rather than specialized knowledge. Knox insists, in fact, that the value of learning varies inversely with its rarity:

> The erudition which is confined to a few libraries, or locked in the bosom of a few professors . . . may be compared to a stagnant pool; large perhaps and deep, but of little utility; while the knowledge which displays itself in popular works may be said to resemble a river, fertilizing, refreshing, and embellishing whole provinces through which its meanders roll their tide.[19]

The analogy of the river alludes to economic circulation as well, for Knox specifies that the 'flow' of English learning depends on 'commercial engagements'. His celebration of global exchange differs not only from antiquarian projects like Thomas Percy's *Reliques of Ancient English Poetry* (1765), which define literature as a national inheritance, but even more radically from the factionalism of Ritson's ballad collections.

The fact that the *Elegant Extracts* happen to be edited by a conservative Anglican clergyman – not, like the *Speaker* or the *Female Speaker*, by a woman, a radical, or a dissenter – suggests how little its commercial model of literary circulation and feminized vision of the literary public depend on any individual anthologist's identity (what Knox himself dismisses as 'private judgement') but how inexorably they follow from the genre of the anthology itself.[20] The anthologist speaks *ex officio* or not at all. Conversely, Knox's self-consciousness about the relations among money, gender, and the circulation of literature reflects more than a biographical mismatch between his own classical education and his readers' presumed lack of it (or between his gentlemanly pretensions and his anthologies' commercial success). Knox's ambivalence looks back to the ambiguous gender of the figure who oversees the transmission of texts and of property in *Sir Charles Grandison*, and forward to George Eliot's hesitation about being excerpted in gift books marketed to girls. Eliot associates anthologies with private exchange among female consumers, Knox with the international trade carried out by classically illiterate men. Both take the anthology as a limit case for the entanglement of esthetics with money.

The convergence that anthologies like Knox's and Enfield's celebrated between the feminization of schooling and the commercialization of literature was soon turned against the genre, however. Hannah More's charge in *Strictures on the Modern System of Female Education* (1799) that 'the swarms of *Abridgments, Beauties*, and *Compendiums*, . . . form too considerable a part of a young lady's library' did not so much reflect facts (since the formal education of boys guaranteed condensers their most centralized and captive audience) as literalize the gendered language that Knox and Enfield had used to define their audience's class position. More adds:

> A few fine passages from the poets (passages perhaps which derived their chief beauty from their position and connection) are huddled together by some extract-maker, whose brief and disconnected patches of broken and discordant materials, while they inflame young readers with the vanity of reciting, neither fill the mind nor form the taste; and it is not difficult to trace back to their shallow sources the hackney'd

quotations of certain *accomplished* young ladies, who will be frequently found not to
have come legitimately by any thing they know: I mean, not to have drawn it from its
true spring, the original works of the author from which some beauty-monger has
severed it . . . If we would purchase knowledge we must pay for it the fair and lawful
price of time and industry.

That attack on 'the hackney'd quotations of certain accomplish'd young ladies' recalls Richardson's revisionary claim that 'seldom did [Clarissa] quote or repeat from' poets – and, more
immediately, More's insistence in *Coelebs in Search of a Wife* that her own feminine paragon, Lucilla
Stanley, 'does not say things to be quoted'.[21] In the *Strictures*, however, More's concern is epistemological as much as moral. Quoting reflects not simply feminine vanity, but feminine imposture.
More's argument draws on three turn-of-the-century esthetic concepts that have fueled the backlash
against anthologies well into the present: originality (the 'true spring', the 'original works'); organic
structure ('position and connection' opposed to 'broken and discordant materials'); and, most of all,
the fear of a mass public.

Yet More protests anthologists' appeal to a frivolous feminine audience only at the expense of
naturalizing it. Compilation is to complete works as women to men: both secondary rather than
'original', both decorative but 'shallow'. Indeed, More's attack on the 'disconnected' structure of
anthologies echoes her description elsewhere of the female mind: 'Both in composition and action
[women] excel in details; but they do not so much generalize their ideas as men . . . Women have
equal parts, but are inferior in *wholeness* of mind, in the integral understanding.' That taste for detail,
including textual beauties, extends from women themselves to feminized men. More's caricature of
a fop

> . . . studied while he dress'd, for true 'tis
> He read Compendiums, Extracts, Beauties
> Abregés, Dictionnaires, Recueils,
> Mercures, Journaux, Extraits, and Feuilles.[22]

Attention to anthology-pieces undermines masculinity as much as does attention to dress.

More appropriates not only Knox's assumptions about gender but his metaphors of community. Her image of the 'swarm' neatly inverts the picture of the busy editorial beehive that
decorates the title-page of his *Extracts*. In Knox, the commonplace stands not only for the hard work
involved in culling literary 'flowers' but for the sociable character of that project. One contemporary editor's conventional defense of the 'extract' makes clear how well the beehive emblematizes
Knox's subordination of the editorial self to the literary community: 'if like the industrious bee I
have cull'd from various flowers my share of Honey, and stored it in the common Hive, I shall have
performed the duties of a good citizen of the Republic of letters.'[23] But More's substitution of a
swarm for a hive turned the apiary image against itself, replacing the republic of letters by the mob.
In 1782 the *London Magazine* had already characterized anthologists as a 'swarm of servile imitators'
guilty of 'invasion of property'.[24] More went farther to hint that unwillingness to pay a 'fair' or
'legitimate' price made anthology-readers receivers of pilfered goods.

More's nervousness about readers' dependence on anthologies provides one measure of their
success. Another can be found in Jane Austen's complaint that critics take novelists less seriously
than 'the man who collects and publishes in a volume some dozen lines of Milton, Pope, and Prior
with a paper from the Spectator, and a chapter from Sterne.'[25] Like Coleridge's, More's and
Austen's hostility testifies to the power which anthologists modestly disclaimed. By the turn of the
nineteenth century, what Lonsdale calls 'the hypnotically influential way in which the eighteent'

entury succeeded in anthologizing itself' had provoked an equally powerful reaction against antho-
ogists and their audience – a public which, like novel-readers, ranked scarcely above illiterates in
critics' estimation.[26]

The difference, however, is that novel-reading went on to become respectable, as anthologies
have yet to do. More than a century later, More's scorn for commercial 'beauty-mongers' and
mechanical 'extract-makers' could still be recognized in Laura Riding and Robert Graves's attack
on 'the all too numerous trade-anthologies that turn poetry into an industrial packet-commodity'.
But their *Pamphlet Against Anthologies* proposes no alternative except a kind of hypertrophied anthol-
gy: a self-sufficient corpus of self-contained *oeuvres*.

> This full Corpus would include all poets who had a certain recognizable minimum of
> credibility . . . If there were any disagreement at all about whether or not a poet
> should be included, he would naturally be included. When it was agreed to include a
> poet, disagreement as to his relative merit would not matter, as each poet would be
> printed entire.[27]

omething close to the 'Corpus' imagined by Riding and Graves has finally been realized in the form
f Chadwyck-Healey's *English Full-Text Poetry Database*, arranged like theirs by author, and delimited
y the 'recognizable minimum of credibility' borrowed (with scattershot additions) from the *New
Cambridge Bibliography of English Literature*. Yet both corpuses are 'full' only in the sense that they
xclude œuvres wholesale rather than piecemeal, omitting minor poets instead of minor poems.
Riding and Graves's metonymic demand for 'each poet entire' simply displaces the canon of
anthology-pieces by a catalogue of signatures. The life replaces the poem as the smallest unit that can
tand on its own. That substitution depends in turn on the exclusion of anonymous texts, which
ecame conventional in literary anthologies (as opposed to antiquarian ones) at the same moment in
hich collections like Knox's *Extracts* systematically began to disclaim their editors' individuality.
Like the *Extracts*, the *Pamphlet* makes authorial subjectivity the precondition of editorial objectivity.
Their doubly impersonal reference to a 'recognizable credibility' spares Riding and Graves from
pecifying who recognizes 'merit' and who is expected to 'credit' that recognition. Both arguments
roject the editor's taste onto readers (Riding and Graves's 'recognizable minimum of credibility',
nox's 'voice of fame' and 'public judgment') at the same time as they replace the editor's
ndividuality with the identity of the authors who sign their raw materials.

At a moment when the editors of the *Norton Anthology of English Literature* are experimenting
ith a *salon des refusés* on the Web – a supplementary collection of texts too unwieldy to fit within its
overs – it is tempting to imagine that the electronic database will eliminate the economic con-
traints which have so long rendered the excerpt unavoidable. But the needs to which the anthology
esponds are hermeneutic, not just logistical. So far at least, Margaret Ezell's hope that exhaustive
ull-text databases will render anthologies of women's writing obsolete looks as utopian as the idea
at genetically modified crops can end famine. Anthologies more often respond to a surfeit of
ccessible texts than to their shortage: what they omit is as crucial as what they include.[28] Indeed,
nthologies like Knox's defined only the minimal limit of an emerging tradition whose maximal
orm had already been marked by the encyclopedic reprint series beginning with Hugh Blair's *British
Poets* (forty-four volumes published between 1773 and 1776).[29] The speed with which Knox's
ecessary canon followed upon Blair's sufficient one reveals how quickly information overload
reates a demand for editors, even for censors – not simply to limit the data available, but to order
. What Paul Duguid has argued of the codex remains even truer for the anthology: 'If books [as
pposed to digital media] can be thought of as "containing" and even imprisoning information, that
formation must, in the last analysis, be understood as inescapably the product of bookmaking.'[30]

Notes

1   Barbara Benedict, *Making the Modern Reader: Cultural Mediation in Early Modern Anthologie* (Princeton: Princeton University Press, 1996), 6, 157–60; Trevor Ross, 'Copyright and th Invention of Tradition', *Eighteenth-Century Studies* 25 (1992): 1–27; see also Douglas Lan Patey, 'The Eighteenth Century Invents the Canon', *Modern Language Studies* 18 (Winte 1988): 17–37, and Julia Wright, ' "The Order of Time": Nationalism and Literary Antholo gies, 1774–1831', *Papers on Language and Literature* 33 (Fall 1997): 339–65. But Richard Terr warns against overstating the novelty of literary-historical self-consciousness in this perio ('The Eighteenth-Century Invention of English Literature: A Truism Revisited', *British Journa for Eighteenth-Century Studies* 19 [Spring 1996]: 47–62), while Marilyn Butler dates the proces instead to the 1820s ('Revising the Canon', *Times Literary Supplement* [4 December 1987] 1349). I'm indebted as well to William St. Clair's unpublished lectures on the parameters c the post-1774 canon ('The Reading Nation in the Romantic Period', University of Cam bridge, 1999); to John Brewer's analysis of cultural retrospection in *The Pleasures of th Imagination: English Culture in the Eighteenth Century* (London: HarperCollins, 1997), 427–9: and to Peter Uwe Hohendahl's exploration of an analogous case in *Building a Nationa Literature: The Case of Germany, 1830–1870* (Ithaca: Cornell University Press, 1989).

2   Lonsdale argues that Robert Anderson's *Works of the British Poets* (13 vols., 1792–95) an Alexander Chalmers's *Works of the English Poets* (21 vols., 1810) established the principle c excluding anonymous texts as well as the work of living and female poets ('Introduction New Oxford Book of Eighteenth-Century Verse*, ed. Roger Lonsdale [Oxford: Oxford Universit Press, 1984], xxxvi). Andrew Ashfield suggests that the canonization of a generation c recently deceased poets in the 1770s set a precedent for excluding living poets ('Introduc tion', *Romantic Women Poets 1770–1838: An Anthology*, ed. Andrew Ashfield [Mancheste: Manchester University Press, 1995], xi). As early as 1784, Vicesimus Knox felt the need t defend his departure from the practice of excluding living poets: see his *Elegant Extracts: useful and entertaining Passages in Prose Selected for the Improvement of Scholars in Classical and oth Schools* (London: Charles Dilly, 1784), v–vi. On the exclusion of the living in later antholo gies, see Sabine Haas, 'Victorian Poetry Anthologies', *Publishing History* 17 (1985): 51–6 (59).

3   Vicesimus Knox, ed., *Elegant Extracts in Prose, Selected for the Improvement of Young Persons*, 10t edn (London, 1816).

4   Vicesimus Knox, *Elegant Extracts: or Useful and Entertaining Pieces of Poetry, Selected for th Improvement of Youth in Speaking, Reading, Thinking, Composing; and in the Conduct of Life* (Londor C. Dilly, 1784), iv–v. On the subordination of individual taste to the public voice, see als John Barrell, *The Political Theory of Painting from Reynolds to Hazlitt* (New Haven: Yale Un versity Press, 1986), 4, 82, and Leo Damrosch, 'Generality and Particularity', in *The Cam bridge History of Literary Criticism. Vol. 4: The Eighteenth Century*, ed. H. B. Nisbet and Claud Rawson (Cambridge: Cambridge University Press, 1997), 381–93 (390).

5   Samuel Johnson, 'Gray', in *Lives of the Poets*, ed. Arthur Waugh (Oxford: Oxford Universit Press, 1975), 463. On the relation of this passage to Gray's *Elegy*, see also John Guillory *Cultural Capital: The Problem of Literary Canon Formation* (Chicago: University of Chicago Pres 1993), 90–91; and, on the origins of Johnson's term, Trevor Ross, 'Just When *Did* "Britis Bards Begin t'Immortalize?" ', *SECC* 19 (1989): 383–98 (389).

6   Knox, *Extracts . . . Poetry* (1784), vi. The quotation is from *Essais*, 3.12.

7   See also Jonathan Brody Kramnick's argument that Johnson's common reader 'is commo not in his or her social status but in his or her lack of particular traits (of class, region, gende and so on)' ('The Making of the English Canon', *PMLA* 112 [October 1997]: 1087–10 [1098]).

8   Knox, *Extracts . . . Poetry* (1784), v.

9   Knox, *Extracts in Prose* (1816), ii.

10   *The Beauties of Shakespeare, selected from his plays and poems* (London: G. Kearsley, 1783), i; Francis Turner Palgrave, ed., *The Golden Treasury of the Best Songs and Poems in the English Language*, ed. Christopher Ricks (Harmondsworth: Penguin, 1991), 5; Cleanth Brooks and Robert Penn Warren, eds, *Understanding Fiction* (New York: F. S. Crofts, 1943), xiii; William Bennett, ed., *The Book of Virtues* (New York: Simon and Schuster, 1993), 11.

11   'Preface', in Frank Kermode and John Hollander, eds, *Oxford Anthology of English Literature* (New York: Oxford University Press, 1973). See also Guillory's argument that 'by suppressing the context of a cultural work's production and consumption, the school produces the illusion that "our" culture (or the culture of the "other") is transmitted simply by contact with the works themselves. But a text tradition is not sufficient in itself either to constitute or to transmit a culture' (*Cultural Capital*, 43).

12   Knox, *Extracts in Prose* (1816), iii. In an earlier preface, Knox bids more explicitly for the widest possible market: 'The title-page describes it as compiled for the use of boys. It is very certain that it is not exclusively adapted to boys . . . Such Books as this are calculated to become the companions of all, without distinction of sex, who are in the course of a polite and comprehensive education' (Knox, *Extracts in Prose* [1783], iv).

13   Knox, *Extracts . . . Poetry* (1784), v.

14   William Enfield, ed., *The Speaker: or Miscellaneous Pieces, Selected from the Best English Writers, and disposed under proper heads, with a view to facilitate the improvement of youth in reading and speaking* (London: Joseph Johnson, 1774), xxxii. The patriotic pedantry of the *Speaker* replaced what Enfield later calls 'the affectation of introducing foreign words and phrases' (*The Speaker* [London: Joseph Johnson, 1803], xliii). On Enfield's pedagogical career, see P. O'Brien, *Warrington Academy, 1757–86* (Wigan: Owl Books, 1989), 71–72; and for Barbauld's relation to both the Academy and to Enfield's *Speaker*, Guillory, *Cultural Capital*, 101–7.

15   Anna Laetitia Barbauld, *The Female Speaker; or, Miscellaneous Pieces in Prose and Verse . . . Adapted to the Use of Young Women* (London: Joseph Johnson, 1811), iv. Barbauld's subsequent recommendation of Boileau over Virgil makes clear that she is distinguishing not so much English from foreign languages as modern languages from ancient ones. I draw here on Nancy Armstrong's argument that 'modern educational institutions continued the project of feminizing the subject as they made what had been a specifically female body of knowledge into a standard for literacy in general' (*Desire and Domestic Fiction: A Political History of the Novel* [New York: Oxford University Press, 1987], 103), as well as Walter Ong's analysis of the relation between classical education and masculinity ('Latin Language Study as a Renaissance Puberty Rite', *Rhetoric, Romance and Technology* [Ithaca: Cornell University Press, 1971]). On collections of women's poetry in this period, see Greg Kucich, 'Gendering the Canons of Romanticism: Past and Present', *Wordsworth Circle* 27 (Spring 1996): 95–102 (which draws a useful distinction between the representation of women in anthologies and miscellanies), and Elizabeth Eger, 'Fashioning a Female Canon: Eighteenth-Century Women Poets and the Politics of the Anthology', in *Women's Poetry in the Enlightenment: The Making of a Canon, 1730–1820*, ed. Isobel Armstrong and Virginia Blain (Basingstoke: Macmillan, 1999), 201–15.

16   Vicesimus Knox, ed., *Elegant Epistles: Being a Copious Collection of Familiar and Amusing Letters, Selected for the Improvement of Young Persons, and for General Entertainment* (London: Longman, 1795), iii.

17   Knox, *Extracts in Prose* (1816), iii.

18   See also Trevor Ross's argument that the late-eighteenth-century debate over literary property reflects the conflict described by Pocock between an older conception of civic virtue founded on private possession and an emerging idea of civilization as the result of economic exchange ('Copyright and the Invention of Tradition', 8).

19 Vicesimus Knox, *Winter Evenings, or, Lucubrations on Life and Letters*, 2 vols (London: Charle: Dilly, 1790), 1.7–9. Knox's association of the modern canon with geopolitical expansior already suggests an awareness of the relation between colonialism and canon formation tha Gauri Viswanathan has argued in *Masks of Conquest: Literary Study and British Rule in India* (New York: Columbia University Press, 1989).

20 For Knox's biography, see Robert W. Uphaus, 'Vicesimus Knox and the Canon of Eighteenth Century Literature', *The Age of Johnson* 4 (1991): 345–61. It may be worth noting tha Enfield's *Speaker* was published by the radical Joseph Johnson.

21 Hannah More, *Coelebs in Search of a Wife*, 2 vols (London: Cadell, 1808), 1.186.

22 Hannah More, *Strictures on the Modern System of Female Education*, 2 vols (London: T. Cadell 1799), 1.7.174–75, 2.26–27; More, *Florio: A Tale, for Fine Gentlemen and Fine Ladies* (London T. Cadell, 1786). Thanks to Elizabeth Eger for the second reference. On the gender of the detail, see also Naomi Schor, *Reading in Detail: Aesthetics and the Feminine* (New York: Methuen 1987).

23 C[lara] R[eeve], *The Progress of Romance*, 2 vols (Colchester: W. Keymer, 1785), 2.98. On the apiary topos, see Ann Moss, *Printed Commonplace-Books and the Structuring of Renaissanc Thought* (Oxford: Clarendon Press, 1996), 12–14.

24 Quoted in Allen T. Hazen, 'The *Beauties of Johnson*', *Modern Philology* 35 (February 1938) 289–95 (290).

25 Jane Austen, *Northanger Abbey*, in *Complete Novels* (Oxford: Oxford University Press, 1994) 1.5.1086. Barbara Benedict argues that this passage ascribes to miscellanies the improbabilit and coarseness for which romance is traditionally faulted (*Making the Modern Reader*, 215).

26 Lonsdale, Roger. 'Gray and "Allusion": The Poet as Debtor', in *Studies in the Eighteenth Centur IV*, ed. R. F. Brissenden and J. C. Eade (Canberra: Australian National University Press, 1979) 31–56. Compare Walter Ong's argument that originality could become the highest literar value only once Enlightenment encyclopedism had rendered the commonplace redundar (*Rhetoric, Romance, and Technology*, 255–83). Ann Moss explains the decline of the commor place over the course of the seventeenth century in rather more nuanced terms by 'a growin, sense that evidence was empirically and scientifically measurable across a spectrum of prob ability' as well as 'a social code of polite behavior and a consensual aesthetic of good tast which was inimical to its primary qualities of abundance and display' (*Printed Commonplace Books*, 275–76).

27 Laura Riding and Robert Graves, *A Pamphlet Against Anthologies* (London: Jonathan Cape 1927), 185.

28 Margaret Ezell, *Writing Women's Literary History* (Baltimore: Johns Hopkins University Press 1993), 164; that Ezell's plea for teachers to replace the anthology by the database comes a the end of a richly nuanced analysis of seventeenth- and eighteenth-century anthologies lend it extra poignancy. See, however, Marjorie Perloff's argument that a canon which professes t expand continually strips canonicity of any meaning ('Why Big Anthologies Make Bad Text books', *Chronicle of Higher Education* 45 [16 April 1999]: B6–B7 [B6]).

29 See Thomas Bonnell, 'Bookselling and Canon-Making: The Trade Rivalry over the Englis Poets, 1776–1783', *Studies in Eighteenth-Century Culture* 19 (1989): 53–89, and 'John Bell' Poets of Great Britain', *Modern Philology* 85 (November 1987): 128–52; Trevor Ross, 'Th Emergence of "Literature": Making and Reading the English Canon in the Eighteenth Cen tury', *ELH* 63 (1996): 397–422; and, on the relation between exhaustive series and selectiv anthologies, Roger Chartier, *The Order of Books*, trans. Lydia Cochrane (Stanford: Stanfor University Press, 1994), 68–69.

30 Paul Duguid, 'Material Matters: The Past and Futurology of the Book', in *The Future of th Book*, ed. Geoffrey Nunberg (Berkeley: University of California Press, 1996), 63–102 (66).

Chapter 25

Jane Tompkins

MASTERPIECE THEATER
The politics of Hawthorne's literary reputation

Because modern commentators have tended to ignore the context within which nineteenth-century authors and critics worked, their view of the criticism that was written on *The Scarlet Letter* in the nineteenth century has failed to take account of the cultural circumstances that shaped Hawthorne's novel for his contemporaries. They evaluate this criticism as if it had been written about the same text that they read, and so produce accounts of that criticism that are unrelated to the issues with which it was actually engaged. For example, three modern scholars of Hawthorne criticism all find George Loring's reply in 1850 to an attack on *The Scarlet Letter* that had appeared in the *North American Review* one of the ablest contemporary discussions of the novel.[1] It is not hard to see why these critics think so highly of Loring's defense. His essay is written in answer to a religions attack on the novel which argues that *The Scarlet Letter* is unchristian because it presents its adulterous heroine in a sympathetic light, sees 'devils and angels [as] alike beautiful', deals with a 'revolting' subject whose 'ugliness' is unredeemed by Hawthorne's 'wizard power over language' and is manifestly untrue to the realities of 'God's moral world'.[2] Because Loring's essay sets itself up in opposition to what seems to the modern critics a narrowly based doctrinal attack, they find the defense admirable. When Loring says, for example, that without sorrow and sin 'virtue cannot rise above innocency', it looks as if he has acknowledged the complex nature of moral problems as the twentieth century views them.[3] When he says that those who think 'vice stands at one pale and virtue at another' betray a 'want of sympathy' which 'the experience of our own temptation should remove', Loring seems to be acknowledging the existence of 'the dark underside of the psyche' with which so much modern criticism has been preoccupied.[4] When he writes that 'in casting [Hester] out, the world had torn from her all the support of its dogmatic teachings, . . . and had compelled her to rely upon that great religious truth which flows instinctively around a life of agony, with its daring freedom', the modern critic discerns a celebration of human individuality and an affirmation of the heroic struggle for personal freedom at all costs.[5]

But Loring's review of *The Scarlet Letter* does not escape the confines of religious controversy; on the contrary, his argument with the reviewer for the *North American* is mounted on specifically doctrinal grounds. . . .

Loring's interpretation of *The Scarlet Letter* arises from the theological controversy (which was also a power struggle) then raging within the New England churches.[6] The very shape of his disagreement with the reviewer for the *North American* shows that the text these critics argued over had been structured by a set of interests and beliefs that we can reconstruct but no longer hold. It is just as impossible for a twentieth-century critic to argue, as Loring does, that the story of Hester's sin demonstrates the existence of a certain 'spot' in the human soul as it would have been for a Transcendentalist to read it, along with Charles Feidelson, as demonstrating the 'anticonventional impulse . . . inherent in symbolism'.[7] This is not simply because each critic looks at the text from a different point of view or with different purposes in mind, but because *looking* is not an activity that is performed outside of political struggles and institutional structures, but arises *from* them.

One such structure is the machinery of publishing and reviewing by means of which an author is brought to the attention of his audience. The social and economic processes that govern the dissemination of a literary work are no more accidental to its reputation, and indeed to its very nature, as that will be perceived by an audience, than are the cultural conceptions (of the nature of poetry, of morality, of the human soul) within which the work is read. The conditions of dissemination interpret the work for its readers in exactly the same way as definitions of poetry in that they flow from and support widely held – if unspoken – assumptions about the methods of distribution proper to a serious (or non-serious) work. The fact that an author makes his or her appearance in the context of a particular publishing practice rather than some other is a fact about the kind of claim he or she is making on an audience's attention and is *crucial* to the success of the claim. Hawthorne's debut as a novelist illustrates this proposition rather strikingly.

In 1970, C. E. Frazer Clark, Jr, published an article that revealed some little-known facts surrounding the publication of *The Scarlet Letter*.[8] Clark observed that despite Hawthorne's habit of referring to himself as 'the most unpopular author in America', he was much better known than he himself was aware. His satires and sketches had been pirated liberally by newspapers up and down the Eastern seaboard; notices, advertisements, and reviews of his work had regularly appeared in the periodical press. And so, when Hawthorne lost his job as surveyor of customs at Salem, it caused a furor in the local papers.[9] The press took up the case of political axing not because such events were so extraordinary – nothing could have been more common with a change of administrations – but because Hawthorne was already newsworthy. This publicity attracted the attention of James T. Fields, shortly to become New England's most influential publisher, who until then had not printed a word of Hawthorne's, but whose business instincts now prompted him to visit Salem on the off-chance that Hawthorne might have something ready for the press. Hawthorne, as it happened, did have something on hand which, very reluctantly, he gave to Fields. It was a story which Fields encouraged him to turn into a novel – novels being more marketable than short fiction. Hawthorne took this suggestion and prefaced the story with an introductory essay on his stint in the customs house to help achieve the desired length. As Fields suspected, Hawthorne's first book to appear after the customs house fiasco sold remarkably well: the advance publicity had guaranteed that *The Scarlet Letter* would be a success.

Encouraged by the attention paid to his novel, and prodded by the ever-vigilant Fields, who saw an opportunity to capitalize on the reputation so recently enlarged, Hawthorne, who until then had not been a prolific writer, turned out two more novels in rapid succession. These received a great deal of favorable attention from well-placed reviewers, with the result that, two years after the publication of *The Scarlet Letter*, Hawthorne was being referred to as a classic American writer – and has been so identified ever since. But the success of *The Scarlet Letter* and of the subsequent novel becomes fully explicable only within a larger frame of reference than the one Clark's essay supplies.

By the 1840s Irving's reputation had sagged and Cooper had alienated large portions of th reading public and the critical establishment with his attacks on American manners and h unpopular political stands. America needed a living novelist whom it could regard as this country answer to Dickens and Thackeray, a novelist who represented both what was essentially America and what was 'best' by some universal criteria of literary value. Hawthorne seemed well suited for the role, since, as almost every critic emphasized, his work made use of characteristically American materials. Hawthorne's feel for the humbler aspects of the American scene made him attractive both as an interpreter of 'spiritual laws' that know no nationality and as a spokesman for the democratic way of life. These qualities, however, were shared equally by novelists like Warner and Stowe who, if anything, outdid him in this respect. What finally distinguished Hawthorne from his popular rivals was his relation to the social and institutional structures that shaped literary opinion; these associations ultimately determined the longevity of his reputation. The parallel but finally divergent careers of Hawthorne and Warner illustrate dramatically how important belonging to the right network was as a precondition for long-standing critical success.

The circle of well-educated, well-connected men and women who controlled New England's cultural life at mid-century thought of themselves as spiritually and culturally suited to raise the level of popular taste and to civilize and refine the impulses of the multitude. Any writer whom they chose as a model of moral and aesthetic excellence, therefore, had to be someone whose work had not already been embraced by the nation at large, but had been initially admired only by the discerning few. Longfellow formulates the prevailing view of Hawthorne as a writer for a cultivated minority in his review of the second edition of *Twice-told Tales*:

> Mr. Hawthorne's . . . writings have now become so well known, and are so justly appreciated, by all discerning minds, that they do not need our commendation. He is not an author to create a sensation, or have a tumultuous popularity. His works are not stimulating or impassioned, and they minister nothing to a feverish love of excitement. Their tranquil beauty and softened tints, which do not win the notice of the restless many, only endear them the more to the thoughtful few.[10]

The 'thoughtful few' to whom Longfellow refers are the people who controlled New England's cultural life before the Civil War. Once Hawthorne's work had been published by Ticknor and Fields, New England's most prominent publisher; once it had been reviewed by E. P. Whipple, a member of Fields' coterie and one of the most influential contemporary reviewers; and had become the subject of long discussions in the *Christian Examiner* and the *North American Review*, periodicals whose editors, in Sydney Ahlstrom's words, 'alone constitute . . . a hall of fame of the New England flowering'; Hawthorne had gained a place in a socio-cultural network that assured his prominence because its own prominence was already an established and self-perpetuating fact.[11]

Lewis Simpson has characterized this group of literary and intellectual men who took the nation's spiritual welfare as their special charge as the 'New England clerisy'.[12] Simpson traces its beginnings in the passage from a theological to a literary clergy in the early years of the nineteenth century, using the career of Joseph Stevens Buckminster, a precocious young theology professor at Harvard, to exemplify the broadening of ecclesiastical authority to include general cultural matters, and especially literature. Buckminster and his associates, who founded the *Monthly Anthology*, America's most serious literary journal at the time, spoke of literature as a 'commonwealth' with its own 'government', that along with church and state fought for civilization against barbarism.[13] As a result of their activity, Simpson writes, 'the image in the New England mind of the old theocratic polity begins to become the image of a literary polity. . . . The *Respublica Christiana* . . . becomes the *Respublica Litterarum*.'[14] The metaphor of the state as a means of conceptualizing literary activity is important because it suggests the need for centralized leadership and control in cultural affairs: the choice of proper reading matter was not something that could be left to the 'restless many', but rightly belonged to the 'thoughtful few' whose training and authority qualified them as arbiters of public taste. The formation of a literary canon in the nineteenth century was not a haphazard affair, but depended on the judgment of a small group of prominent men, the members of the Anthology Society – clergymen, professors, businessmen, judges, and statesmen – who conceived of their task as a civic and moral duty. The power they had to determine who would be read and who would not is dramatically illustrated by the career of Richard Henry Dana, Sr., whose ardent admiration for the English Romantic poets drew scathing criticism from the Boston literati. He failed to be elected to the editorship of the *North American* (the direct descendant of the *Monthly Anthology*), and thereafter refused to contribute to it. When his essays and tales, his long poem, and the collected edition of his poems and prose elicited only a cool response from reviewers, he simply withdrew from the world, devastated by its failure to recognize his genius.[15]

This fate did not befall Nathaniel Hawthorne because he had been taken up by the second generation of the New England clerisy, whose power to shape literary opinion had been inherited from the first through an interlocking network of social, familial, political, and professional connections. William Tudor, an active member of the Anthology Society, the *Monthly Anthology*'s editorial board, became the founding editor of the *North American Review*. John Kirkland, another of the Society's original members, became president of Harvard. Alexander Everett, another member, later a minister to Spain, also went on to edit the *North American*, as did Edward Everett, who had studied German at Göttingen with George Ticknor, both of them original members of the Anthology Society. Ticknor, who preceded Longfellow as Professor of Modern Languages at Harvard, was the cousin of William Ticknor, of Ticknor and Fields, who became one of Hawthorne's lifelong friends. William Emerson, pastor of the First Church of Boston, who edited the *Monthly Anthology* for two years before the Society took over, was Ralph Waldo Emerson's father.[16]

Joseph Buckminster's father had strenuously opposed the liberal theological tendencies of his son, just as the Unitarians of Buckminster's era and beyond would oppose the radical theorizing of Emerson and his circle; but the authority to speak on spiritual and cultural issues passed smoothly down from father to son undiminished by doctrinal differences. The men who thus assumed the role of cultural spokesmen at mid-century – Longfellow, Holmes, Lowell, Whittier, and Emerson – were particularly powerful since by then Boston had become the literary center of the nation.[17] These were the men whom Caroline Ticknor records as gathering to socialize at the Old Corner Bookstore, as Ticknor and Fields was familiarly known.[18] These were the men who in 1857 'all agreed to write for the *Atlantic* and . . . made it immediately . . . the most important magazine in America'.[19] These were the men who, as Sophia Hawthorne left the cemetery after her husband's funeral, stood with bared heads as the carriage passed.[20]

It is hard to overestimate the importance of Hawthorne's connections with these men who outlived him by a score of years and who launched the periodical that would dominate literary activity in the United States for the rest of the nineteenth century. When William Dean Howells returned to Boston in 1866, he became assistant editor of the *Atlantic Monthly* under James T. Fields (Hawthorne's publisher), who had taken over the editorship from Lowell (Hawthorne's good friend). Howells, whom Hawthorne had helped get his start by introducing him to Emerson, took over the editorship from Fields in 1871, and George Persons Lathrop, Hawthorne's son-in-law, became an assistant editor.[21] Lathrop would publish the first full-length study of Hawthorne, which Howells' close friend, Henry James, would challenge three years later in his full-length study. This touched off a critical controversy – notably in an essay by Howells – over whether Hawthorne was an idealist or a realist, so that it was Hawthorne whose texts critics used to argue the merits of literary realism in the 80s and 90s.[22] Meanwhile, several friends published poems commemorating Hawthorne's death; relatives, friends, and associates printed their reminiscences; Sophia published excerpts from Hawthorne's journals; and other admirers wrote pieces with titles such as 'The Homes and Haunts of Hawthorne'.

But most important in assuring Hawthorne's continuing presence in the cultural foreground was James T. Fields. Fields, wanting to make good on his investment, followed his former practice of putting out anything he thought would pique the public's interest in his author and managed to produce eleven posthumous editions of Hawthorne's work between 1864 and 1883. This meant, twenty years after he was dead, that Hawthorne was still being reviewed as a live author. Osgood, the successor to Fields, pushed this strategy further by adding Hawthorne to his 'Little Classics' series, and in 1884, Houghton Mifflin, the successor to Osgood, capped it off by publishing *The Complete Works of Nathaniel Hawthorne* in twelve volumes edited by his son-in-law. Finally, Houghton Mifflin reinforced the image by including Hawthorne in two more series: 'Modern Classics' and 'American Classics for the Schools'. In 1883, the academic establishment put its imprimatur on what the publishers had done. In that year, Yale allowed English literature students for the first time to write their junior essays on 'Hawthorne's Imagination' – the only topic on the list that concerned an American author. Consequently, Hawthorne's texts were 'there' to be drawn upon for ammunition in the debates over the question of realism that raged during the 1880s. By the end of the century, as Edwin Cady observes in his survey of Hawthorne criticism, 'a minor critic might well have doubted his respectability if he failed to cite Hawthorne whether in praise of or attack against any writing in question'.[23]

The prominence of Hawthorne's texts in the post-Civil War era is a natural consequence of his relation to the mechanisms that produced literary and cultural opinion. Hawthorne's initial connections with the Boston literati – his acquaintance with Longfellow at college, his residence next door to Alcott and a half mile from Emerson (his son and Emerson's nephew roomed together at Harvard), his marrying a Peabody, becoming fast friends with Ticknor and Lowell, being published by the indefatigable Fields, socializing with Duyckinck and Whipple – these circumstances positioned Hawthorne's literary production so that it became the property of a dynastic cultural elite which came to identify itself with him.[24] The members of this elite could not fail to keep Hawthorne's reputation alive since it stood for everything they themselves stood for. America's literary establishment, no less than James T. Fields (who was part of it), had an investment in Hawthorne. In short, the friends and associates who outlived Hawthorne kept his fiction up-to-date by writing about it, and then *their* friends took over. Consequently, when the next generation of critics – Howells, James, and their contemporaries – came of age, they redefined his work according to the critical tastes of the new era. And so when the century turned, it seemed appropriate that a volume of Hawthorne criticism should appear in 1904 celebrating the hundredth anniversary of his birth. And 'by then', writes Edwin Cady, 'figures like George Woodberry, William Peterfield Trent, and Paul Elmer More had come to maturity', who, with their 'Arnoldian . . . neo-humanism' would 'project Hawthorne toward the present century's Age of Criticism'.[25]

During the same period, Warner's critical reputation dwindled to nothing. Whereas critics writing before the Civil War had discussed her work alongside that of Hawthorne, Brockden Brown, Cooper, Irving, Longfellow, and Stowe, by the 70s they had ceased to take her novels seriously as literature and finally stopped reviewing them altogether. Under the pressure of new conditions, Warner's work, like Hawthorne's, came to be redefined. The circumstances that created each author's literary reputation were of the same *kind* in either case – that is, they consisted of the writer's relation to centers of cultural domination, social and professional connections, blood relations, friendships, publishing history, and so on – but in Warner's case the circumstances were negative rather than positive.

Warner's connections – such as they were – sprang from New York rather than Boston, which at this particular period put her at a geographical disadvantage. Unlike Hawthorne, Warner had not lived in Concord, did not know Emerson and his circle, was not published by Fields, had not known Longfellow at college, had not roomed with a former President of the United States whose campaign biography she would write and who would get her a consulship when she needed money. Rather, she had been forced by her father's financial failure in the 1830s to retire to an island in the Hudson River where the family owned property, and where, along with her maiden sister, she wrote novels to earn a living. The Warners' poverty and their resulting social isolation affected both what they wrote and the way their work was perceived by contemporary audiences. As a consequence of their social isolation, the Warners threw themselves into church-centered activities and became extremely devout followers of the Reverend Thomas Skinner – a New Light Presbyterian who preached the importance of faith over doctrine in religious conversion. They considered the novels and stories they wrote their best means of doing the Lord's work and – since they had to – of supporting themselves. These conditions (at one point their house was in receivership and creditors took their furniture away) determined not only what they wrote, but how much, how fast, for what kind of audience, and for which publishers.[26] Though they had started out with G. P. Putnam, a large commercial publisher in New York whose founder had been a friend of their father, in the 1860s they gave most of what they wrote to Robert Carter, a highly respected religious publisher who could guarantee a certain number of sales. The audience for religious books was large, stable, and provided an outlet for the Warners that answered their need both to win souls and to have bread on the table. Thus, at a time when changes in the economic and social environment created the context within which literary realism flourished, the Warner sisters guaranteed that their novels would be read as religious rather than literary discourse, labeled with Carter's imprint and with titles – 'Stories on the Lord's Prayer', 'A Story of Small Beginnings', 'The Word' – more reminiscent of tract society pamphlets than of high art.

Given a different cultural milieu, these conditions of production might have guaranteed the Warner sisters lasting fame. If the religious views that characterized the attacks on *The Scarlet Letter* in the 1850s had dominated literary criticism after the war, Hawthorne would have done well to experience a religious conversion and switch to Carter, too. But the moral impulse behind American criticism, which had been evangelical and religious in the ante-bellum years, evolved during the 70s and 80s into a concern for the material conditions of social life. Novels which had previously appeared to contain superb renditions of American character and homely scenes imbued with universal human truths, now seemed to be full of idealized characters, authorial didacticism, and an overt religiosity that marked them as morally false and artistically naive. Warner's work became identified with an outmoded piety and a discredited Romanticism that assured its swift disappearance from the critical scene. It is not that critics suddenly discovered limitations they had previously failed to notice, but that the context within which the work appeared had changed the nature of the work itself. If Warner had had the kinds of connections that kept Hawthorne's works in the public eye, had commanded the attention of influential publishers, editors, and reviewers, her early novels might have remained critically viable as they came to be recast according to the prevailing standards. And in that case *The Wide, Wide World* might have been passed down to us as one of the benchmarks of American literary realism.[27] But when she died in 1885, there were no famous men at her funeral to write poems in her memory for the *Atlantic Monthly* or for Harvard Phi Beta Kappas to hear. She had no publisher whose commercial interests lay in bringing out posthumous editions of her work, whose friends would write retrospective evaluations of her career. There were no surviving relatives whose connections would allow them to publish excerpts from her journals in prestigious places, no son to write three volumes of reminiscences, no son-in-law to write a full-length critical study and then go on to edit her complete works in twelve volumes.

What these facts demonstrate is that an author's relation to the mechanisms by which his or her work is brought before the public determines the status of that work in the world's eyes. Hawthorne's canonization was the result of a network of common interests – familial, social, professional, commercial, and national – that, combined, made Hawthorne a literary and cultural artifact, a national possession. The same combination of circumstances in reverse reconstituted

Warner's best-selling novels as ephemera that catered to the taste of a bygone age. Nor was there a conspiracy involved in keeping Hawthorne's reputation green while Warner's withered. By attributing the canonical status of Hawthorne's work to factors other than its 'intrinsic' merit, I do not mean to suggest that the merits that critics and editors discerned in that work were not real, that they promoted work they believed was worthless or mediocre, or that they deliberately ignored work they believed was good. On the contrary, although a mixture of motives was bound to be present in any individual decision to publish or write about Hawthorne's work – friendship, family feeling, commercial gain, professional advancement – these motives are not distinguishable from a belief in Hawthorne's genius and the conviction that his novels were great works of art. For that conviction is itself a contextual matter; that is, it does not spring from a pure, unmediated perception of an author's work on the part of his admirers and supporters (a kind of perception which, as I argued earlier, is never possible), but is determined by the situation in which they encounter it. The circumstances surrounding Hawthorne's texts in the 70s and 80s – literary, cultural, social, economic, and institutional – presented that work to its readers in such a way that it possessed the marks of greatness. Indeed, Hawthorne's work had by that time become one of the touchstones by which literary excellence could be defined, for canonical texts themselves become the bearers of the particular tradition of quality of which they are the exemplars. To put it another way, the fact that an author's reputation depends upon the context within which his or her work is read does not empty the work of value; it is the context – which eventually includes the work itself – that creates the value its readers 'discover' there. Their reading is an activity arising within a particular cultural setting (of which the author's reputation is a part) that reflects and elaborates the features of that setting simultaneously.

At this point, someone might object that while my description of the way Hawthorne's reputation came into being may support the foregoing account of how Hawthorne's texts were constructed, it does not really furnish grounds for making claims about literary works in general. What about Melville, some readers may ask; how did his work come to be appreciated in the twentieth century if there were no relatives and friends, no critical establishment, working to keep it in the public eye? Conversely, why did Longfellow, who had all of the social and institutional advantages I have ascribed to Hawthorne, lose his place in the canon while Hawthorne maintained his? The cases of Melville and Longfellow, though they differ from Hawthorne's at the particular level, are in principle exactly the same. It is not that their work, unlike Hawthorne's, has been judged on its intrinsic merits, but rather that it has been constituted by a changing series of interpretive frames. These authors' fluctuating reputations (Longfellow is now on the verge of a revival) further illustrate how changing definitions of literary value, institutionally and socially produced, continually refashion the literary canon to suit the culture's needs.

Notes

1 George Bailey Loring, *Massachusetts Quarterly Review*, 3 (September 1850), pp. 484–500, as reprinted in *Hawthorne: The Critical Heritage*, ed. Joseph Donald Crowley (New York: Barnes & Noble, 1970), pp. 168–173. The critics in question are Bertha Faust; Joseph Donald Crowley; and Bernard Cohen, ed., *The Recognition of Nathaniel Hawthorne* (Ann Arbor: University of Michigan Press, 1969).

2 Anne W. Abbott, in *Hawthorne*, ed. Crowley, pp. 165, 166.

3 Loring, in *The Recognition of Hawthorne*, ed. Cohen, p. 48.

4 Loring, in *The Recognition of Hawthorne*, ed. Cohen, p. 48; Henry Nash Smith's characterization of Hawthorne's subject matter in 'The Scribbling Women and the Cosmic Success Story', *Critical Inquiry*, 1 (September 1974), p. 58.

5 Loring, in *Hawthorne*, ed. Crowley, p. 173.

6   For the main outlines of the controversy, see Conrad Wright, 'Introduction', *A Stream of Light, A Sesquicentennial History of American Unitarianism*, ed. Conrad Wright (Boston: Unitarian Universalist Association, 1975).

7   Charles Feidelson, Jr, *Symbolism and American Literature* (Chicago: University of Chicago Press, 1953), p. 15.

8   C. E. Frazer Clark, Jr, 'Posthumous Papers of a Decapitated Surveyor: *The Scarlet Letter* in the Salem Press', *Studies in the Novel*, 2 (1970), pp. 395–419.

9   What happened was that Hawthorne, who had gotten the job through the influence of his old college friends and not through local connections or service to the party, lost his post when the Whigs took office. Because he was accused, in the process, of using his office for partisan ends, he became angry enough to stir up his friends on his behalf – hence the heated exchanges in the Salem and Boston papers. See George Woodberry, *Nathaniel Hawthorne* (Boston: Houghton Mifflin, 1902), pp. 163–177, and Arlin Turner, *Nathaniel Hawthorne, A Biography* (New York: Oxford University Press, 1980), pp. 177–187.

10   Longfellow, *North American Review*, 56 (April 1842), pp. 496–499, as reprinted in *Hawthorne*, ed. Crowley, p. 83.

11   Sydney E. Ahlstrom, *A Religious History of the American People* (New Haven: Yale University Press, 1972), p. 398. Ahlstrom's account of the emergence of Unitarianism is instructive for understanding the literary history of the period.

12   Lewis P. Simpson, *The Man of Letters in New England and the South* (Baton Rouge: Louisiana State University Press, 1973).

13   Simpson, p. 22.

14   Simpson, p. 22.

15   Robert E. Spiller *et al.*, eds, *Literary History of the United States*, 3rd ed. rev. (London: Macmillan, 1963), pp. 286–287.

16   Francis Luther Mott, *A History of American Magazines, 1850–1865* (Cambridge, Mass.: Harvard University Press, 1957) (1930), I, pp. 253–255.

17   Mott, *American Magazines* (1957), II, p. 32.

18   Caroline Ticknor, *Hawthorne and His Publisher* (Boston: Houghton Mifflin, 1913), p. 7.

19   Mott, *American Magazines* (1957), II, pp. 33, 494, 496.

20   Turner, pp. 392–393.

21   *Literary History*, ed. Spiller, p. 888; Mott, *American Magazines* (1957), II, pp. 493 ff.

22   Edwin Cady, ' "The Wizard Hand": Hawthorne, 1864–1900', in *Hawthorne Centenary Essays*, ed. Roy Harvey Pearce (Columbus: Ohio State University Press, 1964), pp. 324 ff.

23   Cady, p. 331.

24   Much of this interesting social information is contained in Julian Hawthorne, *The Memoirs of Julian Hawthorne*, ed. Edith Garrigue Hawthorne (New York: Macmillan, 1938).

25   Cady, p. 334.

26   Anna Warner, *Susan Warner* (New York: G. P. Putnam Sons, 1909), p. 126.

27   Henry James, writing in *The Nation* in 1865, says that in its depiction of rural scenes *The Wide, Wide World* is superior to the realism of Flaubert. But later in the review he expresses exactly that critical doctrine which would eventually disqualify Warner's fiction from serious consideration as art. In reviewing The *Schönberg-Cotta Family*, he says that novels written for both parents and children 'frequently contain . . . an infusion of religious and historical information, and they in all cases embody a moral lesson. This latter fact is held to render them incompetent as novels; and doubtless, after all, it does, for of a genuine novel the meaning and the lesson are infinite; and here they are carefully narrowed down to a special precept' (*The Nation* [September 14, 1865], pp. 344–345). It is interesting to compare James' comment with Brownson's review of *The Scarlet Letter* attacking the novel for failing to be Christian and moral enough.

Chapter 26

John Sutherland

THE VICTORIAN NOVELISTS
Who were they?

I

Awareness of Victorian fiction as an industry is uncommon, even at the level of parenthesis or historical backing to scholarly discussion of canonical texts. And generalizations about 'the Victorian novel' (which are common enough) are often hobbled by their being restricted in range of reference to the dozen writers designated 'major' by the *New Cambridge Bibliography of English Literature* – writers whose extraordinary literary distinction renders them necessarily unrepresentative. Despite fifty years of intense, academically sponsored research into the form, we still make do with only the sketchiest sense of the infrastructure of Victorian fiction – how the bulk of it was produced; who originated, reproduced, distributed and consumed the product. For most critics, commentators and readers, the Victorian novel is something that appears quite magically on the library shelf, or in the 'Literary Classics' section of the bookshop, found, as it were, under the gooseberry bush, the fruit of Dickens's 'genius' or George Eliot's 'moral sensibility' or Thackeray's 'satire' or Henry James's 'art'.

Statistics are an initial area of vagueness. In his monumental *Nineteenth-Century Fiction, A Bibliographical Catalogue* (5 vols, 1982–86), R. L. Wolff estimates that there are some 42,000 published Victorian novels of which – aiming at completeness – he contrived to collect 7,000. The annual statistics of the trade journal the *Publisher's Circular*, 1837–1901, suggest that total book production rose annually from 2,000 to 8,000 new titles over the Victorian period, and that the proportion of fiction concurrently rose from around 12 per cent to about 25 per cent (the increase being largely explained by the recruitment of new reading publics, particularly after the Education Act of 1870). Assuming exponential progressions for both figures over the 64 years, one arrives at a probable total output of around 50,000 novels. But exactness is impossible, given the fuzzy borders of fiction where it shades into religious-tract, educational and ephemeral periodical reading matter. Around 50,000 is, however, at this stage, a good ball-park figure to start from. When the promised 'History of the Book in Britain' project has done its work we shall know more precisely.[1]

This chapter is concerned less with bibliometrics than with the human infrastructure of Victorian fiction, namely the novelists, those largely invisible masses that Dickens called 'my fellow labourers'. Given an average output of 17 novels per novelist (for the justification of this figure, see below), a work-force of around 3,500 may be hazarded. Given an average working life for novelists of around 32 years (see below again), and the fact that many novelists qualify with only one work of fiction, it is a fair guess that two such working forces would populate the period, with the necessary chronological overlaps and a progressive upward scaling to take account of the production increase over the 64 years. At the end of the century, Walter Besant (in his capacity as founder of the Society of Authors) reckoned that there were some 1,200 novelists at work, of whom 200 were entirely self-supporting by their writing. This seems somewhat on the low side and may be biased (especially as regards the self-supporting figure) by Besant's ineradicable gloom about the treatment of the creative writer by philistine English culture. But it is roughly in line with my estimates if one adds the amateurs and one-novel wonders who would have been beneath Besant's notice.

Most of these estimated 3,500 Victorian novelists will never emerge from the obscurity of the statistical mass. Even the most exhaustive investigations can turn up no worthwhile biographical (or sometimes even reliable bibliographical) data. The cult of anonymous authorship which persisted well into the late Victorian period is an often impenetrable screen. Another source of obscurity is the sheer human insignificance of the very minor Victorian novelist. In personal terms, they were of no more consequence than the cabby who drove Dickens to the *All the Year Round* office, or the chambermaid who cleaned the room at the 'Priory', where George Eliot wrote *Felix Holt, the Radical*.

I would guess that some bio-bibliographical profile (dates of birth, death, career details, marital status, total number of novels published) can be readily retrieved for about 1,200 Victorian novelists. For another purpose than this chapter, I have gathered such material on some 878 of them. These represent authors whose records lie close enough to the surface for one to discover salient facts using the resources of the British Library.[2] It is, I think, probably the largest database yet assembled. (The *New Cambridge Bibliography of English Literature*, for instance, has entries on under 200; this will probably be rectified in the third *Cambridge Bibliography*, currently in production.) A lifetime's work could probably turn up a few hundred more, but the majority of Victorian novelists have, I suspect, sunk for ever without trace.

As a sample, 878 cases out of 3,500 is more than substantial enough for statistical analysis, if the sample is not too skewed. But, one must assume, it is manifestly skewed in favour of the 'noteworthy' writer. To have left any record is, in itself, a mark of egregiousness. If the condition of the Victorian novelist is obscurity, to be known is to be in some degree exceptional and to be at all famous (either to one's contemporaries or posterity) is to be a very rare bird indeed. Nevertheless, with the necessary qualifications, 878 novelists is a solid starting point. What I intend to do here is make some preliminary interrogation of this data with the hope of arriving at a set of initially serviceable generalizations about the Victorian novelist, *en masse*.

II

Close up, the corps of Victorian novelists is bewildering in its variety and diversity. All Victorian life seems to be there: from servants, errand-boys and criminals to High Court judges, generals, admirals, bishops, prime ministers and marquises. In the general catalogue they may, like Macbeth's dogs, be cleped novelists, but what rational points of congruence can one find, say, between the following pair?

> LENNOX, Lord William [Pitt] (1799–1881). Born at Winestead Abbey in Yorkshire, Lennox was the fourth son of the fourth Duke of Richmond. His godfather was William Pitt and one of his cousins was Charles James Fox. While still a thirteen-year-old boy at Westminster school, he was gazetted to a cornetcy. He then joined Wellington's staff as an aide-de-camp, remaining in the post until three years after Waterloo.

He missed the battle itself, though in Brussels his mother threw the ball for him which is commemorated in Thackeray's *Vanity Fair*, Byron's *Childe Harold* and Charles Lever's *Charles O'Malley*. If not the author of good literature himself, Lennox was the cause of good literature in others. Lennox sold his commission in 1829, and served as a Whig MP from 1832 to 1834. He was, however, more interested in sport (particularly flat racing) and literature than in public service. The young lord went on to write extensively for the journals and was the author of fashionable novels, which hit the taste of the day but which look very feeble to the modern eye. In his later years, he was a sadly broken-down figure willing to hire himself out for lectures on the theme of 'Celebrities I have known'. Nonetheless his volumes of reminiscences, published in the late 1870s, are lively. His fiction includes: *Compton Audley* (1841), *The Tuft Hunter* (1843), *Percy Hamilton* (1851), *Philip Courtenay* (1855), *The Adventures of a Man of Family* (1864). There are thirteen novels by Lennox deposited in the British Library.

LEVY, Amy (1861–89). Levy was born at Clapham into a cultured and orthodox Jewish family who actively encouraged her literary talents. She was educated at Brighton, and at Newnham College Cambridge, where she was the first Jewish girl to matriculate. At university in 1881 Levy's first volume of poems was published. Entitled *Xantippe* (after Socrates' fabled shrew of a wife) the work indicated her feminist sentiments. The details of Levy's subsequent life are tantalisingly mysterious. She may have taught, or even have worked in a factory from idealistic motives. She was a friend of Olive Schreiner and of the socialist novelist Clementina Black. Her novel *Reuben Sachs* (1888) is the story of a sexually unscrupulous politician. Its depiction of Jewish life in London as grossly materialistic caused a furore, and was widely taken as a race libel, as was Julia Frankau's similarly anti-Semitic *Dr Philips* (1887). Levy's subsequent novel, *Miss Meredith* (1889) was less tendentious. It is the story of an English Governess, who falls in love with the son of the Italian household where she is employed. Its lightness of tone suggests that it may have been written some time before actual publication. Levy also wrote the shorter fiction *The Romance of a Shop* (1888), in which four sisters set up their own business. A prey to melancholy, Levy committed suicide by suffocating herself with charcoal fumes shortly after correcting her fifth and last volume of poems for the press. There are three novels of Levy's deposited in the British Library.[3]

Both these are, in their ways (more particularly in their failures), fascinating and instructive cases. Lennox, if we confuse fact and fiction, was actually *there* when George Osborne made his reckless proposal to Becky Sharp on the night before Waterloo. In fact, as the central figure of that actual ball, he survives for posterity only as one of the far background props in its most famous fictional representations. The pathos of his hawking himself around London as a kind of raree show or literary Prufrock is a parable on the treacherous evanescence of fame. And his career is a powerful reminder of the rule that interesting lives do not, inevitably, make for interesting novels. Lennox's is not, of course, a harrowing end, as is Levy's, even in the starkly skeletal form of a dictionary entry. Her Roman death (accompanied by the final act of literary duty) is an almost unbearably poignant indictment of the cruelty of the sensitive Victorian novelist's lot.

Regarding Levy and Lennox as co-professional writers ('two Victorian novelists'), what can one reasonably claim that they had in common, other than that both lived in nineteenth-century England and wrote what the generic record calls fiction? Clearly, the differences make more sense than the similarities. And the main difference I would draw attention to is that Levy began writing early in life as a direct (almost reflexive) career option. Lennox, by contrast, came to novel writing late and indirectly. He ricocheted into it from an earlier, more promising career in the military (cut short by an inconvenient declaration of peace) and from his clear incompetence in fulfilling his expected class destinies in Parliament (possibly due to the equally inconvenient Reform Bill of 1832). This ricochet route into novel writing is, I suggest, a typical male pattern. The direct route into authorship that Levy followed is, by contrast, typically female. In many ways, the archetypal female novelist is Daisy Ashford (1881–1972), who began writing at the age of nine and had four novels complete by the age of thirteen, when she was packed off to convent school, never to write fiction again. The archetypal male novelist, by contrast, would be William de Morgan (1839–1917) who began life as an art student, worked with William Morris, rediscovered medieval techniques for staining glass, set up a successful ceramics factory at Fulham and retired in 1905. In his retirement, aged 65, he began a successful career writing Victorian (in all but date) novels with *Joseph Vance* (1906). He was initially encouraged to write by his wife, who was worried by his depressed state of mind. De Morgan followed this bestseller with five more, and left two works of fiction incomplete at the time of his death. At its bluntest, one may say that men tended to have lived, loved and worked before writing fiction, women often the other way round.

This is not to say that women could not turn their hand to fiction late in life, if they had to; more particularly if it was the only way they could put bread on the family table. One can cite, for instance, the case of Mrs Trollope (1779–1863) who, finding herself let down by her bankrupt husband in the early 1830s, set to at the age of 55 and wrote 35 sprightly works of fiction to keep the Trollopes in middle-class respectability. As resourceful was Amelia Barr (1831–1919), whose husband dragged her off to America and then died of yellow fever (together with three of his daughters), leaving the widow Barr on the streets of New York with $5 in her purse and three surviving daughters to support. At the age of 54, Mrs Barr set to and went on to write 64 popular novels (among them *Remember The Alamo*, 1888, elements of which resurfaced in the 1960s John Wayne movie). A sizeable band of these resourceful ladies can be assembled who, had the wolf not been at the door, would never have put pen to paper, and certainly not in their grandmotherhood.

Something that one may deduce as having been shared professionally by Amy Levy and William Lennox is a sense of guilt and shame. It must have been wormwood for Lennox to pocket his paltry guineas for lecturing on the celebrities he, anything but a celebrity, had known. What the guilt was that drove Levy to suicide one can only guess. But clearly the male, Lennox, was more able to survive than was the female, Levy. This is a pattern one sees elsewhere in the ranks of the profession. Suicide is uncommon, but pseudonyms and anonymity, for instance, were often used to mask shame at being a novelist. Thus Julia Wedgwood (1833–19 14, an offspring of the Wedgwood-Darwin dynasty) wrote one of her two novels anonymously and one pseudonymously (as 'Florence Dawson'). Evidently her first (*Framleigh Hall*, 1858) was written without her father's knowledge; her second (*An Old Debt*, 1859) was published only after he gave her his patriarchal imprimatur, having read and censored the manuscript. Thereafter, parental disapproval inhibited Julia Wedgwood from writing fiction altogether. Hugh Stowell Scott (1862–1903) ran into similar paternal opposition. His father, a prosperous shipowner in Newcastle upon Tyne, decreed that his son should follow the family business. Ostensibly dutiful, young Hugh complied. But secretly he began writing and publishing novels, at first anonymously, then under the pseudonym 'Henry Seton Merriman' (the overtones of hedonistic release implicit in this pen name – 'the merry man' – are striking). The difference between Scott and Wedgwood is that he did not finally crumple into filial silence. He went on to write 18 bestselling works of fiction. (He also turned his duplicity to good effect in later life by serving as one of the early clandestine agents of the British secret service.) This greater resolution and independence of the male novelist in the face of the stigma attached to writing fiction is generally borne out by mass survey.

Skimming the bio-bibliographies of 878 Victorian novelists yields any number of suggestive primary observations. Not least, the inadequacy of the term 'novelist', implying as it does both someone who merely wrote a novel and someone who devoted their life to (and won their bread by) fiction. It is said that the Eskimo has twenty words for snow. It would be useful to have a similarly discriminating sub-vocabulary for 'Victorian novelist'. As it is loosely applied, the term can legitimately cover someone like Grace Kimmins ('Sister Grace of the Bermondsey Settlement', 1870–1954), whose philanthropy expressed itself primarily in charitable work in the East End, and who in furtherance of that work wrote one successful novel with a purpose, *Polly Of Parker's Rents* (1899). 'Victorian novelist' equally covers the similarly philanthropic, but exclusively literary Miss Evelyn Everett-Green (1856–1932) who has no less than 254 works of fiction deposited in the British Library (many written for the Religious Tract Society). It is hard to imagine that given a 24-hour day and a 76-year life-span Everett-Green ever had time to do anything but write fiction. If quantity means anything, she was a novelist of a quite different stamp from one-shot Grace Kimmins.

A feature that stands out from a cursory scanning of the 878 bio-bibliographical capsules is the clear link between novel writing and certain historical conjunctions. Sea captains in the 1830s, for instance, were recruited in large numbers into the profession (the names of Marryat, Howard, Chamier, Barker, Glascock, and Neale come to mind). Clearly peace, half-pay, and national nostalgia for the Great Victorious War all played a part. But so too did the training and discipline of the officer's life at sea, which was quite different from that of the land-based soldier. Naval service in the early nineteenth century entailed long periods of boredom unmitigated by drink or women. And, unlike their military counterparts, naval commanders were expected to write as a central part of their duty, keeping the log-book being a daily ritual (soldiers, by contrast, were notoriously illiterate). This state of affairs holds up only to the mid-1850s after which (following Crimean reforms) soldiers became better penmen (and more of them wrote novels). With the advent of steam, sailors had less time to spin yarns, in both senses of the term. Apart from the 1830s and 1840s, sea captains rarely feature as active novelists.

Another fact that strikes the casually enquiring eye is the dynastic effect of the great Victorian novelist on those around him/her, particularly close relatives. Thus, for instance, Thackeray had one daughter, Anne Thackeray Ritchie, who went on to be a considerable novelist in her own right. His other daughter was the first wife of Leslie Stephen, father of Virginia Woolf. The woman with whom Thackeray had his (possibly) adulterous love affair in 1851, Jane Octavia Brookfield, went on after 1868 (Thackeray dying in 1863) to write 4 novels. And her son, Arthur Brookfield, went on in his turn to write 5 novels. A Thackeray cousin, Blanche Ritchie, wrote a novel and so did her husband, Francis Warre Cornish (both narratives were pseudo-Thackerayan in tone). To have 6 novelists clustered so closely around a major novelist is a much higher than chance rate. The same clustering phenomenon is found among the Trollopes. There is Anthony, who wrote 47 novels, his mother Frances Milton who wrote 35, his sister Cecilia who before dying of consumption wrote one, a couple of cousins who wrote about a dozen between them. Finally there was Anthony's brother Thomas Adolphus, who wrote 20 novels, and Thomas's second wife, Frances Eleanor Trollope, who wrote 60-odd. Altogether, Trollopes accounted for some 170 Victorian novels, or 0.3 per cent of the Victorian total. Add his present-day descendant, Joanna Trollope, and the total on the dynastic scoreboard soars out of sight.

Frances Eleanor Trollope's maiden name was Ternan, and she was the sister of Dickens's mistress, Ellen Ternan. Dickens's son Charles Jr did not write novels (although he commissioned many, as the editor in succession to his father on *All The Year Round*). But Angela Dickens, Charles Jr's daughter (1863–1946), went on to write nine novels (all noticeably morbid in tone) and she was aunt (I believe) to the twentieth-century novelist, Monica Dickens. Dickens's daughter Kate married Charles Allston Collins, author of two novels and brother of Wilkie, author of 30. Altogether, this Dickens constellation accounts for some 60 Victorian novels.

Charles Kingsley wrote 10 novels of the first rank. Only slightly less far behind in critical standing was his brother Henry Kingsley, with 20. A daughter of Charles, Mary St Leger, whose married name was Harrison and whose pen-name was 'Lucas Malet', wrote 12 novels. A younger sister, Charlotte (married name 'Chanter'), wrote a bestseller, *Over the Cliffs*, in 1860. Altogether, this Kingsley constellation accounts for 45 works of Victorian fiction, all of very high literary quality. Of the 11 children of Frederick Marryat, 4 daughters and one son wrote Victorian novels, running up a family score of around 100 titles.

One could follow these genealogical, or free-masonic, connections much further than I have done here. But it is clear that one of the main predisposing factors to writing Victorian novels was to have a close relative, or intimate acquaintance, who wrote Victorian novels.

III

Looking at individual cases is delightful, yielding the same kind of pleasure as turning over the pages of old photograph albums. And clearly enough it is instructive as well as perplexing to get to know the personnel behind the novels. But I want now to move to quantitative and more systematic analysis of my 878 cases. The questions to which initial answers are sought are: (1) How many Victorian novelists were seriously professional, and how many were amateur or sideline novelists? (2) Given the fact that Victorian fiction was unique in being a profession/industry/hobby in which males and females took part in equal numbers, is there any observable difference in the ways in which men and women were drawn or recruited into writing novels? Put more simply – what made the Victorian a Victorian novelist, and was the process different for men and women?

For multi-factorial research about 40 different fields can be covered by my data, including such factors as class origin, education, religious background, illness or handicap at significant periods of life, career activities, marital status, and so on. For my purposes here, I have collected responses on the following questions: (1) When was s/he born, and when did s/he die? (2) How many novels did s/he write? (3) At what age did s/he start writing? (4)Was there a career previous to writing novels?

Novel writing, I have said, was unique in Victorian society in being a public and professional activity open both to middle-class men and middle-class women on more or less equal terms. Nevertheless, given the social role forced on them, women naturally tended to be more of a modestly submerged component than their male partners. There was clearly more inhibition on women revealing themselves in the public activity of publication, hence they made more use of the pseudonymity and anonymity conventions afforded by the profession. Revealingly enough, their pseudonyms tended to be sexually neutral, or transsexual as in the following: 'John Oliver Hobbes' (Pearl M. T. Craigie), 'George Egerton' (Mrs Chavelita Bright), 'G. B. Brunefille' (Lady Colin Campbell), 'Lucas Malet' (Mary St Leger Harrison), 'Lucas Cleeve' (Adelina Kingscote), 'Cecil Adair' (Evelyn Everett-Green), 'Leslie Keith' (Grace Johnston), 'Michael Fairless' (Margaret Barber), 'Maxwell Gray' (Mary Tuttiett), 'John Law' (Margaret Harkness), and, most famously, Currer, Ellis, and Acton Bell (the Brontë sisters).The process is almost entirely one-way. Although men often used pseudonyms, for a variety of reasons, I have discovered only one male using even a vaguely female pen-name, the obscure nautical novelist Alexander Christie (1841–95), who wrote as 'Lindsay Anderson', an amalgamation of his mother's and his wife's maiden names.

The total of 878 yields 566 men and 312 women. As I suggest above, I imagine this is a function of greater reticence about declaring identity among women writers. Altogether, these 878 authors account for 15,490 fiction titles. At first glance, this looks like an impressively large fraction of the 50,000-or-so hypothetical total. But it needs to be qualified. Given the fact that Victorian authors were, regrettably enough, not all born in 1837 and overlap both ends of the period, the

15,490 figure should in prudence be reduced by as much as a third. The graph in Figure 26.1 shows the birthdates of the 878 novelists, from 1790 to 1870. Many of those born at the very end of the period continued writing, in some cases up to the mid-twentieth century.

Demographically, the sample reveals no great surprises. The average life expectancy of the male novelist was 66; the female novelist slightly longer, at 68.5 years. The average length of writing career (first novel to death) was 29.9 years for men, and 35.2 years for women. The average age of starting to write was 36 for the male novelist, 33 for the female. (Given the difficulty of determining when a writer actually broke into print, I suspect this figure should be adjusted downwards by about 5 years.)

The per-author lifetime total breaks down to 17.6 novels per writer. Sexually, women novelists averaged 21 titles against men's 15.7. This is a high amount in all categories and suggests that the practice of fiction was thoroughly professionalized. At an average payment of around £250, 16–21 novels would make a useful contribution to a life's income and in many circumstances would constitute its bulk. Given the average career lengths, it gives a novel for every 24 months of professional activity. But the per-author output figures rise even higher if one breaks them down. Thus:

878	(100%)	wrote 1 novel or more	(15,490 titles, or 100%)
553	(63%)	wrote 5 novels or more	(14,542, or 93%)
400	(45.5%)	wrote 10 novels or more	(13,352, or 86%)
212	(24%)	wrote 20 novels or more	(10,651, or 68.7%)
141	(16%)	wrote 30 novels or more	(8,883, or 57.3%)
95	(10.8%)	wrote 40 novels or more	(7,277, or 46.9%)
67	(7.6%)	wrote 50 novels or more	(5,992, or 38.6%)
45	(5%)	wrote 60 novels or more	(4,159, or 30.7%)
29	(3.3%)	wrote 70 novels or more	(3,713, or 23.9%)
24	(2.7%)	wrote 80 novels or more	(3,344, or 21.5%)
19	(2.1%)	wrote 90 novels or more	(2,932, or 18.9%)
18	(2%)	wrote 100 novels or more	(2,837, or 18%)

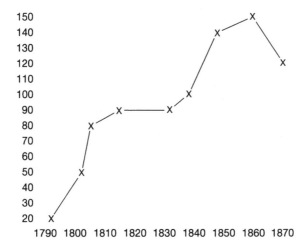

Figure 26.1   Birthdates of Victorian novelists

It is evident from this sample that Victorian fiction was largely the product of a relatively small, active component within a fairly large loosely participatory community (i.e. 7 per cent producing a third of all titles). It is evident too that the canonical novelists could make do on smaller than average outputs (Dickens 15, Gaskell 15, Thackeray 9, Eliot 10) because their work was rewarded more highly than average. And Anthony Trollope, with his 47 fiction titles, is not – given the production rates of the profession – as fertile a writer as commonly believed. Almost half of all Victorian novels seem to have been produced by authors clocking up 40 or more titles.

I have not analysed the class backgrounds in the sample, or other predisposing factors such as higher education. But the prior, or concurrent profession field throws up interesting results. Among the male novelists, all but 57 can be allocated at least one (and in many cases more than one) previous or other gainful line of work. In over half the cases, these are lines of work in which the embryo Victorian novelist has not notably succeeded. The principal stepping-stones to a Victorian man's writing fiction were as follows:

Law (predominantly service at the bar)	110
Journalism	82
Business, civil service	75
Church	57
Army	50
Teaching	37
Navy	21
Medicine	21
Manual, menial	17
Book trade	11
	Total 481

The dominance of law as an entry point into novel writing is the striking feature here. Put simply, one in five (male) Victorian novelists was a lawyer, and in the vast majority of cases a failed barrister. 'Called to the Bar but never practised' is thus the commonest prelude to a career in writing novels. And if one adds lawyer fathers (or, for women, lawyer husbands) the coincidence of a training in law with the Victorian novel is even more pronounced. Nor is it just hacks who turned from law to fiction. Among the great novelists one can cite are: Thackeray (failed barrister), Dickens (articled as a solicitor's clerk in Gray's Inn), Blackmore (called to the Bar but never practised), Stevenson (studied law at Edinburgh), Charles Reade (called to the Bar but never practised), Meredith (articled to a solicitor for a while), Wilkie Collins (called to the Bar but never practised), Harrison Ainsworth (studied law at the Inner Temple).

Some reasons for the law–fiction link may be guessed at. To read for the English Bar, it is necessary to have family money, contacts and (usually) an Oxbridge education. To practise at the Bar was, and is, a top job and one from which the working classes are generally excluded. And, for complex reasons, the British aristocracy have never encouraged younger sons to follow law, directing them instead to the army and the Church. None of this, however, is a convincing explanation of the wide bridge connecting Victorian law and Victorian fiction. A more likely factor is the closeness of the Inns of Court to Fleet Street – journalism often being the transitional stage between law and writing novels. But geographically, some of the main teaching hospitals are even nearer Fleet Street. Yet failed doctors did not drift into novel writing in anything like the same numbers as young lawyers.

The critical factor was, presumably, the peculiar nature of legal training. Reading for the Bar centres on two activities: (1) reading, self-evidently; (2) dining; the law, even more than Parliament, being one of the best clubs in London with the difference that taking dinner a certain number of times is obligatory on trainee barristers. Moreover, the study and practice of law is punctuated by absurdly long vacations. Young doctors, especially during internship, are routinely overworked for 50 weeks of the year. And they do not just read up their professional expertise, which is largely a matter of manual and interpersonal skills. Unlike the newly qualified doctor, the young barrister emerged from his training without any clear next step. He waited, hopefully, for briefs. Often they were slow in coming. Typically, in this awkward interval, the lawyer would marry, incurring new debts. And typically, in this interval, the drift to writing would occur. Finally, although it is a hard link to discern, there is probably an affinity between the mentalities of jurisprudence and Victorian fiction, shaped as both were by the study of individual cases and the canons of (poetic) justice.

Only 32 of the 312 women can be given alternative professional, business or trade activities. Those with no other vocational attribution than 'married woman' or 'spinster' hugely predominate:

Married women	167
Spinsters	113
Journalists	9
Teachers or governesses	8
Actresses or artists	6
Doctors or nurses	4
Book trade	4
Business	1
	Total 312

Not surprisingly, perhaps, the Victorian spinster author was the most productive single category of writer, with an average output of 24 titles.

These findings are very preliminary, and in many cases simply confirm what common sense would anyway suggest. And even where the conclusions are instructive (as in the male-professional and female-amateur finding), they should be treated with some caution. The principal uncertainty can be expressed as a question: do the 878 cases examined mirror the profession, or are they a superstructure of the most successful practitioners self-selected by being that much better than the rest? Granted the sample is probably unrepresentative, but it is less unrepresentative than the invariable dozen or so novelists who furnish the staple material for the study of 'Victorian fiction' in higher education. Beneath that elite handful my 878 novelists form a reasonably sound and now fairly visible foundation. Beneath these 878 is a still invisible sub-stratum (of several thousands) composed, one suspects, of failures, rank amateurs, third-rate hacks and utter nonentities. Some future literary archaeological tool will have to be devised to investigate these lower reaches.

Notes

1   This project was being undertaken by a team of scholars under the general editorship of D. F. McKenzie. Simon Eliot's *Some Patterns and Trends in British Publishing, 1800–1919* (London, 1994) supersedes some of my comments here.

2   The purpose for which the material was collected was *The Longman Companion to Victorian Fiction* (London, 1988).

3   These entries, and 876 like them, will be found in the *Longman Companion*.

Chapter 27

Robert L. Patten

WHEN IS A BOOK NOT A BOOK?

Within a print culture, many forms of communication may not be constructed for or produced in book format. Private letters, state documents, manuscript poetry circulated within a coterie as John Donne's poetry was,[1] and dramatic scripts, are some instances of writing not designed for book publication. Another non-book publication format is the periodical – magazines and newspapers. The fiction issued in nineteenth-century periodicals provides a complex and interesting case where privileging the volume edition over periodical issue distorts the nature of the fiction and the history of the book. And the case is an important exception to the primacy of book publication throughout the century, for, as the eminent literary historian George Saintsbury has said, 'there is no single feature of the English literary history of the nineteenth century . . . which is so distinctive and characteristic as the development in it of periodical literature.'[2]

What is a book? According to the *Oxford English Dictionary*, a book is a 'printed treatise or series of treatises, occupying several sheets of paper or other substance fastened together so as to compose a material whole'.[3] Books are sheets of paper on which something self-contained and internally coherent has been printed; all the printed material relates in some way to the book's title and 'treatise'. The contents of books are fixed in space – 'fastened together so as to compose a material whole', and they are also fixed in time – to a date of completion or publication at which copyright protection commences. Finally, many books are defined by being authored, or edited, by one or more than one person. Indeed, marketing a book by the author's name has been a commercial strategy for centuries: John Grisham's name is probably more important to most customers than the title of his newest book, and when *I Am Charlotte Simmons* was released in paperback after lukewarm reviews of the hard cover edition, Tom Wolfe's name was pasted over the title in hopes of increasing sales.

When, around 1700, magazines were invented in England, the designers started out by creating a character, a persona whose observations constituted the 'printed treatise' of the publication. Thus Joseph Addison and Richard Steele, the editors of the first major eighteenth-century magazine, the *Spectator*, developed the persona of 'Mr. Spectator'. In 1731, the first periodical with the word magazine in the title appeared; its persona was also announced in the title, the *Gentleman's Magazine*. A century later, the proprietors and editors of *Punch* created Mr. Punch, who never quite qualified as a gentleman. Magazines aim to develop their own distinctive personality; editors, designers, writers, and artists all direct their efforts toward that end. For instance, the *New Yorker* has a distinctive personality, complete with a character, Eustace Tilley, who at the end of February every year examines a butterfly through his monocle, and whose portrait, presumably as proprietor, appears on the journal's paychecks. This magazine prints only certain kinds of prose and poetry and cartoons, only certain kinds of 'Talk of the Town'. Magazines, then, like books, often market themselves as coherent texts 'fastened together so as to compose a material whole' and authored by an individual. But magazines are in other ways very different from books.

To illustrate one aspect of the stake our society has in preferring the book, consider this entry in a 1993 bookseller's catalogue: 'AN EXCEPTIONALLY FINE COPY. REMARKABLY CLEAN. DICKENS (Charles) Oliver Twist, . . . 3 volumes, FIRST EDITION. First issue, . . . choicely bound for Hatchards, . . . £1500.'[4] This notice is misleading in fundamental ways. The 'material whole' for sale for £1500 is not the first issue or first edition of most of the text of the novel now known as *Oliver Twist*. It does not print the title by which the story was first identified; it is not a book whose author was named Charles Dickens; and it is not even the 'material whole' it was when it first appeared. This three-volume edition, authored by 'Boz', was originally published in cloth covers by Richard Bentley on 9 November 1838, six months *before Oliver Twist* finished its serialized run in the pages of *Bentley's Miscellany* where it began [see Figure 27.1]. This bookseller's copy has been

Figure 27.1   Six months before *Oliver Twist* finished its serial run in *Bentley's Miscellany*, the publisher Richard Bentley brought out the completed text, with all the illustrations, as a three-volume novel. Although Dickens was known to be the author, the book was still published under the name of 'Boz'. At Dickens's request, a new title page, giving his real name, was substituted within a week of publication day, November 9, 1838. Cruikshank's frontispiece illustrates 'Oliver's reception by Fagin and the boys'. – Berg Collection

rebound in half red morocco with gilt tops and gilt letters: the cloth covers have been stripped off, leather covers substituted, the edges of the pages trimmed, and the tops of the pages gilded to protect them from dust. So this is not 'an exceptionally fine copy' of the first three-volume book edition of the novel, but rather a copy that has been made finer by an expensive bookbinder and book dealer. This copy sells for fifteen hundred pounds because it contains early state title pages, a suppressed plate, and three leaves of publishers' advertisements that have nothing to do with the text of the 'treatise'.

By contrast, battered copies of the monthly numbers or half-yearly volumes of *Bentley's Miscellany* containing the serialized version of *Oliver Twist* could be found on bookstalls for much less. And for a little over half of the £1500 that in 1993 would buy a single novel, the same dealer a year later offered twenty-eight volumes of the *Cornhill Magazine*, 1860–1873, whose first editor was William Makepeace Thackeray, Dickens's great rival as journalist and novelist. Within those twenty-eight volumes are hundreds of stories and articles and the first issue of four serial fictions by Anthony Trollope, two by Thackeray, and one each by Elizabeth Gaskell, Wilkie Collins, and George Eliot.[5] For even less money, $1200, an antiquarian bookseller offered ten volumes of *Bentley's Miscellany*, 1837–1841, containing as the dealer correctly says 'the true first version of *Oliver Twist*'.[6] In addition, these ten volumes contain a half dozen other significant novels, scores of poems and articles, and over a hundred first-issue etchings by George Cruikshank.

But dealers, collectors, museums, libraries, bibliographers, textual scholars, and the general public have been conditioned to think of the book as the substantial, first publication of most serials, from Dickens's *Pickwick Papers* to Thomas Hardy's *Tess of the d'Urbervilles* and Joseph Conrad's *Lord Jim*. Books have authors who are solely responsible for their contents – Charles Dickens, for example, even though those 'early state' title pages of the 'exceptionally fine copy' identify the author not as Charles Dickens but as what was then a well-known pseudonym, 'Boz'. And books get passed down through the generations, while periodicals are tossed out by families or broken up for the prints by dealers or reduced to microfilm, -form, or -fiche by librarians. The book is semipermanent and simply displaces the format in which the text first appears. This is true for virtually every magazine serial, not just fiction, but also history, theology, biography, philosophy, criticism, and other genres which, as Saintsbury reminds us, were often in the nineteenth century first published in installments in periodicals.[7]

Over the last twenty years we have learned a lot about what this preference for the book produces in the way of copytext distortions. But I'm interested here, not in the textual controversies surrounding serialized, machine-printed works, but in the distortions that preferring the book version has imposed on our very conception of periodical fiction. Defining the text as identifiably authored and self-contained obscures the ways in which fiction was affected by the periodicals in which it first appeared. Four aspects of book fiction that are significantly altered by magazine serialization are the convention of single authorship, the genre of fiction itself, the apparent self-containedness of the 'material whole', and the timing and effect of the story's reception.

That magazines are collaborations among proprietors, editors, writers, and sometimes illustrators should not be surprising, since the word 'magazine', from the Arabic *makhazin* meaning storehouses (related to the French *magasin*, department store), denotes a warehouse storing many things. Collaboration among those running a magazine – the editorial 'we' is not always only a convention – is the norm even for the production of periodical fiction. Some of the most amusing, and possibly accurate, accounts of proprietors' constructing their publications are contained in Anthony Trollope's *The Way We Live Now* and George Gissing's *New Grub Street*. But though we have biographies of publishers and publishing houses, and narratives of publishers' interventions in the works of such famous authors as Sir Walter Scott and Dickens, little work has been done on the theory or general practice of proprietorial intervention in periodical texts. However, recently some scholars have studied the kinds of effects editors may have on the medley of materials they assemble and publish. Mark Parker has shown how John Scott, editor of the *London Review* in the 1820s, transmitted Romantic ideology by manipulating the style, tone, subject, and placement of Charles Lamb's and William Hazlitt's essays and by framing them with surrounding essays in each issue so that their political implications were highlighted.[8] Laurel Brake has demonstrated the influence of the differing editorial practices at the *Westminster Review* and the *Fortnightly Review* on the separately published essays that make up Walter Pater's *Renaissance*.[9]

To assess proprietorial and editorial interventions in *Oliver Twist*, we need first to recall that the proprietor, Richard Bentley, had started up his magazine as a rival to his former partner, Henry Colburn's, successful *New Monthly Magazine*. Bentley, determined to outdo the competition, aimed at capturing the market for humor: the *Wit's Miscellany*, he intended to call it at first. Then he changed to a name that links his own to that of the magazine's persona: *Bentley's Miscellany*. (One wag said the title was ominous – Miss Sell Any.) Humor, not politics, was as the 'Prologue' announced the keynote of the venture.[10]

For contributors to this miscellany of papers melded together into 'Bentley's', Richard Bentley bought up the team who were making a decided hit with their humorous pen and pencil sketches of lower-middle-class urban life: Charles Dickens and George Cruikshank. Their success was in the sketch, something either visual or verbal that was quickly executed and quickly absorbed, and that recorded the evanescent and fugitive detail of modern life.

The text of *Oliver Twist*, a long novel that is seldom humorous and that from the beginning attacks political measures, should be understood as a contribution that contrasts to the ostensible purpose and tone of *Bentley's Miscellany* and to the previous publication, *Sketches by Boz*, written by Dickens and illustrated by Cruikshank. The magazine's purpose and tone, in turn, are defined against the competition, archly described in the 'Prologue':

> We do not envy the fame or glory of other monthly publications. Let them all have their room . . . One may revel in the unmastered fun and the soul-touching feeling of Wilson, the humour of Hamilton . . . and the Tory brilliancy of half a hundred contributors zealous in the cause of Conservatism . . . Elsewhere, what can be better than Marryat, Peter Simple, Jacob Faithful, Midshipman Easy, or whatever other title pleases his ear . . . In short, to all our periodical contemporaries we wish every happiness and success . . . We wish that we could catch them all . . .

But, the unsigned 'Prologue' continues, using the editorial first-person plural in this case probably because Dickens and Bentley were agreed about the policy, 'Our path is single and distinct. In the first place, we have nothing to do with politics.'[11]

Out of the context of a magazine promising 'wit' and eschewing 'politics', *Oliver Twist* loses some of its shock value.[12] And unless we keep in mind the opening announcement that this will be a witty non-political miscellany, we may miss some of the underlying tension that surfaced in Richard Bentley's quarrels with Dickens about his contribution to the *Miscellany*.[13] Moreover, proprietor and editor further shaped the contents of the journal by attempting to buy up the writers then making *Fraser's Magazine* so popular. They succeeded in hiring many of the contributors to *Fraser's*, including its outstanding editor William Maginn. And they signaled their intentions in the 'Prologue', hailing 'the wit of our contributor Theodore Hook', 'the fascinating prose or delicious verse of our fairest of *collaborateuses* Miss Landon', and 'the polyglot facetiae of our own Father Prout'. The contents of any issue of *Bentley's*, and of its serial fiction from Samuel Lover's *Handy Andy* to Harrison Ainsworth's *Jack Sheppard*, should be understood in the context of what other journals were publishing and what other writers and illustrators were available. To some extent authors and artists had their own styles, but to some extent too they were melded collectively into a house style, the polyphonic 'miscellany' unifying into a 'material whole'.[14] The best serial fiction in or out of magazines, such as Thackeray's *Vanity Fair*, exploits that verbal and visual polyphony.

Dickens both edited and supplied text for *Bentley's* under the pseudonym 'Boz', the author of *Sketches by Boz* [see Figure 27.2]. At the conclusion of Boz's first story, about the Mayor of the

Figure 27.2 In April of 1837, Dickens posed for Cruikshank. 'I was sitting for my portrait to George Cruikshank . . . to-day,' Dickens told a friend, 'and George being a ticklish subject [I] could not leave him.' Berg Collection

provincial town of 'Mudfog', Boz explains that 'this is the first time we have published any of our gleanings from this particular source', that is, the Mudfog papers. He also suggests that 'at some future period, we may venture to open the chronicles of Mudfog.'[15] This fiction of a manuscript source resembles that preserved through the first numbers of Dickens's concurrent monthly-parts serial, *The Pickwick Papers. Oliver Twist* commences in the February number of *Bentley's*, under the title of *Oliver Twist, or, the Parish Boy's Progress*, by 'Boz'. As the first sentence of the story makes clear, this is a continuation of the Mudfog Papers: Oliver is born in the Mudfog workhouse. Thus naming Dickens as the author of *Oliver Twist*, as the first volume publication and the book dealers' catalogues do, not only distorts the textual record but more importantly obscures the ways in which the narratorial voice, Boz, is constructed out of those voices that precede and surround it.[16]

That distortion was compounded when Dickens's authorized biographer, John Forster, made *Oliver Twist* into the first of three versions of Dickens's own childhood hardships, as if the story had its only origin in Dickens's own life. In fact there were other claimants for the originator of the story. Dickens's 'coadjutor' on *Sketches by Boz*, George Cruikshank, may indeed, as he later said, have suggested to Dickens that they collaborate on a story about the rise of 'a boy from a most humble position up to a high and respectable one'.[17] For fifteen years, Cruikshank had wanted to illustrate a contemporary version of Hogarth's narrative series of twelve pictures, *Industry and Idleness*. Hogarth's pictures track the parallel but contrasted fortunes of two apprentices, one, Francis Goodchild, who through industry rises to 'a high and respectable' position as Lord Mayor of London, and the other, Tom Idle, who through idleness falls into bad company and is eventually sentenced by his former fellow apprentice Goodchild and hanged on Tyburn Hill. A successful recent exhibition of Hogarth's work had made such a project more viable.

If Dickens did adopt Cruikshank's suggestion, which chimed with some of his own ideas for what he told Richard Bentley was 'a capital notion for myself, and one which will bring Cruikshank out',[18] then that resulting story has wider contexts than Dickens's own life. But those wider contexts and those other contributors were deliberately effaced. Charles Dickens constructed himself over the decades as a separable and distinct, unique, author. The promulgation of the figure of the writer Dickens became an immensely powerful merchandising ploy, selling not only his books but also political programs, charitable causes, wines and teas, and hundreds of manufactured products, from printed handkerchiefs to china, deriving from Dickens's work. Dickens's biographers, following John Forster's lead, reinforced the notoriety and singularity of Charles Dickens, author, rather than 'Boz', the editor and collaborator. Severing Dickens's periodical fictions from their magazine contexts allowed them to be reinterpreted as self-referential biographical disclosures. Largely a marketing strategy that made Dickens a household name, a fortune, and a model of a genius generating text out of trauma, this elevation of the book over the serial and its consequences persuaded even George Cruikshank's biographer to say in 1882 that 'In all the range of Dickens's work, there is nothing more essentially his own than "Oliver Twist".'[19] But writers closer to the initial context within *Bentley's*, knowing both Dickens and Cruikshank, were of a different opinion. Samuel Warren, one of the most successful authors of the day, said that the illustrations influenced Dickens, and 'thus the writer follows the caricaturist, instead of the caricaturist following the writer.'[20]

Another writer with a claim on Oliver's paternity is the novelist William Harrison Ainsworth, who was from the 1830s through the end of the century a very popular writer, especially of fiction for boys. Dickens's closest friend, Ainsworth had put Boz in touch with the publishers, artists, and journalists who helped to make Dickens's early reputation. By 1836 Ainsworth had embarked on a series of novels exploring the lives of thieves. The first, *Rookwood*, about the famous highwayman Dick Turpin, had been reissued with illustrations by Cruikshank, who had also been interested for seventeen years in collaborating with some writer on an illustrated life of a thief. The second, *Jack Sheppard*, about a romantic young burglar, overlapped *Oliver Twist* in *Bentley's Miscellany*. Ainsworth collected a lot of written and pictorial material about eighteenth-century miscreants, including James Sykes, a companion of Jack Sheppard and a possible inspiration for Bill Sikes. Dickens and Ainsworth were together frequently, discussing a slew of present and future projects. Yet Ainsworth's contribution to *Oliver Twist* usually goes unnoticed.

The point of all this is that in the magazine context *Oliver Twist*'s authorship is a multiple thing – the proprietor Richard Bentley; the editor Charles Dickens; other journals such as the *New Monthly* and *Fraser's Magazine*; other contributors of articles such as the stable of *Fraser's* writers and those already being published by Bentley; the pseudonymous author 'Boz', known for his 'sketches' of metropolitan scenes, characters, and tales; the illustrator George Cruikshank; pictorial progresses by Hogarth and his successors; and a close friend (and future editor of the *Miscellany*) Harrison Ainsworth, all influenced the subject, style, tone, and content of the serialized fiction. Serialization deconstructs the single author as sole creator, and does so as part of a larger collaborative project within which the serial is framed. Conversely, prioritizing the book as a single-authored material object over the multiply authored serial deconstructs the periodical, erasing all the extratextual influences, turning the voice from polyphonic to monophonic, and connecting the text to one author's imagination rather than to the culture of a magazine and of a historical moment.

Serialization also tends to deconstruct the genre of fiction. *Oliver Twist; or, The Parish Boy's Progress*, beginning as a Mudfog paper, starts as a further instance of the articles and tales Dickens had written for the *Morning* and *Evening Chronicle* and which in turn were partly based on sketches of the city by other journalists and graphic artists. Like the *Old Curiosity Shop,* it begins more as a short story than an extended fiction. Like *Pickwick*, the first Mudfog paper claims affinity with Parliamentary reports, memoirs, and posthumous papers. In *Bentley's Miscellany*, the installments of *Oliver Twist* are interspersed with other serials and with essays and poems about everything from angling in the days of Isaac Walton to an ode upon the birthday of Princess Victoria. It was not unusual for periodical stories to incorporate poems, criticism, philosophy, history, travelogues, or even musical scores.

Most notably, many magazine fictions articulate an affinity with drama. *Oliver Twist* is confessedly constructed according to melodramatic principles: 'It is the custom on the stage,' Boz the narrator tells us, 'in all good, murderous melodramas, to present the tragic and the comic scenes in as regular alternation as the layers of red and white in a side of streaky, well-cured bacon.'[21] The story is situated among many articles about the theater: the very first number of *Bentley's Miscellany* starts with an essay by Theodore Hook on George Colman the Younger. The novel employs a great deal of theatrical characterization and dialogue, such as Sikes's stagy 'Wolves tear your throats!'[22] Like other serials, *Oliver Twist* was on the boards before it was in boards, even before it was completely written: the first dramatization, by Gilbert A'Beckett, appeared after only half the installments had been composed. Cruikshank increasingly directed the illustrations toward their theatrical realization;[23] and for Dickens the prospects, and retrospects, of dramatizing the story significantly affected the text's design [see Figures 27.3 and 27.4]. Knowing, as he did about half the way through composition and publication, that the actor-manager Frederick Yates wanted to stage the story before it was completed in print, Dickens may have enhanced the role of Fagin in the concluding chapters in anticipation of the dramatization. Certainly Dickens wanted his serial readers to respond viscerally, as if in a theater.[24] Further, *Bentley's Miscellany* is itself refigured as a stage rather than a magazine or sheets of printed paper bound up as a 'material whole': the 'Editor's Address' on the completion of the first half-year – bound up as a volume – is couched as the manager's stage address at the end of a theatrical season.

Nor is this the end of the generic ambiguities of serials. As in *Oliver Twist*'s case, the graphic tradition often played a prominent role; this story is sub-titled a 'progress', a term denoting the sort of life-contour, physical and moral, often told through a series of pictures. And mid-way through the

Figure 27.3 'Oliver asking for more', the first Cruikshank illustration to *Oliver Twist*, stands facing the first chapter in the February 1837 number of *Bentley's Miscellany*. The title (which recalls a Hogarth 'progress'), the name of the author ('Boz'), and the reference to 'the town of Mudfog', which relates this story to one that appeared in the January number, were changed in later editions so that the novel would stand on its own as the work of Charles Dickens.

text's composition Dickens renegotiated his author's contracts with Richard Bentley, who was not only the proprietor of the magazine but also the stipulated publisher of Dickens's next two novels. That renegotiation changed the serialized fiction *Oliver Twist* from fulfilling a contractual monthly contribution of sixteen pages for the *Miscellany* into a novel, to be released in three volumes half a year before the serial dragged to a close in the magazine. So even in format *Oliver Twist* was neither conceived of nor produced as a novel for much of its initial appearance. Its affinities with theater, pictures, sketches, journalism, short stories, and Parliamentary proceedings are at least as influential in its initial stages as the generic protocols of the novel. Serial fictions interweave with other genres in immediate, material ways that their later repackaging into self-contained novels conceals.

My third concern is the way serial fictions, not being self-contained, incorporate the times.

Figure 27.4   George Cruikshank's pencil, pen, and watercolor sketch for 'The Last Chance' shows Bill Sikes attempting to escape from the angry mob surrounding a thieves' hideout on Jacob's Island. Charles Dickens told Cruikshank it would be impossible to illustrate this scene, as it 'is so very complicated, with such a multitude of figures, such violent action, and torch-light to boot, that a small plate could not take in the slightest idea of it'. The illustration – pasted into a copy of volume 3 of the 1838 book edition – was translated into set designs for theatrical adaptations of the novel. – Berg Collection

Eminent scholars have identified many topics of the day to which serials make reference.[25] The topicalities of periodical fiction tend to be journalistic, metropolitan, sensational, and narratable. For instance, the gradual spread of a mysterious form of equine hoof-disease might throw the country-side into a panic, but though topical it probably wouldn't become the subject of a successful serial fiction: it wouldn't make the daily newspapers, wouldn't appeal to city dwellers, wouldn't accelerate the pulses of readers seeking sensation, and couldn't be cast as an enthralling narrative.

Murder, on the other hand, fulfills all these requirements, and by the 1850s was a leading subject of periodical fiction.

Magazine serials also circulate references of a more general character than local, topical, and timely ones. Two categories of fundamental referentiality are ideology and aesthetics. (Each of these kinds of reference involves the other, but for present purposes I have separated them.) By ideology, I mean those clusters of ideas, abstract or pragmatic, that issue in the mythologies and expressions of an era.[26] Scholars have studied the political ideology of selected nineteenth-century British journals, from the Whig quarterlies in the first decades of the century to John Stuart Mill's Utilitarian *London Magazine* at mid-century and the imperialism fostered by *Blackwood's Edinburgh Magazine* in the last decade. But little has been done about more diffuse ideological concerns. In the case of *Oliver Twist*, Richard Stein has demonstrated that the story participates in widespread writing about orphanhood and lost identities surfacing at the beginning of Victoria's reign.[27] A population that was becoming more mobile across spaces and classes had vested its proofs of identity in detachable and forgeable adjuncts such as birth and marriage certificates, names, and other tokens. These may fail to confirm identity, legitimacy, property, class, status, rights, and name, as they failed for Oliver and his mother.

There are other anxieties of the late Regency and early Victorian period that ally with this fear of alienable identity. Cruikshank and the *Fraser's* crowd, especially Ainsworth, were as we have seen interested in the lives of thieves [see Figure 27.5]. 'Crime', Martin Wiener recently noted, 'was a central metaphor of disorder and loss of control in all spheres of life.'[28] This interest in crime related to perennial debates about nature versus nurture, that is, whether bad was innate like a bad seed or produced by a bad environment. A related issue vexed Dickens for decades: did parental neglect foster in the child a determination to succeed in respectable society (Charles Dickens) or did it lead to criminality (the Artful Dodger) and/or death (Oliver's orphan friend Dick)? The early Victorian cultural fascination with criminality seemed to find expression particularly in the dramas of incarceration and excarceration. Many critics have noted the cramped, confined world of Dickens's and Cruikshank's collaborations – the sense of structures, persons, environments, laws, and fortune closing down, cramping, deforming the individual.[29] Such paradigms do seem to reflect the cultural emphasis on policing the self that bourgeois industrial capitalism emphasized.

Conversely, and less often noticed, there is in the 1830s an equal interest in escape, excarceration, in how individuals might defy those pressures that could identify and fix them. Nowhere is that escapism more celebrated than in *Jack Sheppard*. This was the serial Harrison Ainsworth wrote, and that began to appear at the front of each issue of *Bentley's Miscellany* after *Oliver Twist* had been published in three volumes but while it was still running in installments in the periodical. The letterpress by Ainsworth and the illustrations by Cruikshank celebrate the eighteenth-century prison escapist Jack Sheppard, who, though an idle and foolish apprentice, is unfairly bedeviled by the law and repeatedly foils its attempts to imprison him. His famous escapes from Newgate prison stage, in the text and pictures and later in the theater, his eel-like ability to slip out of shackles and cells. They also dramatize the site of the old Newgate prison, as Fagin's time in the condemned cell, like the earlier sketch 'A Visit to Newgate' in *Sketches by Boz* brings to life the modern prison.

Had Dickens continued as editor of *Bentley's Miscellany*, and Cruikshank continued as illustrator, their next collaborative serial fiction, following *Jack Sheppard* in the magazine, would have been about the burning of the old Newgate prison, *Barnaby Rudge*. The original title Dickens assigned to that work was *Gabriel Vardon, the Locksmith of London*, a title that again plays on the theme of incarceration and excarceration, since a locksmith can lock or unlock doors. And so, within the pages of *Bentley's Miscellany*, all illustrated by Cruikshank, would have appeared three serial fictions

Figure 27.5 'Oliver introduced to the respectable Old Gentleman', an original etching by George Cruikshank, appeared first in the May 1837 number of *Bentley's Miscellany*. It was reissued in volume one (January-
June 1837) of the collected numbers of the *Miscellany* and reprinted in November 1838 opposite page 132 in
volume one of the first three-volume edition of the novel. – Berg Collection

about crime, dealing in sequence with the modern Newgate, the eighteenth-century prison, and its
destruction during the Gordon Riots. These unrealized plans for a triple serial on prisons illustrate
one way in which magazine publication shows deep ideological currents that separate book publication obscures.[30]

    Victorian periodicals were also much occupied with aesthetic issues. The idea of the aesthetic
comprises a great range of topics, from the typographic design of the journal and the accuracy,
beauty, and instructiveness of its 'illuminations' to debates about the moral (or immoral) function
of literature and the appropriate conduct of readers. As Kelly Mays shows, by mid-century periodicals regularly instructed their customers in the proper – that is, moral – way to read. Critics
denounced desultory, casual, random, escapist, and sensationalistic reading practices; they
condemned short attention spans, skimming, and flitting from topic to topic, and they criticized

mothers for reading while minding their children because the children would grow up to associate reading with surveillance.[31]

At the time of *Oliver Twist*, William Maginn was producing for *Bentley's Miscellany* a series of articles on character in Shakespeare that are, in Kathryn Chittick's judgment, 'of impressive acuteness'.[32] His was another way of directing reading, writing, social, and punitive practices, as well as commenting on theatricality – all themes touched on in this essay. One of Maginn's papers, on the villain Iago in the tragedy of *Othello*, appears in a crucial spot in the journal: between the first chapters of Ainsworth's *Jack Sheppard*, about an eighteenth-century boy thief, and the last chapters of Dickens's *Oliver Twist*, about nineteenth-century boy thieves.[33] In this paper Maginn implicitly argues against Samuel Taylor Coleridge's notion that Iago's actions can only be explained as the product of 'motiveless malignity'. All Shakespeare's characters, he says, 'are real men and women, not mere abstractions'. Their virtues and vices are compounded 'and are not unfrequently blended'. Maginn maintains that wickedness is prompted by the same impulses that stimulate persons 'to the noblest actions – ambition, love of adventure, passion, necessity'. Thus, in an article printed between the opening of *Jack Sheppard* and the chapters of *Oliver Twist* recounting Sikes's last day and Monks's capture, Maginn ventures to say that 'the creatures of Boz's fancy, Fagin or Sikes, did not appear in every circle as the unmitigated scoundrels we see them in Oliver Twist.' It is due to the exigencies of the story, Maginn reasons, that readers see only one side of their characters. 'But, after all, the Jew [Fagin] only carries the commercial, and the housebreaker [Sikes] the military principle to an extent which society cannot tolerate.'[34]

Maginn uncovers an aesthetic that appeals more to empathy and capitalistic entrepreneurship than to social control: the feeling that covers the globe with shipping also animates the breast of thieves and highwaymen. 'Robber, soldier, thief, merchant, are all equally men,' he reasons.[35] (No wonder archconservative Mary Russell Mitford hated the idea of making law-breakers so attractive and the police so venal.) In conclusion Maginn calls for yet another inscription of the Hogarthian 'progress' contrasting industry and idleness: 'It would not be an unamusing task to analyze the career of two persons starting under similar circumstances, and placed in situations not in essence materially different, one ending at the debtors' door of Newgate amid hootings and execrations, and the other borne to his final resting-place in Westminster Abbey, graced by all the pomps that heraldry can bestow.'[36]

Thus Maginn's serial criticism of Shakespeare's characters accomplishes five things. It establishes an aesthetic principle – successfully drawn characters are compounded of good and evil. Second, it derives reading practices from that principle – readers should recognize and empathize with motives that lead to bad actions as well as to good ones. Third, it declares a moral order – 'robber, . . . merchant, are all equally men.' Fourth, it relates dramatic criticism to the magazine's current serial fictions – Fagin and Bill Sikes are also 'equally men', appearing much more lovable and redeemable off-stage, out of the plot. And fifth, Maginn's essay sets an agenda for future writings – another fiction contrasting the industrious and idle apprentice. In such ways this and the many other articles interspersed with poetry and serialized fiction collectively articulate the aesthetic presumptions and reading practices that inform the journal and affect its contributions.

With regard to the last of my concerns, reception, the difference is obvious: novels issued in book form as 'material wholes' on a single publication date get reviewed after the text has been written and printed; serial fictions, which appear periodically in small sections over months or years, tend to get reviewed as each installment is published. Thus amateur and professional readers of serial fiction are encouraged to speculate about the story and the characters, to project the future, and to offer the writer advice. Moreover, magazine fictions are, as we have seen in the case of *Oliver Twist*, frequently dramatized before completion. Readers often bombarded the producers of the periodical or the serial with suggestions for changes, some of which might be adopted, others resisted, so that the narrative, by a kind of back-formation, could revise its own previous trajectory in the course of subsequent installments. (A good example of this back-formation is Dickens's making amends in *David Copperfield* to the outraged original of Miss Mowcher by changing the character in the middle of serialization from a procuress into a nemesis; another proof of Maginn's thesis that outside the plot a villain may be exemplary.) Thus readers of serial fiction could exert influence on the narrative as it was being composed, something readers of books cannot usually do.

There is another way that serial fictions can be affected by serial responses. When a magazine serial becomes popular, it gets copied, imitated, pirated, plagiarized, often before the story has been completed in manuscript, much less in print. Such imitations and anticipations rob the original producers of the story of some of their revenue and some of their options, both for the story and for merchandising the product. Hence Dickens and others were deeply concerned, when *Oliver Twist* was being published, about passing legislation to strengthen copyright. Mark Rose reminds us that *plagiarism* is Latin for kidnapped – a plagiarist appropriates the offspring of a creator's body, the text, just as a kidnapper appropriates the offspring of a parent's body, the child.[37] Dickens resented the fact that his stories were taken over by others – his publishers, dramatists, rival authors, foreign publishing houses. He objected to losing money, to having his story mangled by incompetents, to finding his climaxes anticipated, and to enriching others by his imagination and industry. Dickens's resentment, which he shared with many authors and publishers, found its way into his story of an orphan boy whose identity is stolen at birth by a legion of kidnappers who take Oliver's story and make it their own. Oliver's half-brother Monks tries to ruin Oliver's mother's reputation by rewriting it, and to invoke those clauses in the paternal will that would disinherit Oliver by rewriting him as a criminal. Nancy stages a public scene in which Oliver is her naughty brother, and more privately tries to make him her son, a reinscription of his identity and relationship to Nancy that drives Sikes mad with jealousy. Giles and Brittles, the Maylies' servants, and the surgeon who attends the wounded boy, aver that Oliver is a thief. Even Mr Brownlow constructs many stories about Oliver, sometimes agreeing with Grimwig and Bumble, before he puts together the true narrative of Oliver's past. The story of *Oliver Twist*, therefore, is not just about the loss of personal and familial identity and legitimacy and inheritance. It also absorbs Dickens's and his age's pre-occupation with losing control over one's own story, having it kidnapped – plagiarized – by others. The very popularity of serials made them vulnerable to commercial highwaymen who hijacked them for their own profit.

We have looked at four areas of difference between novels designed to be produced as books and serialized fiction. Serials tend to be multiply authored, being written by the producers, editors, and other contributors to the magazine in which they appear. Serials have permeable generic boundaries, incorporating a miscellany of literary genres and appealing to readers in ways more dynamic and theatrical than contemplative. Serial fictions are topical both specifically and more generally; annotated editions for modern classroom use often pick up particular references but neglect the general ideological and aesthetic resonances. And serials interact, during the course of production, with a wide variety of readers whose responses impact successive installments. When magazine fictions are repackaged as books these points are often obscured or denied or canceled. The result, in case after case of which *Oliver Twist* is only one example, is a significant distortion of the history of the book. To respond to the interrogative title, 'When is a book not a book?', one answer is, 'When it is a serial.' And that can make all the difference.

Notes

First published in *Biblion* 4, 2 (Spring 1996): 35–63, this essay was adapted as an illustrated online course for FATHOM, now defunct, and subsequently revised and published under the title 'Dickens as Serial Author: /

Case of Multiple Identities', in *Nineteenth-Century Media and the Construction of Identities*, ed. Laurel Brake, Bill Bell, and David Finkelstein (Houndmills, Basingstoke: Palgrave, 2000), pp. 137–53.

1   See Richard B. Wollman, 'The "Press and the Fire": Print and Manuscript Culture in Donne's Circle', *SEL* 33, 1 (Winter 1993): 85–97.

2   George Saintsbury, *A History of Nineteenth Century Literature (1780–1895)* (New York: Macmillan, 1896; repr. 1913), p. 166; quoted by Laurel Brake in her essay, 'The "wicked *Westminster*", the *Fortnightly*, and Walter Pater's *Renaissance*', in *Literature in the Marketplace: Nineteenth-Century British Publishing and Reading Practices*, ed. John O. Jordan and Robert L. Patten, Cambridge Studies in Nineteenth-Century Literature and Culture (Cambridge: Cambridge University Press, 1995), pp. 289–305.

3   *OED*, s.v. 'book,' sense 3 *gen.*

4   Charles W. Traylen, catalogue 113 (1993), item 185.

5   Charles W. Traylen, catalogue 114 (1994), item 203.

6   John Windle, list 23, item 96.

7   Saintsbury, p. 166.

8   Mark Parker, 'The Institutionalization of a Burkean–Coleridgean Literary Culture', *SEL* 31, 4 (Autumn 1991): 693–711.

9   Brake, passim.

10   [Dr. Maginn], 'Prologue', *Bentley's Miscellany* 1 (January 1837): 2–6.

11   Kathryn Chittick, *Dickens and the 1830s* (Cambridge: Cambridge University Press, 1990), p. 102, says that Dickens may have written the second part of the 'Prologue', although the table of contents to *Bentley's Miscellany*, vol. 1, identifies Maginn as the sole author. Maginn was unquestionably the author of the passages just quoted.

12   In the 'Introduction' to his *Companion to 'Oliver Twist'* (Edinburgh: Edinburgh University Press, 1992), David Paroissien establishes the novel's principal ideological contexts and argues that 'a determination to respond to contemporary issues shaped Dickens's writing plans' (p. 5).

13   Chittick, pp. 92–113. Her chapter, in a book on all of Dickens's writings in the 1830s, is necessarily brief, but it is the best account of the magazine and of Bentley's proprietorship that we have.

14   Dickens's correspondence with Bentley through the first nine months of editing the *Miscellany* indicates some of the decisions he and his publisher made about which pieces to accept or reject, what to rewrite, and how to arrange the contents of numbers. See Charles Dickens, *Letters*, ed. Madeline House and Graham Storey, vol. 1 (Oxford: Clarendon Press, 1965).

15   Boz, 'Public Life of Mr. Tulrumble, Once Mayor of Mudfog', *Bentley's Miscellany* 1 (January 1837): 49–63, 63.

16   For illuminating discussions of the shaping of narratorial voice in Dickens, see Audrey Jaffe, *Vanishing Points: Dickens, Narrative, and the Subject of Omniscience* (Berkeley: University of California Press, 1991), and for Dickens's unsuccessful struggle to establish a coherent persona for his miscellany *Master Humphrey's Clock*, see Rosemary Mundhenk, 'Creative Ambivalence in Dickens's *Master Humphrey's Clock*', *SEL* 32, 4 (Autumn 1992): 645–61.

17   See Cruikshank's version of the origin of the novel in his letter to *The Times*, 30 December 1871.

18   Dickens, *Letters*, 1:224 (Dickens to Bentley, [?18 January 1837]).

19   Blanchard Jerrold, *The Life of George Cruikshank*, 2 vols. (London: Chatto and Windus, 1882), 1:223–24.

20   Q.Q.Q. [Samuel Warren], 'Dickens's American Notes for General Circulation', *Blackwood's Edinburgh Magazine* 52, 326 (December 1842): 783–801, 785.

21   Charles Dickens, *Oliver Twist*, chapter 17, *Bentley's Miscellany* 2 (November 1837), 437.

22   Dickens, *Oliver Twist*, Book 2, chapter 6, in *Bentley's Miscellany* 3 (April 1838): 313; chapter 28 in the revised 1846 numbering.

23   Jonathan E. Hill, 'Cruikshank, Ainsworth, and Tableau Illustration', *Victorian Studies* 23, 4 (Summer 1980): 429–59.

24   In different ways, the following authors have analyzed aspects of Dickens's theatricality: William Axton, *Circle of Fire: Dickens' Vision and Style and the Popular Victorian Theater* (Lexington: University of Kentucky Press, 1966); Edwin M. Eigner, *The Dickens Pantomime* (Berkeley: University of California Press, 1989); Robert Garis, *The Dickens Theatre, A Reassessment of the Novels* (Oxford: Clarendon Press, 1965); Linda K. Hughes and Michael Lund, *The Victorian Serial* (Charlottesville: University Press of Virginia, 1991); Martin Meisel, *Realizations: Narrative, Pictorial, and Theatrical Arts in Nineteenth-Century England* (Princeton: Princeton University Press, 1983); D. A. Miller, *The Novel and the Police* (Berkeley: University of California Press, 1988); and J. Hillis Miller, *Charles Dickens: The World of His Novels* (Cambridge MA: Harvard University Press, 1959).

25   See Richard Altick, *The Presence of the Present: Topics of the Day in the Victorian Novel* (Columbus: Ohio State University Press, 1991), Rowland McMaster, *Thackeray's Cultural Frame of Reference: Allusion in the Newcomes* (Basingstoke: Macmillan, 1990), and numerous articles by K. J. Fielding on Dickens's topicality published in, among other journals, the *Dickensian*.

26   Cf. *OED*, s. v. ideology, 2: 'The study of the way in which ideas are expressed in language.' Raymond Williams distinguishes between Napoleonic and Marxist usage, where ideology is abstract or false theory not based on experience and materiality, and a more neutral usage meaning the system of ideas appropriate to a particular class (*Keywords: A Vocabulary of Culture and Society* (New York: Oxford University Press, 1966), s. v. ideology).

27   Richard L. Stein, *Victoria's Year: English Literature and Culture, 1837–1838* (New York: Oxford University Press, 1987).

28   Martin J. Wiener, *Reconstructing the Criminal: Culture, Law, and Policy in England, 1830–1914* (Cambridge: Cambridge University Press, 1990), p. 11.

29   See G. K. Chesterton, *Charles Dickens* (New York: Dodd Mead and Co., 1906); J. Hillis Miller, 'The Fiction of Realism: *Sketches by Boz*, *Oliver Twist*, and Cruikshank's Illustrations', *Charles Dickens and George Cruikshank* (Los Angeles: William Andrews Clark Memorial Library, 1971); and Stein.

30   For more about the connections among these three 'Newgate' novels, see my *George Cruikshank's Life, Times, and Art*, vol. 2 (New Brunswick NJ: Rutgers University Press; Cambridge, England: Lutterworth Press, 1996).

31   Kelly J. Mays, 'The Disease of Reading and Victorian Periodicals', in Jordan and Patten, pp. 165–94.

32   Chittick, p. 96.

33   Dr. Maginn, 'Shakespeare Papers. – No. VIII. Iago', *Bentley's Miscellany* 5 (January 1839): 43–50.

34   Maginn, p. 43.

35   Maginn, p. 43.

36   Maginn, pp. 43–4.

37   Mark Rose, *Authors and Owners: The Invention of Copyright* (Cambridge MA: Harvard University Press, 1993).

Chapter 28

James L. W. West III

THE MAGAZINE MARKET

It's all a question of how much a writer can stand to compromise
— Elizabeth Nowell to Vardis Fisher (1935)

During the 1880s and 1890s, modern mass-circulation magazines came into being in the United States. For the author they provided an important outlet for work and a major source of income. Before 1880, serious authors had only a few respectable magazines in which they could publish – *Scribner*'s, *Harper*'s, the *Century*, and three or four others. Such magazines were usually allied with book publishing firms and addressed a relatively well-educated and genteel audience. They tended, in editorial philosophy, to pattern themselves after such British models as *Blackwood*'s, the *Edinburgh Review*, and the *Fortnightly*. In the 1890s and early 1900s, however, editors and publishers like Frank Munsey, S. S. McClure, John Brisben Walker, Edward Bok, and George Horace Lorimer began to produce mass-circulation magazines for a vast middle-to-lowbrow American readership that hitherto had not been addressed successfully. Advances in printing technology – especially in the reproduction of illustrations – made it possible to manufacture visually attractive magazines in huge printing runs and to price them at fifteen cents or a dime, well within reach of these new audiences. During this same period, America was making the final transition from a largely agricultural economy to a predominantly industrial one. Urbanization, growth in average income, better public education, and an increase in leisure time combined to produce a ready audience for magazines that published popular fiction and articles of general interest. During the first half of the twentieth century the American author could publish stories and serialize novels in an unprecedented number and variety of such magazines.

The great boom in national retailing and the growing importance of brand names made mass-circulation magazines the ideal advertising medium for American business. Indeed, it was the partnership between advertising and magazines that made possible the enormous growth of the periodical industry in the United States. Magazine publishers could sell their magazines for less than production costs and still take substantial profits from advertising revenues. Magazine publishers thus became intermediaries between specific groups of businessmen and homogeneous groups of readers. A publisher had to devise an editorial philosophy that would appeal to a particular body of readers and acquire material to fit that philosophy. Then space had to be sold to advertisers who wanted to present their products to that segment of the retail market. Almost every magazine was designed for a well-defined public, large or small, within the total population. As a consequence, the magazine publisher came to be a dealer both in reading matter and in consumer groups.

The great success of magazines such as the *Saturday Evening Post*, *Ladies' Home Journal*, *Redbook*, *Munsey's*, *Collier's*, *Woman's Home Companion*, the *Delineator*, *Cosmopolitan*, *McCall's*, *Liberty*, the various McClure publications, and many other magazines opened up high-paying markets for fiction writers and began to make the services of a good literary agent indispensable. Agents became brokers between magazines and authors, guiding writers to editors who could use their work and introducing editors to authors whose writing would fit the needs of their magazines. Not coincidentally, advertising agencies began to spring up in New York and in other publishing centers at about this time. Such agencies facilitated dealings at another 'interface': they brought businesses in touch with magazines that would reach their particular markets, helped these businesses with copy-writing and layout, and carried out elementary experiments in market analysis.[1]

The important role played by advertising in the magazine industry had an effect on content. A magazine like the *Smart Set*, which addressed a limited and sophisticated readership, could afford to be risqué or controversial because it charged a high price per copy and did not court advertising from name-brand national firms. The drawback for the author was that the *Smart Set* and other magazines of its kind paid low fees – from one hundred to four hundred dollars for a short story and even less for nonfiction. Writers who wanted to publish in mass-circulation magazines and enjoy the financial rewards and wide exposure of such publication had to be ready to tailor their work for those markets. That usually meant turning out a relatively bland product. Much of the material in mass-circulation magazines was written to order. Experienced authors like John P. Marquand and Eric Ambler would receive specific instructions from editors about subject matter, structure, tone, and length. The editor might even dictate the point of the article, story, or poem; the author would write to these specifications for an agreed-upon price, negotiated by the agent.

One writer who worked well within this system was Booth Tarkington, who for over thirty years received top prices for his short fiction and serials from national magazines – particularly from the *Saturday Evening Post*. The editorial philosophy of the *Post* was pro-business and pro-success. The hero of a typical *Post* story used his inborn resourcefulness to overcome difficulties and to achieve high standing in business and fulfillment in love. This philosophy originated in the personal beliefs of George Horace Lorimer, editor of the magazine, who liked to call himself 'The Old Hard-Boiled Self-Made Merchant'. Few deviations from pattern were allowed in the *Post* and an author had to be willing to conform in order to publish there.[2]

Most of the stories Tarkington submitted to the *Post* were readily and even enthusiastically accepted, and Lorimer regularly raised Tarkington's story fee in order to bind him more securely to the magazine. By 1939, Tarkington's price had reached four thousand dollars per story. The self-effacing Gentleman from Indiana was so embarrassed by Lorimer's generosity that he asked, in January 1939, to have his price *cut* – a suggestion that Lorimer laughed down. Tarkington sometimes had to alter his work for the *Post*, however. Political themes, for example, were *verboten*: the *Post* returned Tarkington's story 'Ripley, Try to Be Nice' in April 1939 because 'it is patent anti-New Deal propaganda and we have burnt our fingers on propaganda stories'. Tarkington removed the political references and sold the manuscript to the *Post* on a second try.[3]

Near the end of his life, Tarkington's fiction – heretofore relentlessly upbeat – began to take on slightly darker tones. His novel *The Man of the Family* was turned down for serialization by the *Post* in February 1940 because fiction editor Adelaide W. Neall thought it 'very depressing reading, and it is the fact that it is depressing up to the end that makes us doubt it as a serial for a popular magazine'. For almost the first time in the long history of his dealings with the *Post*, Tarkington was moved to protest. Correspondence followed with Neall about such subjects as 'reality' and 'life', but she was not persuaded. 'I am not prepared to argue with you when you say that none of our lives has a happy ending', she wrote him. Then she added with incontrovertible commercial logic: 'Isn't that perhaps why people want to read stories that suggest that perhaps some of the characters are going to find happiness?' Tarkington gave in and by early March 1940 was revising his serial. He still retained his imaginative facility and his knack for compromise; on 18 March, Neall accepted the revised novel for publication. In her congratulatory letter she told Tarkington, with no apparent irony: 'We have all been admiring the seemingly effortless skill with which you have repaired the weaknesses – from a serial point of view – in MAN OF THE FAMILY.' Neall was not quite finished with the novel, however. When she sent galleys to Tarkington in April, she directed that he cut 'hells or damns or other swear words', all of which she had queried in the margins. He could have a few, she noted, but only a few.[4]

Even a willingness to compromise would not always guarantee a sale, especially if the material in a prospective serial involved a woman of doubtful moral behavior. Zona Gale's novel *Light Woman* dealt with an actress who refused to marry the man with whom she had been living because, after the fashion of the time, she was opposed to the idea of marriage. The manuscript had another drawback as well – it contained a suicide. *Ladies' Home Journal* turned down *Light Woman* in 1934 as did *Cosmopolitan*, even after Gale had offered to change her ending and have her heroine marry the man. Edwin Balmer at *Redbook* stalled, then asked for a new ending; Gale rewrote her conclusion, but Balmer still rejected *Light Woman*. Through Paul Revere Reynolds the novel was offered in succession to *Woman's Home Companion*, *Pictorial Weekly*, *Harper's*, *Scribner's*, *McCall's*, the *Delineator*, *Colliers*, and even the *New York Herald Tribune*, which sometimes printed first-run serials. At that point, Reynolds gave up and returned the manuscript to Gale, who, through a friend, played a long shot and sent the novel to *Liberty*. That magazine, to Gale's great relief, bought the serial rights. Gale had learned a hard lesson about the kind of behavior expected of heroines in popular magazine fiction.[5]

Money from the magazines was extremely important to writers before 1940. Indeed, they often made a good deal more from serial rights than from book royalties. Between 1919 and 1936, F. Scott Fitzgerald earned some $225,784 for his magazine fiction as opposed to only $66,588 for his novels. Theodore Dreiser, in the early 1920s, was still relying heavily on fees for magazine work to meet his day-to-day expenses. Dreiser was by then in his early fifties and was the author of five novels, including *Sister Carrie*, *Jennie Gerhardt*, and *The Financer*, but those books brought him little in the way of dependable income. And Edith Wharton, to take one final example, left Scribners for Appleton in part because the latter house offered more profitable arrangements for serializing her novels in magazines.[6] Serial money, collected in advance, could make it possible to complete a book. A dependable writer whose work was in demand could often contract for serial rights on the basis of a manuscript that was only about one-fourth complete. If an editor liked the finished chapters and the accompanying synopsis of the rest of the story, the magazine would buy the serial rights for a stated figure, payable in installments. An advance of perhaps one-third of the money would be made initially. The author lived on these funds while composing subsequent chapters and collected further checks as later chapters were delivered against specific deadlines. Often the early chapters were running in the magazine before the final chapters had been composed. When these last chapters were delivered, the author received the remainder of the money and was free to begin revising the novel for book publication.

Frequently, however, the author had to pay an artistic price for serial publication. Some novels lend themselves more readily to serialization than others: an episodic story with a chronologically arranged plot, for example, can easily be presented in coherent segments over a five- or six-month period. On the other hand, a novel written within a twenty-four-hour time frame or a narrative with frequent flashbacks and dislocations in chronology will not appear to best advantage in monthly installments. *A Farewell to Arms*, for example, is a relatively straightforward narrative; it was a simple matter for *Scribner's Magazine* to serialize the book in six segments from May to October of 1929.

Tender Is the Night, by contrast, has a complex time frame and employs a major flashback sequence that takes up the middle third of the book. By splitting this three-part novel into four installments, *Scribner's Magazine* made the potentially confusing narrative structure quite difficult to follow. Fitzgerald was convinced that most reviewers of *Tender* had read it as a serial and that they had gotten a negative first impression of the book in that medium.

Authors who were interested in selling serial rights obviously needed to write their novels with serialization in mind from the beginning, taking care to structure the narrative in installments suitable for monthly magazine publication. James Boyd's first novel, a historical adventure about the Revolutionary War entitled *Drums*, had not been written in this fashion, however, and Robert Bridges, editor of *Scribner's Magazine*, turned it down for magazine publication in 1924 because of Boyd's technique of delineating character. 'The very excellence of your method which reproduces the character through a succession of episodes, rather than through the development of a strong story, seems to me to stand in the way of that impelling interest which is necessary in a serial', wrote Bridges to the young author. In composing subsequent novels, Boyd took care to tailor his manuscripts for the serial market. For example, when he sent the first installment of *Roll River* to Maxwell Perkins ten years later, he noted: 'The action is sustained, and the break is logical. I have an idea that the succeeding installments will not only be briefer but more rapid in movement and therefore satisfactory from a serialization standpoint'.[7]

Concessions to taste and decorum also had to be made. *Scribner's Magazine* had to persuade Hemingway to omit numerous words and lines from *A Farewell to Arms* because they were judged too strong for magazine presentation.[8] Pregnancy, even within wedlock, was a delicate subject: Fitzgerald's 1926 novella 'The Rich Boy' was made fit for appearance in *Redbook* by a bumbling editor who removed from the text, without Fitzgerald's permission, all references to the character Paula Hagerty's swollen shape during her pregnancy. One can imagine the confusion in readers' minds when Paula dies in childbirth a few pages later, without its having been mentioned that she is with child. By 1939 Fitzgerald had learned to anticipate such problems. While drafting *The Last Tycoon*, he realized that some of his material would be potentially censorable. He wrote Kenneth Littauer, editor of *Collier's*, that he would compose the central seduction scene two ways: 'Now we have a love affair between Stahr and Thalia, an immediate, dynamic, unusual, physical love affair – and I will write it so that you can publish it. At the same time I will send you a copy of how it will appear in book form somewhat stronger in tone.'[9]

Some authors saw serialization as undignified. Ellen Glasgow, who was much concerned about her literary reputation, all but forbade her agent Paul Revere Reynolds from offering serial rights for her novels to mass-circulation magazines.[10] More business-minded authors simply saw serialization as a source of additional income. In answer to a query from agent Carl Brandt about a serial feeler from England, John P. Marquand sent a simple two-word telegram: 'HOW MUCH?' An author, however, often lost some control over the text in return for serial money. After purchasing North American serial rights to Marquand's *Point of No Return* for sixty thousand dollars, *Ladies' Home Journal* made it clear to Brandt that some cutting and editorial rewriting might be done. 'It is understood', they wrote, 'that we must of necessity be the final judges as to what goes into the magazine.'[11] Even when novels had been written to specifications, authors could end up with maimed texts, especially if they were not close enough to New York to oversee publication. In 1921, English novelist Arnold Bennett wrote angrily from London to Eric Schuler of the Authors League that the *Delineator* had butchered the first four serial installments of *Mr. Prohack*, a one-hundred-thousand-word novel that he had written for the magazine, as directed, in seven installments of some fourteen thousand words each. From the first four installments, totaling fifty-seven thousand words, the *Delineator* had cut more than twenty-six thousand words. Bennett was furious, but there was nothing he could do.[12] A year later, Fitzgerald's second novel, *The Beautiful and Damned*, was treated similarly by Carl Hovey at *Metropolitan Magazine*. Fitzgerald was unhappy, but the only satisfaction he received was in seeing the uncut text published in book form by Scribner's after the serial run was over.[13]

Authors who wrote regularly for mass-circulation magazines sometimes found themselves typecast by previous material. After the great success of her two-volume *Early Life of Abraham Lincoln* in 1900, Ida Tarbell found that there was virtually no way she could stop writing about Lincoln, so insistent were magazine editors that she do follow-up articles on incidents from his life that she had not treated in her biography. People who had known Lincoln or had observed him would contact her with requests that she write up this or that incident; sometimes Tarbell would pay a percentage of her magazine fee to the source of the material. She probably could have made her way easily for the rest of her career by manufacturing little else but spin-off articles on Lincoln, but she very much wanted to work with different material. So eager was she to write on other subjects that she proposed to Reynolds a lengthy article on 'the rise of the hookless fastener' – to us, the zipper. It was a 'rather long and dramatic story', she assured him.[14]

Stephen Vincent Benét's short story 'The Devil and Daniel Webster', published first in the *Saturday Evening Post* on 24 October 1936, brought wide notice to its author and was quickly anthologized in numerous high school textbooks. The story was also adapted for radio and the movies; later a stage play and a television production were mounted. Benét found a ready market thereafter for short fiction based on incidents in American history, but eventually he tired of the material. He complained in a letter to his agent, Carl Brandt, and asked that Brandt try to interest magazine editors in something else. Brandt, however, did not seem to understand the problem: 'I am much interested in the spread of your patriotic writing', he wrote Benét. 'In all seriousness, I don't see how you can get out of it or think you should.'[15] Still, Benét felt trapped by his own success with 'Daniel Webster'.

Something similar happened to William Faulkner in his dealings with *Scribner's Magazine* during the early 1930s. Faulkner sold a cut-down version of 'Spotted Horses' to *Scribner's* in February 1931 and thereafter had difficulty selling them anything else for a time, so determined were they to have another Flem Snopes story. K. C. Crichton, assistant editor of the magazine, wrote Faulkner, 'We regret that it has not been possible to accept more of the stories you have offered us, but on Flem Snopes we are clear. He is our character and we think that in your hands he will become one of the great characters of literature'. Faulkner was probably flattered, but unfortunately for *Scribner's* he had found a higher-paying market for his Flem Snopes material – the *Saturday Evening Post*. In the meantime he sent other stories to *Scribner's*, including 'Rose of Lebanon', 'Idyll in the Desert', and 'All the Dead Pilots', but all were turned down. 'We have become so hipped on the thought of Flem Snopes', wrote Crichton, 'that we are confining all our prayers in the hope that George Horace Lorimer will be struck with lightning just at the time those pieces of yours reach him.'[16]

Fitzgerald must have felt similarly trapped in 1937 when, down on his luck and living in a seedy hotel in Tryon, North Carolina, he was desperately attempting to manufacture amusing love stories, in his old style, for the *Post*. Fitzgerald was heavily in debt to Charles Scribner's Sons, his publisher, and to Harold Ober, his literary agent. He had been in debt before – indeed it was almost a perpetual condition for him after 1920 but he had always been able to rescue himself by writing short fiction for the *Post* and other mass-circulation magazines. In fact he had even tried to have himself declared 'virtually an employee' of the *Post* in 1932 for income tax purposes.[17] By 1937, however, Fitzgerald had lost the knack of turning out salable material for the popular fiction market. This situation was caused in part by his inability to write convincingly about his prototypical Fitzgerald heroine. Young, beautiful, and willfully independent, she had been a feature of nearly all of his magazine fiction since 1919. By 1937, however, Fitzgerald was no longer much interested in her, and his repeated attempts to recreate her in his post-1935 stories were unsuccessful. These stories are puzzling: the familiar matter of his earlier *Post* fiction is there, but the manner is lacking. The heroines are curiously diminished versions of their more engaging, vital sisters from Fitzgerald's earlier stories. As a working author, however, he had to meet the demands of his market, which, as he interpreted it, still wanted his heroine.

In March 1937, living in the Tryon hotel, the weary Fitzgerald began a story of young love entitled 'A Full Life'. The manuscript opened with an improbable incident in which his heroine, named Gwen Davis, donned an inflatable flying suit and floated out the window of a Manhattan skyscraper. This was to be the first occurrence of a motif Fitzgerald wanted to work into the story, a motif of flying and falling. Gwen flies and falls first from the skyscraper window, later from the deck of an ocean liner, and finally from a circus cannon. Had he been able to inject his writing with a suitably light tone, Fitzgerald might have brought off this little fantasy, but as one reads through the surviving draft of the story, one sees that his heart was not in the work. Plotting is artificial, characters are wooden, and motivations are unclear.

About midway through the draft, Fitzgerald apparently realized what was happening and, in disgust, worked a freakish detail into the story. He quite literally filled his heroine with dynamite. Gwen leaves her childhood home because she does not want to 'raise the roof'. Later she marries the son of a gunpowder manufacturer because she has 'always belonged to him'. Still later she becomes a circus daredevil who makes her living by being shot from a cannon. Gwen's performing name is symptomatic of Fitzgerald's dislike for her: he dubs her 'The Human Shell' – and indeed she is an empty character. Discouraged by his inability to bring his dynamite-filled heroine to life and tired of trying to manufacture yet another light romance for the *Post*, Fitzgerald made a macabre private gesture in his manuscript. He blew Gwen up. The explosion killed a man standing next to her and was heard as far away as New York City. This grisly little tale reveals much about Fitzgerald's state of mind during his famous Crack-Up period. He felt victimized by his previous success, locked into writing one kind of story about one type of character – a heroine about whom he no longer cared.[18]

Many authors of novels and short fiction chafed under the formal and structural limitations imposed on them by mass-circulation magazines. They disliked the simplistic, undeviating pattern of the 'formula' story: it began typically with action or dialogue in order to capture the attention of a reader paging through an issue; it was rigidly plotted and moved relentlessly toward an artificial climax; and it ended with a 'final suspiration', often faintly saccharine in tone, usually in the advertising pages at the rear of the magazine.[19] Some writers (Sherwood Anderson, for example) could not adapt to these limitations. Other authors – Fitzgerald, Faulkner, and Dreiser among them – learned to work more or less within the formula and eventually turned out some very good short fiction for the big-audience slicks. Writing for high-paying magazines, however, was not a predict-able business. Editors and staff readers changed with some frequency at the various magazines, and editorial requirements fluctuated. Writing for the magazines took patience, adaptability, and a thick skin. There was no sheet of dos and don'ts for prospective authors to follow; length, subject matter, tone, language, plot, characterization – all had to be negotiated by a complicated system of trial and error, inference and suggestion, submission, rejection, and submission. The work could be frustrat-ing, but the potential financial rewards were large. In fact, most American authors before World War I saw the magazine market as virtually their only source of big money. After the war, however, different ways of publishing one's work, or adapting it to other media, began to emerge. Books could be serialized or abridged or distributed through book clubs or reprinted as paperbacks; story material could be adapted for presentation on the radio, stage, screen, or lecture circuit. Even translation rights could yield significant amounts of money for some books. The author set about tapping these new sources of income and learning how to exploit the full earning potential of what was now beginning to be called a 'literary property'.

Notes

1   Theodore Peterson, *Magazines in the Twentieth Century*, 2d ed. (Urbana: University of Illinois Press, 1964), chaps. 1–5; James Playsted Wood, *Magazines in the United States*, 2d ed. (New York: Ronald Press, 1956), chaps. 9–11, 13, 20–21.

2   John Tebbel, *George Horace Lorimer and the* Saturday Evening Post (Garden City, N.Y.: Doubleday, 1948); 'George Horace Lorimer', in James Playsted Wood, *The Curtis Magazines* (New York: Ronald Press, 1971). In 1901–2, Lorimer wrote an extraordinarily popular epistolary series for the *Post* entitled 'Letters from a Self-made Merchant to His Son' – hence the sobriquet. Also see Bernard Berelson and Patricia J. Salter, 'Majority and Minority Americans: An Analysis of Magazine Fiction', *Public Opinion Quarterly* 10 (1946): 168–90; and Patricke Johns-Heine and Hans H. Gerth, 'Values in Mass Periodical Fiction, 1921–1940', *Public Opinion Quarterly* 13 (1949): 105–13.

3   Adelaide W. Neall (*Post* fiction editor) to Tarkington, 17 April 1939, Tarkington Papers, Princeton University, Princeton, N.J. Literary feuding was also not allowed. In March 1930, Sherwood Anderson sent an article on cotton-mill workers to John Hall Wheelock at *Scribner's Magazine*. The manuscript, entitled 'Labor and Sinclair Lewis', was in part an attack on the author of *Main Street* for his satirical portraits of life in small American towns. Wheelock found Anderson's treatment of Lewis too vehement and personal and required Anderson to rewrite in order to direct his criticisms more generally against a group of anti-small-town writers. (Wheelock to Anderson, 19 March 1930, Scribner Archive, Princeton University, Princeton, N.J.)

4   Neall to Tarkington, 12 and 19 February, 18 March, and 22 April 1940, Tarkington Papers, Princeton University, Princeton, N.J.

5   Zona Gale files, P. R. Reynolds Papers, Butler Library, Columbia University, New York, esp. Reynolds to Gale, 6 September 1934.

6   *As Ever, Scott Fitz – Letters between F. Scott Fitzgerald and His Literary Agent Harold Ober, 1919–1940*, ed. Matthew J. Bruccoli and Jennifer McCabe Atkinson (Philadelphia: Lippincott, 1972), p. xviii; Thomas P. Riggio's introduction to Dreiser's *American Diaries, 1920–1926*, ed. Thomas P. Riggio *et al.* (Philadelphia: University of Pennsylvania Press, 1982), p. 15; Charles A. Madison, 'Charles Scribner and Edith Wharton', in *Irving to Irving: Author–Publisher Relations, 1800–1974* (New York: Bowker, 1974), pp. 140–41.

7   Bridges to Boyd, 13 May 1924; Boyd to Perkins, 20 March 1934, Scribner Archive. In his letter to Perkins, refers to *Roll River* by its working title, 'The Dark Shore'.

8   Michael S. Reynolds, *Hemingway's First War: The Making of* A Farewell to Arms (Princeton: Princeton University Press, 1976), chap. 3.

9   James L. W. West III and J. Barclay Inge, 'F. Scott Fitzgerald's Revision of "The Rich Boy" ', *Proof* 5 (1976): 133; Fitzgerald to Littauer, 29 September 1939, *Correspondence of F. Scott Fitzgerald*, ed. Matthew J. Bruccoli and Margaret M. Duggan (New York: Random House, 1980), p. 547.

10   James B. Colvert, ed., 'Agent and Author: Ellen Glasgow's Letters to Paul Revere Reynolds', *Studies in Bibliography* 14 (1961): 177–96.

11   Marquand to Brandt (cable), 7 December 1948; Hugh M. Kahler (*Ladies' Home Journal*) to Carl Brandt, 21 September 1948, Marquand Collection, Beinecke Library, Yale University, New Haven, Conn.

12   Bennett to Schuler, 14 October 1921, Authors League file, Henry Holt Papers, Princeton University, Princeton, N.J.

13   See Arthur Mizener, *The Far Side of Paradise*, rev. ed. (Boston: Houghton Mifflin, 1963), p. 158.

14   Tarbell to Reynolds, 22 August 1927, P. R. Reynolds Papers.

15   Brandt to Benét, 27 June 1941, Benét Collection, Beinecke Library, Yale University, New Haven, Conn.

16   Crichton to Faulkner, 23 July and 6 August 1931, in James B. Meriwether, ed., 'Faulkner's Correspondence with *Scribner's Magazine*', *Proof* 3 (1973): 268–69.

17   Fitzgerald to Ober, ca. 21 April 1932, *As Ever Scott Fitz*, pp. 190–93.

18   See James L. W. West III, 'Fitzgerald Explodes His Heroine', *Princeton University Library Chronicle* 49 (1988): 159–65.

19   Henry Seidel Canby, 'Free Fiction', *Atlantic Monthly* 116 (July 1915): 60–68.

Chapter 29

Jayne Marek

TOWARD INTERNATIONAL COOPERATION
The literary editing of H.D. and Bryher

The activities of H.D. and of Bryher in literary editing and publishing during the rise of modernism deserve careful examination. Both women affected modernist thought in their contributions to the appreciation of cinematic art as well as through their support for avant garde literature. This chapter treats these two women in tandem because their long-term association led to work that was historically intertwined. . . .

H.D.'s literary work during her first several years in London represents a critical period in her artistic development. During the years following her first appearance in *Poetry* (1913), H.D. became known as the 'premier Imagist'; less well known, however, is the part she played in literary editing and publishing.[1] A good portion of H.D.'s time in England was spent planning the three Imagist anthologies of 1915–17, along with Amy Lowell and Richard Aldington, working with (and without) Aldington at the *Egoist*, and preparing the two Poets' Translation Series with Aldington for the Egoist Press. H.D.'s critical work, in reviews and in editorial choices, connected a sense of the artist's spiritual integrity with new investigations of form and helped to enunciate the parameters of modern thought.

Although Bryher published many critical comments and promoted other writers in a number of ways, her multifaceted support of publishing activities has been largely overlooked. She began her involvement by assisting with production and financial support for the Poets' Translation Series of the Egoist Press. Following her marriage to Robert McAlmon, she supported his publication of Contact Editions, which brought out Hemingway's first book and Stein's *The Making of Americans*, among other innovative works. H.D. brought Bryher to the *Egoist*, the Egoist Press, and other literary connections, and Bryher provided H.D. with years of financial support and an entrée into the world of cinema through *Close Up*. The articles that the two women wrote for that magazine during 1927–33 reflect the aesthetic, social, and political issues raised by the new cinematic art. The long association between the two allowed both to work as writers, editors, and critics helping to push forward the frontiers of twentieth-century thought.

H.D.'s connections with Amy Lowell and with the *Egoist* initiated an important segment of her career. At that time, H.D. was busy and influential within a significant circle of young writers in England. She shared in the spirit of comradeship that characterized the small group of poets in London including herself, her husband Aldington, Ezra Pound, F. S. Flint, and John Cournos. This sharing of mutual excitement over new forms and ideas carried through Lowell's visit to England in

1913 and the appearance of the anthology Pound had compiled, *Des Imagistes* (1914), which aroused some discussion in the United States, although it was less successful in England. Disagreement arose, however, between Pound and the others over what 'Imagism' meant. The argument reached a breaking point during Lowell's return trip in 1914, when Pound provoked Lowell at a dinner party. Lowell and the Aldingtons, by this time good friends, preferred to continue in the spirit of sharing work rather than to reject such poets as John Gould Fletcher and D. H. Lawrence, as Pound would have done.[2] Therefore, when Lowell proposed another anthology based on more democratic ideas – each poet would help decide who would be included, with equitable space allotted to all – Pound refused to participate. As a result, H.D. and Aldington became the chief liaisons between the English group and Lowell.

H.D.'s correspondence during this time demonstrates the confluence of her personal and literary priorities: she was intent on preserving the spirit of collaboration intended for these volumes, she was stimulated by her exchanges with Lowell over possible inclusion and alteration of poems, and she trusted Lowell's judgment and discretion both to see to details of publication and to serve as H.D.'s surrogate in criticizing Aldington's work. In all of these functions, H.D. emphasized the democracy and cooperation that had been missing from *Des Imagistes* and that she supported despite her mixed feelings about the poems included in *Some Imagist Poets*.

Initially, H.D.'s distress over the contretemps with Pound caused her to urge Lowell to dispense with the word 'Imagist' in the title of the 1915 anthology.[3] Pound earlier had made a similar suggestion, but from a desire to protect a movement he considered his own; his suggestion was that Lowell title the book *Vers Libre* in order to detach the term 'Imagisme' from the work of people he did not consider deserving.[4] To H.D., however, the matter carried quite a different import. She wrote to Lowell in December 1914 that she, Aldington, and Flint wanted to 'quit' any association with Pound and offered a significant replacement title, *The Six*.[5] The letter shows impatience with the limitations implied by Pound's dictatorial definitions of 'Imagism'. To H.D., cooperative exchange was more important than the immediate recognition that might be gained by publishing a new book under the Imagist title. In fact, H.D.'s response suggests that she saw the dissent caused by Pound's authoritarianism as more inhibiting than any mutual criticism by the poets could be.

Since H.D. had no intention of being constrained or labeled by what she had written in previous years, she felt no possessiveness about the Imagist name. Indeed, part of the point of maintaining mutual contact between the poets was to help them all mature in their art. H.D.'s letters show her efforts to prepare and publish current poetry and to draw her friends together (especially after the disagreement with Pound) into a stimulating and supportive group. With Lowell back in the United States, H.D. began at once on the preparations for the 1915 volume, assembling materials, sending them to Lowell, and following up with comments and minor emendations.[6] By April 1915, she wrote Lowell that she was taking much pleasure in the book and expressed hope that the anthologies would continue; she was sending poems and articles by herself and Aldington, which Lowell tried to place in American publications while H.D. circulated Lowell's books among her friends.[7]

At one point, H.D. expressed regret over the distance between herself and Lowell, which prevented her sharing fully in the duties of their collaboration: '[It] is very hard arranging things, isn't it [sic], from both sides of the pond? . . . I wish we could share the burden of work, but this old pond does hinder.'[8] Yet physical distance from the machinery of publication forced H.D. to leave some of those details to be resolved as Lowell thought appropriate, which suggests that H.D. had been designated to represent to Lowell the entire group of poets in England. In fact, the English poets may have felt the need to shield themselves from Lowell's powerful personality as they had from Pound's, despite the democratic nature of their undertaking. In this case, H.D. was their diplomat, faced with the delicate problem of making her own and the other London writers' intentions clear while preserving the mutuality of decision-making. When, for instance, H.D. deferred to Lowell the important decision about the final arrangement of H.D.'s poems in the 1916 volume, she indicated that she expected Lowell and Fletcher to work together – an urging apparently intended to preserve the cooperative nature of the volume, even if at H.D.'s expense.[9]

H.D.'s efforts in soliciting contributions and in smoothing the collaboration for the series of anthologies may be considered to account for the existence of the volumes at all. In 1914–15, certainly, the schism with Pound could have interfered with the publication of much good work had H.D. not acted as mediator. This mediation provided some of the important writers of that time with a means of communicating among themselves as well as a way to reach a larger public, while the anthologies provided Lowell as well as H.D. with a means of staying in contact with literary developments that they both found stimulating.

In the meanwhile, H.D. had become involved with the *Egoist* through Aldington's position as assistant editor, which began in 1913. As Cyrena Pondrom notes, H.D. seems to have taken 'an active part in the editing of the *Egoist* even before Aldington's departure for military service', sending Flint a review copy of Lowell's book *Sword Blades and Poppy Seeds* in November 1914 from the *Egoist*'s editorial offices.[10] H.D. saw Harriet Shaw Weaver, the paper's editor, on a regular basis and certainly had been reading some of the submissions.[11] In fact, she solicited submissions for that magazine as she did for the Imagist anthologies. One result of H.D.'s assistance at the *Egoist* was the special number on Imagism that appeared May 1, 1915.

The combined boost of *Some Imagist Poets* and two special numbers of important little magazines helped to establish Imagism in modernist history, culminating more than two years of scattered notices more firmly than Pound's irregular association had. The March 1913 issue of *Poetry* had included two comments signed by Flint and Pound – Flint's brief outline of the history of Imagism, followed by Pound's well-known 'A Few Don'ts by an Imagiste', which sketched the aesthetic tenets of the group. A few other mentions of Imagism had appeared before, for example Alice Corbin Henderson's review of *Des Imagistes* in *Poetry* for October 1914. Mention of Imagism in the *New Freewoman* (precursor of the *Egoist*) in August of that year had been substantially a summary of the articles that had appeared in *Poetry*.[12] Imagism had gained more significant exposure through Lowell's acquaintance with Margaret Anderson, editor of the *Little Review*, which in July 1914 printed Charles Ashleigh's review of the 'Des Imagistes' issue of the *Glebe*; subsequently, the *Little Review* published numerous poems by Lowell, articles discussing vers libre in November and December 1914 and April 1915, and Aldington's article about H.D. in March 1915.

The Imagist number of the *Egoist* for May 1, 1915, offered new poetry by Richard Aldington, H.D., F. S. Flint, D. H. Lawrence, Marianne Moore, and May Sinclair, and included a number of articles addressing the history, aesthetics, and poets of Imagism in more depth than in any previous publication.[13] The issue opened, however, with a lengthy philosophical editorial by *Egoist* founder Dora Marsden, and H.D., who had helped put the issue together, found herself again acting as mediator, this time by placating Lowell. Lowell had agreed to distribute the paper in America and had planned that the issue would coincide with the appearance of *Some Imagist Poets* and with a lecture that Lowell would give to the Poetry Society of America (Hanscombe and Smyers 202). Also, Lowell had arranged for the May 1915 issue of the *Little Review* to include pieces by various Imagists as well as her and John Gould Fletcher's collaborative review of *Some Imagist Poets* (under the pseudonym 'George Lane').[14] After all her work to help establish Imagism in the United States, Lowell was upset about Marsden's article, which Lowell regarded (probably with justice) as a barrier to sales. H.D. attempted to alleviate Lowell's displeasure and redirect her attention to the positive force of the issue: 'R. has done his best for that blooming old Egoist – though I know how disappointed you & Fletcher will be to see Miss M. on the first page. I assure you we both fought hard enough – but

Miss Weaver runs the paper for Dora Marsden – swears by her – and R. is after all only sub-edito
He did work hard. I think the number a great success but for that! – Trust you will!'[15] By stressir
the 'great success' of the number, H.D. encouraged Lowell that the English side of the promotic
was nevertheless continuing well. Considering that many of the Imagists were English, this was a
important reassurance.

The Imagist number of the *Egoist* offered the first extended and collective examination
Imagism and amended what had gone before in several senses. All six of the poets appearing in *Son
Imagist Poets* received detailed critical comment, which drew attention to their particular styles an
thus helped to demonstrate the variety in this form of writing, as distinct from the directive tone
Pound's 'A Few Don'ts'. In addition, the issue included comments that were judicious in tone rathe
than directive or promotional, such as Harold Monro's substantial article placing Imagism's roots
'most of the more important English theorists of the past' as well as in the younger French poet
and located in *Some Imagist Poets* 'a transitionary point in the Imagist movement', particularly fc
H.D.[16] The cumulative effect of the poetry and articles in this issue reiterated these writer
differences from Pound without homogenizing Imagism.

Lowell's continuing support for the Imagists 'promised . . . that there would be a future',
Barbara Guest's phrase, and it is clear that H.D. appreciated the exposure that she and other write:
stood to gain by book publication in America, whether or not Imagism itself continued after th
anthologies as a viable concern.[17] H.D.'s reasons for continuing with the anthologies had less to c
with her own personal success than with her hope that certain kinds of art would stand against th
divisions of a world at war.

H.D.'s caretaking of much of the business for the anthologies in England included distributir
some of the royalties, and in this point – seemingly a minor one – one sees an additional impetus fc
the work. H.D. felt great concern over the well-being of her friends and tried to provide for ther
through the means she had at hand. H.D. herself often was short of funds, like the others in he
circle, yet in February 1916 she offered to share some of the money Lowell had sent her (calling
'royalties') with Flint and Lawrence, saying she had already given some of it to others.[18] In sub
sequent months, when Lawrence was suffering the effects of illness, discouragement, and censo:
ship, she suggested that Lowell send money to the Lawrences directly.[19] Even when in 1917 H.I
agreed with Lowell that the anthologies had served their purpose, she punningly regretted the loss
the '*collective*' work'.[20] Certainly Lowell's regular remittances cheered a number of writers, H.I
among them, during the privations of wartime.

[. . .]

H.D.'s vision of hope and mutual responsibility, expressed privately in her letters as well
publicly in her collaborative efforts to promote the Imagists, also appears in her three reviews
books of poetry for the *Egoist*. It is clear from these pieces for the *Egoist* – her first publishe
comments about her aesthetic values – that she takes quite seriously the issue of the artist
responsibility to society as well as to beauty, clarity, and integrity. She expresses her belief that a
can stand against the selfishness and waste of war. She also indicates her dissatisfaction with author
tative literary standards of the time. Her own interest in modern and avant garde work informed he
readings of the modifications in imagery, language, form, and tradition she found in Mariann
Moore, Charlotte Mew, and John Gould Fletcher, the subjects of her reviews.

Her first critical piece to appear in print was an appreciation of Moore in August 1916. Th
was the earliest full review to herald one of modernism's greatest poets, predating by nearly tw
years Pound's article about Moore in the *Little Review* in 1918, which has been called the first critic
notice of Moore.[21] The two poets' reacquaintance when Moore sent poems to the magazine in 191
led to years of friendship and artistic benefit for Moore, H.D., and Bryher, as these women eager
read, commented upon, and tried to find publication for each other's work.[22]

[. . .]

Having found an individual avant garde sensibility in Moore, H.D. capitalized on the *Egoist*'s opportunity and asked Moore to send her critical articles. 'The Accented Syllable' was printed in October of that year.[23] Just before it appeared, H.D. wrote in a letter of September 1916, 'Miss Weaver, I think I wrote you, liked your article very much. So please do the comparison of Poe, Byron + Bacon. I do wish that the magazine could pay for contributions! It is very generous of you to send us your work.'[24] Although the proposed article on Poe, Byron, and Bacon did not appear in the *Egoist*, H.D. continued to present Moore's work to other writers she knew and began exchanging ideas with Moore about the possibility of publishing a book of Moore's poetry. In the September 1916 letter, H.D. noted that May Sinclair, who had 'a certain amount of influence', was interested in Moore's poetry, and that if John Cournos, another friend, failed in placing 'the book', H.D. would pass the manuscript on to Sinclair; she also mentioned that Aldington wanted to write an article on Moore, although he could not 'work at all now . . . [He] wanted to write on you after he read the book.'[25] These efforts on behalf of Moore's book were occurring at the same time that H.D. was working on her contributions for the first Poets' Translation Series and the Imagist anthologies with Amy Lowell, to say nothing of her own poetry and her critical work for the *Egoist*. H.D. continued to show her initiative and extend her experience by undertaking these promotional activities.

[. . .]

H.D.'s early literary editing and criticism may be read on several levels. On one hand, her collaboration with Lowell and the other Imagists continued to promote the spirit of exchange that had informed her first years in London. In this sense, H.D.'s publishing work may be seen as a means of self-assertion against the many troubles in her marriage and her life during wartime, as well as a positive expression of her aesthetic vision.[26] Most importantly, the different venues in which H.D. was able to present her aesthetic ideas enabled her to affect and effect modern writing in a number of ways. It was very important to her to be able to encourage and publish other writers, to share ideas and criticisms, to draw attention to writers whose work she thought worthy, and to elucidate her disagreements with other poets' writings. That she was so successful in presenting her own work and that of her contemporaries allows us to read H.D.'s critical and editorial work as an enactment of her vision of harmony arising from dissonance.

When the literary editorship of the *Egoist* passed to Eliot's hands in 1917, H.D. expressed little regret because her attention had been increasingly captured by war and personal problems. She left behind solid accomplishment in presenting and analyzing avant garde writing, and took with her several years' experience in editing, reviewing, and planning, which clearly informed her subsequent critical writing and publication.

The year after H.D. left the *Egoist*, she met Bryher. Already an admirer of H.D. and the Imagists through reading Amy Lowell's *Tendencies in Modern American Poetry* (1917), Bryher had obtained H.D.'s address through Clement Shorter, editor of Sir John Ellerman's the *Sphere* and husband of Bryher's friend Doris Banfield (Guest 105). When the two young women met in Cornwall in July 1918, one of their earliest topics of discussion was Lowell. Bryher became an enthusiastic reader of Lowell's poetry, and like H.D. entered into a correspondence with her that lasted until Lowell's death. Whereas H.D. appreciated Lowell's interest in her work, as demonstrated in the Imagist anthologies and *Tendencies in Modern American Poetry*, and kept Lowell informed of the plans for the Poets' Translation Series, Bryher carried on long discussions of literary matters in her letters to Lowell and sought her opinion about original essays and poems. Lowell, in fact, provided a foreword for Bryher's first novel, *Development* (1920).

Bryher's involvement with literary publishing and patronage reflected her consistent concern for high-quality, innovative writing. One of her early projects arose from her association with the Poets' Translation Series of the Egoist Press – a connection forged through H.D. – for which she was invited to translate Antipater of Sidon's 'Six Sea Poems'.[27] A few years later, Bryher helped subsidize the printing at least of Moore's *Poems* and of H.D.'s second book, *Hymen*, both in 1921.[28] Bryher also supported *Contact*, the magazine begun by William Carlos Williams and Robert McAlmon, after her marriage to McAlmon in February 1921, and later McAlmon's Contact Editions.[29]

Once Bryher and McAlmon were established in London, Bryher renewed her friendship with Harriet Weaver of the *Egoist*, and McAlmon's first book, *Explorations*, appeared through the Egoist Press in the winter of 1921. Bryher's publishing connections very likely provided McAlmon with the impetus and the basic knowledge that he later used to achieve his own reputation as a publisher in Paris.[30] His Contact Publishing Company was established there in 1922, and, in conjunction with William Bird's Three Mountains Press, brought out thirty-two volumes through 1929.

Literary historians have tended to give McAlmon credit for supporting, encouraging, and publishing a number of writers. Certainly McAlmon's memoirs were available earlier than Bryher's, and his lifestyle brought him greater attention through being mentioned in numerous other memoirs, but it is also clear that in this case Bryher became an 'invisible' woman. Bryher's importance as supporter of the press has been treated merely as a convenience for McAlmon rather than as the source of vital connections and funds. The vicissitudes of McAlmon's work, in terms of both publishing and writing, suggest rather that Bryher's money was the only thing that allowed him to continue. Her status and previous friendships, as well, brought him into contact with many of the artists and writers who became his companions. Without these connections, the Contact Editions lists would have been extremely thin and might well have been limited to McAlmon's own books and Williams's *Spring and All*. Bryher has yet to receive proper credit for her support, while McAlmon's own lapses in his publishing work – for instance in the fiasco over Gertrude Stein's *The Making of Americans*, which Stein and Jane Heap finally tried to resolve without McAlmon – indicate that it may not have been a business in which he was entirely competent.[31] Even despite their subsequent separation, Bryher remained helpful to McAlmon, reviewing his *Portrait of a Generation* in *Poetry* in 1926 and later still publishing one of his stories in *Life and Letters*.[32]

The most celebrated early project with which Bryher was involved, however, was Marianne Moore's *Poems* of 1921. Bryher had met Moore with H.D. on their trip to America in 1920. They had become friends, although Bryher's sudden marriage of convenience to McAlmon just before sailing home had upset Moore very much. Still, their friendship endured that strain, and Moore may well have attempted to make amends later by claiming that McAlmon was one of the parties (along with H.D. and Bryher) involved in the publication of her *Poems*.

For many years it was said that Moore knew nothing of the compilation of her poems and was surprised when the volume was issued, but the evidence of Moore's collusion with H.D. and Bryher in making plans for such a volume has been clarified by Cyrena Pondrom.[33] Moore's response of surprise and consternation, which scholars have taken to imply that the publication was without her acquiescence, does not express 'modesty' so much as strong feeling about editing and rewriting her own verse, as well as her personal preferences in selecting and arranging her verse, should she have done so herself. Based on the correspondence, one imagines that Moore's concern arose rather from a belief that her writing would be appreciated by only a few readers (H.D. and Bryher among them), that she disliked 'public attention' to pieces that even she felt were highly individualistic, and that in fact she may have preferred to organize her first volume – perhaps at a later date – according to her own choices.

In general, the book seems to have been H.D.'s idea, as she had been collecting Moore's poems for some time, and Bryher's financial project, as she had the resources to see such a publication through; indeed, she had proposed to other writers that books of theirs should be printed under her subsidy. Bryher's efforts for Moore included assembly, support, and distribution even at the expense of Bryher's own book, as is clear from a reference Moore made to Bryher' amusing 'advance on the book-seller' on Moore's behalf; while Moore appreciated the support, she expressed regret that Bryher 'did not have time to inquire for "*Development*" ', Bryher's own novel.[34]

Bryher seems to have been less interested in giving herself credit than with providing other writers and artists with the means to present their works and with continuing to seek out new ideas and vehicles . . .

[. . .]

. . . it is clear that both H.D. and Bryher affected the development of modernist art and thought in a number of significant ways. Each gave generously of time and money as well as writing; each strove to make connections between people, to publish important new work by herself and by other writers, and to work against the despair of wartime as well as the stagnation of outmoded ways of thinking. They were outspoken in their resistance to two world wars, and between them wrote creative and critical pieces presenting their hope that art might help heal humanity's spiritual and intellectual wounds. Together, they refused to accept the imposition of conventional standards on their writing and their lives, and opened the way for much that was new in the world of modernist thought.

Notes

1   Cyrena Pondrom has pointed out H.D.'s extensive activity in that circle of young English writers, in 'Selected Letters' and especially in 'H.D. and the Origins of Imagism', *Sagetrieb* 4.1 (1985): 73–97, reprinted in *Signets: Reading H.D.*, ed. Susan Stanford Friedman and Rachel Blau DuPlessis (Madison: U of Wisconsin P, 1990) 85–109.

2   Holly Baggett believes that Lowell had planned to oust Pound during her 1914 trip, based on Lowell's offer to Margaret Anderson to write a 'London Letter' for the *Little Review* in May of 1914, and on Fletcher's opinion that Lowell's trip was part of a 'campaign'; see his autobiography, *Life Is My Song* (New York: Farrar and Rinehart, 1937) 145. Lowell was certainly capable of such a plan, although Fletcher was equally capable of exaggerating his reading of Lowell; the offer of a 'London Letter' was obviously going to be a short-term proposition in any case. See Holly Ann Baggett, 'Aloof from Natural Laws: Margaret C. Anderson and the "Little Review," 1914–1929' (Diss., University of Delaware, 1992).

3   H.D., letter to Amy Lowell, 17 December 1914, MS Lowell 19, Amy Lowell Papers, Houghton Library, Harvard University. This letter is printed in Scott's *The Gender of Modernism* (134–35).

4   Ezra Pound, letter to Amy Lowell, 1 August 1914, Amy Lowell Papers. In a subsequent letter Pound suggests that Lowell use another title for the book, or if she insisted on using 'Imagisme' that she add a subtitle such as ' "an anthology devoted to Imagisme, vers libre and modern movements in verse" or something of that sort' (letter to Amy Lowell, 12 August 1914, Amy Lowell Papers).

5   H.D., letter to Amy Lowell, 17 December 1914, Amy Lowell Papers.

6   H.D., letter to Amy Lowell, 14 January 1915, Amy Lowell Papers.

7   H.D., letter to Amy Lowell, 23 November 1914; 27 April 1915; 7 October 1915; 30 August 1916, Amy Lowell Papers.

8   H.D., letter to Amy Lowell, February 1916, Amy Lowell Papers.

9   H.D., letter to Amy Lowell, 24 January 1916, Amy Lowell Papers.

10   Pondrom notes that this card is 'postmarked November 23, 1914' ('Selected Letters' 561). Since Weaver and H.D. saw each other frequently, there was not much need for correspondence between them. There is very little material on H.D. among the Harriet Shaw Weaver papers in the British Library.

11   Jane Lidderdale, personal interview, January 1988.

12   In 1913 Pound became literary editor of the *New Freewoman* through the agency of Rebecca

West, who had solicited work from him. The issue of 15 August 1913 found West introducing 'Imagisme' in an article that briefly recapitulated segments of Flint's essay and Pound's 'A Few Don'ts', followed by Pound's 'Contemporania'. The prose works had previously appeared in America in *Poetry*.

13   F. S. Flint, 'The History of Imagism', *Egoist* 2.5 (1915): 70–71; Richard Aldington, 'The Poetry of Ezra Pound', *Egoist* 2.5 (1915): 71–72; F. S. Flint, 'The Poetry of H.D.,' *Egoist* 2.5 (1915): 72–73; Ferris Greenslet, 'The Poetry of John Gould Fletcher', *Egoist* 2.5 (1915): 73; Harold Monro, 'The Imagists Discussed,' *Egoist* 2.5 (1915): 77–80; Richard Aldington, 'The Poetry of F. S. Flint', *Egoist* 2.5 (1915): 80–81; O[livia] Shakespear, 'The Poetry of D. H. Lawrence', *Egoist* 2.5 (1915): 81; John Gould Fletcher, 'The Poetry of Amy Lowell', *Egoist* 2.5 (1915): 81–82.

14   'George Lane' [Amy Lowell and John Gould Fletcher], 'Some Imagist Poets', *Little Review* 2.3 (1915): 27–35. This issue included Aldington's article 'Remy de Gourmont', Lowell's 'The Poetry Bookshop', and Fletcher's prose-poems under the title 'America, 1915', as well as Aldington's review.

15   H.D., letter to Amy Lowell, 27 April 1915, Amy Lowell Papers.

16   Monro 78. Although the context set by this article is useful, Monro's comments about H.D. are less so, since he found her work 'fragile', 'restrained', and too 'petty' or 'small' to represent the direction in which he saw Imagism developing.

17   Barbara Guest, *Herself Defined: The Poet H.D. and Her World* (New York: Quill, 1984) 69.

18   H.D., letter to Amy Lowell, February 1916, Amy Lowell Papers. This letter is printed in *The Gender of Modernism* (135–36).

19   H.D., letters to Amy Lowell, March 1916; 14 August 1916, Amy Lowell Papers.

20   H.D., letter to Amy Lowell, 10 August 1917, Amy Lowell Papers.

21   In *Marianne Moore: A Literary Life* (New York: Atheneum, 1990), Charles Molesworth cites Aldington's mention of Moore's work in the context of a piece on Imagism for *Bruno's Weekly* in 1915 (112, 119); the actual reference is 'The Imagists', *Bruno Chap Books*, special ser. 5, 1915. Aldington mentions Moore in only one sentence: 'Two American girls, Miss C. Shanafeldt and Miss Marianne Moore show promise' (72).

22   This has been amply detailed in Cyrena N. Pondrom, 'Marianne Moore and H.D.: Female Community and Poetic Achievement', *Marianne Moore: Woman and Poet*, ed. Patricia C. Willis (Orono: National Poetry Foundation, 1990) 371–402, which discusses the long-term relationship between H.D., Moore, and Bryher, and establishes, at the very least, Moore's knowledge of her friends' efforts on her behalf.

23   Marianne Moore, 'The Accented Syllable', *Egoist* 3.10 (1916): 151–52.

24   H.D., letter to Marianne Moore, 3 September [1916] (V:23:32), Marianne Moore Papers, the Rosenbach Museum and Library, Philadelphia.

25   H.D., letter to Marianne Moore, 3 September [1916] (V:23:32), Marianne Moore Papers.

26   Rachel Blau DuPlessis writes that H.D. felt constricted by a 'romantic thralldom' in her early work – a powerful love for figures of male power to whom she felt unequal (*Writing Beyond the Ending: Narrative Strategies of Twentieth Century Women Writers* [Boston: G. K. Hall], chapter 5). William Carlos Williams claimed at about this time in the *Little Review* that H.D. always asked him about her early writing: ' "You're not satisfied with me, are you Billy? There's something lacking, isn't there?" ' He follows this passage, however, with a letter from H.D. as assistant editor of the *Egoist* in which she clearly shows artistic self-assurance: 'I trust you will not hate me for wanting to delete from your poem all its flippancies. . . . I consider this business of writing a very sacred thing! . . . I think you have the "spark," am sure of it, and when you speak *direct* are a poet. I feel in the hey-ding-ding touch running through your poem a derivative tendency which, to me, is not *you*. . . . It's very well to *mock* at yourself – it is a spiritual sin to mock at your inspiration' ('Prologue: The Return of the Sun', *Little Review* 5.11 [1919]: 7).

27   Guest credits Aldington with deciding that Bryher, as a possible patron, should be included in the series; in the same paragraph, however, she notes that the sea poems were suggested to Bryher by H.D., and since H.D. was much closer to Bryher than was Aldington, one may suppose that the person who really brought Bryher to the Egoist Press was H.D. (107). Lidderdale and Nicholson note that, subsequently, Weaver and Bryher became genuine friends (177). It is unclear whether the 'Six Sea Poems' actually appeared. Lidderdale, Jane and Mary Nicholson (1970), *Dear Miss Weaver: Harriet Shaw Weaver, 1876–1961* (New York: Viking).

28   Receipts made out by Harriet Shaw Weaver include '£31 for Marianne Moore's *Poems*, from Bryher' and '£30 for *Hymen*, from Bryher' (Lidderdale and Nicholson 461). These writers also state that the Egoist Press's edition of Jean Cocteau's *Cock and Harlequin* (Winter 1920/21) was 'the last of the books paid for by Egoist Press funds', but that Weaver 'was very willing to publish subsidized books. It was not long before several others were added to her list, financed by her new friend Bryher' (177).

29   In her memoir, Bryher notes that her money subsidized McAlmon's publishing (Bryher (1962), *Heart to Artemis: A Writer's Memoirs*, New York: Harcourt, Brace, 201).

30   Lidderdale and Nicholson 177, 464. Bearing in mind H.D. and Bryher's involvement with Egoist Press books, it seems that Weaver's acceptance of McAlmon's book was likely a generous gesture of friendship rather than a strong endorsement of his prose. McAlmon's previous experience with publishing *Contact* seems not to have been demanding, involving mimeographed copies of two sheets each.

31   Robert E. Knoll, 'Robert McAlmon: Expatriate Writer and Publisher', *University of Nebraska Studies* n.s. 18 (1957): 16, 81–84. If Contact Editions was what Knoll calls 'a kind of pump-primer' or a 'showcase for the talents of the expatriates' that eventually 'got American publishers for [its] authors', then Bryher's importance as a backer should not be overlooked, good intentions being one thing and actual productivity another. Knoll persistently refers to McAlmon's impatience, his inability to persevere in detail work, and his migratory tendencies (not to mention his 'errors of convenience' in retyping the 'Penelope' chapter of Joyce's *Ulysses*), all of which would seem to mitigate against finding McAlmon an effective businessman.

        Sanford J. Smoller notes in *Adrift Among Geniuses: Robert McAlmon, Writer and Publisher of the Twenties* (University Park: Pennsylvania State UP, 1975) that when McAlmon left London in 1921 a few months after his marriage, he went to Paris 'with only letters of introduction and the names of people to look up' (56), but he does not emphasize the importance of having those names and letters of introduction.

32   Knoll mentions that, in later years as McAlmon's literary work waned, one of his (reworked) stories appeared in '*Life and Letters*, the distinguished British publication, in 1934', without noting Bryher's connection to the magazine, which probably accounted for the publication (56, 72). Bryher's review was 'The Biography of Continents', *Poetry* 28.5 (1926): 280–82.

33   See Pondrom, 'Marianne Moore and H.D.', and John M. Slatin, who writes, 'Moore's *Poems* was compiled by H.D. and Winifred Ellerman (Bryher). It is usually said that they worked without Moore's knowledge; but the most that can be said is that while Moore did not actively collaborate in producing the volume, she probably gave tacit consent. Laurence Stapleton quotes a letter from Moore to H.D. which shows no surprise at the fact of the book's publication; on the contrary, Moore is surprised only by how well she comes off. See Stapleton, Laurence (1978) *Marianne Moore: The Poet's Advance* (Princeton: Princeton University Press), 28 (*The Savage's Romance: The Poetry of Marianne Moore* [University Park: Pennsylvania State UP, 1986] 266).

34   Marianne Moore, letter to Bryher, 13 December 1920, Bryher Papers, Beinecke Rare Book and Manuscript Library, Yale University.

PART FOUR

Texts and readers

EDITORS' INTRODUCTION

Reception, or to be more accurate the study of reading and reading practices, was once upon a time the Cinderella of book history. However, the agenda set out by Robert Darnton in his 'First Steps Toward a History of Reading' has been taken up by the scholarly community and the survey he offers of work up to that point has been built on and extended in new directions (Darnton 1990: 154–87). Darnton called for further research into a history of reader response: 'comparing readers' accounts of their experience with the protocols of reading in their books and, when possible, with their behaviour'.

We are now, in Darnton's terms, exploring the 'whys' and 'hows' of the history of reading as much as the 'who', 'what', 'where' and 'when'. The sources for this history remain fertile and problematic: the archival material, including booksellers' lists, library records and state registers, offers generalised data which can be used to ascertain patterns and trends which may or may not be localised; and the personal material, including letters, diaries and autobiographies, offers presentations of the reading self which can provide cautious insights into the individual's reading habits and practices. Richard Altick's account of reading in Britain from the late fifteenth until the eighteenth century illustrates the richness and density to be derived from this material as well as alerting us to the need to recreate the mentalité of the culture under review – the 'why' and the 'how'.

Darnton's 'how' includes both the paratextual elements of the printed word (a theme developed by McGann and Genette) and the nature of the act of reading itself. The latter theme was the subject of the school of reader-response criticism which emerged from Germany in the 1970s and in which Wolfgang Iser was the predominant figure. Iser restored the reader to the centre of the act of reading, a position from which a bunkered focus upon the author's 'intentions' and the structures of the text had dislodged him/her. Within Iser's model of reading, the reader becomes an active and creative participant in the creation of meaning from the text. This model might seem then to underline the importance of the historical since it follows that different readers at different periods will derive different meanings from their reading. That different readers will, in fact, arrive at remarkably similar meanings and that a single reader may change his/her view of a text over time are central concerns of Stanley Fish. Fish, although by no means 'of the school of' Iser, reiterates the key point of the reader-response model that the meaning of the text does not exist independently of the reader and the reader's contribution, reflecting his/her experience, to its creation. He extends the model by offering the concept of 'interpretive communities' to account for similarities, if not sameness, in both the way of reading of groups of individuals and the meaning they derive individually from a text.

This notion has proved important in allowing the historian of reading to move from data about individuals to conclusions about audiences – to attempt to refute Darnton's assertion that 'the experience of the great mass of readers lies beyond the range of historical research'. Jonathan Rose moves the focus of inquiry from the individual as solitary reader to the individual as member of an 'audience' to examine how texts affect the lives and intellectual development of the 'common', that is, non-professional, reader. Where Janice Radway had undertaken this for contemporary readers of romance novels, Rose sets out to undertake historical research without the obvious benefit of direct access to the readers themselves. Elizabeth McHenry describes a similar reading 'audience' and community in her in-depth study of African-American literary 'clubs'. The extract reproduced here draws on a wealth of archival and secondary sources to reconstruct the place of these clubs in supporting the development of self-awareness, self-expression and challenges to accepted status amongst black communities in the USA at the beginning of the twentieth century. Radway herself exploits archival material, as well as 'real-time' interviews and observation, to clarify the nature of the selection process for the Book-of-the-Month Club and the role of the Club in creating, relating to and reinforcing an 'interpretive community' of middle-class and aspiring middle-class readers. Where the Book-of-the-Month Club achieved this in a positive manner, the negative means of creating an 'interpretive community' by signalling what will not be read by its members, or the children of its members to be more precise, provides Kate Flint with a key element in her profile of the woman reader in the nineteenth century.

Chapter 30

Wolfgang Iser

INTERACTION BETWEEN TEXT AND READER

Central to the reading of every literary work is the interaction between its structure and its recipient. This is why the phenomenological theory of art has emphatically drawn attention to the fact that the study of a literary work should concern not only the actual text but also, and in equal measure, the actions involved in responding to that text. The text itself simply offers 'schematized aspects'[1] through which the aesthetic object of the work can be produced.

From this we may conclude that the literary work has two poles, which we might call the artistic and the aesthetic: the artistic pole is the author's text, and the aesthetic is the realization accomplished by the reader. In view of this polarity, it is clear that the work itself cannot be identical with the text or with its actualization but must be situated somewhere between the two. It must inevitably be virtual in character, as it cannot be reduced to the reality of the text or to the subjectivity of the reader, and it is from this virtuality that it derives its dynamism. As the reader passes through the various perspectives offered by the text, and relates the different views and patterns to one another, he sets the work in motion, and so sets himself in motion, too.

If the virtual position of the work is between text and reader, its actualization is clearly the result of an interaction between the two, and so exclusive concentration on either the author's techniques or the reader's psychology will tell us little about the reading process itself. This is not to deny the vital importance of each of the two poles – it is simply that if one loses sight of the relationship, one loses sight of the virtual work. Despite its uses, separate analysis would only be conclusive if the relationship were that of transmitter and receiver, for this would presuppose a common code, ensuring accurate communication since the message would only be traveling one way. In literary works, however, the message is transmitted in two ways, in that the reader 'receives' it by composing it. There is no common code – at best one could say that a common code may arise in the course of the process. Starting out from this assumption, we must search for structures that will enable us to describe basic conditions of interaction, for only then shall we be able to gain some insight into the potential effects inherent in the work. . . .

Acknowledgement to Princeton University Press for permission to reprint Wolfgang Iser, 'Interaction between Text and Reader' from Susan K. Suleiman and Inge Crossman, eds, *The Reader in the Text: Essays on Audience and Interpretation*, New Jersey: Princeton University Press, 1980, pp. 106–119. Copyright © 1980 by Princeton University Press. Reprinted by permission of Princeton University Press.

An obvious and major difference between reading and all forms of social interaction is the fact that with reading there is no *face-to-face-situation*.[2] A text cannot adapt itself to each reader it comes into contact with. The partners in dyadic interaction can ask each other questions in order to ascertain how far their images have bridged the gap of the inexperienceability of one another's experiences. The reader, however, can never learn from the text how accurate or inaccurate are his views of it. Furthermore, dyadic interaction serves specific purposes, so that the interaction always has a regulative context, which often serves as a *tertium comparationis*. There is no such frame of reference governing the text–reader relationship; on the contrary, the codes which might regulate this interaction are fragmented in the text, and must first be reassembled or, in most cases, restructured before any frame of reference *can* be established. Here, then, in conditions and intention, we find two basic differences between the text–reader relationship and the dyadic interaction between social partners.

Now, it is the very lack of ascertainability and defined intention that brings about the text–reader interaction, and here there is a vital link with dyadic interaction. Social communication arises out of the fact that people cannot experience how others experience them, and not out of the common situation or out of the conventions that join both partners together. The situations and conventions regulate the manner in which gaps are filled, but the gaps in turn arise out of the inexperienceability and, consequently, function as a basic inducement to communication. Similarly, it is the gaps, the fundamental asymmetry between text and reader, that give rise to communication in the reading process; the lack of a common situation and a common frame of reference corresponds to the 'no-thing', which brings about the interaction between persons. Asymmetry and the 'no-thing' are all different forms of an indeterminate, constitutive blank, which underlies all processes of interaction. With dyadic interaction, the imbalance is removed by the establishment of pragmatic connections resulting in an action, which is why the preconditions are always clearly defined in relation to situations and common frames of reference. The imbalance between text and reader, however, is undefined, and it is this very indeterminacy that increases the variety of communication possible.

Now, if communication between text and reader is to be successful, clearly the reader's activity must also be controlled in some way by the text. The control cannot be as specific as in *face-to-face-situation*, equally it cannot be as determinate as a social code, which regulates social interaction. However, the guiding devices operative in the reading process have to initiate communication and to control it. This control cannot be understood as a tangible entity occurring independently of the process of communication. Although exercised *by* the text, it is not in the text. This is well illustrated by a comment Virginia Woolf made on the novels of Jane Austen:

> Jane Austen is thus a mistress of much deeper emotion than appears upon the surface. She stimulates us to supply what is not there. What she offers is, apparently, a trifle, yet is composed of something that expands in the reader's mind and endows with the most enduring form of life scenes which are outwardly trivial. Always stress is laid upon character . . . The turns and twists of the dialogue keep us on the tenterhooks of suspense. Our attention is half upon the present moment, half upon the future . . . Here, indeed, in this unfinished and in the main inferior story, are all the elements of Jane Austen's greatness.[3]

What is missing from the apparently trivial scenes, the gaps arising out of the dialogue – this is what stimulates the reader into filling the blanks with projections. He is drawn into the events and made to supply what is meant from what is not said. What is said only appears to take on significance as a reference to what is not said; it is the implications and not the statements that give shape and weight to the meaning. But as the unsaid comes to life in the reader's imagination, so the said 'expands' to take on greater significance than might have been supposed: even trivial scenes can seem surprisingly profound. The 'enduring form of life' which Virginia Woolf speaks of is not manifested on the printed page; it is a product arising out of the interaction between text and reader.

Communication in literature, then, is a process set in motion and regulated, not by a given code, but by a mutually restrictive and magnifying interaction between the explicit and the implicit, between revelation and concealment. What is concealed spurs the reader into action, but this action is also controlled by what is revealed; the explicit in its turn is transformed when the implicit has been brought to light. Whenever the reader bridges the gaps, communication begins. The gaps function as a kind of pivot on which the whole text–reader relationship revolves. Hence, the structured blanks of the text stimulate the process of ideation to be performed by the reader on terms set by the text. There is, however, another place in the textual system where text and reader converge, and that is marked by the various types of negation which arise in the course of the reading. Blanks and negations both control the process of communication in their own different ways: the blanks leave open the connection between textual perspectives, and so spur the reader into coordinating these perspectives and patterns – in other words, they induce the reader to perform basic operations *within* the text. The various types of negation invoke familiar and determinate elements or knowledge only to cancel them out. What is cancelled, however, remains in view, and thus brings about modifications in the reader's attitude toward what is familiar or determinate – in other words, he is guided to adopt a position in *relation* to the text.

In order to spotlight the communication process we shall confine our consideration to how the blanks trigger off and simultaneously control the reader's activity. Blanks indicate that the different segments and patterns of the text are to be connected even though the text itself does not say so. They are the unseen joints of the text, and as they mark off schemata and textual perspectives from one another, they simultaneously prompt acts of ideation on the reader's part. Consequently when the schemata and perspectives have been linked together, the blanks 'disappear'.

If we are to grasp the unseen structure that regulates but does not formulate the connection or even the meaning, we must bear in mind the various forms in which the textual segments are presented to the reader's viewpoint in the reading process. Their most elementary form is to be seen on the level of the story. The threads of the plot are suddenly broken off, or continued in unexpected directions. One narrative section centers on a particular character and is then continued by the abrupt introduction of new characters. These sudden changes are often denoted by new chapters and so are clearly distinguished; the object of this distinction, however, is not separation so much as a tacit invitation to find the missing link. Furthermore, in each articulated reading moment, only segments of textual perspectives are present to the reader's wandering viewpoint.

In order to become fully aware of the implication, we must bear in mind that a narrative text, for instance, is composed of a variety of perspectives, which outline the author's view and also provide access to what the reader is meant to visualize. As a rule, there are four main perspectives in narration: those of the narrator, the characters, the plot, and the fictitious reader. Although these may differ in order of importance, none of them on its own is identical to the meaning of the text, which is to be brought about by their constant intertwining through the reader in the reading process. An increase in the number of blanks is bound to occur through the frequent subdivisions of each of the textual perspectives; thus the narrator's perspective is often split into that of the implied author's set against that of the author as narrator. The hero's perspective may be set against that of the minor characters. The fictitious reader's perspective may be divided between the explicit position ascribed to him and the implicit attitude he must adopt to that position.

As the reader's wandering viewpoint travels between all these segments, its constant switching during the time flow of reading intertwines them, thus bringing forth a network of perspectives, within which each perspective opens a view not only of others, but also of the intended imaginary object. Hence no single textual perspective can be equated with this imaginary object, of which it forms only one aspect. The object itself is a product of interconnection, the structuring of which is to a great extent regulated and controlled by blanks.

In order to explain this operation, we shall first give a schematic description of how the blanks function, and then we shall try to illustrate this function with an example. In the time flow of reading, segments of the various perspectives move into focus and are set off against preceding segments. Thus the segments of characters, narrator, plot, and fictitious reader perspectives are not only marshaled into a graduated sequence but are also transformed into reciprocal reflectors. The blank as an empty space between segments enables them to be joined together, thus constituting a field of vision for the wandering viewpoint. A referential field is always formed when there are at least two positions related to and influencing one another – it is the minimal organizational unit in all processes of comprehension,[4] and it is also the basic organizational unit of the wandering viewpoint.

The first structural quality of the blank, then, is that it makes possible the organization of a referential field of interacting textual segments projecting themselves one upon another. Now, the segments present in the field are structurally of equal value, and the fact that they are brought together highlights their affinities and their differences. This relationship gives rise to a tension that has to be resolved, for, as Arnheim has observed in a more general context: 'It is one of the functions of the third dimension to come to the rescue when things get uncomfortable in the second'.[5] The third dimension comes about when the segments of the referential field are given a common framework, which allows the reader to relate affinities and differences and so to grasp the patterns underlying the connections. But this framework is also a blank, which requires an act of ideation in order to be filled. It is as if the blank in the field of the reader's viewpoint had changed its position. It began as the empty space between perspective segments, indicating their connectability, and so organizing them into projections of reciprocal influence. But with the establishment of this connectability the blank, as the unformulated framework of these interacting segments, now enables the reader to produce a determinate relationship between them. We may infer already from this change in position that the blank exercises significant control over all the operations that occur within the referential field of the wandering viewpoint.

Now we come to the third and most decisive function of the blank. Once the segments have been connected and a determinate relationship established, a referential field is formed which constitutes a particular reading moment, and which in turn has a discernible structure. The grouping of segments within the referential field comes about, as we have seen, by making the viewpoint switch between the perspective segments. The segment on which the viewpoint focuses in each particular moment becomes the theme. The theme of one moment becomes the background against which the next segment takes on its actuality, and so on. Whenever a segment becomes a theme, the previous one must lose its thematic relevance[6] and be turned into a marginal, thematically vacant position, which can be and usually is occupied by the reader so that he may focus on the new thematic segment.

In this connection it might be more appropriate to designate the marginal or horizontal position as a vacancy and not as a blank; blanks refer to suspended connectability in the text, vacancies refer to non-thematic segments within the referential field of the wandering viewpoint. Vacancies, then, are important guiding devices for building up the aesthetic object, because they condition the reader's view of the new theme, which in turn conditions his view of previous themes. These modifications, however, are not formulated in the text – they are to be implemented by the reader's ideational activity. And so these vacancies enable the reader to combine segments into a field by reciprocal modification, to form positions from those fields, and then to adapt each position to its successor and predecessors in a process that ultimately transforms the textual perspectives through a whole range of alternating themes and background relationships, into the aesthetic object of the text. . . .

To sum up, then, the blank in the fictional text induces and guides the reader's constitutive activity. As a suspension of connectability between textual perspective and perspective segments, it marks the need for an equivalence, thus transforming the segments into reciprocal projections, which in turn organize the reader's wandering viewpoint as a referential field. The tension that occurs within the field between heterogeneous perspective segments is resolved by the theme-and-background structure, which makes the viewpoint focus on one segment as the theme, to be grasped from the thematically vacant position now occupied by the reader as his standpoint. Thematically vacant positions remain present in the background against which new themes occur; they condition and influence those themes and are also retroactively influenced by them, for as each theme recedes into the background of its successor, the vacancy shifts, allowing for a reciprocal transformation to take place. As the vacancy is structured by the sequence of positions in the time flow of reading, the reader's viewpoint cannot proceed arbitrarily; the thematically vacant position always acts as the angle from which a selective interpretation is to be made.

Two points need to be emphasized: (1) we have described the structure of the blank in an abstract, somewhat idealized way in order to explain the pivot on which the interaction between text and reader turns; (2) the blank has different structural qualities, which appear to dovetail. The reader fills in the blank in the text, thereby bringing about a referential field; the blank arising in turn out of the referential field is filled in by way of the theme-and-background structure; and the vacancy arising from juxtaposed themes and backgrounds is occupied by the reader's standpoint, from which the various reciprocal transformations lead to the emergence of the aesthetic object. The structural qualities outlined make the blank shift, so that the changing positions of the empty space mark out a definite need for determination, which the constitutive activity of the reader is to fulfill. In this sense, the shifting blank maps out the path along which the wandering viewpoint is to travel, guided by the self-regulatory sequence in which the structural qualities of the blank interlock.

Now we are in a position to qualify more precisely what is actually meant by reader participation in the text. If the blank is largely responsible for the activities described, then participation means that the reader is not simply called upon to 'internalize' the positions given in the text, but he is induced to make them act upon and so transform each other, as a result of which the aesthetic object begins to emerge. The structure of the blank organizes this participation, revealing simultaneously the intimate connection between this structure and the reading subject. This interconnection completely conforms to a remark made by Piaget: 'In a word, the subject is there and alive, because the basic quality of each structure is the structuring process itself'.[7] The blank in the fictional text appears to be a paradigmatic structure; its function consists in initiating structured operations in the reader, the execution of which transmits the reciprocal interaction of textual positions into consciousness. The shifting blank is responsible for a sequence of colliding images, which condition each other in the time flow of reading. The discarded image imprints itself on its successor, even though the latter is meant to resolve the deficiencies of the former. In this respect the images hang together in a sequence, and it is by this sequence that the meaning of the text comes alive in the reader's imagination.

Notes

This essay contains a few ideas which are dealt with more comprehensively in my book *The Act of Reading: A Theory of Aesthetic Response* (Baltimore: The Johns Hopkins University Press, 1978).

1   See Roman Ingarden, *The Literary Work of Art*, trans. George G. Grabowicz (Evanston, Ill., 1973), pp. 276ff.

2   E. Goffman, *Interaction Ritual: Essays on Face-to-Face Behavior* (New York, 1967).

3   Virginia Woolf, *The Common Reader: First Series* (London, 1957), p. 174. In this context, it is well worth considering Virginia Woolf's comments on the composition of her own fictional characters. She remarks in her diary:

> I'm thinking furiously about Reading and Writing. I have no time to describe my plans. I should say a good deal about *The Hours* and my discovery: how I dig out beautiful caves behind my characters: I think that gives exactly what I want; humanity, humour, depth. The idea is that the caves shall connect and each comes to daylight at the present moment.
>
> (*A Writer's Diary: Being Extracts from the Diary of Virginia Woolf*, ed. Leonard Woolf (London, 1953), p. 60)

The suggestive effect of the 'beautiful caves' is continued in her work through what she leaves out. On this subject, T. S. Eliot once observed:

> Her observation, which operates in a continuous way, implies a vast and sustained work of organization. She does not illumine with sudden bright flashes but diffuses a soft and placid light. Instead of looking for the primitive, she looks rather for the civilized, the highly civilized, where nevertheless something is found to be left out. And this something is deliberately left out, by what could be called a moral effort of the will. And, being left out, this something is, in a sense, in a melancholy sense, present.
>
> ('T. S. Eliot "Places" Virginia Woolf for French Readers', in *Virginia Woolf: The Critical Heritage*, ed. Robin Majumdar and Allen McLaurin (London, 1975), p. 192)

4   See Aron Gurwitsch, *The Field of Consciousness* (Pittsburgh, 1964), pp. 309–75.

5   Rudolph Arnheim, *Toward a Psychology of Art* (Berkeley and Los Angeles, 1967), p. 239.

6   For a discussion of the problem of changing relevance and abandoned thematic relevance, see Alfred Schütz, *Das Problem der Relevanz*, trans. A. v. Baeyer (Frankfurt am Main, 1970), pp. 104ff., 145ff.

7   Jean Piaget, *Der Strukturalismus*, trans. L. Häfliger (Olten, 1973), p. 134.

Chapter 31

E. Jennifer Monaghan

LITERACY INSTRUCTION AND GENDER
IN COLONIAL NEW ENGLAND

Hanna Newberry, the most prominent mortgage-holder in Windsor, Connecticut, for most of the second quarter of the eighteenth century, was unable to sign the many documents to which she affixed her name. Instead, she subscribed her mark, the initials HN. Her case illustrates, according to Linda Auwers, 'the widespread fact of female illiteracy among women born in the seventeenth century and the difficulty in relating literacy to social class'.[1]

Literacy historians have used signatures and marks as indicators of, respectively, the literacy and illiteracy of ordinary people in the seventeenth and eighteenth centuries in Europe and America.[2] For colonial New England, the best-known study remains that by Kenneth Lockridge, who tabulated the signatures/marks made on over three thousand wills. He found that the proportion of males able to sign their own wills increased from 60 percent in the 1660s to 85 percent by 1760 and to almost 90 percent by 1790. Female signing rates were much lower throughout the entire period. Some 31 percent of the women signed their wills before 1670; this average increased, but only to 46 percent by the 1790s.[3] Three later studies have found a higher rate of signing than Lockridge did, in part by using deeds and other sources in addition to wills, so accessing a larger or less decrepit population.[4] One of these is the study cited above by Auwers, who allocated her signers/markers into birth cohorts and found that the proportion of women in Windsor who could sign their own names to deeds rose from 27 percent for the cohort born between 1650 and 1669 to 90 percent for the 1740–49 cohort.[5]

The equation of literacy possession with signing rests on the assumption that signing ability is roughly equivalent to fluent reading. As reading was taught before writing, the argument runs, the ability to write (as indicated by a signature) also indicates the ability to read. Carl Kaestle has recently summarized the arguments for and against this position, and – after warning us that the relationship between signing and reading may vary by gender, class, place, and period – finally suggests that signature counts indicate roughly the 'minimum number of people who were minimally literate'.[6]

Although scholars have varied in their interpretations of what a signature implies, there has been more general agreement about the mark: it has been viewed as a valid indicator of illiteracy.

Reprinted from Cathy N. Davidson, ed., *Reading in America: Literature and Social History*, pp. 53–80. © 1989 Johns Hopkins University Press. Reprinted with permission of the Johns Hopkins University Press.

Lockridge's figures have therefore contributed to the widely held belief that in New England and elsewhere females were dramatically less literate than males throughout the colonial period, reaching roughly half the literacy level of males.

Several scholars, however, including Lockridge himself, have raised the possibility that some people – particularly women – could read but not write. Margaret Spufford and Victor Neuburg have provided examples of this in the context of seventeenth- and eighteenth-century England.[7] The thesis of the present study is that this was also true of colonial New England. When we examine the contexts in which literacy instruction was conducted, paying close attention to the role played by gender, it will become apparent that the mark cannot be considered an infallible indicator of illiteracy, particularly in the seventeenth century.

The evidence to be presented is qualitative in nature, scattered, and fragmentary; it is also skewed toward the seventeenth century. Further research will be necessary to see if the conclusions to be drawn will stand. Nonetheless, the bits and pieces of the puzzle seem to form a remarkably coherent picture across time and place. In order to support my contention, I first discuss how reading and writing were taught and by whom, then turn to examine how the colonists themselves viewed literacy from the legal and economic standpoints. Next follows an elaboration of the relationship between schooling and gender. Basic to the entire discussion is the concept that literacy was considered by the colonists to comprise a deliberately imparted set of skills, taught in ways that were both widely accepted and precise.

The reading curriculum

The colonial reading curriculum was, of course, brought over to the new continent, along with so much else, from England. The seventeenth-century curriculum followed the outline sketched by John Locke, who in 1693 characterized it as the 'ordinary road of the Hornbook, Primer, Psalter, Testament, and Bible'.[8]

There is plenty of evidence that the colonists followed this 'ordinary road' in the early days of settlement and throughout the seventeenth century. The hornbook formed the novice's introduction to reading. Its name derived from its single page (originally covered with transparent protective horn), which was tacked onto a little wooden paddle. It presented the alphabet, the first few lines of the syllabarium (*ab eb ib ob ub*), and the Lord's Prayer. Often mentioned in the same context as primers, hornbooks turn up here and there in the sources over the course of the seventeenth century, and advertisements for primers and both gilt and plain hornbooks have been found in Philadelphia newspapers as late as 1760.[9] The hornbook was used in dame schools – private schools for small children run by a woman in her own home – as the child's first 'text'. Samuel Sewall mentioned one in just such a context. He recorded in his diary on April 27, 1691, that he had sent his little son Joseph, not yet three years old, to school (obviously for the first time). 'This afternoon had Joseph to school to Capt. Townsend's Mother's, his cousin Jane accompanying him, carried his Horn-book.'[10]

Hornbooks were apparently never manufactured on American soil, but were all imported.[11] Primers, the next step in the reading curriculum, were also imported into the colonies from very early on. They must have been a standard item in any village store. One example of their widespread availability is documented for New Haven, in 1645 – only seven years after it was founded as a separate colony. That year, a Captain Turner was accused by Mistress Stolion before the New Haven Colony Court of having reneged on a deal in which he had promised to give her two cows in exchange for six yards of cloth. Not to be outdone, the captain accused Mrs. Stolion in turn of price gouging: he claimed that 'she sold primmers at 9*d* [nine pence] apeece which cost but 4*d* here in New England'.[12]

Primers were such essential texts for instruction in both reading and religion, however, that their publication on American presses is documented early in the colonial adventure. The oldest extant American primer was composed by John Eliot as part of his efforts to convert the Massachuset Indians. Written in the Massachuset dialect of the Algonquian language and published in 1669 on the Cambridge, Massachusetts, press, the primer admirably sums up, in its title, the dual role it, like the hornbook, played in both reading and religious instruction. The English version reads, *The Indian Primer; or, the Way of Training up of Our Indian Youth in the Good Knowledge of God, in the Knowledge of the Scriptures and in an Ability to Read.*[13]

Primers as a genre became a publishing staple in New England and the middle states as presses increased in number. The *New England Primer*, the most famous of colonial textbooks, has a publishing history that runs from 1690, when it was already in its second impression, to long after the American Revolution. (Its sales up to 1830 have been estimated at between six million and eight million copies.) It contained several pages of instructional material, presenting the syllabarium and words of increasing length, from monosyllables to words of six syllables. Its popularity was enhanced by the inclusion of a catechism.[14] In addition to the *New England Primer*, there were numerous other primers in the marketplace.[15]

The next text in both the religious and reading curriculum was the Psalter (the Book of Psalms). Psalters too were extensively printed on American presses. They were generally published without the addition of any reading instructional material, but we do know of one 1760 Philadelphia edition that indicated that it had been 'Improved by the addition of a variety of lessons in spelling. . . . Likewise, rules for reading. . . . The whole being a proper introduction, not only to learning, but to the training of children in the reading of the holy scriptures in particular.'[16]

One incident that revealed the Psalter's status as a reading instructional text occurred in the context of writing instruction. John Proctor, master of the town-financed North Writing School in Boston from 1731 to 1743, was summoned in 1741 before the Boston selectmen to answer what seems to have been a parental complaint: he was accused of having refused to admit boys from 'Families of low Circumstances' to his school. Proctor replied that he had 'refus'd none of the Inhabitants Children, but such as could not Read in the Psalter'.[17] Clearly, the Psalter was being used as a kind of minimum competency test of reading ability.

The final two stages in the reading curriculum consisted of mastering first the New Testament and then the entire Bible (both Old and New Testaments). Because it was illegal to print these on American presses (John Eliot's *Indian Bible* being a specialized exception), English Bibles were imported until after the American Revolution.

The use of the Scriptures as the climax of the reading curriculum is well known. Two seventeenth-century instances occur in the records of New Haven. The first illustrates the seventeenth-century assumption that reading instruction was supposed to have begun before a child entered the town school. The job description for a New Haven schoolmaster, hired in 1651, was to 'perfect male chilldren in the English, after they can reade in their Testament or Bible, and to learne them to wright', and to bring them on to Latin, if he could.[18] The second involved a school for girls. That same year, the daughter of a Captain How was brought before the New Haven Court and charged with misconduct that included speaking in a blasphemous way of the Scriptures. The girl's mother claimed that her daughter had picked up some of her bad habits at 'Goodwife Wickams', where she went to school. Witnesses testified that they had seen the girl look in a Bible, turn over a leaf, and say that 'it was not worth reading'. It is not too far-fetched to assume that young Miss How had reached the stage of reading the Bible at her school.[19]

Not included in Locke's characterization of the 'ordinary road' was the spelling book. In a major pedagogical shift that cannot be documented here in any detail, the spelling book was introduced into schools, perhaps fairly early in the eighteenth century, as an important beginning text for reading instruction.[20] In the rise of the speller we see the demands of religious content taking second place to the requirements of methodology, in a continuation of a process begun when the first alphabet was added to the primer.[21]

Spelling books as a genre appear at least as early as Edmund Coote's *The English Schoole-Maister*, published in London in 1596, and reprinted fifty-four times by 1737.[22] Moreover, spellers were printed very early on colonial presses: an unidentified speller came off Stephen Daye's press in Cambridge, in the Bay Colony in about 1644.[23] It was not, however, until the eighteenth century that the speller's ascendancy as a school text began. An important clue to its popularity is the frequency with which English spellers were reprinted on American presses. (Unlike primers, some of which reflected colonial circumstances, American spellers were all reproduced verbatim from English copies until after the American Revolution.) When Benjamin Franklin in 1747 reprinted Thomas Dilworth's *A New Guide to the English Tongue*, he ushered onto the American scene a spelling book that would enjoy tremendous popularity in the second half of the eighteenth century ('the nurse of us all', as one user put it), until ousted by Noah Webster's speller after 1783.[24]

The name 'spelling book' was a reflection of the prevailing methodology: spelling was the key to reading. After mastering the letters of the alphabet, the novice reader's next task was to spell out, orally, syllables and words (broken into syllables) from the printed page. Spelling books incorporated exactly the same methodology – the alphabetic method – as primers did. Although some spellers included secular content, a key difference between primers and spellers was that the latter presented the reading curriculum in a more elaborate and systematic fashion. The tables of words were greatly increased in number and were followed by 'lessons' – reading material based in part on vocabulary already introduced.[25]

One key aspect of the alphabetic method was that reading instruction was conducted entirely orally, without requiring the child to write. Progress in learning to read could therefore be gauged simply by listening to the child's oral spelling. As Edmund Coote had put it in the 1596 preface to his speller, the purchaser of his book could sit at the loom or needle, 'and neuer hinder thy worke, to heare thy scholers, after thou hast once made this little booke familiar vntu thee'.[26]

Comprehension was virtually ignored, pedagogically speaking. It would probably be fairer to say that comprehension of the text was assumed. After all, the seventeenth-century reading curriculum was in essence a course in Christianity: the texts used were basic to the religion itself. Not until the spelling books of the eighteenth century would any reference be made to such matters as how easily a child could learn the material.

In sum, the task of the reading teacher throughout the entire colonial period was clearly laid out. Both methodology and content were agreed upon; the curriculum was, in effect, standardized. Moreover, no qualifications for teaching reading were necessary other than being able to read oneself. Not only did the child not write in the course of learning to read; the teacher did not need to know how to write either.

The reading teacher

Because the task of the reading teacher was so well defined and was considered, rightly or wrongly, to be easy, the teaching of reading was more often than not considered to be a female province. In the context of family education, it is significant that in those rare cases when we know who taught the child to read at home, it is the mother who is singled out. A pious mother was particularly motivated to teach her child to read. The Boston minister Increase Mather (father of Cotton Mather) was born in Dorchester, Massachusetts, in 1639, nine years after the town was founded. He wrote that he 'learned to read of my mother' whom he described as a 'very Holy praying woman'. (Significantly, it was his father who taught him to *write*.) Richard Brown, born in 1675, also had 'pious and prudent' mother, who endeavored to instill in him 'the principals of Religion and Holiness'. After 'she had caused me to read well at home, she sent me to school'.[27]

It appears, however, that early in the colonial period children began attending a school to learn to read, either as well as, or instead of, learning from their mothers. Such schools were called dame schools or reading schools. The dame school is well documented for England in the seventeenth and eighteenth centuries.[28] A woman would take small children, both boys and girls, into her own home for a few hours. We even know of one two-year-old girl who drowned on her way to school.[29] While no doubt the dame's major contribution was to afford an overworked mother a few hours of respite from her three- and four-year-olds, ostensibly her purpose was to introduce her charges to reading. In fact, some dame schools taught a substantial amount of reading. John Barnard, born in 1681, recalled that when he was less than six years old his schoolmistress 'made me a sort of usher, appointing me to teach some children that were older than myself, as well as smaller ones; and in which time I had read my Bible through thrice'.[30]

The dame, or reading, school was not funded by the town, but was a private venture. It represented, of course, a most useful source of income for a woman. We meet women as paid teachers of reading in unexpected contexts. The Commissioners of the United Colonies of New England, who disbursed monies sent over from England for missionary work among the Indians, not only employed a woman to teach the Indians to read, but even gave her a raise. As their letter said, in 1653, 'The wife of William Daniell of Dorchester hath for this three yeares last past bestowed much of her time in teaching severall Indians to Read and that shee hath onely Receiued the summe of six pounds towards her paines; [we] thought fitt to allow her nine pounds more for the time past.'[31]

Women are notoriously invisible in colonial records. Even though most townships (Boston, for instance) required private schoolteachers to obtain permission from the town before they were allowed to teach, private women teachers do not appear in the Boston records until the 1730s. In the seventeenth century, therefore, most of our evidence comes from those rare cases in which women teachers were involved with the law, as happened to Goodwife Wickam of New Haven. One can only guess how many women must have earned a few pennies a week as private teachers of reading throughout that century. As we shall see, in the following century women would be called upon to ply their skills in the public arena as well.

Writing instruction

Writing was defined, in the colonial context, as penmanship.[32] In only a few respects did writing instruction resemble reading instruction. Just as 'good' reading was considered to be accurate oral reading, so 'good' writing seemed to be viewed entirely in terms of fine letter formation. Composition seems rarely to have been discussed at all. Similarly, mastery was to be attained by rote and repetition: by the careful reproduction by the learner of the 'copy' set for him by the writing master. As was the case in reading instruction, mastery of the individual letters of the alphabet was the first step in the writing curriculum. Later the learner would copy, five or six times, pithy moral sentences, and then work up to copying poems or texts reproduced by the master from the traditional copybooks such as George Bickham's *The Universal Penman* (1743).[33]

In other respects, however, the contrast between the teaching of the two literacy skills could hardly have been greater. Writing was considered a craft, subject to all the limitations of access that that implied. The gender bias implicit in the term 'penmanship' was not fortuitous: writing was largely a male domain. This was particularly true as it related to the gender of the instructor: men taught writing. The writing master, analogous to the scribe of earlier times, was the possessor of a fairly arcane skill. The most telling evidence that his knowledge was considered specialized was that he had usually had to attain it through the apprenticeship route.[34]

Moreover, unlike textbooks for reading instruction, which were early reproduced on American presses, the texts for writing instruction were, for technical reasons, not reprinted on American presses but imported. Although the successful reproduction of different kinds of 'hands' (scripts) had been made much easier by the invention of copperplate engraving, engraving not only was costly but demanded a great deal of skill; in fact, the best engraving was undertaken by penmen themselves. (George Bickham, for instance, personally engraved the work of some twenty-five masters for his *Universal Penman*.) The closest Americans came to reproducing scripts was in a text like George Fisher's *The Instructor: or, Young Man's Best Companion*, which included a few pages of scripts in its American versions from 1748 on. Not until after the American Revolution would there be copy books penned by Americans and printed on American presses.[35]

Again unlike reading texts, which could be purchased in any colony for mere pennies and were probably in most households, copybooks were costly to purchase and the prized possessions of the writing master. It was clearly not to the best interests of the profession to encourage the notion that anyone could learn from a book, rather than from a person.[36] Writing, in short, unlike reading, was considered a specialized skill, and colonial access to instructional writing texts was far more limited than access to reading texts.

What penmanship was used for, however, was even more important, in terms of who would be taught to write, than its aspect as a specialized skill. Writing was a male job-related skill, a tool for ministers and shipping clerks alike. When the Boston town meeting voted in 1682 to open a town writing school, Bostonians were acknowledging the importance of Boston as a thriving commercial and mercantile center. Hundreds of boys a year passed through the three writing schools that Boston had established by 1720. They mastered the English round hand that had become the international script for commerce, routing the old secretary hand of the seventeenth century.[37] At a time when all clerical and bookkeeping work was a male stronghold, every young man with business aspirations needed to know how to form a legible script. Writing was also, of course, useful for rural concerns. Farmers who wanted to sell surplus produce needed to write in order to keep accounts. Penmanship was therefore both a hallmark of the well-educated and the servant of commerce.

Sequence of instruction

The order, then, of the different components of the literacy curriculum followed the sequence implicit in the 'three R's', a term still glossed today as 'reading, 'riting, and 'rithmetic'. There is nothing accidental about this universally agreed-upon phrase: its wording faithfully reflects the actual order of instruction during the colonial period. Reading instruction preceded, and was independent of, writing instruction. That this was possible was a function of its methodology – reading instruction was, as we have seen, conducted entirely orally. Arithmetic, which involved the endless writing of rules and examples, in turn presupposed the mastery of writing.[38]

It may be difficult for the modern reader/writer to believe reading instruction could be conducted without having the child write. A few examples will have to suffice. In 1660, a master in New Haven was asked whether he had seen to his apprentice's education, as he was legally obliged to do. He responded that the apprentice 'could read pretty well, and that he was now learning to write'. Two years later, one William Potter, who had been accused of (and was subsequently hanged for) the crime of bestiality, was asked by the New Haven Court if he had been educated. 'He answered, well, and was taught to reade'. Had he also been taught to write, he would undoubtedly have said so.[39]

A century later, in 1762, Samuel Giles of New York City advertised his private writing and arithmetic instruction at his evening school. After stating firmly that teaching small children the rudiments had taken up too much of his time, he said that 'for the Future, no Children will be take

but such as have already been taught to Read, and are fit for Writing'. Finally, there is an advertisement that appeared in a Boston newspaper in 1755. In it, the advertiser promised to teach 'persons
of both sexes from twelve to fifty years of age, who never wrote before, to write a good hand in five
weeks, at one hour per day, at his house in Long Lane'.[40]

Literacy and the law

The Dissenters who had made their way over hazardous seas to settle in New England saw themselves as part of a literate culture. At a time when paper itself was precious and scarce, the
meticulous records of the early town secretaries stand as a self-explanatory tribute to a new
settlement's belief in the power of the written word to safeguard its new laws.

The greater importance placed by colonial Americans on the ability to read rather than to
write is well exemplified by the legislation passed in 1642 by the colony of Massachusetts. Religious
and political motives are explicit in this law; economic motives are implicit. The law empowered the
colony's elected representatives, the selectmen, to inquire into the 'calling and implyment' of all
children, 'especially of their ability to read and understand the principles of religion and the capitall
lawes of this country'. Children who were not being trained to a skill or taught to read were liable to
be removed from their parents and apprenticed to someone else for such instruction.[41] While the
provisions in the law for 'putting out' indigent children to apprenticeship were borrowed from
English precedents, the educational provisions were unique to the colonies. As Lawrence Cremin has
put it, the statute was part of 'a vigorous legislative effort to increase the political and economic self-
sufficiency of the colony'.[42]

The Massachusetts law that required that children be taught to read was quickly replicated by
other colonies. Connecticut passed such a provision in 1650, New Haven (then a separate colony) in
1655, New York in 1665, Plymouth in 1671, and Pennsylvania in 1683.[43] The colony of New Haven
was unusual in adding, in 1660, a writing requirement to the law. Significantly, only one of the sexes
was to be taught this skill: 'To the printed law, concerning the education of children, it is now added,
that the sonnes of all the inhabitants within this jurisdiction, shall (vnder the same penalty) be
learned to write a ledgible hand, so soone as they are capable of it.'[44] The only other colony to
require writing initially was Pennsylvania, which in its 1683 ordinance mandated that parents and
guardians should ensure that children 'may be able to read the Scriptures and to write' by the age of
twelve.[45]

The 1642 law on reading was taken seriously by at least several Massachusetts townships.
When the Dorchester selectmen called in Timothy Wales and his sons in 1672, they examined the
boys and found that they were unable to read. The following year Salem conducted its own
investigation, found several families in violation of the law, and initiated – although it may not have
carried out – the process of finding persons to whom the children could be apprenticed.[46] Watertown, Massachusetts, made a particularly consistent effort over successive decades to keep parents up
to the mark. The first recorded Watertown inspection occurred in 1661. Upon surveying their
fellow townsmen to see whether they fulfilled the law that required 'the knowledg of God and
excerising reading to the advancing of Catachising', the selectmen discovered that four families, with
eighteen children among them, had failed in this respect. All the families were poor (so providing an
early example of a correlation between poverty and illiteracy).[47]

Successive versions of what came to be called the Massachusetts Poor Laws continued to
authorize the removal of children, without the consent of their parents, if the parents were considered unable to maintain them. A 1703 supplement to earlier acts reaffirmed the need to provide
apprentices with an education by stipulating that the masters should provide 'for the instructing of
children so bound out, to read and write, if they be capable'. Clearly, as both sexes could be

apprenticed, both sexes were to be taught reading and writing. However, it turned out that the legislators had not intended this. In 1710, an amendment was passed that altered the order to 'males to read and write, females to read'. The act was repeated in the same form once a decade until 1741, when the requirement of 'cyphering' was added to the regulations for males. Finally, in 1771, the legislation was changed once again, and the legislation for children apprenticed under the Poor Laws now stipulated, 'males, reading, writing, cyphering; females, reading, writing'.[48]

In other words, it was not until 1771 that Massachusetts considered the ability to write to be a minimal educational necessity for girls. This is particularly significant because the whole purpose of apprenticing these children was to provide them with a skill with which they could eventually support themselves, so as not to be a burden on the town like their indigent parents. Boys needed to be able to write, girls did not.

Literacy and employment

If legislation on involuntary apprenticeship reveals that children's gender made a difference to the kind of literacy instruction they were required to receive, so too do the terms of apprenticeship agreements that were completely voluntary. In a study of apprenticeship in seventeenth-century Massachusetts, Judith Walter identified 267 apprentices, of whom 32 were girls. For only 31 of all the apprentices was some kind of educational provision specified. For boys, the indenture usually stipulated that the boy be taught to read, write and cipher. James Chichester, for example, when apprenticed at the age of ten, was to be sent to school 'until he can write a leagable hand'. The 1658 indenture of Hopestill Chandler, who was being apprenticed to a blacksmith, required that he be taught to read the Bible and 'to write enough to keep book for his trade'. In contrast, the educational provisions made in 1674 for Sarah Joye of Salem were that she be taught her catechism, and 'to read English, [and] the capital laws of the country', while Sarah Braibrok of Watertown was apprenticed in 1636 to a couple who were to teach her 'to reade the English Tongue' and provide her with religious instruction. In not one case does Walter report finding a writing provision for female apprentices.[49]

The explanation lies in colonial perceptions of the function of writing. Writing was a job-related skill. Because girls were being trained not to hold jobs, but to be successful homemakers, penmanship was an irrelevant acquisition for them. The skill that corresponded, for girls, to what writing was for boys was the ability to sew. In the study just cited, Walter identified some forty different crafts and trades that the boys were to learn during their apprenticeships. There was no indication, however, that girls were to learn anything other than housewifery and, in two cases, sewing or knitting and spinning.[50]

Further evidence on the relationship between jobs and literacy comes from court rulings. In 1635, the Hartford Court ordered the administrators of Thomas Gridley's estate to educate his children, 'learning the sons to read and write, and the daughters to read and sew well'. The next year, the same court interpreted the provisions of Thomas Thomson's will that related to education as follows: 'the sons shall have learning to write plainly and read distinctly in the Bible, and the daughters to read and sew sufficient for the making of their ordinary linen'.[51]

More evidence of sewing as the advanced skill to be acquired by girls in lieu of writing is provided by contemporary records from across the Atlantic. They are particularly instructive because both sexes were being educated in the same institution. Orphaned or needy children between the ages of five and fifteen were admitted to the Great Yarmouth Children's Hospital which was in effect a charitable workhouse. The master of the hospital was expected to see to the children's education, and kept a register of their educational attainments upon entering and leaving the hospital. David Cressy has tabulated the notes in the hospital register on 132 boys and 85 girls admitted to the hospital between 1698 and 1715. The register reveals that several boys were taught to write before they left the hospital. In contrast, 'none of the girls reached the stage of writing', according to Cressy. Their 'highest achievement was to sew well and to read in the testament or Bible'.[52]

The fact that none of the girls was taught to write should, however, surely be interpreted differently. As eleven of the girls were already in either their Testament or Bible on entering the hospital, they were as ready as the thirty-six boys, similarly prepared, for further instruction. That not even these relatively accomplished readers were taught to write suggests that writing instruction was withheld from them because of their gender, not because they had not 'reached the stage of writing'. Mary Clark, for instance, had entered the hospital at the age of nine with the comment, 'can't read at all'. Four years later, she was characterized as reading 'in her testament but indifferently and hath gone through her sampler'.[53] If girls were to form letters, it would be through the medium of thread, not ink.

No wonder Anne Bradstreet, whose first book of poetry appeared in London in 1650, felt that she was incurring odium by stepping outside the role prescribed by society for women, in exchanging her needle for a pen:

> I am obnoxious to each carping tongue
> Who says my hand a needle better fits,
> A Poets pen all scorn I should thus wrong,
> For such despite they cast on female wits.[54]

Nor should gender restrictions on writing instruction be considered simply a seventeenth-century feature. Apprenticeship indentures for sixty poor children 'put out' by the Newbury selectmen between 1743 and 1760 reveal precisely the same differentiation. Forty-nine boys were apprenticed to learn a range of skills from blacksmithing to making periwigs. The eleven girls, however, were to learn only 'women's work' or 'housewifery'. All the apprentices were promised reading instruction, but only the boys were to be taught writing and arithmetic.[55]

There are several cases in which masters of apprentices were hauled into court for not fulfilling their educational obligations toward their apprentices. We have already noted the New Haven master who in 1660 was brought to court for his alleged failure to teach his apprentice his craft, and who was examined on how much literacy education his apprentice had received. A telling instance is provided about a century later by John Adams. In 1761, Adams remarked on the case of Daniel Prat, 'a poor, fatherless Child' who was suing his master, Thomas Colson. The terms of the apprenticeship had required Colson to teach Prat to read, write, and cipher, and to teach him the trade of a weaver. He had done none of these. Adams felt strongly that Prat, as a child without a male parent, was to be favored in the case, 'Because the English Law greatly favours Education. In every English Country, some sort of Education, some Acquaintance with Letters, is necessary, that a Man may fill any station whatever'.[56]

From the earliest days of settlement, then, and throughout the colonial period, the colonists expected that all children ought to be able to read, no matter how low their station or how poor their circumstances.

Schooling and gender

As we have seen, in 1642 the Bay Colony had legislated reading without any mention of either schools or writing. Five years later, in striking contrast, a new law mentioned writing and schoolmaster in the same breath: in 1647, Massachusetts passed its first schooling law. Every township of over fifty families was required to engage a master to 'teach all such children as shall resort to him to write and reade', while towns of over a hundred families were to provide a (Latin) grammar school.[57]

The relationship between writing instruction and schooling is exemplified by Watertown, Massachusetts, which constructed its first schoolhouse in 1649 and soon thereafter hired Richard Norcross as its first schoolmaster. The job description spelled out that he was responsible 'for the teaching of Children to Reed and write and see much of Lattin . . . as also if any of the said towne, haue any maidens, that haue a desire to learne to write that the said Richard, should attend them for the Learning off them; as also that he teac[h]e such as desire to Cast acompt'.[58] The clear implication of this wording is that girls would attend the school only if they wished to learn writing and arithmetic. Obviously, they were supposed to have learned to read at home.

Norcross's contract is also an example of the ambiguity of the word 'children'. To modern ears, the word indicates children of both sexes. In the colonial period, there was a strict separation of roles in the home and workplace by gender, and it was the males who held all the positions of responsibility and power.[59] Male children, therefore, were the prime targets of any town's educational efforts. As a result of this bias, the word 'children' meant, in effect, male children, even though it always retained its broader meaning of children of both sexes. (In discussions of Boston schools, for example, the town records habitually refer to the students of their free schools as 'children'. Yet free schooling in the Boston system was restricted to males until 1789.)[60]

While 'reading' is indeed included in Norcross's job description, as we saw earlier, children were supposed to have mastered initial reading before they reached the town school. The school was expected to 'perfect' them in reading, not introduce them to it. Moreover, girls were often not admitted to town schools, particularly if such schools had any aspirations toward teaching Latin (the hallmark of the true grammar school). The rules and regulations of the Hopkins Grammar School, opened by New Haven in 1684, are a case in point. They insisted that 'noe Boyes be admitted into the said Schoole for the learning of English Books, but such as have ben before taught to spell their letters well and begin to Read, thereby to perfect theire right Spelling, and Reading, or to learne to write, and Cypher . . . and that all others either too young and not instructed in letters and spelling, and all Girles be excluded as Improper and inconsistent with such a Crammer Schoole'.[61]

Walter Small, in his study of some two hundred schools in the colonial period, reported finding only seven schools that definitely admitted girls, and another five that might have. The school in Rehoboth, Massachusetts, was among the seven. In 1699, Robert Dickson contracted with the Rehoboth selectmen 'to do his utmost endeavor to teach *both sexes* of boys and girls to read English and write and cast accounts'. Similarly, Deerfield, in northwestern Massachusetts, obviously allowed girls to enter its town school in 1698, because it warned parents that all heads of families with children between the ages of six and ten, whether male or female, should pay a poll tax to the school, 'whether they send such children or not'. Five years later the town made a similar motion but this time changed the ages of admission. Families of 'boys from four to eight, and girls from four to six years old', were to pay their proportion of ten pounds for the ensuing year.[62] (The shorter timespan for girls suggests that they were to leave school at the point when they were supposed to be able to read, having reached the age for the instruction in writing that they would not receive.)

The comparatively late dates at which these and similar provisions were enacted is significant they suggest that on the boundaries of settlement, as the seventeenth century drew to a close, the town school had two characteristics. In the first place, it did not attempt any education fancier than the three R's, and in the second, it chose not to restrict its education to boys. Indeed the experience of the frontier settlement of Hatfield may prove, with further research, to be characteristic. From 1695 to 1699 there were no girls in Hatfield's town school; in 1700 there were four girls and forty-two boys during the winter term; nine years later there were sixteen girls in a total of sixty-four schoolchildren.[63]

Nevertheless, there were many towns that stood firm against the admission of girls to the master's school throughout the entire seventeenth and even the eighteenth century. Farmington, Connecticut, for example, voted in 1686 to devote twenty pounds to a town school, 'for the instruction of all such children as shall be sent to it, to learn to read and write the English tongue'. Some parents of daughters, it seems, interpreted this too broadly, for the following year the town issued a clarification: '*all* such children as shall be sent is to be understood only *male* children that are through their horning book [hornbook]'. Small found many instances of town schools – Salem, Medford, Haverhill, Gloucester, Hingham, and Charlestown – that, shortly before or even well after the American Revolution, were only just beginning to open their doors to girls. And in these cases, the girls were being admitted only for a couple of hours a day (presumably for writing instruction). As one witness put it, remembering his schooling in Lynn, Massachusetts, 'In all my school days which ended in 1801, I never saw but three females in public schools, and they were there only in the afternoon to learn to write'.[64]

School dames

A new feature in colonial town schooling can be detected as the seventeenth century drew to a close: the towns' formal sponsorship of women to teach reading. One presumes that private dame-school instruction had continued for decades in New England; after 1670, however, we see towns actively seeking female teachers to teach reading to small children. These women were paid a few pennies per week per child, and substantially less than their male colleagues.

Walter Small collected numerous references to such 'school dames'. Among Massachusetts towns, Woburn paid ten shillings to two women in 1673, and the same sum to another in 1686. Cambridge reported in 1680 that 'For English, our school dame is Goodwife Healy; at present but nine scholars.' Two years later, Springfield made an agreement with Goodwife Mirick that, in order to 'encourage her in the good work of training up of children and teaching children to read', she should have three pence per child per week.[65]

After 1700, mention of school dames increases. Small found references to them in records running from 1700 to 1730 for, among others, Waterbury and Windsor in Connecticut, and for Weymouth, Lexington, Charlestown, Salem, and Falmouth, all in Massachusetts. A few of these, as was the case for Charlestown, only involved the town in paying women for the instruction of poor children who could not otherwise attend school. But increasingly, as the eighteenth century wore on, there seems to have been a definite shift in the direction of employing women to teach reading on a regular basis, in specific parts of town, with funds allocated for that purpose from the town treasury. Framingham had voted as early as 1713 to appoint selectmen to 'settle school dames in each quarter of the town'. Worcester in 1731 decided that, because small children could not walk to the school in the center of town, up to five school dames should be hired 'for the teaching of small children to read' and placed in different parts of the town. Wenham, two years later, made an arrangement with its schoolmaster that permitted him to delegate some of his teaching responsibilities to others: he was to be 'allowed to teach little children to read by suitable women, in the several parts of the town, that he shall agree with, by the approbation of the selectmen; also to teach to write by another man in another part of town'.[66]

Marriage was no obstacle for a woman in teaching reading. In fact, there were those who taught for almost the whole of their adult lives. When Abigail Fowler died in Salem, Massachusetts, in 1771, her death was reported affectionately: 'Widow Abigail Fowler, a noted school dame, finished her earthly labors. She was in her 68th year, and began to teach children before she was 18, and continued so to do till her decease, with the exception of a few years after she was married.'[67]

The reason for the towns' new eagerness to employ women seems to have been the continuing failure of parents to carry out their legal responsibility to teach their children to read. For example, at the turn of the century Marblehead undertook a survey on the number of boys who could not read, and who could therefore not be admitted to the master's school. The town found a total of 122 such boys.[68]

Note that there were children who still read too poorly for the master's school despite the fact that standards for admission appear to have been lowered in many schools as the decades progressed. Whereas, formerly, schoolmasters had expected children to be in their Psalter or Bible (still the case in Boston's three elite writing schools, as the incident with John Proctor revealed), now the admission requirement was only, for the New Haven grammar school in 1684, to 'have been taught to spell the letters well and begin to Read', or, for Farmington, Connecticut, two years later, that boys should be through their hornbook.

For many women, the chance to earn money from the town must have been most welcome. Others, as the eighteenth century lengthened, were able to use newspapers successfully to advertise their private literacy instruction.

Conclusion

The arguments made up to this point are as follows:

1.   Reading was considered easy to teach, and reading instruction unaccompanied by writing instruction was the province of women, both at home and at school (private or town-sponsored). Texts for reading instruction were cheap and easy to obtain.
2.   Writing was considered a craft, difficult to teach and taught by men. Texts for writing instruction were comparatively expensive and difficult to obtain.
3.   Reading instruction preceded, and was independent of, writing instruction. Instruction in reading was conducted orally, by means of the oral alphabet method.
4.   Because reading was considered to be important for religious, political, and economic reasons, legislation was passed that required it of all children.
5.   Because writing was considered a job-related skill, society only required that it be taught to boys.
6.   Writing was one of the key components of the curriculum of the town schools, which were taught by men and in many cases restricted to boys. Girls won access to some, but by no means all, of the masters' schools from the 1690s on.
7.   Towns began to employ women (school dames) to teach reading to small children of both sexes from the 1680s on.

      These statements generate further conclusions:

8.   Because reading was required to be taught, and because people could and did learn to read without also learning to write, we cannot assume that all those – particularly women – who only marked documents were totally illiterate.
9.   However, because educational standards in New England were raised over time, marks have to be interpreted in context.

In the seventeenth century, class, gender, and rural location all militated against obtaining writing instruction. In terms of class, the children whose apprenticeships have been mentioned above were at the bottom of the social heap, as were the orphans admitted to the Great Yarmouth Children's Hospital. Even at this low social level, it is clear that boys were offered both reading and writing instruction, but girls were only expected to know how to read and sew. If such girls could not sign when grown women, it was because no one had ever taught them to write.

Of course, then as now, low social class combined with poverty often correlated with illiteracy in reading as well as writing. It is surely no coincidence that the eighteen children found to be unable to read in Watertown in 1661 all came from impoverished families, and that the boys who could not read the Psalter, and who were therefore refused admittance to one of the Boston writing schools in 1741, were the children of 'Families of low Circumstances'.

As we would also expect, high social standing, when combined with an urban setting, was able to erase the restrictions on female access to writing instruction. In cities, the daughters of the higher ranks learned to write because their parents sent them off for private instruction. In Boston, for instance, even in the seventeenth century, girls were taught by private entrepreneurs like the writing master who taught Hannah Sewall (wife of Samuel Sewall) to write. In the eighteenth century, girls could also learn from publicly financed town masters who taught fee-paying female students 'out of hours'.[69] The fact that during the early colonial period rural women, even when wealthy, signed at a lower rate than urban women is surely to be explained by the exclusion of girls from the town school and the relative paucity of private male teachers in rural areas. But in cities, private teachers abounded: at least twenty private writing masters have been documented for Boston during the colonial period.[70]

It is the girls of modest social standing, however, who are of the most importance to my argument. Even in the seventeenth century access to reading instructional materials was easy, and the teaching of reading was considered a female domain. There is every reason to believe that reading at some level was taught widely to girls by women, whereas writing, for a long time considered a male teaching preserve, was not.

Around the turn of the century, several strands were coming together, all of them favoring increasing education in general, and female education in particular. One that should not be ignored is domestic tranquility, bought at considerable cost to both whites and Indians. King Philip's short but bloody war, 1675 to 1676, spelled the end of the political and military power of the Indians. Slaughter and disease had thinned their ranks, and surviving Indian communities passed into obscurity.[71] The colonists were therefore freer to concentrate less on defense and more on such matters as education.

As we have seen, after 1680 women were increasingly incorporated into town educational systems, hired for their skill in teaching beginning reading. (Such women would have had to be taught to write, for they needed to be able to keep school records.) Girls were also winning access to some of the masters' town schools, and so to writing instruction.

There are several other factors that no doubt made their contribution, although proof of these lies beyond the scope of this essay. For instance, eighteenth-century instructional texts in reading improved, thanks to the advent of the spelling book. Similarly, the switch from the secretary hand of the seventeenth century to the eighteenth-century round hand would appear to have made penmanship easier. There were also political changes: some colonies began to put teeth into their education laws. The expansion during the course of the eighteenth century in the availability of secular reading material, including chapbooks and, at the end of the century, novels, was undoubtedly significant.

These speculations aside, it is still possible to take a fresh look at the supposed illiteracy of those who made marks instead of signatures. First, a comment on the mark itself. When we talk today about making a 'mark' on a document, what springs to mind is the traditional X. That is not, however, how most colonists marked documents. When the information is available, marks often turn out to be initials, like the HN used by Hanna Newberry. These initials indicate, at the least, an acquaintance with the alphabet.[72]

We can now reinterpret some of the detailed information provided by Auwers for Windsor, Connecticut. What puzzled Auwers was that she found no correlation between social class and the signatures ('literacy') of Windsor women born before 1690: many rich women, like Hanna

Newberry, only made marks. We can now explain this as a function of gender, which impeded access to writing instruction. Surely Hanna could read: her socioeconomic status alone makes it very unlikely that she would have been truly illiterate.

Windsor forms a useful example in other ways. In 1717 the town employed its first school dame: Sarah Stiles was hired to teach reading in the summer; schooling opportunities improved.[73] The dramatic increase that Auwers found in the percentage of women able to sign their names, as the decades passed, suggests that the right of girls to write in Windsor had been permanently won by the 1740s.

And what of the female will-markers in Lockridge's study, cited so often in defense of claims of massive female illiteracy in colonial New England? The figures from these women are misleading, I believe, in several respects. For one, as Lockridge is the first to point out, the sample of females is small, representing under 15 percent of his total sample and only 5 percent of the population he was investigating.[74] Just as important is the fact that wills were Lockridge's only source. Some women may have been able to sign but chose not to. People often make their wills late in life, and when a mark was as legal as a signature, initialing a will if you were old and ill may have seemed more appealing than struggling to sign. Auwers's study, for instance, identified thirty-one women who had affixed their names to both deeds and wills. Eight of these (26 percent) signed their deeds but marked their wills, only one did the reverse. (This could also be interpreted, with Auwers, as evidence of the marginality of female signing skill.)[75] We can speculate that no stigma would have attached to a woman who chose not to sign her name. In contrast, because society increasingly expected them to write, men by the early eighteenth century might have felt more deeply about the social cachet attached to signing.[76] Even more important is the age at which a person subscribed his or her will. A mark in the 1760s may represent the absence of writing instruction as much as forty or fifty years earlier.

Be that as it may, it is, in any case, likely that many of Lockridge's female will-markers could read, at least to some extent. Further research, ideally using Linda Auwers's birth cohort approach, is likely to produce evidence of higher female signing rates in the eighteenth century similar to those found by Auwers and, later in the century, William Gilmore.[77]

How well could someone read who could read but not write? The colonists themselves were aware that there were differing levels of literacy. Experience Mayhew, a pastor on Martha's Vineyard, discussed in 1727 the literacy of the Christian Indians who could read books published in their own language; he said that such Indians read and wrote only at the 'rate that poor Men among the English are wont to do'.[78] The literacy of nonwriters fits the profile of 'traditional literacy' that David D. Hall has sketched, of readers who approached print with reverential deliberation.[79] Probably, many nonwriters read familiar material without too much trouble. This would have been particularly true of the Scriptures: the advantage was that ministers, heads of households, and other family members were constantly reading from them aloud. Nonwriters would also have been able to decipher writings such as the notes – like those asking for information on strayed animals – that were so often tacked onto the doors of meeting houses.[80] They surely could not, however, as Cathy N. Davidson points out, have been able to read the works of John Locke.[81]

On the other hand, we should not underestimate the pleasure that even a limited reading ability can bring. For a colonial woman, reading must have provided one of the very few sources of satisfaction that was not dependent upon others. In virtually all of the roles identified by Laurel Thatcher Ulrich, whether as housewife, deputy husband, consort, mother, mistress of servants, or neighbor, a woman was looking out for the welfare of others.[82] When she was reading, she was doing something for herself. Above all, if she was a Christian (another of the roles posited by Ulrich), her reading would have been an important and meaningful part of her private devotions.[83] For those who were called upon to teach reading to others, their reading ability transformed itself into a measure of independence. These were small treasures of the mind and spirit that we should not despise.

here is no reason to suppose that the conclusions drawn here for New England are very different from those to be drawn for other parts of colonial America – except, perhaps, for the South, where male tutors on plantations taught children of both genders to read and write. A poem penned by a judge in Philadelphia at the end of the seventeenth century shows that differentiation of schooling by gender was not exclusive to New England:

> Here are schools of divers sorts,
> To which our youth daily resorts,
> Good women, who do very well
> Bring little ones to read and spell,
> Which fits them for writing, and then,
> Here's men to bring them to their pen,
> And to instruct and make them quick
> In all sorts of arithmetick.[84]

otes

his research was supported in part by grant no. 6–64048 from the PSC-CUNY Research Award Program of e City University of New York.

1   Linda Auwers, 'Reading the Marks of the Past: Exploring Female Literacy in Colonial Windsor, Connecticut', *Historical Methods* 13 (1980): 209.

2   See Carl F. Kaestle's summary of literacy studies in 'The History of Literacy and the History of Readers', in *Review of Research in Education*, vol. 12, ed. Edmund W. Gordon (Washington, D.C., 1985), 11–53.

3   Kenneth A. Lockridge, *Literacy in Colonial New England: An Enquiry into the Social Context of Literacy in the Early Modern West* (New York, 1974), 128 n. 4, 13, 38–42, 140 n. 57.

4   Auwers, 'Reading the Marks of the Past'; and Ross W. Beales, Jr., 'Studying Literacy at the Community Level: A Research Note', *Journal of Interdisciplinary History* 9 (1978): 93–102. The largest study to date is that by William Gilmore, who surveyed 10,467 documents dated between 1760 and 1830 from the Upper Connecticut Valley, and found almost universal male signing levels by the 1770s, while female signing began at two-thirds in the late 1770s and rose thereafter: William J. Gilmore, *Elementary Literacy on the Eve of the Industrial Revolution: Trends in Rural New England, 1760–1830* (Worcester, Mass., 1982), 98, 114.

5   Auwers, 'Reading the Marks of the Past', 204–5.

6   Kaestle, 'History of Literacy and the History of Readers', 21.

7   E.g. *ibid.*, 21, 29; Margaret Spufford, *Small Books and Pleasant Histories: Popular Fiction and Its Readership in Seventeenth-Century England* (Cambridge, 1981), 22, 27, 29, 34–35; Victor E. Neuburg, *Popular Education in Eighteenth-Century England* (London, 1971), 55, 93; Geraldine Jonçich Clifford, 'Buch und Lesen: Historical Perspectives on Literacy and Schooling', *Review of Educational Research* 54 (1984): 474–75, and Gerald F. Moran and Maris A. Vinovskis, 'The Great Care of Godly Parents: Early Childhood in Puritan New England', in *History and Research in Child Development*, ed. Alice Boardman Smuts and John W. Hagen, *Monographs of the Society for Research in Child Development* 50, nos. 4–5 (1985): 34. Lockridge himself raises the possibility several times in *Literacy in Colonial New England*, 14, 109, 127, 134 n. 26, but rejects it for the purpose of his analysis, 38.

8   James L. Axtell, ed., *The Educational Writings of John Locke: A Critical Edition with Introduction and Notes* (London, 1968), 260; and Lawrence A. Cremin, *American Education: The Colonial Experience, 1607–1783* (New York, 1970), 277. I would like to acknowledge here my indebtedness to Professor Cremin's bibliography.

9   George A. Plimpton, *The Hornbook and Its Use in America* (Worcester, Mass., 1916). Pla
      and gilt hornbooks were listed in the book inventories of a Boston bookseller in 170
      Worthington C. Ford, *The Boston Book Market, 1679–1700* (rpt. New York, 197:
      177–78.

10   Quoted in Andrew W. Tuer, *History of the Horn Book* (1897; rpt. New York, 1979), 133.

11   Plimpton, *Hornbook and Its Use in America*, 9.

12   Charles J. Hoadly, ed., *Records of the Colony and Plantation of New Haven, from 1638 to 16*
      (Hartford, Conn., 1857), 176. For ease of reading, I have silently expanded all the abbre
      ations in this and other quotations (e.g., 'y^e,' 'y^t,' and 'Testam^t' appear as 'the', 'that', a
      'Testament'), but have preserved the spelling, punctuation, and capitalization of the origina

13   John Eliot, *The Indian Primer* . . . (Cambridge, Mass., 1669).

14   Paul L. Ford, *The New-England Primer: A History of Its Origin and Development with a Reprint of*
      Unique Copy of the Earliest Known Edition (New York, 1897); and Richard L. Venezky,
      History of the American Reading Textbook', *Elementary School Journal* 87, no. 3 (1987): 24
      For a discussion of *The New England Primer* as the vehicle for a set of metaphors on Christi
      obedience, see David H. Watters, ' "Spake as a Child": Authority, Metaphor and *T*
      New-England Primer', *Early American Literature* 20 (1985–86): 193–213.

15   Charles F. Heartman, *American Primers, Indian Primers, Royal Primers, and Thirty-Seven Other Ty*
      of Non-New-England Primers Issued Prior to 1830 (Highland Park, N.J., 1935).

16   Quoted in Nila Banton Smith, *American Reading Instruction* (Newark, Del., 1965), 17–18.

17   Boston, Registry Department, *Records Relating to the Early History of Boston*, vol. 15, *A Report*
      the Record Commissioners of the City of Boston, Containing the Records of Boston Selectmen, 1736
      1742 (Boston, 1886), 288.

18   Franidin B. Dexter, ed., *New Haven Town Records, 1649–1662* (New Haven, Conn., 1917), 9
      Similarly, the Reverend Peter Thacher wrote of a new student in 1680 that he was 'to perfe
      him in reading, and to teach him to write'; quoted in David D. Hall, 'The Uses of Literacy
      New England, 1600–1850', in *Printing and Society in Early America*, ed. William L. Joyce *et*
      (Worcester, Mass., 1983), 24.

19   Dexter, *New Haven Town Records*, 88.

20   For spelling books in Britain, see Neuburg, *Popular Education*, 64–91; R. C. Alston, *A Bib*
      ography of the English Language from the Invention of Printing to the Year 1800, vol. 4, *Spelling Boo*
      (Bradford, England, 1967); and Ian Michael, *The Teaching of English: From the Sixteenth Centu*
      to 1870 (Cambridge, UK, 1987). For spelling books in the American colonies, see Rac
      N. Smith, 'Interest in Language and Languages in Colonial and Federal America', *Proceedir*
      of the American Philosophical Society 123 (1979): 36–38.

21   Venezky, 'History of the American Reading Textbook', 248.

22   William R. Hart, '*The English Schoole-Maister* (1596) by Edmund Coote: An Edition of t
      Text with Critical Notes and Introductions', diss., University of Michigan, 1963, 8.

23   Robert F. Roden, *The Cambridge Press, 1638–1692: A History of the First Printing Press Establish*
      in English America, Together with a Bibliographical List of the Issues of the Press (New York, 190!
      36.

24   E. Jennifer Monaghan, *A Common Heritage: Noah Webster's Blue-Back Speller* (Hamden, Conn
      1983), 31–34; quotation, 26. There were seventy-six editions of Dilworth by 1801, of whi
      forty-three were printed before 1787: Smith, 'Interest in Language and Languages', 36.

25   Monaghan, *Common Heritage*, 33–34; and Smith, *American Reading Instruction*, 25–31.

26   Edmund Coote, *The English Schoole-Maister* (London, 1596), A3; in Hart, '*The English Schoo*
      Maister', 129.

27   M. G. Hall, ed., *The Autobiography of Increase Mather* (Worcester, Mass., 1962), 278; Richa
      Brown is quoted in James Axtell, *The School upon a Hill: Education and Society in Colonial N*
      England (New Haven, Conn., 1974), 174–75. Cf. Hall, 'The Uses of Literacy', 25; and M.

Clanchy, 'Learning to Read in the Middle Ages and the Role of Mothers', *Studies in the History of Reading*, ed. Greg Brooks and A. K. Pugh (Reading, England, 1984), 33–39.

28   Spufford, *Small Books*, 35–36; J. H. Higginson, 'Dame Schools', *British Journal of Educational Studies* 22, no. 2 (1974): 166–81; and D. P. Leinster-MacKay, 'Dame Schools: A Need for Review', *British Journal of Educational Studies* 24, no. 1 (1976): 38–48; cited in Joan N. Burstyn, 'Women in the History of Education', paper presented at the annual meeting of the American Educational Research Association, Montreal, April 1983.

29   Axtell, *School upon a Hill*, 176.

30   'Autobiography of the Rev. John Barnard', *Collections of the Massachusetts Historical Society* 3, no. 5 (1836): 178. Cf. 'The Commonplace Book of Joseph Green', *Publications of the Colonial Society of Massachusetts* 34 (1943): 236.

31   David Pulsifer, ed., *Records of the Colony of New Plymouth, in New England. Acts of the Commissioners of the United Colonies of New England*, vol. 2, *1653–1679* (Boston, 1859), 106.

32   E. Jennifer Monaghan and E. Wendy Saul, 'The Reader, the Scribe, the Thinker: A Critical Look at the History of American Reading and Writing Instruction', in *The Formation of School Subjects: The Struggle for Creating an American Institution*, ed. Thomas S. Popkewitz (New York, 1987), 88.

33   George Bickham, *The Universal Penman, Engraved by George Bickham, London 1743* (New York, 1954). For the writing curriculum, see E. Jennifer Monaghan, 'Readers Writing: The Curriculum of the Writing Schools of Eighteenth-Century Boston', *Visible Language* 21, no. 2 (1987): 167–213.

34   Ray Nash, *American Writing Masters and Copybooks: History and Bibliography through Colonial Times* (Boston, 1959), 13.

35   George Fisher, *The Instructor; or, American Young Man's Best Companion*, 30th ed. (Worcester, Mass., n.d.); and Nash, *American Writing Masters and Copybooks*, 25–34.

36   At least one copybook, however, proclaimed (in 1656) that it was *Set forth for the benefit of poore Schollers, where the Master hath not time to set Copies*: see Nash, *American Writing Masters and Copybooks*, 21–22.

37   Monaghan, 'Readers Writing'.

38   Cremin, *American Education*, 501–3; Patricia Cline Cohen, *A Calculating People: The Spread of Numeracy in Early America* (Chicago, 1982), 120–22.

39   Dexter, *New Haven Town Records*, 438; and Charles J. Hoadly, ed., *Records of the Colony or Jurisdiction of New Haven, from May 1653, to the Union, Together with the New Haven Code of 1656* (Hartford, Conn., 1858), 443.

40   Robert F. Seybolt, *The Evening School in Colonial America* (Urbana, Ill., 1925), 23; advertisement quoted in Walter H. Small, *Early New England Schools* (Boston, 1914), 317.

41   Nathaniel B. Shurtleff, ed., *Records of the Governor and Company of the Massachusetts Boy in New England*, vol. 2, *1642–1649* (Boston, 1853), 6–7.

42   Cremin, *American Education*, 125.

43   *Ibid.*

44   Hoadly, *Records of the Colony or Jurisdiction of New Haven, from May 1653, to the Union*, 376.

45   Quoted in Cremin, *American Education*, 125.

46   Dorchester Antiquarian and Historical Society, *History of the Town of Dorchester, Massachusetts* (Boston, 1859), 223–24; and Salem, Massachusetts, *Town Records of Salem, Massachusetts*, vol. 2, *1659–1680* (Salem, Mass., 1913), 180.

47   Watertown, Massachusetts, *Watertown Records Comprising the First and Second Books of Town Proceedings* (Watertown, Mass., 1894), 71. Subsequent inspections occurred in 1665, 1670, 1672, 1674, 1679, 1680, and later: *ibid.*, 86, 104, 113, 121, 137, 145.

48   Robert F. Seybolt, *Apprenticeship and Apprenticeship Education in Colonial New England and New York* (New York, 1917), 46–47.

49   Judith Walter, 'Apprenticeship Education and Family Structure in Seventeenth Century Massachusetts Bay', M.A. thesis, Bryn Mawr College, 1971, 33–34, 42–43.

50   *Ibid.*, 34.

51   Walter H. Small, 'Girls in Colonial Schools', *Education* 22 (1902): 534.

52   David Cressy, *Literacy and the Social Order: Reading and Writing in Tudor and Stuart England* (Cambridge, 1980), 30–34; quotation, 34.

53   *Ibid.*, 34. For girls taught only reading and sewing in England, see Spufford, *Small Books*, 34–35.

54   Quoted in Thomas Woody, *A History of Women's Education in the United States* (1929; rpt. New York, 1966), I: 132.

55   Laurel Thatcher Ulrich, *Good Wives: Image and Reality in the Lives of Women in Northern New England, 1650–1750* (New York, 1982), 43–44.

56   L. H. Butterffield, ed., *Diary and Autobiography of John Adams*, vol. I, *Diary 1755–1770* (Cambridge, Mass., 1961), 219.

57   Shurtleff, *Records of the Governor and Company of the Massachusetts Bay*, 2: 203.

58   *Watertown Records Comprising the First and Second Books*, 18, 21.

59   Lyle Koehler, *A Search for Power: The 'Weaker Sex' in Seventeenth-Century New England* (Urbana, Ill., 1980).

60   See, for example, the proposal in 1682 to open a free school for the 'teaching of Children to write & Cypher': Boston, Registry Department, *Records Relating to the Early History of Boston*, vol. 7, *A Report of the Record Commissioners of the City of Boston, Containing the Boston Records from 1660 to 1701* (Boston, 1881), 158.

61   *American Journal of Education* 4 (1857): 710.

62   Small, 'Girls in Colonial Schools', 532–33. Small used primary sources such as town records for his study, but did not document his sources. Where I have been able to crosscheck them, I have found them accurate.

63   *Ibid.*, 533.

64   *Ibid.*, 533–37; quotations, 533–34.

65   *Early New England Schools*, 168, 165.

66   *Ibid.*, 165–70; quotations, 179, 168, 170.

67   *Ibid.*, 169.

68   *Ibid.*, 167.

69   Robert F. Seybolt, 'Schoolmasters of Colonial Boston', *Publications of the Colonial Society of Massachusetts* 27 (1928): 137; for an example of female instruction by a writing master, see Alice Morse Earle, ed., *Diary of Anna Green Winslow: A Boston School Girl of 1771* (1894; rpt. Williamstown, Mass., 1974), 12, 92–94.

70   Seybolt, 'Schoolmasters of Colonial Boston'.

71   William C. Sturtevant, ed., *Handbook of North American Indians*, vol. 15, *Northeast*, ed. Bruce G. Trigger (Washington, D.C., 1978), 177.

72   For initials as marks, see, for example, Joseph Underwood's V in 1684 as his mark set to an agreement to teach his male apprentice to read and write: *Watertown Records Comprising the First and Second Books*, 129.

73   Auwers, 'Reading the Marks of the Past', 204.

74   Lockridge, *Literacy in Colonial New England*, 128.

75   Auwers, 'Reading the Marks of the Past', 207.

76   I am indebted to Ross W. Beales, Jr., for this insight.

77   Auwers, 'Reading the Marks of the Past'; and Gilmore, *Elementary Literacy on the Eve of the Industrial Revolution*.

78   Experience Mayhew, *Indian Converts: Or, Some Account of the Lives and Dying Speeches of a Considerable Number of the Christianized Indians of Martha's Vineyard, in New-England* (London, 1727), xxiii.

79   Hall, 'The Uses of Literacy', 21–24. Hall emphasizes the role played by memorization and recitation in learning to read.

80   See, for example, the complaint in 1687 about such notes: Watertown, Massachusetts, *Watertown Records Comprising the Third Book of Town Proceedings and the Second Book of Births Marriages and Deaths to End of 1737* (Watertown, Mass., 1900), 31.

81   Cathy N. Davidson, *Revolution and the Word: The Rise of the Novel in America* (New York, 1986), 59.

82   Ulrich, *Good Wives*, 9–10.

83   Charles F. Hambrick-Stowe, *The Practice of Piety: Puritan Devotional Disciplines in Seventeenth-Century New England* (Williamsburg, Va., 1982), 157–61.

84   Quoted in Carl Bridenbaugh, *Cities in the Wilderness: The First Century of Urban Life in America, 1625–1742* (1938; rpt. Oxford, 1971), 283–84.

Chapter 32

Kate Flint

READING PRACTICES

Reading, prohibition and transgression

Not all accounts of reading are untroubled. Numerous narratives of prohibitions, warnings, and censorship are told, which amount to a substantial body of evidence about the control exercised within some families, particularly concerning the ideas and emotions which were considered suitable for girls to encounter. Such accounts of transgression provide sites for the writer's own assertion of individuality, measures of the distance she has travelled from her family background and the ideological assumptions of her parents, even siblings. Julia Kristeva may claim that the adolescent is one of those mythic figures which has the function of distancing us from certain of our faults by reifying them in the form of someone who has not yet grown up,[1] but the role of the figure of the adolescent reader in many of these writings is to problematize the idea of fault. A symbolic action against family or against dominant social beliefs is not so much distanced from the time of writing as highlighted; presented as an incident which helps form the recognition and assertion of individual identity which leads directly towards the self-confidence necessary for the writing of published autobiography.

Sometimes, these instances of rebellious reading took place in carefully chosen social contexts, like Marie Corelli (b. 1855) deliberately startling her governess with quotations from *Don Juan*,[2] or Mrs Benson, wife of the Headmaster of Wellington College, scandalizing his friends by letting her children read George Eliot, and thrusting *Adam Bede* into the hands of clergymen's wives telling them not to mind being seen reading it.[3] Sometimes they were private ones, like Jean Curtis Brown and her friend Lucy consuming the forbidden magazine *Home Chat*, borrowed from the kitchen on the cook's night out.[4] But the impact of the transgressive act was not necessarily dependent on breaching obvious moral imperatives or crossing class boundaries. It could signify a different form of assertion: access into the domain of parental property. Joan Evans, later to become a historian of medieval art and a well-known Ruskin scholar, was brought up in the 1890s in a house full of books, most of them dating from the early and mid-century: she could claim that she was more familiar with life in England between 1810 and 1850 than with anything happening in her own time. Yet despite the freedom of her access to the fiction of Scott and Thackeray, she was aware that she lacked poetry, of which there was little in the house other than the well-bound wedding presents, belonging to her mother, kept in a glass-fronted bookcase in the drawing room:

> One of my few conscious naughtinesses after I had attained the age of perception was to steal into the drawing-room, when I knew my parents were safe in London, open the case, and take deep delicious draughts of verse. Tennyson and Matthew Arnold are all the sweeter for being read in secret.[5]

Controls over what was, or was not, considered suitable reading focused around certain specific issues. Some of these controls were generically determined, demonstrating, especially, the distrust of novels. 'Lucas Malet', daughter of Charles Kingsley (b. 1852), told a reporter that 'novels were practically forbidden at Eversley Rectory', and that she was not allowed to read even so safe a writer as Charlotte Yonge until she was twenty. Despite the fact that she had the run of Kingsley's library, where she read history, philosophy, and the poets, 'novels were not within my reach', and she never recollects having seen her father open a novel.[6] This is perhaps not entirely surprising, given the attitudes towards women as readers of fiction which her father professed outside the home. In 'Nausicaa in London: Or, The Lower Education of Woman', written in 1879, for example, he paints a particularly dismal picture of the unhealthy modern girl, stunted, pallid, subsisting on tea and bread and taking a novel from the library as her stimulus.[7] On the other hand, Kingsley was not entirely consistent, recognizing elsewhere that women may have needs in their reading which can be met through fiction. He defended his habit of inserting pieces of information into his own novels on the ground that many readers enjoyed them, especially intelligent women who were starved of opportunities for serious discussion.[8] Kingsley's novels themselves, incidentally, were not immune from censure: Edward Pusey considered *Hypatia* 'a work not fit to be read by our wives and our sisters'.[9]

There are plentiful further examples of fiction being regarded with qualified disapproval. Mary Paley Marshall, for example, one of Newnham's first students, recalls her father in the 1860s reading aloud *The Arabian Nights*, *Gulliver's Travels*, the *Iliad* and *Odyssey*, Shakespeare, and, above all, Scott's novels, but she never understood why – unless it was the more pronounced 'religious tone' in Scott – which meant that his novels were allowed whilst Dickens's were forbidden: 'I was grown up before I read *David Copperfield* and then it had to be in secret'.[10] But it is impossible to arrive at any sound generalizations. Dorothy McCall (b. *c.* 1884) recalls that *The Heart of Midlothian* was the one book in her father's library which she and her siblings were forbidden to read: 'he immured it in his dressing room, where we took our baths at night. It was a gentleman's agreement, and we behaved like gentlemen, and never looked inside it'.[11] On the other hand, Julia Grant, leaving for boarding-school for the first time in 1877, was bought a copy of the same novel by her father at the railway station, for reading on the journey.[12] And Anne Thackeray's (b. 1837) memories serve to remind us that what an adult might find unsuitable was in any case often unintelligible to a child: she could not 'imagine how little Em'ly ever was so stupid as to run away from Peggotty's enchanted houseboat'.[13]

The combination, here, of reference to Scott's aura of religiosity on the one hand, and on the other to *David Copperfield*, the novel of Dickens's most commonly considered *risqué*, points to the two most common areas in which familial control was exercised: sexuality and religion. First, sexuality. Like McCall's family, Maurice Baring's sisters were not allowed to read *The Heart of Midlothian* 'which was not, as they said, for the J.P. (jeune personne)'.[14] Frequently forbidden, too, was George Eliot's *Adam Bede*. Whilst Lucy Caroline Lyttelton's grandmother only left out one chapter of this new novel about which 'the world raves . . . a heart-rending book, with its stern true moral of the irrevocableness of sin' when she was reading it aloud to her grandchildren,[15] as late as the 1890s, Harriet Shaw Weaver's mother was shocked when she came upon her adolescent daughter reading *Adam Bede*: the story in part of a girl who had given birth to and disposed of an illegitimate child, written by a woman who herself lived unmarried, with a man. Weaver was sent immediately to her room, and the local vicar was asked to call in order to explain the book's unsuitability. This incident was to remain painful to her for fifty years, since it epitomized, for her, the forthcoming conflict between loyalty to her family and her championing of individual liberties.[16] Slightly less surprisingly, given its content, Yeats forbade his sisters to read George Moore's *A Mummer's Wife*: a proscription which led Susan Mitchell, who lived with the family, to 'gulp . . . guilty pages of it' as she went to bed.[17] Mary Butts's (b. 1890) mother warned her solemnly against the cupboard in her father's room:

> I was not to look at the books in the cupboard. It was full of dreadful books. Books, she went on to explain, that only men read, and she wished indeed that my father would not read them. But I was always to remember that men were different. Also it seemed that even God would have to try specially hard to forgive Daddy for reading some of the books that were in there.

These works included books by Ronsard, Guy de Maupassant, Defoe, Balzac, and Stendhal. On her father's death, Butts's mother ceremoniously burnt the offending texts on a funeral pyre, paying no concern to their potential financial, let alone literary value, so shocked was she by what she knew, or presumed, of their contents: 'Little square old books, the noble pages of Burton in their gold and black, their delicate engravings of fabulous princesses. French memoirs, with their portraits of Ninon and the Dubarry and the great Pompadour'.[18]

It was not only the young who could be presumed to be corrupted, or to think themselves corrupted, by what they read. A letter from Elizabeth Barrett Browning to Arabel Barrett tells of a sixty-year-old woman who believed that her morals had been injured by reading *Aurora Leigh* and that her character would be in danger if it were to become known that she had looked at the poem.[19] Josephine Butler recalled the publication of Elizabeth Gaskell's *Ruth* in 1853 and the voicing of double standards to which it gave rise in Oxford University circles:

> A moral lapse in a woman was spoken of as an immensely worse thing than in a man; there was no comparison to be formed between them. A pure woman, it was reiterated, should be absolutely ignorant of a certain class of evils in the world, albeit those evils bore with murderous cruelty on other women. One young man seriously declared that he would not allow his own mother to read such a book as that under discussion – a book which seemed to me to have a very wholesome tendency, though dealing with a painful subject. Silence was thought to be the great duty of all on such subjects.

This formed one among a growing list of iniquities which led Butler into 'revolt against certain accepted theories in Society'.[20] Gaskell herself recorded how one close Chapel associate of her family 'has forbidden his wife to read it',[21] and expressed to Anna Jameson her sorrow and surprise 'how very many people – good kind people – and *women* infinitely more than men, really & earnestly disapprove of what I have said & express that disapproval at considerable pain to themselves, rather than allow a "demoralizing laxity" to go unchecked'.[22]

Readers more willing to confess to their assertions of independence explicitly indicate how prohibition and censorship in themselves, unsurprisingly, led to inquisitiveness and transgression. These were presented as crucial acts in the development of their consciousness which they could look back to, in some cases, with gratitude. Lady Frances Balfour, for example, was brought up in a highly literary environment: her father and mother both read poetry aloud (she particularly recollected her mother repeating 'How well Horatius kept the bridge in the brave days of old') and at home she listened to Gladstone reading Latin and Italian. The book 'on which my youth was nourished', however, was *Uncle Tom's Cabin*, the plot of which served as an analogy for the liberation of her own bonds of thought and experience. She was forbidden to read the second volume of this 'but human nature cannot be denied, and of course I read it . . . It did its work! A woman's pen, under Divine inspiration touched the iron fetters, the rivets fell apart and "the slave where 'er he cowers" went free'.[23] Netta Syrett recalls how when a pupil at North London Collegiate School, aged about thirteen, Miss Buss confiscated Lemprière's *Classical Dictionary* on the grounds that it was a 'clumsy book' which she did not wish her to read:

> Up to that moment in perfect innocence (if anyone had been so unwise as to set it) I could have passed an examination in the stories of the gods and goddesses, sexual vagaries and all, for I looked upon these as part of the general incomprehensibilty of grown-up people. But when the book was removed I never rested till I knew, at least dimly, why I was not allowed to keep it in my possession.[24]

Autobiographies and letters certainly show that many girls picked up what they knew about sex from what they read, and the patchiness of this knowledge is a vindication in itself for the campaign that greater straightforward information about sex should be given to girls, whether directly by their mothers or, if this proved too intimate and embarrassing, through the written word. H. M. Swanwick, in the late 1870s, absorbed what she could from any available scientific books and medical journals, and puzzled over the Bible, Shakespeare, Chaucer, La Fontaine. Forbidden *David Copperfield*, *Bleak House*, *The Heart of Midlothian*, and *The Vicar of Wakefield*, she read them none the less, 'and my attention was sharpened by the prohibition'. She:

> must have been still a child when I rebelled against the common morality of the day in regard to responsibility in sex relations. These little Em'lys and Hetties and Olivias and Effies – by what divine law was it decreed that they must for ever live a life of abject penitence or, better still, die?[25]

When she was lent Dante Gabriel Russetti's poems by a friend, 'Jenny', which takes a prostitute for its subject-matter, came as a welcome antidote.

The degree to which girls could be protected from 'unsuitable' material could be taken to ridiculous lengths. Mary Stocks (b. 1891) recorded how her Aunt Tiddy made great efforts to preserve her and her siblings from 'indelicacy':

> In Tennyson's poem, 'The Revenge', which was among those she read to us, occurs the line: 'Bearing in her womb that which left her ill-content'. Over the word 'womb' Aunt Tiddy stuck a narrow strip of paper. My family still cherishes the tattered volume of Tennyson showing the marks from which the strip was surreptitiously removed by us to satisfy a curiosity very natural in the young.[26]

Dora Russell, at Sutton High School during the first decade of the twentieth century, knew nothing whatever about sex': she was not aided in any attempt at self-instruction by the fact that books on anatomy and physiology in the school library had 'certain dangerous pages stuck fa together'.[27]

In her biography of Marie Stopes, Ruth Hall indicates that prior to the birth-control reform er's marriage, her only sexual knowledge came from reading Browning, Swinburne, and – ignorin her mother's advice – Shakespeare's sonnets and 'Venus and Adonis', with the addition of novels, an 'the only book on sex that she had read before her marriage', Edward Carpenter's *Love's Coming of Ag* This last figures frequently in her letters. Certainly Carpenter believes that young people should b informed about sex, should be told how 'intoxicating, indeed, how penetrating – like a most preciou wine – is that love which is the sexual transformed by the magic of the will into the emotional an spiritual', and that the young of both sexes should not be kept 'in ignorance and darkness an seclusion from each other'[28] but he includes virtually no physiological detail to support his rhapsod

Some girls obtained straightforward practical information about sexual matters from standar household reference books. Vera Brittain's far from bookish home contained, in addition to th yellow-back novels which formed the main staple of her early reading, a volume entitled *Househo Medicine*: 'the treatment of infectious diseases left me cold, but I was secretly excited at the prospe of menstruation; I also found the details of confinement quite enthralling'. She added the knowledg thus gained to other sources, recalling 'that intensive searching for obstetrical details through th Bible and such school-library novels as *David Copperfield* and *Adam Bede* which appears to have bee customary almost everywhere among the adolescents of my generation'. None the less, she wer into wartime nursing a relative innocent, only learning the details of venereal disease – the 'hidde plague' of newspaper reports – when she had to nurse a case in 1917; her knowledge of Arm doctors and nurses, 'derived entirely from the more idealistic poems of Kipling', in no way helpir her to understand her colleagues' suggestive language and furtive manœuvrings.[29] Other wome add a small number of further texts to this catalogue of sources. The Viscountess Rhondda mentio *Midshipman Easy* as an enabling text, presumably because of the presence of the illegitimate child Jack Easy's wet-nurse, and the general post-Fielding-and-Smollett stress on physical function Cicely Hamilton, the suffragette and actress, claimed that she learnt 'what are sometimes called "th facts of life" . . . fairly early from the Bible'.[30] Hamilton's autobiography also indicates how it w possible to come across potentially controversial material and read it undetected – even under th guise of approval – when she tells how she found a dusty copy of Eugene Sue's *Juif Errant* in cupboard and, with the aid of a dictionary, read it from cover to cover. The fact that 'it containe episodes which those in authority would probably consider unsuitable for juvenile reading' on adding to her enjoyment, for, in this educational context, 'there were only smiles of approval wher was seen with a French book in my hand . . .'.[31]

Despite the considerable furore in the press concerning both sensation and the so-called 'Ne Woman' fiction, and the undesirable degree of explicitness on sexual matters which these genr were criticized for offering, and despite, too, the number of copies of such novels in circulation, fe women noted that they made much of an impact. An exception is provided by Dr Elizabeth Chesse recollecting Glasgow in the 1890s, at a time when the onerous duties of the daughters of profe sional men stretched to dusting the drawing-room and washing the aspidistras. She contrasts t atrophy inherent in this lifestyle with reading 'extraordinary "modern" sexual novels . . . in ope drawers which were shut on the approach of adult footsteps', or hidden under the mattresses. Maud Churton Braby recalls the excitement Grant Allen's *The Woman Who Did* aroused when sh was a schoolgirl, 'and my acute disappointment when it was forcibly commandeered from me an irate governess who apparently took no interest in these enthralling subjects'. But she clair that despite the temporary enthusiasm kindled by this and other fictions in precocious and impre sionable girls, the eventual lure of 'the Ring, the Trousseau, and the House of My Own' almo inevitably won out.[33]

It is worth while bearing in mind, despite all the testimony to the furtive but fascinated arches for sexual information entered into by many of the women who look back at their olescence, that others of them remained unenlightened, despite the breadth of their reading. Nor d they necessarily resent this fact: they represent themselves as having had other priorities. Mary amilton (b. 1884), looking back at her time at Newnham, recalls that during her second year, atthew Arnold was left open on the mantelpiece, to remind her of the vanity of human wishes and e essential loneliness of the heart. Even being in love, for her, 'expressed itself almost exclusively highly spiritual and mental terms; although I had always been allowed, nay encouraged, to read nnivorously, I remained blankly ignorant about sex and its manifestations, even the most normal es'. She refers here to the lesbian relationships within her college which, looking retrospectively, e could recognize, but which, she said, she would not remotely have been able to comprehend at e time. An intense concern for politics, she said, made up for ignorance about sex.[34] There is a ar sense, here, of a young woman, proud of her educational achievements and intellectual terests, separating herself off − unconsciously at the time, consciously in later life − from the ncerns of those whom she did not regard as privileged enough to share the same exalted mental ace.

As this memory hints, not all prohibitions were based around preserving the 'innocence' of e young woman in relation to sexual matters, nor was sexuality the area with which the young oman's mind was necessarily the most consciously concerned. A variety of anxieties centred ound the reading of religious works, or works which might cause the young woman to query portant Christian tenets, or to find religion disturbing rather than affirmative. Elizabeth Sewell d her sister were given a volume of Cardinal Newman's sermons by an Oxford friend of their other William, 'but it was with the caution that there were two sermons which it was better for us t to read'. Whilst the prohibition was ultimately lifted, this was only when the friend had made up mind that the girls were not likely to have their minds disturbed by the new teaching.[35] Laura ight, in 1899, was mystified by being forbidden Foxe's *Book of Martyrs*: 'Just the sort of horrors I ould love to read about − or so I imagined', having been used to enjoying Edgar Allen Poe, the ore gruesome parts of *The Ingoldsby Legends*, and the *Boy's Own Paper*, bought with her weekly penny helping with the housework.[36] And older women, too, could be disturbed by the tone and ntent of works which queried their religious beliefs. Fanny Kemble (b. 1809), for example, called how 'extremely disagreeable' Chambers's *Vestiges of the Natural History of Creation* was to her, hough the knowledge that it dealt with facts, not fiction, gave it 'a thousand times more interest an the best of novels for me'.[37] Mary Howitt wrote to her daughter concerning Harriet Martineau d Henry Atkinson's 'new *infidel* book' *Letters on the Laws on Man's Social Nature and Development* 851): first telling her that the volume was making such an excitement that it was always out from e London Library when she sent for it, and then, with disgust, noting that 'It is to my mind the ost awful book that was ever written by a woman. It made me sick and ill to hear them talk of Jesus a mere clever mesmerist'.[38]

But such disquiet and revulsion are predictable enough. More interesting, from the point of w of the individual's development, are those writers who, when they remember being frightened unsettled by what they read, frequently indicate that a girl's perception of what texts might or ght not be advisable differed from that of adults: troubling effects could not invariably be guarded inst. Margaret Cole claimed that the only reading which was forbidden her was Bram Stoker's cula, Poe's *Tales of Mystery and Imagination*, and *What a Young Mother Ought to Know*, plus 'trashy gazines', but maintained that she read 'all that was forbidden' anyway. Whilst the motherhood nual was an obvious target for prohibition because of the explicitly sexual material it concerned, more deliberately frightening material is introduced by her in the context of what *actually* turbed her. Thus Cole writes that she was scared by Uncle Remus, by a series of American picture stories called the Golliwog books, and by a book of noble deeds, principally rescues from shipwrecks and burning houses: 'Even today I cannot read the words "blind alley" without a faint reminiscent shudder born of a story, whose details I have entirely forgotten, of people fleeing from a burning building into a blind alley with the flames at their heels'.[39] On occasion, the experience of disturbance could derive from texts disapproved of by parents. For example, in the early 1870s, the ten-year-old Annabel Huth Jackson 'was terribly frightened by the episode of the mad woman tearing the wedding veil' in Jane Eyre, although the existence of this incident alone was doubtless insufficient to explain Jackson's mother's horror when she learnt her daughter had read the book.[40] But as many reminiscences, including Cole's, show, the reading which frightened rarely involved the reading material about which parents expressed direct apprehension. Margaret Campbell ('Marjorie Bowen'), for example, was particularly scared by a book – she believes one of Thackeray's novels – which 'had a yellow paper cover of a howling negro running along in terror while a man shot at him', and by Wordsworth's 'Lucy Gray';[41] Winifred Peck claims to have been 'terrified' by a book routinely figuring as a Sunday School prize, Wood's Natural History;[42] Janet Courtney remembers 'as a special terror' Scott's White Lady of Avenel in The Monastery,[43] and Cicely Hamilton, who had read all of Scott by the time she was eleven, wrote that one of his short stories, 'The Tapestry Chamber',

> was a disturber of my rest for years. So too was an illustrated version of The Ingoldsby Legends; I remember the peculiar horror inspired by a devil, arrayed in Elizabethan garb, who danced up the room with a lady and never came down again! And the even greater horror inspired by the Dun Horse ridden by Exciseman Gill, with hell-fire streaming from its nostrils![44]

These instances act as reminders, too, that not all disturbing effects were necessarily linked to gender expectations, nor, in any explicit way, to the gendered experiences of the reader.

Notes

1   Julia Kristeva, 'The Adolescent Novel', in John Fletcher and Andrew Benjamin (eds), Abjection, Melancholia and Lore: The Work of Julia Kristeva (1990), 8.
2   Bertha Vyver, Memoirs of Marie Corelli (1930), 19–20.
3   Amy Cruse, The Victorians and their Books (1935), 278.
4   Jean Curtis Brown, To Tell My Daughter (1948), 67.
5   John Evans, Prelude and Fugue: An Autobiography (1964), 17
6   'Lucas Malet' (Mary St Leger Harrison), interviewed by Sarah A. Tooley, 'Some Women Novelists', Woman at Home, 5 (1897), 187.
7   Charles Kingsley, 'Nausicaa in London: Or, The Lower Education of Woman', Health and Education (1879), 82.
8   See Brenda Colloms, Charles Kingsley: The Lion of Eversley (1975), 130.
9   Quoted by Cruse, The Victorians and their Books, 271.
10   Mary Paley Marshall, What I Remember (1947), 7.
11   Dorothy McCall, When That I Was (1952), 118.
12   Julia M. Grant, Katherine H. McCutcheon, and Ethel F. Sanders, St Leonards School 1877–1927 (1927), 164.
13   Anne Thackeray Ritchie, Chapters from Some Memoirs (1894), 78.
14   Maurice Baring, The Puppet Show of Memory (1922), 49.
15   Diary of Lady Frederick Cavendish, i. 83.
16   Jane Lidderdale and Mary Nicholson, Dear Miss Weaver: Harriet Shaw Weaver 1876–196 (1970), 33.

17   Susan L. Mitchell, *George Moore* (Dublin, 1916), 43.

18   Mary Butts, *The Crystal Cabinet: My Childhood at Salterns* (1937), 102, 111. For Butts and her treatment of the past, see Patrick Wright, *On Living in an Old Country: The National Past in Contemporary Britain* (1985), 93–134.

19   Elizabeth Barrett Browning to Arabel Barrett (19 Feb. 1857), Berg collection, New York Public Library.

20   Josephine F. Butler, *Recollections of George Butler* (Bristol and London, 1893), 96.

21   Elizabeth Gaskell, letter to Eliza Fox (?early Feb. 1853), *The Letters of Mrs Gaskell*, ed. J. A. V. Chapple and Arthur Pollard (Manchester, 1966), 223.

22   Elizabeth Gaskell, letter to Anna Jameson (7 Mar. 1853), *Letters*, 226.

23   Lady Frances Balfour, *Ne Obliviscaris: Dinna Forget*, 2 vols (1930), i. 89.

24   Netta Syrett, *The Sheltering Tree* (1939), 20. Syrett's *The Victorians* (1915), a novel which draws considerably on her own childhood, gives considerable space to the importance played by reading in an adolescent girl's life.

25   H. M. Swanwick, *I Have Been Young* (1935), 83–4.

26   Mary Stocks, *My Commonplace Book* (1970), 12.

27   Dora Russell, *The Tamarisk Tree: My Quest for Liberty and Love* (1975), 24.

28   Edward Carpenter, *Love's Coming of Age* (Manchester, 1896), 11, 102.

29   Vera Brittain, *Testament of Youth* (1933, repr. 1983), 26, 48, 49.

30   Cicely Hamilton, *Life Errant* (1935), 4.

31   *Ibid.* 17.

32   Elizabeth Sloan Chesser, MD, in Countess of Oxford and Asquith (ed.), *Myself When Young, by Famous Women of To-Day* (1938), 81.

33   Maud Churton Braby, *Modern Marriage and How to Bear it* (1909), 6, 8.

34   Mary Agnes Hamilton, *Remembering My Good Friends* (1944), 46–7.

35   Sewell, *Autobiography*, 65.

36   Laura Knight, *Oil Paint and Grease Paint* (1936), 7; *idem, The Magic of a Line* (1965), 56. Angela Brazil, on the other hand, was considerably disturbed by the pictures in the work, especially the final one which showed a half-charred body falling out of lurid flames. The disturbance worked at two levels, stimulating both physical revulsion and self-doubt: 'At night when I lay awake in the dark I saw those fearful pictures, and not the least of their horror was the persuasion that I had not the stuff in me to make a martyr'. *My Own Schooldays* (1925), 164.

37   Frances Anne Kemble, *Records of Later Life*, 3 vols (1882), iii. 242.

38   Margaret Hosvitt (ed.), *Mary Hewitt: An Autobiography* (1889), 67, 69.

39   Cole, *Growing up into Revolution*, 11.

40   Jackson, *A Victorian Childhood*, 58.

41   Margaret Campbell, in Oxford and Asquith, *Myself When Young, by Famous Women of To-Day*, 44, 48.

42   Peck, *A Little Learning*, 34. John George Wood published a large number of volumes on natural history: most probably she refers to his *Natural History Book for Children*, 3 vols (1861–3).

43   Courtney, *Recollected in Tranquillity*, 25.

44   Hamilton, *Life Errant*, 4.

Chapter 33

Jonathan Rose

REREADING THE ENGLISH COMMON READER
A preface to a history of audiences

As a genre, the working-class autobiography originates around 1800 – here too the reading revolution marked a watershed, when common readers began to write about themselves. And they are often wonderfully forthcoming about their reading experiences – not only what they read, but how they comprehended and reacted to their reading.

These sources open up a new scholarly frontier. They will make possible a third generation of reading history – a history of audiences, which would reverse the usual perspective of intellectual historiography. It would first define a mass audience, then determine its cultural diet, and ultimately measure the collective response of that audience not only to particular works of literature, but also to education, religion, art, and any other cultural activity. Whereas reception histories have generally traced the responses of professional intellectuals (literary and social critics, academics, clergymen), audience histories would focus on the common reader – defined as any reader who did not read books for a living. The British working-class reader happens to be my subject, but this essay offers general encouragement and advice for the study of common readers in all classes and all nations. It illustrates some of the questions a history of audiences could tackle, and points out the methodological problems it may involve.

Although autobiographies will probably prove to be the richest sources for a history of audiences, they must be used with caution and balanced against other materials. Memoirists are not entirely representative of their class (whatever that class may be), if only because they were unusually articulate. Autobiographies were produced in every one of the several British working classes, ranging down to tramps and petty criminals, but a disproportionate number were written by skilled workers and especially the self-employed. Only one in ten nineteenth-century workers memoirs were written by women, and the whole sample is skewed to the political left: the twentieth-century volume of the Burnett–Vincent–Mayall bibliography lists many more Communist than Conservatives.[1]

We also must bear in mind that an autobiographer (like any other 'nonfiction' writer) is liabl

Jonathan Rose, 'Rereading the English Common Reader: A Preface to a History of Audiences', *Journal of History of Ideas*, 53 (1992), 47–70. © The Journal of the History of Ideas, Inc. Reprinted with permission of The John Hopkins University Press, 1992.

to forget, misremember, remember selectively, embellish, invent, and rearrange events in the interest of creating an engaging story. The uncertainties are especially troublesome in the case of common readers, since we usually have no other sources to check their memoirs against. Flora Thompson's *Lark Rise* (1939) – perhaps the most widely read of all working-class memoirs, cited by every important historian of Victorian rural life – has been compared with parish, poor law, school, legal, and census records; and there are just enough discrepancies to give one a moment's pause.[2] To crosscheck and augment the data gleaned from memoirs, a historian of audiences could look to library records, reader surveys, the reports of educational bodies, and oral history projects.[3] It is not Micawberish to suggest that, if we look deliberately enough, we may stumble on a documentary gold mine – such as the Lenin Library archive of N. A. Rubakin, a popular educator in late Czarist Russia who corresponded with eleven thousand readers.[4]

A history of audiences could supply tests for the various theories of reading offered by phenomenological, deconstructionist, semiotic, reader-response, and Marxist critics. Already, it is becoming evident that many of these theories do not square with the praxis of reading, especially in connection with the provocative issue of canon formation. Do the 'great books' embody universal moral values, psychological insights, and aesthetic standards; or do they represent an arbitrary cultural hierarchy imposed upon the masses by the ruling classes? Hayden White has argued that 'the comic strip cannot be treated as *qualitatively* inferior to a Shakespeare play or any other classic text'.[5] Janice Radway, who has recently moved on from Harlequin Romances to the Book-of-the-Month Club, asserts that critics have no right to dismiss the latter as 'middlebrow'. If literature professors insist on drawing such prejudiced distinctions, that, Radway concedes, is 'understandable', so long as they do it in the privacy of the classroom; but they must recognize that Book-of-the-Month Club books 'might be valuable to others because they perform functions more in keeping with their own somewhat different social position, its material constraints, and logical concerns'.[6]

Similarly, Barbara Herrnstein Smith (past president of the Modern Language Association) insists that 'The endurance of a classic canonical author such as Homer . . . owes not to the alleged transcultural or universal value of his works but, on the contrary, to the continuity of their circulation in a particular culture.' They survive only because they have been 'repeatedly cited and recited, translated, taught and imitated, and thoroughly enmeshed in the network of intertextuality that continuously *constitutes* the high culture of the orthodoxly educated population of the West'. The classics are irrelevant to people who have not received an orthodox Western education, Smith asserts. It is an undeniable 'fact that Homer, Dante, and Shakespeare do not figure significantly in the personal economies of these people, do not perform individual or social functions that gratify their interests, *do not have value for them*'. It is also unquestionably a 'fact that other verbal artifacts (not necessarily "works of literature" or even "texts") and other objects and events (not necessarily "works of art" or even artifacts) have performed and do perform for them the various functions that Homer, Dante, arid Shakespeare perform for us'.[7]

Here Radway and Smith fall into the error that Radway herself so rightly showed up in *Reading the Romance*: they dogmatize enormously about the sociology of reading without bothering to study actual readers. They really do not know what functions Homer, Book-of-the-Month Club selections, comic books, or any other verbal artifacts perform for their respective audiences. Moreover, their theories cannot explain autodidacts like Will Crooks, the Edwardian Labour Member of Parliament. Growing up in extreme poverty in East London, Crooks stumbled across a copy of the *Iliad*, and was dazzled:

> What a revelation it was to me! Pictures of romance and beauty I had never dreamed of suddenly opened up before my eyes. I was transported from the East End to an enchanted land. It was a rare luxury for a working lad like me just home from work to find myself suddenly among the heroes and nymphs of ancient Greece.[8]

According to Barbara Herrnstein Smith, this should not have happened. Crooks was not orthodoxly educated, and he was not particularly enmeshed in the network of intertextuality that includes classical literature. All the same, Homer spoke to him – and that is about as radical a transcultural leap as one can imagine. Smith claims that we respond to a great book only because it tends to '*shape and create* the culture in which its value is produced and transmitted and, for that reason, to perpetuate the conditions of its own flourishing'.[9] If she wants to defend that argument, she will have to explain how the *Iliad* created the culture of the East End – without using italics as a substitute for evidence.

She will also have to account for other accomplished proletarian classicists: for example, Thomas Cooper, the Chartist shoemaker who authored one of the best-known workers' auto-biographies, and Tom Barclay, Leicester's intellectual bottle-washer.[10] Of course, such autodidacts were hardly typical of the British working class, but they did constitute a fairly substantial minority. In her 1907 sociological study *At the Works*, Lady Bell estimated that one out of eight working-class households in Middlesbrough included someone who 'read books that are absolutely worth reading', and three out of ten families were 'fond of reading'. A decade later Arnold Freeman, a settlement house warden, interrogated 408 Sheffield workers and classified twenty to twenty-six percent of them as intellectually 'well-equipped'.[11]

Throughout the Victorian period and well into the twentieth century, the British working class maintained a vital autodidact culture that, quite independently of ruling-class cultural hege-mony, found inspiration in the canonical works of Western culture. The literary diet of worker intellectuals was sometimes suggested by clergymen, settlement house residents, university-bred instructors in continuing education classes, and periodicals like *Cassell's Popular Educator*. Usually, however, they were introduced to books by friends, schoolmates, teachers, workmates, or relatives – that is, by other members of the working class. Peter Miles has shown how Robert Tressell's socialist novel *The Ragged-Trousered Philanthropists* (1914) was disseminated by word of mouth and by simply passing along battered copies of the book.[12] The same process of grassroots cultural transmission brought *Hamlet* and *The Origin of Species* to the workers.

'Until now intellectual history has chosen to account for the dissemination of ideas and values by the easy trickle-down hypothesis', observes William Gilmore. 'Its foundation assumption is that the dissemination of ideas, and hence of reading, and of specific types of reflection, proceeded in a hierarchical two-step fashion, from elites to the masses and from "high" to "popular" culture.' But as Gilmore illustrates, banks and ideas were actually diffused through a web of cultural institutions and personal networks that were often created and controlled by common readers, who recognized 'high culture' even when no professors were there to point it out to them.[13] In 1815 Vermont's Windsor District had not quite thirty college graduates among a population of seventeen thousand, mostly farmers and workers; but within a few years the area could boast ten lending libraries, two debating societies, several series of public lectures, a theater club, a music society, and a lyceum.[14]

Similarly, by the early twentieth century South Wales was served by a network of Miners' Institutes – worker-run adult education centers offering libraries, evening classes, lectures, and theatrical productions. Will Jon Edwards remembered discussions of Shakespeare, Darwin, Marx and Herbert Spencer down in the pits. At times he heard some fairly incisive literary criticism. 'Meredith is a poet who sings with a harp', one collier observed; 'Kipling is a nobody who sings what he can sing with a mouth-organ although he does talk of tambourines'.[15] This is not to imply that there was a seminar down every mineshaft: you had to gain admission to the right pit. Walter Haydn Davies recalled that, at his mine,

> The conveyor face down the Number 2 Pit was a university, the surface of Number 1
> Pit a den of grossness. Night after night in this Alma Mater, well-read intelligent, clean

minded men discussed the burning topics of the day, the changing religious trend, the theory of evolution, the nature of spiritualism, Christian Socialism, Communism and all the other isms that then did abound. The ideas expressed by Charles Darwin, R. J. Campbell, Sir Oliver Lodge, Keir Hardie, Ramsay Macdonald, Karl Marx, Noah Ablett were treasured in their minds as well as in the books they carried in their pockets.

Incidentally, it was no anomaly that Walter Haydn Davies was named after a classical composer; that was a custom that reflected the musical culture in which Welsh miners were steeped. 'In fact', he remembered, 'in one family there was a Handel, Haydn, Elgar, Verdi, Joseph Parry, Caradog, Mendy (short for Mendelssohn) and an unforgettable Billy Bach, together with an only daughter Rossini (called Rosie for short)'.[16]

As David Vincent demonstrated, the autodidact usually directed his own reading in a highly idiosyncratic and random manner, somehow managing to discover the classics on his own.[17] He might, like young Manny Shinwell, pick up Dickens, Meredith, Hardy, Keats, Burns, Darwin, Huxley, Kant, and Spinoza from rubbish heaps and tuppeny second-hand bookstalls.[18] Like George Howell, the Victorian bricklayer and trade unionist, he could grope his way through the canon 'on the principle that one poet's works suggested another, or the criticisms on one led to comparisons with another. Thus: Milton–Shakespeare; Pope–Dryden; Byron–Shelley; Burns–Scott; Coleridge–Wordsworth and Southey, and later on Spenser–Chaucer, Bryant–Longfellow, and so on through a numerous class of writers.'[19] Working people often made a point of reading the books their employers warned them not to read: that was how Flora Thompson discovered Byron's Don Juan.[20] Far from following hegemonic lines laid down by cultural elites, workers were so independent in their choice of books as to provoke endless hand-wringing among the university-educated. Even Arnold Freeman, who dedicated his life to working-class education, despaired over what he considered to be the unsystematic reading patterns revealed in his 1918 survey.[21]

A concise summary may be found in a 1906 survey of the first large cohort of Labour members of Parliament. The 51 MPs were asked to name the books and authors that had influenced them most, and 45 of them responded as follows:

- John Ruskin
- Charles Dickens
- The Bible
- Thomas Carlyle
- Henry George
- Walter Scott
- John Stuart Mill
- William Shakespeare
- Robert Burns, John Bunyan
- Alfred Lord Tennyson, Giuseppe Mazzini
- Charles Kingsley, T. B. Macaulay, James Russell Lowell
- Adam Smith, William Cobbett, Sidney and Beatrice Webb, W. M. Thackeray; J. R. Green, Charles Darwin, Henry Drummond.

Interestingly, only two MPs mentioned Karl Marx, while five cited at least one of the ancient Greeks or Romans. Granted, the 45 respondents were all politicians, all male, and all on the leftward half of the political spectrum; if our sample had been more representative of the working class, the above list would have included more literature and less politics and economics. Generally, Victorian working-class intellectuals read more American literature and less Greek and Roman literature than their middle-class counterparts.[22]

However, with the exception of Henry Drummond and the Webbs (who may have involved copyright problems) every one of the authors listed above would be included in Everyman's Library, the series of shilling classics launched by J. M. Dent just after this survey was conducted. In other words, the writers cited by these MPs were nearly all canonical, as that term was defined by a major publisher in 1906. Rarely did these men refer to newspapers, the novels of Harrison Ainsworth, or anything commonly labeled 'popular culture'. Five of the forty-five respondents made no pretense to intellectual culture, asserting (a bit defensively) that they had been educated in 'the school of life'. Beyond that, there is no real basis for what Barbara Herrnstein Smith calls 'the fact that other verbal artifacts (not necessarily "works of literature") . . . have performed and do perform for them the various functions that Homer, Dante, and Shakespeare perform for us'. When they were asked what had inspired them to create a new social order, these men pointed to a selection of 'great books'.

A history of audiences could put some sorely needed discipline into the study of popular culture – and it might begin by abolishing the term 'popular culture' as vague and misleading. Morag Shiach has shown that, for as long as intellectuals have discussed 'popular' or 'folk' or 'mass' culture, they have never been able to offer any firm and unslippery definitions of those categories.[23] In attempting such a definition, Ray B. Browne, the dean of American popular culture studies, manages to contradict himself several times in the space of two sentences:

> Popular Culture is the culture of the people, of *all* the people, as distinguished from a select, small elite group. It is also the dominant culture of minorities – of ethnic, social, religious, or financial minorities – simply because their way of life is, by and large, not accepted into the elite culture of the dominant group.[24]

Popular culture, then, is the culture of all the people *and* of minorities. This would presumably include nearly all culture except that of the British working class, which was neither the whole population nor a minority within it. It excludes any 'small elite group', though that is by definition a minority, and rentier intellectuals would certainly qualify as a 'financial minority'. Students of popular culture create this kind of muddle when they try to sort all culture and all audiences into two bins: 'high culture' and social elites are tossed together into one category, while all culture that is not 'high' is labeled 'popular' and is assumed to have a mass audience. Even when great books clearly have a mass readership, they are usually excluded from popular culture monographs: Jeffrey Brooks appreciates that Maxim Gorky and Leonid Andreev were 'genuinely popular' writers, and that Leo Tolstoy was the author most highly regarded among Red Army soldiers, but Brooks deliberately puts them aside to concentrate on cheap tales of romance and banditry.[25]

Ray Browne cannot account for the Victorian workers who attended Shakespearean drama, or for the Victorian aristocrats who frequented boxing matches. A growing number of cultural historians, however, are discovering that what we call 'high' and 'popular' culture can both spill across class lines.[26] A history of audiences would follow Roger Chartier in avoiding 'the simple opposition of *populaire* versus *savant*';[27] rather than start off with that kind of false antithesis, it would reconstruct the cultural diet of a given audience. The term 'popular culture' is only meaningful as quantitative measure of the audience – applying, say, to any novel that sells over a million copies. 'High culture' is not its polar opposite, but rather a qualitative measure of the work – the best that known and thought in the world, leaving open the question of whose criteria we are following. Given those definitions, it is clear that some culture (such as *Sons and Lovers*) is both popular and high and some culture (such as Victorian pornography) is neither.

However we define it, high culture is clearly not enjoyed exclusively by social elites. British

orking-class autobiographers generally drew a clear distinction between 'improving' literature and
ght' or 'low' literature; I have yet to find a single one who defended the latter as anything more
an a good read. Though George Acorn grew up in poverty in late Victorian East London, he
called that, even as a boy, he had 'some appreciation of style' and a sense of literary hierarchies,
ckling all sorts and conditions of books, from "Penny Bloods" to George Eliot'. He was sophisti-
ted enough to understand that a gifted writer could draw on the conventions of trash literature
d work them into a near-classic in this case *Treasure Island*, which he discerningly characterized as
e usual penny blood sort of story, with the halo of greatness about it'.[28]

This is not to say that working-class autodidacts were as hostile to gutter literature as late
ctorian educators and clergymen, who loudly warned that penny dreadfuls were encouraging
enile delinquency.[29] In fact a few proletarian autobiographers did admit that Dick Turpin stories
spired them to commit petty thefts,[30] but the following comment is far more typical: '[My]
dding love of literature . . . I trace to an enthusiastic reading of Penny Dreadfuls which, so far
om leading me into a life of crime, made me look for something better.'[31] The key word here is
etter'. Where middle-class critics reviled penny dreadfuls as dangerous trash, workers read them
harmless trash, perhaps even delightful trash – but trash all the same.

Many cultural historians – most recently John Springhall – read penny dreadfuls with an eye
discerning whether they 'reinforce rather than subvert the existing social and political struc-
res'.[32] Literary critics and journalists commonly subject all sorts of texts, from Hardy novels to
garette ads, to that kind of political examination; but their efforts may be misdirected on two
unts. First, they usually overlook the possibility that these texts were politically innocuous;
ringhall fails to consider that penny dreadfuls may have only entertained their readers and
ercised the reading habit, which is what working-class autobiographers generally suggest. Second,
s and most other exercises in cultural studies founder on the receptive fallacy.[33] As James Smith
len presumes, 'Because literature was recreated by historical audiences, the world view expressed
the novel may well have involved the beliefs of the readers themselves, who were the most
thusiastic about a particular work. In fact the more popular the work, the more likely this is.'[34] In
t because literature was recreated by historical audiences, and may have been recreated in a
hion quite unlike anything envisioned by the author or the critic, the world view of the novel does
t necessarily equal the beliefs of the reader, no matter how popular the work may be. We cannot
en assume that popular fiction does not offend its readers: Janice Radway's interviewees were
en repelled by the violence and brutal sexuality they found in some romance novels. The reaction
one of those romance fans should serve as a salutary reminder to all cultural historians: one
ssible reader response is to toss the text in the garbage bin.[35]

Hayden White, then, is quite wrong to conclude that 'Every text, grand or humble, is seen to
equally representative, equally interpretive of its proper milieu.'[36] We may not treat any text as
presentative of any reader without that reader's authorization. In his day the sensational novelist G.
M. Reynolds outsold Charles Dickens, but in their memoirs Victorian working people repeatedly
l on Dickens to represent them, not Reynolds. Dickens, they recall, was an honored name in their
me;[37] and even in the most extreme poverty, they could be touched and comforted by a cast-off
py of *David Copperfield*.[38] They saw something of themselves in Jo the crossing-sweeper[39] or had
rned to pick pockets like the Artful Dodger.[40] They had attended a school like Dr. Blimber's
ademy[41] or Dotheboys Hall.[42] They recalled that bad actors in cheap theaters were treated just like
. Wopsle in *Great Expectations*;[43] and East End readers praised *A Tale of Two Cities* for transporting
em out of a 'confused kitchen, that reeked still of fish and chips . . ., to France and the
volution'.[44]

Above and beyond that, Dickens played a critically important role in making the British
orking classes articulate. He supplied a fund of allusions, characters, tropes, and situations that

could be drawn upon by people who were not trained to express themselves on paper. In 1869 t
Dundee, Perth, and Forfar People's Journal, which had a huge circulation among Scottish worke■
sponsored a Christmas story competition: readers submitted more than a thousand entries (abo■
one for every hundred subscribers) and many of them clearly reflected the influence of A Christn
Carol.[45] Cotton operative Joseph Burgess was so deeply shocked by the death of Dickens that he w■
driven, almost unconsciously, to compose a poem, and that began his long career as a labor poet a■
journalist.[46] We find the daughter of a Dudley shoe repairer beginning her reminiscences as Dav■
Copperfield began his ('I am born'),[47] and a Devonshire farm boy could point to the tale of 'T
Convict's Return' from The Pickwick Papers to affirm the importance of writing a biography o■
'homely and ordinary life'.[48] Clearly, Dickens provided working people with the inspiration and t
generic literary conventions they needed to tell their own stories.

G. W. M. Reynolds did not have that kind of impact. Except for an occasional dismissi■
comment, his novels are rarely mentioned by working-class memoirists.[49] Equally 'popular' texts ■
not necessarily have equal influence: some transform the lives of their readers, whereas others a■
consumed like literary chewing gum, leaving no taste behind. Properly done, a history of audienc■
could teach us to make that kind of distinction.

Of course, even the most ephemeral literature can leave a mark on the consciousness. Jose■
Burgess traced his optimistic turn of mind to a blackface minstrel song he once heard in Manchest■

> I will live as long as I can, ha! ha!
> Or I'll know de reason why,
> For as long as dere's breff in pore old Jeff,
> Dis nigger will never say die, ha! ha![50]

Henry Coward, who rose from poverty to become an eminent Sheffield choir conduct■
launched his ascent when he read the following in a scrap of newspaper: ' "Men may be divided in■
two classes, leaders and followers, and any one who has the equipment for leadership – brains a■
power of control – will never lack followers if the cause is a just and reasonable one." Eurel■
Eureka! I had found my niche'.[51]

These autobiographies, however, suggest that this is all 'low' culture can do: it can commu■
cate simple formulas. The Iliad, in contrast, did not transmit any pat 'message' to Will Crooks, bu■
did something far more radical and valuable: it revealed a world outside of the East End,
introduced him to new standards of beauty, it aroused desires and dissatisfactions, it explosiv■
expanded the range of his imagination, it inspired him to recreate his world. That kind of epipha■
recurs again and again in working-class autobiographies, and it is usually produced by canoni■
literature, not by any odd verbal artifact. For Arthur Harding, an East End pickpocket, the magi■
book was The Decline and Fall of the Roman Empire.[52] And it was a 'serious novel' that liberat■
housemaid Edith Hall from the cultural hegemony imposed by the popular press of the 1920s, wh■

> Punch and other publications of that kind showed cartoons depicting the servant class as
> stupid and 'thick' and therefore fit subjects for their jokes. The skivvy particularly was
> revealed as a brainless menial. Many of the working-class were considered thus and
> Thomas Hardy wrote in Tess of the D'Urbervilles that 'Labouring farm folk were personi-
> fied in the newspaper press by the pitiable dummy known as Hodge' . . . and it was in
> this book that Hardy told the story of Tess, a poor working girl with an interesting
> character, thoughts and personality. This was the first serious novel I had read up to
> this time in which the heroine had not been of 'gentle birth' and the labouring classes
> as brainless automatons. This book made me feel human and even when my employers

talked at me as though I wasn't there, I felt that I could take it; I knew that I could be a person in my own right.[53]

The crucial difference between middle-class and working-class autobiographers, according to genia Gagnier and Nan Hackett, is that the latter present themselves less as individuals than as embers of a class, 'social atoms' among the masses.[54] That is true up to a point – but only to the int where the proletarian memoirist describes the book that made all the difference, the book that nferred a sense of identity, mastery, and possibility on the reader. In that respect a history of diences could provide as good a test as any for identifying 'great books'. These are the books that what *Tess* did for Edith Hall – they burst the boundaries of the mind, and they have a record of ing that for a broad range of audiences, representing different classes, cultures, and generations.

In an attempt to rehabilitate forgotten nineteenth-century novelists like Harriet Beecher we, Jane Tompkins has argued that their books must be judged not by modernist aesthetic criteria t according to the 'kind of work the text is doing within its particular milieu'.[55] When we look to ders' memoirs, however, it becomes apparent that the quality of work done by canonical and ncanonical texts is very different. In the 1890s Elizabeth Bryson, the daughter of a Dundee tory worker, did indeed find the story of *Uncle Tom's Cabin* quite gripping. *Sartor Resartus*, however, s nothing less than a 'miracle': it incited 'the exciting experience of being kindled to the point of plosion by the fire of words'.[56]

Likewise, as a Tyneside hospital worker in the 1920s, Catherine McMullen enjoyed Elinor yn's *The Career of Catharine Bush*, in which a common girl prepares for marriage into the aris- cracy by studying Lord Chesterfield's letters to his son. But Glyn's novel was valuable to Miss Mullen mainly because it induced her to visit the public library and read Lord Chesterfield: he s the author who transformed her life.

Now here (to anticipate a possible objection) Barbara Herrnstein Smith might step in and im vindication. Catherine, one could argue, read Chesterfield's letters not because they were rinsically great literature but because they were cited in some trashy novel. That is how upper- ss cultural hegemony seduces the poor working girl: it ensnares her in a web of ertextuality.

My first response is that (as noted earlier) working people can recognize great literature when y see it. Winifred Albaya once picked up an old *Strand* magazine and was wonderfully impressed a story set in an industrial town like Sheffield, where she was growing up. Only years later did she rn that the story, 'Tickets Please', was by D. H. Lawrence.[57] Second, while Smith's theories may plain why Catherine McMullen read Lord Chesterfield, they do not account for the emancipating wer of the book. Inspired by its vision of aristocratic splendor ('I would see myself beautifully wned going down a marble staircase on the hand of Chesterfield'), she became (as Catherine okson) an immensely successful author of novels about poor but plucky Northern girls. Even re importantly, she recalled, Lord Chesterfield brought her for the first time into a public library:

And here began my education. With Lord Chesterfield I read my first mythology. I learned my first real history and geography. With Lord Chesterfield I went travelling in the world. I would fall asleep reading the letters and awake around three o'clock in the morning, my mind deep in the fascination of this new world, where people conversed, not just talked. Where the brilliance of words made your heart beat faster. Dear, dear Lord Chesterfield. Snob or not I owe him much.[58]

Marxist critics have long contended that classic literature can persuade workers like Catherine accept social hierarchies and distract them from the business of correcting social injustice. Indeed,

Chris Baldick and Terry Eagleton have argued that English literature was established as an academ[ic] discipline partly for the purpose of social control:

> Since literature, as we know, deals in universal human values rather than in such historical trivia as civil wars, the oppression of women or the dispossession of the English peasantry, it could serve to place in cosmic perspective the petty demands of working people for decent living conditions or greater control over their own lives, and might even with luck come to render them oblivious of such issues in their high-minded contemplation of eternal truth and beauties. . . . Instead of working to change such conditions . . . you can vicariously fulfill someone's desire for a fuller life by handing them *Pride and Prejudice*.[59]

That might have been the intention of some critics and educators, but did literature actua[lly] have such a narcotizing effect on the workers? How then do we explain the fact that another gre[at] fan of Lord Chesterfield's letters was the ultra-radical agitator Richard Carlile?[60] While servi[ng] respective prison sentences, T. A. Jackson read Jane Austen worshipfully; J. T. Murphy devour[ed] Conrad and Macaulay; and Manny Shinwell was consoled by Shakespeare, Walter Scott, Dicke[ns,] Hardy, Keats, Shelley, and Tennyson. All three of these proletarian Marxist intellectuals survived t[he] great books with their ideological loyalties intact.[61] Canonical literature tended to spark insurre[c-] tions in the mind of the working-class reader and was more likely to radicalize than mollify him. [In] Arnold Freeman's Sheffield survey, the population of worker-intellectuals was not identical with t[he] radical activists, but the two groups overlapped very closely. Robert Roberts recalled that the mo[st] militant socialists in Edwardian Salford, the workers who most persistently challenged prevaili[ng] conservative ideologies, were the 'readers of Ruskin, Dickens, Kingsley, Carlyle, and Scott'.[62] At t[he] same time Jewish anarchists in London's East End were sponsoring popular lectures on *Haml[et]*, *Gulliver's Travels*, and Beethoven's Ninth Symphony because they believed that kind of acculturati[on] was essential to political liberation.[63]

This brings us to a corollary of the receptive fallacy: even when working people read boo[ks] approved and provided by the governing classes, there was no guarantee that they would read tho[se] texts as their patrons wished. *Pilgrim's Progress* was a staple of prison and Sunday School libraries, b[ut] nascent Chartists like John James Bezer read it as a radical political allegory:

> My own dear Bunyan! if it hadn't been for you, I should have gone mad, I think, before I was ten years old! Even as it was, the other books and teachings I was bored with [in Sunday School], had such a terrible influence on me, that somehow or other, I was always nourishing the idea that 'Giant Despair' had got hold of me, and that I should never get out of his 'Doubting Castle'. Yet I read, ay, and *fed* with such delight as I cannot *now* describe – though I think I could *then*. Glorious Bunyan, you too were a 'Rebel', and I love you *doubly* for *that*. I read you in Newgate, – so I could, I under-stand, if I had been taken care of in Bedford jail, – your books are in the library of even your Bedford jail. Hurrah for progress![64]

Even an author with a conservative message could be turned to radical uses by working-cla[ss] activists. When Walter Scott was first published, he was denounced as a reactionary by Thom[as] Wooler and Richard Carlile,[65] but among the first Labour MPs he ranked near the top of the char[t.] George Howell read *The Wealth of Nations* as a critique rather than a defense of capitalists: 'Ada[m] Smith, with that clear insight and accurate knowledge of life which he so eminently possesse[d,] pointed out that combinations among masters, either directly or tacitly, enabled them to fix t[he] price of labour or to regulate it'.[66] The land nationalizers inspired by Thomas Spence likewise appropriated John Locke as their champion. After all, Locke had discovered a natural right to property, and had postulated that all land was held in common in the 'state of nature': for the Spenceans, the commonalization of land followed logically from those premises.[67] This does not necessarily mean that C. B. Macpherson was wrong to conclude that Locke 'provides a moral foundation for bourgeois appropriation';[68] but a history of audiences would remind us to ask, 'Provides for whom?' Until we can answer that question, we should forswear the critical habit of pronouncing that texts reinforce or subvert existing social and political structures.

Literary theorists have debated endlessly whether the reader writes the text or the text manipulates the reader. A history of audiences could lead us out of this deadlock by revealing the interactions of specific readers and texts. Already, a pattern is emerging from Carlo Ginzburg's study of a sixteenth-century Italian miller, Margaret Spufford's work on seventeenth-century English peasant readers, Ned Landsman's recent article on popular responses to Presbyterian preachers in eighteenth-century Scotland, Richard Altick's nineteenth-century English common readers, and my own research into twentieth-century students in a British adult education program. Spufford was 'startled' to find laborers and peasants reading and discussing Scripture with striking critical independence. They were, she concluded, 'far from being the docile material which their ministers no doubt desired'. Landsman also found that 'the laity possessed a rather remarkable capacity to integrate seemingly disparate beliefs and actively forge their own understandings of the delivered message and create their own religious symbols', all of which could be quite unlike anything their preachers intended to convey.[69] We have all independently discovered what Roger Chartier calls 'appropriation': the power of an audience – even at the bottom of the social pyramid – to transform received messages, rendering those messages 'less than totally efficacious and radically acculturating'.[70]

Literary theorists may argue, as an epistemological question, whether texts have any fixed meaning; but intellectual historians hardly need to be told that, in practice, all readers are editors – often ruthless and insensitive editors. The Jacques Derrida who worried that wantonly deconstructive criticism 'would risk developing in any direction at all and authorize itself to say almost anything'[71] might have been shocked to learn what common readers can do to texts. They create their own meanings, they mistake the 'unmistakable', they read very selectively. The same workmen who drew inspiration from Ruskin's social criticism, for instance, were apparently baffled by his art criticism. Regarding the latter 'I was frankly a philistine', wrote Frederick Rogers, a bookbinder and self-taught Elizabethan scholar, 'and in this I undoubtedly expressed the feelings of the . . workmen who had read his books'.[72] Likewise, several of the autodidacts who embraced Karl Marx frankly confessed that they could hardly understand him.[73]

We must be equally careful not to underestimate the common reader's level of comprehension. Jonathan Culler states a general postulate that has become a commonplace among reader-response critics: 'Literary works may be quite baffling to those with no knowledge of the special conventions of literary discourse'.[74] That sounds logical, but readers ignorant of the appropriate literary conventions sometimes read difficult works anyway, and thereby manage to puzzle out those conventions. One Edwardian bootmaker's daughter recalled finding her father's Shakespeare in the attic, 'and I tried to kind of get out the plots in my mind, from reading the dialogue, . . . and I didn't ever get them out right, but it was a good help to me, wasn't it, trying to get by myself'. Clearly it was a great help: she expanded her vocabulary and later entered a teacher training college, where she performed in productions of *Twelfth Night* and *Electra*.[75]

Richard Altick recognized that common readers who had not learned the literary conventions the Bible could still read it as a simple collection of stories.[76] As a boy W. F. Adams enjoyed *Pilgrim's Progress*, *Gulliver's Travels*, and the *Arabian Nights* on the same level: 'The religious meaning of

the first, the satirical meaning of the second, and the doubtful meaning of the third were, of cour
not understood. The story was the thing – the trials of Christian, the troubles of Gulliver, t
adventures of Aladdin'.[77] George Acorn may have read George Eliot at age nine, but 'solely for t
story. I used to skip the parts that moralized, or painted verbal scenery, a practice at which I becar
very dextrous'.

That kind of editing, Acorn added, was a defense mechanism that working people had
develop against

> the flood of goody-goody literature which was poured in upon us. Kindly institutions
> sought to lead us into the right path by giving us endless tracts, or books in which the
> comparative pill of religious teaching was clumsily coated by a mild story. It was
> necessary in self-defense to pick out the interesting parts, which to me at the time
> were certainly not those that led to the hero's conversion, or the heroine's first
> prayer.[78]

A striking illustration of this selective reading is the working-class response – or rath
nonresponse – to imperialist propaganda. Patrick Dunae and others have argued that a who
generation of boys were converted to imperialism by the novels of G. A. Henty and similar forms
indoctrination. 'At school, in church groups, in recreational associations – at almost every turn bo
were exposed to the imperial idea': that undeniable fact leads Dunae to the conclusion that 'in t
late nineteenth and early twentieth century most British youths were acutely aware of their imper
heritage. They could scarcely have been otherwise'.[79]

They certainly could have been otherwise. The majority of those youths were working cla
and they seem to have been acutely unaware of their empire. Although John MacKenzie has shov
that imperialist propaganda saturated textbooks, popular literature, and later the cinema, he fails
prove that this message got through to its intended audience.[80] The memoirs of Robert Rober
Willie Gallacher, and Harry Pollitt all document workers' indifference to the empire, except I
brief and exceptional outbursts of jingoism during the First World War.[81] Roberts reports that t
same people who rushed to the colors in August 1914 would have considered it a disgrace to jo
the army in peacetime. Royal jubilees were celebrated as national, not imperial, holidays: 'One f
the coming together of a whole country for a day of contentment and freedom'. Schoolchildr
might well be imperialists on Empire Day, having been taught 'a lot of inconsequential facts on In
[and] parts of Africa, . . . all ruled over by Edward the Peace-maker (pacemaker, my father call
him)'. But, Roberts emphasizes, 'Except in periods of national crisis or celebration, industr
labourers, though Tory, royalist and patriotic, remained uninterested in any event beyond the loc
horse racing excepted.'[82]

That last point is confirmed by the very titles of workers' autobiographies: *A Sheffield Chi
hood*, *My Dorset Days*, *Newlyn Boyhood*, *Memories of Old Poplar*, *Salford Boy*, *Ancoats Lad*, *A Man of Kent
Love for Bermondsey and Its People*, *In a Lancashire Street*, *36 Stewart Street, Bolton*, *Lark Rise*. The scope
these memoirs is almost entirely local. There lies one of the most telling silences in worke
memoirs: they not only fail to express imperialist sentiments, they scarcely mention the empi
Many autobiographers, including several future socialists, do recall that they enjoyed reading He
tyesque stories;[83] but they did not therefore become imperialists. Apparently they did not ev
notice the ideological freight carried by these tales, which were read purely as adventure stories,
which India or Africa was simply an exotic backdrop, not a territory the reader wanted to spend I
life policing.

A history of audiences, then, will have to take into account not only the concrete messag
that readers pick up from texts, but also the degree of credulity, involvement, and critical distan

that readers bring to those texts. Semioticians call this dimension of audience response 'suture', which has been defined by Jacques Alain-Miller as 'the relation of the subject to the chain of its discourse'.[84] Roger Chartier, for example, has tried to fix the relation of readers to the roguery stories published in seventeenth- and eighteenth-century France. He concludes that because these stories combined documentary effects with parody, they may have suspended the reader somewhere between credulity and incredulity:

> Belief in what is read is thus accompanied by a laugh that gives it the lie; the readers' acceptance is solicited, but a certain distance shows literature for what it is. . . . This delicate balance permits multiple readings that fluctuate between a persuasion by literal interpretation and an awareness of and amusement at the parody. . . . Thus the reader could simultaneously know and forget that fiction was fiction.[85]

Perhaps he could, but how do we know that? Lacking more direct evidence of audience involvement, Chartier tries to infer it from an analysis of texts and of editorial decisions made by the publishers; the method is ingenious, but it does not avoid the receptive fallacy. Most students of suture construct their theories on still shakier foundations: Kaja Silverman, for instance, tells us with great assurance what perspectives Hitchcock's film *Psycho* 'obliges' the audience to assume, without interrogating any actual viewer. In this area George Acorn was a superior sociologist: he observed audiences at the Edwardian counterpart of *Psycho* and the roguery tale – 'lurid, streaky melodrama, in which the villain always vowed to steep his hands in the hero's gore' – and found that their involvement with the narrative ran the complete gamut:

> 'Look out!' an overwrought galleryite would shout, ' 'e's going to stab her with a knife'. Or when the poisoned cup was offered to the handsome hero, the action of the play would be delayed by voices anxiously bidding him not to drink it. 'Shut up, Fathead!' some grumpy old chap would say to the nearest possessor of one of those voices; ' 'ow can the play go on if he don't get drugged? Besides, the 'ero's bahnd to win in the end, ain't he?'[86]

Where Chartier and Silverman assume that all audiences have the same relation to a given narrative, Acorn appreciated that individual theatergoers might be 'sutured' very differently. Where Chartier concluded that his readers simultaneously believed and disbelieved, Acorn found his audience sharply divided between the totally credulous and the contemptuously incredulous. Silverman asserts that suture involves 'passive insertions into pre-existing discursive positions', in which the audience 'permits itself to be spoken by the film's discourse'; but part of Acorn's audience quite aggressively tried to insert itself into the narrative and seize control of the discourse, while another section (including Acorn) was wholly divorced from the play and sneered at all its clanking machinery. Anyone who doubts that the common reader can manipulate the text should consider the case of a Victorian actor who, having died an elaborately melodramatic stage death, was loudly urged by his working-class audience to 'Die again!' – and did so.[87]

Given that these audiences were so obstreperous and even dictatorial, the term 'suture' should be scrapped as misleading, since it suggests that the reader is helplessly stitched into the narrative. We should instead be asking questions about the degree of audience *involvement*, which may have been quite active. We might also ask why Silverman and so many other literary theorists habitually treat that audience as a passive vessel, but that is another question for another essay. A brief answer would be that, in a democratic society, this assumption is attractive to both extremes of the political spectrum, because it rationalizes their failure to win broad popular support: they would enjoy that support, if only the masses were not somehow manipulated by the media. Thus cultural studies monographs and the House Un-American Activities Committee have both tried to expose the devilishly subtle political messages embedded in Hollywood movies, and for essentially the same reason.

There is no denying that films and books can be manipulative; but it should be equally obvious that we cannot know whether or when they succeed without somehow questioning the audience. Many literary critics today are understandably anxious to present themselves as sociologists rather than mere belletrists: they are concerned not with what texts mean, but with what texts do, as Stanley Fish has put it.[88] I would reply that it is equally worthwhile to ask what texts do, what texts mean, and which texts are the best texts; my point is that literary criticism cannot answer the first of these questions, while a history of audiences might. In that sense, the reader is outside the text.

Notes

1   John Burnett, David Vincent, and David Mayall (eds), *The Autobiography of the Working Class: An Annotated, Critical Bibliography* (3 vols, New York, 1984–89). For scholars who want to investigate upper- and middle-class readers, the potential sample is even larger, more than 6000 entries in William Matthews, *British Autobiographies* (Hamden, Conn., 1968).

2   Barbara English, 'Lark Rise and Juniper Hill: A Victorian Community in Literature and in History', *Victorian Studies*, 29 (1985), 7–35. Joel Wiener likewise corrected the autobiography of Chartist William Lovett in *William Lovett* (Manchester, 1989), 2.

3   For example, much information on popular reading can be extracted from the oral history project on family, work, and community in Britain before 1918, conducted by Paul Thompson and Thea Vigne and housed at the University of Essex.

4   Jeffrey Brooks, *When Russia Learned to Read: Literacy and Popular Culture, 1861–1917* (Princeton, 1988).

5   Hayden White, 'Method and Ideology in Intellectual History: The Case of Henry Adams', Dominick LaCapra and Steven L. Kaplan (eds), *Modern European Intellectual History: Reappraisals and New Perspectives* (Ithaca, 1982), 307–8.

6   Janice Radway, 'The Book-of-the-Month Club and the General Reader: On the Uses of "Serious" Fiction', *Critical Inquiry*, 14 (1988), 518–19.

7   Barbara Herrnstein Smith, *Contingencies of Value: Alternative Perspectives for Critical Theory* (Cambridge, Mass., 1988), 52–53.

8   George Haw, *The Life Story of Will Crooks, MP* (London, 1917), 22.

9   Smith, *Contingencies*, 50.

10   Thomas Cooper, *The Life of Thomas Cooper* (London, 1882), 5, 33, 59–60; Tom Barclay *Memoirs and Medlies: The Autobiography of a Bottle-Washer* (Leicester, 1934), 19–20.

11   Naturally, Lady Bell and Mr. Freeman were following their subjective Edwardian upper- and middle-class definitions of culture, and Freeman's was a bit generous: he classified as 'well equipped' some workers who were thoroughly respectable but had few intellectual interests. On the other hand, Lady Bell tended to err on the side of restrictiveness: she found that a quarter of working-class families read only novels, and she wrote them all off as culturally deprived. Lady [Florence] Bell, *At the Works* (London, 1907), ch. 7. [Arnold Freeman,] *The Equipment of the Workers* (London, 1919), ch. 3.

12   Peter Miles, 'The Painter's Bible and the British Workman: Robert Tressell's Literary Activism', Jeremy Hawthorn (ed.), *The British Working-Class Novel in the Twentieth Century* (London 1984), 2–10.

13   William J. Gilmore, *Reading Becomes a Necessity of Life: Material and Cultural Life in Rural New England 1780–1835* (Knoxville, 1989), 163.

14 *Ibid.*, 103, 289.

15 Will Jon Edwards, *From the Valley I Came* (London, 1956), 46–48, 67.

16 Walter Haydn Davies, *The Right Place – The Right Time* (Llandybie, 1972), 64–66, 101–5.

17 David Vincent, *Bread, Knowledge and Freedom: A Study of Nineteenth-Century Working Class Auto-biography* (London, 1981), ch. 6.

18 Emmanuel Shinwell, *Conflict without Malice* (London, 1955), 24–25.

19 George Howell, draft autobiography, Bishopsgate Institute, vol. B, b/4, f. 4.

20 Flora Thompson, *Lark Rise to Candleford* (Harmondsworth, 1987), 414–15.

21 Freeman, *Equipment*, ch. 3. A similar observation is made in Bell, *At the Works*, ch. 7.

22 'The Labour Party and the Books That Helped to Make It', *Review of Reviews*, 33 (1906), 568–82.

23 Morag Shiach, *Discourse on Popular Culture* (Cambridge, 1989).

24 Ray B. Browne, 'Popular Culture – New Notes Toward a Definition', in Christopher G. Geist and Jack Nachbar (eds), *The Popular Culture Reader* (3rd ed.; Bowling Green, 1983), 13.

25 Brooks, *Russia Learned to Read*, xvi, 33.

26 See John E. Toews, 'Intellectual History after the Linguistic Turn: The Autonomy of Meaning and the Irreducibility of Experience', *American Historical Review*, 92 (1987), 883–85.

27 Roger Chartier, *The Cultural Uses of Print in Early Modern France*, tr. Lydia G. Cochrane (Princeton, 1987), 3–8.

28 One might doubt Acorn's claim that he appreciated all that at age nine, but he had certainly reached that level of understanding by young adulthood, when he wrote his autobiography. George Acorn, *One of the Multitude* (London, 1911), 49–50.

29 Patrick A. Dunae, 'Penny Dreadfuls: Late Nineteenth-Century Boys' Literature and Crime', *Victorian Studies*, 22 (1979), 133–50.

30 J. H. Howard, *Winding Lanes* (Caernarvon, n.d.), 27; Peter Donnelly, *The Yellow Rock* (London, 1950), 31–32.

31 Alfred Cox, *Among the Doctors* (London, 1950), 17.

32 John Springhall, ' "A Life Story for the People"? Edwin J. Brett and the London "Low-Life" Penny Dreadfuls of the 1860s', *Victorian Studies*, 33 (1990), 225.

33 Lately, a few investigators in this field have come to recognize that fallacy. See Anne Beezer, Jean Grimshaw, and Martin Barker, 'Methods for Cultural Studies Students', David Punter (ed.), *Introduction to Contemporary Cultural Studies* (London, 1986), 97, 109–13.

34 James Smith Allen, 'History and the Novel: *Mentalité* in Modern Popular Fiction', *History and Theory*, 22 (1983), 248–49.

35 Radway, *Romance* (1984b), 63–76.

36 White, 'Method and Ideology', 282.

37 Charles H. Welch, *An Autobiography* (Banstead, 1960), 33.

38 Acorn, *Multitude*, 28–35.

39 Thomas McLauchlan, *The Life of an Ordinary Man* (n.p., 1979), 51.

40 Arthur Harding, *East End Underworld: Chapters in the Life of Arthur Harding*, ed. Raphael Samuel (London 1981), 47, 74–75.

41 Alfred Gilchrist, *Naethin at A'* (Glasgow, n.d.), 14.

42 John Sykes, *Slawit in the 'Sixties* (London, 1926), 23–29.

43 Thomas Wright, *Some Habits and Customs of the Working Classes* (London, 1867), 166.

44 Elizabeth Flint, *Hot Bread and Chips* (London, 1963), 163.

45 William Donaldson, *Popular Literature in Victorian Scotland* (Aberdeen, 1986), 32.

46 Joseph Burgess, *A Potential Poet? His Autobiography and Verse* (Ilford, 1927), 33.

47 Nora Hampton, 'Memories of Baptist End, Netherton, Dudley in the Period 1895–1919', TS, Brunel University Library, p. 1.

48 Richard Pyke, *Men and Memories* (London, 1948), 9.

49   Interestingly, the radical journalist W. F. Adams anticipated in 1903 that changing litera
      standards might bring about Reynolds's rehabilitation: 'With the taste for sensation ar
      salacious details which the modern novelist and modern dramatist have cultivated, it is not
      all unlikely that he would . . . [be] admitted to the hierarchy of fiction'. But as Adams revile
      all the Emile Zolas of contemporary literature, that hardly constituted an endorsement. W.
      Adams, *Memoirs of a Social Atom* (New York, 1968), 102–8, 233–34, ch. 57.
50   Burgess, *Potential Poet*, 70–72.
51   Henry Coward, *Reminiscences of Henry Coward* (London, 1919), 42.
52   Harding, *East End Underworld*, 274.
53   Edith Hall, *Canary Girls and Stockpots* (Luton, 1977), 39–40.
54   Regenia Gagnier, 'Social Atoms: Working-Class Autobiography, Subjectivity and Gender
      Victorian Studies, 30 (1987), 335–63. Nan Hackett, *XIX Century British Working-Cl
      Autobiographies: An Annotated Bibliography* (New York, 1985).
55   Jane Tompkins, *Sensational Designs: The Cultural Work of American Fiction 1790–1860* (Ne
      York, 1985), 38. See Chapter 25 of this Reader.
56   Elizabeth Bryson, *Look Back in Wonder* (Dundee, 1967), 71, 80–82 124–25.
57   Winifred Albaya, *A Sheffield Childhood* (Sheffield, n.d.), 40–41.
58   Catherine Cookson, *Our Kate* (London, 1969), 158–60.
59   Terry Eagleton, *Literary Theory: An Introduction* (Minneapolis, 1983), 22–27; Chris Baldick, *T
      Social Mission of English Criticism 1848–1932* (Oxford, 1983), 63–67.
60   Joel H. Wiener, *Radicalism and Freethought in Nineteenth-Century Britain: The Life of Richa
      Carlisle* (Westport, Conn., 1983), ch. 4.
61   T. A. Jackson, draft autobiography, Marx Memorial Library, 364; J. T. Murphy, *New Horizo
      (London, 1941), 216; Shinwell, *Conflict*, 72–73.
62   Robert Roberts, *The Classic Slum: Salford Life in the First Quarter of the Century* (London, 199C
      177–79.
63   William J. Fishman, *East End Jewish Radicals 1875–1914* (London, 1975), 266.
64   John James Bezer, 'The Autobiography of One of the Chartist Rebels of 1848', in Dav
      Vincent (ed.), *Testaments of Radicalism: Memoirs of Working Class Politicians 1790–1885* (Londo
      1977), 167.
65   Paul Thomas Murphy, ' "Imagination Flaps Its Sportive Wings": Views of Fiction in Briti
      Working-Class Periodicals, 1816–1858', *Victorian Studies*, 32 (1989), 341–53.
66   George Howell, *The Conflicts of Capital and Labour* (2nd ed., London, 1890), ch. 4.
67   Malcolm Chase, *The People's Farm: English Radical Agrarianism 1775–1840* (Oxford, 1988
      143, 181.
68   C. B. Macpherson, *The Political Theory of Possessive Individualism: Hobbes to Locke* (Oxford, 1964
      194–221.
69   Ginzburg, C., *The Cheese and The Worms*, xiv–xxi, 41–50; Spufford, *Small Books*, xvii, 30–3
      Ned Landsman, 'Evangelists and Their Hearers: Popular Interpretation of Revivalist Preac
      ing in Eighteenth-Century Scotland', *Journal of British Studies*, 28 (1989), 120–49; Altic
      The English Common Reader: A Social History of the Mass Reading Public, 1800–1900 (Chicag
      Chicago University Press, 1957), 255–56; Jonathan Rose, 'The Workers in the Worker
      Educational Association, 1903–1950', *Albion*, 21 (1989), 591–608.
70   Chartier, *Cultural Uses of Print*, 3–8.
71   Jacques Derrida, *Of Grammatology*, tr. Gayatri Chakravorty Spivak (Baltimore, 1976), 158.
72   Frederick Rogers, *Life, Labour and Literature* (London, 1913), 61–62.
73   Shinwell, *Conflict*, 25–28.
74   Jonathan Culler, 'Prolegomena to a Theory of Reading', in Susan R. Suleiman and In
      Crossman, eds., *The Reader in the Text: Essays on Audience and Interpretation* (Princeton: Princet
      University Press, 1980), 46–66.

75   University of Essex Oral History Archive, in 'Family, Work and Community Life Before 1918', interview 21.

76   Altick, *Common Reader*, 255–56.

77   Adams, *Memoirs*, 100–101.

78   Acorn, *Multitude*, 49–50.

79   Patrick A. Dunae, 'Boys' Literature and the Idea of Empire, 1870–1914', *Victorian Studies*, 24 (1980), 105–21.

80   John M. MacKenzie, *Propaganda and Empire: The Manipulation of British Public Opinion, 188–1960* (Manchester, 1984), 254.

81   William Gallacher, *Revolt on the Clyde: An Autobiography* (London, 1936), 18–19; Harry Pollitt, *Serving My Time: An Apprenticeship in Politics* (London, 1940), 85–87.

82   Roberts, *Classic Slum*, 140–44, 162–63, 179–82.

83   John Lanigari, 'Thy Kingdom *Did* Come', TS in Brunel University Library, 22, 63; William Holt, *Under a Japanese Parasol* (Halifax, 1933), 111–12; John Allaway in Ronald Goldman (ed.), *Breakthrough: Autobiographical Accounts of the Education of Same Socially Disadvantaged Children* (London, 1968), 7–9; James Griffiths, *Pages from Memory* (London, 1969), 11–12; John Edwin, *I'm Going – What Then?* (Bognor Regis, 1978), 89.

84   For a theoretical discussion of suture, see Kaja Silverman, *The Subject of Semiotics* (New York, 1983), ch. 5.

85   Chartier, *Cultural Uses of Print*, 335–36.

86   Acorn, *Multitude*, 134–36.

87   Wright, *Habits and Customs*, 165.

88   Stanley Fish, *Is There a Text in This Class?* (Cambridge, Mass., 1980), 3. See Chapter 35 in this Reader.

Chapter 34

Richard Altick

THE ENGLISH COMMON READER
From Caxton to the eighteenth century

I

William Caxton set up his printing press in Westminster at a fortunate moment in history. Already the great cultural revolution with which his name is associated was under way. Though most Englishmen still depended upon their ears for their share of the common cultural heritage, or upon their ability to interpret the pictures and statuary they saw in the churches, by 1477 there were substantial hints that in the future the art of reading would have a greater role in their lives. The demand for manuscripts was increasing. Caxton had not yet begun business when John Shirley, a dealer in manuscripts, started to lend out copies of the works of such authors as Chaucer and Lydgate in a sort of primitive circulating-library arrangement. In fifteenth-century inventories and wills, too, one finds mention of books, as if the rising class of country gentlemen and city merchants felt that the possession of a few manuscript volumes would provide them with a certain cachet.[1] The demand threatened soon to exceed the supply – unless, as actually happened, a means were discovered of duplicating books so that, instead of but a single manuscript, there could be hundreds and even thousands of printed copies.

We do not know how large the literate public was in Caxton's time, or in the century that followed. Only a few unsatisfactory scraps of evidence survive. Of 116 witnesses before the consistory court in 1467–76, some 40 per cent were recorded as literate.[2] In 1533 Sir Thomas More said that 'farre more than fowre partes of all the whole divided into tenne coulde never reade englishe yet',[3] an obscure statement which may possibly be interpreted as implying a literacy rate of 50 per cent or so. In 1547, on the other hand, Stephen Gardiner, Bishop of Winchester, observed that 'not the hundredth part of the realme' could read.[4] One modern estimate is that in Shakespeare's London between a third and a half of the people were literate.[5] It is at least certain that the growing commercial life of the nation required men of the merchant class to read and write English in order to transact business, keep records, and interpret legal documents. Some guilds set literacy as a condition of membership. Even women were becoming literate, and servants as well, if their circumstances required and permitted it.[6] Indeed, a recent historian has asserted that in Elizabethan times 'there was a higher level of literacy among women than at any other time until the late nineteenth century'.[7]

Opportunities for education, at least to the extent of learning to read the vernacular increased in the fifteenth and sixteenth centuries and were available to a fairly wide diversity of classes. A youth from even the lowest stratum of freemen had always had the chance of following Chaucer's clerk to the university as a mendicant student. The ideal of extending education to the 'poor' was affirmed in the foundation statutes of the grammar schools. The phase *pauperes et indigentes scholares* in such statutes, it appears, was not simply designed to insure to the school the legal privileges of a charitable institution but means that boys of relatively humble station (say the equivalent of the modern lower-middle class) really were enrolled in some numbers.

No longer, in any event, was education limited, as it had been in the Middle Ages, to those destined for the religious life. Even if the prospects were that they would take up their father's occupation, the children of small tradesmen, farm laborers, and domestic servants had some opportunity to learn to read English. For them, by Henry VIII's time, were provided petty schools, ABC schools, and song schools for the training of choirboys.[8]

These schools were all under the control of the church, and it used to be thought that Henry VIII's expropriation of ecclesiastical property, some of the income from which had been earmarked for teaching purposes, dealt a severe blow to English education. Today, however, it is believed that the dissolution of the churchly establishments did not interfere too much, at least in the long run, with the spread of learning. In time, new schools sprang up to replace those that were wiped out. A favorite practice among those who profited by the nation's prosperity was to endow grammar (that is, classical) schools. Almost every town of any size had at least one such school; in 1600 there were about 360 of them.[9] In addition, many noblemen and other large landowners founded and supported schools for the children of the neighborhood. Some of these were limited to elementary instruction; others, like the one at Stratford-on-Avon which Sir Hugh Clopton re-endowed in 1553, provided an excellent Latin education.

Therefore, since there was as yet little sign of the social exclusiveness that later was to reserve grammar-school and university education largely for children of noble or gentle birth, it was possible for bright boys from the artisan and tradesman class to acquire a thorough schooling. This is suggested by the number of Elizabethan writers who sprang from that station. To mention only a few: Peele was the son of a salter; Marlowe, of a cobbler; Munday, of a draper; Chettle, of a dyer; Herrick, of a goldsmith; Gabriel Harvey, of a ropemaker; Donne, of an ironmonger.[10]

A classical education was, however, the lot of only a minority of those who went to school at all. More numerous were the boys who received an abbreviated education in primary or petty schools. These schools were open not only to those destined to go on to the Latin curriculum but also to those who would begin their apprenticeship immediately after learning to read. While parish clergymen still could be found teaching children their letters, by the middle of the sixteenth century the church's monopoly over elementary education was forever ended. From the humble hand-laborer in a remote parish teaching a few pupils the ABC's, to the professional schoolmaster in the town, laymen became teachers. Their 'private adventure' schools made literacy available to a wide range of society. In addition, a growing number of craft guilds established schools for their members' children.

By the latter part of the sixteenth century the people who could read only English had become so numerous as to require more and more books to be printed in the vernacular. Contemporary writers, apologizing for their use of what was still considered an inferior language, frequently alluded to the 'unskilfull', the 'unacquainted with the latine tounge', the 'unlettered', who nevertheless should share in the age's knowledge. The very fact that this was the great age of translations proves the existence of a sizable audience who knew only English. The translator of a Latin theological work in 1599 remarked that he 'brought into the artificer's shop, [that] which was before in the studies and closets of the learned alone'.[11]

In the country, where most of the people lived, the proportion of literates probably was much smaller than in the towns, partly because there were fewer schools, partly because the conditions of rural life made illiteracy less of a handicap. Most cottagers were wholly indifferent to education, or could not spare their children from labor in field or cottage for even a year or two. Furthermore, by no means all the children who learned to read ever exercised their talent in later life. The boys soon went to the plow or the craftsman's shop, and the girls (of whom there were at least a sprinkling in some of the ABC schools) to the spinning wheel and the rearing of families; and having neither books nor any necessity for them, they lost such small gift as they had once possessed.

When all allowances have been made, however, it seems likely that in the Tudor and Stuart eras the ability to read was more democratically distributed among the English people than it would again be until at least the end of the eighteenth century. But, since there is a vital distinction between the simple possession of literacy and its active, continual exercise, it does not follow that the reading public in the late sixteenth and early seventeenth centuries was either as large or socially as diversified as the apparent extent of literacy in the nation might suggest. Books were not easy to acquire. Their production was artificially limited in several ways. One was the restriction on the number of printers. In 1586, partly to satisfy the printers already in business and partly to ease the ecclesiastical authorities' alarm over the spread of controversial and polemic books, the Star Chamber forbade the establishment of any new press until a vacancy occurred among the already existing ones (twenty-two commercial presses, in addition to the Queen's Printer and the two university presses).[12] Again, to make work for the increasing number of journeymen and apprentices, the Stationers' Company in 1587 limited to 1,250 or 1,500 the number of copies of a book that could be produced from one setting of type, although, in the interests of public morality and enlightenment, 'grammers, Accidences, prymers, and Catechisms' were allowed four impressions annually, of 2,500 to 3,000 copies each.[13] How prices would have been affected had a printer been free to issue as many copies as he foresaw a sale for, we can only speculate.

The book trade was also restricted, at the expense of the reader, by 'privilege' – the vested right accorded to certain booksellers in the printing and sale of specified categories of books. As early as 1559 such patents had been granted, and although in the 1580s some individual patentees transferred their monopolies to Stationers' Company, the practice continued unabated to the end of the Queen's reign. Her successors, James I and Charles I, between them allowed forty-three new patents.[14] The effect this monopoly had upon prices is illustrated by the fact that the London booksellers sold *Aesop's Fables* at 4d. a sheet and Ovid's Epistles at 8d., while in Cambridge the same books, issued by the university press (which was unaffected by 'privilege'), cost respectively 3d. and 5d. a sheet.[15] The university authorities bitterly resented the refusal by members of the Stationers' Company to sell these cheaper books, and in 1621 they obtained a royal injunction against the company's boycott of the Cambridge edition of Lily's *Grammar*.[16] Thus, although there might be a brisk demand for books of a certain kind, the number available was limited to those that the privileged bookseller desired or was able to produce in his own shop. There could be no competition and no healthy multiplication of such books.

The crescendo of public events in the first part of the seventeenth century, as well as the spread of the reading habit on other grounds among the middle class, increased the demand for books. Gradually the Tudor restrictions were lifted, and the market became better supplied. When the Court of the Star Chamber was abolished in 1641, the number of London printers ceased to be limited, and by 1660 there were about sixty printing houses in the city. Although the Licensing Act of 1662 reaffirmed the old regulation, it was for the most part ineffectual.[17] The day when the availability of books could be governed by that kind of maneuver was past, and in the future the government would have to find other ways of regulating the press.

In 1635, the restrictions on the number of copies to be issued from a single setting of type were liberalized to 1,500 or 2,000 for ordinary books, and to 3,000 for books in brevier type and

5,000 in nonpareil.[18] These ceilings were probably adequate for the market. In 1652, during a squabble between members of the Stationers' Company, one party alleged that the usual impression of a book was 1,500 copies, while the other asserted that the figure was too high.[19] Apart from staple items like almanacs (Partridge's *Anglicus* sold 13,500 in 1646, 17,000 in 1647, and 18,500 in 1648) and Lily's imperishable *Grammar* (20,000 copies a year in mid-century), a book would have had to be very popular indeed to sell as many as 5,000 copies in two years, as did the combined edition of Quarles's *Emblems and Hieroglyphikes* in 1639–40.[20] *Paradise Lost* sold 1,300 copies in two years. No edition, according to Milton's agreement with his bookseller, was to consist of more than 1,500 copies.[21] Our information on the prices of new books in the sixteenth and seventeenth centuries is sketchy.[22] In the earlier part of the sixteenth century, the average cost of a book was between two and three sheets for a penny.[23] On this basis, in 1520, Luther's *De potestate papae* cost 3*d.*, the ABC's a penny or 2*d.*, broadside ballads a halfpenny, Christmas carols 1*d.* or 2*d.*, and the book of Robin Hood, 2*d.*[24] In 1541, by royal proclamation, the price of Coverdale's Great Bible was fixed at 10*s.* unbound, 12*s.* bound.

Debasement of the coinage resulted in the doubling of commodity prices between 1540 and 1550, and books shared in the inflation. The cost of a psalter rose from 10*d.* in 1548 to 2*s.* 4*d.* in 1563. But after this increase, the prices of books remained remarkably constant down to 1635, despite another 100 per cent rise in the general price index during that period. In the golden age of Elizabethan literature, Holinshed's *Chronicles* cost £1 6*s.* bound, *Euphues* 2*s.* unbound, Camden's *Britannia* 2*s.* 6*d.*, North's *Plutarch* 14*s.* bound, Spenser's *Shepheardes Calender* 1*s.*, Sidney's *Arcadia* 9*s.* bound, and Hakluyt's *Voyages* 9*s.* unbound. Quarto plays, such as Shakespeare's, were 4*d.* or, more usually, 6*d.*[25]

During the Elizabethan and Jacobean periods, therefore, books were not too expensive when compared with other commodities. But that does not mean that they were easily accessible to a great many would-be readers, for one of the basic facts of English economic history at this time is that wages lagged far behind prices. The ordinary man could afford only the cheapest of books, and not many of these. When an unbound copy of *Hamlet* was selling for 6*d.*, master artisans and handicraftsmen in London – carpenters, joiners, cobblers, smiths – earned about 16*d.* a day. Shopkeepers made about the same. Thus a man who had seen *Hamlet* at the Globe and wanted to read it at his leisure would have had to spend between a quarter and a half of his day's earnings. With that same sixpence he could have bought two dinners or gone back to the Globe (if he was content to stand in the pit) for six more performances.[26]

Even professional men, who would have been more likely to be habitual readers, did not have enough money to buy many books. An ordinary clergyman made between £10 and £20 a year, which means that the purchase of Sidney's *Arcadia* or Hakluyt's *Voyages* would have required the sacrifice of one or two whole weeks' income. A schoolmaster, making, say, £6 9*s.* a year, would have had to spend the equivalent of about three weeks' income.[27]

About 1635, for a reason not yet clear, book prices rose by some 40 per cent.[28] Incomes, however, were rising as well, so that books were relatively no more expensive by the Restoration than they had been in Shakespeare's time. In 1668 folios, meant for the wealthy trade, were priced from 5*s.* to 16*s.*, the majority from 7*s.* to 10*s.* Most newly published books in octavo, the commonest size, ranged from 1*s.* to 4*s.* bound. Unbound plays were regularly published at 1*s.*, and sermons, controversial pamphlets, accounts of trials, and other 'timely' items of restricted length as a rule were 6*d.* The smallest books (12mo) usually were 1*s.* 6*d.*[29] During this general period (there were, of course, variations from year to year) butter sold for 6*d.* a pound, coffee 3*s.* a pound, sugar 6*d.* a pound, and canary wine 7*s.* a gallon.[30] Pepys laid out 24*s.* for a 'nightgown' (i.e., dressing robe) for his wife, and 2*s.* for a pair of kid gloves. Admission to the gallery of a theater where Nell Gwyn was playing cost 12*d.* or 18*d.*, although a citizen out on the town might pay as much as 2*s.* 6*d.* to go into the pit.[31] In 1688 the average income of lesser clergymen was estimated at a little less than a pound week; that of farmers, 16s. 4d.; of shopkeepers, 17s. 4d.; and of artisans and handicraftsmen, 14s. 7d.

Between this time and the first quarter of the eighteenth century, book prices again rose. Whatever the strictly economic reasons behind the increase, it was also a natural development in period when the reading public was contracting instead of expanding. The demand for books, like the writing of them, was limited to a narrower social group. Whether the higher prices charged for books were a contributory cause or merely a symptom of the change, we cannot tell. But as the seventeenth century drew to a close, it is at least plain that books were dearer and readers were fewer.

Books, then, were the possession chiefly of the more prosperous members of the middle class in the sixteenth and seventeenth centuries, as well as of that permanent nucleus of well-educated upper-class readers whose existence will be constantly assumed, though seldom mentioned, in this volume. Among them were the keepers of fair-sized shops and master artisans who, like Simon Eyre in Dekker's comedy *The Shoemaker's Holiday*, had achieved the dignity of being employers of labour. Here and there, members of the class carried their bookishness to the point of becoming collectors on a modest scale. As early as 1575 a London mercer, writing to another, described the library one Captain Cox, a Coventry mason. Eighty years later we find an undersheriff of London giving his office to be free to make his daily round of the bookstalls, and a turner in Eastcheap lining his 'studdy' with books.[33]

Since the printing trade was concentrated in London and transportation and communication were still primitive, there was little commerce in books in the provinces. Only occasionally are books mentioned in yeomen's wills. Most men of that class seem to have read little, or in any event to have owned so few books that it was not worthwhile to include them in the inventories of their personal effects.[34]

II

The people of the Tudor and Stuart eras read books for reasons which would have made excellent sense to their Victorian descendants. John Stuart Mill, in his inaugural address at the University St. Andrews in 1867, spoke of 'the two influences which have chiefly shaped the British character since the days of the Stuarts: commercial money-getting business, and religious Puritanism'. The influences affected reading tastes in Milton's time as profoundly as in Mill's. Their tendency was discourage popular interest in most forms of imaginative literature. 'Business', said Mill, 'demanding the whole of the faculties, and whether pursued from duty or the love of gain, regarding as a loss of time whatever does not conduce directly to the end; Puritanism, which looking upon every feeling of human nature, except fear and reverence for God, as a snare, if not as partaking of sin, looked coldly, if not disapprovingly, on the cultivation of the sentiments'.[35]

Protestantism, in the phrase of Élie Halévy, is a 'book religion'.[36] From the time it began transform English life in the sixteenth century it laid emphasis upon the practice of private reading. With the appearance in 1540 of the Great Bible (Coverdale's revised translation), the first English Bible to be authorized by the Crown, Henry VIII ordered a copy to be placed in every church 'Every body that could', wrote Strype, the early biographer of Cranmer, 'bought the book, or busied read it, or got others to read it to them, if they could not themselves; and divers more elderly people learned to read on purpose. And even little boys flocked among the rest to hear portions of the holy Scripture read . . . When the King had allowed the Bible to be set forth to be read in all churches immediately several poor men in the town of Chelmsford in Essex . . . bought the New Testament and on Sundays sat reading it in the lower end of the Church'.[37] But this novel freedom to read the Bible was short-lived. In 1543 the Reformed Parliament forbade it to all women (except those high birth), artificers, apprentices, journeymen, servingmen, husbandmen, and laborers – an evidence of the social distribution of literacy even at that early date.

However, with the accession of Mary, though the practice of displaying Bibles in the churches was condemned, no attempt was made to interfere with individual reading. Under Elizabeth I, Bibles were restored to the churches, and the idea that men had to be 'authorised and licensed' to read Scripture for themselves was quietly dropped.[38] But only under the Puritans did Scripture become the veritable foundation of Christian faith, achieving, along with the surrounding literature of religion, a place in men's lives that was inconceivable in pre-Reformation England.

It was not, however, only the Protestant, and especially the Puritan, emphasis upon private Bible-reading as a way to religious truth and thus to personal salvation which stimulated the spread of reading. The religious controversies that reached a climax in the Civil War played their part as well. They reached into the minds, and even more the passionate emotions, of great numbers of ordinary people, who were as stirred by them as later generations would be by purely political furor. And the controversies were carried on by floods of tracts and pamphlets, arguments and replies and rejoinders and counterrejoinders – printed matter which found a seemingly limitless market among all classes that could read.[39] With the establishment of the Commonwealth, 'everybody with views to express, from Milton down to the most insignificant crank or fanatic, took a hand'.[40] The London bookseller George Thomason collected some 23,000 books and pamphlets printed between 1641 and 1662.

On the secular side of life, men's interest in books stemmed from motives strikingly prophetic of nineteenth-century utilitarianism. Readers were increasingly concerned to obtain books of practical guidance and information.[41] With the simultaneous spread of a new economy, which required a degree of knowledge unnecessary under the old feudal system, and of a humanism which brought vast new areas of worldly interest to men's attention, books became instruments of utility. Through them, men could learn the things they needed to know as businessmen and functionaries in civil government and could share in the humane learning of the Renaissance. Reading was inextricably associated with 'improvement', with cultivation of the prudential virtues and the more easily acquired amenities of conduct. The books most in request were those which either showed the way to a morality acceptable in the eyes both of God and of Mammon or brought the ideals of humanistic conduct down to the level of the common man. Thus – to adopt the categories described in Louis Wright's encyclopedic account of middle-class reading in the age – the demand was for handbooks of improvement, lessons in diligence and thrift, instruction in domestic relations, guides to godliness, popularized histories (always with useful lessons), translations, travel books, and books on science.

These were the books that the sober, ambitious citizen read. Other kinds were available, as we shall note in a moment; but, though they might be admitted to a Simon Eyre's shelf, they owed their presence there to stealth or rationalization, or both. For the spirit of the time was strongly against books of any lighter quality than the types just mentioned. Over the whole age, affecting even those who were staunchest in their allegiance to orthodox Anglicanism, hung the fervent Puritan opposition to polite letters as un-Christian, frivolous, and demoralizing. From the 1580s to the Root and Branch petition of 1640, which attacked the prevalence of 'lascivious, idle, and unprofitable Books and Pamphlets, Play-Books and Ballads', the Puritan divines ceaselessly denounced the reading of books which offered no more than idle entertainment. We shall hear their voices again – though the rhetorical splendor of Puritan pulpit utterance will be sadly missing – when we look into the effect of evangelicalism, the neo-Puritanism of the industrial age, upon the reading habits of the nineteenth century.

Even the courtesy books, interpreters of humanistic standards of conduct to the middle-class citizen, frowned upon the reading of plays and romances. At best, reading was only a minor one among the many polite activities one might pursue; but if one did read, it should always be with at least a moderately serious purpose.[42]

But the demands of the imagination and the feelings are too strong to be consistently denied. At their disposal always is man's inexhaustible talent for rationalization, and the extent to which it was employed is suggested by the popularity of lighter forms of literature – jestbooks, chapbooks, ballads, and the fiction that Thomas Nashe and Thomas Deloney devised expressly for the common reader. Usually the Elizabethan or Jacobean reader could find a plausible reason for dipping into such dubious books. The reading of jestbooks could be, and was, justified on the ground that they were pills to purge melancholy and thus (since the Elizabethans were firm believers in psychosomatic medicine) could improve one's physical health. Similarly, because the reading of history was recommended as perfectly safe and useful, it was possible to take up with a clear conscience any book, however fantastic, that had the word 'history' displayed on its title page.[43] Thus innumerable chapbooks and debased romances found their way into the hands of pious purchasers. Nor did the factual truth of the travel books have to be scrutinized too carefully. So long as they had an air of genuineness – so long as their authors did not candidly admit that they were spinning tales – they could be read as improving literature, no matter how outrageous their romancing. In such ways as these the reading regimen of the sixteenth- and seventeenth-century public had, despite its surface appearance of austerity, a full seasoning of imagination and escapism.[44]

Even among the strictest of Puritans, whose reading dealt exclusively and unambiguously with the concerns of the soul, imaginative stimulation and satisfaction were by no means lacking. The Bible is unequaled, among all the books of the world, for the variety and splendor of its imaginative and emotional appeal. Between a single pair of covers it offers the cosmic dramas of creation and the Last Judgment, the human pathos of Ruth and the tragedy of Samson; the wars of the Hebrews, the destruction of the Babylonians, the simple charm of the nativity story, the wonder of the miracles, the supreme climax of the Crucifixion and the Resurrection.

Furthermore, as William Haller has pointed out in his study of Puritanism, the Puritan preachers offered in their sermons, which in printed form had a wide circulation, a very acceptable substitute for the forbidden drama. 'They were to discover that their listeners . . . took a livelier interest in sin itself than in its categories, in the psychology of spiritual struggle than in the abstract analysis of moral behavior or even the satirical exposure of vice and folly. . . . So they set out to describe the warfare of the spirit, to portray the drama of the inner life, to expound the psychology of sin and redemption'.[45] Between the Bible itself, and such works as Foxe's *Book of Martyrs*, and these exceedingly dramatic presentations of the conflict of good and evil, the reading hours of even the most rigorous Puritans were seldom dull.

Of another segment of the reading public, which had few such scruples as affected the book choice of the sober middle class, we have little record except that of the books it preferred. This was the lowest stratum of the literate population: the casual, unpurposeful readers, those who, in the phrase of Heming and Condell's dedication in the 1623 Shakespeare folio, 'can but spell'. It was among these people – apprentices, common laborers, peasants, rivermen, and the rest – that the printers of broadside ballads and chapbooks found their chief market. The ballads were the precursors of a later era's sensational newspapers: never was a celebrated highwayman executed or catastrophe visited upon a hapless town but the event was described in crude language and crude woodcuts. They were, as well, the poor man's history: John Aubrey's nurse could recite the whole chronicle of England, from the Conquest to Charles I, in ballads.[46] The chapbooks, vulgarized versions of old chivalric tales, were his fiction – as Milton put it, 'the countryman's *Arcadias*, and his *Monte Mayors*'.[47]

This popular printed literature ran as a continuous thread, however seldom seen in the form of historical records, from Elizabeth's time to Victoria's. The descendants of Autolycus were to found trudging with their packs along every rural road; in the end they would be acquiring fresh stock from the thriving establishment of Jemmy Catnach in London's unsavory Seven Dials. The fact that ballads and chapbooks did not vanish from the English scene until the advent of penny periodicals is assurance enough that the tradition of reading among the poor, in town and country, never wholly disappeared.

But the size of this public fluctuated with the vicissitudes of popular education, and we cannot know how large it was, in Tudor times or later. Though it is pleasant to envision the Elizabethan cottage with its faded and tattered ballads on the wall, and the cottager crouching over the feeble fire spelling out the words of a chapbook of Sir Thopas or an account of a late horrid crime and the ensuing visitation of justice on the malefactor, it would be a mistake to imagine that reading had any but the most incidental place in the life of the masses. For most of them – the fact is inescapable – were illiterate; and, impressive though the spread of reading was among the middle class in these first centuries of printing, it made little headway among the humble in either town or country. Their life still was lived according to the immemorial pattern. The recreations that occasionally lightened their hard lives were those which had been traditional centuries before Caxton – the rude games, the maypole dances, the harvest celebrations, and the other festivals that marked the progress of the seasons. Songs and stories were handed down by word of mouth from generation to generation, with never a page of print intervening. The life of the imagination and the feelings was still attuned to the ear rather than to the eye. The popular tradition, rich in folk heroes and broad humor and proverbial wisdom and memorable events, a strange and fascinating mixture of local legend and the lore of the Bible and the classics and medieval tale, was part of the very soil, and there was as yet no need for the printed word to supplant it.

Notes

1   Bennett, 'The Author and His Public in the Fourteenth and Fifteenth Centuries', pp. 19–23. This and other studies by Bennett (see Bibliography) are the fullest sources for the reading public in Caxton's time and the first century afterward.

2   Sylvia L. Thrupp, *The Merchant Class of Medieval London, 1300–1500* (Chicago, 1948), p. 156.

3   Quoted by Adamson, 'Literacy in England in the Fifteenth and Sixteenth Centuries', p. 45.

4   Bennett (1952), *English Books and Readers*, p. 28.

5   Albert C. Baugh, *A History of the English Language* (New York, 1935), p. 246.

6   Bennett, 'The Author and His Public', pp. 18–19.

7   A. L. Rowse, *The England of Elizabeth: The Structure of Society* (1950), p. 503.

8   Material on Tudor and Stuart schools has been derived from Adamson's article (n. 3 above); Curtis, *History of Education in Great Britain*, chap. ii; Wright, *Middle-Class Culture in Elizabethan England*, chap. iii; Rowse, *The England of Elizabeth*, chap. xii; and general histories of the period. These draw upon specialized earlier studies of the subject, notably those by A. F. Leach.

9   Rowse, p. 496.

10   Wright, pp. 17–18.

11   Richard F. Jones, *The Triumph of the English Language* (Stanford, Calif., 1953), pp. 36 ff.

12   Plant, *The English Book Trade*, p. 83.

13   *Ibid.*, pp. 92–93. Occasionally a printer evaded this regulation by setting aside his types after the legal maximum of copies had been struck off, and then reusing them after a prudent interval for a 'new edition'. But type was too scarce to make this a frequent procedure.

14   *Ibid.*, pp. 100–14.

15   A 'sheet' is a piece of paper one side of which is printed in a single operation. After both sides have been printed, it is folded once or several times to form one unit of the prospective book.

The practice of selling books at retail in individual sheets – that is, a small section at a time – was a common means of 'cheapening' literature during the nineteenth century.

16   S. C. Roberts, *A History of the Cambridge University Press* (Cambridge, 1921), pp. 34–38.

17   Plant, pp. 84–85.

18   *Ibid.*, p. 93; W. W. Greg, *Some Aspects and Problems of London Publishing between 1550 and 1650* (Oxford, 1956), p. 16.

19   Communication by Alcuin Shields, O.F.M., *Times Literary Supplement*, February 22, 1952, p. 141.

20   Stanley Gardner, *Times Literary Supplement*, March 7, 1952, p. 173. This letter and an accompanying one by H. John McLachlan provide much information, garnered from contemporary sources, on the number of copies printed at a single impression in the seventeenth century.

21   David Masson, *The Life of John Milton* (1894), VI, 510, 628.

22   Only after the Restoration did booksellers begin to adopt fixed prices; until then, they asked whatever the customer could be induced to pay. Hence such figures as we have for the period before 1660 are for individual transactions, and they may or may not represent the average selling price. Nor are the records always clear as to whether the price given is for a volume in its bound or unbound state. Binding could as much as double the price of a book.

23   Bennett, *English Books and Readers*, p. 233.

24   *The Day-Book of John Dorne, Bookseller in Oxford, A.D. 1520*, ed. F. Madan, *Collecteana*, Ser. 1, Part III (Oxford Historical Society, 1885).

25   Johnson, 'Notes on English Retail Book-Prices, 1550–1640' (the most detailed survey of the subject, as Bennett's *English Books and Readers* is for the period just preceding); Plant, p. 240.

26   Alfred Harbage, *Shakespeare's Audience* (New York, 1941), pp. 55–62. J. E. Thorold Rogers, *A History of Agriculture and Prices in England* [*1259–1793*] (Oxford, 1866–1902), Vols V and VI, gives masses of figures for sixteenth- and seventeenth-century wages and commodity prices. The prices, unfortunately, are almost always wholesale; very few retail prices are available. Figures for London wages are only approximate, since few city wages for these centuries are known to economic historians. They are reckoned on the assumption that the pay scale in London was at least a third higher than in the country. It may sometimes have been double the country rate.

27   Plant, p. 42.

28   Johnson, p. 93.

29   Based on advertised prices for books published in 1668–69: *Term Catalogues, 1668–1709*, ed. Edward Arber (1903–1906), I, l–7.

30   From household accounts of the Russell family at Woburn: Gladys S. Thomson, *Life in a Noble Household, 1641–1700* (1937), pp. 137, 166–67, 198. This volume gives hundreds of figures for food, clothing, and other expenses in the middle and late seventeenth century.

31   Pepys, *Diary*, under dates of September 7 and 8, 1667, and January 1, 1667/68. Pepys's entries for April 13–17, 1668, contain many records of everyday expenses such as cab fare and meals.

32   Gregory King's estimate of the annual incomes of the various classes of society; frequently reprinted, e.g., in G. N. Clark, *The Later Stuarts* (Oxford, 1934), p. 25.

33   Wright, pp. 76 n., 84–85. On other Elizabethan book collectors, see Phoebe Sheavyn, *The Literary Profession in the Elizabethan Age* (Manchester, 1909), pp. 150–51, and Raymond Irwin in *Library Association Record*, LVI (1954), 195–201.

34   Sheavyn, p. 149; Mildred L. Campbell, *The English Yeoman under Elizabeth and the Early Stuart* (New Haven, 1942), pp. 266–68.

35   *Inaugural Address Delivered to the University of St. Andrews* (1867), p. 89.

36   *History of the English People in 1815*, p. 457.

37 Quoted by David Daiches, *The King James Version of the English Bible* (Chicago, 1941), pp. 38–59.
38 *Ibid.*, *passim*.
39 David Mathew, *The Social Structure in Caroline England* (Oxford, 1948), p. 95.
40 Esmé Wingfield-Stratford, *The History of British Civilization* (1928), I, 563.
41 Bennett (1943), 'Caxton and His Public', *passim*.
42 See John F. Mason, *Gentlefolk in the Making* (Philadelphia, 1935).
43 Wright, pp. 102–3, 301.
44 Pepys permitted himself to read Helot's *L'Escole des Filles* before throwing it into the fire on the ground that, though it was a 'mighty lewd book', yet it was 'not amiss for a sober man once to read over to inform himself in the villainy of the world' (*Diary*, entry for February 9, 1667/68). The rationalization is thoroughly in the spirit of his class and time.
45 William Haller, *The Rise of Puritanism* (New York, 1938), pp. 32–33.
46 *Aubrey's Brief Lives*, ed. O. L. Dick (1949), p. xxix.
47 *Areopagitica*.

Chapter 35

Stanley Fish

INTERPRETING THE *VARIORUM*

Undoing the case for reader-response analysis

The assumptions to which I stand opposed – the assumption that there is a sense, that it is embedded or encoded in the text, and that it can be taken in at a single glance – are, in order, positivist, holistic and spatial, and to have them is to be committed both to a goal and to a procedure. The goal is to settle on a meaning, and the procedure involves first stepping back from the text, and then putting together or otherwise calculating the discrete units of significance it contains. My quarrel with the procedure (and with the assumptions that generate it) is that in the course of following it through the reader's activities are at once ignored and devalued. They are ignored because the text is taken to be self-sufficient – everything is *in* it – and they are devalued because when they are thought of at all they are thought of as the disposable machinery of extraction. In the procedures I would urge, the reader's activities are at the center of attention, where they are regarded not as leading to meaning but as *having* meaning. The meaning they have is a consequence of their not being empty; for they include the making and revising of assumptions, the rendering and regretting of judgments, the coming to and abandoning of conclusions, the giving and withdrawing of approval, the specifying of causes, the asking of questions, the supplying of answers, the solving of puzzles. In a word, these activities are interpretive – rather than being preliminary to questions of value, they are at every moment settling and resettling questions of value – and because they are interpretive, a description of them will also be, and without any additional step, an interpretation, not after the fact but of the fact (of experiencing). It will be a description of a moving field of concerns, at once wholly present (not waiting for meaning but constituting meaning) and continually in the act of reconstituting itself.

As a project such a description presents enormous difficulties, and there is hardly time to consider them here;[1] but it should be obvious how different it is from the positivist-formalist project. Everything depends on the temporal dimension, and as a consequence the notion of mistake, at least as something to be avoided, disappears. In a sequence where a reader first structures the field he inhabits and then is asked to restructure it (by changing an assignment of speaker or realigning attitudes and positions) there is no question of priority among his structurings; no one of them, even if it is the last, has privilege; each is equally legitimate, each equally the proper object of analysis, because each is equally an event in his experience.

The firm assertiveness of this paragraph only calls attention to the questions it avoids. Who is this reader? How can I presume to describe his experiences, and what do I say to readers who report that they do not have the experiences I describe? Let me answer these questions or rather make a beginning at answering them in the context of an example from Milton's *Comus*. In line 46 of *Comus* we are introduced to the villain by way of a genealogy:

> Bacchus that first from out the purple grape,
> Crushed the sweet poison of misused wine.

In almost any edition of this poem, a footnote will tell you that Bacchus is the god of wine. Of course most readers already know that, and because they know it, they will be anticipating the appearance of 'wine' long before they come upon it in the final position. Moreover, they will also be anticipating a negative judgment on it, in part because of the association of Bacchus with revelry and excess, and especially because the phrase 'sweet poison' suggests that the judgment has already been made. At an early point then, we will have both filled in the form of the assertion and made a decision about its moral content. That decision is upset by the word 'misused'; for what 'misused' asks us to do is transfer the pressure of judgment from wine (where we have already placed it) to the abusers of wine, and therefore when 'wine' finally appears, we must declare it innocent of the charges we have ourselves made.

This, then, is the structure of the reader's experience – the transferring of a moral label from a thing to those who appropriate it. It is an experience that depends on a reader for whom the name Bacchus has precise and immediate associations; another reader, a reader for whom those associations are less precise, will not have that experience because he will not have rushed to a conclusion in relation to which the word 'misused' will stand as a challenge. Obviously I am discriminating between these two readers and between the two equally real experiences they will have. It is not a discrimination based simply on information, because what is important is not the information itself, but the action of the mind which its possession makes possible for one reader and impossible for the other. One might discriminate further between them by noting that the point at issue – whether value is a function of objects and actions or of intentions – is at the heart of the seventeenth-century debate over 'things indifferent'. A reader who is aware of that debate will not only have the experience I describe; he will recognize at the end of it that he has been asked to take a position on one side of a continuing controversy; and that recognition (also a part of his experience) will be part of the disposition with which he moves into the lines that follow.

It would be possible to continue with this profile of the optimal reader, but I would not get very far before someone would point out that what I am really describing is the intended reader, the reader whose education, opinions, concerns, linguistic competences, and so on make him capable of having the experience the author wished to provide. I would not resist this characterization because it seems obvious that the efforts of readers are always efforts to discern and therefore to realize (in the sense of becoming) an author's intention. I would only object if that realization were conceived narrowly, as the single act of comprehending an author's purpose, rather than (as I would conceive it) as the succession of acts readers perform in the continuing assumption that they are dealing with intentional beings. In this view discerning an intention is no more or less than understanding, and understanding includes (is constituted by) all the activities which make up what I call the structure of the reader's experience. To describe that experience is therefore to describe the reader's efforts at understanding, and to describe the reader's efforts at understanding is to describe his realization (in two senses) of an author's intention. Or to put it another way, what my analyses amount to are descriptions of a succession of decisions made by readers about an author's intention – decisions that are not limited to the specifying of purpose but include the specifying of every aspect of successively intended worlds, decisions that are precisely the shape, because they are the content, of the reader's activities.

Having said this, however, it would appear that I am open to two objections. The first is that the procedure is a circular one. I describe the experience of a reader who in his strategies is answerable to an author's intention, and I specify the author's intention by pointing to the strategies employed by that same reader. But this objection would have force only if it were possible to specify one independently of the other. What is being specified from either perspective are the conditions of utterance, of what could have been understood to have been meant by what was said. That is, intention and understanding are two ends of a conventional act, each of which necessarily stipulates (includes, defines, specifies) the other. To construct the profile of the informed or at-home reader is at the same time to characterize the author's intention and vice versa, because to do either is to specify the *contemporary* conditions of utterance, to identify, by becoming a member of, a community made up of those who share interpretive strategies.

The second objection is another version of the first: if the content of the reader's experience is the succession of acts he performs in search of an author's intentions, and if he performs those acts at the bidding of the text, does not the text then produce or contain everything – intention *and* experience – and have I not compromised my antiformalist position? This objection will have force only if the formal patterns of the text are assumed to exist independently of the reader's experience, for only then can priority be claimed for them. Indeed, the claims of independence and priority are one and the same; when they are separated it is so that they can give circular and illegitimate support to each other. The question 'do formal features exist independently?' is usually answered by pointing to their priority: they are 'in' the text before the reader comes to it. The question 'are formal features prior?' is usually answered by pointing to their independent status: they are 'in' the text before the reader comes to it. What looks like a step in an argument is actually the spectacle of an assertion supporting itself. It follows then that an attack on the independence of formal features will also be an attack on their priority (and vice versa), and I would like to mount such an attack in the context of two short passages from *Lycidas*.

The first passage (actually the second in the poem's sequence) begins at line 42:

> The willows and the hazel copses green
> Shall now no more be seen,
> Fanning their joyous leaves to thy soft lays.

It is my thesis that the reader is always making sense (I intend 'making' to have its literal force), and in the case of these lines the sense he makes will involve the assumption (and therefore the creation) of a completed assertion after the word 'seen', to wit, the death of Lycidas has so affected the willows and the hazel copses green that, in sympathy, they will wither and die (will no more be seen by *anyone*). In other words, at the end of line 43 the reader will have hazarded an interpretation, or performed an act of perceptual closure, or made a decision as to what is being asserted. I do not mean that he has done four things, but that he has done one thing the description of which might take any one of four forms – making sense, interpreting, performing perceptual closure, deciding about what is intended. (The importance of this point will become clear later.) Whatever he has done (that is, however we characterize it), he will undo it in the act of reading the next line, for here he discovers that his closure, or making of sense, was premature and that he must make a new one in which the relationship between man and nature is exactly the reverse of what was first assumed. The willows and the hazel copses green will in fact be seen, but they will not be seen by Lycidas. It is he who will be no more, while they go on as before, fanning their joyous leaves to someone else's soft lays (the whole of line 44 is now perceived as modifying and removing the absoluteness of 'seen') Nature is not sympathetic, but indifferent, and the notion of her sympathy is one of those 'false surmises' that the poem is continually encouraging and then disallowing.

The previous sentence shows how easy it is to surrender to the bias of our critical language
d begin to talk as if poems, not readers or interpreters, did things. Words like 'encourage' and
isallow' (and others I have used in this essay) imply agents, and it is only 'natural' to assign
ency first to an author's intentions and then to the forms that assumedly embody them. What
ally happens, I think, is something quite different: rather than intention and its formal realiz-
on producing interpretation (the 'normal' picture), interpretation creates intention and its
rmal realization by creating the conditions in which it becomes possible to pick them out. In
her words, in the analysis of these lines from *Lycidas* I did what critics always do: I 'saw' what
y interpretive principles permitted or directed me to see, and then I turned around and
ributed what I had 'seen' to a text and an intention. What my principles direct me to 'see' are
aders performing acts; the points at which I find (or to be more precise, declare) those acts to
ve been performed become (by a sleight of hand) demarcations *in* the text; those demarcations
e then available for the designation 'formal features', and as formal features they can be
legitimately) assigned the responsibility for producing the interpretation which in fact produced
em. In this case, the demarcation my interpretation calls into being is placed at the end of line
; but of course the end of that (or any other) line is worth noticing or pointing out only
cause my model *demands* (the word is not too strong) perceptual closures and therefore
cations at which they occur; in that model this point will be one of those locations, although
) it need not have been (not every line ending occasions a closure) and (2) in another model,
e that does not give value to the activities of readers, the possibility of its being one would not
ve arisen.

What I am suggesting is that formal units are always a function of the interpretive model
e brings to bear; they are not 'in' the text, and I would make the same argument for intentions.
at is, intention is no more embodied 'in' the text than are formal units; rather an intention, like a
rmal unit, is made when perceptual or interpretive closure is hazarded; it is verified by an
terpretive act, and I would add, it is not verifiable in any other way. This last assertion is too large
be fully considered here, but I can sketch out the argumentative sequence I would follow were I to
nsider it: intention is known when and only when it is recognized; it is recognized as soon as you
cide about it; you decide about it as soon as you make a sense; and you make a sense (or so my
odel claims) as soon as you can.

Let me tie up the threads of my argument with a final example from *Lycidas*:

> He must not float upon his wat'ry bier
> Unwept . . .   (13–14)

ere the reader's experience has much the same career as it does in lines 42–44: at the end of line
perceptual closure is hazarded, and a sense is made in which the line is taken to be a resolution
rdering on a promise: that is, there is now an expectation that something will be done about this
fortunate situation, and the reader anticipates a call to action, perhaps even a program for the
dertaking of a rescue mission. With 'Unwept', however, that expectation and anticipation are
sappointed, and the realization of that disappointment will be inseparable from the making of a
w (and less comforting) sense: nothing will be done; Lycidas will continue to float upon his wat'ry
er, and the only action taken will be the lamenting of the fact that no action will be efficacious,
cluding the actions of speaking and listening to this lament (which in line 15 will receive the
eretricious and self-mocking designation 'melodious tear'). Three 'structures' come into view at
ecisely the same moment, the moment when the reader having resolved a sense unresolves it and
akes a new one; that moment will also be the moment of picking out a formal pattern or unit, end
line/beginning of line, and it will also be the moment at which the reader, having decided about

the speaker's intention, about what is meant by what has been said, will make the decision again an in so doing will make another intention.

This, then, is my thesis: that the form of the reader's experience, formal units, and t structure of intention are one, that they come into view simultaneously, and that therefore t questions of priority and independence do not arise. What does arise is another question: wh produces *them*? That is, if intention, form, and the shape of the reader's experience are simp different ways of referring to (different perspectives on) the same interpretive act, what is that act interpretation of? I cannot answer that question, but neither, I would claim, can anyone els although formalists try to answer it by pointing to patterns and claiming that they are availab independently of (prior to) interpretation. These patterns vary according to the procedures th yield them: they may be statistical (number of two-syllable words per hundred words), grammatic (ratio of passive to active constructions, or of right-branching to left-branching sentences, or anything else); but whatever they are I would argue that they do not lie innocently in the world b are themselves constituted by an interpretive act, even if, as is often the case, that act is unacknov ledged. Of course, this is as true of my analyses as it is of anyone else's. In the examples offered he I appropriate the notion 'line ending' and treat it as a fact of nature; and one might conclude that as fact it is responsible for the reading experience I describe. The truth I think is exactly the revers line endings exist by virtue of perceptual strategies rather than the other way around. Historicall the strategy that we know as 'reading (or hearing) poetry' has included paying attention to the line a unit, but it is precisely that attention which has made the line as a unit (either of print or of aur duration) available. A reader so practiced in paying that attention that he regards the line as a bru fact rather than as a convention will have a great deal of difficulty with concrete poetry; if I overcomes that difficulty, it will not be because he has learned to ignore the line as a unit b because he will have acquired a new set of interpretive strategies (the strategies constitutive 'concrete poetry reading') in the context of which the line as a unit no longer exists. In short, wh is noticed is what has been *made* noticeable, not by a clear and undistorting glass, but by interpretive strategy.

This may be hard to see when the strategy has become so habitual that the forms it yiel seem part of the world. We find it easy to assume that alliteration as an effect depends on a 'fact' th exists independently of any interpretive 'use' one might make of it, the fact that words in proximi begin with the same letter. But it takes only a moment's reflection to realize that the sameness, f from being natural, is enforced by an orthographic convention; that is to say, it is the product of interpretation. Were we to substitute phonetic conventions for orthographic ones (a 'reforn traditionally urged by purists), the supposedly 'objective' basis for alliteration would disappe because a phonetic transcription would require that we distinguish between the initial sounds those very words that enter into alliterative relationships; rather than conforming to those relatio ships, the rules of spelling make them. One might reply that, since alliteration is an aural rather th a visual phenomenon when poetry is heard, we have unmediated access to the physical soun themselves and hear 'real' similarities. But phonological 'facts' are no more uninterpreted (or le conventional) than the 'facts' of orthography; the distinctive features that make articulation an reception possible are the product of a system of differences that must be *imposed* before it can I recognized; the patterns the ear hears (like the patterns the eye sees) are the patterns its percept habits make available.

One can extend this analysis forever, even to the 'facts' of grammar. The history of linguisti is the history of competing paradigms, each of which offers a different account of the constituents language. Verbs, nouns, cleft sentences, transformations, deep and surface structures, sem rhemes, tagmemes – now you see them, now you don't, depending on the descriptive apparatus y employ. The critic who confidently rests his analyses on the bedrock of syntactic descriptions resting on an interpretation; the facts he points to *are* there, but only as a consequence of the interpretive (man-made) model that has called them into being.

The moral is clear: the choice is never between objectivity and interpretation but between an interpretation that is unacknowledged as such and an interpretation that is at least aware of itself. It is this awareness that I am claiming for myself.

Interpretive communities

It seems then that the price one pays for denying the priority of either forms or intentions is an inability to say how it is that one ever begins. Yet we do begin, and we continue, and because we do there arises an immediate counterobjection to the preceding pages. If interpretive sets are the source of forms rather than the other way around, why isn't it the case that readers are always performing the same acts or a sequence of random acts, and therefore creating the same forms or a random succession of forms? How, in short, does one explain these two 'facts' of reading? (1) The same reader will perform differently when reading two 'different' (the word is in quotation marks because its status is precisely what is at issue) texts; and (2) different readers will perform similarly when reading the 'same' (in quotes for the same reason) text. That is to say, both the stability of interpretation among readers and the variety of interpretation in the career of a single reader would seem to argue for the existence of something independent of and prior to interpretive acts, something which produces them. I will answer this challenge by asserting that both the stability and the variety are functions of interpretive strategies rather than of texts.

Let us suppose that I am reading *Lycidas*. What is it that I am doing? First of all, what I am not doing is 'simply reading', an activity in which I do not believe because it implies the possibility of pure (that is, disinterested) perception. Rather, I am proceeding on the basis of (at least) two interpretive decisions: (1) that *Lycidas* is a pastoral and (2) that it was written by Milton. (I should add that the notions 'pastoral' and 'Milton' are also interpretations; that is, they do not stand for a set of indisputable, objective facts; if they did, a great many books would not now be getting written.) Once these decisions have been made (and if I had not made these I would have made others, and they would he consequential in the same way), I am immediately predisposed to perform certain acts, to 'find', by looking for, themes (the relationship between natural processes and the careers of men, the efficacy of poetry or of any other action), to confer significances (on flowers, streams, shepherds, pagan deities), to mark out 'formal' units (the lament, the consolation, the turn, the affirmation of faith, and so on). My disposition to perform these acts (and others; the list is not meant to be exhaustive) constitutes a set of interpretive strategies, which, when they are put into execution, become the large act of reading. That is to say, interpretive strategies are not put into execution after reading (the pure act of perception in which I do not believe); they are the shape of reading, and because they are the shape of reading, they give texts their shape, making them rather than, as it is usually assumed, arising from them. Several important things follow from this account:

(1) I did not have to execute this particular set of interpretive strategies because I did not have to make those particular interpretive (pre-reading) decisions. I could have decided, for example, that *Lycidas* was a text in which a set of fantasies and defenses find expression. These decisions would have entailed the assumption of another set of interpretive strategies (perhaps like that put forward by Norman Holland in *The Dynamics of Literary Response*) and the execution of that set would have made another text.

(2) I could execute this same set of strategies when presented with texts that did not bear the title (again a notion which is itself an interpretation) *Lycidas, A Pastoral Monody*. I could decide (it is a decision some have made) that *Adam Bede* is a pastoral written by an author who consciously modeled herself on Milton (still remembering that 'pastoral' and 'Milton' are interpretations, not facts in the

public domain); or I could decide, as Empson did, that a great many things not usually considere
pastoral were in fact to be so read; and either decision would give rise to a set of interpreti
strategies, which, when put into action, would write the text I write when reading *Lycidas*. (Are yc
with me?)

(3) A reader other than myself who, when presented with *Lycidas*, proceeds to put int
execution a set of interpretive strategies similar to mine (how he could do so is a question I will tal
up later), will perform the same (or at least a similar) succession of interpretive acts. He and I the
might be tempted to say that we agree about the poem (thereby assuming that the poem exis
independently of the acts either of us performs); but what we really would agree about is the way
write it.

(4) A reader other than myself who, when presented with *Lycidas* (please keep in mind th
the status of *Lycidas* is what is at issue), puts into execution a different set of interpretive strategi
will perform a different succession of interpretive acts. (I am assuming, it is the article of my fait
that a reader will always execute some set of interpretive strategies and therefore perform son
succession of interpretive acts.) One of us might then be tempted to complain to the other that v
could not possibly be reading the same poem (literary criticism is full of such complaints) and l
would be right; for each of us would be reading the poem he had made.

The large conclusion that follows from these four smaller ones is that the notions of tł
'same' or 'different' texts are fictions. If I read *Lycidas* and *The Waste Land* differently (in fact I c
not), it will not be because the formal structures of the two poems (to term them such is also a
interpretive decision) call forth different interpretive strategies but because my predisposition
execute different interpretive strategies will produce different formal structures. That is, the tw
poems are different because I have decided that they will be. The proof of this is the possibility
doing the reverse (that is why point 2 is so important). That is to say, the answer to the questic
'why do different texts give rise to different sequences of interpretive acts?' is that *they don't have t
an answer which implies strongly that 'they' don't exist. Indeed, it has always been possible to p
into action interpretive strategies designed to make all texts one, or to put it more accurately, to ł
forever making the same text. Augustine urges just such a strategy, for example, in *On Christie
Doctrine* where he delivers the 'rule of faith' which is of course a rule of interpretation. It
dazzlingly simple: everything in the Scriptures, and indeed in the world when it is properly rea
points to (bears the meaning of) God's love for us and our answering responsibility to love ot
fellow creatures for His sake. If only you should come upon something which does not at first see
to bear this meaning, that 'does not literally pertain to virtuous behavior or to the truth of faitł
you are then to take it 'to be figurative' and proceed to scrutinize it 'until an interpretatic
contributing to the reign of charity is produced'. This then is both a stipulation of what meanir
there is and a set of directions for finding it, which is of course a set of directions – of interpreti
strategies – for making it, that is, for the endless reproduction of the same text. Whatever one m
think of this interpretive program, its success and ease of execution are attested to by centuries
Christian exegesis. It is my contention that any interpretive program, any set of interpretive strat
egies, can have a similar success, although few have been as spectacularly successful as this one. (Fe
some time now, for at least three hundred years, the most successful interpretive program has got
under the name 'ordinary language'.) In our own discipline programs with the same characteristic
always reproducing one text include psychoanalytic criticism, Robertsonianism (always threatenir
to extend its sway into later and later periods), numerology (a sameness based on the assumption
innumerable fixed differences).

The other challenging question – 'why will different readers execute the same interpreti
strategy when faced with the "same" text?' – can be handled in the same way. The answer is aga
that *they don't have to*, and my evidence is the entire history of literary criticism. And again th

swer implies that the notion 'same text' is the product of the possession by two or more readers of
milar interpretive strategies.

But why should this ever happen? Why should two or more readers ever agree, and why
ould regular, that is, habitual, differences in the career of a single reader ever occur? What is the
planation on the one hand of the stability of interpretation (at least among certain groups at
rtain times) and on the other of the orderly variety of interpretation if it is not the stability and
riety of texts? The answer to all of these questions is to be found in a notion that has been implicit
my argument, the notion of *interpretive communities*. Interpretive communities are made up of
ose who share interpretive strategies not for reading (in the conventional sense) but for writing
xts, for constituting their properties and assigning their intentions. In other words, these strategies
ist prior to the act of reading and therefore determine the shape of what is read rather than, as is
ually assumed, the other way around. If it is an article of faith in a particular community that there
e a variety of texts, its members will boast a repertoire of strategies for making them. And if a
mmunity believes in the existence of only one text, then the single strategy its members employ
ll be forever writing it. The first community will accuse the members of the second of being
ductive, and they in turn will call their accusers superficial. The assumption in each community
ll be that the other is not correctly perceiving the 'true text', but the truth will be that each
rceives the text (or texts) its interpretive strategies demand and call into being. This, then, is the
planation both for the stability of interpretation among different readers (they belong to the same
mmunity) and for the regularity with which a single reader will employ different interpretive
rategies and thus make different texts (he belongs to different communities). It also explains why
ere are disagreements and why they can be debated in a principled way: not because of a stability
texts, but because of a stability in the makeup of interpretive communities and therefore in the
posing positions they make possible. Of course this stability is always temporary (unlike the
nged for and timeless stability of the text). Interpretive communities grow larger and decline, and
dividuals move from one to another; thus, while the alignments are not permanent, they are always
ere, providing just enough stability for the interpretive battles to go on, and just enough shift and
ppage to assure that they will never be settled. The notion of interpretive communities thus stands
tween an impossible ideal and the fear which leads so many to maintain it. The ideal is of perfect
reement and it would require texts to have a status independent of interpretation. The fear is of
terpretive anarchy, but it would only be realized if interpretation (text making) were completely
ndom. It is the fragile but real consolidation of interpretive communities that allows us to talk to
e another, but with no hope or fear of ever being able to stop.

In other words interpretive communities are no more stable than texts because interpretive
rategies are not natural or universal, but learned. This does not mean that there is a point at which
individual has not yet learned any. The ability to interpret is not acquired; it is constitutive of
ing human. What is acquired are the ways of interpreting and those same ways can also be
rgotten or supplanted, or complicated or dropped from favor ('no one reads that way anymore').
hen any of these things happens, there is a corresponding change in texts, not because they are
ing read differently, but because they are being written differently.

The only stability, then, inheres in the fact (at least in my model) that interpretive strategies
e always being deployed, and this means that communication is a much more chancy affair than we
e accustomed to think it. For if there are no fixed texts, but only interpretive strategies making
em, and if interpretive strategies are not natural, but learned (and are therefore unavailable to a
ite description), what is it that utterers (speakers, authors, critics, me, you) do? In the old model
terers are in the business of handing over ready-made or prefabricated meanings. These meanings
e said to be encoded, and the code is assumed to be in the world independently of the individuals
ho are obliged to attach themselves to it (if they do not they run the danger of being declared

deviant). In my model, however, meanings are not extracted but made and made not by encoded forms but by interpretive strategies that call forms into being. It follows then that what utterers do is give hearers and readers the opportunity to make meanings (and texts) by inviting them to put into execution a set of strategies. It is presumed that the invitation will be recognized, and that presumption rests on a projection on the part of a speaker or author of the moves he would make if confronted by the sounds or marks he is uttering or setting down.

It would seem at first that this account of things simply reintroduces the old objection; for isn't this an admission that there is after all a formal encoding, not perhaps of meanings, but of the directions for making them, for executing interpretive strategies? The answer is that they will only be directions to those who already have the interpretive strategies in the first place. Rather than producing interpretive acts, they are the product of one. An author hazards his projection, not because of something 'in' the marks, but because of something he assumes to be in his reader. The very existence of the 'marks' is a function of an interpretive community, for they will be recognized (that is, made) only by its members. Those outside that community will be deploying a different set of interpretive strategies (interpretation cannot be withheld) and will therefore be making different marks.

So once again I have made the text disappear, but unfortunately the problems do not disappear with it. If everyone is continually executing interpretive strategies and in that act constituting texts, intentions, speakers, and authors, how can any one of us know whether or not he is a member of the same interpretive community as any other of us? The answer is that he can't, since any evidence brought forward to support the claim would itself be an interpretation (especially if the 'other' were an author long dead). The only 'proof' of membership is fellowship, the nod of recognition from someone in the same community, someone who says to you what neither of us could ever prove to a third party: 'we know'. I say it to you now, knowing full well that you will agree with me (that is, understand) only if you already agree with me.

Note

1   See my *Surprised by Sin: The Reader in Paradise Lost* (London and New York: Macmillan, 1967); *Self-Consuming Artifacts: The Experience of Seventeenth-Century Literature* (Berkeley: University of California Press, 1972); *Is There a Text in This Class?* (Cambridge, Mass.: Harvard University Press, 1980): 'What Is Stylistics and Why Are They Saying Such Terrible Things About It?' (chap. 2); 'How Ordinary Is Ordinary Language?' (chap. 3); 'Facts and Fictions: A Reply to Ralph Rader' (chap. 5).

Chapter 36

Elizabeth McHenry

FORGOTTEN READERS
Recovering the lost history of
African American literary societies

'To discover and uncover hidden capacities'

In a June 1895 meditation on black women's 'special and growing interest' in commencement exercises, Fannie Barrier Williams wrote: 'Women who have daughters capable of culture can do nothing better for womankind, as well as for the daughters, than to give them the advantage of a college training, or an education that will have an equivalent value in the quality of their intelligence.' In encouraging black women to do everything in their power to ensure that their daughters were given the most complete education possible, Williams pointed not to the primacy of the university experience itself but to the importance of the 'mental discipline and culture that are the most important furnishings of a university education'. The great majority of black women at the turn of the century were denied access to venues of higher education, and those who did go to college were often offered limited and inferior academic curricula. But developing mental discipline and the skills associated with culture and its acquisition was recognized as essential to black women's public service efforts and their increased visibility at the end of the nineteenth century. Such talents, Williams noted, 'will save us from many humiliating mistakes in our public efforts'.[1] Williams's comments effectively isolate the correlation made by black clubwomen at the turn of the century between their own education and the success of the public work they wished to accomplish. With limited opportunities for black women to educate themselves in formal academic settings, black women's clubs provided an alternative and supplemental context in which to acquire and practice the skills they needed to confidently and effectively enter public and organizational life.

The association that Williams identified between personal betterment and social betterment was at the center of the black women's club movement at the turn of the century. Clubwomen's primary social interests – providing welfare services, building community institutions, defining the position and the capabilities of black women and of African Americans generally, and voicing protests against racial injustice – were integrally linked to their own education and intellectual abilities. In order to effectively perform as public activists, they needed to work individually and collectively to enhance their abilities as articulate speakers, persuasive writers, and critical thinkers.

These skills, clubwomen believed, difficult to measure or document in and of themselves, would form the basis of their more readily measurable and immediately visible material accomplishments. Although material accomplishments were perceived as the outward signs of successful endeavors for the public good, clubwomen understood their self-education and self-improvement exercise to be an equal if not more important gauge of black women's potential for effecting change. 'Some people's measure of good is an entirely material one,' observed clubwoman Florida Ridley in a paper titled 'Opportunity and Privileges of Club Life', delivered at a public meeting sponsored by the membership of Boston's Woman's Era Club in October 1896. 'They recognize little that cannot be seen or handled, and consider nothing an advantage that does not add to material prosperity. We are all too much under the control of material things, and too slow to recognize the power of thought,' Ridley observed. She admitted that a 'woman's club may not build a home for the unfortunate, but if it opens the eyes and the hearts of its members to the condition of these unfortunates, if it considers the ways in which their misfortune might be averted, if it extends its intelligence and influence over the conduct of those who have the institution under management, it is fulfilling its mission.' Ridley's comments underscore black clubwomen's belief that their ability to improve existing conditions depended on preparation and study. Only when armed with a critical understanding of the reasons behind poverty, Ridley insists, can effective strategies be developed to prevent it. And while black clubwomen might not be the ones who build the institution, their ability to effectively lobby those with the power to change policies and appeal to 'those who have the institution under management' may prove a productive means of effecting significant and long-lasting change.[2]

Ridley's comments are a part of an address delivered at the first of a series of public Sunday afternoon meetings that, according to a description in the club's newspaper, 'drew a large crowd of women interested in the work [of the Woman's Era Club] and men, curious to know just what the work [of the club] meant'. Her comments were geared primarily toward this latter group, described as 'skeptical and quite prepared to smile with superior indifference'. It was onlookers like these who often dismissed the organized work of black women with the analysis that their 'women's clubs mean nothing but "talk, talk" '. That Ridley was prepared to respond to this critique acknowledges the assumptions about the nature and value of women's talk against which black clubwomen labored to assert the legitimacy of the many dimensions of their clubwork. Women's talk – most commonly associated then as it remains today with negative and derogatory terms, the most familiar and resonant of which is gossip – was seen as strictly trivial, largely vacuous, and essentially social. In outlining the work of women's clubs, Ridley embraced but critically revalued the association between women and talk: rather than a woman's weakness, she forced her audience to reconsider women's talk in positive terms, as an essential channel of communication and, finally, as a medium for positive communal change. 'It is true the club is all talk,' she told her audience, 'it was created to furnish opportunities to talk.' Calling a woman's 'general felicity of language' her 'strongest medium', Ridley persuaded her audience to imagine an atmosphere in which women's talk constituted substantive work: their talk, she argues, is 'the result of thought'.[3]

The verbal relationships and relationships to language forged in the context of women's club allowed clubwomen to enter a space, both physical and psychological, where they could seriously engage, first, with one another, and then, with the profound issues that surrounded them and threatened to destroy their communities. The twofold nature of this process should not be overlooked, although it was not always embraced with the openness displayed by Florida Ridley. In speaking about their clubwork, black women often devised strategies to emphasize that aspect of their work that was explicitly focused on community service, often downplaying self-education and the component of the club activities that centered on social interaction and their own intellectual advancement. This tendency to suggest that self-education was merely a fortunate by-product of their benevolent activities is well illustrated in the following report on the activities of the Woman

Era Club, the club in which Florida Ridley was a member: 'the work for humanity in [the] way of interesting oneself in public affairs leads to self-culture and an active interest in the laws of education.'[4] In truth, however, black women's significant accomplishments in the realm of public service could not have been possible without the 'self-culture' and practical skills learned and the confidence derived from the educational programs that regularly took place in the intimate setting of the club meeting. Unlike the meetings of men's societies, which historically emphasized public debates and literary competitions, African American women's clubs focused their attention on reading, conversation, and mutual support; their meetings centered on exercises that would nurture the membership, pushing them to acquire and practice the skills that they would put to use in the effective public presentation of their words and their ideas.

The preparation and presentation of club papers is one example of these exercises. Club-women prepared papers to be read orally before the membership on a great variety of subjects. As Florida Ridley's paper on 'Opportunity and Privileges of Club Life' indicates, a self-conscious reflection of the impact and importance of club life for black women was a popular area of exploration, especially as the women's club movement reached its maturity. Meditations on the benefits of club life were one way that black women reflected their primary concern with women and their changing roles. Clubwomen presented papers on the benefits of physical exercise that encouraged women to develop strong bodies to physically support their strength of mind and character.[5] They reflected on every aspect of what they called 'Domestic Science'. While these papers practically addressed black women's traditional responsibilities in the home, they also reim-agined the boundaries of domestic roles, often presenting concrete alternatives to the traditional patterns they saw reflected around them. In her paper on 'Domestic Science', for instance, Ellen Bartelle Deitrick outlined her belief in a 'division of labor'. All household labor, she asserted, 'will be better done when women evolve some plan by which cooking may be done by a highly skilled and scientific cook, laundering by an equally accomplished laundress and general cleaning by another expert specially trained for this branch of work'. Although she believed that 'young women should begin to learn domestic science by going through every operation from cleaning stoves and building fires to the artistic arrangement of a parlor', Deitrick was confident that, banded together, women could make more of their domestic skills, including combining them with business savvy. 'I see no reason why the women of Boston should not, in some . . . fashion, start and build up a co-operative laundry,' she proposed.[6]

Deitrick's paper on domestic science points to the ways in which, through club papers and the discussions they prompted, black women participated in debates through which different ideolo-gies of womanhood were advanced and shaped. Her suggestion that the various domestic tasks be in some sense 'professionalized', not only for greater efficacy but also as a way to form a union of women and turn a profit, is just one example of the way that black clubwomen recognized and embraced their own shifting status and the possibilities and implications of taking on new and different roles. Even as they continued to emphasize the importance of their domestic obligations, for instance, black women like Deitrick actively imagined a world outside of their homes and began to picture the various ways in which they might participate in it. Through their club papers and the discussions that they inspired, black women were able to actively explore just what, in practical terms, Frances E. W. Harper meant when she declared in 1893 that women stood on 'the threshold woman's era'.

Titles of their club papers indicate the extent to which these explorations negotiated a critical balance between asserting new roles for women and affirming traditional responsibilities. Often the tension between women's traditional responsibilities and the goals of the 'new woman' was vividly apparent because these perspectives were literally positioned side by side. For instance, in the fall of 1895, the Tuskegee Woman's Club heard two papers at one meeting, both of which addressed the topic 'Women and her Work'. Miss M. M. Fleming's paper on 'Women in the Home' maintained that 'the ideal woman in a home' was 'worth having'. It was followed by Miss Leonora L. Chapman's paper on 'Woman in Business', which, according to the club's report, 'introduced facts and portrayed the business capacity of the new woman with a zest that created a fervor in the breasts of those who are advocating some of her principles'.[7] From the record of this meeting, there is no indication that these aspects of women's work were considered in opposition with one another, nor was the membership required to favor one paper or its position over another. Rather, by examining the subject from two perspectives, members of the Tuskegee Woman's Club could gain exposure to multiple ideas which they could use to consider their own positioning.

It is worth noting that these papers on women's work were delivered at the Tuskegee Woman's Club's 'first literary meeting of the current year', a fact that underscores the close connection between the clubs' literary endeavors and their political dialogues.[8] What was 'literary' and educational about the club papers was not only their subject matter, although the dissemination of information on a variety of topics was clearly an important aspect of their work. Through the club paper, black women drew on myriad rhetorical skills, all of which they would need to be successful in their public service work. Not the least of these was the ability to work collectively. As clubs investigated a specific topic or concern, they organized their presentations in such a way as to involve as many members as possible. For example, when the Tuskegee Woman's Club discussed 'The Education of Negro Girls', on 7 October 1895, seven members prepared short papers that allowed the women present to conduct an in-depth discussion of the history, present, and future of black women's education. The evening began with Miss Mattie Child's paper, 'The Early Education', in which she

> recalled the days of toil and pain that attended those who struggled in secret for a little learning. 'Present Methods', by Miss Milla Hadley gave a marked contrast over that of years ago and a corresponding feeling of thankfulness was aroused in her hearers. 'Defects in Present System', were strongly pointed out by Mrs. Young, who gave the danger of extremes, one-sidedness, and the lack of simple thoughtfulness in small things. 'Suggestion[s] for Future Improvement' by Miss Sarah Hunt were timely. Miss Hunt gave her hearers some of the benefits she received from her summer course taken at Cottage City. 'Home Training', by Mrs. Irene Bond, struck a keynote that gave no uncertain sound, but vibrated throughout with the idea of its vital importance. 'School Training', by Miss S. Belle Bransford prompted each member to the serious duties that are involved in the work of training our student girls. 'Training for Society', by Miss Eliza Adams, brought out more duties for mothers and others in training the daughters in habits of economy, in modesty, in uprightness and honesty in dealing with others.[9]

All of the components of this presentation required the presenters to conduct research, whether formally or informally, and the division of the larger topic, 'The Education of Negro Girls', into smaller subtopics introduced its own lesson in organization. Because club papers were traditionally read before the membership, they required that their authors demonstrate both written and oral presentation skills. Criteria for judging the quality of papers presented orally before the clubs were extensive. Club women wished to come away from their meetings 'highly entertained and instructed'; they demanded that the content of the papers delivered before them be both 'practical and profitable'.[10] Those who both 'spoke with ease and crowded much thought into [their] . paper[s]' received the highest praise.[11]

It is impossible to underestimate the centrality of the club paper to the mission and the objectives of black women's clubs. Josephine St. Pierre Ruffin, president of Boston's Woman's E

Club, reflected explicitly on this centrality in her address before the membership on the occasion of their second anniversary. Her comments are addressed to the Woman's Era Club specifically but pertain to the importance of the club paper for turn-of-the-century black women's clubs generally. 'The especial aim of this club is to promote and foster a spirit of unity and helpfulness in every needed direction among its members, to discover and uncover hidden capacities,' she began. 'The club paper has done much in this way, bringing to the light talent among our women which had only to be discovered to reflect credit on any people.' Opportunities to produce, present, critique, and discuss club papers provided a black clubwoman with a definitive way to 'realize how much more potent for good she is when she combines with other like-minded women and they utilize the endowments of each for the benefit of all.'[12] The experience of preparing and delivering club papers was directly responsible for giving clubwomen the confidence to pursue other, more ambitious goals. For instance, in 1892, their first year of organization, the women of the Sierra Leone Club of Lawrence, Kansas, interspersed papers on home training and domestic economy with 'Current Topic Talks'. 'The knowledge we gained made a generous impression upon us, and it was concluded that if we could help ourselves in short talks and a few hours of study each day, that much good could be accomplished if we founded an industrial school.' By January 1894 plans for establishing that school were 'moving along nicely', and the women had 'adopted a resolution to the effect that we would use every effort this year to get means to purchase a lot and erect a cottage for the salvation of our girls'. Although the women of the Sierra Leone Club defined themselves as ' "queens of the fireside", as all of us are wives and almost all mothers', their intellectual training and accomplishments moved them well outside of this limited realm.[13]

In addition to being shared among the immediate membership at club meetings, club papers reached an audience beyond that of the local club in three critical ways. At the end of the nineteenth century, as more and more black women's clubs were created, clubwomen who were members of one organization were invited to address the members of other black women's clubs, whether locally or when traveling to another city. Maria Baldwin, a member of Boston's Woman's Era Club, traveled across the river to Cambridge to deliver a paper on 'The True Hold of the Poet on the People'.[14] When visiting New York the president of the Woman's Era, Josephine St. Pierre Ruffin, attended a meeting of New York's Woman's Loyal Union in 1895, where she read 'a very interesting paper'.[15] Such visits offered clubwomen unfamiliar yet still sympathetic audiences before which to present their work. It also allowed clubwomen in various locations to hear the perspectives of others and hear about the work of other clubs.

Second, clubwomen throughout the country were called on to serve as delegates to national conventions. At the first annual meeting of the National Conference of Colored Women, held over a three-day period in July 1895, for instance, eleven clubwomen delivered papers before the audience. In addition to Victoria Earle Matthews's paper on 'The Value of Race Literature', these included Ella L. Smith's paper on 'Woman and the Higher Education', Anna Julia Cooper's paper on the 'Need of Organization' among women, L. C. Carter's paper on 'Industrial Training', and Margaret Murray Washington's paper on 'Individual Work for Moral Education'.[16] In fact, so 'many fine papers prepared for the conference remained unread' that organizers predicted they 'might have been in session a week and then not have exhausted [them]selves'. So impressive was the quality of the papers at this first national conference that organizers suggested that, collected, they 'would make a credible book'.[17] The success of the first convention ensured that national conventions of black clubwomen would convene each summer, each one presenting another opportunity for them to present their work.

Growing interest in the regional organization of clubwomen also offered opportunities for black clubwomen to deliver papers outside the context of the club with which they were locally affiliated. At the first annual meeting of Colorado's Federation of Women's Clubs, for example,

Mrs. Ida DePriest, a member of the Woman's League of Denver, contributed a paper to a conversation on the 'Trend of Popular Literature'. Of all the subjects addressed at the conference, this 'was considered one of the hardest, if not the most difficult subject under discussion'. More challenging still was DePriest's status as one of the few black representatives to attend the meeting; she was 'one of the two colored delegates sent from the Woman's League of Denver'. DePriest's paper posed the question 'to what extent may we accept . . . the conclusions of others without personal investigation' and argued in part that 'only when the motive, intention, and apparent purpose of an act is known, and when a calm and comprehensive survey of the subject is taken, have we any right to express conclusions'. The response to her paper suggests both the value of the intimate context of black women's local organizations and the importance of black women actively seeking venues beyond the space of those local organizations to present their work. Surely the content of DePriest's paper and the quality of its delivery benefited from her past experience preparing and presenting similar papers before the sympathetic membership of her home organization, the Woman's League. More importantly, DePriest's success before an audience composed for the most part of white women at the first annual meeting of the Colorado Federation of Women's Clubs illustrates the extent to which black clubwomen capably represented themselves through their literary work; in doing so, they redefined black womanhood for those who were skeptical about a black woman's intelligence or her capabilities. DePriest's presentation proved 'an agreeable surprise to the women' at the meeting, who found her to be 'equal to the occasion'. The other 'colored delegate' who attended the meeting, Mrs. Lizzie Olden, president of the Woman's League, was also able to alter the audience's perception of black womanhood through the paper she delivered. In 'The Club as a Factor in Bettering Social and Civic Conditions', Olden argued that those 'who are called our best women have little right to their title unless they make use of their talents and their leisure for the benefit of the community'. Her paper was well received, and she was 'frequently applauded'. Both women, in this case, were able to use their literary presentations to help others begin to recognize and appreciate them in terms of their dignified self-presentation and significant intellectual abilities.[18]

Successfully exposing their texts to the scrutiny of others, both those who supported as well as those skeptical about the intellectual abilities of black women, gave African American clubwomen a sense of confidence in their critical writing. It also offered them a tangible sense of the potential impact of its public presentation. Coupled with the skills that clubwomen acquired in the context of conducting research for their club assignments and forming and presenting their opinions before the membership of their local clubs, club papers became the building blocks of other, more public documents that black women produced and disseminated. The creation and dissemination of these public documents, which had their roots in private literary exercises, became central to fulfilling the political objectives of black women's clubs.

The members of Boston's Woman's Era Club, for instance, came to fully appreciate the value of print as a means of widely publicizing injustices and communicating the political position of club members when in 1894 they used a printed text to respond to an especially heinous and, in the last decade of the nineteenth century, seemingly ubiquitous crime: lynching. In response to a particular incident, members of the Woman's Era decided that the time had come to give public voice to their disapproval. In the past they had written resolutions and composed other documents to express their opinions and communicate their outrage; for the most part, however, these documents had not been publicly issued or widely distributed and had therefore not attracted a great deal of attention. This time they composed a leaflet that communicated their protest and provided valuable information on the subject of lynching; these leaflets were printed and 'sent in every direction'. The effectiveness of the members' intervention was apparent from the acknowledgments they received from those who read their leaflet and learned from it. Through widespread dissemination, the leaflet made its way into the hands not only of the general populace but also of influential persons who 'announced their intention of doing something toward awakening public sentiment'. 'Large demands for the leaflets have been made', the club reported, 'two hundred being called for at one time and a postal note being received from St. Louis calling for as many as could be spared.' The success of this effort indicated to members of the Woman's Era that print offered them the means to address a range of issues that affected African Americans in the United States. 'This reception of the leaflets has revealed to the club a line of work which has been little used and which the club can incorporate with its other work with advantage,' they wrote of their experience. 'This is the publication and circulation of matter that refers especially to the race, not alone, but also such matter as shall be for the advancement and encouragement of the race and to quote from our constitution "to collect all facts obtainable, showing the moral, intellectual, industrial and social growth, and attainment of our people".' Their conclusion that 'the receipt of leaflets . . . among the colored people generally South and West could be but a welcome and hope-inspiring feature' of their work suggests that it was a strategy they would turn to again and again in their capacity as public servants.[19]

For other black women's clubs, the dissemination of print was a central mission from their inception, and their accomplishments on this front were significant. The 'object' of the Woman's Loyal Union of Brooklyn and New York, for instance, was 'the diffusion of accurate and extensive information relative to the civil and social status of the Afro-American'. Through print, they believed, African Americans might make 'intelligent assertion[s] of their rights', and turn the 'attention of conscientious, conservative, thinking people at large . . . to the injustice' of the treatment of African Americans.[20] Led by Victoria Earle Matthews, whose own literary ambitions included the 'determination to write a series of text books, historical primers for the youth of the race, which will trace the history of the African and show that he and his descendants have been prominently identified with every phase of this country's history including the landing of Columbus', the tremendous literary achievements of this organization are not surprising. One of their first projects suggests their firm understanding of the power of the printed word and their determination to tap into it to relay accurate information about African Americans to a broader public. 'Realizing the wrongs perpetuated upon our race in the South, the injury occasioned by opinions that have been freely expressed in several leading magazines and newspapers, as to the retrogression of the race morally', the club set out to 'ascertain the truth of such statements' by conducting their own survey. Headed by Matthews herself, the membership of the Woman's Loyal Union 'wrote a set of questions, submitted them to the executive board with the hope of their approval, and expressed the desire to have said questions sent to the ministers, school teachers and other representative men and women throughout the country for the purpose of eliciting from them the true statistics of our people morally'.[21] Praised as 'comprehensive and pointed', the questionnaire was considered an effective tool for fulfilling its design: 'to gather from the most reliable sources facts as to the mental, moral and financial position of our people.' 'The circular is an intelligent step in the right direction', wrote one source in praise of the project; 'the Loyal Union evidently intends gaining a clear understanding of the situation, and without doubt that is the way to undertake any broad work.'[22]

Practice as researchers, writers, and presenters of papers in the intimate setting of club meetings prepared black women for the demands of issuing their writing in more public forums and formats. Statistics offered by the recording secretary at the second anniversary celebration of the Woman's Era, for instance, suggest the extent to which black clubwomen made use of these literacy skills and the authority with which they were associated. In the preceding year, clubwomen had shown their support for the antilynching crusade of Ida B. Wells-Barnett by responding in print to 'all attempts to retard her influence'; their 'letters of protest' had been sent to various individuals as well as to 'the leading papers of New York and Boston'. In addition, they submitted twenty-five petitions 'for the forwarding of the Blair Joint resolution', which they hoped would reach 'the highest officials in the state and prominent citizens'.[23] 'In accordance with that clause of constitution . . . which provides for the dissemination of race literature', the Woman's Loyal Un spent much of its 1899–1900 season circulating 'the important leaflet[,] "An Address to the Peo of the United States", prepared by Prof. Jesse Lawson and issued by the National Afro-Ameri Council'. Organized by the chairman of the literature committee, this effort resulted in the distri tion of over two hundred leaflets. 'The object to be gained by such circulation', they articulated their end-of-year report, was 'to fully furnish that dominant class [with] an accurate statement of true condition and progress of the race'. To accomplish this, their strategy was to send the pampl 'primarily to those who need enlightenment on the present position of the Afro-American[,] sv persons to be reached either directly or through the co-operation of others known to be favora disposed'.[24]

Clubwomen's commitment to the distribution of print and their belief that leaflets, pam lets, and other printed texts could engage multiple communities in the service of African Ameri progress remained at the center of their reform efforts. In 1896 the newly formed governing body African American women's clubs listed 'some of the things clubs in the association are pledged consider this year': 'To attack the chain gang system of the South, the separate car law, to do res work in the alleys and slums of our great cities, and for the plantation woman and child, the found of homes for our indigent, and to show greater interest in the fallen and the wayward.'[25] The cl used every effort to uplift 'the fallen and the wayward' and to criticize legal and extralegal racism America. Toward that end, they distributed their own writing and that of others who shared th politics. Frances E. W. Harper expressed this commitment when, early in 1903, she wrote to Reverend Francis Grimké, pastor of the influential 15th Avenue Presbyterian Church in Washingt D.C., regarding a series of sermons he had delivered on lynching. After thanking Grimké for send her a printed copy of one of these sermons and praising its 'manly refusal to accept the verdict of mob in the cases of lynching', Harper suggested an alternative means of disseminating this powei discourse throughout the white community. 'Do these sermons have a circulation outside of people?' she asked. 'Could there not be some contrivance planned by which your sermons wo reach larger audiences than they do now? Could not the council plan for their circulation, and women's clubs be induced to scatter them among the white people in different localities?' Harpe promise to Grimké that 'after New Year's day I will get a few from you to distribute' may seem a hopelessly small gesture in light of the huge and fast-growing problems with which the bl community grappled at the beginning of the twentieth century, but it serves as a reminder that th seemingly small individual and group actions laid the groundwork for the more widespread form public protest that were to come.[26]

Notes

1   Fannie Barrier Williams, 'Illinois', *Woman's Era*, June 1895, 4.

2   Florida Ridley, 'Opportunity and Privileges of Club Life', *Woman's Era*, October and Nove ber 1896, 10.

3   Ibid.

4   'Report of the Woman's Era Club, Boston, Mass.' (1896); reprinted in *A History of the (Movement among the Colored Women of the United States of America* (Washington, D.C.: Natic Association of Colored Women's Clubs, 1902), 116. The Woman's Era Club met the first third Monday of each month. Members were expected to pay $1.00 annually in dues. By 1\ the membership of the Woman's Era was listed as 133.

5   See, for example, the series of papers by Mary P. Evans printed in the *Woman's Era* in 18 including: 'Health and Beauty from Exercise: Paper No. 1', *Woman's Era*, 1 May 1894

'Health and Beauty from Exercise: Paper No. 2', *Woman's Era*, 1 June 1894, 7; 'Health and Beauty from Exercise: Paper No. 3', *Woman's Era*, July 1894, 7.

6   Ellen Bartelle Deitrick, 'Domestic Science: Paper No. 2', *Woman's Era*, 1 May 1894, 6.

7   Elizabeth E. Lane, 'Tuskegee Woman's Club', *Woman's Era*, November 1895, 4.

8   Ibid.

9   Ibid.

10   Elizabeth Piper Ensley, 'Colorado Club Women', *Woman's Era*, November 1895, 12; 'An Afternoon with the Boston Woman's Era Club', *National Association Notes*, 15 June 1897, 1.

11   Ensley, 'Colorado Club Women', 12.

12   Details of the anniversary celebration, including a summary of Ruffin's comments, are recorded in the *Woman's Era*. See 'England's Attitude', *Woman's Era*, February 1895, 12.

13   Annie King and S. H. Johnson, 'Sierra Leone Club', *Woman's Era*, 1 May 1894, 2.

14   'Club Gossip', *Woman's Era*, 1 May 1894, 4.

15   Katie V. Carmand, 'Report of the Women's [*sic*] Loyal Union of New York and Brooklyn', *Woman's Era*, August 1895, 5.

16   Cooper was a member of Washington, D.C.'s Colored Woman's League, and Washington belonged to the Tuskegee Women's Club. I have been unable to identify the club affiliations of Smith or Carter.

17   In the conference souvenir issue of the *Woman's Era*, the editors of the newspaper lamented that it was only possible to print these papers 'singly, or at most doubly'. They suggested, however, that the 'papers especially prepared for the conference would make a credible book' and expressed their hope that 'in some way or another, at some time or another, they may all be collected in one volume'. See untitled announcement, *Woman's Era*, August 1895, 20.

18   Ensley, 'Colorado Club Women', 12. The inclusion and seeming acceptance of these African American delegates at the meeting of the Colorado Federation of Women's Clubs contradicts the more common depictions of the experience of black women who wished to participate in the activities of and form affiliations with white women's clubs. In 1893 Fannie Barrier Williams was denied admission to the Chicago Woman's Club despite her high social standing and numerous contributions to the women's clubs in Illinois. The *Woman's Era*'s assessment of the situation was cogent: although she was 'well equipped to help on the work the Woman's clubs are formed to do, the modicum of negro [*sic*] blood in her veins outweighed her eminent fitness' ('The Chicago Woman's Club Reject Mrs. Williams', *Woman's Era*, December 1894, 20). As Anne Ruggles Gere notes in her discussion of the women's club movement, social segregation dictated that white women 'saw very little of their African American peers', which allowed them to 'develop and nurture highly distorted images' of them. Excluding black women from their midst was also a way white clubwomen asserted their own privilege and power. See Gere, *Intimate Practices: Literacy and Cultural Work in U.S. Women's Clubs, 1880–1920* (Urbana: University of Illinois Press, 1997), 164. Gere's study of women's clubs and clubwomen in a variety of social locations has been invaluable to my own work on the black women's club movement.

19   'The Woman's Era', *Woman's Era*, 24 March 1894, 4. The event that inspired members of the Woman's Era to create and distribute the leaflets is described as the 'Denmark lynching'. I have been unable to further identify this lynching, or even to determine whether 'Denmark' is a location or proper name.

20   'News from the Clubs', 'New York Letter', *Woman's Era*, 24 March 1894, 2.

21   S. Elizabeth Frazier, 'Profile of Victoria Earle Matthews', *Woman's Era*, 1 May 1894, 1.

22   'Club Gossip', *Woman's Era*, July 1894, 4.

23   'England's Attitude', *Woman's Era*, February 1895, 13. Several times in the 1880s and 1890s Senator Henry W. Blair, a Republican from New Hampshire, introduced before Congress a bill that would provide for the distribution of surplus Federal funds to state schools in

proportion to the prevalence of illiteracy. The bill was never passed. For examples of the kind of resolution the *Woman's Era* might have drafted, see Herbert Aptheker, ed., *A Documentary History of the Negro People in the United States*, vol. 2 (1951; reprint, New York: Carol Publishing Group, 1992), 648, 693–94, 710, 715.

24   'The Work of the Woman's Loyal Union of New York City', *National Association Notes*, April 1900, unpaginated.

25   'Work Suggested by the National Association', *Woman's Era*, October/November 1896, 3.

26   Harper, 'Count on Me as a Subscriber', in *A Brighter Coming Day*, 322–23.

Chapter 37

Janice Radway

A FEELING FOR BOOKS
The Book-of-the-Month Club, literary taste and middle-class desire

Books are for readers

When Harry Scherman laid out his original plan for the Book-of-the-Month Club in 1926, he made it clear that he understood implicitly how the literary field was configured. He also demonstrated a canny sense of how his projected operation would likely challenge the traditional understanding of that configuration. Scherman suggested that he planned to create his committee of selection as a way of acknowledging the dominant view of the literary field as a special domain dealing with a category of printed objects distinctly different from all things commercial.[1] As he himself later put it, 'Obviously, there would be suspicion that the books which would be presented to subscribers would be presented for *commercial* reasons.' To counter that assumption, 'there had to be some real assurance that the books that were going to be sent to them . . . were chosen for their *quality* as really desirable books. That necessitated a committee', he added. 'The members of it had to be known to the public as completely disinterested people.'[2] The original selection committee was established, therefore, to foreground the status of his books as literary objects rather than their role as commodities bound for circulation through the market.

After he hired Henry Canby, Dorothy Canfield Fisher, Heywood Broun, Christopher Morley, and William Allen White, however, Harry Scherman empowered them to do more than function as a concession to the dominant view of publishing. He asked them to provide something other than a mere testimonial to the quality of the merchandise offered by the club. In fact, he asked the committee members to make determinations about the quality of the merchandise itself, and more importantly, he asked them to determine their own criteria for making such determinations in the first place. Neither he nor his partners interfered in their deliberations. They left it to the judges to work out procedures and criteria for selecting the best book of the month. As I have already indicated, however, the committee had its own ideas about how to think about the literary field and about the nature of literary production. Consequently, only a few months into the enterprise, Dorothy Canfield Fisher and her colleagues urged Scherman to rethink some of the basic operating assumptions of the club.

As we have already seen, Fisher was instrumental in promoting reconsideration. She object
to the advertised premise of Harry Scherman's new organization, the idea that one book, better th
all the rest, could be identified every month. She worried that promotion of a single title wou
obscure all the other worthy books published at the same time. And those books, she suggeste
should not necessarily be compared with one another. Books were different, just as readers we
different. Fisher conceived of her role at the club as a kind of scout on behalf of a variety of reade
She was attempting to match prospective readers with titles that would appropriately and effectiv
address their needs. Thus she urged Scherman to allow the judges to recommend more than
designated book of the month.

Fisher and the rest of the judges seem to have worried less about the commercial orientati
of the Book-of-the-Month Club than Harry Scherman did. William Allen White, who express
skepticism about his suitability for a literary undertaking when first approached by Scherman, wr
later in a letter to him that 'now if I am worth anything to you it is [as] a mentor on that side of
merchandising operation'.[3] Joan Rubin has shown that he often pronounced books 'salable' a
expressed concern about how the committee's more literary selections would affect the clu
'business proposition'.[4] Similarly, Christopher Morley's talents as a book promoter, which
displayed with great panache in his column 'The Bowling Green', accorded well with the fun
mental purposes of the Book-of-the-Month Club, which despite Harry Scherman's queasiness a
organizational caveats, was commercial to its very core. Antiquarian and bibliophile though he w
Morley did not envision books as static, shelved, or cherished objects alone. For him they achiev
their true vitality and dynamic promise only in the hands of active readers.

One of Morley's first literary successes was the novel *Parnassus on Wheels*, which chronic
the activities of a peripatetic bookseller devoted to making books accessible to ordinary peopl
And at the end of *Ex Libris Carissimis*, a 1932 collection of his essays, he appended a list of his favor
books, which he troped as 'Golden Florins'. For him classics were not eternal treasures in so
literary museum but value-bearing, circulating currency.[6] Morley also sought to familiarize
readers of his columns with something other than 'the best books'. He discussed all sorts of write
major and minor; the latter category he justified by saying that 'some of the most exquisite pleasu
of print are to be found in pursuit of the smaller names'.[7]

The Book-of-the-Month Club judges, like the organization they were hired to assist (and l
Melvil Dewey, the cheap libraries, and the creators of the Harvard Classics), were devoted to
cause of the circulating book. In their minds the value of a book was not fixed once and for all at
moment of its creation but was established and reestablished anew in the process of exchange ev
time it made its way into the hands of readers who found particular uses for it in keeping with th
own peculiar aims. Even Henry Canby, by all accounts the most literary of the judges, once obser
that 'the primary object of all writing about books is to give them currency'.[8] This was especia
necessary, he believed, in the bewildering and confusing modern age because people relied on bo
and literature to tell them how to make sense of the new forms of life that swirled so meaningles
about them.

In fact, as I have indicated before, Canby left the professoriate to take up the activity of bo
reviewing because he felt that the conservatism of the literary academy prevented him from devot
his attention to the all-important task of searching out a literature appropriate to the modern a
'We are not concerned to know only whether Joyce's "Ulysses" is inferior to Homer's or O'Nei
plays to the tragedies of Euripides,' he once wrote. 'Our chief interest is in interpretations
comparisons. We would know what these modern works . . . are good for, what are their defe
and how they might have been bettered.'[9] Canby's turn to reviewing was motivated by his ferv
belief that the general American public needed to discover a literature that might counter mod
skepticism and materialism without turning its back on every aspect of modernity. 'We shall lis

to no philosopher or critic,' he wrote, 'who out of ignorance is afraid of the results of science, saying pooh! pooh! to the machines, and resorting to the seventeenth century or the fourth A.D. or B.C.' He continued, 'That life is out of control now is notorious, but it will never be brought back by cursing from a hill top. It is better to try to ride the machines than to pretend that they can be disinvented; wiser to guide a civilization than to oppose it utterly.'[10]

In a sense Henry Canby continued to believe in the power and efficacy of words to address modern dilemmas. It was that faith, in fact, that caused him to worry so insistently about the difficulties of finding a literature adequate to the challenges of modernity in a world where so many more books were being churned out by faster presses and sped-up editorial processes at increasingly profit-minded publishing houses. As he put it, 'Books are being published daily, and some one must tell the busy and none too discriminating public what they are worth – not to mention the librarians who are so engaged in making out triple cards and bibliographies and fitting titles to vague recollections that they have no time left to read.'[11] Canby took up newspaper reviewing out of the conviction that '[the newspapers] alone . . . have kept pace with the growing swarm of published books'. Without the reviews first placed on book pages and then collected in book supplements, he argued, 'the public would have . . . only the advertisements and the publishers' announcements to classify, analyze, and in some measure describe the regiment of books that marches in advance of our civilization'.[12] Henry Canby's commitment to regular reviewing and to the distribution goals of the Book-of-the-Month Club was a function of his belief that books could effectively provide the guidance modern people needed to make sense of the unprecedented rate and extent of social change they were forced to confront on a daily basis.

Adumbrated here, it should be clear, is an attitude toward books and, by extrapolation, culture at large that privileges the activities and objectives of circulation and use. Henry Canby was never driven simply by an overwhelming desire to identify the best that had been thought and said in the past. He was motivated by a mission to ensure the utility of books (and other cultural products) by getting them into the hands of people who might best understand them and apply the insights they contained. As he put it, 'The best book is worth nothing at all if it never finds a reader'. He noted as well that 'good reading is a highly personal experience, whose quality depends upon the taste, the intellect, the imagination, and the sensitivity of the individual reader. Still he has to get the books. I find too little in histories of literature and criticism of how books get to readers.'[13]

My point here is that just as Harry Scherman's desire to market new books in an endless stream prompted him to foreground the pleasures and uses of reading as an activity rather than to focus on the particularities of books as singular objects, so the judges' interest in book promotion and their matter-of-fact acquiescence to the market-driven nature of publishing pushed them to focus on the processes of book buying and book reading as well. In effect they installed readers and their differentiated reading activities at the center of their evaluative operation. Not all readers bought books, they knew, and not all book buyers bought books to read. Some books were bought as gifts; some were bought to be displayed. Others were purchased as reference tools or as volumes intended to comprise a personal library. And still others were bought to be read through to the end. In their writings Henry Canby, Dorothy Canfield Fisher, and the others suggested that readers often sought different affective experiences in the act of reading, different relationships to the book they had picked up, and different ends as the goal of the reading process. Ironically, then, despite the larger advertising emphasis on the club's search for the single best book of the month, the judges began to elaborate a practical logic of selection that foregrounded not only the variability of readers and reading but also the variability of the evaluative standards used to find books for them.

Even Henry Canby's more narrow view of specifically 'literary' books accorded with this larger perspective. Although he would continue to believe that the literary had a special role to play in what he called modern civilization, he considered its distinctiveness less a matter of quality and more a difference of kind, function, or purpose. The literary, for Canby, was not necessarily better than other sorts of books, nor was it universally useful. Nor did he believe that all instances of the category 'literature' should be ranked along a single scale of value. Rather, Canby argued that, like works of sociology, psychology, general science, history, and biography, literary books appealed to particular audiences and performed distinct functions. They did so because all books concretized the experience of their authors and because different authors turned their experience to different purposes and goals. Books, like all forms of cultural production, according to Canby, attempted different things for different purposes and with different audiences in mind. Canby felt, therefore, that every book ought to be approached on its own terms if readers would do justice to it and get the most from it that they could. The reviewer's proper task, then, in order to facilitate appropriate connections between books and readers, was to clarify precisely what those terms were. The reviewer's job was to provide an adequate and informative definition of the book as a categorical object of a particular kind.

Canby's earliest collection of 'essays in contemporary criticism' had been issued in 1922 under the title *Definitions* as a way of emphasizing the fact that he offered not a 'sequence of chapters developing a single theme and arriving at categorical conclusions' but, rather, a series of essays, quite literally 'attempts' to illuminate the multiple purposes, means, and achievements of contemporary writers in a confused age.[14] Then, as later, Canby did not consider his criticism an Olympian pronouncement issued from on high, measuring all works against a single, universal standard. Rather, he viewed his essays as a series of attempts to open doors 'through which both writer and reader may enter into a better comprehension of what novelists, poets, and critics have done or are trying to accomplish'.[15] Such a mediating role was necessary, he believed, because the literary world had grown muddied as a consequence of augmented production and because the general business of evaluation and judgment had been thrown into disarray.

Henry Canby differed crucially from cultural critics such as Waldo Frank and Ernest Boyd in that he did not blame the much-remarked-on evaluative confusion of his era on the abandonment of standards altogether. He argued instead that standards had proliferated drastically. Observing that 'one of the common complaints against this slipshod generation is that it has no standards', he countered, 'not a lack of standards but a confusion of standards is our undoing'.[16] And he well understood that such confusion profoundly unsettled the profession of literary criticism as it had previously been conceived. 'Literary criticism', he wrote, 'has become polytheistic and we worship at so many altars that we cannot ourselves name our literary religion'.[17] For Canby the kind of religion of literature promoted by the modernists and the little magazines was a decided anachronism simply because the assumption of a universal standard on which omniscient judgment could be predicated was no longer possible.

The second most powerful judge, Dorothy Canfield Fisher, held views remarkably similar to Henry Canby's. In fact she insisted even more strongly than he did that literary judgments, evaluations, and descriptions needed to vary with their audiences and their objects. Nonetheless, because she believed that there was a fundamental continuity between literature and life, she treated all books as instrumental guides for living and argued that even fiction could enable readers to broaden their experience and to lead richer, more intense, and honorable lives. Similarly, she championed nonfiction titles when they strove to make their technical knowledge both accessible and useful to the general reader. She was known at the club for her interest in continuing education. Fisher was as aware as Henry Canby that readers differed not only in their interests and tastes but in their education and literary preparation as well. Accordingly, she conceptualized her role at the club as promoter of many different kinds of interactions between books and readers, and she conceptualized her duty as a reviewer in a manner distinctly different from the way she thought of the activities of the traditional literary critic.

In a report on a book of poems by Marion Canby, for instance, she once expatiated at length on her understanding of the difference between book reviewing and literary criticism.[18] It is worth quoting several passages of her analysis, for they lay out clearly the thinking that was shared by all of the Book-of-the-Month Club judges, and they suggest that the judges were quite aware they were not functioning as traditional critics. 'People of experience agree that one trouble with book reviews could be eliminated by firmly specifying at the head of each one . . . the kind of person for whom it is intended. One sort of review is written for actual readers of books, people of intelligence and taste not professionally literary in any way who, seeing a new volume would like to find a statement about it that gives them a fairly clear idea what is inside it and whether it is the kind of book they would be apt to find worth reading.' Actual readers, Fisher suggested, were quite different from professional readers. Thus they needed something different from what was generally provided in literary criticism. Since the worth of a book was apparently a function of the content it offered to inquiring readers, a review ought to inform them about what they would find between its covers, and it ought to advise them if they would be likely to derive satisfaction or pleasure from reading it.

Literary criticism, on the other hand, because it was aimed at the professional reader, stressed judgment and evaluation rather than information and advice. Fisher suggested, in fact, that 'the [literary] sort of review is intended, consciously or unconsciously, not at all for mere readers of books, but for other critics, and for professionally literary folk whose self-appointed business it is correctly to appraise and accurately to calculate the position of each new piece of creative writing, in relation with what has gone before and is likely to come after it in the history of literature'. Evaluation and judgment, from her point of view, belonged to the province of the literary professional, whose job it was to provide a critical account of literary history and tradition. Fisher clearly believed that professional reading was organized differently from that practiced by the nonprofessional, and she obviously thought both entirely legitimate. She suggested, in fact, that 'both kinds of reviews are interesting, worth-while and of value – but only when read by those for whom they are intended. Each kind is exasperating and disappointing when read by people who are looking for the other kind'.

Significantly, Fisher concluded her report on Marion Canby's poems with the observation 'that the reviews written for the Book of the Month Club News are of the first kind'.[19] Like Henry Canby, then, who had abandoned literary criticism, he once reported, because he 'had shaken off some pedantic ideas and no longer yearned to publish articles that only scholars could understand, which no one, not even scholars did', Fisher seems to have understood that criticism and the books critics tended to find valuable were closely bound up with the interests and concerns of a highly specialized, often heavily trained, and quite small professional audience.[20] Since ordinary readers could derive benefit from many different kinds of books, she suggested, the judges ought to concern themselves with more than the literary, and they ought to report accurately on the nature of those books for the club's subscribers. Although she was willing to include high literary titles on the club's list, she was as careful as Henry Canby was to ask herself whether a large, general audience might find a given title pleasing, compelling, or useful. If the judgment was no, she would argue vigorously for a report in the News that would characterize the book honestly and that would discourage readers who might not be up to its challenge or likely to find it interesting.

Of the April 1928 main selection, for instance, Elizabeth Bowen's The Hotel, the Book-of-the-Month Club News noted that 'it is a book . . . that calls for a more than usually careful characterization to subscribers'. The report continued, 'It must be described, first, as a subtle book.' Obviously hoping to avoid baffled or irate customers and a mountain of returns, the News cautioned its readers further:

Those who enjoy writers like Joseph Conrad, Anatole France, Henry James – and to come closer to today – writers somewhat like H. M. Tomlinson, Willa Cather, Edith Wharton, will exult in it. It will yield its full delight, like an old and rare wine, only to those who take it in with an appreciative and unhurried attention. Those readers, on the other hand, who prefer the straightforward narrative – as exemplified by such novelists as Galsworthy, Tarkington, Bennett and innumerable others – while they cannot fail to appreciate the color and sparkle of this gem, may not be enthusiastic about it. If one is not in a proper mood, indeed, one may even find *The Hotel* annoying by reason of its subtlety, although this would be unfair to a deft piece of work.[21]

Similarly, the next issue of the *News* warned potential readers straightaway that Henry Canby had reported that *Mr Weston's Good Wine*, by T. F. Powys, should be avoided 'if you cannot endure symbolism' or 'if the earthly humors of the all-too-human race, especially in the pursuit of love, shock you easily'. In that case, the *News* concluded bluntly, 'you are advised not to read it'.[22] Apparently neither Canby nor Fisher had any compunctions about warning the club's subscribers away from books they thought distinct literary achievements yet esoteric.

The commentary of Henry Canby and Dorothy Canfield Fisher suggests that the judges believed the principal aim of the Book-of-the-Month Club was not to place books in the long sweep of literary history but to match readers with the books appropriate to them. Following from this premise, the logic of the evaluative system they established at the club in its early years developed three pointed concerns. The judges tried first to determine what sort of book they had before them. Then they attempted to understand why a reader might select this book rather than another. Finally they explored how best to describe that book to make its relevant features known to readers, who would approach it with previously formed expectations, desires, and needs. In the final analysis, despite their presentation to the public as authorities who could magisterially issue pronouncements on the basis of special literary expertise, the Book-of-the-Month Club judges developed an evaluative process that was thoroughly contingent and fundamentally reader driven. They tended to subordinate the critical act of literary judgment to the activity of recommendation. And recommendation, as they practiced it, was a self-consciously social activity constituted by their effort to understand and to adopt the point of view of their subscribers. Once they managed to understand readers' desires, needs, and tastes, they subsequently strove to match those aims to goods and authors already available in the public marketplace. In a sense the judges constituted themselves as social facilitators or mediators trying to foster connections between readers, books, and their authors. Thus they resisted taking up the usual critical distance and pose of superiority found in traditional criticism. More frequently in their daily practice they tried not to dictate on the basis of their own taste but sought to imagine themselves as the readers they aimed to address. Only after they had managed that act of imagination and identification did they turn to the monthly output of the publishing industry and seek particular books for particular readers.[23]

The planar logic of middlebrow evaluation

Harry Scherman's judges conceived of their business less as a process of evaluation and judgment than as one of definition and sorting. Their job was to read all the books submitted by the trade, to imagine who might find such books interesting or useful, and then to evaluate how well particular books might satisfy those readers most likely to select them. Since the publishers had been instructed by Scherman to send many different kinds of books to the club, the judges quickly recognized that they could not compare apples to oranges or oranges to grapefruits. Not all books were literary books, and even literary books, the judges believed, varied considerably in form function, and intent. As Canby himself observed, 'There is — to take the novel — the story well calculated to pass a pleasant hour but able to pass nothing else; there is the story with a good idea in it and worth reading for the idea only; there is the story worthless as art but usefully catching some current phase of experience; and there is the fine novel which will stand any test for insight, skill, and truth.' He continued, 'Now it is folly to apply a single standard to all these types of story. It can be done, naturally, but it accomplishes nothing except to eliminate all but the shining best.'[24] The project at the club, as a consequence, was to proliferate gauges and to multiply evaluative standards. The judges asked what every book was useful for. Even lesser books, with modest aims and intentions, they believed, deserved their readers, and those books could sometimes satisfy and serve their readers better than more ambitious titles.

In effect, then, Henry Canby and his colleagues treated all books that came to them as instances of multiple and multifarious types, that is, as examples of different classes or genera, each with its own peculiar functions and uses. 'Is this serious fiction', they asked themselves, 'or hammock literature?' 'Is this a sea saga or a small woman's novel?' 'Is it popular history or too specialized for the general reader?' 'Is it literary criticism or literary biography?' Only after determining the category did they ask themselves whether a book was any good or not. Having determined that a particular title was a literary biography, for instance, they then asked themselves, 'Is it a *good* literary biography?' 'Does it fail as an entertaining yarn?' they similarly wondered. 'Will it please readers who are partial to nature books?' To answer this latter question about quality, they additionally had to ask themselves what, exactly, characterized an excellent example of a particular kind of book. 'What makes a good nature book good?' they wondered. 'Is it the same quality or set of features that establishes the excellence of a biography or a work of serious fiction?'

The Book-of-the-Month Club judges focused on the diversity and variety of the literary field and on its ability to generate many different kinds of books with different features and different aims. In spite of Harry Scherman's ritual repetition of the claim that the club sent out the best book of the month, in practice the judges deemed this kind of absolute hierarchical grading an impossible and undesirable task. Their work, consequently, contested a hierarchical and pyramidal view of the literary field. Although they continued to recognize the existence of a special aesthetic category called Literature, which they rendered with a capital *L*, they also thought of the literary field itself as a universe encompassing all kinds of print productions. Accordingly, they differentiated books from one another on the basis of their differential functions and variable appeals to readers. In their view books were only comparable if they were of the same genus or type. It made no sense to judge a popular history lacking because its verbal style was undistinguished. Nor was it justifiable to eliminate a rollicking good story because its characters were superficially delineated. This is not to say that at the club the larger field was conceived as an open, free space, lacking its organization and structure. It was quite structured, in fact, but according to a different logic and in respect of different principles.

As a way of getting at that logic and its supporting principles, it might be useful to quote Henry Canby again on the variability of the literary as a special category unto itself. For although Canby continued to group most fictional texts under the sign of the literary, he also subdivided that body of texts on the basis of the functions they could perform for their readers. His comments here come from an essay about the difference between literary criticism and reviewing, a subject that concerned him throughout his career, as it did Dorothy Canfield Fisher. Criticism, Canby also felt, rightly concerned itself with literary values. Reviewing, on the other hand, which he believed properly functioned to inform readers about new books, needed to approach the question of value more flexibly. 'It is sometimes necessary to remind the austerer critic', he wrote, 'that there are a hundred books of poetry, of essays, of biography, of fiction, which are by no means of the first rank and yet are highly important, if only as news of what the world, in our present, is thinking and feeling. They cannot be judged, all of them on the top plane of perfect excellence; and if we judge them on any other plane, good, better, best, get inextricably mixed.'[25] Canby, at least, was willing to judge books on other planes and thus to contest the very idea of good, better, and best judged on one set of aesthetic criteria. Fiction, for instance, could be evaluated for the news it provided of the contemporary world rather than for its linguistic craftsmanship. Canby continued significantly, 'There is no help except to set books upon their planes and assort them into their categories – which is merely to define them before beginning to criticize'. The crucial move in the evaluative practice of the Book-of-the-Month Club judges was not judgment at all but the activity of categorization, of sorting onto different planes.

The concept of different planes, it should be noted, constructs a vision of a print universe conceived of not as an organic, uniform, hierarchically ordered space. Rather, the print universe appears as a series of discontinuous, discrete, noncongruent worlds. Those worlds bring together readers with particular needs and demands and writers with special forms of expertise capable of addressing both. The role prescribed for the critic in a uniform literary world is that of Solomonic, omniscient judge. The disposition best suited to this more differentiated world of particular and locally specific purposes, desires, and goals is closer to that of a manager who has been charged with the smooth functioning of a complex system. The skills required of this literary manager – with the literary defined very broadly to include virtually all kinds of books and print – are more like those of the modern, professional librarian than the critic. Trained to bring together inquiring readers with the appropriate forms of technical expertise capable of answering their questions, the modern librarian is primarily oriented to the needs and tastes of readers. Relying on the card catalog and the innovations of the Dewey system of classification, this individual approaches the world of print not as a single universe but rather as a world of differentiated knowledge-production where language is put to multiple and different uses, where it is deployed differentially to describe and manipulate the world in highly specific, technically distinct ways.

Given this view of the world of print as a series of contiguous and equivalent domains, it should not be surprising to note that the category of Literature was treated by the Book-of-the-Month Club judges with a certain amount of ambiguity. On one hand the club's rhetoric about best books and future classics tended to evoke a sense of the literary as both sacred and transcendent, as the apex of all cultural achievement. On the other hand their day-to-day selection procedures and habits of description tended to construe the literary as only one more category among many. In practice, literary books were treated as books of a certain sort, as a special taste dependent on a high degree of education and familiarity with the complexities of literary history. The insight and enlightenment associated with the literary was offered at the club not as a superior form of knowledge but as a particular and peculiar sort with its own uses and applications, equivalent to yet different from other sorts of knowledge, such as knowledge to be found in works of science, political affairs, or history. Thus the judges' pragmatic approach to the larger literary field challenged the sacred status of Literature and contested its claim as the best that had been thought and said in the world. This does not seem particularly surprising when we consider that they lived in an ever-more secular world impressed every day by the achievements of modern science and its supporting discourses, which foregrounded the material, the utilitarian, the technological, and the technical.

What I think we see at the Book-of-the-Month Club, then, is a disposition to structure the larger literary field according to a logic congenial to the emergent social group in connection with the debate over the Book-of-the-Month Club – the professional-managerial class. Increasingly educated to think of the world, whether mechanical, social, or natural, as an infinitely complex universe beyond the comprehension of single persons or even single points of view, individuals aspiring to membership in this group of workers were taught by specialized high school and college curricula to divide the universe into discrete domains and particular provinces, such as sociology, political science, the humanities, science, and history. They were asked to think of each of these areas capable of being rendered comprehensible by highly specific and technical ways of knowing. Aiming to labor not with their hands but with their minds, these potential knowledge workers were asked to learn particular forms of technical competence and professional expertise and to use both to facilitate better description and manipulation of all that was encompassed by their own special domain. They were to convey the technical knowledge they commanded as specialists and professionals to people who were nonspecialists, to clients, consumers, or students in need of usable versions of such knowledge for pragmatic decision making and the conduct of everyday life.

The multiple planes of the literary field as conceived by the Book-of-the-Month Club judges, it seems to me, were structured according to this kind of logic, a planar logic that foregrounded the discreteness and particularity of domains and forms of expertise. This view also emphasized the pragmatic disposition of expertise and its fundamentally instrumental orientation in the service of a putatively general population. In effect expertise was constructed as a positivity in relation to a generality, the generality and lack exhibited by Harry Scherman's general reader, that individual who could not reproduce technical competence but who could, out of need and desire, recognize its claims, revere it, and make use of it for practical ends.

This parallel construction is evident in the way Harry Scherman presented his judges to the public. In fact, he did not simply present Canby, Fisher, Morley, Broun, and White as experts. He simultaneously stressed their orientation to the needs of the general reader. In the first prospectus issued for the club in 1926, for instance, he observed that the selecting committee consisted of 'well-known critics and writers, whose complicity of taste and whose judgment as to books have been demonstrated for many years before the public'.[26] Then, beneath full-page portraits of each expert, he listed their professional credentials, stressing equally their special training and competence as well as their devotion to a broad, general taste. Of Broun, Scherman wrote, 'His reporting revealed a rare critical and descriptive faculty which was fully developed when he became a columnist for *The New York Tribune* and afterward *The New York World*. Since then his comment upon things in general as well as upon the special fields of literature and the theater in which he has become an authority, has been followed by the intelligent with constant delight.'[27] Furthermore, Scherman characterized William Allen White as 'one of the most distinguished editors in America' and noted significantly that 'in addition to service on many delegations and foundations, he is a writer of distinction in pure literature as well as journalism'. He continued, 'His admirable sanity, combined with a courageous and progressive attitude in all affairs involving the American mind, has won general recognition.'[28]

The specialist and the generalist were locked together at the club and, more generally, within American culture at this historical moment, in a relation of mutuality, each serving the other. The specialist labored on behalf of the generalist, who in turn obligingly accorded the specialist respect, legitimacy, and ultimately authority itself. What the Book-of-the-Month Club sold, then, along with its subscriptions and endless stream of new books, was a social framework and cognitive map for understanding and organizing the world. In a social formation and economy increasingly driven by the need to generate, to distribute, and to control myriad forms of information and knowledge, the Book-of-the-Month Club performed the important role of acclimating the professional-managerial class and all who aspired to its status to the assumption that books and the experts who wrote them addressed the particular purposes of general readers. Less an innovative force in achieving national distribution of books than an exercise in social training and pedagogy, the Book-of-the-Month Club functioned more significantly, it seems to me, as a key cultural agency constructing the idea of the general reader, yet ironically modeling and thereby promoting belief in the worth of technical expertise and specialized knowledge.

The club promised such a membership the chance to keep up with the ever-advancing production of new knowledge as well as the opportunity to confirm its identity as educated and au

courant. In a sense it assuaged an anxiety instilled by the increasingly specialized and technic
curricula of the colleges and universities; it calmed the fear that once one had cut formal ties
institutions of higher education, one ran the risk of being left behind by relentlessly changing, high
specialized fields of knowledge. Although one's ongoing participation in a profession and its k
associations would enable one to keep up with one's own field, all those other important fields
knowledge might grow increasingly opaque and incomprehensible to the flagging reader. Thus t
Book-of-the-Month Club's many handbooks, outlines, guides, omnibuses, and popularizatio
helped to alleviate this anxiety and, at the same time, to produce a belief in the naturalness
technical knowledge and special competence as well as a sense that these could be translated f
general readers who might thereby benefit practically from their advances and insights.

In dispensing its middlebrow cultural products, then, the club also recommended a particul
orientation to those products and the culture they represented, a habitus suitable to a wor
organized and understood in this way. The club suggested that though knowledge and culture we
the province of experts, they were valuable to the extent that they produced practical results ar
utilitarian effects for general readers. This was true even of fiction, they thought, which aim
sometimes to promote relaxation and escape and at other times to produce aesthetic pleasure. Bo
knowledge and culture were conceived, therefore, in utilitarian and pragmatic fashion. They we
not valuable, in and for themselves, according to the Book-of-the-Month Club, but for what th
could do.

The middlebrow habitus or orientation toward the world that Canby and company taught w
an instrumental one, finally, even when they were speaking about Literature with a capital *L*. Thou
the club began by appropriating an older, genteel view of culture and knowledge as higher forms
learning capable of ennobling all who came in contact with them, it did so in order to market the
forms for its own profit, thereby refuting the notion that culture and intellectual inquiry ought to
thought of as finalities without purposes, as instances of the transcendent. The Book-of-the-Mor
Club extended its own pragmatic, utilitarian disposition to culture to those it addressed as su
scribers by attempting to persuade them that a certain facility with the material contained in boc
could assure them of social success. Thus, while the club selected and sold serious cultural mater
and thereby continued to underwrite the notion of a higher, sacred culture of learning and art, it al
invited its members to take up a relationship to that culture that was troublesome to those who sa
themselves as its authoritative guardians.

For Henry Canby, Dorothy Canfield Fisher, and the rest of the Book-of-the-Month Cl
judges, all books, including fiction, achieved success and even greatness to the degree that they to
up issues of everyday life. Value was also a function of a book's capacity to be used in pragma
fashion to accomplish a particular end or purpose. The judges were wary of the dispassionate, high
intellectualized aesthetic distance associated with experimental forms of literary modernism and t
highly academic criticism that had appeared to legitimate it. As a consequence, their guidi
philosophy of book selection was less anaesthetic, in the sense of a philosophy or theory of art, th
an ethos, a practical disposition or orientation to books that evaluated them according to how w
they harmonized with a reader's moral norms, ethical standards, and expectations about pleasu
The Book-of-the-Month Club judges aimed to distribute more books to more readers not by seeki
to elevate literary or aesthetic taste but by pursuing the possibilities of functional alignment,
attempting to match books and readers through a correlation of their most basic perceptual schem
for structuring 'the everyday perception of everyday existence'.[29]

This attention to the variability of readers and reading aims produced an evaluative practice
the Book-of-the-Month Club that was as attentive to minor works of crime fiction as it was to wor
aspiring to the status of great literature. Although Henry Canby and even Dorothy Canfield Fish
sometimes continued to insist on the value of the literary above all else in their nonclub writings,

their work at the club they treated books as a collection of categorically different objects, each category a subset with its own defining features, operative functions, and potential audience. Together the judges attempted to see the merit in a popular biography just as they tried to describe accurately the potential value in a work of free verse, a volume on foreign affairs, or a book on modern science. Although they continued to try to root out what Henry Canby called cheap vulgarity, none of them were very confident that they knew what that was in an age marked by extreme confusion. Thus they tried to follow the exhortation he had published before in *American Estimates*. Canby wrote, 'Let us fight, then, in despite of time, tide, tendency, against cheap vulgarity in literature. But let us disclaim the reformer's easy distinctions as to what is to be saved and what damned.' He continued significantly, 'If the great first cause has foreordained a vital pictorial art to come from the comic strip, or a new literature from "The Saturday Evening Post," why let them come.'[30] In an age of diversifying audiences, proliferating publications, and the destruction of sure and singular standards, Canby and company felt that it was essential for them as book experts to mill about in the crowd, to take for granted the muddle and confusion, and yet to keep their eyes open to all possibilities.

Not surprisingly, Canby and his colleagues produced an ecumenical practice at the Book-of-the-Month Club that enabled Harry Scherman's distribution machine to send out in 1928 alone Bernard Shaw's *The Intelligent Woman's Guide to Socialism and Capitalism*, Felix Salten's *Bambi*, Stephen Vincent Benét's *John Brown's Body*, Paul de Kruif's *Hunger Fighters*, and a book called *Whither Mankind?* edited by Charles Beard, which the *News* praised both because it represented 'the ripest thought, upon a subject of interest, of some of the leading figures of our day' and because it exhibited 'great readability'.[31] In 1929 they sent out and retracted a book titled *Cradle of the Deep*, which had proved to be a hoax; *The Omnibus of Crime*, edited by Dorothy Sayers; *Kristin Lavransdatter*, by Sigrid Unset, who later won the Nobel Prize; and Walter Lippmann's *A Preface to Morals?*.[32] In subsequent years the selection grew even more diverse as the club's judges moved away from their early predilection for serious fiction and toward a more self-conscious attempt to serve the full range of subscriber taste and to represent the varied output of the publishing industry. They increased the number of popular histories they offered and added more biographies, accounts of scientific developments and public affairs, and even medical manuals aimed at middle-class parents eager to implement the newest theories of child development in their own families.

Notes

1   Harry Scherman, 'Original Outline of Plan for the Book-of-the-Month Club', 4–7.
2   Oral History Research Office, 'Reminiscences of Harry Scherman', 41: emphasis added.
3   Quoted in Rubin, *Making of Middlebrow Culture*, 142.
4   *Ibid*.
5   Morley, *Parnassus on Wheels*.
6   Morley, *Ex Libris Carissimis*.
7   Morley, *Streamlines*, 130, quoted in Wallach and Bracker, *Christopher Morley*, 21.
8   Canby, 'Exacting Art'.
9   Canby, 'Post Mortem'.
0   Canby, 'New Humanists'.
1   Canby, *Definitions*, 199–200.
2   *Ibid.*, 188.
3   Canby, *American Memoir*, 357.
4   Canby, *Definitions*, vii.
5   *Ibid*.

16   Canby, *American Estimates*, 199.
17   *Ibid.*, 201.
18   Dorothy Canfield Fisher, review of *High Mowing*, by Marion Canby, box 26, folder 1, 'Activities', Fisher Collection.
19   *Ibid.*
20   Canby, *American Memoir*, 278.
21   *Book-of-the-Month Club News*, March 1928, 1–2 (unpaginated).
22   *Ibid.*, April 1928, 4.
23   Joan Rubin has been the pioneer in taking middlebrow culture seriously. My account, as a result, is heavily indebted to her work. I should point out, however, that our attributes and approaches to the topic of literary criticism diverge significantly. In her account of the activities of the judges, Rubin acknowledges that she herself believes it important to maintain standards in the face of the judges' abnegation of them. She therefore holds them responsible for failing to teach such standards to their subscribers. In keeping with her assumption, Rubin evaluates the judges' activities by measuring the distance they had moved from the more responsible evaluation and pedagogy of the 'true critic'. Indeed, she accuses them of the 'withholding, or underexercise, of critical authority' in their reports for the *Book-of the-Month Club News* because those reports 'tended to substitute narrative for evaluation, information for aesthetics' (*Making of Middlebrow Culture*, 102). I feel that her assertions are based on the familiar acceptance of the aesthetic as a higher form of human cultural production, of criticism as a higher moral calling, and on a view of standards themselves as in some way obvious, eternal, and universal. I would prefer to see all of these as contingent historical forms serving particular and identifiable social purposes. I want to suggest that the narrative and information supplied in those reports appeared there because the judges were searching for something other than the aesthetically excellent. Thus they were exercising critical authority, but in a form unrecognizable to those who insisted that authority be exercised only as criticism and in the exclusive service of literary and aesthetic values.
24   Canby, *Definitions*, 297.
25   *Ibid.*, 298.
26   Harry Scherman, '*The Book of the Month Club*', 7.
27   *Ibid.*, 6.
28   *Ibid.*, 12.
29   Bourdieu, *Distinction*, 44. I am drawing here on Bourdieu's arguments about the characteristic petit bourgeois approach to art and culture, an approach distinctly related to that of middlebrow culture.
30   Canby, *American Estimates*, 125.
31   *Book-of-the-Month Club News*, October 1928, 1.
32   For the full list of yearly selections to 1957, see Charles Lee, *Hidden Public*, 161–94.

References

Bourdieu, Pierre, *Distinction: A Social Critique of the Judgement of Taste*, trans. Richard Nice Cambridge, Mass.: Harvard University Press, 1984.
Canby, Henry Seidel, *American Estimates*, London: Jonathan Cape, 1929.
—— *American Memoir*, Boston: Houghton Mifflin, 1947.
—— 'An Exacting Art', *Saturday Review of Literature*, March 1, 1930, 32.
—— *Definitions: Essays in Contemporary Criticism*, New York: Harcourt, Brace, 1922.
—— 'The New Humanists', *Saturday Review of Literature*, February 22, 1930, 751.
—— 'Post Mortem', *Saturday Review of Literature*, June 14, 1930, 1122.

Lee, Charles, *The Hidden Public: The Story of the Book-of-the-Month Club*, Garden City, NY: Doubleday, 1938.

Morley, Christopher, *Parnassus on Wheels*, Philadelphia: Lippincott, 1917.

—— *Ex Libris Carissimis*, Philadelphia: University of Pennsylvania Press, 1951.

Oral History Research Office, Butler Library, Columbia University. The Book of the Month Club. Director, Allan Nevins. Interviews by Louis M. Starr, 1955. 'The Reminiscences of Harry Scherman'.

Rubin, Joan Shelley, *The Making of Middlebrow Culture*, Chapel Hill: University of North Carolina Press, 1992.

Scherman, Harry, 'Original Outline of Plan for the Book-of-the-Month Club', Folder D–III, Box 3, Harry Scherman Papers, Rare Book and Manuscript Library, New York: Columbia University.

Scherman, Harry, 'The Book of the Month Club', Original brochure mailed to first interested subscribers, Folder D-III, Box 3, Harry Scherman Papers, Rare Book and Manuscript Library, New York: Columbia University.

Wallach, Mark I., and Jon Bracker, *Christopher Morley*, Boston: Twayne, 1976.

PART FIVE

The future of the book

EDITORS' INTRODUCTION

Book History as a field of study marks both an end and a beginning. It is clear that as we move into an era marked by discussions of the 'new' electronic revolution, the 'old' print revolution, begun in the fifteenth century, assumes a clearer focus and a natural closure. Just as manuscript traditions merged with new print technologies, so too we are now seeing similar mergings and complementarities between new and old media. The embedding of visual culture into cultural formations from the twentieth century onwards (the advance of film, television, the World Wide Web) has meant also a reshaping of print culture to accommodate such media of communication. We can see this in the manner in which books now form a part of contemporary Western cultural industries, where creativity, capitalism and consumption are linked through production of mass media products based on texts (books to films and subsequent film 'novelisations'). It is also evident in the manner in which texts (newspapers, journals) are now only one among many media communication systems competing for the attention of mass audiences. One has only to survey the multiple media through which humanity now communicates to see that print culture is slowly being displaced from the centre of social communication to the periphery, still necessary but no longer the sole form of information in an electronic age.

The history of human communication can be interpreted as comprising three major revolutions: in the movements from orality to literacy, from the written text to the printed text, and from print to computer-generated content. The development of alphabets, and of writing systems generally, provided an enabling technology which empowered minorities within societies. The coming of the printing press took that technology of writing and provided materials for mass consumption within society. The third revolution, through which we are still living, has used digital technology, in Internet-based applications such as websites and blogs, to move from mass consumption to mass creation. Unlike the book, the technologies and economies of which entail that authorship can only ever be a minority pursuit, the computer has been able to turn us all into creators as well as consumers (see Paul Duguid, Mark Poster and Geoffrey Nunberg in this Reader).

Chapter 38

Mark Poster

THE DIGITAL SUBJECT AND CULTURAL THEORY

[. . .]

I hope in this essay to clarify some of the issues at stake in a technological change from print to digital texts. But I hope to do so without . . . the uncritical enthusiasm of prophets of progress who greet each new communication technology, from printing and photography to the telegraph, telephone, radio, film, and television, with a certainty of humanity's imminent perfection, global unification, and eternal peace.[1] And yet one cannot deny that the potential for change enabled by digital writing is vast. The point is not to predict utopia or dystopia but to understand what is happening and attempt to shape the outcome in the best way we can.

My attempt to clarify the issue of digital writing confronts a special difficulty because I deploy a predigital form of presentation: an oral, face-to-face format (in spoken version) and print. Although this essay was written on a computer, with the keyboard input mediated by binary code before becoming a graphic, alphabetic representation as pixels on a screen, then a series of ink marks on paper, the machine product has been appropriated by analogue apparatuses of authorship.[2] If you were reading this essay using a browser on your computer to access an Internet site where the work exists, let us say, in hypertext format, my arguments might be more convincing and my illustration might hit home with greater effect. Instead I am like a reporter returning home from a foreign culture to relate exotic discoveries, except the foreign culture, digital authorship, is right here, to the extent that cyberspace is anywhere. I am not, then, a foreign correspondent but a local informant, and perhaps you the reader, if you have not already shared my experience, are becoming other becoming distant, like all analogue authors, within your own discursive home.

Insisting on the medium

The 1996 Geneva conference of the World Intellectual Property Organization (created in 196? attempted to reform copyright law to reflect computer communications technologies (Samuelso 1997, 61 ff.). The problem for the group was daunting: to adjust laws originally formulated durin the print age of the seventeenth century to the conditions of the digital age. How could the mediu of the Internet be reconciled with the media of print and broadcast? Copyright law presumes wh has become no longer necessarily true: that the reproduction of information requires costly mater casings (books, audio records or tapes, celluloid films), that the dissemination of information enta

expensive construction of channels and apparatuses of transmission, and that the audience of information is unable to alter it in the form in which it is received. In Geneva delegates contrived to
ignore above all these momentous changes in technological form (Browning 1997, 185). This is the
problem I want to address. With the digitization of print, film, radio, and television broadcasts and
their insertion into a global network, the media in which intellectual property appears alters the
message of its legal integument. Put otherwise, the commodity form of cultural objects and the
authorial coherence of individual subjects are shaken by digitization.

A great deal is at stake in the current change of the media of cultural objects, with those most
benefiting from the existing arrangements also most resistant to the change and generally least able
to discern the significance of what is happening. In current debates, the figure of the author becomes
one such rallying point for much ideological jockeying. The television industry, for example, cannot
do without the author because without the author there is no copyright protection, a must for
broadcasting. Even though, properly speaking, there is no author of television shows, the author
stands behind the tube's success (Streeter 1996). In the guise of protecting authors, media moguls –
those who have most exploited authors – raise the banner of copyright protection against what they
see as the anarchic exchange of bytes on the Internet. A 'Copyright Assembly', an extraordinary
meeting of leaders of media industry, on February 17, 2000, witnessed Jack Valenti, spokesman for
Hollywood, defending 'creative works' against 'illegitimate intruders on the Internet who steal
copyrighted works' (Snider 2000). Such self-righteous posturing poorly conceals the helplessness of
the media industry in the face of the sharing of cultural objects on the Net. The meeting ended with
no specific legislative proposals to tame the Internet, a sure sign that the great wealth of the cultural
industry is not enough to alter the basic architecture of cyberspace.

If we set aside the tendentious positions of those who wish only to extend existing copyright
provisions to include new media such as the Internet, we may then ask, What might actually be the
fate of authorship when technology shifts from print to the Internet? Is the figure of the author in
fact a good point of defense against alarming technical innovations? Is cyberspace an occasion of
strengthening or of restructuring or of abandoning authorship?

This chapter brings together an analysis of the technical conditions of authorship in print and
in cyberspace with the theoretical proposals for understanding the question of the construction of
the author. In most cases the discussion of these two related issues fails adequately to connect them:
either one is knowledgeable about technology or one is adept in social and cultural theory. Those
who understand the technology are frequently hampered by an unexamined instrumentalist framework, while theorists who address questions of the media often have limited grasps of their technical
characteristics. By bridging the gap between technology and culture I hope to illuminate the
relations between them.
. . .]

Beyond the author function

The cultural figure of the modern author begins in the eighteenth century, emerging in a confluence
of print technology, a book market, a legal status, and an ideology of individual as creator. Mark
Rose (1993) has shown how the inception of the modern author required the pre-existence of these
elements as well as their convergence into a particular social form (142).[3] The legally defined rights
of the author required a print technology that could reproduce large quantities of texts, a market
system that could determine printed products as objects for sale, and distribution institutions that
could make identical copies available in many places, a discursive regime in which individuals were
understood as agents capable of inventing new things and as proprietors with interests in accumulating capital. The interlocking of each and every one of these elements alone affords authorship both

cultural recognition and social place. Authorship also required, as I shall argue below, a technology of the analogue: a conviction that what was printed in the book was a direct representation of an author's intention, be it in the form of idea, style, or rhetoric; in short, that the book was an analogue reproduction of an original, authentic author.

Before turning to the possible fates of the author in a digital age, I shall explore the characteristics of what I call the analogue author by briefly reviewing Foucault's position. Foucault has presented the most complex and convincing conceptual articulation of the modern author. What is remarkable in his analysis is not only its rigor and comprehensiveness but also its anticipation of digital authorship. To grasp the full extent of the question of the author, I contend that Foucault's insights are essential.

In his influential and well-known essay 'What Is an Author?' ([1969] 1984) (see Chapter 20), Foucault delimits four perspectives on the modern author:

1. The humanist author who governs the meaning of the text. This author expresses, intends, and creates all the meanings that may be read in the text.

2. The structuralist rejection of the humanist author, most notably in Roland Barthes's essay 'The Death of the Author'. In this view, the meaning of the text has no connection with the author. It is a pure synchronic, semiotic object contained within the external materiality of the printed page. Foucault is here not interested in the shift Barthes enacts in the essay to the position of the reader.

3. A poststructuralist move in which Foucault rejects the structuralist annihilation of the author, returning to recognize the importance of the author but not as the humanist understood him or her. Foucault uses the term 'the author function' as the discursive figure and institutional practice of modern society that inscribes the author as a source of meaning. Now the critic can acknowledge the importance of the figure of the author in modern society, but instead of translating his recognition into affirmation, legitimation, and celebration, can turn it rather into an analysis of the construction of the figure. This 'genealogy' of the author, as Foucault calls it, would also serve as a basis for its critique.

4. The last perspective on the author Foucault offers is a most uncharacteristic one for him.[4] Foucault sets forth an alternative, future, utopian nonauthor whose position, presciently, bears remarkable resemblance to the position of authors in cyberspace, or what I call digital authors. I shall examine this discursive move in more detail.

Foucault's effort to delineate a post-author-function future reproduces a theoretical problem he did much to counter in the writings of others and in his own projects. As part of his critique of the modern subject, Foucault opposed as a conservative gesture the penchant of 'the traditional intellectual' to compose metanarratives that totalized the historical field. In this discursive regime the theorist produced a discursive closure either by legitimizing the present as the fulfillment of human essence or by predicting a future ('the tenth epoch' in Condorcet, communism in Marx, 'the transvaluation of all values' in Nietzsche) that served the same purpose. It is most surprising, then to find Foucault making a similar gesture, as when one reads the following in 'What Is an Author?': think that, as our society changes, at the very moment when it is in the process of changing, the author function will disappear, and in such a manner that fiction and its polysemous texts will once again function according to another mode, but still with a system of constraint – one which will no longer be the author, but which will have to be determined or, perhaps, experienced' (1984, 119

(Chapter 19). The passage is maddeningly brief, not indicating which processes are changing or why they will lead to the disappearance of the author function. Yet even in this prescriptive moment of his text, Foucault is careful to indicate that the inconveniences of authorship will be replaced by new constraints. In addition, one cannot, according to him, speculate about the new regime, by time traveling into the future, but must patiently await its appearance to 'experience' it before attempting to name and to outline these impediments to freedom. With these caveats, Foucault offers his 'tenth epoch' beyond the author function.

Foucault's future eviscerates the author's presence from the text, shifting interpretive focus on the relation of the reader to a discourse understood in its exteriority, without resort to a founding creator, without reference to the patriarchal insemination of text with meaning. His picture of writing beyond the author function would seem to contravene both Benjaminian aura and culture industry celebrity. Here in his own words is the Foucauldian heterotopia:

> All discourses . . . would then develop in the anonymity of a murmur. We would no
> longer hear the questions that have been rehashed for so long: Who really spoke? Is it
> really he and not someone else? With what authenticity or originality? And what part
> of his deepest self did he express in his discourse? Instead there would be other
> questions, like these: What are the modes of existence of this discourse? Where has it
> been used, how can it circulate, and who can appropriate it for himself? What are the
> places in it where there is room for possible subjects? Who can assume these various
> subject functions? And behind all these questions, we would hear hardly anything but
> the stirring of an indifference: What difference does it make who is speaking?
>
> (119–20)

If one can imagine the future according to Foucault, where so little interest rests with the author's relation to the text, the question of the transition, the hoary Marxist conundrum, raises its head. How would the author function disappear, especially considering that it has adapted itself so well to the change from print to broadcast media? What social process would work to strip the author from his or her reign over discourse? What conceivable transformation would undo the cultural operations through which the reader, listener, or viewer thinks of little else than 'who is speaking'?

Foucault envisioned his post-author-function culture as a heterotopia, as a different sort of space that functions as a critique of established spatial forms. Heterotopias, in his words, 'have the curious property of being in relation with all the other sites, but in such a way as to suspect, neutralize, or invert the set of relations that they happen to designate, mirror, or reflect' (1986, 24). How then would some new space be established that would serve this function of undoing the author? How would a discourse arise in a space that uncoupled the links between author and text, author and book, author and reader, author and press, author and government that had been so firmly stitched together in the course of the formation of modern society?

I contend that the practice of digital writing, linked to electronic networks, may be the mediation Foucault anticipated but did not recognize.[5] Digital writing in many of its forms separates the author from the text, as does print, but also mobilizes the text so that the reader transforms it, not simply in his or her mind or in his or her marginalia, but in the text itself so that it may be redistributed as another text. Digital writing may function to extract the author from the text, to remove from its obvious meaning his or her intentions, style, concepts, rhetoric, and mind – in short, to disrupt the analogue circuit through which the author makes the text his or her own, through which the mechanisms of property solidify a link between creator and object, a theological link that remains in its form even if its content changes from the age of God to the age of Man. Digital writing may produce the indifference to the question 'Who speaks?' that Foucault dreamed of and may bring to the fore in its place preoccupations with links, associations, and dispersions of meaning throughout the Web of discourse. And this is so not simply for alphabetic text but for sounds and images, as well. The issue rests with the mediation, with the change from analogue to digital techniques.

Foucault's insistence on a 'murmur of indifference' to the question 'Who speaks?' echoes his critique of Cartesian–Hegelian individualism but also raises difficulties for his genealogical method. He produces in his writing, within the domains of the book and the author function, an alternative cultural position. Rather than simply delineating the genealogy of the author function and leaving to his readers the task of conceiving and building an other to it, he breaches the limit of theory, expanding its function to trace a direction for political action. Since Foucault did not, and could not, in the 1970s, recognize networked authorship as his future beyond the author function, one may object that he took on too much.[6] To some extent the direction he indicates is highly suggestive. Without the referent of the practice of digital writing in the world, however, his proposal flirts with inflating again the author function, his own, rendering his text an empty proponent of a new culture. Only by reference to the context of networked computing can the indifference to the question 'Who speaks?' make a link with a line of practice in a contingent domain of relations of forces. Thereby the author function, in this case my own, is recognized but at the same time reduced and available for a critique.[7]

I introduce, then, the term *analogue author* in place of Foucault's *author function* and *digital author* in place of Foucault's *postauthor utopia*. The terms *analogue* and *digital* are taken from the world of technology and their use here suggests the centrality of the machinic mediation. So much I hope is already clear. But I do not mean the terms in an apodictic, transcendental sense by which certain media would necessarily produce certain figures of authorship. I am not making a philo-sophical argument but a historical one: that the figure of the author in the modern period is bound to print technology, while in the more recent, perhaps postmodern, perhaps future, computer-mediated, even networked form of writing produces, amid the contingent world of events, a digital author. The chief difference between the two, I contend, is the degree and shape of alterity in the relation of author to writing. Analogue authors configure a strong bond between the text and the self of the writer, a narcissistic, mirroring relation as the text is fundamentally an expression of the author – his or her style, mind, or feelings. The digital author connotes a greater alterity between the text and the author, due in part to the digital nature of the writing. I claim that digital writing is both a technological inscription of the author and a term to designate a new historical constellation of authorship, one that is emergent, but seemingly more and more predominant. So I borrow from the world of technology the terms *analogue* and *digital*, but I also reconfigure them to designate degrees of otherness in the relation of authors to texts.

[. . .]

The issue at stake in digitization of authorship may now be sharply posed: how is the subject reconfigured in this process? Butler's theory of the performative is useful in exploring the question. Speech acts not only represent things but do things. One thing they do is constitute the subject. But speech acts accomplish this ambiguously, partially, never with certainty, Butler contends (1997: 125). She argues for an analysis of the incompleteness of the performative in constituting the subject, not, as Derrida does, in relation to the formal characteristics of the trace (150) but in the fully social context of enunciation. Speech acts *perform in the world*, Butler reminds us, and there lies political hope: 'The possibility for the speech act to take on a non-ordinary meaning, to function in contexts where it has not belonged, is precisely the political promise of the performative' (161). And performatives are so imbricated in the social in part because they are 'never fully separable from bodily force' (141). The body is fundamental, to Butler, in the performative speech act as both constituting and constituted. The role of the body, she insists further, is at play in writing as well, although she allows for some difference in this regard.

To summarize then: In speech and writing, performatives incompletely but effectively constitute subjects in the world and on the body. Yet if Butler insists on the social and political nature of
the process, she does not indicate how different body–text relations, in speech, in handwriting, in
print, on the radio, in film, on television, and in cyberspace, each configure the performative process
differently and produce, incompletely to be sure, different incarnations of the subject. In one
analysis, the video of the Rodney King beating by police, Butler (1993) relates her theory of
performativity to the medium of video. She points out the dangers in forgetting the medium and
presuming that vision is apolitical: 'To claim that King's victimization is *manifestly* true is to assume
that one is presenting the case to a set of subjects who *know how to see*' (17). She objects to the use by
the defense attorneys of the technique of freeze frame, which rips gestures from their 'temporal
place in the visual narrative' and eliminates the sound track (20). But these examples of Butler's
sensitivity to the medium of the performative do not go far enough. Instead of a more extensive
examination of the role of the medium in speech acts, she contextualizes them. She points out that
'the field of the visible is racially contested terrain' so 'that there is no simple recourse to the visible'
(17). The deconstruction of the visible in this manner is, of course, necessary. Yet Butler deploys it
against naïveté about the medium ('to think that the video "speaks for itself" is, of course, for many
of us, obviously true'; 17) when the medium itself requires sustained analysis in addition to the
social context.

Sandy Stone (1995) makes the argument for the importance of the media and the body in
performativity: 'Most Western theories of the self, even feminist theories, stop just short of
tinkering with the framework upon which the idea of gender itself is based – the framework of the
individual's self-awareness in relation to a physical body' (85). As soon as we consider the relationship between bodies and selves, she continues, we must take into account communications technologies as these mediate social groups and speech acts (88). And in a further clarification Katherine
Hayles (1999) writes, 'Whereas in performative utterances *saying is doing* because the action performed is symbolic in nature and does not require physical action in the world, at the basic level of
computation, *doing is saying* because physical actions also have a symbolic dimension that corresponds
directly with computation' (275). How then does digital authorship differ from analogue authorship
in the performative process of interpellation?

Let us take the example of on-line, synchronous communications in electronic communities
where participation requires that one fashion one's own identity and gender. In these cases individuals type messages on computers at different locations, watching their own words and those of
others on the screen as they are typed. Each individual is a character, and participation is successful
to the extent that the character is believable by others. This is disembodied communication just like
letters and print, where the enunciation is separate from the body of the sender. But the communication in on-line communities is also like speech in that it is simultaneous. The important question is
the way identity is performed in these contexts. Participants are interpellated by each other, suturing
identity in performatives, but the construction of the subject occurs entirely on the screen, determined entirely by the words entered on the keyboard. Participants are authors of themselves as
characters, not simply by acts of consciousness, but by the interactions that take place on the screen.
In these situations, the body, mediated by the interface of computers and the communications
network, enters a new relation with the subject, a dissociated yet actual relation that opens identity
to new degrees of flexible, unstable determination. The body no longer constrains the performativity of speech acts to the extent that it does in face-to-face relations. These digital authors enact an
unprecedented type of performative self-constitution in which the process of interpellation becomes
an explicit question in the communication. Instead of the policeman-teacher-parent-boss hailing the
individual in a manner that conceals the performative nature of the communication, in on-line
communities one invents oneself and one knows that others also invent themselves, while each

interpellates the others through those inventions. Unlike earlier forms of mediated communication, digital authorship is about the performance of self-constitution.

[. . .]

Digression on the indeterminacy of technology

Cultural theorists might raise immediately the objection that I am flirting dangerously with techno-logical determinism by drawing direct conclusions about discourse and practice from the introduc-tion of new techniques. To forestall these skeptics I maintain that technologies are no more mono-semic than language or action, that the impact of technologies is never the linear result of the intention of their creators or of their internal, 'material', capabilities. The Internet, for example, bears not a trace of the U.S. Department of Defense's purpose in developing it: to ensure computer communications in the event of nuclear attack from the Soviet Union. The Soviet Union falls now in the category of proper nouns designated by 'formerly', and the Net seems more a threat to the Department of Defense than an instrument of its design. In my own experience with writing technologies, the same contingencies are evident. In junior high school in the mid-1950s in New York City I was required to take a series of courses introducing me to the practical arts. I took cooking, sewing, carpentry, and typewriting. The curricular intent was to train me in manual skills in the event that a middle-class occupation was not in my future. This training was also highly gendered, since women of my generation with a college degree were often hired in professional fields such as publishing with the reduced status of typists. Even with my academic career these basic skills – or at least some of them – have proven useful. In particular, typewriting, considered at the time a menial practice of secretaries, proved invaluable as this technology changed its social status, becoming acceptable first for academics, then, with the introduction of computing in business, even essential for managers and executives. The technology of the keyboard changed within my lifetime from a machine used by low-level clerks to an essential tool of scientists and leaders of industry With the use of computers in communication, it mutated further into an instrument for sending messages, 'chatting' in electronic meeting places, and such. It has also become the source o crippling diseases like carpal tunnel syndrome. This brief exploration of one technology suffices to indicate the complexity of the relation of machines to humans. . . .

Notes

1   For a discussion and critique of the role of technology in apocalyptic thinking see Quinb 1994 (xix).

2   Case (1996) argues that orally presented academic papers echo 'the condition of havin written the paper elsewhere . . . [and foreground] the stability of print' (24). She sugges that a more improvised performance is more harmonious with poststructuralist theory an digital writing.

3   See also the valuable collection of essays by Jaszi and Woodmansee (1994). For a discussion the position of writing before the author, see Pease 1995. Pease connects the premodern *auct* with the European exploration of the New World.

4   The rare moments where Foucault writes of a future alternative are, to my knowledge, on two: in a conversation with Maoists about the possibility of a system of punishment beyo that of incarceration (1980) and at the end of the first volume of his study of sexuali where he proposes a 'different economy of bodies and pleasures' beyond that of the regime 'sexuality' (1978, 159). Foucault also discusses utopias (1986), but these are spaces of t past and present, not the future, especially bordellos and colonies.

5   Derrida is more sensitive to the technological implications for authorship and the question of the speaking subject. In 'Psyche: Inventions of the Other' (1989), he relates his theory of deconstruction to copyright and patent law relating to new technologies: 'The patent . . . is visibly affected by all sorts of disturbances, especially those resulting from new techniques of reproduction and telecommunication' (45). Because of this, 'deconstruction must assume the task of calling into question the traditional status of invention itself' (43). Foucault then is not at all alone in calling for a critique of the author function.

6   Others have also recognized the value of Foucault's theory for understanding the Internet. See, for example, Boyle 1997.

7   I wish to thank Donald Pease for pointing out this problem in Foucault. On this question see also the interesting essay by Aycock (1999).

Chapter 39

Paul Duguid

MATERIAL MATTERS
The past and futurology of the book

1 Goodbye the book?

With barely the flick of a digital switch, the long era of the 'coming of the book' appears to have given way to the brief period of its going.[1] For it is going, predictions insist, like the telegram, the Bakelite phone, the vinyl record, or the analog computer before it. United only in a shared sense of inevitability, gloomy bibliophiles and triumphant technophiles wave the book goodbye.[2] As elegies are read, eyes turn from history to the future. To be concerned with the past risks appearing like Shakespeare's Salisbury, vainly trying to 'call back yesterday, bid time return', while to talk about the continued relevance of the book can single you out as a modern Erewhonian.[3]

I want to argue, however, that there are good reasons beyond either nostalgia or an insurmountable hatred of technology to question the apparent choice between leaping to the new or drowning with the old. If nothing else, futurologists do have a habit of announcing both deaths and births prematurely. Talking machines, domestic robots, automated language translators, and a host of other 'new technologies' have, for forty years or more, been perennial examples of 'vaporware' always coming yet never coming 'within the next decade'. Even the paperless office, long on the timetable, still shows little sign of arriving. Indeed, many digital offices can't even do without the typewriter, though its 'Nunc Dimittis' was sung years ago. The forward thrust of predictions tends to insist that we don't look back. But past predictions, particularly failed predictions like these, deserve more attention than they get. The point of reexamining them, though, is not to gloat. Rather, it's to understand where predictions go wrong.

[. . .]

So, to explore issues concerning the past and the futurology of the book, I start from the simple fact that, despite lugubrious elegies and triumphant dismissals, the book, like the hinge, still here. Its continued presence raises these related issues of the resilience of artifacts and the frailty of predictions and allows me to suggest that to design robust new artifacts (design being itself an act of prediction), it may be important not to dismiss survival as cussed and irrelevant resistance, but instead to consider, in social and historical terms, the sources of endurance.

Unfortunately, the necessary task of addressing the relation between old and new technologies can be difficult. If, as Benjamin (1969: 257) suggests, the Angel of History goes backward into the future, 'face turned towards the past' and wreckage piling at its feet, technology's angel usually advances facing determinedly the other way, trying to sweep objects and objections from its path.[4] There is much to be gained, I believe, from getting the two angels to see eye to eye. Unfortunately, as I shall argue, this has recently become only more difficult. Technology's angel is engaged in a passing flirtation with 'critical theory', which harbors much of what Jameson calls postmodernism's 'deafness to history'. To add deafness to blindness is not what McLuhan expected when he foretold a return to the synergy of the auditory and the visual, though it may explain why the volume of debate and, in particular, of the demonization of the book has, as a result of this flirtation, been raised a notch or two.[5]

In particular, any idea that old technologies can tell us anything about new ones has been discouraged by two futurological tropes (supported in varying degrees by critical theory) that I intend to examine in some detail. The first is the notion of *supersession* – the idea that each new technological type vanquishes or subsumes its predecessors: 'This will kill that', in the words of Victor Hugo's archdeacon that echo through debates about the book and information technology. The second is the claim of *liberation*, the argument or assumption that the pursuit of new information technologies is simultaneously a righteous pursuit of liberty. Liberationists hold, as another much-quoted aphorism has it, that 'information wants to be free' and that new technology is going to free it. The book, by contrast, appears never to have shaken off its restrictive medieval chains.

Together, ideas of supersession and liberation present a plausibly united front. But this front, I want to suggest, conceals some significant conflicts. First, cultural arguments for supersession lean heavily on the language of postmodernism, while liberationists' arguments about emancipation are laden with the ideas of postmodernism's great antipathy, 'the enlightenment project'. And second, technological ideas of supersession understandably expect progress through technology, while liberation looks for freedom from it.

The latter conflict in particular reflects, I go on to claim, uncertainty about relations between form and content, information and technology. In general, both supersession and liberation assume that information stands aloof from the technology that carries it. Whereas I argue that if books can be thought of as 'containing' and even imprisoning information, that information must, in the last analysis, be understood as inescapably a product of bookmaking. Books, I conclude, are not a hide-bound alternative to the freedoms of the multiply linked items of hypertext, but an important social, political, and historical solution to problems raised by the particularity of such linked items.

So in the end, I suggest, to offer serious alternatives to the book, we need first to understand and even to replicate aspects of its social and material complexity. Indeed, for a while yet, it will probably be much more productive to go by the book than to go on insistently but ineffectually repeating 'goodbye'.

The supersession of the book

The idea of supersession is never too far from discussions of the book, where the words of Hugo's archdeacon are repeated again and again: 'This will kill that. The book will kill the building . . . The press will kill the church . . . printing will kill architecture' (Hugo 1978: 188–189). And though the book notably did not 'kill' architecture, these words are now read against it. The gloom of the archdeacon is transformed into the triumph of the digerati: computer architecture is set to take revenge. Thus it seems fitting that the Dean of Architecture at MIT should envisage a future in which the book will exist only as a sort of methadone treatment, irrelevant except to those 'addicted to the look and feel of tree flakes encased in dead cow (and prepared to pay for it)' (Mitchell 1995).[6]

Of course, futurological predictions that the past is slipping into irrelevance encompass much more than just books. Following Toffler's announcement that society was crossing the greatest divide since barbarism gave way to civilization (a change driven, as he saw it, by the 'great growling engine of technology'), the rhetoric of technological revolution and dismissals of the *ancien régime* have become quite unexceptional. Talk of breaks and disconnections, of paradigm shifts and social transformations, of waves and generations, and of disjunctions between old and new abounds. It's now merely a reflex, more obligatory than provocative, for Negroponte to tell us we're entering a 'radically new culture' propelled by the technological movement from 'atoms to bits'. Under the cumulative weight of these proclamations, it becomes increasingly easy to believe that to fall behind in the technological race is to fall behind in the human race. Technology's path, in this view, is 'inevitable and unavoidable', Negroponte (1995: 4) tells us.[7] To demur or look back could be a symptom of 'lunacy', according to Lanham (1994: 23), of isolation 'in a quaint museum of the intellect', in the view of Feigenbaum and McCorduck (1983), or of clinical 'future shock', those morbid symptoms of the inadequate individual in the face of progress (Toffler 1971: 21).[8]

But if the reach of this revolution concerns humanity as a whole, the book nonetheless forms an important centerpiece. Nor is it merely a symbol of reaction. Accepted by many as an 'agent of change' in the Gutenberg revolution, the book is easily cast as a force of reaction in the information one.[9] Its material lineaments stand accused of foisting a vast amount of ideological baggage on innocent people. Thus Landow (1992) sees its 'center and margin, hierarchy and linearity' as fostering a malign 'conceptual system'. The book is something, he insists with some urgency, 'we must abandon' in order to go through 'this paradigm shift, which marks a revolution in human thought'.

In such accounts of a textual revolution, voices of critical theorists and postmodernists join those of technologists in proclaiming supersession. Undoubtedly, they are well suited for this role, for, in Jameson's words (1994: ix), postmodernism 'looks for breaks' and when it finds them it usually portrays them in suitably supersessive terms. Thus Olsen, who is credited with the first use of 'postmodern', sought complete secession from the past: 'had we not, ourselves (I mean post-modern man) better just leave such things behind us?' (Olsen, quoted in Ford 1995). More famously, Lyotard (1979: 3) announced the 'postmodern condition' by unequivocally dismissing precedent: 'the status of knowledge is altered . . . the general situation is one of temporal disjunction. Perhaps nowhere is the sense that culturally the past has been left behind more evident than in Baudrillard's writing, which repeats on page after page that things are 'no longer', 'no more', 'never again', the way they were: '*ne . . . plus*', '*ne . . . plus*', '*ne . . . plus*' echoes through his writing.[10]

'Only disconnect' seems to have become the united rallying cry of contemporary cultural and technological theorists alike, and this apparent convergence is sometimes offered as independent and cumulative evidence of an epistemological or even ontological shift. I contend, however, that it is more a case of coincidence and opportunism.

To understand what drives the claims of both technologists and compatible cultural theorists we should notice that, while recalling the archdeacon's sense of patricide, they invert his attitude toward it. His was a cry of loss and regret. These new cries of supersession are, to the contrary, triumphantly dismissive. They celebrate escape from the clutches of the past and in so doing reveal that most assertions of supersession are at base declarations of independence. This desire to secede from history and set to work on a newly cleaned *tabula rasa* involves both settling accounts with the old and selling accounts of the new.

[. . .]

On occasion, technology can be seen playing a double role in this process. Where established technology prompts secession by threatening to suffocate a new generation with the legacy of the old, 'new' technology, if sufficiently distinct, can be invoked as a means of escape. Marinetti's 'Manifeste de Futurisme', a classic claim for supersession ('We stand', he declares, 'at the high point between ages!'), provides a clear precedent for this double involvement of technology. Its vision was propelled, as Banham (1967: 100) notes, by a desire for 'the overriding of an old, tradition-bound technology, unchanged since the Renaissance, by a newer one without traditions'. The old, along with 'Time and Space', Marinetti insisted, must be annihilated by the speed of new technology. Museums and academies, which Marinetti dismissed as 'the graveyards of vain endeavor', were to be swept aside to allow the Futurists to set out unburdened. In particular, Marinetti insisted to his followers, 'Go and set fire to the stacks of the libraries'.[11]

If the past cannot easily be physically burned to the ground, it can at least be theoretically or ideologically reduced to ashes. Raymond Williams explores ways in which this has been done. Tracing ideas of temporal disjunction back to Hesiod, Williams (1973: 13–33) shows that claims about the utter newness of the new long antedate both postmodernism and modernism.[12] (Declarations of separation may actually be one of the ties that perennially binds one generation to another. So regularly do generations insist on their utter newness that the first to be truly different may in fact be the generation that does not claim this distinction.) Within this tradition, certain ways of dismissing the past recur. In particular, as Williams argues, the past is repeatedly portrayed in a version of 'pastoral' that extracts idyllic and simple aspects of an earlier age only to contrast them with the assumed complexity and sophistication of the present.[13]

This strategy emerges in contemporary dismissals of the book. Characterizations of the present 'condition' often portray the past, either directly or by implication, as a time in which, for instance, the prelapsarian sign and referent walked hand in hand on their amiable way. For Baudrillard (1981: 5) this was the childlike phase of history in which 'l'image . . . est le reflet d'une réalité profonde'. By contrast with our own, in these pastoral societies the author was apparently both alive and suitably authoritative, and the reader naive and suitably subordinated. The inhabitants of the past saw the book, some have claimed, as 'the natural and only vehicle for a written text' and the text simply 'a transparent window into creative thought' and consequently they suffered beneath the 'tyrannical' voice of print.[14]

We should always be suspicious of the contempt that flows beneath a surface of idealization and concern. And we should note how often the characterization of 'them' is in fact a self-aggrandizement of 'us'. Roger Chartier (1991: 90) describes a similar world 'in which the book was revered and authority was respected' until the book 'lost its charge of sacrality' and 'reverence and obedience gave way to a freer, more casual way of reading'. What distinguishes Chartier's account from these other claims, however, is that he is describing the attitudes of eighteenth-century urban elites towards the pastoral innocence of their rural counterparts and forebears. Significantly, a skepticism we have been led to believe characteristic of the postmodern reader was, it seems, evident even at the start of the enlightenment project. In this light, our claims to a new, technologically mediated epistemological disillusionment seem particularly hollow.[15]

In the end, the apparent convergence of technological futurism and cultural theory fails to distinguish itself with decisive clarity from the very past it attempts to escape. Instead, it primarily recapitulates what it sought to supersede. Of course, we all know that those who forget the past are condemned to repetition, primarily of Santayana's tedious aphorism, but the problems of supersession may require stronger remedies. As a practical matter, naive ideas of supersession may actually be making some forms of repetition difficult rather than inevitable. While our technological superiority has long been taken for granted, high acid paper and silver nitrate film are silently destroying significant regions of twentieth-century cultural production with much more success than Marinetti had destroying the nineteenth. Meanwhile, the rapid, predatory supersession of both hardware and software is rendering recently created digital documents and archives inaccessible or unreadable. To save significant products of our digital being, we may have to move, some suggest, from bits back to atoms.[16]

We need to be cautious about the trivialization and dismissal of the past, however, not simply because we may lose particular documents or artifacts, but because we are also losing valuable cultural insights gained through old communicative technologies, just as we are trying to build new ones. Disinheriting the present from the past rejects a legacy of many and varied strategies that our actual as opposed to idealized predecessors engaged to deal with the problems of the sign, of narrative, of linearity and nonlinearity, of deferral and *différance*, or of authority – problems which the past, pastoralization to the contrary, was insufficiently benign to obscure from its inhabitants. Just as archivists are now resurrecting apparently otiose paper documents to help fathom unreadable digital archives, so we may need to reassess earlier communicative artifacts and forms to revive some of the newer ones.[17]

[. . .]

In all, then, I suggest it's important to resist announcements of the death of the book or the more general insistence that the present has swept away the past or that new technologies have superseded the old. To refuse to accept such claims is not, however, to deny that we are living through important cultural or technological changes. Rather, it's to insist that to assess the significance of these changes and to build the resources to negotiate them, we need specific analysis, not sweeping dismissals. Indeed, as Williams (1973: 21) argues, proclaiming our distance from the past only prevents 'the reality of a major transition' from being fully 'acknowledged and understood'.

In the case of the book, it's helpful to note Foucault's (1977b) remarks on the author function: 'It is not enough to repeat the empty affirmation that the author has disappeared . . . we must locate the space left empty by the author's disappearance, follow the distribution of gaps and breaches, and watch for the openings that this disappearance uncovers' (Foucault 1977b: 121), and again, 'Themes destined to replace the privileged position accorded the author have merely served to arrest the possibility of genuine change' (1977b: 128). A similar case can be made against unguarded assumptions of the death of the book. The theory of technological supersession too easily suggests that there will be no space left empty, no gaps or breaches to worry about, and (as I argue in the following section) that all technological change is progress toward the removal of privilege. Technology, it is assumed, is projecting society into a postmodern, posthistorical plenum where the only problems are caused by Luddites.

3 Liberation technology

Except at their most vaunting, assumptions of supersession tend to run beneath the surface of debate as pressures and tendencies that shape discussion rather than as topics that appear within it. One symptom of this subterranean presence, however, may be the claim of liberation. Leo Marx has argued that, unless protected by claims for simultaneous emancipation, deterministic visions of technological development quickly turn dystopian. Information technology in particular is often painted as either the panopticon or the beacon of liberty. (The famous Apple advertisement during the Superbowl of 1984 presented both by opposing imprisoning Big [Brother] Blue to the liberating rainbow of Macintosh.) The idea that supersession brings with it liberation provides a bulwark against the darker side of this opposition.[18]

So where statements about supersession are often muted, the cry of liberation tends to ring clear. Hence the wide currency of Stuart Brand's extravagant aphorism that 'information wants to be free', which has been picked up by many who want to chase off the imprisoning book. Bolter talks about the 'revolutionary' goal of 'freeing the writing from the frozen structure of the page' and ultimately 'liberating the text'. Barlow claims information 'has to move', Nelson suggests that only with new technology can emerge the 'true structure and interconnectedness of information', while Sterling argues that information 'wants to change . . . [but] for a long time, our static media whether carvings in stone, ink on paper, or dye on celluloid, have strongly resisted the evolutionary impulse'.[19]

This language of liberty moves quickly to such icons of freedom as the market and the frontier. Thus Rheingold evocatively subtitles his book on electronic 'communities', 'Homesteading on the electronic frontier'. The Electronic Frontier Foundation, with which Brand, Barlow, Sterling, and Rheingold are connected, brings many related ideas of liberty together, associating 'electronic' technologies with the frontier and the 'marketplace of ideas' and in so doing casting doubt on preelectronic technologies like the book. Intriguingly, such proclamations occasionally transfer attributes of liberty from people to information. Freedom of information, once a citizen's right to gain access to information, by a sleight of argument becomes the right of information to move freely, free of material impediment. This is not to deny the important First Amendment issues taken up by the Electronic Frontier Foundation. But for a variety of reasons, the language of personal freedom is being attached to information, which as a result is given autonomous desires and an independent existence and evolution. Technological futurology occasionally transfers autonomy and rationality from people and societies to machines. Here, there's a similar exchange. Information is endowed with human attributes and simultaneously a certain independence from human control.[20]

This transference ultimately rests on dualistic assumptions. Where once we had ghosts in machines, now we have information in objects like books. Technology is thus called upon to do for information what theology sought to do for the soul. But this liberation technology is quite distinct from liberation theology, for where the latter turned from tending the soul to tending the body, liberation technology turns in the opposite direction, away from the text's embodiment toward information's pure essence. When the young Wordsworth let out the impassioned cry against the book,

> Oh! why hath not the Mind
> Some element to stamp her image on
> In Nature somewhat nearer to her own?
> (*The Prelude* [1850], V, 45–49)

his more down-to-earth associate replied calmly that this 'was going far to seek disquietude' (L. 53). But now the question is being asked again and more earnestly, and digital information technology is being offered as the answer. The book, no longer its incarnation, has been reduced to the incarceration of the word. But a technological Prospero seems at last to be at hand to free the informational Ariel from the cleft pine (or wood products) in which he has been trapped.[21]

Barlow, an influential popularizer of the electronic future, uses the idea of a wine or spirit stoppered in a bottle as a metaphor for this entrapment. The image goes back at least to Milton's *Areopagitica*: 'books . . . do preserve as in a vial the purest efficacy and extraction of that living intellect bred in them.' But as that last phrase indicates, Milton resisted any simple image of the book as mere container: 'books are not absolutely dead things, but do contain a potency of life in them to be as active as that soul whose progeny they are'. Barlow, however, disdains such qualification. The container, as he sees it, is thoroughly superseded, and, like a good genie, the contents once free will not go back.[22]

Many present this release in near apocalyptic terms. Electronic text will, Lanham argues, disempower . . . the force of linear print' and 'blow . . . wide open' social limits imposed by the index book, in the process democratizing the arts and allowing us 'to create that genuine social self which America has discouraged from the beginning'. Landow agrees it will liberate readers from the tyrannical, univocal voice of the novel' and create the sort of intertextuality that, in Thaïs Morgan's words, will free 'the literary text' from 'psychological, sociological, and historical determinisms'. While for Bolter it will remove a veil of distortion so that 'what is unnatural in print becomes natural in the electronic medium.'[23]

A fair amount of poststructuralist theory is being ingested to provide intellectual support for what is, in fact, the demonization of the book. In particular, Barthes's (1974) powerful distinction between the 'work', servant of one master, and the 'text', an item of pleasure for many, is invoked directly or indirectly to confirm the idea of books as procrustean containers. Electronic technologies are spoken of as if they would shake the 'text' free from the 'work' (though Barthes 1979: 34 himself held 'it would be useless to attempt a material separation'). And more explicitly, Barthes's concept of the *lexia* has proved an influential and tendentious term for the unit of liberated text.

Yet the invocation of Barthes raises some doubts about the convergence of theorists and practitioners. For Barthes, the *lexia* was the arbitrary unit into which he separated text in order to disrupt 'blocks of signification of which reading grasps only the surface, imperceptibly soldered by the movement of sentences, the flowing discourse of narration, the "naturalness" of ordinary language'. Starting with these *lexias*, and with the errors of his structuralist-scientist past clearly in mind, Barthes (1974: 13 *passim*) sets out to explore 'several kinds of criticism (psychological, psychoanalytical, thematic, historical, structural)' which collectively destroy any notion of 'totality' and deny 'naturalness' to the work. As a result of the ensuing dramatic reconstruction of the text, the work is revealed to be an impossibility, a denial of its own assertions.

Barthes's dramatic strategies undoubtedly challenge those who accept the book as writ. In fact, Barthes's ideas seem to challenge more forcefully many of the enthusiasts of electronic hypertexts. For while Barthes's poststructuralist legacy merges easily with the general demonization of the book, it does not fit so easily with ideas of pure, natural information or the grand information-retrieval concepts put forward by, for example, Vannevar Bush and Ted Nelson, the great forefathers of practical hypertext. (Nor is it quite at home with the fairly conventional pedagogical goals of, for example, Lanham and Landow.) Many who embrace poststructuralist forays against the codex to support their arguments for the electronic emancipation of information or society too easily forget that these forays were launched to a significant degree because the book was presented not as a prison, but as a key technology of the grand narratives of emancipation. Dominant strains of postmodernism and ideas of posthistory have long insisted that all such emancipatory narratives, whether they concern books or information technologies, are illusory.[24]

[. . .]

4 Material information

The tangles supersession and liberation get into result, I think, from the dualistic assumptions referred to earlier. In this section, I suggest that, if we avoid the assumption that information and technology, the 'semiotic' and the 'perceptual', in Bolter's (1991: 13) terms, are as distinct and separable as wine and bottles, we avoid the problematic tangles. After discussing this idea of dualism and its connection to the trope of the pastoral a little further, I outline an alternative way to think of information. This alternative, more systemic approach emphasizes the role of material artifacts in both making and warranting information.

Ideas of supersession often rely on a pastoral characterization of the past (or future), and this can help explain both the source and the nature of the problematic dualism. William Empson argues that the pastoral attempts but always fails to depict a reconciliation of the inimical products of mind and matter.[25] It's not surprising, then, to find pastoral visions in debates about the book and its past and future. Ideas about the reconciliation of conceptual and physical, mind and matter, sign and signified provide the common ground between pessimistic and optimistic views of technological development. Extreme pessimistic views suggest that the coming of the computer is destroying previous reconciliation achieved by the book. Extreme optimists hold, by contrast, that any prior sense of harmony was a delusion and that the computer will both dispel those illusions created by the book and in its place achieve true reconciliation, offering the 'real character of information', 'the genuine social self', and so forth.[26]

A significant alternative position shares the optimists' view that the past was an era of delusion, but distinguishes itself by denying the promise of future reconciliation. Harmony, this view suggests, is always a deception; attempts at reconciliation can only end in contradiction. (This view explains why pastoral, like the Queen's jam, is something never achieved today, but only projected into yesterday or tomorrow.) This position escapes the disappointment of the one and the hope of the other, but it nonetheless shares the dualism of both optimist and pessimist. It argues less against their dualistic assumptions than their vision of harmonious reconciliation. So Empson and Barthes, for example, see a pastoral landscape seeded by the intentions of Marvell or Balzac but producing only self-annihilation and contradiction.

Varied though their destinations may be, there is evidently one way to avoid starting down any of these paths and that is to reject the dualism with which they all begin. In the next few paragraphs I sketch an alternative position.[27] Rather than to think of wine in bottles, each of which has a separate identity, it is more useful to consider information and technology as mutually constitutive and ultimately indissoluble. Apt images then would be rivers and banks, Yeats's example of dancer and dance, or Newman's of light and illumination: you don't get one without the other. In this view, information is undoubtedly less autonomous than liberationists would hold; on the other hand, books appear more productive and less like the passive constraints supersessionists make them out to be. Indeed, it can be helpful to think of them as Richards (1960: 1) did when, somewhat uncharacteristically, he declared that 'a book is a machine to think with'.[28]

Viewing the book as a machine, we quickly bridge the supersessive chasm some have dug between new technology and the book, as if one were a machine and the other not. Indeed, the idea of the book as a 'machine to think with' makes it seem much closer to what are standardly called information technologies than either those who idealize it in Miltonic vein as 'the Soul's progeny' or those who demonize it in Mitchell's terms as 'tree flakes encased in dead cow' seem to believe. In the end all information technologies and the information they carry — whether made from trees and cows or sand and petroleum — are not independent, but interdependent.[29]

If books and the information they carry are interdependent, then, as a machine, the book is clearly more than a conduit for ideas produced elsewhere.[30] It is itself a means of production. This concept goes beyond the simple idea of an individual book producing the information it contains. Books are part of a social system that includes authors, readers, publishers, booksellers, libraries, and so forth. Books produce and are reciprocally produced by the system as a whole. They are not, then, simply 'dead things' carrying performed information from authors to readers. They are crucial agents in the cycle of production, distribution, and consumption. This is why, as McGann (1991: 10) puts it, 'readers and audiences are hidden in our texts, and the traces of their multiple presence are scripted at the most material levels.' Recent work by McGann and other 'bibliographic' critics such as McKenzie, Chartier, Genette, and Darnton increasingly acknowledges this systemic relation of the work, the author, and the audience and the role played by the passage of physical books in creating, maintaining, and developing this literary system. Their work and related ideas about cultural production and consumption of cultural artifacts offer fuller and more complex accounts of the book than those implicit in claims of supersession and liberation.[31]

For instance, arguments of Michel de Certeau (1984) and Richard Johnson (1986) help explain how easy it can be to idealize information technology and demonize the book as if the two were not, indeed, both machines. De Certeau and Johnson hold that in attempting to understand cultural artifacts traveling a social circuit, it is essential to distinguish the different cardinal points of the system. To take one and ignore the others inevitably misrepresents the system as a whole and the role of the artifact within it. Similarly, it is a mistake to contrast analyses made from two different points on the circuit. Arguments against the book, for example, often characterize it not in terms of the whole cycle, from writers to readers and back again, but from the point of authorial production alone. Isolating this position allows the book to appear to exert malign, authoritative influences over passive audiences. (Indeed, as de Certeau argues, the isolation of production more generally both leads to and ultimately vitiates many of Foucault's arguments about the efficacy of power.)

Information technology, by contrast, is often characterized in terms of the circulating text or of cultural consumption, but not of production. Privileging the circulating text makes information seem remarkably self-sufficient and the book, by contrast, imprisoning. In the past, 'practical', 'new', and structuralist critics looked from this point of view, granting the text an autonomy distinct from its production or consumption. And this is also essentially the view of those liberationists who defer to the autonomous integrity of information. A third position moves to consumption alone – a stance taken up by Stanley Fish, whose readers appear liberated from all constraints – and, by contrast, devolves all power to the consumer.

By amalgamating the last two positions, supersessionists and liberationists have been able to create an idealized picture of new technologies that makes these appear as complete departures from the book's determined assaults on both texts and readers. But this conclusion is achieved only through incompatible forms of analysis. Furthermore, as we saw, it also leads to the tangle between the two alternative positions, one of which sees the text as becoming independent of technology, while the other sees consumers as becoming independent through technology. Looking at communication technologies in the round, by contrast, circumvents these partial, isolated, and antagonistic accounts. For the book at least, cultural theorists, contemporary bibliographic critics, and literary sociologists have recently begun to do this. It still needs to be done for alternative information technologies.

The attention to the book as a material object involved in a social circuit helps in particular to explain some problems with evolutionary accounts like Sterling's, which view information technologies as progressively removing material encumbrances from the 'true' information assumed to lie beneath them.[32] In Sterling's view, the printed codex can be no more than a material burden on the information 'inside', which technology now permits us to remove. This approach, the essence of what I have called 'liberation technology', discounts the substantial role the book plays in coordinating consumption and production, and so maintaining the social system of information. In so doing such an approach renders the process of publication particularly absurd, for instead of removing material constraints, publishing appears to add them. The manuscript appears as the more authentic form from which the various stages of book production retreat into artificiality and imprisonment.

Considered as part of a larger social system, however, publication is not so easily portrayed as an act of incarceration. It is rather, as McGann describes it, an act of socialization. The production of a book is a shaping of an artifact capable of traveling a public circuit and coordinating production and distal consumption. On their own, manuscripts have a very limited reach and are essentially private documents for local circuits, lacking the forms and warrants that make them more generally consumable. Publication is then very much a process of producing a public artifact and inserting it in a particular social circuit. Indeed, what general intelligibility manuscripts have is due not to the autonomy of information, but to a reader's understanding of the broader literary system. Manuscripts are read not as a purer form of the book, but as incomplete versions, rapid prototypings of the artifact they are intended to become. To turn them into public forms requires more productive work. Consequently, what from the liberationist point of view are looked upon as material constraints, from which text should be 'freed', are more often social resources that, if removed, need be reconstituted or invoked in some other way if the status of the text is to be maintained to a degree.

[. . .]

Acknowledging the coordinating role books play doesn't entail accepting a rigid correspondence between what we think of as 'form' and 'content'. Chartier is right to note that 'meaning changes when form changes' (consequently, irony, the trope of self-denial, travels particularly badly). But within a robust system such as the modern system of lapidary publishing, many changes can be easily negotiated. Despite new forms for old words, it's often possible to recognize a putative form (much as we recognize putative narrators and putative audiences) despite the changes in the actual material. Nevertheless, the changes we are contemplating at the moment concern more than particular inscriptions and may involve the system itself. Faced with the changes at this level, it becomes important to think not idealistically about information, but materially, in terms of what Genette calls the 'ensemble heteroclite' or McGann the 'laced network of linguistic and bibliographic codes'. Systemic changes reach beyond particular semiotic effects, altering our understanding of not just what things might mean, but also why they matter.[33]

5 Future concerns

. . . The advent of multiple new technologies is probably changing not only particular works, but also the social system in relation to which the works were written and read. It will take care and thought to negotiate these changes, and the task will inevitably become more difficult if changes are made in material processes without regard to the social practices they underwrite. Information is taken to be a natural category and its material substrate ultimately immaterial or if supersession is assumed to be inevitably beneficial, the problems will remain invisible, though their effects may be increasingly felt. So, contrary to the convention of ending with solutions, I end by trying to raise two related concerns that seem to me hidden to optimistic eyes (the pessimists, of course, see nothing but problems). I do not pretend that a nondualistic, social-material approach automatically resolves these problems, only that it makes them visible and so open to attention.

Borrowing a portmanteau word coined by Toffler and packing a little more into it, I call the first problem the paradox of demassification. *Demassification* refers to the increasing ease with which socially complex technologies can be made not just for broad masses of people, but for small groups and individuals. Economies of scale, necessary for material-intensive and labor-intensive products, once guaranteed common artifacts. Flexible production of post-Fordism has made this increasingly less important. Less generically Taylored production can be more easily individually tailored. This sort of social demassification or individualization is, to a significant degree, the result of material demassification, which might, indeed, more strictly be called *dematerialization*. As technology is transformed from mechanical to digital-informational, machines shed mass dramatically. Huge mainframes, for instance, have been reduced to individual laptop computers which people can work on alone and, more significantly, separately.

Individuation and separation, two effects of the two kinds of demassification, in the end pull against one another. With large machines, from production lines to time-sharing computers, activities were implicitly coordinated because people worked together in the same place, on the same machine. With dematerialized, portable objects, people no longer need to congregate in single buildings or communicate through central, unifying machines in order to work together. Nonetheless, while they remained uniform, mass-produced artifacts (and books offer one of the earlier examples) continued to support social coordination despite prompting separation. With faithful replication, people had access to what was, for all intents and purposes, the 'same' object, and so, though physically separated, could easily negotiate among themselves coordinated interactions. The more artifacts are tailored to individual users, however, the more such separation becomes problematic. It's hard to share and coordinate practice if you don't share the same physical space. Its much more difficult if you also don't share common artifacts. In brief, centrifugal forces of individualization and separation are coming into conflict with centripetal social needs, which were met previously and unproblematically through shared or common material objects.[34]

Certainly, no one wants to throw away their laptops and move back into the world of time-sharing. But having blown apart the mainframe with personal computers, we have spent a decade or more valiantly struggling to recoordinate or 'network' computational practice. (It's interesting to note that MOOs, which return users to shared space, virtual though it may be, have been compared to time-sharing machines.) To prevent similar problems with other artifacts, it may be more prudent to attend from the first both to material and social needs and the way in which these have been met by the circulation of public forms and to avoid succumbing to ideas of information in the abstract or of consumption as an individual and unfettered practice.

Yet one response to this paradox may be the increasing individuation and personalization of the production of information. Using new technologies, people seem to be trying to produce and consume information with less reliance on impersonal forms and more on personal warrants for legitimation. In this context, it is interesting to consider the coming of hypertext systems, which often seek to replace public, general forms with particularized, individual links. Hypertext also offers to replace linearity with random access, narrative structure with *lexias*, distinctions between reader and writer with an elision of consumption and production. This type of electronic text has been greeted, as I noted earlier, with some extravagant claims, and in keeping with these, hypertext is sometimes portrayed as the means to achieve the triumphant deconstruction of old institutions and forms of authority, in particular those Marinetti attacked, the academy and the library, and with these the publishing houses and the news media. It sometimes appears possible to think of hypertext only in terms of supersession and liberation.[35]

To understand hypertext and its implications, however, we should look back as well as forward. Hypertext is not unprecedented. Hypertext theorists themselves often cite the footnote as a shadowy predecessor, but there is a less obscure and more important one, overlooked not only as a consequence of the forward-looking ideology of supersession, but also as a result of the narrowness of the sociology of literacy and information. If I am right and hypertext has a significant precedent then of course it may lack the novelty to offer either supersession or liberation; on the other hand precedent may offer us some way to understand the social implications of the technological shift to hypertext forms.

For a precedent, we should look beyond the newspaper and related pamphlet and journal forms and beyond the book and its related forms to the robust and enduring forms of 'the books.' For half a millennium, bookkeeping, a system of individual blocks or *lexias* interconnected by multiple links, created and maintained networks of information, 'books mutually dependent on each other' as the *Catechism of Trade and Commerce* called them.[36] A conventional set of account books comprised several generically quite different types of document: the waste book, the journal, the ledger (with its distinct types of account), the letter book (with its many authors), the bill book, the cash book, the sales book, inventories, and so on.[37] The accounting system also embraced several media, including physical objects (goods, merchandise) and complex intermediate representations (tags, tallies, chits, receipts, bills of lading, and the like). Items, books, and sets of books were elaborately linked in ways that connected items not only to those in the other types of book within a single business but to other books in other businesses (for of course every credit in one 'real' account is a debit in someone else's; every bill receivable represents a bill payable elsewhere). With the spread of merchant capital, these links in effect produced a global network with several of the characteristics of hypertext. It was an endless, unfinished, nonsequential, transnational, and highly practical web of circulating information. As with hypertext, there was no single or sequential route through these entries, but only ever-new and perpetually unfinished pathways created by each new reticulating reader-writer. And, as with information technology, the system was triumphant described by great and sober minds as the ultimate rational technology of an ultimately rational society.[38]

Far from an obscure or reserved practice, this system was both geographically and socially widely dispersed. As Braudel shows, from the thirteenth century, the travels of merchants quickly spread the complex form of the *partita doppia* with its necessary accoutrements from the Mediterranean around the world. At its height in the nineteenth century it had in one form or another penetrated (and interconnected) almost all societies at a variety of levels, crossing class, race, and gender boundaries. Household and petty-commodity accounting, for instance, required accounts, and this was done predominantly by women. Consequently, the fishwives who surround Peter Simple's ship in foreign ports and the bourgeois English wife of Pendennis's publisher are bound together by the books they wave. The wealthy of both sexes in both capitalist and feudal societies also kept their books, so we find Colonel Newcome and Anna Karenina (and others that had neither a wife nor servant to do it for them) engaged in the same practice. The countinghouse stool provided early education for many with insufficient social connections (among them Hume and Dickens). Meanwhile poor men long provided the bulk of clerks of one sort or another and probably had more to do with accounting books than discursive ones. Many of the hanged apprentices described in Linbaugh's *London Hanged* appear to have been united not only in death but in the skill of 'casting accompts'.[39]

The history of accounting as a cultural rather than just a business practice is, as yet, too little explored to read too much into the effects of accounting on other types of literacy. But accounting may help explain the diffusion of the common conceptions of 'information' as the content of rational technology. Bookkeeping is a process for producing apparently robust individual items or *lexias* and a social practice that helped naturalize a misleading concept of information as seemingly autonomous items, put into, rather than developed out of, books.

[. . .]

6 Conclusion

The debate about the book is caught between two voices a little like those heard at the opening of *A Tale of Two Cities*, one proclaiming the best of times and the other the worst, one proclaiming the future is our salvation and another pointing back to a lost Eden. I have tried to argue that, with regard to the book, both of these positions too easily separate the past from the future, the simple from the complex, technology from society, and information from technology. To escape both utopian and dystopian oversimplifications, we need first to question such ready separations.

We should, for example, look not at technology in isolation but within its social-material and historical context. Enlarging our viewpoint in this way sets aside ideas of simple supersession (the separation of the past from the future) or liberation (the separation of information from technology) and avoids quasi-Weberian dichotomies between, for instance, progressive technological logic and regressive social illogic or between technologically tractable constraints and socially useful resources. Instead, we discover that the technological and the cultural, constraint and resource are finely and inextricably interwoven. If we consider the book in this light, we should discover that despite its apparent simplicity, it has a great deal to tell us and will, for some time yet, be both a useful, practical tool and a resourceful precedent for designers of alternative technologies to go by.

So if Victor Hugo is to remain our guide in these matters, to the Archdeacon's fatalist prediction of supersession, I prefer a scene from another work – that claustrophobic moment in *Les Misérables* where Valjean lies alive in his coffin and, having expected liberation, hears the unexpected and terrifying clods of earth dropping slowly into the grave. His life, the words on the page seem to say, is over; but, of course, the seven hundred odd pages remaining in our right hand materially insist, to the contrary, that Valjean is quite unlikely to die soon. Nonetheless, as if to caution the overly sanguine, Hugo called this section 'Cemeteries Take What They Are Given'. If nothing else, this offers a useful caution not to permit the burial of what yet has useful life.

Acknowledgments

Thanks to Laura Hartman, Jean Lave, Geoff Nunberg, and Shawn Parkhurst for patiently reading earlier drafts of this paper.

Notes

1   The 'coming of the book' was famously mapped in Febvre and Martin (1984; first published 1958). Its elegy was read just four years later by McLuhan (1962). McLuhan, less a techno- logical determinist than some allow, did not make the 'going' as brief as more contemporary accounts, for he backdates the beginning of the 'going' some 150 years (see McLuhan 1962: 3). Nonetheless, the transition from coming to going remains brief, for this dates the 'going' barely a decade after Febvre and Martin close the 'coming'.

2   For a recent example of the gloomy, see Birkerts (1994); for the triumphant, see Lanham (1994).

3   Butler's Erewhonians destroyed all machines; books then became the only way future gener- ations knew about these malign objects (Butler 1970: chapters 23, 24).

4   Erewhonians lived by a similar image: 'Man is drawn through life with his face to the past instead of the future' (Butler 1970: 181).

5   See, for example, Lanham (1994: 23), who talks of 'this remarkable convergence of social, technological, and theoretical pressures', or Landow (1992); Jameson (1994: xi), McLuhan (1962).

6   Landow rightly points out that bibliophiles will fetishize the book and argue as though all books were incunabula if it helps their argument. This image of Mitchell's makes it clear that technophiles do the very same thing when it suits them. This convergence endorses my central point that in many ways the bibliophiles and the technophiles are more alike than different.

7   Negroponte's idea of a 'new culture' looks modest beside his dominant assumption of the 'new ontology' of 'digital being'.

8   See Toffler (1971: 12), Lanham (1994: 23), and Feigenbaum and McCorduck (1983).

9   See, for example, Eisenstein (1979; 1983). The degree of determinism embraced by Eisen- stein's argument has been much debated (see McNally 1987).

10 See, for example, Baudrillard (1981: e.g., 2ff), where the count is particularly high. Baudrillard has perhaps amassed more cultural capital than Toffler and given postmodernism a grander status than futurology, but his views of simulacra often appear as little more than a frenzied extension of Toffler's early assumption that 'simulated and non-simulated experiences will also become combined in ways that will sharply challenge man's grasp of reality' (Toffler 1971: 213). Baudrillard's trick has been to say this state is here, now, while Toffler, no doubt as a wise professional speculation, set it off in the future.

11 F. T. Marinetti, 'Premier Manifeste du Futurisme', in Ballo, Cachin-Nora, Leymarie, and Russoli (1973). While much of Marinetti's Manifesto sounds quite familiar to postmodern ears, there is one noticeable difference. Where the Manifesto set goals to pursue, more recent supersessive claims often replace iron resolve with digital determinism. Certainly, The Post- modern Condition presents not an option but a fait accompli.

12 As Williams makes clear, a focus on the differences between generations tends to obscure

differences of class. So Negroponte (1995) claims there's no need to worry about social divisions between 'information rich' and 'information poor'; the only significant division, as he sees it, is between the generation of analog adults and digital kids. This, his extrapolative mind tells him in an argument common among the digerati, time will erase. Yet Stuart (1995: 73) points out that in 1989 nearly half of households with an income of $75,000 or more owned computers while under 5 percent of households with an income of under $15,000 had them.

13 The strategy of pastoralization is extremely complex. It plays with both time and space, calling to mind L. P. Hartley's resonant phrase, 'The past is another country.' The post-modern condition, according to Lyotard, is a property of the 'highly developed' alone. So like the past, other countries take on the primitive, pastoral mantle and are subject to similar dismissive judgments. Edward Said's concept of 'orientalism' (Said 1978) elaborates the effects of this elision between the past and the primitive.

14 Quotations from Lanham (1994: 9 and 4) and Landow (1992: 11).

15 The 'coming of the book' involved almost from the start books that made fun of naive and gullible readers.

16 Cf. Rothenberg (1995) and Cook (1995).

17 I discuss some of these issues in section 4 below.

18 Marx (1994: 237–258). Even the dystopic cyberfication of Gibson and others presents both sides. On one are the corporate empires, and on the other the hacker resistance. This conveniently allows all programmers, however large the corporation they work for, to iden-tify with the forces of liberation.

19 The aphorism 'information wants to be free', often quoted, is attributed to Brand in Barlow (1995); Bolter (1991: 21); Nelson quoted in Davis (1993: 613). See Sterling (1995).

20 The influential Vannevar Bush spotted the ideological potential in such rhetoric when he wrote the promotional report *Science. The Endless Frontier* at the request of the president in 1945, about the time he was pondering the possibilities of his influential memex. Cf. Bush (1945b). The report was requested by Roosevelt. See White and Limerick (1994).

21 Futurologists, particularly when they take a flight from simple technological extrapolation, often show dualistic leanings. Thus, for example, Kahn and Weiner break from sensible projec-tions about automatic teller machines and on-line libraries to more exotic ideas about personal flying platforms, changeable sex, and controllable diets and body shapes. All reflect a spiritual yearning to escape the material inertia of the human body. See Kahn and Weiner (1968).

22 J. Milton, *Paradise Lost and Selected Poetry and Prose*, Northrop Frye (ed.) (New York: Reinhart and Co., 1951: 464); Barlow (1995). Barlow's image is more apt for his central issue, the relationship between music and discs and tapes. The relationship between a song and a disc is not the same as that between text and book. The latter relation is more akin to the relation of music to instrument or song to voice. Barlow perhaps also overlooks the point that while good wine can be poured out of bottles, it attains its maturity in them. The quality of wine in the glass is not indifferent to its career in the bottle.

3 Lanham (1994: 21, 105, and 219); Landow (1992: 10–11); Morgan in Landow (1992: 10); Bolter (1991: 143).

4 Cf. Lyotard (1979: esp. 37ff).

5 Here I draw not only on Empson's work, in particular Empson (1947; 1950), but also De Man (1983: 235–41).

5 The influence of dualism on technological thought is not wholly surprising. Information technology in general and artificial intelligence in particular have a long and problematic history of trying to separate mind and matter. For some helpful insight into the pervasiveness of dualistic thinking or 'Cartesianism', see Gumbrecht (1995). Thanks to Shawn Parkhurst for this reference.

27   Some of the ideas offered here are sketched more fully in Seely Brown and Duguid (1994a; 1994b).

28   See Seely Brown and Duguid (1994a) for further reflections on the significance of thinking of books as machines.

29   From this point on, for ease, I refer unashamedly to the content of books as 'information', though my central point is that the two are only conceptually, not materially, separable.

30   See Reddy (1979).

31   McGann (1991), McKenzie (1986), Genette (1987), Chartier (1991; 1992), and Darnton (1979). Though these authors raise related issues, there are clear differences among them. See Sutherland (1989). For comments on the distinctive view of bibliographic criticism, see Chartier (1992).

32   For Sterling's comments, see section 3, above.

33   Chartier (1992); Genette (1987: 8); McGann (1991: 13). McGann assumes that materiality only has significance for literary works, but such a view is far too narrow. Ziman, for instance, has argued that science too is a product of similar social-material processes that create 'public knowledge' and insert it into the system of consumption. Latour and Woolgar's sociology of science reaches similar conclusions. See Ziman (1968), Latour and Woolgar (1986). More generally, the distinction McGann makes between 'noise' and 'information' assumes that constraints can always be distinguished from resources.

34   This paradox is laid out more fully in Seely Brown and Duguid (1994a). As I read it, Derrida's distinction between speech and writing tends to suggest that all distal coordination is not merely problematic but impossible, because communicating artifacts introduce temporal deferral passing beyond immediate negotiation. I am suggesting that in fact social systems of negotiation have allowed coordination that this abstract philosophical skepticism cannot explain away. See Derrida (1977).

35   For the characteristics of modern hypertext, see Landow (1992: 4–5), Bush (1945a), Nelson (1990), Delany and Landow (eds) (1994). For an insightful and more moderate and practical approach, see McGann, 'The rationale of hypertext' (online, available www http://jefferson.village.virginia.edu/public/jjm2f/rationale.html). Landow suggests that the electronic links of modern systems provide a certain ease that supersedes earlier forms. Ease certainly seems important, but not defining. Moreover, the importance of ease is often missing from assaults on the codex book.

36   W. Pinnock, *Catechism of Trade and Commerce: Intended to Lay the Basis of Practical Commercial Knowledge in the Youthful Mind* . . . London: G. & B. Whittaker, 1828: 26.

37   There were two main types of accounting, single and double entry. Usually only large firms (and not all those, the Dutch East India Company being a classic exception) used a full set of books and double-entry accounting. Many businesses and most individuals kept single-entry accounts, but even these usually involved some sort of journal and cash book as well as the accounts themselves. Personal accounts are often an intriguing combination of all three.

38   Weber saw 'rational capital accounting' as the 'most general presupposition for the existence of present-day capitalism' (M. Weber, *General Economic History*, quoted in Giddens and Held (eds) 1982: 81). According to Braudel, Sombart also saw it as the essence of the rationality of capitalist practice, arguing intriguingly that capitalism and bookkeeping were as close to one another as form and content. See Braudel (1992: 573 *passim*) and Yamey (1949). As with other supersessive arguers, both Sombart and Weber have problems with their periodizing, for the technology of bookkeeping long predated the capitalist society they so closely link to it.

39   See Anderson (1976) and Linebaugh (1992).

Chapter 40

Geoffrey Nunberg

FAREWELL TO THE INFORMATION AGE

Paper is just an object that [some] information has been sprayed onto in the past . . .

(Ted Nelson)

And one of the side effects of digital technology is that it makes those containers irrelevant. Books, CDs, filmstrips – whatever – don't need to exist anymore in order to get ideas out. So whereas we thought we had been in the wine business, suddenly we realized that all along we've been in the bottling business.

(John Perry Barlow)

[In cyberspace, communication will be] redeemed from all the inefficiencies, pollutions, and corruptions attendant to the process of moving information attached to *things*.

(Michael Benedikt)

Introduction: The word turned upside-down

Nothing betrays the spirit of an age so precisely as the way it represents the future. Take the picture that appeared in *Popular Mechanics* magazine in 1950 in an article on 'The Home of the Future'. It shows a woman in an apron in the middle of a living room full of furniture with the rounded 'futuristic' forms of the period, which she is spraying with a garden hose. The caption reads, 'Because all her furniture is waterproof, the housewife of the year 2000 can do her cleaning with a hose.' Like most such representations, it gives itself away in two complementary misapprehensions. The first and most obvious comes of taking some recent innovation at the steepest point of its curve and projecting it linearly to a point where it has swept all its predecessors aside. No one makes provision for the inevitable banalization of the new, or for the reactions that it invokes.

The second misapprehension is the opposite of the first. It comes from a failure to appreciate, not how durable some features of the material setting will turn out to be, but rather how contingent and mutable are some of the categories of social life. What is most telling to us now about the *Popular Mechanics* picture is its presupposition that in the year 2000 the household cleaning will still be woman's work – and indeed the function of the picture, wittingly or unwittingly, is to naturalize that assumption. This is a much harder kind of misconception to avoid, because it rests on the unspoken presuppositions of a discourse, and as such is more difficult to bring to consciousness. Or to put it another way: the first sort of error is in seeing the future as being insufficiently like the present, and that is relatively easy to correct for; you just imagine the future furnished like the room you are in, whereas the second sort of error involves seeing the future as insufficiently different from the present, and this we can correct for only by a determined act of imagination: forty-five years from now gender roles will be different . . . how?

Discussions of the future of the book involve both kinds of misapprehensions. For the thematization of material change, we have the picture of electronic media driving the printed book and the institutions of print culture to the margins of discourse. (To paraphrase the closing line of the mad scientist in the movie *Back to the Future*, 'Books? Where we're going we don't need books.') For the present it's enough to observe that there is nothing in the economics of publishing as a whole or the body of practice surrounding the use of the printed book that militates for its disappearance, even over the long term. And while it is certain that many forms and genres will migrate in part or in whole to an electronic mode of existence over the coming years, there are numerous other printed genres that stand to benefit from the new technologies, whether in the form of electronic text preparation, demand printing, Web advertising, or, what may be most important, the computerized inventory systems that have made possible new types of retail distribution that have vastly extended general public access to texts over the past five years in ways that are arguably more significant than the effects of electronic media.[1] There will be a digital revolution, but the printed book will be an important participant in it. And by the same token, there is no reason to expect the digital library to replace the brick-and-mortar library, even less so once we can make a physical replica of any book in the collection of the Gregorian University and put it on the shelves of a university library in Iowa or Lyon at the same time we make it available over the Web in digital form. In all of this we are likely to be seriously misled by analogies to technologies like movable type, which established a privative opposition between two kinds of artifacts. There never was a technology less amenable to determinist arguments than this one.

For the indefinite future, then, there will be printed books, just as surely as there will be wooden shelves and coffee tables to put them on. But none of this should be taken as depreciating the cultural effects of electronic media. Enthusiasts of the new technologies are right to point out that the introduction of these media is bound to be accompanied by sweeping changes in all the features of the modern literary system, to use Carla Hesse's phrase, including the relation between author and reader, the nature of the public, the conception of intellectual property, and the nature of the text itself. It is true, as writers like Jay Bolter and Raffaele Simone point out here, that many of these changes have been prefigured by tendencies in modern print publications, to an extent that visionaries are slow to acknowledge. But the effects of the new media will be profound.

The difficulties, both conceptual and practical, come when we try to spell out the effects of the new technologies in detail. And here, for all the revolutionary talk of the enthusiasts, there is a persistent tendency to yield to the second kind of misapprehension that representations of the future are liable to, where we naturalize contingent features of the current order of things. Indeed, the revolutionary rhetoric of the enthusiasts makes them especially susceptible to this presupposition because the goal of making the material advantages of the new media sound inviting and exciting requires us to assume a continuity of communicative needs and interests. It is not the brief of visionaries to make the New Jerusalem sound like an alien place (the enthusiasm of *Popular Mechanics* readers for the new chemistry might have been more tempered if the designer of that picture had had the prescience to put the hose in the hand of a man).

The tendency is pervasive. When theorists talk about the power of the new media to make everyone an author, for example, or to provide everyone with universal access to potential audiences

millions of readers, they invoke a notion of authorship and a model of access that are more
propriate to traditional print media than to electronic communication. What is an author, after all,
the new media no longer support the legal status or institutional privileges that have traditionally
fined that role? And what real increase is there in the ability of the average citizen to affect public
inion if anyone who wants to gain the attention of a mass audience has to compete for attention
th millions of other 'authors'? There was a telling example of this sort of difficulty not long ago in
story in an academic newsletter about an assistant professor at a Southern university who had
sted on a news list a bibliography of sources on the uses of virtual reality in education and was
dulously keeping a record of all the electronic queries that she had received about her work from
over the world, in the hope of being able to demonstrate to her tenure committee that her work
d 'an international reputation'. But the assumption implicit in that phrase – that the magnitude or
eadth of someone's reputation is proportional to its farthest geographic extension – has no
levance in the electronic world, where it takes no greater investment of resources to make a text
ailable to distant readers than to local ones. Electronic publication implies a new calculus of
putation, which I think no one has yet come to grips with.

One other example. Enthusiasts of the media have sometimes said that a medium like the Web
akes it possible to actualize intertextuality to the point of eradicating all of the boundaries and
visions between texts, so that we arrive, finally, at a perfect Derridean *débordement* of meaning – a
xt, as George Landow (1992) has put it, that cannot shut out other texts. The implication is that
gital technology makes it possible for literature to do in the light of day what it has up to now been
le to do only furtively. It is true that we can have something of this feeling when we are moving
mongst Web documents, where there need be no material difference, say, between the link that
kes us to the subsequent chapter of a text and the link that takes us to one of its predecessors or to
commentary on it, even if these are stored at different sites. But there is a difficulty even in
eaking of 'intertextuality' when the individuation of texts themselves becomes so problematic:
nat could *débordement* signify when there are no *bords* in the first place? Ultimately, this sort of
gument rests on an anachronistic sense of the text that is carried over from our experience of
int. Whereas what electronic media really give us, in the end, is something stranger than that: a
main where there can be intertextuality without transgression.

It's understandable, of course, that it should take a while to accommodate the conceptual
nsequences of any technologies whose effects are so pervasive we have to rethink not just
viously print-based categories like 'publication' and 'authorship', but also notions like 'reputa-
on', with all the temporal and spatial presuppositions it trails in its wake. Perhaps the most basic
d least well examined of these, though, is the notion of content itself. The quotations that I began
is essay with are typical of virtually all the manifestos issued on behalf of the new technologies in
eir assumption that content is a noble substance that is indifferent to the transformation of its
hicles. In the print world it was attached to things or contained in them, but now it can be
erated and manipulated as a kind of pure essence: we can break the bottles and have the wine. In
is essay, I want to show that these metaphors play false to the truth; we are rather in the situation,
Paul Duguid (1996) puts it, of breaking the banks and hoping still to have the river.

Of course writers like these do not usually talk about content as such, but rather as
nformation', a term that incorporates assumptions of nobility and transferability in its meaning, so
at it seems foregone that content will be preserved intact when its material and social supports are
ripped away. But considering how much work we ask the word 'information' to do, we don't
end time thinking critically about what it means. As Philip Agre (1995) has put the point: '. . . the
rm "information" rarely evokes the deep and troubling questions of epistemology that are usually
sociated with terms like "knowledge" and "belief." One can be a skeptic about knowledge but not
out information. Information, in short, is a strikingly bland substance.' The reason for this, Agre

argues, is that information is a category shaped by professional ideologies and, like most ideological terms, is invested with a 'pregiven' character that makes it impervious to interrogation. This is surely right, but it doesn't justify our discounting information as a notion whose interest is exhausted once we've dispelled the forms of semantical false consciousness that it embodies. Agre is certainly right, for example, to say that part of the work that 'information' does for librarians is to flatten and obscure the subjective social topographies of content that are implicit when we speak of the holdings of a library in terms of 'literatures'. And from a different point of view, Dan Schiller (1994) has argued that as used by postindustrial theorists like Daniel Bell, the word 'information' '. . . both covers and covers up much of what was referenced by the anthropological sense of "culture" '. But even granting all this, it doesn't follow that we can simply drop the word 'information' from our vocabularies in favor of 'literatures', 'culture', 'knowledge', or whatever other items it seems to be standing in for.

One simple reason for this is that once we begin the purge we might not know where to stop. Like many of the words that do important ideological work, 'information' is anchored in unexceptionable ordinary usage. It goes without saying that 'information' is not simply a substitute for 'culture' or the rest when we say something like 'Can you give me some information about vacation rentals?' Nor for that matter do we have any right to complain about the technical uses of the word as such, for example when somebody talks about the amount of information in a particular television signal or in the genetic code. But where and how do we draw the distinction, and what kind of distinction is it? Is the suspect use of 'information' merely a 'loose' use of the word or a separate sense? And in either case, what is its relation to the technical and ordinary-language uses of the word? As a kind of propadeutic, then, we have to do a certain amount of philological reconstruction.

The philolology of 'information'

The OED2 gives the word 'information' only two relevant current senses.[2] The first of these is what we can think of as the particularistic sense of the word, the sense it has in an ordinary sentence like 'I'm looking for a book with information about guinea pigs', where it means, as the OED2 puts it:

> Knowledge communicated concerning some particular fact, subject, or event; that of which one is apprised or told; intelligence, news, spec. contrasted with *data*.

(This definition isn't quite as precise or as complete as we might like, but it will do for now.) The second sense given by the OED2 is what we can think of as the naturalistic sense, which arose in the twentieth century when the word was made a term of art in fields like cybernetics and information theory. The OED explains this sense as follows:

> Separated from, or without the implication of, reference to a person informed: that which inheres in one of two or more alternative sequences, arrangements, etc., that produce different responses in something, and which is capable of being stored in, transferred by, and communicated to inanimate things.[3]

The OED makes this second sense a subsense of the first, with the implication that it is really a kind of reconstruction or elaboration of the ordinary use of the word. As it happens, William Weaver explicitly rejected this interpretation of the theory that he and Shannon had developed:

> The word 'information', in this theory, is used in a special sense that must not be confused with its ordinary usage. In particular, information must not be confused with

meaning. In fact, two messages, one of which is heavily loaded with meaning and the other of which is pure nonsense, can be exactly equivalent, from the present view-point, as regards information.

(Weaver 1964: 4)[4]

Weaver's reservations are warranted, though of course if he and Shannon had really wanted to avoid confusion they would have done better to refer to their enterprise as 'entropy theory' or 'signal theory' (both of which were seriously considered for a time), or at least as 'informativeness theory', which would have more closely captured the notion of information as a property of a signal relative to an interpreter. In any case these reservations did not stop postwar social scientists from trying to put the theory to use in their accounts of human communication. More generally, people have come to assume that the 'information' that figures in computer science – the stuff of bits and bandwidths – is the same use of the word that figures in its ordinary usage. As *Business Week* put it in a special number on 'The Information Revolution':

We can glean it from the pages of a book or the morning newspaper and from the glowing phosphors of a video screen. Scientists find it stored in our genes and in the lush complexity of the rain forest. And it's always in the air where people come together, whether to work, play, or just gab.

(Business Week, 1994)

One effect of this is to create the retrospective anachronism that is implicit in that 'contrasted with *data*' clause in the OED2 definition, which suggests that the 'information' that we contrast with 'data' is the same sort of stuff that Lydgate was talking about when he used the word in the fifteenth century, two hundred years before the word *data* entered the language. This trope is ubiquitous in writing about the cultural implications of the new technologies. For example the *Business Week* article goes on to say: '. . . all technologies that "process information" (although they were never described in those terms in the predigital era) affect deeply the societies that use them. Johannes Gutenberg's printing press eventually helped reformers to erode the Catholic Church's political power . . .'. The trope is crucial to the claims of enthusiasts of the technology that it will usher in a new and epochal discursive order. We have to believe, that is, that the substance that computers traffic in, 'informa-tion' in the technical sense of the term, is the same sort of stuff that led to the Reformation and the French Revolution, whether or not contemporaries talked about it in those terms.

But the fact is that the use of 'information' that people have in mind when they talk about 'the information age' or say that information brought about the Reformation is not quite what the OED is describing in its definition of the ordinary particularistic sense of the word – what we get when we call an airline to find out about flight times. They are thinking rather of what I will call the 'abstract' sense of the word, where it refers not to 'knowledge . . . concerning some particular fact, subject, or event', but rather to a kind of intentional substance that is present in the world, a sense that is no longer closely connected to the use of the verb 'inform', anchored in particular speech acts. This is the sense of the word which bears the ideological burden in discussions of the new technologies.

The distinction between the particularistic and abstract senses is not immediately evident, particularly in English – after all, it escaped the attention even of the redoubtable compilers of the OED. And indeed, our first temptation is to say that 'information' in this abstract sense is really the same sort of thing as 'information' in the particularistic sense, only taken in the aggregate; it merely denotes the sum of all the bits of information about particulars that are at large in the world. In this way these general uses of 'information' might be compared to the general uses of a word like 'gossip'. When we say something like 'gossip is unreliable', for example, we are simply taking 'gossip' as a universal that comprises all the instances of particular gossip – gossip about the Smiths, gossip about the new boss, gossip about movie stars, and so on.

It is true that the particularistic sense of 'information' can have something like this aggregate use. When we say that such-and-such a book contains much useful information, for example, we mean that it has numerous bits of useful information about particular things. In the end, though, the story doesn't quite explain the use of the word we are interested in. One way of making this point is to consider how we translate these various phrases into other European languages, where the particularistic sense of 'information' is rendered by count nouns, usually in the plural – French *informations* or *renseignements*, Italian *informazioni*, Modern Greek *plirofories*, and so on. (English too permitted such a usage until the mid-nineteenth century.) So we would translate a sentence like 'The book contains a lot of useful information' into French as *Le livre contient beaucoup de renseigne-ments* (or *informations*) *utiles*. But we would not use the plural to translate a sentence like 'The world is overwhelmed by information', or a phrase like 'the information age' – uses like these are generally translated using either a mass term (as in *l'age d'information*) or sometimes by using an unrelated word like *connaissance*. Of course the fact that French has two words where English has one does not necessarily mean that the English word is ambiguous (they have two words for 'river', after all), but it does suggest that there is a principled distinction to be made.

There is another bit of circumstantial evidence that is relevant to the distinction, which may help to explain why the first edition of the OED did not record it: this abstract sense of the word did not appear in English (or in any other language) until the mid-nineteenth century. Before this period you could not really speak of information in an abstract way. There is a revealing example in *Gulliver's Travels*: 'For he argued thus: that the use of speech was to make us understand one another, and to receive information of facts . . .'. It's notable that Swift could not say simply that the use of speech was 'to receive information' *tout court*, but could only refer to an aggregation of particular propositions (this sentence would be translated into French using a plural). He had no way, that is, to speak of information as a kind of abstract stuff present in the world, disconnected from the situations that it is *about*.

This 'presence' of abstract information is one of the crucial properties that distinguishes it from particularistic information. This is what makes it possible to talk about it as a measurable quantity, particularly in the claims about the 'information explosion' that people like to make with extravagant exactitude. For example, there is a widely repeated claim to the effect that a daily issue of the *New York Times* contains more information than the average seventeenth-century Englishman came across in a lifetime.[5] Now whatever writers have in mind when they make such claims (not a great deal, you suspect), it's clear that they are not talking simply about the sum of individual propositions that are communicated from one agent to another. That seventeenth-century English-man was doubtless informed of any number of things over the course of his life – relatives wrote to tell him when they were coming to visit, a gardener told him that the peaches would be particularly sweet this year. But clearly these things were of no account to whoever made the estimate, since it would be absurd to suppose you could calculate their number. Nor do people who try to quantify information have in mind the naturalistic sort of information that inheres, say, in the markings on a mushroom that indicate it is poisonous or in the darkening sky that announces the imminence of a rainstorm. Clearly there is no way to estimate how much of *that* sort of information there is in the world, nor is it possible or for that matter interesting to know whether there is more of it now than there was a few centuries ago.

When people refer to the amount of information that the average seventeenth-century Englishman came across in a lifetime or say that the amount of information is doubling every five (or twenty, or fifty) years, they are talking about the information in published documents, in the broad sense of the term – documents, that is, that have been made available for unknown others to refer to whether by circulating them or putting them in files or archives. And this way of talking rests on two assumptions. First, they assume a correlation between the size of a text (as measured in characters, bytes, column inches, or whatever) and the amount of content it conveys – a step that implies the commoditization of content that is central to the cultural role we ask information to play. And at the same time they privilege this content communicated in this way at the expense of content communicated privately or irreproducibly.

And indeed, this sense of 'information' was privileged from its inception. As it happens this use of the word is probably not directly derived from the ordinary particularistic sense, but rather from the now-obsolete use of 'information' to mean 'formation or moulding of the mind or character, instruction', a sense that's equivalent to the German *Bildung*. The OED2 has nothing to say about this development (as we saw, it doesn't even recognize the abstract sense at all), but the point is clear enough when we look at early nineteenth-century uses of the word to mean 'instruction' and note how often we are tempted to interpret it in the modern way. The misreading is particularly easy to make when the context involves talk or 'having', 'acquiring' or 'receiving' information, or in phrases like 'man of information'. For example:

> 'Mr. Martin, I suppose, is not a man of information beyond the line of his own business? He does not read?'
>
> (Jane Austen, *Emma*)

> Susan was growing very fond of her, and though without any of the early delight in books which had been so strong in Fanny, with a disposition much less inclined to sedentary pursuits, or to information for information's sake, she had so strong a desire of not *appearing* ignorant . . .
>
> (Jane Austen, *Mansfield Park*)[6]

> I would not be hurried by any love of system, by any exaggeration of instincts, to underrate the Book . . . [G]reat and heroic men have existed, who had almost no other information than by the printed page. I only would say, that it needs a strong head to bear that diet. One must be an inventor to read well . . .
>
> (Ralph Waldo Emerson, *The American Scholar*)[7]

Austen would not have considered it admirable in Fanny to have been interested in 'information for information's sake' if the word for her had entailed no more than knowing the names and dates of all the kings of England. And it would be wholly alien to Emerson's thought in this passage to assume that the 'information' that heroic men might derive from books was merely a matter of knowledge of facts. At the same time, though, each of the uses *could* be misread, with just the slightest change in understanding, so that 'information' was taken to denote not the instruction derived from books, but the content of books from which instruction is derived – the same kind of 'cause for effect' metonymy that has left us with 'mystery' and 'horror' as the names of genres. And this, I suggest, is exactly what contemporaries did in creating the new sense of the word.

Like most of the misreadings that underlie such shifts of meaning, this one was highly strategic. On the one hand, it resituated the agency of instruction in the text and its producers, and reduced the reader to the role of a passive consumer of content, far from Emerson's 'inventor'. Michel de Certeau talks about this process in *The Invention of Everyday Life* under the heading, 'The Ideology of "Information" through Books' (the title plays on a similar polysemy in the French word). He casts it as a stage in the progressive evolution of the Enlightenment belief in a society produced by a textual system [*système 'scripturaire'*], which 'always had as its corollary the assumption . . . of a public shaped by writing (verbal or iconic), but in both cases, a society that starts to resemble that which it takes in, to the point where it is, so to say, *imprinted* by and in the image of the text that is stamped upon it' (de Certeau 1990: 241).

At the same time the shift in the denotation of 'information' from effect to cause facilitated another, no less strategic confusion between abstract and particularistic information, which was conflated under the assumption that the production of 'informed' public consciousness was to be achieved chiefly through the production and dissemination of 'objective' propositional content – the 'information', that is, on whose free exchange the functioning of democratic society, the free marketplace, and the rest are routinely held to depend. And by way of response, the older, particularistic use of information came increasingly to be restricted to the sorts of things you might learn from a book or from an official or institutional source. When your six-year-old daughter tells you that she doesn't like vegetables, for example, you wouldn't ordinarily describe her as having provided you with information about her tastes (not that you'd be lying if you did, but you would open yourself to a charge of archness). We can no longer use the word the way Emily Brontë could in *Wuthering Heights*, to refer to a casual communication about immediate experience:

'A letter from your old acquaintance, the housekeeper at the Grange,' I answered . . .
She would gladly have gathered it up at this information, but Hareton beat her.

This development has contributed to the confusion between the two senses, as particularistic information has come to be treated increasingly as a subtype of abstract information – the particles of propositional content derived from public sources that make up information in the mass.

The modern public sense of 'information', then, has arisen through a conceptual creolization, first of the *Bildung* and particularistic senses, and subsequently of these two with the naturalistic sense provided by information theory. In this sort of situation, any effort to try to extract a coherent conceptual structure for the notion would be not just futile but false to its phenomenology: 'information' is able to perform the work it does precisely because it fuzzes the boundaries between several genetically distinct categories of experience. Ultimately, then, the question we want to ask is phenomenological rather than lexicographical: not, What does 'information' mean? but rather, How is the impression of 'information' constituted out of certain practices of reading and the particular representations that support them?

The phenomenology of information

In 'The Storyteller', Walter Benjamin described information (by which we should understand abstract information) as a 'form of communication' that emerged with 'the full control of the middle class, which has the press as one of its most important instruments in fully developed capitalism' (Benjamin 1936/1969a: 88). The description nicely encapsulates the two kinds of conditions that the phenomenon of information rests on. The first are social: the rise of industrial capitalism and all the apparatus that accompanies it. The second are the particular forms of expression and representation that served as what Benjamin calls the 'instruments' of these social forces, what we can think of as the informational genres. Both Benjamin and Richard Terdiman (1985) lay particular emphasis on the appearance of the modern mass newspaper – ostensibly apolitical, eclectic in content, and sold to a vast readership for a low price on a copy-by-copy basis. The newspaper was, as Terdiman has observed, the first disposable consumer commodity, and it brought with it a new, commercialized conception of content. It was characterized by 'journalistic' objectification and depersonalization of voice; it spoke with (literally) everyday matter-of-factness. But while the modern conception of 'the news' (*les informations* in French) is in many ways the prototype for information in the large, a number of other forms of publication contributed to the same effect. The archetype of these is the modern 'reference work' (a phrase first used in its modern sense in English in 1859, and in French in 1870) – the 'national' dictionaries and encyclopedias of Brockhaus, Webster, and Larousse, the travel guides of Karl Baedeker and John Murray, and the census reports and other government publications that introduced into public discourse the notion of 'statistics' in the original sense of the term. In the private sector, too, the growth of managerial organizations was accompanied by the emergence of printed schedules, work rules, and forms.[8] Finally, there were the genres that exploited and inverted the informational mode of reading, particularly the modern novel, which as Benjamin suggests emerged directly out of the crisis created when information confronted the epic form. It is impossible to imagine Dickens, Twain, Galdós, or Zola in a world without newspapers or newspaper readers. There is very little in modern literature that is not either parasitic on information or in violent reaction against it.

These forms were closely mirrored by a new set of institutions and structures charged with representing the modern world. There were the public libraries, great and small, card catalogs, and the 'library science' (now 'information science') that grew up along with them. There were the public art museums organized 'thematically', by period and nation.[9] There were the museums of natural history that grew out of the eighteenth-century cabinet of curiosities, with rows of labeled exhibits that made them seem the material instantiation of the encyclopedic dictionary. There were the museums of science and industry and the international expositions that inscribed the Baedekers on urban spaces. There were department stores, which as Terdiman observes, mirrored the organization of newspapers in their deliberate scattering of 'articles' and the putative universality of their offerings. There was fiat money.

[. . .]

The future of information

Since its inception, information has managed to colonize every new form of public representation. If you think of communication primarily in terms of its mode – via texts or via sounds and images – then you will see an abrupt break between print and the broadcast media. But the emergence of a form like television seems less consequential from the informational point of view. All the features that sustain the impression of information in print are realized here as well: the blurring of genres; the fragmentation of content into 'bites', segments, programs, and regular editions; the circumscription of a public discourse; and a phenomenal autonomy even more marked than in print, in the sense that the identities of the responsible agents (stations, networks, producers, writers) are almost wholly obscure and irrelevant to the way we interpret what we see.

So it isn't surprising that electronic forms have been informationalized as well. The World Wide Web teems with particularistic information (stock prices, course schedules, the texts of nineteenth-century novels you can search for tokens of the word 'information').[10] And the print and broadcast media that mediate the impression of abstract information have already established important beachheads here: you can call up *Time* magazine, *Webster's Tenth Collegiate*, university catalogs, and the *Encyclopedia Britannica*.

On the face of things, in fact, electronic documents like those on the Web seem not only to preserve the impression of information but to reinforce it. They are highly modular, amenable to abstraction and reorganization, and are much easier to dislodge and decontextualize than print documents are, features that support the sense of corpuscularity and transferability. They can be reformatted and reformulated – you can change the visual presentation or cause a table to be reformulated as a bar graph – which supports the conception of their content as a kind of fungible abstract substance. And the ease with which we can move from one document to another leads to the conception of content as a kind of extended substance, the conception that underlies the metaphors of 'infospace' and the rest.

But while the content of the documents we find on the Web has a lot of the syntactic and formal properties that we ascribe to information, it is less well adapted to supporting the semantic properties that the informational mode of reading requires, particularly the impressions of objectivity and autonomy. The problem, as I suggested at the outset, is that these media don't preserve the social and material boundaries that the informational mode of reading requires. On the one hand, they disrupt the constellation of properties embodied in the notion of 'publishing' – the connections, that is, between accessibility, diffusion, and 'publicity', in the older sense of the term. On the other, they efface the material and phenomenal boundaries of and between both documents and collections.

It's true that neither of these has much effect on the way we interpret the on-line versions of informational publications that are well established in print, which we read, essentially, as transcriptions. But it creates difficulties for the development of new, autochthonous forms of electronic communication. And for various reasons, the Web makes it more difficult to marginalize these forms than has been historically possible, say, in the world of print. Information may be able to colonize the Web, then, but I think it will not be possible for it to establish its imperium there.

Information on the Web

First, for the notion of 'publishing'. To a certain extent, the particularities of the Web in this regard are purely quantitative. A signal virtue of electronic technologies is to remove the capital and institutional impediments to the production and circulation of documents. As we're often reminded, 'anyone' can produce a document and make it accessible to thousands or millions of readers.[11] And indeed, this is exactly what anyone has been doing in increasing numbers. (You think of what someone said about Greenwich Village in the 1950s, that it was home to 50,000 people who had a great letter to the editor in them.) In a certain sense, this could seem to be merely the continuation of a tendency that has been in progress for a long time. Walter Benjamin observed sixty years ago that with the extension of the press and the multiplication of organs, 'an increasing number of readers became writers . . . Today there is hardly a gainfully employed European who could not, in principle, find an opportunity to publish somewhere or other comments on his work, grievances, documentary reports, or that sort of thing' (Benjamin 1936/1969b: 232). And we can find reports to the same effect in Carlyle in the nineteenth century and Johnson in the eighteenth. But while the absolute number of writers and documents has been steadily growing, the *proportion* of writers to readers has remained relatively constant or may even have declined over the centuries, along with the circulation of the average published document. The average first printing of a novel in 1780 was around 1,250, and is perhaps 5,000 or 7,500 today, but most or all of this increase is explained by the fact that a far larger proportion of the eighteenth-century editions would have gone to circulating libraries and book clubs, and by an increase in the number of books that individual readers buy.

This still means, of course, that every generation has had a larger number of documents to cope with. But the consequences for the individual reader have not been as severe as we might be led to believe by the complaints about 'information overload' that seem to come up in every age (though of course that particular way of putting things is recent). Up to now, each successive stage of increase has been met by a corresponding institutionalization and specialization of discourses, which constrain readers' expectations of themselves. A modern graduate student in physics is sure to feel overwhelmed by the volume of material she is responsible for, but not to any greater degree than her nineteenth-century predecessor did. There has always been too much to read.

But electronic discourse promises to disrupt this process. In the first place it sharply increases the proportion of writers to readers. (We might paraphrase Benjamin by saying that 'today there is hardly a gainfully employed European or American who has not published somewhere or other comments on his work, grievances, documentary reports, or that sort of thing' – provided we make access to a computer and modem a precondition to 'gainful employment'.) The increase in the number of documents that any reader has to sort through is for this reason genuinely unprecedented. It could be argued, of course, that the difficulty is partially offset by an increased ease of access that makes it possible for readers to look at many more documents than previously. But the effect of this is chiefly to enable people to go through more documents in search of those that might be interesting or useful – and in the course of things, to waste more time checking out large numbers of documents that are neither. Ease of access tends to exacerbate the impression of overload, rather than relieving it.

The purely quantitative difficulties are exacerbated by qualitative ones. Media like the Web tend to resist attempts to impose the sort of solutions that enable us to manage (even imperfectly) the steady increase in the number of print documents – the ramification of discourses and forms of publication, the imposition of systems of screening or refereeing, the restriction of the right to speak to 'qualified' participants. And at the same time the new forms of circulation can disrupt the long historical development of cataloging and classification systems that Roger Chartier describes in *The Order of Books*, through which emerged '[the] operations thanks to which it became possible to order the world of texts' (Chartier 1992: 7).

For one thing, there are almost no barriers to posting a document on the Web, not even the minimal requirements that have to be satisfied before you can publish your 'comments on work, grievances, documentary reports' in some print organ or another. Many Net discussion groups have moderators, it's true, but their responsibilities are usually limited to screening out blatant incivil- ities. On the Net, there is no strong material or economic incentive to rule out prolixity or to winnow redundant postings, and the breadth and openness of the discussions and the interest in quick turnaround militate against screening for accuracy. The discussions are ruled by the sort of principle that Henry Oldenburg offered when he began the publication of the *Philosophical Transac- tions of the Royal Society* in 1665: *sit penes authorem* [sic] *fides*, 'let it be on the author's head.' And of course there is no need even to submit to the judgment of moderators. Any undergraduate is free to post her night thoughts on Mary Shelley or the Klingon verb to a 'potential audience' of millions (a quick search of the Web turns up numerous examples of both), and there will be nothing in its mode of circulation to distinguish it from communications from better-qualified contributors. Nor, for that matter, is the material form of a document very informative here. If I am willing to make even a small investment of time, I can produce a Web home page that is every bit the graphical equal of the home pages of *Time* magazine or Sun Microsystems.

One effect of all of this is to undercut the autonomy of documents that is essential to the impression of 'information' in the print world. You do a search over the Web on the words 'Alfred Hitchcock', for example, and you come up with twenty or thirty hits, most of them 'professional- looking' pages. Some of them announce their provenance – there is an essay by someone in the English department at the University of Maryland and an undergraduate's senior thesis (at an unnamed university) on *Rear Window*. But there are no material or external clues to help you evaluate the three filmographies, one apparently prepared by a Hitchcock buff in Poitiers, another in Cardiff, and a third, which looks on internal evidence the most authoritative, from someone's site in Mexico.

On the Web, that is, you can never have the kind of experience that you can have with the informational genres of print, the experience of interpreting a text simply *as* a newspaper or encyclopedia article without attending to its author, its publisher, or the reliability of its recom- mender. We read Web documents, that is, not as information but as intelligence, which requires an explicit warrant of one form or another. Sometimes this is provided by a masthead that announces that the document has been produced by a well-known organization or print publication, in which case the content of the document does indeed constitute a kind of derivative information. With primary electronic documents, though, the warrant more often comes, as with the intelligence of old, from sources whose reliability we can judge from personal experience. One of the most striking things about the Web is the secondary traffic in *trouvailles* that it encourages, either in the form of the mail messages that users exchange when they locate an interesting or useful URL (a universal resource locator, the address of a Web page) or of the active links to other sites that users embed in their own Web pages. From these in turn have sprung various electronic reviews, information services, and clearinghouses, most run by enthusiasts but with an increasing number of commercial efforts. And you can find hot tips, too, in print publications from *Wired* to the *New York Times*, and in Silicon Valley, even on highway billboards. It is a phenomenon reminiscent of the response to the multiplication of print forms in the early eighteenth century, when Pope described in the *Dunciad* the pullulation of 'Miscellanies . . . Journals, Medleys, Merc'ries, Magazines', most of them produced by booksellers to publicize the increasing output of print titles.

Over the course of time, services like these will help to address some of the evidential problems that come up when we want to use the Web as source of reliable information in the particularistic sense. But we should bear in mind that they are not really the equivalents of the informational genres of print, which offer themselves as compendia of a circumscribed body of public knowledge – the news, the lexis, the library collection. In the electronic world, this goal of circumscription is chimerical, in the absence of phenomenal boundaries between documents, genres, and discourses. The implications are nicely summed up in an old joke about the *New York Times* to the effect that its slogan 'All the news that's fit to print' would be more appropriately rephrased as 'all the news that fits.' But it is not a joke you could make about a truly electronic newspaper. It isn't just that there are no longer any relevant material limits to the capacity of a document – that we can 'fit' into a newspaper as much content as we like – but that the boundaries of 'news' fall away at the same time. There is no event so trivial or particular that someone might not find it useful, no piece of background that has to be left out for reasons of space. And in the same way there is no word so obscure or technical or slangy that some user mightn't want to find it in a dictionary. This might seem to pose intimidating challenges for the compilers, except that 'compilation' is a different matter when the boundaries between documents are themselves so problematic. A dictionary can be linked to an encyclopedia, for example (the distinction between the two has always been as much a matter of two kinds of books as of two modularities of knowledge). Or an encyclopedia can take us directly into the primary literature (likewise).

At the limit we may want to think of these forms on the model of the new news services and clearinghouses: not as static compendia but rather as dynamic interfaces to an open-ended discourse. They are forms of automated intelligence, that is, rather than informational genres in themselves. So the true electronic 'dictionary' (already taking shape in research projects) might be a tool that pairs a word in an on-line text with a body of citations that match and clarify the sense relevant to its context, without having to pass through the lexicographical processes of distillation and abstraction with their attendant implication of a distinction between language and speech. And the 'digital library' is analogous. Once the notion of a collection is no longer materially constrained, it tends naturally to extend indefinitely. Of course it includes a lot of what most readers will find trivial and ephemeral; when you take down the walls of the library you shouldn't be surprised to find the reading room filling up with street people. But the solution is not to try to close off the collection some arbitrary way, but to provide benign Medeas (both automatic and flesh and blood) who can help users thread their way through the maze. The electronic news service, newspaper, dictionary, and library are still tools for 'information access' in the particularistic sense of the word. But the are no longer the kinds of determinate public limits that are implicit when we talk about 'information' in the abstract sense, and no way to talk about how much of it there is in a copy of the electronic *New York Times*.

After information

But from a cultural if not commercial point of view, the importance of the Net and the Web is not as a convenient if sometimes leaky alternative to the informational functions of print. Rather it lies in the forms of discourse that are emerging in all those Web sites and discussion groups that the electronic referral services are helping us to avoid wasting our time on. One of the most pervasive features of these media is how closely they seem to reproduce the conditions of discourse of the late seventeenth and eighteenth centuries, when the sense of the public was mediated through a series of transitive personal relationships – the friends of one's friends, and so on – and anchored in the immediate connections of clubs, coffee-houses, salons, and the rest. The social aggregations that assemble themselves on the Net may be virtual, but they are in no wise 'imagined' in Benedict Anderson's sense – they aren't groups, that is, whose 'fellow members . . . will never know most of their fellow members, meet them, or even hear of them, yet in [whose minds] lives the image of their communion' (Anderson 1983: 15). It may be true that most participants in Net colloquy will never actually meet each other individually, or even have direct electronic contact, but unlike the members of nations, social classes, or even ethnicities, each of them is immediately and personally accessible to any other.

Perhaps not surprisingly, the forms of discourse that emerge tend to mirror those of the preinformation age. One place where this is very much in evidence is in the professional discussion groups of linguists, historians, literary historians, and the rest, which fall somewhere between the refereed electronic journals (a genre that has so far been slow to take form) and the freewheeling conversations of Net news groups (which can sometimes be rebarbatively brusque). The participants are usually familiar enough with the forms of 'official' communication, if not always in the field that the list is given over to. But their exchanges here don't have the character of the print journals of the modern ages.

There is, first, the opening up of the right to speak. The lists reverse the effects of nineteenth-century immurement and professionalization of the disciplines that Raymond Williams described as a transition from the republic of letters to the bureaucracy of letters, where a writer can no longer speak as himself, but 'must continually declare his style and department, and submit to an examination of his purpose and credentials at the frontier to every field' (Williams 1983: 121). It's not just that the lists permit the participation of interested amateurs (the 'virtuosi' of the age of Pepys and Wren). They also remove the burden of professionalism that was imposed in the nineteenth century to limit the published discourse of the sciences to descriptions of its 'subject matter' and purge it of critical self-consideration. The amateur epistemologizing and sociologizing, the pedagogical and technical lore, the gossip and the professional politics, the anecdotal observations about curiosities that lie outside the realm of current theory – all these come bubbling back up into public view from the orality where they have been repressed for the past two hundred years. The effect is something like that of reading an early number of the *Philosophical Transactions*, which might mix the serious contributions of Boyle or Leeuwenhoeck with a report from a gentleman in Suffolk about a curious and flood or the birth of a monstrous calf. (You wonder whether the more scholarly readers of the *Transactions* tended to skip over the contributions that came in from anyone with an 'Esq.' at the end of his name, the way some readers of scholarly lists give short shrift to postings from anyone whose email address ends with 'compuserve.com'.)

Of course it can be a risky matter to read all this informationally. It often happens that a query will elicit several contradictory answers, leaving the person who posed it in something of a quandary, especially if he is not adept enough in the discourse to be able to sort out the dross either on internal grounds or on the basis of some knowledge of the qualifications of his respondents. (To take an extreme example, someone wrote to the Linguist List not long ago asking for the source of the quotation *Homo sum; homini nihil a me alienum puto*. The answers offered included Cicero, Horace, Plautus, and Virgil, and while Terence did get the most votes, you have the feeling that serious scholarship ought to require some standard more rigorous than mere majority rule.) Predictably, as elsewhere in the electronic sphere, there are frequent complaints about the unevenness and copiousness of the discussions, in tones reminiscent of those of the 1756 critic who taxed the editors of the *Philosophical Transactions* for publishing too many 'crude essays that cannot appear with propriety among the works of the learned'. And with these come attempts to restrict access or fragment the lists into new, more exclusionary discourses.[13] But while it's reasonable enough to look to these discussions to answer certain informational needs, once again it's futile to suppose they can be circumscribed and regimented in the way print discourse can. They are too porous to the personal.

Derrida (1995: 35) makes a point along these lines in *Mal d'archive* about the effects of electronic mail (which seems to include for him the broader range of Net communication):

> . . . Electronic mail is now even more than the fax in the process of transforming all the public and private space of humanity, and first of all the limit between the private, the secret (whether private or public) and the public or phenomenal.

This personalism is the feature that most sharply distinguishes Net discussions from the formal discourses of print. It is implicit in the forms of language, as people speak, not as authors to an anonymous public, but rather in the form of a colloquial conversation between participants who are copresent in the act of speaking. Contributors often address one another directly, a style alien to the letters column of a magazine journal, where antagonists always refer to each other in the third person. And the style of argument admits the personal, the anecdotal, the subjective. If you are willing to make allowances (rather a lot of them), the tone recalls the early eighteenth-century periodicals and the first stirrings of the modern critical spirit. It is a capacity, as Terry Eagleton puts it, that is 'incurably amateur', which draws together 'writer and reader, critic and citizen, multiple literary modes and dispersed modes of inquiry', and whose goal, as Eagleton quotes T. H. Green as saying, 'consists of talking to the public about itself' (Eagleton 1984: 22).

We shouldn't try to make too much of this, as some of its enthusiasts have tried to do (one calls E-mail the 'third revolution' in human communication, the first two having been writing and print). The discussion is very often banal and can on occasion be uncivil; certainly no one would be tempted to say of the language of the Net discussion groups, as Eagleton does of the language of the *Spectator*, that it is 'mannerly and pellucid'. Of course it could be argued that unevenness and lowering of quality are inevitable whenever participation is so wide (and indeed, there are analogous complaints about the decline in standards whenever participation in public discourse seems to be broadened, which go back to Addison and Swift and before).[14] There is some truth to this, though claims about the increased breadth of participation on the Web are greatly exaggerated, just like Defoe's claims that London held 'rarely a Victualing House but you meet with a Tinker, a Cobbler or a Porter, Criticizing upon the Speeches of Majesty, or the writings of the most celebrated Men the Age'.[15] The Web is still the electronic equivalent of a gated suburban community, and shouldn't be surprising that it contains a lot of suburban chatter.

Still, it is unfair to expect electronic media to be the agents of sweeping social revolution even for that matter of a complete over-turning of the present order of discourse. And from the literary point of view, it is early days yet; really the appropriate comparison here is not to the *Tat* or the *Spectator*, but to the seventeenth-century 'news letters' and the like that antedated these forms and made them possible. The chief difference is that these new forms inhabit a public space that is already highly developed and differentiated, so that like other technological innovations (plastic furniture, for example), they will wind up assuming certain specialized functions alongside the established informational genres of print and their derivative electronic representations. This is the only quibble that I have with Derrida's description of the Net as being 'in the process of transforming *all* the public and private space of humanity'. Rather, I think we should look to electronic discourse to provide a counter and complement to the informational forms of print – a domain that privileges the personal, the private, and the subjective against the impersonal, the public, and the objective.

Notes

1   Cities like Brownsville, Texas, Waco, Texas, and Cheyenne, Wyoming, now boast book 'superstores' of between 25,000 and 50,000 square feet, which can offer readers from 30,000 to 60,000 distinct titles; stores in larger cities may offer as many as 150,000 titles.

2   I'm ignoring most of the obsolete and legal uses of the word 'information', as well as the remnants of the use of the word as an action nominal, as in the phrase 'for your information'.

3   The OED2 actually gives two senses for this naturalistic use of the word, the second of them applying to information as a mathematically defined quantity, but it indicates that the two are probably descriptions of the same thing, and for the present purposes the difference needn't concern us.

4   Weaver also acknowledged the 'semantic problem' of information ('How precisely do the transmitted symbols convey the desired meaning?') and the 'effectiveness problem' ('How effectively do the transmitted symbols affect conduct in the desired way?'). Neither of these has been addressed formally in the information-theoretic framework, though something like these problems have been taken up in recent years by philosophers like Fred Dretske, David Israel, and John Perry. For the present purposes it is enough to observe that these have had virtually no effect on popular ways of talking about information, which is what I am concerned with here.

5   A search in several databases of the Dialog Information Services turned up over eighty mentions of this claim in various magazines and newspapers, all of them uncritical.

6   Austen sometimes plays on the ambiguity of the word, as in this conversation between Fanny and Edmund in *Mansfield Park*: 'I speak what appears to me the general opinion; and where an opinion is general, it is usually correct. Though I have not seen much of the domestic lives of clergymen, it is seen by too many to leave any deficiency of information.' 'Where any one body of educated men, of whatever denomination, are condemned indiscriminately, there must be a deficiency of information, or (smiling) of something else . . .'. Fanny uses the word here in its particularistic sense, to mean something like 'intelligence, authoritative reports' whereas Edmund is using it to mean something more like 'moral instruction'.

7   Cf also: 'But though the interest of the labourer is strictly connected with that of the society, he is incapable either of comprehending that interest or of understanding its connection with his own. His condition leaves him no time to receive the necessary information . . .' (Adam Smith, *The Wealth of Nations*). '. . . It is well known that some of the most distinguished members of that Congress, who have been since tried and justly approved for patriotism and abilities, and who have grown old in acquiring political information, were also members of this convention, and carried into it their accumulated knowledge and experience' (Alexander Hamilton, *The Federalist Papers*, 14).
      See, on these, Yates (1989) and Beniger (1986).

9   Jean Clair observed that the museum and the railway station were the nineteenth century's only original forms of public building, the one a representation of the colonization of time, the other of the colonization of space.

10   It is difficult to make any interesting generalizations about the full range of electronic media, given both the welter of emergent forms (CD-ROM, hypertext, multimedia, virtual reality, MUDs and MOOs, and so on) and the increasing difficulty of separating print and electronic documents now that 'traditional' print documents can be electronically distributed and printed locally on demand. For the present purposes I will take the World Wide Web (or more broadly, the Net) as a model. For one thing the Web has already established itself as a means of distributing journalistic, scholarly, commercial, and institutional documents. As of this writing (in August of 1995) there are some 60,000 Web servers, a figure that has increased eightfold over the last year. (This figure is available at http://webcrawler.com/WebCrawler/Facts/Facts. htmlhttp://webcrawler.com/.) I will also assume only the functionalities currently available – that is, the possibility of reading, writing, and interacting in simple ways with hypertextually organized documents which may include audio or video, and which contain active links to other sites. It's clear that within a short period there will be basically nothing you can do on a workstation or local server that you can't do remotely over the Web – you will be able to edit your documents or OCR a text image using software available on a remote server, for example – but while the implications of this increased functionality are considerable, I won't discuss them here.

11   I'm going to assume here that the Web will remain resistant to the kind of monopolization that would make this sort of communication too costly for individual users. This is a big assumption, of course, but I think that even if the Web were bought by a few large commercial interests, it would be difficult or counterproductive to impose a commercial model that limited the accessibility of certain documents, or that militated against the continuing use of distribution lists and similar fora.

12   Over the past century the number of titles published has probably grown at something like two or three times the rate of growth of the reading public itself. In 1945 there were about seven thousand titles published in the US; by 1990 this figure was about fifty thousand. Over the same period the reading public probably no more than trebled (assuming a doubling of the population and an increase of 50 percent in the proportion of the population that buys books) though the difficulty of finding comparable statistics and of assessing what we mean by the 'reading public' makes all such estimates highly speculative. As vague as they are, though, the figures suggest that the proportion of writers to readers has remained constant within an order of magnitude. Figures from earlier periods conform to this principle. Richardson' best-selling novels in the 1740s achieved sales of around 6,500; seventy years later, when the reading public (as measured by newspaper sales) had increased roughly four times, Scott *Marmion* and *Rob Roy* sold around 11,000 each (see Williams 1961).

13   Quoted in Kronick (1991: 161).

14   Cf. the remarks of Aldous Huxley in 1934: '. . . The proportion of trash in the total artistic output is greater now than at any other period. That it must be so is a matter of simple arithmetic. Process reproduction and the rotary press have made possible the indefinite multiplication of writing and pictures. Universal education and relatively high wages have created an enormous public who know how to read and can afford to buy reading and pictorial matter. A great industry has been called into existence in order to supply these commodities . . . The population of Western Europe has little more than doubled during the last century. But the amount of reading – and seeing – matter has increased, I should imagine at least twenty and possibly fifty or even a hundred times.' (The passage is quoted in Benjamin (1936/1969b: 248), who adds: 'This mode of observation is obviously not progressive.') course Huxley was assuming, as Benjamin seems to do, that the proportion of writers

readers was increasing throughout this period, an impression enhanced by the fact that the ephemera of earlier ages tend to be forgotten, so that the overall quality of contemporary writing always seems infinitely more mediocre when it is compared to the works that are still available from earlier periods. Historically, as we have seen, the impression of proportionally increased participation is probably unjustified, but it could in fact be a cause of some change in the overall quality of public writing as we move from print to electronic communication.

15   Quoted in Eagleton (1984: 14).

BIBLIOGRAPHY

Introduction

Adams, Thomas and Barker, Nicolas (1993) 'A New Model for the Study of the Book', in Nicolas Barker, ed., *A Potencie of Life: Books in Society*, London: British Library.

Bowers, Fredson (1949) *Principles of Bibliographical Description*, Princeton: Princeton University Press.

Bradbury, Ray (1953) *Fahrenheit 451*, New York: Ballantine Press.

Darnton, Robert (1990) 'What is the History of Books', in T*he Kiss of Lamourette: Reflections in Cultural History*, New York: Norton, pp. 107–36.

Duguid, Paul (1996) 'Material Matters: The Past and Futurology of the Book', in Geoffrey Nunberg, ed., *The Future of the Book*, Berkeley: University of California Press, pp. 63–101.

Eco, Umberto (1983) *The Name of the Rose*, trans. William Weaver, London: Secker and Warburg.

Eisenstein, Elizabeth (1968) 'Some Conjectures about the Impact of Printing on Western Society and Thought: A Preliminary Report', *Journal of Modern History* 40: 1–56.

Eisenstein, Elizabeth (1979) *The Printing Press as an Agent of Change*, 2 vols, Cambridge: Cambridge University Press.

Eisenstein, Elizabeth (1983) *The Printing Press as an Agent of Change*, 1 vol. edn, Cambridge: Cambridge University Press.

Escarpit, Robert (1958, 1965) *Sociologie de la Littérature / The Sociology of Literature*, trans. Ernest Pick, Painesville, Ohio: Lake Erie College Press.

Febvre, Lucien and Martin, Henri-Jean (1958) *L'Apparition du Livre*, Paris: Albin Michel.

Febvre, Lucien and Martin, Henri-Jean (1976) *The Coming of the Book: The Impact of Printing, 1450– 1800*, English trans., London: Verso.

Greg, W. W. (1966) *Collected Papers*, ed. J. C. Maxwell, Oxford: Clarendon Press.

Johns, Adrian (1998) *The Nature of the Book: Print and Knowledge in the Making*, Chicago: University of Chicago Press.

Jordan, John O. and Patten, Robert L., eds (1995) *Literature in the Marketplace: Nineteenth-Century British Publishing and Reading Practices*, Cambridge: Cambridge University Press.

Landow, George P. (1997) *Hypertext 2.0: The Convergence of Contemporary Critical Theory and Technology* Baltimore and London: Johns Hopkins University Press.

McGann, J. J. (1991) *The Textual Condition*, Princeton: Princeton University Press.

McKerrow, Ronald B. (1927) *An Introduction to Bibliography for Literary Students*, Oxford: Clarendon Press.

Nunberg, Geoffrey (1993) 'The Place of Books in the Age of Electronic Reproduction', *Representations* 42: 13–37.

Tanselle, G. T. (1979) *Selected Studies in Bibliography*, Charlottesville: University Press of Virginia pp. 308–53.

Part 1: What is book history?

Adams, Thomas R. and Barker, Nicolas (1993) 'A New Model for the Study of the Book', in Nicolas Barker, ed., *A Potencie of Life: Books in Society; The Clark Lectures, 1986–1987*, London: British Library, pp. 5–43.

Balsamo, Luigi (1990) *Bibliography: History of a Tradition*, Berkeley, Ca.: B. M. Rosenthal.

Barker, Nicolas (1993a) 'Intentionality and Reception Theory', in Nicolas Barker, ed., *A Potencie of Life: Books in Society*, London: British Library.

Barker, Nicolas, ed. (1993b) *A Potencie of Life: Books in Society: The Clark Lectures 1986–1987*, London: British Library.

Barthes, Roland (1977) *Image Music Text*, London: Fontana Press.

Barzun, Jacques (1986) *On Writing, Editing and Publishing*, Chicago: University of Chicago Press.

Benjamin, Walter (1969) 'The Work of Art in the Age of Mechanical Reproduction', in *Illuminations*, trans. Harry Zohn, New York: Schocken Books.

Birley, Robert (1962) *Sunk Without Trace: Some Forgotten Masterpieces Remembered: The Clark Lectures 1960–1961*, London: Hart-Davis.

Bourdieu, Pierre (1993) *The Field of Cultural Production*, ed. Randal Johnson, Cambridge: Polity Press.

Bowers, Fredson (1949) *Principles of Bibliographical Description*, Princeton: Princeton University Press.

Bowers, Fredson (1952) 'Bibliography, Pure Bibliography, and Literary Studies', *Papers of the Bibliographical Society of America* 46: 186–208.

Bowers, Fredson (1964) *Bibliography and Textual Criticism*, Oxford: Clarendon Press.

Carey, James W. (1992) *Communication as Culture*, New York: Routledge.

Chartier, Roger (1988) *Cultural History: between Practices and Representations*, Cambridge: Polity Press.

Chartier, Roger, ed. (1989) *The Cultures of Print: Power and Uses of Print in Modern Europe*, Cambridge: Polity Press.

Clair, Colin (1960) *Christopher Plantin*, London: Cassell & Company.

Darnton, Robert (1984) *The Great Cat Massacre and Other Episodes in French Cultural History*, New York: Basic Books.

Darnton, Robert (1990) 'What is the History of Books', in *The Kiss of Lamourette: Reflections in Cultural History*, New York: Norton, pp. 107–36.

Davison, Peter, ed. (1992) *The Book Encompassed: Studies in Twentieth Century Bibliography*, Cambridge: Cambridge University Press.

Eisenstein, E. (1983) *The Printing Revolution in Early Modern Europe*, Cambridge: Cambridge University Press.

Elsky, Martin (1989) *Authorizing Words: Speech, Writing and Print in the English Renaissance*, Ithaca: Cornell University Press.

Escarpit, Robert (1958, 1965) *The Sociology of Literature*, trans. Ernest Pick, Painesville, Ohio: Lake Erie College Press.

Escarpit, Robert (1966) *The Book Revolution*, London: George C. Harrap & Co.

Festivals, Robert (1994) 'Histoire du livre et bibliologie', *Canadian Review of Comparative Literature/ Revue Canadienne de Littérature Comparée* 21.3: 457–68.

Feather, John (1980) 'Cross-Channel Currents: Historical Bibliography and l'Histoire du Livre', *Library Series* 62.1: 1–15.

Feather, John (1986a) 'The Book in History and the History of the Book', *Journal of Library History* 21: 12–26.

Feather, John (1986b) *A Dictionary of Book History*, New York and Oxford: Oxford University Press.

Feather, John P. and McKitterick, David (1986) *The History of Books and Libraries: Two Views*, Washington, DC: Library of Congress.

Freeman, R. B. (1977) *The Works of Charles Darwin, An Annotated Bibliographical Handlist*, 2nd edn, Folkestone: Dawson.

Gaskell, Philip (1972) *A New Introduction to Bibliography*, New York and Oxford: Oxford University Press.

Gaskell, Philip (1978) *From Writer to Reader: Studies in Editorial Method*, Oxford: Clarendon Press.

Genette, Gerard (1997) *Paratexts: Thresholds of Interpretation*, trans. Jane F. Lewin, Cambridge: Cambridge University Press.

Greetham, D. C. (1994) *Textual Scholarship: An Introduction*, New York: Garland Press.

Greg, W. W. (1966) *Collected Papers*, ed. J. C. Maxwell, Oxford: Clarendon Press.

Haight, Anne Lyon (1955) *Banned Books*, New York: Bowker.

Hall, David D. (1983) 'On Native Ground: From the History of Printing to the History of the Book', *Proceedings of the American Antiquarian Society* 93: 313–36.

Hall, David D. (1996) *Cultures of Print: Essays in the History of the Book*, Amherst: University of Massachusetts Press.

Hall, David D. and Hench, J. B., eds (1987) *Needs and Opportunities in the History of the Book: America, 1639–1876*, Worcester: American Antiquarian Society.

Hoggart, Richard (1958) *The Uses of Literacy: Changing Patterns in English Mass Culture*, New York: Oxford University Press.

Howard-Hill, T. H. (1993–1995) 'The Institutionalization of Bibliography', *Analytical and Enumerative Bibliography* 7.4: 181–91.

Johns, Adrian (1998) *The Nature of the Book: Print and Knowledge in the Making*, Chicago: Chicago University Press.

Jordan, John O. and Patten, Robert L., eds (1995) *Literature in the Marketplace: Nineteenth-Century British Publishing and Reading Practices*, Cambridge: Cambridge University Press.

Love, Harold (1993) *Scribal Publication in Seventeenth-Century England*, Oxford: Clarendon Press.

Love, Harold (2003) 'Early Modern Print Culture: Assessing the Models', *Parergon* 20.1: 45–64.

Macherey, Pierre (1978) *A Theory of Literary Production*, London.

McGann, Jerome (1983) *A Critique of Modern Textual Criticism*, Chicago: University of Chicago Press.

McGann, Jerome (1985) *The Beauty of Inflections: Literary Investigations in Historical Method and Theory*, Oxford: Clarendon Press.

McGann, J. J. (1991) *The Textual Condition*, Princeton: Princeton University Press.

McKenzie, D. F. (1969) 'Printers of the Mind: Some Notes on Bibliographical Theories and Printing House Practices', *Studies in Bibliography* 22: 1–75.

McKenzie, D. F. (1986) *The Panizzi Lectures, 1985: Bibliography and the Sociology of Texts*, London: British Library.

McKenzie, D. F. (1992) 'History of the Book', in Peter Davidson, ed., *The Bibliographical Society 1892–1992*, Cambridge: Cambridge University Press.

McKerrow, Ronald B. (1927) *An Introduction to Bibliography for Literary Students*, Oxford: Clarendon Press.

McLuhan, Marshall (1962) *The Gutenburg Galaxy: The Making of Typographic Man*, Toronto: University of Toronto Press.

Needham, Paul (1980) 'Review of Eisenstein's *The Printing Press as an Agent of Change*', *Fine Print* 6.1: 23–25, 32–35.

Nunberg, Geoffrey (1993) 'The Place of Books in the Age of Electronic Reproduction', *Representations* 42: 13–37.

Nunberg, Geoffrey, ed. (1996) *The Future of the Book*, Berkeley: University of California Press.

Oliphant, D. and Carver, Larry (1990) *New Directions in Textual Studies*, Austin: University of Texas H. Ransom Center.

Ong, Walter J. (1983) *Orality and Literacy: The Technologizing of the Word*, London: Methuen.

Patten, Robert L. (1996) 'When is a Book not a Book', *Biblion*, Spring: 35–63.

Phelps, Deirdre (1994) 'Theory and the Book: Socio-Cultural Theory of the Novel I', *New England Book and Text Studies* 1: 91–101.

Rawson, David A. (1991) 'Review Essay: New Questions and New Approaches in the Study of the "History of the Book" ', *Eighteenth-century Studies* 15: 103–12.

Rose, Jonathan (1994) 'How to Do Things with Book History', *Victorian Studies* 37: 461–71.

Rose, Jonathan (1996) 'How Historians Teach the History of the Book', *Canadian Review of Comparative Literature/Revue Canadienne de Littérature Comparée* 23.1: 217–24.

Shillingsburg, Peter L. (1986) *Scholarly Editing in the Computer Age*, Athens: University of Georgia Press.

Shillingsburg, Peter L. (1991) 'Text as Matter, Concept, and Action', *Studies in Bibliography* 44: 31–82.

Steinberg, S. H. (1961) [1955] *Five Hundred Years of Printing*, Harmondsworth: Penguin Books.

Sutherland, John (1988) 'Publishing History: A Hole at the Centre of Literary Sociology', *Critical Enquiry* 14.3: 574–89.

Tanselle, C. T. (1981) *The History of Books as a Field of Study*, Chapel Hill: Rare Book Collection, University of North Carolina.

Tanselle, C. T. (1987) *Textual Criticism Since Greg: A Chronicle, 1950–1985*, Charlottesville: University Press of Virginia for the Bibliographical Society of the University of Virginia.

Tanselle, C. T. (1989) *A Rationale of Textual Criticism*, Philadelphia: University of Pennsylvania Press.

Tanselle, C. T. (1990) *Textual Criticism and Scholarly Editing*, Charlottesville: University Press of Virginia for the Bibliographical Society of the University of Virginia.

Willison, I. R. (1991) 'Remarks on the History of the Book in Britain as a Field of Study within the Humanities', *Library Chronicle of the University of Texas* 21: 95–147.

Willison, I. R. (1993) 'The History of the Book in Twentieth-Century Britain and America: Perspective and Evidence', *Proceedings of the American Antiquarian Society* 102: 353–77.

Zaret, David (2000) *Origins of Democratic Culture: Printing, Petitions, and the Public Sphere in Early-Modern England*, Princeton: Princeton University Press.

Part 2: The impact of print

Achebe, Chinua (1961) *No Longer at Ease*, New York: Ivan Obolensky.

Allison, A. F. and Rogers, D. M. (1989) *The Contemporary Printed Literature of the English Counter-Reformation between 1558 and 1640*, Aldershot: Scolar Press.

Armbruster, Carol (1993) *Publishing and Readership in Revolutionary France and America*, Westport, Conn.: Greenwood.

Armstrong, Elizabeth (1986) *Robert Estienne: Royal Printer: An Historical Study of the Elder Stephanus*, rev. edn, Abingdon: Sutton Courtenay Press.

Bailyn, Bernard and Hench, John B., eds (1980) *The Press & the American Revolution*, Worcester, Mass.: American Antiquarian Society.

Barber, Giles (1994) *Studies in the Booktrade of the European Enlightenment*, London: Pindar.

Bekker-Nielsen, Hans, ed. (1986) *From Script to Book*, Odense: Odense University Press.

Bell, David N., ed. (1992) *The Libraries of the Cistercians, Gilbertines and Premonstratensians*, London: British Library.

Bell, David N. (1995) *What Nuns Read: Books and Libraries in Medieval English Nunneries*, Cistercian Studies Series, 158, Kalamazoo: Cistercian Publications.

Bell, H. F. (1936–1937) 'The Price of Books in Medieval England', *The Library*, 4th series, 312–32.

Bell, Susan Groag (1982) 'Medieval Women Book Owners: Arbiters of Lay Piety and Ambassadors of Culture', *Signs* 7.4: 742–68.

Bennett, H. S. (1947) 'The Production and Dissemination of Vernacular Manuscripts in the Fifteenth Century', *The Library*, 5th series, 167–78.

Bennett, H. S. (1952) *English Books and Readers 1475–1557*, Cambridge: Cambridge University Press.

Berkvens-Stevelinck, C., Bots, H., Hoffijzer, P. G. and Lankhorst, O. S., eds (1992) *Le Magasin de l'Univers: The Dutch Republic as the Centre of the European Book Trade: Papers Presented at the International Colloquium Held at Wassenaar, 5–7 July 1990*, Leiden: E. J. Brill.

Bernstein, Basil (1974) *Class, Codes and Control. Theoretical Studies towards a Sociology of Language*, vol. 1, 2nd rev. edn, London: Routledge and Kegan Paul.

Bietenholz, Peter G. (1971) *Basle and France in the Sixteenth Century: The Basle Humanists and Printers in their Contacts with Francophone Culture*, Toronto: University of Toronto Press.

Biller, Peter and Hudson, Anne, eds (1994) *Heresy and Literacy, 100–1530*, Cambridge: Cambridge University Press.

Blake, N. F. (1991) *William Caxton and English Literary Culture*, London: Hambledon Press.

Bloch, Eileen (1965) 'Erasmus and the Froben Press: The Making of an Editor', *Library Quarterly* 35: 109–20.

Boerner, Peter (1969) *Tagebuch*, Stuttgart: J. B. Metzler.

Bologna, Guila (1988) *Illuminated Manuscripts: The Book Before Gutenberg*, New York: Weidenfeld and Nicolson.

Boyle, Leonard (1984) *Medieval Latin Palaeography: A Bibliographical Introduction*, Toronto: University of Toronto Press.

Brant, S. (1968) *Das Narrenschiff*, ed. M. Lemmer, Tübingen.

Brown, Cynthia J. (1995) *Poets, Patrons and Printers: Crisis of Authority in Late Medieval France*, Ithaca: Cornell University Press.

Brownrigg, Linda L. (1990) *Seminar in the History of the Book to 1500: Assessing the Evidence*, Los Altos Hills: Red Gull Press.

Brownrigg, Linda L., ed. (1994) *Making the Medieval Book: Techniques of Production*, Oxford: Oxford University Press.

Buhler, Curt Ferdinand (1960) *The Fifteenth Century Book: The Scribes, the Printers, the Decorators*, Philadelphia: University of Pennsylvania Press.

Bury, R. de (1960 [1345]) *Philobiblon*, trans. F. C. Thomas, ed. M. Maclagan, Oxford: Oxford University Press.

Calkins, Robert G. (1983) *Illuminated Books of the Middle Ages*, Ithaca, NY: Cornell University Press.

Carlson, David R. (1993) *English Humanist Books: Writers and Patrons, Manuscripts and Print 1475–1525*, Toronto: University of Toronto Press.

Carpenter, Kenneth, ed. (1983) *Books and Society in History*, New York: Bowker.

Carter, Harry (1969) *A View of Early Typography up to about 1600*, Oxford: Oxford University Press.

Carter, Thomas Francis (1955) *The Invention of Printing in China and Its Spread Westward*, 2nd edn, rev. by L. Carrington Goodrich, New York: Ronald Press.

Chafe, Wallace L. (1982) 'Integration and Involvement in Speaking, Writing and Oral Literature', in Deborah Tannen, ed., *Spoken and Written Language: Exploring Orality and Literacy*, Norwood, N J: Ablex.

Chappell, Warren (1970) *A Short History of the Printed Word*, New York: Knopf.

Chartier, Roger (1987) *The Cultural Uses of Print in Early Modern France*, trans. Lydia G. Cochrane, Princeton: Princeton University Press.

Chartier, Roger, ed. (1989) *The Culture of Print: Power and the Uses of Print in Early Modern Europe*, trans. Lydia G. Cochrane, Princeton: Princeton University Press.

Chrisman, Miriam Usher (1982) *Lay Culture, Learned Culture: Books and Social Change in Strasbourg 1480–1599*, New Haven: Yale University Press.

Clair, Cohn (1976) *A History of European Printing*, London: Academic Press.

Clanchy, Michael T. (1979) *From Memory to Written Record: England 1066–1307*, Cambridge, Ma and Oxford: B. H. Blackwell.

Coleman, Janet (1981) *Medieval Readers and Writers 1350–1400*, New York: Columbia University Press.

Davies, Martin (1993) *Aldus Manutius: Printer and Publisher of Renaissance Venice*, London: British Library.

Davis, Natalie Zemon (1957) 'The Protestant Printing Workers of Lyons in 1551', *Aspects de la propogande religieuse*, Geneva: Droz, 247–57.

De Hamel, Christopher (1986) *A History of Illuminated Manuscripts*, Oxford: Phaidon.

De Hamel, Christopher (1992) *Scribes and Illuminators*, Toronto.

De Roover, Florence Edler [as Florence Edler] (1937) 'Cost Accounting in the Sixteenth Century: The Books of Accounts of Christopher Plantin, Antwerp, Printer and Publisher', *Accounting Review* 12: 226–37.

De Roover, Florence Edler [as Florence Edler] (1953) 'New Facets on the Financing and Marketing of Early Printed Books', *Bulletin of the Business Historical Society* 27: 222–30.

Diringer, David (1953) *The Alphabet: A Key to the History of Mankind*, 2nd edn rev., New York: Philosophical Library.

Eisenstein, Elizabeth (1968) 'Some Conjectures about the Impact of Printing on Western Society and Thought: A Preliminary Report', *Journal of Modern History* 40: 1–56.

Eisenstein, Elizabeth (1979) *The Printing Press as an Agent of Change: Communications and Cultural Transformations in Early-Modern Europe*, 2 vols, Cambridge: Cambridge University Press.

Eisenstein, Elizabeth (1986) *Print Culture and Enlightenment Thought*, Chapel Hill, NC: Hanes Foundation, Rare Book Collection/ University Library, The University of North Carolina.

Fabian, Bernhard (1992) *The English Book in 18th-Century Germany*, London: British Library.

Febvre, Lucien, and Martin, Henri-Jean (1958) *L'Apparition du Livre*, Paris: Albin Michel.

Febvre, Lucien and Martin, Henri-Jean (1976) *The Coming of the Book: The Impact of Printing, 1450–1800*, trans. David Gerard, London: NLB.

Finnegan, Ruth (1988) *Literacy and Orality*, Oxford: Blackwell.

Flood, John L. and Kelly, William A., eds (1995) *The German Book, 1450–1750*, London: British Library.

Gameson, Richard, ed. (1994) *The Early Medieval Bible: Its Production, Decoration and Use*, Cambridge: Cambridge University Press.

Ganz, Peter, ed. (1986) *The Role of the Book in Medieval Culture*, Tournhout: Brepols.

Garcin de Tassy, J. H. (1870, repr. 1968, New York 1972) *Histoire de la Littérature Hindouie et Hindoustanie*, 4 vols. Paris: Adolphe Labitt.

Gelb, I. J. (1963) *A Study of Writing*, rev. edn, Chicago: University of Chicago Press.

Geldner, F. (1961) 'Zum ältesten Missaidruck', in *Gutenberg-Jahrbuch*, pp. 101–6.

Gellrich, Jesse (1986) *The Idea of the Book in the Middle Ages: Language Theory, Mythology, and Fiction*, Ithaca: Cornell University Press.

Gerson, J. (1973) [1423] 'De laude scriptorum', in J. Gerson, *Oeuvres complètes*, Paris, 9: 423–34.

Gesner, C. (1966) [1545] *Bibliotheca Universalis and Appendix*, Zurich.

Goody, Jack, ed. (1968a) *Literacy in Traditional Societies*, Cambridge: Cambridge University Press.

Goody, Jack (1968b) 'Restricted Literacy in Northern Ghana', in Jack Goody, ed., *Literacy in Traditional Societies*, Cambridge: Cambridge University Press, pp. 198–264.

Goody, Jack (1977) *The Domestication of the Savage Mind*, Cambridge: Cambridge University Press.

Goody, Jack (1987) *The Interface between the Oral and the Written*, Cambridge: Cambridge University Press.

Goody, Jack and Watt, Ian (1968) 'The Consequences of Literacy', in Jack Goody, ed., *Literacy in Traditional Societies*, Cambridge: Cambridge University Press, pp. 27–84.

Grafton, Anthony T. (1980) 'The Importance of Being Printed', *Journal of Interdisciplinary History* 11: 256–86.

Grafton, Anthony (1997) *Commerce with the Classics: Ancient Books and Renaissance Readers*, Ann Arbor: University of Michigan Press.

Greg, W. W. (1956) *Some Aspects and Problems of London Publishing between 1550–1650*, Oxford: Clarendon Press.

Griffiths, Jeremy and Pearsall, Derek, eds (1995) *Book Production and Publishing in Britain, 1375–1475*, Cambridge: Cambridge University Press.

Guxman, M. M. (1970) 'Some General Regularities in the Formation and Development of National Languages', in Joshua A. Fishman, ed., *Readings in the Sociology of Language*, The Hague: Mouton, pp. 773–6.

Harris, Victor (1989) *Ancient Literacy*, Cambridge: Cambridge University Press.

Harvey R., Kirsop, W. and McMullin, B. J., eds (1993) *An Index of Civilization: Studies in Publishing and Printing History in Honour of Keith Maslen*, Clayton, Vic.: Centre for Bibliographical and Textual Studies, Monash University.

Haugen, Einar (1966) 'Linguistics and Language Planning', in William Bright, ed., *Sociolinguistics: Proceedings of the UCLA Sociolinguistics Conference 1964*, The Hague: Mouton, pp. 50–71.

Havelock, Eric A. (1963) *Preface to Plato*, Cambridge, Mass.: Belknap Press of Harvard University Press.

Havelock, Eric A. (1978) *The Greek Concept of Justice: From its Shadow in Homer to its Substance in Plato*, Cambridge, Mass., and London: Harvard University Press.

Havelock, Eric A. (1982) *The Literate Revolution in Greece and Its Cultural Consequences*, Princeton: Princeton University Press.

Havelock, Eric A. and Herschell, Jackson P., eds (1978) *Communication Arts in the Ancient World*, Humanistic Studies in the Communication Arts, New York: Hastings House.

Heidenheimer, H. (1925) 'Das Beglietgedicht zum Justiniani Institutiones-Drucke von 1468', in A. Ruppel, ed., *Gutenberg-Festschrift: Feier des 25 jährigen Bestenhens des Gutenberg-Museums in Mainz Mainz*, pp. 108–17.

Hellinga, Lotte (1983) *Caxton in Focus: The Beginning of Printing in England*, London: British Library.

Hellinga, Lotte and Goldfinch, John, eds (1987) *Bibliography and the Study of 15th-century Civilization*, London: British Library.

Hindman, Sandra, ed. (1991) *Printing the Written Word: The Social History of Books, Circa 1450–1520*, Ithaca and London: Cornell University Press.

Hindman, Sandra and Farquhar, James Douglas (1977) *Pen to Press: Illustrated Manuscripts and Printed Books in the First Century of Printing*, College Park, Maryland: University of Maryland Press.

Hirsch, E. D. Jr. (1977) *The Philosophy of Composition*, Chicago and London: University of Chicago Press.

Hirsch, Rudolph (1974) *Printing, Selling, and Reading, 1450–1550*, Wiesbaden: Otto Harrassowitz.

Hussein, Mohamed A. (1972) *Origins of the Book: Egypt's Contribution to the Development of the Book from Papyrus to Codex*, Greenwich, Conn.: New York Graphic Society.

Ing, Janet (1988) *Johann Gutenberg and His Bible: A Historical Study*, New York: Typophiles.

Jardine, Lisa (1993) *Erasmus, Man of Letters: The Construction of Charisma in Print*, Princeton: Princeton University Press.

Johns, Adrian (1991) 'History, Science and the History of the Book: The Making of Natural Philosophy in Early Modern England', *Publishing History* 30: 5–31.

Johns, Adrian (1998) *The Nature of the Book: Print and Knowledge in the Making*, Chicago: University Chicago Press.

Kenney, E. J. (1974) *The Classical Text: Aspects of Editing in the Age of the Printed Book*, Berkeley: University of California Press.

Kerckhove, Derrick de (1981) 'A Theory of Greek Tragedy', *Sub-stance* (Summer), University Wisconsin, Madison.

Kingdom, Robert M. (1956) 'The Flood Tide: Books from Geneva', in *Geneva and the Coming of Wars of Religion in France, 1553–1563*, Geneva: Droz, pp. 93–105.

Leakey, Richard and Lewin, Roger (1979) *People of the Lake: Mankind and its Beginnings*, Garden City NY: Anchor Press/ Doubleday.

Lévi-Strauss, Claude (1966) *The Savage Mind*, Chicago: University of Chicago Press. Originally published as *La Pensée Sauvage* (1962).

Leyser, Karl (1994) *Communications and Power in Medieval Europe*, Rio Grande, Ohio: Hambledon.

Lowry, Martin (1979) *The World of Aldus Manutius*, Oxford: Blackwell.

Lowry, Martin (1991) *Nicholas Jenson and the Rise of Venetian Publishing*, Oxford: Blackwell.

Lycosthenes, C. (1551) *Elenchus scriptorum omnium*, Basel.

Machlup, Fritz (1978–80) *Information through the Printed Word: The Dissemination of Scholarly, Scientific and Intellectual Knowledge*, 4 vols, New York: Praeger.

Martin, Henri-Jean (1993) *Print, Power and People in 17th Century France*, trans. David Gerard, Metuchen, NJ: Scarecrow Press.

Martin, Henri-Jean (1994) *The History and Power of Writing*, trans. Lydia G. Cochrane. Chicago: University of Chicago Press.

McKenzie, D. F. (1981) 'Typography and Meaning: The Case of William Congreve', in *Wolfenbutteler Schriften zur Geschichte des Buchwesens* 4, Hamburg: Dr. Ernst Hauswedell & Co., pp. 81–125.

McKenzie, D. F. (1984) 'The Sociology of a Text: Orality, Literacy and Print in Early New Zealand', *The Library*: 333–65.

McKitterick, Rosamund (1989) *The Carolingians and the Written Word*, Cambridge: Cambridge University Press.

McKitterick, Rosamund, ed. (1990) *The Uses of Literacy in Early Medieval Europe*, Cambridge: Cambridge University Press.

McMurtrie, Douglas C. (1943) *The Book: The Story of Printing and Bookmaking*, 3rd rev. edn, New York and Oxford: Oxford University Press.

McNally, Peter F., ed. (1987) *The Advent of Printing: Historians of Science Respond to Elizabeth Eisenstein's The Printing Press as an Agent of Change*, Montreal: McGill University Graduate School of Library and Information Studies.

Meggitt, Mervyn (1968) 'Uses of Literacy in New Guinea and Melanesia', in Jack Goody, ed., *Literacy in Traditional Societies*, Cambridge: Cambridge University Press, pp. 300–9.

Mertens, D. (1983) 'Früher Buchdruck und Historiographie', in B. Moeller *et al.*, eds, *Studien zum stadtischen Bildungswesen des späten Mittelalters und der frühen Neuzeit*, Göttingen, pp. 83–111.

Minnis, A. J. (1984) *The Medieval Theory of Authorship*, Toronto.

Moss, Ann (1996) *Printed Commonplace-Books and the Structure of Renaissance Thought*, Oxford: Clarendon Press.

Myers, Robin and Harris, Michael, eds (1990) *Spreading the Word: The Distribution Networks of Print, 1550–1850*, Winchester: St. Paul's Bibliographies.

Needham, Paul (1982) 'Johann Gutenberg and the Catholicon Press', *Papers of the Bibliographical Society of America* 76: 395–456.

Needham, Paul (1992) 'Mainz and Eltville: The True Tale of Three Compositors', *Bulletin du Bibliophile*: 257–304.

Noegel, Scott B. (2004) 'Text, Script, and Media: New Observations on Scribal Activity in the Ancient Near East', in Raimonda Modiano, Leroy F. Searle, and Peter Shillingsburg, eds, *Voice, Text, Hypertext: Emerging Practices in Textual Studies*, Seattle: Walter Chapin Simpson Center for the Humanities in association with University of Washington Press, pp.133–143.

Olson, David R. (1977) 'From Utterance to Text: The Bias of Language in Speech and Writing', *Harvard Educational Review* 47: 257–81.

Olson, David R. (1980) 'On the Language and Authority of Textbooks', *Journal of Communication* 30.4 (Winter): 186–96.

Ong, Walter J. (1958) *Ramus, Method and Decay of Dialogue*, Cambridge, Mass.: Harvard University Press.

Ong, Walter J. (1967) *The Presence of the Word*, New Haven and London: Yale University Press.

Ong, Walter J. (1971) *Rhetoric, Romance and Technology*, Ithaca: Cornell University Press.

Ong, Walter J. (1977) *Interfaces of the Word*, Ithaca and London: Cornell University Press.

Ong, Walter J. (1981) *Fighting for Life: Contest, Sexuality, and Consciousness*, Ithaca and London: Cornell University Press.

Ong, Walter J. (1982) *Orality and Literacy: The Technologizing of the Word*, New York: Methuen.

Parkes, Malcolm (1991) *Scribes, Scripts, and Readers: Studies in the Communication, Presentation and Dissemination of Medieval Texts*, London: Hambledon Press.

Parkes, Malcolm (1992) *Pause and Effect: An Introduction to the History of Punctuation in the West*, Aldershot: Scolar Press.

Parkes, Malcolm and Watson, Andrew G., eds (1978) *Medieval Scribes, Manuscripts, and Libraries*, London.

Pearsall, Derek, ed. (1983) *Manuscripts and Readers in Fifteenth-Century England: The Literary Implications of Manuscript Study: Essays from the 1981 Conference at the University of York*, Cambridge: D. S. Brewer.

Pedersen, Johannes (1984) *The Arabic Book*, Princeton, NJ: Princeton University Press.

Petrucci, Armando (1995) *Writers and Readers in Medieval Italy: Studies in the History of Written Culture*, New Haven: Yale University Press.

Plato (1973) *Phaedrus and Letters VII and VIII*, trans. and intro. Walter Hamilton, Harmondsworth: Penguin Books.

Polidori Vergilii Urbinatis (1502) *De inventoribus rerum opus*, Paris.

Popkin, Jeremy D. (1992) 'Print Culture in the Netherlands on the Eve of the Revolution', in *The Dutch Republic in the Eighteenth Century: Decline, Enlightenment and Revolution*, ed. Margareth C. Jacob and Wijnand W. Mijnhardt, Ithaca: Cornell University Press, pp. 273–91.

Richardson, Brian (1994) *Print Culture in Renaissance Italy: The Editor and the Vernacular Text, 1470–1600*, Cambridge: Cambridge University Press.

Richardson, Malcolm (1980) 'Henry V, the English Chancery, and Chancery English', *Speculum* 55.4 (October): 726–50.

Roberts, Colin H. and Skeat, T. C. (1987) *The Birth of the Codex*, London: Oxford University Press for the British Academy.

Robinson, Pamela R. and Zim, Rivkah, eds (1997) *Of the Making of Books: Medieval Manuscripts, their Scribes and Readers: Essays Presented to M. B. Parkes*, Brookfield: Ashgate.

Rouse, Mary and Rouse, Richard (1991) *Authentic Witnesses: Approaches to Medieval Texts and Manuscripts*, Notre Dame.

Saenger, Paul (1982) 'Silent Reading: Its Impact on Late Medieval Script and Society', *Viator* 13: 367–414.

Scholderer, Victor (1970) *Johann Gutenberg: The Inventor of Printing*, 2nd edn, London: British Museum.

Schottenloher, Karl (1931) 'Handeschriftenforschung und Buchdruck im 15. and 16. Jahrhundert', *Zutenberg-Jahrbuch*, 73–106.

Schottenloher, Karl (1989) *Books and the Western World: A Cultural History*, trans. William D. Boyd and Irmgard H. Wolfe, Jefferson, NC: McFarland.

Schreiner, K. (1984) 'Laienbildung als Herausforderung für Kirche und Gesellschaft', *Zeitschrift für historische Forschung* 11: 257–345.

Scribner, Sylvia and Cole, Michael (1978) 'Literacy without Schooling: Testing for Intellectual Effects', *Harvard Educational Review* 48: 448–61.

Shernan, William H. and Dee, John (1995) *The Politics of Reading and Writing in the English Renaissance*, Amherst: University of Massachusetts Press.

Shuger, Deborah Kuller (1994) *The Renaissance Bible: Scholarship, Sacrifice and Subjectivity*, Berkeley: University of California Press.

Steinberg, S. H. (1974) [1955] *Five Hundred Years of Printing*, 3rd rev. edn, Harmondsworth: Penguin.

Stock, Brian (1990) *Listening for the Text*, Baltimore: Johns Hopkins University Press.

Swierk, A. (1972) 'Johannes Gutenburg als Erfinder in Zeugnissen seiner Zeit', in H. Widmann, ed., *Der gegenwartige Stand der Gutenberg-Forschung 1*, Stuttgart, pp. 79–90.

Tambiah, S. J. (1968) 'Literacy in a Buddhist Village in North-east Thailand', in Jack Goody, ed., *Literacy in Traditional Societies*, Cambridge: Cambridge University Press, pp. 85–131.

Thomas, Marcel (1976) 'Manuscripts', in Lucien Febvre and Henri-Jean Martin, eds, *The Coming of the Book: The Impact of Printing, 1450–1800*, trans. David Gerard, London: Verso, pp. 15–28.

Trapp, J. B., ed. (1983) *Manuscripts in the Fifty Years after the Invention of Printing*, London: Warburg Institute, University of London.

Trithemius, J. (1973) [1494] *De laude scriptorum: Zum Lobe der Schreiber*, ed. and trans. K. Arnold, Wurzburg.

Tyson, Gerald P. and Wagonheim, Sylvia S., eds (1986) *Print and Culture in the Renaissance: Essays on the Advent of Printing in Europe*, Newark: University of Delaware Press.

Widmann, H. (1972) 'Gutenburgh im Urteil der Nachwelt', in H. Widmann, ed., *Der gegenwärtige Stand der Gutenburg-Farschung 1*, Stuttgart, pp. 251–72.

Widmann, H. (1970) 'Kontinuität und Wandel in der Herstellung des Buches', *Archiv für die Geschichte des Buchwesens* 10: xxxv–xlviii.

Wilks, Ivor (1968) 'The Transmission of Islamic Learning in the Western Sudan', in Jack Goody, ed., *Literacy in Traditional Societies*, Cambridge: Cambridge University Press, pp. 162–97.

Wilson, Edward O. (1975) *Sociobiology: The New Synthesis*, Cambridge, Mass.: Belknap Press of Harvard University Press.

Winterich, John T. (1935) *Early American Books and Printing*, Boston: Houghton Mifflin.

Witten, Laurence (1959) 'The Earliest Books Printed in Spain', *Papers of the Bibliographical Society of America* 53: 91–113.

Wolfram, Walt (1972) 'Sociolinguistic Premises and the Nature of Nonstandard Dialects', in Arthur L. Smith, ed., *Language, Communication, and Rhetoric in Black America*, New York: Harper and Row, pp. 28–40.

Zumthor, P. (1983) *Introduction à la poésie orale*, Paris.

Zumthor, P. (1987) *La Lettre et la voix*, Paris.

Part 3: Texts and authors

Albertine, Susan, ed. (1996) *A Living of Words: American Women in Print Culture*, Knoxville: University of Tennessee Press.

Alston, R. C. and Fellner, H. (1992) *Publishing, the Book Trade, and the Diffusion of Knowledge*, Cambridge: Chadwyck-Healey.

Altick, Richard (1962) 'The Sociology of Authorship: The Social Origins, Education and Occupations of 1,100 British Writers, 1800–1935', *Bulletin of the New York Public Library* 66: 389–404.

Anderson, Patricia and Rose, Jonathan, eds (1991) *Dictionary of Literary Biography*, vols 106 and 112: *British Literary Publishing Houses*, Detroit: Gale Research.

Barbert, Biles and Fabian, Bernhard, eds (1981) *Buch und Buchhandel in Europa im achtzehnten Jahrhundert: The Book and the Book Trade in Eighteenth-Century Europe: Wolfenbutteler Symposium, November 1–3, 1977*, Hamburg: Hauswedell.

Barnes, James J. (1964) *Free Trade in Books: A Study of the London Book Trade since 1800*, Oxford: Clarendon Press.

Barnes, James J. (1974) *Authors, Publishers, and Politicians: The Quest for an Anglo-American Copyright Agreement, 1815–1854*, Columbus: Ohio State University Press.

Benedict, Barbara M. (1996) *Making the Modern Reader: Cultural Mediation in Early Modern Literary Anthologies*, Princeton: Princeton University Press.

Blagden, Cyprian (1960) *The Stationers' Company: A History, 1403–1959*, London: Allen & Unwin.

Bonham-Carter, Victor (1978) *Authors by Profession*, 2 vols, London: Society of Authors.

Botein, Stephen (1975) '"Mere Mechanics" and an Open Press: The Business and Political Strategies of Colonial American Printers', *Perspectives in American History* 5: 127–225.

Briggs, Asa, ed. (1974) *Essays in the History of Publishing in Celebration of the 250th Anniversary of the House of Longman, 1724–1974*, London: Longman.

Brown, Richard D. (1989) *Knowledge is Power: The Diffusion of Information in Early America, 1700–1865*, Oxford: Oxford University Press.

Charvat, William (1968) *The Profession of Authorship in America, 1800–1870: The Papers of William Charvat*, ed. Matthew J. Bruccoli, Columbus, Ohio: Ohio State University Press.

Charvat, William (1992) [1959] *Literary Publishing in America, 1790–1850*, Amherst: University of Massachusetts Press.

Coser, Lewis A., Kadushin, Charles and Powell, Walter W. (1982) *Books: The Culture and Commerce of Publishing*, New York: Basic Books.

Coultrap-McQuin, Susan (1990) *Doing Literary Business: American Women Writers in the Nineteenth Century*, Chapel Hill: University of North Carolina Press.

Crawford, Patricia (1985) *Women's Published Writings 1600–1700*, London: Methuen.

Cross, Nigel (1985) *The Common Writer: Life in Nineteenth-Century Grub Street*, Cambridge: Cambridge University Press.

Darnton, Robert (1979) *The Business of Enlightenment: A Publishing History of the Encyclopedie, 1775–1800*, Cambridge, Mass.: Harvard University Press.

Darnton, Robert (1982) *The Literary Underground of the Old Regime*, Cambridge, Mass.: Harvard University Press.

Darnton, Robert (1995) *The Forbidden Best-Sellers of Pre-Revolutionary France*, New York: Norton.

Dooley, Allan C. (1992) *Author and Printer in Victorian England*, Charlottesville: University Press of Virginia.

Dudek, Louis (1960) *Literature and the Press: A History of Printing, Printed Media, and their Relation to Literature*, Toronto: Contact Press.

DuPlessis, Rachel Blau (1985) *Writing Beyond the Ending: Narrative Strategies of Twentieth Century Women Writers*, Bloomington: Indiana University Press.

Dzwonkoski, Peter, ed. (1986) *Dictionary of Literary Biography*, vols 46 and 49: *American Literary Publishing Houses*, Detroit: Gale Research.

Eliot, Simon (1994) *Some Patterns and Trends in British Publishing, 1800–1919*, London: Bibliographical Society.

Feather, John (1988) *A History of British Publishing*, London: Croom Helm.

Feltes, N. N. (1978) *Modes of Production of Victorian Novels*, Chicago: University of Chicago Press.

Feltes, N. N. (1993) *Literary Capital and the Late Victorian Novel*, Madison, WI: University of Wisconsin Press.

Foucault, Michel (1984) 'What is an Author?', in Paul Rabinow, ed., *The Foucault Reader*, trans. Harari, Harmondsworth: Penguin, pp.101–20.

Fritschner, Linda Marie (1980) 'Publishers' Readers, Publishers and their Authors', *Publishing History* 7: 43–100.

Goldsmith, Elizabeth C. and Goodman, Dena, eds (1995) *Going Public: Women and Publishing in Early Modern France*, Ithaca: Cornell University Press.

Griest, Guinevere L. (1970) *Mudie's Circulating Library and the Victorian Novel*, Bloomington: Indiana University Press.

Gross, John (1969, 1991) *The Rise and Fall of the Man of Letters*, Hardmondsworth: Penguin.

Hanscombe, Gillian and Virginia L. Smyers (1987) *Writing for their Lives: The Modernist Women 1910–1940*, Boston: Northeastern University Press.

Hepburn, James (1968) *The Author's Empty Purse and the Rise of the Literary Agent*, London: Oxford University Press.

Hesse, Carla (1992) *Publishing and Cultural Politics in Revolutionary Paris, 1789–1810*, Berkeley: University of California Press.

Hill, Christopher (1991) *The World Turned Upside Down: Radical Ideas during the English Revolution*, Harmondsworth: Penguin Books.

Keating, Peter (1989) *The Haunted Study: A Social History of the English Novel: 1875–1914*, London: Secker and Warburg.

Kiernan, Alvin (1993) *Samuel Johnson and the Impact of Print*, Princeton: Princeton University Press.

Knox, Vicesimus (1784) *Elegant Extracts: or Useful and Entertaining Pieces of Poetry, Selected for the Improvement of Youth in Speaking, Reading, Thinking, Composing; and in the Conduct of Life*, London: C. Dilly.

Knox, Vicesimus, ed. (1816) *Elegant Extracts in Prose, Selected for the Improvement of Young Persons*, 10th edn, London.

Landon, Richard, ed. (1978) *Book Selling and Book Buying: Aspects of the Nineteenth-Century British and North American Book Trade*, Chicago: American Library Association.

Lehmann-Haupt, Hellmut, Wroth, Lawrence C. and Silver, Rollo G. (1951) *The Book in America: A History of the Making and Selling of Books in the United States*, New York: R. R. Bowker.

Lough, J. (1978) *Writer and Public in France from the Middle Ages to the Present Day*, Oxford: Clarendon Press.

McAleer, Joseph (1992) *Popular Reading and Publishing in Britain, 1914–1950*, Oxford: Oxford University Press.

McDonald, Peter (1997) *British Literary Culture and Publishing Practice 1880–1914*, Cambridge: Cambridge University Press.

McDowell, Paula J. (1996) 'Tace Sowle', in James Bracken and Joel Silver, eds, *The British Literary Book Trade, 1475–1700*, Detroit: Gale.

McDowell, Paula (1998) *The Women of Grub Street: Press, Politics, and Gender in the London Literary Marketplace 1678–1730*, Oxford: Oxford University Press.

Marek, Jayne E. (1995) *Women Editing Modernism: 'Little' Magazines & Literary History*, Lexington: University Press of Kentucky.

Martin, Henri-Jean and Roger Chartier, eds (1983) *Histoire de l'Edition Française, Tome 1–4*, Paris: Promodis.

Moss, Ann (1996) *Printed Commonplace-Books and the Structuring of Renaissance Thought*, Oxford: Oxford University Press.

Mumby, Frank Arthur and Norris, Ian (1982) *Publishing and Bookselling: A History from the Earliest Times to the Present Day*, rev. edn, London: Bell & Hyman.

Myers, Robin (1973) *The British Book Trade, from Caxton to the Present Day*, London: Andre Deutsch.

Nowell-Smith, Simon (1968) *International Copyright Law and the Publisher in the Reign of Queen Victoria*, Oxford: Clarendon Press.

O'Malley, Thomas (1982) ' "Defying the Powers and Tempering the Spirit." A Review of Quaker Control over their Publications 1672–1689', *Journal of Ecclesiastical History* 33: 72–88.

Ong, Walter (1971) *Rhetoric, Romance, and Technology: Studies in the Interaction of Expression and Culture*, Ithaca: Cornell University Press.

Parker, George L. (1985) *The Beginnings of the Book Trade in Canada*, Toronto: University of Toronto Press.

Patten, Robert L. (1978) *Charles Dickens and His Publishers*, Oxford: Clarendon Press.

Patten, Robert L. (1996) 'When is a Book not a Book?', *Biblion*, Spring: 35–63.

Plant, Marjorie (1974) [1939] *The English Book Trade: An Economic History of the Making and Sale of Books*, 3rd rev. edn, London: George Allen and Unwin Ltd.

Price, Leah (2003) *The Anthology and the Rise of the Novel: From Richardson to George Eliot*, Cambridge: Cambridge University Press.

Raven, James (1992) *Judging New Wealth: Popular Publishing and Responses to Commerce in England, 1750–1800*, Oxford: Clarendon Press.

Rose, Mark (1993) *Authors and Owners: The Invention of Copyright*, Cambridge, Mass.: Harvard University Press.

Ross, Trevor (1992) 'Copyright and the Invention of Tradition', *Eighteenth-Century Studies* 26.1: 1–27.

Schick, Frank L. (1958) *The Paperbound Book in America: The History of Paperbacks and Their European Background*, New York: R. R. Bowker.

Scott, Bonnie Kime, ed. (1990) *Gender in Modernism*, Bloomington: Indiana University Press.

Shevelow, K. (1989) *Women and Print Culture*, London: Routledge.

Shillingsburg, Peter L. (1992) *Pegasus in Harness: Victorian Publishing and W. M. Thackeray*, Charlottesville: University Press of Virginia.

Sutherland, John (1978) *Victorian Novelists and Publishers*, Chicago: Chicago University Press.

Sutherland, John (1995) *Victorian Fiction: Writers, Publishers, Readers*, Basingstoke: Macmillan Press.

Tebbel, John (1972–81) *A History of Book Publishing in the United States*, 4 vols, New York: R. R. Bowker.

Thomas, Gillian (1992) *A Position to Command Respect: Women and the Eleventh Britannica*, Metuchen, NJ: Scarecrow Press.

Todd, Janet (1984) *Dictionary of British and American Women Writers 1660–1800*, London: Methuen.

Tompkins, Jane P. (1985) *Sensational Designs: The Cultural Works of American Fiction, 1790–1860*, New York: Harvard University Press.

Tuchman, Gaye and Fortin, Nina E. (1989) *Edging Women Out: Victorian Novelists, Publishers and Social Change*, New Haven and London: Yale University Press.

Unseld, Siegfried (1980) *The Author and His Publisher*, trans. Hunter Hannum and Hildegarde Hannum, Chicago: University of Chicago Press.

Vincent, David (1989) *Literacy and Popular Culture: England, 1750–1914*, Cambridge: Cambridge University Press.

Viscomi, Joseph (1993) *Blake and the Idea of the Book*, Princeton: Princeton University Press.

Wall, Wendy (1993) *The Imprint of Gender: Authorship and Publication in the English Renaissance*, Ithaca: Cornell University Press.

Warner, Michael (1990) *Letters of the Republic: Publication and the Public Sphere in Eighteenth-Century America*, Cambridge, Mass.: Harvard University Press.

West III, James L. W. (1988) *American Authors and the Literary Marketplace since 1900*, Philadelphia: University of Pennsylvania Press.

Williams, Raymond (1962) *The Long Revolution*, London: Penguin Books.

Winship, Michael (1995) *American Literary Publishing in the Mid-Nineteenth Century: The Business of Ticknor and Fields*, Cambridge: Cambridge University Press.

Woodmansee, Martha (1994) *The Author, Art, and the Market*, New York: Columbia University Press.

Woodmansee, Martha and Jaszi, Peter, eds (1994) *The Construction of Authorship: Textual Appropriation in Law and Literature*, Durham, NC: Duke University Press.

Zionkowski, Linda (1992) 'Aesthetics, Copyright and "The Goods of the Mind" ', *British Journal of Eighteenth-Century Studies* 15: 163–74.

Part 4: Texts and readers

Adamson, J. W. (1946) 'Literacy in England in the Fifteenth and Sixteenth Centuries', in J. Adamson, *'The illiterate Anglo-Saxon' and other essays an education, medieval and modern*, Cambridge: Cambridge University Press, 33–61.

Allen, James Smith (1991) *In the Public Eye: A History of Reading in Modern France, 1800–1940*, Princeton, NJ: Princeton University Press.

Altick, Richard (1957) *The English Common Reader: A Social History of the Mass Reading Public 1800–1900*, Chicago: University of Chicago Press.

Aycock, Alan (1999) 'Technologies of the Self', *Foucault and Internet Discourse*. Available at http://www.ascuse.org/jcmc/vol 1/issue/aycock.html.

Bennett, H. S. (1938 for 1937) 'The Author and His Public in the Fourteenth and Fifteenth Centuries', *Essays and Studies by Members of the English Association*, xxiii: 7–24.

Bennett, H. S. (1943) 'Caxton and His Public', *Review of English Studies*, xix: 113–19.

Bennett, H. S. (1952) *English Books and Readers, 1475–1557*, Cambridge: Cambridge University Press.

Bennett, H. S. (1965) *English Books and Readers, 1558–1603*, Cambridge: Cambridge University Press.

Bennett, H. S. (1970) *English Books and Readers, 1603–1640*, Cambridge: Cambridge University Press.

Boyarin, Jonathan, ed. (1993) *The Ethnography of Reading*, Berkeley: University of California Press.

Boyle, James (1997) Foucault in Cyberspace: Surveillance, Sovereignty, and Hard-Wired Sensors. Available at http://www.wcl.american.edu/pub/faculty/boyle/foucault.html.

Brooks, Jeffrey (1985) *When Russia Learned to Read*, Princeton: Princeton University Press.

Cavallo, Guglielmo and Chartier, Roger, eds (1999) *A History of Reading in the West*, Cambridge: Polity Press.

Chartier, Roger, ed. (1989) *A History of Private Life: Passions of the Renaissance*, Cambridge, Mass.: Harvard University Press.

Chartier, Roger (1989) 'Texts, Printing, Readings', in Lynn Hunt, ed., *The New Cultural History*, Berkeley: University of California Press, pp. 154–75.

Chartier, Roger (1993) *The Order of Books: Readers, Authors and Libraries in Europe between the 14th and 18th Centuries*, trans. Lydia Cochrane, Cambridge: Polity Press.

Chartier, Roger (1995) *Forms and Meanings: Texts, Performances, and Audiences from Codex to Computer*, Philadelphia: University of Pennsylvania Press.

Cipolla, Carlo M. (1969) *Literacy and Development in the West*, Harmondsworth: Penguin Books.

Cressy, David (1980) *Literacy and the Social Order: Reading and Writing in Tudor and Stuart England*, Cambridge: Cambridge University Press.

Danky, James P. and Wiegand, Wayne, eds (1998) *Print Culture in a Diverse America*, Champaign: University of Illinois Press.

Darnton, Robert (1990) 'First Steps Toward a History of Reading', in *The Kiss of Lamourette*, London: Faber and Faber, pp. 154–90.

Derrida, Jacques (1989) 'Psyche: Inventions of the Other', Trans. Catherine Porter, in Lindsay Waters and Wlad Goozich, eds, *Reading de Man Reading*, Minneapolis: University of Minnesota Press, 25–65.

Eco, Umberto (1979) *The Role of the Reader: Explorations in the Semiotics of Texts*, Bloomington: Indiana University Press.

Fish, Stanley (1980) *Is There a Text in This Class? The Authority of Interpretive Communities*, Cambridge, Mass.: Harvard University Press.

Flint, Kate (1993) *The Female Reader*, Oxford: Oxford University Press.

Flynn, Elizabeth A. and Schweichart, Patrocinio P., eds (1986) *Gender and Reading: Essays on Readers, Texts, and Contexts*, Baltimore: Johns Hopkins University Press.

Foucault, Michel (1978) *The History of Sexuality: An Introduction*, Trans. Robert Harley, Vol 1, New York: Pantheon.

Foucault, Michel (1980) 'On Popular Justice', in Colin Gorden, ed, New York: Pantheon, 1–36.

Foucault, Michel (1986) 'Of Other Spaces', *Diacritics*, Spring, 22–7.

Furet, Francois and Ozouf, Jacques (1982) *Reading and Writing: Literacy in France from Calvin to Jules Ferry*, Cambridge: Cambridge University Press.

Gamble, Harry Y. (1995) *Books and Readers in the Early Church: A History of Early Christian Texts*, New Haven: Yale University Press.

Ginzburg, Carlo (1982) *The Cheese and the Worms: The Cosmos of a Sixteenth-Century Miller*, New York: Penguin Books.

Gross, Robert A. (1996) 'Reading Culture, Reading Books', *Proceedings of the American Antiquarian Society* 106: 59–78.

Halévy, É. (1924) *A History of the English People in 1815*, London: Fisher Unwin.

Iser, Wolfgang (1978a) *The Act of Reading: A Theory of Aesthetic Response*, Baltimore: Johns Hopkins University Press.

Iser, Wolfgang (1978b) *The Implied Reader*, Baltimore: Johns Hopkins.

Jaus, Hans Robert (1982) *Towards an Aesthetic of Reception*, University of Minnesota Press.

Jaszi, Martha and Woodmansee, Peter, eds (1994) *The Construction of Authorship: Textual Appropriation in Law and Literature*, Durham, NC: Duke University Press.

Kaestle, Carl, Damon-Moore, Helen and Stedman, Lawrence C., eds (1991) *Literacy in the United States: Readers and Reading since 1880*, New Haven: Yale University Press.

Kintgen, Eugene R. (1996) *Reading in Tudor England*, Pittsburgh: University of Pittsburgh Press.

Leavis, Q. D. (1932) *Fiction and the Reading Public*, London: Chatto & Windus.

Machor, James L. (1993) *Readers in History: Nineteenth-Century American Literature and the Contexts of Response*, Baltimore: Johns Hopkins University Press.

Manguel, Alberto (1996) *A History of Reading*, New York: Viking.

McHenry, Elizabeth (2002) *Forgotten Readers: Recovering the Lost History of African American Literary Societies*, Durham and London: Duke University Press.

Moylan, Michele and Stiles, Lane, eds (1996) *Reading Books: Essays on the Material Text and Literature in America*, Amherst: University of Massachusetts Press.

Pease, Donald (1995) 'Author', in Frank Lentricchia and Thomas McLaughlin, eds, *Critical Terms for Literary Study*, Chicago: University of Chicago Press, 106–9.

Plant, Marjorie (1974) [1939] *The English Book Trade: An Economic History of the Making and Sale of Books*, 3rd rev. edn, London: George Allen and Unwin Ltd.

Radway, Janice (1984a) 'Interpretive Communities and Variable Literacies: The Functions of Romance Reading', *Daedalus* 113 (Summer): 49–73.

Radway, Janice (1984b) *Reading the Romance: Women, Patriarchy, and Popular Literature*, Chapel Hill: University of North Carolina Press.

Radway, Janice (1997) *A Feeling for Books: The Book-of-the-Month Club, Literary Taste, and Middle-Class Desire*, Chapel Hill: University of North Carolina Press.

Raven, James, Small, Helen and Tadmor, Naomi, eds (1996) *The Practice and Representation of Reading in England*, Cambridge: Cambridge University Press.

Rivers, Isabel, ed. (1982) *Books and Their Readers in Eighteenth-century England*, New York: St Martin's Press.

Suleiman, Susan and Crosman, Inge, eds (1980) *The Reader in the Text: Essays on Audiences and Interpretation*, Princeton: Princeton University Press.

Tompkins, Jane P., ed. (1980) *Reader-Response Cricitism*, Baltimore: Johns Hopkins University Press.

Travis, Molly Abel (1998) *Reading Cultures: The Construction of Readers in the Twentieth Century*, Carbondale: Southern Illinois University Press.

Ward, Albert (1974) *Book Production, Fiction, and the German Reading Public, 1740–1800*, Oxford: Clarendon Press.

Part 5: The future of the book

Agre, P. (1995) 'Institutional Circuitry: Thinking about the Forms and Uses of Information', *Information Technology and Libraries* 14.4: 225–30.

Althusser, L. (1990) *For Marx*, London: Verso.

Anderson, B. (1983) *Imagined Communities*, London: Verso.

Anderson, G. (1976) *Victorian Clerks*, Manchester: Manchester University Press.

Anderson, P. (1992) 'The Ends of History', in *A Zone of Engagement*, London: Verso.

Ballo, G., Cachin-Nora, F., Leymarie, F. and Russoli, F. (1973) *Le Futurisme*, Paris: Editions des Musées Nationaux.

Banham, R. (1967) *Theory and Design in the First Machine Age*, New York: Praeger Publishing, second edition.

Barlow, J. (1995) 'Selling Wine Without Bottles: The Economy of Wine on the Global Net', available FTP or Telnet: ftp.eff.org Directory: on line/Pub/Publication: John-Perry-Barlow: idea-economy-article.

Barthes, R. (1974) *S/Z: An Essay*, New York: Hill & Wang.

Barthes, R. (1979) 'From Work to Text', in J. Harari, ed., *Textual Strategies: Perspectives in Post-Structuralist Criticism*, Ithaca: Cornell University Press.

Bate, W. J. (1970) *The Burden of the Past and the English Poet*, Cambridge, Mass.: Belknap Press.

Baudrillard, J. (1981) *Simulacres et Simulations*, Paris: Edition Galilée.

Benedikt, M. (1991) 'Introduction', in M. Benedikt, ed., *Cyberspace: First Steps*, Cambridge, Mass.: MIT Press.

Beniger, J. R. (1986) *The Control Revolution*, Cambridge, Mass.: Harvard University Press.

Benjamin, W. (1969) 'Theses on the Philosophy of History', in H. Arendt, ed., *Illuminations: Essays and Reflections*, New York: Schocken Books.

Benjamin, W. (1969a) [1936] 'The Storyteller', in H. Arendt, ed., *Illuminations: Essays and Reflections*, New York: Schocken Books.

Benjamin, W. (1969b) [1936] 'The Work of Art in the Age of Mechanical Reproduction', in H. Arendt, ed., *Illuminations: Essays and Reflections*, New York: Schocken Books.

Birkerts, S. (1994) *The Gutenberg Elegies: The Fate of Reading in an Electronic Age*, Boston: Faber & Faber.

Bloom, H. (1975) *The Anxiety of Influence: A Theory of Poetry*, New York: Oxford University Press.

Bolter, J. D. (1991) *Writing Space: The Computer, Hypertext, and the History of Writing*, Hillsdale: Erlbaum Associates.

Braudel, F. (1992) *Civilization and Capitalism. The Wheels of Commerce*, vol. 2, Berkeley: University of California Press.

Braining, J. (1997) 'Africa 1, Hollywood 0', *Wired*, 5.3: 61–2, 64, 185–8.

Bush, V. (1945a) 'As We May Think', *Atlantic Monthly* 176: 101–8.

Bush, V. (1945b) *Science. The Endless Frontier: A Report to the President for Postwar Scientific Research*, Washington: National Science Foundation.

Butler, J. (1993) 'Endangered/Endangering Schematic Racism and White Paranoia', in R. Gooding-Williams, ed., *Reading Rodney King: Reading Urban Uprising*, New York: Routledge, 15–22.

Butler, J. (1997) *Excitable Speech: A Politics of the Performative*, New York: Routledge.

Butler, S. (1970) *Erewhon*, Harmondsworth: Penguin Books.

Carr, E. H. (1964) *What is History: The G.M. Trevelyan Lectures*, Harmondsworth: Penguin Books.

Case, S. E. (1996) *The Domain-Matrix: Performing Lesbian at the End of Print Culture*, Bloomington, Indiana: Indiana University Press.

Chartier, R. (1991) *The Cultural Origins of the French Revolution*, Durham: Duke University Press.

Chartier, R. (1992) *L'Ordre des livres*, Paris: Alinea.

Cook, T. (1995) 'It's 10 O'clock: Do You Know Where Your Data Are?', *Technology Review*, January, on line available www:http://web.mit.edu/afs/athena/org/t/techre-view/www/articles/dec94/cook.html.

Darnton, R. (1979) *The Business of the Enlightenment: The Publishing History of the Encyclopédie*, Cambridge, Mass.: Harvard University Press.

Davis, E. (1993) 'Techgnosis, Magic, Memory, and the Angels of Information', in M. Derby, ed., *Flame Wars: The Discourse of Cyberspace*, special issue of *South Atlantic Quarterly* 92.4: 585–616.

de Certeau, M. (1984) *The Practice of Everyday Life*, Berkeley: University of California Press.

de Certeau, M. (1990) *L'invention du quotidian*, vol. 1, Paris: Gallimaud.

De Landa, M. (1993) 'Virtual Environments and the Emergence of Synthetic Reasoning', in M. Derby, ed., *Flame Wars: The Discourse of Cyberspace*, special issue of *South Atlantic Quarterly* 92.4: 793–815.

Delany, P. and Landow, G., eds (1994) *Hypermedia and Literary Studies*, Cambridge, Mass.: MIT Press.

De Man, P. (1983) *Blindness and Insight: Essays in the Rhetoric of Contemporary Criticism*, Minneapolis: University of Minnesota Press.

Derrida, J. (1977) *Writing and Difference*, Chicago: University of Chicago Press.

Derrida, J. (1995) *Mal d'archive*, Paris: Galilée.

Dretske, F. (1983) 'Précis of Knowledge and the Flow of Information', *The Behavioral and Brain Sciences* 6: 55–90.

Duguid, Paul (1996) 'Material Matters: The Past and Futurology of the Book', in Geoffrey Nunberg, ed., *The Future of the Book*, Berkeley: University of California Press, pp. 63–101.

Eagleton, T. (1984) *The Function of Criticism*, London: Verso.

Eisenstein, E. (1979) *The Printing Press as an Agent of Change: Communications and Cultural Transformations in Early Modern Europe*, Cambridge: Cambridge University Press, 2 vols.

Eisenstein, E. (1983) *The Printing Revolution in Early Modern Europe*, Cambridge: Cambridge University Press.

Empson, W. (1947) *Seven Types of Ambiguity*, London: Chatto & Windus.

Empson, W. (1950) *Some Versions of Pastoral: A Study of the Pastoral Form in Literature*, Norfolk, Conn.: New Directions.

Febvre, L. and Martin, H. J. (1984) *The Coming of the Book: The Impact of Printing, 1450–1800*, London: Verso.

Feigenbaum, E. and McCorduck, P. (1983) *Fifth Generation: Artificial Intelligence and Japan's Computer Challenge to the World*, Reading, UK: Addison-Wesley.

Ford, M. (1995) 'Without a City Wall', *TLS*, 4798.

Foucault, M. (1972) *The Archaeology of Knowledge and the Discourse on Language*, New York: Pantheon.

Foucault, M. (1977a) 'Nietzsche, Genealogy, History', in *Language, Counter-Memory, Practice: Selected Essays and Interviews*, Ithaca: Cornell University Press.

Foucault, M. (1977b) 'What Is an Author?', in *Language, Counter-Memory, Practice: Selected Essays and Interviews*, Ithaca: Cornell University Press.

Genette, G. (1987) *Seuils*, Paris: Seuil.

Giddens, A. and Held, D., eds (1982) *Classes, Power, and Conflict: Classical and Contemporary Debates*, Berkeley: University of California Press.

Gumbrecht, H. (1995) 'A Farewell to Interpretation', in H. Gumbrecht and K. Pfeiffer, eds, *Materialities of Communication*, Stanford: Stanford University Press.

Habermas, J. (1989) *The Structural Transformation of the Public Sphere: An Inquiry into a Category of Bourgeois Society*, Cambridge, Mass.: MIT Press.

Habermas, J. (1994) 'The Information Revolution', special number of *Business Week*.

Hugo, V. (1978) *Notre Dame of Paris*, Harmondsworth: Penguin Books.

Huizinga, J. (1972) *America: A Dutch Historian's Vision from Afar and Near*, New York: Harper Torchbooks.

James, H. (1987) *The American Scene*, London: Granville.

Jameson, F. (1994) *Postmodernism and the Cultural Logic of Late Capitalism*, Durham: Duke University Press.

Johnson, R. (1986) 'The Story So Far and Further Transformations', in D. Punter, ed., *Introduction Contemporary Cultural Studies*, London: Longman.

Kahn, H. and Weiner, A. (1968) 'One Hundred Technical Innovations Likely in the Next 33 Years', in *Toward the Year 2000: Work in Progress*, American Academy of Arts and Sciences, Boston: Beacon Press.

Kronick, D. (1962) *A History of Scientific and Technical Periodicals: The Origins and Development of the Scientific and Technological Press, 1665–1790*, New York: Scarecrow Press.

Kronick, D. (1991) *Scientific and Technical Periodicals of the Seventeenth and Eighteenth Centuries*, Metuchen, NJ: Scarecrow Press.

Landow, G. P. (1992) *Hypertext: The Convergence of Contemporary Critical Theory and Technology*, Baltimore: Johns Hopkins University Press.

Lanham, R. (1994) *The Electronic Word: Democracy, Technology, and the Arts*, Chicago: University of Chicago Press.

Latour, B. and Woolgar, S. (1986) *Laboratory Life: The Construction of Scientific Facts*, Princeton: Princeton University Press.

Linebaugh, P. (1992) *The London Hanged: Crime and Civil Society in the Eighteenth Century*, New York: Cambridge University Press.

Lyotard, F. (1979) *The Postmodern Condition: A Report on Knowledge*, Minneapolis: University of Minnesota Press.

Marvell, A. (1972) 'Horation Ode', in E. Story Donno, ed., *The Complete Poems*, Harmondsworth: Penguin Books.

Marx, L. (1964) *The Machine in the Garden: Technology and the Pastoral Ideal in America*, New York: Oxford University Press.

Marx, L. (1994) 'The Ideology of Technology and "Postmodern" Pessimism', in M. Smith and L. Marx, eds, *Does Technology Drive History? The Dilemma of Technological Determinism*, Boston: MIT Press.

McGann, J. (n.d.) 'The rationale of hypertext' (on line), available www:http://jefferson.village. virginia.edu/public/jjmaf/rationale/html.

McGann, J. (1991) *The Textual Condition*, Princeton: Princeton University Press.

McKenzie, D. (1986) *Bibliography and the Sociology of the Text*, London: British Library.

McLuhan, H. M. (1962) *The Gutenberg Galaxy: Making a Typographic Man*, Toronto: Toronto University Press.

McNally, P., ed. (1987) 'The Advent of Printing: Historians of Science Respond to Elizabeth Eisenstein's *The Printing Press as an Agent of Change*', Occasional Paper 10, Montreal: Graduate School of Library and Information Studies, McGill University.

Mitchell, W. J. T. (1995) *City of Bits: Space, Place, and the Infobahn*, Cambridge, Mass.: MIT Press.

Negroponte, N. (1995) *Being Digital*, New York: Basic Books.

Nelson, T. (1990) *Literary Machines*, Sausalito: Mindful Press.

Niethammer, L. (1992) *Posthistoire: Has History Come to an End?*, London: Verso.

Nunberg, Geoffrey (1996) 'Farewell to the Information Age', in Geoffrey Nunberg, ed., *The Future of the Book*, Berkeley: University of California Press, pp. 103–138.

Ozenfant, A. (1952) *Foundations of Modern Art*, New York: Dover Publications.

Petrosky, H. (1990) *The Pencil: A History of Design and Circumstance*, New York: Alfred A. Knopf.

Poster, Mark (2001) *What's the Matter with the Internet?*, Minneapolis: University of Minnesota Press.

Quinby, L. (1994) *Anti-Apocalypse: Exercises in Genealogical Criticism*, Minneapolis: University of Minnesota Press.

Reddy, M. J. (1979) 'The Conduit Metaphor', in A. Ortney, ed., *Metaphor and Thought*, Boston: Cambridge University Press, pp. 284–324.

Richards, I. A. (1960) *Principles of Literary Criticism*, London: Routledge & Kegan Paul.

Roberts, J., ed. (1994) *Art Has No History: The Making and Unmaking of Modern Art*, London: Verso.

Rothenberg, J. (1995) 'Ensuring the Longevity of Digital Documents', *Scientific American* 272.1: 42–47.

Said, E. (1978) *Orientalism*, London: Routledge & Kegan Paul.

Samuelson, P. (1997) 'Big Media Beaten Back', *Wired*, 5.3: 63ff.

Schaffner, A. (1994) 'The Future of Scientific Journals: Lessons From the Past', *Information Technology and Libraries* 13.4: 239–47.

Schiller, D. (1994) 'From Culture to Information and Back Again: Commoditization as a Route to Knowledge', *Critical Studies in Mass Communication*, 11.1: 93–115.

Schrage, M. (1995) 'Revolutionary Evolutionist', *Wired*, July: 120–24.

Seely Brown, J. and Duguid, P. (1994a) 'Borderline Issues: Social and Material Aspects of Design', *Human Computer Interaction* 9.1: 3–35.

Seely Brown, J. and Duguid, P. (1994b) 'Patrolling the Border: A Reply', *Human Computer Interaction* 9.1: 137–49.

Snider, M. (2000) 'Media vs. Web in Digital Copyright War', *USA Today*, February 17, A1.

Stallybrass, P. and White, A. (1986) *The Politics and Poetics of Transgression*, Ithaca: Cornell University Press.

Sterling, B. (1995) 'Free as Air, Free as Water, Free as Knowledge', on line available FTP or Telnet: ftp.eff.org. Directory:/Pub/Publications:Bruce_Sterling:Free_As_Air.speech.

Stone, A. R. (1995) *The War of Desire and Technology at the Close of the Mechanical Age*, Cambridge, Mass.: MIT Press.

Streeter, T. (1996) *Selling the Air: A Critique of the Policy of Commercial Broadcasting in the United States*, Chicago: University of Chicago Press.

Stuart, R. (1995) 'High-Tech Redlining', *Utne Reader* 68.

Sutherland, J. (1989) 'Publishing History: A Hole in the Centre of Literary Sociology', in P. Desan *et al.*, eds, *Literature and Social Practice*, Chicago: University of Chicago Press, pp. 267–82.

Teichgraeber, R. (1993) ' "A Yankee Diogenes": Thoreau and the Market', in T. Haskell and R. Teichgraeber, eds, *The Culture of the Market: Historical Essays*, New York: Cambridge University Press, pp. 293–325.

Terdiman, R. (1985) *Discourse/Counter-Discourse*, Ithaca, NY: Cornell University Press.

Toffler, A. (1971) *Future Shock*, London: Pan Books.

Toulmin, S. (1972) *Human Understanding: The Collective Use and Evolution of Concepts*, Princeton: Princeton University Press.

Weaver, W. (1964) 'Recent Contributions to the Mathematical Theory of Communication', in *The Mathematical Theory of Communication*, Urbana: University of Illinois Press.

White, R. and Limerick, P. (1994) *The Frontier in American Culture*, Berkeley: University of California Press.

Williams, R. (1961) *The Long Revolution: An Analysis of the Democratic, Industrial, and Cultural Changes Transforming Our Society*, London: Chatto & Windus.

Williams, R. (1973) *The Country and the City*, Oxford: Oxford University Press.

Williams, R. (1974) *Television*, New York: Schocken Books.

Williams, R. (1983) 'David Hume: Reasoning and Experience', in *Writing in Society*, London: Verso.

Wurman, R. S. (1989) *Information Anxiety*, New York: Doubleday.

Yamey, B. S. (1949) 'Scientific Bookkeeping and the Rise of Capitalism', *EHR* (second edition series) 1, 2 and 3: 99–113.

Yates, J. (1989) *Control Through Communication*, Baltimore: Johns Hopkins University Press.

Ziman, J. (1968) *Public Knowledge: An Essay Concerning the Social Dimension of Science*, Cambridge: Cambridge University Press.

INDEX

an instrument of secret and magic power 138, 163; rejection of and hostility towards 123–4, 162–4; relationship with power 124; and social status 159–60; and speech 95, 138; as a technology 136–7; and urban-rural divide 160; and women 159
writing instruction: New England 401–2
written records 140–2
Wroth, L.C. 20
Wroth, Mary 81

xylography 237

Yate, William 213, 214, 216
Yates, Frances 243, 244
Yates, Frederick 360
Yates, Joseph 312
Yeats, W.B. 418
Yeo, Richard 75
'young' writers 107–8

Zaret, David: *Origins of Democratic Culture* 75
Zenger, John Peter 59
Zola, Émile 18, 103, 106, 107, 115
Zumthor, P. 186